DHTML and JavaScript

Gilorien

Cascading Style Sheets, JavaScript Style Sheets, & JavaScripted Layers plus advanced JavaScript 1.2 & 1.3

ISBN 0-13-086334-3

Prentice Hall PTR
Upper Saddle River, NJ 07458
http://www.phptr.com

90000

9 780130 863348

Library of Congress Cataloging-in-Publication Data

Gilorien.
    DHTML and JavaScript / Gilorien.
       p.   cm.
    Includes bibliographical references.
    ISBN 0-13-086334-3
    1. DHTML (Document markup language)   I. Title.
    QA76.76.H94G55   1999   99-40535
    005.7'2--dc21   CIP

Editorial/production supervision: Nicholas Radhuber
Manufacturing manager: Alexis Heydt
Acquisitions editor: Greg Doench
Marketing manager: Bryan Gambrel
Editorial assistant: Mary Traecy
Cover design: Design Source
Cover design director: Jerry Votta

© 2000 Prentice Hall PTR
Prentice-Hall, Inc.
Upper Saddle River, New Jersey 07458

Printed in the United States of America
10 9 8 7 6 5 4 3 2 1

ISBN 0-13-086334-3

Prentice-Hall International (UK) Limited, London
Prentice-Hall of Australia Pty. Limited, Sydney
Prentice-Hall Canada Inc., Toronto
Prentice-Hall Hispanoamericana, S.A., Mexico
Prentice-Hall of India Private Limited, New Delhi
Prentice-Hall of Japan, Inc., Tokyo
Prentice-Hall (Singapore) Pte. Ltd., Singapore
Editora Prentice-Hall do Brasil, Ltda., Rio de Janeiro

Contents

Part I   *Dynamic HTML*

Contents

Contents

Part II   JavaScript 1.2

Contents

Contents

Part III *JavaScript 1.3*

Part IV   *Resources*

Preface

This book is designed to guide the reader in developing web sites that can use the new features and capabilities for using Style Sheets and Layers in both Cascading Style Sheet Syntax and JavaScript Syntax that are reflected in Netscape's Navigator 4.0+ browser. Additionally, it covers all of the new abilities of JavaScript 1.2 and including the Layer Object and advanced Event Handling for capturing Events and using them to dynamically alter the appearance and content of documents. There is also a chapter devoted to the new functionality of JavaScript 1.3 and changes from version 1.2.

If you are a complete beginner, then check out Appendix A in Part IV which will introduce you to all of the basics for using HTML Elements to design your web pages including Images, Area Maps, Tables, Frames, Forms, and Embedded Objects for advanced content like VRML, QTVR, QD3D, and Audio files. Appendix A contains a truncated version of the HTML Elements Primer but there is a much more complete version on the CD-ROM, in both HTML and PDF formats. Both of these online versions have about 100 additional examples that are linked to the documentation from separate files. If you are already deep into web site design, then Appendix A can serve as a reference when you need a quick memory fix.

Part I covers Styles and Layers. It starts with an introduction to using Cascading Style Sheet (CSS) Syntax and the Properties that are used to define Styles for your Elements. Chapter 2 demonstrates how to position Layers, which are Blocks of Content and introduces additional Properties associated with Layers. Chapter 3 moves on to Style Sheets created with JavaScript Syntax, focusing on using JavaScript to manipulate Layers in real-world examples.

The Layer Object in JavaScript is new and has many Properties and Methods that facilitate the manipulation of Layers both programmatically and dynamically from user input. Many of the Methods and Properties of other JavaScript Objects which can enhance this process are covered in both theory and in Sample Listings which are both in the book and in separate files on the CD-ROM for you to run. Generally speaking, you can digest a concept faster if you run the examples in a browser.

Part II covers all the vast array of new features of JavaScript 1.2 and changes to previous Object functionality. There are new Statements to consider and many Objects that required Constructor Functions can now be created with Literal Notation. String Objects, Array Objects and Event Objects have been massively enhanced with a plethora of new Properties and Methods. There is a new RegExp Object which uses Regular Expressions to perform pattern matches in text searches that opens up a whole new range of possibilities.

Additionally, Part II covers many of the essential tools for using JavaScript such as basic and advanced Object Theory, Statements and Operators, Functions, Methods, Expressions, Variables and Properties.

Part III covers the new features and minor changes to JavaScript 1.3. Version 1.2 is a major upgrade but version 1.3 is not. However, one really useful feature of 1.3 is the JavaScript Console that you can use to debug your code from Navigator/Communicator.

Most of the examples in this book will require that you use the Navigator 4.0 version of the browser and make sure that you have JavaScript enabled in the Preferences dialogue box. This book follows the standard conventions of using a fixed-width font (Courier or Geneva) for displaying HTML and JavaScript code except when it occurs in the context of a normal paragraph. In that circumstance, the code is displayed with a bold font. Usually HTML code is displayed in allcaps and JavaScript is either all lowercase or interCap.

Appendix E in Part IV consists of a group of charts that contain a lot of condensed information that can serve as Syntax references. These charts are all in a file named:

```
Charts.pdf
```

on the CD-ROM. It is suggested that you print out the whole file for use while you are learning the book and even more importantly for when you are writing your own code.

In summary, this book thoroughly covers CSS Style Sheets and JavaScript Style Sheets in theory and by example, along with all of the new features of JavaScript versions 1.2 and 1.3. It also serves as a Syntax Reference for these topics. Most importantly, after learning the theory, this book demonstrates how to effectively integrate JavaScript with DHTML to create innovative and advanced web sites. Finally, this book is heavily focused on examples as a learning mechanism; there are over 400 working examples in the book and even more on the CD-ROM.

Have FUN!!

Gilorien

About the Author

Gilorien is a freelance artist in both the 2D and 3D realms, a 3D animator, musician and advanced website designer and consultant. His company, DreamPlay Studios, provides content and consulting for a variety of projects and is currently working on a full-length animation film that is being created exclusively in the 3D digital realm. Still images of his art, along with excerpts of music from his 2 CDs, can be seen/heard and purchased at:

`http://www.erols.com/gilorien`   Contact him at: `gilorien@erols.com`

Regarding HTML Syntax

The way that Syntax (your HTML code) is laid out in this book is with the Element Name first which in this case would be BODY. Then there is a list of the Attribute Names with their respective Value possibilities which compose the NAME="**value**" pair as mentioned previously. When you see a vertical bar (|) between the **values** that means that you have a choice of **value** Types to choose from. The Character (|) just means (or). For the first Attribute Name of TEXT you can choose to use either a HEXADECIMAL Color or a Color Name.

The **value** placeholder names between the quote marks (like **colorName**) are descriptive only and are just an attempt to try to explain what kind of **value** you should replace it with except when it is allcaps, which signifies that it is a Keyword that can be used as is. One exception to this is "URL" (or "URI" if you want to be cutting edge).

Most Attributes are optional and are used to modify the Element to your own tastes. When an Attribute is <u>required</u> for the Element to work I will let you know.

Regarding JavaScript Syntax

The way that Syntax for JavaScript code is displayed in this book is similar to what was just mentioned for HTML Syntax with the following additions. When Brackets [] are used they signify, in most circumstances, that what they surround is/are optional Parameter(s). The one exception to this is when they are used to create an Array with Literal notation.

Curly Braces are used to enclose Statement Blocks in Functions and other types of special Statements like **if()**. They are also used to create an Object with Literal notation.

InterCap words, such as **statementsIfTrue**, usually signify that this is a Parameter that you should replace with your own specification. However, don't confuse that with Keywords, Properties, Methods or Function Names, etc., that use interCap spelling.

For more information on characters and symbols, see Chapter 9 and Chapter 10 on Special Characters in JavaScript.

Regarding Section Header Capitalization

The capitalization scheme for the Section Header Names in this book is somewhat unorthodox. To make it as easy as possible for the reader to identify the topic or whatever s/he is looking for, I have implemented the following general rules:

1.   The first word of each section header is capitalized in all circumstances.

2.   All other normal words are in lowercase letters, which is the most atypical aspect of this scheme. The reason for this is to quickly identify code words.

3.   All CSS, JSS, HTML, and JavaScript Keywords, Properties, Attributes, and Objects, etc., have the capitalization that is appropriate for that particular word when it is used as actual code. If a JavaScript Object such as the **layers[i]** Array is used in a title, then the word **layers** is usually followed by the **[i]** which immediately shows that it is an Array.

Similarly, CSS Properties are usually identified like this: **{ font-size: }**

4.   Ordinarily, underlined words, if any, signify that they are the primary focus of the topic to be discussed. Underlining a word also signals that this is definitely a code word, which is especially useful for lowercase code words like the Keyword <u>**all**</u>. Just in case you are wondering why I don't just make them bold like in regular paragraphs, the answer is simple: The whole header is already bold.

5.   Certain words like Element, while technically aren't code words themselves, are important enough to warrant capitalizing the first letter all the time. Actual HTML Elements are always written in all uppercase letters and are usually surrounded by angle brackets (< >) like this: <SCRIPT>.

6.   Finally, there are some words which are capitalized according to the conventions that seem to have been adopted or initiated. For instance, Netscape started using allcaps for CONTEXTUAL SELECTION CRITERIA and I've continued the tradition.

7.   Regarding the capitalization of the word Layer: Layer and LAYER are only used for emphasis and should be considered interchangeable in most cases; although I do use LAYER for usages of the <LAYER> Element, this is still a conventional choice because HTML is case-insensitive. When LAYER is used in a topic concerning CSS Syntax, it more than likely refers to a NAMED LAYER, but not always. Sometimes it is used that way just to draw attention to it within the surrounding text. When Layer is used, it usually refers to a generic usage.

There are two instances when the spelling of the word "Layer" is case-sensitive. The first is when you access the **layers[i]** Array, and the second is when you create a new Layer with the **Layer()** Constructor Function and the Keyword **new**, like this:

```
myContainer = new Layer(500);
```

See page 199 for **layers[i]** Array and pages 240-241 for **new Layer()**.

About the CD-ROM

All of the more than 400 examples in the book have an associated BBEdit HTML Sample file on the CD-ROM in the folder named <u>DHTML-JS_BOOK-Main_Files</u>. Each of these files starts with the word "Sample" and are intended to be run on the Netscape Navigator/Communicator browser. You can also check out the source code for copying/pasting or alteration in any text editor. If you work on a Macintosh, you might want to get the BBEdit text editor from Bare Bones Software, which is specifically designed to work with HTML and other types of coding.

Netscape's homepage on the web is:

```
http://home.netscape.com/
```

Netscape's "DevEdge" (Developer Edge) on the web is:

```
http://developer.netscape.com/index_home.html?cp=hom07cnde
```

Netscape's "DevEdge - Library" on the web is:

```
http://developer.netscape.com/docs/manuals/index.html
```

Bare Bones Software's homepage on the web is:

```
http://www.bbedit.com/
```

The CD-ROM also contains a wealth of additional information of a technical nature on a variety of subjects including HTML 4.0 white papers, Netscape's final HTML 4.0 Guide, JavaScript 1.2 and 1.3 References and Guides.

See the last two pages of the book, after the Index, for more information about the contents of the CD-ROM.

Acknowledgments

Thanks to the many persons at Prentice Hall's PTR Division for their suggestions and contributions in making this the best book it could be. Of special note at PTR are: Greg Doench, Nicholas Radhuber, Mary Traecy, and Kathy Finch. Special thanks go to my parental units, for their support and patience. This book is dedicated to all practitioners of creativity and exploration everywhere.

Part I
Dynamic HTML

Chapter 1

Style Sheets

Chapter 1
Style Sheets

Contents

∞∞

Introduction to Style Sheets

Style Sheets Overview

Cascading Style Sheets (CSS) and JavaScript Style Sheets used in concert with Scripting is what puts the dynamism in Dynamic HTML. It allows you to precisely format, embellish, and position the content in your documents instead of acquiescing to the whims of each browser's rendering choices. You can also create documents that change by themselves, or in response to user interaction, and have inline animations contained within them. Inline is the key word here because that means faster downloading and no plug-ins to load or have compatibility issues with or annoy the user because, if after downloading seventy-five plug-ins, the one for your content isn't on his/her system. It also means that you can have an image that not only animates but can move around the page instead of being confined to a stationary rectangular space.

You embellish your content by making stylistic choices that affect the color, size, font face, boldness, and other aspects of text markup, and you can create margins and borders for your text. Then you can position your content exactly where you want it to appear in the page instead of the old inline flow method. Transparent and opaque blocks of content are now possible which you can change, move, resize, make appear or disappear on-the-fly, or respond to user input. If so inclined, you could let each user custom design how the website will appear for them.

Time will definitely be saved if you have a particular style that you want to use for your whole site or section of it by creating the Style Sheet just once and saving it in its own file and then accessing it multiple times with one line of code. You just LINK to the Style Sheet when you want it to apply to that specific page.

The text layout paradigm of Style Sheets has been directly ported from the desktop publishing world where programs like QuarkXpress have had Style Sheets for years. If you are familiar with that then you're already halfway home to understanding Cascading Style Sheets in HTML. There are two main differences between Style Sheets as used in Quark and those used in Navigator. The first is that in Quark you are working in a WYSIWYG environment so you just make your choices from radio buttons, text-boxes, and pop-up menus in a dialog window and then Quark does all the post-script coding for you. In HTML with Cascading Style Sheets you have to do the coding yourself but you're doing the same thing to your content and you get very similar results. In fact, getting HTML pages to behave more like documents in the publishing world is half the point. The other difference, and this one goes way beyond desktop publishing, is the dynamic and interactive aspects of Cascading Style Sheets.

Using the TYPE Attribute of <STYLE> Element

When you use the <STYLE> Element, you have to declare with the TYPE Attribute which type of Style Sheet it is, either TYPE="text/CSS" or TYPE="text/JavaScript".

For the purposes of clarity and brevity **CSS syntax** (Cascading Style Sheet syntax) refers to syntax declared as:

```
TYPE="text/CSS"
```

When the term **JavaScript syntax** is used it refers to syntax declared as:

```
TYPE="text/JavaScript"
```

Creating a Style

You can create Styles for your content in several ways. By using the <STYLE> Element, the STYLE Attribute, the CLASS Attribute, the ID Attribute with the CLASS Attribute, or the <SPAN> Element.

Once you get familiar with the new terms and how they are used together, and especially the fact that there is a STYLE Element and a STYLE Attribute, it's easy.

Here's the new <u>Elements</u> (Tags) associated with using Styles:

-    <STYLE>   specifies a Style or Layer or inflow Layer
-    <SPAN>   on-the-fly Style for one section of content in the BODY Element
-    <LINK>   loads a Style Sheet from another Document
-    <LAYER>   specifies a Layer
-    <ILAYER>   specifies an inflow Layer or Offset inflow Layer

Here's the new <u>Attributes</u> that you use with all the old Elements that you're familiar with that are associated with creating Styles:

-    STYLE   on-the-fly Style for one Element only at a time in the BODY Element
-    CLASS   on-the-fly Style for one Element only at a time in the BODY Element that addresses a NAMED CLASS of Style that was created in the HEAD Element
-    ID   on-the-fly NAMED INDIVIDUAL Style EXCEPTION to a CLASS of STYLE addressed by the CLASS Attribute for one Element only at a time in the BODY Element

The Golden Rules for Styles

This is a reference list of the idiosyncrasies and general parameters you will need at your fingertips until you've synaptically burned them in.

Element Names are always case-insensitive.	HTML
Attribute Names are always case-insensitive.	HTML
Attribute Values are generally case-insensitive.	HTML
CLASS Names are case-sensitive.	HTML / CSS Style
ID Names are case-sensitive.	HTML / CSS Style
Style Property Names are always case-sensitive.	CSS / JavaScript Style
Style Property Values are generally case-sensitive.	CSS / JavaScript Style
JavaScript **classes** Names are always case-sensitive.	JavaScript Style
JavaScript **ids** Names are always case-sensitive.	JavaScript Style
Layer Object Properties are always case-sensitive.	JavaScript
Layer Object Method Names are always case-sensitive.	JavaScript

STYLE is used as both an Element and as an Attribute of other Elements.

Only one CLASS of STYLE can be applied to each HTML Element.

There are several ways to apply a STYLE to your document content. They are:

> STYLE as Element
> STYLE as Attribute of most Elements
> CLASS as Attribute of most Elements
> ID as Exception Attribute for the CLASS Attribute
> STYLE with CONTEXTUAL SELECTION CRITERIA
> SPAN Element with STYLE Attribute
> SPAN Element with CLASS Attribute
> SPAN Element with CLASS Attribute and ID Exception Attribute for CLASS

It can be useful to think of:

STYLE as Element as the Cascading Style Sheet or JavaScript Style Sheet where you set all of your global stylistic Attributes for the entire document and which always goes in the HEAD Element.

STYLE as Attribute as a way to add a Style on-the-fly with specific Properties to a single Element that is contained between the BODY start and end Tags.

CLASS as Attribute as a way to add a Style on-the-fly by referencing the NAME of the CLASS of STYLE to a single Element that is contained between the BODY Start and End Tags.

ID as Attribute as a way to add a Style on-the-fly by addressing a reference to a NAMED INDIVIDUAL STYLE which is used to create an EXCEPTION to a CLASS of STYLE.
STYLE with CONTEXTUAL SELECTION CRITERIA creates a Style that is only applicable when a specified Element is nested within other Elements in a prescribed way by the STYLE definition.

These different possibilities vary in their range of applicability or, put another way, in how global they are.

Never put double quotes around the Values in Cascading Style Sheet Attributes. This is the correct way to do it:

```
H2 { color: red; }
```

The one exception to the double quotes rule is when you specify a **font-family** Value Name that is composed of more than one word and separated by a space like this:

```
H2 { font-family:"Brush Script"; }
```

HTML documents usually load faster if you use lowercase letters for Element and Attribute names because the compression algorithms used by the browser software are more efficient at storing data patterns that occur more often than those that are infrequent. In general circumstances lowercase letters occur more frequently than uppercase ones.
Remember that Cascading Style Sheet Syntax is a scripting language that has rules of its own that are distinct from HTML and JavaScript but is designed to interact with HTML and JavaScript. Expect subtle differences in syntax and new capabilities and terms. The same is true for Style Sheets that use JavaScript Syntax.
In an effort to establish distinctions between HTML Syntax and Style Sheet Syntax and in keeping with tradition: When the term *Attribute* is used, it refers to an Attribute of an HTML Element, and when the term *Property* is used, it refers to a Style Sheet Syntax Property. Just remember that in a generic sense they accomplish the same thing but point to different types of code. *Property* also refers to a JavaScript Property of Objects.
All of the Examples have a corresponding Sample HTML file on the CD-ROM so you can see the results in a browser. They are located in the folder named:

```
DHTML-JS_BOOK-Main_Files
```

The name of the Sample File is always listed to the right of the Example Number and above the source code. These Sample files have been tested in version 4.0 of Navigator, but are not guaranteed to work in other browsers.

Cascading Style Sheets & JavaScript Style Sheets

Chapter 1 deals with laying the foundation for creating Style Sheets using Cascading Style Sheet (CSS) Syntax. Then in Chapter 2 we explain how the Layers that are created with Style Sheets or the LAYER Elements are positioned in a browser window. Chapter 3 covers JavaScript Style Sheets and using JavaScript to dynamically manipulate Layers.

When you use the <STYLE> Element, you have to declare with the TYPE Attribute which type of Style Sheet it is, either: **TYPE="text/CSS"** or **TYPE="text/JavaScript"**. In this book, the term:

<u>CSS syntax</u> (Cascading Style Sheet syntax) refers to syntax declared as:

```
TYPE="text/CSS"
```

and when the term **JavaScript syntax** is used it refers to syntax declared as:

```
TYPE="text/JavaScript"
```

Cascading Style Sheets

To create a Cascading Style Sheet, you use CSS syntax to define the parameters of a Style by first specifying the HTML Element that you want to assign a Style to and then, inside of curly braces{}, you list the ATTRIBUTE NAME and VALUE pair or pairs. You separate each NAME and VALUE with a colon like this: <u>NAME:VALUE</u>. Then you separate each <u>NAME:VALUE;</u> pair with a semicolon, even if there is only one pair, like this:

```
{ NAME:VALUE; }
{ NAME:VALUE; NAME:VALUE; NAME:VALUE; }
```

Here are three different examples of real <u>NAME:VALUE;</u> pairs:

```
{ color:red; }
{ text-align:left; float:right; }
{ background-color:purple; margin:10pt; border-style:ridge; }
```

Putting that all together, here's a simple Style that causes all H2 Element headings to be displayed with a font that is sized at 14 point and colored aqua:

```
H2 { font-size:14pt; color:aqua; }
```

and here is the complete syntax using the STYLE Tags, which are always located in the HEAD Element:

```
<HEAD>

<STYLE TYPE="text/CSS">

H2 { font-size: 14pt; color: aqua; }

</STYLE>

</HEAD>
```

Just one more thing: While it isn't required, most people put the <u>CSS</u> Style Definition parameters inside of a Comment Tag (<!-- ... -->) so that they will be hidden from browsers that don't recognize Style Sheets or the STYLE Tags. However, be careful that you don't put the STYLE Tags themselves inside the Comment Tag or they will be ignored even by Style-Savvy browsers like Navigator. Here's how the last example would look when properly placed within a Comment Tag:

```
<HEAD>

<STYLE TYPE="text/CSS">

<!--

        H2 { font-size: 14pt; color: aqua; }

-->

</STYLE>

</HEAD>
```

Special Notice:

It is absolutely critical that you code your syntax correctly. Pay special attention to your colons and semicolons so that they are in the correct place. This is how the browser knows how to distinguish between just an ordinary piece of text and CSS <u>NAME: VALUE;</u> syntax.

Do NOT put the <u>VALUE</u> choice inside of double quote marks like you do for regular HTML Attributes. The Style Sheet Property Names are case-sensitive.

So far we have created a Style Sheet, but we haven't actually applied it to any Elements in the BODY of the document yet. This is the easy part because it works just like normal HTML that you're used to. Expanding on the above example one last time, here is what it looks like when you apply the Style defined for the H2 in the Style Sheet to an actual H2 heading in the BODY section of the document.

Example 1-1:   **Sample201.html**

```
<!DOCTYPE HTML PUBLIC "-//W3C//DTD HTML 3.2//EN">
<HTML>
<HEAD>  <TITLE>          Sample 201 - CSS Example 1-1  </TITLE>

<STYLE TYPE="text/CSS">

<!--
       H2 { font-size: 14pt; color: aqua; }
-->

</STYLE>
</HEAD>

<BODY>
<P>
Style Sheet Use:

<H2>This is a level-two heading that is aqua and sized at 14 points.</H2>

Notice that this text which is not inside the H2 tags is rendered with the default
colors of the BODY Tag.

</BODY>
</HTML>
```

I've included the following charts because when you're trying to organize all this theory inside your head, it's very useful to have the options that you use in the real world at your fingertips to improve how you remember how it all fits together. Just look it over to get a feel for what the possibilities are and then use it for reference when you need a quick memory jog. If you want a printout of all these charts, then print Charts.pdf, in the PDF-Files folder on the CD-ROM. Other charts are in the Charts folder in HTML format.

CSS Syntax Property Chart

Here's a list of all the Property Names and Values that are used to format the content in your Style Sheets using Cascading Style Sheet Syntax. Check the explanatory notes at the top of page 13 if deciphering the chart is initially unwieldy.

∞∞

Property Name CSS Syntax	All Possible Categories	All Possible Values
font-size	absolute-size	xx-small, x-small, small, medium, large, x-large, xx-large
	relative-size	larger, smaller
	length | percentage	10pt, 12pt, 14pt, 20pt, 24pt,... 20%, 25%, 50%, 80%, 120%,150%, 200%,...
font-family	any system font	Helvetica, Times, Geneva, Courier,...
font-weight	keyword | number	normal, bold, bolder, lighter | 100-900
font-style	keyword	normal, italic
line-height	number	multiplied by a number or decimal
	length | percentage	em, ex, px, pt, pc, in, mm, cm | 1%-1000%, ...n%
	keyword	normal
text-decoration	keyword	none, underline, line-through, blink
text-transform	keyword	capitalize, uppercase, lowercase, none
text-align	keyword	left, right, center, justify
text-indent	length | percentage	em, ex, px, pt, pc, in, mm, cm | 1%-1000%, ...n%
margin	length | percentage	em, ex, px, pt, pc, in, mm, cm | 1%-1000%, ...n%
	keyword	auto (is available for all 5 margin Properties)
margin (example)		{ margin: 24pt 30pt 30pt 17pt; } sets each margin to diff. value The order is: top right bottom left
margin-top	length | percentage	em, ex, px, pt, pc, in, mm, cm | 1%-1000%, ...n%
margin-right	length | percentage	em, ex, px, pt, pc, in, mm, cm | 1%-1000%, ...n%
margin-bottom	length | percentage	em, ex, px, pt, pc, in, mm, cm | 1%-1000%, ...n%
margin-left	length | percentage	em, ex, px, pt, pc, in, mm, cm | 1%-1000%, ...n%
padding	length | percentage	em, ex, px, pt, pc, in, mm, cm | 1%-1000%, ...n%
padding (example)		{ padding: 25px 20px 45px 35px; } sets each padding to diff. value
padding-top	length | percentage	em, ex, px, pt, pc, in, mm, cm | 1%-1000%, ...n%
padding-right	length | percentage	em, ex, px, pt, pc, in, mm, cm | 1%-1000%, ...n%
padding-bottom	length | percentage	em, ex, px, pt, pc, in, mm, cm | 1%-1000%, ...n%
padding-left	length | percentage	em, ex, px, pt, pc, in, mm, cm | 1%-1000%, ...n%
color	colorvalue	none, name, #$$$$$$, rgb(0-255,0-255,0-255), rgb(?%,?%,?%)
background-color	colorvalue	none, name, #$$$$$$, rgb(0-255,0-255,0-255), rgb(?%,?%,?%)
the 16 color names are		aqua, black, blue, fuchsia, gray, green, lime, maroon, navy, olive, purple, red, silver, teal, white, yellow
background-image	imageurl	url( ) { background-image: url(JPEG-Images/ExampleImage.jpeg); }
border-style	keyword	none, solid, double, inset, outset, groove, ridge
border-color	colorvalue	none, name, #$$$$$$, rgb(0-255,0-255,0-255), rgb(?%,?%,?%)
border-width	length | percentage	em, ex, px, pt, pc, in, mm, cm | 1%-1000%, ...n%
border-width	same	{ border-width: 20px 30px 40px 50px; } sets each width to diff. value
border-top-width	length | percentage	em, ex, px, pt, pc, in, mm, cm | 1%-1000%, ...n%
border-right-width	length | percentage	em, ex, px, pt, pc, in, mm, cm | 1%-1000%, ...n%
border-bottom-width	length | percentage	em, ex, px, pt, pc, in, mm, cm | 1%-1000%, ...n%
border-left-width	length | percentage	em, ex, px, pt, pc, in, mm, cm | 1%-1000%, ...n%
width	length | percentage	em, ex, px, pt, pc, in, mm, cm | 1%-1000%, ...n%
	keyword	auto
float	keyword	left, right, center, none
clear	keyword	none, left, right, both
display	keyword	block, inline, list-item
list-style-type	keyword	disc, circle, square, decimal, lower-roman, upper-roman, lower-alpha,
	keyword	upper-alpha, none
white-space	keyword	normal, pre { white-space: pre; } { white-space: normal; }

∞∞

CSS & JavaScript Syntax Property Comparison Chart

Property Name CSS Syntax	Property Name JavaScript Syntax	Simple CSS Syntax Examples
font-size	fontSize	{ font-size: 14pt; }
font-family	fontFamily	{ font-family: Helvetica, Times, Geneva, Courier; }
font-weight	fontWeight	{ font-weight: bold; }
font-style	fontStyle	{ font-style: italic; }
line-height	lineHeight	{ line-height: 22pt; }
text-decoration	textDecoration	{ text-decoration: underline; }
text-transform	textTransform	{ text-transform: uppercase; }
text-align	textAlign	{ text-align: right; }
text-indent	textIndent	{ text-indent: 40px; }
margin	margins( )	{ margin: 75px; } sets all 4 margins to same value
margin	margins( )	{ margin: 24pt 30pt 30pt 17pt; } sets each margin to diff. value
		The order is: top right bottom left
margin-top	marginTop	{ margin-top: 40mm; }
margin-right	marginRight	{ margin-right: 4cm; }
margin-bottom	marginBottom	{ margin-bottom: 12pc; }
margin-left	marginLeft	{ margin-left: 1in; }
padding	paddings( )	{ padding: 25px; }
padding	paddings( )	{ padding: 25pt 20px 45pt 35px; }
padding-top	paddingTop	{ padding-top:.5in; }
padding-right	paddingRight	{ padding-right: 25pt; }
padding-bottom	paddingBottom	{ padding-bottom: 15pt; }
padding-left	paddingLeft	{ padding-left: 5pt; }
color	color	{ color: blue; } { color:#0000ff; }
color	color	{ color: rgb(0%, 0%, 100%); } { color: rgb(0,20, 255); }
background-color	backgroundColor	{ background-color: maroon; } same options as color
background-image	backgroundImage	{ background-image: url(JPEG-Images/ExampleImage.jpeg); }
border-style	borderStyle	{ border-style: groove; }
border-color	borderColor	{ border-color:#335a77; }
border-color	borderColor	{ border-color: rgb(20%, 50%, 70%); }
border-color	borderColor	{ border-color: rgb(255, 20, 150); }
border-width	borderWidths( )	{ border-width: 20px; }
border-width	borderWidths( )	{ border-width: 20px 30px 40px 50px; }
border-top-width	borderTopWidth	{ border-top-width: 20px; }
border-right-width	borderRightWidth	{ border-right-width: 30px; }
border-bottom-width	borderBottomWidth	{ border-bottom-width: 40px; }
border-left-width	borderLeftWidth	{ border-left-width: 50px; }
width	width	{ width: 50%; } { width: 500px; } { width: 7in; }
float	align	{ float: left; } { float: right; } { float: center; }
clear	clear	{ clear: left; } { clear: right; } { clear: both; }
display	display	{ display: block; } { display: list-item; }
list-style-type	listStyleType	{ list-style-type: square; } { list-style-type: upper-roman; }
white-space	whiteSpace	{ white-space: pre; } { white-space: normal; }

absolute units		relative units
pt -- points	pc -- picas	em -- the height of the element's font
px -- pixels	in -- inches	ex -- half the height of the element's font
mm -- millimeters	cm -- centimeters	px -- pixels, relative to rendering surface

Note that in the chart on pages 11 and 195, for any of the Properties that have the scenario:

<u>Possible</u> <u>Categories</u>	<u>Possible</u> <u>Values</u>		
length | *percentage*	em, ex, px, pt, pc, in, mm, cm	|	1%-1000%, ...n%

It means that if you use a *length* type Value, then it should be a <u>number</u> suffixed by one of these units of measurement: em, ex, px, pt, pc, in, mm, cm, like this: "200px".

If you use a *percentage* type Value then it should be a <u>number</u> that is followed by a percent (%) sign, like this: "75%".

CSS Layer Properties and <LAYER> Attributes Chart

Notice that the <u>preceding</u> two charts do not include the Properties that are used to POSITION your content. Those are listed in the chart below within the Layers model.
Also note that there are no corresponding Properties in CSS Syntax for the LAYER Attributes of **PAGEX**, **PAGEY**, **ABOVE** and **BELOW** or the five Event Handlers.

∞∞∞

Property Name CSS Syntax	Attribute Name <LAYER> Syntax	Simple CSS Syntax Examples	Simple <LAYER> Syntax Examples
position		{ position: absolute; }	<LAYER></LAYER>
position		{ position: relative; }	<ILAYER></ILAYER>
#myLayerName	ID	{ position: absolute; }	ID="myLayerName"
left	LEFT	{ left: 40px; }	LEFT=40
top	TOP	{ top: 20px; }	TOP=20
	PAGEX		PAGEX=72
	PAGEY		PAGEY=144
width	WIDTH	{ width: 550px; }	WIDTH=550
height	HEIGHT	{ height: 400px; }	HEIGHT=400
clip	CLIP	{ clip: rect('10, 20, 30, 40'); }	CLIP="10, 20, 30, 40"
z-index	Z-INDEX	{ z-index: 3; }	Z-INDEX=3
	ABOVE		ABOVE="myLayerName5"
	BELOW		BELOW="myLayerName7"
visibility	VISIBILITY	{ visibility: show; }	VISIBILITY="SHOW"
background-color	BGCOLOR	{ background-color: purple; }	BGCOLOR="#0000ff"
layer-background-color		{ layer-background-color: blue; }	
background-image	BACKGROUND	{ background-image:url('image1.jpg'); }	BACKGROUND="image3.jpg"
layer-background-image		{ layer-background-image:url('image2.jpg'); }	
include-source	SRC	{ include-source: url('myPage.html'); }	SRC="myPage.html"
	onMouseOver		onMouseOver="JSCode"
	onMouseOut		onMouseOut="JSCode"
	onFocus		onFocus="JSCode"
	onBlur		onBlur="JSCode"
	onLoad		onLoad="JSCode"

∞∞∞

JavaScript Layer Object Properties Chart

∞◇∞

Layer Object Property Name JavaScript Syntax	Simple JavaScript Syntax Examples (assume there is a Layer named **myLayer1**)	Read-Only or Read/Write
document	document.write(document.myLayer1.document);	Read-Only
name	myVar=document.name;	Read-Only
left	document.myLayer1.left=20;	Read-Write
top	document.myLayer1.top=30;	Read-Write
pageX	document.myLayer1.pageX=10;	Read-Write
pageY	document.myLayer1.pageY=15;	Read-Write
zIndex	document.myLayer1.zIndex=7;	Read-Write
visibility	document.myLayer1.visibility="hide";	Read-Write
clip.top	document.myLayer1.clip.top=50;	Read-Write
clip.left	document.myLayer1.clip.left=-200;	Read-Write
clip.right	document.myLayer1.clip.right=700;	Read-Write
clip.bottom	document.myLayer1.clip.bottom=500;	Read-Write
clip.width	document.myLayer1.clip.width=640;	Read-Write
clip.height	document.myLayer1.clip.height=480;	Read-Write
background.src	document.myLayer1.background.src="myImage.jpeg";	Read-Write
bgColor	document.myLayer1.bgColor = "#ff0000";	Read-Write
	document.myLayer1.bgColor = "green";	Read-Write
	document.myLayer1.bgColor = null;	Read-Write
siblingAbove	document.myLayer1.siblingAbove;	Read-Only
siblingBelow	document.myLayer1.siblingBelow;	Read-Only
above	document.myLayer1.above;	Read-Only
below	document.myLayer1.below;	Read-Only
parentLayer	document.myLayer1.parentLayer;	Read-Only
src	document.myLayer1.src="myFile.html";	Read-Write

∞◇∞

Generic { font-family: } Names Chart

These are the *generic* Name Values for the **font-family** Property, followed by an example of each that the browser might select from the user's System Fonts:

Generic font-family Names	Example
serif	Times
sans-serif	Helvetica
cursive	Zapf-Chancery
fantasy	Western
monospace	Courier

Styles Chart for HTML Elements

This is a list of all the Elements, including those in HTML 4.0, that you can use the STYLE Attribute or the CLASS Attribute or the ID Attribute with:

∞∞

A	ACRONYM	ADDRESS	B
BIG	BLOCKQUOTE	BODY	BR
BUTTON	CAPTION	CENTER	CITE
CODE	COL	COLGROUP	DD
DEL	DFN	DIR	DIV
DL	DT	EM	FIELDSET
FORM	H1	H2	H3
H4	H5	H6	HR
I	IMG	INPUT	INS
ISINDEX	KBD	LABEL	LEGEND
LI	LINK	MAP	MENU
OBJECT	OL	OPTION	P
PRE	Q	S	SAMP
SELECT	SMALL	SPAN	STRIKE
STRONG	SUB	SUP	TABLE
TBODY	TD	TEXTAREA	TFOOT
TH	THEAD	TR	TT
U	UL	VAR	XMP

∞∞

You can also use them with the following Elements, but at the time of this writing, they will only work in Navigator 4.0+, but more than likely by the time you read this all the other major browsers will recognize them also. If you use cutting-edge code then you should create parallel code to include in Elements like <NOLAYER> and <NOSCRIPT> and additional pages with alternative content to cover all the cross-browser compatability issues. Note that Internet Explorer does not support Style Sheets with JavaScript Syntax.

ILAYER   LAYER

∞∞

Special Notice:

By default, a LAYER is transparent in the sense that other LAYERs that are beneath it will show through except in the places where the actual content, such as text or images, reside.

The <STYLE> Element

The <STYLE> Element is what you use to declare and define a Style Sheet. It always goes in the header of your document between the <HEAD> Element Start and End Tags. There is only one <u>required</u> Attribute called TYPE and its default Value is **"text/CSS"**, which specifies a Style Sheet in Cascading Style Sheet Syntax. You may also declare it as **TYPE="text/JavaScript"** to create a Style Sheet using JavaScript Syntax.

There are certain Keywords that make life much easier. The Keyword **all** is used when you want to define the same Style for all possible HTML Elements all at once. You can define a Style for as many Elements as you want within the STYLE Element, hence the term "Style Sheet." Each Attribute is covered individually in Chapters 1 and 2.

Syntax:

```
<STYLE
TYPE="text/CSS" | "text/JavaScript"
SRC="URL">

      [ Element { PropertyName: Value; } ]
      [ Element.className { PropertyName: Value;} ]
      [ #IDname { PropertyName: Value; } ]
      [ Element Element ... { PropertyName: Value; } ]
...
</STYLE>
```

Attributes Defined:

TYPE="text/CSS" specifies a Style Sheet in the Cascading Style Sheet Syntax.
TYPE="text/JavaScript" specifies a Style Sheet in the JavaScript Syntax.
SRC="URL" specifies the URL of an external Style Sheet to load. See pages 116-123.

Parameters Defined:

Element specifies an HTML Element to apply a Style to.

PropertyName specifies a CSS Property Name followed by a colon and then a **Value**, which is the specific value parameter for that Property and is followed by a semicolon, and together they form a **Name:Value:** pair that is enclosed within curly braces that defines a Style. If you use multiple **Name:Value:** pairs to define a Style they would all be enclosed within the curly braces as a complete Style Definition for that Element.

className specifies a CLASS of STYLE that can be accessed with the CLASS Attribute of most HTML Elements.

IDname specifies a named Style Exception which is identified as such by the preceding hashmark(#) and which can be called to apply to an Element by the ID Attribute.

Element Element ... this is a special way to apply Styles that is called CONTEXTUAL APPLICATION or you could say that it's implemented by specifying CONTEXTUAL SELECTION CRITERIA. When you have sequential Elements in your definition, or put another way, one Element followed by another Element, like this:

    DIV   BLOCKQUOTE

then the Style that you define will only apply to BLOCKQUOTE Elements that are <u>also</u> contained within DIV Elements. The following mini-example demonstrates this by defining a Style that creates a border that is 20 pixels thick and makes the text blue for <u>only</u> BLOCKQUOTE Elements <u>inside</u> DIV Elements. (See Sample202.html on CD-ROM.)

    DIV   BLOCKQUOTE { color: blue; border-width: 20px; }

The next example defines three Styles. It first creates a Style for all PARAGRAPH Elements, which will have green text at a point size of 20. Next, a Style creates bold red text for all BLOCKQUOTE Elements and another Style creates a purple border that is 10 pixels thick and makes the text blue for all BLOCKQUOTE Elements, which are also inside DIV Elements.

```
P { color: green; font-size: 20pt; }
BLOCKQUOTE  { color: red; font-weight: bold; }
DIV  BLOCKQUOTE  { color: blue; border-width: 10px; border-color: purple; }
```

Here's the complete code:

Example 1-3:   **Sample203.html**

```
<!DOCTYPE HTML PUBLIC "-//W3C//DTD HTML 3.2//EN">
<HTML>
<HEAD><TITLE>  Sample 203 - CSS Example 1-3</TITLE>

<STYLE TYPE="text/CSS">

<!--

        P { color: green; font-size: 20pt; }
        BLOCKQUOTE  { color: red; font-weight: bold; }
        DIV    BLOCKQUOTE { color: blue; border-width: 10px; border-color: purple;  }

-->

</STYLE>
```

```
</HEAD>

<BODY>
<P>
Style Sheet Use for Contextual Selection Criteria:        <BR><BR>
Notice how the P Element has green text sized at 20 point.
</P>

<BLOCKQUOTE>
There are two Blockquotes in this example. This is the first one and as this Style
demonstrates, it has bold and red text for all BLOCKQUOTE Elements.
</BLOCKQUOTE>

<DIV><BLOCKQUOTE>
This Style creates a purple border that is 10 pixels thick and overrides the red
text setting above but does not change the Bold parameter which applies to all
BLOCKQUOTE Elements, even CONTEXTUAL ones. The result is that the text is Bold and
Blue for all BLOCKQUOTE Elements inside of DIV Elements like this one.
</BLOCKQUOTE>
</DIV>

</BODY>
</HTML>
```

The concept of CONTEXTUAL SELECTION CRITERIA is covered in much more detail later in this chapter starting at page 93.

Special Notice:

Putting Comments inside Style Sheets is different from putting them inside HTML code. First, they are not Elements and cannot go inside their own Tag. The syntax is also different: For CSS Syntax you include Comments like this:

```
/*     This is a comment.  It can be on
            as many lines as you need.    */
```

For JavaScript Syntax you have two options and can include Comments like this:

```
/*     This is a comment.  It can be on
            as many lines as you need.    */
//     This is a comment that can only be on one line
```

Just in case you forgot, here is an HTML Comment Element:

```
<!--  This is a comment.  -->
```

Example 1-3   Sample203.html

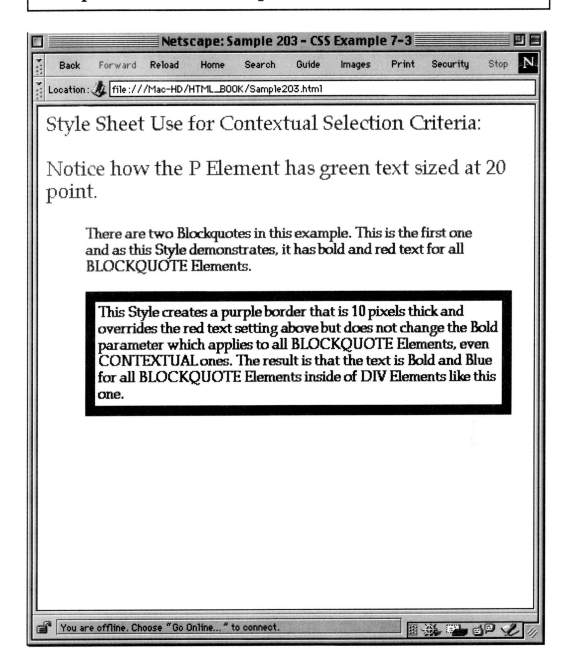

∞∞∞

There are multiple ways to apply CSS Styles to your documents:

- **<STYLE> Element Style**
- **<STYLE> Element with CLASS of STYLE**
- **<STYLE> Element with ID Definition for CLASS Exceptions**
- **<STYLE> Element with CONTEXTUAL SELECTION CRITERIA**
- **STYLE Attribute**
- **<SPAN> Element with CLASS Attribute**
- **<SPAN> Element with ID Attribute for CLASS Exceptions**
- **<LINK> Element to load another document containing an External Style Sheet**
- **<LINK> Elements to load multiple External Style Sheets**
- **Multiple <STYLE> Elements in one document**

Now we'll explore each of these possibilities in detail with lots of examples. It may be helpful to refer to the Properties Chart on pages 11-15 for quick reference and to the more in-depth Property explanations later in this chapter. The Property capabilities are where the real creative possibilities reside. To start all this we'll look at the formatting Properties and then proceed on to the positioning Properties in Chapter 2.

<STYLE> Element Style

The first basic example of this has already been demonstrated in Example 1-1, just to let you know that this isn't a completely new topic. In fact, it's just expanding on the basic syntax contained in the previous section "The <STYLE> Element."

In the following example, we are creating individual Styles for three different Elements: BODY, H2 and DIV.

This is the Style for the BODY Element:

```
BODY   { margin: 50px 20px 25px 72px;
        font-family: Helvetica, Times, Geneva;
        font-size: 12pt;
        font-style: plain;
        background-color: yellow;
       }
```

You should immediately notice that you can declare all four margins with a single Property and that they are <u>not</u> separated by commas.

The margin order is: top-right-bottom-left, so that:

- the   top margin   is 50 pixels thick,
- the   right margin   is 20 pixels thick,
- the   bottom margin   is 25 pixels thick, and
- the   left margin   is 72 pixels thick.

Next, the font is declared by just including the name of the font that you want to use. The reason that more than one font name is supplied is in case the first font isn't in the user's System, Navigator will check and see if the second font listed is available and so on. Listing several fonts that are very similar in look to your first choice will increase your chances of a visual match. If no listed fonts are available, then Navigator will use the default font specified in the user's Preferences.

There is only one way to make sure that the font that you specify is the one that's really used: Use DOWNLOADABLE Fonts. Some fairly safe bets are Helvetica, Courier, and Times. There are five generic **font-family** Property Value <u>Names</u> that will choose something close from the user's System Fonts and they are the **serif**, **sans-serif**, **cursive**, **fantasy**, and **monospace** Families. See the chart at the bottom of page 13 for examples of individual fonts from each category.

Next, the size of the font is specified as 12 point with the **font-size** Property, and then the **font-style** Property specifies that it will be plain. Finally, the background color for the whole document is set to yellow with the **background-color** Property.

Next, the Style for the H1 Element is specified with a Moonlight font that is bold, purple, and sized at 24 point, and the text will be center aligned.

The DIV Element is in 14 point Clarendon font (if available) and it will be bold, green, and indented in the first line only by 72 pixels, which is like having a tab coded in.

Example 1-4:   **Sample204.html**

```
<!DOCTYPE HTML PUBLIC "-//W3C//DTD HTML 3.2//EN">
<HTML><HEAD>    <TITLE>      Sample 204 - CSS Example 1-4  </TITLE>

<STYLE TYPE="text/CSS">
<!--
            /*      The margin order is:    top right bottom left      */

BODY    { margin: 50px 20px 25px 72px;
          font-family: Helvetica, Times, Geneva;
          font-size: 12pt;
          font-style: plain;
          background-color: yellow;
        }

H1      { font-family: Moonlight, Clarendon, Palatino, Helvetica;
          font-size: 24pt;
          text-align: center;
          font-style: bold;
          color:#8800cc;                /*      real purple    */
        }
DIV     { font-family: Clarendon, Palatino, Helvetica;
          font-size: 14pt;
          font-style: bold;
          color: green;
          text-indent: 72px;
        }
-->
```

Example 1-4   Sample204.html

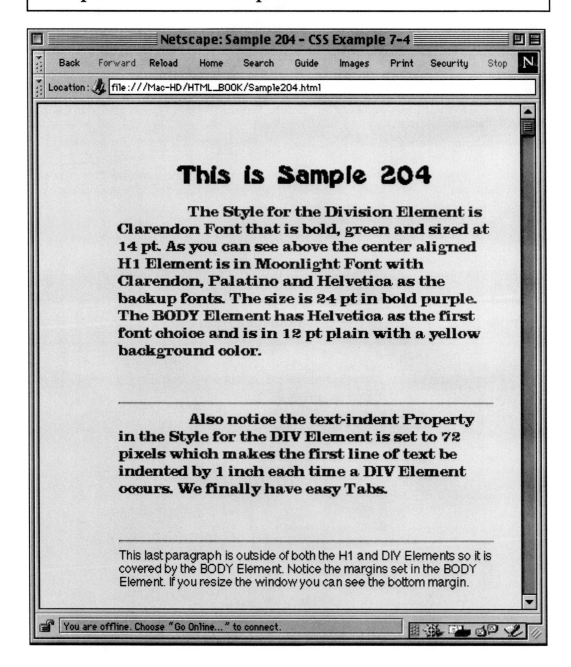

This is Sample 204

The Style for the Division Element is Clarendon Font that is bold, green and sized at 14 pt. As you can see above the center aligned H1 Element is in Moonlight Font with Clarendon, Palatino and Helvetica as the backup fonts. The size is 24 pt in bold purple. The BODY Element has Helvetica as the first font choice and is in 12 pt plain with a yellow background color.

Also notice the text-indent Property in the Style for the DIV Element is set to 72 pixels which makes the first line of text be indented by 1 inch each time a DIV Element occurs. We finally have easy Tabs.

This last paragraph is outside of both the H1 and DIV Elements so it is covered by the BODY Element. Notice the margins set in the BODY Element. If you resize the window you can see the bottom margin.

```
</STYLE>
</HEAD>

<BODY>

<H1>This is Sample 204</H1>

<DIV>
The Style for the Division Element is Clarendon Font that is bold, green and sized
at 14 pt. As you can see above the center aligned H1 Element is in Moonlight Font
with Clarendon, Palatino and Helvetica as the backup fonts. The size is 24 pt in
bold purple. The BODY Element has Helvetica as the first font choice and is in 12
pt plain with a yellow background color.
</DIV><BR><BR><HR>

<DIV>Also notice the text-indent Property in the Style for the DIV Element is set
to 72 pixels which makes the first line of text be indented by 1 inch each time a
DIV Element occurs. We finally have easy Tabs.
</DIV><BR><BR><HR>

This last paragraph is outside of both the H1 and DIV Elements so it is covered by
the BODY Element. Notice the margins set in the BODY Element. If you resize the
window you can see the bottom margin.

</BODY>
</HTML>
```

Cascading Style Sheet Properties

The { font-size: } Property

The **font-size** Property is used to specify the size of your text in one of four ways: **absolute**, **relative**, **length**, or **percentage**. Each of these four categories has its own characteristic strengths of application and is detailed in the syntax below. Personally I find that using the **length** point size is the easiest. The default size is the **absolute** Value of **medium**. If you use standard font sizes like 12, 14, 18 or 24 or if you use **relative** or **percentage** Values you will get more consistent output, especially when printing.

CSS Syntax:

```
{ font-size: absolute|relative|length|percentage; }
```

- *absolute*   uses one of the following seven Keyword options as a fixed size:

  `xx-small, x-small, small, medium, large, x-large, xx-large`

- *relative*   uses one of the following two Keywords to create a size that is relatively larger or smaller than the parent Element's font.

  `larger, smaller`

- *length*   a number followed by a unit of measurement abbreviation. The units of measurement that are recognized by CSS syntax are:

  - `px`   pixels
  - `in`   inches
  - `cm`   centimeters
  - `mm`   millimeters
  - `pt`   points
  - `pc`   picas
  - `em`   height of the font
  - `en`   half the height of the font

- *percentage*   a number followed by a percent sign that creates a size that is a relative percentage of the parent Element's font size.

Here is a usage of each of the four categories:

- *absolute*   `{ font-size: xx-large; }`
- *relative*   `{ font-size: smaller; }`
- *length*   `{ font-size: 24pt; }`
- *percentage*   `{ font-size: 150%; }`

The { font-family: } Property

The **font-family** Property is used to specify any font by name just like the name of font that is contained in your normal System Folder/Font Folder. You are only required to specify one font name, but it's always good practice to list several similar possibilities since the fonts must be contained in the user's System in order for Navigator to use it unless you use Downloadable Fonts. See the Dynamic HTML Guide on the CD-ROM for more info.

There are also five <u>generic</u> safe **font-family** names which aren't specific and are system dependent but offer more variety in terms of appearance. They are: **sans-serif, serif, cursive, fantasy** and **monospace**. Use them as the last font in your list as a fail-safe font if you don't want to rely on the user's Preferences choice which is the default. When you list more than one font, separate each one with a comma and a blank space like so:

`{ font-family: Helvetica, Times, TimesRoman, serif; }`

If the font name that you want to list is composed of two or more words that have a space between them, then you need to enclose the *entire* <u>font name</u> within either quotes or double quotes like this:

```
{ font-family: "Brush Script"; }
```

CSS Syntax:

```
{ font-family: fontName; }
{ font-family: fontName1, fontName2, fontNameN; }
```

The { font-weight: } Property

The **font-weight** Property is used to specify how bold or thick your text will be. You can use a Keyword Name like **bold** or **lighter**, or a whole number from 100 to 900 (in increments of 100) where the larger the number, the bolder the text.

```
{ font-weight:bolder; }
{ font-weight:lighter; }
{ font-weight:500; }
```

CSS Syntax:

```
{ font-weight: normal|bold|bolder|lighter|
           100|200|300|400|500|600|700|800|900; }
```

The { font-style: } Property

The **font-style** Property is used to embellish your text with italics or return it to normal like this:

```
{ font-style:italic; }
{ font-style:normal; }
```

CSS Syntax:

```
{ font-style: normal|italic; }
```

Example 1-5 focuses on the four font Properties that were just explained.

Example 1-5:   Sample205.html

```
<!DOCTYPE HTML PUBLIC "-//W3C//DTD HTML 3.2//EN">
<HTML>
<HEAD>
<TITLE>        Sample 205 - CSS Example 1-5        </TITLE>

<STYLE TYPE="text/CSS">

<!--

H1      { color: olive;
          font-family: Palatino, Moonlight, Clarendon, Helvetica;
          font-size: 30pt;
          font-style: italic;
          font-weight: lighter;
        }
DIV     { color: silver;
          background-color: black;
          font-family: Clarendon, Helvetica;
          font-size: 24pt;
          font-weight: bolder;
        }
-->

</STYLE>
</HEAD>

<BODY>

<H1>This is Sample 205</H1>

<DIV>
        This example focuses on demonstrating font Property characteristics.
</DIV>                                                             <BR><HR>

<DIV>
<IMG SRC="JPEG-FILES/J5-SKY_SPHERE_1.jpg" ALIGN="ABSMIDDLE" WIDTH=360 HEIGHT=245
BORDER=20 HSPACE=10 VSPACE=10 ALT="Sky Sphere">

<H1>    Sky Sphere     </H1>                                      <BR><HR>
        Check out the Image in the Division.
</DIV>                                                             <BR><HR>

<H1>    Do you see the inheritance of the black background color from the DIV Style
to the H1 Element that's inside the DIV Tags which is not applied to this H1.
</H1>

</BODY>

</HTML>
```

The { line-height: } Property

The **line-height** Property is used the same way that leading is used in page layout programs: to set the vertical distance between the baselines of adjacent lines of text. You can only use this Property with block-level Elements. It is specified with a Value that is either the Keyword **normal**, a **number**, **length**, or a **percentage**. The default Value is the Keyword **normal**, which is the normal Value for the current Font that is being used. You can't use negative numbers with any of the following Value types for this Property.

number   When you specify a **number** Value without a unit of measurement, it is the same as multiplying the current Font Size by that **number** and returning that product as the Value of the **line-height** Property. This **number** Value can be a floating point decimal number and it can be less than one but it can't be a negative number. The only real difference between this type of Value and a **percentage** Value is in the way that child Elements will inherit the Value. When using a **number** Value without units attached, the child Element will inherit the actual **number** Value, not the computed Value that is multiplied. When using a **percentage** Value, the child Element will inherit the multiplied Value.

length   Using a **length** type Value means that it is a measurement. This means that it is a number followed by a unit of measurement like **pt** for points or **px** for pixels.
See the charts on pages 11, 12, and 14 on units of measurement for more information on all the possible types of units that are available.

percentage   Using a **percentage** type Value means that the Value that you supply is multiplied by the font size of the current font and that Value is returned as the **line-height** Value. The **percentage** Value is always followed by a percent (%) sign.

Mini-Examples:

Here are a few mini-examples of using the **line-height** Property:

```
{ line-height: normal; }
{ line-height: 1.5; }
{ line-height: 24pt; }
{ line-height: .25in; }
{ line-height: 150%; }
```

CSS Syntax:

```
{ line-height: normal|number|length|percentage; }
```

The { text-decoration: } Property

The **text-decoration** Property is used to embellish your text with one of the following Values:

underline, **line-through**, **blink**, or with the default Value of **none** like this:

Mini-Example: { text-decoration: underline; }

CSS Syntax:

{ text-decoration: none|underline|line-through|blink; }

The { text-transform: } Property

The **text-transform** Property is used to change your text in one of the following four ways and followed by an example. The default Value is **none**.

- **capitalize**   causes the first letter in each word to be in uppercase letters
- **uppercase**   causes all the text to be in uppercase letters
- **lowercase**   causes all the text to be in lowercase letters
- **none**   causes the text to revert to normal, meaning that the inherited Value, if any, is thwarted.

Mini-Example: { text-transform: uppercase; }

CSS Syntax:

{ text-transform: capitalize|uppercase|lowercase|none; }

The { text-align: } Property

The **text-align** Property is used to horizontally align your text with the Keywords of **left**, **right** or it can make the text be centered with **center** or justified with **justify**. The default Value is **left**. Here's a mini-example:

Mini-Example: { text-align: right; }

CSS Syntax:

{ text-align: left|right|center|justify; }

The { text-indent: } Property

The **text-indent** Property is used to indent only the first line of text within an Element. It is specified with either a **length** type Value that is a number followed by a unit of measurement or a **percentage** type Value that is a number followed by a percent (%) sign. When the Value is specifed as a percentage, it is a percentage of the width of the parent Element. The default Value is 0. It only applies to block-level Elements and the Value is inherited. See the charts on pages 11, 12, and 14 on units of measurement for more information on all the possible types of units that are available.

```
{ text-indent: 40px; }   { text-indent: 200%; }
```

CSS Syntax:

```
{ text-indent: length|percentage; }
```

This example focuses on demonstrating the **text-decoration**, **text-transform**, **text-align**, **text-indent**, and **line-height** Properties.

Example 1-6:   **Sample206.html**

```
<!DOCTYPE HTML PUBLIC "-//W3C//DTD HTML 3.2//EN">
<HTML> <HEAD>          <TITLE>         Sample 206 - CSS Example 1-6   </TITLE>

<STYLE TYPE="text/CSS">
<!--
H1      { text-align: center;
          line-height: 50pt;
          text-decoration: line-through;
          text-transform: uppercase;
          text-indent: 40px;
          color: red;
          font-family: Clarendon, Palatino, Helvetica;
          font-size: 24pt;
        }
DIV     { text-align: right;
          line-height: 32pt;
          text-decoration: underline;
          text-transform: capitalize;
          text-indent: 100px;
          color: blue;
          font-family: Palatino, Clarendon, Helvetica;
          font-size: 14pt;
        }
-->
</STYLE>
</HEAD>
```

```
<BODY>

<H1>this is sample 206</H1>

<DIV>   This example focuses on demonstrating text-decoration, text-transform,
text-align, text-indent and line-height.
</DIV>
            <BR><HR>

<DIV>   Notice that the line-height parameter causes the space between the lines to
be greater than normal leading in the DIV tags. The DIV Elements are text-aligned
to the right, blue, underlined and the first letter of each word is capitalized.
</DIV>            <BR><HR>

<DIV>   Also Notice that the text in the H1 Element is all in uppercase letters even
though when it was typed in they were all in lowercase letters.
</DIV>

</BODY>
</HTML>
```

Margins

Margins Overview

This is an overview for the five Properties that deal with setting Margins for your Styles. Each of the individual Margin-type Properties is covered separately after the overview. The group of Margin-type Properties behave differently than you might expect at first glance. They add invisible space around the <u>outside</u> of the Element so that it creates distance <u>between</u> adjacent Elements. When using the **margin** Property you can set all four Margins to have the same Value or they can each have different Values. Don't use negative Margins or else you may get erratic results.

You can also set each one of the Margins individually by using the **margin-top**, **margin-right**, **margin-bottom** and **margin-left** Properties. These Properties are usually used if you don't need a margin around one or more of the sides because you don't have to set all of them; you can just pick and choose the ones you need.

There are six different ways to set the thickness of your Margins for a particular Style by using the following five Properties:

•	**margin**	sets all the Margins at once
•	**margin-top**	sets the top Margin
•	**margin-right**	sets the right Margin
•	**margin-bottom**	sets the bottom Margin
•	**margin-left**	sets the left Margin

The { margin: } Property

The **margin** Property is used to globally set the thickness of your Margins. You can set them all at once to the same value by just specifying one Value like this:

```
{ margin: 20px; }
```

or when you want Margins of different sizes you can set each one all at once by declaring four different Values with a space between each one like this:

```
{ margin: 72px 35px 20px 50px; }
```

so that the:

top margin	is	72 pixels thick
right margin	is	35 pixels thick
bottom margin	is	20 pixels thick
left margin	is	50 pixels thick.

The order of the Margins is always the same and, as shown in the previous code snippet, is:

<u>top-right-bottom-left;</u>

Just think of the order as being clockwise and starting from the top. Note that there are no commas in the Margins list. The possible Value types are **length**, **percentage** and the Keyword **auto**. Note that if you assign a **margin** Property to an Element that has no content in it, then the Margin for that Element is ignored, unless it subsequently is dynamically altered to contain content, then the Margin is implemented.

CSS Syntax:

```
{ margin: length|percentage|auto; }
```

Parameters Defined:

percentage is any positive number suffixed by a percent sign like:

1%-1000%, ...n%

length is a number suffixed by one of the following units of measurement:

```
em, ex, px, pt, pc, in, mm, cm
```

See the charts on page 11, 12, and 14 for more information.

The { margin-top: } Property

The **margin-top** Property is used to set the thickness of the top margin like this:

{ margin-top: 50px; }   { margin-top: 20%; }

CSS Syntax:
{ margin-top: length|percentage; }

The { margin-right: } Property

The **margin-right** Property is used to set the thickness of the right margin like this:

{ margin-right: 20px; }   { margin-right: 25%; }

CSS Syntax:
{ margin-right: length|percentage; }

The { margin-bottom: } Property

The **margin-bottom** Property is used to set the thickness of the bottom margin.

{ margin-bottom: .5in; }   { margin-bottom: 50%; }

CSS Syntax:
{ margin-bottom: length|percentage; }

The { margin-left: } Property

The **margin-left** Property is used to set the thickness of the left margin like this:

{ margin-left: 24pt; }   { margin-left: 40%; }

CSS Syntax:
{ margin-left: length|percentage; }

The following example demonstrates the ability to have individual Margins be of different sizes or omitted altogether. This is accomplished by setting unique **length** Values for the **margin-top, margin-right, margin-bottom** or **margin-left** Properties or by omitting one or more of these properties when any of the four are used in a STYLE.

Example 1-7: **Sample207.html**

```
<!DOCTYPE HTML PUBLIC "-//W3C//DTD HTML 3.2//EN">
<HTML><HEAD><TITLE>   Sample 207 - CSS Example 1-7        Margins        </TITLE>

<STYLE TYPE="text/CSS">

<!--
H1      { margin: 10px;
            text-transform: capitalize; color: red;
            border-style: ridge; border-width: 20px; border-color: purple; }

H2      { margin: 10px 30px 50px 70px;
            text-transform: capitalize; color: red;
            border-style: ridge; border-width: 20px; border-color: blue; }

H3      { margin-top: 35px;
            text-transform: capitalize; color: red;
            border-style: ridge; border-width: 20px; border-color: aqua; }

H4      { margin-right: 177px;
            text-transform: capitalize; color: red;
            border-style: ridge; border-width: 20px; border-color: green; }

H5      { margin-bottom: 2in;
            text-transform: capitalize; color: red;
            border-style: ridge; border-width: 20px; border-color: yellow; }

H6      { margin-left: 100px;
            text-transform: capitalize; color: red;
            border-style: ridge; border-width: 20px; border-color: fuchsia; }

P       { margin-left: 55px; margin-top: 1in; font-size: 17pt;
            border-style: ridge; border-width: 20px; border-color: red; }
-->
</STYLE>
</HEAD>

<BODY>
        <H1>    This is Sample 207      </H1>

<P>Notice that the P Element is set to a left margin of 55 pixels and a top margin
of 1 inch.</P>

<H1>  H1- This is a margin at 10 pixels on all four sides              </H1>
<H2>  H2- This is a margin at 10 30 50 70 pixels for top right bottom left </H2>
<H3>  H3- This is a top margin of 35 pixels                           </H3>
<H4>  H4- This is a right margin of 177 pixels                        </H4>
<H5>  H5- This is a bottom margin of 2 inches                         </H5>
<H6>  H6- This is a left margin of 100 pixels                         </H6>

</BODY>
</HTML>
```

Padding

When you want to create space between the edge or perimeter of an Element and the content inside the Element, you use one of the five Padding Properties. This has the same effect as the CELLPADDING Attribute in a TABLE Element. Think of any Element as consisting of a rectangular block that has an outside, an edge, and an inside. To get your text or image or other content to start and stop at an interior distance from the edge you add Padding space, like an inside margin that applies just to that particular Element. Remember from the last section that the Margin Properties add space to the <u>outside</u> of the Element so that it creates distance <u>between</u> different Elements. The Padding Properties add space to the <u>inside</u> of the Element so that it creates space between the Element edge and the Element content.

When using the **padding** Property you can set all four Paddings to have the same Value or they can each have different Values. You can also set each one of the Paddings individually by using the **padding-top**, **padding-right**, **padding-bottom** and **padding-left** Properties. There are six different ways to set the thickness of your Padding for a particular style by using the following five Properties, which are covered individually afterward:

- **padding**   sets all the Paddings at once
- **padding-top**   sets the top Padding
- **padding-right**   sets the right Padding
- **padding-bottom**   sets the bottom Padding
- **padding-left**   sets the left Padding

The { padding: } Property

The **padding** Property is used to globally set the thickness of your Paddings. You can set them all at once with the same value by just specifying one Value like this:

```
{ padding: 20px; }
```

When you want Paddings of different sizes you can set each one all at once by declaring four different Values with a space between each one, noting there are no commas and the order is <u>top-right-bottom-left</u>:

```
{ padding: 72px 80px 22px 50px; }
```

so that the:

top padding	is	72 pixels thick
right padding	is	80 pixels thick
bottom padding	is	22 pixels thick
left padding	is	50 pixels thick.

CSS Syntax:

```
{ padding: length|percentage; }
```

length is a number suffixed one of these units: em, ex, px, pt, pc, in, mm, cm
percentage is any positive number suffixed by a percent sign like: 1%-1000%, ...n%

The { padding-top: } Property

The **padding-top** Property is used to set the thickness of the top Padding like this:

```
{ padding-top: 50px; }          { padding-top: 20%; }
```

CSS Syntax:

```
{ padding-top: length|percentage; }
```

The { padding-right: } Property

The **padding-right** Property is used to set the thickness of the right Padding.

```
{ padding-right: 20px; }          { padding-right: 25%; }
```

CSS Syntax:

```
{ padding-right: length|percentage; }
```

The { padding-bottom: } Property

The **padding-bottom** Property is used to set the thickness of the bottom Padding.

```
{ padding-bottom: .5in; }          { padding-bottom: 50%; }
```

CSS Syntax:

```
{ padding-bottom: length|percentage; }
```

The { padding-left: } Property

The **padding-left** Property is used to set the thickness of the left Padding.

```
{ padding-left: 24pt; }          { padding-left: 40%; }
```

CSS Syntax:
```
{ padding-left: length|percentage; }
```

This is an example demonstrating the ability to have individual Paddings be of different sizes or omitted altogether. This is accomplished by setting unique **length** Values for the **padding-top, padding-right, padding-bottom,** or **padding-left** Properties or by the omission of one or more of these properties when any of the four are used in a STYLE.

Example 1-8: Sample208.html

```
<!DOCTYPE HTML PUBLIC "-//W3C//DTD HTML 3.2//EN">
<HTML><HEAD><TITLE>   Sample 208 - CSS Example 1-8  Paddings        </TITLE>
<STYLE TYPE="text/CSS">
<!--
H1      { padding: 10px;
          text-transform: capitalize; color: red;
          border-style: ridge; border-width: 20px; border-color: purple; }

H2      { padding: 10px 30px 50px 70px;
          text-transform: capitalize; color: red;
          border-style: ridge; border-width: 20px; border-color: blue; }
H3      { padding-top: 35px;
          text-transform: capitalize; color: red;
          border-style: ridge; border-width: 20px; border-color: aqua; }

H4      { padding-right: 177px;
          text-transform: capitalize; color: red;
          border-style: ridge; border-width: 20px; border-color: green; }

H5      { padding-bottom: 2in;
          text-transform: capitalize; color: red;
          border-style: ridge; border-width: 20px; border-color: yellow; }

H6      { padding-left: 100px;
          text-transform: capitalize; color: red;
          border-style: ridge; border-width: 20px; border-color: fuchsia; }

P       { padding-left: 55px; padding-top: 1in; font-size: 17pt;
          border-style: ridge; border-width: 20px; border-color: red; }
-->
</STYLE>
</HEAD>
<BODY>          <H1>   This is Sample 208     </H1>
<P>Notice that the P Element is set to a left padding of 55 pixels and a top
padding of 1 inch.</P>

<H1>H1- This is a padding at 10 pixels on all four sides                </H1>
<H2>H2- This is a padding at 10 30 50 70 pixels for top right bottom left   </H2>
<H3>H3- This is a top padding of 35 pixels                          </H3>
<H4>H4- This is a right padding of 177 pixels                       </H4>
<H5>H5- This is a bottom padding of 2 inches                        </H5>
<H6>H6- This is a left padding of 100 pixels                        </H6>
</BODY>
</HTML>
```

Color

In CSS Syntax, there are three Properties that allow you to manipulate the color in your styles directly. They all work exactly the same way but operate on different aspects of your document. The **color** Property controls the foreground color, which is the color of the text in the Element that it is applied to. The **background-color** Property controls the background color of the Element it is applied to, and finally there is the **border-color**, Property which changes the color of your border from the default color that it inherits from the foreground color of the BODY Element.

In CSS Syntax, you have more ways to specify the color than in HTML. You can use a recognized color Name, including all the JavaScript color Names (see Appendix B), a Hexadecimal triplet and you can also express it by using the **rgb( )** Function.

The **rgb( )** Function takes the three Arguments of **redArg**, **greenArg**, and **blueArg** which represent the Red, Green, and Blue Values of a total color. They are separated by commas and can be either numbers from 0 to 255 or a percentage from 0 to 100%. If a percentage is used, the percent (%) sign must follow the number for each Argument.

CSS Syntax:

```
rgb(redArg, greenArg, blueArg)
rgb(redArg%, greenArg%, blueArg%)
```

The numbers used in the 0-255 measurement scheme go from the lowest, which represents no color, to 255, which represents full color, so that:

rgb (255, 0, 0)	means:	full red, no green, no blue	=	red
rgb (255, 0, 255)	means:	full red, no green, full blue	=	plum
rgb (0, 0, 255)	means:	no red, no green, full blue	=	blue
rgb (0, 255, 255)	means:	no red, full green, full blue	=	aqua
rgb (0, 255, 0)	means:	no red, full green, no blue	=	lime
rgb (255, 255, 0)	means:	full red, full green, no blue	=	yellow
rgb (255, 255, 255)	means:	full red, full green, full blue	=	white
rgb (0, 0, 0)	means:	no red, no green, no blue	=	black
rgb (100%, 0%, 0%)	means:	full red, no green, no blue	=	red
rgb (100%, 0%, 100%)	means:	full red, no green, full blue	=	plum
rgb (0%, 0%, 100%)	means:	no red, no green, full blue	=	blue
rgb (0%, 100%, 100%)	means:	no red, full green, full blue	=	aqua
rgb (0%, 100%, 0%)	means:	no red, full green, no blue	=	lime
rgb (100%, 100%, 0%)	means:	full red, full green, no blue	=	yellow
rgb (100%, 100%, 100%)	means:	full red, full green, full blue	=	white
rgb (0%, 0%, 0%)	means:	no red, no green, no blue	=	black

The { color: } Property

The **color** Property is quite straightforward; it lets you choose the foreground color of your Element, which changes the color of your text. Here are the four ways to express foreground color:

```
{ color: silver; }              { color:#e35a77; }
{ color: rgb(5, 220, 250); }    { color: rgb(38%, 43%, 69%); }
```

CSS Syntax:

```
{ color: colorname|#$$$$$$|rgb(0-255,0-255,0-255)|
                      rgb(0-100%,0-100%,0-100%); }
```

This example focuses on specifying foreground color using the **color** Property.

Example 1-9:   **Sample209.html**

```
<!DOCTYPE HTML PUBLIC "-//W3C//DTD HTML 3.2//EN">
<HTML>
<HEAD>
<TITLE> Sample 209 - CSS Example 1-9  The color Property     </TITLE>

<STYLE TYPE="text/CSS">
<!--

H1     { color: blue;
         border-style: ridge; border-width: 20px; border-color: purple; }

H2     { color: rgb(155,0,255);
         border-style: ridge; border-width: 20px; border-color: blue; }

H3     { color: rgb(0,57,155);
         border-style: ridge; border-width: 20px; border-color: aqua; }

H4     { color: rgb(0%,50%,0%);
         border-style: ridge; border-width: 20px; border-color: green; }

H5     { color: rgb(90%,0%,5%);
         border-style: ridge; border-width: 20px; border-color: yellow; }

H6     { color:#7705dd;
         border-style: ridge; border-width: 20px; border-color: fuchsia; }

P      { color:#ef4499;
         font-size: 17pt;
         border-style: ridge; border-width: 20px; border-color: red; }
-->
</STYLE>
```

```
</HEAD>

<BODY>

<H1>This is Sample 209</H1>

<P>Notice that the all the different heading types have unique foreground colors
which controls the text color.</P>

<H1>          This is a H1 Heading                    </H1>
<H2>          This is a H2 Heading                    </H2>
<H3>          This is a H3 Heading                    </H3>
<H4>          This is a H4 Heading                    </H4>
<H5>          This is a H5 Heading                    </H5>
<H6>          This is a H6 Heading                    </H6>

</BODY>
</HTML>
```

Example 1-9   Sample209.html

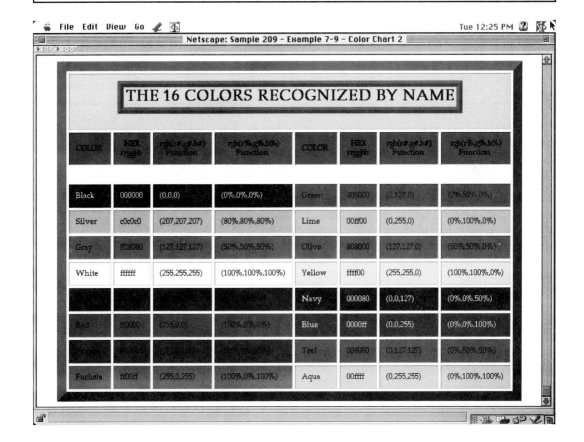

The { background-color: } Property

The **background-color** Property lets you choose the color of the background of each Element. You can use a recognized color Name, Hexadecimal triplet, or you can use the **rgb( )** Function, which allows you to specify an rgb triplet using regular numbers or as a percentage, which may be more familiar to artists, graphic designers, Photoshop users, and other image-editing afficionados. Here are four examples of ways to specify the background color of a Style for an Element with the **background-color** Property:

```
{ background-color: olive; }
{ background-color:#aaca77; }
{ background-color: rgb(155, 120, 50); }
{ background-color: rgb(50%, 0%, 90%); }
```

CSS Syntax:

```
{ background-color: colorname|#$$$$$$|rgb(0-255,0-255,0-255)|
                                  rgb(0-100%,0-100%,0-100%); }
```

Example 1-10 focuses on the **background-color** Property.

Example 1-10:   Sample210.html

```
<!DOCTYPE HTML PUBLIC "-//W3C//DTD HTML 3.2//EN">
<HTML>
<HEAD>

<TITLE> Sample 210 - CSS Example 1-10 The background-color Property </TITLE>

<STYLE TYPE="text/CSS">

<!--

H1      { background-color: blue;
          border-style: ridge; border-width: 20px; border-color: purple; }

H2      { background-color: rgb(155,0,255);
          border-style: ridge; border-width: 20px; border-color: blue; }
```

```
H3        { background-color: rgb(0,57,155);
            border-style: ridge; border-width: 20px; border-color: aqua; }

H4        { background-color: rgb(0%,50%,0%);
            border-style: ridge; border-width: 20px; border-color: green; }

H5        { background-color: rgb(90%,0%,5%);
            border-style: ridge; border-width: 20px; border-color: yellow; }

H6        { background-color:#7705dd;
            border-style: ridge; border-width: 20px; border-color: fuchsia; }

P         { background-color:#ef4499;
            font-size: 17pt;
            border-style: ridge; border-width: 20px; border-color: red; }

-->

</STYLE>

</HEAD>

<BODY TEXT="#eeeeee" BGCOLOR="#000000">

<H1>This is Sample 210</H1>

<P>This example is exactly the same as Sample 208 except that the colors used are
for the background instead of the foreground. Because no foreground color is
specified, all of the Heading Elements inherit it from the BODY Element since they
are contained within it.</P>

<H1>          This is a H1 Heading          </H1>
<H2>          This is a H2 Heading          </H2>
<H3>          This is a H3 Heading          </H3>
<H4>          This is a H4 Heading          </H4>
<H5>          This is a H5 Heading          </H5>
<H6>          This is a H6 Heading          </H6>

</BODY>

</HTML>
```

Check out the color chart in Appendix B on pages 1033-1037 for a huge list of all the JavaScript color Names and their Hexadecimal, and rgb number and percentage Value equivalents. This information is also contained in a file on the CD-ROM named AppendixB-ChartOnly.html, that's in the HTML_BOOK-Online Folder, that's in the DHTML-JS_BOOK-Main_Files Folder. It uses Arrays, a **for()** Loop, and **document.write()** in a JavaScript Script to output the data, and it renders the actual color behind the text. In Appendix B there is also a treatise on additive color theory if you're interested in how color works in the visible light spectrum. There is a color conversion calculator that uses

JavaScript to convert colors to and from a variety of formats on pages 340-350.

The { background-image: } Property

The **background-image** Property lets you choose an image to display behind the content of your Element. You can have a different image for each Element that you create a Style for. This background image will be tiled as many times as is necessary to fill the space that is assigned to that Element. Here's an example of how to code a background image into your Style, noting that (JPEG-FILES) is the folder that contains the actual image and the image file has a relative **urlName** of (ExampleImage.jpeg) :

```
{ background-image: url(JPEG-FILES/ExampleImage.jpeg); }
```

In the syntax note that the "<u>l</u>" in **url** and the <u>left parentheses</u> "<u>(</u>" in **(urlName)** must not be separated by any blank spaces and the **urlName** is not enclosed in quotes.

CSS Syntax:

```
{ background-image: url(urlName); }
```

This example focuses on the **background-image** Property.

Example 1-11:   Sample211.html

```
<!DOCTYPE HTML PUBLIC "-//W3C//DTD HTML 3.2//EN">
<HTML>
<HEAD>
<TITLE> Sample 211 - CSS Example 1-11    Background Images  </TITLE>

<STYLE TYPE="text/CSS">

<!--

BODY    { font-size: 36pt; }

H1      { background-image: url(./JPEG-FILES/icon-BG-asteroids.jpg);
          border-style: ridge; border-width: 20px; border-color: purple; padding: 30px;
          background-color: white;}

H2      { background-image: url(./JPEG-FILES/Icon-Clouds.jpg);
          border-style: ridge; border-width: 20px; border-color: blue; padding: 72px; }
```

```
H3        { background-image: url(./JPEG-FILES/icon-BG-stars.jpg);
            border-style: ridge; border-width: 20px; border-color: aqua; padding: 144px; }
H4        { background-image: url(./JPEG-FILES/icon-FieldStone-Purple.jpeg);
            border-style: ridge; border-width: 20px; border-color: green; padding: 100px; }

H5        { background-image: url(./JPEG-FILES/icon-Paint-Palette.jpg);
            border-style: ridge; border-width: 20px; border-color: yellow; padding: 144px; }

H6        { background-image: url(./dreamplay-website/JPEG-FILES/J2-JERRY_GARCIA-2-RS.jpg);
            border-style: ridge; border-width: 20px; border-color: fuchsia; padding: 50px;
            color: white;}

P         { background-color:#ccccff;
            font-size: 17pt;
            border-style: ridge; border-width: 20px; border-color: red; }

-->

</STYLE>

</HEAD>

<BODY TEXT="#0000ff" BGCOLOR="#000000">

<H1>   This is Sample 211     </H1>

<P>    Make sure that there are no blank spaces between the last letter of (url)
and the first parentheses containing the urlName. This is correct: url(urlName) and
this is wrong: url (urlName).                                      <BR><BR>
Also notice that the image tiles or repeats to fill up the available or assigned
space.</P>

<H1>           This is a H1 Heading               </H1>
<H2>           This is a H2 Heading               </H2>
<H3>           This is a H3 Heading               </H3>
<H4>           This is a H4 Heading               </H4>
<H5>           This is a H5 Heading               </H5>
<H6>           This is a H6 Heading               </H6>

</BODY>
</HTML>
```

Example 1-12 uses a lot of the Properties that have been discussed so far. Check it out and make sure everything in it is familiar. Some details to be aware of are: The BODY Element has a **margin** Property assigned, which causes each of the Elements contained in the BODY to have a 20 pixel Margin around it also.

Since the CITE Element also has a **margin** Property assigned to it, the effect is cumulative; that is, all CITE Elements will have 20 pixels of Margin from the BODY Element added to its own 10 pixels of Margin.

If you look at the example in a browser you will see that there is more distance between Elements that are adjacent to a CITE Element than the others which don't have explicit **margin** Properties within their Style Definition. Also remember that H1 and PRE Elements are BLOCK LEVEL Elements and have a built-in line-break while the CITE and

Example 1-12:   Sample212.html

```
<!DOCTYPE HTML PUBLIC "-//W3C//DTD HTML 3.2//EN">
<HTML>
<HEAD>
<TITLE> Sample 212 - CSS Example 1-12   Compilation  </TITLE>

<STYLE TYPE="text/CSS">

<!--

BODY    { margin: 20px; background-color:#7777cc;}

H3      { font-family: Clarendon, Moonlight, Palatino, Helvetica;
          font-size: 30pt;
          text-align: center;
          font-style: bold;
          color: blue;
          border-width:.25in;
          border-style: groove;
          border-color:#335a77;
          margin: 20px;
          background-color:#755f11;            /*      metallic gold  */
        }
PRE     { font-family: Brush Script,Geneva, Palatino, Helvetica;
          font-size: 19pt;
          font-style: plain;
          color: black;
          text-indent: 45px;
          line-height: 30pt;
          border-width:.25in;
          border-style: inset;
          border-color: blue;
          background-color: aqua;
          margin: 15px;
        }
CITE    { font-family: Bellevue, New York, Geneva, Times;
          font-size: 25pt;
          font-style: italic;
          text-align: center;
          color: red;
          line-hcight: 45pt;
          border-width: 10mm;
          border-style: outset;
          border-color: lime;
          background-color: yellow;
          margin: 10px;
          margin: 20px;
        }
XMP     { font-family: Helvetica, Times, New York, Geneva;
          font-size: 18pt;
          font-style: bold;
          text-align: center;
          color: maroon;
          border-width: 10mm;
```

```
            border-style: ridge;
            border-color: purple;
            background-color: gray;
            margin: 40px;
            white-space: pre;
        }
-->

</STYLE>

</HEAD>

<BODY>

<H3>    This is Sample 212     </H3>

<CITE>  There are a lot of Properties in this example.                    </CITE>
<PRE>   The Site still has their website. You should email them to let the powers
that be know that they should reinstate the show. Bring back Dev.          </PRE>

<XMP>
This example has a lot of
borders in it but the
next example is the one with
all border style possibilities.

If you don't
explicitly code in the
white-space Property to "pre" then even
with an XMP Tag or a PRE Tag the
white-space will collapse because in
Style Sheet syntax white-space is
collapsed by default.

Below are all the
Properties used in the
Style for the XMP Element.


        { font-family: Helvetica, Times, New York, Geneva;
          font-size: 18pt;
          font-style: bold;
          text-align: center;
          color: maroon;
          border-width: 10mm;
          border-style: ridge;
          border-color: purple;
          background-color: gray;
          margin: 40px;
          white-space: pre;
        }
</XMP>

</BODY>
</HTML>
```

Setting Borders

The { border-style: } Property

By using the **border-style** Property you can highlight your content by choosing to surround it with either 2D or 3D raised borders. The **solid** and **double** styles are 2D, and the **inset**, **outset**, **groove**, and **ridge** styles are all 3D shaded. You also have the option of creating borders that have less than four sides if you want to experiment with graphical innovation. Try nesting your content within Elements that all have borders for some very interesting effects. The default value is **none**, which may also be chosen using JavaScript if you are creating Styles that change. Remember to include a **border-width** Property Value as part of your Style Definition or else it will be invisible because by default it has a Value of zero. For more info on setting Border Widths, see pages 52-58.

This is an example of a 3D **border-style**:

```
{ border-style: groove }
```

CSS Syntax:

```
{ border-style: none|solid|double|inset|outset|groove|ridge; }
```

This example covers all the Values of the **border-style** Property except for **none**.

Example 1-13:   **Sample213.html**

```
<!DOCTYPE HTML PUBLIC "-//W3C//DTD HTML 3.2//EN">
<HTML><HEAD>
<TITLE> Sample 213 - CSS Example 1-13          Border Styles  </TITLE>

<STYLE TYPE="text/CSS">
<!--

BODY    { margin: 10px; font-size: 30pt;
          border-style: ridge; border-width: 10px;
          font-family: Clarendon, Moonlight, Palatino, Helvetica;
        }
H1      { border-style: solid;
          border-width: 20px;
          border-color:#ff0000;
          margin: 10px;
          background-color:#755f11;          /*      metallic gold  */
        }
```

```
H2      { border-style: double;
          border-width: 20px;
          border-color: blue;
          margin: 10px;
          background-color:#755f11;         /*      metallic gold  */
        }
H3      { border-style: inset;
          border-width: 20px;
          border-color: green;
          margin: 10px;
          background-color:#755f11;         /*      metallic gold  */
        }
H4      { border-style: outset;
          border-width: 20px;
          border-color: aqua;
          margin: 10px;
          background-color:#755f11;         /*      metallic gold  */
        }
H5      { border-style: groove;
          border-width: 20px;
          border-color: purple;
          margin: 10px;
          background-color:#755f11;         /*      metallic gold  */
        }
H6      { border-style: ridge;
          border-width: 20px;
          border-color: maroon;
          margin: 10px;
          background-color:#755f11;         /*      metallic gold  */
        }
P       { font-size: 14pt;
          border-style: none;
          border-width: 20px;
          border-color: maroon;
          margin: 10px;
          background-color:#755f11;         /*      metallic gold  */
        }
-->
</STYLE>
</HEAD>
<BODY>
<P>    Notice that the P Element is set to a border-style of NONE which contains
this paragraph. Also notice that the font size is globally set in the BODY Style so
it applies to all of the Elements contained within the BODY Tags, even to the
following HEADING Elements which would normally be of different sizes. The BODY
Element even has a border and it's inside of the margins.          </P>

        <H1>    This is a solid border         </H1>
        <H2>    This is a double border        </H2>
        <H3>    This is an inset border        </H3>
        <H4>    This is an outset border       </H4>
        <H5>    This is a groove border        </H5>
        <H6>    This is a ridge border         </H6>
</BODY>
</HTML>
```

The { border-color: } Property

The **border-color** Property is quite straightforward; it lets you choose the color of the border surrounding your Element. In CSS Syntax you have more ways to specify the color than in straight HTML. Using a recognized color Name and the old standby Hexadecimal triplet are both still available but now you can also express it as an **rgb( )** Function triplet using regular numbers or as a percentage. See page 37 or Appendix B for more information on Color. Here are the four ways to express **border-color**:

```
{ border-color: purple; }
{ border-color:#335a77; }
{ border-color: rgb(255, 20, 150); }
{ border-color: rgb(20%, 50%, 70%); }
```

CSS Syntax:

```
{ border-color: colorname|#$$$$$$|rgb(0-255,0-255,0-255)|
                          rgb(0-100%,0-100%,0-100%); }
```

This example focuses on **border-color** examples. At the end of this example there are nested Elements that each have a **border-style** so that it looks like you have nested borders, which is not normally possible using standard Property code.

Example 1-14:   Sample214.html

```
<!DOCTYPE HTML PUBLIC "-//W3C//DTD HTML 3.2//EN">
<HTML>
<HEAD>
<TITLE> Sample 214 - CSS Example 1-14         border-color Properties</TITLE>

<STYLE TYPE="text/CSS">

<!--
                              /*  Remember these are CSS comments  */
H1      { border-style: solid;
          border-width: 20px;
          border-color: blue;
          padding: 10px;
          background-color: rgb(255, 100, 0);        /*      orange        */
        }
H2      { border-style: double;
          border-width: 20px;
          border-color: rgb(55, 200, 50);        /*      medium green   */
          padding: 10px;
          background-color:#755f11;               /*      metallic gold  */
        }
```

```
H3      { border-style: inset;
          border-width: 20px;
          border-color: rgb(50%, 0%, 98%);         /*      purple      */
          padding: 10px;
          background-color: rgb(15%, 0%, 98%);      /*      dark blue   */
        }
H4      { border-style: outset;
          border-width: 20px;
          border-color: rgb(15, 200, 150);          /*      water green */
          padding: 10px;
          background-color: rgb(100%, 0%, 0%);      /*      red         */
        }
H5      { border-style: groove;
          border-width: 20px;
          border-color: rgb(50%, 100%, 20%);        /*      lime green  */
          padding: 10px;
          background-color:#955f31;                 /*      red metallic gold  */
        }
H6      { border-style: ridge;
          border-width: 20px;
          border-color: rgb(155, 0, 250);           /*      plum        */
          padding: 10px;
          background-color:#457e71;                 /*      metallic aqua  */
        }
P       { font-size: 14pt;
          border-style: groove;
          border-width: 20px;
          border-color:#255fa1;                     /*      steel blue  */
          padding: 10px;
          background-color:#959f51;                 /*      metallic green */
        }
-->
</STYLE></HEAD>

<BODY>
<P>    Most of the settings in this example are the same as in the last example to
let you focus on the border-colors. Notice that the following HEADING Elements are
rendered in their normal  sizes this time because there are no overriding
Properties to inherit.</P>

<H1><H2><H3>   This is an inset border H3 inside a double border H2 inside a solid
border H1      </H3></H2></H1>

<H5><H4>       This is an outset border inside a groove border      </H4></H5>

<H4><H5><H6>   This is a ridge border H6 inside a groove border H5 inside an outset
border H4      </H6></H5></H4>

Just below is an empty H6 heading. Very interesting. Spark any graphical insights?
<H6></H6>

</BODY></HTML>
```

Example 1-15 shows nested Elements that each have a **border-style** so that it creates a nested rainbow multiborder.

Example 1-15: **Sample215.html**

```
<!DOCTYPE HTML PUBLIC "-//W3C//DTD HTML 3.2//EN">
<HTML><HEAD><TITLE>   Sample 215 - CSS Example 1-15      Nested Borders   </TITLE>

<STYLE TYPE="text/CSS">
<!--
                                      /*  Remember these are CSS comments  */
H1       { border-style: solid;
           border-width: 20px;
           border-color: rgb(155, 0, 255);
           background-color: blue;                 /*       orange       */
         }
H2       { border-style: double;
           border-width: 20px;
           border-color: blue;                     /*       medium green  */
           background-color: rgb(0%, 100%, 100%);   /*       metallic gold */
         }
H3       { border-style: inset;
           border-width: 20px;
           border-color: rgb(0%, 100%, 100%);       /*       purple       */
           background-color: rgb(0, 255, 0)    ;    /*       dark blue     */
         }
H4       { border-style: outset;
           border-width: 20px;
           border-color: rgb(0, 255, 0);           /*       water green   */
           background-color: rgb(100%, 100%, 0%);   /*       red          */
         }
H5       { border-style: groove;
           border-width: 20px;
           border-color: rgb(100%, 100%, 0%);       /*       lime green    */
           background-color: rgb(255, 0, 0);        /*       red metallic gold  */
         }
H6       { border-style: ridge;
           border-width: 20px;
           border-color: rgb(255, 0, 0);           /*       plum         */
           background-color: red;                   /*       metallic aqua */
           font-size: 24pt;
         }
-->
</STYLE>
</HEAD>

<BODY>
<H1><H2><H3><H4><H5><H6>Rainbow Land</H6></H5></H4></H3></H2></H1>
</BODY>
</HTML>
```

Example 1-16 shows two instances of nested Elements that each have a Property of **border-style** so that it creates a nested rainbow multiple border that has inherited white backgrounds from the BODY Element instead of explicitly specifying them.

Example 1-16:   **Sample216.html**

```
<!DOCTYPE HTML PUBLIC "-//W3C//DTD HTML 3.2//EN">
<HTML>
<HEAD>
<TITLE> Sample 216 - CSS Example 1-16  Nested Rainbow Borders</TITLE>

<STYLE TYPE="text/CSS">

<!--
                                /*  Remember these are CSS comments  */

H1      { border-style: solid;
          border-width: 20px;
          border-color: rgb(255, 0, 255);          /*      plum        */
        }
H2      { border-style: double;
          border-width: 20px;
          border-color: blue;                       /*      medium green */
        }
H3      { border-style: inset;
          border-width: 20px;
          border-color: rgb(0%, 100%, 100%);        /*      purple      */
        }
H4      { border-style: outset;
          border-width: 20px;
          border-color: rgb(0, 255, 0);             /*      water green */
        }
H5      { border-style: groove;
          border-width: 20px;
          border-color: rgb(100%, 100%, 0%);        /*      lime green  */
        }
H6      { border-style: ridge;
          border-width: 20px;
          border-color: rgb(255, 0, 0);             /*      red         */
          font-size: 24pt;
        }

-->

</STYLE>
</HEAD>

<BODY>

<H1><H2><H3><H4><H5><H6>Rainbow Land</H6></H5></H4></H3></H2></H1>

<H6><H5><H4><H3><H2><H1>Rainbow Land</H1></H2></H3></H4></H5></H6>

</BODY>
</HTML>
```

Border Widths

When you use the **border-style** Property to augment your content with a graphical Border of either **solid**, **double**, **inset**, **outset**, **groove**, or **ridge** style, you also must specify one of the five Border Width Properties listed below. The reason for this is that a Border has zero thickness by default, until you specify a width for it. You can set your Borders to all have the same thickness, or each side of the Border can have a unique width. You can even have a three-sided Border where each side has a different width. There are six different ways to set the thickness, that is, the width of your Borders, by using any of the following five Properties:

- **border-width**
- **border-top-width**
- **border-right-width**
- **border-bottom-width**
- **border-left-width**

The { border-width: } Property

The **border-width** Property is used to set the thickness of your borders globally. You can set them all at once with the same value by just specifying one Value like this:

```
{ border-width: 20px; }
```

or you can set them all at once by declaring four different Values with a space between each one like this:

```
{ border-width: 10px 20px 30px 40px; }
```

The order of the borders in this case would be <u>top-right-bottom-left</u>; just think of the order as being clockwise from the top.

CSS Syntax:

```
{ border-width: length|percentage; }
```

length is a number suffixed by one of the following units of measurement:

```
em, ex, px, pt, pc, in, mm, cm
```

See the charts on page 11-12, 14 for more information on units of measurement.

percentage is any positive number suffixed by a percent sign like: 1%-1000%, ...n%

The { border-top-width: } Property

The **border-top-width** Property is used to set the thickness of the top side of your border like this:

```
{ border-top-width: 20px; }
```

CSS Syntax:

```
{ border-top-width: length|percentage; }
```

The { border-right-width: } Property

The **border-right-width** Property is used to set the thickness of the right side of your border like this:

```
{ border-right-width: 20px; }
```

CSS Syntax:

```
{ border-right-width: length|percentage; }
```

The { border-bottom-width: } Property

The **border-bottom-width** Property is used to set the thickness of the bottom side of your border like this:

```
{ border-bottom-width: 20px; }
```

CSS Syntax:

```
{ border-bottom-width: length|percentage; }
```

The { border-left-width: } Property

The **border-left-width** Property is used to set the thickness of the left side of your border like this:

```
{ border-left-width: 20px; }
```

CSS Syntax:

```
{ border-left-width: length|percentage; }
```

This is an example demonstrating the ability to have individual sides of one total border be of different sizes or omitted altogether. This is accomplished by setting unique *length* values for the following Properties or by the omission of one or more of these Properties when any of the four are used in a STYLE:

border-top-width: *length;*
border-right-width: *length;*
border-bottom-width: *length;*
border-left-width: *length;*

It also demonstrate the **border-width** Property.

Example 1-17: Sample217.html

```
<!DOCTYPE HTML PUBLIC "-//W3C//DTD HTML 3.2//EN">
<HTML>
<HEAD><TITLE>  Sample 217 - CSS Example 1-17</TITLE>

<STYLE TYPE="text/CSS">
<!--

BODY    { margin: 10px; font-size: 30pt; background-color:#aaccbb;
          border-style: ridge; border-width: 10px;
          font-family: Bellevue, Clarendon, Moonlight, Helvetica;
        }

H1      { border-style: solid;
          border-top-width: 5px;
          border-right-width: 10px;
          border-bottom-width: 20px;
          border-left-width: 25px;
          border-color:#ff0000;
          margin: 10px;
          background-color:#665599;        /*    metallic purple    */
        }
H2      { border-style: double;
          border-top-width: 20px;
          border-right-width: 20px;
          border-bottom-width: 20px;
          border-color: blue;
          margin: 10px;
          background-color:#665599;        /*    metallic purple    */
        }
H3      { border-style: inset;
          border-top-width: 20px;
          border-right-width: 20px;
          border-color: green;
          margin: 10px;
          background-color:#665599;        /*    metallic purple    */
        }
```

```
H4      { border-style: outset;
          border-right-width: 20px;
          border-left-width: 25px;
          border-color: aqua;
          margin: 10px;
          background-color:#665599;        /*    metallic purple    */
        }
H5      { border-style: groove;
          border-top-width: 20px;
          border-bottom-width: 20px;
          border-color: purple;
          margin: 10px;
          background-color:#665599;        /*    metallic purple    */
        }
H6      { border-style: ridge;
          border-left-width: 20px;
          border-right-width: 20px;
          border-bottom-width: 20px;
          border-color: maroon;
          margin: 10px;
          background-color:#665599;        /*    metallic purple    */
        }
P       { font-size: 18pt;
          border-style: none;
          border-width: 20px;
          border-color: maroon;
          margin: 10px;
          background-color:#665599;        /*    metallic purple    */
        }

-->

</STYLE>
</HEAD>

<BODY>

<P>     This example demonstrates the ability to have the sides of your borders be
of different sizes or omitted. Netscape doesn't seem to have nailed the math down
on getting the borders to match up precisely when certain sides of certain styles
are used, at least on the Mac Platform. If the size of your text in the headings is
not all 30pt, try holding the Shift Key down and hitting the reload button in your
browser.                                  </P>

          <H1>    This is a solid border     </H1>
          <H2>    This is a double border    </H2>
          <H3>    This is an inset border    </H3>
          <H4>    This is an outset border   </H4>
          <H5>    This is a groove border    </H5>
          <H6>    This is a ridge border     </H6>

</BODY>
</HTML>
```

This example shows a chart of the 16 universally recognized color names. On the CD-ROM, there is a color chart in Sample43.html showing those colors. This is a variation of that example which has Border Styles applied to HEADING Elements inside of a TABLE Element and it includes the **rgb()** Function Values for each color. When looking at the code, recognize that each TABLE ROW has 8 CELLS but each CELL has its code on its own line in the text editor. Where the individual instances of the FONT Element are inserted, they provide contrast between the background color of the CELL and the text color.

Example 1-18:   **Sample218.html**

```
<!DOCTYPE HTML PUBLIC "-//W3C//DTD HTML 3.2//EN">
<HTML>

<HEAD>
<TITLE> Sample 218 - Example 1-18  - Color Chart 2   </TITLE>

<STYLE TYPE="text/CSS">

<!--

H1      { border-style: ridge;
          border-width: 10px;
          font-size: 24pt;
          border-color: rgb(255, 0, 0);
          float: center;
        }

H2      { border-style: groove;
          border-width: 15px;
          border-color: rgb(55, 0, 255);
          color: rgb(255, 255, 255);
          background-color: rgb(175, 175, 25);
          padding: 15px;
          font-size: 30pt;
          float: center;
          font-family: Brush Script, Moonlight, Clarendon;
        }

-->

</STYLE>

</HEAD>

<BODY BGCOLOR="#ffffff" TEXT="#000000">

<H2>CSS COLOR CHART</H2>

<TABLE BORDER="15" CELLSPACING="4" CELLPADDING="10"
        BGCOLOR="#00ffff" BORDERCOLOR="#7700ff" ALIGN="CENTER">
```

```
<TR>
<TH COLSPAN="8">
<FONT SIZE="6">          <H1>THE 16 COLORS RECOGNIZED BY NAME</H1>      </FONT></TH>
</TR>


<TR WIDTH="140" BGCOLOR="#755f11">
<TH> COLOR </TH>
<TH> HEX<BR>rrggbb </TH>
<TH> rgb(r#,g#,b#)<BR>Function </TH>
<TH> rgb(r%,g%,b%)<BR>Function </TH>
<TH> COLOR </TH>
<TH> HEX<BR>rrggbb </TH>
<TH> rgb(r#,g#,b#)<BR>Function </TH>
<TH> rgb(r%,g%,b%)<BR>Function </TH>
</TR>



<TR>
<TH></TH>        <!--  This creates the White Bar under the Table Headings   -->
</TR>


<TR WIDTH="140">
<TD BGCOLOR="#000000"><FONT COLOR="#ffffff">Black</FONT></TD>
<TD BGCOLOR="#000000"><FONT COLOR="#ffffff">000000</FONT></TD>
<TD BGCOLOR="#000000"><FONT COLOR="#ffffff">(0,0,0)</FONT></TD>
<TD BGCOLOR="#000000"><FONT COLOR="#ffffff">(0%,0%,0%)</FONT></TD>
<TD BGCOLOR="#008000">Green</TD>
<TD BGCOLOR="#008000">008000</TD>
<TD BGCOLOR="#008000">(0,127,0)</TD>
<TD BGCOLOR="#008000">(0%,50%,0%)</TD>
</TR>


<TR WIDTH="140">
<TD BGCOLOR="#c0c0c0">Silver</TD>
<TD BGCOLOR="#c0c0c0">c0c0c0</TD>
<TD BGCOLOR="#c0c0c0">(207,207,207)</TD>
<TD BGCOLOR="#c0c0c0">(80%,80%,80%)</TD>
<TD BGCOLOR="#00ff00">Lime</TD>
<TD BGCOLOR="#00ff00">00ff00</TD>
<TD BGCOLOR="#00ff00">(0,255,0)</TD>
<TD BGCOLOR="#00ff00">(0%,100%,0%)</TD>
</TR>


<TR WIDTH="140">
<TD BGCOLOR="#808080">Gray</TD>
<TD BGCOLOR="#808080">808080</TD>
<TD BGCOLOR="#808080">(127,127,127)</TD>
<TD BGCOLOR="#808080">(50%,50%,50%)</TD>
<TD BGCOLOR="#808000">Olive</TD>
<TD BGCOLOR="#808000">808000</TD>
<TD BGCOLOR="#808000">(127,127,0)</TD>
<TD BGCOLOR="#808000">(50%,50%,0%)</TD>
</TR>


<TR WIDTH="140">
<TD BGCOLOR="#ffffff">White</TD>
<TD BGCOLOR="#ffffff">ffffff</TD>
<TD BGCOLOR="#ffffff">(255,255,255)</TD>
```

```
<TD BGCOLOR="#ffffff">(100%,100%,100%)</TD>
<TD BGCOLOR="#ffff00">Yellow</TD>
<TD BGCOLOR="#ffff00">ffff00</TD>
<TD BGCOLOR="#ffff00">(255,255,0)</TD>
<TD BGCOLOR="#ffff00">(100%,100%,0%)</TD>
</TR>

<TR WIDTH="140">
<TD BGCOLOR="#800000">Maroon</TD>
<TD BGCOLOR="#800000">800000</TD>
<TD BGCOLOR="#800000">(127,0,0)</TD>
<TD BGCOLOR="#800000">(50%,0%,0%)</TD>
<TD BGCOLOR="#000080"><FONT COLOR="#ffffff">Navy</FONT></TD>
<TD BGCOLOR="#000080"><FONT COLOR="#ffffff">000080</FONT></TD>
<TD BGCOLOR="#000080"><FONT COLOR="#ffffff">(0,0,127)</FONT></TD>
<TD BGCOLOR="#000080"><FONT COLOR="#ffffff">(0%,0%,50%)</FONT></TD>
</TR>

<TR WIDTH="140">
<TD BGCOLOR="#ff0000">Red</TD>
<TD BGCOLOR="#ff0000">ff0000</TD>
<TD BGCOLOR="#ff0000">(255,0,0)</TD>
<TD BGCOLOR="#ff0000">(100%,0%,0%)</TD>
<TD BGCOLOR="#0000ff"><FONT COLOR="#ffffff">Blue</FONT></TD>
<TD BGCOLOR="#0000ff"><FONT COLOR="#ffffff">0000ff</FONT></TD>
<TD BGCOLOR="#0000ff"><FONT COLOR="#ffffff">(0,0,255)</FONT></TD>
<TD BGCOLOR="#0000ff"><FONT COLOR="#ffffff">(0%,0%,100%)</FONT></TD>
</TR>

<TR WIDTH="140">
<TD BGCOLOR="#800080">Purple</TD>
<TD BGCOLOR="#800080">800080</TD>
<TD BGCOLOR="#800080">(127,0,127)</TD>
<TD BGCOLOR="#800080">(50%,0%,50%)</TD>
<TD BGCOLOR="#008080">Teal</TD>
<TD BGCOLOR="#008080">008080</TD>
<TD BGCOLOR="#008080">(0,127,127)</TD>
<TD BGCOLOR="#008080">(0%,50%,50%)</TD>
</TR>

<TR WIDTH="140">
<TD BGCOLOR="#ff00ff">Fuchsia</TD>
<TD BGCOLOR="#ff00ff">ff00ff</TD>
<TD BGCOLOR="#ff00ff">(255,0,255)</TD>
<TD BGCOLOR="#ff00ff">(100%,0%,100%)</TD>
<TD BGCOLOR="#00ffff">Aqua</TD>
<TD BGCOLOR="#00ffff">00ffff</TD>
<TD BGCOLOR="#00ffff">(0,255,255)</TD>
<TD BGCOLOR="#00ffff">(0%,100%,100%)</TD>
</TR>
</TABLE>

</BODY>
</HTML>
```

The { width: } Property

The **width** Property is used specify the horizontal size of an Element. It can be expressed as a *length*, as a *percentage* of the available window space or by the Keyword **auto** which is the default value. If you set up absolute values like pixels and there is a conflict with values set in the **margin** Property, the Margins will have their values assigned first and the leftovers go to the **width** Property. Here are some instant **width** examples:

```
{ width: 500px; }
{ width: 7in; }
{ width: 100%; }
{ width: auto; }
```

CSS Syntax:

```
{ width: length|percentage|auto; }
```

Example 1-19 focuses on rudimentary **width** Property parameters for several Elements. The next example will focus on conflicts and precedence issues pertaining to **width** and **margin** Properties.

Example 1-19:   Sample219.html

```
<!DOCTYPE HTML PUBLIC "-//W3C//DTD HTML 3.2//EN">
<HTML>
<HEAD>
<TITLE> Sample 219 - CSS Example 1-19 Widths</TITLE>

<STYLE TYPE="text/CSS">

<!--

H1      { width: 300px;
          text-transform: capitalize; color: red;
          border-style: ridge; border-width: 20px; border-color: purple; }
H2      { width: 5in; margin: 10px 30px 50px 70px;
          text-transform: capitalize; color: red;
          border-style: ridge; border-width: 20px; border-color: blue; }

H3      { width: 100%; margin-top: 35px;
          text-transform: capitalize; color: red;
          border-style: ridge; border-width: 20px; border-color: aqua; }

H4      { width: 50mm; margin-right: 177px;
          text-transform: capitalize; color: red;
          border-style: ridge; border-width: 20px; border-color: green; }
```

```
H5          { width: 10cm; margin-bottom: 2in;
              text-transform: capitalize; color: red;
              border-style: ridge; border-width: 20px; border-color: yellow; }

H6          { width: 50%; margin-left: 100px;
              text-transform: capitalize; color: red;
              border-style: ridge; border-width: 20px; border-color: fuchsia; }

P           { width: auto; margin-left: 55px; margin-top: 1in; font-size: 17pt;
              border-style: ridge; border-width: 20px; border-color: red; }

-->

</STYLE>
</HEAD>
<BODY>

<H1>this is sample 219</H1>

<P>      This Example is similar to Example 207. It adds different WIDTH sizes to the
various Heading Elements. Notice that the P Element is set to a left margin of 55
pixels and a top margin of 1 inch. It has its WIDTH set to AUTO.
</P>

<H1>     This is a H1 Heading with margins at 10 pixels on all four sides with a
WIDTH set to 300 pixels.
</H1>

<H2>     This is a margin at (10 30 50 70) pixels for (top right bottom left) and a
WIDTH set to 5 inches.
</H2>

<H3>     This is a top margin of 35 pixels with a WIDTH set to 100 percent of the
window. If you resize the window the border will change width.
</H3>

<H4>     This is a right margin of 177 pixels with a WIDTH set to 50 millimeters.
</H4>

<H5>     This is a bottom margin of 2 inches with a WIDTH set to 10 centimeters.
</H5>

<H6>     This is a left margin of 100 pixels with a WIDTH set to 50 percent of the
window.
</H6>

</BODY>
</HTML>
```

Example 1-20 examines some of the conflicts that can arise when settings for the
width Property interact with the **margin** Property, which can vary in relation to how the
user has the window sized. When you run the example, resize the window and see how
that affects the display.

Example 1-20: **Sample220.html**

```
<!DOCTYPE HTML PUBLIC "-//W3C//DTD HTML 3.2//EN">
<HTML><HEAD><TITLE>    Sample 220 - CSS Example 1-20 Widths and Margins</TITLE>
<STYLE TYPE="text/CSS">
<!--
H1      { width: 300px; margin-left: 250px; margin-right: 250px;
          text-transform: capitalize; color: red;
          border-style: ridge; border-width: 20px; border-color: purple; }


H2      { width: 5in; margin: 10px 200px 50px 200px;
          text-transform: capitalize; color: red;
          border-style: ridge; border-width: 20px; border-color: blue; }


H3      { width: 100%; margin-right: 435px;
          text-transform: capitalize; color: red;
          border-style: ridge; border-width: 20px; border-color: aqua; }


H4      { width: 400mm; margin-right: 177px;
          text-transform: capitalize; color: red;
          border-style: ridge; border-width: 20px; border-color: green; }


H5      { width: 100cm; margin-left: 4in; margin-right: 144px;
          text-transform: capitalize; color: red;
          border-style: ridge; border-width: 20px; border-color: yellow; }


H6      { width: 50%; margin-left: 400px;
          text-transform: capitalize; color: red;
          border-style: ridge; border-width: 20px; border-color: fuchsia; }


P       { width: auto; margin-left: 355px; margin-top: 1in; font-size: 17pt;
          border-style: ridge; border-width: 20px; border-color: red; }
-->
</STYLE>
</HEAD>
<BODY> <H1>    this is sample 220     </H1>
<P>     This Example is similar to Example 219. It shows some of the creative uses
and undesirable consequences of conflicts between WIDTH sizes and MARGINS when
applied to the various Heading Elements. Notice that the P Element is set to a left
margin of 355 pixels and a top margin of 1 inch. It has its WIDTH set to AUTO which
can avoid conflict difficulties.                                      </P>
<H1>    This is a H1 Heading with margins set at 250 pixels for the left and right
sides with a WIDTH set to 300 pixels.                        </H1>
<H2>    This is a margin Property set at (10 200 50 200) pixels for (top right
bottom left) margins and a WIDTH set to 5 inches.            </H2>
<H3>    This is a top margin of 435 pixels with a WIDTH set to 100 percent of the
window. If you resize the window the border will change width.     </H3>
<H4>This is a right margin of 177 pixels with a WIDTH set to 400 millimeters.</H4>
<H5>    This is a left margin of 4 inches and a right margin of 144 pixels with a
WIDTH set to 100 centimeters.                                </H5>
<H6>    This is a left margin of 400 pixels with a WIDTH set to 50 percent of the
window.                                                      </H6>
</BODY>
</HTML>
```

Horizontal Alignment, Floating, and Clear

Horizontal Alignment of an Element, Floating an Element, and Clearing a Floating Element are all interrelated. The current syntactical rules are not too confusing but it's less intuitive than it could have been. Here is an overview of the rules; each of these Properties is then covered in subsequent sections.

You use the **float** Property to align your Element. If you align it <u>left</u> or <u>right</u> then it also <u>floats</u>. If you align it <u>center</u> or <u>none</u> then it doesn't <u>float</u>, it repels other Elements. If you assign a **clear** Property to an Element that is adjacent to a **float** Element, then the **clear** Element will repel the **float** Element, which is like saying **clear** has precedence over **float**. There is a chart on page 64 that makes it easier to understand the ramifications of this.

If you specify a **clear** Element adjacent to a <u>nonfloating aligned</u> Property of <u>**none**</u> or <u>**center**</u>, the **clear** Element will repel the other Element also.

The { float: } Property

The **float** Property is used specify the horizontal alignment of an Element. It can be expressed by the any of the four Keywords: **left**, **right**, **center**, or **none**. The default Value is **none**.

If you specify it with the Value of **left** or **right** then the Element floats, which means that text will flow around that Element instead of immediately starting below it. An Element that is floated left will be flush with the left edge of the page or left page-margin, if there is one, and have text flowing around its right side.

If an Element is floated right then it will be flush with the right edge of the page or right page-margin, if there is one, and will have text flowing around its left side.

Never assign a floated Element a <u>Margin</u> because the text-wrapping effect will be disabled or give you bizarre results. The workaround for this is when you want a floated Element to have a Margin just put it inside of another Element like <P> or <DIV> and assign a Style with a Margin to that parent Element.

When you specify a **float** Property to have a Value of **center** or **none** then it will only apply alignment to the Element and is said to be defloated; that is, there will be no text flow around the sides and the text will always begin below that Element.

Here are examples of all the **float** possibilities:

```
{ float: left; }          { float: right; }
{ float: center; }        { float: none; }
```

CSS Syntax:

```
{ float: left|right|center|none; }
```

It should be noted here that for future reference, when we discuss JavaScript Syntax, the CSS Syntax Property of **float** is the same as the JavaScript Syntax Property of **align**. The reason that different words are used for the same Property is that in JavaScript the term <u>float</u> was already a Keyword with a different function.

This example shows several ways of using the **float** Property to align and/or float an Element.

Example 1-21:   Sample221.html

```
<!DOCTYPE HTML PUBLIC "-//W3C//DTD HTML 3.2//EN">
<HTML><HEAD>
<TITLE>    Sample 221 - CSS Example 1-21 Float & Align    </TITLE>

<STYLE TYPE="text/CSS">
<!--

H1      { float: right; color: red;
          border-style: ridge; border-width: 20px; border-color: purple; }

H2      { float: left; color: black;
          border-style: ridge; border-width: 20px; border-color: blue; }
H3      { float: none; color: blue;
          border-style: ridge; border-width: 20px; border-color: aqua; }

H4      { float: center; color: lime;
          border-style: ridge; border-width: 20px; border-color: green; }

P       { font-size: 17pt; }
-->
</STYLE>
</HEAD>
<BODY>
<P>    This Example demonstrates alignment with the float property.       </P>

<H1>   This is a H1 Heading floated right.                               </H1>

<P>    This Example demonstrates alignment with the float property.       </P>

<H2>   This is a H2 Heading floated left.                               </H2>

<P>    This Example demonstrates alignment with the float property.       </P>

<H3>   This is a H3 Heading with no alignment set.                      </H3>

<P>    This Example demonstrates alignment with the float property.       </P>

<H4>   This is a H4 Heading aligned center.                             </H4>
</BODY>
</HTML>
```

The { clear: } Property

The **clear** Property is used to force an Element that is adjacent to a floated Element to start on the next line below the floated Element. How it works depends on two things: the Value of the **clear** Property in one Element and the Value of the **float** Property in another Element that it is adjacent to.

In the following chart, assume that you have two Elements that are next to each other in the document, and one of them has specified a **clear** Property and the other has specified a **float** Property. Then their interaction behaviors are listed in the right column.

When a cleared Element accepts a floated Element, it means that it is allowed to flow or wrap its text around that floated Element. If a cleared Element rejects a floated Element, then it causes the Element with the **clear** Property to start on the next line below the floated Element.

	Element 1		**Element 2**		**How they interact:**
If:	clear=none	and	float=left	Then:	clear Element accepts both floats
If:	clear=none	and	float=right	Then:	clear Element accepts both floats
If:	clear=left	and	float=left	Then:	clear Element accepts right floats and rejects left floats
If:	clear=left	and	float=right	Then:	clear Element accepts left floats and rejects right floats
If:	clear=right	and	float=left	Then:	clear Element accepts left floats and rejects right floats
If:	clear=right	and	float=right	Then:	clear Element accepts right floats and rejects left floats
If:	clear=both	and	float=left	Then:	clear Element rejects both floats
If:	clear=both	and	float=right	Then:	clear Element rejects both floats

---

These are the four **clear** Property Value possibilities:

```
{ clear: none; }          { clear: both; }
{ clear: left; }          { clear: right; }
```

CSS Syntax:

```
{ clear: none|left|right|both; }
```

Example 1-22 focuses on how the **clear** Property interacts with the **float** Property.

Example 1-22:   **Sample222.html**

```
<!DOCTYPE HTML PUBLIC "-//W3C//DTD HTML 3.2//EN">
<HTML>
<HEAD><TITLE> Sample 222 - CSS Example 1-22 Clear, Float & Align</TITLE>

<STYLE TYPE="text/CSS">
<!--

H1      { float: right; color: red;
           border-style: ridge; border-width: 20px; border-color: purple; }

H2      { float: left; color: aqua;
           border-style: ridge; border-width: 20px; border-color: blue; }
H3      { float: right; color: blue;
           border-style: ridge; border-width: 20px; border-color: aqua; }

H4      { float: left; color: lime;
           border-style: ridge; border-width: 20px; border-color: green; }

P       { font-size: 17pt; clear: left; color: red; }

DIV     { font-size: 22pt; clear: right; color: blue; }

-->

</STYLE>

</HEAD>

<BODY>

<P>     This Example demonstrates how to Clear a floated Element.      </P>

<H1>    This is a H1 Heading floated right.                            </H1>

<DIV>   This Example demonstrates how to Clear a floated Element.      </DIV>

<H2>    This is a H2 Heading floated left.                             </H2>

<P>     This Example demonstrates how to Clear a floated Element.      </P>

<H3>    This is a H3 Heading floated right.                            </H3>

<DIV>   This Example demonstrates how to Clear a floated Element.      </DIV>

<H4>    This is a H4 Heading floated left.                             </H4>

<P>     This Example demonstrates how to Clear a floated Element.      </P>

</BODY>
</HTML>
```

The { white-space: } Property

The **white-space** Property is used to specify whether the blank space between words both horizontally and vertically is collapsed to a single character space or is retained and preserved as is. The Value of **pre** preserves white space and the Value of **normal** will collapse white space, which is the default. Since 99% of all Elements have a default value of normal, the only time you use this Property is when you want to preserve white space.

It should be noted that using the **pre** Value is a very imprecise and unreliable way to format your tabular content although it is quick. If appearance is more important than time, then use a TABLE for tabular-oriented data like charts. The **white-space** Property is used with BLOCK LEVEL Elements. It can be very useful for quickly making a paragraph render just the way you originally type it, with indentations and carriage returns intact.

Here are two mini-examples of using the **white-space** Property:

```
{ white-space : normal; }
{ white-space : pre; }
```

CSS Syntax:

```
{ white-space: normal|pre; }
```

This example focuses on how white space is handled in Styles. Of significance are some of the possible caveats and results of less-obvious interaction possibilities. Run the Sample223.html file to see the results and check out the notes in the example for more information.

Example 1-23:　　　　**Sample223.html**

```
<!DOCTYPE HTML PUBLIC "-//W3C//DTD HTML 3.2//EN">
<HTML>
<HEAD>
<TITLE>      Sample 223 - CSS Example 1-23    White Space    </TITLE>

<STYLE TYPE="text/CSS">

<!--
```

```
BLOCKQUOTE      { white-space: normal; font-size: 14pt; color: purple; }

P        { white-space: pre; font-size: 10pt; color: red; font-family: Courier; }

DIV             { white-space: pre; font-size: 20pt; color: blue; }

PRE             { white-space: pre; font-size: 22pt; color: green; }

-->

</STYLE>

</HEAD>

<BODY>

<BLOCKQUOTE>          This is a blockquote with
                     white space set to normal
                     which is the default.
</BLOCKQUOTE>


<P>    This is a Paragraph with white space set to pre. It is boring with
a small chart of Property Values.

margin-top      length | percentage      em, ex, px, pt, pc, in, mm, cm | %
margin-right    length | percentage      em, ex, px, pt, pc, in, mm, cm | %
margin-bottom   length | percentage      em, ex, px, pt, pc, in, mm, cm | %
margin-left     length | percentage      em, ex, px, pt, pc, in, mm, cm | %
</P>


<DIV>                        If you set the white-space Property to
<B>pre</B> for the <B>Paragraph</B> Element it will automatically render
the text in a <B>variable-width</B> font.  If you want it to be in a
<B>fixed-width</B> font like <B>Courier</B> you have to specify that with the
font-family Property.  The same thing is true for the
Division Element.  If you specify the <B>pre</B> Property for the
<B>PRE</B> Element the opposite is true.  It's a good idea to write and
test the pre text with the same font family and size that
it will be rendered at so you will know that the tabs will
match up.  <I><B>Tables are an infinitely more reliable way to display
tabular data.</B></I>
</DIV>


<PRE>
1       2       3       4       5
6       7       8       9       10
11      12      13      14      15
16      17      18      19      20
</PRE>


</BODY>
</HTML>
```

The { list-style-type: } Property

The **list-style-type** Property is used to set the type of bullet or enumeration sequence that will be used for your <LI> LIST ITEM Elements. You might remember from prior HTML knowlege, or if you checked out Appendix A, that LISTS can contain a variety of data types from text and paragraphs to images and even other nested lists. They are used to enumerate and indent the LIST contents or embellish them with graphical bullets. If you want to get fancy, try a symbolic or dingbat font and see what turns up. With Styles you can change the markup or visual characteristics, such as the font colors or font names, for the items in your list if you want to really make them stand out.

These are the nine possibilities for choosing a bullet or enumeration sequence for your Lists:

disc	solid round bullet. Navigator's default value	
square	hollow square bullet with edge color	
circle	hollow round bullet with edge color	
decimal	arabic numerals will vertically enumerate like this:	1, 2, 3, 4, 5...
upper-alpha	uppercase letters will vertically enumerate like this:	A, B, C, D, E...
lower-alpha	lowercase letters will vertically enumerate like this:	a, b, c, d, e...
upper-roman	uppercase roman numerals vertically enumerate:	I, II, III, IV, V...
lower-roman	lowercase roman numerals vertically enumerate:	i, ii, iii, iv, v...
none	no preceding bullet or enumeration sequence	

CSS Syntax:

```
{ list-style-type: disc|square|circle|decimal|upper-roman|
                 lower-roman|upper-alpha|lower-alpha|none; }
```

In the following three Examples of 1-24, 1-24B, and 1-24C, there are a variety of implementations of the **list-style-type** Property. Example 1-24 focuses on using the **disc** bullet within an Unordered List. Example 1-24B focuses on the **upper-roman** numbering sequence in an Ordered List. Example 1-24C demonstrates a **square** bullet Style inside an Unordered List that is nested in the first List Item of an Ordered List which has a Value of a **lower-alpha** sequence in its **list-style-type** Property.

You can also check out Example 1-41 for an advanced demonstration of using the **list-style-type** Property within Styles that use CONTEXTUAL SELECTION CRITERIA.

Example 1-24: **Sample224.html**

```
<!DOCTYPE HTML PUBLIC "-//W3C//DTD HTML 3.2//EN">
<HTML>
<HEAD>
<TITLE>      Sample 224 - CSS  Example 1-24        Lists   </TITLE>

<STYLE TYPE="text/CSS">

<!--

LI      { list-style-type: disc; color: red; }

H1      { float: center; }

UL      { float: center; font-size: 24pt; color: green; text-transform: capitalize;}

P       { color: purple; float: center; font-size: 14pt; }

-->

</STYLE>

</HEAD>

<BODY>

<H1>This is Sample 224</H1>

<P>The following Unordered list is floated Center.</P>

<UL>
        <LI>    item 1
        <LI>    item 2
        <LI>    item 3
        <LI>    item 4
        <LI>    item 5
</UL>

</BODY>
</HTML>
```

Example 1-24B demonstrates two Ordered Lists containing the <LI> Element with a **list-style-type** Property specified in its Style.

Example 1-24B: **Sample224B.html**

```
<!DOCTYPE HTML PUBLIC "-//W3C//DTD HTML 3.2//EN">
<HTML>
<HEAD><TITLE>  Sample 224B - CSS Example 1-24B Lists</TITLE>

<STYLE TYPE="text/CSS">

<!--

H1      { float: center; color: red; }

OL      { list-style-type: upper-roman; color: purple; font-size: 14pt; }

H2      { color: olive; font-size: 24pt; background-color: aqua;}

-->

</STYLE>

</HEAD>

<BODY>

<H1>This is Sample 224B</H1>

<OL>
        <LI>    item 1
        <LI>    item 2
        <LI>    item 3
        <LI>    item 4
        <LI>    item 5
</OL>

<H2>    Gads, is this possible?
        <OL>
        <LI>    item 1 nested in H2
        <LI>    item 2 nested in H2
        <LI>    item 3 nested in H2
        <LI>    item 4 nested in H2
        <LI>    item 5 nested in H2
        </OL>
</H2>

</BODY>
</HTML>
```

Example 1-24C demonstrates nested <LI> Elements with a **list-style-type** Property specified in its Style.

Example 1-24C: Sample224C.html

```
<!DOCTYPE HTML PUBLIC "-//W3C//DTD HTML 3.2//EN">
<HTML>
<HEAD>
<TITLE>       Sample 224C - CSS Example 1-24C       Nested Lists   </TITLE>

<STYLE TYPE="text/CSS">

<!--

H1      { float:center; color:red; }

OL      { list-style-type:lower-alpha; color:green; font-size:24pt; }

UL      { list-style-type:square; color:blue; font-size:17pt; }

-->

</STYLE>

</HEAD>

<BODY>

<H1>This is Sample 224C</H1>

<OL>
        <LI>item 1 has a nested list
                <UL>
                <LI>     item Alpha nested in LI
                <LI>     item Beta nested in LI
                <LI>     item Gamma nested in LI
                <LI>     item Delta nested in LI
                <LI>     item Epsilon nested in LI
                </UL>
        <LI>    item 2
        <LI>    item 3
        <LI>    item 4
        <LI>    item 5
        <LI>    item 6
        <LI>    item 7
</OL>

</BODY>
</HTML>
```

Using Styles in the <STYLE> Element

<STYLE> Element with CLASS of STYLE

Up to this point, all of the theory and examples have applied a STYLE to an Element that would apply to all instances of that Element within a document; that is, every time that Element was used it would have that STYLE attached to it.

By defining a STYLE in the Header STYLE SHEET definition that is <u>named</u> you create a CLASS of STYLE that can be used to apply a different Style to the same Element <u>type</u> each time that you use that particular Element <u>type</u>.

Here's how it works:

First, Define a <u>named</u> CLASS of STYLE and name it **bigRed** and attach it to the H3 Element with <u>dot notation</u>, like this:

```
H3.bigRed    { font-size: 30pt; color: red; }
```

The order from left to right is: (Element) (.) (CLASS NAME) ({definition}).

Next, in order to show that you can apply a different <u>named</u> CLASS of STYLE to the same Element type which in this case is H3, we define another <u>named</u> CLASS of STYLE and name it **bigBlue** and attach it to the H3 Element, like this:

```
H3.bigBlue   { font-size: 48pt; color: blue; }
```

So now you have two different named CLASSes of STYLE that can all be applied to the H3 Element but not at the same time. Remember, you can apply only one Style per Element <u>usage</u>.

Then go into the BODY section of the document and create two H3 heading Elements.

```
<H3 CLASS="bigRed">This is Heading H3 with CLASS bigRed.    </H3>

<H3 CLASS="bigBlue">This is Heading H3 with CLASS bigBlue.  </H3>
```

That's all you have to do. The first H3 Heading, which has the **bigRed** CLASS applied to it, will have red text and a font size of 30 points. The second H3 Heading, which has the **bigBlue** CLASS applied to it, will have a font size of 48 points and will have blue text.

With CLASS Styles, you define the Style just like any other STYLE, but you name it so you can reference it with an Element Attribute for inline usage. It's important to remember that in this example you are also attaching it to the H3 Element by using the dot notation so only that Element can use that CLASS; but this isn't required (see Sample 227).

Be aware that when coding STYLEs like in the first H3 Style that has yellow text in the following example, that this regular Style will automatically apply to all H3 Elements in the document by default unless a CLASS of STYLE or another type of Style is explicitly called to override it from within the Body section or from fancy JavaScript.

Now let's put all that theory, along with a third Style that applies to all H3 Elements in an example that has three different Styles applied to three different usages of the H3 Element:

Example 1-25:   Sample225.html

```
<!DOCTYPE HTML PUBLIC "-//W3C//DTD HTML 3.2//EN">
<HTML>
<HEAD>
<TITLE>Sample 225 - Example 1-25 CLASS of STYLE</TITLE>

<STYLE TYPE="text/CSS">

<!--

H3                     { font-size: 14pt; color: yellow; }
H3.bigRed              { font-size: 30pt; color: red; }
H3.bigBlue             { font-size: 48pt; color: blue; }

-->

</STYLE>

</HEAD>

<BODY BGCOLOR="black">

<H3>This is a regular H3 Heading with STYLE.            </H3><HR>

<H3 CLASS="bigRed">This is Heading H3 with CLASS bigRed.    </H3><HR>

<H3 CLASS="bigBlue">This is Heading H3 with CLASS bigBlue.    </H3>

</BODY>
</HTML>
```

Naming your CLASS of STYLE

Here's a similar example that uses named CLASS STYLES. You can name your CLASSes anything with alphanumeric characters but be aware that the names are always <u>case-sensitive</u> and the first Character in the name must be a letter or the underscore (_) Character, but not a number. After the first Character you can use numbers in the name. You can use uppercase or you can use lowercase letters names or a combination of the two. Just make sure that when you use the name that you type it in exactly the same way when you address it in the BODY section as when you declared it in the HEAD section.

Example 1-26:   **Sample226.html**

```
<!DOCTYPE HTML PUBLIC "-//W3C//DTD HTML 3.2//EN">
<HTML>
<HEAD>
<TITLE> Sample 226 - Example 1-26 CLASS of STYLE</TITLE>

<STYLE TYPE="text/CSS">
<!--

H1.redHeading          { font-size: 40pt; color: red; }

H1.blueHeading         { font-size: 30pt; color: blue; }

DIV                    { font-size: 14pt; color: red; }

DIV.purpleBorder       { font-size: 19pt; width: 300px; color: purple;
            border-style: ridge; border-width: 20px; border-color: purple; }

DIV.blueBorder         { font-size: 24pt; width: 7in; color: blue;
            border-style: ridge; border-width: 20px; border-color: blue; }
-->
</STYLE>
</HEAD>

<BODY>

<H1 CLASS="redHeading">This is Sample 226</H1>

<H1 CLASS="blueHeading">This has CLASS="blueHeading".</H1>

<DIV>This Example is similar to Example 225.</DIV><BR><BR>

<DIV CLASS="purpleBorder">This is a Division with CLASS="purpleBorder".</DIV>

<DIV CLASS="blueBorder">This is a Division with CLASS="blueBorder".</DIV>

</BODY>
</HTML>
```

Defining a CLASS of STYLE
without attaching it to an Element

You can attach the same CLASS to more than one Element in either one of two ways. The first way is to define a named CLASS of STYLE without attaching it to an Element so that it has broader useability; then just put the NAME of the CLASS to the right of the dot(.) and omit the Element to the left like this:

```
.unAttached1        { color: blue; font-size: 22pt; }
```

Then you can assign the Style by name to the CLASS Attribute for <u>any</u> Element like this:

```
<H1 CLASS="unAttached1"> The text to render </H1>
```

See Example 1-29 on page 78.

The Keyword <u>all</u>

Now we introduce the Keyword **all** which is used to define a Style for all Elements at once. Here's an example:

```
all.myCoolStyle { color: purple; background-color: black; }
```

This defines a <u>CLASS of STYLE</u> that is then addressable, that is, assignable by all of your Elements in the whole document by using the <u>CLASS Attribute</u>. Typically you would use the **all** Keyword to define certain Properties that you want to use frequently for many Elements in your document and then fine tune your document with individual, named CLASSes of Styles for specific Elements like this:

```
all.GLOBAL { color:black; font-size:14pt; margin:2em; }
```

This is important: Just because you use the Keyword **all** does not mean that you don't have to still apply the Style with the CLASS <u>Attribute</u> to the Elements contained in the BODY section of the document.

Remember that named CLASS Styles inherit Style Properties from their parent Elements just like regular STYLEs.

Just to make sure there is no confusion, I'll hammer this home; the

CLASS of STYLE   is the <u>Named</u> Style in your Style Sheet Definition which is declared in the Header section of the document, and the

CLASS Attribute   is the way to <u>assign</u> that **CLASS of STYLE**, by Name, to an Element from within the Body section of the document.

Example 1-27:   **Sample227.html**

```
<!DOCTYPE HTML PUBLIC "-//W3C//DTD HTML 3.2//EN">
<HTML>
<HEAD>
<TITLE> Sample 227 - Example 1-27 CLASS of STYLE</TITLE>

<STYLE TYPE="text/CSS">

<!--

all.GLOBAL      { color: black; background-color: white; margin: 2em;
                  font-size: 14pt; font-family: Palatino, Clarendon, serif;
                  text-indent: 40px; line-height: 200%; }

H1.greenSpeak   { color: green; background-color: lime; padding: 15px;
                  font-size: 24pt; font-family: Clarendon, serif; }

H1.aquaSpeak    { color: aqua; background-color: blue; padding: 20px;
                  font-size: 24pt; font-family: Blackoak, serif; }

A.fancyLink     { color: red; background-color: yellow; padding: 40px;
                  font-size: 28pt;
                  font-family: Moonlight, Clarendon, serif; line-height: 125%; }

-->

</STYLE>

</HEAD>

<BODY>

<H1 CLASS="greenSpeak">This is Sample 227<BR> and has CLASS greenSpeak</H1>

<H1 CLASS="aquaSpeak">This has CLASS aquaSpeak.</H1>

<A CLASS="fancyLink" HREF="Sample226.html">This takes you to the last Sample
226</A>

<P CLASS="GLOBAL">CHECK the Link and GLOBAL settings.</P>

</BODY>
</HTML>
```

    If you want to set default Properties for your entire document, then define a STYLE for the BODY Element because all of the Elements contained within the BODY Element will inherit those STYLE Properties.

    This is demonstrated in the following Example 1-28.

Example 1-28: **Sample228.html**

```
<!DOCTYPE HTML PUBLIC "-//W3C//DTD HTML 3.2//EN">
<HTML>
<HEAD>
<TITLE> Sample 228 - Example 1-28 CLASS of STYLE</TITLE>

<STYLE TYPE="text/CSS">

<!--

BODY          { color: aqua; background-color: gray; margin: 2em; font-size: 14pt;
                font-family: Palatino, Clarendon, serif; text-indent: 40px;
                line-height: 125%; }

H1.greenSpeak { color: green; background-color: lime; font-size: 24pt;
                font-family: Clarendon, serif; line-height: 125%; }

H1.aquaSpeak  { color: aqua; background-color: blue; font-size: 24pt;
                font-family: Blackoak, serif; line-height: 150%; }

-->

</STYLE>

</HEAD>

<BODY>

<P>
This example shows STYLE inheritance from the parent BODY Element to the child
Elements it contains. Notice that only the first two H1 Headings have a CLASS Style
applied to them and all the other Elements inherit the STYLE from the BODY Element.
Also notice the amount of space between the lines of text in this paragraph and
that it's 125% bigger than the size of the font. Regarding the text-indent
Property, you should remember that by definition only the first line of the first
Element will be indented which in this case is this paragraph because it's the
first item to occur in the BODY Element.
</P>

<H1 CLASS="greenSpeak"> This is Sample 228<BR> and has CLASS greenSpeak </H1>

<H1 CLASS="aquaSpeak"> This has CLASS aquaSpeak. </H1>

<H1> This Heading has STYLE inherited from the BODY Element. </H1>

<A HREF="Sample227.html">This takes you to the last Sample 227 and also has STYLE
inherited from the BODY Element.</A>

</BODY>

</HTML>
```

Attaching the same CLASS to more than one Element

You can attach the same CLASS to more than one Element. When you want to do that you define a named CLASS of STYLE without attaching it to an Element so that it has broader useability; then just put the NAME of the CLASS to the right of the dot(.) and omit the Element to the left like this:

```
.unAttached1          { color: blue; font-size: 22pt; }
```
or like this:
```
.meUnAttached2        { color: purple; font-size: 44pt; }
```

This has exactly the same effect as in the previous example when the Keyword **all** was used to precede the dot(.) so take your choice.

This example demonstrates how to create CLASSes of STYLE that can be applied to any Element by preceding the CLASS name with a dot(.) in the CLASS Definition but <u>not</u> preceding it with an Element name that would assign it to just that Element. Check out the text inside the <P> </P> Tags inside the example for more hints.

Example 1-29:   **Sample229.html**

```
<!DOCTYPE HTML PUBLIC "-//W3C//DTD HTML 3.2//EN">
<HTML>
<HEAD>
<TITLE> Sample 229 - Example 1-29 CLASS of STYLE      </TITLE>

<STYLE TYPE="text/CSS">
<!--

.navySpeak      { color: navy; background-color: aqua; font-size: 15pt;
                    font-family: Blackoak, serif; line-height: 150%; }

.tealSpeak      { color: teal; background-color: blue; font-size: 22pt;
                    font-family: Clarendon, serif; line-height: 125%; }

.graySpeak      { color: gray; background-color: yellow; font-size: 17pt;
                    font-family: Helvetica, serif; line-height: 125%; }

.redSpeak       { color: red; background-color: silver; font-size: 30pt;
                    font-family:"Brush Script", serif; line-height: 125%; }
-->

</STYLE>
```

```
</HEAD>

<BODY>

<H1 CLASS="redSpeak">This is Sample 229 with CLASS redSpeak</H1>

<P CLASS="graySpeak">This example shows how to define CLASSES of STYLE that can be
used by any Element simply by not assigning them to a specific Element. Notice that
in the code the four CLASSES are each preceded by a dot(.) which is what makes them
applicable to any Element. Remember that in previous examples the same thing was
accomplished by preceding the dot with the keyword (all). They are functionally
equivalent.</P>

<P>Notice in the CLASS redSpeak that the font-family name of Brush Script is
enclosed in quote marks because this is a special case where the font name is
composed of two words instead of one.</P>

<P>It is also reccomended that you use one of the generic font-family
<B>families</B> like (<B>serif</B>) as the last resort font choice to enhance
accurate display of your document.</P>

<H1 CLASS="tealSpeak">This has CLASS tealSpeak.</H1>

<H1 CLASS="navySpeak">This has CLASS navySpeak.</H1>

<A CLASS="redSpeak" HREF="Sample228.html">
This takes you to the last Sample 228 and also has CLASS redSpeak.</A>

</BODY>
</HTML>
```

Revisiting the Keyword <u>all</u>

Let's revisit the Keyword **all** for a moment and look at another useful way to practically employ it. As was previously mentioned, it is used to make a CLASS of STYLE available for all Elements. You can use the Keyword **all** more than once in a Style Definition to define multiple CLASSes of Style that will be assignable to all Elements in your document. To do that just define a CLASS with dot notation and precede it by **all** and then repeat that for as many CLASSes as you want like this:

```
all.firstClass { border-width-left: 10px; border-style: double; }

all.deuxClass  { border-width-right: 30px; border-style: groove; }

all.thirdClass { border-width-bottom: 40px; border-style: ridge; }
```

Example 1-30 demonstrates multiple usages of the Keyword **all**.

Example 1-30:   **Sample230.html**

```
<!DOCTYPE HTML PUBLIC "-//W3C//DTD HTML 3.2//EN">
<HTML>
<HEAD><TITLE>  Sample 230 - Example 1-30 CLASS of STYLE</TITLE>

<STYLE TYPE="text/CSS">

<!--

all.classOne    { border-bottom-width: 30px; border-left-width: 40px;
                  border-style: groove;
                  color: teal; background-color: blue; font-size: 15pt;
                  font-family: Clarendon, serif; line-height: 125%; }

all.classDeux   { border-width: 20px; border-style: double;
                  border-color: rgb(50%, 10%, 100%);
                  background-color: rgb(100%, 90%, 15%); }

all.class3      { border-width: 25px; border-style: ridge;
                  border-color: rgb(250, 120, 100);
                  background-color: rgb(100, 90, 15); }

all.class4      { color: rgb(20, 10, 250); font-size: 32pt;
                  margin: 20px; background-color: rgb(200, 0, 15); }

.graySpeak      { color: gray; background-color: yellow; font-size: 17pt;
                  font-family: Times, serif; line-height: 125%; }
-->

</STYLE>
</HEAD>

<BODY>

<H1 CLASS="classOne">This is Sample 230 with CLASS classOne</H1>

<DIV CLASS="graySpeak">This example shows how to define CLASSes of STYLE that can
be used by any Element simply by using the keyword <B>(all)</B> or by not assigning
them to a specific Element like with CLASS graySpeak. It also demonstrates that you
can repeat the use of the keyword <B>(all)</B> to define more than one CLASS of
STYLE that will be available for <B>(all)</B> Elements.</DIV>

<P CLASS="classDeux">This is a Paragraph Element with CLASS classDeux.</P>

<BLOCKQUOTE CLASS="class3">This BLOCKQUOTE has CLASS class3 assigned to it. It is
still reccomended that you use one of the generic font-family <B>families</B> like
(<B>serif</B>) as the last resort font choice to enhance accurate display of your
document.</BLOCKQUOTE>

<H2 CLASS="graySpeak">This has CLASS graySpeak in a H2 Heading.</H2>

<CENTER CLASS="classDeux">This has CLASS classDeux assigned to the CENTER Element.
</CENTER>
```

```
<A CLASS="class4" HREF="Sample229.html">
     This Link does work and takes you to the last Sample 229 and also has CLASS
class4.</A>

<A CLASS="classOne" HREF="Sample229.html">
     This Link <BLINK>doesn't</BLINK> work because there is a bug with Navigator
so if you want your fancy links to work don't put them inside of a CLASS that has a
border as part of the Style if you use the keyword <B>all</B> .</A>

<BR><BR><BR>

<TABLE BORDER="5" CELLPADDING="5" CELLSPACING="5" WIDTH="200">

<TR>
<TH CLASS="graySpeak">WOW</TH>
</TR>

<TR>
<TH CLASS="graySpeak">You can even assign a CLASS to a TH Element.</TH>
</TR>

</TABLE>

</BODY>
</HTML>
```

Bordered Link workaround example

It should be noted that officially CSS Syntax will not let you directly create fancy Links by any type of STYLE or CLASS of STYLE that has a <u>border</u> as part of the definition for the <A> Element. If you do so, the text will be rendered with the border and other Properties, but the LINK will be unfunctional.

However, there is a workaround. Define a STYLE or CLASS of STYLE that has a border as part of its definition, then use that STYLE on an Element like the H1 Element but nest the Link (the <A> Element) inside that parent H1 Element with the border, and you will then have a Bordered Link.

Example 1-31 demonstrates this workaround. It also demonstrates a nonworking Link when you try to attach a Style to the <A> Element directly. There is more information about the example in its source code. Notice that one Border only has two sides, which is done on purpose.

Example 1-31: **Sample231.html**

```
<!DOCTYPE HTML PUBLIC "-//W3C//DTD HTML 3.2//EN">
<HTML><HEAD>
<TITLE>       Sample 231 - Example 1-31 Bordered Links      </TITLE>

<STYLE TYPE="text/CSS">
<!--

H1.CLASSONE    { border-bottom-width: 30px; border-left-width: 40px;
                 border-style: groove; border-color: rgb(100%, 0%, 50%);
                 color: teal; background-color: blue; font-size: 15pt;
                 font-family: Clarendon, serif; line-height: 125%; }

.CLASSDEUX     { border-width: 20px; border-style: double;
                 border-color: rgb(50%, 10%, 100%);
                 background-color: rgb(100%, 90%, 15%); }

.GRAYTALK         { color: aqua; background-color: gray; font-size: 17pt;
                 font-family: Times, serif; line-height: 125%;
                 text-indent: 40px; }

A.LINK2       { color: yellow; }
-->
</STYLE>
</HEAD>
<BODY>
<H1 CLASS="CLASSONE">
<A HREF="Sample229.html">
This Link does work. Notice it's nested inside of a H1 Element.      </A>
                                        </H1>         <BR><BR><BR>


<H1 CLASS="CLASSONE">
<A CLASS="LINK2" HREF="Sample230.html">
This Link does work. Notice it's nested inside of a H1 Element.      </A>
                                        </H1>         <BR><BR><BR>


<A CLASS="CLASSDEUX" HREF="Sample230.html">
This Link <BLINK>doesn't</BLINK> work because there is a bug with Navigator so if
you want your fancy links to work don't put them inside of a CLASS that has a
border. Instead NEST it inside another Element with a border.         </A>

<P CLASS="GRAYTALK">
Notice that the first link has the regular link color from the preferences. If you
want to change that then you have to change the foreground color with a style and
apply it directly to the A Element like in the second link. The third link is to
show you the pitfall to avoid.                                        </P>

<P CLASS="GRAYTALK">
Just a reminder if you think that the borders in around the top two H1 Headings
aren't working properly, look at the code and you will notice that only the left
and bottom border widths have been specified on purpose for a change of pace.</P>
</BODY>
</HTML>
```

<STYLE> Element with ID Definition for CLASS Exceptions

This is really cool and has a lot of practical use. Let's say you define a CLASS of STYLE that you want to use for a lot of Elements, but there are a few times when you want to change just one or a few things about that CLASS for certain situations. To do that you create a NAMED INDIVIDUAL STYLE, which can be referenced by the ID Attribute of most Elements.

You create a NAMED INDIVIDUAL STYLE just like a CLASS of STYLE with the only difference being that you prefix it with a hashmark (#) like this:

```
#REDEXCEPTION     { color: red; }
```

Now, in order for it to be an <u>exception</u> there has to be a CLASS of STYLE with the general parameters that it will follow. So you create a CLASS of STYLE and then a NAMED INDIVIDUAL STYLE like this:

```
all.GREENTEXT     { color: green; background-color: black;
                       font-size: 20pt; }

#REDEXCEPTION     { color: red; }
```

and then you might call these STYLEs like in the following example.

In this example you should notice that first the Keyword **all** is used to specify that all of the Elements can use the CLASS **GREENTEXT**. Then if you look down at the H1 and DIV Elements, you see that the CLASS **GREENTEXT** is called for both of them, but the DIV Element also has its ID Attribute set to specify that the **REDEXCEPTION** Style is invoked to modify the **GREENTEXT** CLASS, causing the text to be red instead of green.

Example 1-32:   **Sample232.html**

```
<!DOCTYPE HTML PUBLIC "-//W3C//DTD HTML 3.2//EN">
<HTML><HEAD>
<TITLE>  Sample 232 - Example 1-32 Named Individual Style  </TITLE>

<STYLE TYPE="text/CSS">
<!--
      all.GREENTEXT  { color: green; background-color: black; font-size: 20pt; }

      #REDEXCEPTION  { color: red; }
-->
</STYLE>
</HEAD>
```

```
<BODY>
<H1 CLASS="GREENTEXT">        This is Sample 232 with CLASS GREENTEXT</H1>
<DIV CLASS="GREENTEXT" ID="REDEXCEPTION">

This DIVISION has a CLASS GREENTEXT Style and a Named Individual Style of
REDEXCEPTION. You should notice that the background color stays black and the font
size is still 20 points just like in the GREENTEXT CLASS and the only difference is
the red text color which is specified in the REDEXCEPTION Style.   </DIV>

</BODY>
</HTML>
```

This example expands on the NAMED INDIVIDUAL STYLE Exceptions with some options on background images and text contrast caveats. Check out the effect where a P Element has been nested inside of a DIV Element when they both have background images in their Styles.

Example 1-33:   Sample233.html

```
<!DOCTYPE HTML PUBLIC "-//W3C//DTD HTML 3.2//EN">
<HTML><HEAD>
<TITLE>  Sample 233 - Example 1-33 Named Individual Style   </TITLE>

<STYLE TYPE="text/CSS">
<!--

all.RAINBOW    { color: black; font-size: 15pt; text-indent: 45px;
                 padding: 30px; float: center;  text-align: center;
                 background-image: url(./JPEG-FILES/ICON-HorizontalRainbow1.jpg); }

#WHITETEXT     { color: white; }

#RAINBOW2      { color: white;
                 background-image: url(./JPEG-FILES/ICON-HorizontalRainbow4.jpg); }

P.GENERAL      { color: lime; background-color: white; font-size: 14pt;
                 margin-right: 2px;
                 padding: 20px; float: center; text-align: center;
                 background-image: url(./JPEG-FILES/icon-BG-stars.jpg); }
-->

</STYLE>
</HEAD>

<BODY>

<H1 CLASS="RAINBOW">This is Sample 233 with CLASS RAINBOW</H1>

<DIV CLASS="RAINBOW" ID="WHITETEXT">
This DIVISION has a CLASS RAINBOW Style and a Named Individual Style of WHITETEXT.
You should notice that the only difference is the text color which is specified in
the WHITETEXT Style.</DIV>
```

```
<DIV CLASS="RAINBOW" ID="RAINBOW2">
<P CLASS="GENERAL">
This example shows some of the ways to use NAMED INDIVIDUAL STYLES. You should
notice that the text is difficult to read in some of the examples and you might
want to avoid this effect.
</P></DIV>

<BLOCKQUOTE CLASS="RAINBOW" ID="RAINBOW2">
This BLOCKQUOTE has a CLASS RAINBOW Style and a Named Individual Style of RAINBOW2.
You should notice that the only differences are the text color and the background
image which is specified in the RAINBOW2 Style.</BLOCKQUOTE>

</BODY>
</HTML>
```

Styles and Tables

Here's a TABLE example that uses regular Styles that are attached to the TH and TD Elements, a CLASS of STYLE named **GENERAL** that is available to all Elements, and two NAMED INDIVIDUAL STYLEs called **LARGERTEXT** and **RAINBOW2**.

They are primarily intended to show how you can use multiple images for your backgrounds within a Table Cell for interesting effects and to demonstrate the ID Exceptions.

Example 1-34:   Sample234.html

```
<!DOCTYPE HTML PUBLIC "-//W3C//DTD HTML 3.2//EN">
<HTML><HEAD>
<TITLE> Sample 234 - Example 1-34 Named Individual Style</TITLE>

<STYLE TYPE="text/CSS">
<!--

TH              { color: yellow; font-size: 44pt; background-color: blue; }

TD              { color: white; font-size: 34pt;
                    background-image: url(./JPEG-FILES/ICON-HorizontalRainbow4.jpg); }

#LARGERTEXT     { font-size: 40pt; }

#RAINBOW2       { color: white;
                    background-image: url(./JPEG-FILES/ICON-HorizontalRainbow2.jpg); }

.GENERAL        { color: lime; font-size: 34pt;
                    padding: 5px; float: center; text-align: center;
                    background-image: url(./JPEG-FILES/icon-BG-stars.jpg); }

-->
</STYLE>
</HEAD>
```

```
<BODY BGCOLOR="GRAY">

<H1 CLASS="GENERAL">This is Sample 234</H1>

<TABLE BORDER="15" CELLPADDING="5" CELLSPACING="5" WIDTH="500">

<TR>
<TH> 1 </TH> <TH> 2 </TH> <TH> 3 </TH> <TH> 4 </TH> <TH> 5 </TH>
</TR>

<TR>
<TD> 6 </TD> <TD> 7 </TD> <TD> 8 </TD> <TD> 9 </TD> <TD> 10 </TD>
</TR>

</TABLE>

<TABLE BORDER="15" CELLPADDING="5" CELLSPACING="5" WIDTH="500"
                BORDERCOLOR="RED">

<TR>
<TH>

        <BLOCKQUOTE CLASS="GENERAL" ID="RAINBOW2">
                Sing me.
        </BLOCKQUOTE>
</TH>

<TH> 2 </TH>
</TR>

<TR>
<TD>

        <DIV CLASS="GENERAL" ID="LARGERTEXT">
                Sing Me Again
        </DIV>
</TD>

<TD> 4 </TD>

</TR>

</TABLE>
</BODY>
</HTML>
```

As you experiment on your own with TABLEs, be aware that there are definitely limitations with what Style Properties Navigator will let you apply to them. For instance, you <u>cannot</u> directly apply a STYLE or CLASS with a **background-image** Property to a TR or TH Element, but you <u>can</u> to a TD.   If you're sneaky like in the last example and put a CLASS with a **background-image** Propery inside of a BLOCKQUOTE and then put the BLOCKQUOTE inside the TH Element, you can work around the limitation. If you go back and look at the last example in a browser, it's the CELL that says "Sing Me.".

Here are some other limitations and situations to avoid when using STYLEs with TABLEs:

- TH Elements can have their own STYLE or CLASS or ID as long as there is no **background-image** Property in the STYLE definition. See Example 1-35.

- TD Elements can have their own STYLE or CLASS or ID which can include a **background-image** Property in the STYLE definition. See Example 1-35 and 1-36.

- TR Elements cannot have their own STYLE or CLASS or ID. See Example 1-37.

- If you assign a STYLE to all TD Elements in the Style Sheet Definition and then apply a CLASS to an individual TD, the TD will inherit the original STYLE plus any changes that occur from the CLASS. See Example 1-38.

This example demonstrates how TH Elements can have their own STYLE or CLASS or ID as long as there is no **background-image** Property in the STYLE definition. It shows that you get blank cells when you do try to put a **background-image** Property into a TH, and it shows successful implementation into TD cells. The TABLE has 3 rows where the first two rows have TH cells and the last row is all TD cells. These next three examples are all very similar so you can focus on the subtleties of inheritance and caveats to avoid.

Example 1-35: Sample235.html

```
<!DOCTYPE HTML PUBLIC "-//W3C//DTD HTML 3.2//EN">
<HTML>
<HEAD><TITLE> Sample 235 - Example 1-35 Table Style Caveats 1     </TITLE>

<STYLE TYPE="text/CSS">
<!--

TH            { color: red; font-size: 44pt; background-color: black; }

all.BLUETEXT  { color: blue; font-size: 34pt; background-color: aqua; }

all.GENERAL   { color: lime; font-size: 34pt;
                padding: 5px; float: center; text-align: center;
                background-image: url(./JPEG-FILES/icon-BG-stars.jpg); }

all.RAINBOW1  { color: white; font-size: 74pt;
                background-image: url(./JPEG-FILES/ICON-HorizontalRainbow1.jpg); }

#YELLOWTEXT   { color: yellow; font-size: 64pt; background-color: blue; }

#RAINBOW4     { color: black; font-size: 44pt;
                background-image: url(./JPEG-FILES/ICON-HorizontalRainbow4.jpg); }

P             { color: white; font-size: 14pt; text-indent: 45px;}
```

```
-->

</STYLE>
</HEAD>

<BODY BGCOLOR="GRAY">

<H1 CLASS="GENERAL">This is Sample 235</H1>

<TABLE BORDER="15" CELLPADDING="5" CELLSPACING="5" WIDTH="500">

<TR>
<TH>                                        1       </TH>
<TH>                                        2       </TH>
<TH CLASS="BLUETEXT">                       3       </TH>
<TH>                                        4       </TH>
<TH CLASS="BLUETEXT" ID="YELLOWTEXT">       5       </TH>
</TR>

<TR>
<TH CLASS="GENERAL">                        6       </TH>
<TH CLASS="RAINBOW1">                       7       </TH>
<TH CLASS="RAINBOW1" ID="YELLOWTEXT">       8       </TH>
<TH CLASS="RAINBOW1" ID="RAINBOW4">         9       </TH>
<TH CLASS="GENERAL" ID="YELLOWTEXT">        10      </TH>
</TR>

<TR>
<TD CLASS="GENERAL">                        11      </TD>
<TD CLASS="RAINBOW1">                       12      </TD>
<TD CLASS="RAINBOW1" ID="YELLOWTEXT">       13      </TD>
<TD CLASS="RAINBOW1" ID="RAINBOW4">         14      </TD>
<TD CLASS="GENERAL" ID="YELLOWTEXT">        15      </TD>
</TR>

</TABLE>

<P>     The first row shows that TH cells correctly implement the STYLE assigned to
the TH Element for cells 1,2 and 4. The CLASS BLUETEXT in cell 3 and ID YELLOWTEXT
in cell 5 all work correctly also.
</P>

<P>     The second row shows that TH cells DON'T correctly implement the CLASS or ID
Attributes because there are background images contained in their Style
Definitions.
</P>

<P>     The third row has exactly the same CLASSes and IDs as row two but the cells
are TD cells which can handle background images effectively. If you study the code
you can see the inheritence and exceptions.
</P>

</BODY>
</HTML>
```

This example focuses mainly on the TD Elements, which can have their own STYLE or CLASS or ID, which <u>can include</u> a **background-image** Property in the STYLE definition. It also demonstrates how the Exceptions of ID Styles operate in relation to inheriting Properties from a CLASS. Hopefully you are viewing the SAMPLE HTML files in Navigator that go along with the example code in the book. A visual really is worth that thousand words. There are a lot of details about the example within the <P> Elements in the code of the example.

In case you jumped in at the middle of the book and don't know: All of the book examples have a corresponding sample HTML file on the CD-ROM so you can see the results in a browser. They are located in the folder named <u>DHTML-JS BOOK-Main Files</u>. The name of the sample file is always listed to the right of the example number like <u>Sample236.html</u> below.

Example 1-36:   **Sample236.html**

```
<!DOCTYPE HTML PUBLIC "-//W3C//DTD HTML 3.2//EN">
<HTML>
<HEAD><TITLE> Sample 236 - Example 1-36 Table Style Caveats 2</TITLE>
<STYLE TYPE="text/CSS">
<!--

TD              { color: red; font-size: 44pt; background-color: black; }
all.BLUETEXT    { color: blue; font-size: 34pt; background-color: aqua; }

all.GENERAL     { color: lime; font-size: 34pt;
                  padding: 5px; float: center; text-align: center;
                  background-image: url(./JPEG-FILES/icon-BG-stars.jpg); }

all.RAINBOW1    { color: white; font-size: 74pt;
                  background-image: url(./JPEG-FILES/ICON-HorizontalRainbow1.jpg); }

#YELLOWTEXT     { color: yellow; font-size: 64pt; background-color: blue; }

#RAINBOW4       { color: black; font-size: 44pt;
                  background-image: url(./JPEG-FILES/ICON-HorizontalRainbow4.jpg); }

P               { color: black; font-size: 14pt; text-indent: 45px;}

#GREENTEXT      { color: green; }

#FUCHSIATEXT    { color: fuchsia; }

-->
</STYLE></HEAD>

<BODY BGCOLOR="GRAY">

<H1 CLASS="GENERAL">This is Sample 236</H1>
```

```
<TABLE BORDER="15" CELLPADDING="5" CELLSPACING="5" WIDTH="500">

<TR>
<TD>                                          1       </TD>
<TD CLASS="BLUETEXT">                         2       </TD>
<TD CLASS="BLUETEXT"  ID="YELLOWTEXT">        3       </TD>
<TD CLASS="BLUETEXT"  ID="GREENTEXT">         4       </TD>
<TD CLASS="BLUETEXT"  ID="RAINBOW4">          5       </TD>
</TR>

<TR>
<TD CLASS="GENERAL">                          6       </TD>
<TD CLASS="GENERAL"  ID="YELLOWTEXT">         7       </TD>
<TD CLASS="RAINBOW1"  ID="GREENTEXT">         8       </TD>
<TD CLASS="RAINBOW1"  ID="RAINBOW4">          9       </TD>
<TD CLASS="RAINBOW1"  ID="FUCHSIATEXT">       10      </TD>
</TR>

</TABLE>
```

<P>   The first cell gets the STYLE that's attached to all TD cells which is the first Style in the code. All of the other 9 cells have overriding CLASSes and IDs attached to them. Cells 2 through 5 have CLASS BLUETEXT which makes them have 34 point blue text on an aqua background but Cell 3 overrides the CLASS BLUETEXT because it has ID YELLOWTEXT which changes the text to 64 point yellow on a blue background. Cell 4 has ID GREENTEXT which changes only the color of the text to green and the rest of the CLASS BLUETEXT is intact. Cell 5 has ID RAINBOW4 which changes the text to 44 point black and adds a background image.
</P>

<P>   In the second row Cell 6 has CLASS GENERAL. Cell 7 overrides some of the CLASS GENERAL with ID YELLOWTEXT which causes the text to be 64 point yellow. Notice that the background color of blue does not show because the background image of CLASS GENERAL has precedence. In Cell 8 the ID GREENTEXT only changes the color of the text to green and keeps all of CLASS RAINBOW1's other Properites intact. In Cell 9 the background image of ID RAINBOW4 overrides the background image of CLASS RAINBOW1 and the text is changed to black 44 point. In Cell 10 ID FUCHSIATEXT only overrides the text color from white to fuchsia so the rest of the CLASS RAINBOW1 is implemented.
</P>

```
</BODY>
</HTML>
```

Example 1-37 focuses on the fact that, practically speaking, you cannot assign a CLASS of STYLE to a TABLE ROW (TR) Element. It shows what happens when you do, that the background color of the CLASS does get implemented but nothing else. If you have a situation where background color is all you need, then go ahead, but the TH or TD Elements would be more useful.

Example 1-37: **Sample237.html**

```
<!DOCTYPE HTML PUBLIC "-//W3C//DTD HTML 3.2//EN">
<HTML>
<HEAD>
<TITLE> Sample 237 - Example 1-37 Table Style Caveats 3</TITLE>

<STYLE TYPE="text/CSS">

<!--

all.OLIVETEXT          { color: olive; font-size: 24pt; background-color: white; }

all.REDTEXT            { color: red; font-size: 54pt; background-color: black; }

all.BLUETEXT           { color: blue; font-size: 74pt; background-color: aqua; }

P                      { color: black; font-size: 14pt; text-indent: 45px;}
-->

</STYLE>

</HEAD>

<BODY BGCOLOR="GRAY">

<H1 CLASS="REDTEXT">This is Sample 237</H1>

<TABLE BORDER="15" CELLPADDING="5" CELLSPACING="5" WIDTH="500">

<TR CLASS="OLIVETEXT">
<TH>                            1        </TH>
<TH>                            2        </TH>
<TH CLASS="REDTEXT">            3        </TH>
<TH>                            4        </TH>
<TH CLASS="BLUETEXT">           5        </TH>
</TR>

</TABLE>

<P>    Notice that TH Cells with 1,2 and 4 inherit the background color of white
from the OLIVETEXT CLASS but not the text color or font size. Realistically this
severely limits the usefulness of a CLASS for a TR.
</P>

<P>    However the CLASSes in the TH Cells of 3 and 5 work just fine. Remember that
if you want to use a background image in a TH you have to nest it inside another
Element like a BLOCKQUOTE or CITE Element. Use an Element that you won't need for
anything else. The TD Element does not have this limitation so you can include a
background image Property directly in its CLASS.
</P>

</BODY>
</HTML>
```

This example assigns one Style to all TH Elements and another Style to all TD Elements in the STYLE Sheet definition and then applies a CLASS to individual TH and TD cells, causing the TH and TD cells to inherit the original Style plus any changes that occur from the CLASS. This is similar to the way that IDs work, but instead it uses the inheritance of child TH and TD cells from a parent TABLE Element to accomplish the task.

Example 1-38:　　　　　　**Sample238.html**

```
<!DOCTYPE HTML PUBLIC "-//W3C//DTD HTML 3.2//EN">
<HTML>
<HEAD>
<TITLE> Sample 238 - Example 1-38 Tricksie Table Style Inheritance</TITLE>

<STYLE TYPE="text/CSS">

<!--

TH                  { color: red; }

TD           { color: blue; font-size: 20pt; text-decoration: line-through;
                     font-style: italic; font-family: Helvetica;
                     background-color: lime; }

all.FONT54          { font-size: 54pt; }

all.AQUABACK        { background-color: aqua; }

all.TEXTINDENT45    { text-indent: 45px; }

all.TTRANSUP        { text-transform: uppercase; }

P                   { color: black; font-size: 14pt; text-indent: 45px;}
-->

</STYLE>

</HEAD>

<BODY BGCOLOR="SILVER">

<H1 CLASS="FONT54">This is Sample 238</H1>

<TABLE BORDER="15" CELLPADDING="5" CELLSPACING="5" WIDTH="600">

<TR>
<TH>                      1              </TH>
<TH CLASS="FONT54">       2              </TH>
<TH CLASS="AQUABACK">     3              </TH>
<TH CLASS="TEXTINDENT45"> indented 4    </TH>
<TH CLASS="TTRANSUP">     uppercase 5   </TH>
</TR>
```

```
<TR>
<TD>                           6                    </TD>
<TD CLASS="FONT54">            7                    </TD>
<TD CLASS="AQUABACK">          8                    </TD>
<TD CLASS="TEXTINDENT45">      indented 9          </TD>
<TD CLASS="TTRANSUP">          uppercase 10   </TD>
</TR>

</TABLE>
```

```
<P>     In the first row you have TH cells that have a STYLE applied directly to all
of them in the Style Definition which is demonstrated in cell 1.   Then each of the
remaining cells in the first row have a different CLASS of STYLE addressed to it
which makes a minor change to it but the original text color of red is still
applied to all TH cells.
</P>
<P>     In the second row there are TD cells that have a STYLE applied to all of
them that has a lot of Properties in it which are only changed if a CLASS of STYLE
has a Property that explicitly overrides the global settings.   For instance the
font size in cell 7 is changed to 54 point but the rest of the Properties from the
TD STYLE remain intact.
</P>
</BODY>
</HTML>
```

<STYLE> Element with CONTEXTUAL SELECTION CRITERIA

OK, so it looks ominous and it's just slightly tricky to explain, but it's really easy once you see it demonstrated, and it's a really powerful technique that you will use a lot for precise creative control. Way back in the beginning of this section of the book, this concept was defined, and I'll repeat it here as a refresher: This is a special way to apply Styles that is called CONTEXTUAL APPLICATION, or you could say it's implemented by specifying CONTEXTUAL SELECTION CRITERIA. When you have sequential Elements in your Style definition or, put another way, one Element followed by another Element, then that Style will only be applied when the Element appears in that order in the BODY of the document; that is, the Element must be precisely nested.

When you want to apply a Style to a particular Element when that Element is only inside of another Element or Elements, this is called a STYLE with CONTEXTUAL SELECTION CRITERIA because the Style gets applied only when the Element is nested in the context of another Element. The criteria aspect is the actual order of the nested Elements, which you specify in the STYLE definition.

Let's say that you want to create a STRONG Element that has purple text, but only when it's inside a CENTER Element, and when it's not inside a CENTER Element it will be red. First you define a Style for the STRONG Element that applies to it each time it occurs like this:

```
STRONG   { color: red; }
```

Then you define a Style that is applied to a STRONG Element only when it occurs inside a CENTER Element like this:

```
CENTER STRONG  { color: purple; }
```

The reason this works is because a CONTEXTUAL Style always has precedence over a regular Style, so the color purple overrides the color red. Remember to separate the Elements with a space or a tab but not a comma.

Let's put that together in an example like so:

Example 1-39:   Sample239.html

```
<!DOCTYPE HTML PUBLIC "-//W3C//DTD HTML 3.2//EN">
<HTML>
<HEAD>
<TITLE>Sample 239 - CSS Example 1-39 Contextual Selection Criteria</TITLE>

<STYLE TYPE="text/CSS">

<!--

STRONG         { color: red; }

CENTER STRONG  { color: purple; }

-->

</STYLE>

</HEAD>

<BODY>

<H1>This is Sample 239</H1>

<STRONG>
        This is an Element with Strong Emphasis. It's red and bold.
</STRONG><BR><BR>

<CENTER>
<STRONG>
        This is an Element with Strong Emphasis that's contained within a Center
Element therefore it's purple and centered and bold.
</STRONG>
</CENTER>

</BODY>
</HTML>
```

Example 1-40 focuses on Elements that are nested inside one or more other Elements. Example 1-41 demonstrates nested List Elements with CONTEXTUAL Styles and has an indepth explanation on page 97 after the example code.

Example 1-40: **Sample240.html**

```
<!DOCTYPE HTML PUBLIC "-//W3C//DTD HTML 3.2//EN">
<HTML>
<HEAD>
<TITLE>  Sample 240 - CSS Example 1-40 Contextual Selection Criteria    </TITLE>

<STYLE TYPE="text/CSS">

<!--

H4              { color: green; font-size: 40pt; }

DIV H4          { color: navy; font-size: 30pt; }

CITE DIV H4     { color: fuchsia; font-size: 24pt;
                  font-family:"Brush Script", cursive; }

-->

</STYLE>

</HEAD>

<BODY>

<H4>
This is Sample 240.                         <BR><BR>
It's green and has 40 point text.
</H4>

<DIV><H4>
This is an H4 Element nested inside a Division Element that is 30 point navy.
</H4></DIV>
                                    <BR><BR>

<CITE><DIV><H4>

        This is an H4 Element nested inside a Division Element which is then inside
of a Citation Element therefore it is fuchsia, sized at 24 point and is in the
Brush Script font-family.

</H4></DIV></CITE>

</BODY>
</HTML>
```

Example 1-41:   Sample241.html

```
<!DOCTYPE HTML PUBLIC "-//W3C//DTD HTML 3.2//EN">
<HTML><HEAD>
<TITLE>Sample 241 - CSS Example 1-41 Advanced Lists & Contextual Selection</TITLE>

<STYLE TYPE="text/CSS">
<!--
H1                      { float: center; color: red; }

B                       { color: blue; font-size: 17pt; }

DIV                     { color: purple; font-size: 17pt; }

PRE                     { color: green; font-size: 17pt; }

B UL LI                 { list-style-type: disc; color: red; }

DIV UL LI               { list-style-type: circle; color: blue; }

PRE UL LI               { list-style-type: square; color: navy; }
-->
</STYLE>
</HEAD>

<BODY>
<H1>This is Sample 241</H1>
<B>      <UL>
                <LI>    item 1
                <LI>    item 2
                <LI>    item 3
                <LI>    item 4
                <LI>    item 5
         </UL>
</B>
<DIV>    <UL>
                <LI>    item A
                <LI>    item B
                <LI>    item C
                <LI>    item D
                <LI>    item E
         </UL>
</DIV>
<PRE>    <UL>
                <LI>    item i
                <LI>    item ii
                <LI>    item iii
                <LI>    item iv
                <LI>    item v
         </UL>
</PRE>
</BODY>
</HTML>
```

The previous Example 1-41 focuses on creating several LISTS that each have their own bullet type and have bullet colors that are different from the text within the list. First you assign STYLES to the three Elements that will each contain a LIST. Then you use CONTEXTUAL SELECTION CRITERIA to assign a STYLE to a LI Element that is contained within both a UL Element and a parent Element like DIV in this example.

The **list-style-type** Property is set to a Value of **circle** for the LI Elements that are contained inside the DIV Element and so that the UL Element and the LI Elements will have a different Value when they are inside of the other parent Elements of B and PRE.

The explanation for Example 1-42 follows the code below.

Example 1-42: Sample242.html

```
<!DOCTYPE HTML PUBLIC "-//W3C//DTD HTML 3.2//EN">
<HTML>
<HEAD>
<TITLE>Sample 242 - CSS Example 1-42 Contextual Selection Criteria</TITLE>

<STYLE TYPE="text/CSS">
<!--

CITE            { color: red; font-size: 20pt; background-color: yellow; }

DIV             { color: navy; font-size: 30pt; background-color: aqua;
                  text-decoration: line-through; font-family: Helvetica; }

H4              { color: green; font-size: 40pt; }

CITE DIV H4     { color: fuchsia; font-size: 24pt; font-family: cursive;
                  text-decoration: none; }
-->
</STYLE>
</HEAD>
<BODY>
<H4>            This is Sample 242.                      </H4>
<CITE>  This is the CITE part.
<DIV>   This is the DIVISION part.
<H4>
        This is an H4 Element nested inside a Division Element which is then inside
of a Citation Element therefore it is fuchsia, sized at 24 point and is in a
generic cursive font-family. Notice how it inherits the aqua background-color from
the DIV Element but the text-decoration Property of line-through has been
overridden and set to none.
</H4>
</DIV>
</CITE>

</BODY>
</HTML>
```

Inheritance issues for
CONTEXTUAL STYLEs

Example 1-42 demonstrates what happens if you create nested Elements with CONTEXTUAL APPLICATION of a Style where the nested Elements are not terminated by an End Tag before another Element is begun.

If you look at the Elements in the BODY of the document, you will see that the sentence, "<u>This is the CITE part.</u>" is not followed immediately by a CITE End Tag; therefore, the Properties of the Style that are assigned to the CITE Element will continue to be applied to the DIV and H4 Elements, except where they are explicitly overridden with Properties assigned to the DIV and H4 Elements, respectively. This demonstrates Inheritance of Properties from one Element nested inside of another.

Siblings, Ancestors and other relations

Here are some terms you need to know before we go on.

Ancestor   is an Element that contains one or more Elements.
Parent   is an Element that contains one or more Elements (same as Ancestor).
Descendant   is an Element contained by another Element.
Child   is an Element contained by another Element (same as Descendant).
Sibling   is another Child Element contained in the same Parent Element.

Nesting and Inheritance

Child, Sibling and Descendant Elements can be deeply nested and inheritance of Property Values will still carry through.

Contextual Selectors

When you refer to a Style that has a CONTEXTUAL SELECTOR, it's the same as saying that it has CONTEXTUAL SELECTION CRITERIA. This is not a new concept, just a different <u>term</u> to use to make it easier to discuss in the following examples.

Just like before in the most recent mini-example that demonstrated a Style with CONTEXTUAL SELECTION CRITERIA, this is an example of a Style that contains a CONTEXTUAL SELECTOR that applies only to CITE Elements that are nested inside H4 Elements:

```
H4  CITE    { color: green; font-size: 40pt; }
```

CONTEXTUAL SELECTION with CLASSes of STYLE and NAMED INDIVIDUAL STYLEs

Now, CONTEXTUAL SELECTORS can be assigned so that they also include CLASSes of STYLE and NAMED INDIVIDUAL STYLEs in addition to the regular assigned STYLEs that have been demonstrated so far.

Mini-Examples:

Here are four quick mini-examples, followed by explanations:

```
all.BLUETEXT    CITE    { color:blue; text-transform:capitalize; }
.redText        PRE     { color:red; font-weight:bold; font-size:20pt; }
DIV.greenText   H2      { font-size:14pt;}
#PurpleBack     H5      { color:aqua; }
```

Mini-Examples Explained:

In the first of those mini-examples the text would be blue and capitalized for all of the CITE Elements that also had a CLASS of **BLUETEXT** addressed to it. See Example 1-43.

In the second, all PRE Elements would have bold 20 point red text that also had a CLASS of **redText** addressed to it. See Example 1-44.

In the third, all H2 Elements would have 14 point text that are contained within an ancestor that is a DIV Element that has a **greenText** CLASS addressed to it. If the CLASS **greenText** actually specifies the text to be green like in Example 1-45, then the H2 Element would indeed have green text but not green eggs and ham even though Smeagol smells it.

In the fourth, all H5 Elements would have aqua text that are a descendant of any Element that has an ID of **PurpleBack** addressed to it. See Example 1-46.

The next four examples will take one of each of these four mini-examples and demonstrate it fully. The examples will procede in the same order as the mini-examples.

Example 1-43 focuses on the CONTEXTUAL SELECTOR of **all.BLUETEXT CITE**, and it uses several instances of Styles created for the CITE Element when it is used in the context of various Elements.

Example 1-43:   **Sample243.html**

```
<!DOCTYPE HTML PUBLIC "-//W3C//DTD HTML 3.2//EN">
<HTML><HEAD>
<TITLE>Sample 243 - CSS Example 1-43 Contextual Selection Criteria</TITLE>

<STYLE TYPE="text/CSS">
<!--

CITE                    { color: red; font-size: 20pt; background-color: yellow; }

.BLUETEXT               { color: blue; }

all.BLUETEXT   CITE     { color: blue; text-transform: capitalize; }

H4                      { color: green; font-size: 40pt; }

H5                      { font-family: Moonlight, Helvetica; }
-->
</STYLE>
</HEAD>

<BODY>

<H4>            This is Sample 243.                               </H4>


<CITE>  This is a regular CITE.         </CITE>                <BR><BR>

<DIV CLASS="BLUETEXT"> This is the DIVISION part with blue text.
<CITE>
        This is a CITE Element nested inside a Division Element which has
captialized blue text because it overrides the color red, but retains the rest of
the 20 point text and yellow background Properties of the simple Selector CITE
Style.
</CITE>
</DIV>                                                         <BR><BR>

<H5><CITE>
        This is a CITE inside of a H5 Heading. Notice that the font is either
Moonlight if it was available or Helvetica because it was inherited and not
overriden by the CITE Element.
</CITE></H5>

</BODY>
</HTML>
```

Example 1-44 expands on the second mini-example from page 99 in the section on CONTEXTUAL SELECTORs. See the notes in the example code for more information.

Example 1-44:   **Sample244.html**

```
<!DOCTYPE HTML PUBLIC "-//W3C//DTD HTML 3.2//EN">
<HTML>
<HEAD>
<TITLE>Sample 244 - CSS Example 1-44 Contextual Selection Criteria</TITLE>

<STYLE TYPE="text/CSS">

<!--

PRE                 { font-family: Courier, monospace; white-space: normal; }

.redText            { color: red; }

.redText      PRE   { color: red; font-weight: bold; font-size: 20pt; }

.BLUECAPS           { color: blue; text-transform: capitalize; }

.BLUECAPS     PRE   { color: blue; font-size: 24pt; }

H4                  { color: green; font-size: 30pt; }

-->

</STYLE>
</HEAD>

<BODY>

<H4>    This is Sample 244.            </H4>                        <HR>

<PRE>   This is a regular PRE.          </PRE>        <BR><BR>       <HR>

<DIV CLASS="redText"> This is the DIVISION part with red text.
<PRE>
        This is a PRE Element nested inside a Division Element with a CLASS of
'redText' so the CONTEXTUAL STYLE gives it a bold size of 20 point red text. It
also is specified to have white-space set to normal, that is collapsed.
</PRE>
</DIV>                                            <BR><BR>       <HR>

<H4 CLASS="BLUECAPS">This is the H4 part with 30 point blue capitalization.
<PRE>
        This is a PRE inside of a H5 Heading. notice that the text is not
capitalized  because capitalization was not inherited by the PRE Element but the
text is sized at 24 points. Also notice that the text color is not green or 40
points because the H4 simple Selector is not used because the CLASS BLUECAPS is
addressed.
</PRE>
</H4>                                                              <HR>

</BODY>
</HTML>
```

Example 1-45 focuses on mini-example 3 from page 99. The font size of 14 is only applied to H2 Headings that are nested inside of DIV Elements that also have the **greenText** CLASS of STYLE applied to it.

Example 1-45:   Sample245.html

```
<!DOCTYPE HTML PUBLIC "-//W3C//DTD HTML 3.2//EN">
<HTML>
<HEAD>
<TITLE>Sample 245 - CSS Example 1-45 Contextual Selection Criteria</TITLE>

<STYLE TYPE="text/CSS">
<!--

.greenText              { color: green; }

DIV.greenText   H2      { font-size: 20pt; }

H4                      { color: blue; font-size: 30pt; }

-->
</STYLE>
</HEAD>

<BODY>

<H4>           This is Sample 245.                  </H4>          <HR>

<H2>    This is a regular H2.  </H2>                 <BR><BR>      <HR>

<DIV CLASS="greenText">
        This is the DIVISION part with green text from CLASS 'greenText'.
<H2>
        This is a H2 Element nested inside a Division Element with a CLASS of
'greenText' so the CONTEXTUAL STYLE gives it a size of 20 point with inherited
green text.
</H2>
</DIV>

</BODY>
</HTML>
```

Example 1-46 focuses on mini-example 4 of page 99 and points out a deficiency in the ability of Elements to inherit certain Properties in Navigator. It shows two ways of using CONTEXTUAL SELECTION, including the long-hand referencing of CLASSes of STYLE and NAMED INDIVIDUAL STYLEs. See the comments and notes in the example and notice that you can use both short-hand and long-hand referencing.

Example 1-46:   Sample246.html

```
<!DOCTYPE HTML PUBLIC "-//W3C//DTD HTML 3.2//EN">
<HTML>
<HEAD>
<TITLE>Sample 246 - CSS Example 1-46 Contextual Selection Criteria</TITLE>

<STYLE TYPE="text/CSS">

<!--

DIV.indent100          { text-indent: 100px; font-size: 20pt; font-style: italic; }

#PurpleBack            { background-color: purple; }

#PurpleBack    H5      { color: aqua; }

        /*     Technically you would only have to write the following Style:
               DIV.indent100.#PurpleBack     H2              like this:
               #PurpleBack     H2
               but the long hand version shows the actual sequence better.
        */

DIV.indent100.#PurpleBack     H2      { color: yellow; }

H4                              { color: blue; font-size: 30pt; }

-->
</STYLE>
</HEAD>
<BODY>

<H4>           This is Sample 246.                              </H4>   <HR>

<H5>    This is a regular H5.  </H5>                        <BR><BR><HR>

<DIV CLASS="indent100" ID="PurpleBack">
        This is the DIVISION part with 20 point indented text of 100 pixels from
CLASS 'indent100' and a purple background color from ID 'PurpleBack'.

<H5>    This is a H5 Element nested inside a Division Element with a CLASS of
'indent100' and an ID of 'PurpleBack' so the CONTEXTUAL STYLE gives it aqua text
on a purple background and it inherits text that has a size of 20 points.  <BR>

The reason that the text-indent Property and font-style Properties are not
inherited is because Navigator is not sophisticated enough yet.          </H5>

<H2>    This is a H2 Test Heading that has this               <BR>
        "DIV.indent100.#PurpleBack     H2      { color: yellow; }"       <BR>
        CONTEXTUAL STYLE applied.                                        </H2>
</DIV>

</BODY>
</HTML>
```

More Style Uses

The STYLE Attribute

The STYLE Attribute is used to apply a Style directly to an Element in the BODY of the document in an on-the-fly fashion. It's mainly used when you have a Style that you need to use only once or twice. Just so there isn't any confusion, the STYLE Attribute works just like other Attributes of an Element, except that instead of specifying a VALUE within the quote marks, you specify one or more Property <u>NAME: VALUE;</u> Pairs between the double quotes. There is a complete list of all the Elements that the Style Attribute can be used with on page 15. Here are a few mini-examples:

```
<FORM    STYLE="float:center; font-size:14pt;">
<CITE    STYLE="color:olive; font-size:12pt;">
<H1      STYLE="border-style:ridge; color:yellow; border-width:25px;">
<TD      STYLE="background-color:blue; color:white; font-size:15pt;">
<DIV     STYLE="text-indent:50px; font-size:13pt;">
<BODY    STYLE="margin:20px; font-size:14pt;">
<A       STYLE="color:red; font-weight:bold;">
```

Syntax:

```
<ELEMENT    STYLE="PropertyNAME: VALUE; PropertyNAME: VALUE; ...">

***

</ELEMENT>
```

Several usages of the STYLE Attribute within different Elements are demonstrated in this example. Note that the STYLE Element is not used at all in the HEAD of the page. The STYLE Attribute implements the Style on a local Element-by-Element basis.

Example 1-47:   Sample247.html

```
<!DOCTYPE HTML PUBLIC "-//W3C//DTD HTML 3.2//EN">
<HTML><HEAD>
<TITLE>Sample 247 - CSS Example 1-47 Style as Attribute</TITLE>
</HEAD>

<BODY STYLE="margin: 20px; font-size: 19pt;
        border-style: ridge; border-width: 25px;
        border-color: aqua; color: purple;">
```

```
<P>
Just a regular paragraph. Notice that there is no STYLE Element Style Sheet in the
Header. Also notice that this paragraph did not inherit the font-size of 19 pt or
the text color of purple from the BODY Element.
</P>

<CITE STYLE="color: olive; font-size: 22pt;">
The Citation
</CITE>

<H1 STYLE="border-style: ridge; color: blue; border-width: 25px;">  <BR>
The H1.                                                           <BR><BR>
</H1>

<DIV STYLE="text-indent: 50px; font-size: 29pt;">
The Division.
</DIV>                                                            <BR><BR>

<A STYLE="color: red; font-weight: bold;" HREF="Sample248.html">
The Link to the next Sample 248.
</A>

</BODY>
</HTML>
```

The <SPAN> Element

The <SPAN> Element has a different methodology of applying Style than any of the techniques we've used so far and the purpose differs in that it is used to create a Style for a chunk of content itself, instead of for an Element that controls a chunk of content. When you use the SPAN Element, the Style will only be applied to the content between its Start and End Tags. The SPAN Element requires both Start and End Tags.

You use the SPAN Element with only the STYLE Attribute or it can include CLASSes of STYLE that may or may not have ID Exceptions. Using the STYLE Attribute within the SPAN Element is a very quick way of applying Style, but only in the short run if a Style won't be needed very often.

One of the frequently implemented techniques for using the SPAN Element is to highlight a particular word or phrase by changing its color, size, or font or to create an Initial DropCap to start a paragraph, which is demonstrated in Example 1-51.

Obviously you have to use one of the three Attributes listed in the following Syntax in order for the SPAN Element to do anything.

Syntax:

```
<SPAN
      STYLE="PropertyName: Value; PropertyName: Value;..."   |
      CLASS="className"                                      |
      CLASS="className" ID="idName"                          |
>
   ***
</SPAN>
```

The <SPAN> Element with STYLE Attribute

Now we'll explore some techniques for the SPAN Element by using its Attributes of STYLE, CLASS and ID. As previously indicated in the Syntax, when you use the STYLE Attribute with the SPAN Element, you specify the particular CSS Syntax Properties in NAME: VALUE pairs that are separated by a semicolon, which you want to comprise your Style and place them between double quote marks just like any other Attribute Value. Both Start and End Tags are required.

Here is a quick mini-example of the <SPAN> Element used in concert with the STYLE Attribute.

```
<SPAN STYLE="color:blue;"> This text will be blue. </SPAN>
```

And here's another:

```
<SPAN STYLE="background-color: red; font-size: 24pt;">
This text will be on a red background and sized at 24 point.
</SPAN>
```

You should notice that the entire group of Properties listed are contained within only one set of double quotes instead of the possible error of putting each Property in its own set of double quotes. It's also a good idea to check and make sure that you have included the <u>measurement units</u> for Property Values like:

```
font-size:24pt;
```

It's very easy to forget to include them because they aren't required in regular HTML Attribute Syntax. If you're racking your synapses because something's missing when you test your code in a browser, check that first and next check to see if the colons and semicolons are all there and in the right places. Sometimes it's the little gremlins that sabotage the operation.

This example demonstrates the SPAN Element with the STYLE Attribute to change the color and size of text along with background color changes and the creation of a border around a heading.

Example 1-48: **Sample248.html**

```
<!DOCTYPE HTML PUBLIC "-//W3C//DTD HTML 3.2//EN">
<HTML>
<HEAD>
<TITLE>Sample 248 - CSS Example 1-48 SPAN Element with STYLE</TITLE>
</HEAD>

<BODY STYLE="margin: 10px; border-color: lime;
             border-style: groove; border-width: 20px;">

<P>
Just a regular paragraph. Notice that there is no STYLE Element Style Sheet in the
Header. Also notice that

<SPAN STYLE="color:red; background-color:yellow; font-size:24pt;">
this part of the paragraph has the SPAN Element with the STYLE Attribute applied to
it but
</SPAN>

this part does not.
</P>                               <BR>

<H1>
The H1 without SPAN.            <BR>
<SPAN STYLE="border-style: ridge; color: blue; border-width: 25px;">
The H1 with SPAN.
</SPAN>
</H1>                              <BR>

<A HREF="Sample249.html">
<SPAN STYLE="color: purple; font-weight: bold;
 font-size:28pt; background-color:aqua;">
The Link to the next Sample 249 and it is SPAN enhanced.
</SPAN>
</A>

</BODY>
</HTML>
```

This example shows you how to create Initial DropCaps and WordCaps by using the SPAN Element with the STYLE Attribute.

Example 1-49: **Sample249.html**

```
<!DOCTYPE HTML PUBLIC "-//W3C//DTD HTML 3.2//EN">
<HTML>
<HEAD>
<TITLE>Sample 249 - CSS Example 1-49 SPAN Element with STYLE</TITLE>
</HEAD>

<BODY STYLE="border-color: red; margin:0px;
            border-style: double; border-width: 20px;">

<P STYLE="font-size: 20pt; color: blue;">

<SPAN STYLE="color: red; background-color: yellow; font-size: 70pt;">
T
</SPAN>
he first letter has the SPAN Element specified to create an initial-drop-cap that
is often used in the publishing world to start an article but has been a pain to
create up till now.
</P>                                          <BR>

<H1>
<SPAN STYLE="border-style: double; color: blue; border-width: 10px;
            font-size: 150pt; background-color: red; float: left;">
W
</SPAN>

<SPAN STYLE="font-size: 24pt; background-color: red; color: white;">
oah maaaan, that's a big double-u.
</SPAN>
</H1>                                         <BR>

<SPAN STYLE="color: yellow; font-size: 88pt;
        background-color: lime; float: left;">
W
</SPAN>

<SPAN STYLE="font-size: 24pt; background-color: blue; color: white;">
ow another big double-u man.
</SPAN>

<BR CLEAR="ALL"><BR>

<A HREF="Sample250.html">
<SPAN STYLE="color: navy; font-size: 22pt; background-color: silver;">
The Link to the next Sample 250 and it is SPAN enhanced.
</SPAN>
</A>

</BODY>
</HTML>
```

This example shows you how to change the color and size of text for the titles of artwork using the SPAN Element with the STYLE Attribute. It also sets a default Style for the BODY of the document by using the STYLE Attribute with the BODY Element, which puts a Border around the entire viewing area.

Example 1-50: **Sample250.html**

```
<!DOCTYPE HTML PUBLIC "-//W3C//DTD HTML 3.2//EN">
<HTML>
<HEAD>
<TITLE>Sample 250 - CSS Example 1-50 SPAN Element with STYLE</TITLE>
</HEAD>

<BODY STYLE="border-color: rgb(55%,10%,100%); background-color:#bbbbee;
             border-style: outset; border-width: 15px;">

<P STYLE="font-size: 20pt; color: blue;">

<SPAN STYLE="color: rgb(50%,0%,100%); font-size: 30pt;">
<IMG SRC="JPEG-FILES/J5-SpaceDome_27P.jpg" ALT="SpaceDome" ALIGN="ABSMIDDLE">

SpaceDome
</SPAN>                               <BR>
This is a Sci-Fi painting by Gilorien set on a far distant world of the
imagination.                          <HR>

<!--         *************************************************   -->

<SPAN STYLE="color: rgb(50%,0%,100%); font-size: 30pt;">
<IMG SRC="JPEG-FILES/J5-Sedona_Winter_Sphere13.jpg" ALT="Sedona Winter Sphere"
     ALIGN="RIGHT">

<SPACER TYPE="VERTICAL" SIZE="100">

Sedona Winter Sphere<BR><BR>
</SPAN>
This is a Surreal painting by Gilorien inspired by Sedona Arizona.
</P>                                   <BR>

<!--         *************************************************   -->

<A HREF="Sample251.html">
<SPAN STYLE="text-transform: uppercase; color: rgb(255,0,0)">
go to the next sample.
</SPAN>                                </A>

</BODY>
</HTML>
```

The <SPAN> Element with CLASS Attribute

The <SPAN> Element which uses a CLASS Attribute to address a CLASS of STYLE differs from the previous examples only in that you obviously have to create a Style Sheet with the STYLE Element in order to have a CLASS of STYLE. You start by creating and naming a CLASS of STYLE in the STYLE Element in the Header and then addressing it with the CLASS Attribute of an Element to create an on-the-fly Style for a section of content in the Body of the document. Remember that the SPAN Element requires both the Start and End Tags.

Here are a few mini-examples of using the SPAN Element with a CLASS of STYLE:

```
<SPAN     CLASS="NameMe42">      42              </SPAN>

<SPAN     CLASS="blueText">      Blues           </SPAN>

<SPAN     CLASS="DropCap88">     M               </SPAN>
```

which assume you have created the following CLASSes of STYLE:

```
.NameMe42      { font-size: 42pt; background-color: yellow; color: navy; }
.blueText      { color: rgb(0, 0, 255); }
.DropCap88     { font-size: 88pt; line-height: 50%; color: rgb(255, 0, 0); }
```

This example focuses on a variation of the earlier DropCap example, but this time it addresses a CLASS of STYLE within the SPAN Element instead of the STYLE Attribute to accomplish the same thing. It also uses the **rgb( )** Function to set some colors, and there are several other uses of CLASSes of STYLE used within the SPAN Element.

Example 1-51: Sample251.html

```
<!DOCTYPE HTML PUBLIC "-//W3C//DTD HTML 3.2//EN">
<HTML>
<HEAD>
<TITLE>Sample 251 - CSS Example 1-51 SPAN Element with CLASS of STYLE</TITLE>

<STYLE TYPE="text/CSS">

<!--

BODY           { border-color: rgb(15%,0%,80%); background-color:#eeaadd;
                 border-style: outset; border-width: 15px; margin: 0px;
                 padding: 0px; width: 555px; }
```

```
H1              { float:center; color:red; background-color: black;
                  font-size: 42pt; }

P               { color:purple; font-size:17pt; margin: 0px; padding: 0px;
                  font-family: Clarendon, sans-serif; }

all.NameMe42    { font-size: 42pt; background-color: yellow;
                  float: center; color: navy; }

all.blueText    { color: rgb(0, 0, 255); font-size: 44pt; }

all.DropCap88   { font-size: 88pt; float: left;  padding: 0px;
                  color: rgb(255, 0, 0); }

-->

</STYLE>
</HEAD>

<BODY>

<H1>Sample 251</H1>                               <BR><BR><HR>

<!--     ********   The bold text is what is rendered   ********   -->

<SPAN    CLASS="DropCap88">         W</SPAN>           <BR><BR><BR><BR>
```

<P>**hat is the secret of life, the universe and everything according to**

```
<SPAN    CLASS="blueText">         Deep Thought    </SPAN>
```

in the hitch-hiker's guide to the galaxy?</P>

```
<SPAN    CLASS="NameMe42">         42                </SPAN> <BR><HR>

<!--           **************************************************   -->
```

<P>**Play me some**</P>
```
<SPAN    CLASS="blueText">         Blues.            </SPAN> <BR><BR>

<!--           **************************************************   -->

<A HREF="Sample252.html">
<SPAN STYLE="font-style: italic; font-size: 24pt; color: rgb(255,0,250)">
```
go to the next sample.
```
</SPAN>
</A>

</BODY>
</HTML>
```

The <SPAN> Element with ID Attribute for CLASS Exceptions

This works exactly the same way as the last section except that you add the ID Attribute to create exceptions to the inherited Properties of the CLASS of STYLE that are applied to the content.

One thing you will find is that you'll always have more predictably consistent results if you enclose your SPAN Elements inside other Elements like the Division, Paragraph, Preformatted or Heading Elements. It seems to be the nature of the way that Navigator is coded, although the inconsistencies may have been eliminated by the time you read this. Experiment on your own and see what happens.

If you find anything bizarre that you can get repeatable results of then email me the parameters that caused it and I'll include it in the episodic updates in the online followup which comes out about once every few months.

Here's a mini-example:

```
<SPAN   CLASS="redText" ID="Larger">    Bigger Red    </SPAN>
```

based on this CLASS of STYLE:

```
all.redText { color: red; font-size: 12pt; }
```

based on this ID Exception STYLE:

```
#Larger    { font-size: 39pt; }
```

The above SPAN usage would create 'Bigger Red' in red text that is 39pt using the ID Exception to override the 12pt text that is set in the CLASS of STYLE.

This example focuses on a simple implementation of the above mini-example.

Example 1-52:   Sample252.html

```
<!DOCTYPE HTML PUBLIC "-//W3C//DTD HTML 3.2//EN">
<HTML>
<HEAD>

<TITLE>
Sample 252 - CSS Example 1-52 SPAN with ID Exception to CLASS of STYLE
</TITLE>
```

```
<STYLE TYPE="text/CSS">

<!--

BODY            { border-color: rgb(75%,0%,40%); background-color:#cceeff;
                  border-style: inset; border-width: 10px; margin: 0px;
                  padding: 0px; width: 555px; }

H1              { float:center; color:lime; background-color: gray;
                  font-size: 42pt; }

P               { color:purple; font-size:17pt; margin: 0px; padding: 0px;
                  font-family: Clarendon, sans-serif; }

all.blueText    { color: rgb(0, 0, 255); font-size: 20pt; }

all.redText     { color: red; font-size: 12pt; }

#Larger         {font-size: 39pt; }

-->

</STYLE>

</HEAD>

<BODY>

<H1>Sample 252</H1>                                <BR><BR>        <HR>

<!--          **************************************************   -->

<P><SPAN CLASS="blueText">

**Hint** You will always have more consistent results if you enclose your SPAN
Elements inside of other Elements like the Division, Paragraph, Preformatted or
Heading Elements.                                       </SPAN> </P><HR>

<P><SPAN CLASS="redText">     This is CLASS redText.        </SPAN> </P>

<P><SPAN CLASS="redText" ID="Larger"> Big Red             </SPAN> </P>


<P><SPAN CLASS="redText">     had the larger size.        </SPAN> </P>

<!--          **************************************************   -->

<A HREF="Sample253.html">
<SPAN STYLE="font-style: italic; font-size: 24pt; color: rgb(255,0,250)">
go to the next sample.
</SPAN>
</A>

</BODY>
</HTML>
```

External Style Sheets
with the <LINK> Element

There are some major advantages to using External Style Sheets because you can use the same Style Sheet over and over again on multiple documents without having to recode everything. If you have a very large site with lots of pages that use the exact same Style Sheet, even if you need to make minor inline changes, this can save you huge amounts of time. If you plan ahead, you can create a master External Style Sheet or Sheets that have all of your defaults globally set that will work for every page or every page in a section of the site and then just make minor Additions or Exceptions for certain pages that require them.

A typical way to manage a large site effectively is to set global defaults in an External Style Sheet and then use inline SPAN and ID Exceptions to those defaults. The one minor annoyance to this scenario is that the Styles are not at your fingertips if you do need to make changes to the External Style Sheet; but then again, how far away can they be? The seconds you lose will be more than compensated by the hours you save.

Another excellent advantage to this operational paradigm is that you can just make changes to the External Style Sheet without having to alter the documents containing the content. Note the plural form of the word document. If your site has 1000 pages, which isn't really that large, imagine the difference in time it would take to make even three modifications to one External Style Sheet as opposed to 1000 content documents. For a 5-minute correction of 1000 pages, that would translate into 83 hours and 20 minutes.

Obviously the flip side is if you have a lot of different Style Sheets that are only applicable to a few pages, then it's not worth the effort to keep track of External Style Sheets. Just evaluate your needs and be aware of your options and choose wisely.

The <LINK> Element

The <LINK> Element is used to access an External Style Sheet that is contained in another document. The Attributes REL and TYPE are required. The TITLE <u>Attribute</u> (of the LINK Element, not the TITLE Element) is optional and is only used when you want to declare a <u>default</u> Style Sheet, which can then be optionally activated or deactivated by the user. You use the LINK Element in the HEAD Section of your document but not inside the STYLE Element, and you don't even need to declare a STYLE Element, but it is allowed if you want to create additional Style Sheets. Multiple Style Sheets are allowed within a single document, and we'll get to that in the next section. You only use the Start Tag, and the End Tag is forbidden.

This is the typical way that you would specify the <LINK> Element:

```
<LINK REL="STYLESHEET" TYPE="text/CSS" HREF="globalStyles1.html">
```

This is the typical way that you would implement the <LINK> Element:

```
<HEAD>

<TITLE>  My Home Page 2        </TITLE>

<LINK REL="STYLESHEET" TYPE="text/CSS" HREF="globalStyles1.html">

</HEAD>
```

Notice that there is no <STYLE> Element present within the HEAD Element. The reason that the <STYLE> Element is unnecessary is because the information normally conveyed by it to the browser, such as the TYPE="text/CSS" and the fact that it is a Style Sheet, is all contained in the Attributes of the LINK Element.

Syntax:

```
<LINK
REL="STYLESHEET"    | "ALTERNATE STYLESHEET"
TYPE="text/CSS"     | "text/javaScript"
TITLE="name"
HREF="URL">
```

Attributes Defined:

REL="STYLESHEET" | "ALTERNATE STYLESHEET" **Persistent**, **Default** or **Alternate**
This Attribute is used to declare the Relationship of the Style Sheet, whether it is **Persistent**, a **Default**, Style Sheet, or an **Alternate** Style Sheet. If you specify **REL** as:

STYLESHEET, then it is said to be:

Persistent	and will be applied to the document no matter what Style Sheet the user chooses for display (assuming you are offering options).
Default	status is the other possibility but only occurs if you also include the **TITLE** Attribute. If the **TITLE** Attribute is present then this External Style Sheet becomes the <u>Initial</u> Style Sheet used when the document is loaded but can be changed to an ALTERNATE STYLESHEET by the user.

ALTERNATE STYLESHEET   specifies that this Style Sheet be available as a choice for the user to implement as an <u>alternative</u> to the <u>Default Style Sheet</u>. For this Attribute to work there must also be a **TITLE** Attribute present.

TYPE="text/CSS" | "text/JavaScript" works just like in a STYLE Element. If you are creating a Cascading Style Sheet, then specify "text/CSS". If you are creating a Style Sheet using JavaScript Syntax, then specify "text/JavaScript".

TITLE="name" specifies a name for your External Style Sheet that causes it to be the Default Style Sheet when the REL Attribute is set to STYLESHEET. When the REL Attribute is set to ALTERNATE STYLESHEET, it becomes one of the optional alternatives to the Default Style Sheet, which you can dynamically manipulate with JavaScript code or that the user is allowed to choose from.

HREF="URL" specifies the URL of the External Style Sheet to be loaded.

This example is going to demonstrate how to create a **Persistent** External Style Sheet by using the LINK Element. It consists of two parts: The document that contains the LINK to load and apply the External Style Sheet (Sample253.html) and the External Style Sheet itself (Sample253-External-CSS-1.html).

Using a regular type of HTML structure for the External Style Sheet, where the Style Sheet definition is enclosed inside Comment Tags and inside a STYLE Element is not recommended, but it is possible if you want to create some extra work for yourself. All of the External Style Sheet examples in this book will only have the Style Sheet Definition without the extraneous HTML.

Part 1 of Example 1-53 contains the LINK to the External Style Sheet.

Example 1-53 Part 1:   Sample253.html

```
<!DOCTYPE HTML PUBLIC "-//W3C//DTD HTML 3.2//EN">
<HTML>
<HEAD>
<TITLE>Sample 253 - CSS Example 1-53 LINK STYLE SHEET        </TITLE>

<LINK REL="STYLESHEET" TYPE="text/CSS"
      HREF="Sample253-External-CSS-1.html">

</HEAD>

<BODY>

<P>This is a Test of the External Style Sheet Implementation System.</P>

<P>If this is blue 24 point text inside of a magenta border and on a very pale blue
background then it was successful.</P>

</BODY>
</HTML>
```

This file contains the External Style Sheet that is applied to the previous file.

Example 1-53 Part 2:   Sample253-External-CSS-1.html

```
BODY    { border-color: rgb(75%,0%,40%); background-color:#cceeff;
          border-style: inset; border-width: 10px; margin: 0px;
          padding: 0px; width: 555px; }

P       { font-size: 24pt; color: blue; }
```

This example focuses on a simple demonstration of a LINK to an External Style Sheet that is written in CSS Syntax, which is then loaded and applied to this document called Sample254.html in a **Persistent** Relationship to the document; that is, it will always be applied.

Example 1-54 Part 1:   Sample254.html

```
<!DOCTYPE HTML PUBLIC "-//W3C//DTD HTML 3.2//EN">
<HTML>
<HEAD>
<TITLE>Sample 254 - CSS Example 1-54 LINK STYLE SHEET        </TITLE>

<LINK REL="STYLESHEET" TYPE="text/CSS"
      HREF="Sample254-External-CSS-2.html">

</HEAD>

<BODY>

<P>This is the second Test of the External Style Sheet Implementation System.</P>

<P>If this paragraph is 24 point red text inside of a blue border and on a very
pale green background then it was successful. The following division should be in
14 point black text.</P>

<DIV ALIGN=JUSTIFY>
Nothing fancy here but the alignment is set to Justify.
</DIV>

</BODY>
</HTML>
```

This is the External Style Sheet for Example 1-54 and it demonstrates simple Styles for the BODY, P, and DIV Elements by regular Element assignment.

Example 1-54 Part 2:   Sample254-External-CSS-2.html

```
BODY    { border-color: rgb(0%,0%,100%); background-color:#ccffcc;
          border-style: inset; border-width: 10px; margin: 0px;
          padding: 0px; width: 555px; }

P       { font-size: 24pt; color: red; }

DIV     { font-size: 14pt; color: black; }
```

This example shows you a typical use of assigned Styles that can be used as a set of global default Properties for your Elements, which can be kept in an External Style Sheet and then loaded for multiple documents.

Example 1-55 Part 1:   Sample255.html

```
<!DOCTYPE HTML PUBLIC "-//W3C//DTD HTML 3.2//EN">
<HTML>
<HEAD>
<TITLE>Sample 255 - CSS Example 1-55 LINK STYLE SHEET        </TITLE>

<LINK REL="STYLESHEET" TYPE="text/CSS" HREF="Sample255-External-CSS-3.html">

</HEAD>

<BODY>

Here I am just hovering in the Body without another Element.

<P>Hey I got a paragraph to hang out with.</P>
<DIV> That's cool but I'm in a division. Holy mergatroids Batman, this sounds
positively mathematically compartmentalized.</DIV>

<H1>No Prob, I got the major domo Heading 1.</H1>

<H2>Yeah, well I'd rather be blue than big.</H2>

<H3>I may be smaller but my ego isn't in need of surgery.</H3>

</BODY>
</HTML>
```

This is the External Style Sheet part of the example, and it shows a hypothetical set of global Properties that one could use to define most essential Elements, which can then be augmented to your specific requirements.

You might find this useful as a template for your documents after you spice it up a bit. Most of these global parameters are set to render what a normal HTML 2.0 document would look like. Obviously the last five assigned Element Styles are atypical. (Yes, it is possible to assign more than one Style to the same Element within a Style Definition.)

Example 1-55 Part 2:   **Sample255-External-CSS-3.html**

```
BODY    {
                   margin: 5px;
                   font-family: serif;
                   line-height: 1.1;
                   background: white;
                   color: black;
                   font-size: 14pt;
                }

H1, H2, H3, H4, H5, H6, P, UL, OL, DIR, MENU,
DIV, DT, DD, ADDRESS, BLOCKQUOTE, PRE, BR, HR      { display: block }

B, STRONG, I, EM, CITE, VAR, TT,
CODE, KBD, SAMP, IMG, SPAN                         { display: inline }

LI                                                 { display: list-item }

H5, H6                                             { margin-top: 1em }
H1                                                 { text-align: center }
H1, H2, H4, H6                                     { font-weight: bold }
H3, H5                                             { font-style: italic }
H1                                                 { font-size: xx-large }
H2                                                 { font-size: x-large }
H3                                                 { font-size: large }

B, STRONG                                     { font-weight: bolder }
I, CITE, EM, VAR, ADDRESS, BLOCKQUOTE         { font-style: italic }
PRE, TT, CODE, KBD, SAMP                       { font-family: monospace }
PRE                                           { white-space: pre }

ADDRESS                                       { margin-left: 3em }
BLOCKQUOTE                                    { margin-left: 3em; margin-right:3em }

UL, DIR                                       { list-style: disc }
OL                                            { list-style: decimal }
```

```
MENU    { margin: 0 }
LI      { margin-left: 3em }

DT      { margin-bottom: 0 }
DD      { margin-top: 0; margin-left: 3em }

P       { text-indent: 40px; color: purple;
          font-size: 14pt; line-height: 1.2em;
          font-family: Palatino, "New York", Times, serif; }

DIV     { text-indent: 40px; color: navy;
          font-size: 14pt; line-height: 1.2em;
          font-family: Helvetica, Times, "New York", Palatino, serif; }

H1      { color: red; font-size: 30pt; background-color: black;
          border-style: ridge; border-color: #ff5555; border-width: 20px;
          font-family: BlackOak, Moonlight, Clarendon, Cloister, fantasy; }

H2      { color: blue; font-size: 35pt;
          border-style: groove; border-color: aqua; border-width: 20px;
          font-family: Moonlight, BlackOak, Clarendon, Cloister, fantasy; }

H3      { color: green; font-size: 25pt;
          border-style: double; border-color: lime; border-width: 20px;
          font-family: Clarendon, Moonlight, BlackOak, Cloister, fantasy; }
```

Multiple External Style Sheets in one document

You can load multiple External Style Sheets into one document by using a LINK Element for each one. One reason why you might want to do this is if you have a site that has several different External Style Sheets that are each used for a specific type of formatting purpose (created in the past for other individual documents) that you now want to incorporate into a new document at various places. Here's the mini-example:

```
<LINK REL="STYLESHEET" TYPE="text/CSS" HREF="Sample256-External-CSS-4.html">
<LINK REL="STYLESHEET" TYPE="text/CSS" HREF="Sample256-External-CSS-5.html">
<LINK REL="STYLESHEET" TYPE="text/CSS" HREF="Sample256-External-CSS-6.html">
```

External Style Sheet precedence issues

The later an External Style Sheet is loaded, the more precedence it will have in terms of overriding the Style Properties for the various Elements it is assigned to. In other words, the last External Style Sheet in the code sequence will override all previous ones. Styles that are defined locally, that is, in the document in question, will have complete precedence over any conflicting Styles from all External Style Sheets. Be very aware that this can be tricky to keep track of in your head and when trying to debug your code for large and complex sites.

This example uses three different LINK Elements to load in three different External Style Sheets, which are then all applied to the document Sample256.html, which is a very rudimentary example just to get you into the concept. Typically they are much more involved. Just a reminder to notice that the LINK Elements are in the HEAD Element but not within the STYLE Element.

Example 1-56 Part 1:   Sample256.html

```
<!DOCTYPE HTML PUBLIC "-//W3C//DTD HTML 3.2//EN">
<HTML>
<HEAD>
<TITLE>Sample 256 - CSS Example 1-56 LINK Multiple STYLE SHEETs     </TITLE>

<LINK REL="STYLESHEET" TYPE="text/CSS" HREF="Sample256-External-CSS-4.html">

<LINK REL="STYLESHEET" TYPE="text/CSS" HREF="Sample256-External-CSS-5.html">

<LINK REL="STYLESHEET" TYPE="text/CSS" HREF="Sample256-External-CSS-6.html">
```

```
<STYLE TYPE="text/CSS">

<!--

H4       { color: silver; font-size: 50pt;
             border-style: solid; border-color: navy; border-width: 20px;
             font-family: Clarendon, Moonlight, BlackOak, Cloister, fantasy; }

-->

</STYLE>

</HEAD>


<BODY>

<P>Hey can somebody get me out of this paragraph?</P>

<DIV> I thought you liked being in that paragraph.</DIV>

<H1>So passion didn't compensate your intellectual predilections.</H1>

<H2>Grass always greener eh?</H2>

<H3>Wait, that's my line.</H3>

<H4>THE H4 TEST.</H4>

If the preceding bordered H4 Heading is Navy with 50 point silver text then you
know that the Properties in the local document have overridden the Properties from
the External-CSS-6 Style Sheet.

</BODY>
</HTML>
```

This is the first External Style Sheet used in Example 1-56 Part 1. Part 2 gets loaded into Part 1 by the first LINK Element contained in Part 1.

Example 1-56 Part 2:   Sample256-External-CSS-4.html

```
P            { text-indent: 40px; color: purple;
                font-size: 14pt; line-height: 1.2em;
                font-family: Palatino, "New York", Times, serif; }

DIV          { text-indent: 40px; color: navy;
                font-size: 17pt; line-height: 1.2em;
                font-family: Helvetica, Times, "New York", Palatino, serif; }
```

This is the second External Style Sheet used in Example 1-56 Part 1. Part 3 gets loaded into Part 1 by the second LINK Element contained in Part 1.

Example 1-56 Part 3:   **Sample256-External-CSS-5.html**

```
H1          { color: red; font-size: 25pt; background-color: black;
              border-style: ridge; border-color: #ff5555; border-width: 20px;
              font-family: BlackOak, Moonlight, Clarendon, Cloister, fantasy; }

H2          { color: blue; font-size: 35pt;
              border-style: groove; border-color: aqua; border-width: 20px;
              font-family: Moonlight, BlackOak, Clarendon, Cloister, fantasy; }
```

This is the third External Style Sheet used in Example 1-56 Part 1. Part 4 gets loaded into Part 1 by the first LINK Element contained in Part 1.

Example 1-56 Part 4:   **Sample256-External-CSS-6.html**

```
H3          { color: green; font-size: 25pt;
              border-style: double; border-color: lime; border-width: 20px;
              font-family: Clarendon, Moonlight, BlackOak, Cloister, fantasy; }

H4          { color: purple; font-size: 20pt;
              border-style: inset; border-color: olive; border-width: 20px;
              font-family: Clarendon, Moonlight, BlackOak, Cloister, fantasy; }
```

Multiple <STYLE> Elements in one document

You can have more than one STYLE Element in the HEAD of your document. Its intended purpose is to use the SRC Attribute to load in an External Style Sheet so that with multiple STYLE Elements you can have multiple Style Sheets in one document. However, at the time of this writing, it doesn't work for External CSS Style Sheets, but it does work for External JavaScript Style Sheets.

You can also have multiple STYLE Elements in one document without using the SRC Attribute, which can be either CSS Syntax or JavaScript Syntax. This has a limited use if you want to quickly copy a group of Styles from one document to another.

This is just a very simple example to show you that multiple STYLE Elements are possible in one document. It also demonstrates that the **SRC** Attribute works for loading External JavaScript Style Sheets but does not work for External CSS Style Sheets. If it worked for CSS Style Sheets, then the H2 Heading would be blue.

Example 1-57:   **Sample257.html**

```
<!DOCTYPE HTML PUBLIC "-//W3C//DTD HTML 3.2//EN">
<HTML>
<HEAD>
<TITLE>Sample 257 - CSS Example 1-57 Multiple STYLE Elements        </TITLE>

<STYLE TYPE="text/JavaScript" SRC="Sample257-External-JSSS.html"></STYLE>

<STYLE TYPE="text/CSS" SRC="Sample256-External-CSS-5.html"></STYLE>


<STYLE TYPE="text/CSS">

<!--

      H3     { color: red; font-size: 55pt; }

-->

</STYLE>

<STYLE TYPE="text/CSS">

<!--

      H4     { color: purple; font-size: 25pt; }
-->

</STYLE>

</HEAD>

<BODY>

<H5>THE H5 TEST.</H5>

<H2>THE H2 TEST.</H2>

<H3>THE H3 TEST.</H3>

<H4>THE H4 TEST.</H4>

</BODY>
</HTML>
```

Wrapping Up and Looking Ahead

This ends the discussion on Style Sheets created with CSS Syntax. You now have all the information you need to create your own Style Sheets for your documents and a wealth of examples that you can extract code from on the CD-ROM. Feel free to reuse any segments of code from any of the examples.

One final note concerning browsers and Style Sheets: Navigator and Internet Explorer render Style Sheets with varying responses to the official Style Sheet specification. Unfortunately for coders, they are both right in their interpretations, so at least for now, if you want to include Style Sheets in your documents and achieve cross-platform fluidity, you are going to have to research the differences inherent in Explorer and create parallel code to accommodate them.

Chapter 2 deals with positioning blocks of content, which are called Layers and are created by assigning a new Property within the Style Definition called the **position** Property with a Value of either **absolute** or **relative**. There are lots of other new Properties to learn about and use with Layers so let's get on with it.

Part I
Dynamic HTML

Chapter 2

Layers and Styles

Chapter 2
Layers and Styles

Contents

Creating Layers with Styles

Overview

Creating Layers

There are lots of ways to create a LAYER. They are:

- The <STYLE> Element with **position** Property via STYLE Attribute

- The <STYLE> Element with **position** Property via CLASS Attribute

- The <STYLE> Element with **position** Property via ID Attribute

- The <LAYER> Element

- The <ILAYER> Element

- The <SPAN> Element

- The JavaScript **tags** Property of the **document** Object

- The JavaScript **classes** Property of the **document** Object

- The JavaScript **ids** Property of the **document** Object

Essential Requirements

The only thing that is required to turn a Style into a Layer is the inclusion of the **position** Property in the Style Definition and then assigning it a Value of either **absolute** or **relative**. This can be done for a CLASS of STYLE or a Named Exception to a CLASS of STYLE. Additionally the **position** Property can be used in the STYLE Attribute or in the SPAN Element.

You do not use the **position** Property in the LAYER or ILAYER Elements because they are inherently Layers by definition, as a result of the **position** Property being set in the internal code by the browser.

This chapter covers the creation of positioned content, that is, creating Layers by the above methods. Chapter 3 covers the JavaScript aspects of Layers.

Creating Layers with CSS Syntax

Creating a LAYER with the STYLE Attribute

The STYLE Attribute can be used to create a LAYER in most HTML Elements. All you have to do is use the **position** Property to specify whether the Element will be positioned **absolute** or **relative** in the document layout. A relatively positioned LAYER will follow the natural flow of the Elements in the document. An absolutely positioned LAYER will be placed exactly according to the integer coordinates that you specify with the **left** and **top** Properties.

The **left** Property specifies the <u>x-coordinate</u> where the LAYER will start and is measured from the upper-left corner of the Window, or containing LAYER if it's nested, in a rightward direction. The **top** Property specifies the <u>y-coordinate</u> where the LAYER will start and is measured from the upper-left corner of the Window, or containing LAYER if it is nested, in a downward direction.

Just remember that you are using CSS Syntax within an Element Attribute so you don't use the curly braces but you do place the entire group of the Property NAME:VALUE; pairs within one set of double quotes (" ") to the right of the equals (=) sign, which is to the right of the Attribute Name of STYLE, which is to the right of the Element Name, like this:

```
<DIV STYLE="position:absolute; left:50; top:100; color:red;">
```

All of the Properties that were delineated in Chapter 1 can also be used with the STYLE Attribute when it is specified to create a LAYER.

These are the additional Properties that can be used with the STYLE Attribute when you also use the **position** Property to create a LAYER from within an Element when you are using CSS Syntax:

Property Name	{ Property Name with:Possible Values; }
position	{ position:absolute | relative; }
left	{ left:integerLength | integer1%-100%; }
top	{ top:integerLength | integer1%-100%; }
width	{ width:integerLength | integer1%-100% }
height	{ height:integerLength | integer1%-100%; }
clip	{ clip:rect('Y1,X2,Y2,X1'); }
z-index	{ z-index:integer; }
visibility	{ visibility:show | hide | inherit; }
layer-background-color	{ layer-background-color:colorValue; }
layer-background-image	{ layer-background-image:url('imageURL'); }
include-source	{ include-source:url('documentURL'); }

Here's an introductory example just to show you how to create a LAYER by using the STYLE Attribute within the DIV Element. It's defined as an **absolute** LAYER that is positioned at the coordinates ("50,100"), which means that it will start 50 pixels to the right of the left margin and 100 pixels down from the top margin of the Window. It has red text that has a **font-size** of 25 point. Notice that this STYLE is applied in the BODY section of the document.

Example 2-0:   **Sample300.html**

```
<!DOCTYPE HTML PUBLIC "-//W3C//DTD HTML 3.2//EN">
<HTML><HEAD>
<TITLE>Sample 300 - CSS Example 2-0 STYLE as Layer   </TITLE>
</HEAD>

<BODY>

<DIV STYLE="position:absolute; left:50px; top:100px; color:red; font-size:25pt;">

The DIVision test.

</DIV>

</BODY>
</HTML>
```

Creating a LAYER with a CLASS of STYLE

Just define a normal CLASS of STYLE and add the **position** Property like this:

```
<HEAD>
<STYLE TYPE="text/CSS">

DIV.RedText    { position:relative; color:red; }

</STYLE>

</HEAD>

<BODY>
<DIV CLASS="RedText">
        This text will be red in an inflow Layer because the position is relative.
</DIV>
</BODY>
```

The { position: } Property

The **position** Property is what actually causes an Element to become a LAYER. It's the flag that the browser looks for to distinguish it from regular Elements. By setting it to a Value of **absolute,** you are alerting the browser that it should be positioned at a specific location instead of the **relative** designation that causes the LAYER to follow the natural flow of the document order. When you specify a Value of **absolute,** you must also use the **left** and **top** Properties to define where the origin point of the LAYER is. (Technically, you don't have to specify them, but if you don't, the result will be the same as a **relative** LAYER, because the browser will not know where to locate the LAYER and will just bring it in the flow.) When you specify a Value of **relative,** the **left** and **top** Properties are used to assign an offset distance of the LAYER's upper-left corner from its normal inflow location in the document.

Mini-Examples:

```
{ position:absolute; }          { position:relative; }
```

CSS Syntax:

```
{ position:absolute | relative; }
```

The { left: } Property

The **left** Property indicates the horizontal coordinate where the upper-left corner of the LAYER will start. The LAYER will then render down and to the right from that point. You must include the measurement abbreviation to the right of the number that you choose, and the number must be either a positive or negative integer or zero. The default type of measurement scheme is pixels, which is abbreviated (px). Remembering from basic geometry the pair of (x,y) coordinate points in the 2D plane, you can think of the **left** Property as the x-coordinate and the following **top** Property as the y-coordinate. Using percentages renders less-controllable results but there are times when they are preferred.

Mini-Examples:

```
{ left:40px; }     { left:2in; }      { left:25mm; }
```

CSS Syntax:

```
{ left:integerLength | integer1%-100%; }
```

The { top: } Property

The **top** Property indicates the vertical coordinate where the upper-left corner of the LAYER will start. The LAYER will then render down and to the right from that point. You must include the measurement abbreviation to the right of the number that you choose, and the number must be either a positive or negative integer or zero. The default type of measurement scheme is pixels, which is designated with the **px** Keyword, and a unit of measurement must be included. Think of the **top** Property as the <u>y-coordinate</u> of the (x,y) coordinate pair used to position the LAYER.

Mini-Example:

```
{ top:20px; }
```

CSS Syntax:

```
{ top:integerLength | integer1%-100%; }
```

This example demonstrates the use of the **position, left**, and **top** Properties to create two different positioned LAYERs by using the STYLE Attribute for the DIV and P Elements. They both have Borders and other distinguishing Properties and are placed in exact locations with the coordinates specified with the **left** and **top** Properties.

Example 2-1: **Sample301.html**

```
<!DOCTYPE HTML PUBLIC "-//W3C//DTD HTML 3.2//EN">
<HTML>
<HEAD>
<TITLE>Sample 301 - CSS Example 2-1 STYLE Attribute as Layer        </TITLE>
</HEAD>

<BODY>

<DIV STYLE="position:absolute; left:25px; top:100px;
            color:red; font-size:22pt; background-color:blue;
            border-width:25px;  border-style:ridge; border-color:aqua;">

The Division Test.

</DIV>
```

```
<P STYLE="position:absolute; left:150px; top:300px;
        color:blue; font-size:44pt; background-color:lime;
        border-width:25px;  border-style:double; border-color:purple;">

The Paragraph test.
</P>

</BODY>
</HTML>
```

This example demonstrates several inflow LAYERs by specifying the **position** Property to have a Value of **relative**.

Example 2-2:   **Sample302.html**

```
<!DOCTYPE HTML PUBLIC "-//W3C//DTD HTML 3.2//EN">
<HTML>
<HEAD>
<TITLE>Sample 302 - CSS Example 2-2 Relatively Positioned LAYERs     </TITLE>
</HEAD>

<BODY>

<P STYLE="position:relative;
        color:blue; font-size:25pt; background-color:yellow;">

Another Paragraph Test. Notice how both of these Elements follow the natural flow
of the document and in the case of the H1 Heading below the left and top Properties
cause it to be offset by 144 pixels down and to the right of where it would
naturally be, but that is a relative movement of distance to a new location and not
an exact specification of coordinate position.
</P>

<H2 STYLE="position:relative;
        color:purple; font-size:44pt; background-color:teal;
        font-family:Moonlight, fantasy;">

This is Sample 302.
</H2>

<H1 STYLE="position:relative; left:144px; top:144px;
        color:aqua; font-size:35pt; background-color:navy;">

Another H1 Heading Test.
</H1>

</BODY>
</HTML>
```

The NAMED LAYER Style:
Creating a LAYER with the ID Attribute

Another way to create a LAYER is simply to use a NAMED INDIVIDUAL STYLE and include the **position** Property with a specification of either **relative** or **absolute**, which creates a NAMED LAYER. This occurs within a Style Definition using CSS Syntax in the Header of the document. First you Name your LAYER to the right of a hash (#) symbol and then specify which Properties your LAYER will have by using the same Syntax as used to create a regular Style like this:

```
#FirstLayer     { position:relative; color:blue; font-size:50pt; }

#SecondLayer    { position:absolute; left:20px; top:200px;
                  color:red; font-size:20pt; }
```

Then you address that LAYER with the ID Attribute of an Element in the Body of the document so that the LAYER will be inserted and its Properties will be applied to the contents of that Element like this:

```
<DIV ID="FirstLayer"> This is another test. </DIV>

<DIV ID="SecondLayer"> And yet another test. </DIV>
```

Special Notice:

It's important to remember that a NAMED LAYER is addressed differently than a NAMED INDIVIDUAL STYLE. With a NAMED LAYER, you <u>do not have</u> to use the CLASS Attribute at all. You only use the ID Attribute to address or insert the NAMED LAYER into an Element.

Technically you don't have to use the CLASS Attribute of an Element, even when you are implementing a NAMED INDIVIDUAL STYLE; but in that case, you are circumnavigating the intention of the NAMED INDIVIDUAL STYLE so that it is only being used as a regular CLASS of STYLE instead of as an <u>EXCEPTION</u> to a CLASS of STYLE. This defeats its intended purpose, but there's nothing wrong with it.

Note that the two different capitalizations of "Layer" and "LAYER" are only used for emphasis purposes and should be, in all circumstances, considered interchangeable. The only time that the spelling of "Layer" is critical is when using the "layers[i]" Array in JavaScript code.

Example 2-3 creates two NAMED LAYERs and then addresses each one in a DIV Element with their respective ID Attributes.

Example 2-3:   Sample303.html

```
<!DOCTYPE HTML PUBLIC "-//W3C//DTD HTML 3.2//EN">
<HTML>
<HEAD>
<TITLE>        Sample 303 - CSS Example 2-3 NAMED LAYERs     </TITLE>

<STYLE TYPE="text/CSS">

<!--

#FirstLayer     { position:relative; color:blue; font-size:50pt; }

#SecondLayer    { position:absolute; left:20px; top:200px; color:red;
                font-size:20pt; }
-->

</STYLE>

</HEAD>
<BODY>

<DIV ID="FirstLayer"> This is another test.  </DIV>

<DIV ID="SecondLayer">And yet another test.  </DIV>

</BODY>
</HTML>
```

The { width: } Property

The **width** Property is used to specify a horizontal width for the LAYER. You can specify it with a number followed by a unit of measure like inches or pixels, use the **auto** Keyword, or as a percentage of the LAYER followed by a percent (%) sign. The default value for this Property is 100% of the possible space in the browser Window that can be assigned to the LAYER, or if it is a nested LAYER, the contents will wrap to the right edge of the LAYER that immediately contains it.

Mini-Examples:

```
{ width:555px; }            { width:70%; }
```

CSS Syntax:

```
{ width:integerLength | integer1%-100% | auto; }
```

The { height: } Property

The **height** Property is used to specify a vertical height for the LAYER. You can use the **auto** Keyword, specify it with a number followed by a unit of measure such as inches or pixels, or as a percentage of the LAYER followed by a percent (%) sign.

If no height is specified, then by default the LAYER will expand to the minimum height necessary to display all of the content contained within that LAYER.

If you specify a height that is inadequate to properly display the contents, then the LAYER will automatically expand to accommodate the contents.

This Property is primarily intended as a reference for the nested LAYERs that it contains, which express their **height** Values as percentages. For future reference, it also specifies the initial Clipping Rectangle **height**, that is, the **clip.height** Property for a **Layer** Object in JavaScript.

Mini-Examples:

```
{ height:700px; }      { height:13in; }      { height:50%; }
```

CSS Syntax:

```
{ height:integerLength | integer1%-100% | auto; }
```

Special Notice:

You may experience erratic browser rendering when using the **width** or **height** Properties if you create a LAYER by using the STYLE Attribute of an Element that also has BORDER Properties. If you do use either of them in that context, some of your other Properties may be ignored. Once again, this may have been fixed by the time you read this, so test it yourself.

You can see some of the erratic behavior by going into the folder on the CD-ROM named AlternateSamples-NotInBook and loading the file named Sample304-Test.html, which is not in the book.

The **width** and **height** Properties work just fine when using NAMED LAYERs, as is demonstrated with the following Example 2-4.

Example 2-4: **Sample304.html**

```
<!DOCTYPE HTML PUBLIC "-//W3C//DTD HTML 3.2//EN">
<HTML>
<HEAD>

<TITLE>Sample 304 - CSS Example 2-4 Width and Height in NAMED LAYERs        </TITLE>

<STYLE TYPE="text/CSS">

<!--

#ThirdLayer     { position:relative; color:blue; font-size:50pt;
                  width:500px; height:200px;
                  border-style:ridge; border-width:20px; border-color:purple;}

#FourthLayer    { position:absolute; left:70px; top:277px; color:red;
                  width:350px; height:144px; font-size:20pt;
                  border-style:inset; border-width:30px; border-color:blue; }
-->

</STYLE>

</HEAD>

<BODY>

<P ID="ThirdLayer">    This is another test. </P>

<H2 ID="FourthLayer"> And yet another test. </H2>

<P>
Notice that the LAYER Named 'FourthLayer' that is addressed in the H2 heading is
positioned absolutely so that it is 70 pixels to the right of the left margin and
277 pixels down from the top margin and is by its very nature out of the flow of
the rest of the Elements. That's why even though this paragraph is coded in the
HTML document after the H2 Element it shows up in the browser Window before the H2
Element. Obviously this paragraph has the normal inherited attributes from the Body
Element since no Named LAYER was addressed to it.
</P>

</BODY>

</HTML>
```

Be careful when you **position** your LAYERs in an **absolute** fashion because it is very easy to have them overlap with other LAYERS, especially if you create some of them that are relatively positioned. If you change the **top** Property Value to 100 pixels in the previous <u>Sample304.html</u>, you can see the overlap demonstrated.

The { clip: } Property

Before we get started with this Property, at the time of this writing, either Netscape's documentation is wrong or there is a bug in the Navigator 4.0 program, so you're going to bear with two different explanations for the same Property to combat these difficulties. After I've explained how this Property works currently, which is the bugged version, I'm going to put a section in that explains how it is supposed to work, just in case they decide to fix the problems. That way, you will have a guide to the correct theory and application without having to twist the concepts around to accommodate the errors, and you will have a guide to understanding how to make it work with the bugs.

The <u>bugged</u> version of the { clip: } Property

The **clip** Property lets you choose what part of the LAYER is visible and what part is invisible. You do this by defining a Clipping Rectangle Function that first specifies the upper-left corner with an (x1,y1) coordinate point and then the bottom-right corner point with an (x2,y2) coordinate. These four numbers are placed as a group between *single* quotes and then inside a set of parentheses, and each one is separated by a comma. The space inside that Rectangle will be the visible part of the LAYER. If you choose to list them without the *single* quotes, then make sure that not even one blank white space is between the numbers. You can use *double* quotes to enclose the numbers if the **clip** Property is not nested inside of *double* quotes at any point already .

This is how it would look:

```
clip:rect('30,400,275,20');
```

where:		
	30	would be the top coordinate
	400	would be the right coordinate
	275	would be the bottom coordinate
	20	would be the left coordinate

You also have the option of using only two coordinates in the set, which causes the **left** and **top** Properties to both have a default Value of zero. The two-coordinate version, oddly enough, works just fine, without any anomalies. It has the <u>right coordinate</u> first and the <u>bottom coordinate</u> second and looks like this:

```
clip:rect(400,275);
```

which is equivalent to:

```
clip:rect(0,400,275,0);
```

In many instances, you will want to have the beginning of the LAYER visible but hide another part of it to be revealed later on. These clipping coordinates are <u>always</u> measured in pixels so you <u>aren't allowed</u> to put the units abbreviation after the numbers.

The numbers that you specify for the **clip** Property are <u>measured from the edge of the LAYER that contains them</u>, not from the edge of the browser Window. This is always true even when you are working with a top-level container like the BODY Element, but in that circumstance the browser Window is the container.

There are two scenarios for default **clip** Property Values if you choose not to specify them explicitly.

<u>Scenario 1:</u>   is based on the content contained within the LAYER and how it interacts with the WIDTH and HEIGHT Values that you specify.

top coordinate	receives the WIDTH top coordinate
right coordinate	receives the HEIGHT right coordinate
bottom coordinate	receives the HEIGHT bottom coordinate
left coordinate	receives the WIDTH left coordinate

<u>Scenario 2:</u>   is based <u>only</u> on the content contained within the LAYER because you did <u>not</u> specify any Values for the WIDTH and HEIGHT Properties.

top coordinate	defaults to 0
right coordinate	receives the wrapping distance coordinate
bottom coordinate	receives the coordinate that is computed when the vertical space necessary to display all of the contents of the LAYER is calculated.
left coordinate	defaults to 0

SIDE NOTE:

For those of you who aren't JavaScript savvy yet, the use of the double quotes inside a Function causes the numbers to be considered a text String that is composed of a Numeric Literal instead of mathematical entities, which would require conversion if you later needed them for Functions that required them to be real numbers again. In most cases in later versions of JavaScript, this conversion is handled internally, automatically.

The real power of this Property comes into play when you are using JavaScript to dynamically manipulate your pages by having the capability to have parts of the page appear and disappear, shrink or grow, or move around the page. See Chapter 3 on pages 250-263 for examples of dynamically altering the clipping region of a LAYER.

Remember that this is the section that explains how the **clip** Property currently works with the bugs and the <u>order</u> of the clip-set is **top, right, bottom, left**.

CSS Syntax:

```
{ clip:rect("topY1, rightX2, bottomY2, leftX1"); }
```

This example focuses on the way that the **clip** Property currently works, which is incorrect and bugged and which causes the **order** of the clip-set to be **top, right, bottom, left.**

Example 2-5:   Sample305.html

```
<!DOCTYPE HTML PUBLIC "-//W3C//DTD HTML 3.2//EN">
<HTML><HEAD>
<TITLE>Sample 305 - CSS Example 2-5 Clipping in NAMED LAYERs        </TITLE>

<STYLE TYPE="text/CSS">

<!--

#FifthLayer     { position:absolute; left:10px; top:100px;
                  color:blue; font-size:20pt;
                  border-style:ridge; border-width:20px; border-color:purple; }

#SixthLayer     { position:absolute; left:10px; top:300px;
                  color:red; font-size:20pt;
                  border-style:ridge; border-width:20px; border-color:purple;
                  clip:rect('0,150,125,0'); }

                            /*  the order is top, right, bottom, left  */
-->

</STYLE>
</HEAD>

<BODY>
<DIV ID="FifthLayer">
This is what I              <BR>
look like without          <BR>
a clipping rectangle.
</DIV>

<DIV ID="SixthLayer">
This is what I             <BR>
look like with            <BR>
a clipping rectangle.
</DIV>

<P>Notice that the LAYER Named 'FifthLayer' is exactly the same as the LAYER Named
'SixthLayer' except for the color of the text and the CLIP Property in 'SixthLayer'
which causes the right third of that Element to be invisible. Pay strict attention
to the coordinate order in the clip set which is <B>top, right, bottom, left</B>.
This is very <B>counterintuitive</B> but you've got to deal with it.</P>

</BODY>
</HTML>
```

The <u>unbugged</u> version of the { clip: } Property

The **clip** Property lets you choose what part of the LAYER is visible and what part is invisible. You do this by defining a Clipping Rectangle Function that first specifies the upper-left corner with an (x1,y1) coordinate point and then the bottom-right corner point with an (x2,y2) coordinate. These four numbers are placed as a group between *single* quotes and then inside a set of parentheses, and each one is separated by a comma. The space inside that Rectangle will be the visible part of the LAYER. If you choose to list them without the *single* quotes, then make sure that not even one blank white space is between the numbers. You can use *double* quotes to enclose the numbers if the **clip** Property is not nested inside of *double* quotes at any point already .

This is how it would look:

```
clip:rect('20,30,400,275');
```

where: 20   would be the left coordinate
                30   would be the top coordinate
                400   would be the right coordinate
                275   would be the bottom coordinate

You also have the option of using only two coordinates in the set, which causes the **left** and **top** Properties to both have a default Value of zero. Here is a two-coordinate example:

```
clip:rect(400,275);
```

which is equivalent to:

```
clip:rect(0,0,400,275);
```

This can save you typing. In many instances you will want to have the beginning of the LAYER visible but hide another part of it to be revealed later on.

These clipping coordinates are <u>always</u> measured in pixels so you <u>aren't allowed</u> to put the units abbreviation after the numbers.

The numbers that you specify for the **clip** Property are <u>measured from the edge of the LAYER that contains them</u>, not from the edge of the browser Window. This is always true, even when you are working with a top-level container like the BODY Element, but in that circumstance, the browser Window is the container.

There are two scenarios for default **clip** Property Values if you choose not to specify them explicitly:

Scenario 1: is based on the content contained within the LAYER and how it interacts with the WIDTH and HEIGHT values that you specify.

left coordinate	receives the WIDTH left coordinate
top coordinate	receives the WIDTH top coordinate
right coordinate	receives the HEIGHT right coordinate
bottom coordinate	receives the HEIGHT bottom coordinate

Scenario 2: is based <u>only</u> on the content contained within the LAYER because you did <u>not</u> specify any Values for the WIDTH and HEIGHT Properties.

left coordinate	defaults to 0
top coordinate	defaults to 0
right coordinate	receives the wrapping distance coordinate
bottom coordinate	receives the coordinate that is computed when the vertical space necessary to display all of the contents of the LAYER is calculated.

Remember that this is the section that explains how the **clip** Property is supposed to work and the **order** of the clip-set is **left, top, right, bottom**.

CSS Syntax:

```
{ clip:rect("leftX1, topY1, rightX2, bottomY2,"); }
```

The following Example 2-6 focuses on the way that the **clip** Property is supposed to work, which has the order of the clip-set to be **left, top, right, bottom**. It's exactly the same as the previous Example 2-5, except that the clip-set Values are switched to the other order. I can't guarantee its accuracy because it hasn't been tested, and if Netscape hasn't had the bugs fixed then it won't work at all. It's only here for your convenience in case they fixed the bugs. If Netscape hasn't fixed the bugs then the lower Layer will be totally invisible. If the bugs have been fixed then the lower Layer will be partly visible.

Example 2-6:   **Sample306.html**

```
<!DOCTYPE HTML PUBLIC "-//W3C//DTD HTML 3.2//EN">
<HTML>
<HEAD>
<TITLE>Sample 306 - CSS Example 2-6 Clipping in NAMED LAYERs        </TITLE>

<STYLE TYPE="text/CSS">

<!--

#FifthLayer     { position:absolute; left:10px; top:100px;
                  color:blue; font-size:20pt;
                  border-style:ridge; border-width:20px; border-color:purple; }

#SixthLayer     { position:absolute; left:10px; top:300px;
                  color:red; font-size:20pt;
                  border-style:ridge; border-width:20px; border-color:purple;
                  clip:rect('0,0,150,125'); }

                     /*     the order is left, top, right, bottom    */

-->

</STYLE>

</HEAD>

<BODY>

<DIV ID="FifthLayer">
This is what I              <BR>
look like without          <BR>
a clipping rectangle.
</DIV>

<DIV ID="SixthLayer">
This is what I             <BR>
look like with            <BR>
a clipping rectangle.
</DIV>

<P>
Notice that the LAYER Named 'FifthLayer' is exactly the same as the LAYER Named
'SixthLayer' except for the color of the text and the CLIP Property in 'SixthLayer'
which causes the right third of that Element to be invisible. Pay strict attention
to the coordinate order in the clip-set which is <B>left, top, right, bottom</B>.
Hopefully this works because Netscape has fixed the bug. If you try this example
and the second LAYER is totally invisible then that means that Navigator still has
the bug and you should see the Sample305.html instead.
</P>

</BODY>
</HTML>
```

This example is similar to the previous example but demonstrates the **clip** Property for CLASSes of Style, correctly and with bugs and the CLIP Attribute in a LAYER Element. See the Comments in the example. See Chapter 2 on pages 161-172 for LAYER Element details. See Chapter 3 for **Layer** Object details, starting on page 199.

Example 2-7:   Sample307.html

```
<!DOCTYPE HTML PUBLIC "-//W3C//DTD HTML 3.2//EN">
<HTML>
<HEAD>
<TITLE>Sample 307 - CSS Example 2-7   clip Property and Attribute   </TITLE>

<STYLE TYPE="text/CSS">

<!--
       /*      the BUGGY order which currently works in CSS-Syntax is:
               top, right, bottom, left      */

all.alphaL { position:absolute; left:10px; top:10px; color:blue; font-size:20pt;
          width:300; clip:rect(0,450,150,0); }


       /*      the CORRECT order which DOESN'T currently work in CSS-Syntax is:
               left, top, right, bottom      */

all.buggyL { position:absolute; left:200px; top:300px; color:red; font-size:20pt;
          width:300;  clip:rect(0,0,450,150); }
-->

</STYLE>
</HEAD>

<BODY>

<P CLASS="alphaL">This Layer will be visible if there is still a bug.  The obvious
solution is to use the LAYER Element or use JavaScript. </P>

<!--   the CORRECT order which DOES currently work in HTML Attribute-Syntax is:
       left, top, right, bottom  -->

<LAYER LEFT=0 TOP=150 BGCOLOR="cyan" CLIP="0,0,400,150">  There are no bugs in the
LAYER Element.   </LAYER>


<!--  If there is still a bug, then the following Layer won't show up   -->

<DIV CLASS="buggyL">This Layer will be invisible until the bug is fixed.</DIV>

</BODY>
</HTML>
```

The { z-index: } Property

The **z-index** Property uses a positive integer to specify into what position in the stacking order or z-order a LAYER is placed. A LAYER with a **z-index** set to 1 will be underneath all subsequent LAYERs, so it follows that the larger the **z-index**, the higher that LAYER will be in the z-stack. What this does is determine the order of precedence that a LAYER has, which consequently controls the visibility of a LAYER's contents when you have LAYERs that overlap or even occupy the exact same space.

When you set up LAYERs to occupy the same space, you are usually setting all of them but one to be initially hidden, and then using JavaScript to manipulate them or allowing the user to dynamically alter the presentation of the page.

Ordinarily the LAYERs are stacked in the order that they are coded in so that the first LAYER in your code sequence is at the bottom of the z-stack, and the next LAYER coded is the next LAYER in the z-stack, and so on. By using the **z-index** Property, you can change that z-order to accommodate your authoring requirements.

Be advised that this does not affect the stacking order between nested LAYERs and their parent LAYER but only the child LAYERs within a parent LAYER.

Mini-Example:

```
{ z-index:5; }
```

CSS Syntax:

```
{ z-index:integer; }
```

This example demonstrates the **z-index** by creating three Division Elements that each have different colored borders and have absolute coordinates that cause them to overlap one another. Look at the sample file to observe how the stacking order is affected by the **z-index**, causing the first Element coded to have precedence because its **z-index** has the largest integer, instead of the natural way, which would have the opposite effect. This is a very simple example just to detail the concept.

Example 2-8:   **Sample308.html**

```
<!DOCTYPE HTML PUBLIC "-//W3C//DTD HTML 3.2//EN">
<HTML>
<HEAD>
<TITLE>Sample 308 - CSS Example 2-8   z-index </TITLE>

<STYLE TYPE="text/CSS">

<!--

#SeventhLayer   { position:absolute; left:10px; top:100px;
                  z-index:3; color:blue; font-size:20pt; padding:40px;
                  border-style:ridge; border-width:20px; border-color:aqua; }

#EighthLayer    { position:absolute; left:100px; top:258px;
                  z-index:2; color:red; font-size:20pt; padding:40px;
                  border-style:ridge; border-width:20px; border-color:yellow; }

#NinthLayer     { position:absolute; left:280px; top:75px;
                  z-index:1; color:green; font-size:20pt; padding:40px;
                  border-style:ridge; border-width:20px; border-color:lime; }

-->

</STYLE>

</HEAD>

<BODY>

<DIV ID="SeventhLayer">      This is the                  <BR>
                             SeventhLayer Test            <BR>
                             with z-index equals 3.       <BR>
                             It rules!                               </DIV>

<DIV ID="EighthLayer">       This is the                  <BR>
                             EighthLayer Test             <BR>
                             with z-index equals 2.                  </DIV>

<DIV ID="NinthLayer">        This is the                  <BR>
                             NinthLayer Test              <BR>
                             with z-index equals 1.                  </DIV>

<P>     Notice that the Layer Named 'NinthLayer' has z-index of one and it is at the
bottom of the stack while the Layer Named 'SeventhLayer has z-index of three and it
is at the top of the stack and therefore isn't obscured by either of the other
Layers.
</P>

</BODY>
</HTML>
```

Example 2-8   Sample308.html

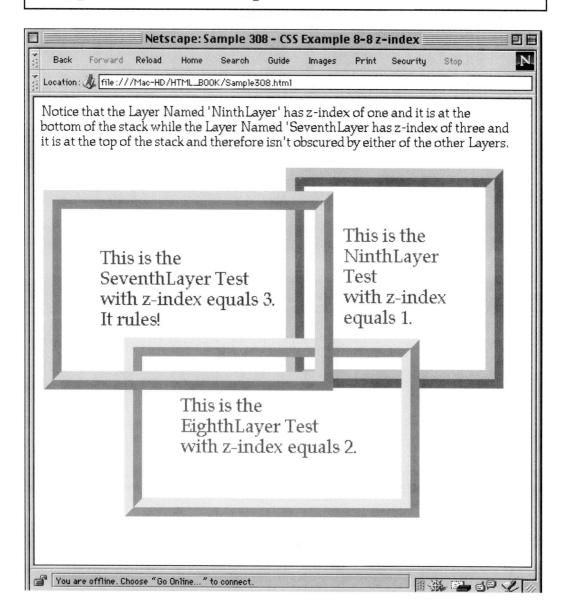

Netscape: Sample 308 - CSS Example 8-8 z-index

Location: file:///Mac-HD/HTML_BOOK/Sample308.html

Notice that the Layer Named 'NinthLayer' has z-index of one and it is at the bottom of the stack while the Layer Named 'SeventhLayer has z-index of three and it is at the top of the stack and therefore isn't obscured by either of the other Layers.

This is the SeventhLayer Test with z-index equals 3. It rules!

This is the NinthLayer Test with z-index equals 1.

This is the EighthLayer Test with z-index equals 2.

You are offline. Choose "Go Online..." to connect.

The { visibility: } Property

The **visibility** Property is closely related to and often used in conjunction with the **z-index** Property, because it determines whether a LAYER is initially visible or hidden when the page is loaded into the browser Window. There are three possible Values, which are **show**, **hide** or **inherit**. The Value of **show** causes the LAYER to be visible and the Value of **hide** causes the LAYER to be invisible, but it still takes up the amount of space in the Window that it normally would and still is available for JavaScript maneuvering.

Specifying a Value of **inherit** causes the LAYER to have the same Value as its parent LAYER. If the LAYER has no parent, it is said to be a top-level LAYER and would inherit a Value of **show** because the Body of the document is always visible. The default Value of a LAYER is that it will have the same Value as its parent LAYER.

Even if a LAYER is set to a Value of **show**, it still may be obscured by another LAYER that has the same positioning coordinates designated or just overlaps it and/or has a higher **z-index** Value.

Mini-Examples:

```
{ visibility:show; }

{ visibility:hide; }

{ visibility:inherit; }
```

CSS Syntax:

```
{ visibility:show | hide | inherit; }
```

The following very simple example just shows those same three Layers from the previous example and adds the **visibility** Property to each one to demonstrate each of its three possible Values of **show**, **hide**, and **inherit**.

Example 2-9: **Sample309.html**

```
<!DOCTYPE HTML PUBLIC "-//W3C//DTD HTML 3.2//EN">
<HTML>
<HEAD>
<TITLE>Sample 309 - CSS Example 2-9   visibility     </TITLE>

<STYLE TYPE="text/CSS">

<!--

#SeventhLayer  { position:absolute; left:10px; top:100px;
                 z-index:3; color:blue; font-size:20pt; padding:40px;
                 border-style:ridge; border-width:20px; border-color:aqua;
                 visibility:show; }

#EighthLayer   { position:absolute; left:100px; top:258px;
                 z-index:2; color:red; font-size:20pt; padding:40px;
                 border-style:ridge; border-width:20px; border-color:yellow;
                 visibility:inherit; }

#NinthLayer    { position:absolute; left:280px; top:75px;
                 z-index:1; color:green; font-size:20pt; padding:40px;
                 border-style:ridge; border-width:20px; border-color:lime;
                 visibility:hide; }

-->

</STYLE>
</HEAD>

<BODY>

<DIV ID="SeventhLayer">
This is the <BR>        SeventhLayer Test <BR>        with z-index equals 3.   <BR>
It rules!                                                                     </DIV>

<DIV ID="EighthLayer">
This is the <BR>        EighthLayer Test <BR>        with z-index equals 2.  </DIV>

<DIV ID="NinthLayer">
This is the <BR>        NinthLayer Test <BR>        with z-index equals 1.   </DIV>

<P>This is exactly the same as Example 307 except that the LAYER Named
'EighthLayer' is designated with the 'inherit' Value and since its parent Layer is
visible it inherits a Value of 'show'. The LAYER Named 'NinthLayer' is designated
as being initially hidden and guess what, you can't see it.

<A HREF="Sample415.html">     Example 3-15   </A>
uses a JavaScript SCRIPT Element to cause these same Layers to disappear and appear
by moving the mouse over them and out from over them. </P>

</BODY>
</HTML>
```

The { layer-background-color: } Property

The **layer-background-color** Property is different from the **background-color** Property that was covered in Chapter 1. As you may recall from many of the previous examples, when you choose a regular <u>background color,</u> say for an H1 Heading Element where only the space that is immediately behind the text gets the background color and the rest of the space that is assigned to that Element has the same color as the BGCOLOR of the BODY Element.

What the **layer-background-color** Property does is take that other available space of an Element in addition to the <u>background color</u> space and assign it all to be the same color. Another way to explain this is to say that it specifies the <u>background color</u> of the entire LAYER instead of just the contents of the LAYER, which usually don't fill up the entire space allotted to the LAYER.

You choose the color just like any other Property, with either a recognized color NAME, a hexadecimal triplet or by using the **rgb()** Function. If you need more information than that because you skipped around, then see the section on COLOR in Chapter 1 on page 37 or see Appendix B, in the "Color Theory" section, starting on page 1030.

This is not a W3C-approved Property. Also it has no corresponding Attribute in the LAYER Element.

Mini-Examples:

```
{ layer-background-color:blue; }
{ layer-background-color:#0000ff; }
{ layer-background-color:rgb(5, 220, 170); }
{ layer-background-color:rgb(45%, 2%, 58%); }
```

CSS Syntax:

```
{ layer-background-color:colorname | #$$$$$$ |
         rgb(0-255,0-255,0-255) | rgb(0-100%,0-100%,0-100%); }
```

Example 2-10 demonstrates the **layer-background-color** Property.

Example 2-10:   Sample310.html

```
<!DOCTYPE HTML PUBLIC "-//W3C//DTD HTML 3.2//EN">
<HTML>
<HEAD>
<TITLE>Sample 310 - CSS Example 2-10  layer-background-color </TITLE>
```

```
<STYLE TYPE="text/CSS">

<!--

#LBCLayer       { position:absolute; left:20px; top:10px;
                  layer-background-color:rgb(45%, 2%, 58%);
                  color:aqua; font-size:25pt; padding:40px;
                  border-style:ridge; border-width:20px; border-color:blue; }

-->
</STYLE>

</HEAD>

<BODY>

<DIV ID="LBCLayer">
This is the LBCLayer Test. <BR>
Notice that the burgundy color completely covers the area inside of the border
instead of just covering the text area.
</DIV>

</BODY>
</HTML>
```

The { layer-background-image: } Property

The **layer-background-image** Property specifies the tiled background image of the entire LAYER, which is slightly different than the regular **background-image** Property that tiles the chosen image over just the contents of the LAYER, which usually doesn't fill up the entire space allotted to the LAYER.

This is not a W3C-approved Property. Also, it has no corresponding Attribute in the LAYER Element.

Mini-Examples:

```
{ layer-background-image:url('JPEG-FILES/icon-BG-stars.jpg'); }

{ layer-background-image:
url('http://www.erols.com/gilorien/JPEG-FILES/icon-BG-stars.jpg');}
```

CSS Syntax:

```
{ layer-background-image:url('fullURL' | 'directory/fileName'); }
```

Example 2-10   Sample310.html

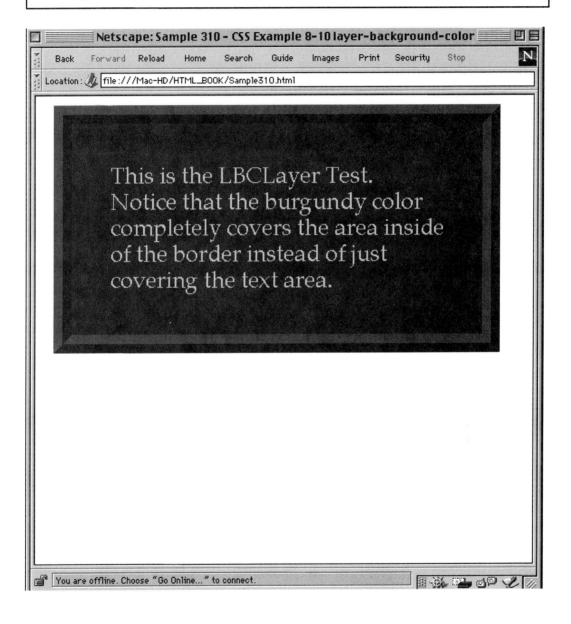

This example shows the difference between the **layer-background-image** Property and the **background-image** Property.

Example 2-11: Sample311.html

```
<!DOCTYPE HTML PUBLIC "-//W3C//DTD HTML 3.2//EN">
<HTML>
<HEAD>
<TITLE>Sample 311 - CSS Example 2-11  layer-background-image </TITLE>

<STYLE TYPE="text/CSS">

<!--

#LBGImage       { position:absolute; left:20px; top:10px;
                  layer-background-image:url('JPEG-FILES/icon-BG-asteroids.jpg');
                  color:aqua; font-size:25pt;
                  border-style:groove; border-width:20px; border-color:green; }

#RegBGImage     { position:absolute; left:20px; top:200px;
                  background-image:url('JPEG-FILES/icon-BG-asteroids.jpg');
                  color:aqua; font-size:25pt;
                  border-style:groove; border-width:20px; border-color:green; }

-->

</STYLE>

</HEAD>

<BODY>

<DIV ID="LBGImage">
This is the LBGImage Test. <BR>
Notice that the tiled image icon completely covers the area inside of the border
instead of just covering the text area.
</DIV>

<P ID="RegBGImage">
This is the RegBGImage Test. <BR>
Notice that the tiled image icon does not completely cover the area inside of the
border.  Instead it just covers the text area.
</P>

</BODY>

</HTML>
```

Example 2-11   Sample311.html

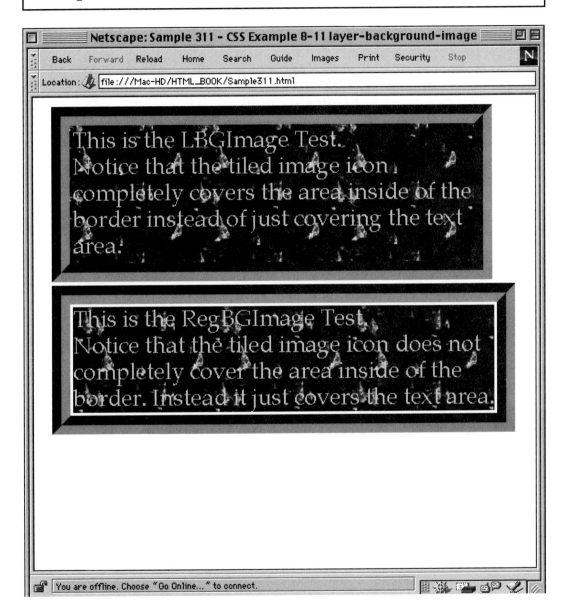

This example shows how to use the **layer-background-image** Property and the **background-color** Property to have text that has a color behind it and have a tiled image behind the color and the text. It also demonstrates that this is not possible by only using the regular **background-image** Property, which will hide the <u>background color</u>.

Example 2-12: Sample312.html

```
<!DOCTYPE HTML PUBLIC "-//W3C//DTD HTML 3.2//EN">
<HTML>
<HEAD>
<TITLE>Sample 312 - CSS Example 2-12  layer-background-image </TITLE>

<STYLE TYPE="text/CSS">

<!--

#LBGImage5      { position:absolute; left:20px; top:10px;
                  layer-background-image:url('JPEG-FILES/icon-CoarseTurf.jpeg');
                  color:red; font-size:25pt; padding:20px;
                  background-color:yellow; }

#BGImage11      { position:absolute; left:20px; top:250px;
                  background-image:url('Sample-ETOC/icon-Ceiling-Tile.jpeg');
                  color:red; font-size:25pt; padding:20px;
                  background-color:blue; }

-->

</STYLE>

</HEAD>

<BODY>

<DIV ID="LBGImage5">
This is the LBGImage5 Test.            <BR>
Notice that the tiled image completely covers the area of the DIV Element and the
background-color covers the text area.
</DIV>

<DIV ID="BGImage11">
This is the BGImage11 Test.            <BR>
Notice that the tiled image for the background-image does not allow the
background-color show through for the text area like the layer-background-image
does.
</DIV>

</BODY>
</HTML>
```

Example 2-12   Sample312.html

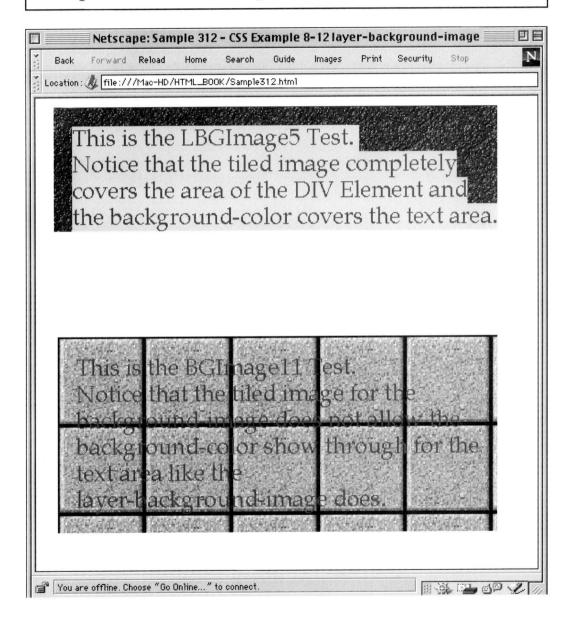

The { include-source: } Property

The **include-source** Property is very different from other Properties, because it allows you to load HTML formatted content into your LAYER from an external document. It can be implemented in the LAYER definition for any valid LAYER by first specifying a **position** Property with a Value of either **absolute** or **relative**. Then, within the LAYER definition, you use the **include-source** Property to specify a Link to an external file that has only __regular HTML__ or **JavaScript** in it, which will be loaded into that LAYER. Remember, though, that you also have to address the LAYER definition with either the CLASS or ID Attribute of the Element that you want to load the external content into. The LAYER's Style Properties will then be applied to any HTML Elements contained in the external file and will be rendered in the current document. This is not a W3C-approved Property. It does have a corresponding LAYER Attribute, which is **SRC**.

Here's how you create a NAMED LAYER with the **include-source** Property:

```
#RedBack      { position:absolute; left:100px; top:300px;
              background-color:red;
              include-source:url("Sample313-External.html");}
```

Then you have to apply that NAMED LAYER to an Element within the Body of the document like this:

```
<DIV ID="RedBack"></DIV>
```

This creates a LAYER with a CLASS of STYLE with the **include-source** Property, which is then applied to the DIV Element with the CLASS Attribute:

```
.myYellow     { position: relative; background-color: yellow;
              include-source:url("Sample313-External.html");}
```

```
<DIV CLASS="myYellow"></DIV>
```

CSS Syntax:

```
{ include-source:url("documentURL"); }
```

Special Notice:

Be very aware that if you want to get predictable and accurate results, do not include any CSS Syntax in any files that you use as __External__ files to be loaded by the __include-source__ Property. Just use regular HTML code or JavaScript in those external files.

This example demonstrates the **include-source** Property that was just presented with the previous mini-examples where the **Redback** NAMED LAYER and the **myYellow** CLASS of STYLE LAYER both load in external files into DIV Elements.

Example 2-13:   **Sample313.html**

```
<!DOCTYPE HTML PUBLIC "-//W3C//DTD HTML 3.2//EN">
<HTML>
<HEAD>
<TITLE>Sample 313 - CSS Example 2-13 include-source Property      </TITLE>

<STYLE TYPE="text/CSS">

<!--

#RedBack       { position: absolute; left: 100px; top: 300px;
                 background-color: red;
                 include-source:url("Sample313-External.html"); }

all.myYellow   { position: absolute; left: 100px; top: 400px;
                 background-color: yellow;
                 include-source:url("Sample313-External.html"); }
-->

</STYLE>

</HEAD>

<BODY>

<P STYLE="position:absolute; left:20px; top:25px; color:blue; font-size:14pt;">

     Notice that both of the DIV Elements below this blue paragraph have content
that is imported from the 'Sample313-External.html' file. The first DIV Element has
a background color of red that is applied to it with the NAMED LAYER named RedBack
which is summoned with the ID Attribute of the DIV Element.            <BR><BR>

     The second uses the CLASS of STYLE named 'myYellow' and has a yellow
background.                                                            <BR><BR>

     Be EXTREMELY careful with the External Files that you load in and make sure
that there is only regular HTML in them and absolutely no CSS Syntax in them or you
will get unpredictable and/or seriously weird results.                </P>

<DIV ID="RedBack"></DIV>

<DIV CLASS="myYellow"></DIV>

</BODY>
</HTML>
```

This example focuses on demonstrating why you should not put any text content within an Element that has a NAMED LAYER addressed to it *with* an **include-source** Property. All of the text (or Properties if you define them for the Element, which I did not do for this example) that you assign to it will be ignored. The NAMED LAYER will still work just fine so that the external content will be displayed. Notice that the text within the DIV Tags does not show up in the browser Window at all.

Example 2-14 Part 1:   Sample314.html

```
<!DOCTYPE HTML PUBLIC "-//W3C//DTD HTML 3.2//EN">
<HTML>
<HEAD>
<TITLE>Sample 314 - CSS Example 2-14 include-source Property Caveat </TITLE>

<STYLE TYPE="text/CSS">
<!--
#RedBack               { position:absolute; left:100px; top:200px;
                         background-color:red;
                         include-source:url('Sample314A.html'); }
-->
</STYLE>
</HEAD>
<BODY>

<DIV ID="RedBack">    This is the ignored text.    </DIV>


<P>This is why putting text inside of an Element that has a NAMED LAYER addressed
to it with an "include-source url" attached, is not a good idea. All of the text or
Properties are ignored and you may get even stranger results than this.</P>

</BODY>
</HTML>
```

Example 2-14 Part 2:   Sample314A.html

```
<!DOCTYPE HTML PUBLIC "-//W3C//DTD HTML 3.2//EN">
<HTML>
<HEAD>
<TITLE>        Sample 314A - CSS Example 2-14A        include-source    </TITLE>
</HEAD>

<BODY>

<H3>This is a H3 Heading.</H3>
<H4>This is a H4 Heading.</H4>

</BODY>
</HTML>
```

CSS Layer Properties and <LAYER> Attributes Chart

This chart is repeated from Chapter 1, on page 13, and it takes the CSS Syntax <u>Properties</u> of Layers created with Positioned Style and compares them with the <u>Attributes</u> of Layers created with the LAYER Element. As you will notice, each way of creating a Layer has some unique capabilities that are not available via the other methodology.

∞∞

Property NAME CSS Syntax	Attribute NAME <LAYER> Syntax	Simple CSS Syntax Examples	Simple <LAYER> Syntax Examples
position		{ position: absolute; }	<LAYER></LAYER>
position		{ position: relative; }	<ILAYER></ILAYER>
#myLayerName	ID	{ position: absolute; }	ID="myLayerName"
left	LEFT	{ left: 40px; }	LEFT=40
top	TOP	{ top: 20px; }	TOP=20
	PAGEX		PAGEX=72
	PAGEY		PAGEY=144
width	WIDTH	{ width: 550px; }	WIDTH=550
height	HEIGHT	{ height: 400px; }	HEIGHT=400
clip	CLIP	{ clip: rect('10, 20, 30, 40'); }	CLIP="10, 20, 30, 40"
z-index	Z-INDEX	{ z-index: 3; }	Z-INDEX=3
	ABOVE		ABOVE="myLayerName5"
	BELOW		BELOW="myLayerName7"
visibility	VISIBILITY	{ visibility: show; }	VISIBILITY="SHOW"
background-color	BGCOLOR	{ background-color: purple; }	BGCOLOR="#0000ff"
layer-background-color		{ layer-background-color: blue; }	
background-image	BACKGROUND	{ background-image:url('image1.jpg'); }	BACKGROUND="image3.jpg"
layer-background-image		{ layer-background-image:url('image2.jpg'); }	
include-source	SRC	{ include-source: url('myPage.html'); }	SRC="myPage.html"
	OnMouseOver		OnMouseOver
	OnMouseOut		OnMouseOut
	OnFocus		OnFocus
	OnBlur		OnBlur
	OnLoad		OnLoad

∞∞

Special Notice:

By default, a LAYER is transparent in the sense that other LAYERs that are beneath it will show through, except in the places where the actual content, such as text or images, are that causes the underlying LAYERs to be obscured.

Creating Layers with the <LAYER> Element

The <LAYER> Element

The <LAYER> Element is the direct way to create a Layer in the Body section of your document. Both the Start and End Tags are required. Functionally, it is equivalent to creating a Layer by using the STYLE Element or the STYLE Attribute of another Element, although there are several additional Attributes available and the Syntax is different for the Attribute Names when compared to the parallel Property Names.

You may have noticed in the preceding chart or the Syntax section below, that the LAYER Element <u>doesn't have</u> a corresponding POSITION Attribute. That's because the Value of **absolute** is built into the LAYER Element and the Value of **relative** is built into the ILAYER Element so it doesn't need to be specified.

Remember that when using the LAYER Element you are back in regular HTML and all of the measurements are in pixels, but you <u>don't</u> put the units abbreviation after the integer number and you <u>do</u> enclose the String Values inside of single or double quotes.

One of the most important concepts to mentally lock down is that the LAYER Element is used primarily to precisely **position** an independent block of content with the LEFT and TOP Attributes. Then you have several options for augmenting the content:

1)   Using additional Attributes within the LAYER Element.
2)   Using the ID or CLASS Attributes to address a NAMED LAYER that you create in the Header using CSS Syntax. This option will give you infinitely more control and creative possibilities than option 1.
3)   Using inline Style with the STYLE Attribute.
4)   Using the SPAN Element for Style on-the-fly.
5)   Using all of the above options. This gives you the most flexibility.

The following Attributes are unique to the LAYER Element and there are no corresponding Properties available in CSS Syntax:

```
PAGEX, PAGEY, ABOVE, BELOW,
OnMouseOver, OnMouseOut, OnFocus, OnBlur, OnLoad
```

A lot of this section on the <LAYER> Element theory is very similar to the previous sections that covered the <u>NAMED LAYER</u> and the <u>STYLE Attribute as LAYER</u>. While it's necessary to repeat this information for completeness, you may want to skim over it to find the aspects that are different than the previous sections and then use it as a reference, which is its primary purpose. The secondary purpose is to give you a way to compare CSS Syntax and HTML LAYER Element Syntax.

Syntax:

```
<LAYER
ID="layerName"
LEFT=integerPixels
TOP=integerPixels
PAGEX=integerPixels
PAGEY=integerPixels
WIDTH=integerPixels | "integer%"
HEIGHT=integerPixels | "integer%"
CLIP="TopInteger,RightInteger,BottomInteger,LeftInteger"
Z-INDEX= positiveInteger
ABOVE="layerName"
BELOW="layerName"
VISIBILITY="SHOW" | "HIDE" | "INHERIT"
BGCOLOR="colorName" | "#$$$$$$"
BACKGROUND="imageURL"
SRC="contentURL"
onMouseOver="function()" | "inlineJavaScript"
onMouseOut="function()" | "inlineJavaScript"
onFocus="function()" | "inlineJavaScript"
onBlur="function()" | "inlineJavaScript"
onLoad="function()" | "inlineJavaScript">
***
</LAYER>
```

Attributes Defined:

ID="layerName"
creates a Name for your LAYER and/or specifies the NAMED STYLE to be addressed and inserted. The Value of the **layerName** must begin with an alphabetic character, not an alphanumeric character. The rest of the **layerName** may contain numbers. Remember that your **layerNames** are always case-sensitive. You can refer to a LAYER by its Name and manipulate it with scripting languages such as JavaScript.

```
<LAYER ID="FirstLayer"> This is another test.   </LAYER>
<LAYER ID="SecondLayer">And yet another test.   </LAYER>
```

LEFT=integerPixels
indicates the horizontal coordinate where the upper-left corner of the LAYER will start to be rendered in the containing LAYER or in the browser Window if it's a top-level LAYER. The LAYER will then render down and to the right. It is always in pixels and must be specified with a positive or negative integer or zero, without the (px) units. This is an optional Attribute, which defaults to the natural flow of the document if unused.

```
<LAYER LEFT=40>              . . .              </LAYER>
```

TOP=integerPixels

indicates the vertical coordinate where the upper-left corner of the LAYER will start to be rendered in the containing LAYER or in the browser Window if it's a top-level LAYER. The LAYER will then render down and to the right. It is always in pixels and must be specified with a positive or negative integer or zero, <u>without</u> the (px) units. This is an optional Attribute, which defaults to the natural flow of the document if unused.

```
<LAYER TOP=20>              . . .    </LAYER>
```

PAGEX=integerPixels

works just like the LEFT Attribute, except that the horizontal starting point for the upper-left corner of this LAYER is the enclosing browser Window in all cases, instead of the containing LAYER.

```
<LAYER PAGEX=55>            . . .    </LAYER>
```

PAGEY=integerPixels

works just like the TOP Attribute, except that the vertical starting point for the upper-left corner of this LAYER is the enclosing browser Window in all cases, instead of the containing LAYER.

```
<LAYER PAGEY=522>           . . .    </LAYER>
```

WIDTH=integerPixels | "integer%"

specifies a horizontal width for the LAYER. You can specify it with a positive integer as pixels or as a percentage of the LAYER followed by a percent (%) sign. Do not use a units suffix for pixels. The default value for this Property is 100% of the possible space in the browser Window that can be assigned to the LAYER, or if it is a nested LAYER, the contents will wrap to the right edge of the LAYER that immediately contains it. If you include an item in a LAYER like an image that cannot be wrapped, and you designate a WIDTH that is too small to contain the item, then the LAYER will expand so that it is wide enough to contain the item. Here are two mini-examples:

```
<LAYER WIDTH=777>...</LAYER>           <LAYER WIDTH="50%">...</LAYER>
```

HEIGHT=integerPixels | "integer%"

specifies a vertical height for the LAYER. You can specify it with a positive integer as pixels or as a percentage of the LAYER followed by a percent (%) sign. If no height is specified, then by default the LAYER will expand to the minimum height necessary to display all of the content contained within that LAYER. If you specify a height that is inadequate to properly display the contents, then the LAYER will automatically expand to accommodate the contents. This Property is primarily intended as a reference for nested LAYERs that it contains, which express their height values as percentages. It also specifies the initial height Value of the clipping area of the **Layer** Object that is used with JavaScript.

```
<LAYER HEIGHT=400>...</LAYER>          <LAYER HEIGHT="75%">...</LAYER>
```

CLIP="TopInteger,RightInteger,BottomInteger,LeftInteger"
chooses what part of the LAYER is initially visible. You do this by defining a Clipping Rectangle by specifying the upper-left corner with an (x1,y1) coordinate point and then the bottom-right corner point with an (x2,y2) coordinate. These four numbers are each separated by a comma and optionally placed as a group between quotes, causing them to be treated as a String. If you omit the quotes, then make sure that there is no white space between any of the numbers or commas. The space inside that Rectangle will be the visible part of the LAYER. The order of the list of coordinates is from left to right; you first have the top coordinate, then the right coordinate, then the bottom coordinate and oddly enough the last one is the left coordinate. It is possible that this order has changed by the time you read this so if you have any problems getting your LAYER to show up try placing the left-coordinate at the beginning of the list, which is how Netscape's documentation says it should be, but is currently in error. These coordinates must be positive or negative integers or zero and always represent pixels. You do not suffix the coordinates with the (px) units of measurement. The **CLIP** Attribute is an optional Attribute that defaults to a completely visible LAYER.

```
<LAYER CLIP="10,200,300,40">        ...     </LAYER>
```

where: 10   is the top coordinate
            200   is the right coordinate
            300   is the bottom coordinate
            40   is the left coordinate

You can also use a Value for the **CLIP** Attribute that only has two numbers in the set of numbers so that it only specifies the right-coordinate and the bottom-coordinate. In this case the top and left coordinates are defaulted to both have a Value of zero like this:

```
<LAYER CLIP="200,300">        ...     </LAYER>
```
which is equivalent to:
```
<LAYER CLIP="0,200,300,0">        ...     </LAYER>
```

Z-INDEX=positiveInteger
uses a positive integer to specify into what position in the stacking order a LAYER is placed. A LAYER with a **Z-INDEX** set to 1 will be underneath all subsequent LAYERs, so it follows that the larger the **Z-INDEX**, the higher that LAYER will be in the z-stack. What this does is determine the order of precedence that a LAYER has, which then controls the visibility of a LAYER's contents when you have LAYERs that overlap or even occupy the exact same space. When you set up different LAYERs to occupy the same space you usually set one with a Value of SHOW and the rest of them have a Value of HIDE and then use JavaScript to manipulate them or allow the user to dynamically alter the page.

Ordinarily, the LAYERs are stacked in the order that they are coded in so that the first LAYER in your code sequence is at the bottom of the z-stack and the next LAYER coded is the next LAYER in the z-stack and so on. By using the **Z-INDEX** Attribute, you can change that z-order to accommodate your authoring requirements.

The **Z-INDEX** Attribute does not affect the stacking order between nested LAYERs and their parent LAYER but only to the sibling LAYERs within a parent LAYER. Also you can only use one **Z-INDEX** Attribute per LAYER. Here is a mini-example:

```
<LAYER Z-INDEX=5>            . . .          </LAYER>
```

ABOVE="layerName"

specifies that this LAYER will be higher in the stacking order than the LAYER that is specified by **layerName**. It is important that the **layerName** LAYER already be an existing LAYER; otherwise, a new LAYER will be created that might cause problems in your JavaScript Scripts or give you unexpected layout results in your HTML page. There is no corresponding CSS Syntax Property for this Attribute. Here is a mini-example:

```
<LAYER ABOVE="myLayer">      . . .          </LAYER>
```

BELOW="layerName"

specifies that this LAYER will be lower in the stacking order than the LAYER that is specified by **layerName**. It's important that the **layerName** LAYER already be an existing LAYER; otherwise, a new LAYER will be created that might cause problems in your JavaScript Scripts or give you unexpected layout results in your HTML page. There is no corresponding CSS Syntax Property for this Attribute. Here is a mini-example:

```
<LAYER BELOW="yourLayer">    . . .          </LAYER>
```

VISIBILITY="SHOW" | "HIDE" | "INHERIT"

determines whether a LAYER is initially visible or hidden when the page is loaded into the browser Window. The Value of SHOW causes the LAYER to be visible. The Value of HIDE causes the LAYER to be invisible but it still takes up the amount of space in the Window that it normally would. This is true even for a LAYER that is inflow; that is, it's defined as inherently absolute but has no LEFT or TOP Values chosen. Note that even if a LAYER has a Value of HIDE, it is still <u>available</u> for JavaScript maneuvering, but it cannot receive Events until the Value of SHOW is assigned. If you want a LAYER to be hidden, but still receive Events, say from the keyboard, then place the LAYER <u>off-screen</u> with the **LEFT** or **TOP** Properties by using negative integers.

Specifying a Value of INHERIT causes the LAYER to have the same Value as its parent LAYER. If the LAYER has no parent, it is said to be a top-level LAYER and it would INHERIT a Value of SHOW because the Body of the document is always visible. The default Value of a LAYER is that it will have the same Value as its parent LAYER.

Even if a LAYER is set to a Value of SHOW it still may be obscured by another LAYER that has the same positioning coordinates designated or just overlaps it and/or has a higher Z-INDEX Value. Here are the mini-examples:

```
<LAYER VISIBILITY="SHOW">      . . .    </LAYER>
<LAYER VISIBILITY="HIDE">      . . .    </LAYER>
<LAYER VISIBILITY="INHERIT">   . . .    </LAYER>
```

BGCOLOR="colorName" | "#$$$$$$"

Not again! Again, use one of the recognized Color Names or use that old reliable red-green-blue Hexadecimal Triplet that is preceded by a hash (#) mark and placed between double quotes.

```
<LAYER BGCOLOR="blue">          ...    </LAYER>
<LAYER BGCOLOR="#22aaff">       ...    </LAYER>
```

BACKGROUND="imageURL"

specifies an image to be tiled (repeated) as the backdrop of a LAYER that is accessed by the URL of the image file. You can also use a GIF89a Animation, or other media type, if you want to get fancy. If you do this, you may want to specify a **padding** Property for the Style of the content for the LAYER.

```
<LAYER BACKGROUND="JPEG-FILES/icon-BG-stars.jpg">       ...
</LAYER>

<LAYER
BACKGROUND="http://www.erols.com/gilorien/JPEG-FILES/
        icon-BG-stars.jpg">  ...
</LAYER>
```

SRC="contentURL"

specifies an external document that contains only HTML content or HTML content and JavaScript that is loaded and placed into this LAYER. Any Layers placed within the LAYER Element from the external file will be treated as child Layers of the containing Layer, which has the SRC Attribute that loads the content. The corresponding CSS Syntax Property for this Attribute is the **include-source** Property.

This can be very useful if you want to dynamically change the content of a LAYER, or it can be used to provide the alternate content for the NOLAYER Element.

```
<LAYER SRC="Sample310.html"> ... </LAYER>

<LAYER SRC="http://www.dreamplay.com/Sample311.html"> ... </LAYER>
```

onMouseOver="function( )" | "inlineJavaScript"

executes this function or inline JavaScript code when the user places the mouse cursor over the space occupied by this LAYER in the document. See Chapter 3, which deals with "JavaScript for Layers" or Chapter 6 on "JavaScript Events and Event Handlers."

onMouseOut="function( )" | "inlineJavaScript"

executes this function or inline JavaScript code when the user places the mouse cursor away from the space occupied by this LAYER in the document. See Chapter 3, which deals with "JavaScript for Layers" or Chapter 6 on "JavaScript Events and Event Handlers."

onFocus="function( )" | "inlineJavaScript"

executes this function or inline JavaScript code when this LAYER in the document gains keyboard focus. See Chapter 3, which deals with "JavaScript for Layers" or Chapter 6 on "JavaScript Events and Event Handlers."

onBlur="function( )" | "inlineJavaScript"

executes this function or inline JavaScript code when this LAYER in the document loses focus. See Chapter 3, which deals with "JavaScript for Layers" or Chapter 6 on "JavaScript Events and Event Handlers."

onLoad="function( )" | "inlineJavaScript"

executes this function or inline JavaScript code after this LAYER has fully loaded into the browser Window. See Chapter 3, which deals with "JavaScript for Layers" or Chapter 6 on "JavaScript Events and Event Handlers."

This example demonstrates three Layers using the LAYER Tags. See the text between the LAYER Tags for more information.

Example 2-15:   Sample315.html

```
<!DOCTYPE HTML PUBLIC "-//W3C//DTD HTML 3.2//EN">
<HTML><HEAD>
<TITLE>Sample 315 - Example 2-15 LAYER Element        </TITLE> </HEAD>
<BODY>

<LAYER LEFT=72 TOP=30>
        This is a simple Layer. It is inherently absolute and placed at 72 pixels to
the right of the left margin of the Body Element and 30 pixels down from the top
margin of the Body Element which contains it.
</LAYER>

<LAYER LEFT=50 TOP=144 BGCOLOR="red" WIDTH=400>
        This Layer is 50 pixels from the left margin and 144 pixels from the top
margin of the Body Element and has a background color of red.
</LAYER>

<LAYER LEFT=10 TOP=244 BGCOLOR="aqua" WIDTH=400>

<FONT SIZE="5" COLOR="blue">
        This Layer is 10 pixels from the left margin and 244 pixels from the top
margin of the Body Element and has a background color of aqua. The text is blue and
sized at 5, but it was specified with the FONT Element and not with CSS Syntax.
</FONT>
</LAYER>

</BODY>
</HTML>
```

This example demonstrates how the LEFT and TOP Attributes behave when their Layer is nested inside of another Layer. Instead of being absolute positioning coordinates, relative to the page, they are relative to the parent Layer. In the third Layer, the LEFT and TOP Attributes are omitted and instead the PAGEX and PAGEY Attributes are used. See the text in the Layers contained in the Example for more details.

Example 2-16: Sample316.html

```
<!DOCTYPE HTML PUBLIC "-//W3C//DTD HTML 3.2//EN">
<HTML>
<HEAD>
<TITLE>        Sample 316 - Example 2-16      LAYER Element   </TITLE>
</HEAD>

<BODY>

<LAYER LEFT=72 TOP=30>

        All three of these Layers have x-coordinates of 72 pixels but the second and
third Layers are both nested inside the first Layer which causes the second Layer
to be 72 pixels to the right of the margin of the first Layer, not just to the
right of the Body Element.           <BR><BR>
        Just to add a little spice to the mix the third Layer is using the PAGEX and
PAGEY Attributes so by definition its coordinates are not applied to the first
Layer but are applied to the margin of the Body Element which causes it to be 72
pixels to the right of the margin of the Body Element and 244 pixels down from the
top of the margin of the Body Element.

<LAYER LEFT=72 TOP=150 BGCOLOR="yellow" WIDTH=400>
        This Layer is 72 pixels from the left margin of the first Layer so it is 144
pixels from the Body Element margin. It 150 pixels from the top margin of the first
Layer which makes it 180 pixels from the top margin of the Body Element and has a
background color of yellow. If it is overlapping the first Layer then resize your
browser window so it is wider.
</LAYER>


<LAYER PAGEX=72 PAGEY=300 BGCOLOR="lime" WIDTH=330>
<FONT SIZE="5" COLOR="blue">
        This Layer is 72 pixels from the left margin and 300 pixels from the top
margin of the Body Element and has a background color of lime. The text is blue and
sized at 5, but it was specified with the FONT Element and not with CSS Syntax.
</FONT>
</LAYER>

                    <!-- Closes the top parent Layer-->
</LAYER>

</BODY>
</HTML>
```

Example 2-16	**Sample316.html**

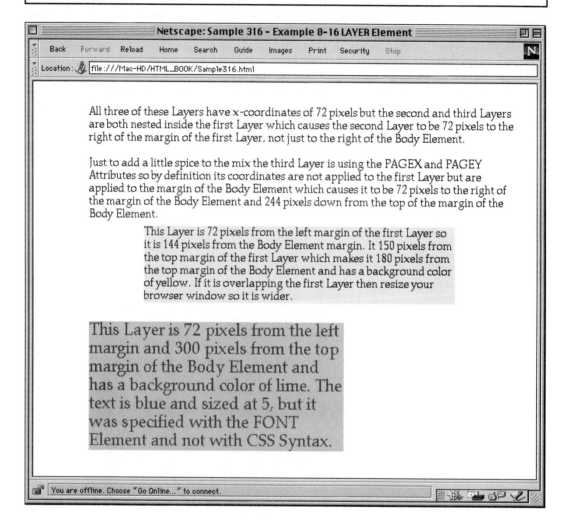

All three of these Layers have x-coordinates of 72 pixels but the second and third Layers are both nested inside the first Layer which causes the second Layer to be 72 pixels to the right of the margin of the first Layer, not just to the right of the Body Element.

Just to add a little spice to the mix the third Layer is using the PAGEX and PAGEY Attributes so by definition its coordinates are not applied to the first Layer but are applied to the margin of the Body Element which causes it to be 72 pixels to the right of the margin of the Body Element and 244 pixels down from the top of the margin of the Body Element.

This Layer is 72 pixels from the left margin of the first Layer so it is 144 pixels from the Body Element margin. It 150 pixels from the top margin of the first Layer which makes it 180 pixels from the top margin of the Body Element and has a background color of yellow. If it is overlapping the first Layer then resize your browser window so it is wider.

This Layer is 72 pixels from the left margin and 300 pixels from the top margin of the Body Element and has a background color of lime. The text is blue and sized at 5, but it was specified with the FONT Element and not with CSS Syntax.

This example demonstrates both the LAYER Element and NAMED LAYERs that are created with CSS Syntax and shows that it is possible to use Attributes within a LAYER Element and inherit Properties from a NAMED LAYER within a single LAYER Element.

Example 2-17:   Sample317.html

```
<!DOCTYPE HTML PUBLIC "-//W3C//DTD HTML 3.2//EN">
<HTML>
<HEAD>
<TITLE>Sample 317 - Example 2-17 LAYER Element        </TITLE>

<STYLE TYPE="text/CSS">

<!--

#LeBodi          { padding:20px; font-size:15pt; }

#LBCLayer        { position:absolute; left:30px; top:170px;
                   layer-background-color:rgb(45%, 2%, 58%);
                   color:aqua; font-size:20pt; padding:20px;
                   border-style:ridge; border-width:20px; border-color:blue; }

#LBCLayer2       { position:absolute; left:25px; top:300px;
                   layer-background-color:rgb(75%, 72%, 8%);
                   color:blue; font-size:25pt; padding:10px;
                   border-style:double; border-width:20px; border-color:lime; }
-->
</STYLE>

</HEAD>

<BODY TEXT="white" BGCOLOR="black">

<LAYER ID="LeBodi" LEFT="45" TOP="40" BGCOLOR="#7700ff" WIDTH="500">
      All of these Layers are specified with the LAYER Element and each address a
NAMED LAYER from the Style Definition. Notice that this Layer also makes use of
LAYER Attributes in addition to the padding Property and font-size Property that it
inherits from the 'LeBodi' NAMED LAYER. <BR><BR>
</LAYER>

<LAYER ID="LBCLayer">
This is the LBCLayer Test. It has a blue border.
</LAYER>

<LAYER ID="LBCLayer2">
This is the LBCLayer2 Test. It has a lime border.
</LAYER>

</BODY>
</HTML>
```

Example 2-17   Sample317.html

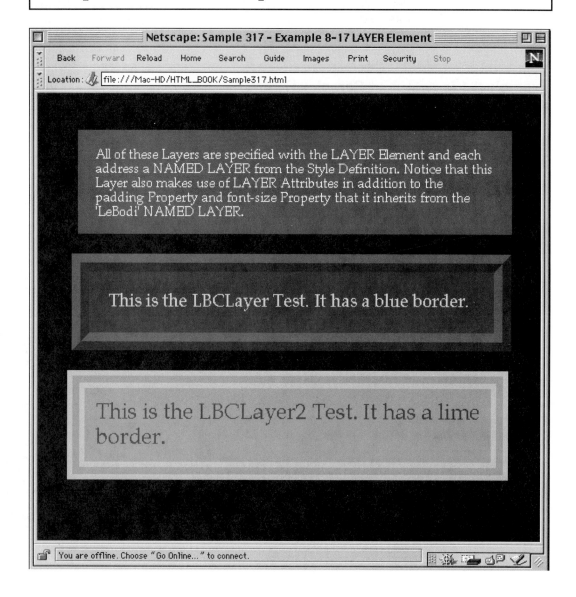

Netscape: Sample 317 – Example 8–17 LAYER Element

Back Forward Reload Home Search Guide Images Print Security Stop

Location: file:///Mac-HD/HTML_BOOK/Sample317.html

All of these Layers are specified with the LAYER Element and each address a NAMED LAYER from the Style Definition. Notice that this Layer also makes use of LAYER Attributes in addition to the padding Property and font-size Property that it inherits from the 'LeBodi' NAMED LAYER.

This is the LBCLayer Test. It has a blue border.

This is the LBCLayer2 Test. It has a lime border.

You are offline. Choose "Go Online..." to connect.

The <ILAYER> Element

The <ILAYER> Element is an inflow and an inline Layer, whereas the LAYER Element is considered out-of-line.

An <ILAYER> Element has all of the same Attributes of a <LAYER> Element, which have identical definitions and work exactly the same except for the LEFT and TOP Attributes. The LEFT and TOP Attributes specify an <u>offset distance</u> from the natural flow of the document instead of an absolute position. There is additional information about these two Attributes after the Syntax for the ILAYER Element. Because the definitions of the other ILAYER Attributes are identical to their LAYER Element counterparts, they are not repeated here, so see the previous section on the LAYER Element for more information.

Syntax:

```
<ILAYER
ID="layerName"
LEFT=integerPixels
TOP=integerPixels
PAGEX=integerPixels
PAGEY=integerPixels
WIDTH=integerPixels | "integer%"
HEIGHT=integerPixels | "integer%"
CLIP="TopInteger,RightInteger,BottomInteger,LeftInteger"
Z-INDEX= positiveInteger
ABOVE="layerName"
BELOW="layerName"
VISIBILITY="SHOW" | "HIDE" | "INHERIT"
BGCOLOR="colorName" | "#$$$$$$"
BACKGROUND="imageURL"
SRC="contentURL"
OnMouseOver="function()" | "inlineJavaScript"
OnMouseOut="function()" | "inlineJavaScript"
OnFocus="function()" | "inlineJavaScript"
OnBlur="function()" | "inlineJavaScript"
OnLoad="function()" | "inlineJavaScript">

* * *

</ILAYER>
```

Attributes Defined:

LEFT=integerPixels

indicates the horizontal offset distance that is measured from the upper-left corner of the space where a Layer would normally flow in the document. This is where the upper-left corner of the ILAYER will start to be rendered in the containing Layer or in the browser Window if it's a top-level Layer.

The ILAYER will then render down and to the right. It is always in pixels and must be specified with a positive or negative integer or zero, <u>without</u> the (px) units. This is an optional Attribute that defaults to the natural flow of the document if unused.

```
<ILAYER LEFT=40>

...  Layer Content  ...

</ILAYER>
```

TOP=integerPixels

indicates the vertical offset distance that is measured from the upper-left corner of the space where a Layer would normally flow in the document. This is where the upper-left corner of the ILAYER will start to be rendered in the containing Layer or in the browser Window if it's a top-level Layer.

The ILAYER will then render down and to the right. It is always in pixels and must be specified with a positive or negative integer or zero, <u>without</u> the (px) units. This is an optional Attribute that defaults to the natural flow of the document if unused.

```
<ILAYER TOP=20>

...  Layer Content  ...

</ILAYER>
```

Example 2-18 is a simple demonstration of two inline ILAYER Elements. In order of appearance, the first ILAYER is purple and the second one is red. They both specify a WIDTH of 500 pixels and each one has a small amount of obvious explanatory text in it.

The point of this example is to have the simplest implementaion of ILAYER Elements for you to use as a reference to compare to when more complicated examples are demonstrated.

Example 2-18: Sample318.html

```
<!DOCTYPE HTML PUBLIC "-//W3C//DTD HTML 3.2//EN">
<HTML>
<HEAD>
<TITLE>        Sample 318 - Example 2-18     ILAYER Element </TITLE>
<BASEFONT SIZE="5">
</HEAD>

<BODY TEXT="white" BGCOLOR="black">

<ILAYER BGCOLOR="#7700ff" WIDTH=500>
This is the first ILAYER Layer.  Without the BR Tags they would stack vertically
snug.
</ILAYER>            <BR><BR>

<ILAYER BGCOLOR="red"  WIDTH=500 HEIGHT=200>
This is the second ILAYER Layer.
</ILAYER>

</BODY>
</HTML>
```

This example demonstrates applying NAMED Styles to ILAYER Elements. Notice that the third ILAYER has LEFT and TOP Attributes, which offset its inflow position by the specified number of pixels.

Example 2-19: Sample319.html

```
<!DOCTYPE HTML PUBLIC "-//W3C//DTD HTML 3.2//EN">
<HTML>
<HEAD>
<TITLE>Sample 319 - Example 2-19      ILAYER Element </TITLE>

<STYLE TYPE="text/CSS">

<!--

#LeBodi        { font-size: 15pt; }

#LBCILAYER     { layer-background-color: rgb(45%, 2%, 58%);
                 color: aqua; font-size: 20pt;
                 border-style:ridge; border-width:20px; border-color:blue; }

#LBCILAYER2    { layer-background-color: rgb(75%, 72%, 8%);
                 color: blue; font-size: 25pt;
                 border-style:double; border-width:20px; border-color:lime; }

-->
```

```
</STYLE>

</HEAD>

<BODY TEXT="white" BGCOLOR="black">

<ILAYER ID="LeBodi" BGCOLOR="#7700ff" WIDTH=500>
      All of these ILAYERs are specified with the ILAYER Element and each address
a NAMED ILAYER from the Style Definition. Notice that this ILAYER also makes use of
ILAYER Attributes. <BR><BR>
</ILAYER>

<ILAYER ID="LBCILAYER">
      This is the LBCILAYER Test. It has a blue border.
</ILAYER>

<ILAYER ID="LBCILAYER2" LEFT=45 TOP=40>
      This is the LBCILAYER2 Test. It has a lime border.
</ILAYER>

</BODY>
</HTML>
```

The <NOLAYER> Element

The <NOLAYER> Element is used to offer information or options to a user that has a non-Layer-capable browser. You put the NOLAYER Element inside of either a LAYER Element or an ILAYER Element or a Layer created with either CSS Syntax or JavaScript Syntax.

Syntax:

```
<NOLAYER>    ***    </NOLAYER>
```

Example 2-20 contains a simple demonstration of the NOLAYER Element, which is contained inside of an ILAYER Element.

Example 2-20:   Sample320.html

```
<!DOCTYPE HTML PUBLIC "-//W3C//DTD HTML 3.2//EN">
<HTML>
<HEAD>
<TITLE>Sample 320 - Example 2-20       NOLAYER Element         </TITLE>
</HEAD>


<BODY TEXT="white" BGCOLOR="black">


<ILAYER>
              <NOLAYER>

<H2>
        Hey Now!!! If you are reading this you are using a LAYER-Challenged-Browser.
For optimal viewing proceed immediately to

<A HREF="http://www.Netscape.com">Netscape's website</A>

 and download version 4.0 or later, of Navigator.
</H2>


<H2>
        Otherwise

<A HREF="myAlternatePage.html">

Enter the Non-Layers Version of the our website.</A>

</H2>


              </NOLAYER>


This is the LAYER Test.

</ILAYER>


</BODY>
</HTML>
```

Part I

Dynamic HTML

Chapter 3

Layers & JavaScript

Chapter 3
Layers & JavaScript

Contents

Introducing JavaScript Layers

Overview

This chapter is primarily focused on Layers created with JavaScript Syntax and using JavaScript with **Layer** Objects. It starts by defining the new JavaScript Properties of the **document** Object that you need to know in order to implement Styles with JavaScript Syntax. The Properties used for JavaScript Syntax Styles are only covered in two charts on pages 194-195 because the information has already been covered in Chapter 1 on CSS. The main difference that you have to be aware of is that the Property Names are different. Then the **Layer** Object Properties and Methods are covered. Next, some additional JavaScript Methods are described and used in examples with a lot of emphasis on the **setTimeout()** Method of the **window** Object to animate Layers.

JavaScript can be used to dynamically modify both the Style of an HTML Element and LAYERs that are created using any of the possible ways of defining a Layer. It doesn't matter whether you define a Layer with the LAYER Element, CLASS of STYLE, the Style Attribute or any of the others, as long as it is a Positioned block of content.

The Properties and Methods of the **Layer** Object provide a powerful set of tools for creative manipulation of your Layers. Used in conjunction with other JavaScript Properties and Methods, you now have an unprecedented level of control for displaying and dynamically altering the content in your page.

Style Sheet Comments
for JavaScript Syntax

When you want to include Comments inside of a STYLE Element that uses JavaScript Syntax, precede Single-line Comments with two forward slashes (//). For Multiple-line Comments precede the first line with one forward slash followed by one asterisk (/*) and follow the last line with one asterisk followed by one forward slash (*/).

JavaScript Syntax:

```
//     Single-line Comments
/*     Multiple-line Comments   */
```

New JavaScript Properties

New <u>document</u> Object Properties

The new Properties for the **document** Object that you need to know in order to use JavaScript Syntax with Styles and Layers are:

> **tags** Property
> **classes** Property
> **ids** Property

The <u>tags</u> Property

JavaScript Syntax:

```
tags.elementName.propertyName="propertyValue";
```

Parameters Defined:

The **tags** Property is used to define a Style for an HTML Element when you are using JavaScript Syntax to create a STYLE SHEET within the <STYLE> Element. It is a Property of the JavaScript **document** Object, which is inherently created when you declare that you are defining your STYLE SHEET to be written in JavaScript Syntax with the **TYPE="text/JavaScript"** Attribute in the <STYLE> Element.

When you use the **tags** Property with dot notation, you are signifying that the HTML Element, specified by the **elementName** Parameter that is suffixed to it, will be assigned a Style by specifying the Property Name via **propertyName** and then its Value by **propertyValue**, like this:

```
document.tags.DIV.fontSize="22pt";
```

The **tags** Property specifies that for this **document** all **DIV** Elements will have the **fontSize** Property designated to set all of the text at 22 point. Here's how that would look inside the <STYLE> Element:

```
<STYLE TYPE="text/JavaScript">

document.tags.DIV.fontSize="22pt";

</STYLE>
```

Now just to make it simpler, when you use the **tags** Property, it can only apply to the **document** Object, so the nice folks at Netscape have thoughtfully coded Navigator so that you don't have to type in **document** each time you use the **tags** Property because it is assumed to be there. This means that the following two mini-examples are equivalent:

```
document.tags.DIV.fontSize="22pt";

tags.DIV.fontSize="22pt";
```

Make sure that you remember to include the semicolon after each designation.

Special Notice:

Do <u>not</u> put your Style Sheets that use <u>JavaScript Syntax</u> inside an HTML Comment (<!-- ... -->) Tag or else you will get an error message.
Use the <NOSCRIPT> ... </NOSCRIPT> Tags for providing alternative content in your pages.

OK, so let's put that all together in a simple example.

Example 3-0:   Sample400.html

```
<!DOCTYPE HTML PUBLIC "-//W3C//DTD HTML 3.2//EN">
<HTML>
<HEAD>
<TITLE>Sample 400 - Example 3-0   tags Property      </TITLE>

<STYLE TYPE="text/JavaScript">

      tags.DIV.fontSize="22pt";

</STYLE>

</HEAD>

<BODY>

<DIV>Live Long and Prosper.</DIV>

</BODY>
</HTML>
```

The <u>classes</u> Property

JavaScript Syntax:

```
classes.className.elementName.propertyName="propertyValue";
```

Parameters Defined:

The **classes** Property is used to define a CLASS of STYLE to apply to an Element as was previously discussed in Chapter 1 on page 72. Here's the Syntax sequence order in dot notation and then some mini-examples to show you how to do it in JavaScript Syntax.

The **classes** Property goes first and then the NAME of the CLASS of STYLE follows immediately after. It, is then followed by the Element Name, which is then followed by the Property Name, then the equals (=) sign followed by the Property Value. The Property Value is enclosed in double quotes (" ") for String Values and not enclosed in double quotes for Number Values or Variables. The final part is a semicolon (;) like this:

```
classes.BlueBlocker.BLOCKQUOTE.color="blue";
```

where:

classes	is the **document** Object Property
BlueBlocker	is the NAME of the CLASS of STYLE
BLOCKQUOTE	is the HTML Element Name
color	is the Style Property Name
blue	is the Style Property Value

which defines a CLASS of STYLE Named **BlueBlocker** which is then applied to all BLOCKQUOTE Elements that will cause the color of the text to be blue.

Here are some more mini-examples:

Mini-Examples:

```
classes.Chunky.H5.fontWeight="bold";
classes.Slanted.DIV.fontStyle="italic";
classes.WhyHelv.PRE.fontFamily="Helvetica";
```

OK, so let's put that all together in a simple example.

Example 3-1:　　　　　　**Sample401.html**

```
<!DOCTYPE HTML PUBLIC "-//W3C//DTD HTML 3.2//EN">
<HTML>
<HEAD>
<TITLE>        Sample 401 - Example 3-1    classes Property  </TITLE>

<STYLE TYPE="text/JavaScript">


        classes.BlueBlocker.BLOCKQUOTE.color="blue";

        classes.Chunky.H5.fontWeight="bold";

        classes.Slanted.DIV.fontStyle="italic";

        classes.WhyHelv.PRE.fontFamily="Helvetica";


</STYLE>

</HEAD>

<BODY>

<BLOCKQUOTE CLASS="BlueBlocker">

The BLOCKQUOTE test.

</BLOCKQUOTE>

<H5 CLASS="Chunky">

The H5 test.

</H5>

<DIV CLASS="Slanted">

The DIV test.

</DIV>

<PRE CLASS="WhyHelv">
The
PRE
test.</PRE>

</BODY>

</HTML>
```

The <u>ids</u> Property

JavaScript Syntax:

```
ids.namedStyleName.propertyName="propertyValue";
```

Parameters Defined:

The **ids** Property is used to create an INDIVIDUAL NAMED STYLE that is used as an Exception to a CLASS of STYLE. You define it like this:

```
ids.PurplishText.color="#7700ff";
```

where **PurplishText** is the **namedStyleName** parameter, which can be any name as long as it begins with an uppercase or lowercase letter or the underscore (_) Character and then followed by any sequence of alphanumeric Characters. In this case, the **propertyName** parameter is **color**, which is a valid Style Sheet Property in JavaScript Syntax.

Then you use the **namedStyleName** parameter as the Value of the ID Attribute. It is usually used in conjunction with the CLASS Attribute in an Element like this:

```
<BLOCKQUOTE CLASS="BlueBlocker" ID="PurplishText">
```

where we used the "**BlueBlocker**" CLASS of STYLE from the previous example.

```
classes.BlueBlocker.BLOCKQUOTE.color="blue";
```

Assigning Additional Properties

When you want to assign another Property to a particular CLASS of STYLE or Named Individual Style, just repeat the process with the additional Property for the same **namedStyleName** parameter.

In preparation for the next example we define a second Property for the "**BlueBlocker**" CLASS so that it is 48 point, like this:

```
classes.BlueBlocker.BLOCKQUOTE.fontSize="48pt";
```

Putting that all together, we have the following Example 3-2:

Example 3-2:   **Sample402.html**

```
<!DOCTYPE HTML PUBLIC "-//W3C//DTD HTML 3.2//EN">
<HTML>
<HEAD>
<TITLE>  Sample 402 - Example 3-2   ids Property  </TITLE>

<STYLE TYPE="text/JavaScript">

        classes.BlueBlocker.BLOCKQUOTE.color="blue";

        classes.BlueBlocker.BLOCKQUOTE.fontSize="48pt";

        ids.PurplishText.color="#7700ff";

</STYLE>

</HEAD>

<BODY>

<BLOCKQUOTE CLASS="BlueBlocker" ID="PurplishText">
Another Purple Example.
</BLOCKQUOTE>

</BODY>
</HTML>
```

Dynamically Change a Property

You can also dynamically change a Property with the **ids** Property within a SCRIPT Element like this:

```
<SCRIPT LANGUAGE="JavaScript1.2">

        document.ids.PurplishText.fontsize="14pt";

</SCRIPT>
```

Special Notice:

JavaScript **ids** Names are case-sensitive.

Additionally, it should be noted for reference and comparison purposes that the **ids** Property is the JavaScript Syntax equivalent to the CSS Syntax usage of prefixing the hash (#) sign to a Name to denote a NAMED INDIVIDUAL STYLE or a NAMED LAYER.

JavaScript Style Sheets

Some of this section is going to be review in terms of the theory but new in terms of the Syntax used. Most of the **CSS Style Sheet Properties** that we have used so far are going to be demonstrated using **JavaScript Style Sheet Syntax**.

When the term **JavaScript Syntax** is used, it refers to <STYLE> Syntax declared as:

```
TYPE="text/JavaScript"
```

Ordinarily when you define STYLES with JavaScript you have to use a full declarative Statement for each Property that you want to assign to an Element, which can get very monotonous, like this:

```
tags.DIV.fontSize="25pt";
tags.DIV.color="aqua";
tags.DIV.textIndent="72px";
tags.DIV.lineHeight="40pt";
tags.DIV.backgroundColor="blue";
```

Using the <u>with()</u> Statement

Alternatively, you can use the Keyword **with** and define them all at once by using the **with( )** Statement, which has the Syntax of:

JavaScript Syntax:

```
with (tags.elementName) {
    propertyName1="propertyValue1";
    propertyName2="propertyValue2";
    propertyNameN="propertyValueN";
}
```

so, rewriting the previous Style Property declarations, we have:

```
with (tags.DIV) {
    fontSize="25pt";
    color="aqua";
    textIndent="72px";
    lineHeight="40pt";
    backgroundColor="blue";
}
```

Putting that together we have this simple example that creates a Style for all DIV Elements by using the **tags.DIV** Argument for the **with( )** Statement.

Example 3-3:   **Sample403.html**

```
<!DOCTYPE HTML PUBLIC "-//W3C//DTD HTML 3.2//EN">
<HTML>
<HEAD>
<TITLE>    Sample 403 - Example 3-3    the with() Statement    </TITLE>

<STYLE TYPE="text/JavaScript">

        with (tags.DIV) {

                fontSize="25pt";
                color="aqua";
                textIndent="72px";
                lineHeight="40pt";
                backgroundColor="blue";
        }

</STYLE>

</HEAD>

<BODY>
        <DIV>   Another Division Example.      </DIV>
        <DIV>   Make sure that you remember to enclose the Properties inside of
curly braces and that each Property is suffixed with a semicolon.    </DIV>

</BODY>
</HTML>
```

The JavaScript Keyword <u>all</u>

The Keyword **all** can also be used in JavaScript to specify that all Elements can have a CLASS of STYLE applied to them like this:

```
classes.UpperRed.all.fontSize="30pt";
classes.UpperRed.all.color="red";
classes.UpperRed.all.textTransform="capitalize";
classes.UpperRed.all.textDecoration="underline";
```

which is demonstrated in the following example:

Example 3-4: **Sample404.html**

```
<!DOCTYPE HTML PUBLIC "-//W3C//DTD HTML 3.2//EN">
<HTML>
<HEAD>
<TITLE>       Sample 404 - Example 3-4 Keyword all  </TITLE>

<STYLE TYPE="text/JavaScript">

        classes.UpperRed.all.fontSize="30pt";
        classes.UpperRed.all.color="red";
        classes.UpperRed.all.textTransform="capitalize";
        classes.UpperRed.all.textDecoration="underline";

</STYLE>
</HEAD>
<BODY>
        <P CLASS="UpperRed">
This Paragraph has Properties assigned with the keyword 'all' in conjunction with
the CLASS of STYLE Named 'UpperRed'.          </P>

</BODY>
</HTML>
```

The <u>contextual()</u> Method

As you recall from Chapter 1, we introduced the concept of CONTEXTUAL SELECTION CRITERIA, where Styles are specified to apply to Elements only when they are in a nested context. To accomplish this using JavaScript Syntax, you use the predefined **contextual()** Method which can look for **tags**, **classes**, **ids** or combinations of them in a comma-separated list inside the parentheses. Use dot notation to assign the Property **PropName** and a **Value** for the Style that is to apply to an Element in that context. Some of the possible combinations are covered in the following Syntax, but not all of them.

JavaScript Syntax:

```
contextual(tags.Element1, ..., tags.ElementN).PropName=Value;
contextual(classes.className.Element1, ..., tags.ElementN).PropName=Value;
contextual(ids.IDName, ..., tags.ElementN).PropName=Value;
contextual(classes.className.Element1, ..., classes.className.Element1).PropName=Value;
contextual(tags.Element1, ..., ids.IDName).PropName=Value;
```

Example 3-5 demonstrates various uses of the **contextual()** Method.

Example 3-5:   **Sample405.html**

```
<!DOCTYPE HTML PUBLIC "-//W3C//DTD HTML 3.2//EN">
<HTML>
<HEAD>
<TITLE>Sample 405 - Example 3-5        contextual() Method    </TITLE>

<STYLE TYPE="text/JavaScript">

        classes.UpperRed.all.fontSize="14pt";
        classes.UpperRed.all.color="red";
        classes.UpperRed.all.textTransform="capitalize";
        classes.GetLarge.all.fontSize="24pt";

        tags.P.backgroundColor="yellow";

        ids.GetBigger.fontSize="40pt";

        contextual(classes.UpperRed.P, tags.H1).color="blue";
        contextual(tags.P, tags.H2).color="green";
        contextual(ids.GetBigger, tags.H3).color="cyan";
    contextual(classes.UpperRed.P, classes.GetLarge.CITE, tags.H4).color="purple";
        contextual(classes.UpperRed.P, classes.OliveText.H1).color="olive";
        contextual(tags.DIV, ids.GoLime).color="lime";

</STYLE>

</HEAD>

<BODY>

<P CLASS="UpperRed">
        This Paragraph has Style Properties assigned to it with the CLASS of STYLE
Named 'UpperRed' which is defined so that the keyword 'all' allows it to be
addressed by any Element.
                        <H1>  This is the blue Heading.</H1>  </P>

<P>Hello.           <H2>  This is the green Heading.</H2> </P>

<P ID="GetBigger"> Hello Again.  <H3>  This is the cyan Heading.</H3>  </P>

<P CLASS="UpperRed">           The P Element
<CITE CLASS="GetLarge">        The CITE Element.
                        <H4>This is the purple Heading.</H4>  </CITE>          </P>

<P CLASS="UpperRed">   Another P Element.
                        <H1 CLASS="OliveText">This is the olive Heading.</H1>   </P>

<DIV>
<BLOCKQUOTE ID="GoLime"> This is the Lime Blockquote Element.</BLOCKQUOTE>  </DIV>

</BODY>
</HTML>
```

JavaScript Style Sheet Layer Properties

The following chart has all of the Properties that are specifically associated with Layers created with JavaScript Style Sheet Syntax in a STYLE Element. The Property Name is listed first, followed by all of the possible Values that can be used, and then an example of each is demonstrated.

JSS Layer Syntax Property	All Possible Values	Simple Example
position=	"absolute" | "relative"	tags.DIV.position="absolute"
left=	"integer em, ex, px, pt, pc, in, mm, cm" | "integer%"	tags.DIV.left="25px"
top=	"integer em, ex, px, pt, pc, in, mm, cm" | "integer%"	tags.DIV.top="50px"
width=	"integer em, ex, px, pt, pc, in, mm, cm" | "integer%"	tags.DIV.width="500px"
zIndex=	integer	tags.DIV.zIndex=2
visibility=	"show" | "hide" | "inherit"	tags.DIV.visibility="show"
clip=	"rect('topInteger,rightInteger,bottomInteger,leftInteger')"	tags.DIV.clip="rect('0,500,300,0')"

JavaScript Style Sheet Properties & Examples Chart

The following chart on page 194 has all of the JavaScript Properties that are used to create Styles with JavaScript Syntax. Most of the simple examples that accompany the Property Names use the DIV Element as the Element that has the STYLE assigned to it. Obviously there are many other Elements that could have been used in the chart but it makes the chart much easier to read for quick reference if the same Element Name is used, so I went with that.

JavaScript Style Sheet Properties & All Values Chart

The second chart, on page 195, has the same JavaScript Property Names on the left and the accompanying list of all the possible Property Values on the right.

Instead of rewriting all of the Theory for the Properties used with JavaScript Syntax for creating Styles, which is nearly identical to the Properties used in CSS Syntax, I've included these charts and then I go on to show examples using JavaScript Syntax. There are a few places where there is some additional Theory to account for slight variations in implementation or capability, which are covered in their own sections.

These two charts can also be printed from the following file on the CD-ROM:

Charts.pdf   in the PDF-Files folder.

For more information about a specific Property used to create Styles or Layers with JavaScript Syntax, go back and review the information about the CSS version of the Property in Chapter 1 or see the Dynamic HTML Guide on the CD-ROM or visit Netscape's website in their DevEdge, (that's Developer's Edge department), at:

http://developer.netscape.com/library/documentation/index.html

Property Name JavaScript Syntax	Simple JavaScript Syntax Examples	
fontSize	tags.DIV.fontSize="14pt";	
fontFamily	tags.DIV.fontFamily="Helvetica, Times, Geneva, Courier";	
fontWeight	tags.DIV.fontWeight="bold";	
fontStyle	tags.DIV.fontStyle="italic";	
lineHeight	tags.DIV.lineHeight="22pt";	
textDecoration	tags.DIV.textDecoration="underline";	
textTransform	tags.DIV.textTransform="uppercase";	
textAlign	tags.DIV.textAlign="right";	
textIndent	tags.DIV.textIndent="40px";	
margins()	tags.DIV.margins("75px");	sets all 4 margins to same value
margins()	tags.DIV.margins("24pt", "30pt", "30pt", "17pt");	each margin with unique value Order is: top right bottom left
marginTop	tags.DIV.marginTop="40mm";	
marginRight	tags.DIV.marginRight="4cm";	
marginBottom	tags.DIV.marginBottom="12pc";	
marginLeft	tags.DIV.marginLeft="1in";	
paddings()	tags.DIV.paddings("25px");	
paddings()	tags.DIV.paddings("25pt", "20px", "45pt", "35px");	
paddingTop	tags.DIV.paddingTop="2in";	
paddingRight	tags.DIV.paddingRight="25pt";	
paddingBottom	tags.DIV.paddingBottom="15pt";	
paddingLeft	tags.DIV.paddingLeft="5pt";	
color	tags.DIV.color="blue";	tags.DIV.color="#0000ff";
color	tags.DIV.color="rgb(0%, 0%, 100%)";	tags.DIV.color="rgb(0,20, 255)";
backgroundColor	tags.DIV.backgroundColor="maroon";	
backgroundImage	tags.DIV.backgroundImage="JPEGImages/ExampleImage.jpeg";	
borderStyle	tags.DIV.borderStyle="groove";	
borderColor	tags.DIV.borderColor="#335a77";	
borderColor	tags.DIV.borderColor="rgb(20%, 50%, 70%)";	
borderColor	tags.DIV.borderColor="rgb(255, 20, 150)";	
borderWidths()	tags.DIV.borderWidths("20px");	
borderWidths()	tags.DIV.borderWidths("20px", "30px", "40px", "50px");	
borderTopWidth	tags.DIV.borderTopWidth="20px";	
borderRightWidth	tags.DIV.borderRightWidth="30px";	
borderBottomWidth	tags.DIV.borderBottomWidth="40px";	
borderLeftWidth	tags.DIV.borderLeftWidth="50px";	
width	tags.DIV.width="50%";	tags.DIV.width="500px";
align	tags.DIV.align="left";	tags.DIV.align="right";
align	tags.DIV.align="center";	tags.DIV.align="none";
clear	tags.DIV.clear="left";	tags.DIV.clear="right";
clear	tags.DIV.clear="both";	tags.DIV.clear="none";
display	tags.DIV.display="block";	tags.LI.display="listitem";
listStyleType	tags.LI.listStyleType="upperroman";	tags.LI.listStyleType="square";
whiteSpace	tags.DIV.whiteSpace="normal";	tags.PRE.whiteSpace="pre";

∞∞

Property Name JavaScript Syntax	All Possible Categories	All Possible Values
fontSize	*absolute-size*	xx-small, x-small, small, medium, large, x-large, xx-large
	relative-size	larger, smaller
	length | percentage	10pt, 12pt, 14pt, 20pt, 24pt,... 20%, 25%, 50%, 80%, 120%,150%, 200%,...
fontFamily	*any system font*	Helvetica, Times, Geneva, Courier,... , (or any available Systemfont)
fontWeight	*keyword | number*	normal, bold, bolder, lighter | 100-900
fontStyle	*keyword*	normal, italic
lineHeight	*number*	multiplied by a number or decimal
	length | percentage	em, ex, px, pt, pc, in, mm, cm　　　|　　1%-1000%, ...n%
	keyword	normal
textDecoration	*keyword*	none, underline, line-through, blink
textTransform	*keyword*	capitalize, uppercase, lowercase, none
textAlign	*keyword*	left, right, center, justify
textIndent	*length | percentage*	em, ex, px, pt, pc, in, mm, cm　　　|　　1%-1000%, ...n%
margins()	*length | percentage*	em, ex, px, pt, pc, in, mm, cm　　　|　　1%-1000%, ...n%
	keyword	auto　　(is available for all 5 margin Properties)
margins()　(example)		margins("24pt", "30pt", "30pt", "17pt");
	sets each margin to diff. value	The order is:　top right bottom left
marginTop	*length | percentage*	em, ex, px, pt, pc, in, mm, cm　　　|　　1%-1000%, ...n%
marginRight	*length | percentage*	em, ex, px, pt, pc, in, mm, cm　　　|　　1%-1000%, ...n%
marginBottom	*length | percentage*	em, ex, px, pt, pc, in, mm, cm　　　|　　1%-1000%, ...n%
marginLeft	*length | percentage*	em, ex, px, pt, pc, in, mm, cm　　　|　　1%-1000%, ...n%
paddings()	*length | percentage*	em, ex, px, pt, pc, in, mm, cm　　　|　　1%-1000%, ...n%
paddings()　(example)		paddings("24px", "30px", "35px", "17px"); sets each padding to diff. value
paddingTop	*length | percentage*	em, ex, px, pt, pc, in, mm, cm　　　|　　1%-1000%, ...n%
paddingRight	*length | percentage*	em, ex, px, pt, pc, in, mm, cm　　　|　　1%-1000%, ...n%
paddingBottom	*length | percentage*	em, ex, px, pt, pc, in, mm, cm　　　|　　1%-1000%, ...n%
paddingLeft	*length | percentage*	em, ex, px, pt, pc, in, mm, cm　　　|　　1%-1000%, ...n%
color	*colorvalue*	none, name, #$$$$$$, 　　rgb(0-255,0-255,0-255), 　　rgb(?%,?%,?%)
backgroundColor	*colorvalue*	none, name, #$$$$$$, 　　rgb(0-255,0-255,0-255), 　　rgb(?%,?%,?%)
(the 16 color names are)		aqua, black, blue, fuchsia, gray, green, lime, maroon, navy, olive, purple, red, silver, teal, white, yellow
backgroundImage	*imageurl*	"url";
backgroundImage	(example)	backgroundImage="JPEG-Images/ExampleImage.jpeg";
borderStyle	*keyword*	none, solid, double, inset, outset, groove, ridge
borderColor	*colorvalue*	none, name, #$$$$$$, 　　rgb(0-255,0-255,0-255), 　　rgb(?%,?%,?%)
borderWidths()	*length | percentage*	em, ex, px, pt, pc, in, mm, cm　　　|　　1%-1000%, ...n%
borderWidths()	*same*	borderWidths("20px", "30px", "40px", "50px");
borderTopWidth	*length | percentage*	em, ex, px, pt, pc, in, mm, cm　　　|　　1%-1000%, ...n%
borderRightWidth	*length | percentage*	em, ex, px, pt, pc, in, mm, cm　　　|　　1%-1000%, ...n%
borderBottomWidth	*length | percentage*	em, ex, px, pt, pc, in, mm, cm　　　|　　1%-1000%, ...n%
borderLeftWidth	*length | percentage*	em, ex, px, pt, pc, in, mm, cm　　　|　　1%-1000%, ...n%
width	*length | percentage*	em, ex, px, pt, pc, in, mm, cm　　　|　　1%-1000%, ...n%
	keyword	auto
align	*keyword*	left, right, center,none
clear	*keyword*	none, left, right, both
display	*keyword*	block, inline, list-item
listStyleType	*keyword*	disc, circle, square, decimal, lower-roman, upper-roman, lower-alpha,
	keyword	upper-alpha, none
whiteSpace	*keyword*	normal, pre

∞∞

JavaScript and Layers

The JSS <u>position</u> Property

To create a Layer using JavaScript Style Sheet Syntax, just include the **position** Property in the Style definition. Here's one way to do it with the **ids** Property:

```
<STYLE type="text/JavaScript">
      ids.testLayer.position="absolute";
      ids.testLayer.left="200px";
      ids.testLayer.top="100px";
      ids.testLayer.width="400px";
</STYLE>
```

and then assign the named Layer of **testLayer** to an Element via the **ID** Attribute like this:

```
<DIV ID="testLayer">  My new Layer is here.  </DIV>
```

The HTML <SCRIPT> Element

The <SCRIPT> Element is what you put your JavaScript or other Scripting Language inside. It requires both the Start and End Tags. You can put this Element within the Body or the Head of the document, but the Head is generally preferred because you want the JavaScript to be fully loaded before a user has a chance to do anything with it to avoid getting errors from lack of content. See page 246 on Localized Layer Scripts for an exception to this. Put your Script in the Body if you need to reference an HTML Element in the code, because the compiler has to read that Element prior to using it in the Script.

Note that even though the TYPE Attribute is required in HTML 4.0, it is poorly supported by most browsers, which continue to support the deprecated LANGUAGE Attribute because it has the capability of specifying a version number and TYPE doesn't. All examples in this book ignore the TYPE Attribute except for those in Chapter 10.

Syntax:

```
<SCRIPT
TYPE="text/JavaScript"|"text/otherMediaType"
LANGUAGE="JavaScript[versionNumber]"|"otherLanguageName"
SRC="URL">
***
</SCRIPT>
```

Attributes Defined:

TYPE="text/JavaScript" | "text/otherMediaType" specifies the media type.

LANGUAGE="JavaScript[versionNumber]" | "otherLanguageName"
identifies the programming language that will be contained within this Element. The default value is JavaScript. If your site is custom designed to have alternative versions that are cognizant of the capabilities and limitations of the different versions of JavaScript, then you can specify for which version of JavaScript a document is to be used. If no version number is indicated, Navigator will read it as being coded for the earliest version of JavaScript.

JavaScript1.3 is for Navigator 4.0.6+   JavaScript1.2 is for Navigator 4.0-4.0.5
JavaScript1.1 is for Navigator 3.0   JavaScript1.0 is for Navigator 2.0

SRC="URL"
specifies an external file that contains JavaScript or other Scripting Language to be loaded in and executed. You should have a suffix on the end of this JavaScript file of (js) to indicate to the browser that it is a JavaScript file, like this: `MyExternalJavaScript.js`

Comment Tag to hide the contents of the <SCRIPT> Element

If you want to hide the contents of the <SCRIPT> Element from browsers that can't interpret JavaScript Scripts, then enclose the text within the Start and End Tags inside of an HTML Comment Tag, noting that due to the complexity of Comment Syntax, you have to precede the last line of the multiline Comment with two forwardslashes (//) such as in the following mini-example.

Also note the backslash (\) character preceding the forwardslash (/) character in the DIV End Tag (<\/DIV>). All HTML End Tags must have their forwardslash character escaped by a backslash character when they are used in **document.write()** Methods if they are inside of an HTML Comment Tag. The reason for this is that technically, the first occurrence of the left-angle bracket followed by a forwardslash (</), which is followed by any letter, is considered to be the End Tag for the SCRIPT Element. If you have a Script that's erratic, this should be checked first. See page 918 for more data on Comment Tags.

```
<SCRIPT LANGUAGE="JavaScript1.2">
<!--BEGIN HIDING FROM NON-JAVASCRIPT SAVVY BROWSERS

    document.write("<DIV>Good Morning All.<\/DIV>");

//END HIDING FROM NON-JAVASCRIPT SAVVY BROWSERS-->
</SCRIPT>
```

This is just the simplest of examples to show that you can use a SCRIPT Element in the Body or the Head Elements.

Example 3-6:   **Sample406.html**

```
<!DOCTYPE HTML PUBLIC "-//W3C//DTD HTML 3.2//EN">
<HTML>
<HEAD>
<TITLE>Sample 406 - Example 3-6      Script </TITLE>

<SCRIPT LANGUAGE="JavaScript1.2"><!--BEGIN HIDING

                document.write("<DIV>Good Morning All.<\/DIV>");
                document.close();
//END HIDING-->
</SCRIPT>

</HEAD>

<BODY>

<SCRIPT LANGUAGE="JavaScript1.2"><!--BEGIN HIDING

                document.write("<DIV>Smile and live longer.<\/DIV>");
                document.close();
//END HIDING-->
</SCRIPT>

</BODY>
</HTML>
```

The JavaScript <u>var</u> Keyword

When you want to define a variable inside of a Function you must use the **var** Keyword. Defining a variable outside of a Function only requires that you assign it a value, but it is still good practice to use the **var** Keyword anyway.

The following Expressions define variables :

```
var myString    = "Hellow World";
var Showcase1   = document.Showcase1;
var myNumber    = 2;
var myBoolean   = true;
var MyText      = document.Showcase1.document.form1.MyText;
var getText     = document.Showcase1.document.form1.MyText.value;
```

The JavaScript <u>Layer</u> Object

For every Layer that you create in an HTML document, there is a corresponding JavaScript **Layer** Object that is virtually created behind the scenes within the JavaScript Compiler of Navigator. Each one of them is manipulable. Just in case you're new to all this, don't think that this is some parallel LAYER that can randomly assert itself visibly into your browser Window. It's a programming entity that has Properties, Methods, Events, and Event Handlers associated with it. This, along with the ability to create your own Functions, allows you to dynamically alter and transform your documents. There's lots more, but let's not get too far ahead just yet.

When you load in an HTML file into the browser, JavaScript automatically creates a top-level **document** Object. For each **document** Object, there is an inherent **layers[i]** **Array** that contains a zero-based integer indexed list of all the top-level LAYERs contained in that Document, and this is called a **layers[i]** Array Property of the **document** Object.

Next, each **Layer** in the **layers[i]** **Array** has its own corresponding **document** Object, which has its own separate **layers** Property, which has a **layers[i]** **Array** of all its top-level LAYERs and so on for all <u>nested</u> LAYERs.

The **document** Object also has many other Properties and Arrays that keep track of what's happening behind the scenes. For now, we are going to concentrate on how to access a LAYER from within JavaScript and then once we know how to get to it, we can change it in all kinds of interesting and creative ways.

If you name your LAYER Element with the ID Attribute, then you can refer to that LAYER by that **layerName** Parameter with the following Syntax:

```
document.layerName;
```

so that for a LAYER that is named with **ID="DreamLayer1"** we would have the following expression that accesses the JavaScript **Layer** Object of that LAYER Element:

```
document.DreamLayer1;
```

The JavaScript <u>layers[i]</u> Array

You can also refer to that same LAYER by using the **layers** Array, which has the following Syntax:

```
document.layers ["layerName"];
```

which is exemplified for the LAYER named **"DreamLayer1"** by:

```
document.layers ["DreamLayer1"];
```

Make sure that you use the double quotes to enclose the Name of the LAYER, which then goes inside the brackets. The brackets are what signifies to the compiler that you are accessing an individual Layer in the **layers[i]** Array.

layers[i] Array <u>index</u> Number

A third way to refer to a LAYER is by accessing it through its **layers[i]** Array **index** number with the following Syntax:

```
document.layers[index];
```

and if a particular LAYER has an index of 5, then here's how that would be expressed:

```
document.layers[5];
```

You can think of the **index** number of the LAYER as being similar but not identical to the **z-index** that you learned about previously. The bottom-most LAYER has an Array **index** of 0 (zero), and the next or second LAYER would have in index of 1, with each of the subsequent LAYERs increasing in its **index** number in order from back to front. Obviously with this numbering scheme the integers must be positive after 0.

Because you can have nested LAYERs, you can therefore have multiple LAYERs in the same document that have the same **z-index** number because you can specify the **z-index** numbers yourself. You can NEVER have two LAYERs in the same document with the same **layers[i]** Array **index** number.

When you start to work on large and complex documents, you will find it useful to keep track of and write down the **index** numbers of your LAYERs as you create them if you need to access them by **index** with the **layers[i]** Array. A LAYER's **index** number is based on the order of its appearance in the HTML. The first LAYER in the HTML code has an **index** of 0 (that's zero) and so on.

Accessing LAYERs via the **index** number is usually used in Functions that have **for()** Statements inside them where the **var i** loops through the **layers[i]** Array. If you want to manipulate an individual LAYER, it is usually easier to reference it by name instead of by **index**.

The two types of <u>document</u> Objects

Now back to the actual **Layer** Object. A **Layer** Object has lots of Properties that can be used to modify it, just like an Element has lots of Attributes. The way that you access these Properties is with dot notation as in the following Syntax:

```
document.layerName.propertyName;
```

or like this for nested Layers:

```
document.layerName.document.layerName2.propertyName;
```

or like this to assign a Value to a Property in a nested Layer:

```
document.layerName.document.layerName2.propertyName="Value";
```

where **layerName** is a **Layer** Object in the top-level **document** Object and **layerName2** is a **Layer** Object that is nested inside of **layerName**. Then, **propertyName** is the Name of the Property that you want to use, like **bgColor** or **visibility** or **left** and **Value** is the Value that you want to assign to that Property like "**blue**" or 300 or "**show**". Remember that there is a **document Object** that is a Property of the **window** Object and a **document Object** that is a **Property** of the **Layer** Object. Remember that you <u>do</u> enclose String Values in quotes but you <u>do not</u> enclose numbers or Variables in quotes.

When you have more than one **layerName** in an expression, like in the first nested Layer Syntax example above, you read it from left to right as: "the **layerName** that contains the **layerName2** that you <u>access</u> the **propertyName** Value <u>of</u>."

Looking at the second nested Layer expression above, you read it from left to right as: "the **layerName** that contains the **layerName2** that has the **propertyName** that you <u>assign</u> the Value <u>to</u>."

Mini-Examples:

Here are some mini-examples to help clarify all this. The following expression has a **layerName** of **DreamLayer1** and a **propertyName** of **bgColor** that returns the **value** of the **bgColor** Property of the **DreamLayer1** Layer so that you can make use of that color Value in subsequent code.

```
document.DreamLayer1.bgColor;
```

The next mini-example has a **layerName** of **DreamLayer1** and has a Property of **visibility**, which has the Value of "**show**" assigned to it, which would make the LAYER named **DreamLayer1** be visible when this Property is set to "**show**" this way.

```
document.DreamLayer1.visibility  = "show";
```

Now let's put some of this together in a simple example that has two LAYERs that are named with the ID Attribute as "**DreamLayer1**" and "**Dream2**", respectively. They are then modified with a SCRIPT Element, which places **DreamLayer1** at 72 pixels down from the **top** of the document margin with a background color of aqua. The **Dream2** LAYER is 288 pixels from the **top** margin and has a lime background color.

Example 3-7: Sample407.html

```
<!DOCTYPE HTML PUBLIC "-//W3C//DTD HTML 3.2//EN">
<HTML>
<HEAD>
<TITLE>Sample 407 - Example 3-7      Script        </TITLE>
</HEAD>

<BODY>

<LAYER ID="DreamLayer1">

<P>     This is a Layer named 'DreamLayer1'.         </P>

<P>     It's important to note that if you put the following JavaScript that is
contained in the SCRIPT Element before the 'DreamLayer1' LAYER then you will get an
error message because the compiler in the browser will not have read the name of
the LAYER with the ID Attribute so it won't know what the layerObject 'DreamLayer1'
within the Script is and the compiler will tell you that it has no Properties.
</P>

</LAYER>


<LAYER ID="Dream2">

<DIV ALIGN=LEFT>
Notice that the Values for top, bgColor and visibility are all specified with the
SCRIPT Element using JavaScript and not within the LAYER Element. The reason that I
didn't include an expression with a visibility Property for the 'Dream2' LAYER was
to demonstrate that the default Value for that Property is 'show', so for simple
uses it isn't needed.
</DIV>

</LAYER>

<SCRIPT LANGUAGE="JavaScript1.2"><!--BEGIN HIDING

          document.DreamLayer1.top = 72;

          document.DreamLayer1.bgColor = "aqua";

          document.DreamLayer1.visibility  = "show";

          document.Dream2.top = 288;

          document.Dream2.bgColor = "lime";

//END HIDING-->
</SCRIPT>

</BODY>
</HTML>
```

Properties of the Layer Object

Properties of the Layer Object — Chart

Here's a chart that lists all of the JavaScript **Layer** Object Properties and assumes in the Mini-Examples that **L1** is a Layer named with ID="L1" and **L2** is a Layer named with ID="L2" and is a nested Layer inside of Layer **L1**:

∞∞∞

Property	Mini-Example	Modifiable
document	document.L1.document.form1.text1.value= "any Text";	No
name	document.L1;	No
left	document.L1.document.L2.left=200;	Yes
top	document.L1.document.L2.top=300;	Yes
pageX	document.L1.pageX=100;	Yes
pageY	document.L1.pageX=150;	Yes
visibility	document.L1.visibility="hide";	Yes
zIndex	document.L1.document.L2.zIndex=5;	Yes
siblingAbove	document.L1.document.L2.siblingAbove;	No
siblingBelow	document.L1.document.L2.siblingBelow;	No
above	document.L1.above;	No
below	document.L1.below;	No
parentLayer	document.L2.parentLayer;	No
clip.top	document.L1.clip.top=50;	Yes
clip.left	document.L1.clip.left=30;	Yes
clip.bottom	document.L1.clip.bottom=450;	Yes
clip.right	document.L1.clip.right=690;	Yes
clip.width	document.L1.clip.width=555;	Yes
clip.height	document.L1.clip.right=444;	Yes
bgColor	document.L1.bgColor="blue";	Yes
background.src	document.L1.background.src="myImage.jpg";	Yes
src	document.L1.src="AnotherPage.html";	Yes

∞∞∞

Special Notice:

JavaScript **Layer** Object Property Names are case-sensitive.

The <u>document</u> Property of the Layer Object

The **document** Property of each **Layer** Object is an Object itself, which is used to access Elements that are contained within the Layer like **images**, **embeds**, **links**, **anchors**, **forms**, nested **layers**, and JavaScript Properties and Values. For example, let's say you have an Image named '**MyImage1**' inside a Layer named '**MyLayer1**'. If you wanted to change the Image via the **src** Property of the Image Object, you would use the following code:

```
document.MyLayer1.document.MyImage1.src = "nextImage.jpg"
```

This next mini-example is <u>not</u> an example of the **document** Property of the **Layer** Object, but it's here to illustrate a common programming error of confusing a **document** Object change of the Window with a **document** Object change of the Layer. If you wanted to change the Background Color of the Layer you would use the following code:

```
document.MyLayer1.bgColor = "purple";
```

OK, you've probably noticed that there was a second **document** in the first of the previous two mini-examples. Here's the rule concerning how to reference **document**, and it's really crucial that you understand the distinction:

If you change something <u>inside</u> the Layer, that is, change the content inside the Layer, then you need that second **document** reference in the code.

If you change the Layer <u>itself</u>, by either assigning a new Value to a Property of the Layer or by Method invocation, you don't need the second **document** reference, because you aren't accessing the **document** Object of the **Layer,** you are accessing only the **Layer** Object of the top-level **document** Object of the **window** Object. Remember, the **window** Object is assumed to be there so you don't have to explicitly reference it each time.

Invoking Methods on a Layer Object

You can invoke Methods on the **Layer** Object to implement changes to the Layer or its contents dynamically or augment a Layer beyond the Attributes established in the LAYER Tag. A full description of all the **Layer** Object Methods starts on page 216. Here's a mini-example that references the Layer named **MyLayer1** via the <u>top-level</u> **document** Object and moves **MyLayer1** to a new position, where the **x**-coordinate is 300 pixels to the right of the left edge of the Window, and the y-coordinate is 400 pixels down from the top of the Window:

```
document.MyLayer1.moveTo(300,400);
```

Special Notice:

Two **Layer** Object Properties have different names than their Style Sheet Property counterparts, which should be investigated when debugging your code. They are:

Layer Object Property		JavaScript Style Sheet Property
bgcolor	=	backgroundColor
background	=	backgroundImage

The Layer Object <u>name</u> Property

The **name** Property of a **Layer** Object is used to identify the Layer that you want to manipulate, and you assign the name with the ID or NAME Attribute in the Layer Element or when you create a Layer with Style Sheet Syntax. The following expression has a Layer with the **name L1** coded to have its **visibility** Property be set to **"hide"**:

```
document.L1.visibility = "hide";
```

The Layer Object <u>left</u> Property

The **left** Property of a **Layer** Object specifies the Horizontal placement of the Layer's left edge. It is intended to work with nested Layers, but if you use it for unnested Layers, it will give you the same results as using the **pageX** Property.

You can have both positive and negative Values, but they must be integers. When you specify a positive Value, Navigator will move the left edge of the Layer to the right by that Value. When you specify a negative Value, Navigator will move the left edge of the Layer to the left by that Value. The default unit of measurement is pixels and you don't append the 'px' suffix. The Value can also be specified as a percentage and you do append the '%' sign. You cannot have negative percentages.

Negative Values will place the left edge outside the parent Layer, but you can still see part of the Layer if its width extends into the parent Layer. To completely hide the Layer, take into account the width of the Layer in your calculations.

If the Layer is nested and has an Absolute Position, then it is offset horizontally by the Value indicated from the parent Layer's left edge. If the Layer is nested and has its **position** Property set to **relative**, then it is offset horizontally by the Value indicated from the natural flow of the Layer in the parent Layer.

Mini-Examples:

In the following three mini-examples, the first has a nested Layer named **L2**, which is offset to the right of the edge of the parent Layer named **L1** by 100 pixels. The second example has the nested Layer named **L2**, offset by 320 pixels to the <u>left</u> of the parent Layer named **L1** so that 320 pixels of its width is hidden. The third example has the nested Layer named **L2**, offset to the right of the left edge of the parent Layer by 50% of the width of the parent Layer so that it <u>starts</u> in the middle of the parent Layer but it <u>isn't centered</u>.

```
document.L1.document.L2.left = 100;
document.L1.document.L2.left = -320;
document.L1.document.L2.left = "50%";
```

The Layer Object <u>top</u> Property

The **top** Property of a **Layer** Object specifies the Vertical placement of the Layer's upper edge. It is intended to work with nested Layers, but if you use it for unnested Layers, it will give you the same results as using the **pageY** Property.

You can have both positive and negative Values but they must be integers. When you specify a positive Value, Navigator will move the top edge of the Layer downward by that Value. When you specify a negative Value, Navigator will move the top edge of the Layer upward by that Value. The default unit of measurement is pixels, and you <u>don't</u> append the 'px' suffix. The Value can also be specified as a percentage, and you <u>do</u> append the '%' sign. You cannot have negative percentages.

Negative Values will place the top edge outside of the parent Layer, but you can still see part of the Layer if its height extends into the parent Layer. If you want to totally hide the Layer, then take into account the height of the Layer in your calculations.

If the Layer is nested and has an Absolute Position, then it is offset vertically by the Value indicated from the parent Layer's top edge. If the Layer is nested and has a **relative position**, then it is offset vertically by the Value indicated from the natural flow of the Layer in the parent Layer.

Mini-Examples:

In the following three mini-examples, the first has a nested Layer named **L2**, which is offset downward from the edge of the parent Layer named **L1** by 400 pixels. The second example has the nested Layer named **L2** offset by 320 pixels upward from the parent Layer named **L1** so that 320 pixels of its width is hidden. The third example has the nested Layer named **L2** offset downward from the top edge of the parent Layer by 25% of the height of the parent Layer.

```
document.L1.document.L2.top = 400;
document.L1.document.L2.top = -320;
document.L1.document.L2.top = "25%";
```

The Layer Object <u>pageX</u> Property

The **pageX** Property of a **Layer** Object specifies the horizontal placement of a Layer in relation to the **window** Object's coordinates. If the Layer has an Absolute Position, it is horizontally offset by the Value indicated from the left edge of the Window. If the Layer has a Relative Position, then it is horizontally offset by the Value indicated from the natural flow of the Layer in the document.

You can have both positive and negative Values, but they must be integers. When you specify a positive Value, Navigator will move the left edge of the Layer to the right of the left edge of the Window by that Value. When you specify a negative Value, Navigator will move the left edge of the Layer to the left of the left edge of the Window by that Value.

Negative Values will place the left edge outside the visible part of the Window, but you still can see the Layer if its width extends into the Window. If you want to completely hide the Layer, then take into account the width of the Layer in your calculations.

The default unit of measurement is pixels, and you <u>don't</u> append the 'px' suffix. The Value can also be specified as a percentage, and you <u>do</u> append the '%' sign. Note that because the '%' sign is also the Modulus Operator in JavaScript, you have to enclose a percentage Value including the '%' inside of quotes. You can't use negative percentages. For now, there is a bug when using percentages, so stick with pixels until they fix it.

Mini-Examples:

Positions the Layer named **L1** 300 pixels to the right of the Window's left edge:

```
document.L1.pageX = 300;
```

Positions the Layer named **L1** 400 pixels to the left of the Window's left edge:

```
document.L1.pageX = -400;
```

Positions the **L1** Layer 75% of the Window width to the right of the Window's left edge:

```
document.L1.pageX = "75%";
```

The Layer Object <u>pageY</u> Property

The **pageY** Property of a **Layer** Object specifies the vertical placement of a Layer in relation to the **window** Object's coordinates.

If the Layer has an Absolute Position, it is vertically offset by the Value indicated from the top edge of the Window. If the Layer has a Relative Position, then it is vertically offset by the Value indicated from the natural flow of the Layer in the document.

You can have both positive and negative Values, but they must be integers. When you specify a positive Value, Navigator will move the top edge of the Layer downward from the top edge of the Window by that Value. When you specify a negative Value, Navigator will move the top edge of the Layer upward from the top edge of the Window by that Value.

Negative Values will place the top edge outside the visible part of the window, but you still can see the Layer if its height extends into the Window. If you want to completely hide the Layer, then take into account the height of the Layer in your calculations.

The default unit of measurement is pixels, and you <u>don't</u> append the 'px' suffix. The Value can also be specified as a percentage and, you <u>do</u> append the '%' sign. You can't have negative percentages.

Mini-Examples:

Positions the Layer named **L1** 111 pixels down from the Window's top edge:

```
document.L1.pageY = 111;
```

Positions the Layer named **L1** 250 pixels up from the Window's top edge:

```
document.L1.pageY = -250;
```

Positions the **L1** Layer 15% of the Window height down from the Window's top edge:

```
document.L1.pageY = "15%";
```

The Layer Object <u>visibility</u> Property

The **visibility** Property of a **Layer** Object causes a Layer to be visible or invisible in the Window or parent Layer. Set the **visibility** Value to **"show"** to make a Layer seen and **"hide"** to make it invisible. The third alternative is setting the Value to **"inherit"**, which causes the Layer to inherit the **visibility** Value of its parent Layer.

If a Layer has Form Elements in it, then even if the Layer is invisible, the Form Elements will be seen. In order to completely hide such Elements, you have to move the Layer off-screen with the **pageX** and/or **pageY** Properties. In the case of a nested Layer, use the **left** and **top** Properties to move the Layer out of view.

If a Layer is set to **"hide"** then it cannot capture Events, even though it will still take up space in the layout of the document.

Mini-Examples:
```
document.L1.visibility = "show";
document.L1.visibility = "hide";
document.L1.visibility = "inherit";
```

The Layer Object <u>zIndex</u> Property

The **zIndex** Property of a **Layer** Object lets you change the stacking order of a Layer in relation to the sibling Layers within a parent Layer. In the case of a top-level Layer, it is in relation to the z-order of all top-level Layers in the Window. The Value must be a positive integer. All sibling Layers with a **zIndex** that is lower than a particular Layer will be stacked below that Layer and therefore obscured. The same is relatively true for top-level Layers. Note that the **zIndex** Property of the JavaScript **Layer** Object is spelled differently from the **z-index** Property in CSS Style Syntax.

Remember that Layers are transparent by default and of course can be different sizes, so a Layer may not be completely obscured by just using the **zIndex** Property alone. Setting background colors and making sure that your Layers are exactly the same size or also using the **visibility** Property can cure many programming gremlins.

Mini-Example:

Here's an obligatory mini-example with the **zIndex** Property set to 5 that places the Layer named **L1** above all Layers with **zIndex** Values from 1 to 4 inclusive, and below all Layers with **zIndex** Values above 5.

```
document.L1.zIndex = 5;
```

The Layer Object <u>siblingAbove</u> Property

The **siblingAbove** Property of a **Layer** Object will **return** the **Layer** Object that is the next one above the indicated Layer in the z-order of all Layers within the same parent Layer. If there is no **siblingAbove** in the parent Layer, the expression will **return null**, which means that this Layer is the top-most Layer within the parent Layer.

Mini-Example:

Looking at the following mini-example, the Layer named **L2** is contained in the parent Layer named **L1**. For the sake of argument, assume that there is another Layer named **L3** that is the next Layer above in the z-order contained within **L1**. This expression would **return** Layer **L3** because it is the sibling Layer that is above Layer **L2**.

```
document.L1.document.L2.siblingAbove;
```

The Layer Object siblingBelow Property

The **siblingBelow** Property of a **Layer** Object will **return** the **Layer** Object that is the next one below the indicated Layer in the z-order of all Layers within the same parent Layer. If there is no **siblingBelow** in the parent Layer, the expression will **return null**, which means that this Layer is the bottom-most Layer within the parent Layer.

Mini-Example:

Looking at the following mini-example, the Layer named **L2** is contained in the parent Layer named **L1**. For the sake of argument, assume that there is another Layer named **MyLayerA** that is the next Layer below in the z-order contained within **L1**. This expression would **return** Layer **MyLayerA** because it is the sibling Layer that is below Layer **L2**.

```
document.L1.document.L2.siblingBelow;        //returns MyLayerA
```

The Layer Object above Property

The **above** Property of a **Layer** Object will **return** the **Layer** Object that is the next one above the indicated Layer in the z-order of all Layers within the **document** Object. If this Layer is the top-most Layer, then the **above** Property will **return** the containing **window** Object.

Mini-Example:

```
document.L1.above;
```

The Layer Object below Property

The **below** Property of a **Layer** Object will **return** the **Layer** Object that is the next one below the indicated Layer in the z-order of all Layers within the **document** Object. If this Layer is the bottom-most Layer, then the **below** Property will **return null**.

Mini-Example:

```
document.L1.below;
```

The Layer Object <u>parentLayer</u> Property

The **parentLayer** Property of a **Layer** Object will **return** the **Layer** Object that is the container of the indicated nested Layer. If the Layer is not nested in another Layer, then the **parentLayer** Property will **return** the **window** Object that contains the Layer.

```
document.L1.parentLayer;
```

The Layer Object and Clipping Rectangles

The next six Properties are used to manipulate the Clipping Rectangle of a Layer, which determines what area of the Layer is visible and what area is hidden. Only the part of the Layer that is inside the Clipping Rectangle is shown. Think of this Rectangle as an opacity Rectangle that is superimposed over the actual Layer and which lets you control the viewable area without having to relayout the HTML. The obvious basic use is to hide part of the Layer initially so that you can reveal the contents later on with a Script. You can also make the Clipping Rectangle larger than the actual dimensions of the Layer.

Clipping Values must be either negative or positive integers or zero. These Values are part of the built-in Properties of the **Layer** Object's Coordinate System, which you can access and test for with **Boolean** Statements.

Mini-Example:

In the following mini-example, the Clipping Properties are assigned Values and then the **DreamLayer1 Layer** Object is written to screen with the **write()** Method:

```
<HTML>
<HEAD>
<TITLE>Sample 407A - Example 3-7A      Clipping Rectangle </TITLE>
</HEAD>
<BODY>

<LAYER ID="DreamLayer1" LEFT=100 TOP=150 WIDTH=500 HEIGHT=400>
<IMG SRC="JPEG-FILES/icon-BG-stars.jpg" WIDTH=150 HEIGHT=75>
</LAYER>

<SCRIPT LANGUAGE="JavaScript1.2"><!--BEGIN HIDING

            document.DreamLayer1.clip.top = 20;
            document.DreamLayer1.clip.left = 30;
            document.DreamLayer1.clip.bottom = 420;
            document.DreamLayer1.clip.right = 530;
            document.DreamLayer1.clip.width = 500;
            document.DreamLayer1.clip.height = 400;

            document.write(document.DreamLayer1);
//END HIDING-->
</SCRIPT>
</BODY>
</HTML>
```

The previous mini-example produces the following output in the browser:

```
{clip:{top:20, left:30, bottom:420, right:530, width:500, height:400}, document:}
```

by using the **write()** Method to render the internal code for the **DreamLayer1 Layer** Object that contains the Property Names and their current Values for the Layer.

Default Values for the Clipping Properties

The default Value for:

`clip.top`	is	0
`clip.left`	is	0
`clip.bottom`	is	the Height of the Layer
`clip.right`	is	the Width of the Layer

The Layer Object <u>clip.top</u> Property

The **clip.top** Property of a **Layer** Object can be modified to show or hide part of a Layer by subtracting or adding pixels from the top edge of the Layer's Clipping Rectangle.

Mini-Example:

//hides the top edge from 0 to 25 pixels

```
document.L1.clip.top = 25;
```

The Layer Object <u>clip.left</u> Property

The **clip.left** Property of a **Layer** Object can be modified to show or hide part of a Layer by subtracting or adding pixels from the left edge of the Layer's Clipping Rectangle.

Mini-Example:

//hides the left edge from 0 to 72 pixels

```
document.L1.clip.left = 72;
```

The Layer Object <u>clip.bottom</u> Property

The **clip.bottom** Property of a **Layer** Object can be modified to show or hide part of a Layer by subtracting or adding pixels from the bottom edge of the Layer's Clipping Rectangle.

Mini-Example:

//hides the bottom edge from 300 to **clip.height**

```
document.L1.clip.bottom = 300;
```

The Layer Object <u>clip.right</u> Property

The **clip.right** Property of a **Layer** Object can be modified to show or hide part of a Layer by subtracting or adding pixels from the right edge of the Layer's Clipping Rectangle.

Mini-Example:

//hides the right edge from 400 to **clip.width**

```
document.L1.clip.right = 400;
```

The Layer Object <u>clip.width</u> Property

The **clip.width** Property of a **Layer** Object is the Width in pixels of the Clipping Rectangle. Modifying it causes the **clip.right** Property to be changed also but has no effect on the **clip.left** Property.

Mini-Example:

```
document.L1.clip.width = 640;
```

The **clip.right** Property is changed with the following formula, which can be observed in <u>Sample407A.html</u>:

```
clip.right = clip.left + clip.width
```

The Layer Object <u>clip.height</u> Property

The **clip.height** Property of a **Layer** Object is the Height in pixels of the Clipping Rectangle. Modifying it causes the **clip.bottom** Property to be changed also but has no effect on the **clip.top** Property.

Mini-Example:

```
document.L1.clip.height  = 480;
```

The **clip.bottom** Property is changed with the following formula, which can be observed in <u>Sample407A.html</u>:

```
clip.bottom = clip.top + clip.height
```

The Layer Object <u>bgColor</u> Property

The **bgColor** Property of a **Layer** Object specifies the background color for the Layer and is the JavaScript equivalent of the JavaScript Style Sheet Syntax Property of **backgroundColor**. You can use the **bgColor** Property to change the background color of a Layer without having to reload the document.

The Value can be "**null**" to make the Layer transparent or a recognized color name or a RGB Hexadecimal color. You can also use a **variable** that contains a pre-defined color based on user actions like MOUSEOVER or CLICK Events or Form Element input, or you can use dynamically evolving Scripts based on time or random numbers.

Mini-Examples:

```
                              //the color name cyan
document.L1.bgColor = "cyan";

                              //real purple
document.L1.bgColor = "#8800ff";

                                //creates a transparent Layer
document.L1.bgColor = "null";

                                //dynamic color variable
document.L1.bgColor = MyColor;
```

The Layer Object <u>background</u> Property

The **background** Property of a **Layer** Object specifies the tiled background image for the Layer and is the JavaScript equivalent of the JavaScript Style Sheet Syntax Property of **backgroundImage**. You have to append the **src** Property with dot notation to access the image so your syntax will always be:

JavaScript Syntax:

```
background.src = "imageURL";
```

Parameters Defined:

where **imageURL** is either the actual URL of the Image or "**null**" if you want to remove the background image or a **var** with a predefined Image URL. Remember that you don't put Variables inside quotes.

Mini-Examples:

```
document.L1.background.src = "./JPEG-FILES/icon-Sun.jpg";
document.L1.background.src = "null";
document.L1.background.src = myBackgroundImageVariable;
```

The Layer Object <u>src</u> Property

The **src** Property of a **Layer** Object is used to specify the source of an external Document that contains content for the Layer. The Value is the URL of the document. It can be either a relative or an absolute URL. It has the following syntax:

JavaScript Syntax:

```
document.layerName.src = "URL";
```

Mini-Examples:

```
document.L1.src = "Sample406.html";

document.L1.src = "http://www.dreamplay.com/Sample406.html";
```

Methods of the Layer Object

All of the JavaScript Methods that work for **Layer** Objects can be used for Layers that are created with the LAYER Element or with JavaScript Style Sheet Syntax or CSS Style Sheet Syntax, and the Method Names are identical.

Currently, there are eight Methods that are specifically available to be invoked on a **Layer** Object to access or modify it. They are:

Method	Mini-Example
moveBy(dx, dy)	document.L1.moveBy(30, -40)
moveTo(x, y)	document.L1.moveTo(20, 90)
moveToAbsolute(x, y)	document.L1.moveToAbsolute(420, 340)
resizeBy(dwidth, dheight)	document.L1.resizeBy(-20, 30)
resizeTo(width, height)	document.L1.resizeTo(550, 350)
moveAbove(layerName)	document.L1.moveAbove(MyLayer5)
moveBelow(layerName)	document.L1.moveBelow(MyLayer3)
load("sourceURL", newPixelWidth)	document.L1.load("Sample400.html", 500)

The JavaScript Syntax to invoke a Method on a **Layer** Object is:

JavaScript Syntax:

```
layerObjectName.methodName(arguments)
```

Parameters Defined:

layerObjectName	The Name of the Layer or an expression that evaluates to a **Layer** Object
methodName	The Name of the Method
arguments	A comma-separated list of Arguments for the Method

Special Notice:

JavaScript **Layer** Object Method Names are case-sensitive.

The <u>moveBy(dx, dy)</u> Method

The **moveBy(dx, dy)** Method moves the Layer by the specified number of pixels, which must be either positive or negative integers or 0. You can also specify **dx** or **dy** with a variable or an expression that evaluates to pixels. A Layer is positioned by taking a set of (x, y) coordinates and placing the upper-left corner of the Layer at these coordinates and then draws the Layer down and to the right from that point. When you invoke the **moveBy( )** Method you supply a set of **(dx, dy)** coordinates which are added to the current coordinates. Obviously, if you supply a negative number, then you are moving the Layer in the opposite direction. Using:

Positive	**dx** Pixels	Moves the Layer to the right
Negative	**dx** Pixels	Moves the Layer to the left
0 (zero)	**dx** Pixels	Does not move the Layer
Positive	**dy** Pixels	Moves the Layer down
Negative	**dy** Pixels	Moves the Layer up
0 (zero)	**dy** Pixels	Does not move the Layer

Mini-Examples:

```
document.L1.moveBy(0, 20);      //Moves Layer L1 20 pixels down
document.L1.moveBy(0, -30);     //Moves Layer L1 30 pixels up
document.L1.moveBy(40, 0);      //Moves Layer L1 40 pixels to the right
document.L1.moveBy(-50, 0);     //Moves Layer L1 50 pixels to the left
document.L1.moveBy(-70, 80);    //Moves Layer L1 70 pixels left and 80 pixels down
```

Mini-Example:

```
document.L1.moveBy(document.L1.clip.width, 0);     //If document.L1.clip.width
                                                     which is the width of the
                                                     Clipping Rectangle evaluates to
                                                     400 pixels, then Layer L1 moves
                                                     by 400 pixels to the right
```

The <u>moveTo(x, y)</u> Method

The **moveTo(x, y)** Method will relocate a Layer with Absolute Position to the specified coordinates of the parent Layer's Coordinate system or document Coordinate system if it is an unnested top-level Layer. For a Layer with Relative Position, it will offset the Layer by the specified amount from the Layer's natural flow Coordinates.

By invoking the **moveTo(x, y)** Method, you are resetting both the **top** and **left** Properties of the **Layer** Object simultaneously.

Negative numbers will place the origin Coordinates of the Layers with Absolute Position out of view but still available for referencing by JavaScript code, as will large positive numbers, depending on the size of the user's monitor screen.

Coordinates must be either positive or negative integers or 0. They may also be a variable or an expression that evaluates to either positive or negative integers or 0.

Mini-Examples:

The first two mini-examples move Layer **L1** to coordinates relative to the **window** Object. The third and fourth mini-examples move Layer **L2** to coordinates that are relative to Layer **L1**.

```
document.L1.moveTo(0, 20)
document.L1.moveTo(0, -30)
document.L1.document.L2.moveTo(200, 100)
document.L1.document.L2.moveTo(-500, -200)
```

The moveToAbsolute(x, y) Method

The **moveToAbsolute(x, y)** Method is the same as the **moveTo()** Method except that you are moving the Layer based on the **window** Object's Coordinate System instead of the parent Layer's Coordinate System. This is the same as simultaneously setting the **pageX** and **pageY** Properties of the **Layer** Object. Even if the Layer is moved outside of the viewable area of the parent Layer, the child Layer is still contained by the parent Layer.

Coordinates must be either positive or negative integers or 0. They may also be a variable or an expression that evaluates to either positive or negative integers or 0.

Mini-Example:

In the following mini-example, there is a Layer named **L2** that is nested inside the Layer **L1**. The **L2** Layer is moved to the new **pageX**, **pageY** Coordinates of (10, 20).

```
document.L1.document.L2.moveToAbsolute(10, 20)
```

The resizeBy(dwidth, dHeight) Method

The **resizeBy(dwidth, dheight)** Method adds (positive integers) or subtracts (negative integers) to the **width** and **height** Properties of the **Layer** Object by the specified **dwidth** and **dheight** Arguments in pixels.

(50, 30)	**(Layerwidth, Layerheight)**
(100, 200)	+ **(dwidth, dheight)**
(150, 230)	= **(newLayerwidth, newLayerheight)**

However, since it does not automatically refresh the HTML, the result is, in effect, a Layer that has more or less of its contents visible, depending on whether you use positive or negative integers. This is the equivalent of simultaneously adding **dwidth** to the **clip.width** Property and **dheight** to the **clip.height** Property of the **Layer** Object.

Even if you get fancy and use the **document.open()**, **document.write()** and **document.close()** Methods to cause Navigator to relayout your HTML page content, the **width** and **height** of your Layer will still be visually rendered with the original **width** and **height** Values. However, the Clipping Rectangle will reflect the new **clip.width** and **clip.height** Values so you will be able to see that specified area of the Layer after the additions or subtractions of the **dwidth** and **dheight** Arguments.

This Method is particularly useful for making part or all of a Layer either visible or invisible in small increments, say a few pixels at a time, but repeating the process rapidly (every 10 to 100 milliseconds is an effective range) so an animation effect of dissolving or revealing the Layer over time is achieved.

Mini-Examples:

```
document.L1.resizeBy(50, 0);
document.L1.resizeBy(0, -70);
document.L1.resizeBy(-50, 100);
```

The <u>resizeTo(width, height)</u> Method

The **resizeTo(width, height)** Method changes the **width** and **height** Properties of the **Layer** Object to the specified **width** and **height** Arguments in pixels, which should be positive integers or zero, since a Layer can't occupy negative space.

However, since it does not automatically refresh the HTML, what you get, in effect, is a Layer that has more or less of its contents visible, depending on the new edges of the Layer. This is the equivalent of simultaneously changing the **Layer** Object's **clip.width** Property to the **width** Argument and the **clip.height** Property to the **height** Argument.

This Method is useful for rapidly making part or all of the contents of a Layer visible or invisible, especially when you need to keep the Layer's **visibility** Property set to **"show"** so that the Layer can receive Events. Setting the Layer's Clipping Rectangle to (0, 0) with the **resizeTo(0, 0)** Method makes the Layer's contents hidden, but the Layer can still receive Events, either programmatically or from the user.

Mini-Example:

Note that in the following mini-example that the **clip.width** Property is also set to 500 pixels and the **clip.height** Property is also set to 400 pixels.

```
document.L1.resizeTo(500, 400);
```

The <u>moveAbove(layerName)</u> Method

The **moveAbove(layerName)** Method changes the z-order of the Layer that the Method is invoked on so that it is <u>above</u> the Layer specified in the **layerName** Argument. The Value for the supplied **layerName** Argument must be a valid **Layer** Object. Remember that this has no effect on the horizontal or vertical position coordinates.

After the **moveAbove(layerName)** Method is evaluated, both Layers will share the same parent Layer, where the parent Layer of the Layer specified in the **layerName** Argument will be the parent Layer for both Layers. Let's clarify that.

Mini-Example:

Suppose you have the following Layer scenario, where:

//**L1** is the parent Layer for **L2** and **L3**

```
<LAYER ID=L1>
<LAYER ID=L2>      </LAYER>
<LAYER ID=L3>      </LAYER></LAYER>
```

//**L4** is the parent Layer for **L5** and **L6**

```
<LAYER ID=L4>
<LAYER ID=L5>      </LAYER>
<LAYER ID=L6>      </LAYER></LAYER>
```

Then if you move **L2** above **L5** with the following code:

```
document.L1.document.L2.moveAbove(document.L4.document.L5);
```

Then **L4** will be the parent Layer for Layers **L5**, **L2**, **L6**.

See <u>Sample411.html</u>, which is Example 3-11.

Mini-Example:

A simple scenario would be to move Layer **L1** above Layer **L4** like this:

```
document.L1.moveAbove(document.L4);
```

The <u>moveBelow(layerName)</u> Method

The **moveBelow(layerName)** Method changes the z-order of the Layer that the Method is invoked on so that it is <u>below</u> the Layer specified in the **layerName** Argument. The Value for the supplied **layerName** Argument must be a valid **Layer** Object. Remember that this has no effect on horizontal or vertical position coordinates.

After the **moveBelow(layerName)** Method is evaluated, both Layers will share the same parent Layer, where the parent Layer of the Layer specified in the **layerName** Argument will be the parent Layer for both Layers.

Mini-Example:

```
document.L5.moveBelow(document.L2);
```

The <u>load("sourceURL", newPixelWidth)</u> Method

The **load("sourceURL", newPixelWidth)** Method changes the contents of a Layer by loading in an external file that is specified by the URL string **"sourceURL"**. It also changes the width of the Layer with the second Argument **newPixelWidth**, which is required and <u>must be</u> specified in pixels. Remember that your **"sourceURL"** <u>must be</u> enclosed by quotes but the **newPixelWidth** Value <u>must not</u> be enclosed by quotes.

Mini-Example:

```
document.L1.load("./Sample406.html", 555);
```

Mini-Example:

If you have a Button in a Form Element with JavaScript code to execute when the Button is clicked, it might look like this, where the **getIt1()** Function is called that was previously defined elsewhere:

```
<INPUT TYPE="button" VALUE="Load External Layer"
    onClick='getIt1(); return false;'>
```

For quick Syntax of the FORM or INPUT Elements, see Appendix A, starting on page 1004. For detailed information and examples on FORM or INPUT Elements, see <u>CH6.html</u> in the <u>HTML BOOK-Online Folder</u>, or any of the HTML specifications on the CD-ROM in the <u>Docs for Book</u> Folder. For more information on Event Handlers, see Chapter 6, starting on page 524.

This example demonstrates how to use the **moveTo()** Method to move a LAYER from one position in a document to another and back again. The two LAYERs are first created, then the Buttons that call the Functions from the SCRIPT Element are added to the FORM Element, and finally the SCRIPT Element is used to define the simple Functions that move the LAYERs around with the **moveTo()** Method.

Example 3-8:   Sample408.html

```
<!DOCTYPE HTML PUBLIC "-//W3C//DTD HTML 3.2//EN">
<HTML><HEAD>
<TITLE>Sample 408 - Example 3-8        Move Layers with Buttons              </TITLE>

<STYLE TYPE="text/JavaScript">

        with(tags.BODY) {
                color="aqua";
                fontFamily="Palatino, cursive";
                fontSize="24pt";
                textAlign="center";
        }

</STYLE>

</HEAD>
<BODY>
<LAYER ID="DreamLayer1" LEFT=30 TOP=350 BGCOLOR="fuchsia">
       <P>
       This is a Layer named DreamLayer1.
       </P>
</LAYER>
<!-- ****************************************************************** -->

<LAYER ID="DreamLayer2" LEFT=72 TOP=288 BGCOLOR="navy">
       <P>
       This is a Layer named DreamLayer2.
       </P>
</LAYER>
<!-- ****************************************************************** -->

<LAYER ID="DreamLayer3" LEFT=10 TOP=15 BGCOLOR="blue">
       <P>
       This is Sample 408.
       </P>
       <FORM NAME="form2">
               <INPUT TYPE=button VALUE="Move Me"

                       onClick='GoThere1();return false;'>

               <INPUT TYPE=button VALUE="Move Me Again"

                       onClick='GoThere2();return false;'>
```

```
          <INPUT TYPE=button VALUE="No, Move Me Instead!"

                  onClick='GoThere3();return false;'>

          <INPUT TYPE=button VALUE="Put Me Back!"

                  onClick='GoBack4();return false;'>

      </FORM>

</LAYER>

<!-- ****************************************************************** -->

<SCRIPT LANGUAGE="JavaScript1.2"><!--BEGIN HIDING

      function GoThere1() {

              document.DreamLayer1.moveTo(50, 150);
      }

      function GoThere2() {

              document.DreamLayer1.moveTo(175, 222);
      }

      function GoThere3() {

              document.DreamLayer2.moveTo(200, 440);
      }

      function GoBack4() {

              document.DreamLayer1.moveTo(30, 350);

              document.DreamLayer2.moveTo(72, 288);
      }

//END HIDING-->
</SCRIPT>

</BODY>

</HTML>
```

The following Example 3-9 demonstrates how to use the **resizeTo()** Method to change a LAYER from one size to another size and back again. The two LAYERs are first created, then the Buttons that call the Functions from the SCRIPT Element are added to the FORM Element, and finally the SCRIPT Element is used to define the Functions that resize the LAYERs to reveal the hidden contents. Notice in the four Screen Capture images, which follow the code, that what is shown are the results of clicking the particular Button that the arrow cursor is over in that image.

Example 3-9:   Sample409.html

```
<!DOCTYPE HTML PUBLIC "-//W3C//DTD HTML 3.2//EN">
<HTML>
<HEAD>
<TITLE>Sample 409 - Example 3-9        Resize Layers with Buttons</TITLE>

<STYLE TYPE="text/JavaScript">

        with(tags.BODY) {
                color="lime";
                fontFamily="Palatino, cursive";
                fontSize="24pt";
                textAlign="center";
        }

</STYLE>

</HEAD>
<!-- ***************************************************************** -->

<BODY>

<LAYER ID="DreamLayer1" LEFT=10 TOP=150 BGCOLOR="green">

        <P>This is a Layer named DreamLayer1.</P><BR><BR>
        <P>I'm the part that you don't see until later.</P>

</LAYER>

<!-- ***************************************************************** -->

<LAYER ID="DreamLayer2" LEFT=10 TOP=350 BGCOLOR="olive">

        <P>    This is a Layer named DreamLayer2.    </P>

</LAYER>

<!-- ***************************************************************** -->

<LAYER ID="DreamLayer3" LEFT=10 TOP=15 BGCOLOR="teal">

        <P>
        This is Sample 409.
        </P>

        <FORM NAME="form2">

                <INPUT TYPE=button VALUE="Resize Me"

                        onClick='GoThere1();return false;'>

                <INPUT TYPE=button VALUE="Resize Me Again"

                        onClick='GoThere2();return false;'>
```

```
                <INPUT TYPE=button VALUE="No, Resize Me Instead!"

                    onClick='GoThere3();return false;'>

                <INPUT TYPE=button VALUE="Put Me Back!"

                    onClick='GoBack4();return false;'>

        </FORM>

</LAYER>

<!-- *********************************************************** -->

<SCRIPT LANGUAGE="JavaScript1.2"><!--BEGIN HIDING

            document.DreamLayer1.resizeTo(72, 72);

            document.DreamLayer2.resizeTo(72, 72);

//END HIDING-->
</SCRIPT>

<!-- *********************************************************** -->


<SCRIPT LANGUAGE="JavaScript1.2"><!--BEGIN HIDING

        function GoThere1() {

            document.DreamLayer1.resizeTo(500, 100);
        }

        function GoThere2() {

            document.DreamLayer1.resizeTo(500, 170);
        }

        function GoThere3() {

            document.DreamLayer2.resizeTo(500, 100);
        }

        function GoBack4() {

            document.DreamLayer1.resizeTo(72, 72);

            document.DreamLayer2.resizeTo(72, 72);
        }

//END HIDING-->
</SCRIPT>

</BODY>
</HTML>
```

Example 3-9   Sample409.html

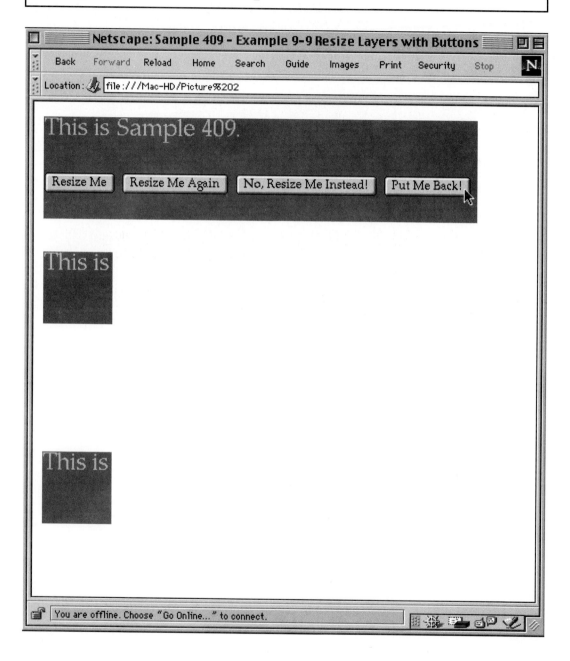

Example 3-9   Sample409.html

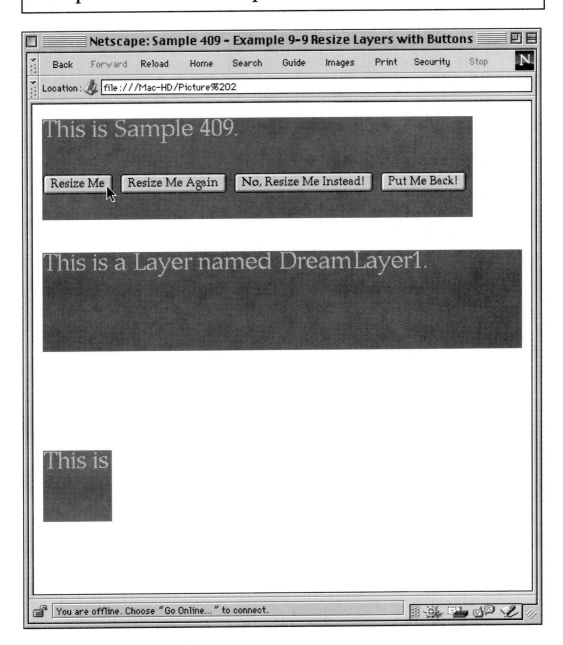

Example 3-9   Sample409.html

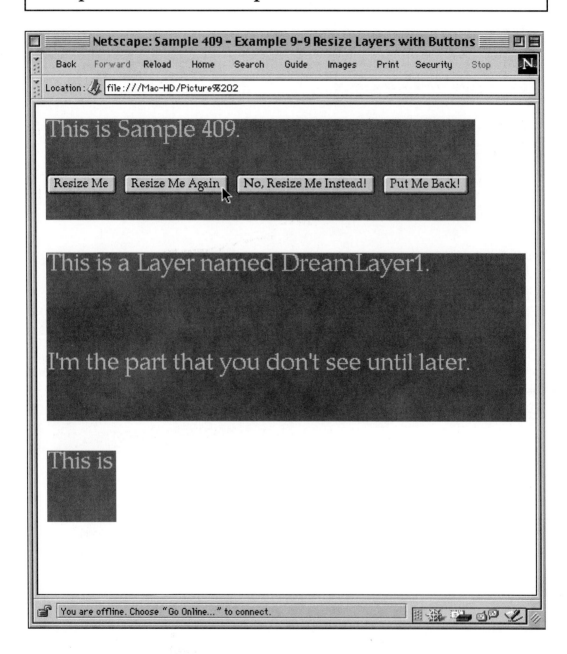

Example 3-9   Sample409.html

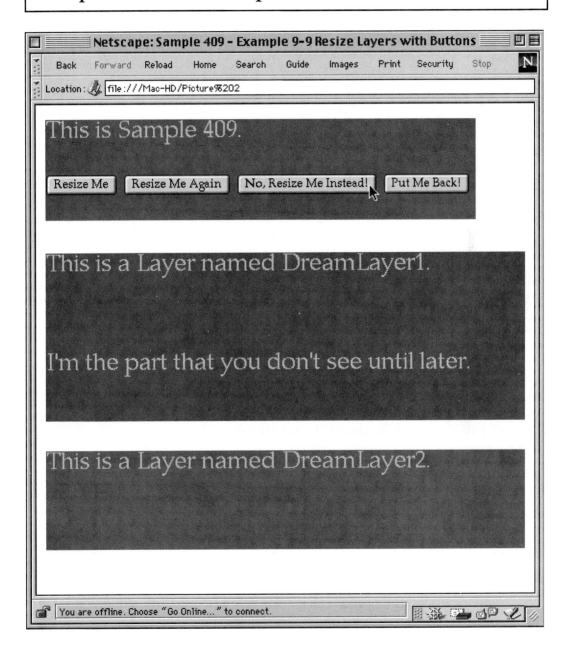

Using JavaScript with Layers

The JavaScript write() Method

This is the quickie version. See the JavaScript Guide for the rest. When you want to include content in a Layer within a SCRIPT Element using JavaScript, you can use the **write()** method with the following Syntax:

```
document.LayerName.document.write (arg, arg | "arg, arg");
```

where the first **document** specifies the **document** Object of the Window, which contains the **Layer** Object that you specify by name in place of **LayerName**. **LayerName** then has its own **document** Object specified by the second use of **document**. This is where you actually create the content with the **write()** method, which has Arguments that can be text or HTML Tags that are enclosed in quotes, or JavaScript Expressions, which are not.

HTML Tags that are contained here will act just like they would if they were not in a SCRIPT Element; that is, if you have text within H1 Tags, you will see an H1 Heading rendered in the browser Window, and if you have a STYLE attached to the H1 Heading, that STYLE will also be rendered.

Regarding other JavaScript Expressions that can be used in the **write()** Method, you can have string, numeric, or logical Expressions that can be implemented with dot notation. You could use the **tags** Property to create a new Style for an Element or nest another Layer within that Layer. The possibilities are endless once you understand the range of JavaScript's capabilities.

Just make sure that after you get done using the **write()** Method you close the document data stream with the **close()** Method like this:

```
document.LayerName.document.close();
```

One final note: When using the **write( )** Method, make sure that you keep all of the Arguments between the parentheses all on the same line in your text editor or you might get errors. Either turn off the soft-wrap capability or use a Variable to assign the text String to and keep adding to the Variable with the **+=** operator. See pages 319, 441.

Using the write() & close() Methods

Example 3-10 demonstrates how to use the **write()** Method to create new content within a Layer, which simultaneously wipes out the previous content when the Button is clicked by the user. Pay attention to the FORM and SCRIPT Elements and don't focus too much on the Styles, which are just the icing on the example. The Functions created in the SCRIPT Element are called by the **onClick** Event Handlers of the Buttons contained in the FORM Element, so that when a user clicks on the Button, the content is written to the Layer.

Example 3-10: **Sample410.html**

```
<!DOCTYPE HTML PUBLIC "-//W3C//DTD HTML 3.2//EN">
<HTML>
<HEAD>
<TITLE>Sample 410 -  Example 3-10 The write() Method </TITLE>

<STYLE TYPE="text/JavaScript">

        with(tags.BODY) {
                color="purple";
                fontFamily="Moonlight, cursive";
                fontSize="34pt";
                textAlign="center";
        }

        with(tags.H1) {
                color="navy";
                fontFamily="Helvetica, serif";
                fontSize="40pt";
                textAlign="center";
                backgroundColor="red";
                borderWidths("25px");
                borderStyle="double";
                borderColor="fuchsia";
        }

        classes.UpperRed.all.fontSize="30pt";
        classes.UpperRed.all.color="red";
        classes.UpperRed.all.textTransform="capitalize";
        classes.UpperRed.all.backgroundColor="yellow";

        classes.Global.all.width="100%";
        classes.Global.all.backgroundColor="lime";
        classes.Global.all.borderWidths("25px");
        classes.Global.all.borderStyle="groove";
        classes.Global.all.textAlign="center";
        classes.Global.all.align="center";
        classes.Global.all.borderColor="green";
        classes.Global.all.color="blue";
        classes.Global.all.fontFamily="Moonlight, cursive";
        classes.Global.all.fontSize="22pt";

</STYLE>

</HEAD>
<BODY>

<P>A Tricky Example 410</P>

<!--  ****************************************************************  -->

<LAYER CLASS="Global" ID="layer2" LEFT=20 TOP=75>

Central
```

```
        <FORM NAME="form2">

                <INPUT TYPE=button VALUE="Site 1"

                onClick='changeSite1();return false;'>

                <INPUT TYPE=button VALUE="Site 2"

                onClick='changeSite2();return false;'>

        </FORM>
Command

</LAYER>

<!--  ************************************************************  -->

<LAYER CLASS="UpperRed" ID="layer1" LEFT=20 TOP=275>

 <P>Pick a Site, any Site for a change of view.<P>

</LAYER>

<!--  ************************************************************  -->

<SCRIPT LANGUAGE="JavaScript1.2"><!--BEGIN HIDING

function changeSite1() {

        document.layer1.document.write("<H1>New Site 1.<\/H1>");

        document.layer1.document.close();
}

function changeSite2() {

        document.layer1.document.write("<H1>The not much New Site 2.<\/H1>");

        document.layer1.document.close();
}

//END HIDING-->
</SCRIPT>

</BODY>
</HTML>
```

Using the <u>moveAbove()</u> Method

The following example demonstrates the **moveAbove()** Method to move one Layer above another in the z-order stack and also changes the parent Layer of the Layer that is moved above the other Layer.

Example 3-10   Sample410.html

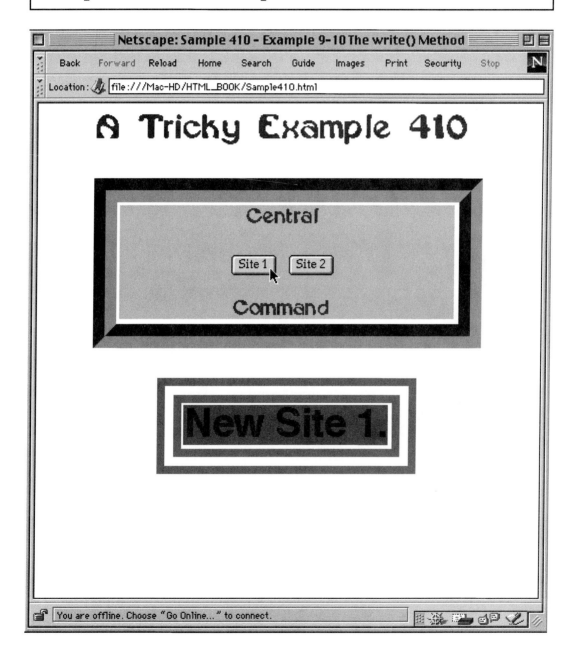

Example 3-11:   **Sample411.html**

```
<!DOCTYPE HTML PUBLIC "-//W3C//DTD HTML 3.2//EN">
<HTML>
<HEAD>

<TITLE>Sample 411 - Example 3-11 moveAbove() Method changes parent Layer</TITLE>
</HEAD>

<BODY>
                <!--  L1 is the parent Layer for L2 and L3  -->

<LAYER ID=L1 BGCOLOR="blue" LEFT=10 TOP=10 WIDTH=500 HEIGHT=200>
        <H1>    This is Layer L1        </H1>

<LAYER ID=L2 BGCOLOR="red" LEFT=10 TOP=50 WIDTH=300 HEIGHT=50>
        <H1>    This is Layer L2. It gets moved above Layer L5 and is relocated so
that Layer L4 is its parent Layer.                       </H1>    </LAYER>

<LAYER ID=L3 BGCOLOR="olive" LEFT=30 TOP=110 WIDTH=200 HEIGHT=80>
        <H1>    This is Layer L3        </H1>                       </LAYER>

</LAYER>

<!--  ***************************************************************  -->
                <!--  L4 is the parent Layer for L5 and L6  -->

<LAYER ID=L4 BGCOLOR="lime" LEFT=10 TOP=240 WIDTH=500 HEIGHT=250>
        <H1>    This is Layer L4        </H1>

<LAYER ID=L5 BGCOLOR="cyan" LEFT=250 TOP=10 WIDTH=220 HEIGHT=100>
        <H1>    This is Layer L5        </H1>                       </LAYER>

<LAYER ID=L6 BGCOLOR="magenta" LEFT=270 TOP=140 WIDTH=190 HEIGHT=70>
        <H1>    This is Layer L6        </H1>                       </LAYER>

</LAYER>

<!--  ***************************************************************  -->

<SCRIPT LANGUAGE="JavaScript1.2"><!--BEGIN HIDING

        //      Then if you move L2 above L5 with the following code:

        document.L1.document.L2.moveAbove(document.L4.document.L5);

        //      Then L4 will be the parent Layer for Layers L5, L2, L6.

//END HIDING-->
</SCRIPT>

</BODY>
</HTML>
```

Example 3-11   Sample411.html

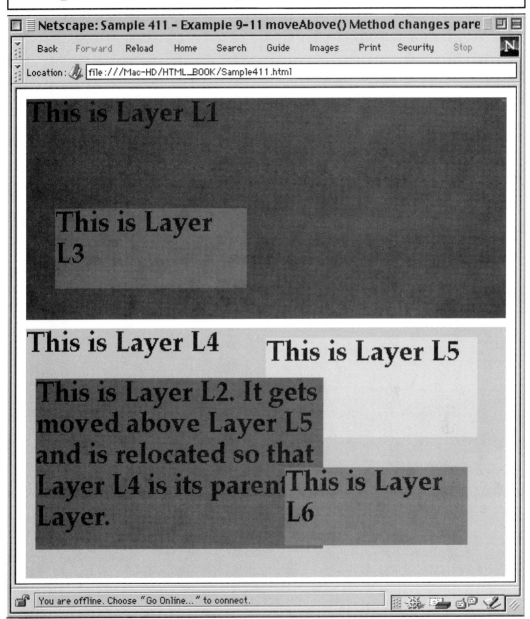

Show & Hide Layers & writing Layer content

Example 3-12 demonstrates the **write()** and **close()** Methods and the **"show"** and **"hide"** Values of the **visibility** Property to write content to Layers and make them appear and disappear.

Example 3-12:   Sample412.html

```
<!DOCTYPE HTML PUBLIC "-//W3C//DTD HTML 3.2//EN">
<HTML>
<HEAD>
<TITLE>Sample 412 - Example 3-12      write() Method and visibility Property</TITLE>

<STYLE TYPE="text/JavaScript">

    with(tags.BODY) {
        color="purple";
        fontFamily="Moonlight, cursive";
        fontSize="34pt";
        textAlign="center";
    }

    with(tags.H1) {
        color="navy";
        fontFamily="Helvetica, serif";
        fontSize="34pt";
        textAlign="center";
        backgroundColor="red";
        borderWidths("25px");
        borderStyle="double";
        borderColor="fuchsia";
    }

    with(tags.H2) {
        textAlign="left";
        borderWidths("30px");
        borderStyle="outset";
        borderColor="green";
    }

    with(tags.H3) {
        color="lime";
        fontFamily="Palatino, sans-serif";
        fontSize="20pt";
        textAlign="right";
        backgroundColor="gray";
        borderWidths("15px");
        borderStyle="inset";
        borderColor="blue";
    }
```

```
        classes.Navy30.all.fontSize="30pt";
        classes.Navy30.all.color="navy";


        classes.Global.all.fontSize="20pt";
        classes.Global.all.fontFamily="Moonlight, Clarendon, serif";
        classes.Global.all.width="100%";
        classes.Global.all.backgroundColor="blue";
        classes.Global.all.borderWidths("20px");
        classes.Global.all.borderStyle="groove";
        classes.Global.all.textAlign="center";
        classes.Global.all.align="center";
        classes.Global.all.borderColor="purple";
        classes.Global.all.color="yellow";

</STYLE>

</HEAD>

<!--  ***************************************************************  -->

<BODY>

<LAYER CLASS="Global" ID="layer2" LEFT=20 TOP=20>


        <FORM NAME="form1">

                Central

                <INPUT TYPE=button VALUE="Site 1"

                onClick='changeSite1(); return false;'>

                <INPUT TYPE=button VALUE="Site 2"

                onClick='changeSite2(); return false;'>

                <INPUT TYPE=button VALUE="Site 3"

                onClick='changeSite3(); return false;'>

                <INPUT TYPE=button VALUE="Site 4"

                onClick='changeSite4(); return false;'>

                <INPUT TYPE=button VALUE="Site 5"

                onClick='changeSite5(); return false;'>

                Command

        </FORM>


</LAYER>
```

```
<!-- ****************************************************** -->

<LAYER CLASS="Navy30" ID="layer1" LEFT=20 TOP=135 VISIBILITY="SHOW">

 <P>    Pick a Site, any Site for a change of view.          <P>

</LAYER>

<!-- ****************************************************** -->

<LAYER ID="layer3" LEFT=20 TOP=135 VISIBILITY="HIDE">        </LAYER>

<LAYER ID="layer4" LEFT=20 TOP=135 VISIBILITY="HIDE">        </LAYER>

<LAYER ID="layer5" LEFT=20 TOP=135 VISIBILITY="HIDE">        </LAYER>

<!-- ****************************************************** -->


<SCRIPT LANGUAGE="JavaScript1.2"><!--BEGIN HIDING


function changeSite1() {

        document.layer1.document.write("<H1><P>New Site 1.<BR

                                    You should notice that not only do you have to
                                    show the layer but you also have to hide all
                                    the the other layers so they don't get in the
                                    way. Of course this is only true if they
                                    occupy the same space.<\/P><\/H1>");

        document.layer1.visibility = 'show';
        document.layer3.visibility = 'hide';
        document.layer4.visibility = 'hide';
        document.layer5.visibility = 'hide';

        document.layer1.document.close();
}

/*----------------------------------------------------------------------*/


function changeSite2() {

        document.layer3.document.write("<H2><P>Do not forget your curly braces or
                                        your semicolons.<\/P><\/H2>");

        document.layer1.visibility = 'hide';
        document.layer3.visibility = 'show';
        document.layer4.visibility = 'hide';
        document.layer5.visibility = 'hide';

        document.layer3.document.close();
}

/*----------------------------------------------------------------------*/
```

```
/*------------------------------------------------------------------------*/

function changeSite3() {

        document.layer4.document.write("<H3><P>The Vorlons always ask,       <BR>
                                        WHO are you???<\/P><\/H3>");

        document.layer1.visibility = 'hide';
        document.layer3.visibility = 'hide';
        document.layer4.visibility = 'show';
        document.layer5.visibility = 'hide';

        document.layer4.document.close();
}

/*------------------------------------------------------------------------*/

function changeSite4() {

        document.layer5.document.write("<H3><P>The Shadows always ask, <BR>
                                        WHAT do you want???<\/P><\/H3>");

        document.layer1.visibility = 'hide';
        document.layer3.visibility = 'hide';
        document.layer4.visibility = 'hide';
        document.layer5.visibility = 'show';

        document.layer5.document.close();
}

/*------------------------------------------------------------------------*/

function changeSite5() {

        document.layer5.document.write("<H1><P>New Site 5.<BR>
                                        Imagine the Possibilities. <\/P><\/H1>");

        document.layer1.visibility = 'hide';
        document.layer3.visibility = 'hide';
        document.layer4.visibility = 'hide';
        document.layer5.visibility = 'show';

        document.layer5.document.close();
}

/*------------------------------------------------------------------------*/

//END HIDING-->
</SCRIPT>

</BODY>

</HTML>
```

The <u>new</u> Operator for creating new Layers in real-time

When you want to create a Layer dynamically, that is, after the page has loaded into the browser, you can do it by using the **new** Operator and the **Layer()** Constructor Function, which has the following Syntax:

JavaScript Syntax:

```
LayerName = new Layer (pixelsWidth, ["optionalParentLayerName"]);
```

Parameters Defined:

LayerName is the name of your Layer, the **pixelsWidth** Argument is how wide in pixels your Layer will render out to, and the second Argument ("which is optional") of **"optionalParentLayerName"**, is the name of the Parent Layer that contains the new Layer. If you do not specify a Parent Layer, then the new Layer will be a top-level Layer by default. Remember that **new Layer** must be spelled exactly as you see it with a capital L. If you use a lowercase 'l', you will get an error. For example:

```
Blue1 = new Layer (400);
```

which creates a new Layer that is named **Blue1** that has a width of 400 pixels, and because the Parent Layer is not specified, the **Blue1** Layer will be a top-level Layer.

Here are three ways to place content into your new Layer:

- Use the **write()** Method on the Layer's **document** Object. See Example 3-13.
- Use the **src** Property to load an external document with content. See Example 3-14.
- Use the **load()** Method to load an external document with content. See Example 3-14.

Special Notice:
- You must wait until your document has fully loaded into the browser before you can dynamically create a **new Layer**.

- You must wait until your document has fully loaded into the browser Window before you open that new Layer's **document** Object and use the **write()** Method to create content.

- You must use the **close()** Method to close a **document** Object after you use the **write()** Method on it.

- You can only have one **document** Object open at a time when using the **write()** Method on it.

Dynamically create <u>new</u> Layers with <u>tags</u> Property Style

The following example demonstrates how to create a **new** Layer when the user clicks on a Button in a FORM Element. There are just a few **Layer** Object Properties that can be directly applied to a Layer, and several of those are specified.

It also shows how to change the Properties of an Element that is used in that Layer with JavaScript by using the **tags** Property, which in this case are immediately applied to the new Layer named **Blue1**. This is how you get around the limitation of not having all of the Style Properties available as **Layer** Object Properties, which will be more critical when you want to let users define their own Styles in real time.

One of most important features to notice in this example is that the **visibility** Property must be set to **show** in order for your **new** Layer **Blue1** to be seen in the document, because the compiler will not automatically make it visible.

Example 3-13: **Sample413.html**

```
<!DOCTYPE HTML PUBLIC "-//W3C//DTD HTML 3.2//EN">
<HTML>
<HEAD>
<TITLE>Sample 413 - Example 3-13      The new Operator to create new Layers</TITLE>

<STYLE TYPE="text/JavaScript">

        with(tags.BODY) {
                color="purple";
                fontFamily="Moonlight, cursive";
                fontSize="34pt";
                textAlign="center";
        }

        with(tags.H1) {
                color="navy";
                fontFamily="Helvetica, serif";
                fontSize="34pt";
                textAlign="center";
                backgroundColor="red";
                borderWidths("25px");
                borderStyle="double";
                borderColor="fuchsia";
        }

        classes.Navy17.all.fontSize="17pt";
        classes.Navy17.all.color="navy";
```

```
        classes.Global.all.fontSize="20pt";
        classes.Global.all.fontFamily="Moonlight, Clarendon, serif";
        classes.Global.all.width="100%";
        classes.Global.all.backgroundColor="blue";
        classes.Global.all.borderWidths("20px");
        classes.Global.all.borderStyle="groove";
        classes.Global.all.textAlign="center";
        classes.Global.all.align="center";
        classes.Global.all.borderColor="purple";
        classes.Global.all.color="yellow";

</STYLE>

</HEAD>
<!-- ****************************************************************** -->
<BODY>

<LAYER CLASS="Global" ID="layer2" LEFT=20 TOP=20>

        <FORM NAME="form1">

                Central

                <INPUT TYPE=button VALUE="Make new Layer"

                onClick='newlayer1(); return false;'>

                <INPUT TYPE=button VALUE="Change new Layer"

                onClick='changelayer1(); return false;'>

                Command

        </FORM>

</LAYER>

<!-- ****************************************************************** -->

<LAYER CLASS="Navy17" ID="layer1" LEFT=20 TOP=135 VISIBILITY="SHOW">

 <P>Click <B>'Make new Layer'</B> first or you will get an error.<P>

</LAYER>

<!-- ****************************************************************** -->

<SCRIPT LANGUAGE="JavaScript1.2"><!--BEGIN HIDING

function newlayer1() {

        document.Blue1 = new Layer(200);
        document.Blue1.left = 20;
        document.Blue1.top = 275;
        document.Blue1.visibility = "show";
        document.Blue1.document.write("<H1>Hi! What's New?<\/H1>");
        document.Blue1.document.close();
}
```

```
/*---------------------------------------------------------------------*/

function changelayer1() {

        document.Blue1.left = 250;
        document.Blue1.top = 175;
        document.Blue1.bgColor = "blue";

        document.tags.H1.fontSize = "50pt";
        document.tags.H1.fontFamily = "Times, Palatino, serif";
        document.tags.H1.color = "yellow";
        document.tags.H1.backgroundColor = "aqua";
        document.tags.H1.borderColor = "lime";
        document.tags.H1.borderStyle = "groove";

        document.Blue1.document.write("<H1>ok so i'm changed.<\/H1>");
        document.Blue1.document.close();
}

//END HIDING-->
</SCRIPT>

</BODY>
</HTML>
```

Example 3-14 has three parts. Part 1 contains the essential section of code, and Parts 2 and 3 are the external files that are loaded into the document when the user clicks on a Button within the document. Part 1 demonstrates a straightforward way to create Layers dynamically by using the Operator **new**, setting the **left** and **top** Properties of the Layer, and then loading content from external files by using the **src** Property in the first Function named **getIt1()** and by using the **load()** Method in the second Function named **getIt2()**. It's similar in structure to the last example but without as much embellishment.

Example 3-14 Part 1:   Sample414.html

```
<!DOCTYPE HTML PUBLIC "-//W3C//DTD HTML 3.2//EN">
<HTML>
<HEAD>
<TITLE>Sample 414 - Example 3-14 new Operator to create layers on-the-fly</TITLE>

<STYLE TYPE="text/JavaScript">

        with(tags.BODY) {
                color="purple";
                fontFamily="Moonlight, cursive";
                fontSize="22pt";
                textAlign="center";
        }

</STYLE>
</HEAD>
```

```
<!--  ********************************************************  -->
<BODY>

<LAYER ID="layer2" LEFT=20 TOP=20>

        <FORM NAME="form1">

                Central Command

                <INPUT TYPE=button VALUE="Load External Layer"

                onClick='getIt1(); return false;'>

                <INPUT TYPE=button VALUE="Load Another External Layer"

                onClick='getIt2(); return false;'>

        </FORM>

</LAYER>

<!--  ********************************************************  -->

<LAYER ID="layer1" LEFT=20 TOP=135 VISIBILITY="SHOW">

 <P>Click a button to make a new Layer and load its content.<P>

</LAYER>

<!--  ********************************************************  -->

<SCRIPT LANGUAGE="JavaScript1.2"><!--BEGIN HIDING

function getIt1() {

        document.ExternalOne = new Layer(200);
        document.ExternalOne.left = 50;
        document.ExternalOne.top = 200;
        document.ExternalOne.src = "Sample414ExternalA.html";
        document.ExternalOne.visibility = "show";
}

function getIt2() {

        document.ExternalTwo = new Layer(50);
        document.ExternalTwo.left = 280;
        document.ExternalTwo.top = 225;
        document.ExternalTwo.load ("Sample414ExternalB.html" , 300);
        document.ExternalTwo.visibility = "show";
}

//END HIDING-->
</SCRIPT>

</BODY>
</HTML>
```

Example 3-14 Part 2:   Sample414ExternalA.html

```
<!DOCTYPE HTML PUBLIC "-//W3C//DTD HTML 3.2//EN">
<HTML>
<HEAD>
<TITLE>Sample 414ExternalA - Example 3-14A    </TITLE>

<STYLE TYPE="text/JavaScript">

        with(tags.BODY) {
                color="blue";
                fontFamily="Helvetica, serif";
                fontSize="44pt";
                textAlign="center";
        }
</STYLE>
</HEAD>
<BODY>
<P>    The First External Content.    <P>
</BODY>
</HTML>
```

Example 3-14 Part 3:   Sample414ExternalB.html

```
<!DOCTYPE HTML PUBLIC "-//W3C//DTD HTML 3.2//EN">
<HTML>
<HEAD>
<TITLE>Sample 414ExternalB - Example 3-14B    </TITLE>

<STYLE TYPE="text/JavaScript">

        with(tags.BODY) {
                color="red";
                fontFamily="Clarendon, Times, fantasy";
                fontSize="24pt";
                textAlign="center";
        }

        classes.darkness.all.color="black";
        classes.greenword.all.color="green";
</STYLE>
</HEAD>
<BODY>
<P>    The Second External Content which uses the

<SPAN CLASS="darkness">        load ( )        </SPAN>

<SPAN CLASS="greenword">        Method        </SPAN>

 to override the width setting for the Layer from 50 pixels to 300 pixels. </P>
</BODY>
</HTML>
```

Localized JavaScript <SCRIPT>s within a Layer

When you use the <SCRIPT> Element <u>within</u> a LAYER, that is, between the Start and End Tags of the LAYER Element, to modify the LAYER with JavaScript, the SCRIPT is said to be Localized because the JavaScript will only work for that particular LAYER. This inherent limitation is useful in large documents when you want to have an easy way to manage your Event Handlers for Mouse movements and clicks. See Example 1-15, which can be viewed in <u>Sample415.html</u>, for a simple example and Example 6-13, which can be viewed in <u>Sample713-Chess.html</u>, for more involved examples. There is an additional file on the CD-ROM that's not in the book, which can viewed in <u>Sample774-Chess-Images.html</u>.

This example focuses on using the **visibility** Property with the **z-index** Property and some simple JavaScript to make Layers appear and disappear. In fact, it is exactly the same as Example 2-8 (from Chapter 2) except that it has additional Functions to handle Mouse Events from within a Localized SCRIPT Element. The Styles for Example 3-15 are written in CSS Syntax, which is different from all the other examples in Chapter 3, which are written in JavaScript Syntax. It also shows that Layers are transparent by default, which is the equivalent of setting the **backgroundColor** Property to **"null"**. There are some additional notes near the end of the source code in the <P> Element.

Example 3-15:   Sample415.html

```
<!DOCTYPE HTML PUBLIC "-//W3C//DTD HTML 3.2//EN">
<HTML>
<HEAD>
<TITLE>Sample 415 - Example 3-15      Localized Scripts, visibility and mouse Events
</TITLE>

<STYLE TYPE="text/CSS">
<!--

#SeventhLayer   { position: absolute; left: 10px; top: 100px;
                    z-index: 3; color: blue; font-size: 20pt; padding: 40px;
                    border-style:ridge; border-width:20px; border-color:aqua;
                    visibility: show; }

#EighthLayer    { position: absolute; left: 100px; top: 258px;
                    z-index: 2; color: red; font-size: 20pt; padding: 40px;
                    border-style:ridge; border-width:20px; border-color:yellow;
                    visibility: show; }
#NinthLayer     { position: absolute; left: 280px; top: 75px;
                    z-index: 1; color: green; font-size: 20pt; padding: 40px;
                    border-style:ridge; border-width:20px; border-color:lime;
                    visibility: show; }
-->
</STYLE>
</HEAD>
```

```
<BODY>
<DIV ID="SeventhLayer">        This is the                    <BR>
                               SeventhLayer Test              <BR>
                               with z-index equals 3.         <BR>
                               It rules!

<SCRIPT LANGUAGE="JavaScript1.2"><!--BEGIN HIDING

        function onMouseOver() { seeNoSee("hide"); }
        function onMouseOut() { seeNoSee("show"); }

        function seeNoSee (WhereAmI) {
                visibility=WhereAmI;
                return false;
        }

//END HIDING-->
</SCRIPT>
</DIV>

<DIV ID="EighthLayer">         This is the                    <BR>
                               EighthLayer Test               <BR>
                               with z-index equals 2.

<SCRIPT LANGUAGE="JavaScript1.2"><!--BEGIN HIDING

        function onMouseOver() { seeNoSee("hide"); }
        function onMouseOut() { seeNoSee("show"); }

        function seeNoSee (WhereAmI) {
                visibility=WhereAmI;
                return false;
        }

//END HIDING-->
</SCRIPT>
</DIV>

<DIV ID="NinthLayer">          This is the                    <BR>
                               NinthLayer Test                <BR>
                               with z-index equals 1.

<SCRIPT LANGUAGE="JavaScript1.2"><!--BEGIN HIDING

        function onMouseOver() { seeNoSee("hide"); }
        function onMouseOut() { seeNoSee("show"); }

        function seeNoSee (WhereAmI) {

                visibility=WhereAmI;
                return false;
        }

//END HIDING-->
</SCRIPT>

</DIV>
```

```
<P>
This is exactly the same as Example 307 except that there is a Localized SCRIPT in
each LAYER that causes it to become hidden when the mouse is placed over it and to
reappear when the mouse is moved out of its space. It'a a little shaky so hold your
mouse steady. If your mouse is over an area where 2 or more LAYERs overlap then the
LAYER with the higher z-index will be the one to get the mouse event and disappear.

</P>

</BODY>
</HTML>
```

Example 3-16 deals with Localized SCRIPTs within LAYER Elements to show that the same Functions with different Values can be independently applied to individual Layers. The **Layer** Object Properties of **clip.right** and **clip.bottom** are used to cause part of a Layer to disappear when the mouse is moved over it and then to reappear when the mouse is moved away from the Layer's assigned space.

Example 3-16:   Sample416.html

```
<!DOCTYPE HTML PUBLIC "-//W3C//DTD HTML 3.2//EN">
<HTML>
<HEAD>
<TITLE>Sample 416 - Example 3-16      Local Scripts & clip Properties</TITLE>

<STYLE TYPE="text/JavaScript">

        with(tags.BODY) {
                color="purple";
                fontFamily="Moonlight, cursive";
                fontSize="22pt";
                textAlign="center";
        }

        classes.Blue22.all.fontSize="22pt";
        classes.Blue22.all.color="blue";
        classes.Blue22.all.width="500px";
        classes.Blue22.all.backgroundColor="aqua";
        classes.Blue22.all.borderWidths("20px");
        classes.Blue22.all.borderStyle="groove";

</STYLE>

</HEAD>

<BODY>
```

```
<!--    *****************************************************************    -->

<LAYER CLASS="Blue22" ID="layer1" LEFT=20 TOP=35 VISIBILITY="SHOW">

 <P>Move the mouse over me and I will shrink.              </P>
 <P>Move the mouse away from                               </P>
 <P>me and I will grow back.                               </P>


<SCRIPT LANGUAGE="JavaScript1.2"><!--BEGIN HIDING

        function onMouseOver() { seeNoSee(370, 130); }

        function onMouseOut() { seeNoSee(500, 200); }

        function seeNoSee (ShrinkingLeft, ShrinkingUp) {

                clip.right=ShrinkingLeft;
                clip.bottom=ShrinkingUp;

        return false;
        }

//END HIDING-->
</SCRIPT>

</LAYER>

<!--    *****************************************************************    -->

<LAYER CLASS="Blue22" ID="layer2" LEFT=20 TOP=222 VISIBILITY="SHOW">

 <P>Move the mouse over me and I will shrink.              </P>
 <P>Move the mouse away from                               </P>
 <P>me and I will grow back.                               </P>

<SCRIPT LANGUAGE="JavaScript1.2"><!--BEGIN HIDING

        function onMouseOver() { seeNoSee(211, 100); }

        function onMouseOut() { seeNoSee(500, 200); }

        function seeNoSee (ShrinkingLeft, ShrinkingUp) {

                clip.right=ShrinkingLeft;
                clip.bottom=ShrinkingUp;
        return false;
        }

//END HIDING-->
</SCRIPT>

</LAYER>

</BODY>
</HTML>
```

Animating a Clipping Rectangle to reveal an Image

The JavaScript <u>setTimeout() Method</u>

The **setTimeout()** Method has two different structures of syntax. One is used to evaluate an <u>Expression</u> after a specified number of **milliseconds** have elapsed. The other is used to call a <u>Function</u> after a specified number of **milliseconds** have elapsed. By itself, the **setTimeout()** Method does not act repeatedly like the **setInterval()** Method. To get it to repeat you must call the same Function that contains the **setTimeout()** Method explicitly as the **functionName** Argument, which is often done inside of a conditional Statement like an **if ()**, which is demonstrated in Examples 3-17 through 3-22. The **anyExpression** or **functionName** Parameters must be inside quote marks or it will be evaluated immediately. When specifying a Function, the comma-separated **arg** Arguments for that Function are optional so you can use **setTimeout()** even if your Function doesn't have any Arguments.

JavaScript Syntax:

```
setTimeout("anyExpression", milliseconds);
setTimeout("functionName()", milliseconds[, arg1, ..., argN]);
```

You must assign a **setTimeout()** Method to a **timeoutID** if you plan to use it in conjunction with the **clearTimeout()** Method like this:

```
timeoutID=setTimeout("functionName()", millisecs);
```

or like this:

```
timeoutID=setTimeout("functionName()", millisecs, arg1, ...,argN);
```

so that you can reference it with the **clearTimeout()** Method like this:

```
clearTimeout(timeoutID);
```

The JavaScript <u>clearTimeout() Method</u>

The **clearTimeout()** Method is used to cancel a previously initiated call to the **setTimeout()** Method that has been assigned to a **timeoutID**.

Syntax:

```
clearTimeout(timeoutID);
```

Animating Clipping Rectangles
and popping Images

In the following Example 3-17, an image can be revealed incrementally, hidden, or popped into view by clicking on one of the three Buttons. It uses the **setTimeout()** Method, the **resizeBy()** Method and the **resizeTo()** Method.

RevealImage()   This Function uses the conditional **if ()** Statement to test if **layer1's** **clip.right** Property is less than 700. If true, then **layer1** is resized so that it is 5 pixels wider and 4 pixels taller. Then the **setTimeout()** Method reinvokes the process by calling the **RevealImage()** Function again and will continue to do so every 20 milliseconds until **layer1's** **clip.right** Property is greater than or equal to 700 pixels wide. It's important to note that the reason the reinvoking continues is because the **setTimeout()** Method calls the **RevealImage()** Function explicitly, which causes the Function to break out at that point and start the loop again. This is in contrast to the **setInterval()** Method (see page 284), which has an inherent reinvoking capability that the **setTimeout()** Method does not.

HideImage()   This Function just resets **layer1** back to its original Clipping **width** and **height**, which only has a small part of the upper-left corner visible by using the **resizeTo()** Method.

PopImage()   This Function instantaneously changes the **width** and **height** of the Clipping Rectangle so that the entire Layer is visible by using the **resizeTo()** Method.

Example 3-17:   **Sample417.html**

```
<!DOCTYPE HTML PUBLIC "-//W3C//DTD HTML 3.2//EN">
<HTML>
<HEAD>
<TITLE>Sample 417 - Example 3-17     SetTimeout Method to Reveal Image</TITLE>

<STYLE TYPE="text/JavaScript">

        classes.Blue22.all.fontSize="22pt";
        classes.Blue22.all.color="blue";
        classes.Blue22.all.width="100%";
        classes.Blue22.all.backgroundColor="aqua";
        classes.Blue22.all.borderWidths("20px");
        classes.Blue22.all.borderStyle="groove";

</STYLE>

</HEAD>

<BODY>
```

```
<!-- ******************************************************************* -->

<LAYER CLASS="Blue22" ID="layer2" LEFT=50 TOP=10 VISIBILITY="SHOW">

<FORM NAME="form1">

                Central Command

                <INPUT TYPE=button VALUE="Reveal Image"

                onClick='RevealImage(); return false;'>

                <INPUT TYPE=button VALUE="Hide Image"

                onClick='HideImage(); return false;'>

                <INPUT TYPE=button VALUE="Pop Image"

                onClick='PopImage(); return false;'>

        </FORM>

</LAYER>

<!-- ******************************************************************* -->

<LAYER CLASS="Blue22" ID="layer1" LEFT=20 TOP=130 CLIP="0,0,100,50"
        VISIBILITY="SHOW">

Wow!<BR><BR>

<CENTER>

 <IMG SRC="JPEG-FILES/J5-SEDONA-SUMMER-7C-HS.jpg" WIDTH="360" HEIGHT="240">

</CENTER>

</LAYER>

<!-- ******************************************************************* -->

<SCRIPT LANGUAGE="JavaScript1.2"><!--BEGIN HIDING

        function RevealImage() {

                var layer1 = document.layer1;

                if (layer1.clip.right < 700)  {
                        layer1.resizeBy(5,4);
                        setTimeout('RevealImage()', 20);
                }

        return false;
        }

/*-----------------------------------------------------------------*/
```

```
/*------------------------------------------------------------------*/
        function HideImage() {

                var layer1 = document.layer1;

                if (layer1.clip.right > 100)  {
                        layer1.resizeTo(100,50);
                }

        return false;
        }

/*------------------------------------------------------------------*/
        function PopImage() {

                var layer1 = document.layer1;

                if (layer1.clip.right < 700)  {
                        layer1.resizeTo(700,500);
                }

        return false;
        }

//END HIDING-->
</SCRIPT>

</BODY>
</HTML>
```

In Example 3-18, the **setTimeout()** Method is used to reveal an image like in the last example, and there is the added functionality of using the **visibility** Property to hide and show other images that have been preloaded into the page but have their **VISIBILITY Attributes** initially set to **"HIDE"** from within the LAYER Element.

Example 3-18: Sample418.html

```
<!DOCTYPE HTML PUBLIC "-//W3C//DTD HTML 3.2//EN">
<HTML>
<HEAD>
<TITLE>Sample 418 - Example 3-18      SetTimeout Method to Reveal Image</TITLE>

<STYLE TYPE="text/JavaScript">

        classes.Blue22.all.fontSize="14pt";
        classes.Blue22.all.color="blue";
        classes.Blue22.all.width="100%";
        classes.Blue22.all.backgroundColor="aqua";
        classes.Blue22.all.borderWidths("20px");
        classes.Blue22.all.borderStyle="groove";
</STYLE>
</HEAD>
```

```
<BODY>
<!-- ****************************************************************** -->

<LAYER CLASS="Blue22" ID="layer2" LEFT=20 TOP=10 VISIBILITY="SHOW">

<FORM NAME="form1">
                Central Command

                <INPUT TYPE=button VALUE="Reveal Image"

                onClick='RevealImage(); return false;'>

                <INPUT TYPE=button VALUE="Hide Image"

                onClick='HideImage(); return false;'>          <BR>

                <INPUT TYPE=button VALUE="Pop Image 1"

                onClick='PopImage(); return false;'>

                <INPUT TYPE=button VALUE="Pop Image 2"

                onClick='PopImage2(); return false;'>
                <INPUT TYPE=button VALUE="Pop Image 3"

                onClick='PopImage3(); return false;'>

                <INPUT TYPE=button VALUE="Pop Image 4"

                onClick='PopImage4(); return false;'>

        </FORM>

</LAYER>
<!-- ****************************************************************** -->

<LAYER CLASS="Blue22" ID="layer1" LEFT=20 TOP=130
CLIP="0,0,100,50" VISIBILITY="SHOW">

Wow!

<CENTER>
  <IMG SRC="JPEG-FILES/J5-SEDONA-SUMMER-7C-HS.jpg" WIDTH=360 HEIGHT=240>
</CENTER>

</LAYER>
<!-- ****************************************************************** -->

<LAYER CLASS="Blue22" ID="layer3" LEFT=20 TOP=130 VISIBILITY="HIDE">

Wow!

<CENTER>
  <IMG SRC="JPEG-FILES/J5-SpaceDome_27P.jpg" WIDTH=360 HEIGHT=240>
</CENTER>

</LAYER>
<!-- ****************************************************************** -->
```

```
<!--    ********************************************************    -->

<LAYER CLASS="Blue22" ID="layer4" LEFT=20 TOP=130 VISIBILITY="HIDE">

Wow!

<CENTER>
 <IMG SRC="JPEG-FILES/J5-MountainScape-Sph-2.jpg" WIDTH=360 HEIGHT=240>
</CENTER>

</LAYER>
<!--    ********************************************************    -->

<LAYER CLASS="Blue22" ID="layer5" LEFT=20 TOP=130 VISIBILITY="HIDE">

Wow!

<CENTER>
 <IMG SRC="JPEG-FILES/J5-SKY_SPHERE_1.jpg" WIDTH=360 HEIGHT=240>
</CENTER>

</LAYER>
<!--    ********************************************************    -->


<SCRIPT LANGUAGE="JavaScript1.2"><!--BEGIN HIDING

function PopImage2() {

        document.layer1.visibility = 'hide';
        document.layer4.visibility = 'hide';
        document.layer5.visibility = 'hide';
        document.layer3.visibility = 'show';
}

/*----------------------------------------------------------------*/

function PopImage3() {

        document.layer1.visibility = 'hide';
        document.layer3.visibility = 'hide';
        document.layer5.visibility = 'hide';
        document.layer4.visibility = 'show';
}

/*----------------------------------------------------------------*/

function PopImage4() {

        document.layer1.visibility = 'hide';
        document.layer3.visibility = 'hide';
        document.layer4.visibility = 'hide';
        document.layer5.visibility = 'show';
}

//END HIDING-->
</SCRIPT>
<!--    ********************************************************    -->
```

```
<SCRIPT LANGUAGE="JavaScript1.2"><!--BEGIN HIDING

        function RevealImage () {

                document.layer1.visibility = 'show';

                var layer1 = document.layer1;

                if (layer1.clip.right < 700)  {
                        layer1.resizeBy(5,4);
                        setTimeout('RevealImage()', 20);

                        document.layer3.visibility = 'hide';
                        document.layer4.visibility = 'hide';
                        document.layer5.visibility = 'hide';
                        document.layer1.visibility = 'show';
                }
        return false;
        }
/*-----------------------------------------------------------------*/
        function HideImage () {

                var layer1 = document.layer1;

                if (layer1.clip.right > 100)  {
                        layer1.resizeTo(100,50);

                        document.layer3.visibility = 'hide';
                        document.layer4.visibility = 'hide';
                        document.layer5.visibility = 'hide';
                        document.layer1.visibility = 'show';
                }
        return false;
        }
/*-----------------------------------------------------------------*/
        function PopImage () {

                document.layer1.visibility = 'show';

                var layer1 = document.layer1;
                layer1.clip.right=0;   //resets to zero to avoid button conflicts

                if (layer1.clip.right < 700)  {
                        layer1.resizeTo(700,500);

                        document.layer3.visibility = 'hide';
                        document.layer4.visibility = 'hide';
                        document.layer5.visibility = 'hide';
                        document.layer1.visibility = 'show';
                }
        return false;
        }
//END HIDING-->
</SCRIPT>
</BODY>
</HTML>
```

Example 3-19 uses the **setTimeout()** Method to move an image by moving its containing Layer named **layer1** as long as **layer1**'s **left** Property is less than 500 pixels. The Button with **VALUE="Move Image"** calls the **MoveImage()** Function when it is clicked, which implements the **setTimeout()** Method.

Example 3-19:   Sample419.html

```
<!DOCTYPE HTML PUBLIC "-//W3C//DTD HTML 3.2//EN">
<HTML>
<HEAD>
<TITLE>Sample 419 - Example 3-19     SetTimeout Method to Animate Image</TITLE>

<STYLE TYPE="text/JavaScript">

        classes.Blue22.all.fontSize="22pt";
        classes.Blue22.all.color="blue";
        classes.Blue22.all.width="100%";
        classes.Blue22.all.backgroundColor="lime";
        classes.Blue22.all.borderWidths("20px");
        classes.Blue22.all.borderStyle="groove";
        classes.Blue22.all.borderColor="green";

</STYLE>

</HEAD>

<BODY>

<!--  ******************************************************** -->

<LAYER CLASS="Blue22" ID="layer2" LEFT=50 TOP=10 VISIBILITY="SHOW">

        <FORM NAME="form1">

                Central Command

                <INPUT TYPE=button VALUE="Move Image"

                onClick='MoveImage(); return false;'>

                <INPUT TYPE=button VALUE="Return Image"

                onClick='ReturnImage(); return false;'>

        </FORM>

</LAYER>

<!--  ******************************************************** -->
```

```
<LAYER ID="layer1" LEFT=20 TOP=130 VISIBILITY="SHOW">

        <IMG SRC="JPEG-FILES/icon-SKULL-BEAR.jpg" WIDTH=106 HEIGHT=144>

</LAYER>

<!-- ***************************************************************** -->

<SCRIPT LANGUAGE="JavaScript1.2"><!--BEGIN HIDING

        function MoveImage (layer1) {

                var layer1 = document.layer1;

                if (layer1.left < 500) {
                        layer1.moveBy(5,1);
                        setTimeout('MoveImage()', 20);
                }

        return false;
        }
/*----------------------------------------------------------------*/
        function ReturnImage (layer1) {

                var layer1 = document.layer1;

                if (layer1.left > 20) {
                        layer1.moveTo(20,130);
                }

        return false;
        }

//END HIDING-->
</SCRIPT>

</BODY>
</HTML>
```

In Example 3-20, one Layer that contains an image is repeatedly animated in a clockwise rectangular motion and another Layer is animated horizontally. Each animation is implemented when a button is clicked.

MoveUpperImage()   This Function tests for the Value of the UpperLayer's **left** and **top** Property coordinates and uses the **moveBy()** Method to move it by the specified pixels if the conditions are true.

MoveLowerImage()   This Function tests for the Value of the LowerLayer's **left** Property coordinates and uses the **moveBy()** Method to move it by the specified pixels if the conditions are true.

ChaseLowerImage()   This Function repositions **LowerLayer** with the **moveTo()** Method.

Example 3-20:   Sample420.html

```
<!DOCTYPE HTML PUBLIC "-//W3C//DTD HTML 3.2//EN">
<HTML>
<HEAD>
<TITLE>Sample 420 - Example 3-20      SetTimeout Method to Animate Image</TITLE>

<STYLE TYPE="text/JavaScript">

        classes.Blue22.all.fontSize="14pt";
        classes.Blue22.all.color="blue";
        classes.Blue22.all.width="100%";
        classes.Blue22.all.backgroundColor="lime";
        classes.Blue22.all.borderWidths("20px");
        classes.Blue22.all.borderStyle="groove";
        classes.Blue22.all.borderColor="green";

</STYLE>
</HEAD>
<BODY>
<!-- *********************************************************** -->

<LAYER CLASS="Blue22" ID="layer1" LEFT=50 TOP=10 VISIBILITY="SHOW">

        <FORM NAME="form1">
                Central Command

                <INPUT TYPE=button VALUE="Move Upper Image"

                onClick='MoveUpperImage(); return false;'>

                <INPUT TYPE=button VALUE="Move Lower Image"

                onClick='MoveLowerImage(); return false;'>

                <INPUT TYPE=button VALUE="Chase Lower Image"

                onClick='ChaseLowerImage(); return false;'>
        </FORM>

</LAYER>
<!-- *********************************************************** -->

<LAYER ID="UpperLayer" LEFT=20 TOP=130 VISIBILITY="SHOW">

 <IMG SRC="JPEG-FILES/J2-Sedona_Winter_Sphere13.jpg" WIDTH=106 HEIGHT=144>

</LAYER>
<!-- *********************************************************** -->

<LAYER ID="LowerLayer" LEFT=20 TOP=300 VISIBILITY="SHOW">

 <IMG SRC="JPEG-FILES/icon-SKULL-BEAR.jpg" WIDTH=106 HEIGHT=144>

</LAYER>
```

```
<!--   ******************************************************************   -->

<SCRIPT LANGUAGE="JavaScript1.2"><!--BEGIN HIDING

function MoveUpperImage() {

        var UpperLayer = document.UpperLayer;

        if (UpperLayer.left < 500  &&  UpperLayer.top == 130)  {
                UpperLayer.moveBy(5,0);                //moves to the right
        }
        if (UpperLayer.left == 500  &&  UpperLayer.top < 300)  {
                UpperLayer.moveBy(0,5);                //moves down
        }
        if (UpperLayer.left > 20  &&  UpperLayer.top == 300)  {
                UpperLayer.moveBy(-5,0);               //moves to the left
        }
        if (UpperLayer.left == 20  &&  UpperLayer.top > 130)  {
                        UpperLayer.moveBy(0,-5);       //moves up
        }

        setTimeout('MoveUpperImage()', 20);
}
/*------------------------------------------------------------------------*/
function MoveLowerImage() {

        var LowerLayer = document.LowerLayer;

        if (LowerLayer.left < 500)  {
                        LowerLayer.moveBy(5,0);
        }
        else {
                LowerLayer.left = 20;
        }

        setTimeout('MoveLowerImage()', 20);
}
/*------------------------------------------------------------------------*/
function ChaseLowerImage() {

        var LowerLayer = document.LowerLayer;

        if (LowerLayer.left > 20)  {

//moves the lower image to the vertical position of the upper image

                LowerLayer.moveTo(20,130);
        }
return false;
}

//END HIDING-->
</SCRIPT>

</BODY>
</HTML>
```

Example 3-21 has four Layers, each of which has an image contained inside. The Layer with the Sun image is stationary while the Layers with the Gif89a animation of a spinning Earth and the comet still-image are animated by reinvoking the **MoveEarth()** Function and **MoveComet()** Functions, respectively. Two of the Layers each have an image of the spinning Earth. The **EarthLayer** Layer is visible in the upper half of the page and the **SecondEarthLayer** Layer is visible in the lower half of the page.

MoveEarth()   This Function basically divides the page in a grid with four sections and uses conditional **if ()** Statements to test for the position coordinates of both the **EarthLayer** and **SecondEarthLayer** Layers and moves them accordingly with the **moveBy()** Method and uses the **visibility** Property to hide or show them. Then the **setTimeout()** Method reinvokes the **MoveEarth()** Function continuously because one of the conditions in one of the **if ()** Statements is always true. This causes the Earth image to move perpetually.

MoveComet()   This Function moves the Layer named **CometLayer** with the image of the comet diagonally from upper-right to lower-left. After a certain point, the image is reset to the original starting point and the animation repeats.

Example 3-21:   Sample421.html

```
<!DOCTYPE HTML PUBLIC "-//W3C//DTD HTML 3.2//EN">
<HTML><HEAD>
<TITLE>Sample 421 - Example 3-21      Sun Earth Animation</TITLE>

<STYLE TYPE="text/JavaScript">

        classes.Blue22.all.fontSize="14pt";
        classes.Blue22.all.color="navy";
        classes.Blue22.all.width="100%";
        classes.Blue22.all.backgroundColor="yellow";

</STYLE>
</HEAD>

<BODY BGCOLOR="black">
<!--   ************************************************************   -->

<LAYER CLASS="Blue22" ID="layer1" LEFT=10 TOP=10 VISIBILITY="SHOW" Z-INDEX=1>

<FORM NAME="form1">
            C&amp;C
            <INPUT TYPE=button VALUE="Start Gravity"

            onClick='MoveEarth(); MoveComet(); return false;'>

    </FORM>

</LAYER>
```

```
<!--    ****************************************************************    -->

<LAYER ID="EarthLayer" LEFT=599 TOP=170 VISIBILITY="SHOW" Z-INDEX=3>

 <IMG SRC="JPEG-FILES/GIFA-EARTH-ANIMATION.gif" WIDTH=100 HEIGHT=100>

</LAYER>

<!--    ****************************************************************    -->

<LAYER ID="SecondEarthLayer" LEFT=30 TOP=195 VISIBILITY=HIDE Z-INDEX=6>

 <IMG SRC="JPEG-FILES/GIFA-EARTH-ANIMATION.gif" WIDTH=100 HEIGHT=100>

</LAYER>

<!--    ****************************************************************    -->

<LAYER ID="SunLayer" LEFT=300 TOP=170 VISIBILITY="SHOW" Z-INDEX=4>

 <IMG SRC="JPEG-FILES/icon-Sun.jpg" WIDTH=144 HEIGHT=144>

</LAYER>

<!--    ****************************************************************    -->

<LAYER ID="CometLayer" LEFT=1000 TOP=100 VISIBILITY="SHOW" Z-INDEX=5>

 <IMG SRC="JPEG-FILES/GIF-Comet.gif" WIDTH=144 HEIGHT=80>

</LAYER>

<!--    ****************************************************************    -->

<SCRIPT LANGUAGE="JavaScript1.2"><!--BEGIN HIDING

function MoveEarth() {

        var EarthLayer = document.EarthLayer;
        var SecondEarthLayer = document.SecondEarthLayer;

                                                //upper-right grid

        if (EarthLayer.left > 320  &&  EarthLayer.top > 0)  {
                EarthLayer.moveBy(-5,-3);
        }
                                                //upper-left grid

else    if (EarthLayer.left <= 320  &&  EarthLayer.top >= 0 )  {
                EarthLayer.moveBy(-5,3);
        }

        if (EarthLayer.left > 20  &&  EarthLayer.left <= 30) {
                EarthLayer.visibility='hide';
                SecondEarthLayer.left = 30;
                SecondEarthLayer.top = 170;
                SecondEarthLayer.visibility='show';
        }
```

```
                                                      //lower-left grid

    if (SecondEarthLayer.left <= 320  &&  SecondEarthLayer.top >= 169)  {
            SecondEarthLayer.moveBy(5,3);
    }


                                                     //lower-right grid

else    if (SecondEarthLayer.left > 320  &&  SecondEarthLayer.top >= 169 )  {
            SecondEarthLayer.moveBy(5,-3);
    }

    if (SecondEarthLayer.left > 598  &&  SecondEarthLayer.left <= 610  &&
            SecondEarthLayer.top >= 169) {
            SecondEarthLayer.visibility='hide';
            EarthLayer.left = 599;
            EarthLayer.top = 170;
            EarthLayer.visibility='show';
    }

setTimeout('MoveEarth()', 20);
}

/*-------------------------------------------------------------------------*/

function MoveComet() {

    var CometLayer = document.CometLayer;

    if (CometLayer.left > -200 )  {
            CometLayer.moveBy(-7,3);
    }

                                    //resets the comet to starting point
    else    {
            CometLayer.left = 600 ;
            CometLayer.top = 100 ;
    }

setTimeout('MoveComet()', 20);
}

//END HIDING-->
</SCRIPT>

</BODY>
</HTML>
```

Some JavaScript Tips

Here are a few tidbits from the trenches. Navigator antialiases the fonts to the background color that is originally set, so if you want to change background colors later on, keep in mind the darkness and lightness factor when making your choices so that you don't get an unsightly antialiased band of color around the font. It is also a good idea to declare any background colors with JavaScript Properties, and if you can, try to set up your Elements so that you aren't constantly overriding background colors and you'll have better and more predictable results. The less you declare with Layer Element Attributes and the more you declare with JavaScript Properties, the fewer headaches you'll have.

If you are authoring pages with minimal or zero paddings you may find that your text is not exactly centered because of tabs and returns that you have in your text editor. Yes, I know it's not supposed to happen, but it does, so if that little discrepancy is critical, then collapse all your white space in the text editor and it should balance out.

Alternatively, you can use that handy <u>nonbreaking space</u> code   to precisely center or balance the paddings of your text if you don't want to collapse your white space in your text editor. In case it's new to you, it's an HTML Entity, and the ampersand and semicolon are part of the code. This <u>nonbreaking space</u> forces the browser to put in a space that won't collapse, no matter how many of them you put in sequence.

One of the main reasons for setting up Global Variables is because it is much easier to read and debug code when looking at Variables rather than a long sequence of dot notation for each expression. You will also find when you create really long and complex pages that Global Variable declaration actually saves you time and space.

If you are preloading large images, be aware of your intended audience and remember to compress the images. Obviously, if you are authoring a website for clients on T1 lines or your viewers expect heavy graphics, this isn't a problem.

Animating control Layers and Images offscreen and onscreen

In Example 3-22, the screen is divided into three areas that visually blend into each other. There is a thin vertical area on the left, a thin horizontal area at the top and the rest of the screen is considered the main viewing area. The Layer named **layerA** is on the left and it's the main control panel. It controls the two Layers **Group1** and **Group2** that are in the top area, animating them into and out of view. Within these two Layers there are Buttons that control the contents of the page, which are art images contained in Layers, that can be animated into and out of view in both preview and large sizes.

The Layer named **Group1** is initially visible at the top of the Window and can be recalled into view by the Button named **BGroup1** in the left Layer named **layerA**. The Layer named **Group2** is initially offscreen at coordinates (120,-110) with the **visibility** Property set to hide. It can be brought into view by clicking on the Button named **BGroup2**, which slides it in with the **moveBy()** Method and the **setTimeout()** Method within the conditional **if ()** and repositions Layer **Group1** with the **moveTo()** Method.

For all of the following Function descriptions, there is more than one in the Script that it applies to with the only difference being the number in the name. For example, there is the **ShowHideGroup1()** Function and the **ShowHideGroup2()** Function with the description below applicable to both, which only have minor differences.

ShowHideGroup1() Functions that change the **visibility, zIndex** and (x,y) Coordinates of the Layers named **Group1** and **Group2**. These Layers contain the main Button groups, which are used to manipulate the **Showcase, ShowcaseSmall,** and **ShowcaseLarge** series of Layers that contain the images.

MoveGroup1() Function that uses the **moveBy()** Method and the **setTimeout()** Method to animate the **Group1** Layer into view from its offscreen coordinates.

The next three Functions are all implemented with one click of the Button named **BPreview1**, which focuses on the first small Preview image.

HideShowLarge1() Function that controls the **visibility** Property of all the Layers and sets the positioning Coordinates for the main parent Layers.

HideShowSmall1() Function that further refines the **visibility** Property and the **zIndex** Property for the sibling Layers contained in the Layer that is selected by the user, so that the sibling Layer with the small image is visible and the sibling Layer with the large image is hidden.

MoveShowcase1() Function that uses the **setTimeout()** Method with the **moveBy()** Method within a conditional **if ()** to animate the parent Layer **Showcase1** into a viewable position.

The next three Functions are all implemented with one click of the Button named **BLargeView1**, which focuses on the first large Art image.

JumpLargeView1() Function that brings the parent Layer **Showcase1** into prominence and changes the **visibility** and **zIndex** Properties of the sibling Layers so that the Layer named **Showcase1Large** with the large image is stacked on top. It also uses the **moveTo()** Method to reposition **Showcase1** to the viewable Coordinates of (120,100).

HideShowLarge1() Function that controls the **visibility** Property of all the Layers and sets the positioning Coordinates for the main parent Layers. Note that this is the same Function that is defined above in the group of Functions associated with the Button named **BPreview1**, but in this case it is called when the **BLargeView1** Button is clicked.

LargeView1() Function that uses the **setTimeout()** Method with the **moveBy()** Method within a conditional **if ()** to progressively reveal the large image contained in the Layer **Showcase1Large**.

Example 3-22	Sample422.html

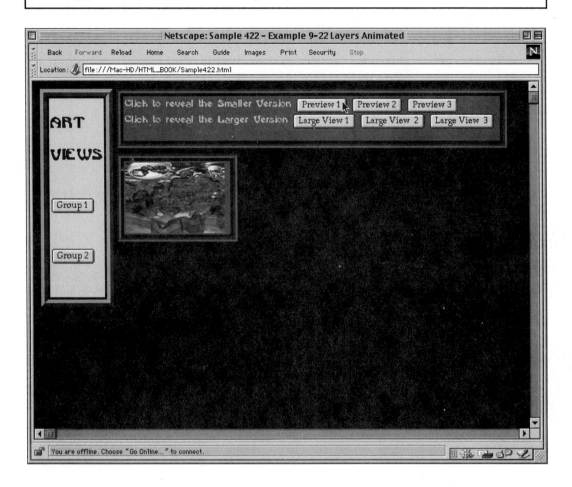

Example 3-22   Sample422.html

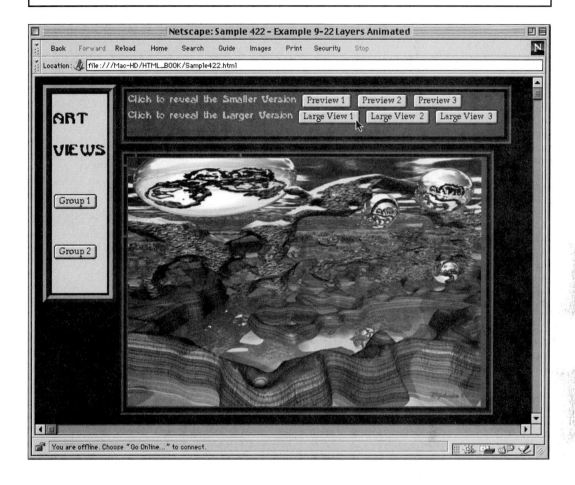

Example 3-22: **Sample422.html**

```
<!DOCTYPE HTML PUBLIC "-//W3C//DTD HTML 3.2//EN">
<HTML>
<HEAD>
<TITLE>Sample 422 - Example 3-22      Layers Animated</TITLE>

<STYLE TYPE="text/JavaScript">

        classes.Blue22.all.fontSize="22pt";
        classes.Blue22.all.color="navy";
        classes.Blue22.all.backgroundColor="aqua";
        classes.Blue22.all.borderWidths("10px");
        classes.Blue22.all.borderStyle="ridge";
        classes.Blue22.all.borderColor="#0077ff";

        with(tags.LAYER) {
                color="lime";
                fontFamily="Moonlight, Helvetica, serif";
                fontSize="14pt";
                borderWidths("7px");
                borderStyle="groove";
                borderColor="#3300ff";
                backgroundColor="#8800ff";
                paddings("2px");
        }

</STYLE>

</HEAD>

<BODY BGCOLOR="black" TEXT="aqua">

<!--  ****************************************************************  -->

<LAYER CLASS="Blue22" ID="layerA" LEFT=10 TOP=10 Z-INDEX=20 WIDTH=100 HEIGHT=500>

<FORM NAME="formA">
                                                               <BR>
        ART                                                    <BR><BR>
        VIEWS                                                  <BR><BR>

        <INPUT TYPE=button NAME="BGroup1" VALUE="Group 1"

                onClick='ShowHideGroup1(); MoveGroup1(); return false;'>   <BR><BR>

        <INPUT TYPE=button NAME="BGroup2" VALUE="Group 2"

                onClick='ShowHideGroup2(); MoveGroup2(); return false;'>   <BR><BR>

        </FORM>

</LAYER>

<!--  ****************************************************************  -->
```

```
<LAYER ID="Group1" LEFT=120 TOP=10 Z-INDEX=10 WIDTH=600 HEIGHT=72>

<FORM NAME="form1">

        Click to reveal the Smaller Version

<INPUT TYPE=button NAME="BPreview1" VALUE="Preview 1"

onClick=' HideShowLarge1(); HideShowSmall1(); MoveShowcase1(); return false;'>

<INPUT TYPE=button NAME="BPreview2" VALUE="Preview 2"

onClick=' HideShowLarge2(); HideShowSmall2(); MoveShowcase2(); return false;'>

<INPUT TYPE=button NAME="BPreview3" VALUE="Preview 3"

onClick=' HideShowLarge3(); HideShowSmall3(); MoveShowcase3(); return false;'><BR>

<!-- ************************************************* -->

        Click to reveal the Larger Version

<INPUT TYPE=button NAME="BLargeView1" VALUE="Large View 1"

onClick='JumpLargeView1(); HideShowLarge1(); LargeView1(); return false;'>

<INPUT TYPE=button NAME="BLargeView2" VALUE="Large View  2"

onClick='JumpLargeView2(); HideShowLarge2(); LargeView2(); return false;'>

<INPUT TYPE=button NAME="BLargeView2" VALUE="Large View  3"

onClick='JumpLargeView3(); HideShowLarge3(); LargeView3(); return false;'>

</FORM>

</LAYER>

<!-- ********************************************************************** -->

<LAYER ID="Group2" LEFT=120 TOP=-110 VISIBILITY="HIDE" Z-INDEX=9 WIDTH=600
HEIGHT=72>

<FORM NAME="form2">

        Click to reveal the Smaller Version

<INPUT TYPE=button NAME="BPreview4" VALUE="Preview 4"

onClick='HideShowLarge4(); HideShowSmall4(); MoveShowcase4(); return false;'>

<INPUT TYPE=button NAME="BPreview5" VALUE="Preview 5"

onClick='HideShowLarge5(); HideShowSmall5(); MoveShowcase5(); return false;'>

<INPUT TYPE=button NAME="BPreview6" VALUE="Preview 6"

onClick='HideShowLarge6(); HideShowSmall6(); MoveShowcase6(); return false;'><BR>
```

```
<!-- ************************************************** -->
        Click to reveal the Larger Version

<INPUT TYPE=button NAME="BLargeView4" VALUE="Large View 4"

onClick='JumpLargeView4(); HideShowLarge4(); LargeView4(); return false;'>

<INPUT TYPE=button NAME="BLargeView5" VALUE="Large View  5"

onClick='JumpLargeView5(); HideShowLarge5(); LargeView5(); return false;'>

<INPUT TYPE=button NAME="BLargeView6" VALUE="Large View  6"

onClick='JumpLargeView6(); HideShowLarge6(); LargeView6(); return false;'>

</FORM>

</LAYER>

<!-- ********************************************************************** -->

<LAYER ID="Showcase1" LEFT=120 TOP=700 VISIBILITY="HIDE" Z-INDEX=19 WIDTH=700
HEIGHT=600>

<LAYER ID="Showcase1Small" Z-INDEX=2>

<IMG SRC="JPEG-FILES/J2-Desert-Arches-2.jpg" ALIGN="ABSMIDDLE" WIDTH=144 HEIGHT=98>

</LAYER>

<LAYER ID="Showcase1Large" Z-INDEX=1 CLIP="0,0,0,0" WIDTH=600>

<IMG SRC="JPEG-FILES/J7-Desert_Arches_2.jpg" ALIGN="ABSMIDDLE" WIDTH=504
HEIGHT=344>

</LAYER>
</LAYER>

<!-- ******************************************************************** -->

<LAYER ID="Showcase2" LEFT=120 TOP=700 VISIBILITY="HIDE" Z-INDEX=18 WIDTH=700
HEIGHT=600>

<LAYER ID="Showcase2Small" Z-INDEX=2>

<IMG SRC="JPEG-FILES/J2-CrystalMtsWinter-14.jpg" ALIGN="ABSMIDDLE" WIDTH=144
HEIGHT=98>

</LAYER>

<LAYER ID="Showcase2Large" Z-INDEX=1 CLIP="0,0,0,0" WIDTH=600>

<IMG SRC="JPEG-FILES/J7-Crystal-Mts-Winter-14.jpg" ALIGN="ABSMIDDLE" WIDTH=504
HEIGHT=344>

</LAYER>
</LAYER>
```

```
<!--    **********************************************************    -->

<LAYER ID="Showcase3" LEFT=1200 TOP=100 VISIBILITY="HIDE" Z-INDEX=17 WIDTH=700
HEIGHT=600>

<LAYER ID="Showcase3Small" Z-INDEX=2>

<IMG SRC="JPEG-FILES/J2-Winter-Arches-15.jpg" ALIGN="ABSMIDDLE" WIDTH=144
HEIGHT=98>

</LAYER>

<LAYER ID="Showcase3Large" Z-INDEX=1 CLIP="0,0,0,0" WIDTH=600>

<IMG SRC="JPEG-FILES/J7-Winter_Arches_15.jpg" ALIGN="ABSMIDDLE" WIDTH=504
HEIGHT=343>

</LAYER>
</LAYER>

<!--    **********************************************************    -->

<LAYER ID="Showcase4" LEFT=120 TOP=700 VISIBILITY="HIDE" Z-INDEX=16 WIDTH=700
HEIGHT=600>

<LAYER ID="Showcase4Small" Z-INDEX=2>

<IMG SRC="JPEG-FILES/J2-SKY_SPHERE_1.jpg" ALIGN="ABSMIDDLE" WIDTH=144 HEIGHT=98>

</LAYER>

<LAYER ID="Showcase4Large" Z-INDEX=1 CLIP="0,0,0,0" WIDTH=600>

<IMG SRC="JPEG-FILES/J5-SKY_SPHERE_1.jpg" ALIGN="ABSMIDDLE" WIDTH=360 HEIGHT=245>

</LAYER>
</LAYER>

<!--    **********************************************************    -->

<LAYER ID="Showcase5" LEFT=120 TOP=700 VISIBILITY="HIDE" Z-INDEX=15 WIDTH=700
HEIGHT=600>

<LAYER ID="Showcase5Small" Z-INDEX=2>

<IMG SRC="JPEG-FILES/J2-SEDONA-SUMMER-7CH.jpg" ALIGN="ABSMIDDLE" WIDTH=144
HEIGHT=99>

</LAYER>

<LAYER ID="Showcase5Large" Z-INDEX=1 CLIP="0,0,0,0" WIDTH=600>

<IMG SRC="JPEG-FILES/J5-SEDONA-SUMMER-7C-HS.jpg" ALIGN="ABSMIDDLE" WIDTH=360
HEIGHT=248>

</LAYER>
</LAYER>
```

```
<!--   ***************************************************************   -->

<LAYER ID="Showcase6" LEFT=120 TOP=700 VISIBILITY="HIDE" Z-INDEX=14 WIDTH=700
HEIGHT=600>

<LAYER ID="Showcase6Small" Z-INDEX=2>

<IMG SRC="JPEG-FILES/J2-MtScape-Spheres-2.jpg" ALIGN="ABSMIDDLE" WIDTH=144
HEIGHT=99>

</LAYER>
<LAYER ID="Showcase6Large" Z-INDEX=1 CLIP="0,0,0,0" WIDTH=600>

<IMG SRC="JPEG-FILES/J7-MtScape_Spheres_2.jpg" ALIGN="ABSMIDDLE" WIDTH=504
HEIGHT=344>

</LAYER>
</LAYER>

<!--   ***************************************************************   -->
<!--   ***************************************************************   -->
<!--   ******   The Next 4 functions control the top layers   *********   -->

<SCRIPT LANGUAGE="JavaScript1.2"><!--BEGIN HIDING

        var Showcase1 = document.Showcase1;
        var Showcase2 = document.Showcase2;
        var Showcase3 = document.Showcase3;
        var Showcase4 = document.Showcase4;
        var Showcase5 = document.Showcase5;
        var Showcase6 = document.Showcase6;

        var Showcase1Small = document.Showcase1.document.Showcase1Small;
        var Showcase2Small = document.Showcase2.document.Showcase2Small;
        var Showcase3Small = document.Showcase3.document.Showcase3Small;
        var Showcase4Small = document.Showcase4.document.Showcase4Small;
        var Showcase5Small = document.Showcase5.document.Showcase5Small;
        var Showcase6Small = document.Showcase6.document.Showcase6Small;

        var Showcase1Large = document.Showcase1.document.Showcase1Large;
        var Showcase2Large = document.Showcase2.document.Showcase2Large;
        var Showcase3Large = document.Showcase3.document.Showcase3Large;
        var Showcase4Large = document.Showcase4.document.Showcase4Large;
        var Showcase5Large = document.Showcase5.document.Showcase5Large;
        var Showcase6Large = document.Showcase6.document.Showcase6Large;

        var Group2 = document.Group2;
        var Group1 = document.Group1;

/*------------------------------------------------------------------*/

function ShowHideGroup1() {

Group2.zIndex=9;        Group2.visibility='hide';        Group2.moveTo(120,-110);
Group1.zIndex=10;       Group1.visibility='show';

return false;
}
```

```
/*--------------------------------------*/

function MoveGroup1() {

                if (document.Group1.top < 10)  {

                        document.Group1.moveBy(0,20);
                        setTimeout('MoveGroup1()', 20);
                }
return false;
}

/*----------------------------------------------------------------*/

function ShowHideGroup2() {

Group2.zIndex=10;       Group2.visibility='show';
Group1.zIndex=8;        Group1.visibility='hide';       Group1.moveTo(120,-110);

return false;
}

/*--------------------------------------*/

function MoveGroup2(Group2) {

                if (document.Group2.top < 10)  {

                        document.Group2.moveBy(0,20);
                        setTimeout('MoveGroup2()', 20);
                }

return false;
}

/*--------------------------------------------------------------------*/
/*--------------------------------------------------------------------*/
/*   The Next 18 functions control the Small and Large images    */

function HideShowSmall1() {

        Showcase1.visibility='show';
        Showcase1Small.visibility='show';
        Showcase1Small.zIndex=2;
        Showcase1Large.visibility='hide';
        Showcase1Large.zIndex=1;
}

/*--------------------------------------*/

function HideShowLarge1() {

        Showcase2.moveTo(120, 700);
        Showcase3.moveTo(1200, 100);   //this is correct
        Showcase4.moveTo(120, 700);
        Showcase5.moveTo(120, 700);
        Showcase6.moveTo(120, 700);
```

```
            Showcase1.visibility='show';
            Showcase2.visibility='hide';
            Showcase3.visibility='hide';
            Showcase4.visibility='hide';
            Showcase5.visibility='hide';
            Showcase6.visibility='hide';

            Showcase1Small.visibility='show';
            Showcase2Small.visibility='hide';
            Showcase3Small.visibility='hide';
            Showcase4Small.visibility='hide';
            Showcase5Small.visibility='hide';
            Showcase6Small.visibility='hide';

            Showcase1Large.visibility='show';
            Showcase2Large.visibility='hide';
            Showcase3Large.visibility='hide';
            Showcase4Large.visibility='hide';
            Showcase5Large.visibility='hide';
            Showcase6Large.visibility='hide';

return false;
}

/*-----------------------------------------*/

function MoveShowcase1() {

            if (document.Showcase1.top > 100)  {

                    document.Showcase1.moveBy(0,-20);
                    setTimeout('MoveShowcase1()', 20);
            }

return false;
}

/*--------------------------------------------------------------------*/

function HideShowSmall2() {

        Showcase2.visibility='show';
        Showcase2Small.visibility='show';
        Showcase2Small.zIndex=2;
        Showcase2Large.visibility='hide';
        Showcase2Large.zIndex=1;
}

/*-----------------------------------------*/

function HideShowLarge2() {

        Showcase1.moveTo(120,700);
        Showcase3.moveTo(1200,100);    //this is correct
        Showcase4.moveTo(120,700);
        Showcase5.moveTo(120,700);
        Showcase6.moveTo(120,700);
```

```
                Showcase1.visibility='hide';
                Showcase2.visibility='show';
                Showcase3.visibility='hide';
                Showcase4.visibility='hide';
                Showcase5.visibility='hide';
                Showcase6.visibility='hide';

                Showcase1Small.visibility='hide';
                Showcase2Small.visibility='show';
                Showcase3Small.visibility='hide';
                Showcase4Small.visibility='hide';
                Showcase5Small.visibility='hide';
                Showcase6Small.visibility='hide';

                Showcase1Large.visibility='hide';
                Showcase2Large.visibility='show';
                Showcase3Large.visibility='hide';
                Showcase4Large.visibility='hide';
                Showcase5Large.visibility='hide';
                Showcase6Large.visibility='hide';

return false;
}

/*----------------------------------------*/

function MoveShowcase2() {

            if (document.Showcase2.top > 100)  {

                    document.Showcase2.moveBy(0,-20);
                    setTimeout('MoveShowcase2()', 20);
            }

return false;
}

/*----------------------------------------*/

function HideShowSmall3() {

        Showcase3.visibility='show';
        Showcase3Small.visibility='show';
        Showcase3Small.zIndex=2;
        Showcase3Large.visibility='hide';
        Showcase3Large.zIndex=1;
}

/*----------------------------------------------------------------*/

function HideShowLarge3() {

        Showcase1.moveTo(120,700);
        Showcase2.moveTo(120,700);
        Showcase4.moveTo(120,700);
        Showcase5.moveTo(120,700);
        Showcase6.moveTo(120,700);
```

```
            Showcase1.visibility='hide';
            Showcase2.visibility='hide';
            Showcase3.visibility='show';
            Showcase4.visibility='hide';
            Showcase5.visibility='hide';
            Showcase6.visibility='hide';

            Showcase1Small.visibility='hide';
            Showcase2Small.visibility='hide';
            Showcase3Small.visibility='show';
            Showcase4Small.visibility='hide';
            Showcase5Small.visibility='hide';
            Showcase6Small.visibility='hide';

            Showcase1Large.visibility='hide';
            Showcase2Large.visibility='hide';
            Showcase3Large.visibility='show';
            Showcase4Large.visibility='hide';
            Showcase5Large.visibility='hide';
            Showcase6Large.visibility='hide';

return false;
}

/*----------------------------------------*/

function MoveShowcase3() {

            if (document.Showcase3.left > 120)  {

                    document.Showcase3.moveBy(-40,0);
                    setTimeout('MoveShowcase3()', 20);
            }

return false;
}

/*---------------------------------------------------------------------*/

function HideShowSmall4() {

        Showcase4.visibility='show';
        Showcase4Small.visibility='show';
        Showcase4Small.zIndex=2;
        Showcase4Large.visibility='hide';
        Showcase4Large.zIndex=1;
}

/*----------------------------------------*/

function HideShowLarge4() {

        Showcase1.moveTo(120,700);
        Showcase2.moveTo(120,700);
        Showcase3.moveTo(1200,100);    //this is correct
        Showcase5.moveTo(120,700);
        Showcase6.moveTo(120,700);
```

```
        Showcase1.visibility='hide';
        Showcase2.visibility='hide';
        Showcase3.visibility='hide';
        Showcase4.visibility='show';
        Showcase5.visibility='hide';
        Showcase6.visibility='hide';

        Showcase1Small.visibility='hide';
        Showcase2Small.visibility='hide';
        Showcase3Small.visibility='hide';
        Showcase4Small.visibility='show';
        Showcase5Small.visibility='hide';
        Showcase6Small.visibility='hide';

        Showcase1Large.visibility='hide';
        Showcase2Large.visibility='hide';
        Showcase3Large.visibility='hide';
        Showcase4Large.visibility='show';
        Showcase5Large.visibility='hide';
        Showcase6Large.visibility='hide';

return false;
}

/*------------------------------------------*/

function MoveShowcase4() {

            if (document.Showcase4.top > 100)   {

                    document.Showcase4.moveBy(0,-20);
                    setTimeout('MoveShowcase4()', 20);
            }

return false;
}

/*----------------------------------------------------------------------*/

function HideShowSmall5() {

      Showcase5.visibility='show';
      Showcase5Small.visibility='show';
      Showcase5Small.zIndex=2;
      Showcase5Large.visibility='hide';
      Showcase5Large.zIndex=1;
}

/*------------------------------------------*/

function HideShowLarge5() {

      Showcase1.moveTo(120,700);
      Showcase2.moveTo(120,700);
      Showcase3.moveTo(1200,100);    //this is correct
      Showcase4.moveTo(120,700);
      Showcase6.moveTo(120,700);
```

```
            Showcase1.visibility='hide';
            Showcase2.visibility='hide';
            Showcase3.visibility='hide';
            Showcase4.visibility='hide';
            Showcase5.visibility='show';
            Showcase6.visibility='hide';

            Showcase1Small.visibility='hide';
            Showcase2Small.visibility='hide';
            Showcase3Small.visibility='hide';
            Showcase4Small.visibility='hide';
            Showcase5Small.visibility='show';
            Showcase6Small.visibility='hide';

            Showcase1Large.visibility='hide';
            Showcase2Large.visibility='hide';
            Showcase3Large.visibility='hide';
            Showcase4Large.visibility='hide';
            Showcase5Large.visibility='show';
            Showcase6Large.visibility='hide';

return false;
}

/*-----------------------------------------*/

function MoveShowcase5() {

            if (document.Showcase5.top > 100)  {

                    document.Showcase5.moveBy(0,-20);
                    setTimeout('MoveShowcase5()', 20);
            }

return false;
}

/*--------------------------------------------------------------------------*/

function HideShowSmall6() {

        Showcase6.visibility='show';
        Showcase6Small.visibility='show';
        Showcase6Small.zIndex=2;
        Showcase6Large.visibility='hide';
        Showcase6Large.zIndex=1;
}

/*-----------------------------------------*/

function HideShowLarge6() {

        Showcase1.moveTo(120,700);
        Showcase2.moveTo(120,700);
        Showcase3.moveTo(1200,100);    //this is correct
        Showcase4.moveTo(120,700);
        Showcase5.moveTo(120,700);
```

```
            Showcase1.visibility='hide';
            Showcase2.visibility='hide';
            Showcase3.visibility='hide';
            Showcase4.visibility='hide';
            Showcase5.visibility='hide';
            Showcase6.visibility='show';

            Showcase1Small.visibility='hide';
            Showcase2Small.visibility='hide';
            Showcase3Small.visibility='hide';
            Showcase4Small.visibility='hide';
            Showcase5Small.visibility='hide';
            Showcase6Small.visibility='show';

            Showcase1Large.visibility='hide';
            Showcase2Large.visibility='hide';
            Showcase3Large.visibility='hide';
            Showcase4Large.visibility='hide';
            Showcase5Large.visibility='hide';
            Showcase6Large.visibility='show';

return false;
}

/*----------------------------------------*/

function MoveShowcase6() {

            if (document.Showcase6.top > 100)  {

                    document.Showcase6.moveBy(0,-20);
                    setTimeout('MoveShowcase6()', 20);
            }

return false;
}

/*----------------------------------------------------------------------*/
/*----------------------------------------------------------------------*/
/*   The Next 12 functions control the main layers with the Large images   */

function JumpLargeView1() {

        Showcase1.visibility='show';
        Showcase1Small.visibility='hide';
        Showcase1Small.zIndex=1;
        Showcase1Large.visibility='show';
        Showcase1Large.zIndex=2;

                    //moves containing layer up if group wasn't clicked first
                    //this is correct, it's coming from left side of the page

            if (Showcase1.top > 100)  {

                    Showcase1.moveTo(120,100);
            }
return false;
}
```

```
/*--------------------------------------------*/

function LargeView1() {

                    //reveals image by resizing the clipping rectangle

            if (Showcase1Large.clip.right < 1000)  {

                    Showcase1Large.resizeBy(7,0);
            }

            if (Showcase1Large.clip.top < 800)  {

                    Showcase1Large.resizeBy(0,5);
            }
setTimeout('LargeView1()', 20);
return false;
}

/*----------------------------------------------------------------------*/

function JumpLargeView2() {

        Showcase2.visibility='show';
        Showcase2Large.visibility='show';
        Showcase2Small.zIndex=1;
        Showcase2Large.zIndex=2;
        Showcase2Small.visibility='hide';

            if (Showcase2.top > 100)  {

                    Showcase2.moveTo(120,100);
            }

return false;
}

/*--------------------------------------------*/

function LargeView2() {

            if (Showcase2Large.clip.right < 1000)  {

                    Showcase2Large.resizeBy(7,0);
            }

            if (Showcase2Large.clip.top < 800)  {

                    Showcase2Large.resizeBy(0,5);
            }
setTimeout('LargeView2()', 20);
return false;
}

/*----------------------------------------------------------------------*/
```

```
/*-----------------------------------------------------------------*/

function JumpLargeView3() {

        Showcase3.visibility='show';
        Showcase3Large.visibility='show';
        Showcase3Small.zIndex=1;
        Showcase3Large.zIndex=2;
        Showcase3Small.visibility='hide';
                                     //this is correct, it's coming from right
                if (Showcase3.left > 120)  {

                        Showcase3.moveTo(120,100);
                }

return false;
}

/*------------------------------------------*/

function LargeView3() {

                if (Showcase3Large.clip.right < 1000)  {

                        Showcase3Large.resizeBy(7,0);
                }
                if (Showcase3Large.clip.top < 800)  {

                        Showcase3Large.resizeBy(0,5);
                }

setTimeout('LargeView3()', 20);
return false;
}



/*-----------------------------------------------------------------*/

function JumpLargeView4() {

        Showcase4.visibility='show';
        Showcase4Large.visibility='show';
        Showcase4Small.zIndex=1;
        Showcase4Large.zIndex=2;
        Showcase4Small.visibility='hide';

                if (Showcase4.top > 100)  {

                        Showcase4.moveTo(120,100);
                }

return false;
}

/*------------------------------------------*/
```

```
/*-------------------------------------------*/

function LargeView4() {

            if (Showcase4Large.clip.right < 1000)  {

                    Showcase4Large.resizeBy(7,0);
            }

            if (Showcase4Large.clip.top < 800)  {

                    Showcase4Large.resizeBy(0,5);
            }

setTimeout('LargeView4()', 20);
return false;
}

/*---------------------------------------------------------------------*/

function JumpLargeView5() {

     Showcase5.visibility='show';
     Showcase5Large.visibility='show';
     Showcase5Small.zIndex=1;
     Showcase5Large.zIndex=2;
     Showcase5Small.visibility='hide';

            if (Showcase5.top > 100)  {

                    Showcase5.moveTo(120,100);
            }

return false;
}

/*-------------------------------------------*/

function LargeView5() {

            if (Showcase5Large.clip.right < 1000)  {

                    Showcase5Large.resizeBy(7,0);
            }

            if (Showcase5Large.clip.top < 800)  {

                    Showcase5Large.resizeBy(0,5);
            }
setTimeout('LargeView5()', 20);
return false;
}

/*-------------------------------------------------------------------*/
```

```
/*----------------------------------------------------------------------*/

function JumpLargeView6() {

        Showcase6.visibility='show';
        Showcase6Large.visibility='show';
        Showcase6Small.zIndex=1;
        Showcase6Large.zIndex=2;
        Showcase6Small.visibility='hide';

                if (Showcase6.top > 100)  {

                        Showcase6.moveTo(120,100);
                }

return false;
}

/*--------------------------------------------*/

function LargeView6() {

                if (Showcase6Large.clip.right < 1000)  {

                        Showcase6Large.resizeBy(7,0);
                }

                if (Showcase6Large.clip.top < 800)  {

                        Showcase6Large.resizeBy(0,5);
                }
setTimeout('LargeView6()', 20);
return false;
}

/*----------------------------------------------------------------------*/

//END HIDING-->
</SCRIPT>

</BODY>
</HTML>
```

The JavaScript <u>setInterval()</u> Method

The **setInterval()** Method has two different structures of syntax. One is used to <u>evaluate an Expression continuously</u> after a specified number of **milliseconds** have elapsed, and the other is used to <u>call a Function continuously</u> after a specified number of **milliseconds** have elapsed.

In the Syntax below, the **anyExpression** Argument specifies the Expression you want to evaluate. In the alternative Syntax, the **functionName** Argument specifies the Name of the Function that you want to call. Any optional Arguments that you need for your Function are specified after the **milliseconds** Argument in a comma-separated list. Your Expression or Function must be inside quote marks or it will be evaluated immediately. The parentheses that follow the **functionName** are required.

After **setInterval()** has been activated, it will continue to fire until you call the **clearInterval()** Method or the Window or Frame is exited by the user, destroyed with the **window.close()** Method, or cleared with the following trio of Methods:

     document.open();, document.write();, document.close();

JavaScript Syntax:

```
setInterval("anyExpression", milliseconds);
setInterval("functionName()", milliseconds[, arg1, ..., argN]);
```

The JavaScript <u>clearInterval()</u> Method

The **clearInterval()** Method is used to cancel a previously initiated call to the **setInterval()** Method that has been assigned to an **intervalID**. For instance, if you have a Function named **myFunction()** that has been created elsewhere, then you assign the **setInterval()** Method to the **myTesterIntervalID**, which can later be called as the Argument for the **clearInterval()** Method like in the following two lines of code:

<u>Mini-Example:</u>

```
myTesterIntervalID = setInterval("myFunction()", 200);
clearInterval(myTesterIntervalID);
```

JavaScript Syntax:

```
clearInterval(intervalID);
```

Three examples to cycle through Background Colors repeatedly

Example 3-23 uses the **setInterval()** Method to repeatedly call the Function **changeColor()**, which uses conditional **if ()** Statements to set up a cycle of changes to the **bgColor Layer** Object Properties for Layers **L1** and **L2**. The **setInterval()** Method is placed inside the **timeColor()** Function, which is called by the **onLoad** Event Handler of the BODY Element so that it starts as soon as the document is fully loaded.

Example 3-23:   **Sample423.html**

```
<!DOCTYPE HTML PUBLIC "-//W3C//DTD HTML 3.2//EN">
<HTML><HEAD>
<TITLE>Sample 423 - Example 3-23     setInterval Method to cycle bgColors</TITLE>
</HEAD>

<BODY onLoad="timeColor();">

<LAYER ID="L1" LEFT=0 TOP=0 WIDTH=40 HEIGHT=400> </LAYER>

<LAYER ID="L2" LEFT=40 TOP=0 WIDTH=400 HEIGHT=40> </LAYER>
<!-- ************************************************************  -->

<SCRIPT LANGUAGE="JavaScript1.2"><!--BEGIN HIDING

     var i=1;

     function changeColor() {

          if (i<9999) {

          document.L1.bgColor = '#ff' + i;
          document.L2.bgColor = '#' + i + 'aa';

          i+=25;
                              //resets i to repeat the cycle
          if (i>=9973) i=1;
          }
     }
/*-----------------------------------------------------------*/

     function timeColor() {
          setInterval('changeColor()', 100);
     }
/*-----------------------------------------------------------*/
//END HIDING-->
</SCRIPT>
</BODY>
</HTML>
```

Examples 3-24 and 3-25 produce exactly the same results but use different coding techniques. Example 3-24 uses the **setInterval()** and **clearInterval()** Methods, while Example 3-25 uses the **setTimeout()** and **clearTimeout()** Methods to animate the background colors of sequential Layers. These two examples will help clarify the differences and tricks that you have to use with these four Methods.

A new Array is created named **colorArray** that has 13 different recognized color names, which are repeated in the same order for a total of 26 Array items. This is because of the way the conditional **if ()** Statement is used in the **changeColor()** Function to cycle through the colors in the Array and assign them to the **bgColor** Property of the eight **Layer** Objects.

The **setInterval()** Method is put inside the **timeColor()** Function, which is then assigned to the **onLoad** Event Handler of the BODY Element that starts the cycle. The **onClick** Event Handler of the Button with Value of "GO" restarts the cycle. The Button with the Value of "STOP" halts the cycle by changing the variable **booleanTest** to false, which kicks in the **clearInterval()** Method inside the **timeColor()** Function.

Example 3-24:   Sample424.html

```
<!DOCTYPE HTML PUBLIC "-//W3C//DTD HTML 3.2//EN">
<HTML>
<HEAD>
<TITLE>Sample 424 - Example9-24      setInterval and clearInterval Methods</TITLE>
</HEAD>

<BODY onLoad="timeColor();">

<LAYER ID="L8" LEFT=20 TOP=200 WIDTH=100 HEIGHT=100>

<FORM NAME="form1">

<INPUT TYPE="button" NAME="b1" VALUE="STOP" onClick="booleanTest=false;">

<INPUT TYPE="button" NAME="b2" VALUE="GO" onClick="booleanTest=true; timeColor();">

</FORM>

</LAYER>

<!-- ****************************************************************** -->

<LAYER ID="L1" LEFT=0 TOP=0 WIDTH=40 HEIGHT=40> </LAYER>

<LAYER ID="L2" LEFT=40 TOP=0 WIDTH=40 HEIGHT=40> </LAYER>

<LAYER ID="L3" LEFT=80 TOP=0 WIDTH=40 HEIGHT=40> </LAYER>

<LAYER ID="L4" LEFT=120 TOP=0 WIDTH=40 HEIGHT=40> </LAYER>

<LAYER ID="L5" LEFT=160 TOP=0 WIDTH=40 HEIGHT=40> </LAYER>
```

```
<LAYER ID="L6" LEFT=200 TOP=0 WIDTH=40 HEIGHT=40> </LAYER>

<LAYER ID="L7" LEFT=240 TOP=0 WIDTH=40 HEIGHT=40> </LAYER>

<LAYER ID="L8" LEFT=280 TOP=0 WIDTH=40 HEIGHT=40> </LAYER>

<!--  ************************************************************  -->

<SCRIPT LANGUAGE="JavaScript1.2"><!--BEGIN HIDING

        var booleanTest=true;
        var i=13;

        colorArray = new Array ('blue','red','yellow','lime','cyan','olive',
'green','steelblue','purple','maroon','orange','navy','black',
                                'blue','red','yellow','lime','cyan','olive',
'green','steelblue','purple','maroon','orange','navy','black');

/*----------------------------------------------------------------------*/

function changeColor() {

        if (booleanTest == true)  {

                if (i<27) {

                document.L1.bgColor = colorArray[i-1];
                document.L2.bgColor = colorArray[i-2];
                document.L3.bgColor = colorArray[i-3];
                document.L4.bgColor = colorArray[i-4];
                document.L5.bgColor = colorArray[i-5];
                document.L6.bgColor = colorArray[i-6];
                document.L7.bgColor = colorArray[i-7];
                document.L8.bgColor = colorArray[i-8];

                i++;

                        if (i==26) i=13;
                }
        }
        else clearInterval(myInterval);
}

/*----------------------------------------------------------------------*/

function timeColor() {

        myInterval = setInterval('changeColor()', 500);
}

/*----------------------------------------------------------------------*/
//END HIDING-->
</SCRIPT>

</BODY>
</HTML>
```

The main difference between Example 3-25 and the last example is that in this example the **setTimeout()** Method is used instead of the **setInterval()** Method and it is contained within the **colorChange()** Function instead of being in the same Function that it calls as an Argument. The **colorChange()** Function is once again called with the **onLoad** Event Handler of the BODY Element and can be called again with the "GO" Button after the "STOP" Button halts the cycle. See page 286 for more information.

Example 3-25: Sample425.html

```
<!DOCTYPE HTML PUBLIC "-//W3C//DTD HTML 3.2//EN">
<HTML>
<HEAD>
<TITLE>Sample 425 - Example 3-25      clearTimeout and setTimeout Methods</TITLE>
</HEAD>

<BODY onLoad="changeColor();">

<LAYER ID="L8" LEFT=20 TOP=200 WIDTH=100 HEIGHT=100>

<FORM NAME="form1">

<INPUT TYPE="button" NAME="b1" VALUE="STOP" onClick="booleanTest=false;">

<INPUT TYPE="button" NAME="b2" VALUE="GO" onClick="booleanTest=true;
changeColor();">

</FORM>

</LAYER>

<!--  **************************************************************  -->

<LAYER ID="L1" LEFT=0 TOP=0 WIDTH=40 HEIGHT=40> </LAYER>

<LAYER ID="L2" LEFT=40 TOP=0 WIDTH=40 HEIGHT=40> </LAYER>

<LAYER ID="L3" LEFT=80 TOP=0 WIDTH=40 HEIGHT=40> </LAYER>

<LAYER ID="L4" LEFT=120 TOP=0 WIDTH=40 HEIGHT=40> </LAYER>

<LAYER ID="L5" LEFT=160 TOP=0 WIDTH=40 HEIGHT=40> </LAYER>

<LAYER ID="L6" LEFT=200 TOP=0 WIDTH=40 HEIGHT=40> </LAYER>

<LAYER ID="L7" LEFT=240 TOP=0 WIDTH=40 HEIGHT=40> </LAYER>

<LAYER ID="L8" LEFT=280 TOP=0 WIDTH=40 HEIGHT=40> </LAYER>

<!--  **************************************************************  -->
```

```
<SCRIPT LANGUAGE="JavaScript1.2"><!--BEGIN HIDING

        var booleanTest=true;
        var i=13;
        myTimeout = setTimeout('changeColor()', 500);

        colorArray = new Array ('blue','red','yellow','lime','cyan','olive',
'green','steelblue','purple','maroon','orange','navy','black',
                        'blue','red','yellow','lime','cyan','olive',
'green','steelblue','purple','maroon','orange','navy','black');

/*-------------------------------------------------------------------*/

function changeColor() {

        if (booleanTest == true)  {

                if (i<27) {

                document.L1.bgColor = colorArray[i-1];
                document.L2.bgColor = colorArray[i-2];
                document.L3.bgColor = colorArray[i-3];
                document.L4.bgColor = colorArray[i-4];
                document.L5.bgColor = colorArray[i-5];
                document.L6.bgColor = colorArray[i-6];
                document.L7.bgColor = colorArray[i-7];
                document.L8.bgColor = colorArray[i-8];

                i++;

                        if (i==26) i=13;
                }
                setTimeout('changeColor()', 500);
        }
        else clearTimeout(myTimeout);
}

//END HIDING-->
</SCRIPT>

</BODY>
</HTML>
```

The following Example 3-26 demonstrates how to load in content for a Layer by using the **src** Property and the **load()** Method to load in External Files that contain images and Layers with JavaScript CLASSes of STYLE attached to them. Notice that the Layers containing the last three large images have different widths, which are specified with the second Argument of the **load()** Method and are always specified in pixels.

Example 3-26 Part 1:   Sample426.html

```
<!DOCTYPE HTML PUBLIC "-//W3C//DTD HTML 3.2//EN">
<HTML>
<HEAD>
<TITLE>Sample 426 - Example 3-26      Layers Loading External Files</TITLE>

<STYLE TYPE="text/JavaScript">

        classes.Lime30.all.color="lime";
        classes.Lime30.all.fontFamily="Moonlight, Helvetica, serif";
        classes.Lime30.all.fontSize="22pt";
        classes.Lime30.all.borderWidths("15px");
        classes.Lime30.all.borderStyle="groove";
        classes.Lime30.all.borderColor="#3300ff";
        classes.Lime30.all.backgroundColor="#8800ff";
        classes.Lime30.all.paddings("2px");

</STYLE>

</HEAD>

<BODY BGCOLOR="black">

<!-- ****************************************************************** -->
<!--   The top layer with the buttons that load the external files   -->

<LAYER CLASS="Lime30" ID="Group1" LEFT=5 TOP=5 WIDTH=700 HEIGHT=72>

<FORM NAME="form1">

            Reveal Art

            <INPUT TYPE=button NAME="BPreview1" VALUE="Previews"

            onClick='LoadPreviews(); return false;'>

<!-- ************************************************** -->

            <INPUT TYPE=button NAME="BLargeView1" VALUE="Art 1"

            onClick='LoadArt1(); return false;'>

            <INPUT TYPE=button NAME="BLargeView2" VALUE="Art  2"

            onClick='LoadArt2(); return false;'>

            <INPUT TYPE=button NAME="BLargeView2" VALUE="Art  3"

            onClick='LoadArt3(); return false;'>

            <INPUT TYPE=button NAME="BLargeView4" VALUE="Art  4"

            onClick='LoadArt4(); return false;'>
```

```
                <INPUT TYPE=button NAME="BLargeView5" VALUE="Art  5"

                onClick='LoadArt5(); return false;'>

                <INPUT TYPE=button NAME="BLargeView6" VALUE="Art  6"

                onClick='LoadArt6(); return false;'>
</FORM>

</LAYER>
<!--  ***************************************************************  -->
<!--  The containing layer that holds images in the external files   -->

<LAYER ID="Showcase1" LEFT=5 TOP=100 WIDTH=700 HEIGHT=600
SRC="Sample426ExternalGroup.html">

</LAYER>
<!--  ***************************************************************  -->

<SCRIPT LANGUAGE="JavaScript1.2"><!--BEGIN HIDING

/*----------------------------------------------------------------------*/
/*  The Next 7 functions load the external files with the images   */

function LoadPreviews() {

        document.Showcase1.src = ('Sample426ExternalGroup.html') ;
}
/*----------------------------------------------------------------------*/

function LoadArt1() {

        document.Showcase1.src = ('Sample426External1.html') ;
}
/*----------------------------------------------------------------------*/

function LoadArt2() {

        document.Showcase1.src = ('Sample426External2.html') ;
}
/*----------------------------------------------------------------------*/

function LoadArt3() {

        document.Showcase1.src = ('Sample426External3.html') ;
}
/*----------------------------------------------------------------------*/

function LoadArt4() {

        document.Showcase1.load('Sample426External4.html', 600) ;
}
/*----------------------------------------------------------------------*/

function LoadArt5() {

        document.Showcase1.load('Sample426External5.html', 600) ;
}
```

```
/*----------------------------------------------------------------*/
function LoadArt6() {

        document.Showcase1.load('Sample426External6.html', 750) ;
}
/*----------------------------------------------------------------*/

//END HIDING-->
</SCRIPT>
</BODY>
</HTML>
```

This is the external file that contains the six small previews of the art.

Example 3-26 Part 2:   Sample426ExternalGroup.html

```
<!DOCTYPE HTML PUBLIC "-//W3C//DTD HTML 3.2//EN">
<HTML>
<HEAD>
<TITLE>
   Sample 426 External Group - Example 3-26 Part 2 Layers in External Files</TITLE>

<STYLE TYPE="text/JavaScript">

        classes.Royalblue30.all.fontSize="30pt";
        classes.Royalblue30.all.color="darkblue";
        classes.Royalblue30.all.borderTopWidth="20px";
        classes.Royalblue30.all.borderRightWidth="20px";
        classes.Royalblue30.all.borderBottomWidth="20px";
        classes.Royalblue30.all.borderLeftWidth="20px";
        classes.Royalblue30.all.borderStyle="groove";
        classes.Royalblue30.all.borderColor="slateblue";
        classes.Royalblue30.all.fontFamily="Moonlight, Helvetica, serif";
        classes.Royalblue30.all.backgroundColor="royalblue";
        classes.Royalblue30.all.paddingTop="10px";
        classes.Royalblue30.all.paddingRight="10px";
        classes.Royalblue30.all.paddingBottom="10px";
        classes.Royalblue30.all.paddingLeft="10px";

</STYLE>
</HEAD>

<BODY>
<LAYER CLASS="Royalblue30">

Art Previews                    <BR><BR>

<IMG SRC="JPEG-FILES/J2-Desert-Arches-2.jpg" WIDTH=144 HEIGHT=98 BORDER=5>

<IMG SRC="JPEG-FILES/J2-CrystalMtsWinter-14.jpg" WIDTH=144 HEIGHT=98 BORDER=5>

<IMG SRC="JPEG-FILES/J2-Winter-Arches-15.jpg" WIDTH=144 HEIGHT=98 BORDER=5>
```

```
<BR><BR>
<IMG SRC="JPEG-FILES/J2-SKY_SPHERE_1.jpg" WIDTH=144 HEIGHT=98 BORDER=5>

<IMG SRC="JPEG-FILES/J2-SEDONA-SUMMER-7CH.jpg" WIDTH=144 HEIGHT=98 BORDER=5>

<IMG SRC="JPEG-FILES/J2-MtScape-Spheres-2.jpg" WIDTH=144 HEIGHT=99 BORDER=5>

</LAYER>

</BODY>
</HTML>
```

This is one of the six external files that contains a large image of the art. The rest of these large images are each in their own external files, which are on the CD-ROM but not in the book because they are so similar. The only difference is obviously the URL of the source image.

Example 3-26 Part 3: Sample426External1.html

```
<!DOCTYPE HTML PUBLIC "-//W3C//DTD HTML 3.2//EN">
<HTML>
<HEAD>
<TITLE>Sample 426 External 1 - Example 3-26A     Layers in External Files</TITLE>

<STYLE TYPE="text/JavaScript">

        classes.Aqua30.all.fontSize="30pt";
        classes.Aqua30.all.color="#0033aa";
        classes.Aqua30.all.borderWidths("15px");
        classes.Aqua30.all.borderStyle="ridge";
        classes.Aqua30.all.borderColor="#0077ff";
        classes.Aqua30.all.fontFamily="Moonlight, Helvetica, serif";
        classes.Aqua30.all.width="100%";
        classes.Aqua30.all.backgroundColor="aqua";

</STYLE>
</HEAD>

<BODY>

<LAYER CLASS="Aqua30">

<IMG SRC="JPEG-FILES/J7-Desert_Arches_2.jpg" WIDTH=504 HEIGHT=344 ALIGN=LEFT>

Desert Arches

</LAYER>

</BODY>
</HTML>
```

Example 3-26   Sample426.html

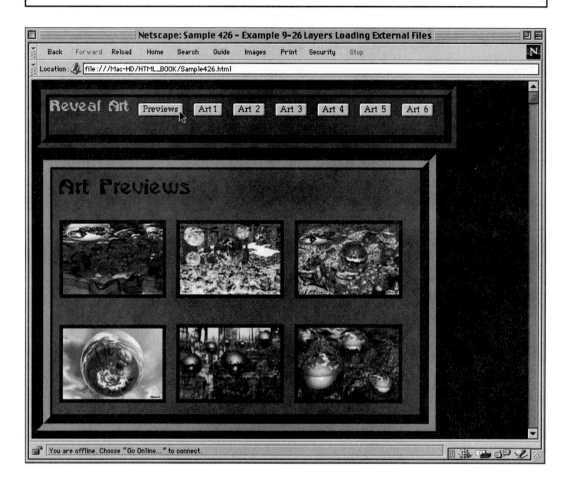

Example 3-26	Sample426.html

A Tic Tac Toe game example

This is the old familiar game of Tic Tac Toe with a twist. The Layers containing the Xs and Os are initially hidden and are animated into view when a Button is clicked in the left Layer named **Control**.

The **revealChoice1X()** through **revealChoice9X()** and **revealChoice1O()** through **revealChoice9O()** Functions control the **visibility** Property and the position coordinates of the Layers.

The **AnimateChoice1X()** through **AnimateChoice9X()** and **AnimateChoice1O()** through **AnimateChoice9O()** Functions control the animation of the Layers with the **moveBy()** and the **setTimeout()** Methods.

The nine Layers that have their BGCOLOR Attribute set to black are used to block out the yellow color of their containing Layer so that the traditional gameboard lines show through. There is another version of this game with a very different programming scheme that allows it to be played from the keyboard. The code for that version is in Chapter 6 on pages 580-585 and can be viewed in the Sample714-TTT-Keys.html file.

Example 3-27:   **Sample427-TTT.html**

```
<!DOCTYPE HTML PUBLIC "-//W3C//DTD HTML 3.2//EN">
<HTML><HEAD>
<TITLE>Sample 427-TTT - Example 3-27       Tic Tac Toe Animated</TITLE>       </HEAD>

        <!--   Note that this example uses CSS Syntax for local Styles on-the-fly      -->

<BODY STYLE='color:white; background-color:black; font-family:Palatino, Moonlight, serif;'>

        <!--   The CONTROL  layer                                                       -->

<LAYER ID="Control" LEFT=5 TOP=5 WIDTH=120 HEIGHT=470 BGCOLOR="LIME">
<FORM NAME="form1">

<SPAN STYLE="font-size:22pt; text-align:center; font-family:Moonlight, cursive;">
<BR><BR>Pick an  <BR>            X or O   <BR>                              </SPAN>  <HR>

<SPAN STYLE="float:center;">

<INPUT TYPE="button" NAME="ChooseX1" VALUE="X1"
onClick='revealChoice1X(); AnimateChoice1X(); return false;'>

<INPUT TYPE="button" NAME="ChooseO1" VALUE="O1"
onClick='revealChoice1O(); AnimateChoice1O(); return false;'>       <BR>

<INPUT TYPE="button" NAME="ChooseX2" VALUE="X2"
onClick='revealChoice2X(); AnimateChoice2X(); return false;'>

<INPUT TYPE="button" NAME="ChooseO2" VALUE="O2"
onClick='revealChoice2O(); AnimateChoice2O(); return false;'>       <BR>

<INPUT TYPE="button" NAME="ChooseX3" VALUE="X3"
onClick='revealChoice3X(); AnimateChoice3X(); return false;'>

<INPUT TYPE="button" NAME="ChooseO3" VALUE="O3"
onClick='revealChoice3O(); AnimateChoice3O(); return false;'>       <BR><BR>       <HR>
```

```
<INPUT TYPE="button" NAME="ChooseX3" VALUE="X4"
onClick='revealChoice4X(); AnimateChoice4X(); return false;'>

<INPUT TYPE="button" NAME="ChooseO3" VALUE="O4"
onClick='revealChoice4O(); AnimateChoice4O(); return false;'>        <BR>

<INPUT TYPE="button" NAME="ChooseX3" VALUE="X5"
onClick='revealChoice5X(); AnimateChoice5X(); return false;'>

<INPUT TYPE="button" NAME="ChooseO3" VALUE="O5"
onClick='revealChoice5O(); AnimateChoice5O(); return false;'>        <BR>

<INPUT TYPE="button" NAME="ChooseX3" VALUE="X6"
onClick='revealChoice6X(); AnimateChoice6X(); return false;'>

<INPUT TYPE="button" NAME="ChooseO3" VALUE="O6"
onClick='revealChoice6O(); AnimateChoice6O(); return false;'>        <BR><BR>        <HR>

<INPUT TYPE="button" NAME="ChooseX3" VALUE="X7"
onClick='revealChoice7X(); AnimateChoice7X(); return false;'>

<INPUT TYPE="button" NAME="ChooseO3" VALUE="O7"
onClick='revealChoice7O(); AnimateChoice7O(); return false;'>        <BR>

<INPUT TYPE="button" NAME="ChooseX3" VALUE="X8"
onClick='revealChoice8X(); AnimateChoice8X(); return false;'>

<INPUT TYPE="button" NAME="ChooseO3" VALUE="O8"
onClick='revealChoice8O(); AnimateChoice8O(); return false;'>        <BR>

<INPUT TYPE="button" NAME="ChooseX3" VALUE="X9"
onClick='revealChoice9X(); AnimateChoice9X(); return false;'>

<INPUT TYPE="button" NAME="ChooseO3" VALUE="O9"
onClick='revealChoice9O(); AnimateChoice9O(); return false;'>        <BR><BR>        <HR>

<INPUT TYPE="button" NAME="StartOver" VALUE="New Game" onClick='StartGame(); return false;'>

</SPAN>
</FORM>
</LAYER>

<!--   The containing layer              -->

<LAYER ID="MainBoard" LEFT=150 TOP=5 WIDTH=470 HEIGHT=470 BGCOLOR="YELLOW">

<!-- The 9 Layers that black out the main Grid to reveal only the Grid Bars    -->

<LAYER LEFT=0 TOP=0 WIDTH=150 HEIGHT=150 BGCOLOR="black"></LAYER>

<LAYER LEFT=160 TOP=0 WIDTH=150 HEIGHT=150 BGCOLOR="black"></LAYER>

<LAYER LEFT=320 TOP=0 WIDTH=150 HEIGHT=150 BGCOLOR="black"></LAYER>

<LAYER LEFT=0 TOP=160 WIDTH=150 HEIGHT=150 BGCOLOR="black"></LAYER>

<LAYER LEFT=160 TOP=160 WIDTH=150 HEIGHT=150 BGCOLOR="black"></LAYER>

<LAYER LEFT=320 TOP=160 WIDTH=150 HEIGHT=150 BGCOLOR="black"></LAYER>

<LAYER LEFT=0 TOP=320 WIDTH=150 HEIGHT=150 BGCOLOR="black"></LAYER>

<LAYER LEFT=160 TOP=320 WIDTH=150 HEIGHT=150 BGCOLOR="black"></LAYER>

<LAYER LEFT=320 TOP=320 WIDTH=150 HEIGHT=150 BGCOLOR="black"></LAYER>
<!--   **************************************************************   -->
```

```
<!-- ***************************************************************** -->


<!-- The 18 Layers that make up the grid with the X and O letters  -->

<LAYER ID="Grid1X" LEFT=0 TOP=0 WIDTH=150 HEIGHT=150 BGCOLOR="blue" VISIBILITY="hide">
<SPAN STYLE="color:white; font-size:115pt; text-align:center;">X</SPAN>
</LAYER>

<LAYER ID="Grid1O" LEFT=0 TOP=0 WIDTH=150 HEIGHT=150 BGCOLOR="red" VISIBILITY="hide">
<SPAN STYLE="color:navy; font-size:115pt; text-align:center;">O</SPAN>
</LAYER>

<!-- ***************************************************************** -->

<LAYER ID="Grid2X" LEFT=160 TOP=0 WIDTH=150 HEIGHT=150 BGCOLOR="blue" VISIBILITY="hide">
<SPAN STYLE="color:white; font-size:115pt; text-align:center;">     X</SPAN>
</LAYER>

<LAYER ID="Grid2O" LEFT=160 TOP=0 WIDTH=150 HEIGHT=150 BGCOLOR="red" VISIBILITY="hide">
<SPAN STYLE="color:navy; font-size:115pt; text-align:center;">O</SPAN>
</LAYER>

<!-- ***************************************************************** -->

<LAYER ID="Grid3X" LEFT=320 TOP=0 WIDTH=150 HEIGHT=150 BGCOLOR="blue" VISIBILITY="hide">
<SPAN STYLE="color:white; font-size:115pt; text-align:center;">X</SPAN>
</LAYER>

<LAYER ID="Grid3O" LEFT=320 TOP=0 WIDTH=150 HEIGHT=150 BGCOLOR="red" VISIBILITY="hide">
<SPAN STYLE="color:navy; font-size:115pt; text-align:center;">O</SPAN>
</LAYER>

<!-- ***************************************************************** -->

<LAYER ID="Grid4X" LEFT=0 TOP=160 WIDTH=150 HEIGHT=150 BGCOLOR="blue" VISIBILITY="hide">
<SPAN STYLE="color:white; font-size:115pt; text-align:center;">X</SPAN>
</LAYER>

<LAYER ID="Grid4O" LEFT=0 TOP=160 WIDTH=150 HEIGHT=150 BGCOLOR="red" VISIBILITY="hide">
<SPAN STYLE="color:navy; font-size:115pt; text-align:center;">O</SPAN>
</LAYER>

<!-- ***************************************************************** -->

<LAYER ID="Grid5X" LEFT=160 TOP=160 WIDTH=150 HEIGHT=150 BGCOLOR="blue" VISIBILITY="hide">
<SPAN STYLE="color:white; font-size:115pt; text-align:center;">X</SPAN>
</LAYER>

<LAYER ID="Grid5O" LEFT=160 TOP=160 WIDTH=150 HEIGHT=150 BGCOLOR="red" VISIBILITY="hide">
<SPAN STYLE="color:navy; font-size:115pt; text-align:center;">O</SPAN>
</LAYER>

<!-- ***************************************************************** -->

<LAYER ID="Grid6X" LEFT=320 TOP=160 WIDTH=150 HEIGHT=150 BGCOLOR="blue" VISIBILITY="hide">
<SPAN STYLE="color:white; font-size:115pt; text-align:center;">X</SPAN>
</LAYER>

<!-- ***************************************************************** -->
<!-- ***************************************************************** -->

<LAYER ID="Grid6O" LEFT=320 TOP=160 WIDTH=150 HEIGHT=150 BGCOLOR="red" VISIBILITY="hide">
<SPAN STYLE="color:navy; font-size:115pt; text-align:center;">O     </SPAN>
</LAYER>
```

```
<!--   ****************************************************************   -->

<LAYER ID="Grid7X" LEFT=0 TOP=320 WIDTH=150 HEIGHT=150 BGCOLOR="blue" VISIBILITY="hide">
<SPAN STYLE="color:white; font-size:115pt; text-align:center;">X</SPAN>
</LAYER>

<LAYER ID="Grid7O" LEFT=0 TOP=320 WIDTH=150 HEIGHT=150 BGCOLOR="red" VISIBILITY="hide">
<SPAN STYLE="color:navy; font-size:115pt; text-align:center;">O</SPAN>
</LAYER>

<!--   ****************************************************************   -->

<LAYER ID="Grid8X" LEFT=160 TOP=320 WIDTH=150 HEIGHT=150 BGCOLOR="blue" VISIBILITY="hide">
<SPAN STYLE="color:white; font-size:115pt; text-align:center;">X</SPAN>
</LAYER>

<LAYER ID="Grid8O" LEFT=160 TOP=320 WIDTH=150 HEIGHT=150 BGCOLOR="red" VISIBILITY="hide">
<SPAN STYLE="color:navy; font-size:115pt; text-align:center;">O</SPAN>
</LAYER>

<!--   ****************************************************************   -->

<LAYER ID="Grid9X" LEFT=320 TOP=320 WIDTH=150 HEIGHT=150 BGCOLOR="blue" VISIBILITY="hide">
<SPAN STYLE="color:white; font-size:115pt; text-align:center;">X</SPAN>
</LAYER>

<LAYER ID="Grid9O" LEFT=320 TOP=320 WIDTH=150 HEIGHT=150 BGCOLOR="red" VISIBILITY="hide">
<SPAN STYLE="color:navy; font-size:115pt; text-align:center;">O</SPAN>
</LAYER>
<!--   ****************************************************************   -->
</LAYER>

<!--   ****************************************************************   -->
<!--   ****************************************************************   -->
<SCRIPT LANGUAGE="JavaScript1.2"><!--BEGIN HIDING

/*----------------------------------------------------------------------*/
/*-----  This section deals with the Functions to show the X and O letters  ------*/

var Grid1X = document.MainBoard.document.Grid1X;
var Grid1O = document.MainBoard.document.Grid1O;

var Grid2X = document.MainBoard.document.Grid2X;
var Grid2O = document.MainBoard.document.Grid2O;

var Grid3X = document.MainBoard.document.Grid3X;
var Grid3O = document.MainBoard.document.Grid3O;

var Grid4X = document.MainBoard.document.Grid4X;
var Grid4O = document.MainBoard.document.Grid4O;

var Grid5X = document.MainBoard.document.Grid5X;
var Grid5O = document.MainBoard.document.Grid5O;
var Grid6X = document.MainBoard.document.Grid6X;
var Grid6O = document.MainBoard.document.Grid6O;

var Grid7X = document.MainBoard.document.Grid7X;
var Grid7O = document.MainBoard.document.Grid7O;

var Grid8X = document.MainBoard.document.Grid8X;
var Grid8O = document.MainBoard.document.Grid8O;

var Grid9X = document.MainBoard.document.Grid9X;
var Grid9O = document.MainBoard.document.Grid9O;

/*-------------------------------------------------------------*/
```

```
/*----------------------------------------------------------*/

function revealChoice1X () {

                Grid1X.visibility="show";
                Grid1O.visibility="hide";
                Grid1X.moveTo(-160,0);
}

function AnimateChoice1X() {

        if (Grid1X.left < 0)  {

                Grid1X.moveBy(20,0);
                setTimeout('AnimateChoice1X()', 20);
        }
return false;
}

/*----------------------------------------*/

function revealChoice1O () {

                Grid1O.visibility="show";
                Grid1X.visibility="hide";
                Grid1O.moveTo(-160,0);
}

function AnimateChoice1O() {

        if (Grid1O.left < 0)  {

                Grid1O.moveBy(20,0);
                setTimeout('AnimateChoice1O()', 20);
        }
return false;
}

/*------------------------------------------------------*/

function revealChoice2X () {

                Grid2X.visibility="show";
                Grid2O.visibility="hide";
                Grid2X.moveTo(160,-160);
}

function AnimateChoice2X() {

        if (Grid2X.top < 0)  {

                Grid2X.moveBy(0,20);
                setTimeout('AnimateChoice2X()', 20);
        }
return false;
}

/*----------------------------------------*/

function revealChoice2O () {

                Grid2O.visibility="show";
                Grid2X.visibility="hide";
                Grid2O.moveTo(160,-160);
}
```

```
function AnimateChoice2O() {

                if (Grid2O.top < 0)  {

                        Grid2O.moveBy(0,20);
                        setTimeout('AnimateChoice2O()', 20);
                }
return false;
}

/*---------------------------------------------------------*/

function revealChoice3X () {

                Grid3X.visibility="show";
                Grid3O.visibility="hide";
                Grid3X.moveTo(320,-160);
}

function AnimateChoice3X() {

                if (Grid3X.top < 0)  {

                        Grid3X.moveBy(0,20);
                        setTimeout('AnimateChoice3X()', 20);
                }
return false;
}

/*-------------------------------------*/

function revealChoice3O () {

                Grid3O.visibility="show";
                Grid3X.visibility="hide";
                Grid3O.moveTo(320,-160);
}

function AnimateChoice3O() {

                if (Grid3O.top < 0)  {

                        Grid3O.moveBy(0,20);
                        setTimeout('AnimateChoice3O()', 20);
                }
return false;
}

/*----------------------------------------------------------*/

function revealChoice4X () {
                Grid4X.visibility="show";
                Grid4O.visibility="hide";
                Grid4X.moveTo(-160,160);
}

function AnimateChoice4X() {

                if (Grid4X.left < 0)  {

                        Grid4X.moveBy(20,0);
                        setTimeout('AnimateChoice4X()', 20);
                }
return false;
}
/*-------------------------------------*/
```

```
/*-----------------------------------------*/

function revealChoice4O () {

                Grid4O.visibility="show";
                Grid4X.visibility="hide";
                Grid4O.moveTo(-160,160);
}

function AnimateChoice4O() {

                if (Grid4O.left < 0)  {

                        Grid4O.moveBy(20,0);
                        setTimeout('AnimateChoice4O()', 20);
                }
return false;
}

/*-------------------------------------------------------*/

function revealChoice5X () {

                Grid5X.visibility="show";
                Grid5O.visibility="hide";
                Grid5X.moveTo(-160,160);
}

function AnimateChoice5X() {

                if (Grid5X.left < 160)  {

                        Grid5X.moveBy(20,0);
                        setTimeout('AnimateChoice5X()', 20);
                }
return false;
}

/*-----------------------------------------*/

function revealChoice5O () {

                Grid5O.visibility="show";
                Grid5X.visibility="hide";
                Grid5O.moveTo(-160,160);
}

function AnimateChoice5O() {

                if (Grid5O.left < 160)  {
                        Grid5O.moveBy(20,0);
                        setTimeout('AnimateChoice5O()', 20);
                }
return false;
}

/*-------------------------------------------------------*/

function revealChoice6X () {

                Grid6X.visibility="show";
                Grid6O.visibility="hide";
                Grid6X.moveTo(480,160);
}
```

```
function AnimateChoice6X() {

                if (Grid6X.left > 320)  {

                        Grid6X.moveBy(-20,0);
                        setTimeout('AnimateChoice6X()', 20);
                }
return false;
}

/*--------------- -----------------------------*/

function revealChoice6O () {

                Grid6O.visibility="show";
                Grid6X.visibility="hide";
                Grid6O.moveTo(480,160);
}

function AnimateChoice6O() {

                if (Grid6O.left > 320)  {

                        Grid6O.moveBy(-20,0);
                        setTimeout('AnimateChoice6O()', 20);
                }
return false;
}

/*-------------------------------------------------------*/

function revealChoice7X () {

                Grid7X.visibility="show";
                Grid7O.visibility="hide";
                Grid7X.moveTo(-160,320);
}

function AnimateChoice7X() {

                if (Grid7X.left < 0)  {

                        Grid7X.moveBy(20,0);
                        setTimeout('AnimateChoice7X()', 20);
                }
return false;
}

/*-----------------------------------------*/

function revealChoice7O () {

                Grid7O.visibility="show";
                Grid7X.visibility="hide";
                Grid7O.moveTo(-160,320);
}

function AnimateChoice7O() {

                if (Grid7O.left < 0)  {

                        Grid7O.moveBy(20,0);
                        setTimeout('AnimateChoice7O()', 20);
                }
return false;
}
```

```
/*----------------------------------------------------------*/

function revealChoice8X () {

                Grid8X.visibility="show";
                Grid8O.visibility="hide";
                Grid8X.moveTo(160,480);
}

function AnimateChoice8X() {

                if (Grid8X.top > 320)  {

                        Grid8X.moveBy(0,-20);
                        setTimeout('AnimateChoice8X()', 20);
                }
return false;
}

/*------------------------------------------*/

function revealChoice8O () {

                Grid8O.visibility="show";
                Grid8X.visibility="hide";
                Grid8O.moveTo(160,480);
}

function AnimateChoice8O() {

                if (Grid8O.top > 320)  {

                        Grid8O.moveBy(0,-20);
                        setTimeout('AnimateChoice8O()', 20);
                }
return false;
}

/*----------------------------------------------------------*/

function revealChoice9X () {

                Grid9X.visibility="show";
                Grid9O.visibility="hide";
                Grid9X.moveTo(480,320);
}

function AnimateChoice9X() {

                if (Grid9X.left > 320)  {

                        Grid9X.moveBy(-20,0);
                        setTimeout('AnimateChoice9X()', 20);
                }
return false;
}

/*------------------------------------------*/

function revealChoice9O () {

                Grid9O.visibility="show";
                Grid9X.visibility="hide";
                Grid9O.moveTo(480,320);
}
```

```
function AnimateChoice90() {

              if (Grid90.left > 320)  {

                      Grid90.moveBy(-20,0);
                      setTimeout('AnimateChoice90()', 20);
              }
return false;
}

/*----------------------------------------------------------*/

function StartGame() {

        Grid1X.visibility="hide"; Grid10.visibility="hide";
        Grid2X.visibility="hide"; Grid20.visibility="hide";
        Grid3X.visibility="hide"; Grid30.visibility="hide";
        Grid4X.visibility="hide"; Grid40.visibility="hide";
        Grid5X.visibility="hide"; Grid50.visibility="hide";
        Grid6X.visibility="hide"; Grid60.visibility="hide";
        Grid7X.visibility="hide"; Grid70.visibility="hide";
        Grid8X.visibility="hide"; Grid80.visibility="hide";
        Grid9X.visibility="hide"; Grid90.visibility="hide";
}

//END HIDING-->
</SCRIPT>

</BODY>

</HTML>
```

Example 3-27	Sample427.html

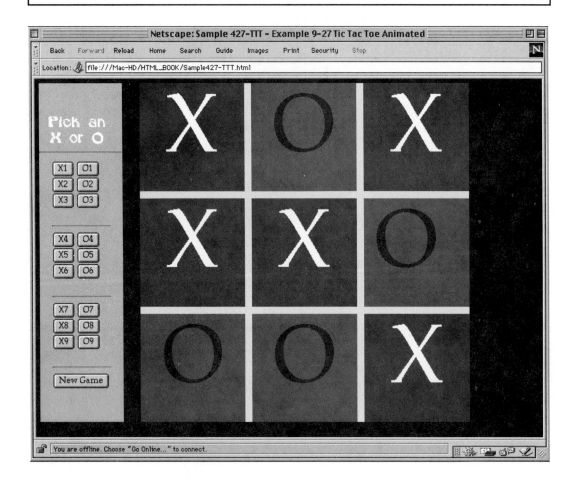

The JavaScript <u>Date</u> Object

The **Date** Object provides a group of Methods to work with dates and times. JavaScript stores **Date** Objects internally as the number of milliseconds that have elapsed since midnight of January 1, 1970. Consequently, when you want to manipulate **Date** data you have to dust off the math cobwebs in your synapses to get useful output. Dates prior to January 1, 1970, are not allowed in JavaScript 1.2, but they are in version 1.3.

The Property and Methods of the **Date** Object that are available for JavaScript1.2 are listed below. Note that in Chapter 10, starting on page 863, there are additional Methods available for the **Date** Object in JavaScript1.3. Also see pages 862-879.

Date Property	Property Description
prototype	Allows you to add and assign your own Properties and Methods when creating a new instance of the **Date** Object.

Date Method	Method Description/Results
getDate()	Returns the day of the month for the specified **Date** Object.
getDay()	Returns the day of the week for the specified **Date** Object.
getHours()	Returns the hour of the specified **Date** Object.
getMinutes()	Returns the minutes of the specified **Date** Object.
getMonth()	Returns the month of the specified **Date** Object.
getSeconds()	Returns the seconds of the specified **Date** Object.
getTime()	Returns the numeric value corresponding to the time for the specified **Date** Object.
getTimezoneOffset()	Returns the time-zone offset in minutes of the specified **Date** Object for the current geographic locale.
getYear()	Returns the year of the specified **Date** Object.
parse()	Returns the number of milliseconds of a **Date** Object String since January 1, 1970, 00:00:00, local time.
setDate(integer)	Sets the day of the month for a specified **Date** Object.
setHours(integer)	Sets the hours for a specified **Date** Object.
setMinutes(integer)	Sets the minutes for a specified **Date** Object.
setMonth(integer)	Sets the month for a specified **Date** Object.
setSeconds(integer)	Sets the seconds for a specified **Date** Object.
setTime(integer)	Sets the value of a **Date** object.
setYear(integer)	Sets the year for a specified **Date** Object.
toGMTString()	Converts a **Date** Object to a String, using the Internet GMT conventions.
toLocaleString()	Converts a **Date** Object to a String, using the current geographic locale's conventions.
UTC()	Returns the number of milliseconds of a **Date** Object since January 1, 1970, 00:00:00, Universal Coordinated Time (GMT).

Creating Date Objects with the four Date Constructors

There are four different **Date Constructors** that you can use to create an instance of the **Date** Object and they are listed below. If you supply no Arguments, then the default version is used with the current date and time in GMT format. The second **Date Constructor** takes a **String** as the Argument in the format listed in the syntax or recognized by the Static **parse()** Method. The third and fourth **Date Constructors** take **integers** as Arguments. The **hours**, **minutes**, and **seconds** Arguments are optional, and zero, if omitted.

Date Constructors Syntax:

```
new Date()                                        //default version
new Date("month day, year [hours:minutes:seconds]")   //String Values
new Date(year, month, day)                        //Integer Values
new Date(year, month, day[, hours, minutes, seconds])   //Integer Values
```

Creating a Time Counter & Displaying the Current Time

Example 3-28 is a simple example that creates a display with the current date and time and the elapsed time that the user has been at the site.

The **initializeTime()** Function constructs a new instance of the **Date** Object with the **new** Operator and the **Date()** Constructor and converts it from the number of milliseconds that have elapsed since January 1, 1970, to a usable format in general use for any particular geographical region by using the **toLocaleString()** Method. It is then assigned to the **value** Property of the Textfield named **TextTime** by calling the **output()** Function. Then the process is repeated so that the time is updated every second by using the **setTimeout()** Method, which calls the **initializeTime()** Function every 1000 milliseconds, which is, of course, every second.

Finally the **BeenHereXT()** Function constructs a new instance of the **Date** Object named **later**, which is always the current time because the **setTimeout()** Method causes a new **Date** Object to be constructed each time it calls the **BeenHereXT()** Function, which is once per second.

There is a third instance of the **Date** Object, named **startTime**, which is constructed when the document loads and remains unchanged. By subtracting **startTime** from **later**, you get the elapsed time that the user has been at the site, which is assigned to the **value** Property of the Textfield named **Visited**. You divide that number by 60000 to convert it from milliseconds to minutes (60 seconds x 1000 milliseconds = 1 minute).

The **setTimeout()** Method updates the elapsed time spent at the site every minute by setting the **milliseconds** Argument to 60000. It calls the **BeenHereXT()** Function, which in turn calls the **visitedUs()** Function, which updates the **Visited** textfield's Value with the **TimeHere** variable.

Note that the **Date** Object by default displays time in the 24-hour military format where 2 PM would be 14, which is how the time is displayed in this example. To get the time into a more familiar format, you have to use some creative coding, which is demonstrated in Example 3-30.

Example 3-28:   **Sample428.html**

```
<!DOCTYPE HTML PUBLIC "-//W3C//DTD HTML 3.2//EN">
<HTML>
<HEAD>
<TITLE>Sample 428 - Example 3-28    Time Counter        </TITLE>

<STYLE TYPE="text/JavaScript">

        tags.BODY.backgroundColor="black";

        classes.Patrol.all.fontSize="24pt";
        classes.Patrol.all.fontFamily="Moonlight, fantasy";
        classes.Patrol.all.color="blue";
        classes.Patrol.all.backgroundColor="#8800ff";
</STYLE>
</HEAD>
<!-- ************************************************ -->
<BODY>
<DIV ALIGN=LEFT CLASS="Patrol">

<FORM NAME="formA">            Hi            <BR>    the Time is:   <BR>
<INPUT TYPE="text" SIZE="22" NAME="TextTime" VALUE="">          <BR>

        You've been    <BR>    here for:            <BR>

<INPUT TYPE="text" SIZE="22" NAME="Visited" VALUE="">           <BR>

            Minutes
</FORM>
</DIV>
<!-- ***************************************************************** -->

<SCRIPT LANGUAGE="JavaScript1.2"><!--BEGIN HIDING

        startTime = new Date();

function output(t) {

        document.formA.TextTime.value=t;
}
/*-------------------------------------------*/
function visitedUs(t2) {

        document.formA.Visited.value=t2;
}
/*-------------------------------------------*/
function initializeTime()  {

        var today = new Date();
        var todayDateTime = today.toLocaleString();
        output (todayDateTime);

        setTimeout('initializeTime()', 1000);
}
```

```
/*-------------------------------------------*/

function BeenHereXT() {

        var later = new Date();
        var TimeHere = Math.round( (later - startTime) / 60000 );

        visitedUs (TimeHere);

        setTimeout('BeenHereXT()', 60000);
}
/*-------------------------------------------*/

                initializeTime();
                BeenHereXT();

//END HIDING-->
</SCRIPT>
</BODY>
</HTML>
```

Creating a Time Counter and Displaying the Current Time in a Frameset

Example 3-29 expands on the previous example by using the **write()** Method, in **parent.display.document.write()**, to dynamically write HTML content, JavaScript Style Syntax, and JavaScript to an external document in a Frame that is contained in the current FRAMESET. In the previous sentence, **parent** calls the container FRAMESET for **display**, and **display** is the name of the FRAME that contains the **document** that you want to **write()** to. The external document with URL of Sample429A.html is just a blank document used as a placeholder for the SRC Attribute of the FRAME, which can't be omitted. All of its content is dynamically generated by the JavaScript code in Sample429.html. The **outputTime(t)** and **initializeTime()** Functions are the heart of this example.

outputTime(t)   This Function uses the **parent.display.document.write()** Method to create the HTML code and JavaScript Styles and then takes the Argument **t** and renders it into the document contained in the FRAME named **display** when it is called by the **initializeTime()** Function.

initializeTime()   This Function has three main differences from the way it was used in the previous example. First, it has a conditional **if ()**, which slows down or speeds up the refresh rate of the **setTimeout()** Method based on whether any of the checkbox Elements are on or off. Second, it has HTML FONT Elements to change the color of the 'Been Here' text to 'red'. Third, the two variables **todayDateTime** and **TimeHere** that contain the text Strings are rendered with the Styles supplied by the **outputTime(t)** Function instead of to the Value parameter of a Textfield. This Function is called as the only item in the SCRIPT Element contained in the BODY Element.

Programming Tips when using the <u>write()</u> Method

There are a couple of things to watch out for when you design your own pages if you're relatively new to JavaScript. First, when you use the **document.write()** Method, you have to make sure that the code between the quotes is all on one line in your text editor or you will likely get some kind of incomprehensible error.

If you have long code to write either break it up into smaller chunks or if that isn't preferred, at least make sure that your text editor isn't soft-wrapping your text because that will cause a problem (in most other circumstances it wouldn't). If you're using BBEdit, go into the Window Options in the Edit Menu and uncheck the 'Soft Wrap Text' checkbox. If you aren't using BBEdit, then you're wasting a lot of your own time.

You will also have to use either single or double quotes to contain the String within the parentheses and the opposite type of quotes for your Attribute Values and/or Property Values contained within the String.

See page 197 for a frequently overlooked, but essential, use of the back-slash (\) character within the **write()** Method.

Example 3-29 Part 1:   Sample429.html

```
<!DOCTYPE HTML PUBLIC "-//W3C//DTD HTML 3.2//EN">
<HTML>
<HEAD>
<TITLE>Sample 429 - Example 3-29    Time Counter     </TITLE>

<STYLE TYPE="text/JavaScript">

        classes.Mainbody.BODY.margins("0px");
        classes.Mainbody.BODY.paddings("0px");
        classes.Mainbody.BODY.backgroundColor="black";
        classes.Mainbody.BODY.color="white";

        classes.SteelBlu.all.margins("0px");
        classes.SteelBlu.all.backgroundColor="steelblue";
        classes.SteelBlu.all.color="navy";
        classes.SteelBlu.all.width="700";
        classes.SteelBlu.all.fontSize="22pt";
        classes.SteelBlu.all.fontFamily="Clarendon, Helvetica, serif";
        classes.SteelBlu.all.paddings("7px");
        classes.SteelBlu.all.borderTopWidth="10px";
        classes.SteelBlu.all.borderRightWidth="30px";
        classes.SteelBlu.all.borderBottomWidth="10px";
        classes.SteelBlu.all.borderLeftWidth="30px";
        classes.SteelBlu.all.borderStyle="inset";
        classes.SteelBlu.all.borderColor="#5555ff";
        classes.SteelBlu.all.lineHeight="28pt";

        classes.RedBox.P.backgroundColor="red";
        classes.RedBox.P.fontSize="17pt";

</STYLE>
```

```
<!--    ***************************************************************    -->

<SCRIPT LANGUAGE="JavaScript1.2"><!--BEGIN HIDING

function outputTime(t){

//Note that you don't have to use the document.open() Method because the
//write() Method does an implicit open for the MIME type for HTML and text.

parent.display.document.write("<HTML><HEAD><TITLE>")
parent.display.document.write("<CLOCK DISPLAY>")
parent.display.document.write("<\/TITLE>")

parent.display.document.write("<STYLE TYPE='text/JavaScript'>")

parent.display.document.write("classes.Mainbody.BODY.margins('0px');")
parent.display.document.write("classes.Mainbody.BODY.paddings('0px');")
parent.display.document.write("classes.Mainbody.BODY.backgroundColor='black';")
parent.display.document.write("classes.Mainbody.BODY.color='white';")

parent.display.document.write("classes.SteelBlu.all.margins('0px');")
parent.display.document.write("classes.SteelBlu.all.backgroundColor='darkblue';")
parent.display.document.write("classes.SteelBlu.all.color='cyan';")
parent.display.document.write("classes.SteelBlu.all.width='700';")
parent.display.document.write("classes.SteelBlu.all.fontSize='24pt';")
parent.display.document.write("classes.SteelBlu.all.fontFamily='Moonlight,
                                          Clarendon, Helvetica, serif';")
parent.display.document.write("classes.SteelBlu.all.paddings('7px');")
parent.display.document.write("classes.SteelBlu.all.borderTopWidth='15px';")
parent.display.document.write("classes.SteelBlu.all.borderRightWidth='40px';")
parent.display.document.write("classes.SteelBlu.all.borderBottomWidth='15px';")
parent.display.document.write("classes.SteelBlu.all.borderLeftWidth='40px';")
parent.display.document.write("classes.SteelBlu.all.borderStyle='groove';")
parent.display.document.write("classes.SteelBlu.all.borderColor='#8800ff';")
parent.display.document.write("classes.SteelBlu.all.lineHeight='24pt';")

parent.display.document.write("<\/STYLE>")
parent.display.document.write("<\/HEAD>")
parent.display.document.write("<BODY CLASS='Mainbody'>")

parent.display.document.write("<LAYER CLASS='SteelBlu' ID='Readout' LEFT=10 TOP='0'
                                          HEIGHT=100>")
parent.display.document.write("<CENTER>")

        parent.display.document.write(t)

parent.display.document.write("<\/CENTER>")
parent.display.document.write("<\/LAYER>")
parent.display.document.write("<\/BODY>")
parent.display.document.write("<\/HTML>")

        parent.display.document.close();
}

/*-------------------------------------------------------------------*/
/*-------------------------------------------------------------------*/
```

```
        startTime = new Date();
        var booleanTest = true;

/*------------------------------------------------------------------*/

function initializeTime()  {

        var today = new Date();
        var todayDateTime = today.toLocaleString();
        later = new Date();
        TimeHere = Math.round( (later - startTime) / 60000 );

        if (booleanTest == true) {

        outputTime(todayDateTime +
                " <FONT COLOR='RED'>   Been Here </FONT> " +
                TimeHere + " Minutes");

        setTimeout('initializeTime()', 1000);
        }

        else {
        outputTime(todayDateTime +
                " <FONT COLOR='RED'>   Been Here </FONT> " +
                TimeHere + " Minutes");

        setTimeout('initializeTime()', 60000);
        }
}

/*------------------------------------------------*/

function slowItDownMon() {

        booleanTest = false;
        }
/*------------------------------------------------*/

function speedItUpMon() {

        booleanTest = true;
        }

//END HIDING-->
</SCRIPT>


</HEAD>
<!-- ****************************************************************** -->
<BODY CLASS="Mainbody">

<SCRIPT LANGUAGE="JavaScript1.2"><!--BEGIN HIDING

        initializeTime();

//END HIDING-->
</SCRIPT>
<!-- ****************************************************************** -->
```

```
<FORM NAME="form3">

<P CLASS="RedBox">Click Me to Slow Time Down.<INPUT TYPE="checkbox" NAME="Slowdown"
onClick="slowItDownMon()"></P>

<P CLASS="RedBox">Click Me to Speed it back Up. Depending on where the setTimeout
was in its cycle, it could take up to 59 seconds to kick back in.<INPUT
TYPE="checkbox" NAME="SpeedUp" onClick="speedItUpMon()"></P>


<DIV ALIGN=CENTER CLASS="SteelBlu">
        If you find this as annoying as I did after the initial coolness then click
on the check box to reduce the refresh rate of the clock from seconds to minutes. I
started it out to refresh in seconds so that you wouldn't have to wait on the
results.
</DIV>


</FORM>
</BODY>
</HTML>
```

This is just the code for the FRAMESET for Example 3-29. Of course, this is the file that you need to run in the browser to get the example to work.

Example 3-29 Part 2:   Sample429Frameset.html

```
<!DOCTYPE HTML PUBLIC "-//W3C//DTD HTML 3.2//EN">
<HTML>
<HEAD>  <TITLE>Frame for Sample 429</TITLE>   </HEAD>

<FRAMESET ROWS="150,*">

        <FRAME MARGINHEIGHT=0 SCROLLING="no" NAME="display" SRC="Sample429A.html">

        <FRAME SCROLLING="auto" NAME="main" SRC="Sample429.html">

</FRAMESET>

</HTML>
```

Example 3-29   Sample429Frameset.html

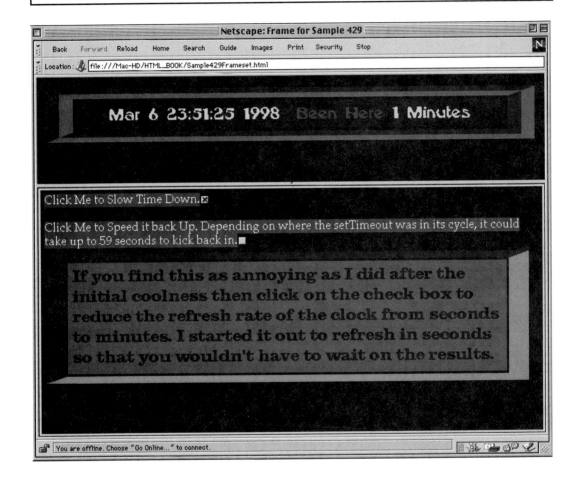

The JavaScript <u>Conditional</u> Operator <u>? :</u>

The **Conditional** Operator **? :** is basically a shorthand version of the Conditional **if ()** Statement. Here's the Syntax and then how it works.

JavaScript Syntax:

```
((booleanCondition) ? expression1 : expression2)
```

Parameters Defined:

booleanCondition   is an expression that evaluates to either true or false
expression1 and **expression2**   are expressions with Values of any type.

If your **booleanCondition** evaluates to **true**, then the Operator returns the Value of **expression1** and if it evaluates to **false** then it returns the Value of **expression2**.

Mini-Example:

For example, suppose you define a variable with a **Date()** Constructor and another variable that extracts the current hours with the **getHours()** Method. Now, because Navigator internally assigns hours from 0 to 23 like military time, you have to manipulate the raw hours to the more conventional mode. So you test the variable **todaysHours**, and if it's greater than 12, you subtract 12 from it, otherwise it stays like it is.

Then you test it again to determine whether to assign PM or AM to the **beforeAfterNoon** variable. Finally, you use the **write()** Method to display the suffixed hours.

```
var today           = new Date();

var todaysHours     = today.getHours();

todaysHours = ((todaysHours > 12)  ?  todaysHours - 12  :  todaysHours);

var beforeAfterNoon = ((todaysHours >= 12)  ?  " PM"  :  " AM");

document.write(todaysHours  +  beforeAfterNoon);
```

Browser Output:

If the time happened to be 22 o'clock, then the output would be like this:

10 PM

Just for comparison purposes, here's what the preceding code would look like if you were to use an **if ()** Statement instead:

```
todaysHours = ((todaysHours > 12)  ?  todaysHours - 12  :  todaysHours);

if (todaysHours > 12)   todaysHours = todaysHours - 12;
else todaysHours;
```

This example is very similar to Example 3-29 except that here the **Comparison Operator ? :** is used several times to modify the raw parameters of a **Date** Object, and there are quite a few Methods of the **Date** Object used to extract useful morsels of data and then display them in a more aesthetically pleasing manner that is also easier to read.

The way that the **showTime** Variable is assigned its Value is also different than has been previously used in that it is repeatedly assigned additional data, which facilitates keeping your code all on one line in your text editor, and it's much easier to read this way.

Example 3-30:   Sample430.html

```
<!DOCTYPE HTML PUBLIC "-//W3C//DTD HTML 3.2//EN">
<HTML>
<HEAD>
<TITLE>Sample 430 - Example 3-30   Advanced Display 2 Time Counter </TITLE>

<STYLE TYPE="text/JavaScript">

        classes.Mainbody.BODY.margins("0px");
        classes.Mainbody.BODY.paddings("0px");
        classes.Mainbody.BODY.backgroundColor="black";
        classes.Mainbody.BODY.color="white";

        classes.SteelBlu.all.margins("0px");
        classes.SteelBlu.all.backgroundColor="steelblue";
        classes.SteelBlu.all.color="navy";
        classes.SteelBlu.all.width="700";
        classes.SteelBlu.all.fontSize="22pt";
        classes.SteelBlu.all.fontFamily="Clarendon, Helvetica, serif";
        classes.SteelBlu.all.paddings("7px");
        classes.SteelBlu.all.borderTopWidth="10px";
        classes.SteelBlu.all.borderRightWidth="30px";
        classes.SteelBlu.all.borderBottomWidth="10px";
        classes.SteelBlu.all.borderLeftWidth="30px";
        classes.SteelBlu.all.borderStyle="inset";
        classes.SteelBlu.all.borderColor="#5555ff";
        classes.SteelBlu.all.lineHeight="28pt";

        classes.RedBox.P.backgroundColor="red";
        classes.RedBox.P.fontSize="17pt";

</STYLE>
```

```
<!--    *************************************************************    -->

<SCRIPT LANGUAGE="JavaScript1.2"><!--BEGIN HIDING

function outputTime(t){

        //Note that you don't have to use the document.open() Method because the
        //write() Method does an implicit open for the MIME type for HTML and text.

parent.display.document.write("<HTML><HEAD><TITLE>")
parent.display.document.write("<CLOCK DISPLAY>")
parent.display.document.write("<\/TITLE>")

parent.display.document.write("<STYLE TYPE='text/JavaScript'>")

parent.display.document.write("classes.Mainbody.BODY.margins('0px');")
parent.display.document.write("classes.Mainbody.BODY.paddings('0px');")
parent.display.document.write("classes.Mainbody.BODY.backgroundColor='black';")
parent.display.document.write("classes.Mainbody.BODY.color='white';")

parent.display.document.write("classes.SteelBlu.all.margins('0px');")
parent.display.document.write("classes.SteelBlu.all.backgroundColor='darkblue';")
parent.display.document.write("classes.SteelBlu.all.color='cyan';")
parent.display.document.write("classes.SteelBlu.all.width='700';")
parent.display.document.write("classes.SteelBlu.all.fontSize='24pt';")
parent.display.document.write("classes.SteelBlu.all.fontFamily='Moonlight,
                                           Clarendon, Helvetica, serif';")
parent.display.document.write("classes.SteelBlu.all.paddings('7px');")
parent.display.document.write("classes.SteelBlu.all.borderTopWidth='15px';")
parent.display.document.write("classes.SteelBlu.all.borderRightWidth='40px';")
parent.display.document.write("classes.SteelBlu.all.borderBottomWidth='15px';")
parent.display.document.write("classes.SteelBlu.all.borderLeftWidth='40px';")
parent.display.document.write("classes.SteelBlu.all.borderStyle='groove';")
parent.display.document.write("classes.SteelBlu.all.borderColor='#8800ff';")
parent.display.document.write("classes.SteelBlu.all.lineHeight='24pt';")

parent.display.document.write("<\/STYLE>")
parent.display.document.write("<\/HEAD>")
parent.display.document.write("<BODY CLASS='Mainbody'>")

parent.display.document.write("<LAYER CLASS='SteelBlu' ID='Readout' LEFT='10'
TOP='0' HEIGHT='100'>")
parent.display.document.write("<CENTER>")

        parent.display.document.write(t)

parent.display.document.write("<\/CENTER>")
parent.display.document.write("<\/LAYER>")
parent.display.document.write("<\/BODY>")
parent.display.document.write("<\/HTML>")

        parent.display.document.close();

}

/*------------------------------------------------------------------*/
/*------------------------------------------------------------------*/
```

```
        startTime = new Date();
        var booleanTest = true;

/*------------------------------------------------------------------*/
/*---------------------------------------------------------------*/
//The getMonth() Method returns a zero to eleven numbering scheme for months
//such that January = 0, February = 1, ..., December = 11,
//so you have to increment the month by 1 if you need January to be 1 instead of 0
//which is used for the todayMonth variable, below.

function initializeTime()  {

        var today              = new Date();
        var todayMonth         = today.getMonth() +1;
        var todayDay           = today.getDate();
        var todayYear          = today.getYear();
        var todaysHours        = today.getHours();
        var todaysMinutes      = today.getMinutes();
        var todaysSeconds      = today.getSeconds();
        var later              = new Date();
        var TimeHere           = Math.round((later - startTime) / 60000);

        todaysHours = ((todaysHours > 12)  ?  todaysHours - 12  :  todaysHours);

        var showTime= "The Date is ***** <FONT COLOR='RED'>"+ todayMonth +"/"
        showTime += todayDay +"/"
        showTime += todayYear + "<\/FONT><BR>"
        showTime += "The Time is ***** <FONT COLOR='RED'>" + todaysHours
        showTime += ((todaysMinutes > 9)  ?  ":"  :  ":0")
        showTime += todaysMinutes
        showTime += ((todaysSeconds > 9)  ?  " :"  :  " :0")
        showTime += todaysSeconds
        showTime += ((todaysHours >= 12)  ?  " PM"  :  " AM")  + "<\/FONT><BR>"
        showTime += "You have been here ***** <FONT COLOR='RED'>"
        showTime += TimeHere + " Minutes.<\/FONT>"

        if (booleanTest == true) {

        outputTime(showTime);

        setTimeout('initializeTime()', 1000);
        }

        else {
        outputTime(showTime);

        setTimeout('initializeTime()', 60000);
        }
}

/*-------------------------------------------------*/

function slowItDownMon() {

        booleanTest = false;
        }
/*-------------------------------------------------*/
```

```
/*----------------------------------------------------*/

function speedItUpMon() {

        booleanTest = true;
        }

//END HIDING-->
</SCRIPT>

</HEAD>

<!-- ****************************************************************** -->

<BODY CLASS="Mainbody">

<SCRIPT LANGUAGE="JavaScript1.2"><!--BEGIN HIDING

        initializeTime();

//END HIDING-->
</SCRIPT>

<!-- ****************************************************************** -->

<FORM NAME="form3">

<P CLASS="RedBox">

Click Me to Slow Time Down.<INPUT TYPE="checkbox" NAME="Slowdown"
onClick="slowItDownMon()">

</P>

<P CLASS="RedBox">

Click Me to Speed it back Up. Depending on where the setTimeout was in its cycle,
it could take up to 59 seconds to kick back in.<INPUT TYPE="checkbox"
NAME="SpeedUp" onClick="speedItUpMon()">

</P>

<DIV ALIGN=CENTER CLASS="SteelBlu">

        If you find this as annoying as I did after the initial coolness then click
on the check box to reduce the refresh rate of the clock from seconds to minutes. I
started it out to refresh in seconds so that you wouldn't have to wait on the
results.

</DIV>

</FORM>

</BODY>
</HTML>
```

The JavaScript <u>Math</u> Object

The **Math** Object is a Core Object, which means it's a top-level predefined JavaScript Object that you can automatically access without having to create it with a Constructor or calling a Method. It has built-in Properties for dealing with mathematical Constants like PI and the Square Root of 2, and Methods for dealing with computational entities like the cosine or absolute value of a number.

All of the Properties and Methods of the **Math** Object are static, which means that they are <u>read-only</u> and you can't change them. **Math** Object Constants are always written in all uppercase letters the same way that Events are. When you want to refer to a **Math** Object Constant like **PI**, you would code it like this:

```
Math.PI
```

When you want to call the Cosine Function with an Argument of **x** for the Method you would code it like this:

```
Math.cos(x)
```

Using the <u>with()</u> Statement with Math Objects

You can use the **with()** Statement to automatically apply **Math** to your Constants and Methods to save your self some typing repetitiveness. For example:

```
with (Math) {

    a = PI * r * r;
    y = tan(theta);
    x = r * cos(theta);
    z = abs(beta);
}
```

is the functional equivalent of:

```
a = Math.PI * r * r;
y = Math.tan(theta);
x = r * Math.cos(theta);
z = Math.abs(beta);
```

Special Notice:

Note that JavaScript is smart enough to recognize Keyword names like **PI** and **cos** that are relevant to the **Math** Object, so it doesn't apply **Math** to non-Math Variables.

Math Object Property Summaries

Math Properties	Description	Approximate Value
E	Euler's constant	2.718281828459045091
LN10	Natural logarithm of 10	2.302585092994045901
LN2	Natural logarithm of 2	0.69314718055994052862
LOG10E	Base 10 logarithm of E	0.43429448190325181467
LOG2E	Base 2 logarithm of E	1.442695040888963387
PI	Ratio of the circumference of a circle to its diameter	3.141592653589793116
SQRT1_2	Square root of 1/2	0.7071067811865475727
SQRT2	Square root of 2	1.414213562373095145

Math Object Method Summaries

Math Methods	Description
abs(x)	Returns the absolute value of x.
acos(x)	Returns the arc cosine of x in radians.
asin(x)	Returns the arc sine of x in radians.
atan(x)	Returns the arc tangent of x in radians.
atan2(y,x)	Returns the arc tangent of the quotient of its Arguments, that is, y/x. This is another way of saying it returns the angle of the Polar Coordinate (y,x).
ceil(x)	Returns the smallest integer greater than or equal to x.
cos(x)	Returns the cosine of x.
exp(x)	Returns e^x, where x is the Argument and e is Euler's constant, the base of the natural logarithms.
floor(x)	Returns the largest integer less than or equal to x.
log(x)	Returns the natural logarithm (base E) of x.
max(x,y)	Returns the greater of the two numbers x and y.
min(x,y)	Returns the lesser of the two numbers x and y.
pow(x,y)	Returns x^y, traditionally base to the exponent power, that is, $base^{exponent}$.
random()	Returns a pseudo-random number between 0 and 1.
round(x)	Returns the value of x rounded to the nearest integer with .50 as cutoff.
sin(x)	Returns the sine of x.
sqrt(x)	Returns the square root of x.
tan(x)	Returns the tangent of x.

Randomly load different Background Images into a Layer

This example demonstrates the **Math.random()** Method and the **setTimeout()** Method to generate random numbers that cause the background image of Layer **L1** and the background color of Layer **L2** to automatically change periodically. For demonstration purposes, the time is set to change relatively fast, but for many practical applications you will want to use a much longer time delay.

Since the **Math.random()** Method always returns a number between 0 and 1, you have to multiply it by a useful number which in the case of Function **randomActs1()** is 7 since there are 7 Elements in the Array **a1**. Because you are using this random number as the **index** of the Array to call that specific Array Element, you must use the **Math.round()** Method to convert the floating-point number to an integer.

Finally, both Functions **randomActs1()** and **randomActs2()** are called with the **onLoad** Event Handler of the BODY Element so that they start when the document is fully loaded. For more information on Arrays see Chapter 7.

Example 3-31: Sample431.html

```
<!DOCTYPE HTML PUBLIC "-//W3C//DTD HTML 3.2//EN">
<HTML>
<HEAD>
<TITLE>Sample 431 - Example 3-31    Random Backgrounds         </TITLE>

<STYLE TYPE="text/JavaScript">

        classes.Mainbody.BODY.margins("0px");
        classes.Mainbody.BODY.paddings("0px");
        classes.Mainbody.BODY.backgroundColor="black";

        tags.LAYER.color="yellow";
        tags.LAYER.fontSize="22pt";

</STYLE>

</HEAD>
<!--   ************************************************************   -->
<BODY CLASS="Mainbody" onLoad="randomActs1(); randomActs2();">

<LAYER ID="L1" LEFT=10 TOP=10 WIDTH=200 HEIGHT=200>
Right now the setTimeout() Method is set to randomly update the background image of
this Layer every 5 seconds.</LAYER>

<LAYER ID="L2" LEFT=220 TOP=10 WIDTH=200 HEIGHT=200>
Right now the setTimeout() Method is set to randomly update the background color of
this Layer every 3 seconds.</LAYER>

<!--   ************************************************************   -->
```

Example 3-31   Sample431.html

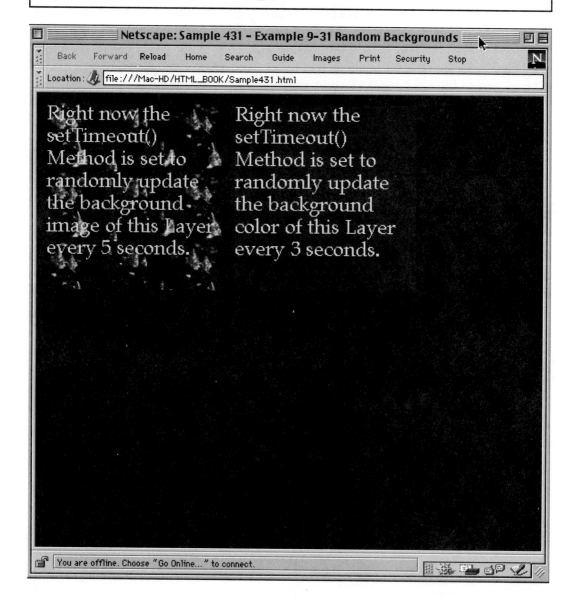

Netscape: Sample 431 – Example 9-31 Random Backgrounds

Back   Forward   Reload   Home   Search   Guide   Images   Print   Security   Stop

Location : file:///Mac-HD/HTML_BOOK/Sample431.html

Right now the setTimeout() Method is set to randomly update the background image of this Layer every 5 seconds.

Right now the setTimeout() Method is set to randomly update the background color of this Layer every 3 seconds.

You are offline. Choose "Go Online..." to connect.

Just so there is no chance of confusion, the rest of the code for Example 3-31 is on the next page.

```
<SCRIPT LANGUAGE="JavaScript1.2"><!--BEGIN HIDING

var L1 = document.L1;
var L2 = document.L2;

a1 = new Array("./JPEG-FILES/icon-BG-asteroids.jpg",
                  "./JPEG-FILES/icon-Sun.jpg",
                  "./JPEG-FILES/ICON-HorizontalRainbow4.jpg",
                  "./JPEG-FILES/icon-BG-stars.jpg",
                  "./JPEG-FILES/icon-CoarseTurf.jpeg",
                  "./JPEG-FILES/icon-FieldStone-Purple.jpeg",
                  "./JPEG-FILES/ICON-HorizontalRainbow2.jpg");

a2 = new Array("blue", "red", "purple", "green", "navy", "olive", "gold", "black");

/*-------------------------------------------------------------------------*/

function randomActs1()  {

        L1.background.src = a1[Math.round(Math.random() * 7)];

        setTimeout('randomActs1()', 5000);
}
/*-------------------------------------*/

function randomActs2()  {

        L2.bgColor = a2[Math.round(Math.random() * 8)];

        setTimeout('randomActs2()', 3000);
}
/*-------------------------------------*/

//END HIDING-->
</SCRIPT>

</BODY>
</HTML>
```

Using Math Methods in a quasi-calculator

In the following example, Sample432.html, all of the Math Methods that take single Arguments are demonstrated in a Table that displays the numbers in a different Frame by using the **document.write()** Method to create the HTML and JavaScript code to update the output as it is generated by the user.

We start by constructing an Array named **numArray** with the Keyword **new** and assigning its length to one, and then in the Function **initiateParam()** we set the Value of the Element at **numArray [0]** to the Numeric String "0". The reason that Strings are used instead of numbers is to allow a simple way to append the additional Values that are added to the Array with the Buttons in the Table.

Next, the Function **getNum(num)** is created, which assigns the **return** Value of the Function **appendNum(num1,num2)** to **numArray[0]** and then calls the Function **output(numerals)** to render the results into the Frame named **display**. This is the critical line of code in the **output(numerals)** Function that actually displays the contents of the Array:

```
parent.display.document.write(numerals.toString())
```

The **showConstant(theConstant)** Function just takes the **theConstant** Argument supplied when the user clicks on a Button with a **Math** Constant and displays it in the **display** Frame. Then, a Function is created for each of the **Math** Object Methods that is called when the user clicks on a Button. Next, the **resetOutput()** Function resets the display back to the starting point when the 'Clear' Button is clicked. Finally, the **initiateParam()** Function is called in a SCRIPT Element when the document is loaded. There is a third part to this example named Sample432A.html which is initially loaded into the top Frame that serves as the initial display for the Calculator.

Example 3-32 Part 1:   Sample432.html

```
<!DOCTYPE HTML PUBLIC "-//W3C//DTD HTML 3.2//EN">
<HTML>
<HEAD>
<TITLE>Sample 432 - Example 3-32   JavaScript Math Methods</TITLE>

<STYLE TYPE="text/JavaScript">

        classes.Mainbody.BODY.margins("0px");
        classes.Mainbody.BODY.paddings("0px");
        classes.Mainbody.BODY.backgroundColor="black";
        classes.Mainbody.BODY.color="white";

</STYLE>

<!--  ********************************************************************  -->

<SCRIPT LANGUAGE="JavaScript1.2"><!--BEGIN HIDING

numArray = new Array(1);

/*----------------------------------------------------*/
function initiateParam(){

        numArray[0] = "0";
}

/*----------------------------------------------------*/

function getNum(num){

        numArray[0] = appendNum(numArray[0], num);
        output(numArray[0]);
}
```

```
/*-------------------------------------------------*/

function appendNum(num1,num2){

        if (num1 == "0") return ""+num2;

        var numerals="";
        numerals += num1;
        numerals += num2;
        return numerals;
}
/*-------------------------------------------------*/
/*-------------------------------------------------*/

function output(numerals){

parent.display.document.write("<HTML>")
parent.display.document.write("<HEAD><TITLE>Calculator Readout<\/TITLE>")
parent.display.document.write("<STYLE TYPE='text/JavaScript'>")

parent.display.document.write("classes.Mainbody.BODY.margins('0px');")
parent.display.document.write("classes.Mainbody.BODY.paddings('0px');")
parent.display.document.write("classes.Mainbody.BODY.backgroundColor='black';")
parent.display.document.write("classes.Mainbody.BODY.color='white';")

parent.display.document.write("classes.SteelBlu.all.margins('0px');")
parent.display.document.write("classes.SteelBlu.all.backgroundColor='steelblue';")
parent.display.document.write("classes.SteelBlu.all.color='lime';")
parent.display.document.write("classes.SteelBlu.all.width='100%';")
parent.display.document.write("classes.SteelBlu.all.fontSize='40pt';")
parent.display.document.write("classes.SteelBlu.all.fontFamily='Moonlight,
                                        Clarendon, Helvetica, serif';")
parent.display.document.write("classes.SteelBlu.all.paddings('7px');")
parent.display.document.write("classes.SteelBlu.all.borderTopWidth='10px';")
parent.display.document.write("classes.SteelBlu.all.borderRightWidth='50px';")
parent.display.document.write("classes.SteelBlu.all.borderBottomWidth='10px';")
parent.display.document.write("classes.SteelBlu.all.borderLeftWidth='50px';")
parent.display.document.write("classes.SteelBlu.all.borderStyle='ridge';")
parent.display.document.write("classes.SteelBlu.all.borderColor='#5555ff';")
parent.display.document.write("classes.SteelBlu.all.lineHeight='40pt';")

parent.display.document.write("<\/STYLE>")
parent.display.document.write("<\/HEAD>")
parent.display.document.write("<BODY CLASS='Mainbody'>")

parent.display.document.write("<LAYER CLASS='SteelBlu' ID='Readout' LEFT=10 TOP=-25
                                        HEIGHT=100>")
parent.display.document.write("<CENTER>")

        parent.display.document.write(numerals.toString())

parent.display.document.write("<\/CENTER>")
parent.display.document.write("<\/LAYER>")
parent.display.document.write("<\/BODY>")
parent.display.document.write("<\/HTML>")

        parent.display.document.close();
}
```

```
/*-----------------------------------------------------------------*/

function showConstant(theConstant){

        numArray[0] = theConstant;
        output(numArray[0]);
}
/*-----------------------------------------------------------------*/

function calcSin() {

        numArray[0] = Math.sin(numArray[0]);
        output(numArray[0]);
}
/*--------------------------------------------------------*/

function calcCos() {

        numArray[0] = Math.cos(numArray[0]);
        output(numArray[0]);
}
/*-----------------------------------------------------*/

function calcTan() {

        numArray[0] = Math.tan(numArray[0]);
        output(numArray[0]);
}
/*---------------------------------------------------*/

function calcAsin() {

        numArray[0] = Math.asin(numArray[0]);
        output(numArray[0]);
}
/*-------------------------------------------------*/

function calcAcos() {

        numArray[0] = Math.acos(numArray[0]);
        output(numArray[0]);
}
/*-----------------------------------------------*/

function calcAtan() {

        numArray[0] = Math.atan(numArray[0]);
        output(numArray[0]);
}
/*---------------------------------------------*/

function calcLog() {

        numArray[0] = Math.log(numArray[0]);
        output(numArray[0]);
}
/*-------------------------------------------*/
```

```
/*-------------------------------------------------*/

function calcExp() {

        numArray[0] = Math.exp(numArray[0]);
        output(numArray[0]);
}
/*-------------------------------------------------*/

function calcSqrt() {

        numArray[0] = Math.sqrt(numArray[0]);
        output(numArray[0]);
}
/*-------------------------------------------------*/

function calcAbs() {

        numArray[0] = Math.abs(numArray[0]);
        output(numArray[0]);
}
/*-------------------------------------------------*/

function calcRound() {

        numArray[0] = Math.round(numArray[0]);
        output(numArray[0]);
}
/*-------------------------------------------------*/

function calcRandom() {

        numArray[0] = Math.random(numArray[0]);
        output(numArray[0]);
}
/*-------------------------------------------------*/

function calcCeil() {

        numArray[0] = Math.ceil(numArray[0]);
        output(numArray[0]);
}
/*-------------------------------------------------*/

function calcFloor() {

        numArray[0] = Math.floor(numArray[0]);
        output(numArray[0]);
}
/*-------------------------------------------------*/

function calcRandom100() {

        numArray[0] = Math.round((Math.random(numArray[0]) * 100));
        output(numArray[0]);
}
/*-------------------------------------------------*/
```

```
function calcPercent() {

        numArray[0] =(parseFloat(numArray[0])) / 100;
        output(numArray[0]);
}
/*--------------------------------------------------*/

function resetOutput() {

        initiateParam();
        output(numArray[0]);
}

//END HIDING-->
</SCRIPT>
</HEAD>

<!--  ************************************************************** -->
<BODY CLASS="Mainbody">

<SCRIPT LANGUAGE="JavaScript1.2"><!--BEGIN HIDING

        initiateParam();

//END HIDING-->
</SCRIPT>
<!--  ************************************************************** -->

<LAYER ID="MainLayer" LEFT=10 TOP=10>

<FORM NAME="FormB">

<TABLE BORDER=10 CELLPADDING=0 CELLSPACING=5 WIDTH="100%" HEIGHT=300
BGCOLOR="yellow" BORDERCOLOR="red">

<TR>
<TH><INPUT TYPE="button" NAME="One" VALUE="1" onClick="getNum(1);"></TH>

<TH><INPUT TYPE="button" NAME="Two" VALUE="2" onClick="getNum(2);"></TH>

<TH><INPUT TYPE="button" NAME="Three" VALUE="3" onClick="getNum(3);"></TH>

<TH BGCOLOR="purple"><INPUT TYPE="button" NAME="thePi" VALUE="pi"
                    onClick="showConstant(Math.PI);"></TH>

<TH BGCOLOR="purple"><INPUT TYPE="button" NAME="theE" VALUE="e"
                    onClick="showConstant(Math.E);"></TH>

<TH BGCOLOR="cyan"><INPUT TYPE="button" NAME="sin" VALUE="sin"
                    onClick="calcSin();"></TH>

<TH BGCOLOR="cyan"><INPUT TYPE="button" NAME="cos" VALUE="cos"
                    onClick="calcCos();"></TH>

<TH BGCOLOR="cyan"><INPUT TYPE="button" NAME="tan" VALUE="tan"
                    onClick="calcTan();"></TH>
</TR>
<!--  ************************************************************** -->
```

```
<!--   ***************************************************************   -->

<TR>
<TH><INPUT TYPE="button" NAME="Four" VALUE="4" onClick="getNum(4);"></TH>

<TH><INPUT TYPE="button" NAME="Five" VALUE="5" onClick="getNum(5);"></TH>

<TH><INPUT TYPE="button" NAME="S0" VALUE="6" onClick="getNum(6);"></TH>

<TH BGCOLOR="purple"><INPUT TYPE="button" NAME="theLog2" VALUE="log2"
                onClick="showConstant(Math.LN2);"></TH>

<TH BGCOLOR="purple"><INPUT TYPE="button" NAME="theLog10" VALUE="log10"
                onClick="showConstant(Math.LN10);"></TH>

<TH BGCOLOR="cyan"><INPUT TYPE="button" NAME="theAsin" VALUE="asin"
                onClick="calcAsin();"></TH>

<TH BGCOLOR="cyan"><INPUT TYPE="button" NAME="theAcos" VALUE="acos"
                onClick="calcAcos();"></TH>

<TH BGCOLOR="cyan"><INPUT TYPE="button" NAME="theAtan" VALUE="atan"
                onClick="calcAtan();"></TH>
</TR>

<!--   ***************************************************************   -->

<TR>
<TH><INPUT TYPE="button" NAME="Seven" VALUE="7" onClick="getNum(7);"></TH>

<TH><INPUT TYPE="button" NAME="Eight" VALUE="8" onClick="getNum(8);"></TH>

<TH><INPUT TYPE="button" NAME="Nine" VALUE="9" onClick="getNum(9);"></TH>

<TH BGCOLOR="purple"><INPUT TYPE="button" NAME="theLog2e" VALUE="log2e"
                onClick="showConstant(Math.LOG2E);"></TH>

<TH BGCOLOR="purple"><INPUT TYPE="button" NAME="theLog10e" VALUE="log10e"
                onClick="showConstant(Math.LOG10E);"></TH>

<TH BGCOLOR="#7700ff"><INPUT TYPE="button" NAME="theLog" VALUE="log"
                onClick="calcLog();"></TH>

<TH BGCOLOR="#7700ff"><INPUT TYPE="button" NAME="theExp" VALUE="exp"
                onClick="calcExp();"></TH>

<TH BGCOLOR="#7700ff"><INPUT TYPE="button" NAME="thesqrt" VALUE="sqrt"
                onClick="calcSqrt();"></TH>
</TR>

<!--   ***************************************************************   -->

<TR>
<TH><INPUT TYPE="button" NAME="Zero" VALUE="0" onClick="getNum(0);"></TH>

<TH COLSPAN="2" BGCOLOR="navy"><INPUT TYPE="button" NAME="Equals" VALUE="."
                onClick="getNum('.');"></TH>
```

```
<TH BGCOLOR="purple"><INPUT TYPE="button" NAME="theSqrt1_2" VALUE="sqrt1/2"
                     onClick="showConstant(Math.SQRT1_2);"></TH>

<TH BGCOLOR="purple"><INPUT TYPE="button" NAME="theSqrt2" VALUE="sqrt2"
                     onClick="showConstant(Math.SQRT2);"></TH>

<TH BGCOLOR="lime"><INPUT TYPE="button" NAME="theAbs" VALUE="abs"
                     onClick="calcAbs();"></TH>

<TH BGCOLOR="lime"><INPUT TYPE="button" NAME="theRound" VALUE="round"
                     onClick="calcRound();"></TH>

<TH BGCOLOR="lime"><INPUT TYPE="button" NAME="theRandom" VALUE="random"
                     onClick="calcRandom();"></TH>
</TR>
<!--  ************************************************************  -->

<TR>
<TH COLSPAN="5" BGCOLOR="blue"><INPUT TYPE="button" NAME="ClearAll" VALUE="Clear"
                     onClick="resetOutput();"></TH>

<TH BGCOLOR="steelblue"><INPUT TYPE="button" NAME="theCeil" VALUE="ceil"
                     onClick="calcCeil();"></TH>

<TH BGCOLOR="steelblue"><INPUT TYPE="button" NAME="theFloor" VALUE="floor"
                     onClick="calcFloor();"></TH>

<TH BGCOLOR="lime">Rounded<BR>
<INPUT TYPE="button" NAME="MyRandom100" VALUE="random*100"
                     onClick="calcRandom100();"></TH>
</TR>
<!--  ************************************************************  -->
</TABLE>
</FORM>
</LAYER>

</BODY>
</HTML>
```

Example 3-32 Part 2:   Sample432Frameset.html

```
<!DOCTYPE HTML PUBLIC "-//W3C//DTD HTML 3.2//EN">
<HTML>
<HEAD>  <TITLE>Frame for Sample 432</TITLE>   </HEAD>

<FRAMESET ROWS="100,*">

      <FRAME MARGINHEIGHT="0" SCROLLING="no" NAME="display" SRC="Sample432A.html">

      <FRAME SCROLLING="auto" NAME="main" SRC="Sample432.html">

</FRAMESET>

</HTML>
```

Example 3-32　　　Sample432Frameset.html

Math Methods of Math.max(x,y), Math.min(x,y) and Math.pow(x,y)

This is a simple example to demonstrate the Math Methods of **Math.max(x,y)**, **Math.min(x,y)** and **Math.pow(x,y)**. The numeric Strings that are input by the user in the Text Boxes are first assigned to **x** and **y** respectively and then converted to Floating Point Numbers with the **parseFloat()** Method. Then one of the above Math Methods is called to perform the calculation depending on which Button is clicked.

Example 3-33:   **Sample433.html**

```
<!DOCTYPE HTML PUBLIC "-//W3C//DTD HTML 3.2//EN">
<HTML>
<HEAD>
<TITLE>Sample 433 - Example 3-33  Math max, min, pow Methods</TITLE>

<STYLE TYPE="text/JavaScript">

        classes.Mainbody.BODY.margins("0px");
        classes.Mainbody.BODY.paddings("0px");
        classes.Mainbody.BODY.backgroundColor="black";
        tags.LAYER.color="yellow";
        tags.LAYER.fontSize="22pt";

</STYLE>
</HEAD>


<BODY CLASS="Mainbody">

<LAYER ID="L1" LEFT=10 TOP=10 WIDTH=500>

max(x,y)        <BR>Returns the greater of the two numbers x and y.<BR><BR>
min(x,y)        <BR>Returns the lesser of the two numbers x and y.<BR><BR>
pow(x,y)        <BR>Returns x to the power of y, that is; x<SUP>y</SUP>.<BR><BR>

<HR>
<FORM NAME="form1">
Input X value          <INPUT TYPE="text" NAME="text1" SIZE=25 VALUE="">   <BR>
Input Y value          <INPUT TYPE="text" NAME="text2" SIZE=25 VALUE="">   <BR>
And the results are:    <INPUT TYPE="text" NAME="text3" SIZE=25 VALUE="">   <BR>

<INPUT TYPE="button" NAME="b1" Value="max(x,y)" onClick="doMax();">
<INPUT TYPE="button" NAME="b2" Value="min(x,y)" onClick="doMin();">
<INPUT TYPE="button" NAME="b3" Value="pow(x,y)" onClick="doPow();">
<INPUT TYPE="button" NAME="b4" Value="Clear All" onClick="clearAll();">

</FORM>
<HR>

</LAYER>
<!--    ************************************************************    -->
```

```
<!--  *************************************************************  -->

<SCRIPT LANGUAGE="JavaScript1.2"><!--BEGIN HIDING

function doMax() {

        var x = document.L1.document.form1.text1.value;
        var y = document.L1.document.form1.text2.value;
        x = parseFloat(x);
        y = parseFloat(y);
        document.L1.document.form1.text3.value = Math.max(x,y);
}

/*----------------------------------------------------------*/

function doMin() {

        var x = document.L1.document.form1.text1.value;
        var y = document.L1.document.form1.text2.value;
        x = parseFloat(x);
        y = parseFloat(y);
        document.L1.document.form1.text3.value = Math.min(x,y);
}

/*----------------------------------------------------------*/

function doPow() {

        var x = document.L1.document.form1.text1.value;
        var y = document.L1.document.form1.text2.value;
        x = parseFloat(x);
        y = parseFloat(y);
        document.L1.document.form1.text3.value = Math.pow(x,y);
}

/*----------------------------------------------------------*/

function clearAll() {

        document.L1.document.form1.text1.value = "";
        document.L1.document.form1.text2.value = "";
        document.L1.document.form1.text3.value = "";
}

/*----------------------------------------------------------*/

//END HIDING-->
</SCRIPT>

</BODY>
</HTML>
```

The following topics are going to be covered, <u>in-brief</u>, as they relate to the next example contained in <u>Sample434.html</u>. For more complete information, see Chapter 8 on **String** Objects or the JavaScript Reference on the CD-ROM.

toString()	Core Method of all Objects	See JavaScript Reference
parseFloat()	Core Function	See JavaScript Reference
parseInt()	Core Function	See JavaScript Reference
isNaN()	Core Function	See JavaScript Reference
charAt()	Method of the **String** Object	See page 759
split()	Method of the **String** Object	See page 782
slice()	Method of the **String** Object	See page 788
length	Property of the **String** Object	See page 750

The JavaScript <u>toString()</u> Method

The **toString()** Method is used to convert an Object into its **text** equivalent. In the case of a **Number** Object, you can use the **radix** to specify a **base** number between 2 and 16 to convert the Value to the numbering system of your choice. The default Value of the **radix** Argument is 10.

In <u>Sample434.html</u> it is used to turn the Array Element **numArray[0]** into a String for display in the browser with the following code:

```
parent.display document.write(numerals.toString())
```

where **numerals** is the Argument passed to the **output(numerals)** Function. It is also used on the **rgbArray[]** Elements **rgbArray[0]**, **rgbArray[1]** and **rgbArray[2]** to convert the numeric Values to Base 16 Hexadecimal Color Values. The following code shows how to convert one Array Element to a Base 16 number that replaces the original Element.

```
rgbArray[0] = (rgbArray[0]).toString(16)
```

If the original Value was **14**   the converted Value in base 16 would be **e**.
If the original Value was **45**   the converted Value in base 16 would be **2d**.
If the original Value was **255**   the converted Value in base 16 would be **ff**.

JavaScript Syntax:

```
objectName.toString()
numberObjectName.toString(radix)
```

The JavaScript <u>parseFloat()</u> Function

The **parseFloat()** Function takes the **myString** String Argument and converts it to a **floating point number** (a number with a decimal in it). If the String contains any Characters other than numerals 0-9, a decimal point, a plus or minus sign, or an exponent it will return all the Characters up to the offending one and omit it and all successive Characters. If the first Character in the String is an offending Character, then 'NaN' is returned. For example, if **numArray[0]** has a Value of a Numeric String of "255" then:

`parseFloat(numArray[0])`	returns the Floating Point Number	255
`parseFloat("142.47@39")`	returns the Floating Point Number	142.47
`parseFloat("-77.25m,g")`	returns the Floating Point Number	-77.25
`parseFloat("ff7725")`	returns	NaN

JavaScript Syntax:

```
parseFloat("myString")
```

The JavaScript <u>parseInt()</u> Function

The **parseInt()** Function takes the **myString** String Argument and converts it to an **Integer** based on the **radix** Argument, which is an integer that designates the base of the numbering system to use. Base 2 is binary, Base 16 is hexadecimal, and Base 10 is normal everyday math. For **radix**es above 10, the letters of the alphabet are substituted for the numbers greater than 9; for example, in Hexadecimal, letters A-F are used for the numbers 10-15. Reading the String from left to right, if the String contains any characters not in the specified **radix**, they are omitted along with any numbers to the right of and including the first offending character. This inherently produces the result that all legitimate values will be truncated to integers, since a decimal would be an offending character.

If the **radix** is omitted or if it is set to 'zero', then the default is 10, unless the first character in the String is '0', which converts the **radix** to 8, or if the first characters are '0x', then the **radix** is 16. If **numArray[0]** = "ff", then:

`parseInt(numArray[0], 16)`	returns the Integer	255	in base 16
`parseInt("FF", 16)`	returns the Integer	255	in base 16
`parseInt("42.57", 10)`	returns the Integer	42	in base 10

JavaScript Syntax:

```
parseInt("myString" ,radix)
```

The JavaScript isNaN() Function

'NaN' is shorthand for 'Not a Number' which is what the **isNaN()** Function tests for. If **testValue** is 'NaN' then **isNaN()** returns **true**. If **testValue** is a number then it returns **false**. For example, if the variable **a1==NaN** in the following code, then the **alert** is called:

```
if (isNaN(a1))          alert('You forgot the green value');
```

JavaScript Syntax:

```
isNaN(testValue)
```

The JavaScript charAt() Method

The **charAt()** Method returns the character of the **myString String** Object at the specified **index** where **index** is an integer from zero to **myString.length - 1**. For any String the Characters are indexed from left to right so that the first Character has an **index** of zero, the second Character has an **index** of one, and the last Character has an **index** of **myString.length - 1**. If you designate an **index** that is larger than the **length** of the String, then an empty String is returned.

If **getChar** is a String Variable with a Value of "fe43a8", then:

```
getChar.charAt(0)              //returns the character f
getChar.charAt(2)              //returns the character 4
```

JavaScript Syntax:

```
myString.charAt(index)
```

The JavaScript split() Method

The **split()** Method is a Method of the **String** Object that searches for the **separator** Argument in the supplied **String** Object and returns an **Array** where each Element in the Array is a String consisting of the string fragment before the occurrence of the **separator**, which is omitted from the substring. The separator can be any character, typically a comma, colon, semicolon, plus sign, or white space, or it can be a **RegExp** (Regular Expression). For more information on usage with **RegExp** Objects, see Chapter 9.

The **optionalLimitInteger** Argument imposes a limit to the number of splits that JavaScript will perform so that you don't get extraneous empty Array Elements.

For instance, if you have a String Variable named **myStr="blue,red,yellow"**, then:

```
myStr.split(",")          //returns an Array with three Elements where:

element[0]="blue"    element[1]="red"    element[2]="yellow"
```

JavaScript Syntax:

```
myString.split("separator", optionalLimitInteger)
```

The JavaScript slice() Method

The **slice()** Method is used to extract a subsection of a **String** Object and return it as a new **String** Object. The **startSliceIndexInteger** Argument specifies the **index** integer to begin the slice where zero would start the slice at the first character and read the String from left to right; 1 would be the second character, and so on. The **endSliceIndexInteger** specifies the **index** integer of the first character after the end of the slice, which means that you slice up to <u>but not including</u> the **endSliceIndexInteger**. If **endSliceIndexInteger** is specified as a negative integer, then it offsets its position from the last character and works from right to left. For example, if **myString** = "123ABC":

```
myString.slice(0, -1)     //extracts all characters in the String except the last one
myString.slice(0, 4)      //would extract characters "123AB" into the new String
myString.slice(2, 5)      //would extract characters "3AB" into the new String
myString.slice(1, 6)      //would extract characters "23ABC" into the new String
```

JavaScript Syntax:

```
myString.slice(startSliceIndexInteger, endSliceIndexInteger)
```

The length Property of String Object

The **length** Property of a **String** Object returns an integer that specifies the number of characters in a **String** Object, which also includes blank spaces in the character count. For example, in the Function **Full1()**, there is a variable named **getChar** that might have a Value of "abcdef", so in that case, the **getChar.length** would be 6.

JavaScript Syntax:

```
myString.length
```

A really cool color conversion calculator

Sample434.html is very useful because you can use it to convert Colors from a variety of formats to another. The following chart shows all of the possible conversions.

Convert From		Convert To		Converted Results
Hexadecimal	to	RGB 0-255	Format	Single Color
Hexadecimal	to	RGB 0-100%	Format	Single Color
RGB 0-255	to	Hexadecimal	Format	Single Color
RGB 0-100%	to	Hexadecimal	Format	Single Color
RGB 0-100%	to	RGB 0-255	Format	Single Color
RGB 0-255	to	RGB 0-100%	Format	Single Color
Hexadecimal	to	RGB 0-255	Format	Full RGB Triplet Color
RGB 0-255	to	Hexadecimal	Format	Full Hex Triplet Color

It also displays the color in the browser in a second Frame in real-time so you can see and verify the results. It starts by Constructing two Arrays named **numArray** and **rgbArray** to hold the color Values that the user chooses with the input Buttons. The **initiateParam()** Function sets all the Elements in both Arrays to an empty String.

Color Value Characters are collected into **numArray** with the **getNum(num)** and **appendNum(num1,num2)** Functions and then the **output(numerals)** Function is called to render the Characters to the Frame named **display** and update its background color.

When updating the background color, there are two tests made; the first to determine if the color Characters are being used for a full RGB to Hex conversion, which would necessitate a comma being in the String. If the **charAt()** Method on the String variable **getColor** returns true, then the update of the background color is essentially stopped and black is used. The color is eventually updated with the **Full3()** Function later on. Second, the **getColor.length** Property tests for the number of Characters in the **String** Object so it can add the appropriate number of zeros to the **bgColor** Value so that the background color updates properly each time a Character is chosen by the user.

TurnHexToRGB255()   This Function uses the **parseInt()** Method with a **radix** of 16 to convert the Hexadecimal color characters String in the **numArray[0]** Element to a RGB Color that ranges from 0 to 255. It's only designed to convert one color at a time; that is, it will convert either the red, green, or blue value but not all three at once. Then the **output(numArray[0])** Function is called to render the results to screen.

TurnHexToRGB100()   This Function uses the **parseInt()** Method with a **radix** of 16 to convert the Hexadecimal color Characters String in the **numArray[0]** Element to a RGB Color that ranges from 0 to 255 and then uses the **Math.round()** Method to truncate the result of dividing that number by 255 and multiplying it by 100, which is the calculation required to convert the value into a percentage.

TurnRGB255toHex()   This Function uses the **parseInt()** Method to first turn the color String contained in **numArray[0]** into a base 10 number so that you can use the **toString(16)** Method with a **radix** of 16 to convert the RGB 255 color into a Hexadecimal color. Because JavaScript refuses to render zeros that are left of the decimal point, you have to force their inclusion in the converted color as a numeric String. To account for converting colors from 1 to 15 you need to insert one zero as a String for final output. To account for converting full black you have to insert two zeros as a String for final output. Yes, I know, no one is going to use this to convert black RGB to black Hexadecimal, but for completeness, it's here. The rest of the Function just tests for character data errata.

TurnRGB100toHex()   This Function is essentially the same as the last Function with the added **Math.round()** Method. It converts a RGB Color percentage into a Hexadecimal color.

TurnRGB255to100()   This Function converts a single RGB Color component, either red, green or blue from the 0 to 255 format into a percentage.

TurnRGB100to255()   This Function converts a single color percentage into a single RGB Color in the 0 to 255 format.

Full1()   This Function converts an entire Hexadecimal color triplet into all three of the RGB components and separates each by a comma and a blank space. It uses the **length** Property of the **String** Object to test for the number of Characters in the String contained in the **numArray[0]** Element so it can use the **charAt()** Method to extract the correct number of Characters and assign each of the red, green, blue color components to its own Element in the **rgbArray[]**. This allows you to individually display them and have them separated by commas and white space. By having a second Array you can also display the original Hexadecimal color for comparison purposes.

Full3()   This Function isn't nearly as complicated as it looks; in fact, the actual conversion is as simple as the **TurnRGB255toHex()** Function. The need for all the **if()...else** Statements is because of the lack of zeros to the left of the decimal when you go to display the converted color and update the background color. Let's clarify that.

    The user is supposed to input three color components that are separated by a comma; one for each of the red, green, and blue Values. You take that raw data and use the **split(',')** Method with a **comma** as the **separator** Argument to split that String into the **rgbArray[]** where each of the Array Elements has one color component. Then you parse the String with the **parseInt(rgbArray[0], 10)** Method for each Element so you can use the **toString(16)** Method to convert the color into Hexadecimal format. This is where the difficulty exists because if:

```
    rgbArray[0] = 5        then    rgbArray[0].toString(16) = "5"    not    "05"
```

and "05" is what you need in order to calculate a proper Hexadecimal Triplet, which then displays the correct background color.

Just in case that wasn't sufficiently clear, if:

```
rgbArray[0] = 2        rgbArray[1] = 7        rgbArray[2] = 15
```

then your new Hexadecimal color would be:

```
"27f"  not    "02070f"
```

which is what you want. It's further complicated when any of the components are zero. This is why you do all of the testing for zeros with the variables **a0**, **a1** and **a2** so you know when and how many zeros to manually code into the output. Numbers from 1 to 15 need one zero manually coded and a color component that is zero needs two zeros manually coded. When you check this example out in the browser be aware that when commas are input by the user, the background color is only updated when the Button with Value of **Full3** is clicked.

clearLastEntry()   This Function uses the **slice(0, -1)** Method to extract all of the Characters except for the last one contained in the String located in the **numArray[0]** Element. Then it calls the **output(numArray[0])** Function to display the results. It's implemented when the user clicks the Button with Value of "Clear Entry".

resetOutput()   This Function just reinitializes all the Array Elements in both Arrays to blank Strings and displays the results.

        Finally the **initiateParam()** Function is called in a separate SCRIPT Element when the document loads. The rest of the code just sets up the HTML for the Table, Buttons and Event Handlers of the Button Elements.

Example 3-34 Part 1:   Sample434.html

```
<!DOCTYPE HTML PUBLIC "-//W3C//DTD HTML 3.2//EN">
<HTML>
<HEAD>
<TITLE>Sample 434 - Example 3-34       Multiple Color Conversion Calculator</TITLE>

<STYLE TYPE="text/JavaScript">

        classes.Mainbody.BODY.margins("0px");
        classes.Mainbody.BODY.paddings("0px");
        classes.Mainbody.BODY.backgroundColor="black";
        classes.Mainbody.BODY.color="white";

</STYLE>

<!-- ******************************************************************* -->

<SCRIPT LANGUAGE="JavaScript1.2"><!--BEGIN HIDING

numArray = new Array(3);

rgbArray = new Array(3);

/*--------------------------------------------------*/
```

```
function initiateParam(){

        numArray[0] = "";
        numArray[1] = "";
        numArray[2] = "";
        rgbArray[0] = "";
        rgbArray[1] = "";
        rgbArray[2] = "";
}
/*--------------------------------------------------*/

function getNum(num){

        numArray[0] = appendNum(numArray[0],num);
        output(numArray[0]);
}
/*--------------------------------------------------*/

function appendNum(num1,num2){

        var numerals="";
        numerals+=num1;
        numerals+=num2;
        return numerals;
}
/*--------------------------------------------------*/
/*--------------------------------------------------*/

function output(numerals){

parent.display.document.write("<HTML>")
parent.display.document.write("<HEAD><TITLE>Calculator Readout<\/TITLE>")
parent.display.document.write("<STYLE TYPE='text/JavaScript'>")

parent.display.document.write("classes.Mainbody.BODY.margins('0px');")
parent.display.document.write("classes.Mainbody.BODY.paddings('0px');")
parent.display.document.write("classes.Mainbody.BODY.backgroundColor='black';")
parent.display.document.write("classes.Mainbody.BODY.color='white';")

parent.display.document.write("classes.SteelBlu.all.margins('0px');")
parent.display.document.write("classes.SteelBlu.all.backgroundColor='steelblue';")
parent.display.document.write("classes.SteelBlu.all.color='lime';")
parent.display.document.write("classes.SteelBlu.all.width='100%';")
parent.display.document.write("classes.SteelBlu.all.fontSize='40pt';")
parent.display.document.write("classes.SteelBlu.all.fontFamily='Moonlight, Clarendon, Helvetica, serif';")
parent.display.document.write("classes.SteelBlu.all.paddings('7px');")
parent.display.document.write("classes.SteelBlu.all.borderTopWidth='10px';")
parent.display.document.write("classes.SteelBlu.all.borderRightWidth='50px';")
parent.display.document.write("classes.SteelBlu.all.borderBottomWidth='10px';")
parent.display.document.write("classes.SteelBlu.all.borderLeftWidth='50px';")
parent.display.document.write("classes.SteelBlu.all.borderStyle='ridge';")
parent.display.document.write("classes.SteelBlu.all.borderColor='#5555ff';")
parent.display.document.write("classes.SteelBlu.all.lineHeight='40pt';")

parent.display.document.write("<\/STYLE>")
parent.display.document.write("<\/HEAD>")
parent.display.document.write("<BODY CLASS='Mainbody'>")

parent.display.document.write("<LAYER CLASS='SteelBlu' ID='Readout' LEFT='10' TOP='-25' HEIGHT='100'>")
parent.display.document.write("<CENTER>")

//This line actually writes the Array data to the document.

        parent.display.document.write(numerals.toString())


        var getColor = numArray[0].toString();

//This disables the color update when using commas in the Full Color Conversion

        if (getColor.charAt(1) == ','  ||  getColor.charAt(2) == ','
        || getColor.charAt(3) == ','  ||  getColor.charAt(4) == ','
        || getColor.charAt(5) == ','  ||  getColor.charAt(6) == ','
        || getColor.charAt(7) == ','  ||  getColor.charAt(8) == ',') {

        parent.display.document.bgColor='black';
        }
```

```
//Allows for continuous color updating for each character input.

else      if (getColor.length == 6)
                   { parent.display.document.bgColor='#'+ getColor;}
else      if (getColor.length == 5)
                   { parent.display.document.bgColor='#'+ getColor + '0';}
else      if (getColor.length == 4)
                   { parent.display.document.bgColor='#'+ getColor + '00';}
else      if (getColor.length == 3)
                   { parent.display.document.bgColor='#'+ getColor + '000';}
else      if (getColor.length == 2)
                   { parent.display.document.bgColor='#'+ getColor + '0000';}
else      if (getColor.length == 1)
                   { parent.display.document.bgColor='#'+ getColor + '00000';}

parent.display.document.write("<\/CENTER>")
parent.display.document.write("<\/LAYER>")
parent.display.document.write("<\/BODY>")
parent.display.document.write("<\/HTML>")

        parent.display.document.close();

}

/*-------------------------------------------------------------------------*/

function TurnHexToRGB255() {

        numArray[0] = parseInt(numArray[0] , 16);

        output(numArray[0]);
}
/*----------------------------------------------------*/

function TurnHexToRGB100() {

        numArray[0] = parseInt(numArray[0] , 16);
        numArray[0] = Math.round((numArray[0] / 255) * 100);

        output(numArray[0]);
}
/*----------------------------------------------------*/

function TurnRGB255toHex() {

        if (numArray[0] >255) {
        alert("While the following conversion will be accurate, if you want a "+
        "useable color you must pick a number from 0 to 255");
        }
else if (isNaN(numArray[0])) {
        alert("YO! The sign said from 0 to 255. You chose:  " + numArray[0]);
        }
else if (numArray[0] == '0'  ||  numArray[0] == '00'  || numArray[0] == '000'){
        output('00');
        }
else if (numArray[0] < 16  &&  numArray[0] > 0){
        numArray[0] = parseInt(numArray[0] , 10);
        numArray[0] =  (numArray[0]).toString(16);
        output('0' + numArray[0]);
        }
else {
        numArray[0] = parseInt(numArray[0] , 10);
        numArray[0] =  (numArray[0]).toString(16);
        output(numArray[0]);
        }
}

/*----------------------------------------------------*/

function TurnRGB100toHex() {

        if (numArray[0] >100  ||  isNaN(numArray[0]) == true) {
        alert("YO! The sign said from 0 to 100. You chose:  " + numArray[0]);
        }
else if (numArray[0] == '0'  ||  numArray[0] == '00'  || numArray[0] == '000'){
        output('00');
        }
```

```
else {
        numArray[0] = parseFloat(numArray[0]);
        numArray[0] = Math.round((numArray[0] * 255) / 100);

                if (numArray[0] < 16  &&  numArray[0] > 0){

                        numArray[0] =  (numArray[0]).toString(16);
                        output('0' + numArray[0]);
                }
                else {
                        numArray[0] =  (numArray[0]).toString(16);
                        output(numArray[0]);
                }
        }
}
/*-------------------------------------------------*/

function TurnRGB255to100() {

        if (numArray[0] >255  ||  isNaN(numArray[0]) == true) {
        alert("YO! The sign said from 0 to 100. You chose:  " + numArray[0]);
        }
else {
        numArray[0] = parseFloat(numArray[0]);
        numArray[0] = Math.round((numArray[0] / 255) * 100);

        output(numArray[0]);
        }
}
/*-------------------------------------------------*/

function TurnRGB100to255() {

        if (numArray[0] >100  ||  isNaN(numArray[0]) == true) {
        alert("YO! The sign said from 0 to 100. You chose:  " + numArray[0]);
        }
else {
        numArray[0] = parseFloat(numArray[0]);
        numArray[0] = Math.round((numArray[0] * 255) / 100);

        output(numArray[0]);
        }
}

/*-------------------------------------------------*/
/*-------------------------------------------------*/


function Full1() {

        var getChar = numArray[0].toString();

        if (getChar.length == 6) {
                rgbArray[0] = getChar.charAt(0) + getChar.charAt(1);
                rgbArray[1] = getChar.charAt(2) + getChar.charAt(3);
                rgbArray[2] = getChar.charAt(4) + getChar.charAt(5);
                rgbArray[0] = parseInt(rgbArray[0] , 16);
                rgbArray[1] = parseInt(rgbArray[1] , 16);
                rgbArray[2] = parseInt(rgbArray[2] , 16);
                output(numArray[0] + ' = ' + rgbArray[0] + ', ' + rgbArray[1] + ', ' + rgbArray[2]);
        }
else if (getChar.length == 5) {
                rgbArray[0] = getChar.charAt(0) + getChar.charAt(1);
                rgbArray[1] = getChar.charAt(2) + getChar.charAt(3);
                rgbArray[2] = getChar.charAt(4);
                rgbArray[0] = parseInt(rgbArray[0] , 16);
                rgbArray[1] = parseInt(rgbArray[1] , 16);
                rgbArray[2] = parseInt(rgbArray[2] , 16);
                output(numArray[0] + ' = ' + rgbArray[0] + ', ' + rgbArray[1] + ', ' + rgbArray[2]);
        }
else if (getChar.length == 4) {
                rgbArray[0] = getChar.charAt(0) + getChar.charAt(1);
                rgbArray[1] = getChar.charAt(2) + getChar.charAt(3);
                rgbArray[0] = parseInt(rgbArray[0] , 16);
                rgbArray[1] = parseInt(rgbArray[1] , 16);
                output(numArray[0] + ' = ' + rgbArray[0] + ', ' + rgbArray[1] + ', 0');
        }
```

```
        else if (getChar.length == 3) {
                    rgbArray[0] = getChar.charAt(0) + getChar.charAt(1);
                    rgbArray[1] = getChar.charAt(2);
                    rgbArray[0] = parseInt(rgbArray[0] , 16);
                    rgbArray[1] = parseInt(rgbArray[1] , 16);
                    output(numArray[0] + ' = ' + rgbArray[0] + ', ' + rgbArray[1] + ', 0');
            }
        else if (getChar.length == 2) {
                    rgbArray[0] = getChar.charAt(0) + getChar.charAt(1);
                    rgbArray[0] = parseInt(rgbArray[0] , 16);
                    output(numArray[0] + ' = ' + rgbArray[0] + ', 0' + ', 0');
            }
        else {
                    rgbArray[0] = getChar.charAt(0);
                    rgbArray[0] = parseInt(rgbArray[0] , 16);
                    output(numArray[0] + ' = ' + rgbArray[0] + ', 0' + ', 0');
            }
}
/*---------------------------------------------------*/

function Full3() {

        var getRGB = numArray[0].toString();

        rgbArray = getRGB.split(',');

        var a0 = parseInt(rgbArray[0] , 10);
        var a1 = parseInt(rgbArray[1] , 10);
        var a2 = parseInt(rgbArray[2] , 10);

        rgbArray[0] = parseInt(rgbArray[0] , 10);
        rgbArray[0] =  (rgbArray[0]).toString(16);
        rgbArray[1] = parseInt(rgbArray[1] , 10);
        rgbArray[1] =  (rgbArray[1]).toString(16);
        rgbArray[2] = parseInt(rgbArray[2] , 10);
        rgbArray[2] =  (rgbArray[2]).toString(16);

/*----------------------------------------------------------------*/

        if (isNaN(a1)) {rgbArray[1] = '00'; alert('You forgot the green value');}
        if (isNaN(a2)) {rgbArray[2] = '00'; alert('You forgot the blue value');}

/*----------------------------------------------------------------*/

        if ( (a0 == 0 || a0 == 00 || a0 == 000)  && (a1 == 0 || a1 == 00 || a1 == 000)  &&
            (a2 == 0 || a2 == 00 || a2 == 000) ) {

            output(numArray[0] + ' = ' + '000000');
            parent.display.document.bgColor='#000000';
        }

/*----------------------------------------------------------------*/

else if ((a0 == 0 || a0 == 00 || a0 == 000) && (a1 == 0 || a1 == 00 || a1 == 000) && (a2 < 16  && a2 > 0))  {

        output(numArray[0] + ' = '    + '0000' + '0' + rgbArray[2]);
        parent.display.document.bgColor='#0000' + '0' + rgbArray[2];
        }

else if ((a0 == 0 || a0 == 00 || a0 == 000) && (a2 == 0 || a2 == 00 || a2 == 000) && (a1 < 16  && a1 > 0))  {

        output(numArray[0] + ' = '    + '00' + '0' + rgbArray[1] + '00');
        parent.display.document.bgColor='#00' + '0' + rgbArray[1] + '00';
        }
else if ((a1 == 0 || a1 == 00 || a1 == 000) && (a2 == 0 || a2 == 00 || a2 == 000) && (a0 < 16  && a0 > 0))  {

        output(numArray[0] + ' = '    + '0' + rgbArray[0] + '0000');
        parent.display.document.bgColor='#0' + rgbArray[0] + '0000';
        }

/*---------------------------------------------------*/

else if ((a0 == 0 || a0 == 00 || a0 == 000)  && (a1 < 16  && a1 > 0)  && (a2 < 16  && a2 > 0))  {

        output(numArray[0] + ' = '    + '00' + '0' + rgbArray[1] + '0' + rgbArray[2]);
        parent.display.document.bgColor='#00' + '0' + rgbArray[1] + '0' + rgbArray[2];
        }
```

```
else if ((a1 == 0 || a1 == 00 || a1 == 000)  &&  (a0 < 16  &&  a0 > 0)  &&  (a2 < 16  &&  a2 > 0))  {

        output(numArray[0] + ' = '    + '0' + rgbArray[0] + '00' + '0' + rgbArray[2]);
        parent.display.document.bgColor='#0' + rgbArray[0] + '00' + '0' + rgbArray[2];
        }
else if ((a2 == 0 || a2 == 00 || a2 == 000)  &&  (a0 < 16  &&  a0 > 0)  &&  (a1 < 16  &&  a1 > 0))  {

        output(numArray[0] + ' = '    + '0' + rgbArray[0] + '0' + rgbArray[1] + '00');
        parent.display.document.bgColor='#0' + rgbArray[0] + '0' + rgbArray[1] + '00';
        }

/*-------------------------------------------------------------------*/

else if ((a0 == 0 || a0 == 00 || a0 == 000)  &&  a1 < 16  &&  a1 > 0)  {

        output(numArray[0] + ' = '    + '00' + '0' + rgbArray[1] + rgbArray[2]);
        parent.display.document.bgColor='#00' + '0' + rgbArray[1] + rgbArray[2];
        }
else if ((a0 == 0 || a0 == 00 || a0 == 000)  &&  a2 < 16  &&  a2 > 0)  {

        output(numArray[0] + ' = '    + '00' + rgbArray[1] + '0' + rgbArray[2]);
        parent.display.document.bgColor='#00' + rgbArray[1] + '0' + rgbArray[2];
        }
else if ((a1 == 0 || a1 == 00 || a1 == 000)  &&  a0 < 16  &&  a0 > 0)  {

        output(numArray[0] + ' = '    + '0' + rgbArray[0] + '00' + rgbArray[2]);
        parent.display.document.bgColor='#0' + rgbArray[0] + '00' + rgbArray[2];
        }
/*------------------------------------------------*/

else if ((a1 == 0 || a1 == 00 || a1 == 000)  &&  a2 < 16  &&  a2 > 0)  {

        output(numArray[0] + ' = '               + rgbArray[0] + '00' + '0' + rgbArray[2]);
        parent.display.document.bgColor='#' + rgbArray[0] + '00' + '0' + rgbArray[2];
        }
else if ((a2 == 0 || a2 == 00 || a2 == 000)  &&  a0 < 16  &&  a0 > 0)  {

        output(numArray[0] + ' = '    + '0' + rgbArray[0] + rgbArray[1] + '00');
        parent.display.document.bgColor='#0' + rgbArray[0] + rgbArray[1] + '00';
        }
else if ((a2 == 0 || a2 == 00 || a2 == 000)  &&  a1 < 16  &&  a1 > 0)  {

        output(numArray[0] + ' = '               + rgbArray[0] + '0' + rgbArray[1] + '00');
        parent.display.document.bgColor='#' + rgbArray[0] + '0' + rgbArray[1] + '00' ;
        }

/*-------------------------------------------------------------------*/

else if (a0 < 16  &&  a0 > 0  &&  a1 < 16  &&  a1 > 0)  {

        output(numArray[0] + ' = '    + '0' + rgbArray[0] + '0' + rgbArray[1] + rgbArray[2]);
        parent.display.document.bgColor='#0' + rgbArray[0] + '0' + rgbArray[1] + rgbArray[2];
        }
else if (a0 < 16  &&  a0 > 0  &&  a2 < 16  &&  a2 > 0)  {

        output(numArray[0] + ' = '    + '0' + rgbArray[0] + rgbArray[1] + '0' + rgbArray[2]);
        parent.display.document.bgColor='#0' + rgbArray[0] + rgbArray[1] + '0' + rgbArray[2];
        }
else if (a1 < 16  &&  a1 > 0  &&  a2 < 16  &&  a2 > 0)  {

        output(numArray[0] + ' = '               + rgbArray[0] + '0' + rgbArray[1] + '0' + rgbArray[2]);
        parent.display.document.bgColor='#' + rgbArray[0] + '0' + rgbArray[1] + '0' + rgbArray[2];
        }

/*------------------------------------------------*/

else if ((a0 == 0 || a0 == 00 || a0 == 000)  &&  (a1 == 0 || a1 == 00 || a1 == 000))  {

        output(numArray[0] + ' = '    + '0000' + rgbArray[2]);
        parent.display.document.bgColor='#0000' + rgbArray[2];
        }

else if ((a0 == 0 || a0 == 00 || a0 == 000)  &&  (a2 == 0 || a2 == 00 || a2 == 000))  {

        output(numArray[0] + ' = '    + '00'+ rgbArray[1] + '00');
        parent.display.document.bgColor='#00'+ rgbArray[1] + '00';
        }
```

```
else if ((a1 == 0 || a1 == 00 || a1 == 000)  && (a2 == 0 || a2 == 00 || a2 == 000))  {

        output(numArray[0] + ' = '            + rgbArray[0] + '0000');
        parent.display.document.bgColor='#'+ rgbArray[0] + '0000';
        }
/*------------------------------------------------------------------*/

else if (a0 == 0 || a0 == 00 || a0 == 000)  {

        output(numArray[0] + ' = '     + '00' + rgbArray[1] + rgbArray[2]);
        parent.display.document.bgColor='#00' + rgbArray[1] + rgbArray[2];
        }
else if (a1 == 0 || a1 == 00 || a1 == 000)  {

        output(numArray[0] + ' = '            + rgbArray[0] + '00' + rgbArray[2]);
        parent.display.document.bgColor='#' + rgbArray[0] + '00' + rgbArray[2];
        }
else if (a2 == 0 || a2 == 00 || a2 == 000)  {

        output(numArray[0] + ' = '            + rgbArray[0] + rgbArray[1] + '00');
        parent.display.document.bgColor='#' + rgbArray[0] + rgbArray[1] + '00';
        }
/*--------------------------------------------------*/

else if (a0 < 16  &&  a0 > 0)  {

        output(numArray[0] + ' = '     + '0' + rgbArray[0] + rgbArray[1] + rgbArray[2]);
        parent.display.document.bgColor='#0' + rgbArray[0] + rgbArray[1] + rgbArray[2];
        }
else if (a1 < 16  &&  a1 > 0)  {

        output(numArray[0] + ' = '            + rgbArray[0] + '0' + rgbArray[1] + rgbArray[2]);
        parent.display.document.bgColor='#' + rgbArray[0] + '0' + rgbArray[1] + rgbArray[2];
        }
else if (a2 < 16  &&  a2 > 0)  {

        output(numArray[0] + ' = '            + rgbArray[0] + rgbArray[1] + '0' + rgbArray[2]);
        parent.display.document.bgColor='#' + rgbArray[0] + rgbArray[1] + '0' + rgbArray[2];
        }
/*----------------------------------------------------------------------------*/

else {
        output(numArray[0] + ' = '  + rgbArray[0] + rgbArray[1] + rgbArray[2]);
        parent.display.document.bgColor='#' + rgbArray[0] + rgbArray[1] + rgbArray[2];
        }
}
/*----------------------------------------------------------------------------*/
/*----------------------------------------------------------------------------*/

function clearLastEntry()  {

        numArray[0] = numArray[0].toString();
        numArray[0] = numArray[0].slice(0,-1);
        output(numArray[0]);
}

function resetOutput() {

        initiateParam();
        output(numArray[0]);
}

//END HIDING-->
</SCRIPT>

</HEAD>
<!-- *************************************************************** -->
<BODY CLASS="Mainbody">

<SCRIPT LANGUAGE="JavaScript1.2"><!--BEGIN HIDING

initiateParam();

//END HIDING-->
</SCRIPT>
<!-- *************************************************************** -->
```

```
<LAYER ID="MainLayer" LEFT="10" TOP="10">

<FORM NAME="FormB">

<TABLE BORDER="10" CELLPADDING="0" CELLSPACING="5" WIDTH="100%" HEIGHT="300" BGCOLOR="yellow"
BORDERCOLOR="red">

<TR>
<TH WIDTH="50"><INPUT TYPE="button" NAME="One" VALUE="1" onClick="getNum(1);"></TH>
<TH WIDTH="50"><INPUT TYPE="button" NAME="Two" VALUE="2" onClick="getNum(2);"></TH>
<TH WIDTH="50"><INPUT TYPE="button" NAME="Three" VALUE="3" onClick="getNum(3);"></TH>
<TH WIDTH="50" BGCOLOR="purple"><INPUT TYPE="button" NAME="letterA" VALUE="a" onClick="getNum('a');"></TH>
<TH WIDTH="50" BGCOLOR="purple"><INPUT TYPE="button" NAME="letterD" VALUE="d" onClick="getNum('d');"></TH>
<TH BGCOLOR="#7700ff">
<INPUT TYPE="button" NAME="HexRGB255" VALUE="Hex to ~~ RGB 0-255" onClick="TurnHexToRGB255();">
</TH>
<TH BGCOLOR="lime"><INPUT TYPE="button" NAME="FullHexRGB255" VALUE="Full 1" onClick="Full1();"></TH>
</TR>

<TR>
<TH><INPUT TYPE="button" NAME="Four" VALUE="4" onClick="getNum(4);"></TH>
<TH><INPUT TYPE="button" NAME="Five" VALUE="5" onClick="getNum(5);"></TH>
<TH><INPUT TYPE="button" NAME="S0" VALUE="6" onClick="getNum(6);"></TH>
<TH BGCOLOR="purple"><INPUT TYPE="button" NAME="letterB" VALUE="b" onClick="getNum('b');"></TH>
<TH BGCOLOR="purple"><INPUT TYPE="button" NAME="letterE" VALUE="e" onClick="getNum('e');"></TH>
<TH BGCOLOR="#7700ff">
<INPUT TYPE="button" NAME="HexRGB100" VALUE="Hex to ~~ RGB 0-100%" onClick="TurnHexToRGB100();"></TH>
</TR>

<TR>
<TH><INPUT TYPE="button" NAME="Seven" VALUE="7" onClick="getNum(7);"></TH>
<TH><INPUT TYPE="button" NAME="Eight" VALUE="8" onClick="getNum(8);"></TH>
<TH><INPUT TYPE="button" NAME="Nine" VALUE="9" onClick="getNum(9);"></TH>
<TH BGCOLOR="purple"><INPUT TYPE="button" NAME="letterC" VALUE="c" onClick="getNum('c');"></TH>
<TH BGCOLOR="purple"><INPUT TYPE="button" NAME="letterF" VALUE="f" onClick="getNum('f');"></TH>
<TH BGCOLOR="#7700ff">
<INPUT TYPE="button" NAME="RGB255Hex" VALUE="RGB 0-255 to ~~ Hex" onClick="TurnRGB255toHex();"></TH>
<TH BGCOLOR="lime"><INPUT TYPE="button" NAME="FullRGB255Hex" VALUE="Full 3" onClick="Full3();"></TH>
</TR>

<TR>
<TH><INPUT TYPE="button" NAME="Zero" VALUE="0" onClick="getNum(0);"></TH>
<TH><INPUT TYPE="button" NAME="Comma" VALUE="," onClick="getNum(',');"></TH>
<TH COLSPAN="2" BGCOLOR="blue">
<INPUT TYPE="button" NAME="ClearEntry" VALUE="Clear Entry" onClick="clearLastEntry();"></TH>
<TH BGCOLOR="red"><INPUT TYPE="button" NAME="ClearAll" VALUE="Clear" onClick="resetOutput();"></TH>
<TH BGCOLOR="#7700ff">
<INPUT TYPE="button" NAME="RGB100Hex" VALUE="RGB 0-100% to ~~ Hex" onClick="TurnRGB100toHex();"></TH>
</TR>

<TR>
<TH COLSPAN="5" BGCOLOR="#7700ff">
<FONT SIZE="4" COLOR="white">
These Conversions are for single colors:            <BR>
Either R, G, or B.....Not RGB.                          </FONT></TH>
<TH BGCOLOR="#7700ff">
<INPUT TYPE="button" NAME="RGB255to100" VALUE="RGB 0-255 to ~~ RGB 0-100%" onClick="TurnRGB255to100();"></TH>
</TR>

<TR>
<TH COLSPAN="5" BGCOLOR="lime">
Buttons
<FONT SIZE="4" COLOR="white">            Full 1     </FONT> and
<FONT SIZE="4" COLOR="white">            Full 3     </FONT> are full Conversions.          <BR>
Hex to rgb: click six sequential digits like this: 8822ff            <BR>
rgb to Hex: separate colors by a comma like this: 42,127,255          </TH>
<TH BGCOLOR="#7700ff">
<INPUT TYPE="button" NAME="RGB100to255" VALUE="RGB 0-100% to ~~ RGB 0-255" onClick="TurnRGB100to255();"></TH>
</TR>

</TABLE>
</FORM>
</LAYER>
</BODY>

</HTML>
```

Example 3-34   Sample434Frameset.html

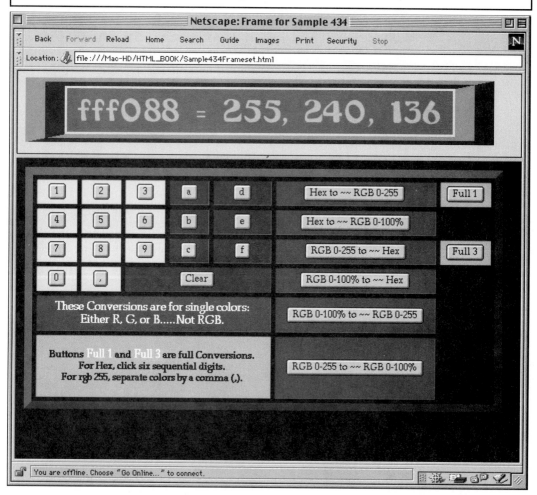

The code for the Frameset for Example 3-34 is on the following page.

All of the recognized JavaScript color names, along with their HEX, rgb% and rgb number value equivalents are in a Chart, starting on page 1033, in Appendix B.
This same information is contained on the CD-ROM in the Sample file:

Sample1100-AllColorValues.html.

If you just want to see all of the actual colors displayed along with the name of each color, then check out Sample1100-AllColorNames.html.

Example 3-34 Part 2:   **Sample434Frameset.html**

```
<!DOCTYPE HTML PUBLIC "-//W3C//DTD HTML 3.2//EN">
<HTML>
<HEAD>  <TITLE>Frame for Sample 434</TITLE>   </HEAD>

<FRAMESET ROWS="140,*">

        <FRAME MARGINHEIGHT=0 SCROLLING="no" NAME="display" SRC="Sample434A.html">

        <FRAME SCROLLING="auto" NAME="main" SRC="Sample434.html">

</FRAMESET>

</HTML>
```

A compilation example with border animation and music

The main purpose of Example 3-35 is to take some of the topics that have been covered so far and use them in a page that you might actually see on the web except for the size of the sound file which is 60 megs. In a real site, you would have links and most likely get a sound-tease with an option to buy, but since this is on a CD-ROM, I included the whole song which I wrote, performed, engineered and recorded. Hope you enjoy it.

This example has a self-updating date, time, and length of stay at the site that displays in the status bar of the window. It also has an embedded sound file of the song "Journeys of Illumination". There are animated rainbow bars that form a moving border at the edges of the page and spinning Earth globes in the four corners of the page.

Two Buttons control a Layer, which animates a banner with text that lists the names of the different movements of the song. Two other Buttons control the animation of the two Layers that contain the image of the CD and the songlist on the CD. MouseOver and MouseOut Events can also show and hide these two Layers.

The audio file is set to play automatically, and the Navigator audio controls are set to be shown by setting the width and height Attributes to 144 and 60, respectively, which are the minimum values required. A Screenshot is on page 361.

Example 3-35 Part 1:   **Sample435.html**

```
<!DOCTYPE HTML PUBLIC "-//W3C//DTD HTML 3.2//EN">
<HTML>
<HEAD>
<TITLE>Sample 435 - Example 3-35  Border Animation and Music          </TITLE>
```

```
<STYLE TYPE="text/JavaScript">

        classes.Mainbody.BODY.margins("0px");
        classes.Mainbody.BODY.paddings("0px");
        classes.Mainbody.BODY.backgroundColor="black";
        classes.Mainbody.BODY.color="white";

        classes.SteelBlu.all.margins("0px");
        classes.SteelBlu.all.backgroundColor="steelblue";
        classes.SteelBlu.all.color="navy";
        classes.SteelBlu.all.fontSize="22pt";
        classes.SteelBlu.all.fontFamily="Clarendon, Helvetica, fantasy";
        classes.SteelBlu.all.paddings("15px");
        classes.SteelBlu.all.borderTopWidth="10px";
        classes.SteelBlu.all.borderRightWidth="30px";
        classes.SteelBlu.all.borderBottomWidth="10px";
        classes.SteelBlu.all.borderLeftWidth="30px";
        classes.SteelBlu.all.borderStyle="inset";
        classes.SteelBlu.all.borderColor="#5555ff";
        classes.SteelBlu.all.lineHeight="28pt";

        classes.RedBox.all.backgroundColor="yellow";
        classes.RedBox.all.fontSize="22pt";
        classes.RedBox.all.color="red";

        ids.L3.fontSize="20pt";
        ids.L3.fontFamily="Moonlight, 'Brush Script', Cloister, cursive";
        ids.L3.color="#8800ff";
        ids.L3.backgroundColor="cyan";

        classes.PurpleBox.all.width="420px";
        classes.PurpleBox.all.borderWidths("15px");
        classes.PurpleBox.all.borderColor="#8800ff";
        classes.PurpleBox.all.fontSize="17pt";
        classes.PurpleBox.all.borderStyle="groove";
        classes.PurpleBox.all.fontFamily="'Brush Script', fantasy";
        classes.PurpleBox.all.paddings("3px");
        classes.PurpleBox.all.color="yellow";
        classes.PurpleBox.all.backgroundColor="mediumblue";

        tags.H1.fontSize="23pt";
        tags.H1.color="red";

        tags.H4.fontSize="14pt";
        tags.H4.color="#007700";
        tags.H4.backgroundColor="#00ff44";
        tags.H4.fontFamily="Palatino, Times, Helvetica, serif";

        classes.LimeIt.all.color="lime";
        classes.LimeIt.all.fontSize="14pt";

        classes.Turqy.all.color="turquoise";

</STYLE>

<!--   ************************************************************   -->
```

```
<SCRIPT LANGUAGE="JavaScript1.2"><!--BEGIN HIDING

        startTime = new Date();

/*-----------------------------------------------------------*/
//The getMonth() Method returns a zero to eleven numbering scheme for months
//such that January = 0, February = 1, ..., December = 11,
//so you have to increment the month by 1 if you need January to be 1 instead of 0
//which is used for the todayMonth variable, below.

function initializeTime()  {

        var today           = new Date();
        var todayMonth      = today.getMonth() +1;
        var todayDay        = today.getDate();
        var todayYear       = today.getYear();
        var todaysHours     = today.getHours();
        var todaysMinutes   = today.getMinutes();
        var todaysSeconds   = today.getSeconds();
        var later           = new Date();
        var TimeHere        = Math.round((later - startTime) / 60000);

        todaysHours = ((todaysHours > 12)  ?  todaysHours - 12  :  todaysHours);

        var showTime= "The Date is:  "+ todayMonth +"/"
        showTime += todayDay +"/"
        showTime += todayYear
        showTime += " *****  The Time is:   " + todaysHours
        showTime += ((todaysMinutes > 9)  ?  " :"  :  " :0")
        showTime += todaysMinutes
        showTime += ((todaysSeconds > 9)  ?  " :"  :  " :0")
        showTime += todaysSeconds
        showTime += ((todaysHours >= 12)  ?  " PM"  :  " AM")
        showTime += " ***** You have been here "
        showTime += TimeHere + " Minutes."

        window.status = showTime;

        setTimeout('initializeTime()', 1000);
}
/*-----------------------------------------------------------*/
//END HIDING-->
</SCRIPT>

</HEAD>
<!-- **************************************************************** -->
<BODY CLASS="Mainbody" onLoad="initializeTime();"
BACKGROUND="JPEG-FILES/icon-BG-asteroids.jpg">

<LAYER CLASS="SteelBlu" ID="L1" LEFT=0 TOP=-10 WIDTH="100%">

<LAYER CLASS="RedBox" ID="L2" LEFT=55 TOP=28>
<NOBR>HI!
<FONT COLOR="#7700ee">Journeys of Illumination</FONT>
has 5 movements. It starts with
<FONT COLOR="#7700ee">Fanfare of Twilight</FONT>
which blends into
<FONT COLOR="#7700ee">Dance of Awakening</FONT>.
```

```
<FONT COLOR="#7700ee">Thought-Travel Meandering in a Time-Free Space-Like
Domain</FONT>
is the third movement which melds into
<FONT COLOR="#7700ee">Dimensional Freefall</FONT>
and the song concludes with
<FONT COLOR="#7700ee">Wanderjahr Ever Onward</FONT>.</NOBR>
</LAYER>


<LAYER CLASS="RedBox" ID="L3" LEFT=0 TOP=80 WIDTH=340>
<FORM NAME="form3">Click to:
<INPUT TYPE="button" NAME="b1" VALUE="Move Banner" onClick="StartBanner();">
<INPUT TYPE="button" NAME="b2" VALUE="Stop Banner" onClick="StopBanner();"><BR><BR>
<EMBED SRC="./Sample-ETOC/Journeys-Of-Illumination.aiff" AUTOSTART="true" WIDTH=144
HEIGHT=60>
<INPUT TYPE="button" NAME="b7" VALUE="Slide Album" onClick="showAlbumText();
slideAlbum();">
<INPUT TYPE="button" NAME="b8" VALUE="Slide Back" onClick="slideAlbumBack();
slideAlbumText(); hideAlbumText();"><BR><BR>

The song that is playing is called <BR>
<FONT COLOR="#2200cc">Journeys of Illumination</FONT> <BR>
which is the title track of the album and was composed, played and recorded in
Sedona, Arizona in 1992.<BR><BR>
<H4>The Date, Time and Length of Stay at this site are down here in the status
bar.</H4>
</FORM></LAYER>


<!-- ********************************* -->
<LAYER CLASS="PurpleBox" ID="L4Text" LEFT=350 TOP=80 VISIBILITY="hide" WIDTH=370
onMouseOut="bringAlbumBack();">
<H1>Journeys of Illumination</H1>
Journeys of Illumination <SPAN CLASS="LimeIt">Song Time 11:02</SPAN><BR>
<SPAN CLASS="Turqy">
Fanfare of Twilight<BR>
Dance of Awakening<BR>
Thought-Travel Meandering in a Time-Free Space-Like Domain<BR>
Dimensional Freefall<BR>
Wanderjahr Ever Onward<BR></SPAN>
Sagacity in Solitude<BR>
Musing Spirals<BR>
Furthur<BR><BR>
</LAYER>


<LAYER CLASS="PurpleBox" ID="L4" LEFT=350 TOP=80 WIDTH=350
onMouseOver="revealAlbumText();">
<IMG SRC="./dreamplay-website/CD-JPEG5-Journeys-Illuminat.jpg" WIDTH=324
HEIGHT=293>
</LAYER>
<!-- ********************************* -->

</LAYER>

<!-- This layer is necessary to have the border on top of the scrolling banner -->

<LAYER CLASS="SteelBlu" ID="L7" LEFT=0 TOP=-10 WIDTH="100%">
</LAYER>


<!-- ****************************************************************** -->
```

```
<SCRIPT LANGUAGE="JavaScript1.2"><!--BEGIN HIDING

        var booleanTest = true;

function ScrollllBanner() {

        if (booleanTest == true) {

                if (document.L1.document.L2.left > -
document.L1.document.L2.clip.width)
                        document.L1.document.L2.moveBy(-10,0);
                else document.L1.document.L2.moveTo(document.L7.clip.width, 28);

                setTimeout('ScrolllllBanner()', 100);
        }
        else document.L1.document.L2.moveTo(document.L1.document.L2.left, 28);
}

function StopBanner() {
        booleanTest = false;
}

function StartBanner() {
        booleanTest = true;
        ScrollllBanner();
}

/*------------------------------------------------------------------------*/
/*------------------------------------------------------------------------*/

function revealAlbumText()  {

        document.L1.document.L4.moveTo(1000,80);
        document.L1.document.L4Text.visibility="show";
        document.L1.document.L4Text.moveTo(350,80);
}

function bringAlbumBack()  {

        document.L1.document.L4.visibility="show";
        document.L1.document.L4Text.visibility="hide";
        document.L1.document.L4.moveTo(350,80);
}
/*--------------------------------------------------*/

function showAlbumText()  {

        document.L1.document.L4Text.visibility="show";
        document.L1.document.L4Text.moveTo(350,80);
}
function slideAlbum()  {

        if (document.L1.document.L4.top < 600) {
        document.L1.document.L4.moveBy(0,20);
        setTimeout('slideAlbum()', 100);
        }
}
/*-------------------------------------------------*/
```

```
function slideAlbumBack() {

        if (document.L1.document.L4.top > 80) {
        document.L1.document.L4.moveBy(0,-20);
        setTimeout('slideAlbumBack()', 100);
        }
}

function slideAlbumText() {

        if (document.L1.document.L4Text.top < 600) {
        document.L1.document.L4Text.moveBy(0,20);
        setTimeout('slideAlbumText()', 100);
        }
}

function hideAlbumText() {

        if (document.L1.document.L4Text.top >= 600) {
        document.L1.document.L4Text.moveTo(350,80);
        document.L1.document.L4Text.visibility="hide";
        }
}
/*----------------------------------------------------------------------*/
//END HIDING-->
</SCRIPT>
</BODY>
</HTML>
```

This part of the example has the spinning Earth in it, and the master Frameset loads it four times so that it is in all four corners of the page.

Example 3-35 Part 2: Sample435-1.html

```
<!DOCTYPE HTML PUBLIC "-//W3C//DTD HTML 3.2//EN">
<HTML><HEAD>  <TITLE> Sample 435-1 - Example 3-35-1   globe in corners   </TITLE>

<STYLE TYPE="text/JavaScript">

        classes.Mainbody.BODY.margins("0px");
        classes.Mainbody.BODY.paddings("0px");
        tags.LAYER.width="100%";
</STYLE>
</HEAD>
<BODY CLASS="Mainbody">

<LAYER ID="L1" LEFT=0 TOP=0>
<IMG SRC="JPEG-FILES/EarthCloudGlobe.gif" WIDTH=20 HEIGHT=20>
</LAYER>

</BODY></HTML>
```

This part of the example has the animated rainbow in the top middle Frame moving from left to right.

Example 3-35 Part 3: Sample435-2.html

```
<!DOCTYPE HTML PUBLIC "-//W3C//DTD HTML 3.2//EN">
<HTML>
<HEAD>
<TITLE>Sample 435-2 - Example 3-35-2   top rainbow   </TITLE>

<STYLE TYPE="text/JavaScript">

        classes.Mainbody.BODY.margins("0px");
        classes.Mainbody.BODY.paddings("0px");
        classes.Mainbody.BODY.backgroundImage="./JPEG-FILES/icon-BG-stars.jpg";

</STYLE>

<SCRIPT LANGUAGE="JavaScript1.2"><!--BEGIN HIDING

function MoveIt2() {

        if (document.L2.left < document.L2.clip.width) document.L2.moveBy(20,0);
        else document.L2.moveTo(-504,0);
        setTimeout('MoveIt2()', 10);
}

//END HIDING-->
</SCRIPT>

</HEAD>

<BODY CLASS="Mainbody">

<LAYER ID="L2" LEFT=0 TOP=0 WIDTH="100%">

<IMG SRC="JPEG-FILES/ICON-HorizontalRainbow1.jpg" WIDTH=504 HEIGHT=18
onLoad="MoveIt2();">

</LAYER>

</BODY>
</HTML>
```

This part of the example has the animated rainbow in the left middle Frame moving from bottom to top.

Example 3-35 Part 4: Sample435-4.html

```
<!DOCTYPE HTML PUBLIC "-//W3C//DTD HTML 3.2//EN">
<HTML><HEAD>    <TITLE>Sample 435-4 - Example 3-35-4    left rainbow </TITLE>

<STYLE TYPE="text/JavaScript">

        classes.Mainbody.BODY.margins("0px");
        classes.Mainbody.BODY.paddings("0px");
        classes.Mainbody.BODY.backgroundImage="./JPEG-FILES/icon-BG-stars.jpg";

</STYLE>

<SCRIPT LANGUAGE="JavaScript1.2"><!--BEGIN HIDING

function MoveIt4() {

        if (document.L4.top > -504) document.L4.moveBy(0,-20);
        else document.L4.moveTo(0, document.L4.clip.height);
        setTimeout('MoveIt4()', 10);
}
//END HIDING-->
</SCRIPT>
</HEAD>

<BODY CLASS="Mainbody">

<LAYER ID="L4" LEFT=0 TOP=0 WIDTH="100%">
<IMG SRC="JPEG-FILES/ICON-VerticalRainbow1L.jpg" WIDTH=18 HEIGHT=504
onLoad="MoveIt4();">
</LAYER>

</BODY></HTML>
```

This part of the example has the animated rainbow in the right middle Frame moving from top to bottom.

Example 3-35 Part 5: Sample435-7.html

```
<!DOCTYPE HTML PUBLIC "-//W3C//DTD HTML 3.2//EN">
<HTML><HEAD><TITLE>Sample 435-7 - Example 3-35-7    right rainbow    </TITLE>

<STYLE TYPE="text/JavaScript">

        classes.Mainbody.BODY.margins("0px");
        classes.Mainbody.BODY.paddings("0px");
        classes.Mainbody.BODY.backgroundImage="./JPEG-FILES/icon-BG-stars.jpg";

</STYLE>
```

```
<SCRIPT LANGUAGE="JavaScript1.2"><!--BEGIN HIDING

function MoveIt7() {

        if (document.L7.top < document.L7.clip.height) document.L7.moveBy(0,20);
        else document.L7.moveTo(0, -504);
        setTimeout('MoveIt7()', 10);
}

//END HIDING-->
</SCRIPT>
</HEAD>

<BODY CLASS="Mainbody">

<LAYER ID="L7" LEFT=0 TOP=0 WIDTH="100%">
<IMG SRC="JPEG-FILES/ICON-VerticalRainbow1R.jpg" WIDTH=18 HEIGHT=504
onLoad="MoveIt7();">
</LAYER>

</BODY>
</HTML>
```

This part of the example has the animated rainbow in the bottom middle Frame moving from right to left.

Example 3-35 Part 6:   Sample435-9.html

```
<!DOCTYPE HTML PUBLIC "-//W3C//DTD HTML 3.2//EN">
<HTML>
<HEAD>
<TITLE>Sample 435-9 - Example 3-35-9    bottom rainbow        </TITLE>

<STYLE TYPE="text/JavaScript">

        classes.Mainbody.BODY.margins("0px");
        classes.Mainbody.BODY.paddings("0px");
        classes.Mainbody.BODY.backgroundImage="./JPEG-FILES/icon-BG-stars.jpg";

</STYLE>

<SCRIPT LANGUAGE="JavaScript1.2"><!--BEGIN HIDING

function MoveIt9() {

        if (document.L9.left > -504) document.L9.moveBy(-20,0);
        else document.L9.moveTo(document.L9.clip.width, 0);
        setTimeout('MoveIt9()', 10);
}

//END HIDING-->
</SCRIPT>
</HEAD>
```

```
<BODY CLASS="Mainbody">

<LAYER ID="L9" LEFT=0 TOP=0 WIDTH="100%">

<IMG SRC="JPEG-FILES/ICON-HorizontalRainbow1B.jpg" WIDTH=504 HEIGHT=18
onLoad="MoveIt9();">

</LAYER>

</BODY>
</HTML>
```

This part of the example has the master Frameset in it.

9-35 Part 7:   Sample435-Frameset.html

```
<!DOCTYPE HTML PUBLIC "-//W3C//DTD HTML 3.2//EN">
<HTML><HEAD>
        <TITLE>Frameset for Sample 435        </TITLE>        </HEAD>

<FRAMESET ROWS="24,*,24" BORDER="0">

        <FRAMESET COLS="24,*,24">
                <FRAME SCROLLING="no" NAME="F1" SRC="Sample435-1.html">
                <FRAME SCROLLING="no" NAME="F2" SRC="Sample435-2.html">
                <FRAME SCROLLING="no" NAME="F3" SRC="Sample435-1.html">
        </FRAMESET>

        <FRAMESET COLS="24,*,24">
                <FRAME SCROLLING="no" NAME="F4" SRC="Sample435-4.html">
                <FRAME SCROLLING="no" NAME="F5" SRC="Sample435.html">
                <FRAME SCROLLING="no" NAME="F7" SRC="Sample435-7.html">
        </FRAMESET>

        <FRAMESET COLS="24,*,24">
                <FRAME SCROLLING="no" NAME="F8" SRC="Sample435-1.html">
                <FRAME SCROLLING="no" NAME="F9" SRC="Sample435-9.html">
                <FRAME SCROLLING="no" NAME="F10" SRC="Sample435-1.html">
        </FRAMESET>

</FRAMESET>
</HTML>
```

Since the information dealing with Layers and Events is fairly long and involved, I've decided to include it in Chapter 6 to prevent redundancy and hopefully to simplify the learning process. If you're confident in your knowledge about JavaScript Objects, Functions, Statements, Operators, and Expressions, or if you just want to learn about Events right now, then skip ahead to Chapter 6 where we cover Events as they relate to Layers and the JavaScript Event Object Model.

Example 3-35	Sample435Frameset.html

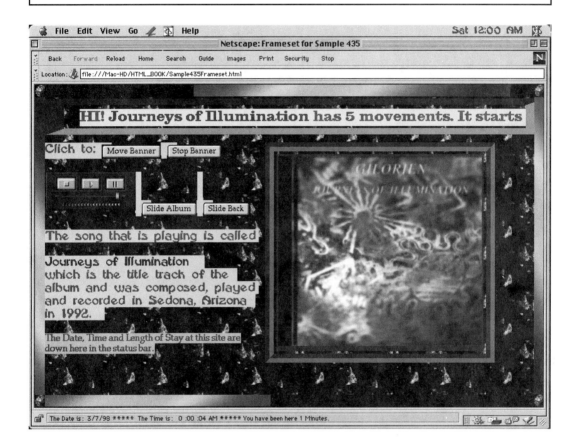

Part II
JavaScript 1.2

Chapter 4

Objects & Functions

Chapter 4
Objects & Functions

Contents

JavaScript Objects

The JavaScript Object Hierarchy

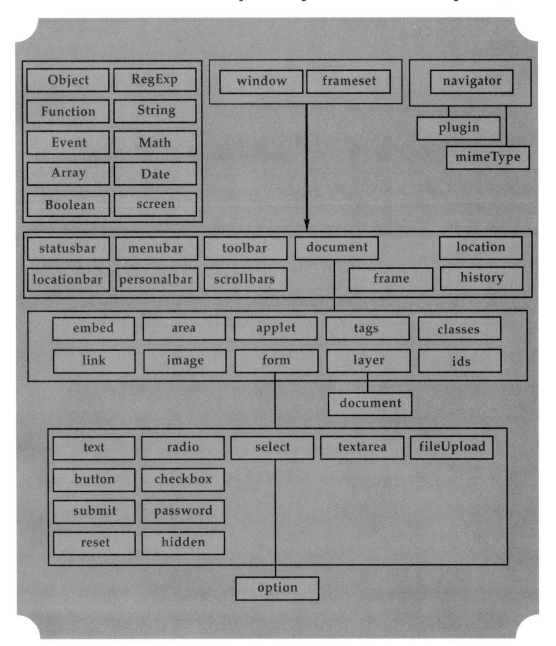

Using JavaScript Objects

Consider this chapter an overview of JavaScript Objects. What it does is lay out the general framework for how Objects operate and how they interrelate to each other and other aspects of JavaScript. This chapter is not going to delineate every single detail of all Objects. For that information see the JavaScript Reference that's on the CD-ROM. This chapter is going to elucidate the essential parameters of Objects and demonstrate some of the more interesting and useful features of some Objects.

Every time you load a page into Navigator, the JavaScript compiler creates certain Objects based on how you wrote the HTML. This minimal Object set is comprised of the **navigator**, **window**, **document**, **location**, and **history** Objects. Depending on what's contained in the page that you authored, there can obviously be other Objects that are also generated by the compiler. All of these Objects exist in an Object hierarchy that can be accessed by calling on the Object with dot notation. The chart on the preceding page demonstrates the structure.

Object Properties and Methods

These Objects all have particular Properties and Methods that are associated with their respective Objects and they can be accessed and manipulated. A Property of an Object is basically a predefined Variable that you can assign a Value to with simple dot notation Syntax like this:

```
objectName.propertyName = value
```

For instance, if you want to change the background color of the **document** Object to blue, you would access the **bgColor** Property and assign the String "blue" to it like this:

```
document.bgColor = "blue"
```

A Method of an Object is just a predefined Function that has already been assigned to an Object by Netscape. You invoke a Method on an Object with the same dot notation like this:

```
objectName.methodName()
```

The **window** Object is the parent Object of all other Objects in a page, which means it's at the top of the hierarchy of all page content, including those that have FRAMESETs and FRAMEs. This means that all other Objects are its descendants or child Objects. Some of the child Objects like the **document** Object are also parent or container Objects for other Objects that are lower down in the hierarchy. All child Objects are said to be Properties of their respective parent Objects and as such they can be referenced and manipulated with JavaScript.

Suppose you want to give focus to the window at some point in your Script. You do that by referencing the **window** Object and calling the **focus()** Method like this:

```
window.focus();
```

Now having demonstrated that, because the **window** Object is always the parent Object, Netscape allows you to omit it from your expressions that involve other Objects, since it is always assumed to be there. This will save you some typing.

The **document** Object is the next major parental unit in the hierarchy. It is the ancestor of most of the other JavaScript Objects. It does not contain the **navigator**, **frame**, **location**, **history**, or **mimeType** Objects.

Suppose you have an **image** Object named **myImage1**, and you want to change the **src** Property by setting it to a different URL. To access the **image** Object, you could call it by name or use the **images[i]** Array, but you also have to get at it through the hierarchy. Here's another way to think about it. Think of the image as having a name and a special position in the page that are specified by its hierarchical name like a family tree. This name is composed of all its ancestors back up to the **document** Object (actually the **window** Object, but remember that you can omit it). So for the **image** named **myImage1** in the **document**, you would change its **src** Property like this:

```
document.myImage1.src = "nextImage2.jpg"
```

If this were the first image in the **document**, you could reference it with the **images[i]** Array like this:

```
document.images[0].src = "nextImage2.jpg"
```

or by its name in the **images[i]** Array like this:

```
document.images["myImage1"].src = "nextImage2.jpg"
```

Changing the <u>value</u> of a <u>text</u> Object

Suppose you had a **form** named **myForm1** that contained an **INPUT TYPE="text"** Object named **myText1**. To change the text string that is displayed in that **text** Object, you would set the **value** Property of the **text** Object like this:

```
document.myForm1.myText1.value = "the new text string";
```

Referencing Objects in a <u>form</u> Object

It gets slightly tricky here. If you have an Object like a **link** in a **form** Object that doesn't have to be in a **form** Object, you still have to reference the **form** Object when you reference the **link** Object. For example, if you wanted to change the **target** Property of the third **link** in your document, and it happened to be in a **form** named **myForm1**, you would access the third element in the **links[i]** Array with a 2 and use the following code:

```
document.myForm1.links[2].target = "mainView";
```

If this **link** were not contained inside of a **form** Object you would code it like this:

```
document.links[2].target = "mainView";
```

Referencing a <u>Layer</u> Object

It gets even trickier when you reference a **Layer** Object, because each **Layer** Object has its own version of a **document** Object inside of it that contains the same kind of data as its outer big brother, but its parameters pertain only to its immediate parent **Layer**. When you reference a **Layer** Object, you always have to reference its parent **document** Object. When you want to reference a Property of a **Layer** Object, you don't reference the **Layer's** interior **document** Object. When you want to reference an Object that is contained inside a **Layer** Object, you always have to reference the interior **document** Object of the **Layer** Object. Here's a demonstration of all three of these possibilities.

Suppose you have a **Layer** named **myLayer1**, you would reference it like this:

```
document.myLayer1
```

Now suppose that you want to change the background color of that **Layer** with its **bgColor** Property, you would code it like this:

```
document.myLayer1.bgColor = "blue";
```

Now suppose that you want to change the text String of a **text** Object named **myText1** inside a **form** Object named **myForm1** that is inside the **Layer** named **myLayer1**. You would have to access the **document** Object <u>of the **myLayer1** Object</u> like this:

```
document.myLayer1.document.myForm1.myText1.value = "Hey Now.";
```

Referencing a <u>select</u> Object

One final example. Suppose you have a **select** Object named **getColor**, and you want to assign the currently selected color Option to a variable you define as **bcolorSel**. Now if the **select** Object is contained inside a **form** named **form1**, which is inside the **document** Object of a **Layer** named **L2**, you are going to have a seriously long line of code to write if you do it all at once. Remember that you are going to have to use the **selectedIndex** Property of the **select** Object as the **index** of the **options[index]** Array, which has its own very long referencing to boot. Here's how the Objects are referenced in a single line of code:

```
var bcolorSel = document.L2.document.form1.getColor.options[document.L2.document. form1.getColor.selectedIndex].value;
```

You can see the advantage of breaking it up into smaller chunks and assigning the chunks to different variables and then substituting the variables appropriately like this:

```
var L2 = document.L2;
var getColor = L2.document.form1.getColor;
var sel = getColor.selectedIndex;
var bcolorSel = getColor.options[sel].value;
```

You can see a very similar implementation of this code in Sample724.html, which is explained in Example 6-24 in Chapter 6, on pages 650-656.

For more information on the **select** Object, see pages 462-465, later in this chapter.

Charts & other upcoming topics

On pages 386-388 there are four charts that lists all of the Predefined JavaScript Objects, the Predefined JavaScript Arrays, the Predefined JavaScript Core Objects, and the Predefined JavaScript Core Functions that Netscape has created for you to use in your Scripts. The Objects that are new to JavaScript 1.2 and some of the more vital or obscure Objects are covered in this book. To detail and examine all of the Objects that are available in JavaScript is beyond the scope of this book and in fact would require an entire book of its own. This chapter will show you how to use existing Objects, how they are created by the JavaScript runtime engine, and how to manipulate content with their Properties and Methods. For more details on JavaScript Objects that aren't covered in the book, see the JavaScript Reference on the CD-ROM.

In addition to the Predefined Objects of JavaScript, you can create your own Objects and define Properties and Methods for them. This process is covered in detail after the Summaries Charts.

You can also create your own Functions, which is one of the essential tools for effectively utilizing JavaScript. In the next section, the process for defining a Function is covered, then the three ways to call a Function, that is, the ways that you can execute the Statements contained within the Function, are covered.

Other topics include the Core JavaScript **Function** Object, the **arguments[i]** Array, and the ability to Nest a Function within a Function so that the Arguments of the outer Function are available to the inner Function (but not vice versa). This is a new capability of Navigator 4.0.

At the very end of this chapter, the two new Functions of **Number** and **String** are introduced for Navigator 4.

JavaScript Functions
Overview

Basically, a Function is a process that incorporates a sequence of JavaScript Statements to accomplish a task. To integrate a Function into your document you have to first define it within a SCRIPT, which is usually contained in the HEAD Element. Then you have to call the Function. Calling the Function can be accomplished in several ways, including the ability to call a Function from within another Function. In many instances the Function is called as the Value of an Event Handler of an HTML Element, which is called Attribute Assignment. The simplest way to call a Function is to use it by name as a Statement. You can use the **return** Statement to return a Value with a Function.

It's usually a good idea to define your Functions in the HEAD of the document so that the Functions are loaded first, before any of the HTML Elements in the BODY have loaded. This precludes the generation of many JavaScript runtime errors due to a Script in one part of the document trying to interact with another Script that hasn't loaded yet. This usually occurs when the user tries to click a Button Object before the page fully loads, and the Button needs that unloaded code before it will work. Since that required code hasn't loaded yet, you get a runtime error. There are exceptions to HEAD Scripts. See pages 367, 392-401 for information on Methods and how they differ from Functions.

Defining a Function with the Function Statement

Defining a Function starts by using the **function** Keyword, which is followed by the name of the Function and then a comma-separated list of Arguments that are enclosed within parentheses. You can define a Function that takes no Arguments, but you still have to include the parentheses. Next comes a sequence of Statements that are semicolon-separated and enclosed within curly braces {}. For instance, the following Function **setColor()** takes no Arguments and sets the background color to purple when it is called:

```
function setColor() {
    document.bgColor = "purple";
}
```

Syntax:

```
function functionName(argument1, argument2, ..., argumentN) {
    statement1;
    statement2;
    statementN;
}
```

Calling a Function by Attribute Assignment

Defining a Function is just the first step in getting a Function to execute its Statements. Next you have to <u>call</u> the Function within a SCRIPT or you have to assign it to an Event Handler of an HTML Element, which is demonstrated in the following scenario:

To start the process for this scenario you could code the previously defined **setColor()** Function so that it was more useful by adding a **color** Argument to it like this:

```
function setColor(color) {
        document.bgColor = color;
}
```

so that when the **setColor()** Function is called, the background will be changed to the **color** Argument that is provided at that time, which can be different each time the Function is called. For instance, suppose you define three Button Objects that each have the **setColor()** Function assigned to its respective **onClick** Event Handler, like this:

```
<INPUT TYPE="button" VALUE="Blue it" onClick="setColor('blue');">
<INPUT TYPE="button" VALUE="Lime it" onClick="setColor('lime');">
<INPUT TYPE="button" VALUE="Red it" onClick="setColor('red');">
```

Then, if the user clicks on the first Button, the **setColor()** Function uses the String 'blue' as the **color** Argument to change the background color to blue. If the user clicks on the second Button, the **onClick** Event Handler uses the same **setColor()** Function but has a different String Value to provide as the **color** Argument so that the background color gets changed to lime. The same is true for the button with '**red**' as the **color** Argument.

Statements in a Function

The Statements within a Function can be practically any type of JavaScript expression and can include (but are not limited to): Variables, Literals, Arrays, Strings, Numbers, Keywords, Objects, Regular Expressions, Operators, and any of the special JavaScript Statements like **if()...else** and **for()**, which are covered in Chapter 5. As was mentioned previously, you can even nest Functions within Functions or call the same Function within itself, which is called a *recursive* Function. The latter of these two possibilities is very useful when using the **setTimeout()** and **setInterval()** Methods, when creating Scripts that perform JavaScript animations, and when using the **Date** Object to display or use the date and time data. See Chapter 3 for examples and details.

Arguments in a Function

The Arguments within a Function are Variables that are placeholders for Values that are passed to the Function and can be Strings, Numbers, Dates, and even other whole Objects.

Calling a Function by Name

There are several scenarios for calling a Function by Name. The first one we'll deal with is when you want to <u>change</u> the HTML layout of the page. In that circumstance, you must call a Function by name, by including the Name of the Function within a SCRIPT in the BODY of the document after the HTML that it references has been loaded into the document. Note that this is not the case when you use a Function to <u>initially</u> layout the document, such as by using the **write()** Method; it's only when you want to change something in the page.

For example: By defining the same **setColor()** Function from before in the HEAD of the document, it is then executed in the BODY of the document in a separate Script by calling it by name. Note that the parentheses are included.

Example 4-0:   **Sample500.html**

```
<!DOCTYPE HTML PUBLIC "-//W3C//DTD HTML 3.2//EN">
<HTML>
<HEAD>
<TITLE>Sample 500 - Example 4-0 Define and Call a Function  </TITLE>

<SCRIPT LANGUAGE="JavaScript1.2"><!--BEGIN HIDING

        function setColor() {
                document.bgColor = "purple";
        }

//END HIDING-->
</SCRIPT>

</HEAD>

<BODY>

<SCRIPT LANGUAGE="JavaScript1.2"><!--BEGIN HIDING

        setColor();

//END HIDING-->
</SCRIPT>

<H2>          The call to the setColor() Function in the second Script actually
changes the background color. Without the explicit call, the Function is only
defined in the HEAD but not executed.
</H2>

</BODY>

</HTML>
```

In Example 4-1, the **setText()** Function is both defined and then called in the HEAD of the document. You could actually call the Function in the BODY of the document, but it's considered good practice to include as much of the Script as possible in the HEAD to avoid runtime errors. The reason that you can call the **setText()** Function in the HEAD is because it is contributing to the layout of the page instead of changing the page after the HTML has been rendered.

This is one of those points of distinction that you need to pay attention to when you are debugging your code.

Example 4-1: Sample501.html

```
<!DOCTYPE HTML PUBLIC "-//W3C//DTD HTML 3.2//EN">
<HTML>
<HEAD>
<BASEFONT SIZE="7">

<TITLE>Sample 501 - Example 4-1 Define and Call a Function  </TITLE>

<SCRIPT LANGUAGE="JavaScript1.2"><!--BEGIN HIDING

        function setText() {

                document.write("Hello out there.");
        }

        setText();

//END HIDING-->
</SCRIPT>

</HEAD>

<BODY>

<H2>
        <FONT COLOR="#FF0000">

Notice that in this case the Function is called in the HEAD of the document because
it <U>isn't changing</U> the layout, it is <U>contributing to the initial
layout</U>.

        </FONT>
</H2>

</BODY>
</HTML>
```

Calling a Function from within a Function

This example demonstrates how to call a Function from within another Function. Since both the **setText()** and the **setDiffText()** Functions make use of references to JavaScript Objects that are created by the JavaScript interpreter after the HTML that creates those Elements in the BODY of the document is loaded, the Script is contained after that relevant HTML in the BODY. The **setText()** Function is first defined and then it is called in the **setDiffText()** Function. Both of these Functions are also assigned to the Event Handlers for the two Links so that the text will change in the text box depending on which link the cursor passes over and away from.

Example 4-2:   **Sample502.html**

```
<!DOCTYPE HTML PUBLIC "-//W3C//DTD HTML 3.2//EN">
<HTML>          <HEAD>          <BASEFONT SIZE="5">
<TITLE>Sample 502 - Example 4-2 Call a Function within a Function</TITLE>   </HEAD>
<BODY BGCOLOR="lime">

<A HREF="Sample502.html" onMouseOver="setText('blue');"
onMouseOut="setDiffText();">
        Test Link Number 1.    </A>     <BR><BR>

<A HREF="Sample502.html" onMouseOver="setText('yellow');"
onMouseOut="setDiffText();">
        Test Link Number 2.    </A>     <BR><BR>

<FORM NAME="form1">    <INPUT TYPE="text" NAME="text1" SIZE=50>       </FORM>

Two Test Links to Change Text in the Text box by moving the mouse over a link and
away from the link.

<SCRIPT LANGUAGE="JavaScript1.2"><!--BEGIN HIDING

function setText(getText) {
        document.form1.text1.value = getText;
}

function setDiffText() {

        var t = document.form1.text1.value;

        if (t == 'blue')       { document.form1.text1.value = 'red'; }

        else { setText('purple'); }
}

//END HIDING-->
</SCRIPT>
</BODY></HTML>
```

Calling a Function by Property Assignment

Calling a Function by Property Assignment is similar to Attribute Assignment with a couple of significant differences. Here a quick mini-example with the explanation following it.

```
<SCRIPT LANGUAGE="JavaScript1.2"><!--BEGIN HIDING

        function setColor() {
                document.bgColor = "purple";
        }

        document.onmouseup=setColor;

//END HIDING-->
</SCRIPT>
```

What you should immediately notice is that the **setColor()** Function that is defined does not have the parentheses attached to the name when it is assigned to the **onmouseup** Event Handler of the **document** Object by Property Assignment. This means that any Arguments that are within the parentheses when the Function is defined are automatically forwarded with the Function internally by the JavaScript interpreter. In some cases, especially when working with **Event** Objects, this can be an advantage. In fact, this ability to not have to manually code in the **event** Keyword Argument is a prime reason to use it when working with Events and Event Handling.

On the other hand, if you have an Argument in your Function that you want to change manually at different points in the Script, it can be a distinct disadvantage, at least to the extent that you will have to write your Functions with a different algorithmic scheme than you might be used to. For example, if you slightly change the **setColor()** Function so that it takes an Argument named **color** like this:

```
        function setColor(color) {
                document.bgColor = color;
        }
```

which is the way a lot of authors normally define Functions when they plan to use them in an Attribute Assignment like this:

```
<INPUT TYPE="button" VALUE="Do it" onClick="setColor('blue');">
```

You probably see the immediate problem with trying to use Property Assignment for this Function, because there is no way to attach the 'blue' String to the **color** Argument. In order to get around this, you need to plan ahead and define your Function in a different way to accommodate the alternate syntax requisites. One solution is demonstrated in the following Example 4-3.

Here's a way to define the Function differently by assigning an Event Argument **e** instead of the **color** Argument and then setting up **if()** Statements to change the background color based on the Value of the Event parameter. The **fromCharCode()** Method of the Core **String** Object is used to extract a String Value from the **which** Property of the **Event** Object **e**, which is then assigned to the **theKey** Variable.

This **theKey** Variable is then Boolean tested against String Literals in the **if()** Statements and executes a background color change when the test is true. Finally the **setColor()** Function is assigned to the **onkeypress** Event Handler for the **document** Object. If you decide to run this Script in the browser, make sure that when you press either of the 1, 2, or 3 Keys, that the main browser Window has focus instead of the location URL bar.

There are numerous additional examples of this type of coding scenario in Chapter 6 on Events.

Example 4-3:   Sample503.html

```
<!DOCTYPE HTML PUBLIC "-//W3C//DTD HTML 3.2//EN">
<HTML>
<HEAD>
<BASEFONT SIZE="5">
<TITLE>Sample 503 - Example 4-3       Function Call by Property Assignment</TITLE>

<SCRIPT LANGUAGE="JavaScript1.2"><!--BEGIN HIDING

//Press either the 1, 2 or 3 Key to change the background color.

        function setColor(e) {

                theKey = String.fromCharCode(e.which);

                if (theKey == "1") { document.bgColor = "purple"; }
                if (theKey == "2") { document.bgColor = "red"; }
                if (theKey == "3") { document.bgColor = "blue"; }
        }

        document.onkeypress=setColor;

//END HIDING-->
</SCRIPT>

</HEAD>

<BODY BGCOLOR="lime" onLoad="window.focus();">

Press either the 1, 2 or 3 Key to change the background color.

</BODY>
</HTML>
```

The JavaScript Core Function Object

JavaScript Syntax:

```
functionObjectName = new Function(["arg1", "arg2", ..., "argN"], "functionBody")
```

Parameters Defined:

functionObjectName

This parameter can be one of three possibilities:
1)   A Variable Name.
2)   A Property of an already Existing Object.
3)   An Object followed by an Event Handler Name, which must be specified in all lowercase characters such as **document.onclick**. In this case, no Arguments are allowed.

arg1, arg2, ..., argN

The Arguments are optional parameters and must be Strings that are used by the Function as formal Argument names.

functionBody

This is a String that contains the Statements of JavaScript code that are to be executed. This would be identical to the Statements contained within the curly braces of a Function that is defined with the Function Statement.

Function Object Origin Differences

Function Objects created with the **Function Constructor** and **Functions** that are declared with the **Function** Statement are similar, but there are two very important distinctions to be aware of. First, when a **Function** Object is assigned to a Variable, then that Variable is said to contain a reference to the **Function** created with the **Function Constructor**, which can be programmatically changed to contain a different Value, while a declared **Function** is static, that is, once it is declared, it will always be that exact **Function**.

Second, a **Function** Object is evaluated every time it is called, which is less efficient than a declared **Function**, which is compiled only once.

Here are two examples of the code you would use to create a **Function** Object and its parallel declared **Function** for comparison purposes:

Function Object

```
myFunction = new Function("document.write('Tennis Rocks');")
```

Declared Function Statement

```
function myFunction() {
      document.write('Tennis Rocks');
}
```

Function Object

```
setColor = new Function("color", "document.bgColor=color;")
```

Declared Function

```
function setColor(color) {
        document.bgColor=color;
}
```

This example demonstrates two implementations of the Core **Function** Object. The first **Function** Object named **setFGColor** uses the **color** Argument, which is assigned to the **fgColor** Property of the **document** Object. When it is called in the next line, it uses the 'red' String as the **color** Argument. The second **Function** Object is assigned to the **onclick** Event Handler of the **document** Object so that the background color of the **document** is changed to lime when it is clicked.

Example 4-4:   Sample504.html

```
<!DOCTYPE HTML PUBLIC "-//W3C//DTD HTML 3.2//EN">
<HTML>
<HEAD>
<BASEFONT SIZE="5">
<TITLE>Sample 504 - Example 4-4      Function Object</TITLE>

<SCRIPT LANGUAGE="JavaScript1.2"><!--BEGIN HIDING

        setFGColor = new Function("color", "document.fgColor=color;")

        setFGColor('red');

        document.onclick = new Function("document.bgColor='lime';")

//END HIDING-->
</SCRIPT>

</HEAD>

<BODY>

Click in the window to change the background color.

</BODY>
</HTML>
```

Function Properties

Property	Description
arguments[i]	An Array containing all of the Arguments passed to a Function and the local Variables of a Function.
arity	Specifies the number of Arguments that the Function expects.
caller	Returns the Name of the outer Function that called the nested Function that is currently being executed. The **caller** Property is only known within the body of a Function. If accessed outside the Function body, the Value is **null**.
prototype	Lets you create your own Properties for a **Function** Object.

Function Methods

Method	Description
toString()	Returns a String containing the inner code for the specified Function.

The <u>arguments[i]</u> Array Property of a Function

JavaScript Syntax:

```
arguments[i]
arguments.argName
arguments.varName
```

JavaScript Syntax for Inner Nested Functions:

```
functionName.arguments[i]
functionName.arguments.argName
functionName.arguments.varName
```

    The **arguments[i]** Array is a Property of a Function where **i** is the zero-based **index** integer from 0 through n where **n=arguments.length-1** and each Array Element contains an Argument of the Function. In the syntax, the **functionName** parameter is the name of the Function that contains the Arguments that are only required if you are accessing a Property of an <u>outer</u> Function from within an <u>inner nested</u> Function. **argName** is the Name of any Argument and **varName** is the Name of any local Variable that you access.

    You can only access the **arguments[i]** Array from within the body of the Function when the Function is declared. A JavaScript runtime error will occur if you attempt to access the **arguments[i]** Array outside the Function declaration.

When referring to Functions and **Function** Objects, you must always refer to them by name, even within the Function body, because the **this** Keyword does not refer to the currently executing Function.

If you call a Function and pass it more Arguments than it was formally declared to accept in the Function Statement declaration, you can use the Arguments Array to deal with the additional Arguments by accessing each Element of the Array.

For example, in the following Script, the **tester()** Function is declared with only one Argument, which is **color**. Then it uses the Arguments Array within the **for()** Statement to write each Argument to screen that is passed to it when it is called.

Example 4-5:   Sample505.html

```
<!DOCTYPE HTML PUBLIC "-//W3C//DTD HTML 3.2//EN">
<HTML>
<HEAD>
<BASEFONT SIZE="5">
<TITLE>Sample 505 - Example 4-5       arguments Array</TITLE>

<SCRIPT LANGUAGE="JavaScript1.2"><!--BEGIN HIDING

function tester(color) {

        for (var i=0; i<tester.arguments.length; i++) {

                document.write(arguments[i] + "<BR>");
        }
}

tester("blue", "red", "green", "yellow");

//END HIDING-->
</SCRIPT>

</HEAD>

<BODY>
</BODY>
</HTML>
```

This Script produces the following output in the browser:

blue
red
green
yellow

arguments[i] Array Properties

Property	Description
length	The number of Arguments in a Function.
argName1, argName2, ..., argNameN	Each Argument in the Function is a Property of the Arguments Array. Note that this capability is only available in Navigator 4.0. In JavaScript 1.3 and Navigator 4.5 it's not just deprecated, the support for it is completely removed and unavailable.
varName1, varName2, ..., varNameN	Each local variable in the Function is a Property of the Arguments Array. Note that this capability is only available in Navigator 4.0. In JavaScript 1.3 and Navigator 4.5 it's not just deprecated, the support for it is completely removed and unavailable.
caller	The Arguments Array of the outer Function. The Value is undefined if there is no outer Function. In JavaScript 1.3 it is deprecated.
callee	A reference to the Function containing the Arguments Array.

Nesting a Function within a Function

As of JavaScript 1.2 for Navigator 4.0 you can now nest a Function within another Function when they are declared with the Function Statement. Note that this is different from just calling a Function from within a Function, which has been possible for quite a while. Nesting a Function means that the Arguments and Variables of the outer Function are available for use by the inner nested Function. However, the reverse is not true; that is, the Arguments and Variables of the inner nested Function are not available for use by the outer Function. The inner Function is unknown outside of the outer Function and cannot be called independently. The following compares nested Functions and called Functions.

Nested Functions

```
function outerTest1() {

    function innerTest2() {
        statements2
    }

    statements1
}
```

Function called from within a Function

```
function myTest1() {
        statements1
}

function myTest2() {
        statements2
        myTest1()
}
```

Example 4-6 demonstrates how to let the Variable **x** of the outer Function named **getColor()** be used by an inner <u>nested</u> Function named **setBGColor()**. Each local Variable is a Property of the **arguments** Array, so to access the Variable **x**, you use dot notation via first the name of the Function where the Variable resides and then via the **arguments** Array.

When you run <u>Sample506.html</u>, just type in a color name and click the button to change the background color of the document. <u>Sample506-Extra.html</u>, which is only on the CD-ROM, uses similar code *without* using a <u>nested</u> Function. Compare the differences. Note that due to nonsupport, this example works in Navigator 4.0, but not version 4.5+.

Example 4-6: Sample506.html

```
<!DOCTYPE HTML PUBLIC "-//W3C//DTD HTML 3.2//EN">
<HTML><HEAD>
<TITLE>Sample 506 - Example 4-6      Nesting Functions</TITLE>
</HEAD>

<BODY>
<FORM NAME="form1">

<INPUT TYPE="text" NAME="text1" SIZE=30> <BR> Type in a Color Name

<INPUT TYPE="button" NAME="b1" VALUE="Do it" onClick="getColor();">
</FORM>

<SCRIPT LANGUAGE="JavaScript1.2"><!--BEGIN HIDING

//Remember that each local variable is a Property of the arguments Array.
//In this case the variable x is the called Property from the outer Function
//and assigned to the variable named color in the inner Function.
//This example works in Navigator 4.0, but not 4.5.

function getColor() {

        var x = document.form1.text1.value;

                function setBGColor() {

                        var color = getColor.arguments.x;

                        document.bgColor = color;
                }

        setBGColor();
}

//END HIDING-->
</SCRIPT>
</BODY>
</HTML>
```

arguments[i] Array Properties Demonstrated

This example demonstrates all of the Properties of the **arguments[i]** Array by using an <u>inner</u> nested Function named **innerTest()** within an <u>outer</u> Function named **outerTest()**.

The **outerTest()** Function is declared with the two Arguments of **arg1** and **arg2** and a String Variable named **myVar2**. The Arguments and Variables are written to screen by accessing their respective Properties of the **callee** Property of the **arguments[i]** Array Property of a Function.

Then the **innerTest()** Function is declared with the two Arguments of **arg3** and **arg4** and a String Variable named **myVar**. Then the **write()** Method is used to display to screen the **length** Property and then the two Elements of the **arguments[i]** Array.

Next, the two Arguments of the **innerTest()** Function, **arg3** and **arg4**, and the String Variable **myVar**, are displayed by accessing them by their names as Properties of the **arguments[i]** Array. Then the **caller** Property is used to access the **arguments[i]** Array of the outer Function **outerTest()** to display its Arguments and Variable. Finally, the **callee** Property is used to display the same Arguments and Variable of the **innerTest()** Function.

Then, the **innerTest()** Function is called from within the **outerTest()** Function so that the contents of all of the **write()** Methods are written to screen. Finally, the **outerTest()** Function is called directly so that it is executed. This example works fine in Navigator 4.0, but it is only partially supported in version 4.5+.

Example 4-7: **Sample507.html**

```
<!DOCTYPE HTML PUBLIC "-//W3C//DTD HTML 3.2//EN">
<HTML><HEAD>
<TITLE>Sample 507 - Example 4-7      arguments Array Properties</TITLE>

<SCRIPT LANGUAGE="JavaScript1.2"><!--BEGIN HIDING

function outerTest(arg1, arg2) {

     var myVar2 = "A test Variable for the outer Function";

     document.write(arguments.callee.arg1 + "<BR>");
     document.write(arguments.callee.arg2 + "<BR>");
     document.write(arguments.callee.myVar2 + "<P>");

     function innerTest(arg3, arg4) {

          var myVar = "A test Variable for the inner Function";

          document.write(arguments.length + "<P>");

          document.write(arguments[0] + "<BR>");
          document.write(arguments[1] + "<P>");

          document.write(arguments.arg3 + "<BR>");
          document.write(arguments.arg4 + "<BR>");
```

```
                document.write(arguments.myVar + "<P>");
                document.write(arguments.caller.arg1 + "<BR>");
                document.write(arguments.caller.arg2 + "<BR>");
                document.write(arguments.caller.myVar2 + "<P>");

                document.write(arguments.callee.arg3 + "<BR>");
                document.write(arguments.callee.arg4 + "<BR>");
                document.write(arguments.callee.myVar + "<P>");
        }

        innerTest("third", "fourth");
}

/*-------------------------------------------------------------------------*/

        outerTest("first", "second");

//END HIDING-->
</SCRIPT>
</HEAD>
<BODY>
</BODY>
</HTML>
```

Which produces the following output in the browser:

first
second
A test Variable for the outer Function

2

third
fourth

third
fourth
A test Variable for the inner Function

first
second
A test Variable for the outer Function

third
fourth
A test Variable for the inner Function

For more information about Arrays, check out Chapter 7.

Summaries Charts
Predefined JavaScript Objects

Here's an alphabetized list of all Predefined JavaScript Objects:

anchor

applet

area

Array   See Chapter 7

Boolean

button

checkbox

Date   See Chapter 3,   page 307

document   See Chapter 4,   page 432

Event   See Chapter 6

fileupload

form

frame

Function   See Chapter 4,   pages 371-385, and Chapter 5,   page 505

hidden

History   See Chapter 4,   page 452

image

Layer   See Chapter 3,   page 199   New in JavaScript 1.2

link

Location   See Chapter 4,   page 447

Math   See Chapter 3,   page 321

mimetype

navigator   See Chapter 4,   page 455

Number   See Chapter 4,   page 460

Object   See Chapter 4,   page 389

option   See Chapter 4,   page 465

password

Plugin

radio

RegExp   See Chapter 9

reset

screen   See Chapter 4,   page 444   New in JavaScript 1.2

select   See Chapter 4,   page 462

String   See Chapter 8

submit

text

textarea

window   See Chapter 4,   page 416

Predefined JavaScript Arrays
as Object Properties

Certain JavaScript Objects have Properties that are actually Arrays of Objects, which are defined by the JavaScript compiler as the page loads, and they are based on the content that you provide. The following table specifies the Array Properties for their respective Objects where **i** is a zero-based integer **index**. These Arrays are also Core Objects.

Predefined JavaScript Arrays

Object	Property	Description
document	**anchors[i]**	An Array reflecting a document's <A> tags that contains a NAME attribute in source order.
	applets[i]	An Array reflecting a document's <APPLET> tags in source order.
	embeds[i]	An Array reflecting a document's <EMBED> tags in source order.
	forms[i]	An Array reflecting a document's <FORM> tags in source order.
	images[i]	An Array reflecting a document's <IMG> tags in source order. (This does not include images created with the Image() Constructor.)
	layers[i]	An Array reflecting a document's <LAYER> tags or Style Sheet Layers in source order.
	links[i]	An Array reflecting a document's <A HREF="..."> tags, <AREA HREF="..."> tags, and Link objects created with the **link()** Method in source order.
Function	**arguments[i]**	An Array reflecting the Arguments to a Function.
form	**elements[i]**	An Array reflecting a form's Elements in source order.
select	**options[i]**	An Array reflecting the <OPTION> tags in a Select object in source order.
window	**frames[i]**	An Array reflecting all the <FRAME> tags in a window containing a <FRAMESET> tag in source order.
	history[i]	An Array reflecting a window's URL history entries.
navigator	**mimeTypes[i]**	An Array reflecting all the MIME types supported by the client, including internal, helper applications, or plug-ins.
	plugins[i]	An Array reflecting all the plug-ins installed on the client in source order.

Predefined JavaScript Core Objects

Certain JavaScript Objects are said to be "top-level" Core Objects because they are built into the language itself. They are:

Predefined Core Objects

Array	See Chapter 7
Boolean	See the JavaScript Reference
Date	See Chapter 3
Function	See Chapter 4
Math	See Chapter 3
Number	See Chapter 4
RegExp	See Chapter 9
String	See Chapter 8

Predefined JavaScript Core Functions

Certain JavaScript Functions are said to be "top-level" Core Functions because they are built into the language itself. They are:

Predefined Core Functions

escape()	See Chapter 4,	page 439
unescape()	See Chapter 4,	pages 439, 442-443
eval()		
isNaN()	See Chapter 3,	page 338
Number()	See Chapter 4,	page 467
parseFloat()	See Chapter 3,	page 337
parseInt()	See Chapter 3,	page 337
String()	See Chapter 4,	page 468
taint()		
untaint()		

The JavaScript Core Object

The JavaScript Core Object Overview

You can create your own JavaScript **object** Objects and then invoke JavaScript Properties and Methods on the Object. You can also define your own Properties and Methods for Objects that you create, which can then be invoked on your created Objects just like JavaScript's predefined Properties and Methods. Oddly enough, the JavaScript Object is completely different from the HTML OBJECT Element, so be sure and don't get them confused.

To create your own Object, you can either use the **Object( )** Constructor Function or use Literal notation, which are both covered in following sections.

There are no parameters for Objects.

Object Properties

Property	Description
constructor	Specifies the Function used to create a particular Object.
prototype	Lets you create your own Properties for an Object.

Object Methods

Method	Description
watch(propertyName, handlerFunction)	Adds a **watchpoint** to a Property of an Object, which causes a call to a **handlerFunction** Function each time that the Property receives a Value.
unwatch(propertyName)	Removes a **watchpoint** from a Property of an Object.
toString()	Returns a String containing the inner code for the specified Object.
valueOf()	Returns the primitive Value for the specified Object.
eval()	Evaluates a String that contains any JavaScript Expression. In Navigator 2.0 and 4.0, **eval()** is a top-level Function. In Navigator 3.0, **eval()** is a Method of every Object.

Creating Objects
with its <u>Constructor</u> Function

JavaScript Syntax: Part 1

```
function objectName(arg1, arg2, ..., argN) {
     propertyName1=value1;
     propertyName2=value2;
     propertyNameN=valueN;
     [methodName1=mValue1;
     methodName2=mValue2;
     methodNameN=mValueN];
}
```

JavaScript Syntax: Part 2

```
objectInstance = new objectName();
```

To create a new JavaScript Object with the Constructor Function, there is a sequence that involves two steps. First, you must define a Function that includes the Object's Name and optionally any Properties. Second, you must create an instance of the Object by using the Keyword **new**. For instance:

```
<SCRIPT LANGUAGE="JavaScript1.2"><!--BEGIN HIDING

     function myObject() {

          this.color = "blue";
          this.size = 42;
          this.time = "now";
     }

     testObject = new myObject();
     document.write(testObject);

//END HIDING-->
</SCRIPT>
```

which would produce the following output in the browser:

{color:"blue", size:42, time:"now"}

The following Script creates an Object by defining a Function with five Arguments and assigns the Values passed to the Function by those Arguments to the five Properties. Notice the use of the Keyword **this** to keep from having to declare variables when creating the Properties. Then an <u>instance</u> of the **myArtObject** Object is created with the **new** Keyword and named **art1**. Finally, **art1** is written to screen and each of its Properties is written to screen mainly to show you that you can access Object Properties that you create the same way as for predefined Objects.

```
<SCRIPT LANGUAGE="JavaScript1.2"><!--BEGIN HIDING

    function myArtObject(title, author, width, height, year) {

            this.title = title;
            this.author = author;
            this.width = width;
            this.height = height;
            this.year = year;
    }

art1 = new myArtObject("Pinnacles", "Gilorien", 24, 36, 1996);

    document.write(art1          + "<P>");

    document.write(art1.title    + "<BR>");
    document.write(art1.author   + "<BR>");
    document.write(art1.width    + "<BR>");
    document.write(art1.height   + "<BR>");
    document.write(art1.year     + "<BR>");

//END HIDING-->
</SCRIPT>
```

This Script produces the following output in the browser:

{title:"Pinnacles", author:"Gilorien",width:24, height:36, year:1996}

Pinnacles
Gilorien
24
36
1996

Creating Methods for an Object

JavaScript Syntax: Part 1

```
function functionName(arg1, arg2, ..., argN) {
     statements1;
     statements2;
     statementsN;
}
```

JavaScript Syntax: Part 2

```
                         //Assigns the Function to the Method
objectName.methodName = functionName;
```

JavaScript Syntax: Part 3

```
                              //Invokes the Method
objectName.methodName([parameters]);
```

The Procedure

A Method is just a Function that is associated with a specific Object. The reason for creating a Method is that when you expect to be using a particular Function a lot for a particular Object, it's more efficient to take the initial extra time to turn it into a Method.

To create and then use a Method for your Object involves a three-part sequence. First, you define a Function using standard Function syntax. Second, you assign the **functionName** to the **methodName** of the Object Instance with **objectName**. Note that you can use the same name for the Method name as for the Function name.

The third part is when you actually invoke the Method on an Instance of the Object just like you would any other Method.

You can also assign the Method to the Object as part of the Object definition. This procedure will be demonstrated in the third of the next three examples.

Example 4-8 will demonstrate all of the steps that are necessary for creating a Method for an Object and then invoking that Method on the Object. It starts by defining the Function **artMethod1**, which will be used as a Method of the **myArtObject** Object from the Script in the last mini-example, which is then defined again in this example.

Next, an Instance of the **myArtObject** named **art1** is instantiated with its attendant Arguments. Then, the Function named **artMethod1** is assigned as a Method for the **art1** Object with the same **methodName** as the Function.

Finally, the **artMethod1** Method is invoked on the **art1** Object, which results in the display of the Object's Properties being written to screen. Check out the code Comments.

Example 4-8: **Sample508.html**

```
<!DOCTYPE HTML PUBLIC "-//W3C//DTD HTML 3.2//EN">
<HTML><HEAD>
<BASEFONT SIZE="5">
<TITLE>Sample 508 - Example 4-8      Method Creation for Object</TITLE>

<SCRIPT LANGUAGE="JavaScript1.2"><!--BEGIN HIDING
                                     //The function that defines the Method
function artMethod1(obj) {

        this.obj = obj;

        document.write(obj.title + "<BR>");
        document.write(obj.author + "<BR>");
        document.write(obj.width + "inches x " + obj.height + "inches" + "<BR>");
        document.write(obj.year);
}
/*-----------------------------------------------------------------------*/
                                     //The function that defines the Object
function myArtObject(title, author, width, height, year) {

        this.title = title;
        this.author = author;
        this.width = width;
        this.height = height;
        this.year = year;
}
/*-----------------------------------------------------------------------*/
                                     //Creates an Instance of the Object

        art1 = new myArtObject("Pinnacles", "Gilorien", 24, 36, 1996);

        art1.artMethod1 = artMethod1;         //Assigns the Method to the Object

        art1.artMethod1(art1);                //Invokes the Method on the Object

//END HIDING-->
</SCRIPT>

</HEAD>
<BODY>
</BODY>
</HTML>
```

The previous example produces the following output in the browser:

Pinnacles
Gilorien
24inches x 36inches
1996

This example is identical to the previous example except that it uses the Keyword **this** to pass the parameters of the **art1** Object to the **artMethod1()** Method instead of passing the whole Object to the Method with the **obj** Argument. The browser output is the same. There are Comments in Example 4-8 that are relevant to Example 4-9.

Example 4-9:   Sample509.html

```
<!DOCTYPE HTML PUBLIC "-//W3C//DTD HTML 3.2//EN">
<HTML>
<HEAD>
<BASEFONT SIZE="5">
<TITLE>Sample 509 - Example 4-9       Method Creation for Object</TITLE>

<SCRIPT LANGUAGE="JavaScript1.2"><!--BEGIN HIDING

function artMethod2() {

        document.write(this.title + "<BR>");
        document.write(this.author + "<BR>");
        document.write(this.width + "inches x " + this.height + "inches" + "<BR>");
        document.write(this.year);
}
/*-------------------------------------------------------------------------*/

function myArtObject(title, author, width, height, year) {

        this.title = title;
        this.author = author;
        this.width = width;
        this.height = height;
        this.year = year;
}
/*-------------------------------------------------------------------------*/

        art1 = new myArtObject("Pinnacles", "Gilorien", 24, 36, 1996);

        art1.artMethod2 = artMethod2;

        art1.artMethod2();

//END HIDING-->
</SCRIPT>
</HEAD>

<BODY>
</BODY>
</HTML>
```

This example demonstrates including a Method as part of an Object definition. It's exactly the same as Example 4-9 except that the Function **artMethod2()** is included as a Method in the definition of the **myArtObject** Object by using the **this** Keyword in an assignment Statement. The output to the browser is the same as in Example 4-8. There is another example of this procedure on the CD-ROM in the file Sample510-Extra.html.

Example 4-10: **Sample510.html**

```
<!DOCTYPE HTML PUBLIC "-//W3C//DTD HTML 3.2//EN">
<HTML>
<HEAD>
<BASEFONT SIZE="5">
<TITLE>Sample 510 - Example 4-10      Method in Object Definition</TITLE>

<SCRIPT LANGUAGE="JavaScript1.2"><!--BEGIN HIDING

function artMethod2() {

        document.write(this.title + "<BR>");
        document.write(this.author + "<BR>");
        document.write(this.width + "inches x " + this.height + "inches" + "<BR>");
        document.write(this.year);
}
/*-------------------------------------------------------------------------*/

function myArtObject(title, author, width, height, year) {

        this.title = title;
        this.author = author;
        this.width = width;
        this.height = height;
        this.year = year;
        this.artMethod2 = artMethod2;          //includes the Method here
}
/*-------------------------------------------------------------------------*/

        art1 = new myArtObject("Pinnacles", "Gilorien", 24, 36, 1996);

        art1.artMethod2();              //invokes the Method on an Object Instance

//END HIDING-->
</SCRIPT>

</HEAD>

<BODY>
</BODY>
</HTML>
```

An Object as a Property in an Object Definition

To include an Object as a Property in the Object definition of another Object, just define the Object that you want to include and then create an Instance of the Object and assign it a name. Then you can include the named Instance Object as a Property of another Object in its definition.

The following example demonstrates the above concept, which is another way of saying that you can pass an Instance of an Object as a parameter of another Object. It expands on the same code that has been used in the last several examples. What's been added is a second Object definition that is created with the Object Function Constructor and is named **includedObject()**. It takes three Arguments and uses the **this** Keyword to define its three Properties that are set to the Values of the three Arguments.

Next, there are two instances of the **includedObject()** Object, which are named **myIO1** and **myIO2**. Then, when the **myArtObject()** Object is defined, there is an additional Argument named **createdBy**, which is assigned to the Property **createdBy** with the **this** Keyword like this:

```
this.createdBy = createdBy;
```

Then when the two Instances of the **myArtObject()** Object are instantiated with the names of **art1** and **art2**, like this:

```
art1 = new myArtObject("Pinnacles", "Gilorien", 24, 36, 1996, myIO1);
art2 = new myArtObject("Chakra Fractal Space", "Gilorien", 17, 11, 1995, myIO2);
```

the **myIO1** and **myIO2** instantiations of **includedObject()** are now part of the **art1** and **art2** Objects, respectively.

Within the **artMethod2()** Method definition, the following three lines of code have been added to the Method as it was used in previous examples:

```
document.write(this.createdBy.artProgram + " ");
document.write(this.createdBy.version + "<BR>");
document.write(this.createdBy.platform + "<P>");
```

which demonstrates the dot notation needed to access the individual Properties of the **includedObject()** Object from within the **artMethod2()** Method.

As an alternative, which is not demonstrated in the example, you could use the following six lines of code to display the individual Properties of the **includedObject()** Object from outside of the **artMethod2()** Method like this:

```
document.write(art1.createdBy.artProgram);
document.write(art1.createdBy.version);
document.write(art1.createdBy.platform);
document.write(art2.createdBy.artProgram);
document.write(art2.createdBy.version);
document.write(art2.createdBy.platform);
```

Note that in the above code:

art1 and **art2**	are instances of the **myArtObject()**.
createdBy	is a Property of the **art1** and **art2** Objects, which is an Object itself.
artProgram	is a Property of the **createdBy** Object Property.
version	is a Property of the **createdBy** Object Property.
platform	is a Property of the **createdBy** Object Property.

Example 4-11: Sample511.html

```
<!DOCTYPE HTML PUBLIC "-//W3C//DTD HTML 3.2//EN">
<HTML>
<HEAD>
<BASEFONT SIZE="3">
<TITLE>Sample 511 - Example 4-11    Include an Object in Object Definition</TITLE>

<SCRIPT LANGUAGE="JavaScript1.2"><!--BEGIN HIDING

function artMethod2() {

        document.write(this.title + "<BR>");
        document.write(this.author + "<BR>");
        document.write(this.width + "inches x " + this.height + "inches" + "<BR>");
        document.write(this.year + "<P>");

        document.write(this.createdBy.artProgram + " ");
        document.write(this.createdBy.version + "<BR>");
        document.write(this.createdBy.platform + "<P>");
}
/*------------------------------------------------------------------------*/

function includedObject(artProgram, version, platform) {

        this.artProgram = artProgram;
        this.version = version;
        this.platform = platform;
}
```

```
myIO1 = new includedObject("Bryce", 3.0, "Macintosh");
myIO2 = new includedObject("Photoshop", 4.0, "Macintosh");

/*-------------------------------------------------------------------------*/

function myArtObject(title, author, width, height, year, createdBy) {

        this.title = title;
        this.author = author;
        this.width = width;
        this.height = height;
        this.year = year;
        this.artMethod2 = artMethod2;        //includes the Method here
        this.createdBy = createdBy;          //includes the Object Property here
}
/*-------------------------------------------------------------------------*/
                                             //Creates Object Instances

art1 = new myArtObject("Pinnacles", "Gilorien", 24, 36, 1996, myIO1);
art2 = new myArtObject("Chakra Fractal Space", "Gilorien", 17, 11, 1995, myIO2);

        art1.artMethod2();         //invokes the Method on an Object Instance
        art2.artMethod2();         //invokes the Method on an Object Instance

//END HIDING-->
</SCRIPT>

</HEAD>

<BODY>
</BODY>
</HTML>
```

The preceding example produces the following output in the browser:

Pinnacles
Gilorien
24inches x 36inches
1996

Bryce 3
Macintosh

Chakra Fractal Space
Gilorien
17inches x 11inches
1995

Photoshop 4
Macintosh

The <u>prototype</u> Property to add a <u>Method</u> to an Object <u>Type</u>

JavaScript Syntax:

```
objectName.prototype.methodName;
objectName.prototype.methodName = functionName;
```

     In the previous section, the process for adding a Method to an Object in the Object definition was demonstrated. In this section, the procedure for adding a Method to the Object Type; that is, to the Object definition after the Object definition has been created. This means that all Instances of that Object Type can invoke that particular added Method, including Instances of the Object that were created <u>before</u> the Method was created with the **prototype** Property.

     It should be noted that the **prototype** Property can be used to create Methods and Properties for Objects that you create and for Predefined JavaScript Objects like the **document** Object or the **Layer** Object, etc. You can also use the **prototype** Property to add new Properties to an Object. This is covered in the next section. In fact, every Object that can be created with a Constructor Function can also use the **prototype** Property to create Methods and Properties for its class.

     This procedure for using the **prototype** Property of the Core Object to add a Method to an Object starts by using the Constructor Function to define a Method. You then invoke the **prototype** Property onto the Object specified by **objectName** that you want to assign the new Method to, while typically assigning the Method defined by **functionName** to the **methodName**, like this:

```
objectName.prototype.methodName = functionName;
```

So that for the Object **myArtObject** that was defined in the previous examples, you could define the following Method with the Function Constructor that would be the **functionName** parameter in the above syntax, like this:

```
function addMethod() {
        if (this.title == "Pinnacles")
                document.bgColor="magenta";
}
```

and then add it to the **myArtObject** with the **prototype** Property, like this:

```
myArtObject.prototype.myAddMethod = addMethod;
```

This example demonstrates adding a Method to an Object Type with the **prototype** Property.

Example 4-12:   Sample512.html

```
<!DOCTYPE HTML PUBLIC "-//W3C//DTD HTML 3.2//EN">
<HTML><HEAD>
<TITLE>Sample 512 - Example 4-12      add Method to Object with prototype</TITLE>

<SCRIPT LANGUAGE="JavaScript1.2"><!--BEGIN HIDING

function artMethod2() {

        document.write(this.title + "<BR>");
        document.write(this.author + "<P>");
}
/*-----------------------------------------------------------------------*/

function addMethod() {
        if (this.title == "Pinnacles")      document.bgColor="magenta";
        if (this.title == "Sedona Winter")  document.bgColor="steelblue";
}
/*-----------------------------------------------------------------------*/

function myArtObject(title, author) {

        this.title = title;
        this.author = author;
        this.artMethod2 = artMethod2;
}
/*-----------------------------------------------------------------------*/
                                                //adds the Method here
        myArtObject.prototype.myAddMethod = addMethod;

        art1 = new myArtObject("Pinnacles", "Gilorien");
        art2 = new myArtObject("Sedona Winter", "Gilorien");

        art1.artMethod2();
        art2.artMethod2();

//END HIDING-->
</SCRIPT>
</HEAD>
<BODY>
<FORM NAME="form1">

<INPUT TYPE="button" NAME="b1" VALUE="Test 1" onClick="art1.myAddMethod();">
<INPUT TYPE="button" NAME="b2" VALUE="Test 2" onClick="art2.myAddMethod();">

</FORM>
</BODY>
</HTML>
```

This example demonstrates how the **prototype** Property can be used to add a Method to a **Number** Object, which is a Predefined JavaScript Object. First, the **addNum()** Function that is to be used as the added Method is defined, and then the Method is named **changeIt()** and added to the **Number** Object with the **prototype** Property. Finally, the **changeIt()** Method is called from within the **doIt()** Function. Notice the dot notation, which calls the Method. This Script adds the number in the text box to the previous total and returns the resulting total back to the text box.

Example 4-13:   Sample513.html

```
<!DOCTYPE HTML PUBLIC "-//W3C//DTD HTML 3.2//EN">
<HTML><HEAD>
<TITLE>Sample 513 - Example 4-13      add a Method to Number Object</TITLE>
</HEAD>

<BODY onLoad="document.form1.t1.focus();">

<FORM NAME="form1">
<INPUT TYPE="text" NAME="t1" VALUE="" SIZE=40>
<INPUT TYPE="button" NAME="b2" VALUE="Add a Number" onClick="doIt();">
</FORM>

<SCRIPT LANGUAGE="JavaScript1.2"><!--BEGIN HIDING

var myNum = new Number(0);

function addNum(n) {

        myNum+=n;
        return myNum;
}
/*-------------------------------------------------------------------------*/

Number.prototype.changeIt = addNum;

function doIt() {

        var nextNum =0;
                                        //converts a String to a Number
        nextNum = myNum.changeIt(parseInt(document.form1.t1.value));

        document.form1.t1.value = nextNum;
        document.form1.t1.select();
}

//END HIDING-->
</SCRIPT>
</BODY>
</HTML>
```

Add a <u>Property</u> to an Object <u>Instance</u> after it is defined

To add a **Property** to an individual **Object Instance** <u>after</u> the **Object Type** has been defined, you just use simple dot notation to assign the **Property** by name and optionally give it a Value with the following Syntax. Note that this does not add the **Property** to the **Object Type**.

JavaScript Syntax:

```
myObjectInstance.myNewProperty;
myObjectInstance.myNewProperty = value;
```

For example, suppose you had an Object named **myBook** and you wanted to add a Property named **chapter** to it, you could do it with either of the following two lines of code:

```
myBook.chapter;
myBook.chapter = 5;
```

The <u>prototype</u> Property to add a <u>Property</u> to an Object <u>Type</u>

JavaScript Syntax:

```
objectName.prototype.propertyName;
objectName.prototype.propertyName = value;
```

To add a Property to an Object Type after the Object has already been defined, you have to use the **prototype** Property of its Function Constructor. This is a relatively simple procedure, which is demonstrated in the following example. However, one aspect of this scenario that isn't particularly intuitive is the fact that when you create a new Instance of the Object, you can't pass an Argument that would be based on the new Property. You have to manually assign the Value to the Property to each Object after you create a new Instance of the Object.

This example uses the **prototype** Property to add the two Properties, **chapter** and **pages**, to the Object Type that is created with the **myBook()** Function Constructor. There are two Instances of the **myBook** Object called **ch7** and **ch10**. Then the **write()** Method is used to display the Property Values of **ch7** and then the actual **ch7** and **ch10** Objects.

Example 4-14: Sample514.html

```
<!DOCTYPE HTML PUBLIC "-//W3C//DTD HTML 3.2//EN">
<HTML>
<HEAD>
<TITLE>Sample 514 - Example 4-14      add a Property to an Object</TITLE>

<SCRIPT LANGUAGE="JavaScript1.2"><!--BEGIN HIDING

function myBook(title, author) {

        this.title = title;
        this.author = author;
}
/*-------------------------------------------------------------------------*/

        ch7 = new myBook("Dynamic HTML", "Gilorien");

        myBook.prototype.chapter;
        myBook.prototype.pages;

        ch7.chapter = 7;
        ch7.pages = 124;

        document.write(ch7.title + "<BR>");
        document.write(ch7.author + "<BR>");
        document.write(ch7.chapter + "<BR>");
        document.write(ch7.pages + "<P>");

        ch10 = new myBook("New JavaScript", "Gil");

        ch10.chapter = 10;
        ch10.pages = 55;

        document.write(ch7 + "<P>");
        document.write(ch10 + "<P>");

//END HIDING-->
</SCRIPT>

</HEAD>
<BODY>
</BODY>
</HTML>
```

The preceding example produces the following output in the browser:

Dynamic HTML
Gilorien
7
124

{title:"Dynamic HTML", author:"Gilorien", chapter:7, pages:124}

{title:"New JavaScript", author:"Gil", chapter:10, pages:55}

Indexing Properties of an Object

When you create Properties for Objects that you create, you can define those Properties by name or by their zero-based **index** number. For instance, in the previous example, the **pages** Property could have been defined for the **ch7** Instance of the **myBook** Object in any of the following three ways:

```
ch7.pages = 7;          //defined by name
ch7["pages"] = 7;       //defined by name
ch7[3] = 7;             //defined by index number
```

What's important to remember is that when you refer to a Property, you must refer to it in the same way that it was defined, that is, by name or **index** number. If you <u>define</u> it by name then you must <u>refer</u> to it by name. If you <u>define</u> it by **index** number then you must <u>refer</u> to it by **index** number. The two ways to refer to it by name that are shown above are considered equivalent and therefor interchangeable.

Equally important is the fact that the above scenario is not true for Objects that are reflected from HTML, such as the **layers[i]** Array or the **images[i]** Array, when the JavaScript interpreter loads a page. The Elements of these Arrays can always be referred to <u>either</u> by name or by their **index** number. For instance, if you had a Layer named **myLayer3** and it was the third Layer in the document, you could refer to it in any of these three ways:

```
document.myLayer3;
document.layers["myLayer3"];
document.layers[2];
```

In case you've forgotten, these Arrays are actually Properties of other Objects. For instance, the **layers[i]** Array is a Property of the **document** Object and the **arguments[i]** Array is a Property of the **Function** Object.

Example 4-15 demonstrates the several ways that you have to define Properties for Instances of an Object and then the proper way to refer to them. Note that in this example, which is similar to the previous example, the **prototype** Property is not used. The Properties that are created after the **myBook** Object is defined are for the individual Instances of the **myBook** Object named **ch7** and **ch8**. Because of that, the **chapter** Property has to be defined for each Instance of the **myBook** Object.

For **ch7**, the fourth Property of that Object is named **pages**. For **ch8**, the fourth Property is not named, but is defined with an **index** of 3 like this:

```
ch8[3]=111;
```

You should notice in the browser output how the Instance Objects of **ch7** and **ch8** are coded internally by JavaScript, which explains why you have to refer to Object's Properties in the same way that they were defined. Specifically the code:

```
document.write(ch7 + "<P>");
```

produces this output in the browser:

{title:"Dynamic HTML", author:"Gilorien", chapter:7, **pages:124**}

while this code:

```
document.write(ch8 + "<P>");
```

produces this output in the browser:

{title:"Layers", author:"Gilorien", chapter:8, **3:111**}

Notice in the bold text that the **pages** name is used in **ch7**, and the **index** number **3** is used in **ch8**.

Example 4-15 is very similar to Example 4-14. In summary, it starts by using the Function Constructor to define an Object named **myBook**, and then two Instances of that Object are created and named **ch7** and **ch8**. Then the individual Properties of **ch7** and **ch8** are written to screen and eventually both of the entire Object Instances are also written to screen.

Example 4-15:   **Sample515.html**

```
<!DOCTYPE HTML PUBLIC "-//W3C//DTD HTML 3.2//EN">
<HTML>
<HEAD>
<TITLE>Sample 515 - Example 4-15        indexing Object Properties</TITLE>

<SCRIPT LANGUAGE="JavaScript1.2"><!--BEGIN HIDING

        function myBook(title, author) {

                this.title = title;
                this.author = author;
        }

/*--------------------------------------------------------------------------*/

        ch7 = new myBook("Dynamic HTML", "Gilorien");

        ch7.chapter = 7;
        ch7.pages = 124;

        document.write(ch7.title + "<BR>");
        document.write(ch7.author + "<BR>");
        document.write(ch7.chapter + "<BR>");
        document.write(ch7.pages + "<P>");

        document.write(ch7 + "<P>");
/*--------------------------------------------------------------------------*/

        ch8 = new myBook("Layers", "Gilorien");

        ch8["chapter"] = 8;              //this is the third Property of the Object
        ch8[3] = 111;                    //this is the fourth Property of the Object

        document.write(ch8.title + "<BR>");
        document.write(ch8.author + "<BR>");
        document.write(ch8.chapter + "<BR>");
        document.write(ch8[3] + "<P>");

        document.write(ch8 + "<P>");

//END HIDING-->
</SCRIPT>
</HEAD>

<BODY>
</BODY>
</HTML>
```

The preceding example produces the following output in the browser:

Dynamic HTML
Gilorien
7
124

{title:"Dynamic HTML", author:"Gilorien", chapter:7, pages:124}

Layers
Gilorien
8
111

{title:"Layers", author:"Gilorien", chapter:8, 3:111}

Creating Objects with <u>Literal</u> Notation

JavaScript Syntax:

```
objectName = {property1:value1, property2:value2, ..., propertyN:valueN}
```

<u>Parameters Defined:</u>

With JavaScript 1.2, you can also create a new Object by using Literal Notation. It takes the same Syntax that you saw in the previous example when an Object was written to screen. It starts with the **objectName** parameter, which is the name of the Object. The **objectName** is then assigned the Object Literal. The entire Object Literal is enclosed in curly braces{}. It consists of a comma-separated list of **property:value** pairs. Each **property** is separated from its **value** by a colon.

For each **property1** through **propertyN** parameter, you choose an identifier for the Property. It can be a name, a number, or a String Literal. The **value1** through **valueN** parameters can be a String, Number, Variable, another Object that you create, or any valid JavaScript Expression.

Even though the syntax separates the **property** and **value** pairs with a colon, the behavior is such that the **value** is assigned to the **property** as if the equals (=) sign is used.
Here's a simple example of creating an Object with Literal notation:

```
myObject = {color:"blue", size:42, year:1999}
```

For comparison purposes, this example rewrites the previous example so that the Objects **ch7** and **ch8** are defined with Literal notation. The output to the browser is exactly the same as in the previous example. Notice how much easier it is to use Literal notation.

Example 4-16:   **Sample516.html**

```
<!DOCTYPE HTML PUBLIC "-//W3C//DTD HTML 3.2//EN">
<HTML>
<HEAD>
<TITLE>Sample 516 - Example 4-16      Creating Objects with Literal notation</TITLE>

<SCRIPT LANGUAGE="JavaScript1.2"><!--BEGIN HIDING

ch7 = {title:"Dynamic HTML", author:"Gilorien", chapter:7, pages:124}

/*-------------------------------------------------------------------------*/

        document.write(ch7.title + "<BR>");
        document.write(ch7.author + "<BR>");
        document.write(ch7.chapter + "<BR>");
        document.write(ch7.pages + "<P>");

        document.write(ch7 + "<P>");
/*-------------------------------------------------------------------------*/

ch8 = {title:"Layers", author:"Gilorien", chapter:8, 3:111}

        document.write(ch8.title + "<BR>");
        document.write(ch8.author + "<BR>");
        document.write(ch8.chapter + "<BR>");
        document.write(ch8[3] + "<P>");

        document.write(ch8 + "<P>");

//END HIDING-->
</SCRIPT>
</HEAD>

<BODY>
</BODY>
</HTML>
```

This example demonstrates an Object created with Literal Notation that has a Property which is itself another Object. The **myCycle** Object is defined with the four Properties of **motorcycle**, **model**, **year**, and **owner**. The **owner** Property is an Object that has the three Properties of **firstName**, **lastName**, and **location**. You should notice the syntax that is used to access a Property of the **owner** Object.

Example 4-17:   **Sample517.html**

```
<!DOCTYPE HTML PUBLIC "-//W3C//DTD HTML 3.2//EN">
<HTML>
<HEAD>
<TITLE>Sample 517 - Example 4-17    Creating Objects with Literal notation</TITLE>

<SCRIPT LANGUAGE="JavaScript1.2"><!--BEGIN HIDING

myCycle = {motorcycle:"Yamaha", model:"YZ-250", year:1997, owner:{firstName:"John",
lastName:"Anderson", location:"Los Angeles"}}

document.write(myCycle.motorcycle + " ");
document.write(myCycle.model + "--");
document.write(myCycle.year + "<BR>");
document.write(myCycle.owner.firstName + " ");
document.write(myCycle.owner.lastName + "<BR>");
document.write(myCycle.owner.location + "<BR>");


//END HIDING-->
</SCRIPT>
</HEAD>

<BODY>
</BODY>
</HTML>
```

The preceding example produces the following output in the browser:

Yamaha YZ-250--1997
John Anderson
Los Angeles

This example demonstrates an Object created with Literal Notation that has one Property named **test1** with a Value of an expression which is **x+y**. The **test2** Property has a Value of the Variable **z**. Since the expression evaluates to 13, the Statements that write the Properties of **myObj** and the Object **myObj** to screen are executed.

Example 4-18:   **Sample518.html**

```
<!DOCTYPE HTML PUBLIC "-//W3C//DTD HTML 3.2//EN">
<HTML>
<HEAD>
<TITLE>Sample 518 - Example 4-18    Creating Objects with Literal notation</TITLE>

<SCRIPT LANGUAGE="JavaScript1.2"><!--BEGIN HIDING

var x=5;
var y=8;
var z=13;

myObj = {test1:x+y, test2:z}

if (myObj.test1 == 13) {

        document.write(myObj.test1 + "<BR>");
        document.write(myObj.test2 + "<BR>");
        document.write(myObj);
}

//END HIDING-->
</SCRIPT>
</HEAD>

<BODY>
</BODY>
</HTML>
```

The preceding example produces the following output in the browser:

```
13
13
{test1:13, test2:13}
```

Deleting an Object

To delete an Object from a Script, just set its Object reference to **null** like this:

```
myObject = null;
```

which removes the Object immediately as part of the assignment expression. It should be noted that there should be no subsequent references to the deleted Object; that is, setting the Object reference to **null** must be the last reference to that Object.

Deleting Objects can be useful in large, complicated Scripts, because it will free up system resources when memory is at a premium and since download times are still abysmally slow for most users.

The <u>watch()</u> Method of the Core Object

JavaScript Syntax:

```
objectName.watch(propertyName, handlerFunction)
```

Parameters Defined:

The **watch()** Method adds a **watchpoint** to a Property specified by **propertyName** of an Object specified by **objectName**, which causes a call to a Function specified by **handlerFunction** each time that the Property receives a Value. This is a new Method for Navigator 4.0.

This is kinda tricky. If you are familiar with the **sort()** Method that has a built-in Function as part of the Method, then you have an edge on comprehension.

Using the <u>handlerFunction</u> Parameter

The **handlerFunction** takes on a specific format but there is a lot of room to custom design it for your own purposes. Note that in the syntax, the **handlerFunction** is not named. The syntax for **handlerFunction** is:

JavaScript Syntax:

```
function (id, oldvalue, newvalue) {
      return somevalue;
}
```

Parameters Defined:

where:

id   is the name of the Property specified by **propertyName**.

oldvalue   starts as the initial Value assigned to the Property and is subsequently the previous Value of the Property each time a new Value is assigned to the Property.

newvalue   takes the first new Value that is assigned to the Property and subsequently takes each new Value that is assigned to the Property. Each time a new Value is assigned to the Property, the current **newvalue** is sent to the **oldvalue** Argument, so that the **newvalue** Argument can take on the next new Value assigned to the Property. This typical scenario assumes that the **somevalue** Argument in the **return** Statement is set to **newvalue**.

somevalue   typically set to **newvalue**, but you can also set it to **oldvalue** or modify **somevalue** in any way that you want.

In its simplest format, the **handlerFunction** would just return the **newvalue** Value to the Property **p** in the Object **o** created with Literal notation like this:

```
o = {p:1}
o.watch("p", function (id, oldvalue, newvalue) {return newvalue ;})
o.p = 2;
document.write(o.p);
```

which would display: 2   in the browser.

With only a slight modification to the **return** Statement, the output to the browser would be 77, like this:

```
o = {p:1}
o.watch("p", function (id, oldvalue, newvalue) {return newvalue + 75 ;})
o.p = 2;
document.write(o.p);
```

The **watchpoint** remains in effect, even if you delete the Property that it was assigned to watch. If you recreate the Property later on in the Script, the **watchpoint** will still work as if the Property had always been there. To remove a **watchpoint**, you have to use the **unwatch()** Method.

To delete a Property use the **delete** Statement like this:

```
delete o.p;
```

To remove a **watchpoint** use the **unwatch()** Method like this:

```
o.unwatch("p");
```

This example demonstrates a simple use of the **watch()** Method by first defining an Object named **o** with Literal notation that has a Property named **p** with a Value of 1. The **watch()** Method is then invoked, so that each time the **p** Property is assigned a Value, the three **write()** Methods are invoked and the **newvalue** Argument is returned as the Value of the **p** Property.

Example 4-19:   **Sample519.html**

```
<!DOCTYPE HTML PUBLIC "-//W3C//DTD HTML 3.2//EN">
<HTML><HEAD>
<TITLE>Sample 519 - Example 4-19     watch Method    </TITLE>

<SCRIPT LANGUAGE="JavaScript1.2"><!--BEGIN HIDING

o = {p:1}
o.watch("p",
        function (id, oldvalue, newvalue) {
                document.write("For the Object o with Property " + id)
                document.write(", the old Value was: " + oldvalue)
                document.write(" and the new Value is: " + newvalue + "<P>")
        return newvalue;
        })

o.p = 2;
o.p = 3;
o.p = 4;

//END HIDING-->
</SCRIPT>
</HEAD>
<BODY>
</BODY>
</HTML>
```

The preceding example produces the following output in the browser:

For the Object o with Property p, the old Value was: 1 and the new Value is: 2

For the Object o with Property p, the old Value was: 2 and the new Value is: 3

For the Object o with Property p, the old Value was: 3 and the new Value is: 4

This example demonstrates a simple use of the **watch()** Method by first defining an Object named **o** with Literal notation that has a Property named **p** with a Value of 1. The **watch()** Method is then invoked so that each time the **p** Property is assigned a Value, the **newvalue** Argument is tested with the **if()** Statement and has either 500 added to it, if it is equal to 7, otherwise 100 is added to it and in both cases it is returned as the Value of the **p** Property.

Example 4-20: **Sample520.html**

```
<!DOCTYPE HTML PUBLIC "-//W3C//DTD HTML 3.2//EN">
<HTML>
<HEAD>
<TITLE>Sample 520 - Example 4-20      watch Method</TITLE>

<SCRIPT LANGUAGE="JavaScript1.2"><!--BEGIN HIDING

o = {p:1}

o.watch("p",
    function (id, oldvalue, newvalue) {

        if (newvalue == 7) {
                document.write("<B>" + "Found the value of 7" + "<\/B><P>");
                return newvalue + 500;
        }
        else {
                document.write("o." + id + " had old Value of " + oldvalue);
                document.write(", now has " + newvalue + "<BR>");
                return newvalue + 100;
        }
    })

o.p = 2;
o.p = 3;
o.p = 4;
o.p = 5;
o.p = 6;
o.p = 7;
o.p = 8;

//END HIDING-->
</SCRIPT>
</HEAD>

<BODY>
</BODY>
</HTML>
```

The preceding example produces the following output in the browser:

---

o.p had old Value of 1, now has 2
o.p had old Value of 102, now has 3
o.p had old Value of 103, now has 4
o.p had old Value of 104, now has 5
o.p had old Value of 105, now has 6
Found the value of 7

o.p had old Value of 507, now has 8

The <u>unwatch()</u> Method of the Core Object

JavaScript Syntax:

```
objectName.unwatch("propertyName")
```

Parameters Defined:

The **unwatch()** Method removes a **watchpoint** from a Property specified by **propertyName** of an Object specified by **objectName**.

Mini-Example:

For example to remove a **watchpoint** for the Object **o** with Property **p**, you could use the following code:

```
o.unwatch("p");
```

Looking Ahead

This ends the section on Objects that you create yourself. The next section deals with some of the Predefined Objects that are included as part of the JavaScript Language. The first Predefined Object that is covered is the **window** Object. In JavaScript1.2, there are new Properties and Methods that are available for increased functionality.

Predefined JavaScript Objects

The JavaScript <u>window</u> Object

The **window** Object covers a lot of ground. It is a top-level Object in the JavaScript Object hierarchy. Specifically, it is the top-level Object for each **document**, **location**, and **history** Objects. A top-level **window** Object is created by the Javascript runtime engine for each BODY or FRAMESET Tag. Additionally, a **window** Object is created for each FRAME Tag that is not a top-level Window. For a Window that is created by a FRAME Tag, the FRAMESET Window is the top-level Window. Finally, a **window** Object is created for each Window that you create by using the **window.open()** Method, which is covered on pages 422-426.

Concerning Frames

Technically speaking, a FRAME is a **window** Object that has behaviors somewhat different than other Windows. There is no separate Frame Object, but there is a **frames[i]** Array that is a Property of the **window** Object. The functionality differences of **window** Objects that are created from FRAME Tags are as follows:

1)   The **parent** and **top** Properties of a top-level Window refer to that same Window. For a Frame Window, the **parent** Property refers to the **parent** Frameset Window. For a Frame Window, the **top** Property refers to the topmost Window.

2)   For a Frame Window, setting the **defaultStatus** or **status** Properties will only display the text message in the status bar when the cursor is over that Frame.

3)   For a Frame Window, the **onfocus** and **onblur** Event Handlers can only be set by Property Assignment, and they must be spelled in all lowercase letters. You can not set these Event Handlers in the HTML Tag of the Frame.

4)   For a Frame Window, the **close()** Method is unavailable.

5)   For a Frame that contains both the SRC and the NAME Attributes, you can refer to that Frame from a sibling Frame by any of the following three ways:

```
parent.frameName
```

```
parent.frames[i]
```

```
parent.frames["frameName"]
```

For instance, if you have a Frame named **myFrame3** that is the third Frame in a Frameset, you could refer to it from another Frame in that Frameset by:

```
parent.myFrame3

parent.frames[2]

parent.frames["myFrame3"]
```

If you wanted to change the background color of the Frame named **myFrame3**, you could do it from within the sibling Frame like this:

```
parent.myFrame3.document.bgColor = "blue";
```

Special Notice:

It should be noted that while you can create **window** Objects with the **open()** Method, you cannot create a Frame or a Frameset as a **window** Object from within JavaScript. They can only be created with HTML. You can get around this limitation by using the **write()** Method of the **document** Object to write HTML directly to the page, and in that context you can create FRAMESET and FRAME Elements. Check out page 456 and Example 4-34 later in this chapter for details on Frame creation. For details on the **write()** Method check out pages 230-232, 434.

These are the Event Handlers for the **window** Object. See Chapter 6 on Events for the definitions and examples.

Window Event Handlers

onBlur
onDragDrop
onError
onFocus
onLoad
onMove
onResize
onUnload

The Properties and Methods of the **window** Object are as follows:

Window Properties

Property	Description
closed	Boolean with a value of true if a Window that you opened is now closed. Once you close a Window, you should not refer to it unless, of course, you reopen it with the **open()** Method.
defaultStatus	A settable Property that specifies the default message to be displayed in the status bar at the bottom of the Window when no priority message specified by the **status** Property is to be displayed, such as when an onMouseOver Event occurs.
document	Accesses the Properties and Methods of the **document** Object to render output to the browser. See the next section on the **document** Object.
frames[i]	An Array that reflects all the Frames in a Window in source order. You can access a Frame by its Name Attribute or by its index number. For the Frame named **myFrame3** that is the third Frame in a Frameset: `parent.frames["myFrame3"]` is equivalent to: `parent.frames[2]` and is equivalent to: `parent.myFrame3` Its **length** Property reflects the number of Frames in the Window. The **name** Property of each Array Element reflects the name of that Frame.
history[i]	An Array reflecting a Window's history of URL entries that the user has visited in source order. Accesses the **History** Object. See Example 4-33.
innerHeight	Specifies in pixels the vertical size of the space reserved for insertion of content for the Window.
innerWidth	Specifies in pixels the horizontal size of the space reserved for insertion of content for the Window.
length	A read-only integer reflecting the number of Frames in the Window. **window.length** is equivalent to **parent.frames.length**
location	Reflects the information about the current URL of the Window contained in the Window's associated **Location** Object. When referring to the **Location** Object, you must use **window.location** instead of just **location**.
locationbar	Represents the location bar of the Window where the URL of the current document is displayed. It has one Property of **visible** which can be set to **"false"** to hide the location bar and **"true"** to show it.**
menubar	Represents the menu bar of the Window where the pull-down menus such as File, Edit, View, and Go reside. It has one Property of **visible**, which can be set to **"false"** to hide the menu bar and **"true"** to show it.**
name	The unique identifier, that is, the name used to refer to a Window. This is a read/write Property as of Navigator 3.0.

** To use this Property requires that the **UniversalBrowserWrite** privilege be secured for security purposes. For more information, see the section on JavaScript Security in the JavaScript Guide or the section on the **window** Object in the JavaScript Reference.

Property	Description
opener	Specifies the name of the Window that is the calling document when the **open()** Method is used to open a new Window. Navigator allows up to 100 open Windows at the same time. To free up system resources, be sure to set the **opener** Property to **null** if you are done with the calling Window.
outerHeight	Specifies, in pixels, the vertical size of the Window's total outside edge, which includes the status bar, scroll bars, menu bar, and tool bars, which are termed the "chrome" elements of a Window.
outerWidth	Specifies, in pixels, the horizontal size of the Window's total outside edge which includes the status bar, scroll bars, menu bar and tool bars which are termed the "chrome" elements of a Window.
pageXOffset	Specifies the horizontal distance that the current position of the page is offset from the upper-left origin point of (0,0) of the document. An integer that can be positive or negative or zero and is measured in pixels.
pageYOffset	Specifies the vertical distance that the current position of the page is offset from the upper-left origin point of (0,0) of the document. An integer that can be positive or negative or zero and is measured in pixels.
parent	The generic synonym for a Frameset Window that contains the current Frame. This allows you to manipulate the contents in one Frame from within another Frame. For multiple nested Framesets use an extra **parent** for each level of nesting such as: **parent.parent.frameName** for 1 nesting.
personalbar	Represents the personal bar of the Window where the user can have easy access to bookmarks. It has one Property of **visible** which can be set to "false" to hide the personal bar and "true" to show it.**
scrollbars	Represents the scroll bars of the Window so the user can scroll the page horizontally and vertically. It has one Property of **visible**, which can be set to **"false"** to hide the scroll bars and **"true"** to show them.**
self	Refers to the current Window. This Property is identical to the **window** Property below, but with an arguably more intuitive name.
status	A settable Property that specifies the priority message to be displayed in the status bar at the bottom of the Window. This is a transient message that temporarily overrides the **defaultstatus** message when an Event such as onMouseOut occurs.
statusbar	Refers to the status bar at the bottom of the browser Window where the default status and status messages are displayed and other icons reside.
toolbar	Represents the tool bar of the Window where the back, forward, home, and other buttons reside. It has one Property of **visible**, which can be set to **"false"** to hide the tool bar and **"true"** to show it.**
top	Refers to the top-most Window, the ancestor of all other child Windows or Frames in the page.
window	Refers to the current Window.

** To use this Property requires that the **UniversalBrowserWrite** privilege be secured for security purposes. For more information see the section on JavaScript Security in the JavaScript Guide or the section on the **window** Object in the JavaScript Reference.

Window Methods

Method	Description
alert("message")	Specifies a **message** String to the user in an Alert dialog box with an OK button when no decision or user feedback is required. To custom design your own Alert dialog box, use the **open()** Method.
back()	Loads the previous URL of the top-level Window. To load the previous URL of the current Window or Frame, use **history.back()**.
blur()	Removes focus from the specified Window or Frame.

captureEvents(Event.EVENTNAME [| Event.EVENTNAME])
> Causes the Window to capture all Events of the specified type. Note that the EVENTNAME such as KEYPRESS or CLICK is always specified in all uppercase and is always preceded by **Event.** and separated by (|) if more than one Event is used. See Chapter 6 on Events for details.

Method	Description
clearInterval(intervalID)	Cancels the timeout specified by **intervalID** that was set with the **setInterval()** Method. See pages 284, 286-287 for details.
clearTimeout(timeoutID)	Cancels the timeout specified by **timeoutID** that was set with the **setTimeout()** Method. See pages 250, 288-289 for details.
close()	Closes the Window specified by a **windowReference** like this: **myWindow.close()**. If no **windowReference** is specified, then the current Window is closed. See page 427 for details.
confirm("message")	Specifies a **message** String to the user in a Confirm dialog box with OK and Cancel buttons when a decision is required by the user.
disableExternalCapture()	Lets you disable external Event capturing that was set by the **enableExternalCapture()** Method.
enableExternalCapture()	Lets you capture Events in Frames that contain pages that have been loaded from different server locations.

find(["searchString"][, casesensitive][, backward])
> Returns true if the specified **searchString** is found in the contents of the specified Window or Frame. The **backward** Argument is a Boolean that, if included, performs a search toward the start of the page and also requires the **casesensitive** Boolean to be included. See the JavaScript Reference on the CD-ROM for details.

Method	Description
focus()	Gives focus to the specified Window or Frame. For Frames, this is indicated by a visual cue like a cyan border on most platforms.
forward()	Simulates the user clicking on the Forward Button in the browser Navigation Bar, which is the same as loading the next URL in the history list. To load the previous URL of the current Window or Frame, use **history.forward()**.

handleEvent(eventArg) Calls the Event handler for the specified **eventArg**. This Method is always used in tandem with the **routeEvent()**
Method.

See Chapter 6 on pages 668-677 on Events for complete details.

home() Loads the URL for the home page that the user specified in the preferences of the browser.

moveBy(x, y) Moves the Window by the specified number of horizontal **x** and vertical **y** pixels, which can be positive or negative integers or zero.

moveTo(x, y) Moves the top-left corner of the Window to the specified horizontal **x** and vertical **y** screen coordinates where (x, y) is measured down and to the right if positive and up and to the left if negative, from a (0, 0) origin at the top-left of the screen. To move any part of the Window off-screen requires that the **UniversalBrowserWrite** privilege be secured in a signed Script.

open("URL", "windowName", "windowFeatures")
Opens a new browser Window. See pages 422-428 for details.

print() Prints the contents of the current Window or Frame that has focus.

prompt("message", [defaultInput])
Specify a **message** String to the user in a Prompt dialog box with an input field for user response data. OK and Cancel buttons respectively allow or disallow the data to be incorporated into a Script although the Script ultimately has control over how the data is used.

releaseEvents(Event.EVENTNAME | Event.EVENTNAME)
Releases the specified Event Types that were set to be captured by the **captureEvents()** Method so they will progress in the Event hierarchy. See Chapter 6 on Events for complete details.

resizeBy(x, y) Resizes the bottom-right corner of the Window by the specified number of horizontal **x** and vertical **y** pixels, which can be positive or negative integers or zero.

resizeTo(x, y) Resizes the entire Window by the specified number of horizontal **x** and vertical **y** pixels that represent the outer width and outer height dimensions.

routeEvent(eventArg) Causes an Event that was captured with the **captureEvents()** Method to be passed along the normal Event hierarchy to its original target, unless another Object captures it along the way. See Chapter 6 on Events for complete details.

scroll(x, y) Deprecated in favor of **scrollBy()** and **scrollTo()**, which have added flexibility and are more intuitively named.

scrollBy(x, y) Scrolls the visible area of the Window by the specified number of horizontal **x** and vertical **y**, positive, negative, or zero pixels.

scrollTo(x, y) Scrolls the visible area of the Window so that the specified (x, y) coordinate becomes the current top-left corner of the Window.

setInterval('expression', milliseconds)
setInterval('functionName()', milliseconds, [arg1, arg2, ..., argN])

> The **setInterval()** Method has two syntax formats. It can evaluate an **expression** or call a Function specified by **functionName()** <u>repeatedly</u> after the specified number of milliseconds have elapsed.
> See pages 284, 286-287 for details and examples.

setTimeout('expression', milliseconds)
setTimeout('functionName()', milliseconds, [arg1, arg2, ..., argN])

> The **setTimeout()** Method has two syntax formats. It can evaluate an **expression** or call a Function specified by **functionName()** <u>once</u> after the specified number of milliseconds have elapsed.
> See pages 250, 288-289 for details and examples.

stop()   Halts the URL that is currently being downloaded.

The <u>open()</u> Method of the <u>window</u> Object

You can use the **open()** Method to create a new browser Window. There are a plethora of features that you can include to custom design the Window, ranging from a full-blown normal-looking Navigator Window down to a simple quasi-Alert dialog box. You can include a URL to load into the Window as part of the **open()** Method or you can open the Window and then use the **write()** Method of the **document** Object to add content to the Window just like any other page. You can even open another Window from the Window that was just opened and repeat the process for up to 100 simultaneously open Windows.

Because of the scoping nature of static Objects in JavaScript, you must specify **window.open()** or **windowName.open()** when this Method is used in Event Handlers. If you don't, that is, if you just specify **open()** without a **window** Object, JavaScript interprets this as **document.open()**.

JavaScript Syntax:

```
window.open("URL", "windowName", ["windowFeatures"]);
windowVarName=window.open("URL", "windowName", ["windowFeatures"]);
```

Parameters Defined:

URL   A String that specifies the URL to load into the new Window. If you don't want to load an existing document, such as when you want to create a custom designed Alert or Prompt Window, then specify an empty String consisting of two adjacent double quote marks like this: "".

windowName   The name of the Window that you can refer to in your Script.

windowFeatures   A String containing a comma-separated list of features to custom-design your Window with. Do not put any spaces in the **windowFeatures** String at all. You cannot use JavaScript to change any of the features after the Window is opened. All of the possible features are listed and described below.

For the features that only require that they be set equal to either yes or no, you can substitute 1 for yes and 0 for no. For these features, you can also just include the name of the feature and it will be treated as a Boolean true, and that will turn the feature on.

If you create a Window and the **windowName** Argument does not specify an already existing Window and the **windowFeatures** Argument is omitted, then all of the features that have a **yes/no** Value option are by default set to **yes**.

Nav4-- means the Feature is new for Navigator 4.0.
*   means the Feature is secure and must be set in a Signed Script.

alwaysLowered   Nav4--* If yes or 1, the new Window will float below other Windows, whether active or inactive. On the Macintosh platform, it floats below all browser Windows but not necessarily below Windows in other applications. On the Windows 95 platform it floats below all other Windows.

alwaysRaised   Nav4--* If yes or 1, the new Window will float above other Windows, whether active or inactive. On the Macintosh platform it floats above all browser Windows but not necessarily above Windows in other applications. On the Windows 95 platform it floats above all other Windows.

dependent   Nav4-- If yes or 1, the new Window is a sibling of the current Window which will close when its parent Window closes.

directories   If yes or 1, the standard directory bar that includes buttons such as What's Cool and Yellow Pages is created. In Navigator 4.0, on some platforms, the directory buttons have been deprecated in favor of putting this data in the Guides Folder under the Bookmarks menu.

hotkeys   Nav4-- If no or 0, most hotkeys, that is; the Command Keys for the new Window, are disabled. It will also have no menu bar. However, the **security** and **quit** hotkeys are still always enabled.

innerHeight   Nav4-- Specifies, in pixels, the height of the viewable area for the Window's content.

innerWidth   Nav4-- Specifies, in pixels, the width of the viewable area for the Window's content.

location   If yes or 1, the Location bar is created for the Window, which displays the current URL and can receive a URL directly from the user which is activated by the Return or Enter Keys.

menubar   If yes or 1, the menu at the top of the screen is created.

outerHeight	Nav4-- Specifies, in pixels, the vertical height of the Window's outer edge.
outerWidth	Nav4-- Specifies, in pixels, the horizontal width of the Window's outer edge.
resizable	If yes or 1, the user has the ability to resize the Window by dragging on the bottom right corner of the Window.
screenX	Nav4-- Specifies, in pixels, how far the Window is positioned from the left edge of the user's screen. To position any portion of the Window off-screen, set this feature in a Signed Script.
screenY	Nav4-- Specifies, in pixels, how far the Window is positioned from the top edge of the user's screen. To position any portion of the Window off-screen, set this feature in a Signed Script.
scrollbars	If yes or 1, the horizontal and vertical scrollbars appear if the content of the Document grows larger than the viewing area of the Window can accommodate.
status	If yes or 1, the status bar at the bottom of the Window is created where priority messages are displayed.
titlebar	Nav4--* If yes or 1, the title bar for the Window is created.
toolbar	If yes or 1, the toolbar is created for the Window.
z-lock	Nav4--* If yes or 1, the new Window is always behind other Windows when it is created.

Mini-Example:

Here's a simple mini-example that calls the **myWindow()** Function in the **onClick** Event Handler of the **b1** Button to open a new Window that loads the file with the relative URL of "Sample1.html". Notice that there are no spaces between the Features in the **windowFeatures** Argument.

```
<SCRIPT LANGUAGE="JavaScript1.2"><!--BEGIN HIDING

function myWindow() {

    myMsg=open("Sample1.html", "myWin",
        "screenX=100,screenY=120,resizable=yes,outerwidth=400,outerheight=300");
}

//END HIDING-->
</SCRIPT>

<FORM NAME="form1">
Click to open a new Window with Sample1.html loaded in it from Chapter 1.

<INPUT TYPE="button" NAME="b1" VALUE="Open Me Up" onClick="myWindow();">
```

</FORM>

This example demonstrates the **open()** Method of the **window** Object to open a Window named **myMsg** when the **myWindow()** Function is called by clicking on the Button named **b1**. Then the **write()** and **close()** Methods of the **document** Object are invoked on **myMsg** to display the message. Make sure that you remember to use the **close()** Method in your own Scripts, otherwise the data stream will not be closed and the contents of the **write()** Methods will not be displayed.

Example 4-21: **Sample521.html**

```
<!DOCTYPE HTML PUBLIC "-//W3C//DTD HTML 3.2//EN">
<HTML>
<HEAD>
<TITLE>Sample 521 - Example 4-21      open Method of window Object</TITLE>

<SCRIPT LANGUAGE="JavaScript1.2"><!--BEGIN HIDING

function myWindow() {

        myMsg=open("", "myWin", "resizable=yes,innerwidth=300,innerheight=200");

        myMsg.document.write("<HTML><HEAD><TITLE>My Window Message<\/TITLE><\/HEAD>");
        myMsg.document.write("<BODY> My first Window Message. <\/BODY><\/HTML>");

        myMsg.document.close();
}

//END HIDING-->
</SCRIPT>

</HEAD>

<BODY>

<FORM NAME="form1">

Click to open the Window.

<INPUT TYPE="button" NAME="b1" VALUE="Open Me Up" onClick="myWindow();">

</FORM>

</BODY>
</HTML>
```

This example focuses on the **opener** Property of the **window** Object. When the **b1** Button is clicked it opens the **myMsg** Window, which contains another Button named **b2** that uses the **opener** Property of the **myMsg** Window to change the background color of the original document, which was the **opener** Window. Notice the use of escaping double-quotes with the backslash (\) Character to provide literal double-quotes for "red".

Example 4-22:   **Sample522.html**

```
<!DOCTYPE HTML PUBLIC "-//W3C//DTD HTML 3.2//EN">
<HTML>
<HEAD>
<TITLE>Sample 522 - Example 4-22      opener Property of window Object</TITLE>

<SCRIPT LANGUAGE="JavaScript1.2"><!--BEGIN HIDING

function myWindow() {

        myMsg=open("", "myWin", "resizable=yes,innerwidth=300,innerheight=200");

        myMsg.document.write("<HTML><HEAD><TITLE>My Window<\/TITLE><\/HEAD>");
        myMsg.document.write("<BODY>");
        myMsg.document.write("<FORM NAME='form2'>");
        myMsg.document.write("<INPUT TYPE='button' NAME='b2' VALUE='Red It'
                          onClick='window.opener.document.bgColor=\"red\";'>");
        myMsg.document.write("<\/FORM>");
        myMsg.document.write("<\/BODY><\/HTML>");

        myMsg.document.close();
}

//END HIDING-->
</SCRIPT>

</HEAD>

<BODY>

<FORM NAME="form1">

Click to open the Message Window.
<INPUT TYPE='button' NAME='b1' VALUE='Open Me Up' onClick='myWindow();'>

</FORM>

</BODY>
</HTML>
```

The close() Method of the window Object

JavaScript Syntax:

```
close();
window.close();
windowName.close();
```

Parameters Defined:

The **close()** Method is used to close the Window that is specified by **windowName**. If no **windowName** reference is supplied, then the current Window is closed. When the **close()** Method is used <u>outside</u> of Event Handlers, **close()** is functionally equivalent to **window.close()**, which closes the current Window.

When used <u>inside</u> an Event Handler you must use **window.close()** or **windowName.close()** because just using **close()** without a Window reference is equivalent to **document.close()**, due to the scoping of static Objects in JavaScript.

Without the **UniversalBrowserWrite** privilege, you can only close Windows that were opened by JavaScript with the **open()** Method. You can still use the **close()** Method in your code without errors to close these other Windows, but a **confirm** Dialog Box will be generated by JavaScript automatically, which gives the user the choice of closing or not closing the Window. This is a security feature.

The exception to this rule is when a Window has only one entry in its **history** Array Property and that document is the current document; you can close the Window without the **confirm** Dialog Box being generated. What this allows you to do is create a document that can open one or more Windows and then dispose of itself to free up system memory and resources.

For more information on the **UniversalBrowserWrite** privilege, Signed Scripts and JavaScript Security see Chapter 1 in the JavaScript Guide on the CD-ROM.

The following example demonstrates using the **close()** Method in two ways to close the **myMsg** Window that is opened when the **b1** Button is clicked. Clicking on either the **b2** Button or **b3** Button will close the Window, but notice the different code that is used in each case.

Example 4-23:   Sample523.html

```
<!DOCTYPE HTML PUBLIC "-//W3C//DTD HTML 3.2//EN">
<HTML>
<HEAD>
<TITLE>Sample 523 - Example 4-23      close Method of window Object</TITLE>

<SCRIPT LANGUAGE="JavaScript1.2"><!--BEGIN HIDING

function myWindow() {

        myMsg=open("", "myWin", "resizable=yes,innerwidth=300,innerheight=200");

        myMsg.document.write("<HTML><HEAD><TITLE>My Window<\/TITLE><\/HEAD>");
        myMsg.document.write("<BODY>");
        myMsg.document.write("<FORM NAME='form2'>");
        myMsg.document.write("<INPUT TYPE='button' NAME='b3' VALUE='Close Me Now'
                                        onClick='window.close();'>");
        myMsg.document.write("<\/FORM>");
        myMsg.document.write("<\/BODY><\/HTML>");

        myMsg.document.close();
}

//END HIDING-->
</SCRIPT>

</HEAD>

<BODY>

<FORM NAME="form1">

Click to open or close the Window.

<INPUT TYPE='button' NAME='b1' VALUE='Open Me Up' onClick='myWindow();'>

<INPUT TYPE='button' NAME='b2' VALUE='Close it' onClick='myMsg.close();'>

</FORM>

</BODY>
</HTML>
```

This example demonstrates the **resizeBy()**, **resizeTo()**, **moveBy()** and **moveTo()** Methods of the **window** Object. It also demonstrates how to use the **status** Property in the **onClick** Event Handler. When using the **status** Property in the **onMouseOver** Event Handler, you also have to include the **return true** Statement for it to work.

Example 4-24:   Sample524.html

```
<!DOCTYPE HTML PUBLIC "-//W3C//DTD HTML 3.2//EN">
<HTML>
<HEAD>
<TITLE>Sample 524 - Example 4-24        some window Methods</TITLE>
</HEAD>

<BODY>
<FORM>

<INPUT TYPE='button' VALUE='Wider'    onClick='resizeBy(100,0);'>
<INPUT TYPE='button' VALUE='Taller'   onClick='resizeBy(0,100);'>
<INPUT TYPE='button' VALUE='Thinner'  onClick='resizeBy(-100,0);'>
<INPUT TYPE='button' VALUE='Shorter'  onClick='resizeBy(0,-100);'>          <BR>

<INPUT TYPE='button' VALUE='400x300'  onClick='resizeTo(400,300);'>
<INPUT TYPE='button' VALUE='640x480'  onClick='resizeTo(640,480);'>
<INPUT TYPE='button' VALUE='832x624'  onClick='resizeTo(832,624);'>          <BR>

<INPUT TYPE='button' VALUE='Go Right' onClick='moveBy(50,0);'>
<INPUT TYPE='button' VALUE='Go Left'  onClick='moveBy(-50,0);'>
<INPUT TYPE='button' VALUE='Go Down'  onClick='moveBy(0,50);'>
<INPUT TYPE='button' VALUE='Go Up'    onClick='moveBy(0,-50);'>              <BR>

<INPUT TYPE='button' VALUE='Down Right' onClick='moveBy(50,50);'>
<INPUT TYPE='button' VALUE='Down Left'  onClick='moveBy(-50,50);'>
<INPUT TYPE='button' VALUE='Up Right'   onClick='moveBy(50,-50);'>
<INPUT TYPE='button' VALUE='Up Left'    onClick='moveBy(-50,-50);'>          <BR>

<INPUT TYPE='button' VALUE='Move To 0,0'      onClick='moveTo(0,0);'>
<INPUT TYPE='button' VALUE='Move To 200,100' onClick='moveTo(200,100);'>  <P>

<INPUT TYPE='button' VALUE='Status Bar Message'
       onClick='window.status="Hi There"'>                                 <BR>

<A HREF="Sample525.html" onMouseOver="status='Notice that (return true) must be
included in the Event Handler.'; return true;">
       Next Sample- Note Status Message.                        </A>

</FORM>

</BODY>
</HTML>
```

The <u>scrollBy()</u> Method of the <u>window</u> Object

JavaScript Syntax:

```
self.scrollBy(x,y);
window.scrollBy(x,y);
windowName.scrollBy(x,y);
```

Parameters Defined:

The **scrollBy()** Method scrolls the contents of the Window by the specified number of pixels. The **x** Argument scrolls in the horizontal direction. Positive **x** integers scroll to the left, and negative **x** integers scroll to the right. The **y** Argument scrolls in the vertical direction. Positive **y** integers scroll the page from the bottom toward the top as if you were holding down the scroll arrow at the bottom of the page. Negative **y** integers scroll from top to bottom.

How this works is that when Navigator loads a document into the browser Window, the very top left of the document has an (x,y) coordinate of (0,0). In a simple document that starts at the normal top-left position, the **pageXOffset** and **pageYOffset** Values would then be 0 and 0. So if you consider these two Properties as a coordinate, you could say that the **scrollBy()** Method creates new coordinates for the document as the result of adding its (**x,y**) Arguments to the (**pageXOffset,pageYOffset**) coordinates.

If you use the **scrollBy()** Method on a Window Reference that you open with the **open()** Method, you must make sure that the **windowFeatures** parameter of **scrollbars** is set to "YES" and the **visibility** Property of **scrollbars** must be set to "true". The **visibility** Property of **scrollbars** is "true" by default so you don't have to be too concerned about it, especially since it requires the **UniversalBrowserWrite** privilege to change it. You just need to be aware of it when you start to get into the security issues requirements.

Example 4-25 focuses on the **scrollBy()** Method that is used in conjunction with the **setInterval()** Method to animate the contents of the Window by automatically scrolling from the top down to bottom. Ordinarily, when the **scrollBy()** Method is used by itself, it scrolls the Window once, by the specified number of pixels. By using the **setInterval()** Method, you call the **scrollDown()** Function repeatedly until the **pageYOffset** Property is less than 1000. There are two buttons that use the **clearInterval()** Method to stop the scrolling process and another two buttons that start it up again from its current location. You could use this technique to create a fancy message Window using the **open()** Method.

There are additional examples on pages 487, 622-624, and 626.

Example 4-25:   Sample525.html

```
<!DOCTYPE HTML PUBLIC "-//W3C//DTD HTML 3.2//EN">
<HTML>
<HEAD>
<TITLE>Sample 525 - Example 4-25      scrollBy and setInterval Methods</TITLE>

<SCRIPT LANGUAGE="JavaScript1.2"><!--BEGIN HIDING


        function scrollDown() {
                if (window.pageYOffset < 1100) {
                        window.scrollBy(0,2);
                }
        }

//END HIDING-->
</SCRIPT>

</HEAD>

<BODY onLoad="t = setInterval('scrollDown()', 50);">
<H1>This is Sample 525</H1>

<ILAYER TOP=50 WIDTH=300 HEIGHT=300 BGCOLOR="red">
<H1>    This page scrolls by itself but you can still use the scrollbars to move the
page.                 </H1>   </ILAYER>

<ILAYER WIDTH=300 HEIGHT=300 BGCOLOR="cyan">
<H1>            This speed is designed so that even slow readers could read the text
and it has start and stop buttons for perusal if you include thought provoking
content in your page. </H1>   </ILAYER>

<FORM>  <INPUT TYPE='button' VALUE='Stop Scroll' onClick='clearInterval(t);'>

<INPUT TYPE='button' VALUE='Continue Scroll'
onClick="t=setInterval('scrollDown()', 50);">                        </FORM>

<ILAYER WIDTH=200 HEIGHT=300 BGCOLOR="yellow">
<H1>You might want to put the buttons in a different Frame so that you would only
need one set of them and so the user doesn't have to chase them, even though the
speed is slow enough that this isn't a problem.</H1></ILAYER>

<FORM>  <INPUT TYPE='button' VALUE='Stop Scroll' onClick='clearInterval(t);'>

<INPUT TYPE='button' VALUE='Continue Scroll'
onClick="t=setInterval('scrollDown()', 50);">

<INPUT TYPE='button' VALUE='Go to Top' onClick="scrollTo(0,0);">        </FORM>

<LAYER LEFT=10 TOP=1050>        <H1>    THE END          </H1>                </LAYER>

</BODY>
</HTML>
```

The JavaScript <u>document</u> Object

JavaScript Syntax:

```
document.propertyName;
document.methodName;
```

The **document** Object is one of the fundamental Objects in JavaScript. Even though it is a descendant of the **window** Object, you do not have to prepend the **document** Object with the **window** Object, because the **window** Object is assumed to be there by JavaScript.

There is only one primary **document** Object for each HTML page, and it is only created by the JavaScript runtime engine from the BODY Element of the page. As the BODY Element contains the main content of a page, so does the **document** Object contain Properties that are references to the Objects created from that content, such as the **forms[i]** Array and **layers[i]** Array, which can then be manipulated.

There are also the more direct Properties, such as the **bgColor** Property, which can be set with **document.bgColor="blue";**. This is one of the few ways to alter the document after it has initially loaded without having to reload it in order for the changes to display. You can also change the **value** Property of a Text Box or Text Area Element without having to reload the page. This procedure is not possible for changing the color of the displayed text, but you can use the **open()**, **write()** and **close()** Methods in a sequence to implement a change to the **fgColor** Property.

When you use the **open()** Method, it causes all of the previous HTML in the page to be cleared out. You then use the **write()** Method to create the content that you want to display in the page and then use the **close()** Method to actually display the content of the **write()** Method to screen. Technically, you don't have to use the **open()** Method when you are creating text or generating HTML or JavaScript within your **write()** Method, because the **write()** Method does an implicit **open()** Method for that type of content by default.

There are many times when you want to write content to the page from within a Script that occurs as part of the original loading of the document. In that case you only need to use the **write()** Method because you don't need to reload the page. Make sure you pay attention to the usage of quotes, double quotes, and escaping quotes in the Strings.

With the addition of **Layers** in Navigator 4, there is also the addition of secondary **document** Objects. Each Layer has its own **document** Object that behaves exactly like the **document** Object that is created with the BODY Tag, except that it applies only to its particular **Layer** and there are additional Properties and Methods available for it. See Chapters 2 and 3 on **Layers**.

Document Properties

Property	Description
alinkColor	A String that contains the Value of the ALINK Attribute.
anchors[i]	An Array reflecting each Anchor in the document in source order.
applets[i]	An Array reflecting each Applet in the document in source order.
bgColor	A String that contains the Value of the BGCOLOR Attribute.
cookie	A Cookie. See pages 436-443 for details and examples.
domain	Specifies the server's domain name that served the current document.
embeds[i]	An Array reflecting each Embed in the document in source order.
fgColor	A String that contains the Value of the TEXT Attribute.
formName	For each named Form in the document, there is a **formName** Property that is specified by that Form's NAME Attribute Value. For instance, for <FORM NAME="myForm1"> the **formName** Property is set to **myForm1**. For a second Form in the document there is also a **formName** Property, so for <FORM NAME="theForm2">, the **formName** Property is **theForm2**.
forms[i]	An Array reflecting each Form in the document in source order.
images[i]	An Array reflecting each Image in the document in source order.
lastModified	A String containing the document's last modification date.
layers[i]	An Array reflecting each Layer in the document in source order.
linkColor	A String that contains the Value of the LINK Attribute.
links[i]	An Array reflecting each Link in the document in source order.
plugins[i]	An Array reflecting each plug-in in the document in source order.
referrer	A String containing the URL of the calling document.
title	A String that contains the content between the TITLE Tags.
URL	A String that contains the document's complete URL.

Document Properties (continued)

Property | Description

vlinkColor   A String that contains the Value of the VLINK Attribute.

The following Methods that are prefaced with three asterisks (***) are new for Navigator 4.0 and you can see Chapter 6 on the **Event** Object for details and examples.

Document Methods

Method | Description

captureEvents() ***Captures all Events of the specified type for the **document** Object.

close()   Closes a data stream and forces the contents of the **write()** or **writeln()** Methods to display.

getSelection()   Returns a string containing the currently selected text that is highlighted by the user or selected by the Script. New for Navigator 4.0.

handleEvent()   ***Calls the Event Handler for the specified Event.

open()   Opens a data stream to collect the contents of the **write()** or **writeln()** Methods.

releaseEvents()   ***Releases the specified Event Types that were set to be captured by the **captureEvents()** Method of the **document** Object so that they will progress naturally in the Event hierarchy.

routeEvent()   ***Forwards a captured Event through the normal Event hierarchy unless it is captured by another Object. Used in conjunction with **handleEvent()**.

write()   Renders HTML expressions, including Dynamic HTML and regular text to the **document** Object for the specified Window or Frame. It will also execute JavaScript code within the context of the newly created HTML. Additionally you can include JavaScript within one or more SCRIPT Elements for the page. Remember that HTML and regular text Strings must be enclosed in quotes or double quotes while executable JavaScript Expressions and Variables are not. This is an extremely useful Method.

writeln()   Same as the **write()** Method with the addition of an automatically appended new line (carriage return) character.

This example demonstrates several ways to use the **write()** Method for displaying content to screen and how to use the **fgColor** Property to change the color of the text in simple scenarios. In complex pages, you need to include in the **write()** Method all of the normal HTML Tags that are required for a page in order for that page to operate smoothly.

Example 4-26: Sample526.html

```
<!DOCTYPE HTML PUBLIC "-//W3C//DTD HTML 3.2//EN">
<HTML>
<HEAD>
      <TITLE>        Sample 526 - Example 4-26   write Method    </TITLE>

<SCRIPT LANGUAGE="JavaScript1.2"><!--BEGIN HIDING

document.fgColor="green";
document.write("<H1>This is Sample 526<\/H1>");

function blueText() {
      document.write("<SCRIPT>");
      document.write(document.fgColor='blue');
      document.write("<\/SCRIPT>");
      document.write("<H1>");
      document.write("Now I'm Blue.");
      document.write("<\/H1>");
      document.close();
}

function redText() {
      document.write("<BODY TEXT='red'>");
      document.write("<H1>");
      document.write("Now I'm Red.");
      document.write("<\/H1>");
      document.write("<\/BODY>");
      document.close();
}

//END HIDING-->
</SCRIPT>
</HEAD>

<BODY>
<FORM>

<INPUT TYPE='button' VALUE='Blue It Now' onClick='blueText();'>
<INPUT TYPE='button' VALUE='Red It Now' onClick='redText();'>

</FORM>

</BODY>
</HTML>
```

The <u>cookie</u> Property of the <u>document</u> Object

A **cookie** is a way to store and retrieve a small piece of persistent data across multiple browser sessions from the client-side of the connection. Persistent data means that the data is available after the user disconnects from the WWW for reuse in the next session, or multiple sessions, if they are prior to the expiration date of the cookie.

When they were first introduced, Cookies were typically used to store the user's name and password for sites that require them, as a courtesy to the user so that the information doesn't have to be resubmitted every time the user logs on to a site. There are lots of other uses that authors have created for them, such as storing user Preferences for text size and color, etc. At a site that is transacting commerce, they could be used to store the items that the user has chosen to purchase like the shopping cart metaphor you've probably seen.

On the Macintosh platform, the Cookies are stored on the user's disk in a file called **MagicCookie** that is located in the <u>System:Preferences:Netscape</u> folder. On the Windows and Unix platforms, they are in a file named **cookies.txt** that is located in the <u>Navigator</u> directory.

Cookies have a syntax that is somewhat different than most traditional JavaScript, so to point that out, I've used a different syntax heading for it. To create a **cookie** Property for the document, you assign it a String by a simple assignment Statement in the following format. The entire String that is assigned to the **cookie** Property must be enclosed in quotes. Also note that the semicolons that are used to separate the Cookie parameters are required.

Cookie Syntax:

```
document.cookie = "cookieName=cookieValue
                   [; EXPIRES=GMTDateString]
                   [; PATH=pathName]
                   [; DOMAIN=domainName]
                   [; SECURE]"
```

Parameters Defined:

cookieName=cookieValue	You assign a name for the Cookie with the **cookieName** parameter and a value for the Cookie with the **cookieValue** parameter. They can be any sequence of characters except a semicolon, comma, or any white space.
PATH=pathName	An optional parameter that specifies the path name.
DOMAIN=domainName	An optional parameter that specifies the domain name.
SECURE	An optional parameter that if included specifies that the Cookie will only be sent over a secure server.

EXPIRES=GMTDateString   Sets an expiration time and date for the Cookie. This is an optional parameter and if it's omitted, then the Cookie expires at the end of the current session. The format of the String that is specified for the **GMTDateString** Value is:

```
Weekday, DD-Mon-YY HH:MM:SS GMT
```

where:

Weekday	The day of the week like Monday.
DD	A two-integer representation of the day of the month like 05 or 22.
Mon	A three-letter abbreviation for the name of the month.
YY	A two-integer representation for the last two numerals of the year like 99.
HH	The hours in military time from 0 to 23.
MM	The minutes like 04 or 33 where the zero is required for less than 10.
SS	The seconds where the zero is required for less than 10.

Note that the comma, dashes, colons, and spaces are necessary parts of the syntax.

Working with Cookies

Navigator can store and retrieve up to 300 total Cookies, and there can be up to 20 Cookies for each domain or server. Each Cookie can have a maximum size of 4 kilobytes. Once the maximum number of Cookies has been reached, the next Cookie created will cause the Cookie that was created the farthest in the past to be deleted so that the new Cookie can be stored.

Creating a Cookie is very simple. Using and manipulating Cookie data is royally difficult. Here is a simple example of creating a Cookie:

```
document.cookie="myCookie1=Eat_A_Cookie";
```

If you were to write the cookie to screen like this:

```
document.write(document.cookie);
```

It would produce the following output in the browser:

myCookie1=Eat_A_Cookie

Massaging Cookie Data

Using Cookies in your Scripts requires some creative manipulation of the text contained in the Cookie String. For instance, if you assign more than one Value to **document.cookie**, then it will contain a single String that contains each of those Values so that each one is separated by a semicolon. One way to access one of those Cookie Values later on is to use the **split(";")** Method of the **String** Object, and use the semicolon Character as the separator Argument, which will return an Array of Strings. Then, access individual Array Elements as needed, which is demonstrated in the following example.

This example creates three Cookies and then assigns the **cookie** Property of the **document** Object to a Variable named **cookieString**. It then uses the **split()** Method to create an Array of Cookie Strings and assigns it to the **cookieArray** Variable. Finally, the entire **cookie** Property is rendered to screen, and each Array Element is rendered to screen so you can see the results.

Example 4-27:   **Sample527.html**

```
<!DOCTYPE HTML PUBLIC "-//W3C//DTD HTML 3.2//EN">
<HTML>
<HEAD>
<TITLE>Sample 527 - Example 4-27      cookie   </TITLE>

<SCRIPT LANGUAGE="JavaScript1.2"><!--BEGIN HIDING

document.cookie="myCookie1=Eat_A_Cookie";
document.cookie="myCookie2=Eat_Another_Cookie";
document.cookie="myCookie3=Throw_A_Cookie";

cookieString = document.cookie;

cookieArray = cookieString.split(";");

document.write(document.cookie + "<P>");

document.write(cookieArray[0] + "<BR>");
document.write(cookieArray[1] + "<BR>");
document.write(cookieArray[2] + "<BR>");

//END HIDING-->
</SCRIPT>
</HEAD>

<BODY>
Make sure that your browser can accept Cookies or this won't work.
</BODY>
</HTML>
```

The previous example produces the following output:

myCookie1=Eat_A_Cookie; myCookie2=Eat_Another_Cookie; myCookie3=Throw_A_Cookie

myCookie1=Eat_A_Cookie
myCookie2=Eat_Another_Cookie
myCookie3=Throw_A_Cookie

Further Massaging of Cookie Data

In order to make the data that goes into the cookie manageable, you have to massage it to get rid of white space, because browsers have the nasty habit of converting blank spaces into (%20). Remember the warning from Chapter 1 about not putting blank spaces in your file names; the same principle applies here. You also have to get rid of any semicolons and commas, which are not allowed in the **cookieName** or **cookieValue**. You can use the **escape()** and **unescape()** Functions to accomplish this or create your own.

Depending on the needs of your Script, you may need to convert the data in the **cookieValue** into a more suitable format. Because the **document.cookie** Property is a String that may contain more than one Cookie, each of which is separated by a semicolon, you may need to get rid of these semicolons as part of the process of extracting an individual Cookie from this **document.cookie** String.

Furthermore, there is additional processing to get the **cookieValue** extracted from the **cookieName=cookieValue** pair. You can use the **split()** Method, which will also extract the equals sign (=) from the **cookieName=cookieValue** pair at the same time.

There are other ways to perform these processes and they will be explored later in other examples. This next example demonstrates one way to perform the above processes.

Example 4-28 has the ability to take the text that is input by the user in the Text Box named **t1** and store it in a Cookie that has a **cookieName** of **testCookie**. After some text transformation processes, the Script displays the **testCookie** Cookie, the **cookieValue**, and an altered **cookieValue** in the Textarea named **ta1**, to verify the results of the Script. All of these procedures are implemented when the user clicks on the Button.

The three Functions, **encodeCookieValue()**, **updateCookie()**, and **processCookie()** do all of the main processing. When the Button is clicked, it passes the text contained in the **value** Property of **t1** as the Argument for the **encodeCookieValue()** Function and assigns it to the String Variable **str1**. Then the Regular Expression **re1** is used in the **replace()** Method to execute a global search in **str1** for any semicolons or commas and replace them with an empty String (""). Then the Regular Expression **re2** is used to search for any white space and replace it with an underscore(_) Character. The result of this Function is that the original text String is processed and returned in the **str3** Variable, which is then assigned to the **cookieString1** Variable in the **updateCookie()** Function.

The **updateCookie()** Function then creates a Cookie that has a **cookieName** of **testCookie** and a **cookieValue** of **cookieString1** with the following code:

```
document.cookie = "testCookie="+cookieString1;
```

Then the **processCookie()** Function is called. Note that for your own Scripts you will probably only need part of this Function, but which part depends on what you are trying to accomplish, hence the variety. This Function uses the **split()** Method to extract the semicolons from **cookieString2** and returns an Array of Strings, which is assigned to **cookieArray1**. Each Element in this Array now has a Cookie in it.

To make use of the **cookieValue** contained in **testCookie**, you first have to locate that Cookie by setting up a **for()** Loop that then tests for the String Literal **testCookie** contained in the Regular Expression **re3** with the **test()** Method of the RegExp Object. If a match is found, then the condition evaluates to **true** and the processing continues for that particular Array Element. The **split("=")** Method is used to extract the equals sign and return an Array where the first two Elements are the **cookieName** and **cookieValue** of **testCookie**, respectively.

At this point, you could just output these values to screen, and in some cases that is all you need to do, such as if you knew there would be no white space in your original text supplied from the user or from your Script. In this case, there is a small amount of additional processing to replace each underscore Character with a blank space so that the text String appears normal. This is accomplished with the **re4** Regular Expression and the **replace()** Method.

Finally, the data is displayed to screen in the **ta1** Textarea, showing the data as it is in different places in the processing procedure so you can compare it and also to verify that the Script is working like it should.

Example 4-28:   Sample528.html

```
<!DOCTYPE HTML PUBLIC "-//W3C//DTD HTML 3.2//EN">
<HTML>
<HEAD>

<TITLE>Sample 528 - Example 4-28      cookie maneuvering   </TITLE>

<BASEFONT SIZE="4">
</HEAD>

<BODY>

<FORM NAME="form1">

Type in some text and click the button to create a cookie.      <BR>

<INPUT TYPE='text' NAME='t1' SIZE=50>                            <BR><BR>

The results are displayed in the Textarea.            <BR>
The testCookie is first.                              <BR>
The cookie Value is next.                             <BR>
The altered cookie Value is last.                     <BR>

<TEXTAREA NAME="ta1" ROWS=7 COLS=50></TEXTAREA>       <BR><BR>

<INPUT TYPE='button' VALUE='Update the Cookie named testCookie'
onClick='updateCookie(this.form.t1.value);'>

</FORM>
```

```
<SCRIPT LANGUAGE="JavaScript1.2"><!--BEGIN HIDING

function encodeCookieValue(s) {

        var str1 = s;
        var re1 = /;+|,+/g;
        var re2 = /\s+/g;
        var str2 = str1.replace(re1, "");
        var str3 = str2.replace(re2, "_");
        return str3;
}

function updateCookie(s) {

        var cookieString1 = encodeCookieValue(s);

        document.cookie = "testCookie="+cookieString1;

        processCookie();
}

function processCookie() {

        var re3 = /testCookie/;
        var cookieString2 = document.cookie;

        cookieArray1 = cookieString2.split(";");

        for (i=0; i<cookieArray1.length; i++) {

                if (re3.test(cookieArray1[i])) {

                        cookieArray2 = cookieArray1[i].split("=");

                        var re4 = /_/g;
                        var str4 = cookieArray2[1].replace(re4, " ");

                        var     showStr = cookieArray1[i] + "\r";
                                showStr += cookieArray2[1] + "\r" + str4;

                        document.form1.ta1.value = showStr;
                }
        }
}

//END HIDING-->
</SCRIPT>

</BODY>
</HTML>
```

Example 4-30   Sample530.html

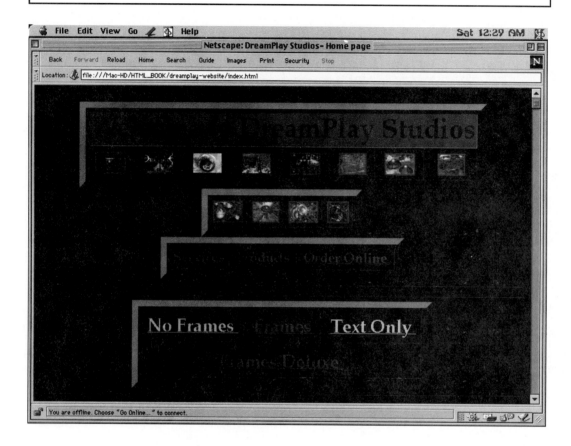

The two main differences between Example 4-29 and the last example is that in the **updateCookie()** Function there is additional code to put in an expiration date for the Cookie that is assigned to the **EXPIRES** parameter. The **myTime** Variable makes it easy for you to input your own amount of time to be added to the current time, which is then used as the expiration date. The same is similarly true for the **myMonth** Variable.

The other difference is the use of the **escape()** and **unescape()** Global Functions to encode the **cookieValue** in the **encodeCookieValue()** Function and then decode the **cookieValue** in the **processCookie()** Function. The advantages to using these Global Functions are that they require less typing and are more streamlined and they encode each character that they can handle in a unique way. The disadvantages are that they do not handle all possible characters, and if you need to further massage the data in unique ways, it's more difficult to keep track of. For most purposes, though, they work fine.

Example 4-29:   Sample529.html

```
<!DOCTYPE HTML PUBLIC "-//W3C//DTD HTML 3.2//EN">
<HTML>
<HEAD>
<TITLE>Sample 529 - Example 4-29        cookie EXPIRES    </TITLE>
<BASEFONT SIZE="4">
</HEAD>

<BODY>

<H2>This Cookie has an Expiration Date.</H2>

<FORM NAME="form1">
First and Last Name.                                     <BR>
<INPUT TYPE='text' NAME='t1' SIZE=70>                    <BR><BR>

The results are displayed in the Textarea.              <BR>
The testCookie is first and shows escaped characters.   <BR>
The cookie Value is next which is now unescaped.        <BR>

<TEXTAREA NAME="ta1" ROWS=7 COLS=70></TEXTAREA>         <BR><BR>

<INPUT TYPE='button' VALUE='Update the Cookie named testCookie'
onClick='updateCookie(this.form.t1.value);'>

</FORM>

<SCRIPT LANGUAGE="JavaScript1.2"><!--BEGIN HIDING

function encodeCookieValue(s) {

      return escape(s);
}
```

```
function updateCookie(s) {

        var cookieString1 = encodeCookieValue(s);
        var now = new Date();
        var expDate = new Date();
                            // Fill in your own time numbers here.
                            // day  hr   min  sec  millisec

        myTime = now.getTime() + (1 * 24 * 60 * 60 * 1000);

                            //Add your month here.
                            //Put 0 or delete + 2 if you don't want
                            //that much time added.
        myMonth = now.getMonth() + 2;
        expDate.setTime(myTime);
        expDate.setMonth(myMonth);
        expDate.toGMTString();

        document.cookie = "testCookie="+cookieString1+"; EXPIRES="+expDate;

        processCookie();
}

function processCookie() {

        var re3 = /testCookie/;
        var cookieString2 = document.cookie;

        cookieArray1 = cookieString2.split(";");

        for (i=0; i<cookieArray1.length; i++) {

                if (re3.test(cookieArray1[i])) {

                        cookieArray2 = cookieArray1[i].split("=");

                        var    showStr = cookieArray1[i] + "\r";
                               showStr += unescape(cookieArray2[1]) + "\r";

                        document.form1.ta1.value = showStr;
                }
        }
}

//END HIDING-->
</SCRIPT>
</BODY>
</HTML>
```

For more detailed information on the syntax of Cookies, see Netscape's Cookie documentation in Appendix C of the JavaScript Guide. You can also check out the:

Cookie Specification; RFC 2109, at: http://www.ietf.org/rfc/rfc2109.txt
Further information on Cookies is at: http://www.cookiecentral.com
Public Domain Cookie Scripts are at: http://www.hidaho.com/cookies/cookies.html

The JavaScript <u>screen</u> Object

The **screen** Object is created automatically by the JavaScript runtime engine, and it contains read-only Properties that convey information about the user's display monitor screen. This can be useful if you want to custom-design your documents based on the capabilities and limitations of each user's monitor. For instance, if a monitor only has 14 inches of viewing space, you might choose to not implement a Frames-based site or possibly choose an alternate Frames-based configuration to accommodate the limited screen real estate. If the user has a 20-inch monitor, you could implement a version of the site that is more spread-out, taking advantage of the additional space.

Screen Properties

<u>Property</u>	<u>Description</u>
availHeight	Specifies, in pixels, the height of the display screen after subtracting the space allotted for any graphical user interface (GUI) features of the operating system that are either permanent or semipermanent.
availWidth	Specifies, in pixels, the width of the display screen after subtracting the space allotted for any graphical user interface (GUI) features of the operating system that are either permanent or semipermanent.
colorDepth	If a color palette is in use, then its bit depth is specified. If no color palette is in use, then **screen.pixelDepth** provides the Value.
height	Specifies, in pixels, the height of the display screen.
pixelDepth	Specifies the resolution of the display screen in bits per pixel.
width	Specifies, in pixels, the width of the display screen.

Screen Methods

There are no Methods for the **screen** Object.

Example 4-30 demonstrates using the **availWidth** and **availHeight** Properties to resize the Window to a desired size based on the available screen size of the user's Monitor and whether the user is currently using the **toolbar** and/or the **locationbar**. The **width** Property is also used to determine which document to load with the **location** Property.

Example 4-30:   Sample530.html

```
<!DOCTYPE HTML PUBLIC "-//W3C//DTD HTML 3.2//EN">
<HTML>
<HEAD>

<TITLE>Sample 530 - Example 4-30      screen Object</TITLE>

<BASEFONT SIZE="4">

<SCRIPT LANGUAGE="JavaScript1.2"><!--BEGIN HIDING

var aw = window.screen.availWidth;
var ah = window.screen.availHeight;

window.moveTo(0, 0);

        if (window.toolbar  &&  window.locationbar)

                { window.resizeTo(aw - 30, ah - 120); }

        else if (window.locationbar)

                { window.resizeTo(aw - 30, ah - 100); }


        if (window.screen.width >= 832)

                { window.location.href = "./dreamplay-website/index.html" }


        else  if (window.screen.width < 832)

                { window.location.href = "./dreamplay-website/welcome2.html" }


//END HIDING-->
</SCRIPT>

</HEAD>

<BODY>
</BODY>
</HTML>
```

The JavaScript __Location__ Object

JavaScript Syntax:

```
location.propertyName;
window.location.propertyName;
windowName.location.propertyName;
```

Working with the __Location__ Object

The **Location** Object contains the complete URL that is loaded into a given **window** Object. A URL is comprised of different components that can be individually accessed by the Properties of the **Location** Object. Typically, you use the **href** Property to set the location, that is, to load a new document, because using other Properties such as **host** or **hostname** for that purpose can generate errors.

To access a Property or Method of the **Location** Object, you do it through the **location** Property of the **window** Object like this: **window.location.hash**. For example, if you wanted to load a document with the **href** Property into the current Window:

```
window.location.href = "http://www.dreamplay.com/welcome.html";
```

You should note that, because the current Window is assumed, the following line of code is functionally equivalent to the previous line of code:

```
location.href = "http://www.dreamplay.com/welcome.html";
```

However, if you want to invoke a Property of the **Location** Object on a **window** Object that you create, you must reference the **window** Object by name like this:

```
myWindow.location.href = "http://www.dreamplay.com/welcome.html";
```

Special Notice:

It's important to note that the **Location** Object is not a Property of the **document** Object. Even though there is currently a **location** Property for the **document** Object, you should not use it, because it has been deprecated in favor of the **URL** Property and will be completely phased out in a future release and there will be no backward compatibility for it.

The alternative is to use the **document.URL** Property, which is a synonym for the **document.location** Property.

Using the location Property inside an Event Handler

When using the **location** Property inside an Event Handler, you must specify **window.location** or **myWindowName.location**; otherwise, if you just specify **location** without a Window reference, it is functionally equivalent to **document.location**, due to the scoping of static Objects in JavaScript.

Dissecting a URL into Components

A URL can be dissected into different parts, which can then be tested for and set. Here is the general syntax for a URL, which is followed by a quick example and a chart that shows the most commonly used **protocol** Property Values and their uses.

See Example 4-31 for a complete breakdown of each component of the URL and its associated **location** Property.

General URL Syntax:

```
protocol//host:port/pathname#hash?search
```

Mini-Example:

```
http://www.dreamplay.com/Examples/Sample1.html#anchor1?x=5&z=8";
```

Chart of URL Protocols and Types

Protocol	URL Type	Example
about:	Navigator info	about: (Same as about Communicator from menu)
		about:cache
		about:plugins
file:/	File	file:///myBook/testFiles/Sample22.html
ftp:	FTP	ftp://ftp.myDomainName.com/myFolder/myFile
gopher:	Gopher	gopher.myHost.com
http:	World Wide Web	http://www.myDomainName.com/
javascript:	JavaScript code	javascript:document.bgColor="blue"
mailto:	MailTo	mailto:gilorien@erols.com
news:	Usenet	news://news.erols.com/vrml
view-source:	source code viewer	view-source:wysiwyg://0/file:/cl/temp/myDoc.html

Location Properties

Property	Description
hash	A String that specifies the Anchor name part of the URL, including the hash (#) sign. Setting the **hash** Property jumps the page to that Anchor without reloading the document, but if the Anchor can't be found, you will get an error; therefore, it is safer to use the **href** Property, which only produces an Alert Window if the Anchor isn't found. The **hash** Property only applies to URLs that are of the HTTP type.
host	A String that specifies the network host, which consists of the server name, subdomain name, and domain name. This is a substring of the **hostname** Property.
hostname	A String that specifies the host:port part of the URL, including the colon.
href	A String that specifies the complete URL.
pathname	A String that specifies the pathname portion of the URL.
port	A String that specifies port part of the URL, which is the communications port that the server uses.
protocol	A String that specifies protocol part of the URL, which is the beginning of the URL, including the colon.
search	A String that specifies a search query, which begins with a question mark and is followed by **variable=value** pairs that are separated by an ampersand sign(**&**). For instance:

```
?x=2&y=5&z=7
```

The **search** Property only applies to URLs that are of the HTTP type.

Location Methods

Method	Description
reload([forceGet])	Reloads the current document into window. Same as **history(0)**. If the optional **forceGet** Boolean is set to **true**, then the server is forced to reload the page unconditionally. Otherwise, the user preferences determine whether the page is reloaded from cache or reloaded from the server.
replace("URL")	Loads the specified URL instead of the current document.

This example demonstrates the Properties of the **Location** Object by writing the Value of each one to screen for the Window named **myWin**. Assigning a URL to a Window after it is opened like this is just to demonstrate the Location Properties.

Example 4-31: **Sample531.html**

```
<!DOCTYPE HTML PUBLIC "-//W3C//DTD HTML 3.2//EN">
<HTML>
<HEAD>
<TITLE>Sample 531 - Example 4-31   Location Object Properties</TITLE>

<SCRIPT LANGUAGE="JavaScript1.2"><!--BEGIN HIDING

myWin = window.open("", "myWin");

myWin.location.href =
             "http://www.dreamplay.com/Examples/Sample1.html#anchor1?x=5&z=8%22;";
document.write("href= " + myWin.location.href + "<BR>");
document.write("protocol= " + myWin.location.protocol + "<BR>");
document.write("port= " + myWin.location.port + "<BR>");
document.write("host= " + myWin.location.host + "<BR>");
document.write("hostname= " + myWin.location.hostname + "<BR>");
document.write("pathname= " + myWin.location.pathname + "<BR>");
document.write("hash= " + myWin.location.hash + "<BR>");
document.write("search= " + myWin.location.search + "<BR>");

//END HIDING-->
</SCRIPT>

</HEAD>
<BODY>
</BODY>
</HTML>
```

The previous example produces the following output in the browser:

href= http://www.dreamplay.com/Examples/Sample1.html#anchor1?x=5&z=8%22;
protocol= http:
port=
host= www.dreamplay.com
hostname= www.dreamplay.com
pathname= /Examples/Sample1.html
hash= #anchor1
search= ?x=5&z=8%22;

This example demonstrates the **reload()** and **replace()** Methods of the **Location** Object. It also demonstrates the **javascript protocol** in a Link with the following code:

```
<A HREF="javascript:window.location.replace(me2);"> Replace with Sample 525 </A>
```

You should notice that when using the **replace()** Method, the URL entry into the **history[i]** Array is also replaced, which can be verified by checking in the "Go" Menu.

The **mailto protocol** has the new **body** Field in it for Navigator 4.0, which lets you include a default message in the body of the message. Note that each Field is separated by an ampersand (&), but the email address is separated from all Fields by a question mark.

Example 4-32:   Sample532.html

```
<!DOCTYPE HTML PUBLIC "-//W3C//DTD HTML 3.2//EN">
<HTML>
<HEAD>
<TITLE>Sample 532 - Example 4-32     replace and reload Methods   </TITLE>
<BASEFONT SIZE="4">

<SCRIPT LANGUAGE="JavaScript1.2"><!--BEGIN HIDING

me1 = "Sample524.html";
me2 = "Sample525.html";

//END HIDING-->
</SCRIPT>
</HEAD>

<BODY>

<FORM NAME="form1">

<INPUT TYPE="button" VALUE="Replace it" onClick="window.location.replace(me1);">

<INPUT TYPE="button" VALUE="Reload it" onClick="window.location.reload(true);">

<A HREF="javascript:window.location.replace(me2);"> Replace with Sample 525 </A>

<P>
<A HREF="mailto:gilorien@erols.com?subject=Just Saying Hi&body=This is where you
put the starter message if any. If you want to include a linebreak %0A in this
message you need to use Hex Encoding %0A which in this case was a 'PercentSign
followed by 0A'."> Send feedback to us. </A>

</FORM>

</BODY>
</HTML>
```

The JavaScript <u>History</u> Object

JavaScript Syntax:

```
window.history;
windowName.history;
```

The **History** Object is an Array that reflects the URLs that the user has visited in a session. It is accessed through the **history** Property of the **window** Object. You can refer to a particular URL by the **index** number of an Element in the Array.

History Properties

<u>Property</u>	<u>Description</u>
current	Specifies the current URL in the **history[i]** Array.
length	Reflects the number of URL entries in the **history[i]** Array.
next	Specifies the next URL in the **history[i]** Array.
previous	Specifies the previous URL in the **history[i]** Array.

History Methods

<u>Method</u>	<u>Description</u>
back()	Loads the previous URL from the **history[i]** Array.
forward()	Loads the next URL from the **history[i]** Array.
go("location")	Loads a URL from the **history[i]** Array where **location** is a String that specifies either a full or partial URL.
go(integer)	Loads a URL from the **history** Array where **integer** is either zero or a positive or negative integer that specifies a relative position in the **history[i]** Array. If zero, the current page is reloaded. If positive, then the URL is loaded that is **integer** number of positions offset from the current URL position in the Array. If negative, the offset is in the opposite direction.

JavaScript Syntax for History Properties

```
window.history.propertyName;
windowName.history.propertyName;
```

JavaScript Syntax for History Methods:

```
window.history.methodName;
windowName.history.methodName;
```

Example 4-33 demonstrates the **back()** and **forward()** Methods of the **History** Object as they are accessed with the **history** Property of the **window** Object. It also demonstrates the **parent** Property of the **window** Object. Because these two Methods are used to control the URLs that are loaded into a sibling Frame, in this example, you have to use the **parent** Property of the **window** Object and then the name of the Frame that you want to load the URL into which in this case is **Upper**.

```
parent.Upper.history.back();
parent.Upper.history.forward();
```

The main code for this example is in the file named Sample533.html. To view this Example load in the file named Sample533Frameset.html.

Example 4-33 Part 1:　　　Sample533.html

```
<!DOCTYPE HTML PUBLIC "-//W3C//DTD HTML 3.2//EN">
<HTML>
<HEAD>
<TITLE> Sample 533 - Example 4-33  back and forward Methods of history</TITLE>
</HEAD>

<BODY>

<FORM>
Back
<INPUT TYPE="button" VALUE="&lt;&lt;Upper"
onClick="parent.Upper.history.back();">

Forward
<INPUT TYPE="button" VALUE="Upper&gt;&gt;"
onClick="parent.Upper.history.forward();">

Back
<INPUT TYPE="button" VALUE="&lt;&lt;Lower"
onClick="parent.Lower.history.back();">
```

```
Forward
<INPUT TYPE="button" VALUE="Lower&gt;&gt;"
onClick="parent.Lower.history.forward();">

</FORM>

These Links load in the Upper Frame.

<A HREF="Sample1.html" TARGET="Upper">        Sample 1        </A>
<A HREF="Sample2.html" TARGET="Upper">        Sample 2        </A>
<A HREF="Sample3.html" TARGET="Upper">        Sample 3        </A>        <P>

These Links load in the Lower Frame.

<A HREF="Sample4.html" TARGET="Lower">        Sample 4        </A>
<A HREF="Sample5.html" TARGET="Lower">        Sample 5        </A>
<A HREF="Sample6.html" TARGET="Lower">        Sample 6        </A>

</BODY>
</HTML>
```

Example 4-33 Part 2:   Sample533Frameset.html

```
<!DOCTYPE HTML PUBLIC "-//W3C//DTD HTML 3.2//EN">
<HTML>
<HEAD>
<TITLE>Frameset for Sample 533</TITLE>
</HEAD>

<FRAMESET COLS="100,*">

        <FRAME SCROLLING="no" NAME="Left" SRC="Sample533.html">

        <FRAMESET ROWS="50%,50%">

                <FRAME SCROLLING="auto" NAME="Upper" SRC="Sample7.html">

                <FRAME SCROLLING="auto" NAME="Lower" SRC="Sample8.html">

        </FRAMESET>

</FRAMESET>

</HTML>
```

There are other examples of using these Methods in a Frame context that are on the CD-ROM. Load the file named welcomeETOC3Bkgd.html, which is in the Sample-ETOC Folder. It's used in that Frameset and deeper into that site; if you click on the "Mats" Link and then on either "Crescent Mats" or "Bainbridge Mats" you can see examples of using the Methods for Frames that didn't initially exist in the main page. Just keep track of the names of your Frames when setting up your own versions.

The JavaScript navigator Object

JavaScript Syntax for navigator Properties:

```
navigator.propertyName;
```

JavaScript Syntax for navigator Methods:

```
navigator.methodName;
```

The **navigator** Object contains data about the browser that is currently being used by the client, which has Properties that can access that data. Furthermore, it has two Properties, the **mimeTypes[i]** Array and the **plugins[i]** Array, which contain information about the MIME Types that are currently supported and the plug-ins that are currently configured, respectively.

All of these Properties are <u>read-only</u>. The **navigator** Object is only created by the JavaScript engine at runtime and it is not a descendant of the **window** Object.

Navigator Properties

Property	Description
appCodeName	Specifies the browser's code name.
appName	Specifies the browser's name.
appVersion	Specifies Navigator's version number.
language	Specifies the language translation for the displayed content, like English.
mimeTypes[i]	An Array reflecting each MIME type supported by the user.
platform	Specifies the machine type, not OS, that Navigator was compiled for. Some possible Values are: Mac68k, MacPPC, Win16, Win32.
plugins[i]	An Array reflecting each plug-in currently configured by the user.
userAgent	Specifies the User Agent header.

Navigator Methods

Method	Description
javaEnabled()	Returns true if Java is enabled. Returns false if Java is not enabled.
plugins.refresh(false)	If **false** supplied, the newly installed plug-ins are made available.
plugins.refresh(true)	If **true** supplied, the newly installed plug-ins are made available and any open documents with EMBED Elements are reloaded.
preference("prefName")	Returns the Value of the **prefName** Preference.
preference("prefName", setValue)	Sets the Value of the **prefName** Preference with the **setValue** Argument and returns that Value. This must be set in a Signed Script.

Creating Frames on-the-fly

This example demonstrates how to use the **appName** and **appVersion** Properties of the **navigator** Object to determine which Frameset you want to load into the page. You use the Values returned from these Properties to determine if the browser in use by the client can interpret Frames or not and to determine if the Methods and Properties of the **window** Object for Navigator 4.0 can be implemented. It uses the **document.write()** Method to create these Frames on-the-fly based on the data that it has previously gathered from the user's browser and monitor.

The **width** Property of the **screen** Object is used to determine how large the user's monitor is and renders Framesets accordingly. If the user has JavaScript disabled in the preferences, then a standard HTML rendering of Framesets is generated. Finally, as a last precaution, the standard HTML Framesets and a NOFRAMES Element are enclosed inside of a NOSCRIPT Element. It's pretty straightforward and should give you some ideas for your own pages.

There is a parallel file named Sample534-NavBUGGED.html on the CD-ROM. It has some minor additional functionality that worked in version 4.0 of Navigator, but for an unfathomed reason, it bugs out in version 4.5 of Navigator. Check it out when Navigator 5.0 comes out and see if it works then. All of the code in Sample534.html is rock solid.

Example 4-34: Sample534.html

```
<!DOCTYPE HTML PUBLIC "-//W3C//DTD HTML 3.2//EN">
<HTML>
<HEAD>
<TITLE>Sample 534 - Example 10-34    navigator Object plus </TITLE>
<BASEFONT SIZE="4">

<SCRIPT LANGUAGE="JavaScript1.2"><!--BEGIN HIDING

var leftP = "dreamplay-website/DP-toc1.html";
var viewP = "dreamplay-website/welcome2.html";
var upperP = "dreamplay-website/BANNER1.html";
var leftP2 = "dreamplay-website/DP-toc2.html";

var brN = navigator.appName;
var ie = "Microsoft Internet Explorer";
var brV = parseFloat(navigator.appVersion);


if (window.screen.width >= 832) {

        document.write('<FRAMESET COLS="200,*">')
        document.write('        <FRAME NAME="toc-icons" SRC="' + leftP + '" ')
        document.write('                SCROLLING=AUTO MARGINHEIGHT=3 MARGINWIDTH=3>')

        document.write('        <FRAMESET ROWS="80,*">')
        document.write('                <FRAME NAME="banner" SRC="' + upperP + '" ')
        document.write('                SCROLLING=AUTO MARGINHEIGHT=5 MARGINWIDTH=5>')

        document.write('                <FRAME NAME="view" SRC="' + viewP + '" ')
        document.write('                SCROLLING=AUTO MARGINHEIGHT=10 MARGINWIDTH=10>')
        document.write('        <\/FRAMESET>')
        document.write('<\/FRAMESET>')
  }

else if (window.screen.width < 832) {

        document.write('<FRAMESET COLS="150,*">')
        document.write('        <FRAME NAME="toc-icons" SRC="' + leftP2 + '" ')
        document.write('                SCROLLING=AUTO MARGINHEIGHT=1 MARGINWIDTH=1>')

        document.write('        <FRAME NAME="view" SRC="' + viewP + '" ')
        document.write('                SCROLLING=AUTO MARGINHEIGHT=5 MARGINWIDTH=5>')
        document.write('        <\/FRAMESET>')
  }


//**************************************************************
```

```
else if ((brN == "Netscape"  ||  brN == ie)  &&  brV >= 2.0) {

        document.write('<FRAMESET COLS="150,*">')
        document.write('      <FRAME NAME="toc-icons" SRC="' + leftP2 + '" ')
        document.write('               SCROLLING=AUTO MARGINHEIGHT=1 MARGINWIDTH=1>')

        document.write('      <FRAME NAME="view" SRC="' + viewP + '" ')
        document.write('               SCROLLING=AUTO MARGINHEIGHT=5 MARGINWIDTH=5>')
        document.write('<\/FRAMESET>')
}

else if ((brN == "Netscape"  ||  brN == ie)  &&  brV < 2.0) {

        document.write('If you do not have access to a browser that ')
        document.write('supports frames, you can view the ')
        document.write('non-frames version of the page by opening')
        document.write('<A HREF="dreamplay-website/welcome2.html">')
        document.write('the alternate homepage.<\/A>.')
}

//END HIDING-->
</SCRIPT>
</HEAD>

<!-- ************************************************************** -->

<!-- IF THE USER HAS JAVASCRIPT DISABLED, DISPLAY DEFAULT FRAMESET -->

<NOSCRIPT>

<FRAMESET COLS="150,*">

    <FRAME NAME="toc-icons" SRC="dreamplay-website/DP-toc1.html"
           SCROLLING=AUTO MARGINHEIGHT=1 MARGINWIDTH=1>

    <FRAME NAME="view" SRC="dreamplay-website/welcome2.html"
           SCROLLING=AUTO MARGINHEIGHT=3 MARGINWIDTH=3>

        <NOFRAMES>

To view this page, your browser must support frames.
<A HREF="http://home.netscape.com/comprod/mirror/index.html">Download</A>
Netscape Navigator 2.0 or later for frames support.

If you do not have access to a browser that supports frames,
you can view the non-frames version of the page by opening
<A HREF="dreamplay-website/welcome2.html">the alternate homepage.</A>.

        </NOFRAMES>

</FRAMESET>

</NOSCRIPT>

</HTML>
```

Example 4-34   Sample534.html

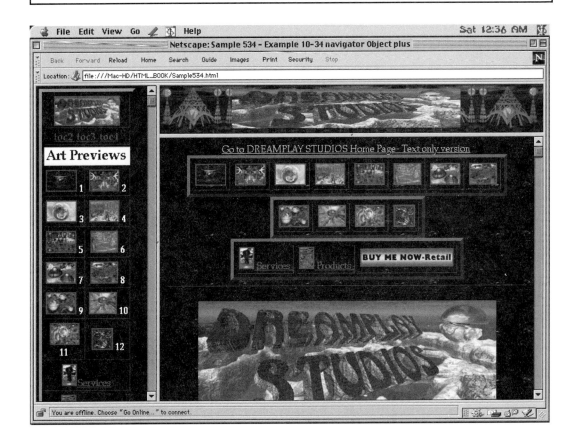

The JavaScript <u>Number</u> Core <u>Object</u>

JavaScript Syntax:

```
new Number(value);
numberName = new Number(value);
```

      To create a **Number** Object, you use the Keyword **new** along with the Number Constructor Function, where **value** is the numeric Value of the Object. This is one of those limited-use Objects that is mainly used when you need to get at the special mathematical Properties that are available with this Object.

Number Properties

<u>Property</u>	<u>Description</u>
MAX_VALUE	Has a Value that is the largest number that JavaScript can represent which is approximately 1.79E+308. It is a read-only Static Property of Number that is always invoked as **Number.MAX_VALUE** instead of as a Property of a Number Object that you have created. Larger numbers overflow to Infinity.
MIN_VALUE	Has a Value that is the smallest number <u>as it approaches zero</u> that JavaScript can represent, which is approximately 2.22E-308. Note that this is not the smallest negative number. It is a read-only Static Property of Number that is always invoked as **Number.MIN_VALUE**. Smaller numbers overflow to zero.
NaN	Has a Value of NaN that represents Not-a-Number which is a Literal that is not enclosed in quotes. It is always unequal to any number and is even unequal to itself. You can't use NaN as a test parameter in a conditional, but you can use the Global Function **isNaN(value)** to test whether a value is a number or NaN.
NEGATIVE_INFINITY	Has a Value of **"-Infinity"**, which represents and behaves like mathematical negative infinity. It is returned on overflow. It is a read-only Static Property of Number that is always invoked as **Number.NEGATIVE_INFINITY**.
POSITIVE_INFINITY	Has a Value of **"Infinity"**, which represents and behaves like mathematical positive infinity. It is returned on overflow. It is a read-only Static Property of Number that is always invoked as **Number.POSITIVE_INFINITY**.
prototype	Lets you create your own Properties for a **Number** Object.

Number Methods

Method	Description
toString([radix])	Converts the **Number** Object to a String and returns that String. The optional **radix** Argument specifies a number from 2 to 16, which is the base for the conversion. If unspecified, the default Value is 10. You can't use this Method on numeric literals.

This example demonstrates some of the Properties of the **Number** Object.

Example 4-35:   Sample535.html

```
<!DOCTYPE HTML PUBLIC "-//W3C//DTD HTML 3.2//EN">
<HTML>
<HEAD>
<TITLE>Sample 535 - Example 4-35      Number Object   </TITLE>

<SCRIPT LANGUAGE="JavaScript1.2"><!--BEGIN HIDING

myNumber1 = new Number(55);
myNumber2 = Number.MAX_VALUE * 10;
myNumber3 = Number.MIN_VALUE / 1000000000000000;
myNumber4 = Number.MIN_VALUE / 10000000000000000;
myNumber5 = Number.MAX_VALUE;
myNumber6 = Number.MIN_VALUE

        document.write("myNumber1 = " + myNumber1 + "<BR>");
        document.write("myNumber2 = " + myNumber2 + "<BR>");
        document.write("myNumber3 = " + myNumber3 + "<BR>");
        document.write("myNumber4 = " + myNumber4 + "<BR>");
        document.write("myNumber5 = " + myNumber5 + "<BR>");
        document.write("myNumber6 = " + myNumber6 + "<BR>");

//END HIDING-->
</SCRIPT>
</HEAD>

<BODY>
<P>
Note that on the Macintosh platform you can create numbers that are smaller than
<B>Number.MIN_VALUE</B> as it approaches zero.  The values for <B>myNumber3</B> and
<B>myNumber4</B> demonstrates this.  Theoretically any number larger than 1 that
divides Number.MIN_VALUE should cause the result to overflow to zero, but look at
how large a number it actually takes to cause the overflow.(10000000000000000)
</P>
</BODY>
</HTML>
```

The JavaScript <u>select</u> Object

JavaScript Syntax:

```
document.formName.selectName;
document.formName.elements[index];
```

A **select** Object is a list of options that can be selected by the user. Depending on the configuration, it can be a scrollable list or a pop-up menu. For more information on the definition of a SELECT Element and its Attributes, see the HTML 40 Guide on the CD-ROM or for just the Syntax see Appendix A on page 1011. See the index for examples.

The **select** Object is a Property of the **form** Object, and the **options[i]** Array is a Property of the **select** Object. The **select** Object cannot be created with JavaScript. You must use HTML syntax to create a **select** Object, along with any optional Event Handlers. The **select** Object will then be created automatically by the JavaScript interpreter and will reflect that SELECT Element. You can use the **document.write()** Method to create a SELECT Element directly from within a JavaScript SCRIPT.

When the JavaScript interpreter creates the **select** Object from the HTML code, it also creates the **options[i]** Array as a Property of the **select** Object. Each Element of the **options[i]** Array contains one **option** Object that reflects an HTML OPTION Element. They are loaded into the Array in source order. You can then access the individual **option** Objects by its **index** number in the **options[i]** Array.

The **option** Objects themselves are <u>read-only</u> Properties, which means that you can't change the **option** by assigning a different Value to it. However, you can change the Value of the **text** Property of the **option**, which will cause the new text String to be displayed in the browser. The **options[i]** Array is covered in more detail in the next section. For more information on **Array** Objects, see Chapter 7.

Because the **select** and **option** Objects are so far down the Object hierarchy, it can be a real pain to get at them with code, that is, to refer to them and access their Properties and Methods. Therefore, it's generally advised to set up variables for different aspects of these Objects and their Properties to make your code more readable. For examples, see pages 501, 650-657.

Select Event Handlers

onBlur
onChange
onFocus

JavaScript Syntax for Select Properties:

```
document.formName.selectName.propertyName;
document.formName.elements[index].propertyName;
```

Select Properties

Property	Description
form	A read-only Property that reflects the **form** Object that contains the current **select** Object.
length	Reflects the number of **option** Object Elements in the **options[i]** Array.
name	Reflects the NAME Attribute of the **select** Object.
options[i]	An Array that reflects an **option** Object in each Array Element.
selectedIndex	An integer that specifies the zero-based index of the currently selected **option** Object. If multiple **option** Objects are selected then the first one in the list is reflected. You can set this Property, which causes a different **option** Object to be currently selected.
type	The Value of **type** is **"select-one"** if the Object is a **select** Object. The Value of **type** is **"select-multiple"** if the Object is a **select** Object and the Boolean MULTIPLE Attribute is included in the HTML SELECT Element. This is a read-only Property.

JavaScript Syntax for Select Methods:

```
document.formName.selectName.methodName(parameters)
document.formName.elements[index].methodName(parameters)
```

Select Methods

Method	Description
blur()	Removes focus from the **select** Object.
focus()	Gives focus to the **select** Object.
handleEvent()	Invokes the Event Handler for the specified Event.

The JavaScript <u>options[i]</u> Array

JavaScript Syntax:

```
document.formName.selectName.optionName;
document.formName.selectName.options[index1];
document.formName.elements[index2].options[index1
```

    The **options[i]** Array is a Property of the **select** Object. It is automatically created by the JavaScript interpreter from the HTML so that each HTML OPTION Element becomes an **option** Object in the **options[i]** Array in its own Array Element.

Deleting an <u>option</u> Object

    To delete an **option** Object from a **select** Object use the following syntax:

JavaScript Syntax:

```
document.formName.selectName.options[index1] = null;
```

Deleting Multiple <u>option</u> Objects

    To delete multiple **option** Objects from the end of a **select** Object's **options** Array use the following syntax to truncate the Array by specifying an **integer**:

JavaScript Syntax:

```
document.formName.selectName.options.length = integer;
```

JavaScript Syntax for options[i] Array <u>Properties</u>:

```
document.formName.selectName.optionName.propertyName;
document.formName.selectName.options[index1].propertyName;
document.formName.elements[index2].options[index1].propertyName;
```

options[i] Array Properties

<u>Property</u>	<u>Description</u>
length	Reflects the number of Options in the Array.
selectedIndex	Reflects the zero-based index number of the currently selected Option.

options[i] Array Element Properties

Property	Description
defaultSelected	Reflects whether an **option** has the SELECTED Attribute or not. If it does the Value is **true** and **false** otherwise.
index	Reflects the zero-based **index** number of the **option**.
selected	Reflects whether the **option** is currently selected or not. This is a Boolean Property that is **true** if the **option** is selected and **false** if not selected.
text	Reflects the text String contained in the VALUE Attribute for the **option**.
value	Reflects the current VALUE Attribute of the **option**, which is returned to the server as a VALUE=value pair if the form is submitted.

The JavaScript <u>option</u> Object

The **option** Object is created with the **Option()** Constructor Function.

To create a new **option** Object use the following Syntax:

JavaScript Syntax:

```
new Option(text, value, defaultSelected, selected);
optionName = new Option(text, value, defaultSelected, selected);
```

Parameters Defined:

text	Argument that specifies the text String to display which is the same as the text that appears between the Start and End Tags of the OPTION Element in the HTML code.
value	Argument that specifies the Value of the VALUE Attribute.
defaultSelected	Argument is optional and specifies if the **option** is initially selected.
selected	Argument is optional and specifies if the **option** is currently selected.
optionName	Variable name that is assigned to the **option** Object.

Adding an <u>option</u> Object to a <u>select</u> Object

To add an **option** Object to a **select** Object use the following Syntax:

JavaScript Syntax:

```
document.formName.selectName.options[indexN] = optionName;
```

option Object Properties

Property	Description
defaultSelected	Specifies the **option**'s initial selection state with a Value of **true** if selected or **false** if it isn't selected.
index	Specifies the zero-based **index** number of the **option**.
prototype	Lets you create new Properties for the **option** Object.
selected	Specifies the **option**'s current selection state. This is a Boolean Property that has a Value of **true** if the **option** is selected and **false** if not selected.
text	Specifies a text String for the **option** that is displayed in the **select** Object.
value	Specifies the current VALUE Attribute of the **option** which is returned to the server as a Value=value pair if the form is submitted.

Here's a list of Sample Files that have a **select** Object used in them. If you want to cross-reference the Samples with code in the book, see Appendix C, on pages 1039+, for page numbers of the examples.

Sample File Name, Line Number	Example Usage
Sample71-SimpleForm.html, line 63:	<SELECT NAME="UPSshippingoptions" SIZE=1>
Sample71-OrderForm.html, line 147:	<SELECT NAME="creditcardtype" SIZE=1>
Sample73.html, line 15:	<SELECT NAME="select2" SIZE=3 MULTIPLE>
Sample724.html, line 23:	<SELECT NAME="getBackColor" SIZE="1" onChange="changeEverything(); return false;">

New JavaScript Core Functions

There are two new Core Functions for JavaScript 1.2 for Navigator 4.0. They are the **Number** Function and the **String** Function. You can also think of the these Functions as Global Functions that are not associated with any particular Object but are part of the JavaScript Language itself. Make sure that you don't confuse them with their Number Object and **String** Object counterparts.

The JavaScript <u>Number</u> Core <u>Function</u>

JavaScript Syntax:

```
Number(x);
```

The **Number** Function is a Core Function that converts the **x** Parameter, which is any Object, to a number. If the **x** Object is a String that doesn't convert to an acceptable number then **NaN** is returned. For example, the following Script:

<u>Mini-Example:</u>

```
<SCRIPT LANGUAGE="JavaScript1.2">

today = new Date();
dateConversion = Number(today);

myMinutes = today.getMinutes();
minutesConversion = Number(myMinutes);

    document.write("dateConversion in milliseconds = " + dateConversion + "<BR>");
    document.write("minutesConversion = " + minutesConversion + "<BR>");

</SCRIPT>
```

has this output in the browser at 3:22 AM, Feb. 16, 1998:

dateConversion in milliseconds = 887617357173
minutesConversion = 22

The JavaScript <u>String</u> Core <u>Function</u>

JavaScript Syntax:

```
String(x);
```

The **String** Function is a Core Function that converts the **x** Parameter, which is any Object, to a String.

This example shows the output for several Objects that are converted to Strings.

Example 4-36:   **Sample536.html**

```
<!DOCTYPE HTML PUBLIC "-//W3C//DTD HTML 3.2//EN">
<HTML>
<HEAD>
<TITLE>Sample 536 - Example 4-36      String Function   </TITLE>
</HEAD>

<BODY>
<H2>Sample 536</H2>

<LAYER ID="L1" LEFT="20" TOP="370" WIDTH=400 HEIGHT=40 BGCOLOR="cyan">
Test Layer </LAYER>

<SCRIPT LANGUAGE="JavaScript1.2"><!--BEGIN HIDING

today = new Date();
todayString = String(today);

dateConversion = Number(today);
dateString = String(dateConversion);

myWindow = String(window);
myLayer = String(document.L1);

        document.write("dateConversion = " + dateConversion + "<BR>");
        document.write("todayString = " + todayString + "<BR>");
        document.write("dateString = " + dateString + "<P>");
        document.write("myWindow = " + myWindow + "<P>");
        document.write("myLayer = " + myLayer + "<P>");

//END HIDING-->
</SCRIPT>

</BODY>
</HTML>
```

The previous example produces the following browser output:

Sample 536

dateConversion = 887619422650
todayString = Mon Feb 16 03:57:02 1998
dateString = 887619422650

myWindow = {length:undefined, frames:undefined, parent:undefined, top:undefined, self:undefined, name:undefined, status:undefined, defaultStatus:undefined, opener:undefined, closed:undefined, innerWidth:undefined, innerHeight:undefined, outerWidth:undefined, outerHeight:undefined, screenX:undefined, screenY:undefined, pageXOffset:undefined, pageYOffset:undefined, secure:undefined, frameRate:undefined, offscreenBuffering:undefined, document:, history:, location:file:///Mac-HD/HTML_BOOK/Sample536.html, crypto:{}, menubar:{visible:undefined}, toolbar:{visible:undefined}, locationbar:{visible:undefined}, personalbar:{visible:undefined}, statusbar:{visible:undefined}, scrollbars:{visible:undefined}, today:Mon Feb 16 03:57:02 1998, todayString:"Mon Feb 16 03:57:02 1998", dateConversion:887619422650, dateString:"887619422650"}

myLayer = {clip:{left:undefined, top:undefined, right:undefined, bottom:undefined, height:undefined, width:undefined}, document:}

Part II
JavaScript 1.2

Chapter 5

Statements &

Operators

Chapter 5
Statements & Operators

Contents

JavaScript Statements

What are JavaScript Statements?

JavaScript Statements are the "behind the scenes action" where the interactivity and serious Scripting potentialities are lurking around the edges of your imagination. The deeper you get into this, the more inherent capabilities of Statements you will discover that aren't immediately obvious. One of the main uses for Statements is to let you Script an action to be performed if a certain condition is true and another action if that condition is false. Loop Statements let you perform the same action repeatedly while a condition is true. In many cases, the action is iterated over all of the Elements in an Array.

Categories of JavaScript Statements

JavaScript Statements can be categorized in the following manner:

Conditional Statements	Loop Statements	Object Manipulation Statements	Comment Statements
if	for	for...in	//single-line comment
if...else	while	with	/*multi-line ...
switch	do while	var	... comment*/
? :	labeled	function	
	break	return	
	continue	export	
		import	
		delete	

The following three Statements <u>don't have names</u> and therefore aren't usually listed as such, but they are Statements nonetheless.

Statement	Terse Definition	Mini-Example
Property Access	Accesses a Property of an Object	myArray1.length
Method Invocation	Invokes a Method on an Object	window.open()
Assignment	Assigns an expression's value to a variable	a = b + c

Chart of all JavaScript Statements

<u>Statement</u>	<u>Terse Definition</u>
break	Ends the current **while** or **for** Loop that contains it and transfers program control to the statement immediately following the terminated Loop.
comment	Explanatory author's notes that are ignored by the JavaScript interpreter.
continue	Halts the block of Statements in a **while** Loop and jumps back to the condition. Halts the block of Statements in a **for** Loop and jumps back to the update Expression.
delete	Destroys the Property of an Object or an Element in an Array.
do...while	As long as the test condition is true, the preceding block of Statements are executed and always executed at least once by preceding the condition.
export	Provides Functions, Objects, and Properties within a Signed Script to other Signed or Unsigned Scripts.
for	Loop Statement that executes a block of Statements based on the parameters of its three optional Expressions, which are inside paretheses and separated by a semicolon.
for...in	Object Manipulation Statement that executes a block of Statements for each Property of an Object using a specified variable.
function	Statement that defines comma-separated, parenthesed Arguments and a named block of Statements that are enclosed in curly braces, which are executed as a unit when called. Arguments can be Strings, Numbers, or Objects. See pages 371-385, 505.
if	Statement that executes a block of statements once, if a specified condition is true or an Expression evaluates to true. If false, nothing happens.
if...else	Statement that executes a block of Statements once, if a specified condition is true or an Expression evaluates to true. If the condition is false, an alternative block of Statements is executed.
? :	Conditional Operator Statement. Shorthand for **if ()...else**.
import	Statement used by a Script to import Functions, Objects, and Properties from a Signed Script that has previously exported them.
labeled	A named Statement with its name separated from its block of Statements by a colon. The **break** or **continue** Statements use this name as the jump point for the program's continuation of Statement execution.
return	Statement specifying the value to be returned by a Function call.
switch	Conditional Statement that executes alternative Statements based on whether an evaluated Expression matches the value of the case labels.
var	Statement declaring a Variable, optionally assigning a value to it.
while	Loop Statement that executes a block of Statements as long as the determining Expression evaluates to true.
with	Statement identifying a default Object to apply a block of Statements to.

Conditional Statements

The JavaScript <u>if ()</u> Statement

JavaScript Syntax:

```
if (condition) {
      statementsIfTrue;
}
```

<u>Parameters Defined:</u>

OK, so technically there is no **if ()** Statement because, strictly speaking, all of them are **if ()...else** Statements, with the optional **else** part omitted. For instructional purposes, it's easier to start this way and the **else** is frequently omitted in real-world use.

An **if ()** Statement will execute the block of Statements that, in the Syntax, are specified by **statementsIfTrue** and inclosed within curly braces, if the **condition** within the parentheses evaluates to **true**. The **condition** can be an **Expression** like (**x >= 5**) or like (**booleanTest**).

You can even test for an Object being present in the page like this:

(**myLayer1**)

where the Statements would execute as long as the **Layer** named **myLayer1** was present in the document.

You can also test for multiple **conditions** like this:

```
if (x >= 0  &&  x <= 77)
```

or like this:

```
if (myLayer.top > 0  ||  myLayer.clip.right < myLayer.width)
```

If the **condition** evaluates to **false**, then the block of Statements do not execute and the program control returns to the Statement following the **if ()** Statements. If you only have one Statement to execute, then you can omit the curly braces. If you want to code in multiple Statements on the same line, you need to separate them with a semicolon. Semicolon Statement separation is optional otherwise. Just pick one way of doing it and stick with it, to make your code easier to debug.

Here's a simple example where the Statement that changes the background color of the document contained within the **if ()** Statement will execute if the Variable **x** is less than or equal to 4, which causes the **condition** to evaluate to true. Since there is only one executable Statement, the curly braces are optional for the **if()** Statement and in this case are omitted. You can use them if it helps you read your code. However, remember that for the function declaration, the curly braces are <u>always required</u>.

```
function changeColor() {
     if (x <= 4)
          document.bgColor = 'purple';
}
```

Here's a simple example where the block of Statements in the **if ()** Statement will execute if the Boolean Variable **booleanTest** evaluates to true:

```
function changeColor() {

     if (booleanTest)  {
          document.myLayer1.clip.width = 500;
          document.myLayer1.clip.height = 400;
          document.myLayer1.visibility = 'show';
          document.myLayer2.visibility = 'hide';
     }
}
```

Here the **clip.right** Property must be less than 800 and the **clip.bottom** Property of the **Layer** named **layer1** must be less than 400 in order for the **condition** to evaluate to true.

```
function LargeView3() {

     if (layer1.clip.right < 800 && layer1.clip.bottom < 400)  {
          document.layer1.moveTo(20, 10);
          document.layer1.resizeBy(8, 4);
          document.layer1.moveAbove(document.layer2);
     }
}
```

You can also test for a false **condition** by using the **logical not** Operator **!** like this:

JavaScript Syntax:

```
if (! condition) {
     statementsIfFalse;
}
```

The JavaScript if ()...else Statement

The **if ()...else** Statement tests for a **condition**, and if the **condition** is an **Expression** that evaluates to true, then the **statementsIfTrue** block of Statements enclosed inside the curly braces will execute. If the **condition** evaluates to false, then the **statementsIfFalse** block of Statements following the **else** will execute. Either of these blocks of Statements can include further nested **if ()...else** Statements, and this potentiality is covered in the next sections. You are going to make serious use of the **if ()...else** Statement in your own code.

JavaScript Syntax:

```
if (condition) {
     statementsIfTrue;
}
else {
     statementsIfFalse;
}
```

Mini-Example:

In this mini-example, if the **myBoolean** Variable is true, then the Layer named **myLayer1** is changed. If the **myBoolean** Variable is false, then a different Layer named **myOtherLayer2** is changed. Obviously there would be other JavaScript lurking about to change the value of the **myBoolean** Variable in order to give the **changeColor()** Function any meaning.

```
function changeColor() {

    if (myBoolean)  {
         document.myLayer1.bgColor = 'purple';
         document.myLayer1.visibility = 'show';
    }
    else  {
         document.myOtherLayer2.bgColor = 'green';
         document.myOtherLayer2.visibility = 'show';
    }
}
```

Nested <u>if ()</u> Statements

JavaScript Syntax:

```
if (condition) {
      statementsIfTrue;

      if (condition2) {
            statementsIfTrue2;
      }
}
```

Parameters Defined:

Sometimes it is either less intuitive, inconvenient or impossible to effectively test for two **conditions** in one **if ()** Statement, so the practical solution is to nest an **if ()** inside of another. This causes the program to first test for the first **condition**, and if the **Expression** evaluates to true, then it proceeds to execute those Statements which in this case consists of a second **if ()** Statement, which proceeds to test for the second **condition2**. If the second **condition2** is also true, then the **statementsIfTrue2** block of Statements is executed. If either of the two **conditions** evaluate to false, then the Script will jump out of the **if ()** and proceed at the next position immediately following the **if ()**.

In this case, the second **if ()** Statement serves as the block of Statements to execute if the first **condition** evaluates to true. You could also have other Statements to execute either before or after the second **if ()** Statement like in the second example in the next section on nested **if ()...else** Statements.

Mini-Example:

In this example, if both Boolean Variables are true, then the text String is written with the **document.write()** Method.

```
if (badHairDayBoolean)   {
      if (seriousHangoverBoolean)   {

            document.write("Reality Bytes, Stay in Bed Today");
}
```

Generally it is considered better programming style to code this with (&&), but sometimes it is improbable to do so when testing for Key Events and Modifiers Keys:

```
if (badHairDayBoolean   &&   seriousHangoverBoolean)
      {document.write("Reality Bytes, Stay in Bed Today"); }
```

Nested <u>if ()</u>...<u>else</u> Statements

JavaScript Syntax:

```
if (condition) {
      statementsIfTrue;

      if (condition2) {
            statementsIfTrue2;
      }
      else {
            statementsIfFalse2;
      }
else   {
      statementsIfFalse;
      }
}
```

Parameters Defined:

When you work with nested **if ()** or **if ()...else** Statements, it's important to know that they can be of any combination of nested or multiple nested **if ()** or **if ()...else** Statements, and you can have up to 255 of them. If you have one nested **if ()...else** Statement inside of another **if ()...else** Statement, here's how the process works.

If the first **condition** evaluates to true, then you execute the following block of Statements. If one of those Statements is an **if ()...else** Statement, then its **condition2** is tested for and if it evaluates to true, then the **statementsIfTrue2** block of Statements is executed, otherwise the **statementsIfFalse2** block is executed.

If the first **condition** evaluates to false, then the Script jumps to the **else** and executes the **statementsIfFalse** block of Statements.

This book uses the terms **if ()** as a shorthand for the **if ()...else** Statement, as is traditional and to save the author some typing.

Mini-Example:

In the following example, if the Boolean Variable **myBoolean1** is true, then the background color of the **document** is changed to yellow. If **myBoolean1** is false, then the background color is changed to red.

If the Boolean Variable **myBoolean1** is true and <u>x is greater than or equal to 5</u>, then the background color of **myLayer1** is changed to olive. If the Boolean Variable **myBoolean1** is true and <u>x is less than 5</u>, then the background color of **myLayer1** is changed to black.

```
if (myBoolean1) {
     document.bgColor = 'yellow';

     if (x >= 5) {
            document.myLayer1.bgColor = 'olive';
     }
     else {
            document.myLayer1.bgColor = 'black';
     }
else   {
     document.bgColor = 'red';
  }
}
```

The ( ) ? : Conditional Operator Statement

JavaScript Syntax:

```
evaluatedResult = (condition) ? expression1 : expression2
```

Parameters Defined:

This is unofficially called the Conditional Operator Statement and is basically a shorthand version of the **if ()** Statement. If the **condition** is true, then **expression1** is returned and assigned to the **evaluatedResult** Variable. If the **condition** is false, then **expression2** is returned and assigned to the **evaluatedResult** Variable. The **condition** can be an expression that evaluates to either true or false. **expression1** and **expression2** can be values of any type including but not limited to: Strings, Variables, Numbers, and Objects.

The two **Expressions** are separated by a colon. The **condition** is optionally inside of parentheses, but it's a good idea to use them.

Mini-Example:

In the following mini-example, if the **wonTheLottery** is true, then the text String "**congratulations**" is assigned to the **myString** Variable. If the **wonTheLottery** is false, then the text String "**condolences**" is assigned to the **myString** Variable.

```
myString = (wonTheLottery)   ?   "congratulations" : "condolences";
```

The <u>switch( )</u> Statement

JavaScript Syntax:

```
switch (expression) {
      case label1 :
              statements;
              [break;]
      case label2 :
              statements;
              [break;]
              ...
      [default :
      statements;]
}
```

Parameters Defined:

The **switch( )** Statement is new for Navigator 4 and is really cool. Its syntax is exactly the same as in Java. One of the best uses for it is to test for ASCII Key values and there are numerous examples in Chapter 6 such as 6-15 on page 588, 6-20 on page 623, 6-21 on page 628, 6-22 on page 632, and 6-23 on page 648, which demonstrate various useful incarnations of this technique. Here's how it works.

First of all, in the following syntax, the Keywords **switch, case, break,** and **default** are not substituted for by the author, that is, code them in exactly as you see them. The rest of the terms are placeholders for you to fill in. The **labels** are separated from the **statements** by a colon. The **break** and **default** Statements are optional. The **break** Statement and the **statements** are each separated by a semicolon, not a colon.

You start with the name **switch** and then an **expression** that is enclosed inside parentheses. Then within curly braces you have all of the following: For each **case** you start with **label1** that is matched against the **expression** in parentheses. If they are equivalent, then the **statements** for that case are executed. The **statements** for that **case** are the ones that immediately follow the colon that follows the **case label1**. If there is an optional **break** Statement, then the program jumps to the end of the **switch ()** Statement. If there is no **break** Statement, the rest of the **statements** in the **switch ()** Statement will execute.

If **label1** does not match the **expression**, then **switch ()** will test and see if **label2** matches the **expression**. If it does, then the **statements** associated with **label2** will execute and break out if **break** is present. This process continues until all of the **case labels** have been tested.

If none of the **case labels** matches the **expression**, then the optional **default** Statement is called and the **statements** associated with it are executed.

In the following example, assume that the Variable **myColor** has some other JavaScript processing that will change it to different colors. The **switch ()** Statement uses **myColor** as the expression to match against the **case labels**. If **myColor** is 'blue', then the Statement **document.layer1.bgColor = 'blue';** is executed and changes the background color of **layer1** to blue, and the **switch ()** Statement is exited due to the **break** Statement.

If **myColor** is not equivalent to 'blue', then **switch ()** continues to test until a match is found or until it reaches the **default** Statement and changes the background color of **layer1** to white.

Make sure that you understand that the 'blue' contained in the Statement:

```
document.layer1.bgColor = 'blue';
```

has no bearing on the test matching that occurs between the Variable **myColor**, which is used as the expression and the **case label** of 'blue'.

```
var myColor;

function changeColor()   {

    switch (myColor) {

        case 'blue' :
            document.layer1.bgColor = 'blue';
            break;

        case 'red' :
            document.layer1.bgColor = 'red';
            break;

        case 'purple' :
            document.layer1.bgColor = 'purple';
            break;

        case 'green' :
            document.layer1.bgColor = 'green';
            break;

        default :
            document.layer1.bgColor = 'white';
    }
}
```

Parameters Defined:

The following syntax is used when you want to execute the same block of **statements** if either one of two case labels matches against the **expression**. The two case labels are separated by a colon. If you want to have more than two cases, then add as many as you want and separate each one by a colon.

JavaScript Syntax:

```
switch (expression) {
     case label1 : case label2 :
          statements;
          [break;]
     case label3 : case label4 :
          statements;
          [break;]
          ...
     [default :
     statements;]
}
```

Mini-Example:

The two cases, such as, **case '188' : case '48' :** cover the two possible ASCII values when their associated number Keys are pressed. This plans for users that have extended keyboards. The **expression e.which.toString()** evaluates to a Numeric String. See Sample721.html for the full version and Chapter 6 for more information on Key Events.

```
function scrollLayers(e)   {
     switch (e.which.toString())   {
                                        //press the ALT + 0 keys
          case '188' : case '48' :
          document.Layer2.moveTo(150,250);
          break;
                                        //press the ALT + 1 keys
          case '193' : case '49' :
          document.Layer2.moveBy(-30,30);
          break;
                                        //press the ALT + 2 keys
          case '170' : case '50' :
          document.Layer2.moveBy(0,30);
          break;

          default : return false;
     }
}
```

Loop Statements

The <u>for( )</u> Statement

JavaScript Syntax:

```
for ([initialExpression]; [condition]; [updateExpression]) {
    statements;
}
```

<u>Parameters Defined:</u>

The **for( )** Statement takes a little getting used to, but once you get it, you recognize that it's really powerful and can save you a lot of typing and time. The first two of the three optional Expressions that are contained inside the parentheses are followed by a semicolon. If it's not immediately obvious, a **condition** is also an Expresion. They are followed by a block of statements, enclosed within curly braces, which are executed based on these Expressions.

The way that authors use the **for( )** Statement most frequently is to use the **initialExpression** to declare and initialize a Variable like this:

```
var i=0;
```

Then the **condition** Expression is declared, which tells the **for ()** Statement the situations under which it is allowed to continue the Loop. Here's a typical implementation:

```
i<4;
```

And finally, the **updateExpression** is used to increment the Variable declared in the **initialExpression**, like this:

```
i++
```

In case you're rusty on your Operator terms:

```
i++
```
        in this case means to increment the Variable **i** by 1.

Putting that all together and adding a statement to execute we have:

```
for (var i=0; i<4; i++)  {
    document.write('The number iterated is ' + i + '<BR>');
}
```

which would produce the following output in the browser:

>The number iterated is 0
>The number iterated is 1
>The number iterated is 2
>The number iterated is 3

The previous **for ()** Statement would be read like this: For the Variable **i** starting at the value of zero, as long as **i** is less than 4, execute the **document.write()** statement. After each iteration, increase the value of **i** by one and repeat the Loop starting at the **condition**, so that if **i** is still less than four, then the Loop continues.

As soon as the **condition** evaluates to false, the Loop is terminated and control returns to the program at the end of the **for ()** Statement.

Programming Tips

The reason that many authors declare the Variable **i** within the **for ()** Statement like this: **var i=0;** is because that way the Variable is only known inside the Function that contains the **for ()** Loop and the same Variable can be reused inside of other Functions, where it will have a separate value and neither of the instances will affect the other.

When you need to use multiple **for()** Statements in the same Function, one option is to use the Variable **i** in the first **for ()** Statement in the Function and the Variable **j** in the second **for ()** Statement and the Variable **k** in the third. This can be useful to help keep track of your parameters and debugging when you are working with multi-level Arrays. The **i**, **j**, and/or **k** Variables can be used to access and manipulate the Array Elements via the Array **index** number. See Chapter 7 for more information on Arrays.

If you want to maximize your memory allocation efficiency, then you can reuse the same Variable **i** in multiple sequential **for()** Loops within the same Function.

Mini-Example:

This example just declares an Array named **myArray** and uses the **for ()** Statement to write each Array Element on its own line.

```
function writeClients()  {

var myArray = new Array('Name', 'Address', 'City', 'State');

    for (var i=0; i<myArray.length; i++) {

        document.write(myArray[i] + '<BR>');
    }
}
```

The <u>while( )</u> Statement

JavaScript Syntax:

```
while (condition) {
      statements;
}
```

Parameters Defined:

The **while( )** Statement creates a Loop that continues as long as the expression in the **condition** Argument evaluates to true. After determining that the **condition** is true, the Loop will execute the block of **statements** and then check to see if the **condition** is still true and repeat the Loop. When the **condition** evaluates to **false**, the Loop is terminated and the Script continues at the end of the **while ()** Statement.

In many instances, you will use this Statement and supply your own increment Statement within the executable block of **statements**. It's crucial that you provide some mechanism within the **statements** that will cause the Loop to eventually become **false**, otherwise you will have an infinite Loop.

Mini-Example:

In the following example, **i** is initialized to zero and **x** is initialized to 5. As long as **i** is less than 4, the Loop will increment **i** by 1 and then add **x** and **i** and then assign the result to **x**.

After the first pass through the Loop,	$x = 6$	and	$i = 1$
After the second pass through the Loop,	$x = 8$	and	$i = 2$
After the third pass through the Loop,	$x = 11$	and	$i = 3$
After the fourth pass through the Loop,	$x = 15$	and	$i = 4$

On the fifth pass, since $i = 4$ at the start of the Loop, this causes the **condition** to evaluate to **false** and the Loop terminates and the final value of **x** remains at 15.

```
i = 0;
x = 5;

while (i < 4) {
      i++;
      x += i;                 //this means        x = x + i;
}
```

Mini-Example:

As long as the **booleanTest** Variable is true, this example will continue to increase the value of **x** by 1. When **x** equals 7, that will cause the **booleanTest** to be changed to **false**, which changes the **condition** to **false** and thus halts the Loop.

```
function myWhileTest()   {

booleanTest = true;
x = 0;

     while (booleanTest) {

          x = x + 1;

          if (x == 7) {
                 booleanTest = false;
          }
     }
}
```

Mini-Example:

This example scrolls the window downward by 50 pixels when both the ALT and CONTROL **modifiers** Keys are pressed in conjunction with the 5 Key being pressed.

Note that the ASCII value for ALT_MASK + CONTROL_MASK is 3, which is what the **e.modifiers** Expression is tested against.

```
document.captureEvents(Event.KEYPRESS)
document.onkeypress=scrollWindow;

function scrollWindow(e)   {

     while (e.modifiers == 3  &&  e.which == 5) {

          window.scrollBy(0, 50);
     }
}
```

The do while( ) Statement

JavaScript Syntax:

```
do {
      statements;
} while (condition)
```

Parameters Defined:

The **do while( )** Statement is very similar to the **while()** Statement. The main difference is that the **statements** are guaranteed to execute at least once because they occur before the **condition** is tested for the first time. After the **statements** are executed the first time, the **condition** is evaluated. If it evaluates to **true**, the **statements** are executed again.

This Loop continues until the **condition** evaluates to **false**, which causes the Loop to terminate and control is returned to the Script at the point after the end of the **do while()** Statement. Once again, it's important that you provide some mechanism within the **statements** that will cause the Loop to eventually become **false** otherwise you will have an infinite Loop.

Mini-Example:

Let's take the previous example and rewrite it using **do while()**. The results are the same with the only difference being that **booleanTest** is evaluated after the **statements** are executed.

```
function myDoWhileTest()   {

booleanTest = true;
x = 0;

      do {
            x = x + 1;

            if (x == 7) {
                  booleanTest = false;
            }
      }
      while (booleanTest)
}
```

Mini-Example:

Here's a simpler example that demonstrates that even though the **while()** **condition** specifies that **x** must be less than zero and evaluates to **false** the very first time, the **statements** are still executed once. The Variable **x** is initialized with a value of 1, then it is incremented by 2 and written to screen with a value of 3. Because 3 is not equal to 1, the Loop then immediately terminates.

```
x = 1;

do {
        x = x + 2;
        document.write(x);
}
while (x == 1)
```

Mini-Example:

This example demonstrates a **do while()** Statement inside the **doItNow()** Function that has a failsafe Alert Dialog to compensate for faulty coding, just to plant a seed for future Scripts. Here's the browser output followed by the code.

```
z=10
z=15
z=20
z=25
```

```
function doItNow() {

        x = 0;
        y = 10;
        z = 0;

        do {
                z = x + y;
                document.write("z=" + z + "<BR>");
                x+=2;
                y+=3;
                if (x >= 50  ||  y >= 50) {
                        alert("Logic Malfunction! Reevaluate.");
                        break;
                }
        }
        while (x <= 10  &&  y <= 20)
}
```

The <u>labeled</u> Statement

JavaScript Syntax:

```
label : {
     statements;
}
```

<u>Parameters Defined:</u>

The **labeled** Statement is not a Loop Statement but it is used in Loop Statements in conjunction with **break** or **continue** Statements. Think of a **labeled** Statement as a block of **statements** that is assigned to an identifying **label**, but instead of using the equals sign for assignment, the syntax requires that a colon be used between the **label** and the block of **statements** enclosed within the curly braces.

When you use the **break** Statement to break out of a **labeled** Loop, you have the option of including the **label** identifier of a **labeled** Statement. This causes the program to break out of the **labeled** Statement that is specified by **label**. This becomes really useful when you have <u>multiple</u> **labeled** Statements in one Loop Statement, because you can tell the Loop which **labeled** Statement you want to break out of, instead of only being able to break out of the entire Loop.

When you use the **continue** Statement inside of a **labeled** Loop Statement, you now have the option of including the **label** identifier of a **labeled** Statement. This causes the program to terminate execution of the current **labeled** Statement and continue at the specified **labeled** Statement. This lets you precisely choose where you want the continuation to reinstigate instead of only being able to continue at the beginning of the Loop.

Remember that in order to use the **label** with a **break** or **continue** Statement, the Statement that contains the **break** or **continue** Statement must be a **labeled** Statement to begin with. Yes, it sounds like circular logic, but it makes sense when you look at the examples and think about it.

There are several examples of using **labeled** Statements in the following sections on the **break** and **continue** Statements.

The <u>break</u> Statement

JavaScript Syntax:

```
break;
break label;
```

Parameters Defined:

The **break** Statement is not a Loop Statement but it can be used inside either a **for()** Loop or a **while()** Loop to terminate execution of that Loop, which returns program control to the Statement following the Loop. If the **break** Statement is used inside a **labeled** Statement, then the optional **label** can be used to specify the particular **labeled** Statement that you want to break out of.

It is possible to use the **break** Statement as part of the executable **statements** of an **if()** Statement but only if the **if()** Statement is contained within a Loop Statement like **for()** or **while()** or inside a **labeled** Statement. See the section on the **switch()** Statement for other uses of the **break** Statement.

Mini-Example:

This example increments **x** by 1 until **x** == 5 and then it adds 100 to **x** and then breaks out of the **while()** Loop.

```
x = 0;

while (x <= 10) {

        if (x == 5) {
                x = x + 100;
                break;
        }
        else   x = x + 1;
}
```

Mini-Example:

Because the following **if()** Statement contains a **break** Statement, and the **if()** is not used inside a Loop Statement, it will generate an error at runtime.

```
if (x==3) {
        document.write(x + 5);
        break;
}
```

This example just demonstrates the use of two **labeled** Statements that have **label Parameters** of **myLabeled1** and **myLabeled2**, respectively. The use of the **break** Statement is also demonstrated such that it makes use of the **label** parameter option to break to a specific **labeled** Statement. Check out the output after the example to follow the logic.

Example 5-0:   Sample600.html

```
<!DOCTYPE HTML PUBLIC "-//W3C//DTD HTML 3.2//EN">
<HTML>
<HEAD>
<TITLE>Sample 600 - Example 5-0     break and labeled Statements     </TITLE>

<SCRIPT LANGUAGE="JavaScript1.2"><!--BEGIN HIDING

x=0;

myLabeled1 :
        while (x < 7) {
                document.write(x + "<BR>");

                myLabeled2 :
                        if (x == 5) {
                                document.write("<B>"+ (x + 5000) +"</B>");
                                break myLabeled1;
                        }
                        else {
                                document.write(x + 10 + "<BR>");
                                break myLabeled2;
                        }
                x++;
        }


//END HIDING-->
</SCRIPT>

</HEAD>

<BODY>
</BODY>
</HTML>
```

The previous example produces the following output:

0
10
1
11
2
12
3
13
4
14
5
5005

Mini-Example:

If you take the previous example and rewrite it with a **for()** Loop instead of a **while()** Loop, it would have identical results and it looks like this:

```
<SCRIPT LANGUAGE="JavaScript1.2"><!--BEGIN HIDING

myLabeled1 :
      for (x=0; x<7; x++) {
            document.write(x + "<BR>");

            myLabeled2 :
                  if (x == 5) {
                        document.write("<B>"+ (x + 5000) +"<\/B>");
                        break myLabeled1;
                  }
                  else {
                        document.write(x + 10 + "<BR>");
                        break myLabeled2;
                  }
      }

//END HIDING-->
</SCRIPT>
```

The <u>continue</u> Statement

JavaScript Syntax:

```
continue;
continue label;
```

Parameters Defined:

The **continue** Statement can be used inside either a **for()** Loop or a **while()** Loop to terminate the execution of the block of **statements** inside the Loop and then continue the execution of the Loop with the next iteration. Don't confuse this with the **break** Statement, which jumps out of the Loop completely. With the **continue** Statement, the Loop is not exited, only the block of **statements** inside the Loop is exited.

When used inside a **for()** Loop the **continue** Statement jumps program control back to the **updateExpression**. When used inside a **while()** Loop, the **continue** Statement jumps program control back to the **condition**.

If the **continue** Statement is used inside a **labeled** Statement, then you can break out of that **labeled** Statement and use the optional **label** to specify the particular **labeled** Statement that you want jump to.

You can use the **continue** Statement as part of the executable **statements** of an **if()** Statement but only if the **if()** Statement is contained within a Loop Statement like **for()** or **while()** or inside a **labeled** Statement.

Mini-Example:

This example writes the **myArray** Element only if it is equivalent to 5:

```
myArray = [2, 7, 13, 11, 5];

for (var i = 0; i < myArray.length; i++) {
      if (myArray[i] == 5) {
            document.write(myArray[i] + "<BR>");
            continue;
      }
}
```

Example 5-1 is a slight variation on the previous Example 5-0. It just replaces the **break** Statement with the **continue** Statement for comparison purposes. Compare the differences in the output and compare the logic of how the **statements** progress between these examples.

Example 5-1:   **Sample601.html**

```
<!DOCTYPE HTML PUBLIC "-//W3C//DTD HTML 3.2//EN">
<HTML>
<HEAD>
<TITLE>Sample 601 - Example 5-1    continue Statement </TITLE>

<SCRIPT LANGUAGE="JavaScript1.2"><!--BEGIN HIDING

        for (x=0; x<7; x++) {
                document.write(x + "<BR>");

                if (x == 5) {
                        document.write("<B>"+ (x + 5000) +"<\/B><BR>");
                        continue;
                }
                else {
                        document.write(x + 10 + "<BR>");
                        continue;
                }
        }

//END HIDING-->
</SCRIPT>

</HEAD>

<BODY>
</BODY>
</HTML>
```

The previous example produces the following output:

0
10
1
11
2
12
3
13
4
14
5
5005
6
16

Mini-Example:

This example uses the **break** Statement to terminate the **while()** Loop when **x** is equivalent to 7; otherwise, the **continue** Statement causes the **while()** Loop to cycle again.

```
x = 0;

while (x <= 10) {

        x = x + 1;
        if (x == 7) {
                x = x + 10;
                document.write("x=" + x + "<BR>");
                break;
        }
        else {
                document.write("x=" + x + "<BR>");
                continue;
        }
}
```

The previous example produces the following output:

x=1
x=2
x=3
x=4
x=5
x=6
x=17

This example demonstrates the use of **labeled** Statements that contain **while()** Statements having **continue** Statements with a **label**. The first use of a continue Statement jumps to the **myLabeled1** Statement and the second use jumps to the **myLabeled2** Statement. Look at the output for this example after the code to facilitate the following of the sequence of the Script.

Example 5-2:   **Sample602.html**

```
<!DOCTYPE HTML PUBLIC "-//W3C//DTD HTML 3.2//EN">
<HTML><HEAD>
<TITLE>Sample 602 - Example 5-2     continue and labeled Statement </TITLE>

<SCRIPT LANGUAGE="JavaScript1.2"><!--BEGIN HIDING

x=0;
y=0;

myLabeled1 :
       while (x < 10) {
               document.write("x=" + x + "<BR>");

               myLabeled2 :
                       while (y < 8) {
                               if (y == 5) {
                                       document.write("y=" + (y + 10) + "<BR>");
                                       y++;
                                       continue myLabeled1;
                               }
                               else {
                                       document.write("y=" + (y + 100) + "<BR>");
                                       y++;
                                       continue myLabeled2;
                               }
                       }
               x+=3;
       }

//END HIDING-->
</SCRIPT>
</HEAD><BODY></BODY></HTML>
```

The previous example produces the following output:

x=0
y=100
y=101
y=102
y=103
y=104
y=15
x=0
y=106
y=107
x=3
x=6
x=9

Object Manipulation Statements

The <u>for...in</u> Statement

JavaScript Syntax:

```
for (var variable in object) {
     statements;
}
```

Parameters Defined:

This Statement is of dubious practical value until you get into advanced scripting.

The **for...in** Statement is technically a Loop Statement but it has a special purpose in that it operates exclusively on the Properties of an Object. The specified **variable** Argument is iterated over all of the Properties of the specified **object** Argument. Then for each unique Property of the **object**, the **statements** block is executed.

Think of the specified **object** so that each Property of that **object** will sequentially be represented by the the **variable** Argument, like an automated Array.

Additionally each Property can have its <u>Value</u> represented as an Array Element where the **variable** Argument can iterate over the Array Elements individually by substituting that **variable** for the **index** integer of its Array Element. This will become more clear by looking at an example.

Note that the **object** Argument is a reference to the Object itself and not to the String Name of the Object. That means don't enclose the **object** Argument in quotes.

Mini-Example:

First an Object named **myObj** is created with Literal notation that has three Properties named **title**, **author** and **pages** respectively. Then the for...in Statement is used to write each Property **i** to screen and then each Property Value **myObj[i]** to screen.

```
<SCRIPT LANGUAGE="JavaScript1.2"><!--BEGIN HIDING

myObj =  {title:"My Book", author:"Gilorien", pages:1100}

for (var i in myObj) {

     document.write("Prop Name = <B>" + i + "<\/B> has Value= ");
     document.write("<B>" + myObj[i] + "<\/B><BR>");
}

//END HIDING-->
</SCRIPT>
```

The preceding Script produces the following output:

Property Name = **title** with Value= **My Book**
Property Name = **author** with Value= **Gilorien**
Property Name = **pages** with Value= **1100**

Mini-Example:

In this next Script, the previous Script is slightly modified to output the Properties and Values of the **document** Object:

```
<SCRIPT LANGUAGE="JavaScript1.2"><!--BEGIN HIDING

for (var i in document) {

    document.write("Prop Name = <B>" + i + "<\/B> has Value= ");
    document.write("<B>" + document[i] + "<\/B><BR>");
}

//END HIDING-->
</SCRIPT>
```

which produces the following output in the browser:

Prop Name = **forms** has Value= **{length:undefined}**
Prop Name = **links** has Value= **{length:undefined}**
Prop Name = **anchors** has Value= **{length:undefined}**
Prop Name = **applets** has Value= **{length:undefined}**
Prop Name = **embeds** has Value= **{length:undefined}**
Prop Name = **images** has Value= **{length:undefined}**
Prop Name = **title** has Value= **Sample 604 - Example 5-4 for...in Statement**
Prop Name = **URL** has Value= **file:///Mac-HD/HTML_BOOK/Sample604.html**
Prop Name = **referrer** has Value=
Prop Name = **lastModified** has Value= **Jan 13 14:12:23 1928**
Prop Name = **cookie** has Value= **testCookie=Gil_Lorien**
Prop Name = **domain** has Value=
Prop Name = **bgColor** has Value= **#ffffff**
Prop Name = **fgColor** has Value= **#000000**
Prop Name = **linkColor** has Value= **#0000ff**
Prop Name = **vlinkColor** has Value= **#9323fd**
Prop Name = **alinkColor** has Value= **#ff0000**
Prop Name = **width** has Value= **519**
Prop Name = **height** has Value= **296**

The <u>with( )</u> Statement

The **with( )** Statement is very practical and will save you a lot of typing when authoring. It is used to specify, once, which Object that your Script is referencing in the subsequent **statements** so that you don't have to repeatedly specify a complete Object reference for each of those Statements in the block. The **object** Argument specifies the default Object for the block of **statements**. It can be any valid Object that the browser has created automatically with the runtime engine or any Objects that are created by the author.

You should basically consider the **with()** Statement as a shorthand way of coding references to an Object for the Properties that are referred to in the **statements** block.

Note that the **object** Argument is a reference to the Object itself and not to the String Name of the Object. That means don't enclose the **object** Argument in quotes.

JavaScript Syntax:

```
with (object) {
      statements;
}
```

Mini-Example:

This example uses the **with()** Statement, where the **document** Object is the default Object, to assign Values to the **bgColor** and **fgColor** Properties. Without using the **with()** Statement they would have to be written like this:

```
document.bgColor = "blue";
document.fgColor = "white";
```

and then rewriting them using the **with()** Statement:

```
with (document) {

      bgColor = "blue";
      fgColor = "white";
}
```

Mini-Example:

This example uses the **with()** Statement, where **document.form1** is the default Object. It is used to add three **option** Objects to the **select** Object named **select1** in the **form** Object named **form1**.

```
<FORM NAME="form1">
<SELECT NAME="select1" >
<OPTION VALUE="purple" SELECTED>      Choose Purple
<OPTION VALUE="orange">               Choose Orange
<OPTION VALUE="yellow">               Choose Yellow
<OPTION VALUE="green">                Choose Green
</SELECT>
</FORM>

<SCRIPT LANGUAGE="JavaScript1.2"><!--BEGIN HIDING

     option5 = new Option("Choose Blue", "blue");
     option6 = new Option("Choose Red", "red");
     option7 = new Option("Choose Lime", "lime");

     with (document.form1) {

          select1[4] = option5;
          select1[5] = option6;
          select1[6] = option7;

     }

//END HIDING-->
</SCRIPT>
```

Mini-Example:

If the above Form named **form1** were located in a Frame named **main**, you could use the **parent.main.document.form1** default Object in the **with()** Statement to add the Options to the Select Object from within a different document contained in the same Frameset.

```
     with (parent.main.document.form1) {

          select1[4] = option5;
          select1[5] = option6;
          select1[6] = option7;

     }
```

The <u>with( )</u> Statement in a <STYLE> Element

JavaScript Syntax:

```
with (tags.elementName) {

        stylePropertyName1 = stylePropertyValue1;
        stylePropertyName2 = stylePropertyValue2;
             . . .
        stylePropertyNameN = stylePropertyValueN;
}
```

Parameters Defined:

As mentioned in previous chapters on Styles, you can use the **with()** Statement where the **tags** Object is the default Object and you also specify the name of the particular HTML Element that you want to assign Style Properties to with **elementName**. In this case, the block of Statements are all of the **stylePropertyName1 = stylePropertyValue1** assignment pairs. Remember that this can only be done inside of the <STYLE> Element, and the TYPE Attribute must be set to "**text/JavaScript**".

Mini-Example:

Here's a quick reminder example, so you don't have to flip pages:

```
<STYLE TYPE="text/JavaScript">

    with (tags.H2) {

            fontSize="42pt";

            color="blue";

            borderStyle="groove";

            borderWidths("25px");

            borderColor="aqua";
    }

</STYLE>
```

The <u>var</u> Statement

JavaScript Syntax:

```
var identifier;
var identifier = expression;
identifier = expression;
```

Parameters Defined:

Basically, a Variable is a named holder for a Value in your Script, like a crackerbox is a container of crackers with a name of saltines on the outside of the box.

The **var** Keyword is used to declare a Variable. If used inside a Function then the **var** Keyword must be used. If used outside a Function then it is optional and is said to be a global Variable. Variables that are declared inside a Function are said to be local and are not recognized outside that Function. If you choose not to use the **var** Keyword outside a Function then you must assign it an **expression** when you declare it. Note that the **expression** Parameter can be a simple Value.

You can assign practically anything to a Variable, including but not limited to: Strings, Numbers, Booleans, Objects and Numeric Literals.

The **identifier** is the name of the Variable. It must start with either an uppercase or lowercase letter or an underscore(_) Character. After that, the subsequent Characters may also be numbers. Remember that JavaScript is case-sensitive, unlike HTML, so when you refer to a Variable, the reference must be spelled exactly the same as when it was declared or you will generate an error.

Data Type Conversion

On a different note, because JavaScript is a loosely-typed Language, you can define a Variable with one type of Value, like a String, and later in the Script you can assign the same Variable a Number without generating an error. This means that the data type does not have to be declared when the Variable is declared. (Actually you can't declare the data type even if you wanted to.) JavaScript does the data type-conversion internally and automatically. Note that this is different from Java, which is a strongly-typed language.

External Referencing of Variables

You can reference Variables by name from another Frame or Window by specifying the name of the containing Frame or Window with normal Object Hierarchy referencing. For instance, if you have a Variable named **myVar1** in a Frame named **myFrame1** and you wanted to assign it a new Value from another Frame in the same Frameset, you would use this code:

```
parent.myFrame1.myVar1 = "whatever value";
```

Mini-Examples:

Here are a few examples of declaring Variables:

```
var myColor = "blue";
var myNumber = 42;
var x;
var myOtherNumber = x + 55;
var myNumericString = "7777";
myAlbum = "Wake of the Flood";
```

This example demonstrates Global Variables.

Example 5-3:   Sample603.html

```
<!DOCTYPE HTML PUBLIC "-//W3C//DTD HTML 3.2//EN">
<HTML>
<HEAD>
<TITLE>Sample 603 - Example 5-3   Global Variables   </TITLE>
<BASEFONT SIZE="7">
</HEAD>
<BODY TEXT="#ffffff">

<LAYER ID="layer1" LEFT="10" TOP="200" WIDTH="300" BGCOLOR="magenta">
        Test Layer 1    </LAYER>

<LAYER ID="layer2" LEFT="10" TOP="300" WIDTH="450" BGCOLOR="navy">
        Test Layer 2    </LAYER>

<FORM NAME="form1">
<INPUT TYPE="button" VALUE="Hide L1" onClick="hideLayers(L1);">
<INPUT TYPE="button" VALUE="Hide L2" onClick="hideLayers(L2);">

<INPUT TYPE="button" VALUE="Show L1" onClick="showLayers(L1);">
<INPUT TYPE="button" VALUE="Show L2" onClick="showLayers(L2);">
</FORM>

<SCRIPT LANGUAGE="JavaScript1.2"><!--BEGIN HIDING

        var L1 = document.layer1;
        var L2 = document.layer2;

function hideLayers(h)  { h.visibility = "hide"; }

function showLayers(s)  { s.visibility = "show"; }

//END HIDING-->
</SCRIPT>
</BODY>
</HTML>
```

The <u>function</u> Statement

JavaScript Syntax:

```
function functionName([argument1, argument2, ..., argumentN]) {
    statements;
}
```

Parameters Defined:

The **function** Statement was covered in Chapter 4 but for completeness it is also reviewed here, with additional information. Remember from Chapter 4 that there are more ways to declare a Function than just with the **function** Statement, which is all that is covered here. The **return** Statement was only mentioned briefly in Chapter 4, so it will be examined here as it is used in the **function** Statement.

The **Arguments** of **argument1** through **argumentN** are optional and are used as placeholders to pass data Values to the block of **statements** in the Function when the Function is called. You <u>must</u> name your Function with the **functionName** parameter.

Mini-Example:

The following Function **returns** z, which in this case has the value of 1024 because the two Arguments that are passed to the Function are 24 and 1000. When the **write()** Method calls the **calculate(24,1000)** Function, it passes the two number values of 24 and 1000 as the Arguments **a** and **b**, respectively. Then, **a** and **b** are assigned to the **x** and **y** Variables, respectively. The Variable **z** is declared as the sum of **x + y**. Last, the **z** Variable is returned as the end result of the **calculate(24,1000)** Function.

Make sure that you understand that the **write()** Method, not the **calculate()** Function, is what actually renders the number 1024 to screen. The **calculate()** Function only **returns** 1024.

```
function calculate(a,b) {

    var x = a;
    var y = b;
    var z = x + y;

    return z;
}

    document.write(calculate(24,1000));
```

The <u>return</u> Statement

JavaScript Syntax:

```
return expression;
```

Parameters Defined:
The **return** Statement is used to specify the Value that is to be returned by a Function. The **expression** Parameter can be any valid Expression.

Mini-Examples:
Here are a few examples of valid Expressions that can be used in the **return** Statement:

```
return x + y;
return true;
return false;
return myArray[1];
return myStringVariable;
return 0;
return 5;
return "Have a Good One";
```

The <u>export</u> Statement

JavaScript Syntax:

```
export name1, name2, ..., nameN;
export *;
```

Parameters Defined:

The **export** Statement is used within a Signed Script to export, that is, to make Objects, Properties, and Functions available for use in other external Signed or Unsigned Scripts. The **name1** through **nameN** Parameters are a comma-separated list of the names of any Objects, Properties, or Functions that you want to export. You can optionally use the asterisk (*) in place of individual names that will export all of the Objects, Properties, and Functions in the entire Script.

In order for the receiving Script to make use of the exported data, it must use the **import** Statement. The **import** Statement is covered in the next section.

For more information on Signed Scripts, see the chapter on JavaScript Security in the JavaScript Reference on the CD-ROM.

The <u>import</u> Statement

JavaScript Syntax:

```
import objectName.name1, objectName.name2, ..., objectName.nameN;
import objectName.*;
```

Parameters Defined:

The **import** Statement is used to make Objects, Properties, and Functions available for use in a Script that have been exported from an external Signed Script with the **export** Statement. In the syntax, the **objectName** Parameter is the name of the Object that will be assigned the imported Objects, Properties, and Functions, which are specified individually by the **name1** through **nameN** Parameters. Alternatively, you can assign all of the Objects, Properties, and Functions from the exported Script to an Object, all at once, by using the asterisk (*) in place of a **nameN** Parameter.

In order for you to use the **import** Statement, you first have to load the entire Script that contains the **export** Statement into either a Layer, Frame, or Window. Only then can you use the **import** Statement to import the previously exported Objects, Properties, or Functions.

For more information on Signed Scripts, see the chapter on JavaScript Security in the JavaScript Reference on the CD-ROM.

Mini-Example:

For instance, if you used the **export** Statement to export the following Functions and Property:

```
export myFunction1, myFunction2, myProperty1;
```

then for an Object named **myObject1** and another Object named **myObject2** in a receiving Script you could use the **import** Statement in the following way:

```
import myObject1.myFunction1, myObject1.myProperty1;
import myObject2.myFunction2;
```

or if you wanted to assign all of the exported items to **myObject3**, do it like this:

```
import myObject3.*;
```

The <u>delete</u> Statement

JavaScript Syntax:

```
delete objectName.propertyName;
delete objectName[index];
delete arrayName[index];
```

Parameters Defined:

The **delete** Statement is technically a delete Operator and is new in Navigator 4. It is used to delete a Property of an Object or an Array Element. It cannot be used to delete Objects themselves or Variables. To delete an Object, you only have to set its Object reference to **null**. See Chapter 4 on Objects on page 411.

The **objectName** Parameter is the name of Object that you want to delete the Property from that is specified by **propertyName**. The **arrayName** Parameter is the name of the Array that you want to delete the Element from that is specified by the **index** Parameter, which is the zero-based integer **index** of the Array.

There is a fourth form of syntax that is possible to use, but it can only be used in the context of a **with()** Statement like this:

JavaScript Syntax:

```
with(objectName) { delete propertyName; }
```

Comment Statements

Single & multiple-line Comment Statements

JavaScript Syntax:

```
//put your single line commment here
/*put your multiple line comment here*/
```

Comment Statements are explanatory notes that the author uses within the Script to delineate the purpose of a particular line or section of code or to overview the entire Script. These Comments are ignored by the browser. There are two types of Comment Statements. Those that must be confined to one line are preceded by two sequential forward slashes(//). Multiple-line Comments are preceded by one forward slash and then an asterisk like this: (/*) and are followed by an asterisk and then a forward slash like this: (*/). These are exactly the same as Java Comments.

JavaScript Operators

What are JavaScript Operators?

The most basic definition of an Operator is that it is an action that is performed on one or more receivers that are called operands. Usually they are symbolic Characters like (+, -, *, /), but there are Special text Operators that have been created as Keywords in the JavaScript Language like **new** and **this**. In JavaScript, there are Unary and Binary Operators and one Ternary Operator (**( ) ? :**), which was covered earlier in this chapter.

Binary Operators must have two operands in order to work, like this:

```
operand1     Operator     operand2
```

For example:

```
a + b
2 * 5
```

Unary Operators only require one operand to work. In this case, the Operator can be either before or after the operand, like this:

```
operand     Operator
```

or like this:

```
Operator     operand
```

For example:

```
i++
--j
-22
```

Don't get confused about there being two plus signs. It's just a shorthand way of saying that you are adding one to the operand.

JavaScript Operators come in several categories, which are listed in the following Chart and further delineated in this section:

JavaScript Operators Categories

Special Operators
Comparison Operators
Arithmetic Operators
String Operators
Logical Operators
Assignment Operators
Bitwise Operators

Special Operators

The Keyword <u>new</u> Operator

You can use the Keyword **new** as an Operator to create an Object with each Object's unique Constructor Function or you can create your own **object** Object. Here is a list of all the predefined **objectType** Object types:

```
Array, Boolean, Date, Function, Image, Number,
Object, Option, RegExp, String
```

Mini-Examples:

Here are some examples of using the **new** Operator to create several different types of Objects.

```
myDate = new Date();
myString = new String("My text goes here");
myArray = new Array(1, 2, 3, 4, 5);
```

JavaScript Syntax:

```
objectName = new objectType ( [param1] [,param2] ...[,paramN] )
```

The Keyword <u>this</u> Statement

The **this** Keyword is used to refer to the current Object or to an optionally specified Property of the current Object. Typically, the **this** Keyword is used to refer to the calling Object in a Method invocation.

JavaScript Syntax:

```
this.object
this.object[.propertyName]
```

This example demonstrates the use of the **this** Keyword to reference the current **form** Object, which is named **form1**. That Statement further specifies that the **value** of the **t1** Textbox that is in that **form** is passed as the Argument in the **doIt()** Function, which then changes the background color of the **document** to that Value.

Example 5-4:   Sample604.html

```
<!DOCTYPE HTML PUBLIC "-//W3C//DTD HTML 3.2//EN">
<HTML>
<HEAD>
<TITLE>Sample 604 - Example 5-4   this Statement      </TITLE>
</HEAD>
<BODY>
<FORM NAME="form1">

Type in a valid color.                                    <BR>

<INPUT TYPE='text' NAME='t1' SIZE=40>                     <BR><BR>

<INPUT TYPE='button' VALUE='Change background color now.'
onClick='doIt(this.form.t1.value);'>

</FORM>

<SCRIPT LANGUAGE="JavaScript1.2"><!--BEGIN HIDING

        function doIt(c) {

                document.bgColor = c;
        }

//END HIDING-->
</SCRIPT>
</BODY>
</HTML>
```

The Keyword <u>typeof</u> Operator

JavaScript Syntax:

```
typeof operand;
typeof (operand);
```

Parameters Defined:

You can use the **typeof** Operator to return a String that represents the JavaScript Class Type of the unevaluated **operand** Argument. Unevaluated means that the **operand** Argument in this context does not get evaluated by the JavaScript runtime engine and is used solely to have its Class Type specified by the **typeof** Operator.

The **operand** Argument can be a Boolean, Number, String, Function, Variable, Array, or any valid JavaScript Object. Most Keywords can also be used. The parentheses are optional but it's a good idea to use them for readability.

Mini-Examples:

Here are some examples of the Strings that **typeof** returns for various operands:

<u>typeof</u>	<u>operand</u>	<u>Returned String</u>
typeof	true	boolean
typeof	false	boolean
typeof	null	object
typeof	this	object
typeof	777	number
typeof	"test message"	string
typeof	"555"	string
typeof	document.form1.text1.value	string
typeof	document.bgColor	string
typeof	window.width	number
typeof	window	object
typeof	document	object
typeof	Date	function
typeof	Function	function
typeof	Array	function
typeof	Number	function
typeof	window.moveTo	function
typeof	moveTo	function

General <u>typeof</u> returns Rules

For Methods, Functions and Predefined Objects, **typeof** returns **function**.

For Object Instances, **typeof** returns **object**.

For Properties, **typeof** returns the type for the particular Value in that Property.

For Variables, **typeof** returns the type for the particular data type contained in that Variable which, of course, can vary.

<u>Mini-Examples:</u>

For the following Variables:

```
var myArray = [1,2,3,4,5];
var myString ="Hi there.";
var myNumber = 5;
var booleanTest = true;
var myDate = new Date();
var to2 = typeof (myString);
```

typeof returns the following String:

<u>typeof</u>	<u>var operand</u>	<u>Returned String</u>
typeof	myArray	object
typeof	myString	string
typeof	myNumber	number
typeof	booleanTest	boolean
typeof	myDate	object
typeof	to2	string

The Keyword <u>void</u> Operator

You can use the **void** Operator to evaluate an expression without returning a value. This is mainly used when you want to make use of the Event Handlers of a Link without letting the Link actually jump to a new page. In that case, you would include an expression like 0 that will have no effect on the Link when the **void** Keyword is used as the Value of the HREF Property. For instance:

Mini-Example:

```
<A HREF="javascript:void(0)"
onMouseOver="window.status='Put Message Here'; return true;">
Mouse me for status info.</A>
```

Note that JavaScript **void** does not have the same capabilities and is not used in the same way as Java **void**.

JavaScript Syntax:

```
javascript:void (expression);
javascript:void expression;
```

The (**,**) Comma Operator

The comma Operator (,) is specified by only the comma Character (,), not by or together with the word comma. It evaluates both of its operands and returns the value of the second operand. Its primary use is in a **for()** Statement when you want to increment two different Variables in the same Statement. For instance:

Mini-Example:

```
for(var i=0, j=0; j<5; i++, j++) {

        document.write(i + j);
}
```

Note that you can also use the comma Character (**,**) to declare more than one Variable with a single **var** Keyword like this:

```
var myNum1=5, myNum2=42, myNum3=77;
```

Comparison Operators

Comparison Operators compare the two **operands** and return a Boolean **true** or **false** based on that comparison. The **operands** can be Numbers, Strings, or an Expression that evaluates to a Number or String. Because they return a Boolean Value, they are often used in **if()** Statements as part of the **condition**.

Operator		Description
==	Equal to	Returns true if the operands are equal.
!=	Not equal to	Returns true if the operands are not equal.
>	Greater than	Returns true if the left operand is greater than right operand.
>=	Greater than or equal to	Returns true if the left operand is greater than or equal to the right operand.
<	Less than	Returns true if the left operand is less than the right operand.
<=	Less than or equal to	Returns true if the left operand is less than or equal to the right operand.

Arithmetic Operators

The Arithmetic Operators return a single value after performing the particular operation on the two **operands**. In this case the **operands** can be Numbers or Variables.

Operator		Description
+	Addition	Normal addition
-	Subtraction	Normal subtraction
-	Unary Negation	Causes a positive number to be negative and vice versa. Note that when negating a negative number you must enclose the negative operand inside of parentheses, otherwise JavaScript will perform a decrement (--) operation instead.
*	Multiplication	Normal multiplication
/	Division	Normal division

%	Modulus	Returns the remainder of a Division Operation on two operands where the first operand is divided by the second operand.

++   Increment

A Unary Operator that adds one to its operand.
When used before its operand like this: ++x
it <u>returns</u> the Vaue of the operand <u>before</u> adding one.
When used after its operand like this: x++
it <u>returns</u> the Vaue of the operand <u>after</u> adding one.

--   Decrement

A Unary Operator that subtracts one from its operand.
When used before its operand like this: --x
it <u>returns</u> the Vaue of the operand <u>before</u> adding one.
When used after its operand like this: x--
it <u>returns</u> the Vaue of the operand <u>after</u> adding one.

String Operators

The String Operators take two String operands and join them together and return that concatenated String. For example, if:

       myString1 = "Hello"   and   **myString2** = "there"

then:

       `myString1 + myString2 = "Hello there"`

+	String Concatenation	Adds two **String** Objects.
+=	Concatenation & Assignment	Adds two **String** Objects and assigns the new Concatenated **String** Object to the first operand. This is just a shorthand version of x = x + y.

Logical Operators

The Logical Operators return a Boolean Value of true or false based on the two Boolean operands that are evaluated.

&&	Logical AND	Returns true if both logical operands are true. Returns false if either logical operand is false.
| |	Logical OR	Returns true if either logical expression is true. Returns false if both are false.
!	Logical negation	Returns true if its single operand is false. Returns false if its single operand is true.

Assignment Operators

The basic Assignment Operator is the equals (=) sign. The operand on the right side of the equals sign is assigned to the operand on the left side of the equals sign. The rest of the Assignment Operators follow this paradigm and are shorthand versions of standard operations.

=	The first operand is assigned the value of the second operand.
+=	The first and second operands are added and assigned to the first operand.
-=	The second operand is subtracted from the first operand, and the result is assigned to the first operand.
*=	Multiplies two numbers and assigns the result to the first operand.
/=	The first operand is divided by the second operand, and the result is assigned to the first operand.
%=	The modulus of two numbers is computed and the result is assigned to the first operand.
&=	A bitwise AND is performed and the first operand is assigned the result.
^=	A bitwise XOR is performed and the first operand is assigned the result.
|=	A bitwise OR is performed and the first operand is assigned the result.
<<=	A left shift is performed and the first operand is assigned the result.
>>=	A sign-propagating right shift is performed and the first operand is assigned the result.
>>>=	A zero-fill right shift is performed and the first operand is assigned the result.

Bitwise Operators

The Bitwise Operators operate on operands that are composed of bits, that is, zeros and ones. However, they return standard JavaScript numbers. It will probably be a long time, if ever, that you actually use these things.

&	(Bitwise AND)	If bits of both operands are ones, then it returns a one in each bit position.
^	(Bitwise XOR)	If bits of either one but not both operands are one, then it returns a one in a bit position.
|	(Bitwise OR)	If bits of either operand is one it returns a one in a bit.
~	(Bitwise NOT)	Reverses the bits of its operand. (A bit-flipper)
<<	(Left shift)	The second operand shifts the first operand to the left by its specified number of bits using binary representation, that is, shifting in zeros from the right.
>>	(Sign-propagating right shift)	The second operand shifts the first operand to the right by its specified number of bits using binary representation, that is, discarding bits shifted off.
>>>	(Zero-fill right shift)	The second operand shifts the first operand to the right by its specified number of bits using binary representation, that is, discarding bits shifted off and shifting in zeros from the left.

JavaScript Expressions

An Expression is any sequence of Variables, Literals, Operators, and even other Expressions that eventually evaluates to a single Value. They can have Values of Strings, Numbers, Numeric Strings, or Booleans. You can even have a Variable that is assigned an Array Element. Additionally you can have a Variable with a **null** Value, which is different from a Variable that has not been assigned a Value, which would be **undefined**.

Note that if you have a Variable that is **undefined**, and in the course of the Script you inadvertently try to use it as if it actually had a number in it, you will generate a runtime error. In complex Scripts, you should set up your code to account for error generation.

Array Elements that have not yet been assigned a Value will evaluate to **false**, not **undefined**.

Mini-Examples:

Here are some examples of Expressions:

```
x = 5

x= y + 2

myVariable  ==  false

22 + 55

myStr = myStr2 + myStr3

myString = "hi" + "there"

e.which == 7
```

Part II

JavaScript 1.2

Chapter 6

JavaScript Events

Chapter 6
JavaScript Events

Contents

Event Objects & Handlers

The JavaScript Event Model

If you are completely unfamiliar with the Event Model, you may need to refer to the JavaScript 1.2 Guide or the JavaScript 1.2 Reference from Netscape, which is free to download from their website. Netscape will always have the most current version, but for a quick fix, there is version 1.2 and 1.3 of the JavaScript Guide, the JavaScript 1.2 and 1.3 Reference, and the DHTML Guide on the enclosed CD-ROM.

This is an overview of the Event Model with more detailed explanations for some of the more interesting and useful capabilities, especially the new stuff in version 1.2. This is not a complete reference work on JavaScript.

Overview

All Events such as CLICK or KEYPRESS are **Event** Objects in JavaScript, and as such, they have Properties associated with them that provide information about the Event. There are no Methods associated with **Event** Objects, but there are Methods such as **captureEvents()** that are available for other Objects like the **document** Object that are used to manipulate Events. There are also Event Handlers such as **onClick** and **onKeyPress**, which basically specify an action or sequence of actions to occur when an Event happens.

Aside from the Stylistic embellishments, JavaScript is essentially Event-Driven, that is, you use Events and Event Handlers to manipulate your documents. Events occur when users click on a Link or a Button in a FORM Element or when the user moves the mouse over or away from an Image or Link. With the new **captureEvents()**, Method you can actually capture Events in a **Layer** or nested **Layer** before the Event gets to the containing Window or its intended target and script actions for it.

This chapter lays out the groundwork for understanding how Events and Event Handlers work. It includes detailed explanations of the **Event** Object, and a lot of practical Examples and Sample Files to show you how to implement Events into your code. There are also some examples that go through some of the drudge work in determining the behind-the-scenes information necessary to use Events effectively, but which isn't readily available elsewhere.

You can create code that will allow the user to drag and reposition **Layers** so that the page can be totally custom designed or manipulate the contents of the page in playing a game like Chess. (There is a working Chess Program in this chapter.) You can Script the page so that the user can use keystrokes to accomplish menu commands just like in normal programs. There are almost endless possibilities, so let's get started.

One final note: The Properties that are listed in the Event Properties Chart on page 526 is a complete list of all possible Properties for all Events. All of these Properties are not available for each Event. Check the subsequent chart on page 529 to see which Properties are associated and available for that particular Event.

JavaScript Event Objects and Event Handlers

The following is a list of the JavaScript **Event** Objects and **Event** Handlers. Remember that JavaScript is case-sensitive; if you are writing code specifically for versions of JavaScript prior to version 1.2, then both the **Event** Object and the **Event** Handler must be in all lowercase. Netscape claims that since JavaScript1.2 you can write the **Event** Handlers in the more familiar interCap way as seen below, but I've found it buggy and unreliable to do so for Events that are assigned by <u>Property Assignment</u>. For Events that are assigned by <u>Attribute Assignment</u>, it is still fine. See pages 530-533 for information on <u>Property Assignment</u> and <u>Attribute Assignment</u> of Events. Note that the **dblclick** Event is not implemented on the Macintosh platform.

<u>Event Object</u>	<u>Event Handler</u>	<u>Objects the Event is built-in for, (uncaptured):</u>
abort	onAbort	images
blur	onBlur	windows (<BODY>), layers, form elements
change	onChange	text fields, textareas, select lists
click	onClick	all types of buttons
		documents, links, checkboxes
dblclick	onDblClick	documents, areas, links
dragdrop	onDragDrop	windows
error	onError	images, windows
focus	onFocus	windows (<BODY>), layers, form elements
keydown	onKeyDown	documents, images, links, textareas
keypress	onKeyPress	documents, images, links, textareas
keyup	onKeyUp	documents, images, links, textareas
load	onLoad	windows (<BODY>), images, layers
mousedown	onMouseDown	documents, buttons, links
mousemove	onMouseMove	nothing by default
mouseout	onMouseOut	areas, links, layers
mouseover	onMouseOver	areas, links, layers
mouseup	onMouseUp	documents, buttons, links
move	onMove	windows
reset	onReset	forms
resize	onResize	windows
select	onSelect	text fields, textareas
submit	onSubmit	forms
unload	onUnload	windows (<BODY>)

JavaScript Syntax:

```
event.propertyName
```

Event Properties Summaries Chart

Event Properties:

Property	Description
type	Returns a String that represents the type of Event like **"click"**, **"mousedown"**, or **"keypress"**.
target	Returns a Reference that represents the Object to which the Event was originally sent. For a Button named "b1", (**event.target.name == "b1"**) would return true when that Button is clicked. Note that you access the **target** Property via its **name** Property.
layerX	Returns a Number that specifies the cursor's horizontal **x**-coordinate in pixels relative to the <u>Layer</u> in which the Event occurred, unless the **resize** Event occurs. In that case, it passes the Object's Width when passed along with the **resize** Event.
layerY	Returns a Number that specifies the cursor's vertical **y**-coordinate in pixels relative to the <u>Layer</u> in which the Event occurred, unless the **resize** Event occurs. In that case it passes the Object's Height when passed along with the **resize** Event.
width	Same as **layerX** but more intuitive syntax for the **resize** Event.
height	Same as **layerY** but more intuitive syntax for the **resize** Event.
x	Same as **layerX**.
y	Same as **layerY**.
pageX	Returns a Number that specifies the cursor's horizontal **x**-coordinate in pixels, relative to the page.
pageY	Returns a Number that specifies the cursor's vertical **y**-coordinate in pixels relative to the page.
screenX	Returns a Number that specifies the cursor's horizontal **x**-coordinate in pixels, relative to the screen.
screenY	Returns a Number that specifies the cursor's vertical **y**-coordinate in pixels, relative to the screen.
data	Returns an Array of Strings consisting of the URLs of all Objects that are dropped into the Window and passes them with the **dragdrop** Event.
which	Returns an Integer that specifies the ASCII Value of a Key that was pressed or the ASCII Value of the mouse button that was pressed.
modifiers	Returns an Integer that specifies the ASCII Value of the **modifiers** Key that was pressed in association with a mouse or Key Event. The **modifiers** Key Constant Values are: ALT_MASK, CONTROL_MASK, SHIFT_MASK, and META_MASK. Their associated ASCII Integer Values when used both individually and in various combinations are listed in the following chart.

Modifiers Keys and ASCII Values Chart

This chart shows the ASCII Value that is returned to the **modifiers** Property when a mouse or keystroke Event occurs. If no Modifiers Key is used, then **modifiers=0**.

Modifiers Key and/or combination		ASCII Value
ALT_MASK	(the Apple Option Key) =	1
CONTROL_MASK	=	2
ALT_MASK + CONTROL_MASK	=	3
SHIFT_MASK	=	4
ALT_MASK + SHIFT_MASK	=	5
CONTROL_MASK + SHIFT_MASK	=	6
ALT_MASK + CONTROL_MASK + SHIFT_MASK	=	7
META_MASK	(the Apple Command Key) =	8
META_MASK + ALT_MASK	=	9
META_MASK + CONTROL_MASK	=	10
META_MASK + ALT_MASK + CONTROL_MASK	=	11
META_MASK + SHIFT_MASK	=	12
META_MASK + SHIFT_MASK + ALT_MASK	=	13
META_MASK + SHIFT_MASK + CONTROL_MASK	=	14
META_MASK + SHIFT_MASK + CONTROL_MASK + ALT_MASK	=	15
If no Modifiers Keys are used for an Event, then **modifiers**	=	0

The Structure of an Event Object

This is what a typical **mouseup Event** Object looks like that is produced by the JavaScript Interpreter in Navigator, which shows its Properties and Values:

```
{type:"mouseup", x:385, y:235, width:undefined, height:undefined,
layerX:385, layerY:235, which:1, modifiers:0, data:undefined,
pageX:395, pageY:245, screenX:494, screenY:323, target:}
```

This is a typical **keyup** Event when the Modifiers Keys of META and CONTROL are pressed and the "**t**" Key is pressed producing the Event **e**:

```
{type:"keyup", x:329, y:116, width:undefined, height:undefined,
layerX:329, layerY:116, which:20, modifiers:10, data:undefined,
pageX:329, pageY:116, screenX:428, screenY:194, target:}
```

where **e.which** = 20   because 20 is the ASCII Integer Value for "t"
and   where **e.modifiers** = 10 because 10 is the ASCII Integer Value for META+CONTROL

Knowing how an Event is organized makes it easier to understand how to test for conditions within Statements when you want to base your code options around Events.

For example, you can test for the condition of the ALT Key being pressed with the **modifiers** Property of the Event and have code to execute if that condition is true like this:

```
if (e.modifiers == Event.ALT_MASK)
        alert ("The Alt key was down for the event.");
```

This assumes that you are using the "**e**" as the Event Argument in a Function so that it passes the Event to the Function. For example:

```
function myEventTester(e) {
        if (e.modifiers == Event.CONTROL_MASK)
                alert ("The CONTROL key was pressed.");
}
```

Here are two other ways to test for the ALT Key being pressed with the first using the Bitwise AND "&" Operator and the second using the more familiar Comparison Equals "==" Operator:

```
if (e.modifiers & Event.ALT_MASK)
```

```
if (e.modifiers == 1)
```

If you remember from the previous chart on Modifiers Keys, the ASCII Value that is returned to the **modifiers** Property is **1** when the ALT Key is pressed.

Specifying an Event by name with dot notation

You specify an Event with dot notation by referring to an **Event Constant** to call an Event in an Expression. The **Event Constant** is always typed in allcaps, *not* interCap, and must be prepended with the word **Event**, like this:

```
Event.MOUSEDOWN
Event.MOUSEUP
Event.MOUSEMOVE
Event.KEYPRESS
```

For instance, when capturing Events (see page 543+ on the **captureEvents()** Method) for a Layer named **myLayer**, you specify which Event or Events (separate each by a vertical bar (|) character) you want to capture, like this:

```
document.myLayer.document.captureEvents(Event.CLICK)
document.myLayer.document.captureEvents(Event.KEYUP|Event.KEYDOWN)
```

Available Event Properties for each Event Object

The following Chart specifes the **Event** Object Properties that are available for each **Event** Object. Once again, the **dblclick** Event is not implemented on the Macintosh.

Event Object   Available Event Properties

abort	type, target
blur	type, target
change	type, target
click	type, target, which, modifiers

Note: When a Link, Layer or the Document or Window is clicked, the following six Properties represent the mouse cursor location, but are unused if a Button is clicked:

layerX, layerY, pageX, pageY, screenX, screenY

dblclick	type, target, which, modifiers, layerX, layerY, pageX, pageY, screenX, screenY
dragdrop	type, target, data
error	type, target
focus	type, target
keydown	type, target, which, modifiers, layerX, layerY, pageX, pageY, screenX, screenY
keypress	type, target, which, modifiers, layerX, layerY, pageX, pageY, screenX, screenY
keyup	type, target, which, modifiers, layerX, layerY, pageX, pageY, screenX, screenY
load	type, target
mousedown	type, target, which, modifiers, layerX, layerY, pageX, pageY, screenX, screenY
mousemove	type, target, layerX, layerY, pageX, pageY, screenX, screenY
mouseout	type, target, layerX, layerY, pageX, pageY, screenX, screenY
mouseover	type, target, layerX, layerY, pageX, pageY, screenX, screenY
mouseup	type, target, which, modifiers, layerX, layerY, pageX, pageY, screenX, screenY
move	type, target, screenX, screenY
reset	type, target
resize	type, target, width, height
select	type, target
submit	type, target
unload	type, target

Defining Event Handlers

You can define your Event Handlers with either the <u>Property Assignment</u> or the HTML Element <u>Attribute</u> approach. The latter approach is used more frequently by authors and has the benefit of increased flexibility. There is one major difference between these two techniques that must be remembered: When you assign a Function to an Event Handler as a JavaScript <u>Property</u> the **event** Argument is automatically included. When you add an Event Handler as an <u>Attribute</u> in an HTML Tag, the Function's **event** Argument must be supplied by you with the **event** Keyword. <u>Property Assignment</u> is demonstrated in Example 6-0 and <u>Attribute Assignment</u> is demonstrated in Example 6-1.

Special Notice:

I've found that using the <u>interCap</u> spelling for Event Handlers when using the <u>Property Assignment</u> approach can cause minor bugs in your program, so for now stick with the all lowercase spelling like this: **onmousedown**, until Netscape fixes it.

Defining Event Handlers by <u>Property Assignment</u>

When you assign a Function to an Event Handler by <u>Property Assignment</u>, it is a very straightforward process. Just write the name of the Event Handler and set it equal to the Function that you want to assign to it, making sure that you <u>*don't*</u> include the normally occurring parentheses. The reason that the parentheses are omitted is that a <u>reference</u> to the Function is being supplied to the Event Handler because Event Handlers cannot take Arguments. For instance, the Function **keyTest(e)** in Example 6-0 is assigned to the **onmousedown** Event Handler of the **document** Object like this:

```
document.onmousedown = keyTest;
```

Testing for <u>Modifiers</u> Keys in Conditionals

In the following Example 6-0, the Function **keyTest(e)** is used to trigger **alert** Windows with different messages when each of the Modifiers Keys are pressed in concert with a **mousedown** Event. The Function **keyTest2(e)** is used to trigger **alert** Windows that contain information about the **type**, **which**, **layerX**, **layerY**, and **modifiers** Properties of the **keydown** Event. Both Functions are initially defined in a SCRIPT in the HEAD of the document and then assigned to their respective Event Properties in a separate SCRIPT in the BODY of the document.

Example 6-0:   Sample700.html

```
<!DOCTYPE HTML PUBLIC "-//W3C//DTD HTML 3.2//EN">
<HTML>
<HEAD>
<TITLE>Sample 700 - Example 6-0      Key Events, Modifier Keys and Alerts </TITLE>

<SCRIPT LANGUAGE="JavaScript1.2"><!--BEGIN HIDING

function keyTest(e) {          .

 if (e.modifiers == Event.ALT_MASK)
  alert ("The Alt key was down for the event which is the option key to Macs.");

 else if (e.modifiers == Event.CONTROL_MASK)
  alert ("The Control key was down for the event.");

 else if (e.modifiers == Event.SHIFT_MASK)
  alert ("The Shift key was down for the event.");

 else if (e.modifiers == Event.META_MASK)
  alert ("The Meta key was down for the event which is the Command key to Macs.");

 else
  alert ("There was no modifiers key held down for the event.");

 return true;
}

/*----------------------------------------------------------------------------*/
/*----------------------------------------------------------------------------*/

function keyTest2(e) {

 if (e.modifiers == Event.ALT_MASK  &&  e.which) {
  alert ("Your Document got an Event of type:  " + e.type);
  alert ("Your Document also had the key pressed with the value of:  " + e.which)
  alert ("The modifiers Key used was:  " + e.modifiers);
 }
 else {
  alert ("Your Document got an Event of type:  " + e.type);
  alert ("The modifiers Key used was:  " + e.modifiers);
  alert ("The x position of the Mouse was:  " + e.layerX);
  alert ("The y position of the Mouse was:  " + e.layerY);
 }
 return true;
}

/*--------------------------------------------------------------------------*/

//END HIDING-->
</SCRIPT>

</HEAD>
```

```
<BODY BGCOLOR="BLACK" TEXT="WHITE">

<LAYER ID="TestLayer" LEFT="10" TOP="10" WIDTH="400" BGCOLOR="red">
<SPAN STYLE="color:black; font-size:22pt;">
        This is a simple example which shows you how to test for and use the
Modifier Keys to control what happens when onMouseDown and onKeyDown Events occur.
Try clicking the mouse

<SPAN STYLE="color:white;">   outside        </SPAN>

of the Layer with the red background or pressing a key on the keyboard with or
without the Alt, Control, Shift or Command keys to see what happens.

</SPAN>
</LAYER>

<!--   ********************************************************************   -->

<SCRIPT LANGUAGE="JavaScript1.2"><!--BEGIN HIDING

            document.onmousedown = keyTest;
            document.onkeydown = keyTest2;

//END HIDING-->
</SCRIPT>

</BODY>
</HTML>
```

Defining Event Handlers by <u>Attribute Assignment</u>

The JavaScript <u>event</u> Keyword

When you assign a Function with an Event Argument to an Attribute of an HTML Element you have to manually supply the **Event** Object by using the **event** Keyword as the Argument parameter. The reason for this is that the **Event** Object <u>Reference</u> does not get passed automatically by the JavaScript compiler, so you have to do it explicitly.

This is demonstrated in the following example where the Function **buttonTest1(e)** tests for the ALT and SHIFT Modifiers Keys, and if either of them are pressed when the Button **b1** is clicked, the background color of the document gets changed to a different color.

Example 6-1:   Sample701.html

```
<!DOCTYPE HTML PUBLIC "-//W3C//DTD HTML 3.2//EN">
<HTML>
<HEAD>
<TITLE>Sample 701 - Example 6-1       Key Events </TITLE>

<SCRIPT LANGUAGE="JavaScript1.2"><!--BEGIN HIDING

function buttonTest1(e) {

        if (e.modifiers == Event.ALT_MASK)
              document.bgColor = "blue";

        if (e.modifiers == Event.SHIFT_MASK)
              document.bgColor = "#7700ff";

 return true;
}
/*-------------------------------------------------------------------------*/
//END HIDING-->
</SCRIPT>
</HEAD>

<BODY BGCOLOR="BLACK" TEXT="WHITE">

<LAYER ID="TestLayer" LEFT="10" TOP="10" WIDTH="400" BGCOLOR="steelblue">
<SPAN STYLE="color:black; font-size:22pt;">

        Hold down the Option/Alt Key and click the button to change the background
color to

<SPAN STYLE="color:blue;">     blue    </SPAN>.<BR><BR>

        Hold down the Shift Key and click the button to change the background color
to real

<SPAN STYLE="color:#7700ff;"> purple  </SPAN>.</SPAN>

<!--It's important to note that the event argument is supplied in
        buttonTest1(event)
        for the onClick Event Handler and has to be spelled in all lowercase!!!-->
<HR>
<FORM NAME="form1">

<INPUT TYPE="button" NAME="B1" VALUE="Change the Background Color"
onClick="buttonTest1(event);">

</FORM>
<HR>
</LAYER>

</BODY>
</HTML>
```

Testing for Multiple Modifiers Keys in Conditionals

This example expands on the previous example by testing for the pressing of <u>multiple</u> Modifiers Keys to change the background color of a Layer. It uses the **event** Keyword in the **onMouseDown** Event Handler of the button named **b1** to pass the **Event** Object to the Function **buttonTest2(e)** for processing.

Example 6-2:   **Sample702.html**

```
<!DOCTYPE HTML PUBLIC "-//W3C//DTD HTML 3.2//EN">
<HTML><HEAD>
<TITLE>Sample 702 - Example 6-2 KeyPress Events </TITLE></HEAD>

<BODY BGCOLOR="BLACK" TEXT="WHITE">

<HR>
<FORM NAME="form1">

<INPUT TYPE="button" NAME="b1" VALUE="Change the Layer Background Color"
onMouseDown="buttonTest2(event);">
</FORM> <HR>

<LAYER ID="TestLayer" LEFT="10" TOP="150" WIDTH="550" BGCOLOR="cyan">
<SPAN STYLE="color:black; font-size:15pt; text-align:right;">

Press one of the following modifiers keys and click the button to change the
background color of the TestLayer Layer.<BR><BR>

ALT_MASK                          =    1      red background         <BR>
META_MASK + SHIFT_MASK            =    12     yellow background      <BR>
META_MASK + SHIFT_MASK + ALT_MASK =    13     lime background        <BR>
META_MASK + SHIFT_MASK + CONTROL_MASK = 14    blue background    <BR></SPAN>

</LAYER>
<!-- ***************************************************************** -->

<SCRIPT LANGUAGE="JavaScript1.2"><!--BEGIN HIDING

function buttonTest2(e) {

        if (e.modifiers == Event.ALT_MASK) {document.TestLayer.bgColor= 'red';}
        if (e.modifiers == 12) {document.TestLayer.bgColor= 'yellow';}
        if (e.modifiers == 13) {document.TestLayer.bgColor= 'lime';}
        if (e.modifiers == 14) {document.TestLayer.bgColor= 'blue';}

 return true;
}
//END HIDING-->
</SCRIPT>
</BODY>
</HTML>
```

Testing for Modifiers Keys
pressed during Mouse Events

This example uses the <u>Property Assignment</u> approach to assign the **keyTest(e)** Function to the **onmousedown** Event Handler of the **document** Object. The **keyTest(e)** Function tests the **modifiers** Property Value and changes the background color of the Layer named **TestLayer** according to which **modifiers** Key is pressed when the **mousedown** Event occurs.

Example 6-3:   **Sample703.html**

```
<!DOCTYPE HTML PUBLIC "-//W3C//DTD HTML 3.2//EN">
<HTML><HEAD>
<TITLE>Sample 703 - Example 6-3 Key Events with MouseDown changes bgColor </TITLE>
</HEAD>
<BODY BGCOLOR="BLACK" TEXT="white">

<LAYER ID="TestLayer" LEFT="10" TOP="70" WIDTH="400" BGCOLOR="LIME">

<SPAN STYLE="color:black; font-size:22pt;">
        This is a simple example which shows you how to use the Modifier Keys to
control the background color of this Layer.  Click the mouse somewhere
<SPAN STYLE="color:white;">    outside         </SPAN>
of the Layer and then click the mouse while any of the Alt, Shift, Control or
Command keys are pressed or just click the mouse to get results.         </SPAN>
</LAYER>
<!-- ************************************************************** -->
<SCRIPT LANGUAGE="JavaScript1.2"><!--BEGIN HIDING

function keyTest(e) {
        if (e.modifiers == Event.ALT_MASK)
             document.TestLayer.bgColor="blue";

 else if (e.modifiers == Event.META_MASK)
             document.TestLayer.bgColor="gray";

 else if (e.modifiers == Event.SHIFT_MASK)
             document.TestLayer.bgColor="purple";

 else if (e.modifiers == Event.CONTROL_MASK)
             document.TestLayer.bgColor="red";

 else   document.TestLayer.bgColor="olive";

 return true;
}
/*-----------------------------------------------------------------*/
             document.onmousedown = keyTest;
/*-----------------------------------------------------------------*/
//END HIDING-->
</SCRIPT>
</BODY></HTML>
```

The <u>load()</u> Method of the Layer Object with Key Events

In this example the **keyTest(e)** Function tests for whether any Modifiers Keys have been pressed, via **e.modifiers**, and executes code accordingly. It has been assigned to the **onclick** Event Handler of the **document** Object by Property assignment. The **keyTest2(e)** Function tests if the CONTROL Key and the **'z'** Key have been pressed together and, if true, executes code. This Function has been assigned to the **onkeypress** Event Handler of the **document** Object. Note that the ASCII Value for the **'z'** Key is 26, when pressed while the CONTROL Key is also pressed. To review the **load()** Method, start with page 221.

Example 6-4:   **Sample704.html**

```
<!DOCTYPE HTML PUBLIC "-//W3C//DTD HTML 3.2//EN">
<HTML><HEAD>
<TITLE>Sample 704 - Example 6-4    Key Events change bgColor </TITLE></HEAD>

<BODY BGCOLOR="BLACK" TEXT="white">

<LAYER ID="TestLayer" LEFT="10" TOP="10" WIDTH="400" BGCOLOR="LIME">
<SPAN STYLE="color:black; font-size:17pt; padding-top:30px; padding-right:30px;
padding-bottom:50px; padding-left:50px;">

        This is a simple example which shows you how to use the Modifier Keys to
control the background color of this Layer.  Click the mouse somewhere

<SPAN STYLE="color:white;">    outside        </SPAN>

of the Layer to see what happens and then click with any of the modifier keys
(except for the Control Key) pressed to get different results.

</SPAN>
</LAYER>
<!--  ***************************************************************  -->

<LAYER ID="TestLayer2" LEFT="10" TOP="200" WIDTH="500" HEIGHT="200"
BGCOLOR="green">
<SPAN STYLE="font-size:30pt;">Hey, I want another job.</SPAN>
</LAYER>
<!--  ***************************************************************  -->

<LAYER ID="TestLayer3" LEFT="10" TOP="200" WIDTH="500" HEIGHT="200" BGCOLOR="aqua">
<SPAN STYLE="font-size:30pt;">The reason that the CONTROL Key wasn't used in the
keyTest function is because of a bug in Navigator which causes the JavaScript to be
ignored if the CONTROL Key is used in conjunction with the onClick Event.</SPAN>
</LAYER>
<!--  ***************************************************************  -->

<LAYER ID="TestLayer4" LEFT="10" TOP="200" WIDTH="500" HEIGHT="200"
BGCOLOR="steelblue">
```

```
<SPAN STYLE="font-size:30pt;">Just to show you that the CONTROL Key isn't useless,
click on the CONTROL Key and the 'z' Key to change the background color of
TestLayer3 to red.</SPAN>
</LAYER>

<!--   ******************************************************************   -->

<SCRIPT LANGUAGE="JavaScript1.2"><!--BEGIN HIDING

function keyTest(e) {

        if (e.modifiers == Event.ALT_MASK) {
                document.TestLayer.load('Sample406.html', 500);
        }
else if (e.modifiers == Event.META_MASK) {
                document.TestLayer.load('Sample400.html', 500);
                document.TestLayer3.zIndex="4";
                document.TestLayer4.zIndex="3";
                document.TestLayer2.zIndex="5";
                document.TestLayer2.bgColor="blue";
        }
else if (e.modifiers == Event.SHIFT_MASK) {
                document.TestLayer2.zIndex="3";
                document.TestLayer4.zIndex="4";
                document.TestLayer3.zIndex="5";
                document.TestLayer3.bgColor="purple";
        }
        else {
                document.TestLayer2.zIndex="4";
                document.TestLayer3.zIndex="3";
                document.TestLayer4.zIndex="5";
                document.TestLayer4.bgColor="olive";
        }
 return true;
}
/*---------------------------------------------------------------------------*/

function keyTest2(e) {

        if (e.modifiers == Event.CONTROL_MASK  &&  e.which == 26) {
                document.TestLayer2.zIndex="3";
                document.TestLayer4.zIndex="4";
                document.TestLayer3.zIndex="5";
                document.TestLayer3.bgColor="red";
        }
}
/*---------------------------------------------------------------------------*/

        document.onclick = keyTest;
        document.onkeypress = keyTest2;

//END HIDING-->
</SCRIPT>

</BODY>
</HTML>
```

The <u>fromCharCode()</u> Method
of the String Object with Key Events

You can use this example to determine the ASCII Value of any Key that is pressed while the ALT Key is also pressed. It also uses the **fromCharCode()** Method of the **String** Object to extract the actual letter, number, or symbol of the Key. An **alert** message shows you what both Values are for comparison purposes. For more information on the **fromCharCode()** Method, see pages 763-765 in Chapter 8 on **String** Objects.

The Function **keyTest2(e)** is assigned to the **onkeydown** Event Handler of the **document** Object by Property Assignment at the end of the SCRIPT. The **focus()** Method is called for the **window** Object in the **onLoad** Event Handler in the BODY Tag so you don't have to click in the window before the Function will work the first time.

Example 6-5:   **Sample705.html**

```
<!DOCTYPE HTML PUBLIC "-//W3C//DTD HTML 3.2//EN">
<HTML><HEAD>  <TITLE>  Sample 705 - Example 6-5      get ALT Key numbers </TITLE>
</HEAD>
<BODY BGCOLOR="BLACK" onLoad="window.focus();">

<LAYER ID="TestLayer" LEFT="10" TOP="10" WIDTH="400" BGCOLOR="red">
<SPAN STYLE="font-size:22pt;">
        Press the Alt or Option Key along with any other regular key to get an alert
with the key that was pressed and the ASCII number that represents it which you can
use in other functions.                        </SPAN>
</LAYER>
<!--  ****************************************************************  -->

<SCRIPT LANGUAGE="JavaScript1.2"><!--BEGIN HIDING

function keyTest2(e) {
        if (e.modifiers == Event.ALT_MASK) {

//Make sure the alert String is all on one line in your text editor

                if (e.which) {
                        alert ("Your Document also had the: " +
                        String.fromCharCode(e.which) + "\r\r" +
                        "key pressed with the ASCII Value of: " + e.which)
                }
        }
 return true;
}
/*--------------------------------------------------------------------*/
                document.onkeydown = keyTest2;
/*--------------------------------------------------------------------*/
//END HIDING-->
</SCRIPT>
</BODY></HTML>
```

This example accomplishes the same thing as the last example, except that it tests for the CONTROL Key instead of the ALT Key.

Example 6-6:   **Sample706.html**

```
<!DOCTYPE HTML PUBLIC "-//W3C//DTD HTML 3.2//EN">
<HTML>
<HEAD>
<TITLE>  Sample 706 - Example 6-6 get CONTROL Key numbers     </TITLE>
</HEAD>

<BODY BGCOLOR="black" onLoad="window.focus();">

<LAYER ID="TestLayer" LEFT="10" TOP="10" WIDTH="400" BGCOLOR="purple">

<SPAN STYLE="color:white; font-size:22pt;">

        Press the Control Key along with any other regular key to get an alert with
the key that was pressed and the ASCII number that represents it which you can use
in other functions.

</SPAN>
</LAYER>

<!-- ************************************************************** -->

<SCRIPT LANGUAGE="JavaScript1.2"><!--BEGIN HIDING

function keyTest2(e) {

        if (e.modifiers == Event.CONTROL_MASK && e.which) {

                alert ("Key pressed: " + String.fromCharCode(e.which) + "\r\r" +
                    "ASCII Value: " + e.which)
 }

 return true;
}

/*------------------------------------------------------------------*/

        document.onkeyup = keyTest2;

/*------------------------------------------------------------------*/

//END HIDING-->
</SCRIPT>

</BODY>
</HTML>
```

Using Modifiers Keys with Regular Keys to Trigger Events

This example demonstrates how to execute code when both the CONTROL and ALT Keys are pressed together with another regular Key. You have to test for the ASCII Value of CONTROL + ALT, which is equal to 3, in your **if ()** Statement. The backslash '\' Key plus the '**r**' Key ('**\r**') is just shorthand for a carriage return.

Example 6-7: **Sample707.html**

```
<!DOCTYPE HTML PUBLIC "-//W3C//DTD HTML 3.2//EN">
<HTML><HEAD>
<TITLE> Sample 707 - Example 6-7   get ALT + CONTROL Key numbers </TITLE> </HEAD>

<BODY BGCOLOR="BLACK" TEXT="WHITE" onLoad="window.focus();">

<LAYER ID="TestLayer" LEFT="10" TOP="10" WIDTH="400" BGCOLOR="olive">
<SPAN STYLE="font-size:22pt;">

      Press the ALT and CONTROL Keys along with any other regular key to get an
alert with the Key that was pressed and the ASCII Value that represents that Key
and the ASCII Value of the MODIFIERS Keys.

</SPAN>
</LAYER>

<!--  **********************************************************************  -->

<SCRIPT LANGUAGE="JavaScript1.2"><!--BEGIN HIDING

function keyTest2(e) {

//e.modifiers Tests for Event.ALT_MASK  &&  Event.CONTROL_MASK == 3
       if (e.modifiers == 3) {
              if (e.which) {
                     alert ("Key Pressed = " + String.fromCharCode(e.which) +
                            "\r\r" + "e.which = " + e.which +
                            "\r\r" + "e.modifiers = " + e.modifiers)
              }
       }
 return true;
}


/*--------------------------------------------------------------------------*/
              document.onkeydown = keyTest2;
/*--------------------------------------------------------------------------*/

//END HIDING-->
</SCRIPT>
</BODY>
</HTML>
```

Determining the ASCII Value of a Pressed Key

This example demonstrates how to test for a specific Key that is pressed when either the ALT or CONTROL Key is also pressed by testing for the ASCII Value of the pressed Key. JavaScript code is then executed that loads various external documents into the Layer named **TestLayer** based on which Key was pressed. See the instructions in the example for more details.

Example 6-8: **Sample708.html**

```
<!DOCTYPE HTML PUBLIC "-//W3C//DTD HTML 3.2//EN">
<HTML>
<HEAD>
<TITLE>Sample 708 - Example 6-8 MODIFIERS and Key Events to load documents</TITLE>
</HEAD>

<BODY BGCOLOR="BLACK" TEXT="white">

<LAYER ID="TestLayer" LEFT="10" TOP="10" BGCOLOR="cyan"></LAYER>
<LAYER ID="staticLayer" LEFT="10" TOP="200" WIDTH="500" BGCOLOR="lime">

<SPAN STYLE="color:black; font-size:17pt; padding-top:20px; padding-right:20px;
padding-bottom:20px; padding-left:20px;">

        This is a simple example which shows you how to use the ALT or CONTROL
Modifier Keys to load in an external document.  Press the ALT key or CONTROL key
and either the z, x, c, or v key to load a document into the Layer named TestLayer.

<P><HR> <SPAN STYLE="color:blue;">
Ignore the text in the documents that are loaded in because they are from previous
Examples.
</SPAN><HR>     </P>

</SPAN>
</LAYER>

<!-- ********************************************************************  -->

<SCRIPT LANGUAGE="JavaScript1.2"><!--BEGIN HIDING

function keyTest2(e) {

        //      189 is the ASCII Event number for the ALT or OPTION key + z key
        //      197 is the ASCII Event number for the ALT or OPTION key + x key
        //      141 is the ASCII Event number for the ALT or OPTION key + c key
        //      195 is the ASCII Event number for the ALT or OPTION key + v key

        //      26 is the ASCII Event number for the CONTROL key + z key
        //      24 is the ASCII Event number for the CONTROL key + x key
        //       3 is the ASCII Event number for the CONTROL key + c key
        //      22 is the ASCII Event number for the CONTROL key + v key
/*-------------------------------------------------------------*/
```

```
/*---------------------------------------------------------*/

        if (e.modifiers == Event.ALT_MASK  && e.which == 189)
            document.TestLayer.load('Sample400.html', 500);

        if (e.modifiers == Event.ALT_MASK  && e.which == 197)
            document.TestLayer.load('Sample401.html', 500);

        if (e.modifiers == Event.ALT_MASK  && e.which == 141)
            document.TestLayer.load('Sample402.html', 500);

        if (e.modifiers == Event.ALT_MASK  && e.which == 195)
            document.TestLayer.load('Sample404.html', 500);

/*---------------------------------------------------------*/

        if (e.modifiers == Event.CONTROL_MASK  && e.which == 26)
            document.TestLayer.load('Sample400.html', 300);

        if (e.modifiers == Event.CONTROL_MASK  && e.which == 24)
            document.TestLayer.load('Sample401.html', 300);

        if (e.modifiers == Event.CONTROL_MASK  && e.which == 3)
            document.TestLayer.load('Sample402.html', 300);

        if (e.modifiers == Event.CONTROL_MASK  && e.which == 22)
            document.TestLayer.load('Sample404.html', 300);
}

/*-------------------------------------------------------------------*/

        document.onkeydown = keyTest2;

/*-------------------------------------------------------------------*/

//END HIDING-->
</SCRIPT>

</BODY>
</HTML>
```

Granted those last eight examples were pretty boring, but they laid a foundation of essential information that will be frequently implemented in more complex work of your own.

The next section is going to teach you how to capture and release Events so that you can manipulate them, along with your Layers, for results that haven't been available before in JavaScript. You will be able to drag images and Layers around with the mouse, and control them via the Keyboard or with Button clicks. A Chess game with pieces that can be positioned around the game board, in real time, without page-refreshing, is now possible, without having to resort to Java. The Chess game starts on page 556.

Capturing & Releasing Events

The JavaScript <u>captureEvents()</u> Method

The **captureEvents()** Method is available for **window**, **document**, and **Layer** Objects and allows you to capture Events before they reach their intended target. The result of this is that you can use JavaScript to compensate for the lack of certain JavaScript Event Handlers or HTML Attribute Event Handlers that you want to manipulate. For instance, a LAYER doesn't have an **onClick** Event Handler, so in order to get a LAYER to respond to a **click** Event, you can use the **captureEvents()** Method to capture the **click** Event before it reaches its natural target. For example, if you have a Layer named **L1**:

```
document.L1.captureEvents(Event.CLICK)
```

will cause all **click** Events to be routed to Layer **L1** for processing until **releaseEvents()** is called like this:

```
document.L1.releaseEvents(Event.CLICK)
```

To capture more than one Event at a time, you separate each Event with the vertical bar ('|') character like this (remembering that Event Constants are spelled in allcaps):

```
window.captureEvents(Event.MOUSEDOWN | Event.MOUSEUP)
```

JavaScript Syntax:

```
window.captureEvents(Event.eventName | Event.eventName)
document.captureEvents(Event.eventName | Event.eventName)
document.layerName.captureEvents(Event.eventName | Event.eventName)
document.layerName.document.layerName2.captureEvents(
                        Event.eventName| Event.eventName)
```

Capturing Events in Nested Layers

To capture all **click** Events for a nested Layer named **L2** inside a Layer named **L1**, you would use the following code:

```
document.L1.document.L2.captureEvents(Event.CLICK)
```

The JavaScript <u>releaseEvents()</u> Method

The **releaseEvents()** Method is available for **window**, **document** and **Layer** Objects and allows you to turn off the **captureEvents()** Method so that Events will progress naturally through the hierarchy. In many cases, you will want to create a Function that calls **captureEvents()** at the beginning of the Function, process the Event with cool code, and then call **releaseEvents()** at the end of Function.

For example, if you wanted to release the **keydown** and **keyup** Events that had previously been captured for the Layer named **myLayer** you would use this code:

```
document.myLayer.releaseEvents(Event.KEYDOWN | Event.KEYUP)
```

JavaScript Syntax:

```
window.releaseEvents(Event.eventName | Event.eventName)
document.releaseEvents(Event.eventName | Event.eventName)
document.layerName.releaseEvents(Event.eventName | Event.eventName)
document.layerName.document.layerName2.releaseEvents(
                          Event.eventName| Event.eventName)
```

Using the <u>type</u> Property and captureEvents() Method on a Layer

In the following example, the **captureEvents()** Method is used to capture all **mousedown** Events for the Layer named **L1** with this code:

```
document.L1.captureEvents(Event.MOUSEDOWN);
```

Next, the **onmousedown** Event Handler for **L1** is assigned the Function **getL1Events(e)** with this code:

```
document.L1.onmousedown = getL1Events;
```

The Function **getL1Events(e)** tests the **Event** Object by comparing it to the **type** Property, and if it is a **mousedown** Event and no **modifiers** Keys are pressed, it calls the **changeL1()** Function, which changes the background color of **L1** to blue and its **clipping width** to 400. If the ALT Key is pressed, then it calls the **changeL1Back()** Function, which changes the background color of **L1** back to purple and the **clipping width** back to 200.

Example 6-9   Sample709.html

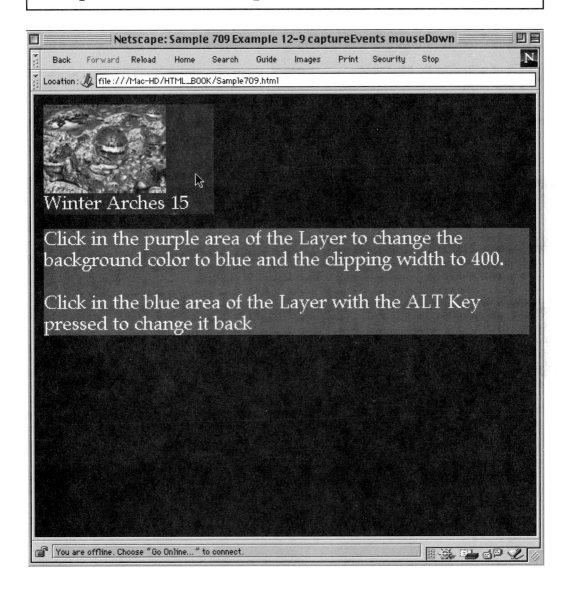

Example 6-9:   Sample709.html

```
<!DOCTYPE HTML PUBLIC "-//W3C//DTD HTML 3.2//EN">
<HTML><HEAD><TITLE> Sample 709   Example 6-9 captureEvents mouseDown</TITLE>

<STYLE TYPE="text/JavaScript">

        classes.Mainbody.BODY.margins("0px");
        classes.Mainbody.BODY.paddings("0px");
        classes.Mainbody.BODY.backgroundColor="navy";
        classes.Mainbody.BODY.color="white";
        classes.Mainbody.BODY.fontSize="22pt";

</STYLE>
</HEAD>

<BODY CLASS="Mainbody">

<LAYER ID="L1" LEFT="10" TOP="10" WIDTH="200" BGCOLOR="purple">
<IMG SRC="JPEG-FILES/J2-Winter-Arches-15.jpg" WIDTH="144" HEIGHT="100"><BR>
Winter Arches 15</LAYER>

<LAYER ID="L2" LEFT="10" TOP="150" WIDTH="570" BGCOLOR="olive">
Click in the purple area of the Layer to change the background color to blue and
the clipping width to 400.<BR><BR>
Click in the blue area of the Layer with the ALT Key pressed to change it back
</LAYER>
<!--  *****************************************************************  -->

<SCRIPT LANGUAGE="JavaScript1.2"><!--BEGIN HIDING

document.L1.captureEvents(Event.MOUSEDOWN);
document.L1.onmousedown = getL1Events;

/*-------------------------------------------------------------*/

function getL1Events(e)  {
                                  //make sure no modifiers key pressed
        if (e.type == 'mousedown' &&  e.modifiers == 0)  {
                changeL1();
                return false;
        }                                 //test for ALT Key
        else if (e.type == 'mousedown' &&  e.modifiers == 1)  {
                changeL1Back();
                return false;
        }
}
/*-------------------------------------------------------------*/

function changeL1()  {

        document.L1.bgColor = 'blue';
        document.L1.clip.width = 400;
}
/*-------------------------------------------------------------*/
```

```
function changeL1Back()   {

        document.L1.bgColor = 'purple';
        document.L1.clip.width = 200;
}
/*------------------------------------------------------------------------*/

//END HIDING-->
</SCRIPT>
</BODY>
</HTML>
```

Dragging an Image with the Mouse

This example shows you how to drag an image with the mouse and reposition it to a different location in the browser window. You accomplish this by setting up code to drag the Layer that contains the image with **captureEvents()** and **releaseEvents()** Methods.

First, you use the **ids** Property to create a Style named **division** that is assigned to the DIV Element with the **ID** Attribute, which causes it to be a Layer by virtue of it having a **position** Property and which is set to **absolute**.

Next, you create some global Variables to make the code more legible and save yourself some typing. Then, the **division** Layer is set to capture all **mousedown** and **mouseup** Events. The **division.onmousedown** Event Handler is assigned the **begindrag(e)** Function and the **division.onmouseup** Event Handler is assigned the **enddrag(e)** Function.

The **begindrag(e)** Function starts the process by testing if the left mouse button is down, and if true, it uses the **captureEvents()** Method to capture all **mousemove** Events that occur in the **division** Layer. Next, the **onmousemove** Event Handler for the **division** Layer is assigned the **drag(e)** Function by Property Assignment. Note the absence of parentheses and **e** Argument, which are not allowed in Property Assignment.

The **drag(e)** Function first tests to make sure that **mousemove** Events are being captured, and if true, it uses the **moveBy()** Method to move the **division** Layer by the specified pixels. If you remember, the **moveBy(x,y)** Method takes two Arguments: the number of pixels in both of the **x** and **y** directions.

By assigning the **e.pageX - previousX** Expression to the **x** Argument, you take the current **pageX** Property of the Event and subtract the previous **pageX** Property of the Event, which has been assigned to the Variable **previousX**, and then move the **division** Layer by that number of pixels in the horizontal **x** direction. The same scenario is implemented in the vertical direction with the **e.pageY - previousY** Expression assigned to the **y** Argument.

Finally, when the mouse button is released, the **enddrag(e)** Function is called to release the **mousemove** Event from the **division** Layer with the **releaseEvents()** Method. The **onmousemove** Event Handler is set to the **null** Keyword to prevent any extraneous Functions from being called after this Function completes its operation.

Note that at the end of the above three Functions, they **return false** to stop Event Handling for the Event at that point.

Example 6-10:   Sample710.html

```
<!DOCTYPE HTML PUBLIC "-//W3C//DTD HTML 3.2//EN">
<HTML><HEAD>
<TITLE>Sample 710 - Example 6-10      Drag an Image </TITLE>

<STYLE type="text/JavaScript">

        ids.division.position="absolute";
        ids.division.left="200";
        ids.division.top="200";
        ids.division.width="200";
        ids.division.height="150";
        ids.division.borderWidths("15px");
        ids.division.borderColor="#7700ff";
        ids.division.borderStyle="groove";

</STYLE>

</HEAD>

<BODY BGCOLOR="BLACK" TEXT="white">

<DIV ID="division"> <CENTER>
<IMG SRC="JPEG-FILES/J2-Winter-Arches-15.jpg" VSPACE="10" WIDTH="144" HEIGHT="99">
</CENTER></DIV>

<!--  *********************************************************************  -->

<SCRIPT LANGUAGE="JavaScript1.2"><!--BEGIN HIDING

var division = document.division;

        division.captureEvents(Event.MOUSEUP|Event.MOUSEDOWN);
        division.onmousedown = begindrag;
        division.onmouseup = enddrag;

var previousX;
var previousY;
var booleanDrag;

/*----------------------------------------------------------------------*/

function begindrag(e) {
                        //e.which tests for the left mouse button being pressed
        if (e.which == 1) {
                division.captureEvents(Event.MOUSEMOVE);
                division.onmousemove = drag;
                previousX = e.pageX;
                previousY = e.pageY;
                booleanDrag = true;
                return false;
        }
}
/*----------------------------------------------------------------------*/
```

```
function drag(e) {
                    //tests to make sure that mousemoves are being captured
       if (booleanDrag) {

              division.moveBy(e.pageX - previousX, e.pageY - previousY);
              previousX = e.pageX;
              previousY = e.pageY;
              return false;
       }
}
/*-------------------------------------------------------------------*/

function enddrag(e) {

       if (e.which == 1) {

              division.releaseEvents(Event.MOUSEMOVE);
              division.onmousemove = null;
              booleanDrag = false;
              return false;
       }
}

//END HIDING-->
</SCRIPT>

</BODY>
</HTML>
```

The <u>name</u> Property of the <u>target</u> Property of the <u>Event</u> Object

You can test for the Name of the Target Object of an Event Argument by using the **name** Property of the **target** Property of the **Event** Object, like this:

```
       if (e.target.name == "myImage") execute this JavaScript code
```

where: **e** is the Event Argument passed with the Function
and: **"myImage"** is the unique NAME Attribute of an <IMG> Element like this:

```
<IMG SRC="Arches.jpg" NAME="myImage" WIDTH="144" HEIGHT="99">
```

JavaScript Syntax:

```
eventArg.target.name
```

The next example is just a slight variation on the previous example. It is here mainly for two reasons: to show you how to test for the **name** Property of the **target** Property of the **Event** Object in an **if ()** Statement and to show an inherent limitation in capturing the **mousemove** Event with the **onmousemove** Event Handler for multiple **Layer** Objects. This limitation is a direct result of Layers having **z-Index** Properties, which prevent the Event from reaching its desired target when the mouse that is dragging a Layer with a lower **z-Index** is dragged into the space of a Layer with a higher **z-Index**. (In Example 3-12 there's a sneaky way to get around this limitation.)

It is very easy to clarify this by loading <u>Sample711.html</u> into your browser and then trying to drag the top image across either of the other two images. While the mouse is in their space, it can't move the top image because top image has the lowest **z-Index**.

This is the line of code that tests for the left mouse button being held down and for the **name** of the Image that is the **target** of the Event:

```
if (e.which == 1  &&  e.target.name == "myImage")
```

In this case, by requiring that the **target** of the Event be an Image, you prevent the Layer that contains the Image from being dragged if the mouse is pressed down on the Layer border or background. It can only be dragged if the mouse presses down on the space occupied by the Image. This, of course, works for all three images because there is executable code prepared for all three of those **target** circumstances.

Example 6-11:   Sample711.html

```
<!DOCTYPE HTML PUBLIC "-//W3C//DTD HTML 3.2//EN">
<HTML>
<HEAD>
<TITLE>Sample 711 - Example 6-11       Drag any of three Images </TITLE>

<STYLE type="text/JavaScript">

       tags.DIV.position="absolute";
       tags.DIV.left="10";
       tags.DIV.top="50";
       tags.DIV.width="174";
       tags.DIV.height="135";
       tags.DIV.borderWidths("15px");
       tags.DIV.borderColor="#7700ff";
       tags.DIV.borderStyle="groove";

       ids.division2.left="10";
       ids.division2.top="200";

       ids.division3.left="250";
       ids.division3.top="200";
```

```
</STYLE>

</HEAD>

<BODY BGCOLOR="BLACK" TEXT="white">

<DIV ID="division">
<IMG SRC="JPEG-FILES/J2-Winter-Arches-15.jpg" NAME="myImage" WIDTH="144"
HEIGHT="99"></DIV>

<DIV ID="division2">
<IMG SRC="JPEG-FILES/J2-SpaceDome_27P.jpg" NAME="myImage2" WIDTH="144"
HEIGHT="99"></DIV>

<DIV ID="division3">
<IMG SRC="JPEG-FILES/J2-SKY_SPHERE_1.jpg" NAME="myImage3" WIDTH="144"
HEIGHT="99"></DIV>


<!--  *****************************************************************  -->

<SCRIPT LANGUAGE="JavaScript1.2"><!--BEGIN HIDING

/*----------------------------------------------------------------------*/
var division = document.division

        division.captureEvents(Event.MOUSEDOWN|Event.MOUSEUP);
        division.onmousedown=begindrag;
        division.onmouseup=enddrag;

var division2 = document.division2

        division2.captureEvents(Event.MOUSEDOWN|Event.MOUSEUP);
        division2.onmousedown=begindrag;
        division2.onmouseup=enddrag;

var division3 = document.division3

        division3.captureEvents(Event.MOUSEDOWN|Event.MOUSEUP);
        division3.onmousedown=begindrag;
        division3.onmouseup=enddrag;

var previousX;
var previousY;
var booleanDrag;

/*----------------------------------------------------------------------*/

function begindrag(e) {

        if (e.which == 1  &&  e.target.name == "myImage") {
                division.captureEvents(Event.MOUSEMOVE);
                division.onmousemove=drag;
                previousX=e.pageX;
                previousY=e.pageY;
                booleanDrag=true;
                return false;
        }
```

```
        else if (e.which == 1  &&  e.target.name == "myImage2") {
                division2.captureEvents(Event.MOUSEMOVE);
                division2.onmousemove=drag;
                previousX=e.pageX;
                previousY=e.pageY;
                booleanDrag=true;
                return false;
        }
        else if (e.which == 1  &&  e.target.name == "myImage3") {
                division3.captureEvents(Event.MOUSEMOVE);
                division3.onmousemove=drag;
                previousX=e.pageX;
                previousY=e.pageY;
                booleanDrag=true;
                return false;
        }
}
/*-----------------------------------------------------------------------*/

function drag(e) {

        if (booleanDrag) {
                if (e.which == 1  &&  e.target.name == "myImage") {
                        division.moveBy(e.pageX-previousX, e.pageY-previousY);
                        previousX = e.pageX;
                        previousY = e.pageY;
                        return false;
                }
                else if (e.which == 1  &&  e.target.name == "myImage2") {
                        division2.moveBy(e.pageX-previousX, e.pageY-previousY);
                        previousX = e.pageX;
                        previousY = e.pageY;
                        return false;
                }
                else if (e.which == 1  &&  e.target.name == "myImage3") {
                        division3.moveBy(e.pageX-previousX, e.pageY-previousY);
                        previousX = e.pageX;
                        previousY = e.pageY;
                        return false;
                }
        }
}
/*-----------------------------------------------------------------------*/

function enddrag(e) {

        if (e.which == 1  &&  e.target.name == "myImage") {
                division.releaseEvents(Event.MOUSEMOVE);
                division.onmousemove=null
                booleanDrag=false;
                return false;
        }
        else if (e.which == 1  &&  e.target.name == "myImage2") {
                division2.releaseEvents(Event.MOUSEMOVE);
                division2.onmousemove=null
                booleanDrag=false;
                return false;
        }
```

```
        else if (e.which == 1  &&  e.target.name == "myImage3") {
             division3.releaseEvents(Event.MOUSEMOVE);
             division3.onmousemove=null
             booleanDrag=false;
             return false;
        }
}

//END HIDING-->
</SCRIPT>

</BODY>
</HTML>
```

Capturing Events for the <u>window</u> Object to Drag an Image

The only difference between this example and the previous example is that in the **begindrag(e)** and the **enddrag(e)** Functions you capture the **mousemove** Event for the **window** Object instead of the three **Layer** Objects. This is one of the lines of code from the previous example where **division** is the name of a Layer:

```
        division.captureEvents(Event.MOUSEMOVE);
```

which has been replaced by the following line of code:

```
        window.captureEvents(Event.MOUSEMOVE);
```

What this accomplishes is the ability to uninterruptedly drag a Layer with a lower **z-Index** around the Window, *even* when it is behind a Layer with a <u>higher</u> **z-Index** Value.

Example 6-12:   Sample712.html

```
<!DOCTYPE HTML PUBLIC "-//W3C//DTD HTML 3.2//EN">
<HTML><HEAD>
<TITLE>Sample 712 - Example 6-12      Drag any of three Images </TITLE>

<STYLE type="text/JavaScript">

        tags.DIV.position="absolute";
        tags.DIV.left="10";
        tags.DIV.top="50";
        tags.DIV.width="174";
        tags.DIV.height="135";
        tags.DIV.borderWidths("15px");
        tags.DIV.borderColor="#7700ff";
        tags.DIV.borderStyle="groove";
```

```
            ids.division2.left="10";
            ids.division2.top="200";

            ids.division3.left="250";
            ids.division3.top="200";

</STYLE>

</HEAD>

<BODY BGCOLOR="BLACK" TEXT="white">

<DIV ID="division">
<IMG SRC="JPEG-FILES/J2-Winter-Arches-15.jpg" NAME="myImage" WIDTH="144"
HEIGHT="99"></DIV>

<DIV ID="division2">
<IMG SRC="JPEG-FILES/J2-SpaceDome_27P.jpg" NAME="myImage2" WIDTH="144"
HEIGHT="99"></DIV>

<DIV ID="division3">
<IMG SRC="JPEG-FILES/J2-SKY_SPHERE_1.jpg" NAME="myImage3" WIDTH="144"
HEIGHT="99"></DIV>

<!--  ***************************************AA**********************  -->

<SCRIPT LANGUAGE="JavaScript1.2"><!--BEGIN HIDING

/*---------------------------------------------------------------------*/

var division = document.division

        division.captureEvents(Event.MOUSEDOWN|Event.MOUSEUP);
        division.onmousedown=begindrag;
        division.onmouseup=enddrag;

var division2 = document.division2

        division2.captureEvents(Event.MOUSEDOWN|Event.MOUSEUP);
        division2.onmousedown=begindrag;
        division2.onmouseup=enddrag;

var division3 = document.division3

        division3.captureEvents(Event.MOUSEDOWN|Event.MOUSEUP);
        division3.onmousedown=begindrag;
        division3.onmouseup=enddrag;

var previousX;
var previousY;
var booleanDrag;

/*---------------------------------------------------------------------*/

//This is where this example is different from Example 6-11.
//Instead of capturing the MOUSEMOVE Event for the 'Layer'.
//you capture it for the 'window'.
//You do the same thing in the enddrag() Function below.
```

```
/*----------------------------------------------------------------------*/

function begindrag(e) {

        if (e.which == 1  &&  e.target.name == "myImage") {
                window.captureEvents(Event.MOUSEMOVE);
                window.onmousemove=drag;
                previousX=e.pageX;
                previousY=e.pageY;
                booleanDrag=true;
                return false;
        }
        else if (e.which == 1  &&  e.target.name == "myImage2") {
                window.captureEvents(Event.MOUSEMOVE);
                window.onmousemove=drag;
                previousX=e.pageX;
                previousY=e.pageY;
                booleanDrag=true;
                return false;
        }
        else if (e.which == 1  &&  e.target.name == "myImage3") {
                window.captureEvents(Event.MOUSEMOVE);
                window.onmousemove=drag;
                previousX=e.pageX;
                previousY=e.pageY;
                booleanDrag=true;
                return false;
        }
}

/*----------------------------------------------------------------------*/

function drag(e) {

        if (booleanDrag) {

                if (e.which == 1  &&  e.target.name == "myImage") {
                        division.moveBy(e.pageX-previousX, e.pageY-previousY);
                        previousX = e.pageX;
                        previousY = e.pageY;
                        return false;
                }
                else if (e.which == 1  &&  e.target.name == "myImage2") {
                        division2.moveBy(e.pageX-previousX, e.pageY-previousY);
                        previousX = e.pageX;
                        previousY = e.pageY;
                        return false;
                }
                else if (e.which == 1  &&  e.target.name == "myImage3") {
                        division3.moveBy(e.pageX-previousX, e.pageY-previousY);
                        previousX = e.pageX;
                        previousY = e.pageY;
                        return false;
                }
        }
}

/*----------------------------------------------------------------------*/
```

```
function enddrag(e) {

     if (e.which == 1  &&  e.target.name == "myImage") {
          window.releaseEvents(Event.MOUSEMOVE);
          window.onmousemove=null
          booleanDrag=false;
          return false;
     }
     else if (e.which == 1  &&  e.target.name == "myImage2") {
          window.releaseEvents(Event.MOUSEMOVE);
          window.onmousemove=null
          booleanDrag=false;
          return false;
     }
     else if (e.which == 1  &&  e.target.name == "myImage3") {
          window.releaseEvents(Event.MOUSEMOVE);
          window.onmousemove=null
          booleanDrag=false;
          return false;
     }
}


//END HIDING-->
</SCRIPT>
</BODY>
</HTML>
```

Using Localized Scripts to Drag an Image

The Chess Game Example

You probably noticed in Example 6-11 that if your mouse wasn't over the image or Layer during the dragging process (because the drag-Layer was behind another Layer by default **zIndex**), the dragging would halt because of the **e.target.name == "myImage"** code. One way to get around this when assigning code to your Layers is to use **Localized Scripts**. You might remember from Chapter 3 that this is a Script that is contained within the Layer's Start and End Tags and only applies to that particular Layer.

This next example is a JavaScript Chess Game that demonstrates the dragging of Layers that contain the chess pieces by using **Localized Scripts**. It's a very long example, but a lot of the code is repetitive and it uses the same code structure as in the last example, but is repeated 32 times in **Localized Scripts**, once for each chess piece.

The code in the file Sample713-Chess.html is much easier to read so you might want to print it out and refer to it instead of the code in the book. There is also a version of the Chess Game that contains small images of the Chess pieces that is in the file named Sample774-Chess-Images.html, which is not in the book but is on the CD-ROM, in the DHTML-JS_BOOK-Main_Files folder.

Example 6-13   Sample713.html

Example 6-13:   Sample713-Chess.html

```
<!DOCTYPE HTML PUBLIC "-//W3C//DTD HTML 3.2//EN">
<HTML><HEAD>
<TITLE>Sample 713-Chess - Example 6-13     Drag Chess </TITLE>

<STYLE type = "text/JavaScript">

        classes.theControl.all.fontSize = "22pt";
        classes.theControl.all.fontFamily = "Moonlight, cursive";
        classes.theControl.all.textAlign = "center";
        classes.theControl.all.align = "center";
        classes.Largefont.all.fontFamily = "Courier";
        classes.Largefont.all.fontSize = "44pt";
        classes.Largefont.all.color = "black";
        classes.Largefont.all.textAlign = "center";
        classes.Largefont.all.lineHeight = "12pt";
        classes.Whitefont.all.fontFamily = "Courier";
        classes.Whitefont.all.fontSize = "44pt";
        classes.Whitefont.all.color = "white";
        classes.Whitefont.all.textAlign = "center";
        classes.Whitefont.all.lineHeight = "12pt";

</STYLE>
</HEAD>
<BODY BGCOLOR="BLACK" TEXT="white">
<!-- ****************  The CONTROL layer      ***************  -->
<LAYER CLASS="theControl" ID="Control" LEFT="5" TOP="5" WIDTH="100" HEIGHT="100"
BGCOLOR="steelblue">
<FORM NAME="form1">             CHESS     <BR>
<INPUT TYPE="button" NAME="StartOver" VALUE="New Game"
onClick='StartGame(); return false;'>
</FORM></LAYER>
<!-- ******************************************************************** -->
<!--  Notice that Showcase2 through Showcase34 are nested inside ShowcaseA   -->
<LAYER ID="ShowcaseA" LEFT="120" TOP="5" WIDTH="700">
<!-- ******************************************************************** -->

<TABLE BORDER="5" CELLSPACING="2" BORDERCOLOR="#8800ff">
<TR BGCOLOR="red">
<TH WIDTH="50" HEIGHT="50">                             Q-r8           </TH>
<TH WIDTH="50" HEIGHT="50" BGCOLOR="black">             Q-n8           </TH>
<TH WIDTH="50" HEIGHT="50">                             Q-b8           </TH>
<TH WIDTH="50" HEIGHT="50" BGCOLOR="black">             Q8             </TH>
<TH WIDTH="50" HEIGHT="50">                             K8             </TH>
<TH WIDTH="50" HEIGHT="50" BGCOLOR="black">             K-b8           </TH>
<TH WIDTH="50" HEIGHT="50">                             K-n8           </TH>
<TH WIDTH="50" HEIGHT="50" BGCOLOR="black">             K-r8           </TH>
</TR>
<TR BGCOLOR="red">
<TH WIDTH="50" HEIGHT="50" BGCOLOR="black">             Q-r7           </TH>
<TH WIDTH="50" HEIGHT="50">                             Q-n7           </TH>
<TH WIDTH="50" HEIGHT="50" BGCOLOR="black">             Q-b7           </TH>
<TH WIDTH="50" HEIGHT="50">                             Q7             </TH>
<TH WIDTH="50" HEIGHT="50" BGCOLOR="black">             K7             </TH>
```

```
<TH WIDTH="50" HEIGHT="50">                       K-b7          </TH>
<TH WIDTH="50" HEIGHT="50" BGCOLOR="black">       K-n7          </TH>
<TH WIDTH="50" HEIGHT="50">                       K-r7          </TH>
</TR>
<TR BGCOLOR="red">
<TH WIDTH="50" HEIGHT="50">                       Q-r6          </TH>
<TH WIDTH="50" HEIGHT="50" BGCOLOR="black">       Q-n6          </TH>
<TH WIDTH="50" HEIGHT="50">                       Q-b6          </TH>
<TH WIDTH="50" HEIGHT="50" BGCOLOR="black">       Q6            </TH>
<TH WIDTH="50" HEIGHT="50">                       K6            </TH>
<TH WIDTH="50" HEIGHT="50" BGCOLOR="black">       K-b6          </TH>
<TH WIDTH="50" HEIGHT="50">                       K-n6          </TH>
<TH WIDTH="50" HEIGHT="50" BGCOLOR="black">       K-r6          </TH>
</TR>
<TR BGCOLOR="red">
<TH WIDTH="50" HEIGHT="50" BGCOLOR="black">       Q-r5          </TH>
<TH WIDTH="50" HEIGHT="50">                       Q-n5          </TH>
<TH WIDTH="50" HEIGHT="50" BGCOLOR="black">       Q-b5          </TH>
<TH WIDTH="50" HEIGHT="50">                       Q5            </TH>
<TH WIDTH="50" HEIGHT="50" BGCOLOR="black">       K5            </TH>
<TH WIDTH="50" HEIGHT="50">                       K-b5          </TH>
<TH WIDTH="50" HEIGHT="50" BGCOLOR="black">       K-n5          </TH>
<TH WIDTH="50" HEIGHT="50">                       K-r5          </TH>
</TR>
<TR BGCOLOR="red">
<TH WIDTH="50" HEIGHT="50">                       Q-r4          </TH>
<TH WIDTH="50" HEIGHT="50" BGCOLOR="black">       Q-n4          </TH>
<TH WIDTH="50" HEIGHT="50">                       Q-b4          </TH>
<TH WIDTH="50" HEIGHT="50" BGCOLOR="black">       Q4            </TH>
<TH WIDTH="50" HEIGHT="50">                       K4            </TH>
<TH WIDTH="50" HEIGHT="50" BGCOLOR="black">       K-b4          </TH>
<TH WIDTH="50" HEIGHT="50">                       K-n4          </TH>
<TH WIDTH="50" HEIGHT="50" BGCOLOR="black">       K-r4          </TH>
</TR>
<TR BGCOLOR="red">
<TH WIDTH="50" HEIGHT="50" BGCOLOR="black">       Q-r3          </TH>
<TH WIDTH="50" HEIGHT="50">                       Q-n3          </TH>
<TH WIDTH="50" HEIGHT="50" BGCOLOR="black">       Q-b3          </TH>
<TH WIDTH="50" HEIGHT="50">                       Q3            </TH>
<TH WIDTH="50" HEIGHT="50" BGCOLOR="black">       K3            </TH>
<TH WIDTH="50" HEIGHT="50">                       K-b3          </TH>
<TH WIDTH="50" HEIGHT="50" BGCOLOR="black">       K-n3          </TH>
<TH WIDTH="50" HEIGHT="50">                       K-r3          </TH>
</TR>
<TR BGCOLOR="red">
<TH WIDTH="50" HEIGHT="50">                       Q-r2          </TH>
<TH WIDTH="50" HEIGHT="50" BGCOLOR="black">       Q-n2          </TH>
<TH WIDTH="50" HEIGHT="50">                       Q-b2          </TH>
<TH WIDTH="50" HEIGHT="50" BGCOLOR="black">       Q2            </TH>
<TH WIDTH="50" HEIGHT="50">                       K2            </TH>
<TH WIDTH="50" HEIGHT="50" BGCOLOR="black">       K-b2          </TH>
<TH WIDTH="50" HEIGHT="50">                       K-n2          </TH>
<TH WIDTH="50" HEIGHT="50" BGCOLOR="black">       K-r2          </TH>
</TR>
<TR BGCOLOR="red">
<TH WIDTH="50" HEIGHT="50" BGCOLOR="black">       Q-r1          </TH>
<TH WIDTH="50" HEIGHT="50">                       Q-n1          </TH>
<TH WIDTH="50" HEIGHT="50" BGCOLOR="black">       Q-b1          </TH>
<TH WIDTH="50" HEIGHT="50">                       Q1            </TH>
<TH WIDTH="50" HEIGHT="50" BGCOLOR="black">       K1            </TH>
<TH WIDTH="50" HEIGHT="50">                       K-b1          </TH>
<TH WIDTH="50" HEIGHT="50" BGCOLOR="black">       K-n1          </TH>
<TH WIDTH="50" HEIGHT="50">                       K-r1          </TH>
</TR>
</TABLE>
```

```
<!-- ********************************************************** -->

<LAYER CLASS="Largefont" ID="Showcase2" LEFT="13" TOP="10" WIDTH="40" HEIGHT="40">R

<SCRIPT LANGUAGE="JavaScript1.2"><!--BEGIN HIDING

        Showcase2.bgColor = 'white';
        Showcase2.captureEvents(Event.MOUSEDOWN|Event.MOUSEUP);
        Showcase2.onmousedown = beginDrag;
        Showcase2.onmouseup = endDrag;
  var previousX;
  var previousY;
  var booleanDrag;
/*-------------------------------------------------*/
function beginDrag(e) {
  if (e.which == 1) {
        window.captureEvents(Event.MOUSEMOVE);
        window.onmousemove = drag;
        previousX = e.pageX;
        previousY = e.pageY;
        booleanDrag = true;
        return false;
  }
}
/*-------------------------------------------------*/
function drag(e) {
  if (booleanDrag) {
        moveBy(e.pageX - previousX, e.pageY - previousY);
        previousX = e.pageX;
        previousY = e.pageY;
        return false;
  }
}
/*-------------------------------------------------*/
function endDrag(e) {
  if (e.which == 1) {
        window.releaseEvents(Event.MOUSEMOVE);
        window.onmousemove = null;
        booleanDrag = false;
        return false;
  }
}
/*-----------------------------------------------------------*/
//END HIDING-->
</SCRIPT>
</LAYER>
<!-- ********************************** -->
<LAYER CLASS="Largefont" ID="Showcase3" LEFT="70" TOP="10" WIDTH="40" HEIGHT="40">N
<SCRIPT LANGUAGE="JavaScript1.2"><!--BEGIN HIDING
  Showcase3.bgColor = 'white';
  Showcase3.captureEvents(Event.MOUSEDOWN|Event.MOUSEUP);
  Showcase3.onmousedown = beginDrag;
  Showcase3.onmouseup = endDrag;
   var previousX, previousY, booleanDrag;
/*-------------------------------------------------*/
```

```
function beginDrag(e) {
  if (e.which == 1) {
        window.captureEvents(Event.MOUSEMOVE);      window.onmousemove = drag;
        previousX = e.pageX;                          previousY = e.pageY;
        booleanDrag = true;                           return false;
  }
}       /*-------------------------------------------------*/
function drag(e) {
  if (booleanDrag) {
        moveBy(e.pageX - previousX, e.pageY - previousY);
        previousX = e.pageX;                                previousY = e.pageY;
        return false;
  }
}       /*-------------------------------------------------*/
function endDrag(e) {
  if (e.which == 1) {
        window.releaseEvents(Event.MOUSEMOVE);      window.onmousemove = null;
        booleanDrag = false;                          return false;
  }
}       /*-----------------------------------------------------------------------*/
//END HIDING-->
</SCRIPT>
</LAYER>
<!-- ******************************** -->
<LAYER CLASS="Largefont" ID="Showcase4" LEFT="125" TOP="10" WIDTH="40" HEIGHT="40">B
<SCRIPT LANGUAGE="JavaScript1.2"><!--BEGIN HIDING
 Showcase4.bgColor = 'white';
 Showcase4.captureEvents(Event.MOUSEDOWN|Event.MOUSEUP);
 Showcase4.onmousedown = beginDrag;
 Showcase4.onmouseup = endDrag;
  var previousX, previousY, booleanDrag;
/*-------------------------------------------------*/
function beginDrag(e) {
  if (e.which == 1) {
        window.captureEvents(Event.MOUSEMOVE);      window.onmousemove = drag;
        previousX = e.pageX;                          previousY = e.pageY;
        booleanDrag = true;                           return false;
  }
}       /*-------------------------------------------------*/
function drag(e) {
  if (booleanDrag) {
        moveBy(e.pageX - previousX, e.pageY - previousY);
        previousX = e.pageX;                                previousY = e.pageY;
        return false;
  }
}       /*-------------------------------------------------*/
function endDrag(e) {
  if (e.which == 1) {
        window.releaseEvents(Event.MOUSEMOVE);      window.onmousemove = null;
        booleanDrag = false;                          return false;
  }
}       /*-----------------------------------------------------------------------*/
//END HIDING-->
</SCRIPT>
</LAYER>
```

```
<!-- ************************************************************** -->
<LAYER CLASS="Largefont" ID="Showcase5" LEFT="182" TOP="10" WIDTH="40" HEIGHT="40">Q
<SCRIPT LANGUAGE="JavaScript1.2"><!--BEGIN HIDING
 Showcase5.bgColor = 'white';
 Showcase5.captureEvents(Event.MOUSEDOWN|Event.MOUSEUP);
 Showcase5.onmousedown = beginDrag;
 Showcase5.onmouseup = endDrag;
  var previousX, previousY, booleanDrag;
/*------------------------------------------------*/
function beginDrag(e) {
  if (e.which == 1) {
        window.captureEvents(Event.MOUSEMOVE);      window.onmousemove = drag;
        previousX = e.pageX;                         previousY = e.pageY;
        booleanDrag = true;                         return false;
  }
}        /*------------------------------------------------*/
function drag(e) {
  if (booleanDrag) {
        moveBy(e.pageX - previousX, e.pageY - previousY);
        previousX = e.pageX;                         previousY = e.pageY;
        return false;
  }
}        /*------------------------------------------------*/
function endDrag(e) {
  if (e.which == 1) {
        window.releaseEvents(Event.MOUSEMOVE);      window.onmousemove = null;
        booleanDrag = false;                        return false;
  }
}        /*----------------------------------------------------------------*/
//END HIDING-->
</SCRIPT>
</LAYER>
<!-- ********************************* -->
<LAYER CLASS="Largefont" ID="Showcase6" LEFT="237" TOP="10" WIDTH="40" HEIGHT="40">K
<SCRIPT LANGUAGE="JavaScript1.2"><!--BEGIN HIDING
 Showcase6.bgColor = 'white';
 Showcase6.captureEvents(Event.MOUSEDOWN|Event.MOUSEUP);
 Showcase6.onmousedown = beginDrag;
 Showcase6.onmouseup = endDrag;
  var previousX, previousY, booleanDrag;
/*------------------------------------------------*/
function beginDrag(e) {
  if (e.which == 1) {
        window.captureEvents(Event.MOUSEMOVE);      window.onmousemove = drag;
        previousX = e.pageX;                         previousY = e.pageY;
        booleanDrag = true;                         return false;
  }
}        /*------------------------------------------------*/
function drag(e) {
  if (booleanDrag) {
        moveBy(e.pageX - previousX, e.pageY - previousY);
        previousX = e.pageX;                         previousY = e.pageY;
        return false;
  }
}        /*------------------------------------------------*/
```

```
function endDrag(e) {
  if (e.which == 1) {
        window.releaseEvents(Event.MOUSEMOVE);     window.onmousemove = null;
        booleanDrag = false;                                 return false;
  }
}        /*--------------------------------------------------------------------*/
//END HIDING-->
</SCRIPT>
</LAYER>
<!-- ***************************************************************** -->
<LAYER CLASS="Largefont" ID="Showcase7" LEFT="294" TOP="10" WIDTH="40" HEIGHT="40">B
<SCRIPT LANGUAGE="JavaScript1.2"><!--BEGIN HIDING
 Showcase7.bgColor = 'white';
 Showcase7.captureEvents(Event.MOUSEDOWN|Event.MOUSEUP);
 Showcase7.onmousedown = beginDrag;
 Showcase7.onmouseup = endDrag;
  var previousX, previousY, booleanDrag;
/*------------------------------------------------*/
function beginDrag(e) {
  if (e.which == 1) {
        window.captureEvents(Event.MOUSEMOVE);     window.onmousemove = drag;
        previousX = e.pageX;                                previousY = e.pageY;
        booleanDrag = true;                                return false;
  }
}        /*------------------------------------------------*/
function drag(e) {
  if (booleanDrag) {
        moveBy(e.pageX - previousX, e.pageY - previousY);
        previousX = e.pageX;                        previousY = e.pageY;
        return false;
  }
}        /*------------------------------------------------*/
function endDrag(e) {
  if (e.which == 1) {
        window.releaseEvents(Event.MOUSEMOVE);     window.onmousemove = null;
        booleanDrag = false;                                 return false;
  }
}        /*--------------------------------------------------------------------*/
//END HIDING-->
</SCRIPT>
</LAYER>
<!-- ************************************* -->
<LAYER CLASS="Largefont" ID="Showcase8" LEFT="350" TOP="10" WIDTH="40" HEIGHT="40">N
<SCRIPT LANGUAGE="JavaScript1.2"><!--BEGIN HIDING
 Showcase8.bgColor = 'white';
 Showcase8.captureEvents(Event.MOUSEDOWN|Event.MOUSEUP);
 Showcase8.onmousedown = beginDrag;
 Showcase8.onmouseup = endDrag;
  var previousX, previousY, booleanDrag;
/*------------------------------------------------*/
function beginDrag(e) {
  if (e.which == 1) {
        window.captureEvents(Event.MOUSEMOVE);     window.onmousemove = drag;
        previousX = e.pageX;                                previousY = e.pageY;
        booleanDrag = true;                                return false;
  }
}        /*------------------------------------------------*/
```

```
function drag(e) {
  if (booleanDrag) {
        moveBy(e.pageX - previousX, e.pageY - previousY);
        previousX = e.pageX;                                    previousY = e.pageY;
        return false;
  }
}         /*--------------------------------------------------*/
function endDrag(e) {
  if (e.which == 1) {
        window.releaseEvents(Event.MOUSEMOVE);     window.onmousemove = null;
        booleanDrag = false;                                    return false;
  }
}         /*-----------------------------------------------------------------------*/
//END HIDING-->
</SCRIPT>
</LAYER>

<!--  ******************************************************************  -->

<LAYER CLASS="Largefont" ID="Showcase9" LEFT="406" TOP="10" WIDTH="40" HEIGHT="40">R

<SCRIPT LANGUAGE="JavaScript1.2"><!--BEGIN HIDING
 Showcase9.bgColor = 'white';
 Showcase9.captureEvents(Event.MOUSEDOWN|Event.MOUSEUP);
 Showcase9.onmousedown = beginDrag;
 Showcase9.onmouseup = endDrag;
  var previousX, previousY, booleanDrag;
/*--------------------------------------------------*/
function beginDrag(e) {
  if (e.which == 1) {
        window.captureEvents(Event.MOUSEMOVE);     window.onmousemove = drag;
        previousX = e.pageX;                                    previousY = e.pageY;
        booleanDrag = true;                                    return false;
  }
}         /*--------------------------------------------------*/
function drag(e) {
  if (booleanDrag) {
        moveBy(e.pageX - previousX, e.pageY - previousY);
        previousX = e.pageX;                                    previousY = e.pageY;
        return false;
  }
}         /*--------------------------------------------------*/
function endDrag(e) {
  if (e.which == 1) {
        window.releaseEvents(Event.MOUSEMOVE);     window.onmousemove = null;
        booleanDrag = false;                                    return false;
  }
}         /*-----------------------------------------------------------------------*/
//END HIDING-->
</SCRIPT>
</LAYER>
<!--  ***********************************  -->
```

```
<!--    ***************************************************************  -->
<LAYER CLASS="Largefont" ID="Showcase10" LEFT="13" TOP="65" WIDTH="40" HEIGHT="40">P
<SCRIPT LANGUAGE="JavaScript1.2"><!--BEGIN HIDING
 Showcase10.bgColor = 'white';
 Showcase10.captureEvents(Event.MOUSEDOWN|Event.MOUSEUP);
 Showcase10.onmousedown = beginDrag;
 Showcase10.onmouseup = endDrag;
  var previousX, previousY, booleanDrag;
/*--------------------------------------------------*/
function beginDrag(e) {
  if (e.which == 1) {
        window.captureEvents(Event.MOUSEMOVE);     window.onmousemove = drag;
        previousX = e.pageX;                          previousY = e.pageY;
        booleanDrag = true;                          return false;
  }
}       /*--------------------------------------------------*/
function drag(e) {
  if (booleanDrag) {
        moveBy(e.pageX - previousX, e.pageY - previousY);
        previousX = e.pageX;                          previousY = e.pageY;
        return false;
  }
}       /*--------------------------------------------------*/
function endDrag(e) {
  if (e.which == 1) {
        window.releaseEvents(Event.MOUSEMOVE);     window.onmousemove = null;
        booleanDrag = false;                         return false;
  }
}       /*------------------------------------------------------------------*/
//END HIDING-->
</SCRIPT>
</LAYER>
<!--    ***************************************************************  -->
<LAYER CLASS="Largefont" ID="Showcase11" LEFT="70" TOP="65" WIDTH="40" HEIGHT="40">P
<SCRIPT LANGUAGE="JavaScript1.2"><!--BEGIN HIDING
 Showcase11.bgColor = 'white';
 Showcase11.captureEvents(Event.MOUSEDOWN|Event.MOUSEUP);
 Showcase11.onmousedown = beginDrag;
 Showcase11.onmouseup = endDrag;
  var previousX, previousY, booleanDrag;
/*--------------------------------------------------*/
function beginDrag(e) {
  if (e.which == 1) {
        window.captureEvents(Event.MOUSEMOVE);     window.onmousemove = drag;
        previousX = e.pageX;                          previousY = e.pageY;
        booleanDrag = true;                          return false;
  }
}       /*--------------------------------------------------*/
function drag(e) {
  if (booleanDrag) {
        moveBy(e.pageX - previousX, e.pageY - previousY);
        previousX = e.pageX;                          previousY = e.pageY;
        return false;
  }
}       /*--------------------------------------------------*/
```

```
function endDrag(e) {
  if (e.which == 1) {
        window.releaseEvents(Event.MOUSEMOVE);      window.onmousemove = null;
        booleanDrag = false;                                 return false;
  }
}        /*----------------------------------------------------------------------*/
//END HIDING-->
</SCRIPT>
</LAYER>
<!-- ********************************  -->
<LAYER CLASS="Largefont" ID="Showcase12" LEFT="125" TOP="65" WIDTH="40" HEIGHT="40">P
<SCRIPT LANGUAGE="JavaScript1.2"><!--BEGIN HIDING
 Showcase12.bgColor = 'white';
 Showcase12.captureEvents(Event.MOUSEDOWN|Event.MOUSEUP);
 Showcase12.onmousedown = beginDrag;
 Showcase12.onmouseup = endDrag;
  var previousX, previousY, booleanDrag;
/*-------------------------------------------------*/
function beginDrag(e) {
  if (e.which == 1) {
        window.captureEvents(Event.MOUSEMOVE);      window.onmousemove = drag;
        previousX = e.pageX;                                previousY = e.pageY;
        booleanDrag = true;                                 return false;
  }
}        /*-------------------------------------------------*/
function drag(e) {
  if (booleanDrag) {
        moveBy(e.pageX - previousX, e.pageY - previousY);
        previousX = e.pageX;                                previousY = e.pageY;
        return false;
  }
}        /*-------------------------------------------------*/
function endDrag(e) {
  if (e.which == 1) {
        window.releaseEvents(Event.MOUSEMOVE);      window.onmousemove = null;
        booleanDrag = false;                                 return false;
  }
}        /*----------------------------------------------------------------------*/
//END HIDING-->
</SCRIPT>
</LAYER>
<!-- *****************************************************************  -->
<LAYER CLASS="Largefont" ID="Showcase13" LEFT="182" TOP="65" WIDTH="40" HEIGHT="40">P
<SCRIPT LANGUAGE="JavaScript1.2"><!--BEGIN HIDING
 Showcase13.bgColor = 'white';
 Showcase13.captureEvents(Event.MOUSEDOWN|Event.MOUSEUP);
 Showcase13.onmousedown = beginDrag;
 Showcase13.onmouseup = endDrag;
  var previousX, previousY, booleanDrag;
/*-------------------------------------------------*/
function beginDrag(e) {
  if (e.which == 1) {
        window.captureEvents(Event.MOUSEMOVE);      window.onmousemove = drag;
        previousX = e.pageX;                                previousY = e.pageY;
        booleanDrag = true;                                 return false;
  }
}        /*-------------------------------------------------*/
```

```
function drag(e) {
  if (booleanDrag) {
       moveBy(e.pageX - previousX, e.pageY - previousY);
       previousX = e.pageX;                             previousY = e.pageY;
       return false;
  }
}       /*--------------------------------------------------*/
function endDrag(e) {
  if (e.which == 1) {
       window.releaseEvents(Event.MOUSEMOVE);    window.onmousemove = null;
       booleanDrag = false;                          return false;
  }
}       /*--------------------------------------------------------------------*/
//END HIDING-->
</SCRIPT>
</LAYER>
<!-- ********************************** -->
<LAYER CLASS="Largefont" ID="Showcase14" LEFT="237" TOP="65" WIDTH="40" HEIGHT="40">P
<SCRIPT LANGUAGE="JavaScript1.2"><!--BEGIN HIDING
 Showcase14.bgColor = 'white';
 Showcase14.captureEvents(Event.MOUSEDOWN|Event.MOUSEUP);
 Showcase14.onmousedown = beginDrag;
 Showcase14.onmouseup = endDrag;
  var previousX, previousY, booleanDrag;
/*--------------------------------------------------*/
function beginDrag(e) {
  if (e.which == 1) {
       window.captureEvents(Event.MOUSEMOVE);    window.onmousemove = drag;
       previousX = e.pageX;                          previousY = e.pageY;
       booleanDrag = true;                          return false;
  }
}       /*--------------------------------------------------*/
function drag(e) {
  if (booleanDrag) {
       moveBy(e.pageX - previousX, e.pageY - previousY);
       previousX = e.pageX;                          previousY = e.pageY;
       return false;
  }
}       /*--------------------------------------------------*/
function endDrag(e) {
  if (e.which == 1) {
       window.releaseEvents(Event.MOUSEMOVE);    window.onmousemove = null;
       booleanDrag = false;                          return false;
  }
}       /*--------------------------------------------------------------*/
//END HIDING-->
</SCRIPT>
</LAYER>
```

```
<!-- ****************************************************************** -->
<LAYER CLASS="Largefont" ID="Showcase15" LEFT="294" TOP="65" WIDTH="40" HEIGHT="40">P
<SCRIPT LANGUAGE="JavaScript1.2"><!--BEGIN HIDING
 Showcase15.bgColor = 'white';
 Showcase15.captureEvents(Event.MOUSEDOWN|Event.MOUSEUP);
 Showcase15.onmousedown = beginDrag;
 Showcase15.onmouseup = endDrag;
  var previousX, previousY, booleanDrag;
/*-----------------------------------------------*/
function beginDrag(e) {
  if (e.which == 1) {
        window.captureEvents(Event.MOUSEMOVE);      window.onmousemove = drag;
        previousX = e.pageX;                             previousY = e.pageY;
        booleanDrag = true;                              return false;
  }
}        /*-----------------------------------------------*/
function drag(e) {
  if (booleanDrag) {
        moveBy(e.pageX - previousX, e.pageY - previousY);
        previousX = e.pageX;                             previousY = e.pageY;
        return false;
  }
}        /*-----------------------------------------------*/
function endDrag(e) {
  if (e.which == 1) {
        window.releaseEvents(Event.MOUSEMOVE);      window.onmousemove = null;
        booleanDrag = false;                             return false;
  }
}        /*----------------------------------------------------------------*/
//END HIDING-->
</SCRIPT>
</LAYER>
<!-- ****************************************************************** -->
<LAYER CLASS="Largefont" ID="Showcase16" LEFT="350" TOP="65" WIDTH="40" HEIGHT="40">P
<SCRIPT LANGUAGE="JavaScript1.2"><!--BEGIN HIDING
 Showcase16.bgColor = 'white';
 Showcase16.captureEvents(Event.MOUSEDOWN|Event.MOUSEUP);
 Showcase16.onmousedown = beginDrag;
 Showcase16.onmouseup = endDrag;
  var previousX, previousY, booleanDrag;
/*-----------------------------------------------*/
function beginDrag(e) {
  if (e.which == 1) {
        window.captureEvents(Event.MOUSEMOVE);      window.onmousemove = drag;
        previousX = e.pageX;                             previousY = e.pageY;
        booleanDrag = true;                              return false;
  }
}        /*-----------------------------------------------*/
function drag(e) {
  if (booleanDrag) {
        moveBy(e.pageX - previousX, e.pageY - previousY);
        previousX = e.pageX;                             previousY = e.pageY;
        return false;
  }
}        /*-----------------------------------------------*/
```

```
function endDrag(e) {
  if (e.which == 1) {
        window.releaseEvents(Event.MOUSEMOVE);       window.onmousemove = null;
        booleanDrag = false;                          return false;
  }
}        /*------------------------------------------------------------------*/
//END HIDING-->
</SCRIPT>
</LAYER>
<!-- ******************************************************************** -->
<LAYER CLASS="Largefont" ID="Showcase17" LEFT="406" TOP="65" WIDTH="40" HEIGHT="40">P
<SCRIPT LANGUAGE="JavaScript1.2"><!--BEGIN HIDING
 Showcase17.bgColor = 'white';
 Showcase17.captureEvents(Event.MOUSEDOWN|Event.MOUSEUP);
 Showcase17.onmousedown = beginDrag;
 Showcase17.onmouseup = endDrag;
  var previousX, previousY, booleanDrag;
/*------------------------------------------------*/
function beginDrag(e) {
  if (e.which == 1) {
        window.captureEvents(Event.MOUSEMOVE);       window.onmousemove = drag;
        previousX = e.pageX;                          previousY = e.pageY;
        booleanDrag = true;                           return false;
  }
}        /*------------------------------------------------*/
function drag(e) {
  if (booleanDrag) {
        moveBy(e.pageX - previousX, e.pageY - previousY);
        previousX = e.pageX;                          previousY = e.pageY;
        return false;
  }
}        /*------------------------------------------------*/
function endDrag(e) {
  if (e.which == 1) {
        window.releaseEvents(Event.MOUSEMOVE);       window.onmousemove = null;
        booleanDrag = false;                          return false;
  }
}        /*------------------------------------------------------------------*/
//END HIDING-->
</SCRIPT>
</LAYER>
<!-- ******************************************************************** -->
<LAYER CLASS="Whitefont" ID="Showcase18" LEFT="13" TOP="390" WIDTH="40" HEIGHT="40">R
<SCRIPT LANGUAGE="JavaScript1.2"><!--BEGIN HIDING
 Showcase18.bgColor = 'black';
 Showcase18.captureEvents(Event.MOUSEDOWN|Event.MOUSEUP);
 Showcase18.onmousedown = beginDrag;
 Showcase18.onmouseup = endDrag;
  var previousX, previousY, booleanDrag;
/*------------------------------------------------*/
function beginDrag(e) {
  if (e.which == 1) {
        window.captureEvents(Event.MOUSEMOVE);       window.onmousemove = drag;
        previousX = e.pageX;                          previousY = e.pageY;
        booleanDrag = true;                           return false;
  }
}        /*------------------------------------------------*/
```

```
function drag(e) {
  if (booleanDrag) {
        moveBy(e.pageX - previousX, e.pageY - previousY);
        previousX = e.pageX;                              previousY = e.pageY;
        return false;
  }
}       /*-------------------------------------------------*/
function endDrag(e) {
  if (e.which == 1) {
        window.releaseEvents(Event.MOUSEMOVE);    window.onmousemove = null;
        booleanDrag = false;                             return false;
  }
}       /*----------------------------------------------------------------------*/
//END HIDING-->
</SCRIPT>
</LAYER>
<!-- ************************************************************** -->
<LAYER CLASS="Whitefont" ID="Showcase19" LEFT="70" TOP="390" WIDTH="40" HEIGHT="40">N
<SCRIPT LANGUAGE="JavaScript1.2"><!--BEGIN HIDING
 Showcase19.bgColor = 'black';
 Showcase19.captureEvents(Event.MOUSEDOWN|Event.MOUSEUP);
 Showcase19.onmousedown = beginDrag;
 Showcase19.onmouseup = endDrag;
  var previousX, previousY, booleanDrag;
/*-----------------------------------------------*/
function beginDrag(e) {
  if (e.which == 1) {
        window.captureEvents(Event.MOUSEMOVE);    window.onmousemove = drag;
        previousX = e.pageX;                             previousY = e.pageY;
        booleanDrag = true;                              return false;
  }
}       /*-------------------------------------------------*/
function drag(e) {
  if (booleanDrag) {
        moveBy(e.pageX - previousX, e.pageY - previousY);
        previousX = e.pageX;                             previousY = e.pageY;
        return false;
  }
}       /*-------------------------------------------------*/
function endDrag(e) {
  if (e.which == 1) {
        window.releaseEvents(Event.MOUSEMOVE);    window.onmousemove = null;
        booleanDrag = false;                             return false;
  }
}       /*----------------------------------------------------------------*/
//END HIDING-->
</SCRIPT>
</LAYER>
<!-- *********************************** -->
```

```
<LAYER CLASS="Whitefont" ID="Showcase20" LEFT="125" TOP="390" WIDTH="40" HEIGHT="40">B
<SCRIPT LANGUAGE="JavaScript1.2"><!--BEGIN HIDING
 Showcase20.bgColor = 'black';
 Showcase20.captureEvents(Event.MOUSEDOWN|Event.MOUSEUP);
 Showcase20.onmousedown = beginDrag;
 Showcase20.onmouseup = endDrag;
  var previousX, previousY, booleanDrag;
/*-------------------------------------------------*/
function beginDrag(e) {
  if (e.which == 1) {
        window.captureEvents(Event.MOUSEMOVE);     window.onmousemove = drag;
        previousX = e.pageX;                               previousY = e.pageY;
        booleanDrag = true;                               return false;
  }
}       /*-------------------------------------------------*/
function drag(e) {
  if (booleanDrag) {
        moveBy(e.pageX - previousX, e.pageY - previousY);
        previousX = e.pageX;                               previousY = e.pageY;
        return false;
  }
}       /*-------------------------------------------------*/
function endDrag(e) {
  if (e.which == 1) {
        window.releaseEvents(Event.MOUSEMOVE);     window.onmousemove = null;
        booleanDrag = false;                              return false;
  }
}       /*----------------------------------------------------------------*/
//END HIDING-->
</SCRIPT>
</LAYER>
<!-- ************************************************************** -->
<LAYER CLASS="Whitefont" ID="Showcase21" LEFT="182" TOP="390" WIDTH="40" HEIGHT="40">Q
<SCRIPT LANGUAGE="JavaScript1.2"><!--BEGIN HIDING
 Showcase21.bgColor = 'black';
 Showcase21.captureEvents(Event.MOUSEDOWN|Event.MOUSEUP);
 Showcase21.onmousedown = beginDrag;
 Showcase21.onmouseup = endDrag;
  var previousX, previousY, booleanDrag;
/*-------------------------------------------------*/
function beginDrag(e) {
  if (e.which == 1) {
        window.captureEvents(Event.MOUSEMOVE);     window.onmousemove = drag;
        previousX = e.pageX;                               previousY = e.pageY;
        booleanDrag = true;                               return false;
  }
}       /*-------------------------------------------------*/
function drag(e) {
  if (booleanDrag) {
        moveBy(e.pageX - previousX, e.pageY - previousY);
        previousX = e.pageX;                               previousY = e.pageY;
        return false;
  }
}       /*-------------------------------------------------*/
```

```
function endDrag(e) {
  if (e.which == 1) {
        window.releaseEvents(Event.MOUSEMOVE);       window.onmousemove = null;
        booleanDrag = false;                                  return false;
  }
}       /*--------------------------------------------------------------------*/
//END HIDING-->
</SCRIPT>
</LAYER>
<!--   ********************************  -->
<LAYER CLASS="Whitefont" ID="Showcase22" LEFT="237" TOP="390" WIDTH="40" HEIGHT="40">K
<SCRIPT LANGUAGE="JavaScript1.2"><!--BEGIN HIDING
 Showcase22.bgColor = 'black';
 Showcase22.captureEvents(Event.MOUSEDOWN|Event.MOUSEUP);
 Showcase22.onmousedown = beginDrag;
 Showcase22.onmouseup = endDrag;
  var previousX, previousY, booleanDrag;
/*------------------------------------------------*/
function beginDrag(e) {
  if (e.which == 1) {
        window.captureEvents(Event.MOUSEMOVE);     window.onmousemove = drag;
        previousX = e.pageX;                             previousY = e.pageY;
        booleanDrag = true;                              return false;
  }
}       /*------------------------------------------------*/
function drag(e) {
  if (booleanDrag) {
        moveBy(e.pageX - previousX, e.pageY - previousY);
        previousX = e.pageX;                               previousY = e.pageY;
        return false;
  }
}       /*------------------------------------------------*/
function endDrag(e) {
  if (e.which == 1) {
        window.releaseEvents(Event.MOUSEMOVE);     window.onmousemove = null;
        booleanDrag = false;                              return false;
  }
}       /*--------------------------------------------------------------------*/
//END HIDING-->
</SCRIPT>
</LAYER>
<!--   *****************************************************************  -->
<LAYER CLASS="Whitefont" ID="Showcase23" LEFT="294" TOP="390" WIDTH="40" HEIGHT="40">B
<SCRIPT LANGUAGE="JavaScript1.2"><!--BEGIN HIDING
 Showcase23.bgColor = 'black';
 Showcase23.captureEvents(Event.MOUSEDOWN|Event.MOUSEUP);
 Showcase23.onmousedown = beginDrag;
 Showcase23.onmouseup = endDrag;
  var previousX, previousY, booleanDrag;
/*------------------------------------------------*/
function beginDrag(e) {
  if (e.which == 1) {
        window.captureEvents(Event.MOUSEMOVE);     window.onmousemove = drag;
        previousX = e.pageX;                             previousY = e.pageY;
        booleanDrag = true;                              return false;
  }
}       /*------------------------------------------------*/
```

```
function drag(e) {
  if (booleanDrag) {
      moveBy(e.pageX - previousX, e.pageY - previousY);
      previousX = e.pageX;                              previousY = e.pageY;
      return false;
  }
}        /*--------------------------------------------------*/
function endDrag(e) {
  if (e.which == 1) {
      window.releaseEvents(Event.MOUSEMOVE);     window.onmousemove = null;
      booleanDrag = false;                              return false;
  }
}        /*----------------------------------------------------------------------*/
//END HIDING-->
</SCRIPT>
</LAYER>
<!-- ************************************ -->
<LAYER CLASS="Whitefont" ID="Showcase24" LEFT="350" TOP="390" WIDTH="40" HEIGHT="40">N
<SCRIPT LANGUAGE="JavaScript1.2"><!--BEGIN HIDING
 Showcase24.bgColor = 'black';
 Showcase24.captureEvents(Event.MOUSEDOWN|Event.MOUSEUP);
 Showcase24.onmousedown = beginDrag;
 Showcase24.onmouseup = endDrag;
  var previousX, previousY, booleanDrag;
/*------------------------------------------------*/
function beginDrag(e) {
  if (e.which == 1) {
      window.captureEvents(Event.MOUSEMOVE);     window.onmousemove = drag;
      previousX = e.pageX;                              previousY = e.pageY;
      booleanDrag = true;                              return false;
  }
}        /*------------------------------------------------*/
function drag(e) {
  if (booleanDrag) {
      moveBy(e.pageX - previousX, e.pageY - previousY);
      previousX = e.pageX;                              previousY = e.pageY;
      return false;
  }
}        /*------------------------------------------------*/
function endDrag(e) {
  if (e.which == 1) {
      window.releaseEvents(Event.MOUSEMOVE);     window.onmousemove = null;
      booleanDrag = false;                              return false;
  }
}        /*----------------------------------------------------------------*/
//END HIDING-->
</SCRIPT>
</LAYER>
```

```
<!--   ********************************************************  -->
<LAYER CLASS="Whitefont" ID="Showcase25" LEFT="406" TOP="390" WIDTH="40" HEIGHT="40">R
<SCRIPT LANGUAGE="JavaScript1.2"><!--BEGIN HIDING
 Showcase25.bgColor = 'black';
 Showcase25.captureEvents(Event.MOUSEDOWN|Event.MOUSEUP);
 Showcase25.onmousedown = beginDrag;
 Showcase25.onmouseup = endDrag;
  var previousX, previousY, booleanDrag;
/*-----------------------------------------------*/
function beginDrag(e) {
  if (e.which == 1) {
        window.captureEvents(Event.MOUSEMOVE);     window.onmousemove = drag;
        previousX = e.pageX;                          previousY = e.pageY;
        booleanDrag = true;                           return false;
  }
}       /*-----------------------------------------------*/
function drag(e) {
  if (booleanDrag) {
        moveBy(e.pageX - previousX, e.pageY - previousY);
        previousX = e.pageX;                          previousY = e.pageY;
        return false;
  }
}       /*-----------------------------------------------*/
function endDrag(e) {
  if (e.which == 1) {
        window.releaseEvents(Event.MOUSEMOVE);     window.onmousemove = null;
        booleanDrag = false;                          return false;
  }
}       /*----------------------------------------------------------*/
//END HIDING-->
</SCRIPT>
</LAYER>
<!--   *********************************  -->
<!--   *********************************************************  -->
<!--   ********************************************************  -->
<LAYER CLASS="Whitefont" ID="Showcase26" LEFT="13" TOP="335" WIDTH="40" HEIGHT="40">P
<SCRIPT LANGUAGE="JavaScript1.2"><!--BEGIN HIDING
 Showcase26.bgColor = 'black';
 Showcase26.captureEvents(Event.MOUSEDOWN|Event.MOUSEUP);
 Showcase26.onmousedown = beginDrag;
 Showcase26.onmouseup = endDrag;
  var previousX, previousY, booleanDrag;
/*-----------------------------------------------*/
function beginDrag(e) {
  if (e.which == 1) {
        window.captureEvents(Event.MOUSEMOVE);     window.onmousemove = drag;
        previousX = e.pageX;                          previousY = e.pageY;
        booleanDrag = true;                           return false;
  }
}       /*-----------------------------------------------*/
function drag(e) {
  if (booleanDrag) {
        moveBy(e.pageX - previousX, e.pageY - previousY);
        previousX = e.pageX;                          previousY = e.pageY;
        return false;
  }
}       /*-----------------------------------------------*/
```

```
function endDrag(e) {
  if (e.which == 1) {
        window.releaseEvents(Event.MOUSEMOVE);     window.onmousemove = null;
        booleanDrag = false;                       return false;
  }
}       /*--------------------------------------------------------------------*/
//END HIDING-->
</SCRIPT>
</LAYER>
<!--  ********************************************************************  -->
<LAYER CLASS="Whitefont" ID="Showcase27" LEFT="70" TOP="335" WIDTH="40" HEIGHT="40">P
<SCRIPT LANGUAGE="JavaScript1.2"><!--BEGIN HIDING
 Showcase27.bgColor = 'black';
 Showcase27.captureEvents(Event.MOUSEDOWN|Event.MOUSEUP);
 Showcase27.onmousedown = beginDrag;
 Showcase27.onmouseup = endDrag;
  var previousX, previousY, booleanDrag;
/*-------------------------------------------------*/
function beginDrag(e) {
  if (e.which == 1) {
        window.captureEvents(Event.MOUSEMOVE);     window.onmousemove = drag;
        previousX = e.pageX;                        previousY = e.pageY;
        booleanDrag = true;                        return false;
  }
}       /*-----------------------------------------------*/
function drag(e) {
  if (booleanDrag) {
        moveBy(e.pageX - previousX, e.pageY - previousY);
        previousX = e.pageX;                       previousY = e.pageY;
        return false;
  }
}       /*-----------------------------------------------*/
function endDrag(e) {
  if (e.which == 1) {
        window.releaseEvents(Event.MOUSEMOVE);     window.onmousemove = null;
        booleanDrag = false;                       return false;
  }
}       /*--------------------------------------------------------------------*/
//END HIDING-->
</SCRIPT>
</LAYER>
<!--  ********************************  -->
<LAYER CLASS="Whitefont" ID="Showcase28" LEFT="125" TOP="335" WIDTH="40" HEIGHT="40">P
<SCRIPT LANGUAGE="JavaScript1.2"><!--BEGIN HIDING
 Showcase28.bgColor = 'black';
 Showcase28.captureEvents(Event.MOUSEDOWN|Event.MOUSEUP);
 Showcase28.onmousedown = beginDrag;
 Showcase28.onmouseup = endDrag;
  var previousX, previousY, booleanDrag;
/*-------------------------------------------------*/
function beginDrag(e) {
  if (e.which == 1) {
        window.captureEvents(Event.MOUSEMOVE);     window.onmousemove = drag;
        previousX = e.pageX;                        previousY = e.pageY;
        booleanDrag = true;                        return false;
  }
}       /*-----------------------------------------------*/
```

```
function drag(e) {
  if (booleanDrag) {
        moveBy(e.pageX - previousX, e.pageY - previousY);
        previousX = e.pageX;                                    previousY = e.pageY;
        return false;
  }
}       /*--------------------------------------------------*/
function endDrag(e) {
  if (e.which == 1) {
        window.releaseEvents(Event.MOUSEMOVE);     window.onmousemove = null;
        booleanDrag = false;                                   return false;
  }
}       /*------------------------------------------------------------------------*/
//END HIDING-->
</SCRIPT>
</LAYER>
<!--  ************************************************************  -->
<LAYER CLASS="Whitefont" ID="Showcase29" LEFT="182" TOP="335" WIDTH="40" HEIGHT="40">P
<SCRIPT LANGUAGE="JavaScript1.2"><!--BEGIN HIDING
 Showcase29.bgColor = 'black';
 Showcase29.captureEvents(Event.MOUSEDOWN|Event.MOUSEUP);
 Showcase29.onmousedown = beginDrag;
 Showcase29.onmouseup = endDrag;
  var previousX, previousY, booleanDrag;
/*--------------------------------------------------*/
function beginDrag(e) {
  if (e.which == 1) {
        window.captureEvents(Event.MOUSEMOVE);     window.onmousemove = drag;
        previousX = e.pageX;                                   previousY = e.pageY;
        booleanDrag = true;                                    return false;
  }
}       /*--------------------------------------------------*/
function drag(e) {
  if (booleanDrag) {
        moveBy(e.pageX - previousX, e.pageY - previousY);
        previousX = e.pageX;                                   previousY = e.pageY;
        return false;
  }
}       /*--------------------------------------------------*/
function endDrag(e) {
  if (e.which == 1) {
        window.releaseEvents(Event.MOUSEMOVE);     window.onmousemove = null;
        booleanDrag = false;                                   return false;
  }
}       /*------------------------------------------------------------------*/
//END HIDING-->
</SCRIPT>
</LAYER>
```

```
<!--    *********************************   -->
<LAYER CLASS="Whitefont" ID="Showcase30" LEFT="237" TOP="335" WIDTH="40" HEIGHT="40">P
<SCRIPT LANGUAGE="JavaScript1.2"><!--BEGIN HIDING
 Showcase30.bgColor = 'black';
 Showcase30.captureEvents(Event.MOUSEDOWN|Event.MOUSEUP);
 Showcase30.onmousedown = beginDrag;
 Showcase30.onmouseup = endDrag;
  var previousX, previousY, booleanDrag;
/*------------------------------------------------*/
function beginDrag(e) {
  if (e.which == 1) {
        window.captureEvents(Event.MOUSEMOVE);     window.onmousemove = drag;
        previousX = e.pageX;                        previousY = e.pageY;
        booleanDrag = true;                         return false;
  }
}       /*------------------------------------------------*/
function drag(e) {
  if (booleanDrag) {
        moveBy(e.pageX - previousX, e.pageY - previousY);
        previousX = e.pageX;                        previousY = e.pageY;
        return false;
  }
}       /*------------------------------------------------*/
function endDrag(e) {
  if (e.which == 1) {
        window.releaseEvents(Event.MOUSEMOVE);     window.onmousemove = null;
        booleanDrag = false;                        return false;
  }
}       /*-----------------------------------------------------------------------*/
//END HIDING-->
</SCRIPT>
</LAYER>
<!--    *****************************************************************   -->
<LAYER CLASS="Whitefont" ID="Showcase31" LEFT="294" TOP="335" WIDTH="40" HEIGHT="40">P
<SCRIPT LANGUAGE="JavaScript1.2"><!--BEGIN HIDING
 Showcase31.bgColor = 'black';
 Showcase31.captureEvents(Event.MOUSEDOWN|Event.MOUSEUP);
 Showcase31.onmousedown = beginDrag;
 Showcase31.onmouseup = endDrag;
  var previousX, previousY, booleanDrag;
/*------------------------------------------------*/
function beginDrag(e) {
  if (e.which == 1) {
        window.captureEvents(Event.MOUSEMOVE);     window.onmousemove = drag;
        previousX = e.pageX;                        previousY = e.pageY;
        booleanDrag = true;                         return false;
  }
}       /*------------------------------------------------*/
function drag(e) {
  if (booleanDrag) {
        moveBy(e.pageX - previousX, e.pageY - previousY);
        previousX = e.pageX;                        previousY = e.pageY;
        return false;
  }
}       /*------------------------------------------------*/
function endDrag(e) {
  if (e.which == 1) {
        window.releaseEvents(Event.MOUSEMOVE);     window.onmousemove = null;
        booleanDrag = false;                        return false;
  }
}       /*-----------------------------------------------------------------------*/
//END HIDING-->
</SCRIPT>
</LAYER>
```

```
<!-- ********************************* -->
<LAYER CLASS="Whitefont" ID="Showcase32" LEFT="350" TOP="335" WIDTH="40" HEIGHT="40">P
<SCRIPT LANGUAGE="JavaScript1.2"><!--BEGIN HIDING
 Showcase32.bgColor = 'black';
 Showcase32.captureEvents(Event.MOUSEDOWN|Event.MOUSEUP);
 Showcase32.onmousedown = beginDrag;
 Showcase32.onmouseup = endDrag;
  var previousX, previousY, booleanDrag;
/*-----------------------------------------------*/
function beginDrag(e) {
  if (e.which == 1) {
        window.captureEvents(Event.MOUSEMOVE);     window.onmousemove = drag;
        previousX = e.pageX;                            previousY = e.pageY;
        booleanDrag = true;                             return false;
  }
}         /*-----------------------------------------------*/
function drag(e) {
  if (booleanDrag) {
        moveBy(e.pageX - previousX, e.pageY - previousY);
        previousX = e.pageX;                            previousY = e.pageY;
        return false;
  }
}         /*-----------------------------------------------*/
function endDrag(e) {
  if (e.which == 1) {
        window.releaseEvents(Event.MOUSEMOVE);     window.onmousemove = null;
        booleanDrag = false;                            return false;
  }
}         /*----------------------------------------------------------*/
//END HIDING-->
</SCRIPT>
</LAYER>
<!-- ***************************************************************** -->
<LAYER CLASS="Whitefont" ID="Showcase33" LEFT="406" TOP="335" WIDTH="40" HEIGHT="40">P
<SCRIPT LANGUAGE="JavaScript1.2"><!--BEGIN HIDING
 Showcase33.bgColor = 'black';
 Showcase33.captureEvents(Event.MOUSEDOWN|Event.MOUSEUP);
 Showcase33.onmousedown = beginDrag;
 Showcase33.onmouseup = endDrag;
  var previousX, previousY, booleanDrag;
/*-----------------------------------------------*/
function beginDrag(e) {
  if (e.which == 1) {
        window.captureEvents(Event.MOUSEMOVE);     window.onmousemove = drag;
        previousX = e.pageX;                            previousY = e.pageY;
        booleanDrag = true;                             return false;
  }
}         /*-----------------------------------------------*/
function drag(e) {
  if (booleanDrag) {
        moveBy(e.pageX - previousX, e.pageY - previousY);
        previousX = e.pageX;                            previousY = e.pageY;
        return false;
  }
}         /*-----------------------------------------------*/
function endDrag(e) {
  if (e.which == 1) {
        window.releaseEvents(Event.MOUSEMOVE);     window.onmousemove = null;
        booleanDrag = false;                            return false;
  }
}         /*----------------------------------------------------------*/
//END HIDING-->
</SCRIPT>
</LAYER>
<!-- ********************************* -->
</LAYER>
```

```
<!--  **************************************************************  -->
<SCRIPT LANGUAGE="JavaScript1.2"><!--BEGIN HIDING
/*-------------------------------------------------------------------------*/
/*----------       This section deals with the New Game Button      ----------*/
function StartGame() {
        document.ShowcaseA.        document.Showcase2.moveTo (13, 10);
        document.ShowcaseA.        document.Showcase3.moveTo (70, 10);
        document.ShowcaseA.        document.Showcase4.moveTo (125, 10);
        document.ShowcaseA.        document.Showcase5.moveTo (182, 10);
        document.ShowcaseA.        document.Showcase6.moveTo (237, 10);
        document.ShowcaseA.        document.Showcase7.moveTo (294, 10);
        document.ShowcaseA.        document.Showcase8.moveTo (350, 10);
        document.ShowcaseA.        document.Showcase9.moveTo (406, 10);
        document.ShowcaseA.        document.Showcase10.moveTo (13, 65);
        document.ShowcaseA.        document.Showcase11.moveTo (70, 65);
        document.ShowcaseA.        document.Showcase12.moveTo (125, 65);
        document.ShowcaseA.        document.Showcase13.moveTo (182, 65);
        document.ShowcaseA.        document.Showcase14.moveTo (237, 65);
        document.ShowcaseA.        document.Showcase15.moveTo (294, 65);
        document.ShowcaseA.        document.Showcase16.moveTo (350, 65);
        document.ShowcaseA.        document.Showcase17.moveTo (406, 65);
        document.ShowcaseA.        document.Showcase18.moveTo (13, 390);
        document.ShowcaseA.        document.Showcase19.moveTo (70, 390);
        document.ShowcaseA.        document.Showcase20.moveTo (125, 390);
        document.ShowcaseA.        document.Showcase21.moveTo (182, 390);
        document.ShowcaseA.        document.Showcase22.moveTo (237, 390);
        document.ShowcaseA.        document.Showcase23.moveTo (294, 390);
        document.ShowcaseA.        document.Showcase24.moveTo (350, 390);
        document.ShowcaseA.        document.Showcase25.moveTo (406, 390);
        document.ShowcaseA.        document.Showcase26.moveTo (13, 335);
        document.ShowcaseA.        document.Showcase27.moveTo (70, 335);
        document.ShowcaseA.        document.Showcase28.moveTo (125, 335);
        document.ShowcaseA.        document.Showcase29.moveTo (182, 335);
        document.ShowcaseA.        document.Showcase30.moveTo (237, 335);
        document.ShowcaseA.        document.Showcase31.moveTo (294, 335);
        document.ShowcaseA.        document.Showcase32.moveTo (350, 335);
        document.ShowcaseA.        document.Showcase33.moveTo (406, 335);
}
//END HIDING-->
</SCRIPT>
</BODY>
</HTML>
```

Capturing and using
KEYPRESS and KEYUP Events

Tic Tac Toe played from the Keyboard

From now on, the Events in this book will be written in all uppercase letters so it will be easier to identify them. Just remember that they really use lowercase Syntax, and that for best results, your Event Handlers should also use lowercase Syntax.

This example focuses on the KEYPRESS and KEYUP Events with code to play the Tic Tac Toe game from the Keyboard. It uses the **captureEvents()** Method on the **document** Object like this:

```
document.captureEvents(Event.KEYPRESS);
document.captureEvents(Event.KEYUP);
```

and then assigns the **keyJump(e)** Function to the KEYPRESS Event and the **keyNewGame(e)** Function to the KEYUP Event like this:

```
document.onkeypress = keyJump;
document.onkeyup = keyNewGame;
```

The **keyJump(e)** Function is what controls the X and O images in their Layers by testing with the **modifiers** Property for whether the ALT Key or the CONTROL Key was pressed, and testing with the **which** Property for which of the Keys from 1 to 9 are pressed, if any. In the following code, if the CONTROL Key is pressed and the number 1 Key is pressed (the ASCII Value for the "1" Key is 49 when the CONTROL Key is also pressed), then the **Showcase2** Layer is moved to the (x,y) coordinates of (10,10), and it is moved above **Showcase3** in the **zindex** stacking order so it is the visible Layer.

```
if (e.modifiers == Event.CONTROL_MASK  &&  e.which == 49)
{ Showcase2.moveTo(10,10); Showcase2.moveAbove(Showcase3); }
```

The same principle applies to the next two lines of code, except that you are testing for the ALT Key, and you have to test for either of two ASCII Values for the "1" Key because there are two different "1" Keys on extended keyboards, and each one has a unique ASCII Value. The ASCII Value for "1" that is on with the "!" Key is 193, and the Value for "1" in the Keypad on the far right side of the keyboard, is 49, when used with the ALT Key.

```
if (e.modifiers == Event.ALT_MASK  &&  (e.which == 193 || e.which == 49))
{ Showcase3.moveTo(10,10); Showcase3.moveAbove(Showcase2); }
```

This process is repeated for all of the Layers that contain the X and O images. Finally, the **keyNewGame(e)** Function is used to reset all the Layers to their original coordinates to start a new game when the "n" Key is pressed with the CONTROL Key.

Example 6-14:   **Sample714-TTT-Keys.html**

```
<!DOCTYPE HTML PUBLIC "-//W3C//DTD HTML 3.2//EN">
<HTML><HEAD>
<TITLE>Sample 714 - Example 6-14      Control and Alt Key Tic Tac Toe </TITLE>

<STYLE type = "text/JavaScript">

        classes.theControl.all.fontSize = "16pt";
        classes.theControl.all.fontFamily = "Moonlight, cursive";
        classes.theControl.all.textAlign = "center";
        classes.theControl.all.align = "center";
        classes.theControl.all.color = "blue";
        classes.theControl.all.backgroundColor = "lime";

</STYLE>

</HEAD>

<BODY BGCOLOR="BLACK" TEXT="blue">

<!-- ***************    The CONTROL  layer       ***************  -->

<LAYER CLASS="theControl" ID="Control" LEFT="0" TOP="0" WIDTH="100"> <BR>
<FORM NAME="form1">

CONTROL Key plus 1-9 <BR>pops an X                      <BR><BR><HR>
ALT <BR>Key plus 1-9 <BR>pops an O                      <BR><HR>
CONTROL Key plus 'n' <BR>starts a New Game              <BR><HR>

<INPUT TYPE="button" NAME="StartOver" VALUE="New Game"
onClick='StartGame(); return false;'>

</FORM>
</LAYER>

<!-- *********************************************************************  -->
<!--   Notice that Showcase2 through Showcase11 are nested inside ShowcaseA   -->

<LAYER ID="ShowcaseA" LEFT="100" TOP="5" WIDTH="700" HEIGHT="470" BGCOLOR="yellow">


<!--  The 9 Layers that black out the main Grid to reveal only the Grid Bars   -->

<LAYER LEFT="0" TOP="0" WIDTH="150" HEIGHT="150" BGCOLOR="black"> </LAYER>

<LAYER LEFT="160" TOP="0" WIDTH="150" HEIGHT="150" BGCOLOR="black"> </LAYER>

<LAYER LEFT="320" TOP="0" WIDTH="150" HEIGHT="150" BGCOLOR="black"> </LAYER>

<LAYER LEFT="0" TOP="160" WIDTH="150" HEIGHT="150" BGCOLOR="black"> </LAYER>

<LAYER LEFT="160" TOP="160" WIDTH="150" HEIGHT="150" BGCOLOR="black"> </LAYER>

<LAYER LEFT="320" TOP="160" WIDTH="150" HEIGHT="150" BGCOLOR="black"> </LAYER>
```

```
<LAYER LEFT="0" TOP="320" WIDTH="150" HEIGHT="150" BGCOLOR="black"> </LAYER>

<LAYER LEFT="160" TOP="320" WIDTH="150" HEIGHT="150" BGCOLOR="black"> </LAYER>

<LAYER LEFT="320" TOP="320" WIDTH="150" HEIGHT="150" BGCOLOR="black"> </LAYER>

<LAYER LEFT="470" TOP="0" WIDTH="230" HEIGHT="470" BGCOLOR="black"> </LAYER>

<!-- ***************************************************************** -->
<!-- ***************************************************************** -->

<LAYER ID="Showcase2" LEFT="480" TOP="10" WIDTH="130" HEIGHT="130">
<IMG SRC="JPEG-FILES/X-TicTacToe.jpg" NAME="myImage2" WIDTH="130" HEIGHT="130">
</LAYER>

<LAYER ID="Showcase3" LEFT="480" TOP="310" WIDTH="130" HEIGHT="130">
<IMG SRC="JPEG-FILES/O-TicTacToe.jpg" NAME="myImage3" WIDTH="130" HEIGHT="130">
</LAYER>

<LAYER ID="Showcase4" LEFT="480" TOP="10" WIDTH="130" HEIGHT="130">
<IMG SRC="JPEG-FILES/X-TicTacToe.jpg" NAME="myImage4" WIDTH="130" HEIGHT="130">
</LAYER>

<LAYER ID="Showcase5" LEFT="480" TOP="310" WIDTH="130" HEIGHT="130">
<IMG SRC="JPEG-FILES/O-TicTacToe.jpg" NAME="myImage5" WIDTH="130" HEIGHT="130">
</LAYER>

<LAYER ID="Showcase6" LEFT="480" TOP="10" WIDTH="130" HEIGHT="130">
<IMG SRC="JPEG-FILES/X-TicTacToe.jpg" NAME="myImage6" WIDTH="130" HEIGHT="130">
</LAYER>

<LAYER ID="Showcase7" LEFT="480" TOP="310" WIDTH="130" HEIGHT="130">
<IMG SRC="JPEG-FILES/O-TicTacToe.jpg" NAME="myImage7" WIDTH="130" HEIGHT="130">
</LAYER>

<LAYER ID="Showcase8" LEFT="480" TOP="10" WIDTH="130" HEIGHT="130">
<IMG SRC="JPEG-FILES/X-TicTacToe.jpg" NAME="myImage8" WIDTH="130" HEIGHT="130">
</LAYER>

<LAYER ID="Showcase9" LEFT="480" TOP="310" WIDTH="130" HEIGHT="130">
<IMG SRC="JPEG-FILES/O-TicTacToe.jpg" NAME="myImage9" WIDTH="130" HEIGHT="130">
</LAYER>

<LAYER ID="Showcase10" LEFT="480" TOP="10" WIDTH="130" HEIGHT="130">
<IMG SRC="JPEG-FILES/X-TicTacToe.jpg" NAME="myImage10" WIDTH="130" HEIGHT="130">
</LAYER>

<LAYER ID="Showcase11" LEFT="480" TOP="310" WIDTH="130" HEIGHT="130">
<IMG SRC="JPEG-FILES/O-TicTacToe.jpg" NAME="myImage11" WIDTH="130" HEIGHT="130">
</LAYER>

<LAYER ID="Showcase12" LEFT="480" TOP="10" WIDTH="130" HEIGHT="130">
<IMG SRC="JPEG-FILES/X-TicTacToe.jpg" NAME="myImage12" WIDTH="130" HEIGHT="130">
</LAYER>

<LAYER ID="Showcase13" LEFT="480" TOP="310" WIDTH="130" HEIGHT="130">
<IMG SRC="JPEG-FILES/O-TicTacToe.jpg" NAME="myImage13" WIDTH="130" HEIGHT="130">
</LAYER>
```

```
<LAYER ID="Showcase14" LEFT="480" TOP="10" WIDTH="130" HEIGHT="130">
<IMG SRC="JPEG-FILES/X-TicTacToe.jpg" NAME="myImage14" WIDTH="130" HEIGHT="130">
</LAYER>

<LAYER ID="Showcase15" LEFT="480" TOP="310" WIDTH="130" HEIGHT="130">
<IMG SRC="JPEG-FILES/O-TicTacToe.jpg" NAME="myImage15" WIDTH="130" HEIGHT="130">
</LAYER>

<LAYER ID="Showcase16" LEFT="480" TOP="10" WIDTH="130" HEIGHT="130">
<IMG SRC="JPEG-FILES/X-TicTacToe.jpg" NAME="myImage16" WIDTH="130" HEIGHT="130">
</LAYER>

<LAYER ID="Showcase17" LEFT="480" TOP="310" WIDTH="130" HEIGHT="130">
<IMG SRC="JPEG-FILES/O-TicTacToe.jpg" NAME="myImage17" WIDTH="130" HEIGHT="130">
</LAYER>

<LAYER ID="Showcase18" LEFT="480" TOP="10" WIDTH="130" HEIGHT="130">
<IMG SRC="JPEG-FILES/X-TicTacToe.jpg" NAME="myImage18" WIDTH="130" HEIGHT="130">
</LAYER>

<LAYER ID="Showcase19" LEFT="480" TOP="310" WIDTH="130" HEIGHT="130">
<IMG SRC="JPEG-FILES/O-TicTacToe.jpg" NAME="myImage19" WIDTH="130" HEIGHT="130">
</LAYER>


</LAYER>
<!--    ******************************************************************    -->

<SCRIPT LANGUAGE="JavaScript1.2"><!--BEGIN HIDING

var Showcase2    =    document.ShowcaseA.document.Showcase2
var Showcase3    =    document.ShowcaseA.document.Showcase3
var Showcase4    =    document.ShowcaseA.document.Showcase4
var Showcase5    =    document.ShowcaseA.document.Showcase5
var Showcase6    =    document.ShowcaseA.document.Showcase6
var Showcase7    =    document.ShowcaseA.document.Showcase7
var Showcase8    =    document.ShowcaseA.document.Showcase8
var Showcase9    =    document.ShowcaseA.document.Showcase9
var Showcase10   =    document.ShowcaseA.document.Showcase10
var Showcase11   =    document.ShowcaseA.document.Showcase11
var Showcase12   =    document.ShowcaseA.document.Showcase12
var Showcase13   =    document.ShowcaseA.document.Showcase13
var Showcase14   =    document.ShowcaseA.document.Showcase14
var Showcase15   =    document.ShowcaseA.document.Showcase15
var Showcase16   =    document.ShowcaseA.document.Showcase16
var Showcase17   =    document.ShowcaseA.document.Showcase17
var Showcase18   =    document.ShowcaseA.document.Showcase18
var Showcase19   =    document.ShowcaseA.document.Showcase19


/*------------------------------------------------------------------------*/
```

// These next two statements are what new author's tend to forget but they are crucial.
// If you don't capture the Events then your keyNewGame() and StartGame() functions won't work.

```
document.captureEvents(Event.KEYPRESS);
document.captureEvents(Event.KEYUP);
/*------------------------------------------------------------------------*/
```

```
/*--------------------------------------------------------------------*/

        document.onkeypress = keyJump;
        document.onkeyup = keyNewGame;
/*--------------------------------------------------------------------*/

function keyJump(e) {

 if (e.modifiers == Event.CONTROL_MASK  &&  e.which == 49)
 { Showcase2.moveTo(10,10); Showcase2.moveAbove(Showcase3); }            //grid 1


                                                    //tests for numbers on extended
Keyboards

 if (e.modifiers == Event.ALT_MASK  &&  (e.which == 193 || e.which == 49))
 { Showcase3.moveTo(10,10); Showcase3.moveAbove(Showcase2); }

 if (e.modifiers == Event.CONTROL_MASK  &&  e.which == 50)
 { Showcase4.moveTo(170,10); Showcase4.moveAbove(Showcase5); }           //grid 2

 if (e.modifiers == Event.ALT_MASK  &&  (e.which == 170 || e.which == 50))
 { Showcase5.moveTo(170,10); Showcase5.moveAbove(Showcase4); }

 if (e.modifiers == Event.CONTROL_MASK  &&  e.which == 51)
 { Showcase6.moveTo(330,10); Showcase6.moveAbove(Showcase7); }           //grid 3

 if (e.modifiers == Event.ALT_MASK  &&  (e.which == 163 || e.which == 51))
 { Showcase7.moveTo(330,10); Showcase7.moveAbove(Showcase6); }

 if (e.modifiers == Event.CONTROL_MASK  &&  e.which == 52)
 { Showcase8.moveTo(10,170); Showcase8.moveAbove(Showcase9); }           //grid 4

 if (e.modifiers == Event.ALT_MASK  &&  (e.which == 162 || e.which == 52))
 { Showcase9.moveTo(10,170); Showcase9.moveAbove(Showcase8); }

 if (e.modifiers == Event.CONTROL_MASK  &&  e.which == 53)
 { Showcase10.moveTo(170,170); Showcase10.moveAbove(Showcase11); }        //grid 5

 if (e.modifiers == Event.ALT_MASK  &&  (e.which == 176 || e.which == 53))
 { Showcase11.moveTo(170,170); Showcase11.moveAbove(Showcase10); }

/*--------------------------------------------------------------------*/

 if (e.modifiers == Event.CONTROL_MASK  &&  e.which == 54)
 { Showcase12.moveTo(330,170); Showcase12.moveAbove(Showcase13); }        //grid 6

 if (e.modifiers == Event.ALT_MASK  &&  (e.which == 164 || e.which == 54))
 { Showcase13.moveTo(330,170); Showcase13.moveAbove(Showcase12); }

 if (e.modifiers == Event.CONTROL_MASK  &&  e.which == 55)
 { Showcase14.moveTo(10,330); Showcase14.moveAbove(Showcase15); }         //grid 7

 if (e.modifiers == Event.ALT_MASK  &&  (e.which == 166 || e.which == 55))
 { Showcase15.moveTo(10,330); Showcase15.moveAbove(Showcase14); }

 if (e.modifiers == Event.CONTROL_MASK  &&  e.which == 56)
 { Showcase16.moveTo(170,330); Showcase16.moveAbove(Showcase17); }        //grid 8
```

```
if (e.modifiers == Event.ALT_MASK  &&  (e.which == 165 || e.which == 56))
{ Showcase17.moveTo(170,330); Showcase17.moveAbove(Showcase16); }

if (e.modifiers == Event.CONTROL_MASK  &&  e.which == 57)
{ Showcase18.moveTo(330,330); Showcase18.moveAbove(Showcase19); }          //grid 9

if (e.modifiers == Event.ALT_MASK  &&  (e.which == 187 || e.which == 57))
{ Showcase19.moveTo(330,330); Showcase19.moveAbove(Showcase18); }

}

/*------------------------------------------------------------------------------*/

function keyNewGame(e) {

// the Character code for letter 'n'  with the CONTROL key pressed is 14

        if (e.modifiers == Event.CONTROL_MASK  &&  e.which == 14 )
        {StartGame();}
}

/*------------------------------------------------------------------------------*/
/*------------------------------------------------------------------------------*/
/*----------       This section deals with the New Game Button      ----------*/

function StartGame() {

        document.ShowcaseA.document.Showcase2.moveTo (480, 10);
        document.ShowcaseA.document.Showcase3.moveTo (480, 310);
        document.ShowcaseA.document.Showcase4.moveTo (480, 10);
        document.ShowcaseA.document.Showcase5.moveTo (480, 310);
        document.ShowcaseA.document.Showcase6.moveTo (480, 10);
        document.ShowcaseA.document.Showcase7.moveTo (480, 310);
        document.ShowcaseA.document.Showcase8.moveTo (480, 10);
        document.ShowcaseA.document.Showcase9.moveTo (480, 310);
        document.ShowcaseA.document.Showcase10.moveTo (480, 10);
        document.ShowcaseA.document.Showcase11.moveTo (480, 310);
        document.ShowcaseA.document.Showcase12.moveTo (480, 10);
        document.ShowcaseA.document.Showcase13.moveTo (480, 310);
        document.ShowcaseA.document.Showcase14.moveTo (480, 10);
        document.ShowcaseA.document.Showcase15.moveTo (480, 310);
        document.ShowcaseA.document.Showcase16.moveTo (480, 10);
        document.ShowcaseA.document.Showcase17.moveTo (480, 310);
        document.ShowcaseA.document.Showcase18.moveTo (480, 10);
        document.ShowcaseA.document.Showcase19.moveTo (480, 310);
}

//END HIDING-->
</SCRIPT>

</BODY>
</HTML>
```

Using the JavaScript <u>switch()</u> Statement & KEYDOWN, KEYPRESS, and KEYUP Events

Using the **switch()** Statement is an extremely convenient way to test for KEYUP, KEYPRESS, and KEYDOWN Events. A typical implementation would be to test for one of those Events by setting up a String Variable and then use the String Method of **String.fromCharCode()** to extract a String from the **which** Property of an Event and assign that String to the Variable like this:

```
var whichKey = String.fromCharCode(e.which);
```

Then you can test for which KEYPRESS Event occurs using the **switch()** Statement inside a Function like this:

```
function moveALayer(e)   {

    var whichKey      = String.fromCharCode(e.which);
    var Layer1        = document.Layer1;

    switch (whichKey)   {
     case '1' : Layer1.moveBy(-20,20);          break;
     case '2' : Layer1.moveBy(0,20);            break;
     case '3' : Layer1.moveBy(20,20);           break;
     default : return false;
    }
}
```

Using <u>return false</u> as the <u>default</u> case

By using <u>return false</u> as the **default** case, you end the Event Handling for this Event if none of the Keys that you have assigned code to are pressed. Remember, of course, that you have to capture the KEYPRESS Events with the **captureEvents()** Method and assign them to an **onkeypress** Event Handler like this:

```
document.captureEvents(Event.KEYPRESS);
document.onkeypress = moveALayer;
```

Example 6-15   Sample715.html

Moving Layers using the <u>switch()</u> Statement

This example demonstrates the above concepts by defining the **moveALayer(e)** Function to test for the **modifiers** CONTROL Key and Keys 1-9 KEYPRESS Events. Depending on which Keys are pressed, there is code that will move the Layers named **L1** and **L2** by using the **moveBy()** and **moveTo()** Methods. Look at the explanation in the example code for the directions that explain how the Keys move the Layers. The screen shot for Example 6-15 is on the previous page.

Example 6-15:   **Sample715.html**

```
<!DOCTYPE HTML PUBLIC "-//W3C//DTD HTML 3.2//EN">
<HTML>
<HEAD>
<TITLE> Sample 715    Example 6-15 Move Layers using Switch Statement</TITLE>

<STYLE TYPE="text/JavaScript">

        classes.Mainbody.BODY.margins("0px");
        classes.Mainbody.BODY.paddings("0px");
        classes.Mainbody.BODY.backgroundColor="navy";
        classes.Mainbody.BODY.color="white";
        classes.Mainbody.BODY.fontSize="22pt";

        ids.L3.fontSize="14pt";
        ids.L3.color="yellow";
        ids.L3.fontSize="14pt";

        tags.DIR.color="red";

</STYLE>

<!-- ********************************************************************* -->

<SCRIPT LANGUAGE="JavaScript1.2"><!--BEGIN HIDING

function moveALayer(e)   {

        var whichKey   = String.fromCharCode(e.which);
        var L1         = document.L1;
        var L2         = document.L2;

//The moveBy numbers make sense if you use the number pad on the right side of the
keyboard.
```

```
/*----------------------------------------------------------------------*/
  if (e.modifiers == Event.CONTROL_MASK)  {

      switch (whichKey)  {
        case '1' : L2.moveBy(-20,20);        break;  //press the CONTROL + 1 keys
        case '2' : L2.moveBy(0,20);          break;  //press the CONTROL + 2 keys
        case '3' : L2.moveBy(20,20);         break;  //press the CONTROL + 3 keys
        case '4' : L2.moveBy(-20,0);         break;  //press the CONTROL + 4 keys
        case '5' : L2.moveTo(10,150);        break;  //press the CONTROL + 5 keys
        case '6' : L2.moveBy(20,0);          break;  //press the CONTROL + 6 keys
        case '7' : L2.moveBy(-20,-20);       break;  //press the CONTROL + 7 keys
        case '8' : L2.moveBy(0,-20);         break;  //press the CONTROL + 8 keys
        case '9' : L2.moveBy(20,-20);        break;  //press the CONTROL + 9 keys
      }
  }
  else {
      switch (whichKey)  {
        case '1' : L1.moveBy(-20,20);        break;  //press the 1 key
        case '2' : L1.moveBy(0,20);          break;  //press the 2 key
        case '3' : L1.moveBy(20,20);         break;  //press the 3 key
        case '4' : L1.moveBy(-20,0);         break;  //press the 4 key
        case '5' : L1.moveTo(10,10);         break;  //press the 5 key
        case '6' : L1.moveBy(20,0);          break;  //press the 6 key
        case '7' : L1.moveBy(-20,-20);       break;  //press the 7 key
        case '8' : L1.moveBy(0,-20);         break;  //press the 8 key
        case '9' : L1.moveBy(20,-20);        break;  //press the 9 key
        default : return false;
      }
  }
}


/*----------------------------------------------------------------------*/

      document.captureEvents(Event.KEYPRESS);
      document.onkeypress = moveALayer;
/*----------------------------------------------------------------------*/

//END HIDING-->
</SCRIPT>

</HEAD>

<BODY CLASS="Mainbody">

<LAYER ID="L1" LEFT="10" TOP="10">

<IMG SRC="JPEG-FILES/J2-Winter-Arches-15.jpg" WIDTH="144" HEIGHT="100"
NAME="myImage1"><BR>
Winter Arches 15
                </LAYER>

<LAYER ID="L2" LEFT="10" TOP="150">

<IMG SRC="JPEG-FILES/J2-SpaceDome_27P.jpg" WIDTH="144" HEIGHT="100"
NAME="myImage2"><BR>
SpaceDome 27P
                </LAYER>
```

```
<!--  This just contains directions on how to use the Keys  -->

<LAYER ID="L3" LEFT="200" TOP="10">
<UL TYPE=circle>
        <LI>Press  1 -- L1 Go Down and Left
        <LI>Press  2 -- L1 Go Down
        <LI>Press  3 -- L1 Go Down and Right
        <LI>Press  4 -- L1 Go Left
        <LI>Press  5 -- L1 Reset
        <LI>Press  6 -- L1 Go Right
        <LI>Press  7 -- L1 Go Up and Left
        <LI>Press  8 -- L1 Go Up
        <LI>Press  9 -- L1 Go Up and Right
</UL>
<DIR>
        <LI>Press Control +  1 -- L2 Go Down and Left
        <LI>Press Control +  2 -- L2 Go Down
        <LI>Press Control +  3 -- L2 Go Down and Right
        <LI>Press Control +  4 -- L2 Go Left
        <LI>Press Control +  5 -- L2 Reset
        <LI>Press Control +  6 -- L2 Go Right
        <LI>Press Control +  7 -- L2 Go Up and Left
        <LI>Press Control +  8 -- L2 Go Up
        <LI>Press Control +  9 -- L2 Go Up and Right
</DIR>

</LAYER>

</BODY>
</HTML>
```

Animating Layers and Images

By using some creative JavaScript along with the **captureEvents()** Method, you can animate Images that are contained in Layers, setting up a pre-Scripted presentation that still relies on user choices. You can animate the Layers so that they disappear off-screen in any direction. In the case of Layers disappearing either up or left, you have to use negative numbers.

Several working examples are included that are easily adaptable to your own needs. One example includes Layers that have additional controls in them that are initially <u>off-screen</u> and can only be accessed by clicking an image in a sibling Frame.

Animating Layers automatically and by clicking on an Image

Example 6-16 is the first in a series of examples that use mouse clicks and a variety of Methods within seven Functions to animate and reveal Layers with Art images (that were created by the author).

Here's what you should expect to see when you run the script. When you click on the image icon in the upper-left corner of the screen, a small bordered preview image will start sliding across the screen from right to left at the bottom of the screen. It will then start rising straight upward until it halts and begins to disappear as if it's being eaten away. When it completely disappears, the large image of the art begins to be revealed as if an invisible veil is being removed. Finally, if you click the icon again, the large image will erase itself from view and the entire process will repeat from the beginning.

The JavaScript starts by defining three Boolean Variables. Then, four Variables are defined, each with a Layer assigned to it. Next, the MOUSEDOWN and MOUSEUP Events are both captured with the **captureEvents()** Method when it's called by the **Control** Layer. Then the **booleanTest1(e)** Function is applied to the **onmousedown** Event Handler, and the **hideLargeClippedImage()** Function is applied to the **onclick** Event Handler.

```
Control.captureEvents(Event.MOUSEDOWN | Event.MOUSEUP);
Control.onmousedown = booleanTest1;
Control.onclick = hideLargeClippedImage;
```

booleanTest1(e)　　　　　This Function captures the CLICK Event for the **Control** Layer, and if the mouse is pressed and the **target** of the Event is the image named **myImage1**, then **imageBoolean = true** and **imageBoolean3 = false**; Layer **L1** gets its **visibility** Property set to '**show**' and it's moved almost offscreen, at bottom-right, with the **moveTo(main.clip.width, main.clip.height-120)** Method. The reason that the **y** Argument of the **moveTo()** Method is set to 120 pixels less than the **clipping height** of the main Layer is so that it will be visible as it horizontally slides into view from right to left at the bottom of the browser Window. Finally, it calls the **revealSmallImage()** Function.

revealSmallImage()　　　　　This Function tests **L1** Layer's **clip.right** and **clip.top** Properties, and because they will always be less than or equal to zero, it always resizes **L1** to 180 pixels wide by 120 pixels tall when it's called.

hideLargeClippedImage()　　　　　This Function is called whenever there is a CLICK Event captured by the **L1** Layer. If **imageBoolean3 == false**, then if either of the clipping **top** or **right** Properties is greater than zero, it resizes the clipping rectangle by (-20, -12) which shrinks it. The **setTimeout()** Method then calls its container Function which, of course, is **hideLargeClippedImage()**, and the process repeats until the image is hidden. When the clipping rectangle gets to (0,0), then **imageBoolean** is set to '**true**' and the **timeWasterLeft()** Function is called.

timeWasterLeft()   Slides Layer **L1** to the **left** of the window until its **left** Property is less than or equal to zero when the **setTimeout()** Method repeatedly reinvokes the **timeWasterLeft()** Function. Then it calls the **timeWasterTop()** Function.

timeWasterTop()   This Function slides Layer **L1** from roughly the bottom left corner of the **main** Layer upward, while its **top** Property is greater than zero by the **setTimeout()** Method continually calling the **timeWasterTop()** Function. When the Layer reaches its final upper-left destination, the **clipSmallImage()** Function is called.

clipSmallImage()   This Function decreases the size of the Clipping Rectangle until the small image disappears by testing for the Values of the **clip.right** and **clip.top** Properties and using the **resizeBy()** Method in conjunction with the **setTimeout()** Method. Once the small image is hidden, the **LLi1** Layer, which contains the large image of the art, has its **visibility** Property set to '**show**'. At this point, Layer **LLi1** still can't be seen because its Clipping Rectangle has been previously set to (0,0) by the **hideLargeClippedImage()** Function. That's why you call the **revealLargeClippedImage()** Function at this point.

revealLargeClippedImage()   This Function reveals the large art image contained in Layer **LLi1** by testing that Layer's **clip.right** and **clip.top** Properties. As long as they are still hiding any part of the Layer, they will be expanded with the **setTimeout()** Method, calling its container Function, which is **revealLargeClippedImage()**.

Example 6-16:   Sample716.html

```
<!DOCTYPE HTML PUBLIC "-//W3C//DTD HTML 3.2//EN">
<HTML>
<HEAD>
<TITLE>Sample 716 - Example 6-16     Click an Image to start sequence </TITLE>

<STYLE type = "text/JavaScript">

       classes.Largefont.all.fontSize = "120pt";

       classes.theControl.all.fontSize = "22pt";
       classes.theControl.all.fontFamily = "Moonlight, cursive";
       classes.theControl.all.borderWidths("7px");
       classes.theControl.all.borderColor="#7700ff";
       classes.theControl.all.borderStyle="groove";

</STYLE>
</HEAD>

<BODY BGCOLOR="BLACK" TEXT="white">
<!--   *********************************************************   -->

<LAYER CLASS="theControl" ID="Control" LEFT="5" TOP="5" WIDTH="100" HEIGHT="100">
<IMG SRC="JPEG-FILES/J2-Winter-Arches-15.jpg" WIDTH="72" HEIGHT="50"
NAME="myImage1">
</LAYER>
```

```
<!--   *********************************  -->

<LAYER ID="main" LEFT="110" TOP="5" WIDTH="540" HEIGHT="380">

<LAYER CLASS="theControl" ID="L1" LEFT="5" TOP="5" VISIBILITY="hide">
<IMG SRC="JPEG-FILES/J2-Winter-Arches-15.jpg" WIDTH="144" HEIGHT="98"
NAME="I1A"></LAYER>

<LAYER CLASS="theControl" ID="LLi1" LEFT="5" TOP="5" CLIP="0,0">
<IMG SRC="JPEG-FILES/J7-Winter_Arches_15.jpg" WIDTH="504" HEIGHT="343"
NAME="myImage1A"></LAYER>

</LAYER>

<!--   **************************************************************  -->

<SCRIPT LANGUAGE="JavaScript1.2"><!--BEGIN HIDING

var imageBoolean;
var imageBoolean2;
var imageBoolean3;
var Control     = document.Control;                    //Layer ID=Control
var main        = document.main;                       //Layer ID=main
var L1          = document.main.document.L1;           //Layer ID=L1
var LLi1        = document.main.document.LLi1;         //Layer ID=LLi1

Control.captureEvents(Event.MOUSEDOWN | Event.MOUSEUP);
Control.onmousedown = booleanTest1;
Control.onclick = hideLargeClippedImage;

/*-------------------------------------------------------------------------*/

function booleanTest1(e)   {

        Control.captureEvents(Event.CLICK);

        if (e.which == 1  &&  e.target.name == "myImage1")   {

                imageBoolean = true;
                imageBoolean3 = false;

                L1.visibility = 'show';
                L1.moveTo(main.clip.width, main.clip.height-120);
                revealSmallImage();
         }
}

/*-------------------------------------------------------------------------*/

function revealSmallImage()   {

        if (L1.clip.right <= 0  ||  L1.clip.top <= 0)   {
                L1.resizeTo(180,120);
        }
}

/*-----------------------------------------------*/
```

```
function hideLargeClippedImage()  {

     if (imageBoolean3 == false)  {

          if (LLi1.clip.right > 0  ||  LLi1.clip.top > 0)  {
               LLi1.resizeBy(-20,-12);
               setTimeout('hideLargeClippedImage()', 20);
          }
          else if (LLi1.clip.right <= 0  ||  LLi1.clip.top <= 0)  {
               imageBoolean = true;
               timeWasterLeft();
          }
     }
}
/*-------------------------------------------------------------------------*/

function timeWasterLeft()  {

     if (imageBoolean == true)  {

          if (L1.left > 0) {
               L1.moveBy(-20,0);
               setTimeout('timeWasterLeft()', 20);
          }
          else if (L1.left <= 0) {
               timeWasterTop();
          }
     }
}
/*----------------------------------------------*/

function timeWasterTop()  {

     if (imageBoolean == true)  {

          if (L1.top > 0) {
               L1.moveBy(0,-20);
               setTimeout('timeWasterTop()', 20);
          }
          else if (L1.top <= 0)  {
               imageBoolean2 = true;
               clipSmallImage();
          }
     }
}
/*-------------------------------------------------------------------------*/

function clipSmallImage()  {

     if (imageBoolean2 == true)  {

          if (L1.clip.right > 0  ||  L1.clip.top > 0)  {
               L1.resizeBy(-10,-6);
               setTimeout('clipSmallImage()', 20);
          }
          else if (L1.clip.right <= 0  &&  L1.clip.top <= 0)  {
               imageBoolean2 = false;
               imageBoolean3 = true;
```

```
                        LLi1.visibility = 'show';
                        revealLargeClippedImage();
                }
        }
}
/*-------------------------------------------*/

function revealLargeClippedImage()  {

        if (imageBoolean3 == true)  {

                if (LLi1.clip.right < main.clip.width  ||
                        LLi1.clip.top < main.clip.height)  {

                        LLi1.resizeBy(20,12);
                        setTimeout('revealLargeClippedImage()', 20);
                }
        }
}


//END HIDING-->
</SCRIPT>
</BODY>
</HTML>
```

Animating Layers with the
<u>e.target.name</u> Property

This example expands on the previous example by having four images to choose from and uses the **name** Property of the **target** Property of the CLICK **Event** Object to determine what code to execute based on which of the images was clicked like this:

```
if (e.which == 1  &&  e.target.name == "myImage1")
```

The main Functions are nearly identical to the last example, except that you have to change the **visibility** Property of the Layers based on which image was clicked, and the **booleanTest(e)** Function determines which of the **revealSmallImage()** Functions to call. There are four versions of each of these six Functions, which are fully explained in the previous Example 6-16, on pages 591 and 592:

revealSmallImage()
hideLargeClippedImage()
timeWasterLeft()
timeWasterTop()
clipSmallImage()
revealLargeClippedImage()

Example 6-17:   **Sample717.html**

```
<!DOCTYPE HTML PUBLIC "-//W3C//DTD HTML 3.2//EN">
<HTML>
<HEAD>
<TITLE>Sample 717 - Example 6-17      Click to Reveal Images </TITLE>

<STYLE type = "text/JavaScript">

        classes.Largefont.all.fontSize = "120pt";

        classes.theControl.all.fontSize = "22pt";
        classes.theControl.all.fontFamily = "Moonlight, cursive";
        classes.theControl.all.borderWidths("7px");
        classes.theControl.all.borderColor="#7700ff";
        classes.theControl.all.borderStyle="groove";

</STYLE>

</HEAD>

<BODY BGCOLOR="BLACK" TEXT="white">

<!--    *******************************************************************  -->

<LAYER CLASS="theControl" ID="Control" LEFT="5" TOP="5" WIDTH="100" HEIGHT="500">

<IMG SRC="JPEG-FILES/J2-Winter-Arches-15.jpg" WIDTH="72" HEIGHT="50" NAME="myImage1">

<IMG SRC="JPEG-FILES/J2-SpaceDome_27P.jpg" WIDTH="72" HEIGHT="50" NAME="myImage2">

<IMG SRC="JPEG-FILES/J2-SKY_SPHERE_1.jpg" WIDTH="72" HEIGHT="50" NAME="myImage3">

<IMG SRC="JPEG-FILES/J2-TimeTunSkySphere.jpg" WIDTH="72" HEIGHT="50" NAME="myImage4">
</LAYER>



<LAYER ID="main" LEFT="110" TOP="5" WIDTH="540" HEIGHT="380">

<LAYER CLASS="theControl" ID="L1" LEFT="5" TOP="5" VISIBILITY="hide">
<IMG SRC="JPEG-FILES/J2-Winter-Arches-15.jpg" WIDTH="144" HEIGHT="98" NAME="SmImage1A">
</LAYER>

<LAYER CLASS="theControl" ID="LLi1" LEFT="5" TOP="5" CLIP="0,0">
<IMG SRC="JPEG-FILES/J7-Winter_Arches_15.jpg" WIDTH="504" HEIGHT="343" NAME="LgImage1A">
</LAYER>



<LAYER CLASS="theControl" ID="L2" LEFT="5" TOP="5" VISIBILITY="hide">
<IMG SRC="JPEG-FILES/J2-SpaceDome_27P.jpg" WIDTH="144" HEIGHT="98" NAME="SmImage2A">
</LAYER>

<LAYER CLASS="theControl" ID="LLi2" LEFT="5" TOP="5" CLIP="0,0">
<IMG SRC="JPEG-FILES/J5-SpaceDome_27P.jpg" WIDTH="360" HEIGHT="245" NAME="LgImage2A">
</LAYER>
```

```
<LAYER CLASS="theControl" ID="L3" LEFT="5" TOP="5" VISIBILITY="hide">
<IMG SRC="JPEG-FILES/J2-SKY_SPHERE_1.jpg" WIDTH="144" HEIGHT="98" NAME="SmImage3A">
</LAYER>

<LAYER CLASS="theControl" ID="LLi3" LEFT="5" TOP="5" CLIP="0,0">
<IMG SRC="JPEG-FILES/J5-SKY_SPHERE_1.jpg" WIDTH="360" HEIGHT="245" NAME="LgImage3A">
</LAYER>


<LAYER CLASS="theControl" ID="L4" LEFT="5" TOP="5" VISIBILITY="hide">
<IMG SRC="JPEG-FILES/J2-TimeTunSkySphere.jpg" WIDTH="144" HEIGHT="98" NAME="SmImage4A">
</LAYER>

<LAYER CLASS="theControl" ID="LLi4" LEFT="5" TOP="5" CLIP="0,0">
<IMG SRC="JPEG-FILES/J5-TimeTunSkySphere.jpg" WIDTH="360" HEIGHT="245" NAME="LgImage4A">
</LAYER>


</LAYER>

<!--   *****************************************************************   -->

<SCRIPT LANGUAGE="JavaScript1.2"><!--BEGIN HIDING

var imageBoolean;
var imageBoolean2;
var imageBoolean3;

var Control    = document.Control;
var main       = document.main;
var L1         = document.main.document.L1;
var LLi1       = document.main.document.LLi1;
var L2         = document.main.document.L2;
var LLi2       = document.main.document.LLi2;
var L3         = document.main.document.L3;
var LLi3       = document.main.document.LLi3;
var L4         = document.main.document.L4;
var LLi4       = document.main.document.LLi4;

Control.captureEvents(Event.MOUSEDOWN | Event.MOUSEUP);
Control.onmousedown = booleanTest1;

/*-------------------------------------------------------------------------*/

function booleanTest1(e)   {

        Control.captureEvents(Event.CLICK);

        if (e.which == 1  &&  e.target.name == "myImage1")   {

                imageBoolean3 = false;
                L1.visibility = 'show';
                L2.visibility = 'hide';
                L3.visibility = 'hide';
                L4.visibility = 'hide';
                L1.moveTo(main.clip.width, main.clip.height-120);
                revealSmallImage();
        }
```

```
        if (e.which == 1  &&  e.target.name == "myImage2")  {

                imageBoolean3 = false;
                L1.visibility = 'hide';
                L2.visibility = 'show';
                L3.visibility = 'hide';
                L4.visibility = 'hide';
                L2.moveTo(main.clip.width, main.clip.height-120);
                revealSmallImage2();
         }
        if (e.which == 1  &&  e.target.name == "myImage3")  {

                imageBoolean3 = false;
                L1.visibility = 'hide';
                L2.visibility = 'hide';
                L3.visibility = 'show';
                L4.visibility = 'hide';
                L3.moveTo(main.clip.width, main.clip.height-120);
                revealSmallImage3();
        }
        if (e.which == 1  &&  e.target.name == "myImage4")  {

                imageBoolean3 = false;
                L1.visibility = 'hide';
                L2.visibility = 'hide';
                L3.visibility = 'hide';
                L4.visibility = 'show';
                L4.moveTo(main.clip.width, main.clip.height-120);
                revealSmallImage4();
        }
}


/*----------------------------------------------------------------------*/

function revealSmallImage()  {

        hideLargeClippedImage();

        if (L1.clip.right <= 0  ||  L1.clip.top <= 0)  {
                L1.resizeTo(180,120);
        }
}

function hideLargeClippedImage()  {


        if (imageBoolean3 == false)  {

                LLi2.visibility = 'hide';
                LLi3.visibility = 'hide';
                LLi4.visibility = 'hide';
                LLi1.resizeTo(0,0);
                LLi1.visibility = 'hide';
                imageBoolean = true;
                timeWasterLeft();
        }
}
```

```
function timeWasterLeft()  {

     if (imageBoolean == true)  {

          if (L1.left > 0) {
               L1.moveBy(-20,0);
               setTimeout('timeWasterLeft()', 20);
          }
          else if (L1.left <= 0) {
               timeWasterTop();
          }
     }
}

function timeWasterTop()  {

     if (imageBoolean == true)  {

          if (L1.top > 0) {
               L1.moveBy(0,-20);
               setTimeout('timeWasterTop()', 20);
          }
          else if (L1.top <= 0)  {
               imageBoolean2 = true;
               clipSmallImage();
          }
     }
}

function clipSmallImage()  {

     if (imageBoolean2 == true)  {

          if (L1.clip.right > 0  ||  L1.clip.top > 0)  {
               L1.resizeBy(-10,-6);
               setTimeout('clipSmallImage()', 20);
          }
          else if (L1.clip.right <= 0  &&  L1.clip.top <= 0)  {
               imageBoolean2 = false;
               imageBoolean3 = true;
               LLi1.visibility = 'show';
               revealLargeClippedImage();
          }
     }
}

function revealLargeClippedImage()  {

     if (imageBoolean3 == true)  {

          if (LLi1.clip.right < main.clip.width
          ||  LLi1.clip.top < main.clip.height)  {

               LLi1.resizeBy(20,12);
               setTimeout('revealLargeClippedImage()', 20);
          }
     }
}
```

```
/*-------------------------------------------------------------------*/

function revealSmallImage2()  {

       hideLargeClippedImage2();

       if (L2.clip.right <= 0  ||  L2.clip.top <= 0)  {
              L2.resizeTo(180,120);
       }
}

function hideLargeClippedImage2()  {


       if (imageBoolean3 == false)  {

              LLi1.visibility = 'hide';
              LLi3.visibility = 'hide';
              LLi4.visibility = 'hide';
              LLi2.resizeTo(0,0);
              LLi2.visibility = 'hide';
              imageBoolean = true;
              timeWasterLeft2();
       }
}

function timeWasterLeft2()  {

       if (imageBoolean == true)  {

              if (L2.left > 0) {
                     L2.moveBy(-20,0);
                     setTimeout('timeWasterLeft2()', 20);
              }
              else if (L2.left <= 0) {
                     timeWasterTop2();
              }
       }
}

function timeWasterTop2()  {

       if (imageBoolean == true)  {

              if (L2.top > 0) {
                     L2.moveBy(0,-20);
                     setTimeout('timeWasterTop2()', 20);
              }
              else if (L2.top <= 0)  {
                     imageBoolean2 = true;
                     clipSmallImage2();
              }
       }
}
```

```
function clipSmallImage2() {

        if (imageBoolean2 == true) {

                if (L2.clip.right > 0 || L2.clip.top > 0) {
                        L2.resizeBy(-10,-6);
                        setTimeout('clipSmallImage2()', 20);
                }
                else if (L2.clip.right <= 0 && L2.clip.top <= 0) {
                        imageBoolean2 = false;
                        imageBoolean3 = true;
                        LLi2.visibility = 'show';
                        revealLargeClippedImage2();
                }
        }
}

function revealLargeClippedImage2() {

        if (imageBoolean3 == true) {

                if (LLi2.clip.right < main.clip.width || LLi2.clip.top <
main.clip.height) {
                        LLi2.resizeBy(20,12);
                        setTimeout('revealLargeClippedImage2()', 20);
                }
        }
}

/*-------------------------------------------------------------------*/

function revealSmallImage3() {

        hideLargeClippedImage3();

        if (L3.clip.right <= 0 || L3.clip.top <= 0) {
                L3.resizeTo(180,120);
        }
}

function hideLargeClippedImage3() {


        if (imageBoolean3 == false) {

                LLi1.visibility = 'hide';
                LLi2.visibility = 'hide';
                LLi4.visibility = 'hide';
                LLi3.resizeTo(0,0);
                LLi3.visibility = 'hide';
                imageBoolean = true;
                timeWasterLeft3();
        }
}
```

```
function timeWasterLeft3()  {

      if (imageBoolean == true)  {

            if (L3.left > 0) {
                  L3.moveBy(-20,0);
                  setTimeout('timeWasterLeft3()', 20);
            }
            else if (L3.left <= 0) {
                  timeWasterTop3();
            }
      }
}

function timeWasterTop3()  {

      if (imageBoolean == true)  {

            if (L3.top > 0) {
                  L3.moveBy(0,-20);
                  setTimeout('timeWasterTop3()', 20);
            }
            else if (L3.top <= 0)  {
                  imageBoolean2 = true;
                  clipSmallImage3();
            }
      }
}

function clipSmallImage3()  {

      if (imageBoolean2 == true)  {

            if (L3.clip.right > 0  ||  L3.clip.top > 0)  {
                  L3.resizeBy(-10,-6);
                  setTimeout('clipSmallImage3()', 20);
            }
            else if (L3.clip.right <= 0  &&  L3.clip.top <= 0)  {
                  imageBoolean2 = false;
                  imageBoolean3 = true;
                  LLi3.visibility = 'show';
                  revealLargeClippedImage3();
            }
      }
}

function revealLargeClippedImage3()  {

      if (imageBoolean3 == true)  {

            if (LLi3.clip.right < main.clip.width ||
                        LLi3.clip.top < main.clip.height)  {
                  LLi3.resizeBy(20,12);
                  setTimeout('revealLargeClippedImage3()', 20);
            }
      }
}
```

```
/*-------------------------------------------------------------------*/

function revealSmallImage4()  {

        hideLargeClippedImage4();

        if (L4.clip.right <= 0  ||  L4.clip.top <= 0)  {
                L4.resizeTo(180,120);
        }
}

function hideLargeClippedImage4()  {


        if (imageBoolean3 == false)  {

                LLi1.visibility = 'hide';
                LLi2.visibility = 'hide';
                LLi3.visibility = 'hide';
                LLi4.resizeTo(0,0);
                LLi4.visibility = 'hide';
                imageBoolean = true;
                timeWasterLeft4();
        }
}

function timeWasterLeft4()  {

        if (imageBoolean == true)  {

                if (L4.left > 0) {
                        L4.moveBy(-20,0);
                        setTimeout('timeWasterLeft4()', 20);
                }
                else if (L4.left <= 0) {
                        timeWasterTop4();
                }
        }
}

function timeWasterTop4()  {

        if (imageBoolean == true)  {

                if (L4.top > 0) {
                        L4.moveBy(0,-20);
                        setTimeout('timeWasterTop4()', 20);
                }
                else if (L4.top <= 0)  {
                        imageBoolean2 = true;
                        clipSmallImage4();
                }
        }
}
```

```
function clipSmallImage4()   {

       if (imageBoolean2 == true)   {

              if (L4.clip.right > 0   ||   L4.clip.top > 0)   {
                     L4.resizeBy(-10,-6);
                     setTimeout('clipSmallImage4()', 20);
              }
              else if (L4.clip.right <= 0   &&   L4.clip.top <= 0)   {
                     imageBoolean2 = false;
                     imageBoolean3 = true;
                     LLi4.visibility = 'show';
                     revealLargeClippedImage4();
              }
       }
}
function revealLargeClippedImage4()   {

       if (imageBoolean3 == true)   {

              if (LLi4.clip.right < main.clip.width   ||
                            LLi4.clip.top < main.clip.height)   {
                     LLi4.resizeBy(20,12);
                     setTimeout('revealLargeClippedImage4()', 20);
              }
       }
}


//END HIDING-->
</SCRIPT>
</BODY>
</HTML>
```

Animating Layers in a Frameset Environment

Example 6-18 accomplishes the same thing as the previous example, but it does so within a FRAMESET environment. Sample718Frameset.html contains the FRAMESET that divides the Window into two FRAMES, with the left FRAME named **display**, which loads the Sample718.html document, and the right FRAME named **view**, which loads the Sample718A.html document. The **display** FRAME has the Layer with ID of **Control** and captures the CLICK, MOUSEDOWN, and MOUSEUP Events and processes them based on which of the image icons are clicked. Once again, the **booleanTest1(e)** Function is assigned to the **onmousedown** Event Handler of the **Control** Layer, but this time it uses the **location** Property of the **view** FRAME to load an external document based on the **e.target.name** conditions (which image the user clicks) like this:

```
       if (e.which == 1   &&   e.target.name == "myImage1")   {

              view.location.href = 'Sample718A.html';
                     . . .
       }
```

It should be noted that **view** had been previously defined as:

```
var view = parent.view;
```

Otherwise, the previous code would have to be written as:

```
parent.view.location.href = 'Sample718A.html';
```

The four external files that can be loaded into the **view** FRAME each have their own animation SCRIPTs, just like the previous example. See Example 6-16, starting at page 591, and Example 6-17, starting at page 595, for details.

Example 6-18 Part 1:   Sample718.html

```
<!DOCTYPE HTML PUBLIC "-//W3C//DTD HTML 3.2//EN">
<HTML>
<HEAD>
<TITLE>Sample 718 - Example 6-18      Click to Reveal Images </TITLE>

<STYLE type = "text/JavaScript">

        classes.theControl.all.fontSize = "22pt";
        classes.theControl.all.fontFamily = "Moonlight, cursive";
        classes.theControl.all.borderWidths("7px");
        classes.theControl.all.borderColor="#22ffff";
        classes.theControl.all.borderStyle="groove";

</STYLE>
</HEAD>

<BODY BGCOLOR="BLACK" TEXT="white"
BACKGROUND="JPEG-FILES/ICON-HorizontalRainbow4.jpg">

<LAYER CLASS="theControl" ID="Control" LEFT="5" TOP="5" WIDTH="100" HEIGHT="500">

<IMG SRC="JPEG-FILES/J2-Winter-Arches-15.jpg" WIDTH="72" HEIGHT="50" NAME="myImage1">

<IMG SRC="JPEG-FILES/J2-SpaceDome_27P.jpg" WIDTH="72" HEIGHT="50" NAME="myImage2">

<IMG SRC="JPEG-FILES/J2-SKY_SPHERE_1.jpg" WIDTH="72" HEIGHT="50" NAME="myImage3">

<IMG SRC="JPEG-FILES/J2-TimeTunSkySphere.jpg" WIDTH="72" HEIGHT="50" NAME="myImage4">

</LAYER>

<SCRIPT LANGUAGE="JavaScript1.2"><!--BEGIN HIDING

var imageBoolean;
var imageBoolean2;
var imageBoolean3;
var Control    = document.Control;
var view       = parent.view;
```

```
Control.captureEvents(Event.MOUSEDOWN | Event.MOUSEUP);
Control.onmousedown = booleanTest1;

function booleanTest1(e)   {

        Control.captureEvents(Event.CLICK);

        if (e.which == 1  &&  e.target.name == "myImage1")   {

                view.location.href ='Sample718A.html';
        }

        if (e.which == 1  &&  e.target.name == "myImage2")   {

                view.location.href ='Sample718B.html';
         }

        if (e.which == 1  &&  e.target.name == "myImage3")   {

                view.location.href ='Sample718C.html';
        }

        if (e.which == 1  &&  e.target.name == "myImage4")   {

                view.location.href ='Sample718D.html';
        }
}


//END HIDING-->
</SCRIPT>

</BODY>
</HTML>
```

This is one of the four external documents that are loaded into the **view** Frame. The other three are Sample718B.html, Sample718C.html, and Sample718D.html, which are on the CD-ROM, but not in the book because they are virtually identical. In this version of the animation sequence, the large image is not eaten away, which saves some time. Therefore, the **hideLargeClippedImage()** Function has been omitted. After some very minimal code compensation for this Function omission, the rest of the Functions for the animation sequence are identical to the previous Example 6-17.

Example 6-18 Part 2:   Sample718A.html

```
<!DOCTYPE HTML PUBLIC "-//W3C//DTD HTML 3.2//EN">
<HTML>
<HEAD>
<TITLE>Sample 718A - Example 6-18A   Click to Reveal Images </TITLE>

<STYLE type = "text/JavaScript">
```

```
        classes.theControl.all.fontSize = "22pt";
        classes.theControl.all.fontFamily = "Moonlight, cursive";
        classes.theControl.all.borderWidths("7px");
        classes.theControl.all.borderColor="#7700ff";
        classes.theControl.all.borderStyle="groove";

</STYLE>
</HEAD>
<BODY BGCOLOR="BLACK" TEXT="white" onLoad="revealSmallImage();"
BACKGROUND="JPEG-FILES/icon-BG-asteroids.jpg">

<LAYER ID="main" LEFT="5" TOP="5" WIDTH="540" HEIGHT="380">

<LAYER CLASS="theControl" ID="L1" LEFT="5" TOP="5" VISIBILITY="hide">
<IMG SRC="JPEG-FILES/J2-Winter-Arches-15.jpg" WIDTH="144" HEIGHT="98" NAME="SmImage1A">
</LAYER>

<LAYER CLASS="theControl" ID="LLi1" LEFT="5" TOP="5" CLIP="0,0">
<IMG SRC="JPEG-FILES/J7-Winter_Arches_15.jpg" WIDTH="504" HEIGHT="343" NAME="LgImage1A">
</LAYER>

</LAYER>

<SCRIPT LANGUAGE="JavaScript1.2"><!--BEGIN HIDING

var imageBoolean;
var imageBoolean2;
var imageBoolean3;
var main = document.main;
var L1 = document.main.document.L1;
var LLi1 = document.main.document.LLi1;
/*-------------------------------------------------------------------*/

function revealSmallImage()  {

        L1.moveTo(main.clip.width, main.clip.height-120);
        L1.visibility = 'show';

        if (L1.clip.right <= 0  ||  L1.clip.top <= 0)  {
                L1.resizeTo(180,120);
        }
        imageBoolean = true;
        timeWasterLeft();
}

function timeWasterLeft()  {

        if (imageBoolean == true)  {

                if (L1.left > 0) {
                        L1.moveBy(-20,0);
                        setTimeout('timeWasterLeft()', 20);
                }
                else if (L1.left <= 0) {
                        timeWasterTop();
                }
        }
}
```

```
function timeWasterTop()  {

      if (imageBoolean == true)  {

            if (L1.top > 0) {
                  L1.moveBy(0,-20);
                  setTimeout('timeWasterTop()', 20);
            }
            else if (L1.top <= 0)  {
                  imageBoolean2 = true;
                  clipSmallImage();
            }
      }
}

function clipSmallImage()  {

      if (imageBoolean2 == true)  {

            if (L1.clip.right > 0  ||  L1.clip.top > 0)  {
                  L1.resizeBy(-10,-6);
                  setTimeout('clipSmallImage()', 20);
            }
            else if (L1.clip.right <= 0  &&  L1.clip.top <= 0)  {
                  imageBoolean2 = false;
                  imageBoolean3 = true;
                  LLi1.visibility = 'show';
                  revealLargeClippedImage();
            }
      }
}

function revealLargeClippedImage()  {

      if (imageBoolean3 == true)  {

            if (LLi1.clip.right < main.clip.width ||
                        LLi1.clip.top < main.clip.height)  {
                  LLi1.resizeBy(20,12);
                  setTimeout('revealLargeClippedImage()', 20);
            }
      }
}

//END HIDING-->
</SCRIPT>

</BODY>
</HTML>
```

This is the Frameset for Example 6-18.

Example 6-18 Part 3:　　　　　**Sample718Frameset.html**

```
<!DOCTYPE HTML PUBLIC "-//W3C//DTD HTML 3.2//EN">
<HTML>
<HEAD>

<TITLE>Frameset for Sample 718</TITLE>

</HEAD>

<FRAMESET COLS="120,*">

        <FRAME SCROLLING="no" NAME="display" SRC="Sample718.html">

        <FRAME SCROLLING="auto" NAME="view" SRC="Sample718A.html">

</FRAMESET>

</HTML>
```

Controlling an External Frame Document with JavaScript

When you want to manipulate the contents of a document that is contained in one FRAME from another FRAME that is contained within the same FRAMESET, you have to reference the external FRAME by its **name** Property and its container FRAMESET with the **parent** Keyword like this:

```
parent.view.document.bgColor = "blue";
```

where **view** is the Name of the FRAME that you want to change, and the **bgColor** Property is to be changed to blue.

Now let's say you have a FRAME Named **view** that contains a Layer Named **main**. Here's how you would change the **visibility** Property to '**show**' if the code is contained in a FRAME Named **display** that is in the same FRAMESET as the **view** FRAME.

```
parent.view.document.main.visibility = 'show';
```

Now let's say that you have a FRAME Named **view** and a Layer Named **main**, which contains a nested Layer Named **L2**. Here's how you would move Layer **L2** to the new coordinates of (240,20) with the **moveTo()** Method from an external FRAME.

```
parent.view.document.main.document.L2.moveTo(240,20);
```

Finally, let's say that you have a FRAME Named **view** and a Layer Named **main**, which contains a FORM Element named **form1** that contains a TEXT INPUT Element named **text1**. To change the text String that is displayed in **text1**, you change its **value** Property. To do this from an external FRAME, use this code:

```
parent.view.document.main.document.form1.text1.value = "Hi there.";
```

The JavaScript <u>linkColor</u>, <u>alinkColor</u>, and <u>vlinkColor</u> Properties

You can use the **linkColor**, **alinkColor**, and **vlinkColor** Properties to change the color of your links, active links, and visited links by simply assigning a new color via the **color** Parameter in the following Syntax. This is demonstrated in a small SCRIPT in the HEAD Element of Example 6-19 on page 619.

JavaScript Syntax:

```
document.linkColor = color;
document.alinkColor = color;
document.vlinkColor = color;
```

Using Key Events to <u>hide</u> and <u>show</u> Layers

This is the final example in the series that deals with capturing Events by Layers to animate other Layers with images. It uses the same FRAMESET environment as the last example and has the additional capabilities of hiding and showing Layers when KEYPRESS Events are captured by the **document** Object in the **display** FRAME.

One distinguishing feature in this example is that each image icon is contained in its own separate Layer, so you have to capture MOUSEDOWN, MOUSEUP, and CLICK Events for each Layer. There are also the four Functions that deal with loading an external document: one for the **onmousedown** Event Handler for each of the four Layers with icons. They essentially parallel the **booleanTest1(e)** Functions from the previous example.

They are:

loadItUp1(e)   loadItUp2(e)   loadItUp3(e)   loadItUp4(e)

The following eleven Functions deal with the KEYPRESS Events and demonstrate most notably how to reach into an External FRAME and manipulate its contents with JavaScript code based on user input from the Keyboard as discussed in the above section.

keyJump(e)   Because there are four different documents that can be loaded into the **display** FRAME, this Function tests for which document is loaded by using **if ()** Conditionals that only execute if a particular Layer is present, because that Layer is unique to each document. For example:

```
if (parent.view.document.main.document.LLi1)
```

tests to see if the Layer named **LLi1** is present in the Layer named **main** in the FRAME named **view**. This prevents the JavaScript errors of trying to manipulate Layers that don't exist because the wrong document is loaded into the FRAME. Think about it this way. If the document that contains the **LLi2** Layer is loaded into the FRAME, and the code tries to access the **LLi1** Layer that is not in the document in the FRAME, you will get an error. Using the above **if ()** Conditional prevents that from happening, because it refuses to allow any execution of code that pertains to a Layer that isn't loaded into the **view** FRAME.

Having tested for that condition, if it returns **true**, then it proceeds to test for the CONTROL Key with any of the 1, 2, 3, or 4 Keys being pressed. (Programming Note: If you don't like testing for Number Values, then use the **String.fromCharCode(x)** Method. Personally I like to work with the numbers, because it's easier to read the code and keep track of the Values, but it's apples and oranges. Find what works best for your mindset.)

So if the **LLi1** Layer is in the **view** FRAME and **e.which == 49**, which is the **1** Key, then: the **visibility** Property of Layer **LLi1** is set to 'show'.

If **e.which == 50**, which is the **2** Key, then the **previewImageA()** Function is called.
If **e.which == 51**, which is the **3** Key, then the **previewAllImages()** Function is called.
If **e.which == 52**, which is the **4** Key, then the **hideAllPreviewImages()** Function is called.

This process is repeated for each of the other three documents that could be loaded into the **view** FRAME.

previewAllImages()   This Function sets the **visibility** Property of the four Layers that contain the small preview images to 'show', resizes and repositions them into a grid.

hideAllPreviewImages()   This Function just hides all of the small preview images.

previewImageA(), previewImageB(), previewImageC(), previewImageD()
These four Functions use the **visibility** Property and the **moveTo()** and **resizeTo()** Methods to display the desired preview image based on which Keys are pressed or with any of the Layers' **L1, L2, L3,** or **L4 onMouseOver** Attribute Event Handlers.

hidePreviewImageA(), hidePreviewImageB(), hidePreviewImageC(), hidePreviewImageD()
These four Functions change their respective Layer's **visibility** Property to "**hide**" based on which Keys are pressed or with any of Layers' **L1, L2, L3,** or **L4 onMouseOut** Attribute Event Handlers.

This example also has a HELP document that loads into a new browser Window when the link is clicked. Its URL is <u>Sample719HELP.html</u> and is on the CD-ROM.

Example 6-19 Part 1: Sample719.html

```
<!DOCTYPE HTML PUBLIC "-//W3C//DTD HTML 3.2//EN">
<HTML>
<HEAD>
<TITLE>Sample 719 - Example 6-19      Click to Reveal Images </TITLE>

<STYLE type = "text/JavaScript">

        classes.theControl.all.fontSize = "22pt";
        classes.theControl.all.fontFamily = "Moonlight, cursive";
        classes.theControl.all.borderWidths("7px");
        classes.theControl.all.borderColor = "#00ff00";
        classes.theControl.all.borderStyle = "groove";
        classes.theControl.all.width = "120px";

        ids.LayerA.borderColor = "cyan";
        ids.LayerB.borderColor = "#00ccff";
        ids.LayerC.borderColor = "#0088ff";
        ids.LayerD.borderColor = "#0022ff";

        ids.LayerA.width = "90px";
        ids.LayerB.width = "90px";
        ids.LayerC.width = "90px";
        ids.LayerD.width = "90px";

        ids.LayerH.width = "100px";
        ids.LayerH.borderColor = "yellow";
        ids.LayerH.backgroundColor = "yellow";
        ids.LayerH.paddings("4px");

</STYLE>

<SCRIPT LANGUAGE="JavaScript1.2"><!--BEGIN HIDING

        document.linkColor = "lime";
        document.alinkColor = "darkblue";
        document.vlinkColor = "red";

//END HIDING-->
</SCRIPT>
</HEAD>
```

```
            <!--The left frame must have focus for KeyPress Events to work.-->

<BODY BGCOLOR="BLACK" TEXT="white" onLoad="window.focus();"
BACKGROUND="JPEG-FILES/ICON-HorizontalRainbow4.jpg">

<LAYER CLASS="theControl" ID="LayerA" LEFT="15" TOP="15"
onMouseOver="previewImageA();" onMouseOut="hidePreviewImageA();">
<IMG SRC="JPEG-FILES/J2-Winter-Arches-15.jpg" WIDTH="72" HEIGHT="50"
NAME="myImage1"></LAYER>

<LAYER CLASS="theControl" ID="LayerB" LEFT="15" TOP="90"
onMouseOver="previewImageB();" onMouseOut="hidePreviewImageB();">
<IMG SRC="JPEG-FILES/J2-SpaceDome_27P.jpg" WIDTH="72" HEIGHT="50"
NAME="myImage2"></LAYER>

<LAYER CLASS="theControl" ID="LayerC" LEFT="15" TOP="165"
onMouseOver="previewImageC();" onMouseOut="hidePreviewImageC();">
<IMG SRC="JPEG-FILES/J2-SKY_SPHERE_1.jpg" WIDTH="72" HEIGHT="50"
NAME="myImage3"></LAYER>

<LAYER CLASS="theControl" ID="LayerD" LEFT="15" TOP="240"
onMouseOver="previewImageD();" onMouseOut="hidePreviewImageD();">
<IMG SRC="JPEG-FILES/J2-TimeTunSkySphere.jpg" WIDTH="72" HEIGHT="50"
NAME="myImage4"></LAYER>

<LAYER CLASS="theControl" ID="LayerH" LEFT="15" TOP="325">
<A HREF="./Sample719HELP.html" TARGET="_blank">      HELP!!  </A>      </LAYER>


<SCRIPT LANGUAGE="JavaScript1.2"><!--BEGIN HIDING

var LayerA      = document.LayerA;
var LayerB      = document.LayerB;
var LayerC      = document.LayerC;
var LayerD      = document.LayerD;

var view        = parent.view;


LayerA.captureEvents(Event.MOUSEDOWN | Event.MOUSEUP);
LayerA.onmousedown = loadItUp1;

LayerB.captureEvents(Event.MOUSEDOWN | Event.MOUSEUP);
LayerB.onmousedown = loadItUp2;

LayerC.captureEvents(Event.MOUSEDOWN | Event.MOUSEUP);
LayerC.onmousedown = loadItUp3;

LayerD.captureEvents(Event.MOUSEDOWN | Event.MOUSEUP);
LayerD.onmousedown = loadItUp4;

                                //-------THIS IS CRITICAL CODE
document.captureEvents(Event.KEYPRESS);
document.onkeypress = keyJump;          //-------THIS IS CRITICAL CODE


/*-------------------------------------------------------------------*/
```

```
function loadItUp1(e)  {

        LayerA.captureEvents(Event.CLICK);
        if (e.which == 1  &&  e.target.name == "myImage1")
                { view.location.href = 'Sample719A.html'; }
}

function loadItUp2(e)  {

        LayerB.captureEvents(Event.CLICK);
        if (e.which == 1  &&  e.target.name == "myImage2")
                { view.location.href ='Sample719B.html'; }
}

function loadItUp3(e)  {

        LayerC.captureEvents(Event.CLICK);
        if (e.which == 1  &&  e.target.name == "myImage3")
                { view.location.href ='Sample719C.html'; }
}

function loadItUp4(e)  {

        LayerD.captureEvents(Event.CLICK);
        if (e.which == 1  &&  e.target.name == "myImage4")
                { view.location.href ='Sample719D.html'; }
}

/*----------------------------------------------------------------------*/

function keyJump(e) {

        if (parent.view.document.main.document.LLi1)  {

                if (e.modifiers == Event.CONTROL_MASK  &&  e.which == 49 ) {
                        parent.view.document.main.document.LLi1.visibility = 'show';
                }
                else if (e.modifiers == Event.CONTROL_MASK  &&  e.which == 50 ) {
                        previewImageA();
                }
                else if (e.modifiers == Event.CONTROL_MASK  &&  e.which == 51 ) {
                        parent.view.document.main.document.LLi1.visibility = 'hide';
                        previewAllImages();
                }
                else if (e.modifiers == Event.CONTROL_MASK  &&  e.which == 52 ) {
                        hideAllPreviewImages();
                }
        }
        if (parent.view.document.main.document.LLi2)  {

                if (e.modifiers == Event.CONTROL_MASK  &&  e.which == 49 ) {
                        parent.view.document.main.document.LLi2.visibility = 'show';
                }
                else if (e.modifiers == Event.CONTROL_MASK  &&  e.which == 50 ) {
                        previewImageB();
                }
```

```
                    else if (e.modifiers == Event.CONTROL_MASK  &&  e.which == 51 ) {
                            parent.view.document.main.document.LLi2.visibility = 'hide';
                            previewAllImages();
                    }
                    else if (e.modifiers == Event.CONTROL_MASK  &&  e.which == 52 ) {
                            hideAllPreviewImages();
                    }
            }
            if (parent.view.document.main.document.LLi3)  {

                    if (e.modifiers == Event.CONTROL_MASK  &&  e.which == 49 ) {
                            parent.view.document.main.document.LLi3.visibility = 'show';
                    }
                    else if (e.modifiers == Event.CONTROL_MASK  &&  e.which == 50 ) {
                            previewImageC();
                    }
                    else if (e.modifiers == Event.CONTROL_MASK  &&  e.which == 51 ) {
                            parent.view.document.main.document.LLi3.visibility = 'hide';
                            previewAllImages();
                    }
                    else if (e.modifiers == Event.CONTROL_MASK  &&  e.which == 52 ) {
                            hideAllPreviewImages();
                    }
            }
            if (parent.view.document.main.document.LLi4)  {

                    if (e.modifiers == Event.CONTROL_MASK  &&  e.which == 49 ) {
                            parent.view.document.main.document.LLi4.visibility = 'show';
                    }
                    else if (e.modifiers == Event.CONTROL_MASK  &&  e.which == 50 ) {
                            previewImageD();
                    }
                    else if (e.modifiers == Event.CONTROL_MASK  &&  e.which == 51 ) {
                            parent.view.document.main.document.LLi4.visibility = 'hide';
                            previewAllImages();
                    }
                    else if (e.modifiers == Event.CONTROL_MASK  &&  e.which == 52 ) {
                            hideAllPreviewImages();
                    }
            }
}
/*-------------------------------------------------------------------*/

function previewAllImages()  {

        parent.view.document.main.document.L2.visibility = 'show';
        parent.view.document.main.document.L3.visibility = 'show';
        parent.view.document.main.document.L4.visibility = 'show';
        parent.view.document.main.document.L1.visibility = 'show';

        parent.view.document.main.document.L1.resizeTo(180,120);
        parent.view.document.main.document.L1.moveTo(20,20);

        parent.view.document.main.document.L2.resizeTo(180,120);
        parent.view.document.main.document.L2.moveTo(240,20);

        parent.view.document.main.document.L3.resizeTo(180,120);
        parent.view.document.main.document.L3.moveTo(20,240);
```

```
        parent.view.document.main.document.L4.resizeTo(180,120);
        parent.view.document.main.document.L4.moveTo(240,240);
}

function hideAllPreviewImages()  {

        parent.view.document.main.document.L1.visibility = 'hide';
        parent.view.document.main.document.L2.visibility = 'hide';
        parent.view.document.main.document.L3.visibility = 'hide';
        parent.view.document.main.document.L4.visibility = 'hide';
}


/*----------------------------------------------------------------------*/

function previewImageA()  {

        if (parent.view.document.main.document.LLi1)  {

                parent.view.document.main.document.LLi1.visibility = 'hide';
                parent.view.document.main.document.L2.visibility = 'hide';
                parent.view.document.main.document.L3.visibility = 'hide';
                parent.view.document.main.document.L4.visibility = 'hide';
                parent.view.document.main.document.L1.visibility = 'show';
                parent.view.document.main.document.L1.resizeTo(180,120);
                parent.view.document.main.document.L1.moveTo(100,100);
        }
}

function hidePreviewImageA()  {

        parent.view.document.main.document.L1.visibility = 'hide';
}
/*----------------------------------------------------------------------*/

function previewImageB()  {

        if (parent.view.document.main.document.LLi2)  {

        parent.view.document.main.document.LLi2.visibility = 'hide';
        parent.view.document.main.document.L1.visibility = 'hide';
        parent.view.document.main.document.L3.visibility = 'hide';
        parent.view.document.main.document.L4.visibility = 'hide';
        parent.view.document.main.document.L2.visibility = 'show';
        parent.view.document.main.document.L2.resizeTo(180,120);
        parent.view.document.main.document.L2.moveTo(100,100);
        }
}

function hidePreviewImageB()  {

        parent.view.document.main.document.L2.visibility = 'hide';
}
/*----------------------------------------------------------------------*/
```

```
function previewImageC()   {

        if (parent.view.document.main.document.LLi3)   {

        parent.view.document.main.document.LLi3.visibility = 'hide';
        parent.view.document.main.document.L1.visibility = 'hide';
        parent.view.document.main.document.L2.visibility = 'hide';
        parent.view.document.main.document.L4.visibility = 'hide';
        parent.view.document.main.document.L3.visibility = 'show';
        parent.view.document.main.document.L3.resizeTo(180,120);
        parent.view.document.main.document.L3.moveTo(100,100);
        }
}

function hidePreviewImageC()   {

        parent.view.document.main.document.L3.visibility = 'hide';
}
/*-------------------------------------------------------------------*/

function previewImageD()   {

        if (parent.view.document.main.document.LLi4)   {

        parent.view.document.main.document.LLi4.visibility = 'hide';
        parent.view.document.main.document.L1.visibility = 'hide';
        parent.view.document.main.document.L2.visibility = 'hide';
        parent.view.document.main.document.L3.visibility = 'hide';
        parent.view.document.main.document.L4.visibility = 'show';
        parent.view.document.main.document.L4.resizeTo(180,120);
        parent.view.document.main.document.L4.moveTo(100,100);
        }
}

function hidePreviewImageD()   {

        parent.view.document.main.document.L4.visibility = 'hide';
}

//END HIDING-->
</SCRIPT>

</BODY>
</HTML>
```

This is one of the four External documents that can be loaded into the **display** FRAME. The **revealSmallImage()** Function is assigned to the **onLoad** Event Handler as an Attribute in the BODY Element so that the animation sequence starts as soon as the page has fully loaded, including the images. The only real difference between this document and Sample718A.html that was used in the previous example is that all four of the small preview images are preloaded and initially hidden in all four of the External documents. Therefore, three of the four previews have to be hidden during the animation sequence, and this is taken care of in the **hideLargeClippedImage()** Function. It also hides the large art image.

Example 6-19 Part 2:   Sample719A.html

```
<!DOCTYPE HTML PUBLIC "-//W3C//DTD HTML 3.2//EN">
<HTML><HEAD>
<TITLE>Sample 719A - Example 6-19A    Click to Reveal Images </TITLE>
<STYLE type = "text/JavaScript">

        classes.theControl.all.fontSize = "22pt";
        classes.theControl.all.fontFamily = "Moonlight, cursive";
        classes.theControl.all.borderWidths("7px");
        classes.theControl.all.borderColor="#7700ff";
        classes.theControl.all.borderStyle="groove";

</STYLE>
</HEAD>
        <!--onLoad="revealSmallImage();"  Starts the animation sequence.-->

<BODY BGCOLOR="BLACK" TEXT="white" onLoad="revealSmallImage();"
BACKGROUND="JPEG-FILES/icon-BG-asteroids.jpg">

<LAYER ID="main" LEFT="5" TOP="5" WIDTH="540" HEIGHT="380">

<LAYER CLASS="theControl" ID="L1" LEFT="5" TOP="5" VISIBILITY="hide">
<IMG SRC="JPEG-FILES/J2-Winter-Arches-15.jpg" WIDTH="144" HEIGHT="98"
NAME="SmImage1A"></LAYER>

<LAYER CLASS="theControl" ID="L2" LEFT="5" TOP="5" VISIBILITY="hide">
<IMG SRC="JPEG-FILES/J2-SpaceDome_27P.jpg" WIDTH="144" HEIGHT="98"
NAME="SmImage2A"></LAYER>

<LAYER CLASS="theControl" ID="L3" LEFT="5" TOP="5" VISIBILITY="hide">
<IMG SRC="JPEG-FILES/J2-SKY_SPHERE_1.jpg" WIDTH="144" HEIGHT="98"
NAME="SmImage3A"></LAYER>

<LAYER CLASS="theControl" ID="L4" LEFT="5" TOP="5" VISIBILITY="hide">
<IMG SRC="JPEG-FILES/J2-TimeTunSkySphere.jpg" WIDTH="144" HEIGHT="98"
NAME="SmImage4A"></LAYER>

<LAYER CLASS="theControl" ID="LLi1" LEFT="5" TOP="5" CLIP="0,0">
<IMG SRC="JPEG-FILES/J7-Winter_Arches_15.jpg" WIDTH="504" HEIGHT="343"
NAME="LgImage1A"></LAYER>

</LAYER>

<SCRIPT LANGUAGE="JavaScript1.2"><!--BEGIN HIDING

var imageBoolean;
var imageBoolean2;
var imageBoolean3;
var main = document.main;
var L1 = document.main.document.L1;
var L2 = document.main.document.L2;
var L3 = document.main.document.L3;
var L4 = document.main.document.L4;
var LLi1 = document.main.document.LLi1;
```

```
/*-------------------------------------------------------------------*/

function revealSmallImage()  {

        imageBoolean3 = false;
        hideLargeClippedImage();

        L1.moveTo(main.clip.width, main.clip.height-120);
        L1.visibility = 'show';

        if (L1.clip.right <= 0  ||  L1.clip.top <= 0)  {
                L1.resizeTo(180,120);
        }
}

function hideLargeClippedImage()  {

        if (imageBoolean3 == false)  {

                L2.visibility = 'hide';
                L3.visibility = 'hide';
                L4.visibility = 'hide';
                LLi1.resizeTo(0,0);
                LLi1.visibility = 'hide';
                imageBoolean = true;
                timeWasterLeft();
        }
}

function timeWasterLeft()  {

        if (imageBoolean == true)  {

                if (L1.left > 0) {
                        L1.moveBy(-20,0);
                        setTimeout('timeWasterLeft()', 20);
                }
                else if (L1.left <= 0) {
                        timeWasterTop();
                }
        }
}

function timeWasterTop()  {

        if (imageBoolean == true)  {

                if (L1.top > 0) {
                        L1.moveBy(0,-20);
                        setTimeout('timeWasterTop()', 20);
                }
                else if (L1.top <= 0)  {
                        imageBoolean2 = true;
                        clipSmallImage();
                }
        }
}
```

```
function clipSmallImage()  {

        if (imageBoolean2 == true)  {

                if (L1.clip.right > 0  ||  L1.clip.top > 0)  {
                        L1.resizeBy(-10,-6);
                        setTimeout('clipSmallImage()', 20);
                }
                else if (L1.clip.right <= 0  &&  L1.clip.top <= 0)  {
                        imageBoolean2 = false;
                        imageBoolean3 = true;
                        LLi1.visibility = 'show';
                        revealLargeClippedImage();
                }
        }
}

function revealLargeClippedImage()  {

        if (imageBoolean3 == true)  {

                if (LLi1.clip.right < main.clip.width  ||  LLi1.clip.top <
main.clip.height)  {
                        LLi1.resizeBy(20,12);
                        setTimeout('revealLargeClippedImage()', 20);
                }
        }
}


//END HIDING-->
</SCRIPT>
</BODY>
</HTML>
```

This is the Frameset part of the example.

Example 6-19 Part 3:   Sample719Frameset.html

```
<!DOCTYPE HTML PUBLIC "-//W3C//DTD HTML 3.2//EN">
<HTML>
<HEAD>  <TITLE>Frameset for Sample 719</TITLE>         </HEAD>

<FRAMESET COLS="130,*">

        <FRAME SCROLLING="no" NAME="display" SRC="Sample719.html">

        <FRAME SCROLLING="auto" NAME="view" SRC="Sample719A.html">

</FRAMESET>

</HTML>
```

Example 6-19	Sample719Frameset.html

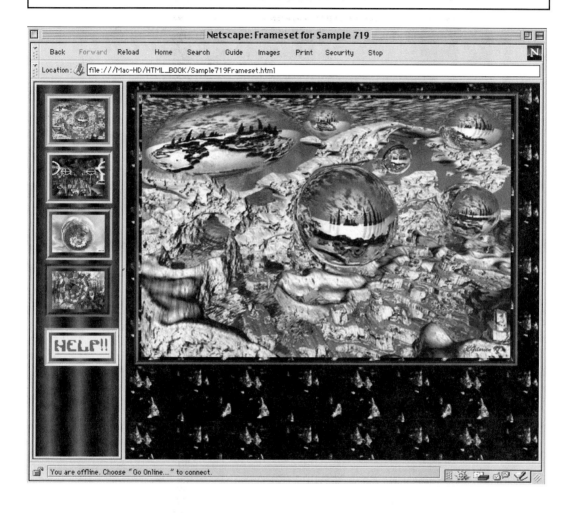

Scrolling, Resizing, & Moving Windows with Key Events

The JavaScript scrollBy() Method

The **scrollBy()** Method of the **window** Object can be used to both horizontally and vertically scroll through the contents of a Window by a specified number of pixels. It takes the two Arguments of **horizontalPixels** and **verticalPixels**, which can be either positive or negative integers or zero. Positive **horizontalPixels** scroll right and negative scroll left. Positive **verticalPixels** scroll down and negative scroll up. The Keyword **self** refers to the current Window. For example:

```
window.scrollBy(100,0);
self.scrollBy(0,-50);
myNewWindow.scrollBy(125,125);
```

JavaScript Syntax:

```
windowReference.scrollBy(horizontalPixels, verticalPixels)
```

The JavaScript scrollTo() Method

The **scrollTo()** Method can be used to horizontally and vertically scroll to a new (x,y) Coordinate in a Window so that this Coordinate becomes the top left corner of the visible area. It takes the two Arguments of **x-Coordinate** and **y-Coordinate**, which can be either positive or negative integers or zero. Because you have the capability to position your Layers off-screen, there may be times when you want to scroll the viewing area of the Window so that they can be seen, and that's where using the negative integers comes in. For example:

```
window.scrollTo(0,700);
self.scrollTo(-400,-550);
```

JavaScript Syntax:

```
windowReference.scrollTo(x-Coordinate, y-Coordinate)
```

Controlling your Window
with a variety of Methods

Example 6-20 does several things. It demonstrates the **scrollBy()**, **scrollTo()**, **moveBy()**, **moveTo()**, **resizeBy()**, and **resizeTo()** Methods of the **window** Object by using the **captureEvents()** Method to capture KEYDOWN Events and execute code using the **switch()** Statement in the **scrollLayers(e)** Function. The **switch()** Statement takes the **e.which** Expression as its **label** Argument and executes code if the CONTROL + ALT Modifiers Keys are pressed along with any of the 0-9 Keys. This Function also defines two Variables named **availSW** and **availSH** that demonstrate two of the **screen** Object's Properties of **availWidth** and **availHeight**, like this:

```
var availSW = ((screen.availWidth) -20);
var availSH = ((screen.availHeight) -100);
```

which are used by the **resizeTo(availSW, availSH)** Method on the **window** Object that is referenced by the Keyword **self**. The **scrollLayers(e)** Function is assigned by **Property Assignment** to the **onkeydown** Event Handler of the **document** Object.

The **showKey(e)** Function is assigned to the **onkeyup** Event Handler of the **document** Object and first sets all of the Text Boxes to a **null** String. Then it defines Variables that get most of the Properties of the **Event** Object and another Variable that uses the **String.fromCharCode()** Method to extract a String from the **e.which** Value. These Variables are then assigned to their respective Text Boxes' **value** Properties, so that every time an Event occurs, the Event's Property **value**s are displayed in the browser Window.

The TABLE in this example just contains a set of directions for testing out the SCRIPT when it's rendered in the browser.

For more information on the **moveBy()**, **moveTo()**, **resizeBy()**, and **resizeTo()** Methods of the **window** Object and the **availWidth** and **availHeight** Properties of the **screen** Object, see Chapter 4 on Objects.

Example 6-20: **Sample720.html**

```
<!DOCTYPE HTML PUBLIC "-//W3C//DTD HTML 3.2//EN">
<HTML><HEAD>
<TITLE> Sample 720   Example 6-20  Modifier Keys to Scroll, Move and Resize the
Window</TITLE>

<STYLE TYPE="text/JavaScript">

        classes.Mainbody.BODY.margins("0px");
        classes.Mainbody.BODY.paddings("0px");
        classes.Mainbody.BODY.backgroundColor="darkcyan";
        classes.Mainbody.BODY.color="white";
        classes.Mainbody.BODY.fontSize="17pt";
```

```
        tags.TD.fontSize="12pt";
        ids.L2.paddings("7px");
        ids.L3.paddings("7px");

</STYLE>
<!--  ************************************************************  -->

<SCRIPT LANGUAGE="JavaScript1.2"><!--BEGIN HIDING

function scrollLayers(e)  {

        var L2          = document.L2;
        var L3          = document.L3;

                //SCREEN is a new object in Navigator 4
                //-20 and -100 Takes into account the browser space
                //around the Window if no pictures are used in button bar

        var availSW     = ((screen.availWidth) -20);
        var availSH     = ((screen.availHeight) -100);

  if (e.modifiers == 3)  {                      //ALT_MASK + CONTROL_MASK = 3

        switch (e.which)  {

case 48 : window.scrollBy(0,50);        break; //press the ALT + CONTROL + 0 keys
case 49 : window.scrollBy(0,-50);       break; //press the ALT + CONTROL + 1 keys

case 50 : self.scrollTo(0,500);         break; //press the ALT + CONTROL + 2 keys
case 51 : self.scrollTo(0,0);           break; //press the ALT + CONTROL + 3 keys

case 52 : window.moveBy(20,0);          break; //press the ALT + CONTROL + 4 keys
case 53 : window.moveBy(-20,0);         break; //press the ALT + CONTROL + 5 keys

case 54 : self.moveTo(0,0);             break; //press the ALT + CONTROL + 6 keys

case 55 : self.resizeBy(-64,-48);       break; //press the ALT + CONTROL + 7 keys

case 56 : self.resizeTo(700,500);       break; //press the ALT + CONTROL + 8 keys
case 57 : self.resizeTo(availSW,availSH); break;   //press ALT + CONTROL + 9 keys
default : return false;
        }
   }
}
/*------------------------------------------------------------------------*/

function showKey(e)  {

        document.form1.T1.value  = "";
        document.form1.T2.value  = "";
        document.form1.T3.value  = "";
        document.form1.T4.value  = "";
        document.form1.T5.value  = "";
        document.form1.T7.value  = "";
        document.form1.T8.value  = "";
        document.form1.T9.value  = "";
        document.form1.T10.value = "";
        document.form1.T11.value = "";
```

```
        var whichKey2        = String.fromCharCode(e.which);
        var whichKey3        = e.which;
        var modifiersKey     = e.modifiers;
        var eventType        = e.type;
        var eventLayerX      = e.layerX;
        var eventLayerY      = e.layerY;
        var eventPageX       = e.pageX;
        var eventPageY       = e.pageY;
        var eventScreenX     = e.screenX;
        var eventScreenY     = e.screenY;

        document.form1.T1.value   = whichKey2;
        document.form1.T2.value   = whichKey3;
        document.form1.T3.value   = modifiersKey;
        document.form1.T4.value   = eventType;
        document.form1.T5.value   = eventLayerX;
        document.form1.T7.value   = eventLayerY;
        document.form1.T8.value   = eventPageX;
        document.form1.T9.value   = eventPageY;
        document.form1.T10.value  = eventScreenX;
        document.form1.T11.value  = eventScreenY;
}
/*-------------------------------------------------------------------------*/

document.captureEvents(Event.KEYDOWN | Event.KEYUP);
document.onkeydown = scrollLayers;
document.onkeyup = showKey;


//END HIDING-->
</SCRIPT>

<!--  *******************************************************************  -->

</HEAD>

<BODY CLASS="Mainbody" onLoad="window.focus();">

<FORM NAME="form1">

<INPUT TYPE="text" NAME="T1" SIZE="15">        String.fromCharCode(e.which)  <BR>
<INPUT TYPE="text" NAME="T2" SIZE="15">        e.which                       <BR>
<INPUT TYPE="text" NAME="T3" SIZE="15">        e.modifiers                   <BR>
<INPUT TYPE="text" NAME="T4" SIZE="15">        e.type                        <BR>

<INPUT TYPE="text" NAME="T5" SIZE="15">        e.layerX                      <BR>
<INPUT TYPE="text" NAME="T7" SIZE="15">        e.layerY                      <BR>
<INPUT TYPE="text" NAME="T8" SIZE="15">        e.pageX                       <BR>
<INPUT TYPE="text" NAME="T9" SIZE="15">        e.pageY                       <BR>
<INPUT TYPE="text" NAME="T10" SIZE="15">       e.screenX                     <BR>
<INPUT TYPE="text" NAME="T11" SIZE="15">       e.screenY                     <BR><BR>

</FORM>

<LAYER ID="L2" LEFT="250" TOP="120" WIDTH="450" BGCOLOR="navy">

This shows you the internal workings of the Event Object.

</LAYER>
```

```
<LAYER ID="L3" LEFT="10" TOP="220" WIDTH="460" BGCOLOR="lime">

<TABLE BGCOLOR="yellow">

<TR><TH COLSPAN="2">Click the ALT and CONTROL Keys with numbers 0-9.</TH></TR>

<TR>
<TD>    case 48 : self.scrollBy(0,50)             </TD>
<TD>    press the ALT + CONTROL + 0 keys          </TD></TR>
<TR>
<TD>    case 49 : self.scrollBy(0,-50)            </TD>
<TD>    press the ALT + CONTROL + 1 keys          </TD></TR>

<TR>
<TD>    case 50 : self.scrollTo(0,500)            </TD>
<TD>    press the ALT + CONTROL + 2 keys          </TD></TR>
<TR>
<TD>    case 51 : self.scrollTo(0,0)              </TD>
<TD>    press the ALT + CONTROL + 3 keys          </TD></TR>

<TR>
<TD>    case 52 : window.moveBy(20,0)             </TD>
<TD>    press the ALT + CONTROL + 4 keys          </TD></TR>
<TR>
<TD>    case 53 : window.moveBy(-20,0)            </TD>
<TD>    press the ALT + CONTROL + 5 keys          </TD></TR>

<TR>
<TD>    case 54 : self.moveTo(0,0)                </TD>
<TD>    press the ALT + CONTROL + 6 keys          </TD></TR>
<TR>
<TD>    case 55 : self.resizeBy(-64,-48)          </TD>
<TD>    press the ALT + CONTROL + 7 keys          </TD></TR>

<TR>
<TD>    case 56 : self.resizeTo(700,500)          </TD>
<TD>    press the ALT + CONTROL + 8 keys          </TD></TR>
<TR>
<TD>    case 57 : self.resizeTo(availSW,availSH)  </TD>
<TD>    press the ALT + CONTROL + 9 keys          </TD></TR>

</TABLE>
</LAYER>


<LAYER ID="L4" LEFT="50" TOP="700" WIDTH="450" BGCOLOR="#8800ff">

        Yep the scrollTo() Method works.              <BR>

        Click ALT + CONTROL + 3 to go back up.

</LAYER>

</BODY>
</HTML>
```

Example 6-20   Sample720.html

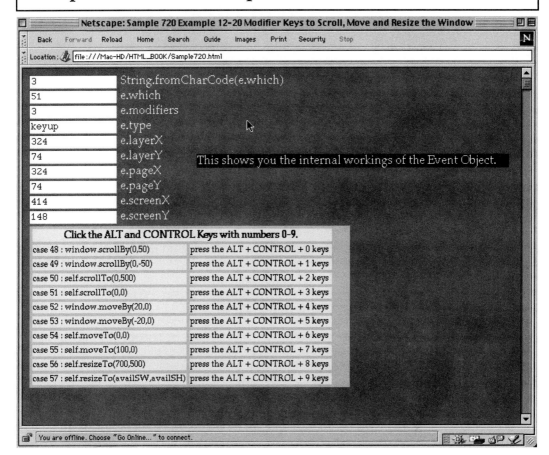

ASCII Values for the which Property
of the Event Object

Examples 6-21 and 6-22 are primarily designed for you to have reusable code and a reference for all of the **ASCII Values** of most of the Key **Constants** on the Keyboard when they are used in conjunction with the **modifiers** Key Constants. They are set up in **switch()** Statements so you can copy and paste chunks of code and then substitute your own JavaScript Statements. The ability to reposition a Layer in this example is secondary and relatively irrelevant.

Example 6-21 covers the individual use of the ALT, CONTROL, and SHIFT Keys, and then Example 6-22 (starting on page 632) covers all of the possible combinations of the **modifiers** Keys such as ALT + CONTROL and the individual use of the META Key.

They are fairly long, dry, and repetitive, but you will find them very convenient as a reference, and they will save you lots of typing if you copy and paste from the CD-ROM.

Example 6-21: Sample721.html

```
<!DOCTYPE HTML PUBLIC "-//W3C//DTD HTML 3.2//EN">
<HTML>
<HEAD>
<TITLE> Sample 721   Example 6-21 Move Layers using Hot Keys</TITLE>

<STYLE TYPE="text/JavaScript">

classes.Mainbody.BODY.margins("0px");
classes.Mainbody.BODY.paddings("0px");
classes.Mainbody.BODY.backgroundColor="navy";
classes.Mainbody.BODY.color="white";
classes.Mainbody.BODY.fontSize="17pt";

</STYLE>

<!--  *********************************************************************  -->

<SCRIPT LANGUAGE="JavaScript1.2"><!--BEGIN HIDING

var whichKey;

function scrollLayers(e)  {

        whichKey        = String.fromCharCode(e.which);
        var L1          = document.L1;
        var L2          = document.L2;
        var L3          = document.L3;

//The moveBy numbers make sense if you use the number pad on the right side of the keyboard.

  if (e.modifiers == Event.CONTROL_MASK)  {
```

```
    switch (whichKey)  {
    case '0' : L1.moveTo(250,250);                    break;   //press the CONTROL + 0 keys
    case '1' : L1.moveBy(-20,20);                     break;   //press the CONTROL + 1 keys
    case '2' : L1.moveBy(0,20);                       break;   //press the CONTROL + 2 keys
    case '3' : L1.moveBy(20,20);                      break;   //press the CONTROL + 3 keys
    case '4' : L1.moveBy(-20,0);                      break;   //press the CONTROL + 4 keys
    case '5' : L1.moveTo(10,350);                     break;   //press the CONTROL + 5 keys
    case '6' : L1.moveBy(20,0);                       break;   //press the CONTROL + 6 keys
    case '7' : L1.moveBy(-20,-20);                    break;   //press the CONTROL + 7 keys
    case '8' : L1.moveBy(0,-20);                      break;   //press the CONTROL + 8 keys
    case '9' : L1.moveBy(20,-20);                     break;   //press the CONTROL + 9 keys
    }
    switch (e.which.toString())  {
    case '1' : L1.moveBy(-20,20);                     break;   //press the CONTROL + a keys
    case '2' : L1.moveBy(0,20);                       break;   //press the CONTROL + b keys
    case '3' : L1.moveBy(20,20);                      break;   //press the CONTROL + c keys
    case '4' : L1.moveBy(-20,0);                      break;   //press the CONTROL + d keys
    case '5' : L1.moveBy(-20,0);                      break;   //press the CONTROL + e keys
    case '6' : L1.moveBy(20,0);                       break;   //press the CONTROL + f keys
    case '7' : L1.moveBy(-20,-20);                    break;   //press the CONTROL + g keys
    case '8' : L1.moveBy(0,-20);                      break;   //press the CONTROL + h keys
    case '9' : L1.moveBy(20,-20);                     break;   //press the CONTROL + i keys
    case '10' : L1.moveBy(-20,20);                    break;   //press the CONTROL + j keys
    case '11' : L1.moveBy(0,20);                      break;   //press the CONTROL + k keys
    case '12' : L1.moveBy(0,20);                      break;   //press the CONTROL + l keys
    case '13' : L1.moveBy(20,20);                     break;   //press the CONTROL + m keys
    case '14' : L1.moveBy(-20,0);                     break;   //press the CONTROL + n keys
    case '15' : L1.moveBy(-20,0);                     break;   //press the CONTROL + o keys
    case '16' : L1.moveBy(20,0);                      break;   //press the CONTROL + p keys
    case '17' : L1.moveBy(-20,-20);                   break;   //press the CONTROL + q keys
    case '18' : L1.moveBy(0,-20);                     break;   //press the CONTROL + r keys
    case '19' : L1.moveBy(20,-20);                    break;   //press the CONTROL + s keys
    case '20' : L1.moveBy(-20,20);                    break;   //press the CONTROL + t keys
    case '21' : L1.moveBy(0,20);                      break;   //press the CONTROL + u keys
    case '22' : L1.moveBy(20,20);                     break;   //press the CONTROL + v keys
    case '23' : L1.moveBy(-20,0);                     break;   //press the CONTROL + w keys
    case '24' : L1.moveBy(-20,0);                     break;   //press the CONTROL + x keys
    case '25' : L1.moveBy(20,0);                      break;   //press the CONTROL + y keys
    case '26' : L1.moveBy(-20,-20);                   break;   //press the CONTROL + z keys
    }
}
else if (e.modifiers == Event.ALT_MASK)  {

          //The two cases cover the numbers in the row above QWERTY letters
          //and the calulator pad numbers on the far right of extended keyboards.

    switch (e.which.toString())  {
    case '188' : case '48' : L2.moveTo(150,250);      break;   //press the ALT + 0 keys
    case '193' : case '49' : L2.moveBy(-30,30);       break;   //press the ALT + 1 keys
    case '170' : case '50' : L2.moveBy(0,30);         break;   //press the ALT + 2 keys
    case '163' : case '51' : L2.moveBy(30,30);        break;   //press the ALT + 3 keys
    case '162' : case '52' : L2.moveBy(-30,0);        break;   //press the ALT + 4 keys
    case '176' : case '53' : L2.moveTo(50,350);       break;   //press the ALT + 5 keys
    case '164' : case '54' : L2.moveBy(30,0);         break;   //press the ALT + 6 keys
    case '166' : case '55' : L2.moveBy(-30,-30);      break;   //press the ALT + 7 keys
    case '165' : case '56' : L2.moveBy(0,-30);        break;   //press the ALT + 8 keys
    case '187' : case '57' : L2.moveBy(30,-30);       break;   //press the ALT + 9 keys

    case '140' : L2.moveBy(30,30);                    break;   //press the ALT + a keys
    case '186' : L2.moveBy(30,30);                    break;   //press the ALT + b keys
    case '141' : L2.moveBy(30,30);                    break;   //press the ALT + c keys
    case '182' : L2.moveBy(30,30);                    break;   //press the ALT + d keys
    case '171' : L2.moveBy(30,30);                    break;   //press the ALT + e keys
    case '196' : L2.moveBy(-30,-30);                  break;   //press the ALT + f keys
    case '169' : L2.moveBy(-30,-30);                  break;   //press the ALT + g keys
    case '250' : L2.moveBy(-30,-30);                  break;   //press the ALT + h keys
```

```
            case '246' : L2.moveBy(-30,-30);           break;   //press the ALT + i keys
            case '198' : L2.moveBy(-30,-30);           break;   //press the ALT + j keys
            case '251' : L2.moveBy(30,30);             break;   //press the ALT + k keys
            case '194' : L2.moveBy(30,30);             break;   //press the ALT + l keys
            case '181' : L2.moveBy(30,30);             break;   //press the ALT + m keys
            case '247' : L2.moveBy(30,30);             break;   //press the ALT + n keys
            case '191' : L2.moveBy(30,30);             break;   //press the ALT + o keys
            case '185' : L2.moveBy(-30,-30);           break;   //press the ALT + p keys
            case '207' : L2.moveBy(-30,-30);           break;   //press the ALT + q keys
            case '168' : L2.moveBy(-30,-30);           break;   //press the ALT + r keys
            case '167' : L2.moveBy(-30,-30);           break;   //press the ALT + s keys
            case '160' : L2.moveBy(-30,-30);           break;   //press the ALT + t keys
            case '172' : L2.moveBy(30,30);             break;   //press the ALT + u keys
            case '195' : L2.moveBy(30,30);             break;   //press the ALT + v keys
            case '183' : L2.moveBy(30,30);             break;   //press the ALT + w keys
            case '197' : L2.moveBy(30,30);             break;   //press the ALT + x keys
            case '180' : L2.moveBy(30,30);             break;   //press the ALT + y keys
            case '189' : L2.moveBy(30,30);             break;   //press the ALT + z keys
            }
    }
    else if (e.modifiers == Event.SHIFT_MASK)  {

                //The two cases cover the numbers in the row above QWERTY letters
                //and the calulator pad numbers on the far right of extended keyboards.

        switch (e.which.toString()) {
        case '33' : case '48' : L3.moveTo(150,250);        break;   //press the SHIFT + 0 keys
        case '64' : case '49' : L3.moveBy(-50,50);         break;   //press the SHIFT + 1 keys
        case '35' : case '50' : L3.moveBy(0,50);           break;   //press the SHIFT + 2 keys
        case '36' : case '51' : L3.moveBy(50,50);          break;   //press the SHIFT + 3 keys
        case '37' : case '52' : L3.moveBy(-50,0);          break;   //press the SHIFT + 4 keys
        case '94' : case '53' : L3.moveTo(50,350);         break;   //press the SHIFT + 5 keys
        case '38' : case '54' : L3.moveBy(50,0);           break;   //press the SHIFT + 6 keys
        case '42' : case '55' : L3.moveBy(-50,-50);        break;   //press the SHIFT + 7 keys
        case '40' : case '56' : L3.moveBy(0,-50);          break;   //press the SHIFT + 8 keys
        case '41' : case '57' : L3.moveBy(50,-50);         break;   //press the SHIFT + 9 keys

        case '65' : L3.moveBy(50,50);             break;   //press the SHIFT + a keys
        case '66' : L3.moveBy(50,50);             break;   //press the SHIFT + b keys
        case '67' : L3.moveBy(50,50);             break;   //press the SHIFT + c keys
        case '68' : L3.moveBy(50,50);             break;   //press the SHIFT + d keys
        case '69' : L3.moveBy(50,50);             break;   //press the SHIFT + e keys
        case '70' : L3.moveBy(-50,-50);           break;   //press the SHIFT + f keys
        case '71' : L3.moveBy(-50,-50);           break;   //press the SHIFT + g keys
        case '72' : L3.moveBy(-50,-50);           break;   //press the SHIFT + h keys
        case '73' : L3.moveBy(-50,-50);           break;   //press the SHIFT + i keys
        case '74' : L3.moveBy(-50,-50);           break;   //press the SHIFT + j keys
        case '75' : L3.moveBy(50,50);             break;   //press the SHIFT + k keys
        case '76' : L3.moveBy(50,50);             break;   //press the SHIFT + l keys
        case '77' : L3.moveBy(50,50);             break;   //press the SHIFT + m keys
        case '78' : L3.moveBy(50,50);             break;   //press the SHIFT + n keys
        case '79' : L3.moveBy(50,50);             break;   //press the SHIFT + o keys
        case '80' : L3.moveBy(-50,-50);           break;   //press the SHIFT + p keys
        case '81' : L3.moveBy(-50,-50);           break;   //press the SHIFT + q keys
        case '82' : L3.moveBy(-50,-50);           break;   //press the SHIFT + r keys
        case '83' : L3.moveBy(-50,-50);           break;   //press the SHIFT + s keys
        case '84' : L3.moveBy(-50,-50);           break;   //press the SHIFT + t keys
        case '85' : L3.moveBy(50,50);             break;   //press the SHIFT + u keys
        case '86' : L3.moveBy(50,50);             break;   //press the SHIFT + v keys
        case '87' : L3.moveBy(50,50);             break;   //press the SHIFT + w keys
        case '88' : L3.moveBy(50,50);             break;   //press the SHIFT + x keys
        case '89' : L3.moveBy(50,50);             break;   //press the SHIFT + y keys
        case '90' : L3.moveBy(50,50);             break;   //press the SHIFT + z keys
            }
    }
```

```
     else {
           switch (whichKey)  {
           case '0' : L1.moveTo(10,100);              break;   //press the 0 key
           case '1' : L1.moveBy(-20,20);              break;   //press the 1 key
           case '2' : L1.moveBy(0,20);                break;   //press the 2 key
           case '3' : L1.moveBy(20,20);               break;   //press the 3 key
           case '4' : L1.moveBy(-20,0);               break;   //press the 4 key
           case '5' : L1.moveTo(150,100);             break;   //press the 5 key
           case '6' : L1.moveBy(20,0);                break;   //press the 6 key
           case '7' : L1.moveBy(-20,-20);             break;   //press the 7 key
           case '8' : L1.moveBy(0,-20);               break;   //press the 8 key
           case '9' : L1.moveBy(20,-20);              break;   //press the 9 key

           case 'q' : case 'Q' : L1.moveBy(20,20);             break;   //press the q key
           case 'w' : case 'W' : L1.moveBy(20,20);             break;   //press the w key
           case 'e' : case 'E' : L1.moveBy(20,20);             break;   //press the e key
           case 'r' : case 'R' : L1.moveBy(-20,-20);           break;   //press the r key
           case 't' : case 'T' : L1.moveBy(-20,-20);           break;   //press the t key
           case 'y' : case 'Y' : L1.moveBy(-20,-20);           break;   //press the y key
           default : return false;
           }
    }
}
/*-------------------------------------------------------------------------*/

function showKey(e)  {

        document.form1.T1.value = "";
        document.form1.T2.value = "";

        var T1           = document.form1.T1;
        whichKey2                = String.fromCharCode(e.which);
        whichKey3                = e.which.toString();

        document.form1.T1.value = whichKey2;
        document.form1.T2.value = whichKey3;
}

/*-------------------------------------------------------------------------*/

document.captureEvents(Event.KEYPRESS | Event.KEYUP);
document.onkeypress = scrollLayers;
document.onkeyup = showKey;

//END HIDING-->
</SCRIPT>
<!-- ************************************************************** -->
</HEAD>

<!--The window.focus() Method takes the automatic focus from the location bar and
puts it in the window so you don't have to click in it first to get the keys to work.-->

<BODY CLASS="Mainbody" onLoad="window.focus();">

<FORM NAME="form1">
String.fromCharCode(e.which)       <SPACER TYPE="horizontal" SIZE="70">  e.which.toString()<BR>
<INPUT TYPE="text" NAME="T1" SIZE="30">
<INPUT TYPE="text" NAME="T2" SIZE="30">
</FORM><HR>

<LAYER ID="L1" LEFT="10" TOP="100" WIDTH="300" BGCOLOR="black">
Use the CONTROL Key plus letters A-Z or numbers 0-9 to move this Layer.<BR>
Try just using the numbers on the keypad or keyboard without modifier keys.
The main goal is to show you what to test for in your functions and the usefulness of the
Switch Statement.
</LAYER>
```

```
<LAYER ID="L2" LEFT="410" TOP="300" WIDTH="300" BGCOLOR="red">
Use the ALT Key plus letters A-Z or numbers 0-9 to move this Layer. <BR>
Note that you get different values in the textfield display for keypad numbers on
extended keyboards than the regular numbers on the keyboard.
</LAYER>

<LAYER ID="L3" LEFT="410" TOP="50" WIDTH="300" BGCOLOR="blue">
Use the SHIFT Key plus letters A-Z or numbers 0-9 to move this Layer.<BR>
Notice that the <B>fromCharCode</B> Method gives you the actual key value while the
<B>toString</B> Method gives you the ASCII Value associated with the event.
</LAYER>

</BODY>
</HTML>
```

Example 6-22 covers the circumstances when you want to use **if()** and **switch()** Statements to test for <u>multiple</u> **modifiers** Keys being pressed before certain actions are taken by the Script. See the preamble to Example 6-21, on page 628, and tips in the Layer text of the example code on page 646, for more information.

Example 6-22:   Sample722.html

```
<!DOCTYPE HTML PUBLIC "-//W3C//DTD HTML 3.2//EN">
<HTML>
<HEAD>
<TITLE> Sample 722 -  Example 6-22          Move Layers with Multiple modifiers Keys</TITLE>

<STYLE TYPE="text/JavaScript">

classes.Mainbody.BODY.margins("0px");
classes.Mainbody.BODY.paddings("0px");
classes.Mainbody.BODY.backgroundColor="darkcyan";
classes.Mainbody.BODY.color="white";
classes.Mainbody.BODY.fontSize="17pt";

ids.L3.fontSize="14pt";

</STYLE>
<!-- ******************************************************************** -->

<SCRIPT LANGUAGE="JavaScript1.2"><!--BEGIN HIDING

function scrollLayers(e) {
         var L1   = document.L1;
         var L2   = document.L2;
         var L3   = document.L3;
```

```javascript
if (e.modifiers == 3) {                    //ALT_MASK + CONTROL_MASK = 3

    switch (e.which.toString()) {

        case '48' : L1.moveTo(410,220);    break;    //press the ALT + CONTROL + 0 keys
        case '49' : L1.moveBy(-90,90);     break;    //press the ALT + CONTROL + 1 keys
        case '50' : L1.moveBy(0,90);       break;    //press the ALT + CONTROL + 2 keys
        case '51' : L1.moveBy(90,90);      break;    //press the ALT + CONTROL + 3 keys
        case '52' : L1.moveBy(-90,0);      break;    //press the ALT + CONTROL + 4 keys
        case '53' : L1.moveTo(410,50);     break;    //press the ALT + CONTROL + 5 keys
        case '54' : L1.moveBy(90,0);       break;    //press the ALT + CONTROL + 6 keys
        case '55' : L1.moveBy(-90,-90);    break;    //press the ALT + CONTROL + 7 keys
        case '56' : L1.moveBy(0,-90);      break;    //press the ALT + CONTROL + 8 keys
        case '57' : L1.moveBy(90,-90);     break;    //press the ALT + CONTROL + 9 keys

        case '1' : L1.moveBy(90,90);       break;    //press the ALT + CONTROL + a keys
        case '2' : L1.moveBy(90,90);       break;    //press the ALT + CONTROL + b keys
        case '3' : L1.moveBy(90,90);       break;    //press the ALT + CONTROL + c keys
        case '4' : L1.moveBy(90,90);       break;    //press the ALT + CONTROL + d keys
        case '5' : L1.moveBy(90,90);       break;    //press the ALT + CONTROL + e keys
        case '6' : L1.moveBy(-90,-90);     break;    //press the ALT + CONTROL + f keys
        case '7' : L1.moveBy(-90,-90);     break;    //press the ALT + CONTROL + g keys
        case '8' : L1.moveBy(-90,-90);     break;    //press the ALT + CONTROL + h keys
        case '9' : L1.moveBy(-90,-90);     break;    //press the ALT + CONTROL + i keys
        case '10' : L1.moveBy(-90,-90);    break;    //press the ALT + CONTROL + j keys
        case '11' : L1.moveBy(90,90);      break;    //press the ALT + CONTROL + k keys
        case '12' : L1.moveBy(90,90);      break;    //press the ALT + CONTROL + l keys
        case '13' : L1.moveBy(90,90);      break;    //press the ALT + CONTROL + m keys
        case '14' : L1.moveBy(90,90);      break;    //press the ALT + CONTROL + n keys
        case '15' : L1.moveBy(90,90);      break;    //press the ALT + CONTROL + o keys
        case '16' : L1.moveBy(-90,-90);    break;    //press the ALT + CONTROL + p keys
        case '17' : L1.moveBy(-90,-90);    break;    //press the ALT + CONTROL + q keys
        case '18' : L1.moveBy(-90,-90);    break;    //press the ALT + CONTROL + r keys
        case '19' : L1.moveBy(-90,-90);    break;    //press the ALT + CONTROL + s keys
        case '20' : L1.moveBy(-90,-90);    break;    //press the ALT + CONTROL + t keys
        case '21' : L1.moveBy(90,90);      break;    //press the ALT + CONTROL + u keys
        case '22' : L1.moveBy(90,90);      break;    //press the ALT + CONTROL + v keys
        case '23' : L1.moveBy(90,90);      break;    //press the ALT + CONTROL + w keys
        case '24' : L1.moveBy(90,90);      break;    //press the ALT + CONTROL + x keys
        case '25' : L1.moveBy(90,90);      break;    //press the ALT + CONTROL + y keys
        case '26' : L1.moveBy(90,90);      break;    //press the ALT + CONTROL + z keys
    }

}
```

```
else if (e.modifiers == 5)  {                    //ALT_MASK + SHIFT_MASK = 5

    //The two cases cover the numbers in the row above QWERTY letters
    //and the calulator pad numbers on the far right of extended keyboards.

    switch (e.which.toString())  {

        case '226' : case '48' : L2.moveTo(150,250);break;   //press the ALT + SHIFT + 0 keys
        case '218' : case '49' : L2.moveBy(-30,30);  break;   //press the ALT + SHIFT + 1 keys
        case '219' : case '50' : L2.moveBy(0,30);    break;   //press the ALT + SHIFT + 2 keys
        case '220' : case '51' : L2.moveBy(30,30);   break;   //press the ALT + SHIFT + 3 keys
        case '221' : case '52' : L2.moveBy(-30,0);   break;   //press the ALT + SHIFT + 4 keys
        case '222' : case '53' : L2.moveTo(50,350);  break;   //press the ALT + SHIFT + 5 keys
        case '223' : case '54' : L2.moveBy(30,0);    break;   //press the ALT + SHIFT + 6 keys
        case '224' : case '55' : L2.moveBy(-30,-30); break;   //press the ALT + SHIFT + 7 keys
        case '161' : case '56' : L2.moveBy(0,-30);   break;   //press the ALT + SHIFT + 8 keys
        case '225' : case '57' : L2.moveBy(30,-30);  break;   //press the ALT + SHIFT + 9 keys

        case '129' : L2.moveBy(30,30);              break;   //press the ALT + SHIFT + a keys
        case '245' : L2.moveBy(30,30);              break;   //press the ALT + SHIFT + b keys
        case '130' : L2.moveBy(30,30);              break;   //press the ALT + SHIFT + c keys
        case '235' : L2.moveBy(30,30);              break;   //press the ALT + SHIFT + d keys
        case '171' : L2.moveBy(30,30);              break;   //press the ALT + SHIFT + e keys
        case '236' : L2.moveBy(-30,-30);            break;   //press the ALT + SHIFT + f keys
        case '253' : L2.moveBy(-30,-30);            break;   //press the ALT + SHIFT + g keys
        case '238' : L2.moveBy(-30,-30);            break;   //press the ALT + SHIFT + h keys
        case '246' : L2.moveBy(-30,-30);            break;   //press the ALT + SHIFT + i keys
        case '239' : L2.moveBy(-30,-30);            break;   //press the ALT + SHIFT + j keys
        case '240' : L2.moveBy(30,30);              break;   //press the ALT + SHIFT + k keys
        case '241' : L2.moveBy(30,30);              break;   //press the ALT + SHIFT + l keys
        case '229' : L2.moveBy(30,30);              break;   //press the ALT + SHIFT + m keys
        case '247' : L2.moveBy(30,30);              break;   //press the ALT + SHIFT + n keys
        case '175' : L2.moveBy(30,30);              break;   //press the ALT + SHIFT + o keys
        case '184' : L2.moveBy(-30,-30);            break;   //press the ALT + SHIFT + p keys
        case '206' : L2.moveBy(-30,-30);            break;   //press the ALT + SHIFT + q keys
        case '228' : L2.moveBy(-30,-30);            break;   //press the ALT + SHIFT + r keys
        case '234' : L2.moveBy(-30,-30);            break;   //press the ALT + SHIFT + s keys
        case '255' : L2.moveBy(-30,-30);            break;   //press the ALT + SHIFT + t keys
        case '172' : L2.moveBy(30,30);              break;   //press the ALT + SHIFT + u keys
        case '215' : L2.moveBy(30,30);              break;   //press the ALT + SHIFT + v keys
        case '227' : L2.moveBy(30,30);              break;   //press the ALT + SHIFT + w keys
        case '254' : L2.moveBy(30,30);              break;   //press the ALT + SHIFT + x keys
        case '231' : L2.moveBy(30,30);              break;   //press the ALT + SHIFT + y keys
        case '252' : L2.moveBy(30,30);              break;   //press the ALT + SHIFT + z keys
    }
}
```

```
else if (e.modifiers == 6)  {                    //CONTROL_MASK + SHIFT_MASK = 6

    switch (e.which.toString())  {

        case '48' : L3.moveTo(410,220);    break;    //press the SHIFT + CONTROL + 0 keys
        case '49' : L3.moveBy(-90,90);     break;    //press the SHIFT + CONTROL + 1 keys
        case '50' : L3.moveBy(0,90);       break;    //press the SHIFT + CONTROL + 2 keys
        case '51' : L3.moveBy(90,90);      break;    //press the SHIFT + CONTROL + 3 keys
        case '52' : L3.moveBy(-90,0);      break;    //press the SHIFT + CONTROL + 4 keys
        case '53' : L3.moveTo(410,50);     break;    //press the SHIFT + CONTROL + 5 keys
        case '54' : L3.moveBy(90,0);       break;    //press the SHIFT + CONTROL + 6 keys
        case '55' : L3.moveBy(-90,-90);    break;    //press the SHIFT + CONTROL + 7 keys
        case '56' : L3.moveBy(0,-90);      break;    //press the SHIFT + CONTROL + 8 keys
        case '57' : L3.moveBy(90,-90);     break;    //press the SHIFT + CONTROL + 9 keys

        case '1' : L3.moveBy(90,90);       break;    //press the SHIFT + CONTROL + a keys
        case '2' : L3.moveBy(90,90);       break;    //press the SHIFT + CONTROL + b keys
        case '3' : L3.moveBy(90,90);       break;    //press the SHIFT + CONTROL + c keys
        case '4' : L3.moveBy(90,90);       break;    //press the SHIFT + CONTROL + d keys
        case '5' : L3.moveBy(90,90);       break;    //press the SHIFT + CONTROL + e keys
        case '6' : L3.moveBy(-90,-90);     break;    //press the SHIFT + CONTROL + f keys
        case '7' : L3.moveBy(-90,-90);     break;    //press the SHIFT + CONTROL + g keys
        case '8' : L3.moveBy(-90,-90);     break;    //press the SHIFT + CONTROL + h keys
        case '9' : L3.moveBy(-90,-90);     break;    //press the SHIFT + CONTROL + i keys
        case '10' : L3.moveBy(-90,-90);    break;    //press the SHIFT + CONTROL + j keys
        case '11' : L3.moveBy(90,90);      break;    //press the SHIFT + CONTROL + k keys
        case '12' : L3.moveBy(90,90);      break;    //press the SHIFT + CONTROL + l keys
        case '13' : L3.moveBy(90,90);      break;    //press the SHIFT + CONTROL + m keys
        case '14' : L3.moveBy(90,90);      break;    //press the SHIFT + CONTROL + n keys
        case '15' : L3.moveBy(90,90);      break;    //press the SHIFT + CONTROL + o keys
        case '16' : L3.moveBy(-90,-90);    break;    //press the SHIFT + CONTROL + p keys
        case '17' : L3.moveBy(-90,-90);    break;    //press the SHIFT + CONTROL + q keys
        case '18' : L3.moveBy(-90,-90);    break;    //press the SHIFT + CONTROL + r keys
        case '19' : L3.moveBy(-90,-90);    break;    //press the SHIFT + CONTROL + s keys
        case '20' : L3.moveBy(-90,-90);    break;    //press the SHIFT + CONTROL + t keys
        case '21' : L3.moveBy(90,90);      break;    //press the SHIFT + CONTROL + u keys
        case '22' : L3.moveBy(90,90);      break;    //press the SHIFT + CONTROL + v keys
        case '23' : L3.moveBy(90,90);      break;    //press the SHIFT + CONTROL + w keys
        case '24' : L3.moveBy(90,90);      break;    //press the SHIFT + CONTROL + x keys
        case '25' : L3.moveBy(90,90);      break;    //press the SHIFT + CONTROL + y keys
        case '26' : L3.moveBy(90,90);      break;    //press the SHIFT + CONTROL + z keys
    }

}

//The number that represents the ALT + CONTROL + SHIFT keys being pressed simultaneously is 7.
//So testing if the Event e modifers is equal to 7, is shorthand for those keys.
```

```
else if (e.modifiers == 7) {                //ALT_MASK + CONTROL_MASK + SHIFT_MASK = 7

    switch (e.which.toString()) {

        case '48' : L1.moveTo(410,220);    break;    //press the ALT + CONTROL + SHIFT + 0 keys
        case '49' : L1.moveBy(-90,90);     break;    //press the ALT + CONTROL + SHIFT + 1 keys
        case '50' : L1.moveBy(0,90);       break;    //press the ALT + CONTROL + SHIFT + 2 keys
        case '51' : L1.moveBy(90,90);      break;    //press the ALT + CONTROL + SHIFT + 3 keys
        case '52' : L1.moveBy(-90,0);      break;    //press the ALT + CONTROL + SHIFT + 4 keys
        case '53' : L1.moveTo(410,50);     break;    //press the ALT + CONTROL + SHIFT + 5 keys
        case '54' : L1.moveBy(90,0);       break;    //press the ALT + CONTROL + SHIFT + 6 keys
        case '55' : L1.moveBy(-90,-90);    break;    //press the ALT + CONTROL + SHIFT + 7 keys
        case '56' : L1.moveBy(0,-90);      break;    //press the ALT + CONTROL + SHIFT + 8 keys
        case '57' : L1.moveBy(90,-90);     break;    //press the ALT + CONTROL + SHIFT + 9 keys

        case '1' : L1.moveBy(90,90);       break;    //press the ALT + CONTROL + SHIFT + a keys
        case '2' : L1.moveBy(90,90);       break;    //press the ALT + CONTROL + SHIFT + b keys
        case '3' : L1.moveBy(90,90);       break;    //press the ALT + CONTROL + SHIFT + c keys
        case '4' : L1.moveBy(90,90);       break;    //press the ALT + CONTROL + SHIFT + d keys
        case '5' : L1.moveBy(90,90);       break;    //press the ALT + CONTROL + SHIFT + e keys
        case '6' : L1.moveBy(-90,-90);     break;    //press the ALT + CONTROL + SHIFT + f keys
        case '7' : L1.moveBy(-90,-90);     break;    //press the ALT + CONTROL + SHIFT + g keys
        case '8' : L1.moveBy(-90,-90);     break;    //press the ALT + CONTROL + SHIFT + h keys
        case '9' : L1.moveBy(-90,-90);     break;    //press the ALT + CONTROL + SHIFT + i keys
        case '10' : L1.moveBy(-90,-90);    break;    //press the ALT + CONTROL + SHIFT + j keys
        case '11' : L1.moveBy(90,90);      break;    //press the ALT + CONTROL + SHIFT + k keys
        case '12' : L1.moveBy(90,90);      break;    //press the ALT + CONTROL + SHIFT + l keys
        case '13' : L1.moveBy(90,90);      break;    //press the ALT + CONTROL + SHIFT + m keys
        case '14' : L1.moveBy(90,90);      break;    //press the ALT + CONTROL + SHIFT + n keys
        case '15' : L1.moveBy(90,90);      break;    //press the ALT + CONTROL + SHIFT + o keys
        case '16' : L1.moveBy(-90,-90);    break;    //press the ALT + CONTROL + SHIFT + p keys
        case '17' : L1.moveBy(-90,-90);    break;    //press the ALT + CONTROL + SHIFT + q keys
        case '18' : L1.moveBy(-90,-90);    break;    //press the ALT + CONTROL + SHIFT + r keys
        case '19' : L1.moveBy(-90,-90);    break;    //press the ALT + CONTROL + SHIFT + s keys
        case '20' : L1.moveBy(-90,-90);    break;    //press the ALT + CONTROL + SHIFT + t keys
        case '21' : L1.moveBy(90,90);      break;    //press the ALT + CONTROL + SHIFT + u keys
        case '22' : L1.moveBy(90,90);      break;    //press the ALT + CONTROL + SHIFT + v keys
        case '23' : L1.moveBy(90,90);      break;    //press the ALT + CONTROL + SHIFT + w keys
        case '24' : L1.moveBy(90,90);      break;    //press the ALT + CONTROL + SHIFT + x keys
        case '25' : L1.moveBy(90,90);      break;    //press the ALT + CONTROL + SHIFT + y keys
        case '26' : L1.moveBy(90,90);      break;    //press the ALT + CONTROL + SHIFT + z keys
    }
}
//Be advised that most of the normal Command Keys in Navigator already have code assigned to them
//which is either difficult or impossible to override so your JavaScript code will be ignored.
//However, use of the META_MASK is hassle-free if you create your own window object without a title
```

```
//bar and set the HOTKEYS Property to true which turns off all native hotkeys except for Quit and
//Security.

  else if (e.modifiers == 8) {          //META_MASK = 8  which is the Apple Command key

      switch (e.which.toString()) {

          case '48' : L2.moveTo(410,220);    break;    //press the META + 0 keys
          case '49' : L2.moveBy(-90,90);     break;    //press the META + 1 keys
          case '50' : L2.moveBy(0,90);       break;    //press the META + 2 keys
          case '51' : L2.moveBy(90,90);      break;    //press the META + 3 keys
          case '52' : L2.moveBy(-90,0);      break;    //press the META + 4 keys
          case '53' : L2.moveTo(410,50);     break;    //press the META + 5 keys
          case '54' : L2.moveBy(90,0);       break;    //press the META + 6 keys
          case '55' : L2.moveBy(-90,-90);    break;    //press the META + 7 keys
          case '56' : L2.moveBy(0,-90);      break;    //press the META + 8 keys
          case '57' : L2.moveBy(90,-90);     break;    //press the META + 9 keys

          case '97' : L2.moveBy(90,90);      break;    //press the META + a keys
          case '98' : L2.moveBy(90,90);      break;    //press the META + b keys
          case '99' : L2.moveBy(90,90);      break;    //press the META + c keys
          case '100' : L2.moveBy(90,90);     break;    //press the META + d keys
          case '101' : L2.moveBy(90,90);     break;    //press the META + e keys
          case '102' : L2.moveBy(-90,-90);   break;    //press the META + f keys
          case '103' : L2.moveBy(-90,-90);   break;    //press the META + g keys
          case '104' : L2.moveBy(-90,-90);   break;    //press the META + h keys
          case '105' : L2.moveBy(-90,-90);   break;    //press the META + i keys
          case '106' : L2.moveBy(-90,-90);   break;    //press the META + j keys
          case '107' : L2.moveBy(90,90);     break;    //press the META + k keys
          case '108' : L2.moveBy(90,90);     break;    //press the META + l keys
          case '109' : L2.moveBy(90,90);     break;    //press the META + m keys
          case '110' : L2.moveBy(90,90);     break;    //press the META + n keys
          case '111' : L2.moveBy(90,90);     break;    //press the META + o keys
          case '112' : L2.moveBy(-90,-90);   break;    //press the META + p keys
          case '113' : L2.moveBy(-90,-90);   break;    //press the META + q keys
          case '114' : L2.moveBy(-90,-90);   break;    //press the META + r keys
          case '115' : L2.moveBy(-90,-90);   break;    //press the META + s keys
          case '116' : L2.moveBy(-90,-90);   break;    //press the META + t keys
          case '117' : L2.moveBy(90,90);     break;    //press the META + u keys
          case '118' : L2.moveBy(90,90);     break;    //press the META + v keys
          case '119' : L2.moveBy(90,90);     break;    //press the META + w keys
          case '120' : L2.moveBy(90,90);     break;    //press the META + x keys
          case '121' : L2.moveBy(90,90);     break;    //press the META + y keys
          case '122' : L2.moveBy(90,90);     break;    //press the META + z keys
      }

  }
```

```
else if (e.modifiers == 9)  {              //META_MASK + ALT_MASK = 9

    //The two cases cover the numbers in the row above QWERTY letters
    //and the calulator pad numbers on the far right of extended keyboards.

    switch (e.which.toString())  {

        case '188' : case '48' : L3.moveTo(150,250);break;   //press the META + ALT + 0 keys
        case '193' : case '49' : L3.moveBy(-30,30);  break;   //press the META + ALT + 1 keys
        case '170' : case '50' : L3.moveBy(0,30);    break;   //press the META + ALT + 2 keys
        case '163' : case '51' : L3.moveBy(30,30);   break;   //press the META + ALT + 3 keys
        case '162' : case '52' : L3.moveBy(-30,0);   break;   //press the META + ALT + 4 keys
        case '176' : case '53' : L3.moveTo(50,350);  break;   //press the META + ALT + 5 keys
        case '164' : case '54' : L3.moveBy(30,0);    break;   //press the META + ALT + 6 keys
        case '166' : case '55' : L3.moveBy(-30,-30); break;   //press the META + ALT + 7 keys
        case '165' : case '56' : L3.moveBy(0,-30);   break;   //press the META + ALT + 8 keys
        case '187' : case '57' : L3.moveBy(30,-30);  break;   //press the META + ALT + 9 keys

        case '140' : L3.moveBy(30,30);         break;   //press the META + ALT + a keys
        case '186' : L3.moveBy(30,30);         break;   //press the META + ALT + b keys
        case '141' : L3.moveBy(30,30);         break;   //press the META + ALT + c keys
        case '182' : L3.moveBy(30,30);         break;   //press the META + ALT + d keys
        case '171' : L3.moveBy(30,30);         break;   //press the META + ALT + e keys
        case '196' : L3.moveBy(-30,-30);       break;   //press the META + ALT + f keys
        case '169' : L3.moveBy(-30,-30);       break;   //press the META + ALT + g keys
        case '250' : L3.moveBy(-30,-30);       break;   //press the META + ALT + h keys
        case '246' : L3.moveBy(-30,-30);       break;   //press the META + ALT + i keys
        case '198' : L3.moveBy(-30,-30);       break;   //press the META + ALT + j keys
        case '251' : L3.moveBy(30,30);         break;   //press the META + ALT + k keys
        case '194' : L3.moveBy(30,30);         break;   //press the META + ALT + l keys
        case '181' : L3.moveBy(30,30);         break;   //press the META + ALT + m keys
        case '247' : L3.moveBy(30,30);         break;   //press the META + ALT + n keys
        case '191' : L3.moveBy(30,30);         break;   //press the META + ALT + o keys
        case '185' : L3.moveBy(-30,-30);       break;   //press the META + ALT + p keys
        case '207' : L3.moveBy(-30,-30);       break;   //press the META + ALT + q keys
        case '168' : L3.moveBy(-30,-30);       break;   //press the META + ALT + r keys
        case '167' : L3.moveBy(-30,-30);       break;   //press the META + ALT + s keys
        case '160' : L3.moveBy(-30,-30);       break;   //press the META + ALT + t keys
        case '172' : L3.moveBy(30,30);         break;   //press the META + ALT + u keys
        case '195' : L3.moveBy(30,30);         break;   //press the META + ALT + v keys
        case '183' : L3.moveBy(30,30);         break;   //press the META + ALT + w keys
        case '197' : L3.moveBy(30,30);         break;   //press the META + ALT + x keys
        case '180' : L3.moveBy(30,30);         break;   //press the META + ALT + y keys
        case '189' : L3.moveBy(30,30);         break;   //press the META + ALT + z keys
    }

}
```

```
else if (e.modifiers == 10)  {              //META_MASK + CONTROL_MASK = 10

        switch (e.which.toString())  {

            case '48' : L1.moveTo(410,220);   break;    //press the META + CONTROL + 0 keys
            case '49' : L1.moveBy(-90,90);    break;    //press the META + CONTROL + 1 keys
            case '50' : L1.moveBy(0,90);      break;    //press the META + CONTROL + 2 keys
            case '51' : L1.moveBy(90,90);     break;    //press the META + CONTROL + 3 keys
            case '52' : L1.moveBy(-90,0);     break;    //press the META + CONTROL + 4 keys
            case '53' : L1.moveTo(410,50);    break;    //press the META + CONTROL + 5 keys
            case '54' : L1.moveBy(90,0);      break;    //press the META + CONTROL + 6 keys
            case '55' : L1.moveBy(-90,-90);   break;    //press the META + CONTROL + 7 keys
            case '56' : L1.moveBy(0,-90);     break;    //press the META + CONTROL + 8 keys
            case '57' : L1.moveBy(90,-90);    break;    //press the META + CONTROL + 9 keys

            case '1' : L1.moveBy(90,90);      break;    //press the META + CONTROL + a keys
            case '2' : L1.moveBy(90,90);      break;    //press the META + CONTROL + b keys
            case '3' : L1.moveBy(90,90);      break;    //press the META + CONTROL + c keys
            case '4' : L1.moveBy(90,90);      break;    //press the META + CONTROL + d keys
            case '5' : L1.moveBy(90,90);      break;    //press the META + CONTROL + e keys
            case '6' : L1.moveBy(-90,-90);    break;    //press the META + CONTROL + f keys
            case '7' : L1.moveBy(-90,-90);    break;    //press the META + CONTROL + g keys
            case '8' : L1.moveBy(-90,-90);    break;    //press the META + CONTROL + h keys
            case '9' : L1.moveBy(-90,-90);    break;    //press the META + CONTROL + i keys
            case '10' : L1.moveBy(-90,-90);   break;    //press the META + CONTROL + j keys
            case '11' : L1.moveBy(90,90);     break;    //press the META + CONTROL + k keys
            case '12' : L1.moveBy(90,90);     break;    //press the META + CONTROL + l keys
            case '13' : L1.moveBy(90,90);     break;    //press the META + CONTROL + m keys
            case '14' : L1.moveBy(90,90);     break;    //press the META + CONTROL + n keys
            case '15' : L1.moveBy(90,90);     break;    //press the META + CONTROL + o keys
            case '16' : L1.moveBy(-90,-90);   break;    //press the META + CONTROL + p keys
            case '17' : L1.moveBy(-90,-90);   break;    //press the META + CONTROL + q keys
            case '18' : L1.moveBy(-90,-90);   break;    //press the META + CONTROL + r keys
            case '19' : L1.moveBy(-90,-90);   break;    //press the META + CONTROL + s keys
            case '20' : L1.moveBy(-90,-90);   break;    //press the META + CONTROL + t keys
            case '21' : L1.moveBy(90,90);     break;    //press the META + CONTROL + u keys
            case '22' : L1.moveBy(90,90);     break;    //press the META + CONTROL + v keys
            case '23' : L1.moveBy(90,90);     break;    //press the META + CONTROL + w keys
            case '24' : L1.moveBy(90,90);     break;    //press the META + CONTROL + x keys
            case '25' : L1.moveBy(90,90);     break;    //press the META + CONTROL + y keys
            case '26' : L1.moveBy(90,90);     break;    //press the META + CONTROL + z keys
        }
}
```

```
else if (e.modifiers == 11) {              //META_MASK + ALT_MASK + CONTROL_MASK = 11

    switch (e.which.toString()) {

        case '48' : L2.moveTo(410,220);   break;   //press the META + ALT + CONTROL + 0 keys
        case '49' : L2.moveBy(-90,90);    break;   //press the META + ALT + CONTROL + 1 keys
        case '50' : L2.moveBy(0,90);      break;   //press the META + ALT + CONTROL + 2 keys
        case '51' : L2.moveBy(90,90);     break;   //press the META + ALT + CONTROL + 3 keys
        case '52' : L2.moveBy(-90,0);     break;   //press the META + ALT + CONTROL + 4 keys
        case '53' : L2.moveTo(410,50);    break;   //press the META + ALT + CONTROL + 5 keys
        case '54' : L2.moveBy(90,0);      break;   //press the META + ALT + CONTROL + 6 keys
        case '55' : L2.moveBy(-90,-90);   break;   //press the META + ALT + CONTROL + 7 keys
        case '56' : L2.moveBy(0,-90);     break;   //press the META + ALT + CONTROL + 8 keys
        case '57' : L2.moveBy(90,-90);    break;   //press the META + ALT + CONTROL + 9 keys

        case '1' : L2.moveBy(90,90);      break;   //press the META + ALT + CONTROL + a keys
        case '2' : L2.moveBy(90,90);      break;   //press the META + ALT + CONTROL + b keys
        case '3' : L2.moveBy(90,90);      break;   //press the META + ALT + CONTROL + c keys
        case '4' : L2.moveBy(90,90);      break;   //press the META + ALT + CONTROL + d keys
        case '5' : L2.moveBy(90,90);      break;   //press the META + ALT + CONTROL + e keys
        case '6' : L2.moveBy(-90,-90);    break;   //press the META + ALT + CONTROL + f keys
        case '7' : L2.moveBy(-90,-90);    break;   //press the META + ALT + CONTROL + g keys
        case '8' : L2.moveBy(-90,-90);    break;   //press the META + ALT + CONTROL + h keys
        case '9' : L2.moveBy(-90,-90);    break;   //press the META + ALT + CONTROL + i keys
        case '10' : L2.moveBy(-90,-90);   break;   //press the META + ALT + CONTROL + j keys
        case '11' : L2.moveBy(90,90);     break;   //press the META + ALT + CONTROL + k keys
        case '12' : L2.moveBy(90,90);     break;   //press the META + ALT + CONTROL + l keys
        case '13' : L2.moveBy(90,90);     break;   //press the META + ALT + CONTROL + m keys
        case '14' : L2.moveBy(90,90);     break;   //press the META + ALT + CONTROL + n keys
        case '15' : L2.moveBy(90,90);     break;   //press the META + ALT + CONTROL + o keys
        case '16' : L2.moveBy(-90,-90);   break;   //press the META + ALT + CONTROL + p keys
        case '17' : L2.moveBy(-90,-90);   break;   //press the META + ALT + CONTROL + q keys
        case '18' : L2.moveBy(-90,-90);   break;   //press the META + ALT + CONTROL + r keys
        case '19' : L2.moveBy(-90,-90);   break;   //press the META + ALT + CONTROL + s keys
        case '20' : L2.moveBy(-90,-90);   break;   //press the META + ALT + CONTROL + t keys
        case '21' : L2.moveBy(90,90);     break;   //press the META + ALT + CONTROL + u keys
        case '22' : L2.moveBy(90,90);     break;   //press the META + ALT + CONTROL + v keys
        case '23' : L2.moveBy(90,90);     break;   //press the META + ALT + CONTROL + w keys
        case '24' : L2.moveBy(90,90);     break;   //press the META + ALT + CONTROL + x keys
        case '25' : L2.moveBy(90,90);     break;   //press the META + ALT + CONTROL + y keys
        case '26' : L2.moveBy(90,90);     break;   //press the META + ALT + CONTROL + z keys
    }

}
```

```
else if (e.modifiers == 12) {        //META_MASK + SHIFT_MASK = 12

    switch (e.which.toString()) {

        case '48' : L3.moveTo(410,220);   break;   //press the META + SHIFT + 0 keys
        case '49' : L3.moveBy(-90,90);    break;   //press the META + SHIFT + 1 keys
        case '50' : L3.moveBy(0,90);      break;   //press the META + SHIFT + 2 keys
        case '51' : L3.moveBy(90,90);     break;   //press the META + SHIFT + 3 keys
        case '52' : L3.moveBy(-90,0);     break;   //press the META + SHIFT + 4 keys
        case '53' : L3.moveTo(410,50);    break;   //press the META + SHIFT + 5 keys
        case '54' : L3.moveBy(90,0);      break;   //press the META + SHIFT + 6 keys
        case '55' : L3.moveBy(-90,-90);   break;   //press the META + SHIFT + 7 keys
        case '56' : L3.moveBy(0,-90);     break;   //press the META + SHIFT + 8 keys
        case '57' : L3.moveBy(90,-90);    break;   //press the META + SHIFT + 9 keys

        case '97' : L3.moveBy(90,90);     break;   //press the META + SHIFT + a keys
        case '98' : L3.moveBy(90,90);     break;   //press the META + SHIFT + b keys
        case '99' : L3.moveBy(90,90);     break;   //press the META + SHIFT + c keys
        case '100' : L3.moveBy(90,90);    break;   //press the META + SHIFT + d keys
        case '101' : L3.moveBy(90,90);    break;   //press the META + SHIFT + e keys
        case '102' : L3.moveBy(-90,-90);  break;   //press the META + SHIFT + f keys
        case '103' : L3.moveBy(-90,-90);  break;   //press the META + SHIFT + g keys
        case '104' : L3.moveBy(-90,-90);  break;   //press the META + SHIFT + h keys
        case '105' : L3.moveBy(-90,-90);  break;   //press the META + SHIFT + i keys
        case '106' : L3.moveBy(-90,-90);  break;   //press the META + SHIFT + j keys
        case '107' : L3.moveBy(90,90);    break;   //press the META + SHIFT + k keys
        case '108' : L3.moveBy(90,90);    break;   //press the META + SHIFT + l keys
        case '109' : L3.moveBy(90,90);    break;   //press the META + SHIFT + m keys
        case '110' : L3.moveBy(90,90);    break;   //press the META + SHIFT + n keys
        case '111' : L3.moveBy(90,90);    break;   //press the META + SHIFT + o keys
        case '112' : L3.moveBy(-90,-90);  break;   //press the META + SHIFT + p keys
        case '113' : L3.moveBy(-90,-90);  break;   //press the META + SHIFT + q keys
        case '114' : L3.moveBy(-90,-90);  break;   //press the META + SHIFT + r keys
        case '115' : L3.moveBy(-90,-90);  break;   //press the META + SHIFT + s keys
        case '116' : L3.moveBy(-90,-90);  break;   //press the META + SHIFT + t keys
        case '117' : L3.moveBy(90,90);    break;   //press the META + SHIFT + u keys
        case '118' : L3.moveBy(90,90);    break;   //press the META + SHIFT + v keys
        case '119' : L3.moveBy(90,90);    break;   //press the META + SHIFT + w keys
        case '120' : L3.moveBy(90,90);    break;   //press the META + SHIFT + x keys
        case '121' : L3.moveBy(90,90);    break;   //press the META + SHIFT + y keys
        case '122' : L3.moveBy(90,90);    break;   //press the META + SHIFT + z keys
    }

}
```

```
    else if (e.modifiers == 13) {            //META_MASK + SHIFT_MASK + ALT_MASK = 13

        //The two cases cover the numbers in the row above QWERTY letters
        //and the calulator pad numbers on the far right of extended keyboards.

        switch (e.which.toString())  {

case '226' : case '48' : L1.moveTo(150,250);break;       //press the META + SHIFT + ALT + 0 keys
case '218' : case '49' : L1.moveBy(-30,30);  break;      //press the META + SHIFT + ALT + 1 keys
case '219' : case '50' : L1.moveBy(0,30);    break;      //press the META + SHIFT + ALT + 2 keys
case '220' : case '51' : L1.moveBy(30,30);   break;      //press the META + SHIFT + ALT + 3 keys
case '221' : case '52' : L1.moveBy(-30,0);   break;      //press the META + SHIFT + ALT + 4 keys
case '222' : case '53' : L1.moveTo(50,350);  break;      //press the META + SHIFT + ALT + 5 keys
case '223' : case '54' : L1.moveBy(30,0);    break;      //press the META + SHIFT + ALT + 6 keys
case '224' : case '55' : L1.moveBy(-30,-30); break;      //press the META + SHIFT + ALT + 7 keys
case '161' : case '56' : L1.moveBy(0,-30);   break;      //press the META + SHIFT + ALT + 8 keys
case '225' : case '57' : L1.moveBy(30,-30);  break;      //press the META + SHIFT + ALT + 9 keys

case '129' : L1.moveBy(30,30);              break;      //press the META + SHIFT + ALT + a keys
case '245' : L1.moveBy(30,30);              break;      //press the META + SHIFT + ALT + b keys
case '130' : L1.moveBy(30,30);              break;      //press the META + SHIFT + ALT + c keys
case '235' : L1.moveBy(30,30);              break;      //press the META + SHIFT + ALT + d keys
case '171' : L1.moveBy(30,30);              break;      //press the META + SHIFT + ALT + e keys
case '236' : L1.moveBy(-30,-30);            break;      //press the META + SHIFT + ALT + f keys
case '253' : L1.moveBy(-30,-30);            break;      //press the META + SHIFT + ALT + g keys
case '238' : L1.moveBy(-30,-30);            break;      //press the META + SHIFT + ALT + h keys
case '246' : L1.moveBy(-30,-30);            break;      //press the META + SHIFT + ALT + i keys
case '239' : L1.moveBy(-30,-30);            break;      //press the META + SHIFT + ALT + j keys
case '240' : L1.moveBy(30,30);              break;      //press the META + SHIFT + ALT + k keys
case '241' : L1.moveBy(30,30);              break;      //press the META + SHIFT + ALT + l keys
case '229' : L1.moveBy(30,30);              break;      //press the META + SHIFT + ALT + m keys
case '247' : L1.moveBy(30,30);              break;      //press the META + SHIFT + ALT + n keys
case '175' : L1.moveBy(30,30);              break;      //press the META + SHIFT + ALT + o keys
case '184' : L1.moveBy(-30,-30);            break;      //press the META + SHIFT + ALT + p keys
case '206' : L1.moveBy(-30,-30);            break;      //press the META + SHIFT + ALT + q keys
case '228' : L1.moveBy(-30,-30);            break;      //press the META + SHIFT + ALT + r keys
case '234' : L1.moveBy(-30,-30);            break;      //press the META + SHIFT + ALT + s keys
case '255' : L1.moveBy(-30,-30);            break;      //press the META + SHIFT + ALT + t keys
case '172' : L1.moveBy(30,30);              break;      //press the META + SHIFT + ALT + u keys
case '215' : L1.moveBy(30,30);              break;      //press the META + SHIFT + ALT + v keys
case '227' : L1.moveBy(30,30);              break;      //press the META + SHIFT + ALT + w keys
case '254' : L1.moveBy(30,30);              break;      //press the META + SHIFT + ALT + x keys
case '231' : L1.moveBy(30,30);              break;      //press the META + SHIFT + ALT + y keys
case '252' : L1.moveBy(30,30);              break;      //press the META + SHIFT + ALT + z keys
        }
    }
```

```
else if (e.modifiers == 14) {              //META_MASK + SHIFT_MASK + CONTROL_MASK = 14

        switch (e.which.toString()) {

case '48' : L2.moveTo(410,220);    break;    //press the META + SHIFT + CONTROL + 0 keys
case '49' : L2.moveBy(-90,90);     break;    //press the META + SHIFT + CONTROL + 1 keys
case '50' : L2.moveBy(0,90);       break;    //press the META + SHIFT + CONTROL + 2 keys
case '51' : L2.moveBy(90,90);      break;    //press the META + SHIFT + CONTROL + 3 keys
case '52' : L2.moveBy(-90,0);      break;    //press the META + SHIFT + CONTROL + 4 keys
case '53' : L2.moveTo(410,50);     break;    //press the META + SHIFT + CONTROL + 5 keys
case '54' : L2.moveBy(90,0);       break;    //press the META + SHIFT + CONTROL + 6 keys
case '55' : L2.moveBy(-90,-90);    break;    //press the META + SHIFT + CONTROL + 7 keys
case '56' : L2.moveBy(0,-90);      break;    //press the META + SHIFT + CONTROL + 8 keys
case '57' : L2.moveBy(90,-90);     break;    //press the META + SHIFT + CONTROL + 9 keys

case '1' : L2.moveBy(90,90);       break;    //press the META + SHIFT + CONTROL + a keys
case '2' : L2.moveBy(90,90);       break;    //press the META + SHIFT + CONTROL + b keys
case '3' : L2.moveBy(90,90);       break;    //press the META + SHIFT + CONTROL + c keys
case '4' : L2.moveBy(90,90);       break;    //press the META + SHIFT + CONTROL + d keys
case '5' : L2.moveBy(90,90);       break;    //press the META + SHIFT + CONTROL + e keys
case '6' : L2.moveBy(-90,-90);     break;    //press the META + SHIFT + CONTROL + f keys
case '7' : L2.moveBy(-90,-90);     break;    //press the META + SHIFT + CONTROL + g keys
case '8' : L2.moveBy(-90,-90);     break;    //press the META + SHIFT + CONTROL + h keys
case '9' : L2.moveBy(-90,-90);     break;    //press the META + SHIFT + CONTROL + i keys
case '10' : L2.moveBy(-90,-90);    break;    //press the META + SHIFT + CONTROL + j keys
case '11' : L2.moveBy(90,90);      break;    //press the META + SHIFT + CONTROL + k keys
case '12' : L2.moveBy(90,90);      break;    //press the META + SHIFT + CONTROL + l keys
case '13' : L2.moveBy(90,90);      break;    //press the META + SHIFT + CONTROL + m keys
case '14' : L2.moveBy(90,90);      break;    //press the META + SHIFT + CONTROL + n keys
case '15' : L2.moveBy(90,90);      break;    //press the META + SHIFT + CONTROL + o keys
case '16' : L2.moveBy(-90,-90);    break;    //press the META + SHIFT + CONTROL + p keys
case '17' : L2.moveBy(-90,-90);    break;    //press the META + SHIFT + CONTROL + q keys
case '18' : L2.moveBy(-90,-90);    break;    //press the META + SHIFT + CONTROL + r keys
case '19' : L2.moveBy(-90,-90);    break;    //press the META + SHIFT + CONTROL + s keys
case '20' : L2.moveBy(-90,-90);    break;    //press the META + SHIFT + CONTROL + t keys
case '21' : L2.moveBy(90,90);      break;    //press the META + SHIFT + CONTROL + u keys
case '22' : L2.moveBy(90,90);      break;    //press the META + SHIFT + CONTROL + v keys
case '23' : L2.moveBy(90,90);      break;    //press the META + SHIFT + CONTROL + w keys
case '24' : L2.moveBy(90,90);      break;    //press the META + SHIFT + CONTROL + x keys
case '25' : L2.moveBy(90,90);      break;    //press the META + SHIFT + CONTROL + y keys
case '26' : L2.moveBy(90,90);      break;    //press the META + SHIFT + CONTROL + z keys
        }

  }
```

```
                          //META_MASK + SHIFT_MASK + CONTROL_MASK + ALT_MASK = 15
    else if (e.modifiers == 15) {

            switch (e.which.toString()) {

case '48' : L3.moveTo(410,220);      break;    //press the META + SHIFT + CONTROL + ALT + 0 keys
case '49' : L3.moveBy(-90,90);       break;    //press the META + SHIFT + CONTROL + ALT + 1 keys
case '50' : L3.moveBy(0,90);         break;    //press the META + SHIFT + CONTROL + ALT + 2 keys
case '51' : L3.moveBy(90,90);        break;    //press the META + SHIFT + CONTROL + ALT + 3 keys
case '52' : L3.moveBy(-90,0);        break;    //press the META + SHIFT + CONTROL + ALT + 4 keys
case '53' : L3.moveTo(410,50);       break;    //press the META + SHIFT + CONTROL + ALT + 5 keys
case '54' : L3.moveBy(90,0);         break;    //press the META + SHIFT + CONTROL + ALT + 6 keys
case '55' : L3.moveBy(-90,-90);      break;    //press the META + SHIFT + CONTROL + ALT + 7 keys
case '56' : L3.moveBy(0,-90);        break;    //press the META + SHIFT + CONTROL + ALT + 8 keys
case '57' : L3.moveBy(90,-90);       break;    //press the META + SHIFT + CONTROL + ALT + 9 keys

case '1' : L3.moveBy(90,90);         break;    //press the META + SHIFT + CONTROL + ALT + a keys
case '2' : L3.moveBy(90,90);         break;    //press the META + SHIFT + CONTROL + ALT + b keys
case '3' : L3.moveBy(90,90);         break;    //press the META + SHIFT + CONTROL + ALT + c keys
case '4' : L3.moveBy(90,90);         break;    //press the META + SHIFT + CONTROL + ALT + d keys
case '5' : L3.moveBy(90,90);         break;    //press the META + SHIFT + CONTROL + ALT + e keys
case '6' : L3.moveBy(-90,-90);       break;    //press the META + SHIFT + CONTROL + ALT + f keys
case '7' : L3.moveBy(-90,-90);       break;    //press the META + SHIFT + CONTROL + ALT + g keys
case '8' : L3.moveBy(-90,-90);       break;    //press the META + SHIFT + CONTROL + ALT + h keys
case '9' : L3.moveBy(-90,-90);       break;    //press the META + SHIFT + CONTROL + ALT + i keys
case '10' : L3.moveBy(-90,-90);      break;    //press the META + SHIFT + CONTROL + ALT + j keys
case '11' : L3.moveBy(90,90);        break;    //press the META + SHIFT + CONTROL + ALT + k keys
case '12' : L3.moveBy(90,90);        break;    //press the META + SHIFT + CONTROL + ALT + l keys
case '13' : L3.moveBy(90,90);        break;    //press the META + SHIFT + CONTROL + ALT + m keys
case '14' : L3.moveBy(90,90);        break;    //press the META + SHIFT + CONTROL + ALT + n keys
case '15' : L3.moveBy(90,90);        break;    //press the META + SHIFT + CONTROL + ALT + o keys
case '16' : L3.moveBy(-90,-90);      break;    //press the META + SHIFT + CONTROL + ALT + p keys
case '17' : L3.moveBy(-90,-90);      break;    //press the META + SHIFT + CONTROL + ALT + q keys
case '18' : L3.moveBy(-90,-90);      break;    //press the META + SHIFT + CONTROL + ALT + r keys
case '19' : L3.moveBy(-90,-90);      break;    //press the META + SHIFT + CONTROL + ALT + s keys
case '20' : L3.moveBy(-90,-90);      break;    //press the META + SHIFT + CONTROL + ALT + t keys
case '21' : L3.moveBy(90,90);        break;    //press the META + SHIFT + CONTROL + ALT + u keys
case '22' : L3.moveBy(90,90);        break;    //press the META + SHIFT + CONTROL + ALT + v keys
case '23' : L3.moveBy(90,90);        break;    //press the META + SHIFT + CONTROL + ALT + w keys
case '24' : L3.moveBy(90,90);        break;    //press the META + SHIFT + CONTROL + ALT + x keys
case '25' : L3.moveBy(90,90);        break;    //press the META + SHIFT + CONTROL + ALT + y keys
case '26' : L3.moveBy(90,90);        break;    //press the META + SHIFT + CONTROL + ALT + z keys
            default : return false;
            }
    }
}
```

```
/*-----------------------------------------------------------------------*/


function showKey(e)  {

            document.form1.T1.value = "";
            document.form1.T2.value = "";
            document.form1.T3.value = "";

//I left in the toString() Method so it wouldn't be confusing but for readout purposes you don't need it.
//It is necessary in the above Switch Statements because you have to compare it to a STRING in the
CASE LABEL.

            var whichKey2     = String.fromCharCode(e.which);
            var whichKey3     = e.which.toString();
            var modifiersKey  = e.modifiers.toString();

            document.form1.T1.value = whichKey2;
            document.form1.T2.value = whichKey3;
            document.form1.T3.value = modifiersKey;
}

document.captureEvents(Event.KEYPRESS | Event.KEYUP);
document.onkeypress = scrollLayers;
document.onkeyup = showKey;

//END HIDING-->
</SCRIPT>

</HEAD>

<!--The window.focus() Method takes the automatic focus from the location bar and
puts it in the window so you don't have to click in it first to get the keys to work.-->

<BODY CLASS="Mainbody" onLoad="window.focus();">

<FORM NAME="form1">

String.fromCharCode(e.which)        <SPACER TYPE="horizontal" SIZE="75">  e.which
<SPACER TYPE="horizontal" SIZE="145">e.modifiers<BR>

<INPUT TYPE="text" NAME="T1" SIZE="33">
<INPUT TYPE="text" NAME="T2" SIZE="30">
<INPUT TYPE="text" NAME="T3" SIZE="30">

</FORM>
```

```
<LAYER ID="L1" LEFT="550" TOP="50" WIDTH="144" BGCOLOR="magenta">
<FONT COLOR="navy">
Notice that the <B>          fromCharCode</B> Method gives you the actual key value while the
<B>toString</B> Method gives you the
HTML number associated with the event.


</FONT><BR><BR>
Combine the META, SHIFT, ALT, and CONTROL Keys with letters A-Z and numbers 0-9. Note that with
certain modifier combinations you get different values in the textfield display for keypad numbers on
extended keyboards than the regular numbers on the keyboard.
</LAYER>


<LAYER ID="L2" LEFT="10" TOP="370" WIDTH="450" BGCOLOR="navy">
The Switch Statement is especially useful for testing the HTML number associated with a Modifier Key
to determine if JavaScript code should be implemented, like in this example.  You can grab chunks of
code from this example and the previous example to save yourself a lot of typing and testing. To avoid
headaches don't use the META Key because it accesses Navigator Command code even when it
shouldn't.
</LAYER>


<LAYER ID="L3" LEFT="10" TOP="50" WIDTH="520" BGCOLOR="green">
Here's the numbers that correspond to the modifier keys used both individually and in
combination.<BR><BR>
<UL TYPE=DISC>
        <LI>1  = ALT_MASK
        <LI>2  = CONTROL_MASK
        <LI>3  = ALT_MASK + CONTROL_MASK
        <LI>4  = SHIFT_MASK
        <LI>5  = ALT_MASK + SHIFT_MASK
        <LI>6  = CONTROL_MASK + SHIFT_MASK
        <LI>7  = ALT_MASK + CONTROL_MASK + SHIFT_MASK
        <LI>8  = META_MASK
        <LI>9  = META_MASK + ALT_MASK
        <LI>10 = META_MASK + CONTROL_MASK
        <LI>11 = META_MASK + ALT_MASK + CONTROL_MASK
        <LI>12 = META_MASK + SHIFT_MASK
        <LI>13 = META_MASK + SHIFT_MASK + ALT_MASK
        <LI>14 = META_MASK + SHIFT_MASK + CONTROL_MASK
        <LI>15 = META_MASK + SHIFT_MASK + CONTROL_MASK + ALT_MASK
</UL>
</LAYER>


</BODY>
</HTML>
```

Example 6-22   Sample722.html

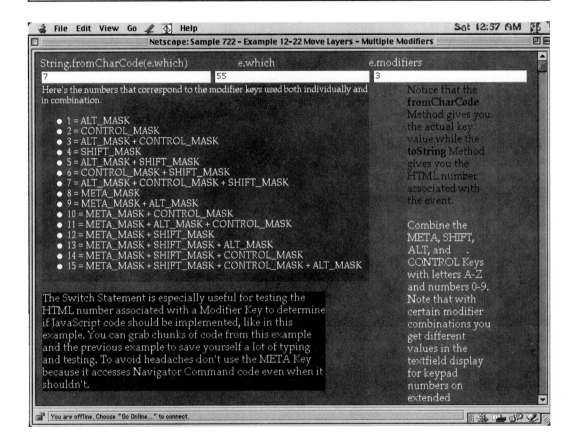

String.fromCharCode(e.which)	e.which	e.modifiers
7	55	3

Here's the numbers that correspond to the modifier keys used both individually and in combination:

- 1 = ALT_MASK
- 2 = CONTROL_MASK
- 3 = ALT_MASK + CONTROL_MASK
- 4 = SHIFT_MASK
- 5 = ALT_MASK + SHIFT_MASK
- 6 = CONTROL_MASK + SHIFT_MASK
- 7 = ALT_MASK + CONTROL_MASK + SHIFT_MASK
- 8 = META_MASK
- 9 = META_MASK + ALT_MASK
- 10 = META_MASK + CONTROL_MASK
- 11 = META_MASK + ALT_MASK + CONTROL_MASK
- 12 = META_MASK + SHIFT_MASK
- 13 = META_MASK + SHIFT_MASK + ALT_MASK
- 14 = META_MASK + SHIFT_MASK + CONTROL_MASK
- 15 = META_MASK + SHIFT_MASK + CONTROL_MASK + ALT_MASK

The Switch Statement is especially useful for testing the HTML number associated with a Modifier Key to determine if JavaScript code should be implemented, like in this example. You can grab chunks of code from this example and the previous example to save yourself a lot of typing and testing. To avoid headaches don't use the META Key because it accesses Navigator Command code even when it shouldn't.

Notice that the fromCharCode Method gives you the actual key value while the toString Method gives you the HTML number associated with the event.

Combine the META, SHIFT, ALT, and CONTROL Keys with letters A-Z and numbers 0-9. Note that with certain modifier combinations you get different values in the textfield display for keypad numbers on extended

Using Key Events to open a new Window

This example defines a Function named **openSesame(e)**, which uses the **switch()** Statement to create and open a new **window** Object by using the **open()** Method when the ALT + CONTROL + 1 Keys are pressed. Remember that your comma-separated list of **windowfeatures** cannot have any spaces between each feature. For more information on the **open()** Method (starting on page 422), see the section on the **window** Object (starting on page 416) in Chapter 4 on JavaScript Objects.

The KEYPRESS Event is captured for the **document** Object by the **captureEvents()** Method, and the **openSesame(e)** Function is assigned to the **onkeypress** Event Handler for the **document** Object.

The **window.focus()** Method is assigned to the **onLoad** Event Handler of the BODY Element to give focus to the **window** as soon as the document is fully loaded.

Example 6-23:   **Sample723.html**

```
<!DOCTYPE HTML PUBLIC "-//W3C//DTD HTML 3.2//EN">
<HTML>
<HEAD>
<TITLE> Sample 723    Example 6-23   Create a new window      </TITLE>

<STYLE TYPE="text/JavaScript">

        classes.Mainbody.BODY.margins("0px");

        classes.Mainbody.BODY.paddings("0px");

        classes.Mainbody.BODY.backgroundColor="lightsteelblue";

        classes.Mainbody.BODY.color="white";

        classes.Mainbody.BODY.fontSize="17pt";


        ids.L1.paddings("7px");


</STYLE>


<!--   ********************************************************************   -->


<SCRIPT LANGUAGE="JavaScript1.2"><!--BEGIN HIDING

/*-------------------------------------------------------------------------*/
```

```
function openSesame(e)   {

        var L1 = document.L1;

        var W1;

  if (e.modifiers == 3)   {                         //ALT_MASK + CONTROL_MASK = 3

        switch (e.which.toString())   {

                case '49' :             //press the ALT + CONTROL + 1 keys

                W1 = window.open('Sample406.html', 'testWindow', 'menubar=no,
scrollbars=no,hotkeys=no,status=no,innerWidth=400,innerHeight=200,screenX=20,
screenY=100,resizable=no');

                break;

                default : return false;
        }
  }
}


/*-------------------------------------------------------------------------*/

document.captureEvents(Event.KEYPRESS);

document.onkeypress = openSesame;

/*-------------------------------------------------------------------------*/


//END HIDING-->
</SCRIPT>

</HEAD>

<BODY CLASS="Mainbody" onLoad="window.focus();">

<LAYER ID="L1" LEFT="100" TOP="5" WIDTH="270" BGCOLOR="red">

        Try clicking ALT + CONTROL + 1 to open a new Window.

</LAYER>

</BODY>

</HTML>
```

Creating user-customizable Documents

Example 6-24 deals with Functions that allow the user to choose the parameters of Style Sheet Properties to create customized web pages in real-time. To do this, you make extensive use of the **document.write()** Method. Basically, you provide the user with some SELECT Menu Elements so that there are choices for Background Color, Text Color, Layer Background Color, Font, Font Point-Size, Border Thickness, and Border Color. When the user makes a choice, then the document in the main viewing FRAME named **display** is updated with the **changeEverything()** Function, which is assigned to all of the **onChange** Event Handlers for all of the SELECT Elements.

There are four parts in this example. The FRAMESET divides the window into three FRAMES. The left FRAME named **display** has all the SELECTION Elements for user preferences. The top FRAME named **input** has the TEXTFIELD for user text input, and the bottom FRAME named **main** is the area where the preferences and text input are rendered into view.

changeEverything()   This Function implements the changes by writing content to the **display** FRAME by first defining all of the Variables that are going to contain the user choices from the SELECT Elements. For example, the Variable **getBackColor** is assigned the SELECT Element named **getBackColor** that is in the FORM Element named **form1**, which is in the Layer named **L2**. Then, the **sel** Variable is assigned the integer Value of the **selectedIndex** Property of the **getBackColor** SELECT Element. It is then used as the **index** of the **options[index]** Array to get the **value** of the current selection and assign it to the **bcolorSel** Variable.

```
var getBackColor = L2.document.form1.getBackColor;
var sel = getBackColor.selectedIndex;
var bcolorSel = getBackColor.options[sel].value;
```

The reason for coding this in a somewhat roundabout way is to make it easier to understand what's going on. It could have been coded in one statement like this:

```
var bcolorSel=document.L2.document.form1.getBackColor.options[document.L2.document.form1.getBackColor.selectedIndex].value;
```

which is way harder to read and comprehend.

Further along in the Function, the **bcolorSel** Variable, which contains the color that the user has selected for the background color, is implemented with the following line of code:

```
parent.main.document.bgColor = bcolorSel;
```

which accesses the FRAME named **main** and uses the **bgColor** Property to implement the new background color. This procedure is exactly duplicated for the foreground color. The rest of the user choices also follow this process with one minor difference in the way that the Variables are set up. Basically the first two lines of code have been combined into one so there are only two lines total like this:

```
var sel3 = L2.document.form1.fontSelection.selectedIndex;
var c3 = L2.document.form1.fontSelection.options[sel3].value;
```

The rest of the Function just uses the **document.write()** Method to create the HTML for the document and implement the user preferences. There are some Comment sections in the example that you can check out for minor clarification.

An alternative version of Example 6-24

There is a parallel file named <u>Sample724B-hasLayerBGColor.html</u> which has some additional functionality of a minor nature. The user can choose between implementing:

```
parent.main.document.L1.bgColor = c4;
```

which, in effect, causes the background color for the Layer to *behave like* the CSS Property of **layer-background-color**; or the alternative choice of:

```
parent.main.document.ids.L1.backgroundColor = c4;
```

which causes it to behave normally. This is accomplished in the **whichTypeBG()** Function with the checkbox named **chbx1**.

If you want to run that version then make sure you load in the file named <u>Sample724-B-Frameset.html</u> instead of <u>Sample724Frameset.html</u>. Additional capabilities are explained below.

whichTypeBG() This Function just changes the Boolean Variables depending on whether the CHECKBOX Element named **chbx1** is checked or unchecked. If **booleanTest** is **false**, then the **changeEverything()** Function implements the **backgroundColor** choice for the Layer **L1** like this:

```
parent.main.document.ids.L1.backgroundColor = c4;
```

If **booleanTest** is **true** then:

```
parent.main.document.L1.bgColor = c4;
```

showPoem() This Function just lets the user decide if a small poem should be displayed along with the user's text. The poem is here so that when you want to test the SCRIPT out, you don't have to continually type in text in the TEXTAREA to get results.

Example 6-24 Part 1:   Sample724.html

```
<!DOCTYPE HTML PUBLIC "-//W3C//DTD HTML 3.2//EN">
<HTML>
<HEAD>
<TITLE> Sample 724   Example 6-24 User Customizable Sites</TITLE>

<STYLE TYPE="text/JavaScript">

        classes.Mainbody.BODY.margins("0px");
        classes.Mainbody.BODY.paddings("0px");
        classes.Mainbody.BODY.backgroundColor="purple";
        classes.Mainbody.BODY.color="white";
        classes.Mainbody.BODY.fontSize="12pt";

</STYLE>
</HEAD>

<BODY CLASS="Mainbody">

<LAYER ID="L2" LEFT="10" TOP="10">

<FORM NAME="form1">

Pick a new <BR>       Background Color       <BR>

<SELECT NAME="getBackColor" SIZE="1" onChange="changeEverything(); return false;">

<OPTION  VALUE="cornsilk" SELECTED>         cornsilk            </OPTION>
<OPTION  VALUE="bisque">                    bisque              </OPTION>
<OPTION  VALUE="black">                      black               </OPTION>
<OPTION  VALUE="blue">                       blue                </OPTION>
<OPTION  VALUE="blueviolet">                 blueviolet          </OPTION>
<OPTION  VALUE="coral">                      coral               </OPTION>
<OPTION  VALUE="cornflowerblue">             cornflowerblue      </OPTION>
<OPTION  VALUE="crimson">                    crimson             </OPTION>
<OPTION  VALUE="cyan">                        cyan                </OPTION>
<OPTION  VALUE="darkblue">                    darkblue            </OPTION>
<OPTION  VALUE="darkcyan">                    darkcyan            </OPTION>
<OPTION  VALUE="darkgoldenrod">              darkgoldenrod       </OPTION>
<OPTION  VALUE="darkgreen">                   darkgreen           </OPTION>
<OPTION  VALUE="darkkhaki">                   darkkhaki           </OPTION>
<OPTION  VALUE="darkmagenta">                darkmagenta         </OPTION>
<OPTION  VALUE="darkturquoise">              darkturquoise       </OPTION>
<OPTION  VALUE="darkviolet">                 darkviolet          </OPTION>
<OPTION  VALUE="goldenrod">                   goldenrod           </OPTION>
<OPTION  VALUE="gray">                        gray                </OPTION>
<OPTION  VALUE="green">                       green               </OPTION>
<OPTION  VALUE="indianred">                  indianred           </OPTION>
</SELECT>

<!-- ***************************************************************** -->
<BR><HR>

Pick a new <BR>       Foreground Color<BR>
```

```
<SELECT NAME="getForeColor" SIZE="1" onChange="changeEverything(); return false;">

<OPTION  VALUE="lightseagreen" SELECTED>lightseagreen            </OPTION>
<OPTION  VALUE="lightskyblue">              lightskyblue        </OPTION>
<OPTION  VALUE="lightslategray">            lightslategray       </OPTION>
<OPTION  VALUE="lightsteelblue">            lightsteelblue       </OPTION>
<OPTION  VALUE="mediumblue">                mediumblue           </OPTION>
<OPTION  VALUE="mediumorchid">              mediumorchid         </OPTION>
<OPTION  VALUE="mediumpurple">              mediumpurple         </OPTION>
<OPTION  VALUE="mediumseagreen">            mediumseagreen       </OPTION>
<OPTION  VALUE="mediumslateblue">           mediumslateblue      </OPTION>
<OPTION  VALUE="mediumspringgreen">         mediumspringgreen    </OPTION>
<OPTION  VALUE="mediumturquoise">           mediumturquoise      </OPTION>
<OPTION  VALUE="mediumvioletred">           mediumvioletred      </OPTION>
<OPTION  VALUE="midnightblue">              midnightblue         </OPTION>
<OPTION  VALUE="plum">                      plum                 </OPTION>
<OPTION  VALUE="powderblue">                powderblue           </OPTION>
<OPTION  VALUE="purple">                    purple               </OPTION>
<OPTION  VALUE="red">                       red                  </OPTION>
<OPTION  VALUE="rosybrown">                 rosybrown            </OPTION>
<OPTION  VALUE="royalblue">                 royalblue            </OPTION>
<OPTION  VALUE="steelblue">                 steelblue            </OPTION>
<OPTION  VALUE="tan">                       tan                  </OPTION>
<OPTION  VALUE="teal">                      teal                 </OPTION>
<OPTION  VALUE="thistle">                   thistle              </OPTION>
<OPTION  VALUE="tomato">                    tomato               </OPTION>
</SELECT>
<!-- ***********************************************************  -->
<HR>
Pick a new <BR>      Font                          <BR>

<SELECT NAME="fontSelection" SIZE="1" onChange="changeEverything(); return false;">

<OPTION  VALUE="Helvetica" SELECTED> Font     </OPTION>
<OPTION  VALUE="Helvetica">                 Helvetica            </OPTION>
<OPTION  VALUE="Times">                     Times                </OPTION>
<OPTION  VALUE="Western">                   Western              </OPTION>
<OPTION  VALUE="Courier">                   Courier              </OPTION>
<OPTION  VALUE="Palatino">                  Palatino             </OPTION>
<OPTION  VALUE="Moonlight">                 Moonlight            </OPTION>
<OPTION  VALUE="Clarendon">                 Clarendon            </OPTION>
<OPTION  VALUE="cursive">                   cursive generic      </OPTION>
<OPTION  VALUE="fantasy">                   fantasy generic      </OPTION>
<OPTION  VALUE="serif">                     serif generic        </OPTION>
</SELECT>
<!-- ***********************************************************  -->
<HR>
Pick a new <BR>      Layer Background Color <BR>

<SELECT NAME="getLayerBackColor" SIZE="1" onChange="changeEverything(); return false;">

<OPTION  VALUE="navajowhite" SELECTED>      navajowhite          </OPTION>
<OPTION  VALUE="bisque">                    bisque               </OPTION>
<OPTION  VALUE="black">                     black                </OPTION>
<OPTION  VALUE="blue">                      blue                 </OPTION>
<OPTION  VALUE="blueviolet">                blueviolet           </OPTION>
<OPTION  VALUE="coral">                     coral                </OPTION>
<OPTION  VALUE="cornflowerblue">            cornflowerblue       </OPTION>
```

```
<OPTION  VALUE="cornsilk">                    cornsilk              </OPTION>
<OPTION  VALUE="crimson">                     crimson               </OPTION>
<OPTION  VALUE="cyan">                         cyan                  </OPTION>
<OPTION  VALUE="darkblue">                     darkblue              </OPTION>
<OPTION  VALUE="midnightblue">                 midnightblue          </OPTION>
<OPTION  VALUE="mintcream">                    mintcream             </OPTION>
<OPTION  VALUE="mistyrose">                    mistyrose             </OPTION>
<OPTION  VALUE="moccasin">                     moccasin              </OPTION>
<OPTION  VALUE="navy">                         navy                  </OPTION>
<OPTION  VALUE="powderblue">                   powderblue            </OPTION>
<OPTION  VALUE="purple">                       purple                </OPTION>
<OPTION  VALUE="red">                          red                   </OPTION>
</SELECT>
<BR>

<!-- ********************************************************************* -->
<HR>
Pick a new <BR>        Font Size                      <BR>

<SELECT NAME="getFontSize" SIZE="1" onChange="changeEverything(); return false;">

<OPTION  VALUE="22" SELECTED>         Font Size                      </OPTION>
<OPTION  VALUE="12">                     12                          </OPTION>
<OPTION  VALUE="14">                     14                          </OPTION>
<OPTION  VALUE="18">                     18                          </OPTION>
<OPTION  VALUE="20">                     20                          </OPTION>
<OPTION  VALUE="22">                     22                          </OPTION>
<OPTION  VALUE="24">                     24                          </OPTION>
<OPTION  VALUE="26">                     26                          </OPTION>
<OPTION  VALUE="28">                     28                          </OPTION>
<OPTION  VALUE="30">                     30                          </OPTION>
<OPTION  VALUE="32">                     32                          </OPTION>
<OPTION  VALUE="34">                     34                          </OPTION>
<OPTION  VALUE="40">                     40                          </OPTION>
<OPTION  VALUE="48">                     48                          </OPTION>
<OPTION  VALUE="55">                     55                          </OPTION>
<OPTION  VALUE="60">                     60                          </OPTION>
<OPTION  VALUE="77">                     77                          </OPTION>
<OPTION  VALUE="111">                    111                         </OPTION>
</SELECT>

<!-- ********************************************************************* -->
<HR>
Pick a new <BR>        Border Color    <BR>

<SELECT NAME="getBorderColor" SIZE="1" onChange="changeEverything(); return false;">

<OPTION  VALUE="blueviolet" SELECTED> blueviolet            </OPTION>
<OPTION  VALUE="lightseagreen">                lightseagreen         </OPTION>
<OPTION  VALUE="lightskyblue">                 lightskyblue          </OPTION>
<OPTION  VALUE="lightslategray">               lightslategray        </OPTION>
<OPTION  VALUE="lightsteelblue">               lightsteelblue        </OPTION>
<OPTION  VALUE="lightyellow">                  lightyellow           </OPTION>
<OPTION  VALUE="limegreen">                    limegreen             </OPTION>
<OPTION  VALUE="linen">                        linen                 </OPTION>
<OPTION  VALUE="magenta">                      magenta               </OPTION>
<OPTION  VALUE="mediumaquamarine">             mediumaquamarine      </OPTION>
<OPTION  VALUE="purple">                       purple                </OPTION>
```

```
<OPTION   VALUE="red">                         red                  </OPTION>
<OPTION   VALUE="seagreen">                    seagreen             </OPTION>
<OPTION   VALUE="seashell">                    seashell             </OPTION>
<OPTION   VALUE="sienna">                      sienna               </OPTION>
<OPTION   VALUE="silver">                      silver               </OPTION>
<OPTION   VALUE="skyblue">                      skyblue              </OPTION>
<OPTION   VALUE="slateblue">                    slateblue            </OPTION>
<OPTION   VALUE="slategray">                    slategray            </OPTION>
<OPTION   VALUE="snow">                         snow                 </OPTION>
<OPTION   VALUE="springgreen">                  springgreen          </OPTION>
<OPTION   VALUE="steelblue">                    steelblue            </OPTION>
<OPTION   VALUE="tan">                          tan                  </OPTION>
<OPTION   VALUE="teal">                         teal                 </OPTION>
<OPTION   VALUE="thistle">                      thistle              </OPTION>
</SELECT>

<!--   ***********************************************************   -->
<HR>
Pick a new <BR>        Border Width                   <BR>

<SELECT NAME="getBorderWidths" SIZE="1" onChange="changeEverything(); return false;">

<OPTION   VALUE="22" SELECTED>        Border Widths          </OPTION>
<OPTION   VALUE="2">                            2             </OPTION>
<OPTION   VALUE="5">                            5             </OPTION>
<OPTION   VALUE="7">                            7             </OPTION>
<OPTION   VALUE="10">                   10                    </OPTION>
<OPTION   VALUE="12">                   12                    </OPTION>
<OPTION   VALUE="14">                   14                    </OPTION>
<OPTION   VALUE="20">                   20                    </OPTION>
<OPTION   VALUE="22">                   22                    </OPTION>
<OPTION   VALUE="25">                   25                    </OPTION>
<OPTION   VALUE="26">                   26                    </OPTION>
<OPTION   VALUE="28">                   28                    </OPTION>
<OPTION   VALUE="30">                   30                    </OPTION>
<OPTION   VALUE="32">                   32                    </OPTION>
<OPTION   VALUE="35">                   35                    </OPTION>
<OPTION   VALUE="40">                   40                    </OPTION>
<OPTION   VALUE="50">                   50                    </OPTION>
<OPTION   VALUE="55">                   55                    </OPTION>
</SELECT>

</FORM>

</LAYER>

<!--   ***********************************************************   -->

<SCRIPT LANGUAGE="JavaScript1.2"><!--BEGIN HIDING


        if (booleanTest == false) { booleanTest = true; }
        else if (booleanTest == true) { booleanTest = false; }
}


/*------------------------------------------------------------------*/
```

```
/*----------------------------------------------------------------------*/

function changeEverything()  {

        var L2 = document.L2;

        var getBackColor = L2.document.form1.getBackColor;
        var sel = getBackColor.selectedIndex;
        var bcolorSel = getBackColor.options[sel].value;

        var getForeColor = L2.document.form1.getForeColor;
        var sel2 = getForeColor.selectedIndex;
        var fcolorSel = getForeColor.options[sel2].value;

        var sel3 = L2.document.form1.fontSelection.selectedIndex;
        var c3 = L2.document.form1.fontSelection.options[sel3].value;

        var sel4 = L2.document.form1.getLayerBackColor.selectedIndex;
        var c4 = L2.document.form1.getLayerBackColor.options[sel4].value;

        var sel5 = L2.document.form1.getFontSize.selectedIndex;
        var c5 = L2.document.form1.getFontSize.options[sel5].value;

        var sel7 = L2.document.form1.getBorderColor.selectedIndex;
        var c7 = L2.document.form1.getBorderColor.options[sel7].value;

        var sel8 = L2.document.form1.getBorderWidths.selectedIndex;
        var c8 = L2.document.form1.getBorderWidths.options[sel8].value;

        var c11 = parent.input.document.form3.textArea1.value;


        parent.main.document.open();
        parent.main.document.write('<HTML><HEAD><TITLE> Test Layer <\/TITLE>');

        parent.main.document.write('<STYLE TYPE="text/JavaScript">');


        parent.main.document.write('tags.BODY.fontSize = "10pt";');
        parent.main.document.write('ids.L1.width="100%";');
        parent.main.document.write('ids.L1.paddingRight="20px";');
        parent.main.document.write('ids.L1.paddingLeft="20px";');
        parent.main.document.write('ids.L1.borderWidths("30px");');
        parent.main.document.write('ids.L1.borderStyle="groove";');

        parent.main.document.write('<\/STYLE>');

        parent.main.document.write('<\/HEAD>');
        parent.main.document.write('<\/BODY>');


/*----------------------------------------------------------------------*/

//Notice that there are no Write Methods
//in the next lines of code with Variables that change Properties

/*----------------------------------------------------------------------*/
```

```
//This is the line that implements the background color change

        parent.main.document.bgColor = bcolorSel;
/*----------------------------------------------------------------------*/

//This is the line that implements the foreground color change

        parent.main.document.fgColor = fcolorSel;
/*----------------------------------------------------------------------*/

//This is the line that implements the font family change

        parent.main.document.ids.L1.fontFamily = c3;
/*----------------------------------------------------------------------*/

//This is the line that implements the LAYER Background Color change

                parent.main.document.ids.L1.backgroundColor = c4;

/*----------------------------------------------------------------------*/

//This is the line that implements the Font Size change

        parent.main.document.ids.L1.fontSize = c5;
/*----------------------------------------------------------------------*/

//This is the line that implements the Border Color change

        parent.main.document.ids.L1.borderColor = c7;
/*----------------------------------------------------------------------*/

//This is the line that implements the Border Widths change

        parent.main.document.ids.L1.borderWidths(c8);

/*----------------------------------------------------------------------*/

        parent.main.document.write('<LAYER ID="L1" LEFT="0" TOP="0">');

        parent.main.document.writeln('<BR>' + c11 + '<BR><BR>');

        parent.main.document.write('<\/LAYER>');

/*----------------------------------------------------------------------*/

        parent.main.document.write('<\/BODY><\/HTML>');
        parent.main.document.close();
}

/*----------------------------------------------------------------------*/

//END HIDING-->
</SCRIPT>

</BODY>
</HTML>
```

This is just the code for the document that goes in the top FRAME named **input**. It has the TEXTAREA named **textArea1** for user input.

Example 6-24 Part 2:　　　　Sample724A.html

```
<!DOCTYPE HTML PUBLIC "-//W3C//DTD HTML 3.2//EN">
<HTML>
<HEAD>
<TITLE>       Sample 724A    Example 6-24A   </TITLE>
</HEAD>

<BODY>

<FORM NAME="form3">

<TEXTAREA NAME="textArea1" ROWS=8 COLS=55 WRAP="hard">

Put your poem or text here and then choose from the pop-up selection menus in the
left frame to render the results.

</TEXTAREA>

</FORM>

</BODY>
</HTML>
```

This gets initially loaded into the FRAME named **main** and basically serves as just a *placeholder* document that gets overridden by user choices.

Example 6-24 Part 3:　　　　Sample724Right.html

```
<!DOCTYPE HTML PUBLIC "-//W3C//DTD HTML 3.2//EN">
<HTML>
<HEAD>
<TITLE>       Sample 724Right    Example 6-24Right   </TITLE>
</HEAD>

<BODY>

<H1>        Children speak the ancient rhyme...   </H1>

</BODY>
</HTML>
```

This is just the FRAMESET for Example 6-24.

Example 6-24 Part 4:   **Sample724Frameset.html**

```
<HTML>
<HEAD>
<TITLE>        Frameset for Sample 724        </TITLE>
</HEAD>

<FRAMESET COLS="220,*">

        <FRAME MARGINHEIGHT=0 SCROLLING="no" NAME="display" SRC="Sample724.html">


        <FRAMESET ROWS="100,*">

                <FRAME MARGINHEIGHT="0" SCROLLING="auto" NAME="input"
                                        SRC="Sample724A.html">

                <FRAME SCROLLING="auto" NAME="main" SRC="Sample724Right.html">

        </FRAMESET>

</FRAMESET>

</HTML>
```

Example 6-24	Sample724Frameset.html

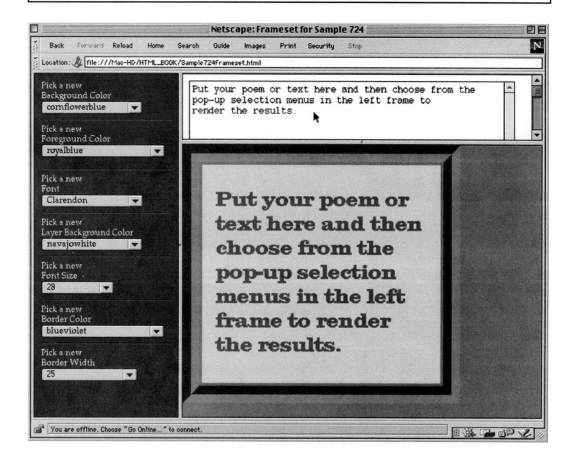

Drag on a Layer to Resize it

In the Dynamic HTML Guide from Netscape, there is an example that is generally correct in theory but it has some coding errors in it which make it behave erratically. I've fixed those anomalies and it's presented in reworked form in Sample725.html.

The basic structure is similar to previous examples from early in this chapter that dealt with repositioning a Layer by dragging on it. In this case, instead of the **pageX** Coordinate being constantly updated by the **mousemove** Events and then forwarded into the **moveBy()** Method where it is altered, the **pageX** coordinate is fed into the **changeWidth()** Function, where it is assigned to the **layerWidth** Variable and massaged with the **delta** Argument so that it changes the **width** of the Layer when it is reloaded into the document with the **load()** Method of the **Layer** Object.

Remember that the **load()** Method takes the URL Argument and has the optional second Argument of assigning a new width to the URL when it is loaded which is used in this case. The external file that is loaded in has a URL of Sample725A.html, which is not in the book. Note that it is initially loaded into the Layer named **Showcase1** with the **SRC** Attribute. If you want to compare the two different types of examples check out Example 6-10 on page 548.

Example 6-25: **Sample725.html**

```
<!DOCTYPE HTML PUBLIC "-//W3C//DTD HTML 3.2//EN">
<HTML>
<HEAD>
<TITLE>Sample 725 - Example 6-25      Drag Mouse to Resize a Layer</TITLE>

</HEAD>

<BODY BGCOLOR="black" TEXT="white">

      <!--   The containing layer that loads the external file   -->

<LAYER ID="Showcase1" LEFT="5" TOP="100" BGCOLOR="blue" SRC="Sample725A.html">
</LAYER>

<!--   ************************************************************   -->

<SCRIPT LANGUAGE="JavaScript1.2"><!--BEGIN HIDING

/*-------------------------------------------------------------------*/
```

```
var layerWidth = 800;
var oldX;
var Showcase1 = document.Showcase1;

Showcase1.captureEvents(Event.MOUSEDOWN|Event.MOUSEUP);

Showcase1.onmousedown=begindrag;
Showcase1.onmouseup=enddrag;
Showcase1.onLoad=resetcapture;
/*--------------------------------------------*/

function resetcapture() {
 Showcase1.captureEvents(Event.MOUSEDOWN|Event.MOUSEUP|Event.MOUSEMOVE);
}

/*--------------------------------------------*/

function begindrag(e) {

        Showcase1.captureEvents(Event.MOUSEMOVE);
        Showcase1.onmousemove=drag;
        oldX=e.pageX;
 return false;
}

/*--------------------------------------------*/

function drag(e) {
        changeWidth(Showcase1, e.pageX - oldX);
        oldX = e.pageX;
 return false;
}

/*--------------------------------------------*/

function changeWidth(thelayer, delta) {

        layerWidth = layerWidth + delta;
        if (delta != 0)
        Showcase1.load('Sample725A.html', layerWidth);
}

/*--------------------------------------------*/

function enddrag(e) {
        Showcase1.onmousemove=0;
        Showcase1.releaseEvents(Event.MOUSEMOVE);
 return false;
}

//END HIDING-->
</SCRIPT>

</BODY>
</HTML>
```

Routing & Handling Events

The JavaScript <u>routeEvent(e)</u> Function

To recap a bit first, the following Methods are available for **window**, **document**, and **Layer** Objects:

```
window.captureEvents(e)
window.releaseEvents(e)
document.captureEvents(e)
document.releaseEvents(e)
layerObject.captureEvents(e)
layerObject.releaseEvents(e)
```

The **routeEvent(e)** Function is used to call the Event Handler that is next in the Event hierarchy. For instance, if you have used the **captureEvents()** Method to capture the **onclick** Event Handler for the **window**, **document**, and a Layer Named **L1** in a page, then when a CLICK Event occurs, it will be captured by the **window** Object first. If the JavaScript code that is assigned to **window.onclick** has **routeEvent(e)** in it appropriately, then it will route the **Event e** to the **document** Object's **onclick** Event Handler for further processing and so on to the **Layer** Object.

Once an Event has been processed by all Objects that use **captureEvents()** to force an Event into their domain, JavaScript looks for the Event Handler of the Event's original Target such as a Link or a Button and completes the processing.

This progression through the hierarchy may seem a bit backward, and it is, but JavaScript, like HTML, is designed from the top on down so that sibling Objects inherit from their parent Objects and Event Handling follows that paradigm. Be careful when using these Methods that you don't inadvertently route an Event so that it sets up an Event feedback loop, which can totally crash your system.

Using the JavaScript <u>routeEvent(e)</u> Function

This example demonstrates the use of the **routeEvent(e)** Function. Button **B1** is inside Layer **L1** and Button **B2** is inside Layer **L2**. Both Buttons have their own **onClick** Event Handler code as an HTML Attribute. The **document** Object is set to capture CLICK Events and Layer **L1** is set to capture CLICK Events. The **myClicker(e)** Function is assigned to the **onclick** Event Handler for the **document** Object and the **myLayerClicker(e)** Function is assigned to the **onclick** Event Handler for the Layer **L1**.

myClicker(e)   This Function is designed to walk you through the beginning of the Event progression by first showing an **alert** when any CLICK Event occurs. In this page, the **document** Object has top priority because the **window** is not set to capture Events.

Then, if you have clicked in the background of the document, the second **alert** will activate. In the case of clicking the Button **B1**, the Event will be routed with **routeEvent(e)** to the Layer **L1** for processing.

If Button **B2** was clicked, the Event will be routed with **routeEvent(e)** directly to the **onClick** Event Handler of Button **B2**, because **B2** is inside Layer **L2**; therefore, it doesn't inherit Events from Layer **L1**. Note that Layer **L2** is not set to capture Events.

```
function myClicker(e) {

        alert ("This event was captured by the document first and may
be routed to... ");

                                //Prevents an Event Feedback Loop
        if (e.target == document)   {
                alert ("The 'if' Statement prevents an Event Feedback
                        Loop if you click in the document.");
                return;
        }

routeEvent(e);
}
```

myLayerClicker(e)   This Function shows the user that it has been activated by the **alert** Window and the change to the background color of Layer **L2**. It then routes the Event to its next possible destination, if any. If the Button **B1** is clicked, then **routeEvent(e)** will route the Event on to that Button's **onClick** Event Handler for processing. In this example, that's the only time that **routeEvent(e)** is implemented in this Function.

```
function myLayerClicker(e) {

        alert ("This event was captured second, by Layer L1; it turns
                Layer L2 to cyan and may be routed to... ");
        document.L2.bgColor = 'cyan';
        routeEvent(e);

}
```

Example 6-26: Sample726.html

```
<!DOCTYPE HTML PUBLIC "-//W3C//DTD HTML 3.2//EN">
<HTML>
<HEAD>
<TITLE>        Sample 726   Example 6-26  routeEvent() Function      </TITLE>

<SCRIPT LANGUAGE="JavaScript1.2"> <!--BEGIN HIDING

function myClicker(e) {

alert ("This event was captured by the document first and may be routed to... ");

                        //Prevents an Event Feedback Loop

        if (e.target == document)  {

                alert ("The 'if' Statement prevents an Event Feedback Loop if you
                        click in the document.");
                return;
        }

routeEvent(e);
}


        document.captureEvents(Event.CLICK);
        document.onclick=myClicker;


//END HIDING-->
</SCRIPT>

</HEAD>

<BODY>
<LAYER ID="L1" LEFT="25" TOP="10">

<FORM NAME="form1">

<INPUT TYPE="button" NAME="B1" VALUE="Button 1"
onClick="alert('me. I am Button 1, at your service.'); return false;">     <BR>

</FORM>
</LAYER>

<LAYER ID="L2" LEFT="25" TOP="70" BGCOLOR="#8888ff">
<H3>Here's the sequence of Events:</H3>

<B>Button 1:</B> The document captures the Event first and routes it to Layer L1
and then routes it to Button B1<BR><BR>

<B>Button 2:</B> The document captures the Event first and routes it to Button B2.

<BR><BR>
```

```
<B>This Layer L2:</B> The document captures the Event first and that ends the Event
Handling.<BR><BR>

<B>Document:</B> The document captures the Event first and that ends the Event
Handling.

<BR><BR><HR><BR>

<H3>It's important to note that when you set up your own documents that you don't
route your Events to create a feedback loop. If Layer L1 were large enough to click
in its background instead of just on a button, there would be an Event feedback
loop. The next two examples show you how to prevent feedback loops. If you create
one of these things and have to FORCE QUIT  Navigator several times you will
probably corrupt your Finder's Preference File, which you will have to trash.
</H3>

<BR><BR>

<FORM NAME="form2">

<INPUT TYPE="button" NAME="B2" VALUE="Button 2"
onClick="alert('me. I am Button 2, at your service.'); return false;">

<BR>

</FORM>

</LAYER>


<SCRIPT LANGUAGE="JavaScript1.2"> <!--BEGIN HIDING

function myLayerClicker(e) {

        alert ("This event was captured second, by Layer L1; it turns Layer L2 to
                cyan and may be routed to... ");

        document.L2.bgColor = 'cyan';
        routeEvent(e);
}

/*----------------------------------------------------------------------*/

        document.L1.captureEvents(Event.CLICK);

        document.L1.onclick=myLayerClicker;

/*----------------------------------------------------------------------*/

//END HIDING-->
</SCRIPT>

</BODY>
</HTML>
```

Example 6-26   Sample726.html

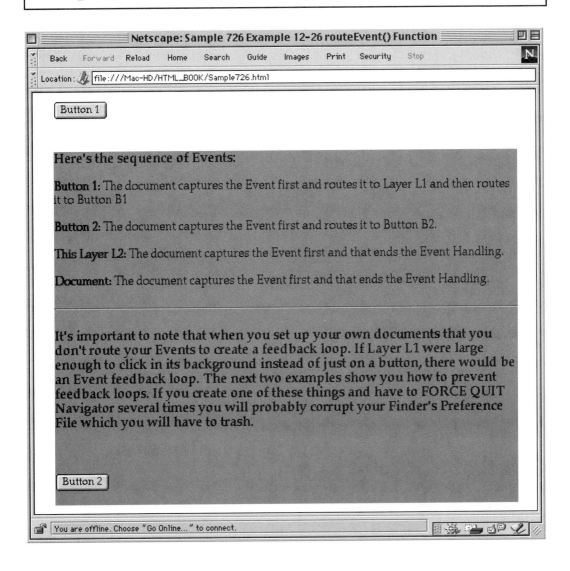

Netscape: Sample 726 Example 12-26 routeEvent() Function

Back Forward Reload Home Search Guide Images Print Security Stop

Location: file:///Mac-HD/HTML_BOOK/Sample726.html

Button 1

Here's the sequence of Events:

Button 1: The document captures the Event first and routes it to Layer L1 and then routes it to Button B1

Button 2: The document captures the Event first and routes it to Button B2.

This Layer L2: The document captures the Event first and that ends the Event Handling.

Document: The document captures the Event first and that ends the Event Handling.

It's important to note that when you set up your own documents that you don't route your Events to create a feedback loop. If Layer L1 were large enough to click in its background instead of just on a button, there would be an Event feedback loop. The next two examples show you how to prevent feedback loops. If you create one of these things and have to FORCE QUIT Navigator several times you will probably corrupt your Finder's Preference File which you will have to trash.

Button 2

You are offline. Choose "Go Online..." to connect.

The JavaScript <u>handleEvent(e)</u> Method

The **handleEvent(e)** Method is used by an Event receiver to circumnavigate the Event Capturing hierarchy by explicitly calling the Event Handler of a particular Event. Think of an Event that is traveling on its way through the natural chain of captured Events. When it encounters a **handleEvent(e)** Method, it breaks out of the flow and jumps to the Object that is calling it with the **handleEvent(e)** Method and proceeds to be processed there. For example, suppose you define a Button named **B2** in a Form named **form1** like this:

```
<INPUT TYPE="button" NAME="B2" VALUE="Button 2"
onClick="alert('I am Button 2, at your service.');">
```

Then you could use a conditional **if ()** to test for that Button being clicked and if true, call **handleEvent(e)** to immediately invoke its **onClick** Event Handler to trigger the **alert** like this:

```
if (e.target.name == "B2") {
      e.target.handleEvent(e);
}
```

Because the conditional **if ()** requires that the target always be Button **B2**, you can use the shorthand way of calling **handleEvent(e)** on the **target** Property of the Event as demonstrated in the above code. You could also code it in the more familiar way like this:

```
if (e.target.name == "B2") {
      document.form1.B2.handleEvent(e);
}
```

or like this:

```
if (e.target.name == "B2") {
      document.form1.elements["B2"].handleEvent(e);
}
```

When you start working with Elements that are multinested, you can see the advantages of the shorthand way of coding.

Using the JavaScript <u>handleEvent(e)</u> Method

Example 6-27 demonstrates the **handleEvent(e)** Method and the **routeEvent(e)** Function. It's structurally similar to the previous example, but more involved. It starts with two Layers named **limeLayer1** and **L2**. There are three Buttons created inside of **limeLayer1** named **B1**, **B2**, and **B3**. Both the **document** Object and the **limeLayer1** Layer use **captureEvents()** to capture the CLICK Event.

The **myClicker(e)** Function is assigned to the **onclick** Event Handler of the **document** Object, and the **myLayerClicker(e)** Function is assigned to the **onclick** Event Handler of **limeLayer1**. The **buttonColors(event)** Function is assigned to the **onClick** Event Handler Attributes of both the **B2** and **B3** Buttons. Notice that the **event** Keyword Argument must be explicitly passed when the Function is called in an Attribute.

myClicker(e) This Function has the added functionality from the previous example by calling the **handleEvent(e)** Method on the **target** Property when the **target** of the Event is Button **B2**. It ends with **routeEvent(e)**, which forwards Events to the **onclick** Event Handler of **limeLayer1**.

myLayerClicker(e) This Function also performs some additional processing from the previous example. If Button **B3** is clicked, then **handleEvent(e)** is called to forward the Event directly to **B3**; otherwise, the Event is processed by **limeLayer1** with the **alert** and the background color change to **L2**. That ends the Event Handling because **routeEvent(e)** is not called in this Function.

buttonColors(event) This Function changes the background color of the **L2** Layer depending on whether Button **B2** or **B3** is clicked.

Example 6-27: Sample727.html

```
<!DOCTYPE HTML PUBLIC "-//W3C//DTD HTML 3.2//EN">
<HTML>
<HEAD>
<TITLE> Sample 727   Example 6-27   routeEvent and handleEvent Method</TITLE>

<SCRIPT LANGUAGE="JavaScript1.2"> <!--BEGIN HIDING

function myClicker(e) {

        if (e.target == document)  {
                alert ("The document captures CLICK Events first in the hierarchy.
The 'return false' in this 'if' ends the Event Handling.");
                return false;
        }
```

```
        alert ("This event was captured by the document first and may be routed
to... ");

        if (e.target.name == "B2") {
                e.target.handleEvent(e);
                return false;
        }

routeEvent(e);
return false;
}

document.captureEvents(Event.CLICK);
document.onclick=myClicker;

//END HIDING-->
</SCRIPT>

</HEAD>

<BODY>
<LAYER ID="limeLayer1" LEFT="25" TOP="10" BGCOLOR="lime" WIDTH="500">
<FORM NAME="form1">

<INPUT TYPE="button" NAME="B1" VALUE="Button 1">      <BR>

<INPUT TYPE="button" NAME="B2" VALUE="Button 2"
onClick="alert('me. I am Button 2, at your service.'); buttonColors(event); return
false;">        <BR>

<INPUT TYPE="button" NAME="B3" VALUE="Button 3"
onClick="alert('me. I am Button 3, at your service.'); buttonColors(event); return
false;">        <BR>

</FORM>
</LAYER>

<LAYER ID="L2" LEFT="25" TOP="120" BGCOLOR="#8888ff">
Here's the sequence of Events:                             <BR><BR>

<B>Button 1:</B> The document captures the Event first and routes it to limeLayer1
where the Event ends so that in this scenario Button B1 never gets the Event
because limeLayer1 does not route Events and there is no handleEvent for Button
B1.<BR><BR>

<B>Button 2:</B> The document captures the Event first and Button 2 handles the
Event directly with handleEvent.<BR><BR>

<B>Button 3:</B> The document captures the Event first and routes it to limeLayer1
and then Button 3 handles the Event directly with handleEvent.<BR><BR>

<B>This Layer L2:</B> The document captures the Event first and that ends the Event
Handling.<BR><BR>

<B>Document:</B> The document captures the Event first and that ends the Event
Handling. <BR><BR><HR><BR>
```

```
<H3>Notice that <B>'limeLayer1'</B> is capturing Click Events, not Layer L2 which
is this Layer.</H3>

<H3>It's important to note that when you set up your own documents that you don't
route your Events to create a feedback loop.</H3>
</LAYER>


<SCRIPT LANGUAGE="JavaScript1.2"> <!--BEGIN HIDING

function myLayerClicker(e) {

        if (e.target.name == "B3") {
                alert ("This event was captured second, by the Layer limeLayer1. It
changes Layer L2 to cyan and then uses e.target.handleEvent to send the event
directly to...");
                document.L2.bgColor = 'cyan';
                document.limeLayer1.document.form1.B3.handleEvent(e);
                return false;
        }
        else {
                alert ("This event was captured second, by the Layer limeLayer1. It
changes Layer L2 to cyan and is not routed.");
                document.L2.bgColor = 'cyan';
                return false;
        }
return false;
}

/*-------------------------------------------------------------------------*/

function buttonColors(e)   {
        if (e.target.name == 'B2')   { document.L2.bgColor='orange'; }
        if (e.target.name == 'B3')   { document.L2.bgColor='yellow'; }
}

/*-------------------------------------------------------------------------*/

        document.limeLayer1.captureEvents(Event.CLICK);
        document.limeLayer1.onclick=myLayerClicker;

/*-------------------------------------------------------------------------*/

//END HIDING-->
</SCRIPT>

</BODY>
</HTML>
```

Example 6-27   Sample727.html

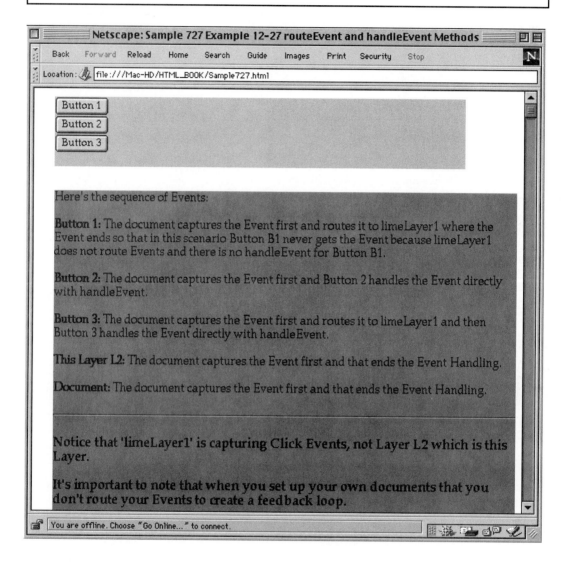

Handling and Routing Events in Nested and Unnested Layers

This example is very similar to the previous example. The differences are that the **window** Object is also set to capture Events, and Button **B1** is in the **document** Object instead of **limeLayer1**. There is also an additional Button named **B4**, which is inside of Layer **L2**.

myWindowClicker(e)   This Function is assigned to the **onclick** Event Handler of the **window** Object, and because it's at the top of the Event hierarchy, all Events go here first, which triggers the **alert** message, and then the Event is routed to the **onclick** Event Handler for the **document** Object, which is next in the hierarchy.

The **myClicker(e)** and **myLayerClicker(e)** Functions, which are equivalent to those used in the previous example, are explained in detail, starting on page 669.

You should notice the sequence of Events when the **B4** Button, which is inside of Layer **L2**, is clicked. The Event gets sent to the **window** first, and to the **document** Object second, but *does not* get forwarded from the **document** Object to the **limeLayer1** Layer. From the **document** Object, the Event gets routed to **B3** Button. This progression isn't exactly intuitively obvious, so be aware of it in your own Scripts.

Example 6-28:   **Sample728.html**

```
<!DOCTYPE HTML PUBLIC "-//W3C//DTD HTML 3.2//EN">
<HTML>
<HEAD>
<TITLE> Sample 728   Example 6-28  Handling Events in Nested Layers</TITLE>

<SCRIPT LANGUAGE="JavaScript1.2"> <!--BEGIN HIDING

function myWindowClicker(e) {

alert ("This event was captured by the window first and may be routed to... ");

routeEvent(e);
return false;
}

/*-------------------------------------------------------------------*/

window.captureEvents(Event.CLICK);
window.onclick=myWindowClicker;

/*-------------------------------------------------------------------*/
```

```
function myClicker(e) {

        if (e.target == document)  {
                alert ("The document captures CLICK Events second in the hierarchy.
The 'return false' in this 'if' ends the Event Handling.");
                return false;
        }

        alert ("This event was captured by the document second and may be routed
to... ");

        if (e.target.name == "B2") {
                e.target.handleEvent(e);
                return false;
        }

routeEvent(e);
return false;
}

/*------------------------------------------------------------------------*/

document.captureEvents(Event.CLICK);
document.onclick=myClicker;

//END HIDING-->
</SCRIPT>

</HEAD>

<BODY>

<FORM NAME="form1">

<INPUT TYPE="button" NAME="B1" VALUE="Button 1"
onClick="alert('me. I am Button 1, at your service.'); buttonColors(event);
return false;">        <BR>
</FORM>

<!--   ******************************************************************   -->

<LAYER ID="limeLayer1" LEFT="25" TOP="50" BGCOLOR="lime" WIDTH="500">
<FORM NAME="form2">

<INPUT TYPE="button" NAME="B2" VALUE="Button 2"
onClick="alert('me. I am Button 2, at your service.'); buttonColors(event);
return false;">        <BR>

<INPUT TYPE="button" NAME="B3" VALUE="Button 3"
onClick="alert('me. I am Button 3, at your service.'); buttonColors(event);
return false;">        <BR>
</FORM>


</LAYER>

<!--   ******************************************************************   -->
```

```
<!--  ********************************************************************  -->


<LAYER ID="L2" LEFT="25" TOP="120" BGCOLOR="#8888ff">


<FORM NAME="form3">

<INPUT TYPE="button" NAME="B4" VALUE="Button 4"
onClick="alert('me. I am Button 4, at your service.'); buttonColors(event); return
false;">        <BR>
</FORM>
<!--  ***********************************************  -->

<B>Here's the sequence of Events:</B>                        <BR><BR>

<B>Button 1:</B> The window captures the Event first and routes it so that the
document captures the Event second and it finally reaches Button B1 with its alert
and magenta color for Layer 2.<BR><BR>

<B>Button 2:</B> The window captures the Event first and routes it so that the
document captures the Event second and uses handleEvent to send it to Button
B2.<BR><BR>

<B>Button 3:</B> The window captures the Event first and routes it so that the
document captures the Event second and routes it to limeLayer1 which uses
handleEvent to send it to Button B3.<BR><BR>

<B>Button 4:</B> The window captures the Event first and routes it so that the
document captures the Event second and routes it to Button B4.<BR><BR>

<B>Layer limeLayer1:</B> The window captures the Event first and routes it so that
the document captures the Event second and routes it to limeLayer1 where it ends
after processing.<BR><BR>

<B>This Layer L2:</B> The window captures the Event first and routes it so that the
document captures the Event second that ends the Event Handling.<BR><BR>

<B>Document:</B> The window captures the Event first and routes it so that the
document captures the Event second and that ends the Event Handling.
<BR><BR><HR><BR>

<H3>Notice that <B>'limeLayer1'</B> is capturing Click Events, not Layer L2 which
is this Layer.</H3>

<H3>It's important to note that when you set up your own documents that you don't
route your Events to create a feedback loop.</H3>

</LAYER>

<!--  ********************************************************************  -->
```

```
<!-- ******************************************************************** -->

<SCRIPT LANGUAGE="JavaScript1.2"> <!--BEGIN HIDING

function myLayerClicker(e) {

        if (e.target.name == "B3") {
                alert ("This event was captured third, by the Layer limeLayer1. It
                        changes Layer L2 to cyan and then uses e.target.handleEvent
                        to send the event directly to...");
                document.L2.bgColor = 'cyan';
                e.target.handleEvent(e);
                return false;
        }
        else {
                alert ("This event was captured third, by the Layer limeLayer1. It
                        changes Layer L2 to cyan and is not routed.");
                document.L2.bgColor = 'cyan';
                return false;
        }
return false;
}


/*------------------------------------------------------------------------*/


function buttonColors(e)  {
        if (e.target.name == 'B1')  { document.L2.bgColor='magenta'; }
        if (e.target.name == 'B2')  { document.L2.bgColor='orange'; }
        if (e.target.name == 'B3')  { document.L2.bgColor='yellow'; }
        if (e.target.name == 'B4')  { document.L2.bgColor='pink'; }
}


/*------------------------------------------------------------------------*/


        document.limeLayer1.captureEvents(Event.CLICK);
        document.limeLayer1.onclick=myLayerClicker;


/*------------------------------------------------------------------------*/


//END HIDING-->
</SCRIPT>

</BODY>
</HTML>
```

Example 6-28   Sample728.html

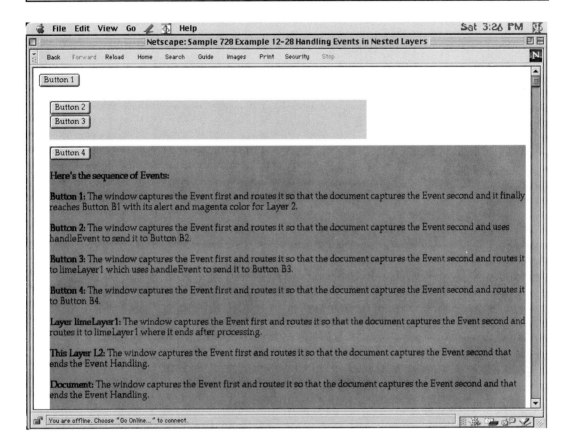

Part II
JavaScript 1.2

Chapter 7

JavaScript Arrays

Chapter 7
JavaScript Arrays

Contents

JavaScript Array Objects

The JavaScript Array Object

JavaScript Syntax:

```
arrayObjectName = new Array(arrayLength);
arrayObjectName = new Array(element0, element1, ..., elementN);
arrayObjectName = [element0, element1, ..., elementN];
```

An **Array** Object is one of JavaScript's Predefined Core Objects. Usually, an Array is assigned to an **arrayObjectName** when the Array is created. An Array is comprised of an ordered set of Values, each of which is called an Element. Each Element of an Array has a unique **index** number that allows you to reference that particular Element. The **index** numbers start at zero, are always integers, and go in the positive direction. So the first Element in your Array would have an **index** of zero, and the second Element in your Array would have an **index** of 1, and so on. There is no limit to the number of Elements you can have in an Array. If you're familiar with Java, then it might be useful to note that a JavaScript Array is more like a Java Vector than a Java Array, because the **length** of a JavaScript Array is flexible, based on use. Array Element Values can be anything.

Arrays can be created with either the **Array Object Constructor** or with **Literal** notation. Using **Literal** notation is new to Navigator 4 and JavaScript 1.2.

Create an Array
with the Array Object Constructor

To create an Array with the **Array Object Constructor**, you start by choosing a name for your Array. Then, using the Keyword **new**, you either define the **length** of your Array by choosing the number of Elements that will be initiated, or create a **dense** Array with a comma-separated list of its actual Elements. This is an example of a regular Array that is initiated to have five Elements; that is, a **length** of 5:

```
myArray1 = new Array(5);
```

You could then optionally proceed to define each Element of the Array by using the Element's **index** number and assigning that Element a Value like this:

```
myArray1[0] = "blue";
myArray1[1] = "red";
myArray1[2] = "purple";
myArray1[3] = "lime";
myArray1[4] = "yellow";
```

You would read the first of these five Elements as the Array Element at **index** 0 of the Array named **myArray1**, having a Value of the text String "blue". Now suppose you wanted to change the Value of Element 0 to the text String "gold"; you would code it like this:

```
myArray1[0] = "gold";
```

You can also reference an Array Element by specifying its Value within the **Array Object** syntax like this:

```
myArray1["blue"]
```

so that this line of code:

```
myArray1[0] = "gold";
```

is equivalent to:

```
myArray1["blue"] = "gold";
```

You *cannot* reference an <u>Array that you create</u> in the hierarchy like this:

document.myArray1[0].

However, you should not get this confused with the built-in Core Object Arrays that are Properties of other Objects. For instance, the **forms[i]** Array is a Property of the **document** Object and is always referenced in the Object hierarchy like this: **document.forms[i]**. See Chapter 4 for more information on Object Arrays.

You can also create an Array with **length** equal to zero, which basically initializes an Array with no Elements that you can populate with Values later in the Script. Here's an example:

```
anotherArray = new Array();
```

JavaScript will automatically extend the **length** of the Array each time you initialize a new Element for the Array. This is true even if the Array **length** is initially fixed when you create the Array.

Here is an example of an Array that is created by the Array Constructor with a **length** of 0, which is subsequently extended in size so that it has eight Elements with a **length** of 8 by initializing an Element at **index** 7.   It is then extended again by initializing another Element at **index** 222, which causes it to now have a **length** of 223 and thus 223 Elements. The Value of all of the Elements that do not have Values explicitly assigned are **undefined** when extending the **length** of an Array in this manner.

```
musicArray = new Array();                    //length=0
musicArray[7] = "Close to the Edge";         //length=8
musicArray[222] = "Yessongs";                //length=223
```

Create a <u>dense</u> Array

You create a **dense** Array that is identical to the previous **myArray1** with one line of code like this, noting that the commas are required but the space is optional:

```
myArray1 = new Array("blue", "red", "purple", "lime", "yellow");
```

To render an Array Element to Screen

If you wanted to display a particular Array Element in the browser, you would use the **document.write()** Method by referencing the Element by its **index** number like this:

```
document.write(myArray1[0]);
```

which would render the following output:

```
blue
```

To render an Array to Screen

If you use the **document.write()** Method with just the name of the Array as the Argument, you will get one long text String, enclosed by brackets, that's composed of each Element of the Array like this:

```
document.write(myArray1);
```

which would render the following output, noting that JavaScript does not store the optional space between Elements, but it does store the comma separator:

```
["blue","red","purple","lime","yellow"]
```

You can check out Sample805.html if you want to see this demonstrated.

When you have an Array with a relatively small number of Elements, it is quite efficient to go ahead and declare them in a **dense** Array. If you need to keep track of the **index** position of your various Elements, then you will probably want to declare the Elements individually.

Using the for() Statement with Array Elements

If you wanted to output each Element of the Array individually and create some additional markup, you could set up a **for ()** Statement like this:

```
for (var i=0;  i < myArray1.length;  i++) {

     document.write(myArray1[i] + "<BR>");
}
```

This would take each Element of the Array and render it on its own line in the browser so that the output would look like this:

blue
red
purple
lime
yellow

The previous concepts are formalized in Example 7-0 and can be viewed in Sample800.html.

Example 7-0:　　　　　**Sample800.html**

```
<!DOCTYPE HTML PUBLIC "-//W3C//DTD HTML 3.2//EN">
<HTML>
<HEAD>
<TITLE> Sample 800    Example 7-0 Array Element display</TITLE>

<SCRIPT LANGUAGE="JavaScript1.2"> <!--BEGIN HIDING

myArray1 = new Array("blue", "red", "purple", "lime", "yellow");


        for (var i=0;  i < myArray1.length;  i++) {

                document.write(myArray1[i] + "<BR>");
        }

//END HIDING-->
</SCRIPT>

</HEAD>

<BODY>
</BODY>
</HTML>
```

Create an Array with Literal notation

When you create an Array with **Literal** notation, you name it and set the name equal to a bracket-enclosed list of Values that are comma-separated, which become the Elements of the Array. The **length** of the Array is equal to the number of Values listed. However, you don't actually have to specify all of the Elements in an Array when it is first created. If you code in two commas sequentially, JavaScript will create a blank placeholder Element at that **index** number.

Here's how to create an Array by using **Literal** notation so that the Array is named **a2** with its five Elements specified like this:

```
a2 = ["green", "gray", "black", "white", "olive"];
```

JavaScript Syntax:

```
arrayObjectName = [element0, element1, ..., elementN];
```

This just demonstrates how to create an Array with **Literal** notation and output the Elements in the browser twice by using the **for ()** Statement to loop through the Elements and by manually using **document.write()** on each Element by referencing its index. This just lets you compare the two techniques.

Example 7-1:   Sample801.html

```
<!DOCTYPE HTML PUBLIC "-//W3C//DTD HTML 3.2//EN">
<HTML>
<HEAD>
<TITLE> Sample 801    Example 7-1 Literal Array Creation</TITLE>

<SCRIPT LANGUAGE="JavaScript1.2"> <!--BEGIN HIDING


a2 = ["green", "gray", "black", "white", "olive"];


        for (var i=0;  i < a2.length;  i++) {

                document.write(a2[i] + "<BR>");
        }


/*----------------------------------------------------------------*/

document.write("<P> This outputs the same Literal Array a2 as above but by a
different technique.<P>");

document.write(a2[0] + "<BR>");

document.write(a2[1] + "<BR>");

document.write(a2[2] + "<BR>");

document.write(a2[3] + "<BR>");

document.write(a2[4] + "<BR>");


//END HIDING-->
</SCRIPT>

</HEAD>

<BODY>
</BODY>
</HTML>
```

Here's how to code in blank Elements in an Array so that there is a blank Element at **index** 2, **index** 5, and **index** 7. Remember that the **index** numbers start at zero.

```
a2 = ["green", "gray",,"black", "white",,"olive",,];
```

<u>Index Hint</u>   <u>0</u>   <u>1</u> <u>2</u>   <u>3</u>   <u>4</u>   <u>5</u>   <u>6</u> <u>7</u>
(This is not part of the code.)

The blank Elements have the Value of **undefined**.

Special Notice:

When you create an Array with **Literal** notation in a top-level SCRIPT, JavaScript will interpret the **Array** Object every time the Expression that contains the **Array Literal** is evaluated. If an **Array Literal** is used within a Function, it is recreated each time that the Function is called.

Creating Two-Dimensional Arrays

An Array can contain Elements that have different Value <u>types</u> in the same Array, which is distinctly different from most other scripting or programming languages. For instance, an Array might have one Element that is a text String, another Element that is a Variable, and a third Element that is a number. Array Elements can also contain Objects, Boolean Literals, and even other Arrays. Using an Array as an Element of another Array is the process for creating quasi-multidimensional Arrays.

To create a two-dimensional Array, just define two Arrays and assign one of the Arrays as an Element of the other Array. To access the Elements of the nested Array, you use a second set of **index** subscripts like in the following example:

```
myArray1 = new Array("alpha", "beta", "gamma");
myArray2 = new Array("eeny", "meeny", "miney", myArray1);
```

where the Elements of **myArray2** are:

```
myArray2[0] = "eeny";
myArray2[1] = "meeny";
myArray2[2] = "miney";
myArray2[3] = myArray1;
```

and the Elements of **myArray1** are:

```
myArray1[3] [0] = "alpha";
myArray1[3] [1] = "beta";
myArray1[3] [2] = "gamma";
```

An example of creating Two-Dimensional Arrays

Here's an example that uses a nested **for ()** loop inside of another **for ()** loop to create a two-dimensional Array. You start by defining an Array named **a1** with a **length** of 2 and then use a **for ()** loop assign a new Array of **length** 5 to each <u>Element of Array **a1**</u>. Then you use a second **for ()** loop to assign a Value to each Element of the second dimension Array.

This Value is composed of (**i** + ", " +**j**) so that the Values of the Variables **i** and **j** are separated by a comma and become a single entry for each Element. Next the **document.write()** Method is used to render the first Array **a1** to screen, but remember that now the first Array **a1** is an Array of Arrays, where each of its Elements is an Array.

The next **document.write()** Method is used to output the series of nested Array Elements that comprise the second dimension of the Array. They are accessed by the second set of subscripts. Remember that the nested Array Elements are not Arrays and will not appear in Array syntax.

The text Strings in the **document.write()** Methods are to help you keep track of the nested Arrays and second-dimensional Elements as you try to follow the logic when looking at the output in the browser.

Example 7-2: **Sample802.html**

```html
<!DOCTYPE HTML PUBLIC "-//W3C//DTD HTML 3.2//EN">
<HTML>
<HEAD>
<TITLE> Sample 802   Example 7-2 Nested Arrays</TITLE>

<SCRIPT LANGUAGE="JavaScript1.2"> <!--BEGIN HIDING

a1 = new Array(2);

for (var i=0;  i<2;  i++) {

        //creates a new Array in each Element of Array a1

        a1[i] = new Array(5);

        for (var j=0; j<5; j++)  {

        //assigns a value to each Element of the second dimension Array

                a1[i][j] = i + ",  " +j;

        //displays the values for the first dimension Array of Arrays

document.write(a1[i] + "    First Dimension Array <BR>")

        //displays the values for the second dimension Array Elements

document.write(a1[i][j] + "    Second Dimension Array Element <BR><BR>")
        }
}


//END HIDING-->
</SCRIPT>

</HEAD>

<BODY>

</BODY>
</HTML>
```

Creating Three-Dimensional Arrays

Preamble to Example 7-3

Example 7-3 starts by defining four Arrays that each have four text Strings as Elements. Then there is a fifth Array named **myArray5** that takes one of the previously defined Arrays for each of its Elements so that it's a two-dimensional Array. Next, there is a sixth Array named **myArray6**, which has as its first Element the two-dimensional Array **myArray5**, which in turn causes **myArray6** to be a three-dimensional Array. The other three Elements of **myArray6** are just numbers.

The rest of the example is just outputting the Arrays to the browser so you can see what they look like and make it easier to see which Element index numbers do what.

This is the output you would get when you write Element **myArray6 [0]**, because this particular Element is **myArray5**, which is a two-dimensional Array inside **myArray6**.

[["alpha", "beta", "gamma", "delta"], ["blue", "red", "gold", "silver"], ["one", "two", "three", "four"], ["www", "xxx", "yyy", "zzz"]]

This is the output you would get when you write Element **myArray6 [0] [0]**, because this particular Element is the Array **a1**.

["alpha", "beta", "gamma", "delta"]

This is the output you would get when you write Element **myArray6 [0] [0] [0]**

alpha

This may seem counterintuitive at first, having to use three subscripts to index what seems to be the very first Element of **myArray6**, but alpha isn't the first Element of **myArray6**. It's the first Element of Array **a1**, and **a1** is the first Element of **myArray5** and **myArray5** is the first Element of **myArray6**. So you can see the progression now.

Preamble to Example 7-4

Example 7-4 is similar to Example 7-3. The main difference is that **myArray100** is a full <u>three-dimensional </u>Array, where each Element in it is an Array, and each of those Arrays has another Array for each of its Elements.

```
myArray100 = new Array(myArray10, myArray11, myArray12);
myArray10 = new Array(a1, a2, a3);
myArray11 = new Array(a4, a5, a6);
myArray12 = new Array(a7, a8, a9);
```

Example 7-3:   **Sample803.html**

```
<!DOCTYPE HTML PUBLIC "-//W3C//DTD HTML 3.2//EN">
<HTML>
<HEAD>
    <TITLE> Sample 803   Example 7-3 three-dimensional Array</TITLE>

<SCRIPT LANGUAGE="JavaScript1.2"> <!--BEGIN HIDING

        //These four Arrays are all text Strings

a1 = new Array("alpha", "beta", "gamma", "delta");
a2 = new Array("blue", "red", "gold", "silver");
a3 = new Array("one", "two", "three", "four");
a4 = new Array("www", "xxx", "yyy", "zzz");

        //myArray5 is composed of the 4 previously defined Arrays

myArray5 = new Array(a1, a2, a3, a4);

        //myArray6 is composed of myArray5 and numbers

myArray6 = new Array(myArray5, 2, 3, 4);

for (var i=0;  i<4;  i++) {
                                        //outputs Array a1
        document.write(a1[i] + "<P>");
}

for (var i=0;  i<4;  i++) {
                                        //outputs Array myArray5
        document.write(myArray5[i] + "<P>");
}

for (var i=0;  i<4;  i++) {
                                        //outputs Array myArray6
        document.write("<BR><P>" + myArray6[i]);
}

document.write("<HR><P>" + "The next line is ELEMENT<B>myArray6 [0] [0] [0]<\/B>");

document.write("<P>" + myArray6[0][0][0]);

document.write("<HR><P>" + "The next line is ELEMENT<B> myArray6 [0] [0]<\/B>");
document.write("<P>" + myArray6[0][0]);

document.write("<P>" + myArray6[0]);

//END HIDING-->
</SCRIPT>
</HEAD>
<BODY>
</BODY>
</HTML>
```

Example 7-4:   **Sample804.html**

```html
<!DOCTYPE HTML PUBLIC "-//W3C//DTD HTML 3.2//EN">
<HTML>
<HEAD>
   <TITLE> Sample 804   Example 7-4 three-dimensional Array   </TITLE>

<SCRIPT LANGUAGE="JavaScript1.2"> <!--BEGIN HIDING

      //These nine Arrays all have Strings in their Elements

a1 = new Array("alpha", "beta", "gamma", "delta");
a2 = new Array("blue", "red", "gold", "silver");
a3 = new Array("one", "two", "three", "four");

a4 = new Array("AAA", "BBB", "CCC", "DDD");
a5 = new Array("EEE", "FFF", "GGG", "HHH");
a6 = new Array("WWW", "XXX", "YYY", "ZZZ");

a7 = new Array("111", "222", "333", "444");
a8 = new Array("555", "777", "888", "999");
a9 = new Array("123", "456", "789", "ABC");

      //these 3 Arrays are composed of 3 previously defined Arrays

myArray10 = new Array(a1, a2, a3);
myArray11 = new Array(a4, a5, a6);
myArray12 = new Array(a7, a8, a9);

      //myArray100 is composed of the myArray10, myArray11, myArray12 Arrays

myArray100 = new Array(myArray10, myArray11, myArray12);

document.write("<HR><P>" + "This outputs each Element of Array<B> myArray100 <\/B>");

for (var i=0;  i<3;  i++) {
                                        //outputs Array myArray100
      document.write("<BR><P>" + myArray100[i]);
}

document.write("<HR><P>" + "The next line is ELEMENT<B> myArray100 [0]<\/B>");
document.write("<P>" + myArray100[0]);

document.write("<HR><P>" + "The next line is ELEMENT<B> myArray100 [0] [0]<\/B>");
document.write("<P>" + myArray100[0][0]);

document.write("<HR><P>" + "The next line is ELEMENT<B> myArray100 [0] [0] [0]<\/B>");
document.write("<P>" + myArray100[0][0][0]);

//END HIDING-->
</SCRIPT>
</HEAD>
<BODY>
</BODY></HTML>
```

Array Property Summaries

Property	Description
index	The zero-based integer index of the match to a String for an Array that is created as a result of a Regular Expression match.
input	Represents the original String that matched the Regular Expression for an Array that is created as a result of a Regular Expression match.
length	An Integer representing the precise number of Elements in an Array. It can be set to truncate Elements but not to extend the number of Elements.
prototype	Used to create your own Properties for all **Array** Objects in a Script.

Array Method Summaries

Method	Description
concat()	Combines two Arrays and returns a new Array that's "one level deep".
join()	Takes all Elements of an Array and converts them into one String where each Element is separated by a comma or, optionally, your own separator.
pop()	Removes and returns the last Element of an Array, changing its **length**.
push()	Adds Element(s) to the end of an Array, returns the last added Element, and changes the **length** of the Array.
reverse()	Reverses the physical order of the Elements in an Array.
shift()	Extracts the first Element of an Array and returns that Element.
slice()	Extracts a selectable portion of an Array and returns a new Array.
splice()	Optionally adds, removes, or <u>adds and removes</u> Elements from an Array.
sort()	Sorts the Elements of an Array lexicographically or by your Function.
toString()	Returns a String that represents the calling **Array** Object or Element.
unshift()	Adds one or more Elements before the first Element of an Array and returns the new **length** of the Array. Does <u>not</u> return the first Element.

An Overview Example that uses all of the Array Methods

This example is a quick introduction to all of the Methods of the **Array** Object. The Methods are further explored and defined individually after this example. Basically, there are two Arrays that are defined and populated with Strings that happen to be colors. Then the various Methods of the **Array** Object are invoked on the Arrays, and the results are then displayed in the browser.

Example 7-5:   **Sample805.html**

```
<!DOCTYPE HTML PUBLIC "-//W3C//DTD HTML 3.2//EN">
<HTML><HEAD>
        <TITLE> Sample 805   Example 7-5 Array Methods</TITLE>

<STYLE TYPE="text/JavaScript">

classes.Mainbody.BODY.margins("0px");
classes.Mainbody.BODY.paddings("0px");
classes.Mainbody.BODY.backgroundColor="navy";
classes.Mainbody.BODY.color="white";
classes.Mainbody.BODY.fontSize="14pt";

tags.P.color="yellow";
tags.H3.color="red";
tags.B.color="lime";

</STYLE>
<!--  ****************************************************************  -->

<SCRIPT LANGUAGE="JavaScript1.2"> <!--BEGIN HIDING

a1 = new Array("blue", "red", "purple", "lime", "yellow");

a2 = ["green", "gray", "black", "white", "olive"];

                //-----Note that a2 is an Array created with literal notation.
//END HIDING-->
</SCRIPT>
</HEAD>
<BODY CLASS="Mainbody">
<!--  ****************************************************************  -->

<SCRIPT LANGUAGE="JavaScript1.2"> <!--BEGIN HIDING

var str = "";

str += '<P>Array a1 has these Elements: <B>' + a1 + '</B></P>';
str += 'Array a2 has these Elements: <B>' + a2 + '</B><BR>';
str += '<P>Array a1 concat a2: <B>' + a1.concat(a2) + '</B></P>';
```

```
str += '<P>Array a1 with the Join Method: <B>' + a1.join(', ') + '</B></P>';

str += 'Array a2 with the Join Method: <B>' + a2.join(', ') + '</B><BR><BR>';

str += '<P>Array a1 Lexicographically Sorted is: <B>' + a1.sort() + '</B><BR>';
str += 'Array a1 Lex. Sorted and Joined is: <B>' + a1.join(', ') + '</B><BR><BR>';

str += 'Array a1 Sorted and Reversed is: <B>' + a1.reverse() + '</B><BR>';
str += 'Array a1 Sorted, Reversed and Joined is: <B>' + a1.join(', ') + '</B></P>';

str += 'Array a2 with the Push Method: <B>' + a2.push('cyan', 'maroon') +
       '</B><BR>';
str += 'Array a2 after the Push Method: <B>' + a2 + '</B><BR><BR>';

str += '<H3>-----Note that the Unshift Method ';
str += 'returns the number of Elements in the Array</H3>';

str += 'Array a2 with  the Unshift Method: <B>' + a2.unshift('navy',"violet") +
       '</B><BR>';

str += 'Array a2 after the Unshift Method: <B>' + a2 + '</B><BR><BR>';

str += 'Array a2 with  the Pop Method: <B>' + a2.pop() + '</B><BR>';
str += 'Array a2 after the Pop Method: <B>' + a2 + '</B><BR><BR>';

str += 'Array a2 with  the Shift Method: <B>' + a2.shift() + '</B><BR>';
str += 'Array a2 after the Shift Method: <B>' + a2 + '</B><BR><BR>';

str += 'Array a2 with  the Slice Method: <B>' + a2.slice(2,5) + '</B><BR>';

str += '<H3>-----Note that the Slice Method does not alter ';
str += 'the Array but returns a new Array</H3>';

str += 'Array a2 after the Slice Method: <B>' + a2 + '</B><BR><BR>';

str += 'Array a2 with  the Splice Method: <B>' + a2.splice(3,2, 'gold','darkblue')
       + '</B><BR>';

str += '<H3>-----Note that the colors gold and darkblue are ';
str += 'added in place of black and white</H3>';

str += 'Array a2 after the Splice Method: <B>' + a2 + '</B><BR><BR>';

str += 'Array a2 with  the Splice Method: <B>' + a2.splice(1,4) + '</B><BR>';

str += '<H3>-----Note that since no new colors are specified, ';
str += 'Elements are simply removed</H3>';

str += 'Array a2 after the Splice Method: <B>' + a2 + '</B><BR><BR>';

document.write(str);

//END HIDING-->
</SCRIPT>
</BODY>
</HTML>
```

Array Object Methods
The <u>concat()</u> Method of the Array Object

JavaScript Syntax:

```
arrayObjectName1.concat(arrayObjectName2);
```

Parameters Defined:

The **concat()** Method returns a new Array that consists of the Elements of **arrayObjectName1** and then the Elements of **arrayObjectName2**. Note that this new Array is a "one-level-deep" copy of the original Elements of both Arrays and does not alter the original Arrays in any way.

The first Element of the new combined Array is equal to the first Element of the **arrayObjectName1** Array. The second Element of the new combined Array is equal to the second Element of the **arrayObjectName1** Array, and so on. For instance, if you have two Arrays named **a1** and **a2** like this:

```
a1 = new Array(1,2,3);
a2 = new Array(4,5,6);

myNewArray = a1.concat(a2);
```

would be equal to:

```
myNewArray = [1,2,3,4,5,6];
```

JavaScript copies Array Elements from the original Arrays into the new Array in different ways depending on what type of Values the Elements are. When an Object is an Element in the original Array, then JavaScript copies a reference of that Object and not the Object itself, and therefore both the original and the new Array still refer to the same Object. If that referenced Object is altered in any way, then those changes are reflected in both the original and new Arrays as well.

When JavaScript copies Strings and Numbers to the new Array with the **concat()** Method, the actual Strings and Numbers are copied, not references. Note that this does not apply to **String** Objects and **Number** Objects, which would be covered under the Object behaviors in the previous paragraph. Any changes to the String or Number in one Array has no effect on the other Array.

If you add an Element to either the new Array or the old Array, then the other Array will <u>*not*</u> have that added Element and is completely unaffected.

This example starts by defining two **dense** Arrays by specifying their Elements within the Array Constructor Function. They are named **a1** and **a2**, respectively. Then the Array **a1** invokes the **concat()** Method with Array **a2** as the Argument and assigns the new Array to **a3**. All three of these Arrays are then written to the browser so you can view the results.

Example 7-6: Sample806.html

```
<!DOCTYPE HTML PUBLIC "-//W3C//DTD HTML 3.2//EN">
<HTML><HEAD>  <TITLE> Sample 806    Example 7-6 concat Method</TITLE>

<SCRIPT LANGUAGE="JavaScript1.2"> <!--BEGIN HIDING


a1 = new Array("one", "two", "three", "four");

a2 = new Array(1, 2, 3, 4);

a3 = a1.concat(a2);

/*-------------------------------------------------------------*/

document.write("<H3>The next line is Array a1<\/H3>");
document.write("<P>" + a1 + "<HR>");

document.write("<H3>The next line is Array a2<\/H3>");
document.write("<P>" + a2 + "<HR>");

document.write("<H3>The next line is Array a3 = a1.concat(a2)<\/H3>");
document.write("<P>" + a3 + "<HR>");

/*-------------------------------------------------------------*/
//END HIDING-->
</SCRIPT>
</HEAD>
<BODY>  </BODY></HTML>
```

The preceding example produces the following output:

The next line is Array a1
["one", "two", "three", "four"]

The next line is Array a2
[1, 2, 3, 4]

The next line is Array a3 = a1.concat(a2)
["one", "two", "three", "four", 1, 2, 3, 4]

This example starts by defining two **dense** Arrays by specifying their Elements within the Array Constructor Function. They are named **a1** and **a2**, respectively. Then the Array **a1** invokes the **concat()** Method with Array **a2** as the Argument and assigns the new Array to **a3**. All three of these Arrays are then written to the browser so you can view the results. Next a new Element is added to **a2**. Then Arrays **a2** and **a3** are both written to the browser so you can see that **a2** shows the change of the added Element to its Array but **a3** is unaffected.

Example 7-7:   Sample807.html

```
<!DOCTYPE HTML PUBLIC "-//W3C//DTD HTML 3.2//EN">
<HTML>
<HEAD>
<TITLE> Sample 807   Example 7-7 concat Method add Element</TITLE>

<SCRIPT LANGUAGE="JavaScript1.2"> <!--BEGIN HIDING

a1 = new Array("alpha", "beta", "gamma", "delta");

a2 = new Array("blue", "red", "gold", "silver");

a3 = a1.concat(a2);


document.write("<P>" + a1);

document.write("<P>" + a2);

document.write("<P>" + a3);



          //Adds a new Element to a2

a2[4] = "PLATINUM";

          //Notice a2 is changed but a3 is not changed

document.write("<P>" + a2);

document.write("<P>" + a3);


//END HIDING-->
</SCRIPT>
</HEAD>

<BODY>
</BODY>
</HTML>
```

The preceding example produces the following output:

["alpha", "beta", "gamma", "delta"]

["blue", "red", "gold", "silver"]

["alpha", "beta", "gamma", "delta", "blue", "red", "gold", "silver"]

["blue", "red", "gold", "silver", "PLATINUM"]

["alpha", "beta", "gamma", "delta", "blue", "red", "gold", "silver"]

Let's explore some of this theory with an example, where the Array **a1** invokes the **concat()** Method with Array **a2** as the Argument and assigns the new Array to **a3**. All three of these Arrays are then written to the browser. Next, the **length** Property is used to change the **length** of **a2** from 4 to 2, which effectively deletes the last two Elements of **a2**. Then both the **a2** and **a3** Arrays are written to the browser again to show that indeed **a2** is changed but **a3** is unaffected. Note that if you were to **concat()** **a1** with **a2** again, then the changes would be implemented in **a3**.

Example 7-8:   **Sample808.html**

```
<!DOCTYPE HTML PUBLIC "-//W3C//DTD HTML 3.2//EN">
<HTML>
<HEAD>
<TITLE> Sample 808    Example 7-8 concat Method delete Element</TITLE>

<SCRIPT LANGUAGE="JavaScript1.2"> <!--BEGIN HIDING

a1 = new Array("alpha", "beta", "gamma", "delta");
a2 = new Array("blue", "red", "gold", "silver");

a3 = a1.concat(a2);

document.write("<P>" + a1);
document.write("<P>" + a2);
document.write("<P>" + a3);

            //changes length from 4 to 2 thus deleting 2 Elements

a2.length = 2;

            //Notice a2 is changed but a3 is not changed

document.write("<P>" + a2);
document.write("<P>" + a3);
```

```
//END HIDING-->
</SCRIPT>

</HEAD>

<BODY>

</BODY>
</HTML>
```

The preceding example produces the following output:

["alpha", "beta", "gamma", "delta"]

["blue", "red", "gold", "silver"]

["alpha", "beta", "gamma", "delta", "blue", "red", "gold", "silver"]

["blue", "red"]

["alpha", "beta", "gamma", "delta", "blue", "red", "gold", "silver"]

This example deals with the **concat()** Method of the **Array** Object when Objects created by using **Literal** notation are the Values of the Array Elements. The premise as stated in the previous theory is that because JavaScript copies a reference of the Objects that are concatenated, any changes to the Objects will be reflected in the original Array and the new concatenated Array.

We start by creating three different types of Objects with **Literal** notation, naming them by assignment, and then defining them with Properties and Values like this:

```
stringObject1 = {theString:"my second string object"};
numberObject1 = {theNumber:8};
computerObject = {make:"Mac", model:8100, ram:264, harddrive:"internal 4Gig"};
```

Next, two **dense** Arrays are created with the Array Constructor Function and a third Array is created by assigning the concatenation of Arrays **a1** and **a2** to **a3**, like this:

```
a1 = new Array("one", "two");

a2 = new Array(stringObject1, numberObject1, computerObject);

a3 = a1.concat(a2);
```

Next, all three Arrays are written to screen with the **document.write()** Method so we can compare them later on. Then some changes are made to the Properties of the Objects like this:

```
stringObject1.theString = "MY CHANGED SECOND STRING OBJECT";
numberObject1.theNumber = 777;
computerObject.model = 9600;
computerObject.ram = 512;
computerObject.harddrive = "external 9Gig";
```

And, finally, the Arrays **a2** and **a3** are written to screen again to show that indeed the changes to the Objects have been reflected in both the original Array **a2** and in the new Array **a3**, which is **a1.concat(a2)**.

Example 7-9:   **Sample809.html**

```
<!DOCTYPE HTML PUBLIC "-//W3C//DTD HTML 3.2//EN">
<HTML>
<HEAD>
<TITLE> Sample 809   Example 7-9 concat Method with Objects</TITLE>

<SCRIPT LANGUAGE="JavaScript1.2"> <!--BEGIN HIDING

//Create three Objects with Literal notation.

stringObject1 = {theString:"my second string object"};

numberObject1 = {theNumber:8};

computerObject = {make:"Mac", model:8100, ram:264, harddrive:"internal 4Gig"};


/*-------------------------------------------------------------*/

a1 = new Array("one", "two");

a2 = new Array(stringObject1, numberObject1, computerObject);

a3 = a1.concat(a2);

/*-------------------------------------------------------------*/

document.write("<H3>The next line is Array a1<\/H3>");
document.write("<P>" + a1);

document.write("<H3>The next line is Array a2<\/H3>");
document.write("<P>" + a2);

document.write("<H3>The next line is Array a3 = a1.concat(a2)<\/H3>");
document.write("<P>" + a3 + "<HR>");
```

```
/*-------------------------------------------------------------------*/

        //Notice when a2 Objects are changed then a3 Objects reflect the change


stringObject1.theString = "MY CHANGED SECOND STRING OBJECT";

numberObject1.theNumber = 777;

computerObject.model = 9600;

computerObject.ram = 512;

computerObject.harddrive = "external 9Gig";


/*-------------------------------------------------------------------*/


document.write("<H3>The next line is Array a2 after the <I>OBJECT<\/I>
changes<\/H3>");

document.write("<P>" + a2);


/*-------------------------------------------------------------------*/


document.write("<P><H3><FONT COLOR='red'>Notice when a2 " +
        "Objects are changed " +
        "then a3 Objects reflect the change.<\/FONT> <\/H3>");


/*-------------------------------------------------------------------*/


document.write("<H3>The next line is Array a3 after the changes<\/H3>");

document.write("<P>" + a3);


//END HIDING-->
</SCRIPT>

</HEAD>

<BODY>

</BODY>
</HTML>
```

The preceding example produces the following output:

The next line is Array a1

["one", "two"]

The next line is Array a2

[{theString:"my second string object"}, {theNumber:8}, {make:"Mac", model:8100, ram:264, harddrive:"internal 4Gig"}]

The next line is Array a3 = a1.concat(a2)

["one", "two", {theString:"my second string object"}, {theNumber:8}, {make:"Mac", model:8100, ram:264, harddrive:"internal 4Gig"}]

The next line is Array a2 after the OBJECT changes

[{theString:"MY CHANGED SECOND STRING OBJECT"}, {theNumber:777}, {make:"Mac", model:9600, ram:512, harddrive:"external 9Gig"}]

The next line is Array a3 after the changes

["one", "two", {theString:"MY CHANGED SECOND STRING OBJECT"}, {theNumber:777}, {make:"Mac", model:9600, ram:512, harddrive:"external 9Gig"}]

The <u>join()</u> Method of the Array Object

JavaScript Syntax:

```
arrayObjectName.join();
arrayObjectName.join("separatorString");
```

Parameters Defined:

The **join()** Method returns a single text String that is composed of each Element of an Array. The optional **separatorString** is used to separate each Element in the text String. If no **separatorString** is supplied, JavaScript by default should separate each Element with a comma. Note that there is a bug in Navigator 4 that causes the output to be an **Array Literal** if no **separatorString** is supplied. If necessary, JavaScript will convert the **separatorString** Argument into a String. Note that the original Array is unaffected.

This example just demonstrates the **join()** Method of the **Array** Object with a few twists on how to use the **separatorString** Argument. Nothing fancy, just create a **dense** Array and use the **join()** Method several times with a variety of **separatorStrings**, which are placed inside of the **write()** Method so you can see the results in the browser.

Example 7-10:   Sample810.html

```
<!DOCTYPE HTML PUBLIC "-//W3C//DTD HTML 3.2//EN">
<HTML>
<HEAD>
        <TITLE> Sample 810    Example 7-10 join Method</TITLE>

<SCRIPT LANGUAGE="JavaScript1.2"> <!--BEGIN HIDING

a1 = new Array("one","two","three","four","five");

var fuzzy1 = "<FONT COLOR='purple'>";
var fuzzy2 = "<\/FONT>";
var fuzzy3 = " _____ ";

document.write("<H3>" + a1.join() + "...NOTE THE BUG<\/H3>");
document.write("<H3>" + a1.join(' + ') + "<\/H3>");
document.write("<H3>" + a1.join(' ***** ') + "<\/H3>");
document.write("<H3>" + a1.join(fuzzy1 + ' plus ' + fuzzy2) + "<\/H3>");
document.write("<H3>" + a1.join(fuzzy3) + "<\/H3>");

//END HIDING-->
</SCRIPT>

</HEAD>
<BODY>
</BODY>
</HTML>
```

The preceding example produces the following output:

["one", "two", "three", "four", "five"]...NOTE THE BUG

one + two + three + four + five

one ***** two ***** three ***** four ***** five

one plus two plus three plus four plus five

one _____ two _____ three _____ four _____ five

The <u>pop()</u> Method of the Array Object

JavaScript Syntax:

```
arrayObjectName.pop();
```

The **pop()** Method extricates, that is, removes the last Element in an Array and returns it. This has the added effect of changing the **length** of the Array, you guessed it, to one less than it was.

If your intent is just to remove an Element, then just invoke the **pop()** Method on a particular Array via its name like this:

```
myArray.pop();
```

If you want to make use of the returned Element, then assign the invoked **pop()** Method to a Variable like this:

```
myPopped = myArray.pop();
```

This simple example just demonstrates the **pop()** Method by creating a **dense** Array named **a1**, writing it and the **length** to screen. It continues by performing the **pop()** Method on **a1** and assigning the returned Element to the Variable **myPopped**. Then it writes **myPopped** to screen and writes **a1** to screen again to show that the last Element was removed. Finally, it writes the **length** of the Array to screen again to show that the **length** is one less than before the **pop()**.

Example 7-11:   **Sample811.html**

```
<!DOCTYPE HTML PUBLIC "-//W3C//DTD HTML 3.2//EN">
<HTML>
<HEAD>

<TITLE> Sample 811   Example 7-11 pop Method</TITLE>

<SCRIPT LANGUAGE="JavaScript1.2"> <!--BEGIN HIDING

a1 = new Array("one","two","three","four","five");
```

```
document.write("Before pop<H3>" + a1 + "<\/H3>");

document.write("<H3>The length is: " + a1.length + "<\/H3>");


myPopped = a1.pop();

document.write("popped<H3>" + myPopped + "<\/H3>");


document.write("After pop<H3>" + a1 + "<\/H3>");

document.write("<H3>The length is: " + a1.length + "<\/H3>");


//END HIDING-->
</SCRIPT>

</HEAD>

<BODY>

</BODY>
</HTML>
```

The previous example produces the following output:

Before pop

["one", "two", "three", "four", "five"]

The length is: 5

popped

five

After pop

["one", "two", "three", "four"]

The length is: 4

The <u>push()</u> Method of the Array Object

JavaScript Syntax:

```
arrayObjectName.push(element1, element2, ..., elementN);
```

Parameters Defined:

The **push()** Method adds as many Elements as you want to the <u>end</u> of the Array and returns the last Element added. This changes the **length** of the Array by how many Elements were added. As usual, each Element must be separated by a comma, but the white space after the comma is optional, for readability.

This example creates the Array **a1** with **Literal** notation and then writes it and its **length** to screen. It then adds three String Elements to **a1** and assigns the returned last Element added to the Variable **myPushed**. The Variable **myPushed** is then written to screen and then **a1** is written to screen again to show the results of the **push()** Method.

Example 7-12:   **Sample812.html**

```
<!DOCTYPE HTML PUBLIC "-//W3C//DTD HTML 3.2//EN">
<HTML>
<HEAD>

<TITLE> Sample 812   Example 7-12 push Method</TITLE>

<SCRIPT LANGUAGE="JavaScript1.2"> <!--BEGIN HIDING


a1 = ["one","two","three","four","five"];

document.write("Before push<H3>" + a1 + "<\/H3>");

document.write("<H3>The length is: " + a1.length + "<\/H3>");


myPushed = a1.push("SIX", "SEVEN", "EIGHT");

document.write("myPushed<H3>" + myPushed + "<\/H3>");

document.write("After push<H3>" + a1 + "<\/H3>");
document.write("<H3>The length is: " + a1.length + "<\/H3>");
```

```
//END HIDING-->
</SCRIPT>

</HEAD>

<BODY>

</BODY>
</HTML>
```

The previous example produces the following output:

Before push

["one", "two", "three", "four", "five"]

The length is: 5

myPushed

EIGHT

After push

["one", "two", "three", "four", "five", "SIX", "SEVEN", "EIGHT"]

The length is: 8

The <u>shift()</u> Method of the Array Object

JavaScript Syntax:

```
arrayObjectName.shift();
```

The **shift()** Method is used to remove the first Element of an Array and return that Element. This Element is equivalent to **arrayObjectName[0]**. This Method also changes the **length** of the Array to one less than before the Method was invoked.

This simple example just demonstrates the **shift()** Method by creating an Array named **a1** with **Literal** notation and then writing it and the **length** to screen. It continues by performing the **shift()** Method on **a1** and assigning the returned Element to the Variable **myShifted**. Then it writes **myShifted** to screen and writes **a1** to screen again to show that the first Element was removed. Finally, it writes the **length** of the Array to screen again to show that the **length** is one less than before the **shift()**.

Example 7-13: **Sample813.html**

```
<!DOCTYPE HTML PUBLIC "-//W3C//DTD HTML 3.2//EN">
<HTML>
<HEAD>
<TITLE> Sample 813   Example 7-13 shift Method</TITLE>

<SCRIPT LANGUAGE="JavaScript1.2"> <!--BEGIN HIDING

a1 = ["one","two","three","four","five"];


document.write("Before shift:<H3>" + a1 + "<\/H3>");
document.write("<H3>The length is: " + a1.length + "<\/H3>");

myShifted = a1.shift();

document.write("myShifted value is:<H3>" + myShifted + "<\/H3>");

document.write("After shift:<H3>" + a1 + "<\/H3>");
document.write("<H3>The length is: " + a1.length + "<\/H3>");

//END HIDING-->
</SCRIPT>
```

```
</HEAD>

<BODY>

</BODY>
</HTML>
```

The previous example produces the following output:

Before shift:

["one", "two", "three", "four", "five"]

The length is: 5

myShifted value is:

one

After shift:

["two", "three", "four", "five"]

The length is: 4

The <u>unshift()</u> Method of the Array Object

JavaScript Syntax:

```
arrayObjectName.unshift(element1, element2, ..., elementN);
```

Parameters Defined:

The **unshift()** Method is used to add as many Elements as you want before the first Element of an Array specified by **arrayObjectName**. This Method returns the new **length** of the Array, not an Element. The **elementN** Arguments are the Elements to be added to the front of the Array.

This simple example just demonstrates the **unshift()** Method by creating an Array named **a1** with **Literal** notation and then writing it and the **length** to screen. It continues by performing the **unshift()** Method on **a1**, adding three Elements, and assigning the returned **length** to the Variable **myReturnedLength**. Then it writes **myReturnedLength** to screen and writes **a1** to screen again to show that the three added Elements are now in the Array and at the beginning of the Array. Finally, it writes the **length** of the Array to screen again to show that the **length** reflects the current number of Elements after the **unshift()** Method was invoked.

Example 7-14: Sample814.html

```
<!DOCTYPE HTML PUBLIC "-//W3C//DTD HTML 3.2//EN">
<HTML>
<HEAD>
<TITLE> Sample 814   Example 7-14 unshift Method</TITLE>

<SCRIPT LANGUAGE="JavaScript1.2"> <!--BEGIN HIDING


a1 = ["one","two","three","four","five"];


document.write("Before unshift:<H3>" + a1 + "<\/H3>");
document.write("<H3>The length is: " + a1.length + "<\/H3>");

myReturnedLength = a1.unshift("minusTwo", "minusOne", "zero");

document.write("myReturnedLength value is:<H3>" + myReturnedLength + "<\/H3>");

document.write("After unshift:<H3>" + a1 + "<\/H3>");
document.write("<H3>The length is: " + a1.length + "<\/H3>");
```

```
//END HIDING-->
</SCRIPT>

</HEAD>

<BODY>

</BODY>
</HTML>
```

The previous example produces the following output:

Before unshift:

["one", "two", "three", "four", "five"]

The length is: 5

myReturnedLength value is:

8

After unshift:

["minusTwo", "minusOne", "zero", "one", "two", "three", "four", "five"]

The length is: 8

The <u>slice()</u> Method of the Array Object

JavaScript Syntax:

```
arrayObjectName.slice(startIndex, [endIndex]);
```

Parameters Defined:

The **slice()** Method is used to extract a sequential group of Elements from an Array and return a new Array comprised of those Elements. The **startIndex** Argument is an integer that serves as the <u>zero-based</u> **index** at which you start the slice. For instance, if **startIndex** is 0, the **slice()** starts at the first Element, and the first Element is included in the **slice()**. If **startIndex** is 4, the **slice()** starts at the fifth Element, and so on.

The **endIndex** Argument is an optional <u>zero-based</u> **index** that is either a positive or negative integer that is used to end the **slice()**. Pay attention here!! The **slice()** Method extracts up to but does <u>not</u> include the Element specified at **endIndex**. For instance, if you have **myArray1.slice(0, 4)**, this would extract the first, second, third, and fourth Elements but not the fifth. If you had **myArray1.slice(2, 5)**, this would extract the third, fourth and fifth Elements, which would be the **myArray[2]**, **myArray[3]** and **myArray[4]** Elements.

If **endIndex** is used as a <u>negative</u> integer, then JavaScript starts the count from the end of the Array and works backward. For instance, if **endIndex** is -1, the **slice()** would extract up to and include the next-to-last Element. So if you had the following Array:

```
al = ["one","two","three","four","five"];
```

then for:

```
al.slice(1, -1)
```

the returned Array would include the Elements "two", "three" and "four".

If you had:

```
al.slice(0, -2)
```

the returned Array would include the Elements "one", "two" and "three".

If **endIndex** is omitted, then **slice()** will extract from **startIndex** all the way to the end of the Array, <u>including</u> the last Element.

JavaScript copies Array Elements from the original Array into the new Array in different ways depending on what type of Values the Elements are. When an Object is an Element in the original Array, then JavaScript copies a reference of that Object and not the Object itself, and therefore both the original and the new Array still refer to the same Object. If that referenced Object is altered in any way, then those changes are reflected in both the original and new Arrays as well.

When JavaScript copies Strings and Numbers to the new Array with the **slice()** Method, the actual Strings and Numbers are copied, not references. Note that this does not apply to **String** Objects and **Number** Objects, which would be covered under the Object behaviors in the previous paragraph. Any changes to the String or Number in one Array has no effect on the other Array.

If you add an Element to either the new Array or the old Array, then the other Array will _not_ have that added Element and is completely unaffected.

Note that there is a **slice()** Method of the **String** Object that extracts Characters from a String and returns a new String. See Chapter 8 on Methods of the **String** Object, starting on page 788.

This example demonstrates four different uses of the **slice()** Method to extract different Elements of the Array named **a1** which is created with **Literal** notation. After each **slice()** Method is invoked, the returned Array is written to screen to check the results.

Example 7-15:   Sample815.html

```
<!DOCTYPE HTML PUBLIC "-//W3C//DTD HTML 3.2//EN">
<HTML>
<HEAD>

<TITLE> Sample 815   Example 7-15 slice Method</TITLE>

<SCRIPT LANGUAGE="JavaScript1.2"> <!--BEGIN HIDING


a1 = ["one","two","three","four","five","six","seven"];


document.write("Before slice:<H3>" + a1 + "<\/H3>");



mySlice = a1.slice(0, 2);

document.write("mySlice Array after slice(0, 2):<H3>" + mySlice + "<\/H3>");
```

```
mySlice = a1.slice(1, -1);

document.write("mySlice Array after slice(1, -1):<H3>" + mySlice + "<\/H3>");


mySlice = a1.slice(0, -3);

document.write("mySlice Array after slice(0, -3):<H3>" + mySlice + "<\/H3>");


mySlice = a1.slice(3);

document.write("mySlice Array after slice(3):<H3>" + mySlice + "<\/H3>");

//END HIDING-->
</SCRIPT>

</HEAD>

<BODY>

</BODY>
</HTML>
```

The previous example produces the following output:

Before slice:

["one", "two", "three", "four", "five", "six", "seven"]

mySlice Array after slice(0, 2):

["one", "two"]

mySlice Array after slice(1, -1):

["two", "three", "four", "five", "six"]

mySlice Array after slice(0, -3):

["one", "two", "three", "four"]

mySlice Array after slice(3):

["four", "five", "six", "seven"]

The <u>splice()</u> Method of the Array Object

JavaScript Syntax:

```
arrayObjectName.splice(startIndex, removeQty[, addElt1,..., addEltN])
```

Parameters Defined:

The **splice()** Method is used to simultaneously remove Elements and add new Elements to an Array. This may change the **length** of the Array.

The **startIndex** Argument is the <u>zero-based</u> **index** specifying the Element where you want to start removing Elements. This is also where any new Elements specified will start to be inserted.

The **removeQty** Argument is the number of Elements that you want to remove from the Array. It must be a positive integer or zero. If zero is specified, then you should add at least one Element, or errors may occur. If **removeQty** is set to one, then that Element is returned. If **removeQty** is greater than one, then an Array containing all of the removed Elements is returned.

The **addElt1**, ..., **addEltN** Arguments are a comma-separated list of new Elements that you want to add to the Array. This is optional. If you choose not to add any Elements, then **splice()** will simply remove the specified Elements.

This example demonstrates several implementations of the **splice()** Method on the Array named **a1**. Unlike many of the previous examples, **a1** is continuously changed as the Script progresses, so when you look at the output, keep track of what the previous invocation of the **splice()** Method has done to the Array. Basically, the Array is created and populated with **Literal** notation, then the **splice()** Method is performed and the returned Array is written to screen, and **a1** is written to screen after each **splice()**.

Pay attention to which Elements are being removed and where the new Elements are being inserted. Also, notice that if no Elements are removed with the **removeQty** Argument, then the return Value is **undefined**.

Example 7-16:   **Sample816.html**

```
<!DOCTYPE HTML PUBLIC "-//W3C//DTD HTML 3.2//EN">
<HTML>
<HEAD>

<TITLE> Sample 816   Example 7-16      splice Method </TITLE>

<SCRIPT LANGUAGE="JavaScript1.2"> <!--BEGIN HIDING


a1 = ["one","two","three","four","five"];

document.write("Before splice:<H3>" + a1 + "<\/H3>");

/*----------------------------------------------------------------*/

mySplice = a1.splice(0, 2, 'six','seven');

document.write("mySplice Array after splice(0,2,'six','seven'):<H3>" + mySplice +
            "<\/H3>");

document.write("Array a1 after splice(0,2,'six','seven'):<H3>" + a1 + "<\/H3>");

/*----------------------------------------------------------------*/

mySplice = a1.splice(4, 1, 'eight','nine');

document.write("mySplice returns one Element after splice(4,1,'eight','nine'):" +
            "<H3>" + mySplice + "<\/H3>");

document.write("Array a1 after splice(4,1,'eight','nine'):<H3>" + a1 + "<\/H3>");

/*----------------------------------------------------------------*/

mySplice = a1.splice(3, 0, 'ten','eleven');

document.write("mySplice is undefined if zero Elements are removed " +
            "like splice (3,0,'ten','eleven'):<H3>" + mySplice + "<\/H3>");

document.write("Array a1 after splice(3,0,'ten','eleven'):<H3>" + a1 + "<\/H3>");


//END HIDING-->
</SCRIPT>

</HEAD>

<BODY>

</BODY>
</HTML>
```

The previous example produces the following output:

Before splice:

["one", "two", "three", "four", "five"]

mySplice Array after splice(0,2,'six','seven'):

["one", "two"]

Array a1 after splice(0,2,'six','seven'):

["six", "seven", "three", "four", "five"]

mySplice returns one Element after splice(4,1,'eight','nine'):

five

Array a1 after splice(4,1,'eight','nine'):

["six", "seven", "three", "four", "eight", "nine"]

mySplice is undefined if zero Elements are removed like splice (3,0,'ten','eleven'):

undefined

Array a1 after splice(3,0,'ten','eleven'):

["six", "seven", "three", "ten", "eleven", "four", "eight", "nine"]

The <u>toString()</u> Method of the Array <u>Object</u>

JavaScript Syntax:

```
arrayObjectName.toString();
```

Parameters Defined:

There is currently a bug in the **toString()** Method in Navigator 4 when it is used with the **Array** Object, so don't use it. Use the **join()** Method instead. Theoretically, it is supposed to concatenate all of the Elements in an Array into one **String** Object, where each Element is separated by a comma. For the Array **a1** = ["one", "two", "three"], the **toString()** Method should render the following String:

one,two,three

What it actually renders now is:

["one","two","three"]

This has been fixed in JavaScript1.3. See page 860 in Chapter 10. Also see page 859 on the new **toSource()** Method.

The <u>toString()</u> Method of the Array <u>Element</u>

JavaScript Syntax:

```
arrayObjectName[index].toString([optionalRadix]);
(arrayObjectName[index]).toString([optionalRadix]);
arrayObjectName[elementValue].toString([optionalRadix]);
(arrayObjectName[elementValue]).toString([optionalRadix]);
```

Parameters Defined:

The **toString()** Method works just fine for an individual Element of an Array. This Method is used to convert any type of Value contained in an Array Element into its **text** equivalent, that is, a text String. In the case of a **Number** Object, you can use the **optionalRadix** Argument to specify a **base** number between 2 and 16 to convert the Value to the numbering system of your choice. If no **radix** is specified, then the default Value of the **optionalRadix** Argument is 10. The parentheses enclosing the calling Element, such as **(arrayObjectName[index])**, are optional, as is indicated by the multiple formats of Syntax.

Example 7-17:   Sample817.html

```
<!DOCTYPE HTML PUBLIC "-//W3C//DTD HTML 3.2//EN">
<HTML>
<HEAD>
<TITLE> Sample 817    Example 7-17       toString Method of Array Element   </TITLE>

<SCRIPT LANGUAGE="JavaScript1.2"> <!--BEGIN HIDING


a1 = ["one","two","three","four","five"];

a2 = [1,2,3,4,5,14,22,55,222,255,333];


/*----------------------------------------------------------------*/
document.write("Array a1:<H3>" + a1 + "<\/H3>");
document.write("Array a2:<H3>" + a2 + "<\/H3>");

/*----------------------------------------------------------------*/
var str1 = a1.toString();
var str2 = a2.toString();

var str3 = a2[5].toString();
var str4 = a2[5].toString(16);
var str5 = a2[9].toString(16);

/*----------------------------------------------------------------*/

document.write("<H3>" + str1 + ".... THIS IS A BUG DEMO<\/H3>");

document.write("<H3>" + str2 + ".... THIS IS A BUG DEMO<\/H3>");

document.write("<H3>" + str3 + "<\/H3>");

document.write("<H3>" + str4 + "<\/H3>");

document.write("<H3>" + str5 + "<\/H3>");


//END HIDING-->
</SCRIPT>

</HEAD>

<BODY>

</BODY>
</HTML>
```

The previous example demonstrates the **toString()** Method when called on an Array in order to point out the bug. It also calls the **toString()** Method on individual Array Elements and writes the output to screen. It uses the default **radix** of 10 and then uses a **radix** of 16 to output the same Element in base 16 math so you can compare them. Note that the letter "**e**" is the base 16 equivalent of 14.

The previous example produces the following output:

Array a1:

["one", "two", "three", "four", "five"]

Array a2:

[1, 2, 3, 4, 5, 14, 22, 55, 222, 255, 333]

["one", "two", "three", "four", "five"].... **THIS IS A BUG DEMO**

[1, 2, 3, 4, 5, 14, 22, 55, 222, 255, 333].... **THIS IS A BUG DEMO**

14

e

ff

For more examples of the **toString()** Method used with Array Elements see:

Sample434.html, line 272:   var getRGB = numArray[0].toString();
Sample434.html, line 458:   numArray[0] = numArray[0].toString();

which are located in Example 3-34 on pages 346 and 348, respectively. The preamble to Example 3-34 starts on page 342.

The <u>reverse()</u> Method of the Array Object

JavaScript Syntax:

```
arrayObjectName.reverse();
```

Parameters Defined:

The **reverse()** Method is used to transpose the order of all of the Elements in an Array, that is, the last Element becomes the first, the first Element is last, and so on. It does not sort the Elements, it just reverses their **index** order. For example, in the Array **a1**:

```
a1 = new Array("one","two","three","four","five");

a1.reverse();
```

would order the Elements like this:

```
a1[0]        has the Value of        "five"
a1[1]        has the Value of        "four"
a1[2]        has the Value of        "three"
a1[3]        has the Value of        "two"
a1[4]        has the Value of        "one"
```

The <u>sort()</u> Method of the Array Object

JavaScript Syntax:

```
arrayObjectName.sort([compareFunction]);
```

Parameters Defined:

The **sort()** Method basically alphabetizes the order of the Elements in an Array. How the **sort** is implemented depends on the optional **compareFunction** Argument. If no **compareFunction** is supplied, then JavaScript will **sort** the Elements lexicographically, which is in "dictionary-order". This means that the number 700 will **sort** so that it occurs <u>before </u>the number 8. Otherwise, it follows the normal alphabetical sorting for letters.

For instance, suppose you have the following Array **a1**:

```
a1 = ["one","two","three","four",8,700,5,"five","six","seven"];
```

Then: **a1.sort()** would produce the following output:

```
[5, 700, 8, "five", "four", "one", "seven", "six", "three", "two"]
```

This type of sorting is based on the ASCII collating sequence where numbers are sorted based on their String Value and not their numeric Value, due to the fact that JavaScript converts the Array Elements to Strings before sorting. On the other hand, a **numeric sort** would have 700 coming after 8 as you would expect it to.

The <u>compareFunction</u> Function

When you supply a **compareFunction** Argument to increase the flexibility of the **sort()** Method, it must have two Arguments, typically **a** and **b**, so that a Value is returned based on the comparison of **a** and **b**. From that point, there are many ways to proceed. For example, the following Function can work with Elements that have String, Numeric String, and Number Values:

```
function compareSort(a, b) {

    if (a > b)   { return 1; }
    if (a == b)  { return 0; }
    if (a < b)   { return -1; }
}
```

The preceding Function **compareSort(a, b)** has the effect of causing the **sort** to be "numeric" instead of "dictionary-type" lexicographical, so that numbers **sort** normally. When you use a **compareFunction** Argument in the **sort()** Method, you have to strip off the parentheses and no **(a, b)** Arguments are manually supplied. Basically, the internal JavaScript handles it for you, so you would invoke **sort()** with the above **compareSort(a, b)** Function like this:

```
myArray1.sort(compareSort)
```

Example 7-18 produces a **numeric sort** by using the **compareSort(a, b)** Function within the **sort()** Method for the Array **myArray1**. Then it writes the sorted Array to screen. Next, a **for()** loop is used to write each sorted Element of the Array to screen. Note that the **numeric sort** has 700 sorted after 8.

Example 7-18:   **Sample818.html**

```
<!DOCTYPE HTML PUBLIC "-//W3C//DTD HTML 3.2//EN">
<HTML><HEAD>
<TITLE> Sample 818    Example 7-18 sort Method of Array Object</TITLE>

<SCRIPT LANGUAGE="JavaScript1.2"> <!--BEGIN HIDING

myArray1 = new Array("one","two","three","four",8,700,5,"five","six","seven");

function compareSort(a,b) {

        if (a > b)     { return 1; }
        if (a == b)    { return 0; }
        if (a < b)     { return -1; }
}

document.write(myArray1 + "<P>");

document.write(myArray1.sort(compareSort) + "<P>");

        for (var i=0; i<myArray1.length; i++) {

                document.write(myArray1[i] + "<BR>");
        }

//END HIDING-->
</SCRIPT>
</HEAD>
<BODY>
</BODY>
</HTML>
```

The previous example produces the following output:

["one", "two", "three", "four", 8, 700, 5, "five", "six", "seven"]

[5, 8, 700, "five", "four", "one", "seven", "six", "three", "two"]

5
8
700
five
four
one
seven
six
three
two

Sorting Number Values

You could create a different Function to be used for the **compareFunction** Argument that is specifically designed to work with **Number** Values so that the smallest number is always returned when they are compared, like this:

```
function compareNumbers(a, b) {

        return a - b;
}
```

Example 7-19 uses the above **compareNumbers(a, b)** Function as an Argument in the **sort()** Method for the Array **myArray1**. The original Array, the sorted Array, and then each sorted Element are output to screen, to verify the results.

Example 7-19:   **Sample819.html**

```
<!DOCTYPE HTML PUBLIC -//W3C//DTD HTML 3.2//EN>
<HTML>
<HEAD>
<TITLE> Sample 819    Example 7-19 more sort Method</TITLE>

<SCRIPT LANGUAGE="JavaScript1.2"> <!--BEGIN HIDING

myArray1 = new Array(4000,30,33,2,8,700,5,-33,0,10);

        function compareNumbers(a,b) {

                return a - b;
        }

document.write(myArray1 + "<P>");

document.write(myArray1.sort(compareNumbers) + "<P>");

        for (var i=0; i<myArray1.length; i++) {

                document.write(myArray1[i] + "<BR>");
        }

//END HIDING-->
</SCRIPT>
</HEAD>

<BODY>
</BODY>
</HTML>
```

The previous example produces the following output:

[4000, 30, 33, 2, 8, 700, 5, -33, 0, 10]

[-33, 0, 2, 5, 8, 10, 30, 33, 700, 4000]

-33
0
2
5
8
10
30
33
700
4000

Performing a reverse Numeric Sort

You could use the following Function to perform a <u>reverse</u> **numeric sort,** so that the larger number is always returned when the comparison occurs:

```
function reverseCompareNumbers(a,b) {

        return b - a;
}
```

If the Array **myArray1** = new Array(4000,30,33,2,8,700,5,-33,0,10);

Then **myArray1.sort(reverseCompareNumbers)** would be output as:

[4000, 700, 33, 30, 10, 8, 5, 2, 0, -33]

If you wanted to use the **sort()** Method to put all of the odd numbers above all of the even numbers <u>without</u> putting them in numerical order, you could do it with the **compareFunction** of **compareEvenOdd(a,b)**, which is demonstrated in the next example:

```
function compareEvenOdd(a,b) {

        if (a%2 == 0  &&  b%2 != 0)   { return 1; }
        if (a == b)                   { return 0; }
        if (a%2 != 0  &&  b%2 == 0)   { return -1; }
}
```

Example 7-20: **Sample820.html**

```
<!DOCTYPE HTML PUBLIC -//W3C//DTD HTML 3.2//EN>
<HTML><HEAD>
<TITLE> Sample 820    Example 7-20 sort odd and even Method</TITLE>

<SCRIPT LANGUAGE="JavaScript1.2"> <!--BEGIN HIDING

myArray1 = new Array(4000,30,33,2,8,701,5,-33,0,111);

document.write(myArray1 + "<P>");

function compareEvenOdd(a,b) {

        if (a%2 == 0  &&  b%2 != 0)    { return 1; }
        if (a == b)                    { return 0; }
        if (a%2 != 0  &&  b%2 == 0)    { return -1; }
}

document.write(myArray1.sort(compareEvenOdd) + "<P>");

        for (var i=0; i<myArray1.length; i++) {

                document.write(myArray1[i] + "<BR>");
        }

//END HIDING-->
</SCRIPT>
</HEAD>
<BODY>
</BODY>
</HTML>
```

The previous example produces the following output:

[4000, 30, 33, 2, 8, 701, 5, -33, 0, 111]

[5, 33, 701, -33, 111, 2, 30, 0, 8, 4000]

5
33
701
-33
111
2
30
0
8
4000

Sorting by String length

This example sorts the Strings in the Array according to their **length**, that is, by how many Characters are in each String. The fewer the Characters in the String, the closer it will be to the Element with an **index** of **[0]**, that is, lower in the Array.

Example 7-21:   **Sample821.html**

```
<!DOCTYPE HTML PUBLIC -//W3C//DTD HTML 3.2//EN>
<HTML>
<HEAD>
<TITLE> Sample 821   Example 7-21 sort by length</TITLE>

<SCRIPT LANGUAGE="JavaScript1.2"> <!--BEGIN HIDING

myArray1 = new Array('fffffffff','aaa','a','bbbbb','c','ccccccc','dd','eee',
                     'eeee','gg');

function compareLengths(a,b) {

        if (a.length > b.length)           { return 1; }
        if (a.length == b.length)          { return 0; }
        if (a.length < b.length)           { return -1; }
}


document.write(myArray1 + "<P>");

myLengthArray = myArray1.sort(compareLengths);

document.write(myLengthArray + "<P>");

//END HIDING-->
</SCRIPT>

</HEAD>

<BODY>
</BODY>
</HTML>
```

The previous example produces the following output:

["fffffffff", "aaa", "a", "bbbbb", "c", "ccccccc", "dd", "eee", "eeee", "gg"]

["c", "a", "dd", "gg", "eee", "aaa", "eeee", "bbbbb", "ccccccc", "fffffffff"]

Working with <u>returned</u> Arrays
Working with <u>returned</u> Arrays
and Regular Expressions

There are three Methods that result in a <u>returned</u> <u>Array</u> if a match is found in a **String** to the **pattern** in a **Regular Expression**. One is the **exec()** Method, which is a Method of Individual Regular Expressions. The other two are the **match()** and **split()** Methods of the **String** Object. This <u>returned</u> <u>Array</u> contains Elements and Properties based on the results of the match, but they differ according to which Method was actually called.

For a <u>returned</u> <u>Array</u> named **myArray**, the **index** and **input** Properties and the Elements at **myArray[0]** and **myArray[1]** to **myArray[n]** are delineated in the following sections. See Chapters 14 and 15 for more background information on returned Arrays.

In the following sections, assume that **myString** is a String Variable and **myRE** is the name of a **Regular Expression**. Also assume that **myArray** is the name of the <u>returned</u> <u>Array</u> as a result of the Method invocation being discussed.

The <u>returned</u> <u>Array</u> from the
<u>match()</u> Method of String Objects

JavaScript Syntax:

```
myArray = anyString.match(regularExpression);
```

For an Array named **myArray** that is returned as a result of invoking the **match()** Method on a **String** Object, the Array Element at **index** zero **[0]** reflects the first and only matched SubString of the calling String named **myString**, that is:

    myArray[0]   =   the first and only matched SubString in **myString**

Furthermore, any <u>Parenthesized SubString matches</u> that are remembered are reflected in the Elements in the Array that are indexed from **[1]** to **[n]** such that:

    myArray[1]   =   the first Parenthesized SubString match in **myString**
    myArray[2]   =   the second Parenthesized SubString match in **myString**
    myArray[n]   =   the last Parenthesized SubString match in **myString**

Finally the **input** and **index** Properties for **myArray** are as follows:

    myArray.input =   the original String **myString**
    myArray.index =   the zero-based Character index of the first matched
                           SubString of **myString**

Example 7-22 demonstrates a <u>returned</u> <u>Array</u> from the **match()** Method, which is assigned to **myArray**. Its Array Elements are then written to screen along with the Values of the **input** and **index** Properties. The browser output follows the code.

Example 7-22:   Sample822.html

```
<!DOCTYPE HTML PUBLIC -//W3C//DTD HTML 3.2//EN>
<HTML>
<HEAD>
<TITLE> Sample 822   Example 7-22 returned Array of match Method</TITLE>

<SCRIPT LANGUAGE="JavaScript1.2"> <!--BEGIN HIDING

        myString = "aaA+B+cc";

        myRE = /(A)(+)(B)/;

        myArray = myString.match(myRE);

        document.write("myArray = " + myArray +  "<P>");

        document.write("myArray[0] = " + myArray[0] +  "<BR>");
        document.write("myArray[1] = " + myArray[1] +  "<BR>");
        document.write("myArray[2] = " + myArray[2] +  "<BR>");
        document.write("myArray[3] = " + myArray[3] +  "<P>");

        document.write("myArray.input = " + myArray.input +  "<BR>");
        document.write("myArray.index = " + myArray.index +  "<BR>");

//END HIDING-->
</SCRIPT>
</HEAD>
<BODY>
</BODY>
</HTML>
```

The previous example produces the following output:

```
myArray       =       ["A+B", "A", "+", "B"]

myArray[0]    =       A+B
myArray[1]    =       A
myArray[2]    =       +
myArray[3]    =       B

myArray.input =       aaA+B+cc
myArray.index =       2
```

The <u>returned</u> <u>Array</u> from the <u>match()</u> Method with the "g" flag

JavaScript Syntax:

```
myArray = anyString.match(/regularExpression/g);
```

Parameters Defined:

For an Array named **myArray** that is returned as a result of invoking the **match()** Method on a **String** Object, which executes a <u>global search</u> over the entire **anyString** and is specified by the "**g**" **flag** Argument in the Regular Expression named **myRE**, the following conditions apply:

myArray[0]	=	the first matched SubString in **myString**
myArray[1]	=	the second matched SubString in **myString**
myArray[2]	=	the third matched SubString in **myString**
myArray[n]	=	the last matched SubString in **myString**

Furthermore, no <u>Parenthesized SubString matches</u> are reflected in the Array.

Finally the **input** and **index** Properties for **myArray** are both **undefined**.

myArray.input =	**undefined**
myArray.index =	**undefined**

The following Example 7-23 is only slightly different from the previous example. The String contained in **myString** is:

"aaA+BccA+B+eeeA+B"

and the Regular Expression **myRE** performs a <u>global search</u> indicated by the "**g**" **flag**.

Unlike the previous example that contained <u>Parenthesized SubString matches</u> in the <u>returned Array</u> **myArray**, this example contains none of them, but it does have all three of the matches found in the <u>global search</u>.

The results of the example are displayed after the code.

Example 7-23:   **Sample823.html**

```
<!DOCTYPE HTML PUBLIC -//W3C//DTD HTML 3.2//EN>
<HTML>
<HEAD>
<TITLE> Sample 823   Example 7-23 returned Array of match Method with g</TITLE>

<SCRIPT LANGUAGE="JavaScript1.2"> <!--BEGIN HIDING

        myString = "aaA+BccA+B+eeeA+B";

        myRE = /(A)(+)(B)/g;


        myArray = myString.match(myRE);


        document.write("myArray = " + myArray +  "<P>");

        document.write("myArray[0] = " + myArray[0] +  "<BR>");
        document.write("myArray[1] = " + myArray[1] +  "<BR>");
        document.write("myArray[2] = " + myArray[2] +  "<P>");

        document.write("myArray.input = " + myArray.input +  "<BR>");
        document.write("myArray.index = " + myArray.index +  "<BR>");


//END HIDING-->
</SCRIPT>

</HEAD>

<BODY>
</BODY>
</HTML>
```

The previous example produces the following output, noting that the vertical alignment of the equals sign and subsequent text in each line is a contrivance of the author, for easier readability:

myArray	=	["A+B", "A+B", "A+B"]
myArray[0]	=	A+B
myArray[1]	=	A+B
myArray[2]	=	A+B
myArray.input	=	undefined
myArray.index	=	undefined

The <u>returned</u> Array from the exec() Method of RegExp Objects

JavaScript Syntax:

```
myArray = regExpName.exec([myString]);
```

Parameters Defined:

The following information is true when the "**g**" **flag** is used to perform a global search with the **exec()** Method <u>and</u> when the "**g**" **flag** is <u>not</u> used, so that a regular search is performed. This is unlike the **match()** Method of the **String** Object, which has different resulting Array Elements, depending on whether the "**g**" **flag** is used or not.

For an Array that is returned as a result of invoking the **exec()** Method on an Individual **RegExp** Object named **myRE**, the Element at **index** zero reflects the <u>first and only</u> matched <u>SubString</u> of the String Argument **myString**.

For Array **Elements** indexed from **[1]** to **[n]**, they reflect any <u>Parenthesized Substring</u> matches specified by the Regular Expression and found in the String Argument that are remembered for later use.

The above paragraphs are summarized in the following chart:

myArray[0] = the first and only matched <u>SubString</u> in **myString**

Furthermore, any <u>Parenthesized SubString matches</u> that are remembered are reflected in the Elements in the Array that are indexed from **[1]** to **[n]** such that:

myArray[1] = the first <u>Parenthesized SubString match</u> in **myString**
myArray[2] = the second <u>Parenthesized SubString match</u> in **myString**
myArray[n] = the last <u>Parenthesized SubString match</u> in **myString**

Finally the **input** and **index** Properties for **myArray** are as follows:

myArray.input = the original String **myString**
myArray.index = the zero-based Character **index** of the first matched <u>SubString</u> of **myString**

The above information is demonstrated in the following example, which is only slightly different from the previous two examples. In this example, there are two Regular Expressions that differ only in that one performs a global search and the other doesn't. The resulting Arrays and Elements for both invocations of the **exec()** Method are displayed in the browser, so that you can see that exactly the same results occur whether or not the "**g**" **flag** is used.

Example 7-24:   **Sample824.html**

```
<!DOCTYPE HTML PUBLIC -//W3C//DTD HTML 3.2//EN>
<HTML>
<HEAD>
<TITLE> Sample 824    Example 7-24 returned Array of exec Method</TITLE>

<SCRIPT LANGUAGE="JavaScript1.2"> <!--BEGIN HIDING

        myString = "aaA+BccA+B+eeeA+B";

        myRE = /(A)(+)(B)/;

        myArray = myRE.exec(myString);

        document.write("myArray = " + myArray +  "<P>");

        document.write("myArray[0] = " + myArray[0] +  "<BR>");
        document.write("myArray[1] = " + myArray[1] +  "<BR>");
        document.write("myArray[2] = " + myArray[2] +  "<BR>");
        document.write("myArray[3] = " + myArray[3] +  "<P>");

        document.write("myArray.input = " + myArray.input +  "<BR>");
        document.write("myArray.index = " + myArray.index +  "<P>");


/*----------------------------------------------------------------*/


document.write("<B>This section deals with the global search.<\/B><P>");

        myRE2 = /(A)(+)(B)/g;

        my2Array = myRE2.exec(myString);

        document.write("my2Array = " + my2Array +  "<P>");

        document.write("my2Array[0] = " + my2Array[0] +  "<BR>");
        document.write("my2Array[1] = " + my2Array[1] +  "<BR>");
        document.write("my2Array[2] = " + my2Array[2] +  "<BR>");
        document.write("my2Array[3] = " + my2Array[3] +  "<P>");

        document.write("my2Array.input = " + my2Array.input +  "<BR>");
        document.write("my2Array.index = " + my2Array.index +  "<BR>");


//END HIDING-->
</SCRIPT>

</HEAD>

<BODY>
</BODY>
</HTML>
```

The previous example produces the following output:

myArray	=	["A+B", "A", "+", "B"]
myArray[0]	=	A+B
myArray[1]	=	A
myArray[2]	=	+
myArray[3]	=	B
myArray.input	=	aaA+BccA+B+eeeA+B
myArray.index	=	2

This section deals with the global search.

my2Array	=	["A+B", "A", "+", "B"]
my2Array[0]	=	A+B
my2Array[1]	=	A
my2Array[2]	=	+
my2Array[3]	=	B
my2Array.input	=	aaA+BccA+B+eeeA+B
my2Array.index	=	2

The <u>index</u> Property of the Array Object

The **index** Property represents the zero-based Character **index** of the searched String where the match to the **pattern** in the Regular Expression is made. For instance, in the following String named **myString** and the Regular Expression named **myRegExp**:

```
myString = "All the world's a Stage";
myRegExp = /world/;
myArray  = myRegExp.exec(myString);
```

Then for the <u>returned Array</u> **myArray**, resulting from the match to the **pattern** in **myRegExp**, **myArray.index** would be equal to 8, because the first Character of "world" is located at the Character **index** of 8 as you count the Characters in **myString** from left to right, where the **index** of the first Character is 0, the second Character is 1, and so on.

The <u>returned</u> <u>Array</u> from the <u>split()</u> Method of String Objects

JavaScript Syntax:

```
myArray = myString.split([separator], [limit]);
```

<u>Parameters Defined:</u>

For an Array named **myArray** that is returned as a result of invoking the **split()** Method on a **String** Object, it is completely different from the returned Arrays of the previous Methods of **match()** and **exec()**. If there are *no* <u>Parenthesized SubExpressions</u> in the Regular Expression, then the Array Elements from **index [0]** to **[n]** reflect SubStrings between the Regular Expression **separator** Argument of the calling String named **myString** like this:

myArray[0]	=	the first SubString extracted from **myString**
myArray[1]	=	the second SubString extracted from **myString**
myArray[2]	=	the third SubString extracted from **myString**
myArray[n]	=	the last SubString extracted from **myString**

Furthermore, any <u>Parenthesized SubExpression separators</u> that are Remembered are reflected in the Elements of the Array that are indexed from **[0]** to **[n]** such that they are interspersed with the **split** SubStrings in the same order that they occur in the original **myString** as it is read from left to right.

myArray[0]	=	the first SubString <u>*or*</u> Remembered separator extracted
myArray[1]	=	the second SubString <u>*or*</u> Remembered separator extracted
myArray[2]	=	the third SubString <u>*or*</u> Remembered separator extracted
myArray[n]	=	the last SubString <u>*or*</u> Remembered separator extracted

Finally the **input** and **index** Properties for **myArray** are both **undefined**.

myArray.input =	**undefined**
myArray.index =	**undefined**

The following example demonstrates the **split()** Method in two scenarios. The first deals with a Regular Expression used as the separator Argument that has no remembered separators, and the second Regular Expression does have the remembered separator Character of "%", which is specified by (%).

The Regular Expression named **myRE** splits on the "+" Character followed by a space Character. The Regular Expression named **myRE2** splits on the "%" Character, which is remembered, followed by a space Character.

The **split()** Method is called on the String Variables **str** and **str2**, and then the resulting Arrays **splitArray** and **split2Array** and their Elements are rendered to screen.

Example 7-25: Sample825.html

```
<!DOCTYPE HTML PUBLIC -//W3C//DTD HTML 3.2//EN>
<HTML><HEAD>
<TITLE> Sample 825   Example 7-25 returned Array of split Method</TITLE>

<SCRIPT LANGUAGE="JavaScript1.2"> <!--BEGIN HIDING

str = "1 + 2 + 3 + 4 + 5"

      //myRE splits on "+" followed by a space.

myRE = /+\s/;

splitArray = str.split(myRE);

document.write("<B>" + splitArray + "<\/B><P>");

document.write(splitArray[0] + "<BR>");
document.write(splitArray[1] + "<BR>");
document.write(splitArray[2] + "<BR>");
document.write(splitArray[3] + "<BR>");
document.write(splitArray[4] + "<P>");
/*----------------------------------------------------------------------*/

str2 = "1% 2% 3% 4%"

//myRE2 splits on "%" followed by a space and "%" is remembered
//and therefore each occurrence is in an Array Element.
//Note that myRE2 does not match the "%" after "4" because there is no space.

myRE2 = /(%)\s/;

split2Array = str2.split(myRE2);

document.write("<B>" + split2Array + "<\/B><P>");

document.write(split2Array[0] + "<BR>");
document.write(split2Array[1] + "<BR>");
document.write(split2Array[2] + "<BR>");
document.write(split2Array[3] + "<BR>");
document.write(split2Array[4] + "<BR>");
document.write(split2Array[5] + "<BR>");
document.write(split2Array[6] + "<P>");

document.write(split2Array.index + "<BR>");
document.write(split2Array.input + "<BR>");

//END HIDING-->
</SCRIPT>
</HEAD>
<BODY>
</BODY>
</HTML>
```

The preceding example produces the following results in the browser. Notice that in the second Array named **split2Array** that the last Element at **index [6]** is "4%"; the Regular Expression **myRE2** does not match the "%" after "4", because there is no space Character after the "%" Character. This means that the "4%" String is a split String and <u>not</u> a Remembered separator.

["1 ", "2 ", "3 ", "4 ", "5"]

1

2

3

4

5

["1", "%", "2", "%", "3", "%", "4%"]

1

%

2

%

3

%

4%

undefined

undefined

For more information on Arrays and how they interact with Strings and Regular Expressions, see Chapter 8 on **String** Objects and Chapter 9 on **RegExp** Objects.

The <u>input</u> Property of the Array Object

When you use the **exec()** Method of a Regular Expression or the **match()** Method of a **String** Object, if a match to the **pattern** contained in the Regular Expression is found in the searched String, then an Array is returned that contains the last match and certain Properties are either set or updated. One of these Properties is the **input** Property, which represents the original String that matched the Regular Expression.

<u>Mini-Example:</u>

For example, suppose you have the String variable **myString** set to:

```
myString = "All the world's a Stage";
```

and you have a Regular Expression named **myRegExp** created with **Literal** notation:

```
myRegExp = /world/;
```

Then using the **exec()** Method on **myRegExp** returns an Array assigned to **myArray**:

```
myArray = myRegExp.exec(myString);
```

so that:

```
document.write(myArray);
```

outputs to the browser:

```
["world"]
```

and:

```
document.write(myArray.input);
```

outputs to the browser:

```
"All the world's a Stage"
```

Using Arrays to fill
\<TABLE> Element Data Dynamically

The next example uses a FRAMESET with two FRAMES. The document that is loaded into the top FRAME named **display** contains all of the pertinent code. The page that is loaded into the FRAME named **main** is just a placeholder, because all the relevant code for that FRAME is created on-the-fly with the **makeTable()** Function, which is assigned to the **onClick** Event Handler of the Button named **B1**.

This example does several things. It demonstrates how you can create a TABLE Element on-the-fly using JavaScript, where the number of rows in the TABLE are based on user input. The data for the Cells of the TABLE is stored in two Arrays. One Array holds Elements that consist of JavaScript color names, and the other Array has Hexadecimal color Values. The data is arranged in two Arrays so that the Element at the **index** number of one Array holds the color name that corresponds to its Hexadecimal equivalent, which is contained in the other Array at exactly the same **index** number. For example, in the two Arrays **Array1** and **Array2**:

```
Array1[0] = "aqua";
Array2[0] = "00ffff";
```

The Script starts with the **makeTable()** Function, which defines Variables for the Layer named **L2**, the TextBox named **Text6**, and an integer Variable named **NumRows** that uses the **parseInt()** Method to convert the numeric String from the **value** Property of **Text6**, which is input by the user, to an integer in base 10. The Value of **NumRows** is used to determine the number of Rows that will be in the TABLE that is created.

Next, the two **dense** Arrays named **Array1** and **Array2** are created with all of the Elements defined at the outset by using the Array Constructor.

Then the **document** Object of the **main** FRAME is opened, and the basic HTML is coded to start the page, which is followed by the Style Sheet code. Next, the code to start the TABLE Element is written. The crux of the Script is the **for()** Statement, nested inside an **if()** Statement that only works if the number of Rows selected by the user is greater than 0 and less than 16. You test the user input because a TABLE with no Rows is irrelevant, and because you only have 15 Rows worth of data in your Arrays, you don't want any Rows in your TABLE to say "undefined".

The **for()** Statement loops through the var **j** from 0 through **NumRows**, and for each var **j**, a Row in the TABLE is created that has two TD Cells. Each of these TD Cells contains an \<ILAYER>. An Array Element from **Array1** in the left \<ILAYER> and an Array Element from **Array2** in the right \<ILAYER>.

If the user chooses any Characters other than 1 to 15, then an **alert** Window sends a message to pick a number from 1 to 15. The FRAMESET for this example is contained in Sample826Frameset.html, and the useful code is contained in Sample826.html.

Example 7-26 Part 1: **Sample826.html**

```
<!DOCTYPE HTML PUBLIC "-//W3C//DTD HTML 3.2//EN">
<HTML>
<HEAD>
<TITLE> Sample 826   Example 7-26 Creating a Color Table</TITLE>

<STYLE TYPE="text/JavaScript">

        classes.Mainbody.BODY.margins("0px");
        classes.Mainbody.BODY.paddings("0px");
        classes.Mainbody.BODY.backgroundColor="purple";
        classes.Mainbody.BODY.color="white";
        classes.Mainbody.BODY.fontSize="20pt";

</STYLE>

<SCRIPT LANGUAGE="JavaScript1.2"><!--BEGIN HIDING

function makeTable()  {

        var L2 = document.L2

        var Text6 = L2.document.form1.Text6;
        var NumRows = parseInt(Text6.value);

        var Array1 = new Array("aqua", "blue", "green", "yellow", "red", "purple",
"orange", "maroon", "black", "white", "plum", "darkgreen", "mediumblue",
"lightblue", "steelblue");

        var Array2 = new Array("00ffff", "0000ff", "008000", "ffff00", "ff0000",
"800080", "ffa500", "800000", "000000", "ffffff", "dda0dd", "006400", "0000cd",
"add8e6", "4682b4");

/*---------------------------------------------------------------------*/

        parent.main.document.open();
        parent.main.document.write('<HTML><HEAD><TITLE> Test Table <\/TITLE>');
        parent.main.document.write('<STYLE TYPE="text/JavaScript">');

        parent.main.document.write('tags.BODY.fontSize = "6pt";');
        parent.main.document.write('tags.LAYER.borderWidths("20px");');
        parent.main.document.write('tags.LAYER.borderStyle = "groove";');
        parent.main.document.write('tags.LAYER.borderColor = "lime";');

        parent.main.document.write('tags.ILAYER.borderWidths("10px");');
        parent.main.document.write('tags.ILAYER.borderStyle = "ridge";');
        parent.main.document.write('tags.ILAYER.borderColor = "#8800ff";');
        parent.main.document.write('tags.ILAYER.width="200px";');
        parent.main.document.write('tags.ILAYER.fontSize = "20pt";');

        parent.main.document.write('ids.L1.width="450px";');
        parent.main.document.write('ids.L1.margins("0px");');

        parent.main.document.write('<\/STYLE>');
```

```
            parent.main.document.write('<\/HEAD>');
            parent.main.document.write('<BODY BGCOLOR="mediumblue" TEXT="black">');

            parent.main.document.write('<LAYER ID="L1" LEFT="20" TOP="20" BGCOLOR="red">');
            parent.main.document.write('<TABLE BORDER="20" WIDTH="420">');
/*----------------------------------------------------------------------*/

if (NumRows > 0  &&  NumRows < 16) {

            for (var j=0; j<NumRows; j++) {

                    parent.main.document.write('<TR>');

                    parent.main.document.write('<TD>');
                    parent.main.document.write('<ILAYER BGCOLOR="yellow">');
                    parent.main.document.write(Array1[j]);
                    parent.main.document.write('<\/ILAYER>');
                    parent.main.document.write('<\/TD>');

                    parent.main.document.write('<TD>');
                    parent.main.document.write('<ILAYER BGCOLOR="orange">');
                    parent.main.document.write(Array2[j]);
                    parent.main.document.write('<\/ILAYER>');
                    parent.main.document.write('<\/TD>');

                    parent.main.document.write('<\/TR>');
            }
}
else { alert("Pick a number from 1 to 15") }

/*----------------------------------------------------------------------*/

            parent.main.document.write('<\/TABLE>');
            parent.main.document.write('<\/LAYER>');
            parent.main.document.write('<\/BODY><\/HTML>');
            parent.main.document.close();
 }


/*----------------------------------------------------------------------*/
//END HIDING-->
</SCRIPT>
</HEAD>
<BODY CLASS="Mainbody">

<LAYER ID="L2" LEFT="20" TOP="20">                          <FORM NAME="form1">

<INPUT TYPE="button" NAME="B1" VALUE="Create Table" onClick="makeTable();">

<INPUT TYPE="text" NAME="Text6" VALUE="" SIZE="2">

How many Rows of Color Information do you want?<BR>
Pick a number from 1 to 15 and click the button to render the Table.     </FORM>

</LAYER>
</BODY>
</HTML>
```

Example 7-26   Sample826Frameset.html

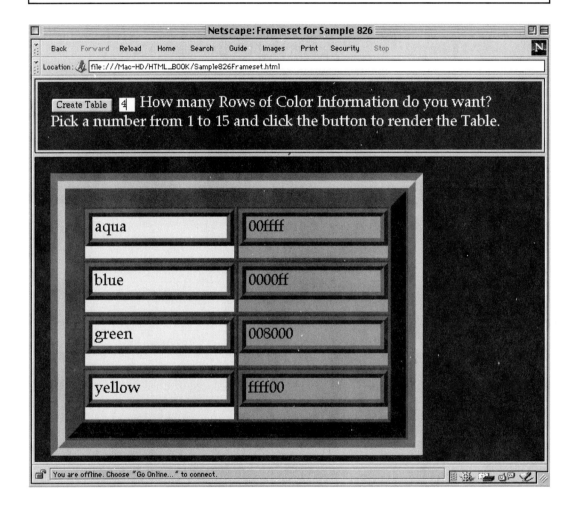

This is the Frameset for Example 7-26.

Example 7-26 Part 2:   Sample826-Frameset.html

```
<!DOCTYPE HTML PUBLIC "-//W3C//DTD HTML 3.2//EN">
<HTML>
<HEAD>
      <TITLE>Frameset for Sample 826</TITLE>
</HEAD>

<FRAMESET ROWS="100,*">

      <FRAME SCROLLING="auto" NAME="display" SRC="Sample826.html">

      <FRAME SCROLLING="auto" NAME="main" SRC="Sample826Main.html">

</FRAMESET>

</HTML>
```

This is the code for Sample826Main.html, which is just used as a placeholder file in the Sample826-Frameset.html file, which contains the Frameset used in Example 7-26. Note that this placeholder file is actually necessary because the SRC Attribute for the FRAME Elment is required.

Example 7-26 Part 3:   Sample826Main.html

```
<!DOCTYPE HTML PUBLIC "-//W3C//DTD HTML 3.2//EN">
<HTML>
<HEAD>
      <TITLE>  Sample 826Main   Example 13-26Main  </TITLE>
</HEAD>

<BODY>

</BODY>
</HTML>
```

Chart of Sample Files that use Arrays

Here are some other Samples from the book that use Arrays in addition to the ones in Chapter 7. You can find the page number that the Sample code is located on by going to the Chart in Appendix C, on pages 1039-1048, which contains the page number reference for all Examples and Samples contained in the book.

If you open a Sample from a CD-ROM in a text editor like BBEdit, you can easily find the Array Usage by going to the Line # listed below.

Sample File , Line #   Array Usage

Sample File , Line #	Array Usage
Sample424.html, Line 46:	colorArray = new Array
Sample425.html, Line 57:	document.L1.bgColor = colorArray[i-1];
Sample431.html, Line 34:	a1 = new Array("./JPEG-FILES/icon-BG-asteroids.jpg", ...
Sample432.html, Line 31:	numArray[0] = appendNum(numArray[0], num);
Sample432.html, Line 173:	numArray[0] = Math.round(numArray[0]);
Sample434.html, Line 20:	rgbArray = new Array(3);
Sample434.html, Line 226:	rgbArray[0] = getChar.charAt(0) + getChar.charAt(1);
Sample434.html, Line 229:	rgbArray[0] = parseInt(rgbArray[0] , 16);
Sample434.html, Line 289:	if (isNaN(a1)) {rgbArray[1] = '00';
Sample434.html, Line 335:	'#0' + rgbArray[0] + '0' + rgbArray[1] + '00';
Sample456.html, Line 59:	if (Array1[j] == "") alert("You forgot to fill in a field.");
Sample456.html, Line 62:	parent.main.document.write(Array2[j]);
Sample912.html, Line 8:	gotItArray = str.match(myRegExp);
Sample912.html, Line 10:	document.write(gotItArray);
Sample1004.html, Line 17:	var myArray = myRE1.exec();
Sample1005.html, Line 11:	myArray = myRE.exec(myStr);
Sample1006.html, Line 18:	var myArray = myRE1.exec(str);
Sample1007.html, Line 14:	myMatchArray = str1.match(myRE1);
Sample1008.html, Line 14:	myExecArray = myRE1.exec(str1);
Sample1011.html, Line 26:	var myArray = myRE1.exec(str);

Part II
JavaScript 1.2

Chapter 8

JavaScript Strings

Chapter 8
JavaScript Strings

Contents

JavaScript String Objects

The JavaScript String Object

Put simply, a **String** Object consists of text. There are two ways to create a **String** Object. You can use the **String** Object Constructor or you can use Literal notation. Additionally, you can define a String and assign it as the Value of a Variable. Strings that are created with Literal notation are also considered **String** Objects.

Each **String** Object has two Properties: the **length** Property and the **prototype** Property. The **length** Property specifies the number of Characters in a String and cannot be changed, so it is said to be <u>read-only</u>. The **prototype** Property is used to create new Properties for your **String** Object, which you can define to your own specifications.

String Objects obviously consist of Characters. These Characters are stored in JavaScript in a Character Array that you can access by calling an Element of the Character Array by its **index** number. The Characters appear in the Array so that as the String is read from left to right, they will appear in the Array from top to bottom; that is, the Character at Element **index** 0 will be the first Character in the String. It should be noted that this Character count does include white space, so that the String "Hey Now" would have seven Characters, not six.

There are a variety of Methods that you can use to work with your **String** Objects. The Methods of the **String** Object fall into the two general categories of text decoration that parallel HTML Attributes and text manipulation that gets into the fancy behind-the-scenes JavaScript. These Manipulative Methods all return a String or an Array of Strings at the end of their processing. The **anchor** and **link** Methods don't fit either category.

The <u>Decorative</u> Methods are:

big, blink, bold, fixed, fontcolor, fontsize, italics, small, strike, sub, sup, toLowerCase, toUpperCase

The <u>Manipulative</u> Methods are:

charAt, charCodeAt, concat, fromCharCode, indexOf, lastIndexOf, match, replace, search, slice, split, substr, substring

The following Methods were implemented in or changed in Navigator 4.0:

charCodeAt, concat, fromCharCode, replace, search, slice, split, substr, substring

String Object Property Summaries

Property	Description
length	Reflects the number of Characters in a String. This is <u>read-only</u>.
prototype	Lets you create your own Properties for the **String** Object.

String Object Method Summaries

Method	Description
anchor()	Parallels the \<A\> Tag creating an anchor that is used as a hypertext target.
big()	Parallels the \<BIG\> Tag to display a bigger String.
blink()	Parallels the \<BLINK\> Tag to display a blinking String.
bold()	Parallels the \<B\> Tag to display a boldface String.
charAt()	Returns a String containing the Character at the specified **index** within the calling String.
charCodeAt()	Returns a number that specifies the ISO-Latin-1 codeset Value of the Character at the indicated **index** within the calling String.
concat()	Returns a String that is the combination of two specified Strings.
fixed()	Parallels the \<TT\> Tag to display a fixed-width String.
fontcolor()	Parallels the \<FONT COLOR="color"\> Tag to change the color of the specified String.
fontsize()	Parallels the \<FONT SIZE=size\> Tag to change the size of the specified String.
fromCharCode()	Converts one or more numbers that are ISO-Latin-1 codeset Values into ASCII Characters and returns them as a String.
indexOf()	Returns a numeric String that is the **index** number within the calling String for the <u>*first*</u> occurrence of the specified pattern that is found inside that calling String.

italics()	Parallels the <I> Tag to display an italicized String.
lastIndexOf()	Returns a numeric String that is the **index** number within the calling String for the *last* occurrence of the specified pattern that is found inside that calling String.
link()	Parallels the <A> Tag transforming a String into an HTML hypertext link to a specified URL.
match()	Matches a Regular Expression pattern against the calling String and returns an Array of Strings reflecting the matches.
replace()	Matches a Regular Expression pattern against the calling String and replaces the matched Substring with a new Substring.
search()	Matches a Regular Expression pattern against the calling String and returns the **index** within the calling String of the match.
slice()	Returns a new String that consists of a part of the calling String.
small()	Parallels the <SMALL> Tag to display a smaller String.
split()	Returns an Array of Substrings resulting from splitting up the calling String based on a separator that can be a String or a Regular Expression.
strike()	Parallels the <STRIKE> Tag to display a strikeout String.
sub()	Parallels the <SUB> Tag to display a subscripted String.
substr()	Returns a String consisting of Characters that are specified by a starting **index** and an optional number that specifies the quantity of Characters to extract from the calling String.
substring()	Returns a String consisting of Characters that are specified by a starting **index** and an optional ending **index** that specifies the Characters to extract from the calling String.
sup()	Parallels the <SUP> Tag to display a superscripted String.
toLowerCase()	Converts the calling String to lowercase Characters and returns it.
toUpperCase()	Converts the calling String to uppercase Characters and returns it.

Chapter 9 goes into great detail concerning **RegExp** Objects and how they interact with **String** Objects and **Array** Objects. For now, only the rudimentary aspects of the **RegExp** Object will be used in this chapter.

Using the String Object Constructor Function

To create a String with the **String** Object Constructor, you use the Keyword **new** and the **String** Object Constructor Function, where the Argument **anyString** is the Value of the **String** Object, like this:

Mini-Examples:

```
new String("anyString");
```

Typically you would assign it to a Variable like this:

```
myString = new String("Let's Play");
```

so that the Variable **myString** has a Value of "Let's Play" and has a **length** of 10.

Create a String Object with Literal notation

String Objects can be created with **Literal** notation simply by enclosing the text inside double quotes or single quotes. It doesn't matter which version of the quote marks that you use, but you must be consistent in that if you start enclosing a String with double quotes, then you must also end the String with double quotes. Pretty simple conceptually, but we've all had to go back and make changes in complicated Statements that employ numerous quotes of both types, because it's tricky to track all of them in your head.

You can even have numbers inside of your **String** Objects. If a **String** Object is composed entirely of numeral Characters, then it is said to be a Numeric String. If a String has a combination of letters and numbers, it is said to be a Mixed Numeric String.

Mini-Examples:

Here are several examples of **String** Objects:

```
"Mountains on the Moon"
'DreamPlay Studios'
'blue'
"555"
"451 Ocean Boulevard"
```

JavaScript Special Characters in Strings

There are several Characters that have a special meaning when they are preceded by a backslash Character in JavaScript. They are:

Character	Definition
\b	backspace
\f	form feed
\n	new line
\r	carriage return
\t	tab
\\	backslash Character

One typical use for them would be when you create an **alert** Window, and you want to augment the text that is to be displayed. An **alert** Window does not respond to HTML tags, carrige returns, tabs, and so on, when they are entered from your keyboard in your text editor. Consequently, if you want to format the **alert**, you have to use these Special Character designations.

Mini-Example:

For example if you had the following **alert**:

```
alert("Close to the Edge," +
    " Down by the River.")
```

it would render in the browser **alert** Window like this:

Close to the Edge, Down by the River.

But if you have the following **alert**:

```
alert("Close to the Edge, \rDown by the River.")
```

it would render in the browser **alert** Window like this:

Close to the Edge,
Down by the River.

The String Object Character Array

Every **String** Object has an associated Character Array that contains all of the Characters in the String, so that each Character of the String is assigned to one Element of the Array. This means that each Element in the Character Array has precisely one Character in it. The **String** Object is read from left to right, and the leftmost Character is the first Element in the Character Array. The next Character in the String is the next Element in the Character Array and so on. A blank space in a text String counts as a Character.

<u>Mini-Example:</u>

For example if you had the following String:

```
myString = new String("DreamPlay Studios");
```

its **length** would be 17; that is, there would be 17 Characters and 17 Elements in the Character Array because the blank space between the two words counts as one Character. The Elements in the Character Array would be equal to the following chart:

```
myString[0]  = "D";
myString[1]  = "r";
myString[2]  = "e";
myString[3]  = "a";
myString[4]  = "m";
myString[5]  = "P";
myString[6]  = "l";
myString[7]  = "a";
myString[8]  = "y";
myString[9]  = " ";
myString[10] = "S";
myString[11] = "t";
myString[12] = "u";
myString[13] = "d";
myString[14] = "i";
myString[15] = "o";
myString[16] = "s";
```

Special Notice:

It should be noted that these Character Array Elements are <u>read-only</u>, which means that you can test for them or display them, but you can't change them.

Manipulative String Object Methods

The <u>concat()</u> Method of String Object

JavaScript Syntax:

```
stringName1.concat(stringName2);
("stringLiteral1").concat("stringLiteral2");
```

<u>Parameters Defined:</u>

The **concat()** Method returns a new **String** Object that combines the text of **stringName1** and **stringName2**. Any changes to one of the **String** Objects will have no effect on the other **String** Object. The only reason there are two versions of the syntax is to remind you that if you use actual text, signified by **stringLiteral1** and **stringLiteral2**, instead of a text Variable, then you need to enclose it in quotes or double quotes. Forgetting to quote your text is one of the most frequent minor "space-outs" in coding.

For instance, if you have the String "Carpe Diem means: " and another String "Seize the Day.", then to concatenate those two Strings you would code it like this:

```
("Carpe Diem means: ").concat("Seize the Day.")
```

which would produce the following String:

```
Carpe Diem means: Seize the Day.
```

If you have the following two Strings assigned to String Variables:

var **str1** = "Tales from "
var **str2** = "Topographic Oceans"

Then, to join those two Strings with the **concat()** Method, code it like this:

```
str1.concat(str2)
```

which would return the following String:

```
Tales from Topographic Oceans
```

Example 8-0 creates a Function named **concatIt()** and defines two String Variables, **myString1** and **myString2**, by assigning each one a String Literal. Next, it uses the **concat()** Method to join these two Strings and assigns the result to the **value** Property of the text box named **text1**. Finally the **concatIt()** Function is assigned to the **onClick** Event Handler of the button named **B1**, which implements the concatenation and renders it to screen.

Example 8-0:   **Sample900.html**

```
<!DOCTYPE HTML PUBLIC -//W3C//DTD HTML 3.2//EN>
<HTML> <HEAD> <TITLE> Sample 900    Example 8-0 concat Method </TITLE>

<SCRIPT LANGUAGE="JavaScript1.2"> <!--BEGIN HIDING

        function concatIt() {

                var myString1 = "Have a ";
                var myString2 = "great day.";

                document.form1.text1.value = "";

                document.form1.text1.value = myString1.concat(myString2);
        }

//END HIDING-->
</SCRIPT>
</HEAD>
<BODY>
<FORM NAME="form1">

<INPUT TYPE="button" NAME="B1" VALUE="concat the Strings" onClick="concatIt();">

<INPUT TYPE="text" NAME="text1" SIZE="30" VALUE="Greetings">

</FORM>
</BODY>
</HTML>
```

Example 8-1 demonstrates the **concat()** Method inside of the Function named **concatIt()** by first creating three String Variables named **myString1**, **myString2**, and **myString3**. The first two String Variables each get assigned a **value** Property from one of the text Elements named **text1** and **text2**. Next, **myString3** is assigned the String resulting from concatenating **myString1** with **myString2**, which is then assigned to the **value** Property of **text3**.

Finally, the **concatIt()** Function is assigned to the **onClick** Event Handler of the button **B1** so that when it is clicked, the text is collected from the first two text boxes and joined together and displayed in the third text box. The **focus()** Method just puts the cursor in the first text box to start the next input session. The reason for the **null** Strings is to prevent a String buildup. This way you start each joining with a blank String.

Example 8-1: **Sample901.html**

```
<!DOCTYPE HTML PUBLIC -//W3C//DTD HTML 3.2//EN>
<HTML>
<HEAD>
<TITLE> Sample 901   Example 8-1 concat Method</TITLE>

<SCRIPT LANGUAGE="JavaScript1.2"> <!--BEGIN HIDING

        function concatIt() {

                var myString1 = document.form1.text1.value;
                var myString2 = document.form1.text2.value;
                var myString3 = myString1.concat(myString2);

                document.form1.text1.value = "";
                document.form1.text2.value = "";
                document.form1.text3.value = myString3;
                document.form1.text1.focus();
        }

//END HIDING-->
</SCRIPT>

</HEAD>

<BODY>

<FORM NAME="form1">

First Text String...
<INPUT TYPE="text" NAME="text1" SIZE="30" VALUE="Hey ">              <BR>

Second Text String...
<INPUT TYPE="text" NAME="text2" SIZE="30" VALUE="Now">              <BR>

<INPUT TYPE="button" NAME="B1" VALUE="concat the Strings" onClick="concatIt();">

<BR>

<INPUT TYPE="text" NAME="text3" SIZE="30" VALUE="">

</FORM>

</BODY>
</HTML>
```

Example 8-2 very simply demonstrates that a change made to one String does not change the other String that was joined to it, nor does it change the resulting concatenated String.

Example 8-2:   Sample902.html

```
<!DOCTYPE HTML PUBLIC -//W3C//DTD HTML 3.2//EN>
<HTML>
<HEAD>
<TITLE>        Sample 902    Example 8-2       concat Method          </TITLE>


<SCRIPT LANGUAGE="JavaScript1.2"> <!--BEGIN HIDING

        var myString1 = "Hello, ";

        var myString2 = "My Name is ";

        var myString3 = myString1.concat(myString2);


        document.write(myString3 +  "<P>");

//Notice that the change to myString1 does not change myString2 or myString3.

        myString1 = "Greetings ";


        document.write(myString1 +  "<P>");

        document.write(myString2 +  "<P>");

        document.write(myString3 +  "<P>");


//Notice that the change to myString1 does change myString3
//if you concat the two strings again.


        myString3 = myString1.concat(myString2);

        document.write(myString3 +  "<P>");


//END HIDING-->
</SCRIPT>

</HEAD>

<BODY>

</BODY>
</HTML>
```

The <u>charAt()</u> Method of String Object

JavaScript Syntax:

```
stringName.charAt(index);
("stringLiteral").charAt(index);
```

Parameters Defined:

Every **String** Object has an inherent Character Array associated with it. The **charAt()** Method accesses this Character Array and returns the Character residing in the Array Element that is specified by the **index** Argument. When JavaScript creates the Character Array internally, it indexes the String from left to right and then assigns each Character to its own Element, starting from vertical top to bottom in the Character Array. Note that, technically, they start from bottom to top, because the bottom of the Array starts at **index** 0, but since we code from page top to bottom in text editors, this is counterintuitive.

The **index** of the first Character is 0 (zero), the second Character has an **index** of 1 and so on. The last Character would have an **index** of **length - 1**. For example, the String named **starString** would have its last Character with the **index** of **starString.length - 1**. This can be used within a **for()** Loop as the condition to test for if you wanted to display all of the Characters in a String with the **charAt()** Method like this:

```
for( var i=0; i<starString.length-1; i++) {

        document.write(starString.charAt(i) + "<BR>");
}
```

If **starString** had the Value of "STAR", then the preceding **for()** Loop would output:

```
S
T
A
R
```

The following code:

```
myString = new String("DreamPlay Studios");

document.write(myString.charAt(0) + "<BR>");
document.write(myString.charAt(1) + "<BR>");
document.write(myString.charAt(2) + "<BR>");
document.write(myString.charAt(3) + "<BR>");
document.write(myString.charAt(4) + "<BR>");
```

would display in the browser like this:

D
r
e
a
m

Out of Bounds index Property Behavior

If you supply an **index** to the **charAt()** Method that is larger than one less than the number of Characters in the String, JavaScript will return an empty String. Remember that the **index** numbers start at zero, so if you have a String with 13 Characters the **index** range would be from 0 to 12.

This example uses the **charAt()** Method to test for the Value of the Character at **index** 0 and changes the background color of the document when the user clicks on one of the two Buttons that supplies the **color** Argument to the Function **changeIt()**.

Example 8-3: Sample903.html

```
<!DOCTYPE HTML PUBLIC -//W3C//DTD HTML 3.2//EN>
<HTML>
<HEAD>
<TITLE> Sample 903    Example 8-3 charAt Method</TITLE>

<SCRIPT LANGUAGE="JavaScript1.2"> <!--BEGIN HIDING

        function changeIt(color) {

                var myString = color;
                if (myString.charAt(0) == 'b') document.bgColor='blue';
                if (myString.charAt(0) == 'r') document.bgColor='red';
        }

//END HIDING-->
</SCRIPT>
</HEAD>
<BODY>
<FORM NAME="form1">

<INPUT TYPE="button" NAME="B1" VALUE="blue" onClick="changeIt('blue');">
<INPUT TYPE="button" NAME="B2" VALUE="red" onClick="changeIt('red');">

</FORM>

</BODY>
</HTML>
```

The <u>charCodeAt()</u> Method of String Object

JavaScript Syntax:

```
stringName.charCodeAt([index]);
("stringLiteral").charCodeAt([index]);
```

Parameters Defined:

The **charCodeAt()** Method returns the number that represents the ISO-Latin-1 codeset Value of the Character at the specified **index** Argument. The **index** Argument is optional and if unspecified, the default Value is 0 (zero). Acceptable Values for the **index** are integers from 0 to **stringName.length - 1**, that is, one less than the number of Characters in the String.

The ISO-Latin-1 codeset numbers range from 0-255, with the numbers 0-127 being identical to the ASCII Character set. For the complete listing of ISO-Latin-1 and ASCII codeset Values, you can try visiting the website of "Best Business Solutions" (BBS) at <u>http://www.bbsinc.com</u>. The Chart is at <u>http://www.bbsinc.com/symbol.html</u> or on the CD-ROM in the file named <u>ISO-Latin-1-Char-Entities.html</u> in the "<u>html-Character-Codes</u>" Folder in the "<u>Docs_for_Book</u>" Folder.

This example defines a String Variable named **str** and assigns it the Value of "abcde" and then uses the **charCodeAt()** Method within the **write()** Method to display the ISO-Latin-1 codeset Value of each Character in **str**. Next, it repeats the technique for the String Literal "ABCDE".

Example 8-4:   **Sample904.html**

```
<!DOCTYPE HTML PUBLIC -//W3C//DTD HTML 3.2//EN>
<HTML>
<HEAD>
<TITLE> Sample 904    Example 8-4 charCodeAt Method</TITLE>

<SCRIPT LANGUAGE="JavaScript1.2"> <!--BEGIN HIDING

str = "abcde";

document.write(str.charCodeAt(0) + " is the number for 'a'<P>");

document.write(str.charCodeAt(1) + " is the number for 'b'<P>");

document.write(str.charCodeAt(2) + " is the number for 'c'<P>");
```

```
document.write(str.charCodeAt(3) + " is the number for 'd'<P>");

document.write(str.charCodeAt(4) + " is the number for 'e'");


document.write(("ABCDE").charCodeAt(0) + " is the number for 'A'<P>");

document.write(("ABCDE").charCodeAt(1) + " is the number for 'B'<P>");

document.write(("ABCDE").charCodeAt(2) + " is the number for 'C'<P>");

document.write(("ABCDE").charCodeAt(3) + " is the number for 'D'<P>");

document.write(("ABCDE").charCodeAt(4) + " is the number for 'E'<P>");
//END HIDING-->
</SCRIPT>

</HEAD>

<BODY>
</BODY>
</HTML>
```

The previous example produces the following output:

65 is the number for 'A'

66 is the number for 'B'

67 is the number for 'C'

68 is the number for 'D'

69 is the number for 'E'

97 is the number for 'a'

98 is the number for 'b'

99 is the number for 'c'

100 is the number for 'd'

101 is the number for 'e'

The <u>fromCharCode()</u> Static Method of String

JavaScript Syntax:

```
String.fromCharCode(num1, num2, ..., numN);
String.fromCharCode(expression);
```

Parameters Defined:

The **fromCharCode()** Method is a <u>Static</u> Method of String and not a Method of a **String** Object that you create. Consequently it is always coded so that it is prepended by "String" and never by a String Variable or a String Literal. This Method always returns a String and not a **String** Object. The **num1** through **numN** Parameters are integers that represent ISO-Latin-1 codeset Values and range from 0-255. For instance, the following code would return the letter "d".

```
String.fromCharCode(100);
```

This example just demonstrates the return of a String that is extracted with the **fromCharCode()** Method for several number Arguments and then displays them to screen.

Example 8-5:   **Sample905.html**

```
<!DOCTYPE HTML PUBLIC -//W3C//DTD HTML 3.2//EN>
<HTML><HEAD>
<TITLE> Sample 905   Example 8-5 fromCharCode Method</TITLE>

<SCRIPT LANGUAGE="JavaScript1.2"> <!--BEGIN HIDING

document.write(String.fromCharCode(65) + " is the character for '65'<P>");
document.write(String.fromCharCode(66) + " is the character for '66'<P>");
document.write(String.fromCharCode(67) + " is the character for '67'<P>");
document.write(String.fromCharCode(68) + " is the character for '68'<P>");
document.write(String.fromCharCode(69) + " is the character for '69'<P>");
document.write(String.fromCharCode(97) + " is the character for '97'<P>");
document.write(String.fromCharCode(98) + " is the character for '98'<P>");
document.write(String.fromCharCode(99) + " is the character for '99'<P>");
document.write(String.fromCharCode(100)+ " is the character for '100'<P>");
document.write(String.fromCharCode(101)+ " is the character for '101'");

//END HIDING-->
</SCRIPT>
</HEAD>
<BODY>
</BODY>
</HTML>
```

The previous example produces the following output:

A is the character for '65'
B is the character for '66'
C is the character for '67'
D is the character for '68'
E is the character for '69'
a is the character for '97'
b is the character for '98'
c is the character for '99'
d is the character for '100'
e is the character for '101'

Testing for ISO-Latin-1 codeset Values

The **fromCharCode()** Method becomes really useful when you use an Expression that evaluates to an ISO-Latin-1 codeset Value and test for it within an **if()** Statement or a **switch()** Statement with code to execute based on the results of the test condition. This is demonstrated in the following example.

Example 8-6 uses the Method **String.fromCharCode(e.which)** in two different ways to ultimately change the background color of the document. First, let's explain how the Method itself works. To start with, the **keyTest2(e)** Function is defined so that it takes the one Argument of **e**, which will grab the **Event** Object when the KEYPRESS Event occurs. Then, the **which** Property of the **Event** Object **e** is called, and it becomes the Argument for the **String.fromCharCode()** Method like this:

```
String.fromCharCode(e.which)
```

Here's what this does: **e.which** extracts the raw ASCII number Value of the Key that was pressed and passes it to **fromCharCode()**, which then converts the ASCII number into a String representing the actual Key Character.

This Character is then tested for, within the condition of the **if()** Statement, so that if a certain Key is pressed with a Character Value that matches one of the **if()** equality parameters, then the appropriate **bgColor** Property change is executed.

Just to show you a couple of ways to implement the test, the first way uses explicit code in the first five uses of **String.fromCharCode(e.which)**. The other way is to assign **String.fromCharCode(e.which)** to the Variable **testKey** and then use **testKey** within the **if()** Statement.

Finally, the **keyTest2()** Function is assigned to the **onkeypress** Event Handler for the **document** Object, and the **String.fromCharCode(e.which)** is assigned to the **value** Property of the TextBox named **text1** so that it is displayed in the browser after each Key is pressed to verify the results.

Example 8-6: **Sample906.html**

```
<!DOCTYPE HTML PUBLIC -//W3C//DTD HTML 3.2//EN>
<HTML>
<HEAD>
<TITLE> Sample 906   Example 8-6 fromCharCode Method</TITLE>

<SCRIPT LANGUAGE="JavaScript1.2"><!--BEGIN HIDING

function keyTest2(e) {

        var testKey = String.fromCharCode(e.which);
        document.form1.text1.value = testKey;

        if (String.fromCharCode(e.which) == "a") { document.bgColor = 'red'; }
        if (String.fromCharCode(e.which) == "b") { document.bgColor = 'blue'; }
        if (String.fromCharCode(e.which) == "c") { document.bgColor = 'purple'; }
        if (String.fromCharCode(e.which) == "d") { document.bgColor = 'cyan'; }
        if (String.fromCharCode(e.which) == "e") { document.bgColor = 'lime'; }

        if (testKey == "A") { document.bgColor = 'yellow'; }
        if (testKey == "B") { document.bgColor = 'steelblue'; }
        if (testKey == "C") { document.bgColor = 'gold'; }
        if (testKey == "D") { document.bgColor = 'olive'; }
        if (testKey == "E") { document.bgColor = 'green'; }
}

/*--------------------------------------------------------------------------*/

            document.onkeypress = keyTest2;

/*--------------------------------------------------------------------------*/

//END HIDING-->
</SCRIPT>

</HEAD>

<BODY onLoad="window.focus();">
                                            <FONT POINT-SIZE="17">
      Press any of the: a, b, c, d, e, A, B, C, D, E      <BR><BR>
      Keys to change the background color of the document.   <BR>
<P>     Notice that:
<P>     testKey = String.fromCharCode(e.which)            <BR><BR>
        is displayed in the text box.              </FONT>
<FORM NAME="form1">

<INPUT TYPE="text" NAME="text1" SIZE="30" VALUE=""><BR>

</FORM>

</BODY>
</HTML>
```

For more examples of the **fromCharCode()** Method, see the following Sample documents. You can find the page number that the Sample code is located on by going to the Chart in Appendix C, on pages 1039-1048.

Sample File , Line #	fromCharCode() Method Usage
Sample705.html, Line 26:	String.fromCharCode(e.which)
Sample706.html, Line 23:	alert ("Key pressed: " + String.fromCharCode(e.which))
Sample707.html, Line 28:	alert ("Key Pressed = " + String.fromCharCode(e.which))
Sample715.html, Line 26:	var whichKey = String.fromCharCode(e.which);
Sample720.html, Line 72:	var whichKey2 = String.fromCharCode(e.which);
Sample721.html, Line 22:	whichKey = String.fromCharCode(e.which);
Sample722.html, Line 580:	var whichKey2 = String.fromCharCode(e.which);

The next two Methods, the **indexOf()** Method and **lastIndexOf()** Method, are used to extract information about a **String** Object concerning its Character content, that is, where a particular part of a String that you are looking for is located. As the names imply, an **index** number of the located match is returned.

The <u>indexOf()</u> Method of String Object

JavaScript Syntax:

```
anyString.indexOf("searchString", [fromIndex]);
```

Parameters Defined:

The **indexOf()** Method returns the location **index** within the String specified by **anyString** for the <u>first</u> occurrence of the search parameter specified by **searchString**. Each Character in **anyString** is indexed from left to right with a number starting at 0 (zero) and ending at **anyString.length - 1**. (That's read **length** minus 1.)

When you supply a **searchString**, the **indexOf()** Method will look for an exact <u>case-sensitive</u> match for it within the calling String **anyString**. If it finds a match, it will return the **index** number of the first Character where the match was found. If no match is found, the Method returns **-1** (negative one). If **anyString** contains an empty ("") or null String, then **indexOf()** returns an empty String.

If the optional **fromIndex** Argument is supplied, then the Method will start the search from that **index** integer and ignore any preceding Characters. Acceptable Values are from zero to **anyString.length - 1**. The default value is 0 (zero). The **fromIndex** Argument can save you some processing time, but make sure you don't inadvertently omit relevant data.

Here's an example that demonstrates the **indexOf()** Method by first defining the String Variable **str1** and then using it as the calling String to perform the search of several **searchString** Arguments. The returned **index** integers are then displayed with the **write()** Method. Notice that in the second use of **indexOf()** the return Value is **-1** because the case-sensitive search does not match 'red'.

Example 8-7:   **Sample907.html**

```
<!DOCTYPE HTML PUBLIC -//W3C//DTD HTML 3.2//EN>
<HTML>
<HEAD>
        <TITLE> Sample 907    Example 8-7 indexOf Method       </TITLE>

<SCRIPT LANGUAGE="JavaScript1.2"><!--BEGIN HIDING

        str1 = "The Colors to search for are Lime, Green, Red and Purple";


        document.write(str1.indexOf('Red', 11) + "<BR>");

        document.write(str1.indexOf('red') + "<BR>");

        document.write(str1.indexOf('Purple', 10) + "<BR>");

        document.write(str1.indexOf('Lime') + "<BR>");

//END HIDING-->
</SCRIPT>

</HEAD>

<BODY>
</BODY>
</HTML>
```

The previous example produces the following output:

42
-1
50
29

This example uses the **changeColor()** Function to change the background color of the document by obtaining text supplied by the user from the text box Element and testing it to see if it matches any of the **searchString** Arguments of the **indexOf()** Method. For instance, if the user types in "red", then that String is matched by the **indexOf()** Method because it returns the **index** of **0**, which is equivalent to (==) **0** in the **if()** Statement. Because the **if()** evaluates to **true**, the next Statement is executed and the background color is changed to red. The same is true for "green" and "purple", but if the user types in a color that isn't tested for, then nothing happens.

Example 8-8: **Sample908.html**

```
<!DOCTYPE HTML PUBLIC -//W3C//DTD HTML 3.2//EN>
<HTML>
<HEAD>
        <TITLE> Sample 908    Example 8-8 indexOf Method</TITLE>

<SCRIPT LANGUAGE="JavaScript1.2"><!--BEGIN HIDING

function changeColor() {

        str2 = document.form1.text1.value;

        if ( str2.indexOf('red') == 0)         document.bgColor = "red";
        if ( str2.indexOf('green') == 0)       document.bgColor = "green";
        if ( str2.indexOf('purple') == 0)      document.bgColor = "purple";

        document.form1.text1.value = "";
        document.form1.text1.focus();
}

//END HIDING-->
</SCRIPT>
</HEAD>

<BODY onLoad="document.form1.text1.focus();">         <FONT POINT-SIZE="17">

        Type in the color red, green or purple in all lowercase letters and click
the button or hit the Tab Key.
</FONT>

<FORM NAME="form1">

<INPUT TYPE="button" NAME="b1" VALUE="Do it Now" onClick="changeColor();"><BR>

<INPUT TYPE="text" NAME="text1" SIZE="30" VALUE=""onBlur="changeColor();"><BR>

</FORM>
</BODY>
</HTML>
```

The <u>lastIndexOf()</u> Method of String Object

JavaScript Syntax:

```
anyString.lastIndexOf("searchString", [fromIndex]);
```

Parameters Defined:

The **lastIndexOf()** Method works exactly the same as the **indexOf()** Method, except that it returns the **index** of the <u>last</u> occurrence of the search parameter specified by **searchString** within the calling String **anyString**. There is currently a bug in this Method when you use the optional **fromIndex** Argument, which causes the Method to perform the search from right to left, instead of from left to right, so don't use it.

Mini-Example:

This demonstrates the bug in the Method.

```
str1 = "AAACCC";

document.write(str1.lastIndexOf('C', 0) + "<BR>");
document.write(str1.lastIndexOf('C', 1) + "<BR>");
document.write(str1.lastIndexOf('C', 2) + "<BR>");
document.write(str1.lastIndexOf('C', 3) + "<BR>");
document.write(str1.lastIndexOf('C', 4) + "<BR>");
document.write(str1.lastIndexOf('C', 5) + "<BR>");
```

which produces the following output in the browser:

```
-1
-1
-1
3
4
5
```

This is what the output should look like in the browser:

```
5
5
5
5
5
5
```

This example demonstrates the use of the **lastIndexOf()** Method on the calling String Variable **str1** and displays the results to screen.

Example 8-9: **Sample909.html**

```
<!DOCTYPE HTML PUBLIC -//W3C//DTD HTML 3.2//EN>
<HTML>
<HEAD>
       <TITLE> Sample 909   Example 8-9 lastIndexOf Method</TITLE>

<SCRIPT LANGUAGE="JavaScript1.2"><!--BEGIN HIDING

       str1 = "AAABBBCCCDDD";

       document.write(str1.lastIndexOf('A') + "<BR>");
       document.write(str1.lastIndexOf('a') + "<BR>");
       document.write(str1.lastIndexOf('B') + "<BR>");
       document.write(str1.lastIndexOf('C') + "<BR>");
       document.write(str1.lastIndexOf('D') + "<BR>");

//END HIDING-->
</SCRIPT>

</HEAD>

<BODY>
</BODY>
</HTML>
```

This causes the output to look like this:

2
-1
5
8
11

String Object Methods used with Regular Expressions

The **search()**, **match()**, **replace()**, and **split()** Methods deal with interactions between Strings and **RegExp** Objects.

The <u>search()</u> Method of String Object

JavaScript Syntax:

```
anyString.search(regularExpression);
```

Parameters Defined:

The **search()** Method returns the **index** number of the first occurrence of a match to the **regularExpression** Argument that it finds in the calling String **anyString**. The **regularExpression** Argument can be either a Regular Expression Literal, a Variable name, or a String Literal. If no match is found, then the Method returns **-1**. Basically, this is a fancy version of the **indexOf()** Method with the added ability to use a Regular Expression as a search parameter in addition to a String Literal.

This Method is typically used when you need only a minimum amount of information, such as for use in a Conditional Statement when you only need to know if the search found a match or not, which would result in a Boolean true or false within an **if()** or **switch()** Statement.

If you need an Array returned that contains the matched results, then use the **match()** Method, which is covered in the next section.

Mini-Example:

Consider the **write()** Method for the following String Variable **str1**:

```
str1 = "AAABBBCCCDDD";

document.write(str1.search('A') + "<BR>");
document.write(str1.search('B') + "<BR>");
document.write(str1.search('C') + "<BR>");
document.write(str1.search('D') + "<BR>");
document.write(str1.search('a') + "<BR>");
```

which would produce the following results:

```
0
3
6
9
-1
```

This example uses the **search()** Method to match the String that is input by the user, which, according to the instructions in the browser page, should be one of the five specified colors. If the match is found, then the background color of the **document** is changed to that color String.

Example 8-10:   Sample910.html

```
<!DOCTYPE HTML PUBLIC -//W3C//DTD HTML 3.2//EN>
<HTML>
<HEAD>
        <TITLE> Sample 910    Example 8-10    search Method    </TITLE>

<SCRIPT LANGUAGE="JavaScript1.2"><!--BEGIN HIDING

function changeColor() {

        str2 = document.form1.text1.value;

        if (str2.search('aqua') != -1)        document.bgColor = "aqua";
        if (str2.search('azure') != -1)       document.bgColor = "azure";
        if (str2.search('beige') != -1)       document.bgColor = "beige";
        if (str2.search('bisque') != -1)      document.bgColor = "bisque";
        if (str2.search('red') != -1)         document.bgColor = "red";

        document.form1.text1.value = "";
        document.form1.text1.focus();
}

//END HIDING-->
</SCRIPT>

</HEAD>

<BODY onLoad="document.form1.text1.focus();">        <FONT POINT-SIZE="17">

        Type in the color aqua, azure, beige, bisque or red in all lowercase letters
and hit the Tab Key.

</FONT>

<FORM NAME="form1">

<INPUT TYPE="text" NAME="text1" SIZE="30" VALUE="" onBlur="changeColor();"><BR>

</FORM>

</BODY>
</HTML>
```

This example uses the **search()** Method and some simple Regular Expressions within two **if()** Statements to change the background color of the document. The RegExp **re1** is created with Literal notation and means to search for the pattern of "red" or "aqua" or "green" and uses the **i flag** to ignore case, so if the user types in "red" or "Red" or "AAAQua" or "gGgreEnNN" the match will still be true.

The first **if()** Statement tests to see if *any* of the three color Strings match, and if true, the second **if()** tests for an individual color. For more information on Regular Expressions, see Chapter 9.

Example 8-11:   **Sample911.html**

```
<!DOCTYPE HTML PUBLIC -//W3C//DTD HTML 3.2//EN>
<HTML><HEAD> <TITLE> Sample 911   Example 8-11 search Method</TITLE>

<SCRIPT LANGUAGE="JavaScript1.2"><!--BEGIN HIDING

function changeColor() {

        str = document.form1.text1.value;
        re1 = /red|aqua|green/i;
        re2 = /red/i;
        re3 = /aqua/i;
        re4 = /green/i;

        if (str.search(re1) != -1)  {

                if (str.search(re2) != -1)         document.bgColor = "red";

                else if (str.search(re3) != -1)    document.bgColor = "aqua";

                else if (str.search(re4) != -1)    document.bgColor = "green";
        }
        document.form1.text1.value = "";
        document.form1.text1.focus();
}

//END HIDING-->
</SCRIPT>
</HEAD>
<BODY onLoad="document.form1.text1.focus();">        <FONT POINT-SIZE="17">
        Type in the color red, aqua or green in any combination of uppercase and
lowercase letters and hit the Tab Key.                </FONT>

<FORM NAME="form1">
<INPUT TYPE="text" NAME="text1" SIZE="30" VALUE="" onBlur="changeColor();"> <BR>

</FORM>
</BODY>
</HTML>
```

The <u>match()</u> Method of String Object

JavaScript Syntax:

```
anyString.match(regularExpression);
```

Parameters Defined:

The **match()** Method is used to match the **regularExpression** Argument against the calling **anyString**. Think of the **match()** Method as the advanced version of the **search()** Method, because it returns an <u>Array</u> of a <u>String match</u> or <u>String matches</u> and other useful information, depending on how you set up the **regularExpression**, instead of an **index** integer. If no match is found, the Method returns "**null**" (without the quotes).

Think of a **RegExp** Object as a fancy search **pattern** to look for in the calling String. You can define an extremely simple **RegExp** with **Literal** notation with a String Literal as the **pattern** and assign it to a Variable like this, noting that you don't enclose <u>red</u> in quotes:

myRegExp = /red/;

which can then be used to search for the text String **red** within the String Variable **str** with the **match()** Method like in the following example, which renders **["red"]** to screen as the only Element in the returned Array named **gotItArray**:

Example 8-12:   **Sample912.html**

```
<!DOCTYPE HTML PUBLIC -//W3C//DTD HTML 3.2//EN>
<HTML>
<HEAD>
<TITLE> Sample 912   Example 8-12 match Method</TITLE>

<SCRIPT LANGUAGE="JavaScript1.2"><!--BEGIN HIDING

        str = "The red fox went into the red house";
        myRegExp = /red/;
        gotItArray = str.match(myRegExp);

        document.write(gotItArray);

//END HIDING-->
</SCRIPT>

</HEAD>
<BODY>
</BODY>
</HTML>
```

Example 8-13 explores the two **flags** Arguments, **i** and **g**, which have special meaning when used in **RegExp** Objects. The **i flag** means <u>ignore case</u>, which specifies that the search is <u>case-insensitive</u>. The **g flag** means <u>global</u>, which causes the search to find all of the occurrences of a particular match instead of just the first one. When the **g** flag is used in a **RegExp** with the **match()** Method, the Array that is returned contains a separate Element for each occurrence of the matched String.

The **RegExp** that is created with:

```
re = /red|green|blue/gi
```

means that if <u>red or green or blue</u> is found in the calling String, in any combination of uppercase and lowercase letters, then for each occurrence, the matched String is assigned to an Element in the returned Array. The **red|green|blue** pattern conforms to the **x|y** Special Character Sequence, and means, "<u>search for x or y</u>", and can have as many <u>or</u> (|) possibilities as you like. See page 808 in Chapter 9 for more information on <u>global</u> searches with Regular Expressions.

Example 8-13:   **Sample913.html**

```
<!DOCTYPE HTML PUBLIC -//W3C//DTD HTML 3.2//EN>
<HTML><HEAD>  <TITLE> Sample 913   Example 8-13 match Method</TITLE>

<SCRIPT LANGUAGE="JavaScript1.2"><!--BEGIN HIDING

function changeColor() {

        str = document.form1.ta1.value;
        re = /red|green|blue/gi;
        gotIt = str.match(re);

        if (str.match(re) != null)  {
               document.form1.ta1.value = gotIt;
        }
        else document.form1.ta1.value = "Try Again";
}

//END HIDING-->
</SCRIPT>
</HEAD>
<BODY>  <FONT POINT-SIZE="17">
        Type in the strings red, green or blue as many times as you want in
lowercase and/or uppercase letters and click outside the Textarea. </FONT>

<FORM NAME="form1">
<TEXTAREA NAME="ta1" ROWS=12 COLS=80 NAME="ta1" onBlur="changeColor();">
rrrrRed green BLUE bluEeeeeeee                                 </TEXTAREA>
</FORM>
</BODY>
</HTML>
```

Mini-Example:

For the **RegExp** created with Literal notation and assigned to the Variable **re**:

```
re = /\w* \d+/gi;
```

The **RegExp** Special Characters mean:

\w	matches [A-Z a-z 0-9]
*	means 'zero or more times'
\d	matches numbers 0-9
+	means 'one or more times'
\w*	matches [A-Z a-z 0-9] zero or more times
\d+	matches numbers 0-9 one or more times

The above RegExp **re** is used in the following example within the Function **foundIt()** to test the user input text and return an Array of matches. This is set up just like the previous example but with a different Regular Expression **pattern**. This **pattern** tries to match a <u>zero or more</u> quantity of alphanumeric Characters, followed by a <u>space</u> and followed by <u>one or more</u> numbers.

Example 8-14:   Sample914.html

```
<!DOCTYPE HTML PUBLIC -//W3C//DTD HTML 3.2//EN>
<HTML>
<HEAD>
       <TITLE> Sample 914    Example 8-14 match Method</TITLE>

<SCRIPT LANGUAGE="JavaScript1.2"><!--BEGIN HIDING

function foundIt() {

           //Just for reference:
           //Note that    \w       matches [A-Z a-z 0-9]
           //Note that    *        means 'zero or more times'
           //Note that    \d       matches numbers 0-9
           //Note that    +        means 'one or more times'

      str = document.form1.ta1.value;

           //      \w*           matches [A-Z a-z 0-9] zero or more times
           //      \d+           matches numbers 0-9 one or more times
           //      g             means a global search
           //      i             means ignore case
```

```
        re = /\w* \d+/gi;

        gotIt = str.match(re);


        if (str.match(re) != null)  {
                document.form1.ta1.value = gotIt;
        }
        else document.form1.ta1.value = "Try Again";


        document.form1.ta1.focus();
        document.form1.ta1.select();
}

//END HIDING-->
</SCRIPT>

</HEAD>

<BODY>  <FONT POINT-SIZE="17">

        This Regular Expression pattern recognizes multiple occurrences of any
combination of numbers and characters followed by a space and followed by 1 or more
numbers. Click outside the Textarea for Array results.        </FONT>

<FORM NAME="form1">

<TEXTAREA NAME="ta1" ROWS=12 COLS=80 NAME="ta1" onBlur="foundIt();">
Sample1
</TEXTAREA>

</FORM>


<SCRIPT LANGUAGE="JavaScript1.2"><!--BEGIN HIDING

document.form1.ta1.focus();
document.form1.ta1.select();

//END HIDING-->
</SCRIPT>

</BODY>
</HTML>
```

There are more examples using the **match()** Method in Chapter 9 on pages 833, 840, 845, and 847. The associated Sample files for these examples are:

Sample1007.html
Sample1012.html
Sample1014.html
Sample1015-SearchEngine1.html

The <u>replace()</u> Method of String Object

JavaScript Syntax:

```
anyString.replace(regularExpression, "newSubString");
```

Parameters Defined:

The **replace()** Method accomplishes two things simultaneously. First it is used to find a match between the **regularExpression** Argument and the calling String **anyString**. Then the Substring contained in the **newSubString** Argument is used to replace the Substring that is matched in **anyString**. However, it should be noted that the **replace()** Method does not alter the original calling String **anyString** in any way. What it does is return a new String consisting of **anyString** with the matched substitutions.

The **regularExpression** Argument can be a Literal or a Variable name. The global **flag g** can be used to execute a global search and the ignore case **flag i** can be used to execute a case-insensitive search. They can be used individually or together as **gi**.

The **newSubString** Argument can be a Literal, a Variable name, or any of the following **RegExp** Properties, which are defined on page 807. Note that **$1** to **$9** are <u>not</u> prepended with **RegExp** when used in the **newSubString** Argument in the **replace()** Method and must be inside quotes. This is true only when using the **replace()** Method.

$1, $2, ..., $9		Not prepended with **RegExp** and must be inside quotes
lastMatch,	**$&**	Is prepended with **RegExp**, outside quotes with String addition +
lastParen,	**$+**	Is prepended with **RegExp**, outside quotes with String addition +
leftContext,	**$`**	Is prepended with **RegExp**, outside quotes with String addition +
rightContext,	**$'**	Is prepended with **RegExp**, outside quotes with String addition +

The following Script uses the **replace()** Method to return a new String, which is assigned to **replaceIt** where the SubString "Monday, boo!" is substituted for "Friday" followed by a <u>space</u>, followed by one or more <u>word</u> Characters, followed by a <u>period</u> in the String Variable **str**.

```
<SCRIPT LANGUAGE="JavaScript1.2">

        str = "The day of the week is Friday, yeah.";
        re = /Friday,\s\w+./;
        replaceIt = str.replace(re, "Monday, boo!");

        document.write(replaceIt);

</SCRIPT>
```

This outputs:　　　　　The day of the week is Monday, boo!

Mini-Example:

The following Script uses the **replace()** Method to return a new String which is assigned to **replaceIt** where the SubString "Music" is substituted for each occurrence of the SubString "Rock climbing" in the String Variable **str**. Without both of the **gi flags**, the second occurrence of "rock climbing" would not be replaced.

```
<SCRIPT LANGUAGE="JavaScript1.2">

str = "Rock climbing is fun and rock climbing is challenging.";
re = /Rock climbing/gi;
replaceIt = str.replace(re, "Music");

document.write(replaceIt);

</SCRIPT>
```

This outputs: Music is fun and Music is challenging.

Mini-Example:

The following Script uses the **replace()** Method to return a new String, which is assigned to **replaceIt** where the SubString "minus" is substituted for each match to the Regular Expression **re** in the String Variable **str**. Without the **g flag**, only the first match would be replaced.

The Regular Expression **re** matches either a "+" sign, the word "plus", or a "*" sign. Notice that because the "+" sign is normally a Special Character, you have to escape it with the backslash "\" Character so that it is treated as a real "+" sign instead of meaning 'match one or more of the preceding Character'. You also have to escape the "*" Character.

This Regular Expression is of the form:

x|y|z   which means match either x or y or z

```
<SCRIPT LANGUAGE="JavaScript1.2"><!--BEGIN HIDING

    str = "One + Two + Three plus Four * Five.";
    re = /\+|plus|\*/g;
    replaceIt = str.replace(re, "minus");

    document.write(replaceIt);

//END HIDING-->
</SCRIPT>
```

This outputs: One minus Two minus Three minus Four minus Five.

The following example uses the **replace()** Method to return a new String, which is assigned to **replaceIt** where the SubString "Sunday, January $1, 19$2" is substituted for the match to the Regular Expression **re** in the String Variable **str**. The Regular Expression **re** matches one or more digits, followed by a dash, followed by one or more digits that are remembered, followed by a dash, followed by one or more digits that are remembered.

The **newSubString** Argument uses the first remembered Parenthesized SubString match, specified by **$1**, and the second one specified by **$2**, to put back the day of the month and the last two digits of the year, so that in this example **$1** = 11 and **$2** = 98.

Example 8-15: Sample915.html

```
<!DOCTYPE HTML PUBLIC -//W3C//DTD HTML 3.2//EN>
<HTML>
<HEAD>
        <TITLE> Sample 915   Example 8-15 replace Method</TITLE>

<SCRIPT LANGUAGE="JavaScript1.2"><!--BEGIN HIDING

        str = "The date is 1-11-98.";

        re = /\d+-(\d+)-(\d+)/;

        replaceIt = str.replace(re, "Sunday, January $1, 19$2");


        document.write(replaceIt);


//END HIDING-->
</SCRIPT>

</HEAD>

<BODY>
</BODY>
</HTML>
```

In the preceding example, after the **replace()** Method is called, the String **replaceIt** is equal to:

The date is Sunday, January 11, 1998.

The following example uses the **replace()** Method to return a new String, which is assigned to **replaceIt** where the compound **newSubString** Argument of:

```
"$2 $1 " + RegExp.lastParen + "/$3"
```

replaces the match to the Regular Expression **re** in the String Variable **str**. The Regular Expression **re** matches one or more <u>word</u> Characters that are remembered, followed by a <u>space</u>, followed by one or more <u>word</u> Characters that are remembered, followed by one or more digits that are remembered, followed by a forward slash, followed by one or more digits that are remembered.

The **newSubString** Argument uses the remembered Parenthesized SubString matches that are specified by **$1**, **$2**, and **$3** and the **lastParen** Properties of the Core **RegExp** Object. Note that the **lastParen** Property, is equal to 500, is not enclosed inside parentheses and is added to the String with the String addition operator. Also note that **lastParen** is prepended with **RegExp.**

The Value of the **replaceIt** String after the **replace()** Method is executed is:

The Apple Macintosh 9600/500 rules.

Example 8-16:   Sample916.html

```
<!DOCTYPE HTML PUBLIC -//W3C//DTD HTML 3.2//EN>
<HTML>
<HEAD>
        <TITLE> Sample 916    Example 8-16 replace Method     </TITLE>

<SCRIPT LANGUAGE="JavaScript1.2"><!--BEGIN HIDING

        str = "The Macintosh Apple 500/9600 rules.";

        re = /(\w+) (\w+) (\d+)\/(\d+)/;

        replaceIt = str.replace(re, "$2 $1 " + RegExp.lastParen + "/" + "$3");


        document.write(replaceIt);

//END HIDING-->
</SCRIPT>

</HEAD>
<BODY>
</BODY>
</HTML>
```

The <u>split()</u> Method of String Object

JavaScript Syntax:

```
anyString.split([separator], [limit]);
```

Parameters Defined:

The **split()** Method is used to break up the calling String **anyString** into SubStrings and return an Array where each Element in the Array is one of these SubStrings. If the optional **separator** Argument is supplied, then it is used as the breakpoint for splitting **anyString**; that is, each time the separator is found, the Characters preceding it are collected into a Substring and placed in an Array Element.

The **separator** is extracted and is not part of the Substring that is placed in the Array. The original String **anyString** is not altered though, so the **separator** aspect of it is also unchanged. If the **separator** Argument is omitted, then the Array that is returned contains just one Element consisting of the entire **anyString**.

In Navigator 4.0, the **separator** Argument can also be a Regular Expression. If you include any parentheses in your Regular Expression, they will cause SubMatches in the Array. Think about it this way: Parentheses in a Regular Expression cause the Regular Expression to remember a SubMatch, that is, a Match that pertains to only a portion of the code contained within the entire Regular Expression. (It's like getting two or more Regular Expressions for the price of one.) This SubMatch is also output to its own Array Element just like the rest of the full Matches. If you specify:

```
<SCRIPT LANGUAGE="JavaScript1.2">
```

then:

```
anyString.split(" ")
```

will produce a split on any sequence of 1 or more white space Characters, including spaces, tabs, carriage returns, and line feeds. If you don't specify "JavaScript1.2", then it will only split on a *single* space Character.

The optional **limit** Argument is also new to Navigator 4.0 and allows you to specify a positive integer that will place an upper boundary on the number of splits that can occur. What this does is give you a way to avoid empty, and therefore "**undefined**", Array Elements in your <u>returned Array</u>.

Mini-Example:

Consider the following mini-example for the String Variable **str** and the returned Array assigned to **splitArray** when the **split()** Method is invoked on **str** with the "**&**" ampersand Character as the **separator** Argument.

The **write()** Method displays **splitArray** after the **split()** Method is invoked, and you should expect all of the "**&**" Characters to have been extracted out of **str**. Then each Element of **splitArray** is written to screen so that it's easier to see what's been done.

```
<SCRIPT LANGUAGE="JavaScript1.2">

    str = "The Characters 1 & 2 & E & 3";

    splitArray = str.split("&");

    document.write("<B>" + splitArray + "<\/B><P>");

    document.write(splitArray[0] + "<BR>");

    document.write(splitArray[1] + "<BR>");

    document.write(splitArray[2] + "<BR>");

    document.write(splitArray[3] + "<BR>");

</SCRIPT>
```

This produces the following output in the browser:

["The Characters 1 ", " 2 ", " E ", " 3 "]

The Characters 1
2
E
3

Mini-Example:

Consider the following mini-example for the String Variable **str** and the returned Array assigned to **splitArray** when the **split()** Method is invoked on **str.** The Regular Expression created with Literal notation is used as the **separator** Argument. It means to search for the Characters "red", followed by a <u>space</u>, followed by one or more <u>word</u> Characters. Therefore the **split()** Method will extract "red rabbit" and "red fox" from **str** and return **splitArray** with three Elements.

```
<SCRIPT LANGUAGE="JavaScript1.2"><!--BEGIN HIDING

str = "The red rabbit ran rapidly from the rabid red fox.";

splitArray = str.split(/red\s\w+/);

document.write("<B>" + splitArray + "<\/B><P>");

document.write(splitArray[0] + "<BR>");
document.write(splitArray[1] + "<BR>");
document.write(splitArray[2]);

//END HIDING-->
</SCRIPT>
```

This produces the following output in the browser. Notice that the <u>period</u> Character that ends the sentence has its own Array Element.

["The ", " ran rapidly from the rabid ", "."]

The
ran rapidly from the rabid

.

Example 8-17 demonstrates the **split()** Method twice, on two different Strings and two different Regular Expressions. Both of the returned Arrays and their respective Elements are output to screen and shown in the book after this description. The Regular Expression specified by:

```
/\s&\s\D/
```

splits on a <u>space</u>, followed by "&", followed by a <u>space</u>, followed by any non-Digit Character. The Regular Expression specified by:

```
/blue\s\w+/
```

splits on "blue", followed by a <u>space</u>, followed by one or more <u>word</u> Characters.

Example 8-17:   Sample917.html

```
<!DOCTYPE HTML PUBLIC -//W3C//DTD HTML 3.2//EN>
<HTML>
<HEAD>  <TITLE> Sample 917    Example 8-17 split Method</TITLE>

<SCRIPT LANGUAGE="JavaScript1.2"><!--BEGIN HIDING

str = "The Characters 1 & 2 & A & 3 & 4 & B & 5 & 6 & E & 7";
str2 = "The blue bird ate the blue fish flying in blue sky above blue water";

splitArray2 = str.split(/\s&\s\D/);

splitArray3 = str2.split(/blue\s\w+/);

document.write("<B>" + splitArray2 + "<\/B><P>");

document.write(splitArray2[0] + "<BR>");
document.write(splitArray2[1] + "<BR>");
document.write(splitArray2[2] + "<BR>");
document.write(splitArray2[3] + "<P>");

document.write("<B>" + splitArray3 + "<\/B><P>");

document.write(splitArray3[0] + "<BR>");
document.write(splitArray3[1] + "<BR>");
document.write(splitArray3[2] + "<BR>");
document.write(splitArray3[3]);

//END HIDING-->
</SCRIPT>
</HEAD>
<BODY>  </BODY>
</HTML>
```

The preceding example produces the following output:

["The Characters 1 & 2", " & 3 & 4", " & 5 & 6", " & 7"]

The Characters 1 & 2
& 3 & 4
& 5 & 6
& 7

["The ", " ate the ", " flying in ", " above "]

The
ate the
flying in
above

Example 8-18 demonstrates the **split()** Method, where a Parenthesized Remembered SubExpression is part of the Regular Expression used as the **separator** Argument. The Regular Expression specified by:

```
/(\d)\sand/
```

splits on any <u>digit</u> which is remembered, followed by a <u>space</u>, followed by "<u>and</u>".

\d	matches a digit, that is, a number from 0 to 9
(\d)	remembers the digit
\s	matches a space Character
and	matches the normal Characters "and"

Therefore, the <u>returned Array</u> **splitArray** will have a separate Element for each *remembered* <u>digit</u>. Note that <u>digits</u> that occur but are not part of the total Regular Expression are *not* remembered. In this case, that would be "3" and "7", which are part of the last Substring.

Once again, the resulting Array **splitArray** is rendered to screen after the **separator** Characters have been extracted and each Element of the Array is rendered to screen.

Example 8-18:   **Sample918.html**

```
<!DOCTYPE HTML PUBLIC -//W3C//DTD HTML 3.2//EN>
<HTML>
<HEAD>
<TITLE> Sample 918   Example 8-18 split Method remembered substrings</TITLE>

<SCRIPT LANGUAGE="JavaScript1.2"><!--BEGIN HIDING

str = "The Characters 1 and blue plus 2 and green plus 3 minus 7."

splitArray = str.split(/(\d)\sand/);

document.write("<B>" + splitArray + "<\/B><P>");

document.write(splitArray[0] + "<BR>");
document.write(splitArray[1] + "<BR>");
document.write(splitArray[2] + "<BR>");
document.write(splitArray[3] + "<BR>");
document.write(splitArray[4] + "<BR>");

//END HIDING-->
</SCRIPT>

</HEAD>

<BODY>
</BODY>
</HTML>
```

The preceding example produces the following output noting that 3 and 7 are *not* remembered.

["The Characters ", "1", " blue plus ", "2", " green plus 3 minus 7."]

The Characters
1
blue plus
2
green plus 3 minus 7.

More String Object Methods

The <u>slice()</u> Method of String Object

JavaScript Syntax:

```
anyString.slice(startSlice, endSlice);
```

<u>Parameters Defined:</u>

The **slice()** Method is used to extract a sequential group of Characters from a String and return a new String comprised of those Characters. The **startSlice** Argument is an integer that serves as the <u>zero-based</u> **index** at which you start the slice. For instance, if **startSlice** is 0, the **slice()** starts at the first Character and the first Character is included in the **slice()**. If **startSlice** is 4, the **slice()** starts at the fifth Character, and so on. You should note that a blank space is considered one Character.

The **endSlice** Argument is an optional <u>zero-based</u> **index** that is either a positive or negative integer that is used to end the **slice()**. Pay attention here!! The **slice()** Method extracts up to, but does *not* include the Character specified at **endSlice**. For instance, if you have **myString.slice(0, 4)**, this would extract the first, second, third, and fourth Characters, but not the fifth. If you had **myString1.slice(2, 5)**, this would extract the third, fourth, and fifth Characters.

If **endSlice** is used as a negative integer, then JavaScript starts the count from the end of the String and works backward. For instance, if **endSlice** is **-1**, the **slice()** would extract up to and include the next to last Character. So if you had the following String:

```
str1 = "one two three four five";
```

then for:

```
str1.slice(1, -1)
```

the returned String would be:

```
ne two three four fiv
```

If you had:

```
str1.slice(0, -2)
```

the returned String would be:

```
one two three four fi
```

If **endSlice** is omitted, then **slice()** will extract from **startSlice** all the way to the end of the String, including the last Character.

This example demonstrates several implementations of the **slice()** Method.

Example 8-19:   Sample919.html

```
<!DOCTYPE HTML PUBLIC -//W3C//DTD HTML 3.2//EN>
<HTML><HEAD>    <TITLE> Sample 919    Example 8-19 slice Method</TITLE>

<SCRIPT LANGUAGE="JavaScript1.2"><!--BEGIN HIDING

        str1 = "one two three four five";

        str2 = str1.slice(0, 2);
        str3 = str1.slice(0);
        str4 = str1.slice(4);
        str5 = str1.slice(8, 13);

        str6 = str1.slice(3, -1);
        str7 = str1.slice(3, -2);
        str8 = str1.slice(3, -3);
        str9 = str1.slice(3, -4);

        document.write(str2 + "<BR>");
        document.write(str3 + "<BR>");
        document.write(str4 + "<BR>");
        document.write(str5 + "<P>");

        document.write(str6 + "<BR>");
        document.write(str7 + "<BR>");
        document.write(str8 + "<BR>");
        document.write(str9 + "<BR>");

//END HIDING-->
</SCRIPT>
</HEAD>
<BODY> </BODY>
</HTML>
```

The preceding example produces the following output:

on
one two three four five
two three four five
three

two three four fiv
two three four fi
two three four f
two three four

The <u>substring()</u> Method of String Object

JavaScript Syntax:

```
anyString.substring(indexA, [indexB]);
```

Parameters Defined:

The **substring()** Method has two major differences from the **slice()** Method. First, you can't use negative numbers for the **indexA** and **indexB** Arguments in **substring()**, but there is more flexibility in how JavaScript deals with them, when they are Variables, in terms of one being larger than the other at any given time during the running of the Script.

The **substring()** Method extracts a portion of the calling String **anyString** and returns a new String without altering the original String in any way. The extraction is specified by the **indexA** and optionally the **indexB** Arguments. Generally, the extraction starts at **indexA**, and as the Characters in the String are read from left to right, extracts up to but not including **indexB**. As a reminder, in the following definitions, the **length** Property is the number of Characters in the String, including white space.

indexA	is a positive integer between 0 and 1 less than **anyString.length**
indexB	is a positive integer between 0 and 1 less than **anyString.length**

Table of Interactions for <u>indexA</u> and <u>indexB</u>

The specifics of the interactions for various Values for **indexA** and **indexB** are:

If	**indexA** < 0	JavaScript interprets **indexA** as being 0.
If	**indexA** == **indexB**	**substring()** returns an empty String.
If	**indexB** > **anyString.length - 1**	JavaScript interprets **indexB** such that **indexB** == **anyString.length -1**.
If	**indexB** is omitted	**substring()** extracts Characters from **indexA** to the end of **anyString**.
With	<SCRIPT LANGUAGE="JavaScript1.2">	
If	**indexA** > **indexB**	JavaScript produces an "out-of-memory" runtime error.
Without	<SCRIPT LANGUAGE="JavaScript1.2">	
If	**indexA** > **indexB**	**substring()** returns a String starting at **indexB** and ending at **indexA - 1**.

This example demonstrates several implementations of the **substring()** Method.

Example 8-20: **Sample920.html**

```
<!DOCTYPE HTML PUBLIC -//W3C//DTD HTML 3.2//EN>
<HTML>
<HEAD>
<TITLE> Sample 920   Example 8-20 substring Method</TITLE>

<SCRIPT LANGUAGE="JavaScript1.2"><!--BEGIN HIDING

        str1 = "one two three four five";

        str2 = str1.substring(0, 2);
        str3 = str1.substring(0);
        str4 = str1.substring(4);
        str5 = str1.substring(8, 13);
        str6 = str1.substring(-5, 15);
        str7 = str1.substring(3, 3);
        str8 = str1.substring(3, 55);

        document.write(str2 + "<BR>");
        document.write(str3 + "<BR>");
        document.write(str4 + "<BR>");
        document.write(str5 + "<BR>");
        document.write(str6 + "<BR>");
        document.write(str7 + ".....Note that str7 is an empty string.<BR>");
        document.write(str8 + "<BR>");

//END HIDING-->
</SCRIPT>

</HEAD>

<BODY>
</BODY>
</HTML>
```

The preceding example produces the following output:

on
one two three four five
two three four five
three
one two three f
.....Note that str7 is an empty string.
two three four five

The <u>substr()</u> Method of String Object

JavaScript Syntax:

```
anyString.substr(startIndex, [characterQuantity]);
```

Parameters Defined:

The **substr()** Method extracts a portion of the calling String **anyString** and returns a new String without altering the original String in any way. The extraction is specified by the **startIndex** and optionally the **characterQuantity** Arguments. Characters in the String are indexed from left to right so that the first Character has an **index** of 0 (zero), the second Character has an **index** of 1, and so on, up to the last Character, which has an **index** equal to one less than the number of Characters in the String, which is equivalent to the Expression **anyString.length - 1**. The **length** Property specifies the number of Characters in the String, including white space.

The **substr()** Method begins the extraction at the **index** number specified by the **startIndex** Argument and extracts the exact number of Characters specified in the **characterQuantity** Argument. If no **characterQuantity** Argument is specified, then the extraction continues to the end of **anyString**.

startIndex	is a positive or negative integer or zero.
characterQuantity	is a positive or negative integer or zero.

Table of Interactions for <u>startIndex</u> and <u>characterQuantity</u>

If   **startIndex >= anyString.length**   substr() returns no Characters.

If   **characterQuantity** $<= 0$ substr() returns no Characters.

If   **characterQuantity** is omitted   substr() extracts Characters from **startIndex** to the end of **anyString**.

If   **startIndex** < 0 substr() uses **startIndex** to start the **index** count from the end of **anyString** instead of the beginning.

If   (**startIndex** < 0 && Math.abs(**startIndex**) > **anyString.length**)

                        substr() uses 0 for **startIndex**.

If **startIndex** = -20 and there are only 15 Characters in the String, then if you count backward from the end, you will run out of String Characters before you run out of **index** numbers, and JavaScript isn't equipped to handle that type of negative Character entity.

This example demonstrates several implementations of the **substr()** Method.

Example 8-21: **Sample921.html**

```
<!DOCTYPE HTML PUBLIC -//W3C//DTD HTML 3.2//EN>
<HTML><HEAD><TITLE> Sample 921   Example 8-21 substr Method</TITLE>

<SCRIPT LANGUAGE="JavaScript1.2"><!--BEGIN HIDING

        str1 = "one two three four five";

        str2 = str1.substr(0);
        str3 = str1.substr(4, 15);
        str4 = str1.substr(-5);
        str5 = str1.substr(-19, 13);

        str6 = str1.substr(3, 55);
        str7 = str1.substr(-8, 7);
        str8 = str1.substr(5, 0);
        str9 = str1.substr(5, -7);
        str10 = str1.substr(35);

        document.write(str2 + "<BR>");
        document.write(str3 + "<BR>");
        document.write(str4 + "<BR>");
        document.write(str5 + "<P>");

        document.write(str6 + "<BR>");
        document.write(str7 + "<BR>");
        document.write(str8 + ".....Note that str8 is an empty string.<BR>");
        document.write(str9 + ".....Note that str9 is an empty string.<BR>");
        document.write(str10 + ".....Note that str10 is an empty string.<BR>");

//END HIDING-->
</SCRIPT>
</HEAD><BODY>   </BODY></HTML>
```

The preceding example produces the following output:

one two three four five
two three four
five
two three fou

two three four five
our fiv
.....Note that str8 is an empty string.
.....Note that str9 is an empty string.
.....Note that str10 is an empty string.

Creating Anchors & Links

The <u>anchor()</u> Method of String Object

JavaScript Syntax:

```
displayString.anchor(anchorName);
```

Parameters Defined:

The **anchor()** Method lets you create an HTML Anchor within a Script that you can then render to screen with the **write()** or **writeln()** Methods. The **anchorName** Argument specifies the name of the Anchor that you can refer to in your script and is equivalent to the NAME Attribute Value in an <A> tag like this:

```
<A NAME="anchorName">
```

You use the **displayString** Argument to assign the text that you want to appear when the Anchor is rendered, just like the text that appears between the start and end <A> Tags. For instance:

```
var myString1 = "I'm the usually hidden anchor.";
var myTopAnchor = "pageTopAnchor";

document.write(myString1.anchor(myTopAnchor));
```

This would be the HTML equivalent of:

```
<A NAME="pageTopAnchor">I'm the usually hidden anchor.</A>
```

Creating a hidden Anchor

If you want to create a hidden Anchor, then assign a **null** String to the String Variable like this:

```
var myString1 = "";
```

Anchors in the <u>anchors[i]</u> Array

Any Anchors that are created with the **anchor()** Method are automatically assigned to **document** Object's **anchors[i]** Array, which for the above Anchor named **pageTopAnchor**, if it was the first Anchor in the **document**, could be accessed like this:

```
document.anchors[0];
```

See <u>Sample922.html</u> on page 796, after the **link()** Method section, which uses both the **anchor()** and **link()** Methods in a Script.

The <u>link()</u> Method of String Object

JavaScript Syntax:

```
displayString.link(href);
```

Parameters Defined:

The **link()** Method lets you create an HTML Link within a Script that you can then render to screen with the **write()** or **writeln()** Methods. The **href** Argument specifies the absolute or relative URL of the document that you want to link to and is equivalent to the HREF Attribute Value in an <A> Tag like this:

```
<A HREF="URL">
```

You use the **displayString** Argument to assign the text that you want to appear when the Link is rendered, just like the text that appears between the start and end <A> Tags. For instance:

```
var myString2 = "Go to Gilorien's Home page.";

var myLink2 = "http://www.erols.com/gilorien";

document.write(myString2.link(myLink1));
```

would produce the following output in the browser:

<u>Go to Gilorien's Home page.</u>

This would be the HTML equivalent of:

```
<A HREF="http://www.erols.com/gilorien">
Go to Gilorien's Home page.          </A>
```

Links in the <u>links[i]</u> Array

Any Links that are created with the **link()** Method are automatically assigned to **document** Object's **links[i]** Array, which for the above Link, if it was the first Link in the **document**, could be displayed to screen like this:

```
document.write(document.links[0]);
```

This example uses the **anchor()** and **link()** Methods of the **String** Object to create an Anchor for the **document** and then a Link that links to the previous Anchor. Notice the Value of the Variable **myTopLink**, which uses String addition to, in effect, prepend a hash symbol (#) to the **myTopAnchor** Variable. The **myTopLink** Variable is then used as the **href** Argument in the subsequent **link()** Method.

When you run this example in your browser, the SPACER Element causes the Link that is created with the **link()** Method to be down the page and out of view. Scrolling down to it and clicking it will return you to the top of the page, where the Anchor is.

Example 8-22:   **Sample922.html**

```
<!DOCTYPE HTML PUBLIC -//W3C//DTD HTML 3.2//EN>
<HTML>
<HEAD>
<TITLE> Sample 922    Example 8-22      anchor and link Methods      </TITLE>

<SCRIPT LANGUAGE="JavaScript1.2"><!--BEGIN HIDING

        var myString1 = "I'm the usually hidden anchor.";

        var myTopAnchor = "pageTopAnchor";


        var myString2 = "Go to the Top of the Page";

        var myTopLink = "#"+myTopAnchor;



        document.write(myString1.anchor(myTopAnchor) + '<BR><BR>');


        document.write("Scroll down to the link and click it.");

        document.write("<SPACER TYPE='vertical' SIZE=800>");


        document.write(myString2.link(myTopLink));


//END HIDING-->
</SCRIPT>

</HEAD>

<BODY>

</BODY>
</HTML>
```

Decorative Methods of String Object

Overview

Here is a list of all of the Decorative Methods of the **String** Object:

big(), **blink()**, **bold()**, **fixed()**, **fontcolor("color")**, **fontsize(size)**, **italics()**, **small()**, **strike()**, **sub()**, **sup()**, **toLowerCase()**, and **toUpperCase()**

All of the following Decorative Methods of the **String** Object take the String contained in the **anyString** Argument and change it so that it reflects a particular enhanced characteristic. The syntax chart below shows the HTML Element counterpart. Use the **write()** Method or the **writeln()** Method of the **document** Object to display the text to screen. See Sample923.html for an example of each of the Decorative Methods.

JavaScript Syntax: HTML Syntax Equivalent:

```
anyString.big();          <BIG>      anyString   </BIG>
anyString.blink();        <BLINK>    anyString   </BLINK>
anyString.bold();         <B>        anyString   </B>
anyString.fixed();        <TT>       anyString   </TT>
anyString.italics();      <I>        anyString   </I>
anyString.small();        <SMALL>    anyString   </SMALL>
anyString.strike();       <STRIKE>   anyString   </STRIKE>
anyString.sub();          <SUB>      anyString   </SUB>
anyString.sup();          <SUP>      anyString   </SUP>
```

The toLowerCase() Method of String Object

JavaScript Syntax:

```
anyString.toLowerCase();
```

Parameters Defined:

The **toLowerCase()** Method changes the text String contained in the **anyString** Argument so that it is in all lowercase Characters.

The <u>toUpperCase()</u> Method of String Object

JavaScript Syntax:

```
anyString.toUpperCase();
```

Parameters Defined:

The **toUpperCase()** Method changes the text String contained in the **anyString** Argument so that it is in all uppercase Characters.

The <u>fontcolor()</u> Method of String Object

JavaScript Syntax:

```
anyString.fontcolor("color");
```

Parameters Defined:

The **fontcolor()** Method changes the text String contained in the **anyString** Argument to the color contained in the **color** Argument, which can be a recognized JavaScript color name or a Hexadecimal Triplet. If you use a Hexidecimal Triplet, you have to enclose it, including the hash (#) sign, in either single or double quotes.

The <u>fontsize()</u> Method of String Object

JavaScript Syntax:

```
anyString.fontsize(size);
```

Parameters Defined:

The **fontsize()** Method changes the size of the text String contained in the **anyString** Argument to that of the **size** Argument. The **size** Argument can be either an integer ranging from 1 to 7 or a String Literal that ranges from "-7" to "+7" (that's negative 7 to positive 7, and the quotes are required).

When **size** is used as an <u>integer</u>, it changes the size of **anyString** to one of the 7 predefined sizes. When **size** is specified as a <u>String Literal</u>, then it changes the size in relation to the size set in the BASEFONT Element. BASEFONT has a default Value of 3.

This example demonstrates all of the <u>Decorative</u> Methods of the **String** Object.

Example 8-23:   **Sample923.html**

```
<!DOCTYPE HTML PUBLIC -//W3C//DTD HTML 3.2//EN>
<HTML>
<HEAD>
<TITLE> Sample 923   Example 8-23 decorative string methods </TITLE>

<BASEFONT SIZE="5">

<SCRIPT LANGUAGE="JavaScript1.2"><!--BEGIN HIDING


       var str1 = "My test string.";


       document.write(str1.big() + '<BR>');
       document.write(str1.blink() + '<BR>');
       document.write(str1.bold() + '<BR>');
       document.write(str1.fixed() + '<BR>');
       document.write(str1.italics() + '<BR>');
       document.write(str1.small() + '<BR>');

       document.write(str1 + str1.sub() + '<BR>');
       document.write(str1 + str1.sup() + '<BR>');

       document.write(str1.toLowerCase() + '<BR>');
       document.write(str1.toUpperCase() + '<BR>');

       document.write(str1.fontcolor('red') + '<BR>');
       document.write(str1.fontcolor('#2244ff') + '<BR>');

       document.write(str1.fontsize('-2') + '<BR>');
       document.write(str1.fontsize('+2') + '<BR>');
       document.write(str1.fontsize(6) + '<BR>');


//END HIDING-->
</SCRIPT>

</HEAD>

<BODY>

</BODY>
</HTML>
```

Part II
JavaScript 1.2

Chapter 9

JavaScript RegExps

Chapter 9
JavaScript RegExps

Contents

JavaScript RegExp Objects

Regular Expression Objects Overview

Regular Expressions are new to JavaScript 1.2 and Navigator 4.0. Netscape has modeled their **RegExp** Object based on the rules and syntactical grammars of Regular Expressions from the Perl programming language.

A Regular Expression is basically used to search for specified text in a String or **String** Object and then manipulate the text and the Script based on the results of the search. This is an extremely powerful tool in your programming palette. You can create your own **RegExp** Objects, which will have Methods and Properties to let you use the Regular Expression to interact with **String** Objects. There are also Methods and Properties of the **String** Object that are specifically designed to work with Regular Expressions.

Predefined and Individual RegExp Object Differences

Additionally, there is the Predefined **RegExp** Core Object, which has Properties that are updated every time that you use an Individual **RegExp** Object. It's important to note that all but two of these Predefined **RegExp** Core Object Properties are Static, which means that even though they are updated at compilation, you can't change them yourself and they are read-only. See the Chart on page 807 for read-only or read-write status.

It's important to understand the difference between an Individual **RegExp** Object and the Predefined **RegExp** Core Object. One way to think about it is that the Predefined **RegExp** Core Object is the master Object that reflects information about a particular Individual **RegExp** Object being used at any given time in the course of a Script. As a Script progresses, the Predefined **RegExp** Core Object will update its Properties to reflect the current parameters of the Individual **RegExp** Object being evaluated. You can have more than one Regular Expression in a document and still be assured of the integrity of the Property Values for each Regular Expression as each one is updated, due to the internal structure of JavaScript's thread execution.

Individual **RegExp** Objects have their own Properties that are distinct from the Properties of the Predefined **RegExp** Core Object. Individual **RegExp** Objects have Methods but the Predefined **RegExp** Core Object has no Methods.

Individual Regular Expression Objects can be created with either the **RegExp** Constructor Function or with Literal notation. Most of the examples in this chapter will create Regular Expressions with Literal notation. I use the terms RegExp and Regular Expression interchangeably, but for the most part, Regular Expression refers to an Individual Regular Expression that you create.

Predefined RegExp Object
The <u>Predefined</u> RegExp Core Object

JavaScript Syntax:

```
RegExp.propertyName
```

Overview

Every separate Script in the browser Window is assigned its own <u>Predefined</u> **RegExp** Core Object so that when you have multiple Scripts in one document, the integrity of the Values contained in the Properties of the <u>Predefined</u> **RegExp** Core Objects are maintained, that is, they do not get overwritten by another Script. The reason this works is because each Script is executed inside of its own separate thread inside of JavaScript.

The <u>Predefined</u> **RegExp** Core Object is used in concert with <u>Individual</u> **RegExp** Objects that you create to manipulate String data in your Scripts.

Setting Properties

All of the Properties of the <u>Predefined</u> **RegExp** Core Object are set during the execution of the **exec()** and **test()** Methods of <u>Individual</u> **RegExp** Objects and during the **match()** and **replace()** Methods of the **String** Object. The **input** and **multiline** Properties can be preset prior to a Method invocation.

Accessing Properties

Properties of the <u>Predefined</u> **RegExp** Core Object are always accessed like this:

```
RegExp.input
RegExp.multiline
RegExp.$2
RegExp.leftContext
RegExp.$+
```

Regarding Methods

There are no Methods for the <u>Predefined</u> **RegExp** Core Object; however, there are Methods for <u>Individual</u> Regular Expressions.

The **input** and **multiline** Properties are covered next, and the rest of the Properties of the <u>Predefined</u> **RegExp** Core Object are covered afterwards, in the Property Summaries.

The <u>input</u> Property
of the Predefined RegExp Core Object

JavaScript Syntax:

```
RegExp.input
RegExp.$_
```

The **input** Property, which has the alternative short name of **$_**, is a Read/Write Property of the Predefined **RegExp** Core Object and is always accessed like this:

```
RegExp.input
```
or like this:
```
RegExp.$_
```

It reflects the String that a **pattern** in an Individual Regular Expression attempts to match. If the **exec()** or **test()** Method does not provide an explicit String Argument to match against, then the **input** Property Value is automatically called as the default, provided it has been preset to have a Value. This would be a circumstance where the Script provides the Value.

When the Browser Provides the <u>input</u> Property Value

The browser itself can also provide the Value for the **input** Property. There are four situations when this occurs, all depending on the String Argument not being explicitly supplied in the **exec()** or **test()** Methods. They are:

1)   The Value for the **input** Property is set to the **value** Property of a Text Box (the contained text inside of an <INPUT TYPE="text"> Element) when an Event Handler is called for that Text Box.

2)   The Value for the **input** Property is set to the current text contained inside of a TEXTAREA Element when an Event Handler is called for that TEXTAREA. The Boolean Property **multiline** is also set to **"true"** automatically.

3)   The Value for the **input** Property is set to the text contained in the current selection of a SELECT Element when an Event Handler is called for that SELECT.

4)   The Value for the **input** Property is set to the text contained between the Start and End Tags for an <A> Element when an Event Handler is called for a Link Object like this: <A HREF="url"> the snagged text for input </A>

It should be noted that in all four of the above circumstances, the Value of the **input** Property is cleared after the Event Handler completes its execution.

The <u>multiline</u> Property
of the Predefined RegExp Core Object

JavaScript Syntax:

```
RegExp.multiline
RegExp.$*
```

The **multiline** Property, which has the alternative short name of **$***, is a Read/Write Property of the <u>Predefined</u> **RegExp** Core Object and is always accessed like this:

```
RegExp.multiline
```

or like this:

```
RegExp.$*
```

It is a Boolean Property that specifies a search across multiple lines of text in the Script or the text contained in a TEXTAREA Element if it is set to **"true"**. If it's set to **"false"**, then the search is performed to the end of the first line of text and goes no further.

This Property can be preset by the Script or it can be set by the browser. The browser will set the **multiline** Property to **"true"** when an Event Handler is called on a TEXTAREA Element. This is always done, and the only way to get around it is to use the **select()** Method of the TEXTAREA Element to select the text, assign it to a Variable, and then perform the search over the Variable, if you want to perform a single line search over text contained inside a TEXTAREA Element.

Special Notice:

Note that after the Event Handler is finished, the Value of **multiline** is changed back to its previous state. If it was preset to **"false"** before the Event, then it will be reset to **"false"** after the Event.

Property Summaries
of the Predefined RegExp Core Object

Six of the following Properties are duplicates; that is, the same Property has two different names that refer to exactly the same Value. The first is the spelled-out, longhand version, and the other is the abbreviated, shorthand, "Perl-esque", name (paralleling the Perl programming language). Make sure to remember that these are Properties of the <u>Predefined</u> **RegExp** Core Object and are *not* available to <u>Individual</u> Regular Expressions even though they carry information *about* <u>Individual</u> Regular Expressions. You access these Properties by prepending **RegExp** to them like this: **RegExp.input**

<u>Property</u>	<u>Status</u>	<u>Description</u>
$_	Read/Write	Same as **input**.
$*	Read/Write	Same as **multiline**.
$&	Read-only	Same as **lastMatch**.
$+	Read-only	Same as **lastParen**.
$`	Read-only	Same as **leftContext**.
$'	Read-only	Same as **rightContext**.

Property	Status	Description
input	Read/Write	Contains the String that a **RegExp** attempts to match.
multiline	Read/Write	Boolean Property designating a search across multiple lines of text if true and a single line of text if false.
lastMatch	Read-only	String containing the last matched Characters.
lastParen	Read-only	String containing the last Parenthesized SubString match.
leftContext	Read-only	Contains the SubString before the most recent match.
rightContext	Read-only	Contains the next SubString after the most recent match.

Property	Status	Description
$1, **$2**, **$3**, **$4**, **$5**, **$6**, **$7**, **$8**, **$9**	Read-only	The last nine Parenthesized SubString matches, if any. To access any additional matches, use the indexed Elements of the <u>returned Array</u> from the **exec()** Method. **$9** is the last match. If less than ten matches are made, **$1** will have the first match. The number of possible Parenthesized SubString matches is unlimited, but the <u>Predefined</u> **RegExp** Core Object can only hold the last nine for easy access.

Individual RegExp Objects

RegExp Objects created with Literal notation

JavaScript Syntax:

```
regExpName = /pattern/[flags]
```

Parameters Defined:

The syntax for a **RegExp** Object created with Literal Notation uses the **pattern** Argument to define a <u>pattern of text</u> to search for in a **String** Object. This **pattern** can be Literal Characters like "abcde" or "purple" or "The Secret is 42". The **pattern** can also contain Special Characters like:

?	which means match the preceding Character zero or one times.
\r	which means match a carriage return.

The complete list of Special Characters and their definitions are on pages 814-818.

Never enclose Characters in the **pattern** and **flags** Arguments inside of quotes when creating a **RegExp** Object with <u>Literal notation</u>. The opposite is true when using the <u>Constructor Function</u>.

The optional **flags** Argument can be one of three Character designation Values consisting of **i**, **g**, or **gi** and are special instructions for the **RegExp** Object.

i	means <u>ignore case</u> so that the **pattern** search is case-insensitive.
g	means <u>global</u> so that the **pattern** search looks for all occurrences of the **pattern** in the String instead of stopping after the first match.
gi	means both <u>global</u> and <u>ignore case</u>. Don't use **ig**.

The **regExpName** parameter is just the Name of the Regular Expression so that you can refer to it or call it in an Expression.

When you create a **RegExp** Object with Literal notation, JavaScript compiles the Regular Expression once, when it is evaluated. Therefore, you should use Literal notation when you know what the Regular Expression is and that it won't be changing. It's the more efficient of the two possibilities in terms of processing time. For instance, if you use a **RegExp** in a **for()** loop, the Regular Expression won't be recompiled each time the loop iterates the sequence.

RegExp Objects
created with its Constructor Function

JavaScript Syntax:

```
regExpName = new RegExp("pattern", ["flags"])
```

Parameters Defined:

The Arguments are the same for a **RegExp** Object created with its Constructor Function as for one created with Literal notation. However, there are some important differences in compilation and how the syntax is written. First of all, when the Constructor Function is used, the single or double quotes that enclose the **"pattern"** and **"flags"** Arguments, *are* necessary, and they indicate Strings to the **RegExp** Constructor.

Second, all of the normal <u>String Escape Rules</u> must be adhered to for Special Characters that are used in the **pattern** Argument. If you remember, when you want a Character to be interpreted <u>literally</u> when it normally has a Special meaning you prepend it with a backslash "\" Character. This is true even for the backslash Character itself.

For Example, noting that the **pattern** is in boldface:

<u>RegExp created by</u> <u>Literal notation</u>	is equivalent to	<u>RegExp created by the</u> <u>Constructor Function</u>
re = /**\d***/		re = new RegExp("**\\d***")
re = /**abc\de**/		re = new RegExp("**abc\\de**")
re = /**"abc\de"**/		re = new RegExp("**\"abc\\de\"**")

Note in the third mini-example above that you are searching for <u>Literal</u> double quotes at the start and end of the **pattern**, which have to be <u>Escaped</u> when using the Constructor Function.

Runtime Compilation Issues

The Constructor for a **RegExp** Object compiles the Regular Expression at runtime. Therefore, if you don't know what the **pattern** will be because it is user supplied or if you do know that the **pattern** will be changing due to the Variable nature of the Script, then use the Constructor to create your Regular Expression. Once the **pattern** has been set in the Script, you can use the **compile()** Method to compile it for efficient reuse. When you use the **compile()** Method to force compilation, it prevents the Constructor from automatically compiling the Regular Expression each time it's called. If you are using the Regular Expression inside of a **for()** loop with a lot of iterations, this will save a lot of processing time. See the section on the **compile()** Method later in this chapter for working examples and more info on page 830.

Patterns in Regular Expressions

A **pattern** is basically the text that you want to find a match for when you search in a String. The text that you are looking for is called a SubString of the original String. When you define a **pattern** that is used in a **RegExp** Object created with Literal notation, you always enclose the **pattern** with a forward-slash (/) at the start and end. Never use quote marks in Regular Expressions created with Literal notation. Here's how to do it:

```
/pattern/
```

Literal Characters in **Patterns** in Regular Expressions

The **pattern** can contain Literal Characters like this:

```
/blue/
/12345/
/Arwen/
```

These are simple **patterns** that you use when you want to find a SubString that is a direct match of Characters in the calling String. For instance:

/blue/	matches	'blue'	in	"The blue bird"
/12345/	matches	'12345'	in	"numbers are 012345678"
/Arwen/	matches	'Arwen'	in	"The Lady Arwen"

Notice in the following that:

/blue/	matches nothing		in	"Blue Fish"

because a lowercase 'b' does not match an uppercase 'B'.

/12345/	matches nothing		in	"numbers are 01234 5"

because there are two white space Characters between the 4 and the 5.

/blue bird/	matches nothing		in	"The bluebird flew."

because there is no space Character between the Characters 'blue' and 'bird'.

Special Characters in Patterns in Regular Expressions

You can create more complex **patterns** that contain Special Characters when you are trying to match a SubString that can't be or would be cumbersome to match directly with Literal Characters. Some Special Characters are designated as such by prepending them with a backslash "\" Character like this:

/\r/	This **pattern** matches a carriage return.
/\d/	This **pattern** matches any number.

For instance:

/\d/	matches	'4'	in	"The number is 42."

Ordinarily a **pattern** will just find the first match in a String as the String is read from left to right. If the global **g flag** is used with the Regular Expression, then the **pattern** will find all occurrences of the SubString it is trying to match. For instance, if the **g flag** is used in the previous example, the **pattern** would match both the '4' and the '2' like this:

/\d/g	matches	'4' and '2'	in	"The number is 42."

Other Special Characters include Brackets "[ ]" or Curly Braces "{ }" or a variety of other Characters for specific types of search **patterns**. You can also use a combination of Literal Characters and Special Characters in your **pattern**.

/[^abc]/	Oppositional **pattern** matches anything but 'abc'.
/a{3}/	This **pattern** matches exactly three sequential occurances of 'a'.

For instance:

/a{3}/	matches	'aaa'	in	"baba waaawa"

All of the Special Characters are listed and defined, along with several examples, on pages 814-818.

Parentheses in Patterns in Regular Expressions

Using parentheses around a portion of a **pattern** causes that part of the **pattern** to be remembered so that it can be recalled for later use. All occurrences of Parenthesized SubStrings are stored internally, and the first nine can be accessed by the Script via the **RegExp.$1**, ..., **RegExp.$9** Properties of the <u>Predefined</u> **RegExp** Object. You can access all of the Parenthesized SubStrings by accessing the individual Elements of the <u>returned Array</u> when using the **exec()** Method.

Parenthesized SubStrings

Let's explore Parenthesized SubStrings a bit. Suppose you have the following Regular Expression created with Literal notation that performs a global search because of the **g flag** for a **pattern** that matches two occurrences of the letter L, followed by a single white space Character, followed by any number from 0 to 9. Additionally, any of the Parenthesized SubString **(\d)** matches of a number from 0 to 9 are remembered.

```
/LL\s(\d)/g
```

Then assign it to the **myRE** Variable like this:

```
myRE = /LL\s(\d)/g
```

Next, suppose you have the following String Variable **myStr**:

```
myStr = "ALL 5 LLAMAS GO TO HALL 4."
```

Then, if you use the **exec()** Method to execute the search for the **pattern** in the Regular Expression **myRE** in the String Variable **myStr** like this:

```
myRE.exec(myStr)
```

then the first Parenthesized SubString Match would be: 5
and the second Parenthesized SubString Match would be: 4

which could be accessed with the **RegExp.$1** and the **RegExp.$2** Properties so that:

the **RegExp.$1** Property would have a Value of: 5

and the **RegExp.$2** Property would have a Value of: 4

Exploring Regular Expressions

Mini-Example:

Consider the following very simple Regular Expression that uses "purple" as the **pattern** to search for in another String of text:

```
myRE = /purple/
```

If you have a String such that:

```
"The sky is purple on planet Neon"
```

then using the **exec()** Method to search for the "purple" **pattern** in that String like this:

```
myRE.exec("The sky is purple on planet Neon")
```

would return an Array with one Element consisting of the String "purple".

Mini-Example:

Consider the following where the **pattern L{2}** means to find a match when the Character L occurs exactly two times in succession:

```
myString = "STELLA BLUE."

myRegExp = /L{2}/

myResults = myRegExp.exec(myString)
```

would match the "LL" in STELLA but not the "L" in BLUE, so that **myResults** would be an Array with the one Element of "LL".

Mini-Example:

Suppose you have a Boolean Variable **booleanCheck**. You could assign it an Expression that uses the **test()** Method to determine if the **pattern** "purple" contained in the **myRE** Regular Expression is matched in a String. In the following code, the **test()** Method returns a Value of **true**, which is assigned to **booleanCheck**.

```
myRE = /purple/

booleanCheck = myRE.test("The sky is purple on planet Neon")
```

Chart of all Special Characters for Regular Expressions

On the next few pages are the listings for all of the Special Characters that can be used in Regular Expressions. The Special Character is listed on the left, with a description on the right. Then several Mini-Examples are given.

<u>Special Character</u>   <u>Description</u>

\   This Character has a dual purpose. If the Character it precedes is normally *not* a Special Character, then it changes it so that it *is* a Special Character and is *not* to be interpreted literally.

For instance:
/d/   Normally matches the Character 'd'
/\d/   Matches any number from 0 to 9
          because the backslash Character '\' precedes 'd'

          ---or alternatively---

          If the Character it precedes *is* normally a Special Character, then it changes it so that it is *not* a Special Character and it *should be* interpreted literally.

For instance:
+   Normally means match the preceding Character occurring one or more times.
/A+/   Normally means match the Character 'A' occurring one or more times.
/A\+/   Matches the Literal Characters 'A+' as in: "I got an A+ on my report."

---

^   Matches the start of an input or a new line.
          For instance: /^A/
          matches: 'A'   in   "An apple for the teacher."
          doesn't match: 'A'   in   "I got an A on my report."

$ Matches the end of an input or the end of a line.
          For instance: /a$/
          matches: 'a'   in   "On the sea"
          doesn't match: 'a'   in   "Sailing on water"

---

*   Matches the preceding Character zero or more times.
          For instance: /he*/
          matches: 'heeeee'   in   "heeeeey there"
          matches: 'h'   in   "those musicians"
          matches nothing: in   "See bears be free"   (Hint: no "h")

+   Matches the preceding Character one or more times. Same as {1,}.

                  For instance: /o+/

matches:	'o'	in	"Turn on the light"
matches:	'oooo'	in	"Varoooom"
doesn't match:	'O'	in	"An Orange"

?   Matches the preceding Character zero or one time.

                  For instance: /su?/

matches:	'su'	in	"submarine"
matches:	's'	in	"song"
matches:	'su'	in	"Black Holes suuuuuck"

.   (Period) Matches any individual Character except the newline Character.

                  For instance: /.m/

matches:	'om'	in	"Go home Trevor."
matches:	'am'	in	"A dog named Toby."
doesn't match:	'^m'	in	"^meager delineation."

(x)   Matches 'x' being any sequence of Characters and remembers the match.

                  For instance: /(her)/

matches and remembers:	'her'	in	"red herring"

                  The matched SubString can be referenced from the
<u>returnedArray</u> Elements **[1]** to **[n]**, or from the
<u>Predefined</u> **RegExp** Object's Properties **$1** to **$9**.

---

x | y   Matches either 'x' or 'y', which can be any sequence of Characters.
For more options just separate each one with a vertical bar Character "|".

                  For instance: /blue|black/

matches:	'blue'	in	"I had blueberry pie."
matches:	'black'	in	"I had blackberry cobbler."
doesn't match:	'Black'	in	"Caution, Black ice ahead."

{n}   Matches exactly 'n' occurrences of the preceding Character where 'n' is a
positive integer.

                  For instance: /yu{3}/

matches:	'yuuu'	in	"Pineapple on pizza is yuuucky."
matches:	'yuuu'	in	"yuuuuuuuuum."
doesn't match:	'yu' or 'yuu'	in	"To yum or not to yuum."

{n,}	Matches at least 'n' occurrences of the preceding Character where 'n' is a positive integer.

For instance: /u{3,}/
matches: 'uuu'   in   "Pineapple on pizza is yuuucky."
matches: 'uuuuuuu'   in   "yuuuuuuum."
doesn't match: 'u' or 'uu' in   "To yum or not to yuum."

{n,m}	Matches at least 'n' and no more than 'm' occurrences of the preceding Character where 'n' and 'm' are positive integers.

For instance: /u{2,4}/
matches: 'uu'   in   "yuucky."
matches: 'uuu'   in   "yuuum."
matches: 'uuuu'   in   "yuuuum."
doesn't match: 'u' or 'uuuuu' in "To yum or not to yuuuuum."

[xyz]	Matches any single Character of the bracketed Character Set. To specify a range of Characters, use a hyphen between the start and end Characters.

For instance: /[abcdefg]/   is equivalent to: /[a-g]/
matches: 'e'   in   "prose"
matches: 'g'   in   "goo"

[^xyz]	Oppositional Character Set. Matches any Character that is not specified in the enclosing brackets after the '^' Character. To specify a range of Characters, use a hyphen between the start and end Characters, after '^'.

For instance: /[^abcdefg]/ is equivalent to: /[^a-g]/
matches: 'r'   in   "bear"
matches: 'y'   in   "bye"

[\b]	Matches a backspace Character (Don't confuse with \b).

\b	Matches a word boundary, like tab or space (Don't confuse with [\b]). Note that spaces, etc., get deleted out of the Strings in the <u>returned Array</u>.

For instance: /\bg/
matches: ' g'   in   "elliptical galaxy"
doesn't match: 'g'   in   "the shaggy dog"
For instance: /g\b/
matches: 'g '   in   "the dog barked"
doesn't match: 'g'   in   "the shaggy pup"

\B	Matches a non-word boundary.

For instance: /\Bg/
matches: 'g'   in   "Shagrat was an Ork"
For instance: /g\B\w/
matches: 'gg'   in   "the shaggy pup"

\cX	Matches a Control Character, where X is a Control Character. For instance: /\cE/ matches the Control Key + the 'E' or 'e' Key in a String. See Example 9-6.

\d	Matches a numerical Character. Same as [0-9]. For instance: /\d/ or /[0-9]/ matches: '5' in "Babylon 5"

\D	Matches any non-numerical Character. Same as [^0-9]. For instance: /\D/ or /[^0-9]/ matches: 'B' in "Babylon 5"

\f	Matches the first form feed.

\n	Matches a line feed.

\r	Matches a carriage return.

\s	Matches any single white space Character like space, tab, vertical tab, carriage return, form feed, and line feed. Same as [\f\n\r\t\v]. For instance: /\s\w+/ matches: ' name' in "The name of the place is"

\S	Matches any single Character other than white space Characters. Same as [^ \f\n\r\t\v]. For instance: /\S/ matches: 'T' in "The name of the place is" matches: 'r' in "rock"

\t	Matches a tab.

\v	Matches a vertical tab.

\w	Matches any alphanumeric Character and the underscore Character '_'. Same as [A-Za-z0-9_]. For instance: /\w/ or /[A-Za-z0-9_]/ matches: 'b' in "blue" matches: '2' in "#2300fe" matches: '_' in "_top"

\W	Matches any non-alphanumeric Character except the underscore. Same as [^A-Za-z0-9_]. For instance: /\W/ or /[^A-Za-z0-9_]/ matches: '#' in "#8800ff"

\n	<u>Where 'n' is a positive integer</u>. When you enclose a SubSection of the Regular Expression within parentheses, that SubSection is remembered and can be referenced as a SubString. The parenthesized SubSections of the Regular Expression are counted from left to right starting at 1. Therefore, 'n' is the nth parenthesized SubSection back-reference to the last SubString that is remembered.

(The simple explanation is that if you want to match text that you know is going to be repeated in the String, then you can use the '\n' to look for it instead of repeating the syntax explicitly in the Regular Expression.)

For instance:	/(red)\1/		
matches:	'red red '	in	"The colors blue red red green."

For instance:	/(3)(+)4\2/		
matches:	'3+4+'	in	"1+2+3+4+5+6+7"

For instance:	/eagle(\sand)\shawk\1/		
matches:	'eagle and hawk and '	in	"eagle and hawk and emu"

Notice that if the number of parenthesized SubSections is less than the number specified in 'n', then 'n' is interpreted as an octal escape Value that is defined next.

See <u>Sample1009.html</u> on pages 835-836 for a working example of this Special Character.

\ooctal	Matches 'ooctal' where 'ooctal' is any octal escape Value. Lets you include ASCII code Values directly into Regular Expressions.

\xhex	Matches 'xhex' where 'xhex' is any hexadecimal escape Value. Lets you include ASCII code Values directly into Regular Expressions.

\dec	Matches 'dec' where 'dec' is any decimal escape Value. Lets you include ASCII code Values directly into Regular Expressions.

Method Summary of
Individual RegExp Objects

The Methods of <u>Individual</u> **RegExp** Objects that you create are:

Method	Description
test()	Used to search for a match between the Regular Expression and the specified String. Returns **true** if a match is found and **false** if no match is found.
exec()	Used to search for a match between the Regular Expression and the specified String. If a match is found, the Method returns an Array of SubStrings and updates the Properties of both the <u>Individual</u> Regular Expression and the <u>Predefined</u> **RegExp** Object. Returns '**null**' if no match is found.
compile()	Used for efficiency to force compilation of a Regular Expression created with the **RegExp** Constructor Function so that it is not continually recompiled during execution. Also used to change the Regular Expression during execution.

Summary of <u>String</u> <u>Methods</u> used with
Individual RegExp Objects

The Methods of **String Objects** that you can use to interact with and manipulate <u>Individual</u> **RegExp** Objects are:

Method	Description
search()	Matches a Regular Expression **pattern** against the calling String and returns the **index** within the calling String of the match.
match()	Matches a Regular Expression **pattern** against the calling String and returns an Array of Strings reflecting the matches.
replace()	Matches a Regular Expression **pattern** against the calling String and replaces the matched SubString with a new SubString.
split()	Returns an Array of SubStrings resulting from splitting up the calling String, based on a **separator** that can be a String or a Regular Expression.

For more information and examples of these String Methods, see Chapter 8 on **String** Objects on pages 770-787, and later on in Chapter 9.

Property Summary of
Individual RegExp Objects

The Properties of <u>Individual</u> **RegExp** Objects that you create are:

<u>Property</u>	<u>Description</u>
global	A <u>read-only</u> Boolean Property that has a Value of '**true**' if the **g flag** was used in the Regular Expression and '**false**' if it wasn't. The **g flag** specifies that the Regular Expression must find all the possible matches in the String. Without the **g flag**, the Regular Expression stops after the first match. Note that this Property cannot be changed explicitly, but it may possibly be changed as a result of calling the **compile()** Method.
ignoreCase	A <u>read-only</u> Boolean Property that has a Value of '**true**' if the **i flag** was used in the Regular Expression and '**false**' if it wasn't. The **i flag** specifies that the Regular Expression should ignore case, so the search is case-insensitive when looking for a match in a String. Note that this Property cannot be changed explicitly, but it may possibly be changed as a result of calling the **compile()** Method.
lastIndex	A <u>read/write</u> integer Property that is only applicable and set if the **g flag** is set to specify a global search. It indicates the **index** where the Regular Expression should start the next search. See page 832 for more information.
source	A <u>read-only</u> Property that contains the **pattern** Argument of the Regular Expression. Note that this does <u>*not*</u> include either of the enclosing forward slashes '/' or the suffixed **i** or **g flags**. Note that this Property cannot be changed explicitly, but it may possibly be changed as a result of calling the **compile()** Method. See page 828 for an example.

The <u>test()</u> Method of <u>Individual</u> RegExp Objects

JavaScript Syntax:

```
regExpName.test(anyString);
```

Parameters Defined:

The **test()** Method of <u>Individual</u> **RegExp** Objects searches for a match in the String **anyString** to the **pattern** contained in the **regExpName** Regular Expression. If a match is found, then the Method returns **true**. Additionally, the Properties of the **regExpName** and the Properties of the <u>Predefined</u> **RegExp** Core Object are set; or updated if previously set. If no match is found, then the Method returns **false**. The **regExpName** can be a Variable name or a **RegExp** Literal.

The **anyString** Argument is optional. If it isn't specified, then the **test()** Method uses the **RegExp.input** Value as the default Argument Value.

When to <u>test()</u> or <u>exec()</u>

The **test()** Method is primarily used when you only need to know if a match was found or not. Therefore, you usually embed it inside of an **if()** or **switch()** Statement and base the executable Statements on the Boolean return of **test()**. This Method is functionally similar to the **search()** Method of the **String** Object.

Because the **test()** Method executes faster than the **exec()** Method, it's the preferred choice when you don't need the additional Property data provided by the **exec()** Method.

Example 9-0 demonstrates the **test()** Method by first defining a String Variable **str1** and then defining a Regular Expression named **myRE1** by setting it to **/crypt/**. Next, it defines a Boolean Variable named **booleanTest** and assigns it the following Expression, which uses the **test()** Method to determine if the **pattern** contained in the Regular Expression is found in the String **str1**.

```
booleanTest = myRE1.test(str1);
```

Because the **pattern** is matched, the **document.write()** Method will output the Value of "**true**" to screen.

Example 9-0:   **Sample1000.html**

```
<!DOCTYPE HTML PUBLIC -//W3C//DTD HTML 3.2//EN>
<HTML>
<HEAD>
<TITLE>        Sample 1000    Example 9-0 test Method </TITLE>
<BASEFONT SIZE="5">

<SCRIPT LANGUAGE="JavaScript1.2"> <!--BEGIN HIDING

        str1 = "cryptical envelopment";

        myRE1 = /crypt/;

        booleanTest = myRE1.test(str1);

        document.write(booleanTest);

//END HIDING-->
</SCRIPT>

</HEAD>

<BODY>
</BODY>
</HTML>
```

Example 9-1 demonstrates the **test()** Method by first defining a String Variable **str1** and then defining a Regular Expression named **myRE1** by setting it to **/galaxy/**. Next, it defines a Boolean Variable named **booleanTest** and assigns it the following Expression, which uses the **test()** Method to determine if the **pattern** contained in the Regular Expression is found in the String **str1**.

```
        booleanTest = myRE1.test(str1);
```

Then **booleanTest** is used as the **condition** in an if() Statement, and because it evaluates to **true**, the **document** background color is changed to blue and the attendant text is written to screen.

Example 9-1:   **Sample1001.html**

```
<!DOCTYPE HTML PUBLIC -//W3C//DTD HTML 3.2//EN>
<HTML>
<HEAD>
<TITLE>        Sample 1001    Example 9-1    test Method     </TITLE>

<BASEFONT SIZE="5">
</HEAD>

<BODY TEXT='white'>

<SCRIPT LANGUAGE="JavaScript1.2"> <!--BEGIN HIDING

      str1 = "elliptical galaxy";

      myRE1 = /galaxy/;

      booleanTest = myRE1.test(str1);

      if (booleanTest) {

             document.bgColor = "blue";
             document.write("Since true, the document is blue.");
      }

//END HIDING-->
</SCRIPT>

</BODY>
</HTML>
```

Example 9-2 assigns the **tester()** Function to the **onClick** Event Handler for the Button named **b1**. The **tester()** Function starts by assigning the Value Attribute of the text field named **text1** to a String Variable named **str1**. Next, a Regular Expression is defined so that it tries to match one or more digits and is assigned to the Variable **myRE1**. Then, the **booleanTest** Variable is assigned the Expression that invokes the **test()** Method on **myRE1** with **str1** as the String Argument like this:

```
var booleanTest = myRE1.test(str1);
```

The **booleanTest** Variable is used as the **condition** in the **if()** Statement so that if the **pattern** in **myRE1** is matched in **str1**, then the matched SubString is displayed in **text1** by using the **lastMatch** Property of the **RegExp** Core Object within the **write()** Method. If no match is made, the "Try again" message is displayed in **text1**.

Example 9-2:   **Sample1002.html**

```html
<!DOCTYPE HTML PUBLIC -//W3C//DTD HTML 3.2//EN>
<HTML>
<HEAD>
<TITLE>       Sample 1002    Example 9-2      test Method     </TITLE>

<BASEFONT SIZE="5">

<SCRIPT LANGUAGE="JavaScript1.2"> <!--BEGIN HIDING

function tester() {

        var str1 = document.form1.text1.value;

                        //matches 1 or more digits

        var myRE1 = /\d+/;

        var booleanTest = myRE1.test(str1);

        if (booleanTest) {

                document.form1.text1.value = "Congrats, you matched: " +
                                        RegExp.lastMatch;
        }

        else document.form1.text1.value = "Try again";

        document.form1.text1.focus();
        document.form1.text1.select();
}

//END HIDING-->
</SCRIPT>

</HEAD>

<BODY onLoad="document.form1.text1.focus();">

Type numbers to match \d+ and click the button.

<FORM NAME="form1">

<INPUT TYPE="text" NAME="text1" SIZE="40" VALUE="">                <BR>

<INPUT TYPE="button" NAME="b1" VALUE="Test it now" onClick="tester();">

</FORM>

</BODY>
</HTML>
```

The <u>exec()</u> Method of
<u>Individual</u> RegExp Objects

JavaScript Syntax:

```
regExpName.exec([anyString]);
regExpName.([anyString]);            //The shortcut version
```

Parameters Defined:

The **exec()** Method of <u>Individual</u> **RegExp** Objects searches for a match in the String **anyString** to the **pattern** contained in the **regExpName** Regular Expression. If a match is found, then the Method returns an Array of SubStrings, where each Element in the Array is a separate SubString, and if there are any Parenthesized SubString matches, then those are returned as well. Additionally, the Properties of the **regExpName** and the Properties of the <u>Predefined</u> **RegExp** Core Object are set; or updated if previously set. The **exec()** Method updates them each time it is invoked. In fact, the **test()** Method and the **match()** and **replace()** Methods of the **String** Object all update these Properties.

If only one match is found, then an Array is returned that has only one Element.

If no match is found, then the Method returns "**null**". The **regExpName** can be a Variable name or a Literal.

The **anyString** Argument is optional. If it isn't specified, then the **exec()** Method uses the **RegExp.input** Value as the default Argument Value.

The **exec()** Method is much more versatile than the **test()** Method, but it does require more processing time. However, until you start programming serious number crunching, the additional processing time is negligible.

The **i flag** causes the matched String returned in the Array at Element [0] to be changed so that it reflects only lowercase Characters of the **pattern**. The remembered Parenthesized SubStrings however, accurately reflect uppercase and lowercase Characters.
When the **g flag** is used with the **exec()** Method, the <u>returned Array</u> at Element [0] reflects the last matched SubString and does not include any other matched SubStrings except for the Parenthesized SubStrings, which are remembered in Elements [1] to [n].
The **match()** Method of the **String** Object will not return the remembered Parenthesized SubStrings in the Array when the **g flag** is used for a global search, but it will return all of the matches found in the search. You can still access the last nine Parenthesized SubString matches that are remembered by using the **RegExp.$1** to **RegExp.$9** Properties when using the **match()** Method. See Example 9-12 on page 840.

This example demonstrates the **exec()** Method for four different Regular Expressions on three String Variables. The results of invoking the **exec()** Method on the Strings are written to screen, and then in the BODY of the **document** the text shows what part of the String was matched to the **pattern**.

Example 9-3: **Sample1003.html**

```
<!DOCTYPE HTML PUBLIC -//W3C//DTD HTML 3.2//EN>
<HTML>
<HEAD>
<TITLE> Sample 1003    Example 9-3 exec Method</TITLE>

<SCRIPT LANGUAGE="JavaScript1.2"> <!--BEGIN HIDING

        str1 = "elliptical galaxy";
        str2 = "the dog barked";
        str3 = "the shaggy pup";

                myRE1 = /\bg/;
                myRE2 = /g\b/;

                myRE3 = /\w\Bg/;
                myRE4 = /g\B\w/;

        document.write(myRE1.exec(str1) +  "<P>");
        document.write(myRE2.exec(str2) +  "<P>");
        document.write(myRE3.exec(str3) +  "<P>");
        document.write(myRE4.exec(str3) +  "<P>");


//END HIDING-->
</SCRIPT>

</HEAD>

<BODY>
        For instance:  /\bg/                                      <BR>
        matches:                ' g'        in      "elliptical galaxy"  <P>

        For instance:  /g\b/                                      <BR>
        matches:                'g '        in      "the dog barked"     <P>

        For instance:  /\w\Bg/                                    <BR>
        matches:                'ag'        in      "the shaggy pup"     <P>

        For instance:  /g\B\w/                                    <BR>
        matches:                'gg'        in      "the shaggy pup"     <BR>

</BODY>
</HTML>
```

This example demonstrates that when a Value is set for the **input** Property and no String is specified in the **exec()** Method, then the **input** Property Value is used as the String Argument by default. If the user-supplied **input** from the Text Box **text1** matches one or more digits, then the **lastMatch** Property displays the match; else, "Try again" is displayed.

Example 9-4:   **Sample1004.html**

```
<!DOCTYPE HTML PUBLIC -//W3C//DTD HTML 3.2//EN>
<HTML>
<HEAD>
<TITLE> Sample 1004   Example 9-4 exec Method and input Property</TITLE>
<BASEFONT SIZE="5">

<SCRIPT LANGUAGE="JavaScript1.2"> <!--BEGIN HIDING

function tester() {

        RegExp.input = document.form1.text1.value;

                             //matches 1 or more digits
        var myRE1 = /\d+/;
                             //since no String is supplied, RegExp.input is used
        var myArray = myRE1.exec();

        if (myArray != null) {

                document.form1.text1.value = "Congrats, you matched: " +
                                     RegExp.lastMatch;
        }

        else document.form1.text1.value = "Try again";

        document.form1.text1.focus();
        document.form1.text1.select();
}

//END HIDING-->
</SCRIPT>
</HEAD>

<BODY onLoad="document.form1.text1.focus();">
        Type numbers to match \d+ and click the button.

<FORM NAME="form1">
<INPUT TYPE="text" NAME="text1" SIZE="40" VALUE=""><BR>
<INPUT TYPE="button" NAME="b1" VALUE="Test it now" onClick="tester();">

</FORM>
</BODY>
</HTML>
```

This example uses the **exec()** Method to search for the **pattern** containing '**aa**' and followed by exactly two **b**'s and followed by one or more **c**'s.

The output that follows this example shows the Values for the Properties and Objects that are associated with the Regular Expression when it is executed in the Script.

Example 9-5: Sample1005.html

```
<!DOCTYPE HTML PUBLIC -//W3C//DTD HTML 3.2//EN>
<HTML><HEAD>
<TITLE> Sample 1005    Example 9-5 exec Method</TITLE>
<BASEFONT SIZE="5">

<SCRIPT LANGUAGE="JavaScript1.2"> <!--BEGIN HIDING

        myStr = "Sizzle your aabbccc's today";

        myRE  = /(aa)(b{2})(c+)/;

        myArray = myRE.exec(myStr);

        document.write("myArray      = " + myArray    + "<P>");

        document.write("myArray.index = " + myArray.index + "<BR>");
        document.write("myArray.input = " + myArray.input + "<BR>");

        document.write("myArray[0]    = " + myArray[0] + "<BR>");
        document.write("myArray[1]    = " + myArray[1] + "<BR>");
        document.write("myArray[2]    = " + myArray[2] + "<BR>");
        document.write("myArray[3]    = " + myArray[3] + "<P>");

        document.write("myRE.global          = " + myRE.global     + "<BR>");
        document.write("myRE.ignoreCase      = " + myRE.ignoreCase + "<BR>");
        document.write("myRE.lastIndex       = " + myRE.lastIndex  + "<BR>");
        document.write("myRE.source          = " + myRE.source     + "<P>");

        document.write("RegExp.lastMatch     = " + RegExp.lastMatch     + "<BR>");
        document.write("RegExp.lastParen     = " + RegExp.lastParen     + "<BR>");
        document.write("RegExp.leftContext   = " + RegExp.leftContext   + "<BR>");
        document.write("RegExp.rightContext  = " + RegExp.rightContext  + "<BR>");

        document.write("RegExp.$1 = "     + RegExp.$1    + "<BR>");
        document.write("RegExp.$2 = "     + RegExp.$2    + "<BR>");
        document.write("RegExp.$3 = "     + RegExp.$3    + "<BR>");

//END HIDING-->
</SCRIPT>
</HEAD>
<BODY>
</BODY>
</HTML>
```

The previous example produces the following data in the browser. It has been spread out and tab-enhanced in the book to make it more chartlike and easier to read.

myArray	=	["aabbccc", "aa", "bb", "ccc"]
myArray.index	=	7
myArray.input	=	Sizzle aabbccc's today
myArray[0]	=	aabbccc
myArray[1]	=	aa
myArray[2]	=	bb
myArray[3]	=	ccc
myRE.global	=	false
myRE.ignoreCase	=	false
myRE.lastIndex	=	0
myRE.source	=	(aa)(b{2})(c+)
RegExp.lastMatch	=	aabbccc
RegExp.lastParen	=	ccc
RegExp.leftContext	=	Sizzle
RegExp.rightContext	=	's today
RegExp.$1	=	aa
RegExp.$2	=	bb
RegExp.$3	=	ccc

The <u>compile()</u> Method of <u>Individual</u> RegExp Objects

JavaScript Syntax:

```
regExpName.compile("pattern", ["flags"]);
```

Parameters Defined:

The **compile()** Method is used to compile a Regular Expression created with the **RegExp** Constructor Function. It forces compilation *once and only once* so that the Regular Expression isn't constantly being recompiled by the Constructor Function each time the Script calls it, which is the default behavior of the Constructor Function. Note in the Syntax that both the **pattern** and the optional **flags** Arguments *must be* enclosed in quotes when used in the **compile()** Method.

Use the **compile()** Method at a point in the Script after the **pattern** of the Regular Expression has been received, from whatever source, and you know that it will be used again and won't be changing later on in the Script. If the **pattern** is going to be changing later on in the Script, you can always **compile** it again later after it has been reset.

The **flags** Argument can take one of the following three parameters:

"g"   Perform a global search.
"i"   Ignore case and thus perform a case-insensitive search.
"gi"   Perform a global case-insensitive search. (Using **"ig"** is an error.)

When this Method is called, the Values of the **global**, **ignoreCase**, and **source** Properties of <u>Individual</u> **RegExp** Objects are updated.

Example 9-6 expands slightly on Example 9-5 and is only designed to show the basic mechanics of using the **compile()** Method. It's not a real-world example where it would be efficiency enhancing to the Script.

Basically, it lets the user supply a String in a Text Box named **text1** and a Regular Expression in another Text Box named **reText**. Those Values are supplied to the String Variables **str** and **reStr**, respectively.

Then a new Regular Expression is created and assigned to **myRE1** that uses the **reStr** Value as the **pattern** for the Regular Expression. The **compile()** Method is then invoked on **myRE1** to compile the **pattern** in the Regular Expression.

Then the **exec()** Method is invoked on **myRE1** with the Value in **str** as the String Argument, and the <u>returned Array</u> is assigned to **myArray**. Finally, in the **if()** Statement the Value of **myArray** will not be equal to **null** if a match is found and **RegExp.lastMatch** displays that match in the Text Box **text1**: otherwise, "Try again" is displayed.

Example 9-6: Sample1006.html

```
<!DOCTYPE HTML PUBLIC -//W3C//DTD HTML 3.2//EN>
<HTML>
<HEAD>
        <TITLE> Sample 1006    Example 9-6 compile Method</TITLE>
<BASEFONT SIZE="5">

<SCRIPT LANGUAGE="JavaScript1.2"> <!--BEGIN HIDING

function tester() {

        var str = document.form1.text1.value;
        var reStr = document.form1.reText.value;

        var myRE1 = new RegExp(reStr);

        myRE1.compile(reStr);

        var myArray = myRE1.exec(str);

        if (myArray != null) {

                document.form1.text1.value = "Congrats, you matched: " +
                                        RegExp.lastMatch;
        }

        else document.form1.text1.value = "Try again";

        document.form1.text1.focus();
        document.form1.text1.select();
}

//END HIDING-->
</SCRIPT>
</HEAD>
<BODY onLoad="document.form1.text1.focus();">

<FORM NAME="form1">

Type in a Text String.
<INPUT TYPE="text" NAME="text1" SIZE="40" VALUE="">  <BR>

Type in your Regular Expression.
<INPUT TYPE="text" NAME="reText" SIZE="40" VALUE=""> <BR>

<INPUT TYPE="button" NAME="b1" VALUE="Test it now" onClick="tester();">    <BR><BR>

Click the button to see if your Regular Expression finds a match in your Text
String.
</FORM>

</BODY>
</HTML>
```

The <u>lastIndex</u> Property of <u>Individual</u> RegExp Objects

JavaScript Syntax:

```
regExpName.lastIndex;
```

The **lastIndex** Property is a read/write Property of an <u>Individual</u> Regular Expression Object. It is only set and therefore relevant, if the **g flag** is specified to execute a global search.

read and write Issues

As a <u>read</u> Property, that is, if you read its Value as it naturally occurs, it indicates the Character **index** immediately following the most recent match.

As a <u>write</u> Property, that is, you choose to set its Value within the Script, you determine the Character **index** where the Regular Expression should start the next search.

read Conditions Chart

As a <u>read</u> Property, the following conditions apply to the **lastIndex** Property for any Regular Expression named **re** and any String named **str**:

If: `re.lastIndex > str.length`   Then: `re.exec()` returns `null`
                                              `re.test()` returns `false`
                                              `re.lastIndex = 0`

If: `re.lastIndex == str.length`   <u>and</u>
If: `re` matches the empty String   Then: `re` matches `re.input` starting at `re.lastIndex`

If: `re.lastIndex == str.length`   <u>and</u>
If: `re` doesn't match the empty String   Then: `re` doesn't match `re.input` and `re.lastIndex` resets to 0

If: None of the above are true   <u>and</u>
If: `re.lastIndex` is not explicitly set   Then: `re.lastIndex` sets to the Character **index** after the most recent match

Example 9-7 employs the Special Characters \D, which matches any non-digit Character and {n,m} where n and m are both positive integers, so that the preceding Character must occur at least n times but no more than m times.

So in the String named **str1**, any non-digit Character followed by at least two c's and at most four c's will match the Regular Expression named **myRE1**, which is also set to perform a global search with the **g flag**.

The **match()** Method of the **String** Object is invoked on **str1**, and the resulting Array is assigned to the **myMatchArray** Variable, which is then written to screen as an Array Literal with the **write()** Method.

Example 9-7 produces this output for **myMatchArray** in the browser:

["Acc", "Bccc", "Dcccc", "Ecccc"]

Example 9-7:   Sample1007.html

```
<!DOCTYPE HTML PUBLIC -//W3C//DTD HTML 3.2//EN>
<HTML>
<HEAD>
<TITLE> Sample 1007   Example 9-7  \D and {n,m} Special Characters</TITLE>

<SCRIPT LANGUAGE="JavaScript1.2"> <!--BEGIN HIDING


        str1 = "aAccaBcccDccccEccccc";

//      \D              matches any non-digit Character
//      c{2,4}          matches c when it occurs at least 2 and at most 4 times

        myRE1 = /\Dc{2,4}/g;

        myMatchArray = str1.match(myRE1);

        document.write(myMatchArray);


//END HIDING-->
</SCRIPT>

</HEAD>

<BODY>
</BODY>
</HTML>
```

This example demonstrates the Special Character **\d**, which matches any digit Character and the Special Characters **{n,}**, which matches at least **n** occurrences of the preceding Character. In the **myRE1** Regular Expression Literal, **n=3**, so the preceding Character "c", must occur at least three times. Note that it actually matches all five of the c's in the String named **str1**, not just the minimum of three occurrences of "c".

The resulting Array **myExecArray** has the one Element of:

["7ccccc"]

Example 9-8:   Sample1008.html

```
<!DOCTYPE HTML PUBLIC -//W3C//DTD HTML 3.2//EN>
<HTML>
<HEAD>
<TITLE> Sample 1008    Example 9-8       {n,} Special Character      </TITLE>

<SCRIPT LANGUAGE="JavaScript1.2"> <!--BEGIN HIDING


        str1 = "a1ca2cc7ccccc";

//      \d              matches any digit Character
//      c{3,}           matches c when it occurs at least 3 times

        myRE1 = /\dc{3,}/;

        myExecArray = myRE1.exec(str1);

        document.write(myExecArray);


//END HIDING-->
</SCRIPT>

</HEAD>

<BODY>
        Note that it matches all five occurrences of c instead of just the required
minimum of three.

</BODY>
</HTML>
```

This example demonstrates the Special Character \n, where **n** is a positive integer that specifies a remembered SubString match to find in the String being searched.

For **myRE1**, the **pattern** searched for is "red " followed by the remembered SubString of "red ".

For **myRE2**, the **pattern** searched for is "3" followed by "+" followed by "4" followed by the second remembered SubString of "+".

For **myRE3**, the **pattern** searched for is "eagle" followed by a space followed by "and" followed by a space followed by the first remembered SubString of a space followed by "and". There is more data about this example on the next page, including output.

Example 9-9:   Sample1009.html

```
<!DOCTYPE HTML PUBLIC -//W3C//DTD HTML 3.2//EN>
<HTML>
<HEAD>
        <TITLE> Sample 1009   Example 9-9  Special Character \n </TITLE>

<SCRIPT LANGUAGE="JavaScript1.2"> <!--BEGIN HIDING


        str1 = "The colors blue red red green.";
        str2 = "1+2+3+4+5+6+7";
        str3 = "eagle and hawk and emu";

        myRE1 = /(red )\1/;
        myRE2 = /(3)(+)4\2/;
        myRE3 = /eagle(\sand)\shawk\1/;

        document.write(myRE1.exec(str1) +  "<P>");
        document.write(myRE2.exec(str2) +  "<P>");
        document.write(myRE3.exec(str3) +  "<P>");


//END HIDING-->
</SCRIPT>
</HEAD>

<BODY>
        For instance:   /(red )\1/                      <BR>
        matches:        'red red '                      <P>

        For instance:   /(3)(+)4\2/                     <BR>
        matches:        '3+4+'                          <P>

        For instance:   /eagle(\sand)\shawk\1/          <BR>
        matches:        'eagle and hawk and '

</BODY>
</HTML>
```

The **exec()** Method is called by the **myRE1** Regular Expression and searches the **str1** String for a match. Note that the resulting Array is not assigned to a Variable, but is written directly to screen with the **write()** Method. This process is repeated for both of the other two Strings and Regular Expressions. The three <u>returned Arrays</u> resulting from the three searches, containing their respective match and remembered SubString or SubStrings, are:

<u>This Expression</u>	<u>Returns</u>	<u>This Array</u>
`myRE1.exec(str1)`	<u>returns</u>	`["red red ", "red "]`
`myRE2.exec(str2)`	<u>returns</u>	`["3+4+", "3", "+"]`
`myRE3.exec(str3)`	<u>returns</u>	`["eagle and hawk and", " and"]`

Example 9-9 produces the following output in the browser. Check the notes in the output below for more information about the matches found in the search.

["red red ", "red "]

["3+4+", "3", "+"]

["eagle and hawk and", " and"]

For instance:	/(red)\1/
matches:	'red red '

For instance:	/(3)(+)4\2/
matches:	'3+4+'

For instance:	/eagle(\sand)\shawk\1/
matches:	'eagle and hawk and '

Example 9-10 demonstrates the Special Character \cX, where **X** is a Control Character, which in this example, **X** is equal to the Control Character "R". Check out the notes in the BODY of the example for more information on the matches.

The resulting Arrays from the **exec()** Method being invoked with the three String Arguments of **str1**, **str2**, and **str3** are as follows:

```
        myRE1.exec(str1)    =        ["\022"]

        myRE1.exec(str2)    =        ["\022"]

        myRE1.exec(str3)    =        ["\022"]
```

Example 9-10:   Sample1010.html

```html
<!DOCTYPE HTML PUBLIC -//W3C//DTD HTML 3.2//EN>
<HTML>
<HEAD>
        <TITLE> Sample 1010   Example 9-10 matching Control Characters</TITLE>

<SCRIPT LANGUAGE="JavaScript1.2"> <!--BEGIN HIDING

        str1 = " galaxy";
        str2 = " galaxy";
        str3 = " galaxy";

        myRE1 = /\cR/;

        document.write(myRE1.exec(str1) +  "<P>");
        document.write(myRE1.exec(str2) +  "<P>");
        document.write(myRE1.exec(str3));

//END HIDING-->
</SCRIPT>

</HEAD>

<BODY>

        For instance:  /\cR/                                        <P>

matches:        'control + r'                 in:.....    " galaxy"  <P>

matches:        'control + shift + R'         in:.....    " galaxy"  <P>

matches:        'control + CapsLock + R'      in:.....    " galaxy"  <P>

</BODY>
</HTML>
```

Example to verify phone number using Regular Expressions

This example uses the Regular Expression created with Literal notation and assigned to **myRE1**, such that:

myRE1 = /\(?**(\d{3})**\)?**([-\/\.]*)**(\d{3})**([-\/\.]*)**(\d{4})/

The alternating plain and bold text in the **pattern** above is so that you can easily see the individual <u>parts</u> of the **pattern** when you check the Comments in the Sample code below for individual explanations of those <u>parts</u>.

The Function **tester()** is used to verify the phone number that is input by the user into the Text Box **text1**.

If a match is found to the **pattern**, then if none of the Separator Characters of dash, period, or forward slash are is, then a **confirm** dialog renders the remembered numbers in the **pattern** and separates each with a dash. If the user confirms that the numbers are correct, then they are displayed in **text1**. If **confirm** is false, the message "Try again" is displayed in **text1**.

If the user has separated the numbers with dashes, periods, or forward slashes, then those Characters are remembered and are rendered along with the remembered numbers in the **confirm** dialog. If the user confirms that they are accurate, then all five of the remembered SubStrings are displayed in **text1**, else, "Try again" is displayed in **text1**.

The remembered SubStrings are accessed by the **RegExp.$1** through **RegExp.$5** Properties.

Example 9-11:   **Sample1011.html**

```
<!DOCTYPE HTML PUBLIC -//W3C//DTD HTML 3.2//EN>
<HTML><HEAD>
<TITLE> Sample 1011    Example 9-11 match and verify phone number</TITLE>
<BASEFONT SIZE="5">

<SCRIPT LANGUAGE="JavaScript1.2"> <!--BEGIN HIDING

function tester() {

        var str = document.form1.text1.value;

//      In the Regular Expression myRE1, the following sections of the pattern mean:

//      \(?            MEANS                 Zero or one parentheses
//      (\d{3})        MEANS   REMEMBER      3 sequential digits
//      \(?            MEANS                 Zero or one parentheses
//      ([-\/\.]*)     MEANS   REMEMBER      a dash or forward slash or period
//      (\d{3})        MEANS   REMEMBER      3 sequential digits
//      ([-\/\.]*)     MEANS   REMEMBER      a dash or forward slash or period
//      (\d{4})        MEANS   REMEMBER      4 sequential digits
```

```
        var myRE1 = /\(?(\d{3})\)?([-\/\.]*)(\d{3})([-\/\.]*)(\d{4})/;

        var myArray = myRE1.exec(str);

        if (myArray != null) {

                if (RegExp.$2 == ""  ||  RegExp.$4 == "") {

                        if (confirm("Is your Phone Number: " +
                                RegExp.$1 + "-" + RegExp.$3 + "-" + RegExp.$5)) {

                                document.form1.text1.value = RegExp.$1 + "-"
                                + RegExp.$3 + "-" + RegExp.$5;
                        }
                        else document.form1.text1.value = "Try again.";
                }

                else { if (confirm("Is your Phone Number: " +
                                RegExp.$1 + RegExp.$2 + RegExp.$3 +
                                RegExp.$4 + RegExp.$5))  {

                                document.form1.text1.value = RegExp.$1 + RegExp.$2 +
                                RegExp.$3 + RegExp.$4 + RegExp.$5;
                        }
                        else document.form1.text1.value = "Try again.";
                }
        }

        else alert("Try again.");

        document.form1.text1.focus();
        document.form1.text1.select();
}


//END HIDING-->
</SCRIPT>

</HEAD>

<BODY onLoad="document.form1.text1.focus();">

<FORM NAME="form1">

Type in your Phone Number.

<INPUT TYPE="text" NAME="text1" SIZE="40" VALUE=""> <BR>

<INPUT TYPE="button" NAME="b1" VALUE="Test it now" onClick="tester();">    <BR><BR>

Click the button to verify the phone number.

</FORM>

</BODY>
</HTML>
```

exec() & match() Method differences

Example 9-12 demonstrates the differences between the **exec()** Method of Regular Expressions and the **match()** Method of the **String Object** in terms of the data returned in the Elements of the returned Array when a global search is indicated with the **g flag**.

When the **g flag** is used with the **exec()** Method, the returned Array at Element **[0]** reflects the last matched SubString and does not include any other matched SubStrings except for the Parenthesized SubStrings that are remembered in Elements **[1]** to **[n]**.

The **match()** Method of the **String** Object will not return the remembered Parenthesized SubStrings in the Array when the **g flag** is used for a global search, but it will return all of the matches found in the search. You can still access the last nine Parenthesized SubString matches that are remembered by using the **RegExp.$1** through **RegExp.$9** Properties when using the **match()** Method.

The **match()** Method is covered first with the Regular Expression named **myRE1** that has four different Parenthesized SubStrings to remember. The **myMatchArray** is assigned the returned Array when the **match()** Method is executed. Then **myMatchArray** is written to screen as are all of the Elements of that Array and the appropriate Parenthesized SubStrings with the **$1, $2, $3**, and **$4** Properties of the Core **RegExp** Object.

Next, the **exec()** Method is covered with the Regular Expression named **myRE2** that has twelve different Parenthesized SubStrings to remember. The **myExecArray** is assigned the returned Array when the **exec()** Method is executed. Then **myExecArray** is written to screen as are all of the Elements of that Array and all nine of the Parenthesized SubString matches.

Notice the differences in what is output in each of the two returned Arrays.

Example 9-12:   **Sample1012.html**

```
<!DOCTYPE HTML PUBLIC -//W3C//DTD HTML 3.2//EN>
<HTML>
<HEAD>
<TITLE> Sample 1012   Example 9-12   exec vs. match Array Elements </TITLE>

<SCRIPT LANGUAGE="JavaScript1.2"> <!--BEGIN HIDING

      strA = "A+B+A+B+A+B+A+B+A+B+A+4";

      myRE1 = /(A)(+)(B)(+)/g;

      myMatchArray = strA.match(myRE1);

      document.write(myMatchArray +  "<P>");
```

```
        document.write(myMatchArray[0] +  "<BR>");
        document.write(myMatchArray[1] +  "<BR>");
        document.write(myMatchArray[2] +  "<BR>");
        document.write(myMatchArray[3] +  "<BR>");
        document.write(myMatchArray[4] +  "<P>");

        document.write(RegExp.$1 +  "<BR>");
        document.write(RegExp.$2 +  "<BR>");
        document.write(RegExp.$3 +  "<BR>");
        document.write(RegExp.$4 +  "<P>");

/*-------------------------------------------------------------------*/

        str2 = "1+2+1+2+1+2+1+2+1+2+4444+1+2+1+2+1+2+1+2+1+2+";

        myRE2 = /(1)(+)(2)(+)(1)(+)(2)(+)(1)(+)(2)(+)/g;

        myExecArray = myRE2.exec(str2);

        document.write(myExecArray +  "<P>");
        document.write(myExecArray[0] +  "<BR>");
        document.write(myExecArray[1] +  "<BR>");
        document.write(myExecArray[2] +  "<BR>");
        document.write(myExecArray[3] +  "<BR>");
        document.write(myExecArray[4] +  "<BR>");
        document.write(myExecArray[5] +  "<BR>");
        document.write(myExecArray[6] +  "<BR>");
        document.write(myExecArray[7] +  "<BR>");
        document.write(myExecArray[8] +  "<BR>");
        document.write(myExecArray[9] +  "<BR>");
        document.write(myExecArray[10] +  "<BR>");
        document.write(myExecArray[11] +  "<BR>");
        document.write(myExecArray[12] +  "<P>");


        document.write(RegExp.$1 +  "<BR>");
        document.write(RegExp.$2 +  "<BR>");
        document.write(RegExp.$3 +  "<BR>");
        document.write(RegExp.$4 +  "<BR>");
        document.write(RegExp.$5 +  "<BR>");
        document.write(RegExp.$6 +  "<BR>");
        document.write(RegExp.$7 +  "<BR>");
        document.write(RegExp.$8 +  "<BR>");
        document.write(RegExp.$9 +  "<BR>");


//END HIDING-->
</SCRIPT>

</HEAD>

<BODY>

</BODY>
</HTML>
```

The previous example produces the following output:

["A+B+", "A+B+", "A+B+", "A+B+", "A+B+"]

A+B+
A+B+
A+B+
A+B+
A+B+

A
+
B
+

["1+2+1+2+1+2+", "1", "+", "2", "+", "1", "+", "2", "+", "1", "+", "2", "+"]

1+2+1+2+1+2+
1
+
2
+
1
+
2
+
1
+
2
+

1
+
2
+
1
+
2
+
1

Example to verify name & address using Regular Expressions

Example 9-13 uses the **myRE1**, **myRE2**, **myRE3**, **myRE4**, and **myRE5** Regular Expressions, to respectively verify, the Name, Address, City, State, and Zip Code that the user inputs into each of the five appropriate Text Boxes. The Regular Expressions cover some of the possibilities, but they don't attempt to anticipate all of the address variations.

The **tester()** Function has all the important code and is assigned to the **onClick** Event Handler of Button **b1**. The Value of each Text Box is assigned to its, own String Variable. Then there are five Regular Expressions designed to test for the anticipated text from the user in the Text Boxes.

The **if()** Statement checks to make sure that each of the five Regular Expressions found a match, and if true, it asks the user to **confirm** that the data are accurate. If it is, the match to the user input is displayed back into the Text Boxes. If not, an **alert** tells the user to try again. In a real-world application, when the address is confirmed, the user would most likely be advanced to the next page in the sequence of a **form** progression, usually a purchase, but there are lots of possible adaptations for you to use.

Example 9-13:   **Sample1013.html**

```
<!DOCTYPE HTML PUBLIC -//W3C//DTD HTML 3.2//EN>
<HTML>
<HEAD>
<TITLE> Sample 1013   Example 9-13 match and verify name, address</TITLE>

<BASEFONT SIZE="5">

<SCRIPT LANGUAGE="JavaScript1.2"> <!--BEGIN HIDING

function tester() {

        var str1 = document.form1.text1.value;
        var str2 = document.form1.text2.value;
        var str3 = document.form1.text3.value;
        var str4 = document.form1.text4.value;
        var str5 = document.form1.text5.value;

        myRE1 = /\D+\s+\D+/;
        myRE2 = /\d+\s\w+\s\w+|\d+\s\w+\s\w+\s\w+|\w+\s\w+/;
        myRE3 = /\D+|\D+\s\D+|\D+\s\D+\s\D+/;
        myRE4 = /\D+|\D+\s\D+/;
        myRE5 = /\d{5}|\d{5}-\d{4}/;

        myArray1 = myRE1.exec(str1);
        myArray2 = myRE2.exec(str2);
        myArray3 = myRE3.exec(str3);
        myArray4 = myRE4.exec(str4);
        myArray5 = myRE5.exec(str5);
```

```
        if (myArray1 != null  &&  myArray2 != null  &&  myArray3 != null  &&
            myArray4 != null  &&  myArray5 != null) {

            if (confirm("Is this address correct? " +  "\r" +  "\r" +
                    myArray1[0] + "\r" + myArray2[0] + "\r" + myArray3[0] +
                    ", " + myArray4[0] + " " + myArray5[0])) {

                    document.form1.text1.value = myArray1[0];
                    document.form1.text2.value = myArray2[0];
                    document.form1.text3.value = myArray3[0];
                    document.form1.text4.value = myArray4[0];
                    document.form1.text5.value = myArray5[0];
            }
            else  alert("Try again.")
        }
        else alert("Try again. Format anomaly found.");

document.form1.text1.focus();
document.form1.text1.select();
}


//END HIDING-->
</SCRIPT>

</HEAD>

<BODY onLoad="document.form1.text1.focus();">

<FORM NAME="form1">

Name
<INPUT TYPE="text" NAME="text1" SIZE="40" VALUE=""> <BR>

Address
<INPUT TYPE="text" NAME="text2" SIZE="40" VALUE=""> <BR>

City
<INPUT TYPE="text" NAME="text3" SIZE="40" VALUE=""> <BR>

State
<INPUT TYPE="text" NAME="text4" SIZE="40" VALUE=""> <BR>

Zip Code
<INPUT TYPE="text" NAME="text5" SIZE="40" VALUE=""> <BR>

<INPUT TYPE="button" NAME="b1" VALUE="Test it now" onClick="tester();">    <BR><BR>

Click the button to verify the Address.

</FORM>

</BODY>
</HTML>
```

A full Regular Expression example

Example 9-14 demonstrates how to perform a simple search using a Regular Expression to find a match for a chapter number that is input by the user and then display Links that are the Sample files associated with that chapter. It's basically an introductory precursor to Example 9-15, which creates a Search Engine that is completely self-contained within client-side JavaScript.

It starts by defining an Array named **a1** with the Array Constructor and defining all of the Elements of the Array with the appropriate URL Strings. The **searchFor()** Function contains the main code and starts by assigning the String from the Text Box named **text1** to a String Variable named **str**. The Regular Expression **re** searches for one or more digits and remembers the match.

As long as the **match()** Method doesn't return **null**, the Script creates appropriate links using the **link()** Method of the **String** Object. It does this by opening the **document** Object in the Frame named **main** and writes the links based on the Value in the **RegExp.$1** Property and the Value of the **i** Variable in the **for()** loop.

The essential code for this example is contained in the Sample1014.html file and the FRAMESET for this example is located within the Sample1014Frameset.html file. Even though Sample1014Main.html is just a placeholder file, it is necessary.

Example 9-14:   **Sample1014.html**

```
<!DOCTYPE HTML PUBLIC -//W3C//DTD HTML 3.2//EN>
<HTML> <HEAD>  <TITLE> Sample 1014   Example 9-14 Simple Search </TITLE>

<SCRIPT LANGUAGE="JavaScript1.2"><!--BEGIN HIDING

a1      = new Array();
a1[0] = "Sample0.html";
a1[1] = "Sample1.html";
a1[2] = "Sample2.html";
a1[3] = "Sample3.html";
a1[4] = "Sample4.html";
a1[5] = "Sample200.html";
a1[6] = "Sample201.html";
a1[7] = "Sample202.html";
a1[8] = "Sample203.html";
a1[9] = "Sample204.html";
a1[10] = "Sample300.html";
a1[11] = "Sample301.html";
a1[12] = "Sample302.html";
a1[13] = "Sample303.html";
a1[14] = "Sample304.html";
a1[15] = "Sample400.html";
a1[16] = "Sample401.html";
a1[17] = "Sample402.html";
a1[18] = "Sample403.html";
a1[19] = "Sample404.html";
```

```
/*----------------------------------------------------------------*/

function searchFor()  {

        str = document.form1.text1.value;
        re = /(\d+)/;
        gotIt = str.match(re);


        if (str.match(re) != null)  {

                parent.main.document.open();
                parent.main.document.write("<HTML><HEAD>");
                parent.main.document.write("<TITLE>TEST</TITLE><\/HEAD>");
                parent.main.document.write("<BODY>");

                for (i=0; i<a1.length; i++) {

                        if (RegExp.$1 == "1"  &&  i>=0  &&  i<5)
                        parent.main.document.write((a1[i]).link(a1[i]) + "<BR>");

                        else if (RegExp.$1 == "2"  &&  i>=5  &&  i<10)
                        parent.main.document.write((a1[i]).link(a1[i]) + "<BR>");

                        else if (RegExp.$1 == "3"  &&  i>=10  &&  i<15)
                        parent.main.document.write((a1[i]).link(a1[i]) + "<BR>");

                        else if (RegExp.$1 == "4"  &&  i>=15  &&  i<20)
                        parent.main.document.write((a1[i]).link(a1[i]) + "<BR>");
                }

                parent.main.document.write("<\/BODY><\/HTML>");
                parent.main.document.close();
        }
        else alert("No such Sample exists. Try again.");
}


//END HIDING-->
</SCRIPT>

</HEAD>

<BODY>
<FORM NAME="form1">

Type in a Chapter number from 1 to 4:

<INPUT TYPE="text" NAME="text1" SIZE="7" VALUE="">

<INPUT TYPE="button" NAME="B1" VALUE="Get Sample Links" onClick="searchFor();"><BR>

</FORM>

</BODY>
</HTML>
```

Creating a Search Engine example

Example 9-15 demonstrates how to create a Search Engine that is fully contained in client-side JavaScript; that is, there is no server-side JavaScript or exchange of data with CGI Scripting via the server. To run the Script, load in Sample1015Frameset.html which contains the FRAMESET, whereas Sample1015-SearchEngine1.html has the pertinent code.

The Script starts by defining an Array named **a**, which contains the descriptions for the Links and an Array named **a2**, which contains the URLs for the Links. Next, the **descriptionsYN()** Function is used to suppress the rendering of the Link descriptions based on whether the checkbox named **ckbx1** is checked or not by changing the Value of the Boolean Variable **noDescriptions**. If **noDescriptions** is false, then the **searchFor()** Function assigns the Elements of Array **a** to Array **b** so that the descriptions will be rendered. Otherwise the Elements of **b** are assigned a null String of "".

The **searchFor()** Function takes the key word to search for, which is provided by the user in the Text Box named **text1** and assigns it to the String Variable **str**. Then the Regular Expression **re** is used to test for a match in **str** with the **match()** Method. If a match is found, then the **gotIt** Array will not be equal to **null** and the **if()** Statement continues by opening the **document** contained in the **main** FRAME and writes to it with the **write()** Method.

The **for()** loop runs through all of the Link URLs contained in Array **a2**, and then the sequence of **if()...else** Statements compares the match contained in **Element [0]** of **gotIt** against the individual Strings that are mapped to the URLs. When a comparison is equivalent, and the **i** Variable is within the proper range, a Link is written to screen by using the **link()** Method of the **String** Object.

For instance: If **gotIt[0]** is equivalent to "layer" and the Variable **i** is greater than or equal to 8 and less than 10, then a Link is written, where the Element at **a2[i]** is both the String and URL of the Link:

```
else if ((gotIt[0] == "layer")  &&  (i>=8  &&  i<10))

parent.main.document.write((a2[i]).link(a2[i]) + "<BR>" + b[i] + "<P>");
```

If **noDescriptions** is false, that is, if the checkbox **ckbx1** is unchecked, then the description contained in **a[i]** is assigned to **b[i]** and is also written to screen.

The **keyShiftESearch(e)** Function just allows you to implement the search by using the keyboard when the Command + Shift + E Keys are pressed. For this to work, you have to make sure that the Frame named **display** has focus. This is accomplished by calling the **focus()** Method on the Text Box named **text1** in the **onLoad** Event Handler of the BODY Element, which also sets the cursor to the search Key input box for the user.

The **loadKeywords()** Function just makes it easier to test the Script by reloading all the Keywords that actually work in the Script so you don't have to remember them.

Finally, if you want to adapt this Script for your own use, just substitute your own URLs in Array **a2** and your own descriptions into Array **a**. You also have to substitute in your own Keywords to match in the nested **if...else** Statements and make sure that the **i** Variables have the proper range of applicability. Once you understand the logic behind this Script, it is much easier to keep track of than by using multi-dimensional Arrays.

Example 9-15: **Sample1015-SearchEngine1.html**

```
<!DOCTYPE HTML PUBLIC -//W3C//DTD HTML 3.2//EN>
<HTML><HEAD><TITLE> Sample 1015   Example 9-15 Search Engine</TITLE>

<SCRIPT LANGUAGE="JavaScript1.2"><!--BEGIN HIDING

a = new Array();            //This Array contains your link descriptions

a[0] = "Introductory HTML-The Global Structure";
a[1] = "Introduction to Links";
a[2] = "Introduction to Images";
a[3] = "How to create Tables";
a[4] = "How to create Frames";
a[5] = "Introduction to CSS Style Sheets";
a[6] = "CSS Style Sheets 2";
a[7] = "CSS Style Sheets 3";
a[8] = "Introduction to Layers and Styles";
a[9] = "Layers and Styles 2";
a[10] = "Introduction to JavaScript and Layers";
a[11] = "JavaScript and Layers 2";
a[12] = "Introduction to Events";
a[13] = "Events 2";
a[14] = "Introduction to Arrays";
a[15] = "Arrays 2";
a[16] = "Introduction to the concat Method of the String Object";
a[17] = "The second example of the concat Method of the String Object";
a[18] = "Introduction to Regular Expressions";
a[19] = "Regular Expressions 2";
a[20] = "QTVR QuickTime VR - Master Frameset with multiple movies to choose from";
/*-------------------------------------------------------------------*/
                  //This Array contains the link URLs
a2 = new Array();

a2[0] = "Sample0.html";                 //html
a2[1] = "Sample30.html";                //Links
a2[2] = "Sample34.html";                //Images
a2[3] = "Sample43.html";                //Tables
a2[4] = "Sample50-Frameset-1.html";     //Frames
a2[5] = "Sample200.html";               //CSS Style Sheets
a2[6] = "Sample201.html";
a2[7] = "Sample202.html";
a2[8] = "Sample301.html";               //Layers
a2[9] = "Sample302.html";
a2[10] = "Sample401.html";              //JavaScript and Layers
a2[11] = "Sample402.html";
a2[12] = "Sample701.html";              //Events
a2[13] = "Sample702.html";
a2[14] = "Sample801.html";              //Arrays
a2[15] = "Sample802.html";
a2[16] = "Sample901.html";              //Strings
a2[17] = "Sample902.html";
a2[18] = "Sample1001.html";             //Regular Expression
a2[19] = "Sample1002.html";
a2[20] = "Sample455Frameset.html";      //qtvr
```

```
/*-----------------------------------------------------------------*/

var noDescriptions = false;

function descriptionsYN() {

        if (noDescriptions == true) noDescriptions = false;
        else if (noDescriptions == false) noDescriptions = true;
}

        //This is the shadow Array when the Sample Descriptions are repressed.
        //Notice that this is the length of the "a" Array, not "b" or "a2".

b = new Array(a.length);

        for (i=0; i<a.length; ++i) {

                b[i] = "";
        }

/*-----------------------------------------------------------------*/

function searchFor()   {

var str = document.form1.text1.value;
        re = /\w+/i;
        gotIt = str.match(re);

  if (gotIt != null)   {

        parent.main.document.open();
        parent.main.document.write("<HTML><HEAD>");
        parent.main.document.write("<TITLE>TEST</TITLE><\/HEAD>");
        parent.main.document.write("<BODY>");

                for (i=0; i<a2.length; ++i) {

                        if (noDescriptions == false)  b[i] = a[i];
                        else b[i] = "";

                        if ((   gotIt[0] == "html"  ||
                                gotIt[0] == "link"  ||
                                gotIt[0] == "image" ||
                                gotIt[0] == "table" ||
                                gotIt[0] == "frame")  &&
                                (i>=0  &&  i<5))

        parent.main.document.write((a2[i]).link(a2[i]) + "<BR>" + b[i] + "<P>");

                else if ((      gotIt[0] == "dynamic"  ||
                                gotIt[0] == "css"  ||
                                gotIt[0] == "cascading"  ||
                                gotIt[0] == "style"  ||
                                gotIt[0] == "sheet")  &&
                                (i>=5  &&  i<8))

        parent.main.document.write((a2[i]).link(a2[i]) + "<BR>" + b[i] + "<P>");
```

```
        else if ((    gotIt[0] == "layer")  &&
                (i>=8  &&  i<10))

parent.main.document.write((a2[i]).link(a2[i]) + "<BR>" + b[i] + "<P>");

        else if ((    gotIt[0] == "javascript")  &&
                (i>=10  &&  i<12))

parent.main.document.write((a2[i]).link(a2[i]) + "<BR>" + b[i] + "<P>");

        else if ((    gotIt[0] == "event")  &&
                (i>=12  &&  i<14))

parent.main.document.write((a2[i]).link(a2[i]) + "<BR>" + b[i] + "<P>");

        else if ((    gotIt[0] == "array")  &&
                (i>=14  &&  i<16))

parent.main.document.write((a2[i]).link(a2[i]) + "<BR>" + b[i] + "<P>");

        else if ((    gotIt[0] == "string"  ||
                gotIt[0] == "text")  &&
                (i>=16  &&  i<18))

parent.main.document.write((a2[i]).link(a2[i]) + "<BR>" + b[i] + "<P>");

        else if ((    gotIt[0] == "regular"  ||
                gotIt[0] == "expression"  ||
                gotIt[0] == "regexp"  ||
                gotIt[0] == "re")  &&
                (i>=18  &&  i<20))

parent.main.document.write((a2[i]).link(a2[i]) + "<BR>" + b[i] + "<P>");

        else if ((    gotIt[0] == "qtvr"  ||
                gotIt[0] == "quicktime"  ||
                gotIt[0] == "vr"  ||
                gotIt[0] == "virtual"  ||
                gotIt[0] == "reality")  &&
                (i>=20  &&  i<21))

parent.main.document.write((a2[i]).link(a2[i]) + "<BR>" + b[i] + "<P>");
            }

    parent.main.document.write("<\/BODY><\/HTML>");
    parent.main.document.close();
    }

document.form1.text1.focus();
document.form1.text1.select();
}


/*----------------------------------------------------------------*/
```

```
/*----------------------------------------------------------------*/

function keyShiftESearch(e)   {

        var theKey = String.fromCharCode(e.which);

                                //Command + Shift + the "e" or "E" keys

        if (e.modifiers  ==  12  &&  (theKey == "e"  ||  theKey == "E"))  {

                searchFor();
        }
}

/*----------------------------------------------------------------*/
        document.onkeypress = keyShiftESearch;
/*----------------------------------------------------------------*/

function loadKeywords() {

        parent.main.location.href = "Sample1015Main.html";
}

//END HIDING-->
</SCRIPT>
</HEAD>
<BODY onLoad="document.form1.text1.focus();">
<FORM NAME="form1">

Type in a key word to search:

<INPUT TYPE="text" NAME="text1" SIZE="50" VALUE=""
onBlur="parent.display.focus();"> <BR>

<INPUT TYPE="button" NAME="B1" VALUE="Get Sample Links" onClick="searchFor();">

Then click the button or hit Tab and then Command + Shift + E

<INPUT TYPE="button" NAME="B1" VALUE="Reload Keywords" onClick="loadKeywords();">
<BR>
<INPUT TYPE="checkbox" NAME="ckbx1" VALUE="true" onClick="descriptionsYN();">

To repress link descriptions click the checkbox.
</FORM>
</BODY>
</HTML>
```

The previous example was written primarily to demonstrate how to incorporate RegExps into a Search Engine. On the CD-ROM, in Sample1016-SearchEngine3.html, there is an example of a better Search Engine. It's faster, more intuitive, and offers an easier methodology for incorporating your own Links and Key words for searching databases. Load in the Sample1016Frameset.html file, which contains the FRAMESET for the Sample; to run it. Between its internal Comments and similarity to the previous example, you should be able to figure out how it works by this time, without an explanation.

Part III
JavaScript 1.3

Chapter 10

What's New & Changed

Chapter 10
What's New & Changed

Contents

What's New in JavaScript 1.3 & Changed in JavaScript 1.2

Overview of Features

Chapter 10 examines the new feature-set in JavaScript 1.3, and what has been changed from JavaScript 1.2. Unlike the vast array of new features and capabilities that were implemented in version 1.2 of JavaScript, version 1.3 is a minor upgrade, that offers a relatively minimal set of new enhancements, but mostly refines preexisting standards.

Having said that, there are a substantial number of new Methods that are now available for the **Date** Object, along with additional parameters for previously available Methods. In all of the following Syntax it should be remembered that:

"Syntax for JavaScript 1.3"

refers to JavaScript that is contained within a SCRIPT Element that has the Value for its LANGUAGE Attribute set to **"JavaScript1.3"** like this:

```
<SCRIPT LANGUAGE="JavaScript1.3">
```

and that:

"JavaScript 1.2 Syntax"

refers to JavaScript that is contained within a SCRIPT Element that has the Value for its LANGUAGE Attribute set to **"JavaScript1.2"** like this:

```
<SCRIPT LANGUAGE="JavaScript1.2">
```

Browser support issues concerning the TYPE and LANGUAGE Attributes of the SCRIPT Element are covered on pages 196-197.

JavaScript 1.3 and ECMA-262 Compliance

JavaScript 1.3 is fully compliant with the ECMA-262 Standard. The European Computer Manufacturers Association has devised an international programming language standard that is based on core JavaScript and this version of JavaScript is known as ECMAScript. For more information on ECMA-262, see Chapter 1 of the JavaScript 1.3 Guide from Netscape that's on the CD-ROM.

JavaScript 1.3 and Unicode

You can now use the Unicode character set for any encoding, and all Unicode Escape Sequences are now recognized and interpreted properly in String Literals. However, Unicode is not supported in the Top-Level Functions of **escape()** and **unescape()**. It should be noted that Unicode is not supported in any versions of JavaScript prior to JavaScript 1.3.

The Unicode character set is a universal character coding standard that uniquely represents the letters, symbols, and mathematical and technical symbols of many modern and ancient languages, including those of North and South America, Europe, the Middle East, Africa, India, Asia, and Pacifica. Even though version 2.0 of Unicode contains 38,885 recognized characters, it still does not cover all languages past and present. Fortunately there is still plenty of room within the coding scheme for additions.

The purpose of Unicode is to solve the problem of multilingual computing. It is initially based around the American Standard Code for Information Interchange (ASCII) character set, and the first 0-127 characters are identical in both schemes. Each character is given a unique four-digit hexadecimal number that is preceded by the letter U and a name that represents that character. For instance:

U+0041	has the name	LATIN CAPITAL LETTER A	A
U+0042	has the name	LATIN CAPITAL LETTER B	B
U+0061	has the name	LATIN SMALL LETTER A	a
U+0062	has the name	LATIN SMALL LETTER B	b
U+0026	has the name	AMPERSAND	&
U+003C	has the name	LESS-THAN SIGN	<
U+003E	has the name	GREATER-THAN SIGN	>
U+0030	has the name	DIGIT ZERO	0
U+0031	has the name	DIGIT ONE	1

In order to use a Unicode Escape Sequence in a String Literal, you need to use a group of six ASCII characters. You always start with: **\u** and follow that by the four-digit hexadecimal number that represents the Unicode character that you want to escape. For instance, to escape the ampersand character (&), you would use: **\u0026** so that the following code, assigned to **myString**, would return: "Crimson & Clover".

```
myString = "Crimson \u0026 Clover";
```

For more information on Unicode and to see the most recent version of the Charts of all Unicode characters, go to the Unicode Consortium website at:

```
http://www.unicode.org
```

Unicode Character Escape Sequences

Here are some of the more useful of the over 38000 Unicode Escape Sequences, along with their ASCII and HTML Entity equivalents. Note that ASCII Escape Sequences that consist of only two characters in this list are also JavaScript Special characters.

Unicode Escape	HTML Entity	ASCII Escape	Name -Value	Format Name
\u0009		\t	Tab	<TAB>
\u000B			Vertical Tab	<VT>
\u000C		\f	Form Feed	<FF>
\u0020			Space	<SP>
\u00A0			Non-Breaking Space	
\u000A		\n	New Line Feed	<LF>
\u000D		\r	Carriage Return	<CR>
\u000b		\b	Backspace	<BS>
\u0022	&quot;	\"	Double Quote	"
\u0027		\'	Single Quote	'
\u005C		\\	Backslash	\
\u0023		\0x23	Number Sign	#
\u0024		\0x24	Dollar Sign	$
\u0025		\0x25	Percent Sign	%
\u0026	&amp;	\0x26	Ampersand	&
\u0028		\0x28	Left Parenthesis	(
\u0029		\0x29	Right Parenthesis	)
\u002A		\0x2A	Asterisk	*
\u002B		\0x2B	Plus Sign	+
\u002C		\0x2C	Comma	,
\u002D		\0x2D	Hyphen-Minus	-
\u002F		\0x2F	Forward Slash	/
\u003A		\0x3A	Colon	:
\u003B		\0x3B	Semicolon	;
\u003C	&lt;	\0x3C	Less-Than Sign	<
\u003D		\0x3D	Equals Sign	=
\u003E	&gt;	\0x3E	Greater-Than Sign	>
\u003F		\0x3F	Question Mark	?
\u0040		\0x40	Commercial At	@
\u005B		\0x5B	Left Square Bracket	[
\u005D		\0x5D	Right Square Bracket	]
\u007B		\0x7B	Left Curly Bracket	{
\u007C		\0x7C	Vertical Line		
\u007D		\0x7D	Right Curly Bracket	}
\u00B0	&deg;	\0xA1	Degrees Sign	°
\u00AE	&reg;	\0xA8	Registered Sign	®
\u00A9	&copy;	\0xA9	Copyright Sign	©

Changes to Objects

Changes to the Array Object

There are only a few changes to the **Array** Object and they consist mostly of changes to Methods of the **Array** Object. The following Methods have minor changes in their functionality: **push()**, **splice()**, and **toString()**. The **length** Property is also changed. One new Method has been added and it's called the **toSource()** Method. The only other change is to the Array Constructor. These changes are all discussed next.

It should be remembered that in the following syntax, the brackets ([ ]) that enclose the Element list are part of the code for creating an Array with Literal notation, and they are not an indication of an optional Argument. It should be noted that even though the syntax for the Array Constructor is identical in versions 1.2 and 1.3 of JavaScript, the behaviors are different.

Changes to the <u>Array Constructor</u>

Syntax for JavaScript 1.3:

```
arrayObjectName = new Array(arrayLength);
arrayObjectName = new Array(element0, element1, ..., elementN);
arrayObjectName = [element0, element1, ..., elementN];
```

JavaScript 1.2 Syntax:

```
arrayObjectName = new Array(arrayLength);
arrayObjectName = new Array(element0, element1, ..., elementN);
arrayObjectName = [element0, element1, ..., elementN];
```

In version 1.3 of JavaScript, when you use the Array Constructor to create a new Array and specify the Value for the **arrayLength** Argument with one numeric parameter, you are declaring the initial **length** of the Array. For instance, an Array with **arrayLength**=22 has an initial **length** of 22, *not* an initial **length** of 1. The Array initially has no Elements, and it definitely *does not* have a first **element0** of 22:

```
myArray = new Array(22);
```

The opposite is true in version 1.3 of JavaScript when you specify a Value for the **arrayLength** Argument with a single parameter that is <u>anything other than a number</u>. Then the **length** is 1 and **element0** is that specified parameter, which in the following example would be "butterfly", like this:

```
myArray = new Array("butterfly");
```

In version 1.2 of JavaScript, if you specify the Value for the **arrayLength** Argument with one numeric parameter (or anything else), you are declaring an Array with a **length** of 1, and that parameter is the Value of **element0**. So that an Array:

```
myArray = new Array(15);
```

would have an initial **length** of 1 and **element0** would be the number 15, and it would be the only Element in the Array.

Change to the <u>length</u> Property of Array Object

There are no changes to the syntax for the **length** Property.

In version 1.3 of JavaScript, the **length** Property is an unsigned 32-bit integer that has a positive sign and must be less than 2^{32} (that's 2 to the 32 power), which means that the Array can have up to 4,294,967,295 Elements.

In version 1.2 of JavaScript, the **length** Property had no upper limit. In other words, you could have as many Array Elements as you wanted.

New <u>toSource()</u> Method of Array Object

Syntax for JavaScript 1.3:

```
arrayObjectName.toSource();
```

The new **toSource()** Method of the **Array** Object returns a String that represents the source code of the Array. For instance:

```
myArray = new Array("one", "two", "three", "four");

myVar = myArray.toSource();
```

returns:

```
["one", "two", "three", "four"]
```

Note that in version 1.2 of JavaScript, this functionality was achieved by using the **toString()** Method, which has been changed in JavaScript 1.3.

Change to the <u>toString()</u> Method of Array Object

Syntax for JavaScript 1.3:

```
arrayObjectName.toString();
```

JavaScript 1.2 Syntax:

```
arrayObjectName.toString();
```

The **toString()** Method, in version 1.3 of JavaScript, concatenates; that is, it joins all of the Elements of an Array and returns a String that consists of a comma-separated list of each Element. In version 1.2 of JavaScript, the **toString()** Method returned a String that contained the source code of the Array. In JavaScript 1.3, the functionality of returning the source code of the Array is provided by the **toSource()** Method.

In the following example, the Array named **myArray** has four Elements, and when the **toString()** Method is called on it, the resulting String is assigned to **myString**:

```
myArray = new Array("one", "two", "three", "four");
myString = myArray.toString();
```

The following String is assigned to **myString**:

```
"one,two,three,four"
```

Change to the <u>push()</u> Method of Array Object

Syntax for JavaScript 1.3:

```
arrayObjectName.push(element1, element2, ..., elementN);
```

JavaScript 1.2 Syntax:

```
arrayObjectName.push(element1, element2, ..., elementN);
```

In JavaScript 1.3, the **push()** Method returns the new **length** of the Array after the specified number of comma-separated Elements have been added to the Array. This Method changes the **length** of the Array.

In JavaScript 1.2, the **push()** Method returns the last Element added to the Array from the specified comma-separated list of Elements.

Change to the <u>splice()</u> Method of Array Object

Syntax for JavaScript 1.3:

```
arrayObjectName.splice(startIndex, removeQty, addElt1, ..., addEltN)
```

JavaScript 1.2 Syntax:

```
arrayObjectName.splice(startIndex, removeQty, addElt1, ..., addEltN)
```

In JavaScript 1.3 the **splice()** Method returns an Array that consists of all of the Elements that have been removed from the Array, including the circumstance when only one Element is removed. The number of Elements to be removed is specified by the **removeQty** Argument, starting at the ordinal **index** number specified by the **startIndex** Argument.

In JavaScript 1.2, if only one Element was removed by the **splice()** Method, then an Array was not returned, but the removed Element was returned.

Changes to the Date Object

Date Objects now exhibit uniform behavior across all platforms.

UTC or Universal Coordinated Time, specifies time according to the number of milliseconds that have elapsed since January 1, 1970, 00:00:00 from GMT position.

Date Objects now have a much larger range of days. The range is from:

-100,000,000 days before January 01, 1970 UTC

to:

+100,000,000 days after January 01, 1970 UTC

It should be noted that in JavaScript version 1.2 and earlier, you could not use dates prior to January 01, 1970.

Changes to the <u>Date Constructor</u>

Syntax for JavaScript 1.3:

```
new Date()
new Date("month day, year hours:minutes:seconds")                    //String Values
new Date(milliseconds)                                               //Integer Values
new Date(year, month, day)                                           //Integer Values
new Date(year, month, day[, hours, minutes, seconds, milliseconds]) //Integer Values
```

JavaScript 1.2 Syntax:

```
new Date()
new Date("month day, year hours:minutes:seconds")                    //String Values
new Date(year, month, day)                                           //Integer Values
new Date(year, month, day[, hours, minutes, seconds])               //Integer Values
```

In JavaScript 1.3, the **Date** Constructor has an optional **milliseconds** parameter that can be specified when creating a **Date** Object.

Coding Hints: There are 86,400,000 milliseconds contained in one day. You should always specify the year with four digits in your dates to ensure no Y2K difficulties.

New Methods for the Date Object

In JavaScript 1.3, the following Methods have been added to the **Date Object**:

Date Method	Method Description/Results
getFullYear()	Returns the year of the specified **Date** Object. Replaces the deprecated **getYear()** Method.
getMilliseconds()	Returns the milliseconds of the specified **Date** Object.
setFullYear()	Sets the year of the specified **Date** Object. Replaces the deprecated **setYear()** Method.
setMilliseconds()	Sets the milliseconds of the specified **Date** Object.
getUTCFullYear()	Returns the UTC year of the specified **Date** Object.
getUTCMonth()	Returns the UTC month of the specified **Date** Object.
getUTCDate()	Returns the UTC day of the month for the specified **Date** Object.
getUTCDay()	Returns the UTC day of the week for the specified **Date** Object.
getUTCHours()	Returns the UTC hours of the specified **Date** Object.
getUTCMinutes()	Returns the UTC minutes of the specified **Date** Object.
getUTCSeconds()	Returns the UTC seconds of the specified **Date** Object.
getUTCMilliseconds()	Returns the UTC milliseconds of the specified **Date** Object.
setUTCFullYear()	Sets the UTC year of the specified **Date** Object.
setUTCMonth()	Sets the UTC month of the specified **Date** Object.
setUTCDate()	Sets the UTC day of the month for the specified **Date** Object.
setUTCHours()	Sets the UTC hours of the specified **Date** Object.
setUTCMinutes()	Sets the UTC minutes of the specified **Date** Object.
setUTCSeconds()	Sets the UTC seconds of the specified **Date** Object.
setUTCMilliseconds()	Sets the UTC milliseconds of the specified **Date** Object.
toUTCString()	Converts the specified **Date** Object into a string in UTC format. Replaces the deprecated **toGMTString()**Method.

Each of the preceding new Methods of the **Date** Object will now be individually covered in detail.

The getFullYear() Method

JavaScript 1.3 Syntax:

```
dateObjName.getFullYear();
```

The **getFullYear()** Method returns the year of the specified **Date** Object according to local time. It always returns the actual full year, not a truncated two-digit version as with the deprecated **getYear()** Method, which **getFullYear()** replaces. For dates from the years 1000 to 9999, the **getFullYear()** Method always returns a four-digit number. You should always use this Method to ensure that your code will properly handle dates for the year 2000 and beyond.

Mini-Example:

Here's a quick example that would return the number 1999 if the code were run in a browser during the year that this book was first published:

```
var myYear;
myDate = new Date();
myYear = myDate.getFullYear();
```

The getMilliseconds() Method

JavaScript 1.3 Syntax:

```
dateObjName.getMilliseconds();
```

The **getMilliseconds()** Method returns the number of milliseconds of the specified **Date** Object according to local time. The possible Values that can be returned from this Method are integers from 0 to 999 inclusive.

Mini-Example:

The Date Constructor created the new **Date**: Thu Jun 17 23:59:35 GMT-0400 (1999, and it was assigned to **myDate**. **myMilliseconds** was then assigned 934 after calling the **getMilliseconds()** Method on **myDate**.

```
var myMilliseconds;
myDate = new Date();
myMilliseconds = myDate.getMilliseconds();
```

The <u>setFullYear()</u> Method

JavaScript 1.3 Syntax:

```
dateObjName.setFullYear(yearInteger[, monthInteger, dayInteger]);
```

Parameters Defined:

The **setFullYear()** Method sets the full year via the required **yearInteger** parameter for the specified **Date** Object of **dateObjName** according to local time. If the optional **monthInteger** Value is not specified, then it's internally supplied by the **getMonth()** Method. If the optional **dayInteger** Value is not specified, the **getDay()** Method supplies it internally.

The **yearInteger** parameter is an integer that represents the full year such that dates from the years 1000 to 9999 must be specified by a four-digit number.

The **monthInteger** parameter is an integer from 0-11 inclusive where 0 represents January, 1 represents February, and so on.

The **dayInteger** parameter is an integer from 1 to 31 inclusive, which represents the day of the month. If you do specify a **dayInteger** parameter, then the **monthInteger** parameter is required.

If the Value that you supply for either or both of the **monthInteger** or **dayInteger** parameters is outside of the expected range of Values, you will not get an error, but the **setFullYear()** Method will attempt to update the specified **Date** Object accordingly.

For instance, if you specify a **dayInteger** Value of 34, then **monthInteger** would be incremented by 1, and **dayInteger** would have a Value of 3 for the **Date** Object parameters.

Mini-Example:

In the following Example, the **setFullYear()** Method is used to set the **Date** Object named **myDate** to August 15, 2012.

```
myDate = new Date();
myDate.setFullYear(2012, 8, 15);
```

The <u>setMilliseconds()</u> Method

JavaScript 1.3 Syntax:

```
dateObjName.setMilliseconds(millisecondsInteger);
```

Parameters Defined:

The **setMilliseconds()** Method is used to set the milliseconds via the required **millisecondsInteger** parameter for the specified **Date** Object of **dateObjName** according to local time. The range of Values is an integer from 0 to 999 inclusive.

If the Value that you supply for the **millisecondsInteger** parameter is outside of the expected range of Values, the specified **Date** Object is updated to reflect that condition.

For instance, if you specify a **millisecondsInteger** Value of 1022, then the seconds parameter would be incremented by 1, and **millisecondsInteger** would have a Value of 23.

Mini-Example:

Here the **setMilliseconds()** Method is used to set the milliseconds parameter of the **Date** Object named **myDate** to 555:

```
myDate = new Date();
myDate.setMilliseconds(555);
```

The getUTCFullYear() Method

JavaScript 1.3 Syntax:

```
dateObjName.getUTCFullYear();
```

Parameters Defined:

The **getUTCFullYear()** Method returns the year of the specified **Date** Object according to universal time. It always returns an absolute number representing the full year, which is Y2K compliant. For dates from the years 1000 to 9999, the **getUTCFullYear()** Method will always return a four-digit number. You should always use this Method instead of the deprecated **getYear()** Method to ensure that your code will properly handle dates for the year 2000 and beyond.

Mini-Example:

Here's a quick example that assigns the number of the full year for the **Date** Object named **myDate** to the variable named **myYear**, according to universal time:

```
var myYear;
myDate = new Date();
myYear = myDate.getUTCFullYear();
```

The <u>getUTCMonth()</u> Method

JavaScript 1.3 Syntax:

```
dateObjName.getUTCMonth();
```

Parameters Defined:

The **getUTCMonth()** Method returns an integer Value that represents the month parameter of the specified **Date** Object according to universal time. The possible Values that can be returned from this Method are integers from 0 to 11 inclusive, such that:

0   represents January,
1   represents February, and so on, to
11   representing December.

Mini-Example:

Here's a quick example that assigns the month parameter for the **Date** Object named **myDate** to the variable named **myMonth**, according to universal time:

```
myDate = new Date();
var myMonth = myDate.getUTCMonth();
```

The <u>getUTCDate()</u> Method

JavaScript 1.3 Syntax:

```
dateObjName.getUTCDate();
```

Parameters Defined:

The **getUTCDate()** Method returns an integer from the range of 1-31 inclusive, which represents the <u>day of the month</u> according to universal time for the specified **Date** Object. Note that the **getUTCDay()** Method returns the <u>day of the week</u>.

Mini-Example:

```
myDate = new Date();
var myDayOfTheMonth = myDate.getUTCDate();
```

The <u>getUTCDay()</u> Method

JavaScript 1.3 Syntax:

```
dateObjName.getUTCDay();
```

Parameters Defined:

The **getUTCDay()** Method returns an integer from the range of 0-6 inclusive, which represents the <u>day of the week</u> according to universal time, for the specified **Date** Object. In this scheme, 0 is for Sunday, 1 is for Monday, 2 is for Tuesday, 3 is for Wednesday, 4 is for Thursday, 5 is for Friday, and 6 is for Saturday.

Note that the **getUTCDate()** Method returns the <u>day of the month</u>.

Mini-Example:

In the following example, if the day of the week is Friday for **myDate**, then the Value assigned to the Variable **myDayOfTheWeek** would be 5.

```
var myDayOfTheWeek;
myDate = new Date();
myDayOfTheWeek = myDate.getUTCDay();
```

The <u>getUTCHours()</u> Method

JavaScript 1.3 Syntax:

```
dateObjName.getUTCHours();
```

Parameters Defined:

The **getUTCHours()** Method returns an integer from the range of 0-23 inclusive, which represents the hour according to universal time for the specified **Date** Object. In this scheme, 0 is for 12:00 midnight, 1 is for 1:00 AM, 2 is for 2:00 AM, 12 is for 12:00 noon, and so on to 23 is for 11:00 PM, which is identical to military time.

The <u>getUTCMinutes()</u> Method

JavaScript 1.3 Syntax:

```
dateObjName.getUTCMinutes();
```

Parameters Defined:

The **getUTCMinutes()** Method returns an integer from the range of 0-59 inclusive, which represents the minutes according to universal time for the specified **Date** Object.

The <u>getUTCSeconds()</u> Method

JavaScript 1.3 Syntax:

```
dateObjName.getUTCSeconds();
```

Parameters Defined:

The **getUTCSeconds()** Method returns an integer from the range of 0-59 inclusive, which represents the seconds according to universal time for the specified **Date** Object.

The <u>getUTCMilliseconds()</u> Method

JavaScript 1.3 Syntax:

```
dateObjName.getUTCMilliseconds();
```

Parameters Defined:

The **getUTCMilliseconds()** Method returns an integer from the range of 0-999 inclusive, which represents the milliseconds according to universal time for the specified **Date** Object.

The <u>setUTCFullYear()</u> Method

JavaScript 1.3 Syntax:

```
dateObjName.setUTCFullYear(yrInteger[, monthInteger, dayInteger]);
```

Parameters Defined:

The **setUTCFullYear()** Method sets the full year by using the required **yrInteger** parameter for the specified **Date** Object of **dateObjName** according to universal time. If the optional **monthInteger** or **dayInteger** Value is not specified, then it is supplied by the **getMonth()** and **getDay()** Method, respectively.

The **yrInteger** parameter is an integer that represents the full year such that dates from the years 1000 to 9999 must by specified by a four-digit number. Remember that the range of dates is -100,000,000 to +100,000,000 days from midnight, January 1, 1970 UTC.

The **monthInteger** parameter is an integer from 0 to 11 inclusive where 0 represents January, 1 represents February, and so on.

The **dayInteger** parameter is an integer from 1 to 31 inclusive, which represents the day of the month. If you do specify a **dayInteger** parameter, then the **monthInteger** parameter is required.

If the Value that you supply for either or both of the **monthInteger** or **dayInteger** parameters is outside of the expected range of Values, you will not get an error, but the **setUTCFullYear()** Method will attempt to update the specified **Date** Object accordingly.

For instance, if you specify a **dayInteger** Value of 34, then **monthInteger** would be incremented by 1, and **dayInteger** would have a Value of 3 for the **Date** Object parameters.

Mini-Example:

In the following Example, the **setUTCFullYear()** Method is used to set the **Date** Object named **myDate** to December 31, 1999, in universal time.

```
myDate = new Date();
myDate.setFullUTCYear(1999, 11, 31);
```

The <u>setUTCMonth()</u> Method

JavaScript 1.3 Syntax:

```
dateObjName.setUTCMonth(monthInteger[, dayInteger]);
```

Parameters Defined:

The **setUTCMonth()** Method sets the month by using the required **monthInteger** parameter for the specified **Date** Object of **dateObjName** according to universal time.

If the optional **dayInteger** Value is not specified, it is internally supplied by the **getUTCDate()** Method.

The **monthInteger** parameter is an integer from 0 to 11 inclusive where 0 represents January, 1 represents February, and so on.

The **dayInteger** parameter is an integer from 1 to 31 inclusive, which represents the day of the month.

If the Value that you supply for either or both of the **monthInteger** or **dayInteger** parameters is outside of the expected range of Values, you will not get an error, but the **setUTCMonth()** Method will attempt to update the specified **Date** Object accordingly.

Mini-Example:

For instance, if you specify a **monthInteger** Value of 20, then the year parameter would be incremented by 1, and the month parameter would have a Value of 8.

```
myDate = new Date();
myDate.setUTCMonth(2);
```

The <u>setUTCDate()</u> Method

JavaScript 1.3 Syntax:

```
dateObjName.setUTCDate(dayOfMonthInteger);
```

Parameters Defined:

The **setUTCDate()** Method sets the month via the required **dayOfMonthInteger** parameter for the specified **Date** Object of **dateObjName** according to universal time.

The **dayOfMonthInteger** parameter is an integer from 1 to 31 inclusive, representing the day of the <u>month</u>, *not* the day of the week.

If the Value that you supply for the **dayOfMonthInteger** parameter is outside of the expected range of Values, you will not get an error, but the **setUTCDate()** Method will attempt to update the specified **Date** Object accordingly.

Mini-Example:

For instance, if you specify a **dayOfMonthInteger** Value of 42, then the month parameter would be incremented by 1, and the day of the month parameter of **dateObjName** would have a Value of 11.

```
myDate = new Date();
myDate.setUTCDate(25);
```

The <u>setUTCHours()</u> Method

JavaScript 1.3 Syntax:

```
dateObjName.setUTCHours(hoursInteger[, minsInt, secsInt, msInt]);
```

Parameters Defined:

The **setUTCHours()** Method sets the hours by using the required **hoursInteger** parameter for the specified **Date** Object of **dateObjName** according to universal time. If the optional **minsInt** Value is not specified, then it is internally supplied by the **getUTCMinutes()** Method. If the optional **secsInt** Value is not specified, then it is internally supplied by the **getUTCSeconds()** Method. If the optional **msInt** Value is not specified, then it is internally supplied by the **getUTCMilliseconds()** Method.

The required **hoursInteger** parameter is an integer within the range of 0 to 11 inclusive that specifies the hours for the specified **Date** Object.

The optional **minsInt** parameter is an integer from 0 to 59 inclusive, which specifies the number of minutes for the specified **Date** Object.

The optional **secsInt** parameter is an integer from 0 to 59 inclusive, which specifies the number of seconds for the specified **Date** Object. If you do specify a **secsInt** parameter, then the **minsInt** parameter is required.

The optional **msInt** parameter is an integer from 0 to 999 inclusive, which specifies the number of milliseconds for the specified **Date** Object. If a **msInt** parameter is specified, then the **secsInt** parameter is required.

If the Value that you supply for any of the parameters is outside of the expected range of Values, you will not get an error, but the **setUTCHours()** Method will attempt to update the specified **Date** Object accordingly.

Mini-Example:

```
myDate = new Date();
myDate.setUTCHours(2, 15, 30, 500);
```

The <u>setUTCMinutes()</u> Method

JavaScript 1.3 Syntax:

```
dateObjName.setUTCMinutes(minutesInteger[, secsInt, msInt]);
```

Parameters Defined:

The **setUTCMinutes()** Method sets the minutes via the required **minutesInteger** parameter for the specified **Date** Object of **dateObjName** according to universal time. If the optional **secsInt** Value is not specified, then it is internally supplied by the **getUTCSeconds()** Method. If the optional **msInt** Value is not specified, then it is internally supplied by the **getUTCMilliseconds()** Method.

The **minutesInteger** parameter is an integer from 0 to 59 inclusive.
The optional **secsInt** parameter is an integer from 0 to 59 inclusive, which specifies the number of seconds for the specified **Date** Object.
The optional **msInt** parameter is an integer from 0 to 999 inclusive, which specifies the number of milliseconds for the specified **Date** Object. If you do specify a **msInt** parameter, then the **secsInt** parameter is required.
If the Value that you supply for any of the parameters is outside of the expected range of Values, you will not get an error, but the **setUTCMinutes()** Method will attempt to update the specified **Date** Object accordingly.

Mini-Example:

```
myDate = new Date();
myDate.setUTCMinutes(8, 14, 200);
```

The <u>setUTCSeconds()</u> Method

JavaScript 1.3 Syntax:

```
dateObjName.setUTCSeconds(secondsInteger[, millisecondsInteger]);
```

Parameters Defined:

The **setUTCSeconds()** Method sets the seconds via the required **secondsInteger** parameter for the specified **Date** Object of **dateObjName** according to universal time. If the optional **millisecondsInteger** Value is not specified, then it is internally supplied by the **getUTCMilliseconds()** Method.

The **secondsInteger** parameter is an integer from 0 to 59 inclusive.
The optional **millisecondsInteger** parameter is an integer from 0 to 999 inclusive, which specifies the number of milliseconds for the specified **Date** Object.
If the Value that you supply for any of the parameters is outside of the expected range of Values, you will not get an error, but the **setUTCSeconds()** Method will attempt to update the specified **Date** Object accordingly.

The <u>setUTCMilliseconds()</u> Method

JavaScript 1.3 Syntax:

```
dateObjName.setUTCMilliseconds(millisecondsInteger);
```

Parameters Defined:

The **setUTCMilliseconds()** Method sets the milliseconds via the required **millisecondsInteger** parameter for the specified **Date** Object of **dateObjName** according to universal time.

If the Value that you supply for the **millisecondsInteger** parameter is outside of the expected range of Values, you will not get an error, but the **setUTCMilliseconds()** Method will attempt to update the specified **Date** Object accordingly. For instance, if you set the **millisecondsInteger** parameter Value to 1500, then the seconds parameter will be incremented by 1 and the milliseconds parameter will be 500.

The <u>toUTCString()</u> Method

JavaScript 1.3 Syntax:

```
dateObjName.toUTCString();
```

Parameters Defined:

The **toUTCString()** Method converts a specified **Date** Object to a String according to universal time. The actual format of this String may vary from platform to platform.

On the Macintosh platform the formatting has this structure:

Mon, 22 Feb 1999 13:03:11 GMT

which is a result of the following code:

```
var myUTCDateString;
myDate = new Date();
myUTCDateString = myDate.toUTCString();
document.write(myUTCDateString);
```

Changes to preexisting Methods of the Date Object

The following changes have been made to Methods that have been previously available for the **Date** Object. After they are listed here in brief, they will immediately be discussed individually in detail, along with the syntax for version 1.3 and version 1.2.

The **day** parameter has been added to the **setMonth()** Method.

The **minutes, seconds**, and **milliseconds** parameters have been added to the **setHours()** Method.

The **seconds** and **milliseconds** parameters have been added to the **setMinutes()** Method.

The **milliseconds** parameter has been added to the **setSeconds()** Method.

The **milliseconds** parameter has been added to the **UTC()** Method.

The **getYear(), setYear()**, and **toGMTString()** Methods have been deprecated in favor of the **getFullYear(), setFullYear()**, and **toUTCString()** Methods, respectively.

For backward compatibility info on **getYear(), setYear()**, and **toGMTString()**, see the **Date** Object in Chapter 1 in the JavaScript 1.3 Reference on the CD-ROM.

For more info on **getFullYear()**,   see page 864.
For more info on **setFullYear()**,   see page 865.
For more info on **toUTCString()**,   see page 874.

setMonth() Method Changes

Syntax for JavaScript 1.3:

```
dateObjName.setMonth(monthInteger[, dayInteger]);
```

JavaScript 1.2 Syntax:

```
dateObjName.setMonth(monthInteger);
```

Parameters Defined:

The **setMonth()** Method sets the specified **Date** Object to the supplied parameter Values of **monthInteger** and optionally **dayInteger** in accordance with local time.

The required **monthInteger** Value is an integer from 0 to 11, which represents the months of January through December, where January is represented by 0, February by 1, and so on in sequence. The optional **dayInteger** Value is an integer from 1 to 31, which represents the day of the month. If you do not specify the **dayInteger** Value, then the Value that is returned from the **getMonth()** Method is used.

If the Value that you supply for either or both of the **monthInteger** or **dayInteger** parameters is outside of the expected range of Values, you will not get an error, but the **setMonth()** Method will attempt to update the specified **Date** Object accordingly.

For instance, if you specify a **monthInteger** Value of 29, then the year parameter would be incremented by 2 and the month parameter would have a Value of 5. It does this by subtracting multiples of 12 from the **monthInteger** Value (assuming the Value supplied is 12 or greater), adds those multiples of 12 to the year, and uses the remainder for the month parameter.

setHours() Method Changes

Syntax for JavaScript 1.3:

```
dateObjName.setHours(hoursInteger[, minsInt, secInt, msInt]);
```

JavaScript 1.2 Syntax:

```
dateObjName.setHours(hoursInteger);
```

Parameters Defined:

In JavaScript 1.3, the optional **minutes**, **seconds**, and **milliseconds** parameters have been added to the **setHours()** Method.

The **setHours()** Method sets the hours with the required **hoursInteger** parameter for the specified **Date** Object of **dateObjName** according to local time. If the optional **minsInt**, **secsInt**, or **msInt** Value is not specified, then it is internally supplied by the **getMinutes()**, **getSeconds()**, and **getMilliseconds()** Method, respectively.

The **hoursInteger** parameter is an integer within the range of 0 to 11 inclusive, which specifies the hours for the specified **Date** Object.

The optional **minsInt** parameter is an integer from 0 to 59 inclusive, which specifies the number of minutes for the specified **Date** Object.

The optional **secsInt** parameter is an integer from 0 to 59 inclusive, which specifies the number of seconds for the specified **Date** Object. If you do specify a **secsInt** parameter, then the **minsInt** parameter is required.

The optional **msInt** parameter is an integer from 0 to 999 inclusive, which specifies the number of milliseconds for the specified **Date** Object. If a **msInt** parameter is specified, then the **secsInt** parameter is required.

If the Value that you supply for any of the parameters is outside the expected range of Values, you will not get an error, but the **setHours()** Method will attempt to update the specified **Date** Object accordingly.

setMinutes() Method Changes

Syntax for JavaScript 1.3:

```
dateObjName.setMinutes(minutesInteger[, secsInt, msInteger]);
```

JavaScript 1.2 Syntax:

```
dateObjName.setMinutes(minutesInteger);
```

Parameters Defined:

The **seconds** and **milliseconds** parameters have been added to the **setMinutes()** Method.

The **setMinutes()** Method sets the minutes by using the required **minutesInteger** parameter for the specified **Date** Object of **dateObjName** according to local time. If the optional **secsInt** or **msInt** Values is not specified, then it is internally supplied by the **getSeconds()** and **getMilliseconds()** Methods, respectively.

The **minutesInteger** parameter is an integer within the range of 0 to 59 inclusive, which specifies the minutes for the specified **Date** Object.

The optional **secsInt** parameter is an integer from 0 to 59 inclusive, which specifies the number of seconds for the specified **Date** Object. If you do specify a **secsInt** parameter, then the **minsInt** parameter is required.

The optional **msInt** parameter is an integer from 0 to 999 inclusive, which specifies the number of milliseconds for the specified **Date** Object. If a **msInt** parameter is specified, then the **secsInt** parameter is required.

If the Value that you supply for any of the parameters is outside of the expected range of Values, you will not get an error, but the **setMinutes()** Method will attempt to update the specified **Date** Object accordingly.

setSeconds() Method Changes

Syntax for JavaScript 1.3:

```
dateObjName.setSeconds(secondsInteger[, msInteger]);
```

JavaScript 1.2 Syntax:

```
dateObjName.setSeconds(secondsInteger);
```

Parameters Defined:

The **milliseconds** parameter has been added to the **setSeconds()** Method.

The **setSeconds()** Method sets the seconds by using the required **secondsInteger** parameter for the specified **Date** Object of **dateObjName** according to local time. If the optional **msInt** Value is not specified, then it is internally supplied by the **getMilliseconds()** Method.

The **secondsInteger** parameter is an integer from 0 to 59 inclusive, which specifies the number of seconds for the specified **Date** Object.

The optional **msInt** parameter is an integer from 0 to 999 inclusive, which specifies the number of milliseconds for the specified **Date** Object.

If the Value that you supply for any of the parameters is outside of the expected range of Values, you will not get an error, but the **setSeconds()** Method will attempt to update the specified **Date** Object accordingly.

UTC() Method Changes

Syntax for JavaScript 1.3:

```
Date.UTC(year, month, day[, hours, mins, secs, milliseconds]);
```

JavaScript 1.2 Syntax:

```
Date.UTC(year, month, day[, hours, mins, secs]);
```

Parameters Defined:

In JavaScript 1.3 the **milliseconds** parameter has been added to the **UTC()** Method.

The **UTC()** Method returns the number of milliseconds that have transpired since January 1, 1970 at 12:00 midnight (January 1, 1970, 00:00:00), in a **Date** Object, based on all of the supplied parameters. This integer is returned in universal time. Three of the seven possible parameters are required and the other four are optional. All of these parameters must be integers.

The required parameters are **year**, **month**, and **day**.

The optional parameters are **hours**, **mins**, **secs**, and **milliseconds**.

The date parameters that you supply must be a comma-separated list.

When specifying the **year** parameter, you should always use a full year and it should be a year after 1899. If you do specify a year between 0 and 99, the **UTC()** Method will convert it to a year in the 1900s by adding 1900 to your year.

month is an integer from 0 to 11 inclusive, specifying the month.

day is an integer from 0 to 31 inclusive, specifying the day of the month.

hours is an integer from 0 to 23 inclusive, specifying the number of hours.

mins is an integer from 0 to 59 inclusive, specifying the number of minutes.

secs is an integer from 0 to 59 inclusive, specifying the number of seconds.

milliseconds is an integer from 0 to 999 inclusive, which specifies the number of milliseconds.

If the Value that you supply for any of the parameters is outside of the expected range of Values, the **UTC()** Method will update your entire supplied list of parameters.

The **UTC()** Method is a Static Method and is always preceded by (**Date.**) as opposed to using it as a named **Date** Object that you have created like this:

```
Date.UTC()
```

Mini-Example:

Here's a quick example where **Date.UTC()** returns 1329301364555 milliseconds:

```
myTimeQtyInMS = Date.UTC(2012, 1, 15, 10, 22, 44, 555);
```

Changes to the Function Object

In JavaScript 1.3, there are two new Methods available for the **Function** Object: the **apply()** Method and the **call()** Method. The formal Arguments and local Variables of a Function are *not* Properties of the **arguments[i]** Array; that is, this previous capability is no longer supported at all. The **arguments.caller** Property has been deprecated.

The apply() Method of the Function Object

JavaScript 1.3 Syntax:

```
callingObject.apply(methodName[, argumentsArray[i]]);
```

Parameters Defined:

callingObject   The Object (usually a Function or Method) that is calling the **apply()** Method.

methodName   You can use the Keyword **this** to refer to the current Object that is the calling Object **callingObject**, or you can reference a previously defined Function/Method by specifying its name.

argumentsArray[i]   An Arguments Array that supplies the Arguments for the **callingObject**. It can take on one of three formats:

An **Array** Object, **Array** Literal, or the **arguments** Property.

The **arguments** Property of all **Function** Objects is a local variable that allows you to pass all of the previously specified arguments of **methodName**, *to* **callingObject** within the **apply()** Method, without having to list them individually.
See pages 380-385 and the examples on the following pages that demonstrate the **apply()** Method.

The **apply()** Method lets you apply a Method of an Object within the context of a different Object, so that you don't have to redefine an identical duplicate Method. This means that you can define a Method once, and then that Method can be inherited by any other Object. The only difference between the **apply()** and **call()** Methods is that with the **call()** Method, the Arguments for the calling Object **callingObject** can only be supplied by a comma-separated list.

Syntax Variations for the <u>apply()</u> Method

Here are the six specific variations of syntax formats for the **apply()** Method:

JavaScript 1.3 Syntax:

```
callingObject.apply(this[, new Array(arg1, arg2, ..., argN)]);      //Array Object

callingObject.apply(this[, [arg1, arg2, ..., argN]]);               //Array Literal

callingObject.apply(this[, arguments]);                            //arguments Property

callingObject.apply(methodName[, new Array(arg1, arg2, ..., argN)]);   //Array Obj

callingObject.apply(methodName[, [arg1, arg2, ..., argN]]);         //Array Literal

callingObject.apply(methodName[, arguments]);                      //arguments Property
```

An <u>apply()</u> Method Example

In the following example, the **checkX(x)** Function tests for the Value of the **x** Argument and updates it accordingly and then returns the result.

Then the **evaluateQ(x, z)** Function uses the **apply()** Method to call the **checkX(x)** Function, adds the returned result to **z**, and assigns that result to the variable **q**. Then the **document.write()** Method displays the Value of **q** to screen.

Finally, two instances of the **evaluateQ(x, z)** Function are created and named **testItOut()** and **testItOut2()**, respectively, and then their source code is displayed to screen with the **toSource()** Method. See <u>Sample10000.html</u> on the CD-ROM.

This Script produces the following results in the Navigator 4.5 browser:

13200

8200

{x:200, z:8000}

{x:100, z:8000}

```
<SCRIPT TYPE="text/javascript" LANGUAGE="JavaScript1.3">

<!--

function checkX(x)   {

     this.x = x;

     if (x < 150) { x = x + 100;     }

     else x = x + 5000;

     return x;
}


function evaluateQ(x, z)   {

     this.x = x;
     this.z = z;

     var q;

     q = z + checkX.apply(checkX, arguments);

     document.write(q + "<P>");
}


testItOut = new evaluateQ(200, 8000);

testItOut2 = new evaluateQ(100, 8000);


document.write(testItOut.toSource() + "<P>");

document.write(testItOut2.toSource() + "<P>");


//-->

</SCRIPT>
```

Another <u>apply()</u> Method Example

This example demonstrates the capability of using the **apply()** Method so that the Arguments of a different Function from the calling Object are passed to the calling Object. What this means in the context of this example is that within the Function **evaluateK(x,y)**, when the following code is used:

```
i = checkY.apply(checkX, [x]);
```

The Value of the Argument **x** (which in this case is 75) is passed to the **checkY(y)** Function and is used as the Value for **y**, so that because 75 is greater than 50, **y** is then assigned the Value of 75 + 3000 = 3075, which is then assigned to the **i** Variable.

Then in the following code:

```
j = checkX.apply(checkY, [y]);
```

The Value of the Argument **y** (which in this case is 300) is passed to the **checkX(x)** Function and is used as the Value for **x**, so that because 300 is greater than 150, **x** is then assigned the Value of 300 + 5000 = 5300, which is then assigned to the **j** Variable.

For the **q** and **r** Variables, the process is more intuitive. In the following code:

```
q = checkX.apply(checkX, [x]);
```

The Value of the Argument **x** (which in this case is 75) is passed to the **checkX(x)** Function and is used as the Value for **x**, so that because 75 is less than 150, **x** is then assigned the Value of 75 + 100 = 175, which is then assigned to the **q** Variable.

Then in the following code:

```
r = checkY.apply(checkY, [y]);
```

The Value of the Argument **y** (which in this case is 300) is passed to the **checkY(y)** Function and is used as the Value for **y**, so that because 300 is greater than 50, **y** is then assigned the Value of 300 + 3000 = 3300, which is then assigned to the **r** Variable.

The rest of the example is mostly devoted to formatting the output to screen, so you can verify the results in the browser in a step-by-step basis.

The results of this Script as displayed in the Navigator browser are shown after the code for the Script. See <u>Sample10001.html</u> on the CD-ROM.

```
<SCRIPT TYPE="text/javascript" LANGUAGE="JavaScript1.3">
<!--

function checkX(x)  {

     this.x = x;

     if (x < 150) { x = x + 100;      }

     else x = x + 5000;

     return x;
}

function checkY(y)  {

     this.y = y;

     if (y >= 50)  { y = y + 3000; }

     else y = y + 44;

     return y;
}

function evaluateS(x, y)  {

     this.x = x;
     this.y = y;

     var q;
     var r;
     var s;

     q = checkX.apply(checkX, [x]);
     document.write("q = " + q + "<P>");

     r = checkY.apply(checkY, [y]);
     document.write("r = " + r + "<P>");

     s = q + r;
     document.write("s = q + r = " + s + "<P><BR>");
}
```

```
function evaluateK(x, y)   {

        this.x = x;
        this.y = y;

        var i;
        var j;
        var k;

        i = checkY.apply(checkX, [x]);
        document.write("i = " + i + "<P>");

        j = checkX.apply(checkY, [y]);
        document.write("j = " + j + "<P>");

        k = i + j;
        document.write("k = i + j = " + k + "<P><BR>");
}

testItOut = new evaluateS(75, 300);

testItOut2 = new evaluateK(75, 300);

document.write(testItOut.toSource() + "<P>");

document.write(testItOut2.toSource());

//-->
</SCRIPT>
```

The previous Script produces the following output to the browser:

q = 175

r = 3300

s = q + r = 3475

i = 3075

j = 5300

k = i + j = 8375

{x:75, y:300}

{x:75, y:300}

The <u>call()</u> Method of the Function Object

JavaScript 1.3 Syntax:

```
callingObject.call(methodName[, arg1, arg2, ..., argN]);
```

Parameters Defined:

callingObject	The Object (usually a Function or Method) that is calling the **call()** Method.
methodName	You can use the Keyword **this** to refer to the current Object that is the calling Object **callingObject**, or you can reference a previously defined Function/Method by specifying its name.
arg1, arg2, ..., argN	A comma-separated list of Arguments to be passed to the **callingObject**.

Using the <u>call()</u> Method

The **call()** Method lets you apply a Method of an Object within the context of a different Object, so that you don't have to redefine an identical duplicate Method. This means that you can define a Method once, and then that Method can be inherited by any other Object.

The only difference between the **apply()** and **call()** Methods is that with the **call()** Method, the Arguments for the calling Object **callingObject** can only be supplied by a comma-separated list. With the **apply()** Method, you have the three choices of using an **Array** Object, an **Array** Literal, or the **arguments** Property of all **Function** Objects.

In the next example, the Function **inventoryItem(name, price, saleBoolean)** uses the **call()** Method to call the previously defined **saleItem(price, saleBoolean)** Function to determine if an item is on sale or not. If the item is on sale, then the **price** Argument is multiplied by 90% (.9) and returned. If the item is not on sale, then the **price** Argument is unaltered and assigned to **this.price** and then returned.

Then, based on the **saleBoolean** Argument, **inventoryItem()** determines which type of output to the browser is used via the **document.write()** Method. The browser output is shown after the Script. You can check out the example in <u>Sample10002.html</u>.

```
<SCRIPT TYPE="text/javascript" LANGUAGE="JavaScript1.3">
<!--

function saleItem(price, saleBoolean)  {

      this.price = price;

      if (saleBoolean) { this.price = price * .9;      }

      else this.price = price;

      return this.price;
}

function inventoryItem(name, price, saleBoolean)  {

      this.name = name;

      this.price = saleItem.call(saleItem, price, saleBoolean);


      if (saleBoolean)

      document.write(this.name + "<BR> Sale Price= $" +
            this.price + ".00 -----Discounted 10% off. <P><BR>");

      else

      document.write(this.name + "<BR> Price= $" +
            this.price + ".00");
}


item1 = new inventoryItem("Power Mac G3/400", 3000, true);

item2 = new inventoryItem("Power Mac G3/350", 2500, false);


//-->

</SCRIPT>
```

The previous Script produces the following output to the browser:

Power Mac G3/400
Sale Price= $2700.00 -----Discounted 10% off.

Power Mac G3/350
Price= $2500.00

Changes to the String Object

In JavaScript 1.3, the following changes have been implemented for **String** Objects.

In JavaScript 1.3, the Methods of **charCodeAt()** and **fromCharCode()** of **String** Objects, now return Unicode Values instead of ISO-Latin-1 Values. Note that the first 128 characters, that is, from 0 to 127, represented by Unicode, are identical to the first 0-127 characters of ASCII and ISO-Latin-1.

Also note that there are 65,535 possible Unicode Values, and as of version 2.1 of Unicode, there are over 38,000 supported characters.

For more information on the **charCodeAt()** Method see pages 761-762.

For more information on the **fromCharCode()** Method see pages 763-766.

For more information on Unicode, see page 856 or the JavaScript 1.3 Guide from Netscape which is on the CD-ROM, or go to the Unicode Consortium website at:

`http://www.unicode.org`

In JavaScript 1.3, you can now nest a Function as an option for the second Argument in the **replace()** Method. In the syntax for the **replace()** Method, which is listed on the following page, this would be the **myFunction** Argument.

This enhanced functionality for the **replace()** Method, along with the new syntax that accompanies it, will require both some review and a substantial amount of explaining to cover all of the details. So, here we go.

Changes to the <u>replace()</u> Method of String Object

Syntax for JavaScript 1.3:

```
anyString.replace(regularExpression, "newSubString");
anyString.replace(regularExpression, myFunction);
```

JavaScript 1.2 Syntax:

```
anyString.replace(regularExpression, "newSubString");
```

Parameters Defined:

As of JavaScript 1.3, the **replace()** Method can optionally use a Function for the **myFunction** Argument instead of only being able to provide a replacement SubString, as in version 1.2 of JavaScript.

All of the previous functionality of the **replace()** Method is retained from JavaScript 1.2 and won't be reiterated here. If you need to refresh your memory, check back in Chapter 8 on Strings on pages 778-781. However, some of the essential details should be at your fingertips, so here's a quick reminder about **replace()**, before we get into the intricacies of the **myFunction** Argument.

The **replace()** Method finds a match between the **regularExpression** Argument and the calling String **anyString**. Then the SubString contained in the **newSubString** Argument is used to replace the SubString that is matched in **anyString**. However, it should be noted that the **replace()** Method does not alter the original calling String **anyString** in any way. It returns a new String consisting of **anyString** with the matched substitutions.

The **newSubString** Argument can be a Literal, a Variable name, or any of the following **RegExp** Properties, which are defined in Chapter 9. Note that $1 - $9 are not prepended with **RegExp** when used in the **newSubString** Argument in the **replace()** Method and must be inside quotes. This is true only when using the **replace()** Method.

$1, $2, ..., $9		Not prepended with **RegExp** and must be inside quotes
lastMatch,	$&	Is prepended with **RegExp**, outside quotes with String addition +
lastParen,	$+	Is prepended with **RegExp**, outside quotes with String addition +
leftContext,	$`	Is prepended with **RegExp**, outside quotes with String addition +
rightContext,	$'	Is prepended with **RegExp**, outside quotes with String addition +

The **regularExpression** Argument can be a Literal or a Variable name. The global **flag g** can be used to execute a <u>global</u> search and the <u>ignore case</u> **flag i** can be used to execute a case-insensitive search. They can be used individually or together as **gi**.

Parameters Defined (continued):

That's it for the review. Let's move on to the **myFunction** Argument.

When you specify a Function for the second Argument in **replace()**, (the **myFunction** Argument), it is invoked after the match between **regularExpression** and **anyString** has executed. The **myFunction** Function is used to dynamically generate the replacement SubString by using the **return** Statement to return the results to the **replace()** Method as the conclusion to the Function call.

Before we go any further, let's do a more detailed delineation of the Syntax for the **myFunction** Argument.

Syntax for JavaScript 1.3:

```
anyString.replace(regularExpression,
        function myFunction(fullMatchedSubString, rememberedSubStr1,
            rememberedSubStr2, ..., rememberedSubStr9, ) {

            Statements;
            return replacementSubString;
        }
);
```

Parameters Defined (continued):

When the **myFunction** Function is specified, its first Argument of **fullMatchedSubString** is always the holder of the complete SubString match from the **regularExpression** Argument. The next Argument of **myFunction** is **rememberedSubStr1** and contains the first parenthesized remembered SubString. The rest of the possible Arguments hold the rest of the parenthesized remembered SubStrings as they occur in order from 2 to 9.

The **Statements** parameters are any valid JavaScript Statements to execute in order to manipulate the matched SubString and its remembered SubStrings into a final **replacementSubString**, which is then returned via the **return** Statement. The **replacementSubString** is the SubString that replaces the match found in the calling **anyString**.

Within the **myFunction** Function, that is, any of the Statements contained within the Function, may make use of the Array returned from the **exec()** Method of the **RegExp** Object. What this means is that you can use the **RegExp** Properties of **$1-$9** to access the parenthesized remembered SubStrings in an efficient manner to massage the replacement String before returning it. You may also use the **RegExp** Property of **input**. See Chapter 9 on pages 803-807 for more information on **RegExp** Properties.

The following example converts kilometers to Light Years by using the **replace()** Method on the String in the **km** Argument. The **RegExp** Literal searches for a match of one or more digits, followed by zero or one decimal, followed by zero or more digits, and this group comprises the only remembered Submatch; followed by white space, followed by the characters of "Kilometers".

The replacement String is provided by the **getLightYears()** Function. The **$1** Argument holds the remembered Submatch, and its Value is used to calculate an equivalent in Light Years. **$1** is next used to create a number equivalent in order to determine whether " Light Years" should be plural or singular.

This Script is contained in <u>Sample10003.html</u>.

```
<SCRIPT TYPE="text/javascript" LANGUAGE="JavaScript1.3">
<!--

function displayLightYears(km)   {

        var LY = km.replace(
                /(\d+\.?\d*)\sKilometers/,

                        function getLightYears(fullMatchedSubString, $1) {

                                var lightYears = $1 / (9.46 * 1000000000000);

                                checkYear = new Number($1);

                                if (checkYear == 9460000000000) {
                                        return lightYears + " Light Year";
                                }
                                else {
                                        return lightYears + " Light Years";
                                }
                        }
                );

        document.write(LY + "<BR>");

}


displayLightYears("9460000000000 Kilometers");
displayLightYears("9460000000000.0 Kilometers");
displayLightYears("9460000000000.5 Kilometers");
displayLightYears("18920000000000 Kilometers");
displayLightYears("25757500558885555.52 Kilometers");

//-->

</SCRIPT>
```

The previous Script produces the following output to the browser:

1 Light Year
1 Light Year
1.0000000000000528 Light Years
2 Light Years
2722.7801859287056 Light Years

New Method

The <u>toSource()</u> Method for several Objects

The **toSource()** Method returns a String, which represents the source code of the Object that it is called on. It is a new Method as of JavaScript 1.3 for all of the following Objects:

Array, **Boolean**, **Date**, **Function**, **Number**, **Object**, **RegExp**, and **String**.

For more information on the **toSource()** Method of the **Array** Object, go to pages 859-860. The rest of the Objects for which it available, are now individually covered.

Syntax for JavaScript 1.3:

```
Boolean.toSource();
booleanObjectName.toSource();

Date.toSource();
dateObjectName.toSource();

Function.toSource();
functionObjectName.toSource();

Number.toSource();
numberObjectName.toSource();

Object.toSource();
objectObjectName.toSource();

RegExp.toSource();
regExpObjectName.toSource();

String.toSource();
stringObjectName.toSource();
```

The **toSource()** Method is generally only useful for debugging purposes, in order to examine the contents of an Object at various points in a troublesome Script. Otherwise, it is usually only called internally by JavaScript, not explicitly with code.

For all of the previously mentioned Objects, if **toSource()** is called on the top-level built-in Object, then a String is returned in the following format, indicating that the native code is unavailable for display: Specifically for the **RegExp** Object, **RegExp.toSource()** would return the following String:

```
function RegExp() {
        [native code]
}
```

For all of the previously mentioned Objects, if **toSource()** is called on an instance of that Object, then the source code of that particular instance is returned, which is the same as saying that an Object Literal is returned. For example, if you had the following instance of a **RegExp** Object:

```
myRegExp = /(\d+)-(\d+)-(\d+)/;
```

then:

```
myRegExp.toSource();
```

returns the **RegExp** Literal:

```
/(\d+)-(\d+)-(\d+)/
```

If you had the following Object named **Computer()**:

```
function Computer(name,model,speed,ram,year) {
this.name=name
this.model=model
this.speed=speed
this.ram=ram
this.year=year
}
```

then for the following instance of **Computer()** named **myNewComputer**:

```
myNewComputer = new Computer("PowerMac","G3/",700,"2Gig","2000");
myNewComputer.toSource()
```

returns the Object Literal:

```
{name:"PowerMac", model:"G3/", speed:700, ram:"2Gig", year:"2000"}
```

New Top-Level Properties

In JavaScript 1.3, there are three new Top-Level Properties that are Core Properties and aren't associated with any particular Object. They are:

Infinity, **NaN**, and **undefined**.

Infinity Property

Syntax for JavaScript 1.3:

```
Infinity;
```

The **Infinity** Property is a numeric Value that represents mathematical positive infinity. Its initial Value is the same as **Number.POSITIVE_INFINITY**. It is larger than any other number including itself. It also behaves like mathematical positive infinity in that any number that is multiplied by **Infinity** is **Infinity** and any number that is divided by **Infinity** is 0 (zero).

In JavaScript 1.2, **Infinity** was only accessed as a Property of the **Number** Object. See page 460, on the **Number** Object for more information.

NaN Property

Syntax for JavaScript 1.3:

```
NaN;
```

The **NaN** Property is a Value that represents Not-A-Number. In JavaScript 1.3, it is a Top-Level Property so it is accessed by itself, whereas in JavaScript 1.2, **NaN** was only accessed as a Property of the **Number** Object like this: **Number.NaN**. See page 460, on the **Number** Object for more information.

undefined Property

Syntax for JavaScript 1.3:

```
undefined;
```

The **undefined** Property has a Value of **undefined**. For any Variable that you have created that does not have a Value assigned to it, it has the Value of **undefined**. Any Methods, Functions, or Statements that return a Variable that has not been assigned a Value will return **undefined**.

You can compare **undefined** against a Variable to determine if it has a Value or not.

Mini-Example:

For instance, if you had the Variable **myX**:

```
var myX;

if (myX == undefined) { execute Statements; }
```

New Top-Level Function

isFinite() Function

Syntax for JavaScript 1.3:

```
isFinite(number);
```

The **isFinite()** Function is a Top-Level Function and is not associated with any Object. The **number** Argument is tested to determine if it is finite or not. If it is finite then **true** is returned. If the **number** Argument is positive infinity, negative infinity, or **NaN**, then **false** is returned.

Changes to Top-Level Functions

eval() Function

Syntax for JavaScript 1.3:

```
eval("string" | stringVariable);
```

In JavaScript 1.3, the **eval()** Function is still a Top-Level Function and only has one minor change to its functionality. You should always use it directly and never use it in an indirect manner, such as by assigning it to a Variable. For more information on the use of the **eval()** Function, see the JavaScript 1.3 Reference on the CD-ROM.

New Operators

The === Operator

In JavaScript 1.3, the === Operator is called the Strict Equal Operator because it returns true only if both operands are equal and are of the same type. For instance, if you compare a String of "5543" and a Number of 5543, then the comparison would return **false** because they aren't of the same type.

Contrast that with the behavior of the Equal Operator ==, which would return **true** because they have the same Value and that is all that is required.

For more information on Operators and Object Types, see the section on Operators in the JavaScript 1.3 Reference on the CD-ROM.

The !== Operator

In JavaScript 1.3, the !== Operator is called the Strict Not Equal Operator because it returns true if both operands are not equal and/or are not of the same type. In other words, only one of the conditions has to be true in order for the comparison to return true.

Changes to Operators

The == Operator

When the == Operator (Equal Operator) is used in JavaScript 1.3, if the two operands are not of the same type, JavaScript will attempt to internally convert them to the same type for the purposes of the comparison. This does not change the actual type of either operand. This behavior reverts to that exhibited in version 1.1 of JavaScript. For more information on the JavaScript 1.2 implementation, see page 515.

The != Operator

When the != Operator (Not Equal Operator) is used in JavaScript 1.3, if the two operands are not of the same type, JavaScript will attempt to internally convert them to the same type for the purposes of the comparison. This does not change the actual type of either operand. This behavior reverts to that exhibited in version 1.1 of JavaScript. For more information on the JavaScript 1.2 implementation, see page 515.

Changes to Conditional Test Behaviors

Assignment Behaviors

In version 1.3 of JavaScript, if you inadvertently use an Assignment Operator instead of a Conditional Operator in a Conditional test, you will generate a runtime error. For instance:

```
if (a = b) { Statements; }
```

generates an error. The correct usage would be:

```
if (a == b) { Statements; }
```

In JavaScript 1.2 and earlier, JavaScript would have converted the oversight into the correct usage automatically.

<u>null</u> and <u>undefined</u> Values for Objects

When passing an Object to a Conditional Statement, that Object will always have a Value of **true** unless it has a Value of **null** or **undefined**. This is true even for Boolean Objects that have a Value of **false**.

Using the JavaScript Console to debug your code

The JavaScript Console is a separate window that displays the bugs in your JavaScript code. The offending character(s) is highlighted in red and the Console tells you the line number that the error occurred on. The easiest way to get the JavaScript Console to appear is to type in **javascript:** in the location bar of the browser. Note that the colon is necessary. See the JavaScript 1.3 Guide on the CD-ROM for more info.

Wrapping Up and Moving On

It's been quite an adventure. If you understand everything that's been covered in the book, then you have all the tools necessary to create a variety of innovative, useful and fun websites with Styles, Layers and advanced JavaScript. The sky's the limit to express your own creations.

The next section of the book is devoted to a Primer on HTML for those who are just starting out on website design or for quick syntax reference. Note that the HTML Primer on the CD-ROM is an expanded version, both in theory, Element delineation and Examples. There are over 70 additional Sample files, with full explanations, just on the topic of regular HTML, on the CD-ROM. There are working examples of QTVR, VRML, music, QuickTime movies, QD3D 3D EMBED files, along with working FORMs for data collection and order forms. Specifically, there is a lot of additional information on the FORM Element, EMBED Element, OBJECT Element and Elements that can be contained in FORM Elements.

Appendix B contains some useful information on Color Theory and a chart of the recognized JavaScript Color Names, their HEX equivalents, RGB percentage Values and RGB number Values.

Appendix C contains a chart with all of the Examples and Sample files used in the book plus some bonus Samples that are only on the CD-ROM. This chart lists the page number that each Example starts on in the book, the number of the Example and the name of the associated Sample file on the CD-ROM and the topic that is covered.

Appendix D contains a chart of Language Abbreviations for the LANGUAGE Attribute of most HTML Elements.

Appendix E is a sequence of charts that contain a lot of useful information in one location that have been collected from scattered sources throughout the book. Note that it can be printed from the file on the CD-ROM named:

Charts.pdf

You might find it very useful to keep a printout of this file at your fingertips when writing your own code, for reference.

Finally, after the Index, there is some information about the files contained in the CD-ROM. This entire book is included in both HTML and PDF formats so that you have the option of learning the material in an interactive way, noting that all of the examples are linked so that you can run them easily, from within the explanations.

Part IV
Resources

Appendix A

HTML Primer

Foreword to Appendix A

This is a primer for HTML. It is not a complete work on all of HTML or even all of the Elements available for HTML 4.0 or the subset that is supported by Navigator. What it does is provide the Syntax for all of the Elements of HTML 4.0 that are supported by Navigator 4.x.

Additionally, it does provide a lot of useful information that is both instructive in using the Elements of HTML and as a reference when you need to verify what Attributes and Values are available for particular Elements and if they are being used correctly within other Elements.

Certain Elements such as the IMG, FRAME, FRAMESET, and TABLE Elements are covered in much more detail than most other Elements because they are more complicated, and it is generally less obvious empirically as to the methods for utilizing them correctly.

There is a lot more information available on the CD-ROM about HTML 4.0. Both the PDF and the HTML versions of Part IV of the book have additional pages that were part of the original version of the book but had to be scrapped due to topic focus and length considerations. Believe me, this book could very easily have been over 2000 pages long. There are lots of additional examples and Sample files in both the HTML and PDF versions. The HTML version starts with

the file named:	**CH1.html**
which is in the folder named:	**HTML_BOOK-Online**

If you are going to print out that document, then print from the PDF version, because the HTML version has Style Sheets and Layers and you can't print those yet due to the lack of current browser support. The following file is Part IV of the book and has all of the Appendixes in it, including Appendix A, which is this HTML Primer, in PDF format:

DHTML BOOK-IV-All ApxS.pdf

The folder from Netscape has the complete documentation of HTML 4.0 for Navigator 4.x, which goes into more detail, especially concerning the Navigator-specific extensions. Load in the **index.html** document from their folder to start it off.

The folder from the Web Design Group (WDG) has complimentary and sometimes overlapping data about all of Elements for HTML 4.0, including Elements that Navigator does not support but are part of the official HTML 4.0 Specification. Load in the **index.html** document from their folder to start it off.

Finally, this section of the book is primarily written for those just getting starting with HTML, so you old-hands using it for reference, skip the obvious.

What is HTML anyway?

HTML is an acronym for Hypertext Markup Language. It consists of Elements and Tags that describe or define the content of the document by suggesting to the web browser how the content should be displayed. It should be noted that "suggesting" is the operative word here; browsers have significant discretion in how they display pages, and all browsers have their idiosyncrasies.

HTML documents can contain text, Tags, image references, audio references, animation references, links, JavaScript, Java Applets, and lots of other cool embedded input that can be accessed via the World Wide Web.

When you save your HTML files, remember to add the suffix (.html) or (.htm) to the end of the file name. The dot(.) in the suffix is necessary for most servers even though it isn't strictly required by the HTML specifications.

Also— and this will save you huge amounts of headaches to know it right at the beginning: DO NOT PUT WHITE SPACE IN YOUR FILE NAMES because the server will change it into a percent (%20) Hex sign, and none of your links will work because the file names will have changed when you upload them and the browser won't be able to find them. Use an Underscore (_) or a Hyphen (-) character instead.

Example A1-1:

```
Name_That_File.html            Correct Naming of a File
Name-That-File.html            Correct Naming of a File
NameThatFile.html              Correct Naming of a File

Name That File.html            TOTALLY WRONG Naming of a File
```

Tags and Elements

Most Elements are composed of three parts. A Start Tag at the beginning, content, and then an End Tag. Some Elements such as the
 (line-break), which do not contain content, do not have an End Tag. Other Elements such as the <LI> (list item) give you the option of using an End Tag or not using it, because the End Tag is implied by either the next usage of the <LI> Start Tag or by the end of the actual list. Usually the End Tag is required, so assume that it is unless it's indicated as forbidden or optional in this book.

A Start Tag is a NAME enclosed by angle brackets (< >) that signifies to a browser the start of an Element. The End Tag is the same NAME preceded by a forward slash(/) and also enclosed by angle brackets, which indicates the end of that Element. The Start and End Tags surround the content that you want to mark up by that particular Element.

It doesn't matter if the Start Tag, the Text, and the End Tag are all on one line or on two or more separate lines. More succinctly put: Spacing is irrelevant in HTML. Element NAMES are always case-insensitive; so <BR> equals <bR> equals <br> equals <Br>.

Example A1-2:

```
<CENTER>
This text will be in the center of the page.
</CENTER>
```

Example A1-3:

```
<CENTER>This text will also be in the center of the page.</CENTER>
<H1>  This will be a very large heading.  </H1>
```

HTML Document Type Declaration

Let's jump right in. Each HTML page needs to declare which version of HTML that it adheres to, and this is accomplished with the Document Type Declaration. If you are writing for version 3.2 of HTML, then you can use this DOCTYPE:

```
<!DOCTYPE HTML PUBLIC "-//W3C//DTD HTML 3.2//EN">
```

However, if you are writing for version 4.0 of HTML then there are three flavors to choose from and each one has its own unique DOCTYPE:

HTML 4.0 Strict

This truncated version of HTML does not allow frames, targeted links, or any of the deprecated Elements or Attributes, which include most presentational Attributes. It is theoretically relying on Style Sheets to do the job of presentational formatting. However, many browsers poorly support Style Sheets, so it is recommended that you use HTML 4.0 Transitional until wider support for Style Sheets is achieved.

Here's the DOCTYPE for HTML 4.0 Strict:

```
<!DOCTYPE HTML PUBLIC "-//W3C//DTD HTML 4.0//EN"
        "http://www.w3.org/TR/REC-html40/strict.dtd">
```

HTML 4.0 Transitional

In addition to all of the capabilities of HTML 4.0 Strict, HTML 4.0 Transitional includes all deprecated Elements, presentational Attributes, and targeted links.

Here's the DOCTYPE for HTML 4.0 Transitional:

```
<!DOCTYPE HTML PUBLIC "-//W3C//DTD HTML 4.0 Transitional//EN"
        "http://www.w3.org/TR/REC-html40/loose.dtd">
```

HTML 4.0 Frameset

This is a slightly different version of HTML 4.0 Transitional, specifically designed for pages that use Framesets instead of the Body Element.

Here's the DOCTYPE for HTML 4.0 Frameset:

```
<!DOCTYPE HTML PUBLIC "-//W3C//DTD HTML 4.0 Frameset//EN"
      "http://www.w3.org/TR/REC-html40/frameset.dtd">
```

Basic HTML Document Structure

All HTML documents follow the same basic structure:

```
<!DOCTYPE HTML PUBLIC "-//W3C//DTD HTML 4.0 Transitional//EN"
      "http://www.w3.org/TR/REC-html40/loose.dtd">
<HTML>
<HEAD>
<TITLE> My Home Page or whatever    </TITLE>
      ***    Put other head content in here      ***
</HEAD>

<BODY>
      ***    Put the body content in here        ***
</BODY>
</HTML>
```

The <HTML> Element

The first Element after the Document Type Declaration is the <HTML> Element. Its Start and End Tags enclose everything in the entire document except the DOCTYPE. This tells a browser like Netscape Navigator that all the HTML code contained between these Start and End Tags (except for the content of the Comment and <XMP> Tags) will be interpreted as HTML code and displayed accordingly.

The first Element contained within the HTML Element is the HEAD Element which is then followed by the BODY Element, except for documents that replace the BODY Element with one or more FRAMESET Elements.

Contents   In HTML4.0 Strict and Transitional: HEAD then BODY
                    In HTML4.0 Frameset: HEAD then FRAMESET

Contained in   Not contained in any Element because HTML is a top-level Element

Syntax:

```
<HTML>
     ***   the entire document except the DOCTYPE goes here   ***
</HTML>
```

The <HEAD> Element

The <HEAD> Element is the first Element contained within the HTML Element. Generally it is used for optional, descriptive data that is useful for search engines by containing the META Element or advanced options like Cascading Style Sheets with the STYLE Element or JavaScript with the SCRIPT Element which we'll get to later on.

The only Element required in the HEAD is the TITLE Element.

Other Elements that can be contained within the HEAD Element are the BASE, BASEFONT, ISINDEX, and OBJECT Elements, which are covered on pages 1021, 925, 1024, and 1021, respectively. The LINK Element is also contained in the HEAD Element, but it was covered back on pages 114-123, in Chapter 1.

Contents   One and only one required TITLE Element,
                      optional BASE, BASEFONT and ISINDEX Elements, and
                      zero or more LINK, META, OBJECT, SCRIPT, or STYLE Elements
Contained in   HTML Element

Syntax:

```
<HEAD
LANG="ISOLanguageAbbreviation">
     ***    Elements    ***
</HEAD>
```

The <TITLE> Element

The <TITLE> Element is used to describe the contents of the page. It will appear in the title bar of the browser Window, not in the document itself.

Contents   none
Contained in   HEAD Element

Syntax:

```
<TITLE>
     My Home Page or whatever
</TITLE>
```

The <BODY> Element

This is where most of the fun stuff happens. The <BODY> Element is where you put most of the <u>Content</u> of your document that you want to have displayed in the browser Window. The <u>Content</u> can be text, images, animations, VRML, QuickTime movies, QTVR, music or other audio, Shockwave files, Streaming Video, and lots more. You put the <u>Content</u> between the BODY Start and End Tags. Unless you are using Style Sheets or Scripts that generate HTML, this is where most of the text markup occurs, that is, where you format and structure the <u>Content</u> with global parameters and other individual HTML Elements. First we'll show you how to set up the BODY Element and then move on to procedures for text markup, document layout, images, and Embedded Objects.

Up until now, all the Tags have been used without any Attributes or with just the unnamed defaults. An Attribute is just a method to modify an Element to your specific display desires. You accomplish this with a NAME="**value**" pair, where the NAME is the name of the Attribute you want to use and the "**value**" is how you choose to modify the content. Always enclose the "**value**" inside of double quote marks when it contains any non-alphanumeric character such as a percent (%) sign. When a "**value**" contains only alphanumeric characters, the double quotes are optional. Many people use lowercase letters for easier code readability but it should be noted that there are some "**value**" Values which are case-sensitive. Element and Attribute Names are always case-insensitive.

Some Quick Color Theory

In HTML, you can specify color either by using one of the sixteen recognized color Names or by using a Hexadecimal RGB Triplet Color (both of which have the advantage of being more widely supported and therefore more consistent across platforms). (Note that in the Navigator specification you can also use the JavaScript Color Names for HTML color Values.) For more on Color Theory, see Appendix B.

The sixteen universally recognized color Names are:

aqua, black, blue, fuchsia, gray, green, lime, maroon,
navy, olive, purple, red, silver, teal, white, yellow

Here's a quickie color overview. In order to understand how color is handled in HTML you have to know that Hexadecimal Triplet RGB color is built on Base 16 math. The dollar signs in the Syntax on page 909 are replaced by you with numbers 0 through 9 and letters A through F because in Base 16 math:

A=10, B=11, C=12, D=13, E=14, F=15

Red values are represented by the first two digits.
Green values are represented by the second two digits.
Blue values are represented by the third two digits.

For Instance:

#RRGGBB	**=**	**Color**
#000000	=	black
#ffffff	=	white
#333333	=	darkgray
#ff0000	=	red
#00ff00	=	lime
#0000ff	=	blue
#ffff00	=	yellow
#9300ee	=	purple

Mini-Example:

This is an example of specifying a magenta-ish HEX color with the TEXT Attribute, noting that it is always preceded with a hash (#) sign like this (remember double quotes):

```
TEXT="#fa13de"
```

The way that Syntax (your HTML code) is laid out in this book is with the Element Name first, which in this case would be BODY. Then there is a list of the Attribute Names with their respective Value possibilities which compose the NAME="**value**" pair as mentioned previously. When you see a vertical bar(|) between the **values** that means that you have a choice of **value** Types to choose from. The Character (|) just means (or). For the first Attribute Name of TEXT you can choose to use either a HEXADECIMAL Color or a Color Name.

The **value** placeholder names between the quote marks (like **colorName**) are descriptive only and are just an attempt to try and explain what kind of **value** that you should replace it with except when it is in all-Caps, which signifies that it is a Keyword that can be used as is. One exception to this is "URL".

Most Attributes are optional and are used to modify the Element to your own tastes. When an Attribute is <u>required</u> for the Element to work, I will let you know. The BODY Element has no required Attributes. For minimal default Attributes just use the BODY Start Tag and End Tag like this: <BODY>   </BODY>

Contents	In HTML4.0 Strict: any block-level Elements or SCRIPT Element
	In HTML4.0 Transitional: any block-level Elements or inline Elements
Contained in	In HTML4.0 Strict or Transitional: HTML
	In HTML4.0 Frameset: NOFRAMES

Syntax:

```
<BODY
TEXT="#$$$$$$"|"colorName"
BGCOLOR="#$$$$$$"|"colorName"
LINK="#$$$$$$"|"colorName"
ALINK="#$$$$$$"|"colorName"
VLINK="#$$$$$$"|"colorName"
BACKGROUND="imageURL"
ONFOCUS="focusJavaScriptCode"
ONBLUR="blurJavaScriptCode"
ONLOAD="loadJavaScriptCode"
ONUNLOAD="unloadJavaScriptCode"
LANG="ISOLanguageAbbreviation"
STYLE="Property:Value; Property:Value; ..."
CLASS="nameOfClass"
ID="nameOfClassException">

        ***    Elements     ***
</BODY>
```

TEXT="#$$$$$$"|"colorName" specifies the color for normal text in your document using either a recognized color Name or a Hexadecimal red-green-blue Triplet. If you don't choose a color, then the default value is black, which can also be overridden by the user in the Preferences Menu of the browser. See the section on Color Theory on pages 1030+.

BGCOLOR="#$$$$$$"|"colorName" specifies the color for the background of the document, which has a default value of white and can also be overridden by the user in the Preferences Menu of the browser. See the section on Color Theory on pages 1030+.

LINK="#$$$$$$"|"colorName" specifies the color for the unvisited Links in your document. They have a default value of blue and are underlined. The user can change the Link color and turn off the underline feature in the Preferences Menu of the Navigator browser but you can't disable the underline feature with HTML. The LINK color is also applied to a default two-pixel-thick border around Linked Images or to the thickness set by the BORDER Attribute of the IMG Element unless the BORDER Attribute is set to zero, which results in no border at all.

ALINK="#$$$$$$"|"colorName" specifies the color for the ACTIVE Links contained in your document, which have a default value of red and are underlined. An ACTIVE Link is only active for the precise amount of time that the user clicks on it so that only during that short interval is the color change visible.

VLINK="#$$$$$$" | "colorName" specifies the color for the VISITED Links contained in your document, which have a default value of magenta and are underlined. The user can change the VISITED Link color and turn off the underline feature in the Preferences Menu of the browser. A VISITED Link is one that the user has gone to previously, and so it changes color by default as a memory jog for the user.

BACKGROUND="imageURL" specifies the URL of an image or GIF89a Animation that is used as a background image for the document. The image is tiled, that is, it's repeated to fill in the entire WINDOW or FRAME, and it will retile if the WINDOW is resized by the user.

ONFOCUS="focusJavaScript Code" executes this JavaScript code when the WINDOW of the document gains FOCUS. FOCUS is when a component or feature of a FORM has been selected for input by the user, and in this case that FORM would be contained inside of this document. See the advanced section on JavaScript for theory and examples dealing with Event Handlers in Chapter 6.

ONBLUR="blurJavaScript Code" executes this JavaScript code when this document loses FOCUS. See the advanced section on JavaScript for theory and examples dealing with Event Handlers in Chapter 6.

ONLOAD="loadJavaScript Code" executes this JavaScript code after the document has fully loaded into the browser WINDOW. See the advanced section on JavaScript for theory and examples dealing with Event Handlers in Chapter 6.

ONUNLOAD="unloadJavaScript Code" executes this JavaScript code after the document has fully exited from the browser WINDOW. See the advanced section on JavaScript for theory and examples dealing with Event Handlers in Chapter 6.

LANG="ISOLanguageAbbreviation" specified by the ISO abbreviation such as "**en**" for English or "**fr**" for French, is the language to be used for the Attribute Values and all of the rendered text for that Element and all contained Elements that do *not* indicate their own LANG Attribute.

STYLE="Property:Value; Property:Value; ..." specifies an inline Style for an Element by using one or more **Property:Value;** pairs. See Part I -- Dynamic HTML for details.

CLASS="nameOfClass" specifies an inline CLASS of STYLE to an Element by addressing that previously NAMED CLASS of STYLE. See Part I -- Dynamic HTML for details.

ID="nameOfClassException " specifies a NAMED INDIVIDUAL Style as an Exception to a NAMED CLASS of STYLE --or-- a location. See Part I -- Dynamic HTML for details.

The <DIV> Element

Used to create Divisions of text; usually with other Elements such as Paragraph.

Contents   All block-level Elements and inline Elements
Contained in   APPLET, BLOCKQUOTE, BODY, CENTER, DD, DIV, FORM,
                LI, MAP, NOFRAMES, NOSCRIPT, OBJECT, TD, TH Elements

Syntax:

```
<DIV
ALIGN="LEFT"|"CENTER"|"RIGHT"
LANG="ISOLanguageAbbreviation"
STYLE="Property:Value; Property:Value; ..."
CLASS="nameOfClass"
ID="nameOfClassException">
...
</DIV>
```

The <P> Element

Used to create Paragraphs of text.

Contents   All inline Elements
Contained in   ADDRESS, APPLET, BLOCKQUOTE, BODY, CENTER, DD, DIV,
                FORM, LI, MAP, NOFRAMES, NOSCRIPT, OBJECT, TD, TH Elements

Syntax:

```
<P
ALIGN="LEFT|CENTER|RIGHT"                        (deprecated)
LANG="ISOLanguageAbbreviation"
STYLE="Property:Value; Property:Value; ..."
CLASS="nameOfClass"
ID="nameOfClassException">
...
</P>
```

The <PRE> Element

Creates Preformatted text where all white space is preserved.

Contents   Inline Elements except: BASEFONT, APPLET, BIG, FONT,
                                         IMG, OBJECT, SMALL, SUB, SUP
Contained in   APPLET, BLOCKQUOTE, BODY, CENTER, DD, DIV, FORM,
                LI, MAP, NOFRAMES, NOSCRIPT, OBJECT, TD, TH Elements

Syntax:

```
<PRE
WRAP
COLS="numberColumns"
LANG="ISOLanguageAbbreviation"
STYLE="Property:Value; Property:Value; ..."
CLASS="nameOfClass"
ID="nameOfClassException">
...
</PRE>
```

The <MULTICOL> Element

Creates MultiColumn text where the number of columns can be specified. This is a Netscape Navigator extension and is not W3G approved.

Contents   Most block-level Elements and inline Elements
Contained in   Most block-level Elements and inline Elements

Syntax:

```
<MULTICOL
COLS="number"
WIDTH="pixels"
GUTTER="pixels"
LANG="ISOLanguageAbbreviation"
STYLE="Property:Value; Property:Value; ..."
CLASS="nameOfClass"
ID="nameOfClassException">
...
</MULTICOL>
```

The <SPACER> Element

Creates horizontal and vertical blocks of white space, which in effect, creates space between its adjacent Elements. See CH1.html in the online Guide for useful information about the TYPE and ALIGN Attributes. This is a Netscape Navigator extension and is not W3G approved.

Contents   None
Contained in   Most block-level Elements

Syntax:

```
<SPACER
TYPE="HORIZONTAL"|"VERTICAL"|"BLOCK"
WIDTH="pix"
HEIGHT="pix"
SIZE="pix"
ALIGN="LEFT"|"RIGHT"|"TOP"|"ABSMIDDLE"|"ABSBOTTOM"|
          "TEXTTOP"|"MIDDLE"|"BASELINE"|"BOTTOM">
```

The <H1> Element

All of the H1 to H6 Elements are for Headings, with H1 using the largest size font.

Contents   Inline Elements
Contained in   APPLET, BLOCKQUOTE, BODY, CENTER, DD, DIV, FORM,
                   LI, MAP, NOFRAMES, NOSCRIPT, OBJECT, TD, TH Elements

Syntax:

```
<H1
ALIGN="LEFT"|"CENTER"|"RIGHT"
LANG="ISOLanguageAbbreviation"
STYLE="Property:Value; Property:Value; ..."
CLASS="nameOfClass"
ID="nameOfClassException">
...
</H1>
```

The <H2> Element

Contents   Inline Elements
Contained in   APPLET, BLOCKQUOTE, BODY, CENTER, DD, DIV, FORM,
                   LI, MAP, NOFRAMES, NOSCRIPT, OBJECT, TD, TH Elements

Syntax:

```
<H2
ALIGN="LEFT"|"CENTER"|"RIGHT"
LANG="ISOLanguageAbbreviation"
STYLE="Property:Value; Property:Value; ..."
CLASS="nameOfClass"
ID="nameOfClassException">
...
</H2>
```

The \<H3\> Element

Contents   Inline Elements
Contained in   APPLET, BLOCKQUOTE, BODY, CENTER, DD, DIV, FORM,
                   LI, MAP, NOFRAMES, NOSCRIPT, OBJECT, TD, TH Elements

Syntax:

```
<H3
ALIGN="LEFT"|"CENTER"|"RIGHT"
LANG="ISOLanguageAbbreviation"
STYLE="Property:Value; Property:Value; ..."
CLASS="nameOfClass"
ID="nameOfClassException">
...
</H3>
```

The \<H4\> Element

Contents   Inline Elements
Contained in   APPLET, BLOCKQUOTE, BODY, CENTER, DD, DIV, FORM,
                   LI, MAP, NOFRAMES, NOSCRIPT, OBJECT, TD, TH Elements

Syntax:

```
<H4
ALIGN="LEFT"|"CENTER"|"RIGHT"
LANG="ISOLanguageAbbreviation"
STYLE="Property:Value; Property:Value; ..."
CLASS="nameOfClass"
ID="nameOfClassException">
...
</H4>
```

The \<H5\> Element

Contents   Inline Elements
Contained in   APPLET, BLOCKQUOTE, BODY, CENTER, DD, DIV, FORM,
                   LI, MAP, NOFRAMES, NOSCRIPT, OBJECT, TD, TH Elements

Syntax:

```
<H5
ALIGN="LEFT"|"CENTER"|"RIGHT"
LANG="ISOLanguageAbbreviation"
STYLE="Property:Value; Property:Value; ..."
CLASS="nameOfClass"
ID="nameOfClassException">
...
</H5>
```

The <H6> Element

Contents	Inline Elements
Contained in	APPLET, BLOCKQUOTE, BODY, CENTER, DD, DIV, FORM, LI, MAP, NOFRAMES, NOSCRIPT, OBJECT, TD, TH Elements

Syntax:

```
<H6
ALIGN="LEFT"|"CENTER"|"RIGHT"
LANG="ISOLanguageAbbreviation"
STYLE="Property:Value; Property:Value; ..."
CLASS="nameOfClass"
ID="nameOfClassException">
...
</H6>
```

The
 Element

Used to force-insert line-breaks in the natural text flow. Only a Start Tag is needed.

Contents	None
Contained in	All inline Elements and block-level Elements

Syntax:

```
<BR
CLEAR="LEFT"|"RIGHT"|"ALL"
STYLE="Property:Value; Property:Value; ..."
CLASS="nameOfClass"
ID="nameOfClassException">
```

The <HR> Element

Used to insert a Horizontal Rule in the natural text flow. You only need to use a Start Tag. The HR Element can be specified with both vertical and horizontal dimensions with the SIZE and WIDTH Attributes, respectively. Include the Boolean Attribute NOSHADE to create a HR without 3D shading applied.

Contents   None
Contained in APPLET, BLOCKQUOTE, BODY, CENTER, DD, DIV, FORM,
                  LI, MAP, NOFRAMES, NOSCRIPT, OBJECT, TD, TH Elements

Syntax:

```
<HR
ALIGN="LEFT"|"CENTER"|"RIGHT"
SIZE="verticalPixels"
WIDTH="horizontalPixels"
NOSHADE
STYLE="Property:Value; Property:Value; ..."
CLASS="nameOfClass"
ID="nameOfClassException">
```

The <CENTER> Element

The <CENTER> Element is used to horizontally center the Elements enclosed within its Start and End Tags between the margins of the Window or containing Layer.

Contents   All block-level Elements and inline Elements
Contained in APPLET, BLOCKQUOTE, BODY, CENTER, DD, DIV, FORM,
                  LI, MAP, NOFRAMES, NOSCRIPT, OBJECT, TD, TH Elements

Syntax:

```
<CENTER
LANG="ISOLanguageAbbreviation"
STYLE="Property:Value; Property:Value; ..."
CLASS="nameOfClass"
ID="nameOfClassException">
  ...
</CENTER>
```

The <NOBR> Element

The <NOBR> Element is used to prevent a line-break from occurring for the text that is contained within its Start and End Tags. This is a Netscape Navigator extension and is not W3G approved.

Contents   Most inline Elements
Contained in   All block-level Elements

Syntax:

```
<NOBR
LANG="ISOLanguageAbbreviation"
STYLE="Property:Value; Property:Value; ..."
CLASS="nameOfClass"
ID="nameOfClassException">
  ...
</NOBR>
```

The <WBR> Element

This is a Netscape Navigator extension and is not W3G approved. The End Tag is optional and typically omitted. The <WBR> Element is usually used inside of <NOBR> to prevent really long passages from becoming unwieldy.

Contents   Most inline Elements but typically none
Contained in   All block-level Elements and NOBR

Syntax:

```
<WBR
LANG="ISOLanguageAbbreviation"
STYLE="Property:Value; Property:Value; ..."
CLASS="nameOfClass"
ID="nameOfClassException">
```

White Space

White space is defined simply as the blank horizontal and vertical space between words and Tags in the coding environment of your text editor program like BBEdit (Bare Bones Edit) or a WYSIWYG visual editing program like CyberStudio. It includes carriage returns, tabs, line-breaks, and multiple spaces created with the spacebar, which will be collapsed to a single character space when rendered by the browser. The reason this is done is to afford the coder or programmer the ability to lay out the code with sufficient white space to allow the code to be easily read and debugged. As mentioned earlier, the exception to this rule is when you use the <PRE> or <XMP> Element, all white space is retained and rendered as is by the browser. Use one ** ** (non-breaking space) HTML entity code, for each sequential space that you want to preserve, for a quick fix.

The <!-- Comment --> Tag

The actual syntax of a Comment Tag is quite complicated but can be roughly distilled with the following rule: Start your Comment with (<!--) and end it with (-->) and don't use two sequential hyphens (--) inside it.

When you want to put text into your document that will be ignored and therefore not rendered by the browser, you can put the text inside a Comment Tag like so:

```
<!--  put your comment in here   -->
```

Your comments can be on one line or multiple lines. This is very useful to write notes to yourself or others that explain what the code is for, what you are trying to accomplish, or just to separate a section of code with a line of characters to make the code more readable and to keep track of what section you are working on, especially in long or very complex documents.

The traditional capabilities of Comment Tags have been carried over from real programming languages like Java and C where commenting your code is absolutely essential for readability, conceptual comprehension, remembering what you were coding previously, allowing others in your team to understand the code, and for debugging purposes.

Other pertinent uses for Comment Tags are the special cases when you want to hide JavaScript <SCRIPT> code or Cascading Style Sheet <STYLE> code inside a Comment Tag to keep nonJavaScript or nonStyles savvy browsers from displaying the code as if it were regular text. There are some additional capabilities for Comment Tags used in JavaScript, which were explained earlier in the JavaScript Chapters.

Make sure that you don't nest your Comments, that is, don't put one Comment Tag inside of another Comment Tag.

Syntax:

```
<!--  ...  -->

<!--  This is what to do if you want to
put comments on multiple lines.  -->
```

Text Markup

These Elements are very straightforward. When you want to mark up your text with a specific style like *italic* or **bold**, just enclose the text inside the Start and End Tags of the appropriate Element. These Tags, such as <I> </I> for *italic*, and <B> </B> for **bold**, can be placed inside of most other Tags; in fact, they usually are at least placed within the <DIV> or <P> Tags.

One note of caution is that BLINKing text is considered very annoying and is the most reviled Element in all of HTML. Use at your own risk. Granted, there are some instances when it is genuinely used to caution someone against risky actions that it will actually be appreciated, but those circumstances are extremely rare. Of course, if your intention is to be patently irritating to your intended audience, then blink away.

The <B> Element

The <B> and </B> Tags are used to enclose text that you want to be rendered with a **boldface** display.

Contents   All inline Elements
Contained in   All block-level Elements and inline Elements

Syntax:

```
<B
LANG="ISOLanguageAbbreviation"
STYLE="Property:Value; Property:Value; ..."
CLASS="nameOfClass"
ID="nameOfClassException">
  ...
</B>
```

The <I> Element

The <I> and </I> Tags are used to enclose text that you want to be rendered with an *italic* display.

Contents   All inline Elements
Contained in   All block-level Elements and inline Elements

Syntax:

```
<I
LANG="ISOLanguageAbbreviation"
STYLE="Property:Value; Property:Value; ..."
CLASS="nameOfClass"
ID="nameOfClassException">
  ...
</I>
```

The <U> Element

The <U> and </U> Tags are used to enclose text that you want to be rendered with an <u>underline</u> display.

Contents   All inline Elements
Contained in   All block-level Elements and inline Elements

Syntax:

```
<U
LANG="ISOLanguageAbbreviation"
STYLE="Property:Value; Property:Value; ..."
CLASS="nameOfClass"
ID="nameOfClassException">
  ...
</U>
```

The \<S> Element

The \<S> and \</S> Tags are used to enclose text that you want to be rendered with a ~~strikeout~~ display.

Contents   All inline Elements
Contained in   All block-level Elements and inline Elements

Syntax:

```
<S
LANG="ISOLanguageAbbreviation"
STYLE="Property:Value; Property:Value; ..."
CLASS="nameOfClass"
ID="nameOfClassException">
  ...
</S>
```

The \<STRIKE> Element

The \<STRIKE> and \</STRIKE> Tags are used to enclose text that you want to be rendered with a ~~strikeout~~ display.

Contents   All inline Elements
Contained in   All block-level Elements and inline Elements

Syntax:

```
<STRIKE
LANG="ISOLanguageAbbreviation"
STYLE="Property:Value; Property:Value; ..."
CLASS="nameOfClass"
ID="nameOfClassException">
  ...
</STRIKE>
```

The <SUB> Element

The _{and} Tags are used to enclose text that you want to be rendered with a subscript display, such as X_2.

Contents   All inline Elements
Contained in   All block-level Elements and inline Elements

Syntax:

```
<SUB
LANG="ISOLanguageAbbreviation"
STYLE="Property:Value; Property:Value; ..."
CLASS="nameOfClass"
ID="nameOfClassException">
  ...
</SUB>
```

The <SUP> Element

The ^{and} Tags are used to enclose text that you want to be rendered with a superscript display, such as Y^2.

Contents   All inline Elements
Contained in   All block-level Elements and inline Elements

Syntax:

```
<SUP
LANG="ISOLanguageAbbreviation"
STYLE="Property:Value; Property:Value; ..."
CLASS="nameOfClass"
ID="nameOfClassException">
  ...
</SUP>
```

The <TT> Element

The <TT> and </TT> Tags are used to enclose text that you want to be rendered with a typewriter display, which is a fixed-width monospaced font, such as "Courier", that is set by the user in the preferences of the browser. This is typically used, by convention, when the author wants to display computer programming or HTML code in the document. A prime example would be any of the example code used in the HTML online version of this book. An instant example would be the font that is used to display the syntax in this book. Note that this Element does *not* preserve white space.

Contents   All inline Elements
Contained in   All block-level Elements and inline Elements

Syntax:

```
<TT
LANG="ISOLanguageAbbreviation"
STYLE="Property:Value; Property:Value; ..."
CLASS="nameOfClass"
ID="nameOfClassException">
  ...
</TT>
```

The <SMALL> Element

The <SMALL> and </SMALL> Tags render text with a small display.

Contents   All inline Elements
Contained in   All block-level Elements and inline Elements

Syntax:

```
<SMALL
LANG="ISOLanguageAbbreviation"
STYLE="Property:Value; Property:Value; ..."
CLASS="nameOfClass"
ID="nameOfClassException">
  ...
</SMALL>
```

The <BIG> Element

The <BIG> and </BIG> Tags render text with a Big display.

Contents   All inline Elements
Contained in All block-level Elements and inline Elements

Syntax:

```
<BIG
LANG="ISOLanguageAbbreviation"
STYLE="Property:Value; Property:Value; ..."
CLASS="nameOfClass"
ID="nameOfClassException">
   ...
</BIG>
```

The <BLINK> Element

The <BLINK> and </BLINK> Tags render text that blinks repeatedly.

Contents   All inline Elements
Contained in All block-level Elements and inline Elements

Syntax:

```
<BLINK
LANG="ISOLanguageAbbreviation"
STYLE="Property:Value; Property:Value; ..."
CLASS="nameOfClass"
ID="nameOfClassException">
   ...
</BLINK>
```

The \<BASEFONT> Element

The \<BASEFONT> Element can go in the HEAD or the BODY of the document and can be used multiple times. It's used to establish the initial size of the text for the document and overrides the setting in the user Preferences. The Value for the SIZE Attribute is a number from 1 to 7. The End Tag is forbidden.

Any subsequent FONT Elements will be rendered *relative* to the SIZE set in the BASEFONT, but only when the FONT Element uses the relative numbering system, which by definition includes prepending the number with either a plus "+" or minus "-" sign. If the FONT Element uses the POINT-SIZE Attribute or a *non-relative* number with the SIZE Attribute, then the text is *not* rendered relative to the BASEFONT.

Contents   None
Contained in   HEAD, BODY, and all block-level Elements except PRE
        and all inline Elements

Syntax:

```
<BASEFONT
SIZE="1|2|3|4|5|6|7"
ID="nameOfClassException">
```

The \<FONT> Element

Used to specify the size, color, boldness, and font face of its enclosed text.

Contents   All inline Elements
Contained in   All block-level Elements except PRE and all inline Elements

Syntax:

```
<FONT
FACE="fontOne,fontTwo,fontThree,...,fontLast"
POINT-SIZE="integer"
COLOR="#$$$$$$"|"colorName"
WEIGHT="100-900"
SIZE="1|2|3|4|5|6|7|-7|-6|-5|-4|-3|-2|-1|+0|+1|+2|+3|+4|+5|+6|+7"
LANG="ISOLanguageAbbreviation"
STYLE="Property:Value; Property:Value; ..."
CLASS="nameOfClass"
ID="nameOfClassException">
    ...
</FONT>
```

Phrasal Elements

The Phrasal Elements are special case blocks of text that are rendered in a variety of ways to accommodate various publishing needs. Technically, they function as a way to augment text fragments with structural information.

The <BLOCKQUOTE> Element

This Element usually specifies a longer quotation. The quote is treated as a block of text and it is all indented in plain text.

Contents	In HTML4.0 Strict:	block-level Elements or SCRIPT
	In HTML4.0 Transitional:	inline Elements or block-level Elements
Contained in	APPLET, BLOCKQUOTE, BODY, CENTER, DD, DIV, FORM, LI, MAP, NOFRAMES, NOSCRIPT, OBJECT, TD, TH	

Syntax:

```
<BLOCKQUOTE
LANG="ISOLanguageAbbreviation"
STYLE="Property:Value; Property:Value; ..."
CLASS="nameOfClass"
ID="nameOfClassException">
    ...
</BLOCKQUOTE>
```

The <CITE> Element

This Element is used to specify a short quotation; in *italics*, but not indented.

Contents	All inline Elements
Contained in	All block-level Elements and inline Elements

Syntax:

```
<CITE
LANG="ISOLanguageAbbreviation"
STYLE="Property:Value; Property:Value; ..."
CLASS="nameOfClass"
ID="nameOfClassException">
    ...
</CITE>
```

The <EM> Element

The <EM> Element suggests that a block of text should be rendered with Emphasis, that is, in *italics*.

Contents   All inline Elements
Contained in   All block-level Elements and inline Elements

Syntax:

```
<EM
LANG="ISOLanguageAbbreviation"
STYLE="Property:Value; Property:Value; ..."
CLASS="nameOfClass"
ID="nameOfClassException">
     ...
</EM>
```

The <STRONG> Element

The <STRONG> Element suggests that a block of text should be rendered with Strong Emphasis, that is, in **boldface**.

Contents   All inline Elements
Contained in   All block-level Elements and inline Elements

Syntax:

```
<STRONG
LANG="ISOLanguageAbbreviation"
STYLE="Property:Value; Property:Value; ..."
CLASS="nameOfClass"
ID="nameOfClassException">
     ...
</STRONG>
```

The <XMP> Element

The <XMP> Element renders actual HTML code as if it were regular text. Put a different way, it's the most convenient mechanism for you to take a whole section of actual HTML code, and have the browser actually display the Tags, white space, and the text, instead of marking up the text according to the Tags. The code will be displayed in a monospaced fixed-width font that is chosen by the user in the Preferences of Navigator. The Start and End Tags are both required. This is a Netscape Navigator extension and is not W3G approved.

Contents   All Elements
Contained in   All block-level Elements

Syntax:

```
<XMP
LANG="ISOLanguageAbbreviation"
STYLE="Property:Value; Property:Value; ..."
CLASS="nameOfClass"
ID="nameOfClassException">
            . . .
</XMP>
```

The <SAMP> Element

According to the documentation provided by Netscape the <SAMP> Element and the <XMP> Element mentioned above should behave identically. They *don't* as of the time of this writing. Both Netscape Navigator 4.0 and MicroSoft Internet Explorer 3.0 render text using the <SAMP> Element in a fixed-width font, but that is where the similarity with <XMP> ends. All Tags enclosed by the <SAMP> Element are fully implemented and are definitely *not ignored*. All white space is collapsed.

Contents   All inline Elements
Contained in   All block-level Elements and inline Elements

Syntax:

```
<SAMP
LANG="ISOLanguageAbbreviation"
STYLE="Property:Value; Property:Value; ..."
CLASS="nameOfClass"
ID="nameOfClassException">
        . . .
</SAMP>
```

The <KBD> Element

The <KBD> Element is used to render text as if it were entered from a Keyboard. The World Wide Web Consortium (W3C) intended it to allow input and output of code to be distinguishable from each other but most browsers render this as a fixed-width font just like the CODE Element does. White Space is not preserved. The Start and End Tags are both required.

Contents   All inline Elements
Contained in   All block-level Elements and inline Elements

Syntax:

```
<KBD
LANG="ISOLanguageAbbreviation"
STYLE="Property:Value; Property:Value; ..."
CLASS="nameOfClass"
ID="nameOfClassException">
          . . .
</KBD>
```

The <VAR> Element

The <VAR> Element is used to display a Variable Name in programming code or in reference material. It is generally rendered in *italics*. The Start and End Tags are both required.

Contents   All inline Elements
Contained in   All block-level Elements and inline Elements

Syntax:

```
<VAR
LANG="ISOLanguageAbbreviation"
STYLE="Property:Value; Property:Value; ..."
CLASS="nameOfClass"
ID="nameOfClassException">
          . . .
</VAR>
```

The <CODE> Element

The <CODE> Element is used to display small sections of real computer code from programming languages like Java, C++, and Fortran. White space is not preserved, so if you need the exact formatting of the code to be preserved, use the <PRE> Tag instead. As expected, the CODE Element renders the text in the user specified fixed-width font chosen in the preferences of the browser. The Start and End Tags are both required.

Contents   All inline Elements
Contained in   All block-level Elements and inline Elements

Syntax:

```
<CODE
LANG="ISOLanguageAbbreviation"
STYLE="Property:Value; Property:Value; ..."
CLASS="nameOfClass"
ID="nameOfClassException">
      ...
</CODE>
```

The <DFN> Element

The <DFN> Element is used to represent the Definition, that is, the defining instance of a term, and renders the text in either **boldface** or *italic boldface*. The Start and End Tags are both required. This Element isn't widely implemented and currently Navigator ignores it.

Contents   All inline Elements
Contained in   All block-level Elements and inline Elements

Syntax:

```
<DFN
LANG="ISOLanguageAbbreviation"
STYLE="Property:Value; Property:Value; ..."
CLASS="nameOfClass"
ID="nameOfClassException">
          ...
</DFN>
```

The <ADDRESS> Element

The <ADDRESS> Element is used to give the author's address or business address, and other contact information. It is also used to convey authorship information, such as when the document was created, or what programs were used to create the images or other content. Navigator renders this data in *italics*. The Start and End Tags are both required.

Contents   All inline Elements
Contained in   All block-level Elements and inline Elements

Syntax:

```
<ADDRESS
LANG="ISOLanguageAbbreviation"
STYLE="Property:Value; Property:Value; ..."
CLASS="nameOfClass"
ID="nameOfClassException">
      ...
</ADDRESS>
```

LISTS

The <LI> Element

The <LI> specifies a List Item for List Elements.

Contents   Block-level Elements   (except for LIs when used in DIR and MENU, which don't permit block-level Elements)

               All inline Elements
Contained in   DIR, MENU, OL, UL

Syntax:

```
<LI
TYPE=       "DISC"|"SQUARE"|"CIRCLE"           used in <UL> only
            |
            "1"|"A"|"a"|"I"|"i"                used in <OL> only
VALUE="startNumber"                            used in <OL> only
LANG="ISOLanguageAbbreviation"
STYLE="Property:Value; Property:Value; ..."
CLASS="nameOfClass"
ID="nameOfClassException">
```

The <OL> Element

The <OL> Element specifies an Ordered List.

Contents   One or more LI Elements
Contained in APPLET, BLOCKQUOTE, BODY, CENTER, DD, DIV, FORM,
              LI, MAP, NOFRAMES, NOSCRIPT, OBJECT, TD, TH

Syntax:

```
<OL
TYPE="1"|"A"|"a"|"I"|"i"
START="number"
COMPACT
LANG="ISOLanguageAbbreviation"
STYLE="Property:Value; Property:Value; ..."
CLASS="nameOfClass"
ID="nameOfClassException">


...
</OL>
```

The <UL> Element

The <UL> Element specifies an Unordered List.

Contents   One or more LI Elements
Contained in APPLET, BLOCKQUOTE, BODY, CENTER, DD, DIV, FORM,
              LI, MAP, NOFRAMES, NOSCRIPT, OBJECT, TD, TH

Syntax:

```
<UL
TYPE="DISC"|"SQUARE"|"CIRCLE"
COMPACT
LANG="ISOLanguageAbbreviation"
STYLE="Property:Value; Property:Value; ..."
CLASS="nameOfClass"
ID="nameOfClassException">


...
</UL>
```

The \<DL\> Element

The \<DL\> Element specifies a Definition List.

Contents   One or more DD or DT Elements
Contained in APPLET, BLOCKQUOTE, BODY, CENTER, DD, DIV, FORM,
                 LI, MAP, NOFRAMES, NOSCRIPT, OBJECT, TD, TH

Syntax:

```
<DL
COMPACT
LANG="ISOLanguageAbbreviation"
STYLE="Property:Value; Property:Value; ..."
CLASS="nameOfClass"
ID="nameOfClassException">
...
</DL>
```

The \<DT\> Element

The \<DT\> Element specifies a Definition Term for your Definition List \<DL\>.

Contents   Inline Elements
Contained in DL

Syntax:

```
<DT
LANG="ISOLanguageAbbreviation"
STYLE="Property:Value; Property:Value; ..."
CLASS="nameOfClass"
ID="nameOfClassException">
```

The <DD> Element

The <DD> Element specifies a Definition Definition to follow your Definition Term <DT>, and they are both inside your Definition List <DL>.

Contents   Block-level Elements and inline Elements
Contained in   DL

Syntax:

```
<DD
LANG="ISOLanguageAbbreviation"
STYLE="Property:Value; Property:Value; ..."
CLASS="nameOfClass"
ID="nameOfClassException">
```


The <DIR> Element

The <DIR> Element is a Directory List and even though it's undocumented in Netscape's Literature, it behaves either like a Definition List or an Unordered List with the bullet capability. It all depends on whether you use the <LI> Element within it, or the <DT> and <DD> Elements.

Contents   One or more LI Elements (which don't contain any block-level Elements)
Contained in APPLET, BLOCKQUOTE, BODY, CENTER, DD, DIV, FORM,
                 LI, MAP, NOFRAMES, NOSCRIPT, OBJECT, TD, TH

Syntax:

```
<DIR
LANG="ISOLanguageAbbreviation"
STYLE="Property:Value; Property:Value; ..."
CLASS="nameOfClass"
ID="nameOfClassException">


...
</DIR>
```

The <MENU> Element

The <MENU> Element works just like the <UL> Unordered List Element.

Contents   One or more LI Elements (which don't contain any block-level Elements)
Contained in   APPLET, BLOCKQUOTE, BODY, CENTER, DD, DIV, FORM,
                   LI, MAP, NOFRAMES, NOSCRIPT, OBJECT, TD, TH

Syntax:

```
<MENU
LANG="ISOLanguageAbbreviation"
STYLE="Property:Value; Property:Value; ..."
CLASS="nameOfClass"
ID="nameOfClassException">
...
</MENU>
```

The <A> Element

The <A> Element as Anchor

The <A> Element can be used to create an Anchor in a document that can then be linked to by another <A> Element that is created as a Link with the proper HREF.

Contents   All inline Elements except the A Element
Contained in   All block-level Elements and inline Elements except the A Element

Syntax:

```
<A
NAME="anchorName"
LANG="ISOLanguageAbbreviation"
STYLE="Property:Value; Property:Value; ..."
CLASS="nameOfClass"
ID="nameOfClassException">
...
</A>
```

The <A> Element as Link

When used to create a Link, the <A> Element creates a hypertext Link that can be applied to text or images, which propels the user to a different document or to a different place in the same document, when it is clicked.

There is a lot more information about this Element in <u>CH3.html</u>, which is in the <u>HTML_BOOK-Online</u> folder, in the <u>DHTML-JS_BOOK-Main_Files</u> folder, on the CD-ROM.

Contents   All inline Elements except the A Element
Contained in   All block-level Elements and inline Elements except the A Element

Syntax:

```
<A
HREF="locationURL"
TARGET="frameName"
NAME="anchorName"
ONCLICK="clickJavaScriptCode"
ONMOUSEOUT="mouseOutJavaScriptCode"
ONMOUSEOVER="mouseOverJavaScriptCode"
LANG="ISOLanguageAbbreviation"
STYLE="Property:Value; Property:Value; ..."
CLASS="nameOfClass"
ID="nameOfClassException">
...
</A>
```

TARGET="frameName" is the destination Window or FRAME for the Linked document or object that is being retrieved. The Linked document or object is specified by the HREF Attribute. If you have a FRAMESET that contains three different FRAMES that all have a NAME assigned to them, then you can TARGET a Link so that it will appear in the FRAME you select by specifying its **frameName** in the TARGET Attribute.

There are certain reserved words for the TARGET Attribute that make it easier to load a document into various Windows or FRAMES, based on relationship. Noting that the underscore (_) character is part of the name, they are:

_parent   loads into the Window or Frame <u>containing</u> the current Frame

_self   loads into the current Frame

_blank   loads into a new additional Window

_top   loads into the top-most Window, which is not contained by any other Window or Frame

Images

Overview

These are the Image File Formats currently supported by Netscape Navigator 4.0.

GIF **(Graphics Interchange Format)**

JPEG **(Joint Photographic Experts Group)** (Technically this is **JFIF**, which stands for **JPEG File Interchange Format**)

XPM **(X PixMap)**

XBM **(X BitMap)**

Always add a suffix to your image file names because it helps you keep track of all your files and it speeds up downloading time. Like this:

```
image1.jpeg          image4.gif
Image2.jpg           image5.xpm
image3.jpe           image6.xbm
```

When deciding which image file formats to use for particular situations, the main rule of thumb is that the JFIF version of JPEG is the format of choice for art and photos where there is a lot of detail and subtle color gradations and hence a large color palette. This format has full 24-bit color and offers the best image quality available for direct access over the multiple platforms used on the web. However, it should be noted that there is still a very slight image degradation inherent to JPEGs, but it's negligible compared with GIFs.

A Progressive JPEG has the advantage of downloading in successive algorithmic passes, so there is almost instantaneous transmission of a blurred version of the image until the rest of the image is downloaded and the final image is then updated to maximum clarity.

The GIF format is only 8-bit and should only be chosen when your image has few colors and therefore large areas of solid color. This format is fast becoming obsolete because of poor quality.

Oddly enough there is a format called GIF89A, which is still suffixed with only **.gif** and has the capability of coding animations that are used within the IMAGE Element and not the EMBED Element. GIF89A files are called Interlaced GIFs and behave similarly to Progressive JPEGs in terms of download characteristics, but like regular GIFs they have restricted color palette capacity.

Certain types of animations lend themselves well to GIF89A format, like dancing logos, and can save you huge amounts of download time. Check out the DreamPlay Logo Animation in <u>Sample35Art.html</u>. There is a freeware program called <u>GifBuilder</u> that will convert your QuickTime movies into GIF89a Animations. You can download it at:

```
http://iawww.epfl.ch/Staff/Yves.Piguet/clip2gif-home/GifBuilder.html
```

A color palette is just the amount of colors that the formatting algorithm has available to it when coding the file for later display. When saving an image in GIF format, there is a variable limited palette of 256 colors to choose from, which is why GIF files are smaller and take up less space on the hard drive and are quicker to download.

Before changing an image to a GIF format in Adobe PhotoShop, you have to convert it from RGB or any other Mode to INDEX COLOR Mode, which is in the Mode Menu. However, there are many options in PhotoShop to try and increase the quality of your image while balancing file size considerations when using INDEX COLOR Mode and then saving a file in the GIF format using the SAVE AS command. Files can also be converted in batches with the Debabelizer Program.

Conversely, JPEG files have virtually unlimited palette colors available at the Maximum Setting and various coding schemes to choose from, which will affect the image quality, size, and download time. You can do file conversions in PhotoShop by choosing SAVE AS from the FILE menu, and a list of options will be presented to you. In version 5.0 of PhotoShop, you can save image files as Progressive JPEGs, including the ability to set the number of passes for the image.

XBM files are called Bitmap because they are only 1-bit files and only used for black and white images. There is no grayscale capability. Just pure black and pure white with jagged edges on all curves. The file sizes are very small but they look awful for art or anything but a rectangle.

XPM files (XPixMap) contain an ASCII image format and a C library. This library provides a set of functions that convert, store, and retrieve images both to and from XPM format data. The format defines how to store the color images. For more information on the XPM format, go to:

```
http://www.inria.fr/koala/lehors/xpm.html
```

The <IMG> Element

Finally the FUN begins. Images, Icons, Picons, Photos, Line Art, Graphics, Single Images that you can move around the page by themselves with JavaScript or change when the mouse moves over them, real animations, and multiple HyperLinked Images are just some of the possibilities.

Some quick considerations. Always include a specified WIDTH and HEIGHT Attribute with your IMAGE Element because it helps speed up the downloading time. Yes indeed, downloading time: the scourge of all who use the web who don't have a T1 Connection. Image file size is always a consideration. To compress or not to compress. To gif or jpeg or bitmap. To take the time to include alternate text with the ALT Attribute for surfers that have image downloading suppressed or may be visually impaired.

Remember that only the Start Tag is used with the Image Element, and the End Tag is totally Forbidden. If you use it, the Image won't show up because the browser will ignore it. The SRC Attribute is the only required Attribute in Navigator, but ALT is required in HTML 4.0. In versions of HTML prior to 4.0, the ALT Attribute was optional.

The Attributes used to modify the <IMG> Element are as follows:

SRC	--	**Required URL Source Location**
SUPPRESS	--	**Boolean Identifier as True if Present**
WIDTH	--	**Image Width in Pixels**
HEIGHT	--	**Image Height in Pixels**
ALIGN	--	**Vertical or Horizontal Alignment Options**
ALT	--	**Alternate Text to Display if Image Doesn't Load**
BORDER	--	**Image Border in Pixels**
HSPACE	--	**Horizontal Margin around Image**
VSPACE	--	**Vertical Margin around Image**
ONABORT	--	**JavaScript Code if Image Aborts**
ONERROR	--	**JavaScript Code if Error Occurs**
ONLOAD	--	**JavaScript Code After Image Loads**
LOWSRC	--	**URL Source for Low Resolution Placeholder**
USEMAP	--	**URL# Source Location for Map Coordinates**
ISMAP	--	**Boolean Identifier as True if Present**
LANG	--	**Chooses the Language for Text Rendering**
STYLE	--	**Chooses a Style for an Element**
CLASS	--	**Chooses a CLASS of STYLE for an Element**
ID	--	**Reformats a CLASS of STYLE for an Element**
NAME	--	**Identifier for Reference in JavaScript, Links**

After the following syntax for the IMG Element, all of these Attributes are covered in detail.

Contents   None
Contained in   All block-level Elements except the PRE Element and All inline Elements

Syntax:

```
<IMG
SRC="imageURL"                                    required Attribute
SUPPRESS
WIDTH="pixelsWidth"|"number%"
HEIGHT="pixelsHeight"|"number%"
ALIGN="LEFT|RIGHT|TOP|TEXTTOP|MIDDLE|
      ABSMIDDLE|BOTTOM|ABSBOTTOM|BASELINE"
ALT="alternateText"                               required in HTML 4.0
BORDER="pixelsThick"
HSPACE="pixelsHorizontalMargin"
VSPACE="pixelsVerticalMargin"
ONABORT="imageAbortJavaScriptCode"
ONERROR="errorJavaScriptCode"
ONLOAD="imageLoadJavaScriptCode"
LOWSRC="lowResolutionImageURL"
USEMAP="URL#MapName"
ISMAP
LANG="ISOLanguageAbbreviation"
STYLE="Property:Value; Property:Value; ..."
CLASS="nameOfClass"
ID="nameOfClassException"
NAME="imageIdentifierName">
```

SRC="imageURL" specifies the URL (Universal Resource Locator) of the IMAGE. If you remember, a URL is the web address of the IMAGE File, which can be coded in one of two ways, either Full or Relative. A Relative URL is almost always used for IMAGES. The nontechnical description of how to code in a Relative URL is to start with the name of the file like:

       MyFirstImage.jpeg   (Don't forget to put the suffix, which in this case
                                 is either jpeg or jpg, at the end of the file name.)

If your IMAGE File is in the same folder (or, in webspeak, the same directory) as your HTML document that wants to access it (has the image coded into the document using the IMG Tag), then just copy the file name and put it between the quote marks like so:

       `<IMG SRC="MyFirstImage.jpeg">`

If your IMAGE File is nested in another folder then you must put the name of that folder to the left of the name of your IMAGE File Name and separate both names with a forward slash character (/). This is a required Attribute.

Let's say that the previously named IMAGE is located in a folder called:

```
JPEG-Images
```

then your URL would be:

```
JPEG-Images/MyFirstImage.jpeg
```

and your IMAGE Element would be:

```
<IMG SRC="JPEG-Images/MyFirstImage.jpeg">
```

SUPPRESS is a Boolean Attribute of either TRUE or FALSE that tells Navigator to either render or suppress the placeholder icon and associated image-frame (not FRAME or FRAMESET) in the space reserved for the IMAGE while it is being downloaded. It also determines if the Tool Tips will be active or inactive. If a Progressive JPEG-formatted IMAGE is being downloaded, then the placeholder aspect of this Attribute is irrelevant.

This Attribute works simply by including it by name within the Element with no equal sign or value attached. So if you include SUPPRESS, then it's TRUE and the placeholder icon and image-frame is suppressed and Tool Tips is deactivated. If you don't put SUPPRESS in the IMAGE Element, then it is FALSE by default (and absence) and the placeholder icon and image-frame will be displayed and Tool Tips will be enabled.

WIDTH="pixelsWidth" | "number%" sets the horizontal width of the IMAGE. It can be expressed in pixels or as a percentage of the total width of the window or frame that contains the image. To determine the width of your image, open it in a paint program like PhotoShop and go to the Image Menu and select the Image Size... item. When the Dialog Window pops ups, you will see the Width and Height Values near the bottom. Make sure that the pop-up menu to the right of the Width value says Pixels because the WIDTH must be specified in pixels (as opposed to inches, etc.) if using a measurement scheme. You should also make sure that the resolution is at 72 pixels/inch. If no WIDTH is indicated, then by default Netscape will display the image at its actual width, but this will increase the download time. Always specify a WIDTH for fastest downloading.

If for some reason you want to have your image displayed at a width that is smaller or larger than its actual width, then just put in the width size that you want and Netscape will resize the image for you. This procedure will increase download time.

When expressing the WIDTH as a percentage, make sure you include the % sign to the right of the number. This can be useful if you want to compensate for the many different monitor sizes that users have available. Generally, you have to make sure that the image is large enough so that if the percentage value used causes the image to be displayed at maximum size there will not be any degradation of quality. Plan your strategy so that the image will only be resized smaller than its actual size to fit into smaller monitor environments.

HEIGHT="pixelsHeight" | "number%" sets the vertical height of the IMAGE. It can be expressed in pixels or as a percentage of the total height of the window or frame that contains the image. See the above section on WIDTH for info on how to determine the HEIGHT of your image. Always specify a HEIGHT for fastest downloading.

ALIGN="LEFT | RIGHT | TOP | TEXTTOP | MIDDLE | ABSMIDDLE | BOTTOM | ABSBOTTOM | BASELINE" specifies how an image will align itself to the surrounding text. There are two distinctly different results to this alignment. If either the LEFT or RIGHT value is indicated, then the image is said to <u>float</u> and the text will <u>flow around the side of the image.</u> If any of the other values are used, the text will not Float and only one line of text will display between the top and bottom of the image; after that one line the text will continue beneath the image. See Example A1-13 on page 921.

LEFT	floats an IMAGE and aligns it flush left with the left margin. Text will then flow around the right side of the IMAGE.
RIGHT	floats an IMAGE and aligns it flush right with the right margin. Text will then flow around the left side of the IMAGE.
TOP	specifies the <u>top of the image</u> to align with the <u>top</u> of the <u>highest object</u> in the line containing the image.
TEXTTOP	specifies the <u>top of the image</u> to align with the <u>top</u> of the <u>tallest text</u> in the line containing the image.
MIDDLE	specifies the <u>middle of the image</u> to align with the <u>baseline</u> of the text in the line containing the image.
ABSMIDDLE	specifies the <u>middle of the image</u> to align with the <u>middle</u> of the text in the line containing the image.
BOTTOM	specifies the default value and is identical to BASELINE.
ABSBOTTOM	specifies the <u>bottom of the image</u> to align with the <u>bottom</u> of the <u>lowest object</u> in the line containing the image.
BASELINE	specifies the <u>bottom of the image</u> to align with the <u>baseline</u> of the text in the line containing the image.

If you want to align an image in the horizontal center of a page, either put the image between the `<CENTER>`   `</CENTER>`   Tags or between the `<DIV ALIGN="CENTER">`   `</DIV>`   Tags or use Style Sheets.

ALT="alternateText" is used to provide text that is displayed in place of the image while the image is downloading or if the image does not download because of an error or for visually impaired surfers who have text-only transmission. Be advised that many users turn off the browser's automatic image downloading capability because of long download times for images, so it is crucial to include it, especially if the image contains instructions or text headings within the graphics that will otherwise be unavailable. Keep the text short and to the point. Required for Strict HTML 4.0 but not by Navigator.

BORDER="pixelsThick" puts a 2D graphical solid border around the image using the same color as the text color, which is also the foreground color of the page. The thickness of the border is measured in pixels. Technically, you can't change the color of the image BORDER within the IMAGE Element, but there is a sneaky workaround. Put the IMAGE inside a TABLE that only has one CELL and set the BGCOLOR of the TABLE to whatever color you want to be the BORDER COLOR. Set the CELLPADDING value to the thickness you want the BORDER around your image to be. What you're doing is substituting the normal use of CELLPADDING for your use as an IMAGE BORDER. Make sure you set the TABLE BORDER to zero and the IMAGE BORDER should be completely omitted. Pay close attention to that last sentence and make sure you don't confuse TABLE BORDER with IMAGE BORDER to get just an image with a different 2D IMAGE BORDER color and not one with a 3D TABLE BORDER around it also. Example A3-3 demonstrates this.

Example A3-3:   Sample33.html

```
<!DOCTYPE HTML PUBLIC "-//W3C//DTD HTML 3.2//EN">
<HTML>
<HEAD>
<TITLE> Sample 33 - Image Example A1  </TITLE></HEAD>

<BODY BGCOLOR="#ffffff" TEXT="#ff0000">

<DIV ALIGN="LEFT">

<TABLE BORDER="0" CELLPADDING="25" BGCOLOR="#00ff00">
<TR>
<TH><IMG SRC="JPEG-FILES/J2-Sedona_Winter_13B.jpg"
      ALT="Sedona Winter" WIDTH="144" HEIGHT="100">
</TH>
</TR>
</TABLE>

</DIV>
</BODY>
</HTML>
```

HSPACE="pixelsHorizontalMargin" sets the amount of horizontal empty SPACE that surrounds the left and right sides of an IMAGE, which is used as a buffer zone so your documents don't look cluttered. It's measured in pixels and there are 72 pixels in an inch.

VSPACE="pixelsVerticalMargin" sets the amount of vertical empty SPACE that surrounds the top and bottom of an IMAGE and is measured in pixels.

ONABORT="imageAbortJavaScriptCode" executes this JavaScript code if and when an Image stops loading because of user action. See the advanced section on JavaScript for theory and examples dealing with Event Handlers in Chapter 6.

ONERROR="errorJavaScriptCode" executes this JavaScript code if and when an error occurs and is detected by previous JavaScript code that has the capability of handling that type of event. See the advanced section on JavaScript for theory and examples dealing with Event Handlers in Chapter 6.

ONLOAD="imageLoadJavaScriptCode" specifies the JavaScript Event Handler to be called after the IMAGE has fully loaded, which will then execute predetermined actions. See the advanced section on JavaScript for theory and examples dealing with Event Handlers in Chapter 6.

LOWSRC="lowResolutionImageURL" specifies the URL location of an IMAGE that is of a much lower resolution and therefore much smaller file size to be used as a proxy or a substitute image while the higher resolution file is being downloaded. At this time, it is somewhat antiquated for file types other than large GIFs.

This Attribute was devised before some really smart programmers created the Progressive JPEG file format, which has a built-in downloading algorithm coded into the image that displays the image in a progressively higher resolution in multiple download passes. Think about it this way. If you have a 24-bit image with 3 channels, that means that each of the red, green, and blue channels each has 8 bits of color information assigned to it. (A bit is the smallest piece of code information and is either zero=off or one=on, in binary-speak.) So 8 bits of color information gives the program more accurate data with which to display an image than 4 bits.

Ok, let's say that when a Progressive JPEG is saved to disk, the bits that describe the image are stored in a way that lets the computer have very fast access to just the first 8 bits, which it will then display, so that you have the equivalent of a blurred image in place while the computer then goes and gets the next 8 bits and then updates the image with the extra 8 bits and you have a more focused image.

Next it goes and gets the last 8 bits of data and updates the image again and now you have the final image displayed perfectly. The theory here is that looking at an image that isn't perfect is more interesting than a blank rectangle and if you don't like what is being downloaded you can abort the process without having to wait for the whole image to download. Considering the abysmal nature of image download times, this is an excellent innovation.

USEMAP="URL#mapName" indicates that the image is to be used as a client-side IMAGE MAP, and there must be an associated MAP file available that contains the MAP definition, which includes the MAP types, coordinates and Links.

The USEMAP Attribute must contain the URL location of this associated MAP file (which is usually suffixed by .map in the file name), and then the # symbol that precedes the NAME of the MAP file. Make sure you understand the distinction between the URL of a file and the NAME of a file. If you go to page 984 in this section and check out the MAP Element, you will notice an Attribute called NAME="mapName". The "mapName" that you choose is what identifies or references the MAP file by the USEMAP Attribute in this IMAGE Element.

So if your URL is: URL=MyFirstMapFile.map

and the NAME of your MAP is: NAME=TheFirstExampleMap

then the USEMAP Attribute is coded like this:

```
USEMAP="MyFirstMapFile.map#TheFirstExampleMap"
```

Remember to include the hash (#) sign after the URL.

This is a really cool amalgamation of capabilities incorporating Images, JavaScript, and HyperLinks for the adventurous. Most of the setup is done in the MAP and AREA Elements, which are fully explained and illustrated later on in this section of Appendix A on pages 984-989.

ISMAP indicates that the IMAGE is to be used as a server-side IMAGE MAP. This is not the recommended, preferred, or efficient way to create multiple HyperLinks within one image. Instead, use the previously mentioned USEMAP Attribute, which operates faster and creates a client-side IMAGE MAP.

LANG="ISOLanguageAbbreviation" specifies the language you want the text to appear in. It is indicated by a two-letter abbreviation. For English, use "EN" or "en". For a complete list of language abbreviations, see Appendix D, on pages 1050-1051, or you can download the current version at: `http://ds.internic.net/rfc/rfc1766.txt`

STYLE="Property:Value; Property:Value; ..." specifies a STYLE for the image. It is important to understand that STYLE is used here as an Attribute of the IMAGE Element and not as the STYLE Element itself. These are two very different situations. As an Attribute, it is used to modify the image within the IMAGE Tag, which is then contained in the BODY Element. When used as the STYLE Element, it is placed within the HEAD Element and is used to set the styles for many other Elements. See the advanced section on Dynamic HTML for more information on the STYLE Attribute on page 104 and the STYLE Element on pages 16-103.

CLASS="nameOfClass" specifies a CLASS of STYLE for an IMAGE. See the section on Dynamic HTML for more information on the CLASS Attribute on pages 72-75.

ID="nameOfClassException" specifies exceptions to a previously formatted STYLE. See the section on Dynamic HTML for more information on the ID Attribute on pages 83-84.

NAME="imageIdentifierName" specifies an identifier name for an IMAGE, which is different from the file name and is used by JavaScript code to refer to or reference an IMAGE during an executable code sequence. See pages 551, 554, 582, 589, 593, 596, and elsewhere, for examples of using the NAME Attribute. Note that it is required for JavaScript Image Rollovers.

Example A3-4:   Sample34.html

```
<!DOCTYPE HTML PUBLIC "-//W3C//DTD HTML 3.2//EN">
<HTML>

<HEAD>

<TITLE> Sample 34 - Image Example A3  </TITLE>

<BASEFONT SIZE="5">

</HEAD>

<BODY BGCOLOR="#000000" TEXT="#009900">


<DIV ALIGN="CENTER">


<IMG SRC="JPEG-FILES/J7-Desert_Arches_2.jpg" BORDER="25"
      ALT="Desert Arches" WIDTH="504" HEIGHT="344">

<P>
      This is Gilorien's art referenced as

<BR>

<BR>

<FONT SIZE="7" COLOR="#0000ff">      Desert Arches 15      </FONT>

</P>

</DIV>

</BODY>

</HTML>
```

Special Notice:

There is a good chance that the file sizes of your images are actually larger on your hard drive than they will be on your server's hard drive, so you may save some space and time. The reason for this is that there are advanced formatting algorithms available that the general public usually doesn't bother with, which will format a hard drive so that the tiny blocks that accept file data are of a smaller size than normal. You can check this out by copying a small file from your hard drive to a floppy disk and comparing the file size.

Images and Multiple HyperLinks

The <MAP> Element

Contents   One or more AREA Elements or one or more block-level Elements
Contained in   block-level Elements or inline Elements

Syntax:

```
<MAP
NAME="mapName"
LANG="ISOLanguageAbbreviation"
STYLE="Property:Value; Property:Value; ..."
CLASS="nameOfClass"
ID="nameOfClassException">
...
</MAP>
```

The <AREA> Element

A client-side Image MAP is just an image that has multiple hyperlinks assigned to it, so that if you click on one region within the image, it will jump to a new Link, and by clicking on a different region, you will go to a different Link. It is composed of three main Elements: The <MAP> Element, the <AREA> Element, and the <IMG> Element.

The <AREA> Elements are always placed between the <MAP> Tags and you can have as many <AREA> Elements as you want. The <IMG> Element is always located outside the <MAP> Element. This is the basic structure of an Image MAP:

```
<BODY>
<MAP>

        <AREA>
        <AREA>
        <AREA>

</MAP>
<IMG>
</BODY>
```

This is the basic structure of an Image MAP with the required Attributes for its various Elements:

```
<BODY>
<MAP NAME="mapName">

        <AREA SHAPE="shape" COORDS="x1,y1,x2,y2" HREF="URL">
        <AREA SHAPE="shape" COORDS="x1,y1,x2,y2" HREF="URL">
        <AREA SHAPE="shape" COORDS="x1,y1,x2,y2" HREF="URL">

</MAP>

<IMG SRC="URL">

</BODY>
```

When creating an Image MAP, it makes sense to create your IMAGE first, because that's where you formulate strategy to effectively synergize a visually appealing graphic with the functional nature of the hyperlinks. Think of the image as a control panel that has multiple capabilities, and plan out in advance exactly what you want the image to do and how to convey that information visually to the user through the image. You might be surprised to see how often a simple graphic of descriptive text is used on the web because the author has control over color, font, and size selection that way, and it doesn't get in the way of the information he or she is trying to make available to the user.

An Image MAP is the most useful when it is used in a group of FRAMES because you can keep the MAP in one FRAME so it is always available to the user and TARGET your LINKS in the MAP to a different FRAME as they change based on user selection.

Ok, let's say you have your finished image ready and it's named "ImageMap1". As an example, let's say that you designed it with nine regions that each have a solid color within that region and the background of the image is white. In this case, there are four rectangles, four circles, and one triangle, which is by definition a polygon.

Now you want to define an AREA Tag for each one of these nine regions so that each region will cause the user to go to a different web page when the user clicks inside it. You define a clickable region for an AREA Tag by specifying a SHAPE Attribute and then a set of COORDINATES with the COORDS Attribute to state where that SHAPE occurs within the Image MAP.

A SHAPE can be either a Rectangle, Circle, Polygon, or Default. Polygons can include triangles, pentagons, or any other 2D multisided geometric shape. The Default SHAPE is a special case, where it is the part of the image that is not actually defined with a specific SHAPE. Think of all the SHAPES that you define as being the foreground and what's not defined is the background and the background is the Default.

The COORDINATES to be used are different for each type of SHAPE as follows:

SHAPE	SHAPE code	COORDINATES
Rectangle	RECT	"x1,y1,x2,y2"
Circle	CIRCLE	"xCenter,yCenter,radius"
Polygon	POLY	"x1,y1,x2,y2,x3,y3,...,x100,y100"
Default	DEFAULT	NONE

Noting that the POLY SHAPE can have up to 100 sides.

Contents	One or more AREA Elements or one or more block-level Elements
Contained in	Block-level Elements or inline Elements

Syntax:

```
<AREA
HREF="locationURL"
TARGET="FrameName"
NOHREF
SHAPE="RECT|CIRCLE|POLY|DEFAULT"
COORDS="x1,y1,x2,y2"|"xCenter,yCenter,radius"|
                    "x1,y1,x2,y2,x3,y3..."
NAME="AreaName"
ALT="alternateText"
ONMOUSEOVER="mouseoverJavaScriptCode"
ONMOUSEOUT="mouseoutJavaScriptCode"
ONCLICK"clickJavaScriptCode"
LANG="ISOLanguageAbbreviation"
STYLE="Property:Value; Property:Value; ..."
CLASS="nameOfClass"
ID="nameOfClassException">
```

Example A3-6 demonstrates the AREA Element.

Example A3-6:   Sample36.html

```
<!DOCTYPE HTML PUBLIC "-//W3C//DTD HTML 3.2//EN">
<HTML>
<HEAD>
     <TITLE>Sample 36 - Image Map Area Example A1</TITLE>
</HEAD>

<BODY>
```

```
<MAP NAME="FirstMap">

<!--Purple Rectangle-->
<AREA COORDS="0,0,144,72" HREF="Sample9.html">

<!--Red Rectangle-->
<AREA COORDS="0,216,144,288" HREF="Sample10.html">

<!--Green Rectangle-->
<AREA SHAPE="RECT" COORDS="288,0,432,72" HREF="Sample11.html">

<!--Blue Rectangle-->
<AREA SHAPE="RECT" COORDS="288,216,432,432" HREF="Sample12.html">

<!--Purple Circle-->
<AREA SHAPE="CIRCLE" COORDS="216,216,71" HREF="Sample13.html">

<!--Red Circle-->
<AREA SHAPE="CIRCLE" COORDS="360,144,71" HREF="Sample14.html">

<!--Green Circle-->
<AREA SHAPE="CIRCLE" COORDS="72,144,71" HREF="Sample15.html">

<!--Blue Circle-->
<AREA SHAPE="CIRCLE" COORDS="216,72,71" HREF="Sample16.html">

<!--Cyan Polygon-->
<AREA SHAPE="POLY" COORDS="149,113,186,144,149,168" HREF="Sample17.html">

<!--default-->
<AREA SHAPE="DEFAULT" HREF="Sample30.html" TARGET="TABLE1">

</MAP>

<!--This is the Image Map 1
Notice the USEMAP value below is the NAME value of the MAP Element Above-->

<IMG SRC="JPEG-FILES/ImageMap1.jpg" USEMAP="#FirstMap"
     BORDER="0" ALT="Image for Map 1" WIDTH="432" HEIGHT="288">

<P><FONT SIZE="5">If you click on the same region of space in either of the two
images the same link will be jumped to. The easiest way to check this is by holding
the mouse over a section of the image and check the STATUS BAR at the bottom of the
window and see the name of the link displayed.</FONT><BR>

<!--   This is the Image Map 2
Notice the USEMAP value below is the NAME value of the MAP Element Above.
The same MAP can be used for more than one image but the real point is that it
doesn't matter what the image looks like for it to work but it should make sense to
the user for it to be functional-->

<IMG SRC="JPEG-FILES/ImageMap2.jpg" USEMAP="#FirstMap"
     BORDER="0" ALT="Image for Map 2" WIDTH="432" HEIGHT="288">

</BODY>
</HTML>
```

HREF="locationURL" chooses the URL, which is the web address of the document that you want to link to when the user clicks into the AREA specified by the SHAPE Attribute and COORDS Attribute below. There should be one and only one URL for each AREA and usually there are at least two AREA Tags inside each MAP Element.

TARGET="FrameName" specifies the Window, Frame, or Layer that the link will be loaded into. Usually it will be loaded into a Frame or Layer, as they are the most useful.

NOHREF demands that when a user clicks into an AREA with this Attribute that there not be any URL loaded. This creates a null zone within the Image MAP.

SHAPE="RECT I CIRCLE I POLY I DEFAULT" specifies the type of SHAPE that a given AREA Element will have, which is then further clarified with the COORDS Attribute that specifies the coordinates, each of which has its own characteristics. There are four types of SHAPES to choose from and they are:

RECT	indicates a rectangular SHAPE.
CIRCLE	indicates a circular SHAPE.
POLY	indicates a polygonal SHAPE, which can have from 3 to 100 sides.
DEFAULT	indicates the SHAPE that is left over after all of the other SHAPES have been created. It has no declared coordinates and thus the COORDS Attribute is not used for this Attribute. You can still assign a Link to the DEFAULT SHAPE.

COORDS="x1,y1,x2,y2" I "xCenter,yCenter,radius" I "x1,y1,x2,y2,x3,y3..." specifies the exact coordinates in comma separated **x,y** points.

All images have their (zero,zero) coordinates at the top left corner and they get larger moving down and to the right. These coordinates are always specified in pixels and there are always 72 pixels in one inch.

"x1,y1,x2,y2" specifies the rectangular coordinates, where the first **x1,y1** coordinate pair represents the top left corner of the SHAPE Attribute when it has a Value of RECT. The second **x2,y2** coordinate pair represents the bottom right corner of the RECT SHAPE. You have to use exactly four numbers to represent a rectangle.

"xCenter,yCenter,radius" specifies the circular CIRCLE coordinates, where the first two numbers represent the center of the CIRCLE, and the third number represents the radius of the CIRCLE. You only use a total of three numbers to represent a CIRCLE.

"x1,y1,x2,y2,x3,y3" specifies the polygonal POLY coordinates, which can have as few as three sides up to as many as 100 sides. Polygonal shapes can be geometric like an equilateral triangle or an eight-sided stop-sign shaped octagon or they can be irregular with sides that are of all different sizes. The first pair of **x,y** coordinates represents the starting point of your polygon.

The second pair connects to the first pair and forms a side of the polygon. The third pair connects to the second pair and so on. The last pair of **x,y** coordinates will connect back to the first pair to enclose the shape so you don't have to restate the first pair as an end point. NetScape does that for you. It doesn't matter at which corner point you start, but you do have to follow the sides in sequence.

One way to figure out what the **x,y** coordinates are (if it's not one of those obvious ones that you do in your head like 0,0,100,100,0,100) is to create a selection in PhotoShop on a different layer and fill it in with a color and then position the mouse over a corner point and write down the **x,y** coordinates that are displayed in the INFO Palette. Make sure that the readout in the INFO Palette is set to pixels. The easiest way, of course, is to use a WYSIWYG HTML coder that does the math for you.

NAME="AreaName" designates a NAME for the AREA not the Link. This Attribute is rarely used except in fancy JavaScript by the Area Object.

ALT="alternateText" is used to provide text that is displayed in place of the image in the same way as it is used for the IMG Element. See page 977. Required for Strict HTML but not by Navigator.

ONMOUSEOVER="mouseOverJavaScriptCode" executes this JavaScript code when the user places the mouse cursor over the space occupied by the AREA in the IMAGE. See the section on JavaScript for theory and examples dealing with Event Handlers in Chapter 6.

ONMOUSEOUT="mouseOutJavaScriptCode" executes this JavaScript code when the user places the mouse cursor outside the space occupied by the AREA in the IMAGE. See the section on JavaScript for theory and examples dealing with Event Handlers in Chapter 6.

ONCLICK="clickJavaScriptCode" executes this alternative JavaScript code when the user clicks on the Link specified by the AREA in the IMAGE. Ordinarily, clicking on a Link will load it into the Window, but this action may be overridden by ONCLICK JavaScript code. See the section on JavaScript for theory and examples dealing with Event Handlers in Chapter 6.

LANG="ISOLanguageAbbreviation" specified by the ISO abbreviation such as "**en**" for English or "**fr**" for French, is the language to be used for the Attribute Values and all of the rendered text for that Element and all contained Elements that do *not* indicate their own LANG Attribute.

STYLE="Property:Value; Property:Value; ..." specifies an inline Style for an Element by using one or more **Property:Value;** pairs. See Part I -- Dynamic HTML for details.

CLASS="nameOfClass" specifies an inline CLASS of STYLE to an Element by addressing that previously NAMED CLASS of STYLE. See Part I -- Dynamic HTML for details.

ID="nameOfClassException " specifies a NAMED INDIVIDUAL Style as an Exception to a NAMED CLASS of STYLE --or-- a location. See Part I -- Dynamic HTML for details.

Tables & the <TABLE> Element

The <TABLE> Element is used when you want precise control over the structure of your Text, Images, and other types of data like GIF89a Animations. TABLEs can stand alone or they can be used within FORMs, LAYERs, or STYLEs, or within a variety of other Elements. They can contain practically anything. You can set them up to be invisible so that only the structure or formatting of the TABLE affects its contained objects or visible with control over border, width, table color, individual cell background color, text color, alignment, and JavaScript controlled HyperLinks.

A Nested TABLE, that is, a TABLE contained within a TABLE, is easy once you understand that it is accomplished by taking one TABLE and just placing it within one individual Cell of the encompassing TABLE (see Example A4-2, starting on page 959). They can also have more than one column, which is the default.

Basically a TABLE is composed of ROWS, which then contain Cells, which then contain the actual text or objects you want to display. Let's run that by you in reverse, starting with the simplest component of the TABLE.
A <TD> </TD>Element is a TABLE DATA Cell, which is the smallest container in a TABLE, and it is what you put your text or data into, like this:

```
<TD>  My first Table Data Cell       </TD>
```

Next, you put one or more TABLE DATA Cells inside a <TR></TR>TABLE ROW Element, like this:

```
<TR>
<TD>  My first Table Data Cell       </TD>
<TD>  My second Table Data Cell      </TD>
</TR>
```

Then you put all of those Elements inside a <TABLE> Element like this:

```
<TABLE>
<TR>
<TD>  My first Table Data Cell       </TD>
<TD>  My second Table Data Cell      </TD>
</TR>
</TABLE>
```

and you have a TABLE. Granted it isn't going to look particularly fancy, because we haven't covered the bells and whistles yet, but rest assured, you have immense quantities of creative control with TABLEs. In this book, and especially on the CD-ROM, there are lots of examples with TABLEs that you can use as templates and modify for your own pages.

As you sift through all this theory, keep in mind that you are creating ROWS of Cells that stack up vertically.

TABLES are always contained within the <BODY> Element. OK, a quick example just to get you started: Remember that the text within the <!-- ... --> Tags to the right are just Comment explanations.

```
<TABLE BORDER="10">          <!--  The Table Start Tag   -->
<TR>                         <!--  The Table Row Start Tag   -->
<TD>                         <!--  The Table Data Start Tag    -->
My First Table               <!--  Your actual Text   -->
</TD>                        <!--  The Table Data End Tag    -->
</TR>                        <!--  The Table Row End Tag    -->
</TABLE>                     <!--  The Table End Tag    -->
```

Many authors would code the above TABLE the following way for readability:

Example A4-0:   **Sample40.html**

```
<TABLE BORDER="10" BGCOLOR="#ff0000">
    <TR>  <TD>  My First Table                    </TD> </TR>
</TABLE>
```

A <TH></TH> TABLE HEADER Element is exactly the same as a TABLE DATA Element except that the default values are different. They both are Cells that can hold all of the same data types. They only reason HTML was created with both types of Cells was because two different sets of defaults make for quicker coding.

The TABLE HEADER Cells are ostensibly used as headings in the first row for the subsequent columns or in the entire first column for a chart-type TABLE, because they have default values that render text that is bold and centered within the cell.

The TABLE DATA Cell has default values that render text plain and aligned to the left, which has a lot of application for data one would normally put into a TABLE. Think about how many charts, price lists, or forms you've seen that have categories in the top row that are highlighted in some way with columns of spreadsheet data, prices per item, and so forth, and it makes sense.

Example A4-1:   **Sample41.html**

```
<TABLE BORDER=25 CELLSPACING=7 CELLPADDING=10
       BGCOLOR="#ff0000" WIDTH=500 HEIGHT=300>

        <TR>    <TH>    This is Row 1 Cell 1            </TH>
                <TH>    This is Row 1 Cell 2            </TH>
                <TH>    This is Row 1 Cell 3            </TH>    </TR>
        <TR>    <TD>    This is Row 2 Cell 1            </TD>
                <TD>    This is Row 2 Cell 2            </TD>
                <TD>    This is Row 2 Cell 3            </TD>    </TR>
        <TR>    <TD>    This is Row 3 Cell 1            </TD>
                <TD>    This is Row 3 Cell 2            </TD>
                <TD>    This is Row 3 Cell 3            </TD>    </TR>
</TABLE>
```

Not particularly exciting but that was just to get the basic idea across. Notice how the code is laid out so that the Tags that are similar are written so that they line up vertically. This isn't required and it certainly isn't going to make the page look any differently in the browser or on the web but it does make the code much easier to read and easier to check for coding errors.

You will also find that if you use file names that are very similar and make judicious use of copy and paste you can reuse a lot of code without having to type out repetitive code over and over again.

Now is a great time to point out that if you are constantly making use of the innovations and improvements of HTML as it evolves, then at some point you will be coding HTML by hand and probably in "BBEdit" on the Mac or "HomeSite" on Windows. My reasoning is this: HTML and Navigator are constantly being expanded and upgraded and there is always going to be lag time of roughly 7-18 months while the programmers rewrite the WYSIWYG programs to implement the enhancements. That's just way too long to wait if you want to be current. None of the GUI programs cover all the possibilities, but Adobe's Go Live CyberStudio or Macromedia's DreamWeaver are good bets.

I'm not recommending that you never use WYSIWYG programs; in fact most authors use both types of programs for their respective strengths. For those of you who are just getting starting with HTML, and fear that very concept, be consoled that HTML is very easy to do and once you get the hang of it, it's just as fast to do most of it by hand as it is in a graphical environment. Note that creating COORDS Attributes for MAP Elements is not one of those places.

I repeat here in case you missed it before. Do not put blank spaces in your file names because when you upload your files your links will all be broken.

Now that you understand the basic layout of a TABLE, augmenting TABLEs with the plethora of Attributes that are available will be covered after listing the syntax.

Contents	Optional CAPTION followed by zero or more TR, TH, TD Elements
Contained in	APPLET, BLOCKQUOTE, BODY, CENTER, DD, DIV, FORM, LI, MAP, NOFRAMES, NOSCRIPT, OBJECT, TD, TH

Syntax:

```
<TABLE
ALIGN="LEFT|RIGHT|CENTER"
BGCOLOR="#$$$$$$"|"colorName"
BORDER="pixelsThick"
BORDERCOLOR="#$$$$$$|colorName"
CELLSPACING="pixels"
CELLPADDING="pixels"
COLS="numberColumns"
WIDTH="pixels|number%"
HEIGHT="pixels|number%"
HSPACE="pixelsHorizontalSpace"
VSPACE="pixelsVerticalSpace"
LANG="ISOLanguageAbbreviation"
STYLE="Property:Value; Property:Value; ..."
CLASS="nameOfClass"
ID="nameOfClassException">


. . .
</TABLE>
```

Note that there is currently no way to globally change the color of the text within a TABLE if you want it to be different from the global TEXT Attribute you set in the BODY Element unless you use Style Sheets. However, you can modify selected text within the Cell by using the:

```
<FONT COLOR="#$$$$$$">  text  </FONT > Tags
```

For more info on the FONT Element and other Text Elements see pages 930-933. Also see <u>CH2.html</u> in the online Guide on the CD-ROM. For examples of modifying **text** within a TABLE, check out <u>Sample43.html</u>, on the CD-ROM, or see <u>Sample230.html</u> on page 81, and <u>Sample234.html</u> on page 86.

The Attributes for the TABLE Element are covered next, with some interspersed examples, and then the Elements that were specifically designed for use in TABLE Elements are covered.

ALIGN="LEFT I RIGHT I CENTER" designates the horizontal alignment of the TABLE:

LEFT   which aligns the TABLE flush left with the left margin. This is the default. Text will then flow around the right of the TABLE at a distance of 72 pixels from the edge of the TABLE.

RIGHT   which aligns the TABLE flush right with the right margin. Text will then flow around the left of the TABLE at a distance of 72 pixels from the edge of the TABLE.

CENTER   which aligns the TABLE in the center of the page with no text flow around either side. Only available in Navigator 4.x.

If no text is present immediately after the first TABLE and another TABLE is the next item to flow into the page, that next TABLE is automatically positioned on a new line so that its top will be flush to the bottom of the first TABLE.

When coding for pre-Navigator 4.x, and you want to align a TABLE to CENTER, put the TABLE between the <CENTER> </CENTER> Tags or alternatively you can use <DIV ALIGN="CENTER"> </DIV> Tags.

See Chapter 1 for using the **float** Property with CSS Style Sheets and Chapter 3 for using the **align** Property with JavaScript Style Sheets, for center-aligning a TABLE.

Text will flow around a TABLE by default, which cannot be changed by the ALIGN Attribute (unless you use the CENTER value), so if you want the text to begin on a new line you must use a line-break Element <BR CLEAR="value"> and set the value to either LEFT, RIGHT, or ALL, or use the default version like this: <BR>.

BGCOLOR="#$$$$$$" I "colorName" sets the background color for the whole TABLE using either a hexadecimal triplet or one of the 16 color Names that are recognized by most browsers. You can override the BGCOLOR for individual ROWS or Cells by using another BGCOLOR Attribute within a <TR>, <TH>, or <TD> Tag. Some very excellent graphical effects can be achieved by contrasting the text color with the color of individual cells. When setting up charts, it can be very visually helpful for the viewer if you code the top row and/or the left column of cells to different background colors from the cells of the rest of the TABLE. See Appendix B or load in Sample43.html for the list of recognized color names and Hexadecimal color theory info.

BORDER="pixelsThick" sets the thickness of the BORDER, which encompasses the entire perimeter of the TABLE and is measured in pixels. Netscape renders TABLE BORDERS in a 3D shaded mode so that it looks as if a light is shining on the TABLE from the top-left at an angle of 45 degrees counterclockwise from vertical north. The top and left BORDERS are rendered in the color you specify in the BORDERCOLOR or BGCOLOR Attribute, and the right and bottom BORDERS are shaded darker than the specified color as if the light was not as bright there as it is in real life.

If you set the TABLE BORDER="0", then there will be more space for your TABLE to be displayed in and that BORDER space will be allocated to TABLE space and your CELLSPACING BORDERS will be invisible also. This can be very useful if you want the formatting qualities of the TABLE but not the graphical effects; that is, you want the ability to structure your text or images in chartesque type layout without the bells and whistles. If you're new to HTML, you might be surprised at how often this technique is used.

BORDERCOLOR="#$$$$$$ | colorName" sets the color for the BORDER indicated by either a hexadecimal triplet or one of the 16 color Names that are recognized by most browsers.

If no color is specified here, then the color set in the BGCOLOR Attribute is used by default. If no color is specified in the TABLE BGCOLOR, then the BGCOLOR Attribute set in the BODY Tag is used. If the BODY BGCOLOR is unspecified, it will default to the user's choice set in the preferences of the browser.

CELLSPACING="pixels" sets the width of the space between the individual Cells of your TABLE and is measured in pixels. This space is transparent, so if a BGCOLOR is specified in the TABLE or BODY Tags, it will show through and become the color of the CELLSPACING width. A TABLE BGCOLOR will override a BODY BGCOLOR setting. If a Background Image is specified in the BODY Tag, you will be able to see it through the CELLSPACING width. The default value is 2 pixels.

CELLPADDING="pixels" sets the amount of space between the text or object in the cell and the edge of the cell. You can think of it as setting all four margins for each cell all at once with a global cell value that is measured in pixels. There is currently no way to change this setting for individual cells. The default value is 1 pixel.

COLS="numberColumns" sets the number of columns for the TABLE, which is mostly used to speed up the display time, because Netscape can use that number as a starting point when calculating how to render large quantities of cells.

WIDTH="pixels" | "number%" sets the horizontal width of the entire TABLE. You can specify it in pixels or as a percentage of the window or frame that contains the TABLE. Remember that the % symbol must be used to indicate a percentage value; otherwise, a plain number will indicate pixels. If no WIDTH is indicated, then by default Netscape will calculate an optimized TABLE based on the contents of all the Cells and the parameters of the window or frame containing the TABLE. If the user resizes the page, Netscape will recalculate the TABLE and display a new version of it. If the minimum size to display all the combined Cells is smaller than the specified WIDTH, then Netscape will increase the amount of space for each Cell proportionally to fill the TABLE WIDTH.

Navigator will scan your code and for each column it will find the Cell with the largest object or longest text for that column and create a Cell wide enough to accommodate it. Next, Navigator will create a column of Cells that all have that same maximum WIDTH. Then it repeats that sequence of events for the next column and so on. Therefore, for any given column, all the Cells in that column will have the same width as each other. Columns can still have different WIDTHS in the same TABLE. If you want to circumnavigate Cell Normalization, then use the WIDTH Attribute or use the ROWSPAN or COLSPAN Attributes in the <TD> or <TH> Elements. If the combined width of all the content is larger than the WIDTH of the TABLE, then Navigator usually soft wraps the text in the least amount of Cells necessary to fit the TABLE within that WIDTH. Check out Example 1-18, on pages 56-58 and Example 3-32 on pages 325-333, or see Sample43.html or CH4.html on the CD-ROM.

If you inadvertently produce errors in your code, like including an unbreakable Element such as an Image inside a Cell with a WIDTH specified that's smaller than the width of the Image, Netscape will automatically enlarge that Cell to accommodate the Image, which will in turn enlarge all the Cells in that column to the larger size.

Another source of errors is when you miscalculate the total WIDTH of your TABLE and you specify a smaller TABLE WIDTH than needed to accommodate the sum of all of your specified Cell and CELLSPACING widths. In that scenario, if you specified the number of COLS, then Navigator will resize the TABLE larger to accommodate the requested WIDTHS. If you did not specify a number of COLS, then Navigator will shrink the size of the Cells in order to preserve the specified TABLE WIDTH.

HEIGHT="pixels" | "number%" sets the vertical height that the TABLE will be scaled to fit. It can be expressed in pixels or as a percentage of the page. If you specify a HEIGHT that is smaller than needed to minimally contain the data in all the Cells, Navigator will automatically resize the TABLE so that it will contain all of your coded content.

HSPACE="pixelsHorizontalSpace" sets the amount of horizontal empty SPACE that surrounds the TABLE, which is used as a buffer zone so that your documents don't look cluttered. It's measured in pixels and there are 72 pixels in an inch. Save yourself some time and make a note with all the multiplication results for 72 times 3 through 20.

VSPACE="pixelsVerticalSpace" sets the amount of vertical empty SPACE that surrounds the TABLE and is measured in pixels.

Example A4-2:   **Sample42.html**

```
<!DOCTYPE HTML PUBLIC "-//W3C//DTD HTML 3.2//EN">
<HTML>
<HEAD>
<TITLE> Sample 42 - Table Example A3   </TITLE>

<BASEFONT SIZE="4">
</HEAD>

<BODY BGCOLOR="#002222" TEXT="#0044ff">

<TABLE ALIGN="RIGHT" BORDER="15" BGCOLOR="#55ff00" WIDTH="400"
           HEIGHT="300" HSPACE="0" BORDERCOLOR="#00ff00">
```

```
<TR>      <TH BGCOLOR="#00ffff">

          <!--    This is the nested table inside a TH cell.      -->

          <TABLE BORDER="15" CELLSPACING="4" CELLPADDING="10"
                          BGCOLOR="#ff0000" BORDERCOLOR="#7700ff">
          <TR>    <TH>    Cell 1  </TH>
                  <TH>    Cell 2  </TH>
                  <TH>    Cell 3  </TH>    </TR>
          <TR>    <TD>    Cell 4  </TD>
                  <TD>    Cell 5  </TD>
                  <TD>    Cell 6  </TD>    </TR>
          <TR>    <TD>    Cell 7  </TD>
                  <TD>    Cell 8  </TD>
                  <TD>    Cell 9  </TD>    </TR>
          <TR>    <TD>    Cell 10         </TD>
                  <TD>    Cell 11         </TD>
                  <TD>    Cell 12         </TD>    </TR>
          </TABLE>

</TH></TR>
</TABLE>
```

To try some interesting effects with color and borders nest a TABLE inside the first TD Cell of an outer table and set the BGCOLOR of the TD Cell of the outer TABLE or the TABLE BGCOLOR to the COLOR that you want to use as a CELLSPACING COLOR as you can see in the example to the right.   <P>

```
<FONT COLOR="#ffff22">
```
Notice that there is an inherent 72 pixel vertical and horizontal space between the TABLE and the text which flows around the TABLE even though the HSPACE is set to zero. Adjust your calculations accordingly.</FONT><P>

```
<FONT COLOR="#ff0055">
```
Notice that the reason that the text is flowing around the table is because the TABLE ALIGN Attribute is set to RIGHT.</FONT><P>

```
<FONT COLOR="#00ff77">
```
For even more color flexibility do a double-nesting where the outer TABLE mentioned above is then also nested inside the first TD Cell of another TABLE. </FONT>

```
</BODY>
</HTML>
```

Special Notice:

If you code in Text adjacent to a TABLE: There is an inherent 72-pixel vertical and horizontal space around the left, right, and bottom sides (but not the top) between the TABLE and the Text that flows around the TABLE, even if the HSPACE and VSPACE is set in code to zero. The one exception to this is when you code in a <CAPTION ALIGN="TOP"> Element inside the <TABLE> Element, which triggers a VSPACE 72-pixel margin above the TABLE and places a caption above that margin. Adjust your calculations accordingly if you want more than that one inch of space.

Special Notice:

If you code in two adjacent TABLEs: They will automatically stack vertically and touch at the edges unless you either code in vertical space with the VSPACE Attribute or use a line-break <BR>. Obviously, the bottom of the upper first TABLE will touch the top of the second lower TABLE. Usually it looks better if there is space between the TABLEs but not always.

Special Notice:

Extremely complex TABLEs are usually slow to download, so to optimize Netscape's efficiency at rendering them, you should always include the WIDTH Attribute for all of the TABLE, TD, and TH Elements and include the COLS Attribute for the TABLE Element. Make sure that the Cell WIDTH Attributes that are vertically stacked in a column have identical values. When you stack a lot of rows on top of each other, you get Cells that form vertical columns. So if all the cells in a particular column have identical WIDTHs, then there is less need for Netscape to recalculate the TABLE in order to get it to display correctly. Just remember that setting this WIDTH is done as a Cell Attribute of TD or TH and not with the COL Attribute, which is only used to specify the number of columns, not the width.

Avoid nested TABLEs if speed is an issue. Nested TABLEs can look awesome though if you have more artistic predilections.

Special Notice:

If you're reading this book straight through, you've already read the following paragraph, so skip it.

If you set the TABLE BORDER=0, then there will be more space for your TABLE to be displayed in and that border space will be allocated to table space and your CELLSPACING borders will be invisible also. This can be very useful if you want the formatting qualities of the TABLE but not the graphical effects; that is, you want the ability to structure your text or images in chartesque type layout without the bells and whistles. If you're new to the web or HTML, you might be surprised how often this technique is used.

You can also use LAYERs in conjunction with STYLE SHEETs instead of TABLEs, which will give you more control and flexibility and even more types of BORDERs. See Chapters 2 and 3 on LAYERs or Chapter 1 on STYLE SHEETs for more info.

STYLE SHEETs and LAYERs are the next major innovation in website design, and in conjunction with the new JavaScript capabilities, there are radical new possibilities for elegant and productive coding.

The <CAPTION> Element

The <CAPTION> Element is used to place a caption, that is, a title above or below your TABLE. This placement is achieved with the ALIGN Attribute and it has the default value of TOP, which places the caption above the TABLE. When writing the code for the caption, you must put the <CAPTION> Element somewhere within the <TABLE> Element but not within a TABLE ROW or TABLE Cell. Make sure you understand the distinction here. When "caption" is used in the first sentence of this paragraph in lowercase letters, it refers to the actual caption that would by rendered by Navigator like:

"My First Table"

and when "CAPTION" is written in all uppercase letters and/or within the <> Characters, it is referring to the <CAPTION> Tags that surround the text to be marked up.

The caption will be rendered outside the VSPACE parameter if one is specified and will be wrapped to as many lines of text as necessary to render the entire caption. The TABLE will not be resized to try and fit the caption on one line. If no VSPACE parameter is set, the caption will be rendered on the closest line above or below the TABLE as indicated by the ALIGN Attribute.

Contents   All inline Elements
Contained in   TABLE

Syntax:

```
<CAPTION
ALIGN="BOTTOM|TOP"
LANG="ISOLanguageAbbreviation"
STYLE="Property:Value; Property:Value; ..."
CLASS="nameOfClass"
ID="nameOfClassException">
  ...
</CAPTION>
```

ALIGN="BOTTOM|TOP" indicates the alignment of the caption, which is placed outside the BORDER of the TABLE but that is technically still within the entire scope of the TABLE. It is placed either above or below the TABLE. If unspecified, **TOP** is the default.

    BOTTOM   aligns the CAPTION below the TABLE.

    TOP   aligns the CAPTION above the TABLE.

The <TR> Element

The <TR> Element creates a new ROW in a TABLE every time it is used. You can designate the horizontal alignment of the contents of all the Cells in a single ROW by setting the ALIGN Attribute to either LEFT, CENTER, or RIGHT. Similarly, the vertical alignment can be set by specifying the VALIGN Attribute to either TOP, MIDDLE, BOTTOM, or BASELINE for all the Cells in any ROW. To set the background color for all the Cells in a ROW, just use the BGCOLOR Attribute and specify either a Hexadecimal Red-Green-Blue triplet or use one of the 16 recognized color names. See the section on Color Theory in Appendix B. You cannot globally change the color of the text in a ROW, but you can change the text color using the <FONT COLOR="#$$$$$$"> Element in an individual <TD> or <TH> Cell. See the section on FONTs on page 934 for more info.

Contents   One or more of either or both TH or TD Elements
Contained in   TABLE

Syntax:

```
<TR
ALIGN="LEFT|CENTER|RIGHT"
VALIGN="TOP|MIDDLE|BOTTOM|BASELINE"
BGCOLOR="#$$$$$$|ColorName"
LANG="ISOLanguageAbbreviation"
STYLE="Property:Value; Property:Value; ..."
CLASS="nameOfClass"
ID="nameOfClassException">
...
</TR>
```

ALIGN="LEFT I CENTER I RIGHT" sets the horizontal alignment of all the Cells in the entire ROW. Remember that the CELLPADDING Attribute of TABLE determines how much horizontal and vertical space there is between the edge of the Cell and where the text or object begins, which in effect makes it the Cell margin.

LEFT	aligns the Cell contents with the Cell left margin for each Cell that is contained in the entire ROW. This is the default.
CENTER	centers the Cell contents between the Cell left and right margins for each Cell that is contained in the entire ROW.
RIGHT	aligns the Cell contents with the Cell right margin for each Cell that is contained in the entire ROW.

VALIGN="TOP | MIDDLE | BOTTOM | BASELINE" sets the vertical alignment for all the Cells in a ROW . Remember that the CELLPADDING Attribute determines how much horizontal and vertical space there is between the edge of the Cell and where the text or object begins which in effect makes it the Cell margin.

TOP   aligns the Cell contents with the top of the Cell top margin.

MIDDLE   centers the Cell contents vertically which is the default.

BOTTOM   aligns the Cell contents with the bottom of the Cell bottom margin.

BASELINE   constrains text in all Cells in that ROW so that it aligned vertically with the baseline of the text, which is positioned so that it is aligned with the bottom of the Cell margin. For all practical purposes, BASELINE is the same as BOTTOM in HTML syntax.

Historical Note: Text baseline is an invisible line underneath the text which is used in programming to change the amount of vertical space (distance) between lines of text (Leading). The terminology has been carried over to HTML.

BGCOLOR="#$$$$$$" | "ColorName" sets the background color for the whole ROW using either a hexadecimal triplet or one of the 16 color Names that are recognized by most browsers. You can override the BGCOLOR for individual Cells by using another BGCOLOR Attribute within a <TH> or <TD> Tag (TABLE HEADER or TABLE DATA).

The <TH> Element

The <TH> Element is a TABLE HEADER Cell, which is the smallest container of text or other types of data like images. You can have an unlimited number of them and they are placed within the TABLE ROW Element(<TR></TR>). You should always specify a WIDTH value so your TABLE will download faster.

Using the COLSPAN Attribute you can force a Cell to be wider and therefore to expand across more than one column. Using the ROWSPAN Attribute you can force a Cell to be taller and cause it to vertically span across more than one ROW. Here is where you can change the background color of just one Cell to be different from any of the other global settings used in the TR or TABLE Elements. Very useful if you are setting up some kind of color chart.

Text in a TABLE is always rendered at the default variable-width font value, which is set by the user in the preferences of Navigator, and the only way to change the SIZE or FACE is by manually coding the changes within each individual Cell. If you want to change other markup or formatting of your text, you also have to do it within a Cell and you can use any of the FONT Elements, H1-H6 Elements, Markup Elements like bold or italic or phrasal Elements like BLOCKQUOTE. Changing the COLOR and SIZE by <FONT> is especially useful, even though it's annoying not to be able to set the values globally.

It should be noted that by using STYLEs, this problem has been obviated for most Elements, but you can't use it on the TABLE or TR Elements. However, STYLEs can be used on a global basis for the TH or TD Elements, by implementing the **tags** Property of the **document** Object in JavaScript STYLEs, or by assigning a STYLE to those Elements with CSS Syntax. STYLEs and LAYERs are extremely powerful tools with excellent new capabilities. See Chapters 1-3.

TH Elements may be empty: That is, they may contain no data, which is sometimes useful as a placeholder or as a graphical construct, because when rendered they will add a small amount of Cell-border between other Cells, which is like having a bold-Cell divider. This is hard to explain in words but is obvious when you see it demonstrated.

Run Sample43.html on the CD-ROM, and notice how there is one CELLSPACING border that is thicker than the rest of them. Just to clarify, the CELLSPACING border is the slightly raised line or divider between the Cells.

The only difference between a TH Cell and a TD Cell is that their default values are different.

TH Cell	has its default values set at **Bold** text that is horizontally centered.

TD Cell	has its default values set at Plain text that is horizontally aligned to the left margin of the individual Cell.

Consequently, TH Cells are typically used in the first Row or as the first Cell of each subsequent Row (which would in effect create the first column) as the headings for a chart or table, because they are emphasized in appearance.

Contents	All block-level Elements and inline Elements
Contained in	TR

Syntax:

```
<TH
COLSPAN="number"
ROWSPAN="number"
WIDTH="pixels"|"number%"
ALIGN="LEFT"|"CENTER"|"RIGHT"
VALIGN="TOP"|"MIDDLE"|"BOTTOM"|"BASELINE"
BGCOLOR="#$$$$$$"|"colorName"
NOWRAP
LANG="ISOLanguageAbbreviation"
STYLE="Property:Value; Property:Value; ..."
CLASS="nameOfClass"
ID="nameOfClassException">

...
</TH>
```

COLSPAN="number" Let's try a little visualization for this one. Remember your old multiplication table from elementary school. Got it in your head. Remember 5 over and 5 down and you see 25. OK, now imagine that you wanted to take the cell that contains 25 and expand it so that it was wide enough to be under the columns of 5, 6, and 7 instead of just column 5, which in TABLE jargon would be its default. To do that you use the COLSPAN Attribute and set the number value to 3. That's it; now your Cell is three times its normal size. The **number** value should be a positive integer.

This technique is very useful when you have an odd number and an even number of Cells that you want to put into different ROWS; that is, when two or more ROWS are coded by you to not have the same number of Cells because of the type or amount of data you have to display.

This happens a lot when you set up a TABLE to act as a Control Panel within a FORM Element, or if you set up a TABLE within a FORM Element to get information from a customer when taking an order.

Other fancy uses could be for graphical emphasis in the same way that bold text is more visually prominent than plain text. It is almost always used when you want to create a caption for your TABLE and have it appear within the TABLE BORDER, which is not possible using the CAPTION Element.

ROWSPAN="number" specifies the number of ROWS that a Cell will be vertically enlarged to span or extend across. This is just the vertical version of COLSPAN.

WIDTH="pixels" | "number%" sets the horizontal width of the Cell. You can specify it in pixels or as a percentage of the total width of the TABLE. Remember that the % symbol must be used to indicate a percentage value; otherwise, a plain number will indicate pixels. If no WIDTH is indicated, then by default Netscape will calculate the minimum WIDTH necessary to create the TABLE based on the content in the Cell.

ALIGN="LEFT" | "CENTER" | "RIGHT" sets the horizontal alignment of just that Cell. Remember that the CELLPADDING Attribute determines how much horizontal and vertical space there is between the edge of the Cell and where the text or object begins, which in effect makes it the Cell margin. The default Value is LEFT.

LEFT   aligns the Cell contents with the Cell's left margin.

CENTER   centers the Cell contents between the Cell's left and right margins.

RIGHT   aligns the Cell contents with the Cell's right margin.

VALIGN="TOP" | "MIDDLE" | "BOTTOM" | "BASELINE" sets the vertical alignment for the Cell. Remember that the CELLPADDING Attribute determines how much horizontal and vertical space there is between the edge of the Cell and where the text or object begins, which in effect makes it the Cell margin. The default value is MIDDLE.

TOP	aligns the Cell contents with the top of the Cell top margin.
MIDDLE	centers the Cell contents vertically, which is the default.
BOTTOM	aligns the Cell contents with the bottom of the Cell bottom margin.
BASELINE	constrains text in that Cell so that it aligned vertically with the baseline of the text, which is positioned so that it is aligned with the bottom of the Cell margin. For all practical purposes, BASELINE is the same as BOTTOM in HTML syntax.

BGCOLOR="#$$$$$$" | "ColorName" sets the background color for the Cell using either a hexadecimal triplet or one of the 16 color Names that are recognized by most browsers. You can override the BGCOLOR for individual Cells by using another BGCOLOR Attribute within a <TH> or <TD> Tag (TABLE HEADER or TABLE DATA).

NOWRAP forces all the text in a Cell to be rendered on one line; that is, no carriage returns are permitted.

The <TD> Element

The only difference between a TH Cell and a TD Cell is that their default values are different.

TD	has its default values set at Plain text that is horizontally aligned to the left margin.
TH	has its default values set at Bold text that is horizontally centered.

Consequently TD Cells are typically used after the first ROW or the first Cell of each subsequent ROW (which would in effect create the first column), because they are less emphasized in appearance. They are the workhorse Cells used for the bulk of the TABLE contents.

See the definitions for the TH Attributes for more information about the Attributes of the TD Element.

Contents	All block-level Elements and inline Elements
Contained in	TR

Syntax:

```
<TD
COLSPAN="number"
ROWSPAN="number"
WIDTH="pixels"|"number%"
ALIGN="LEFT"|"CENTER"|"RIGHT"
VALIGN="TOP"|"MIDDLE"|"BOTTOM"|"BASELINE"
BGCOLOR="#$$$$$$"|"colorName"
NOWRAP
LANG="ISOLanguageAbbreviation"
STYLE="Property:Value; Property:Value; ..."
CLASS="nameOfClass"
ID="nameOfClassException">


...
</TD>
```

Here's an excerpt from Sample43.html, which is only on the CD-ROM. It shows how to include the CAPTION Element and demonstrates the typical uses of the TH and TD Elements in a TABLE.

```
<TABLE BORDER="15" CELLSPACING="4" CELLPADDING="10"
        BGCOLOR="#00ffff" BORDERCOLOR="#7700ff" WIDTH="600">

<CAPTION>      <FONT SIZE="6">THE 16 COLORS RECOGNIZED BY NAME</FONT> </CAPTION>

<TR WIDTH="140">
<TH>COLOR</TH>          <TH>HEXADECIMAL<BR>rrggbb</TH>
<TH>COLOR</TH>          <TH>HEXADECIMAL<BR>rrggbb</TH>                        </TR>

<TR WIDTH="140">
<TD>Black</TD>          <TD>000000</TD> <TD>Green</TD>          <TD>008000</TD> </TR>
<TR WIDTH="140">
<TD>Silver</TD>         <TD>c0c0c0</TD> <TD>Lime</TD>           <TD>00ff00</TD> </TR>
<TR WIDTH="140">
<TD>Gray</TD>           <TD>808080</TD> <TD>Olive</TD>          <TD>808000</TD> </TR>
<TR WIDTH="140">
<TD>White</TD>          <TD>ffffff</TD> <TD>Yellow</TD>         <TD>ffff00</TD> </TR>
<TR WIDTH="140">
<TD>Maroon</TD>         <TD>800000</TD> <TD>Navy</TD>           <TD>000080</TD> </TR>
<TR WIDTH="140">
<TD>Red</TD>            <TD>ff0000</TD> <TD>Blue</TD>           <TD>0000ff</TD> </TR>
<TR WIDTH="140">
<TD>Purple</TD>         <TD>800080</TD> <TD>Teal</TD>           <TD>008080</TD> </TR>
<TR WIDTH="140">
<TD>Fuchsia</TD>        <TD>ff00ff</TD> <TD>Aqua</TD>           <TD>00ffff</TD> </TR>

</TABLE>
```

Frames & Framesets

Overview

This section deals with the creation of FRAMEs as an alternate type of window display system. When FRAMEs were first introduced, it was the first time that you could divide the browser Window up into distinct sections that could each contain a unique URL, which would display simultaneously and allow you to control each one separately and control how they interacted with each other.

Here's the basic scenario: A FRAME contains the URL of the document that you want to display. Then you put each FRAME that you create inside a FRAMESET, which can contain as many FRAMEs as you want. So when you load a document that contains a FRAMESET, Navigator takes each individual FRAME and loads its URL into the browser window in its own section. The way that the FRAMEs are sectioned off is determined by how the FRAMESET Attributes are defined.

When creating your FRAMESET Tag, the only requirement is that you include either the COLS or ROWS Attribute. You must have either COLS or ROWS but you can also have both in the same FRAMESET. Because FRAMESETs can contain other nested FRAMESETs, you can and usually do have a situation where the first FRAMESET in a page has COLS specified, and a second nested FRAMESET will have ROWS specified.

Up to this point, the BODY Element has contained the bulk of the content to be displayed by the browser. In order to display FRAMEs, the BODY Element must be replaced by the FRAMESET Element. Always make sure that there is no BODY Element in a document containing FRAMESETs. If you inadvertently put the BODY Tags inside of a FRAMESET, they will be ignored. If you mistakenly put your FRAMESET Tags inside the BODY Tags, your FRAMESET will be ignored and most likely you will get a blank page showing in your browser.

The basic layout of a document containing FRAMEs is like this:

```
<HTML>
<HEAD>
<TITLE></TITLE>
</HEAD>
        <FRAMESET>
                <FRAME>
                <FRAME>
        </FRAMESET>
</HTML>
```

Example 5-0	Sample50-Frameset-1.html

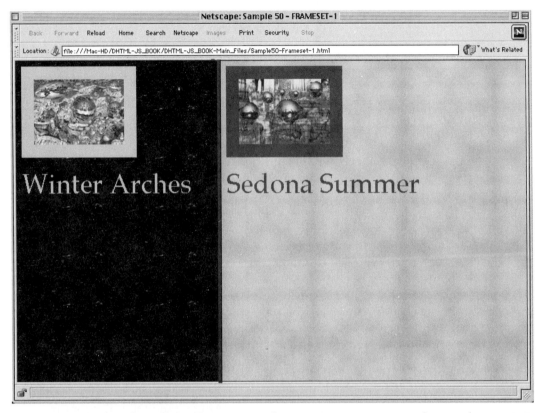

Notice that the FRAMESET Element has Start and End Tags whereas the FRAME Element has only a Start Tag. Notice that there is no BODY Element and that it has been replaced by the FRAMESET Element.

The only required Attribute that must be used with your FRAME is the SRC Attribute, which is demonstrated in the following example, which you can view in the browser by loading in the file named Sample50-Frameset-1.html from the CD-ROM. Note that the Screenshot for this example is at the top of this page.

Example A5-0:   **Sample50-Frameset-1.html**

```
<!DOCTYPE HTML PUBLIC "-//W3C//DTD HTML 3.2//EN">
<HTML>
<HEAD>
        <TITLE>Sample 50 - FRAMESET-1 </TITLE>
</HEAD>
```

```
<FRAMESET COLS="40%,60%" BORDERCOLOR="#ff0000">

        <FRAME SRC="Sample50-A.html">

        <FRAME SRC="Sample50-B.html">

</FRAMESET>

</HTML>
```

The COLS Attribute is set so that it specifies the sizes of the two columns created by the two FRAME Elements below it. The sizes are such that the first FRAME will be given 40 percent of the available Window space, and the second FRAME will occupy the remaining 60 percent of the Window space. No matter how small or large the user resizes the browser Window, these percentages will be followed. The two SRC Attributes point to the URL of the page that is to be loaded into each respective FRAME.

This may seem obvious, but the order that you code the FRAMEs in is the same order that the FRAMEs will load into the browser Window, and FRAMEs are brought in from left to right and then from top to bottom. Following this principle, the first WIDTH value that you specify for the COLS Attribute will apply to the first FRAME, the second WIDTH value will apply to the second FRAME, and so on. Make sure this is understood because later in this section when dealing with Nested FRAMESETs, it will significantly simplify the comprehension process.

So, in order to create the above example, you would have to have three different HTML documents. The first document would be the above example, which creates the FRAMESET, which then holds and specifies via the FRAME Element how the other two documents are displayed. Here's a visual way of saying the same thing:

One of the most useful ways to implement FRAMEs is to set up a FRAME in the left side of your Window that isn't very wide (about 144 pixels, which equals 2 inches) and never changes, which is full of Links that TARGET their contents into a second FRAME that fills the rest of the right side of the Window. This has been termed "Left-Frame Navigation", by users and observers. Think of the left FRAME as the table of contents that is used as a control panel that has all of the site's most important Links or categories all in one place for easy access, because it's always there. Before FRAMEs came along, if you wanted to have important Links available to the user at all times, they had to be included in every page in the site, which is quite annoying when you have to update 1000 pages.

A variation on the above scenario would be to add another FRAME at the top of the Window that's also relatively small and displays horizontally with a company logo or other graphic image or maybe buttons that are JavaScripted to help navigate the site. You would do this with a Nested FRAMESET. See Example A5-5 on page 980.

The <FRAMESET> Element

The <FRAMESET> Element is the container Element for your FRAMEs. If any Tags or Elements that would normally be contained within the BODY Element are placed before the FRAMESET Element, then the FRAMESET will be completely ignored and you will get an empty Window in Navigator unless you have a NOFRAMES Element inside the FRAMESET; then, the content of only the NOFRAMES Element will be displayed.

The only time you can have more than one FRAMESET in a document is when you include one or more <u>nested</u> FRAMESETs inside the master FRAMESET. If you accidentally code in two sequential unnested FRAMESETs, the second one will be ignored by the browser.

Contents   FRAME, FRAMESET, or NOFRAMES
Contained in HTML

Syntax:

```
<FRAMESET
COLS="ColumnWidthNumberList"   =        "numberPixels|number%|number*"
ROWS="RowHeightNumberList"      =        "numberPixels|number%|number*"
FRAMEBORDER="YES"|"NO"
BORDER="pixelWidth"
BORDERCOLOR="color"
FRAMESPACING="pixels"                             //Undocumented Attribute
ONLOAD="loadJavaScriptcode"
ONUNLOAD="unloadJavaScriptcode"
ONFOCUS="focusJavaScriptcode"
ONBLUR="blurJavaScriptcode"
STYLE="Property:Value; Property:Value; ..."
CLASS="nameOfClass"
ID="nameOfClassException">


...

</FRAMESET>
```

COLS="ColumnWidthNumberList" declares the Widths of the FRAMEs contained within the FRAMESET. Either COLS or ROWS must be used in each FRAMESET and you can use <u>both</u> in the same FRAMESET. You must separate each Width with a comma, and there are three types of measurements to choose from, which are: pixels, percentage, and relative: specified with the following Arguments: **numberPixels**, **number%**, and **number***. You can and usually do mix and match types of measurements in your list.

      numberPixels When you use a plain number to declare a Width it specifies an exact number of pixels wide the FRAME will be. You do not suffix the number with the word pixels. You can only use positive integers. No Fractions or decimals.

      number% When you use a number that is suffixed with a percent sign %, then that FRAME will have that percentage of the current Window space assigned to it. If the user resizes the browser Window, then the FRAME will be scaled proportionately. The possible values are from positive 1% to 100%. If all the Widths in your List are percentages then they should add up to 100% for obvious reasons. If they add up to more than 100% then Netscape will scale down each Width by the same amount until they do. If they add up to less than 100% then Netscape will scale up each Width by the same amount until they do unless you have a relative* Width in your list, which would be assigned the extra space instead because it has precedence.

      number* When you use a number that is suffixed with an asterisk *, then that FRAME will have a relative or proportional amount of the current Window space assigned to it. For example:

"*,2*"	would give 1/3 of the space to the 1st FRAME and 2/3 to the 2nd FRAME.
"3*,1*"	would give 3/4 of the space to the 1st FRAME and 1/4 to the 2nd FRAME.
"2*,3*"	would give 2/5 of the space to the 1st FRAME and 3/5 to the 2nd FRAME.
"4*,3*"	would give 4/7 of the space to the 1st FRAME and 3/7 to the 2nd FRAME.
"*,2*,*"	would give 1/4 of the space to the 1st FRAME and 2/4 to the 2nd FRAME and 1/4 of the space to the 3rd FRAME.
"2*,1*,3*"	would give 2/6 of the space to the 1st FRAME and 1/6 to the 2nd FRAME and 3/6 of the space to the 3rd FRAME.

      Do you see the pattern? Just add all the numbers together and use that as the lower number of your fraction (dividend) and use the value for each respective relative width as the upper number of your fraction (divisor). I didn't reduce the fractions like 3/6 to 1/2 because it's easier to see the pattern that way.

      Notice in the first mini-example above "*,2*" that there is no number in front of the asterisk. That's normal. The 1 is optional and is understood to be there even if you don't type it in. When a single asterisk * is assigned to a FRAME and used in conjunction with other types of measurements in the same list, it causes the browser to assign all of the unassigned space to the FRAME with the * width. Let's say you have three FRAMEs and you assign the COLS widths like this:

```
COLS="25%,*,35%"
```

which would give: 25% of the space to the 1st FRAME, then 40% to the 2nd FRAME, and 35% to the 3rd FRAME, because 40% is all of the remaining space after the assigned space of 25% + 35%=60% is allotted.

Another example would be:

```
COLS="150,20%,*"
```

which would give 150 pixels of space to the 1st FRAME, then 20% of the remaining space after subtracting 150 pixels from the total Window space would go to the 2nd FRAME, and all of the remaining space would go to the 3rd FRAME, which is relative to the user's choice of sizing the browser Window, hence the name.

If you had three FRAMEs in your FRAMESET, you could declare their widths like this:

```
FRAMESET COLS="144,432,200"
```

which would be 144 pixels for the first FRAME, 432 pixels for the second, and 200 pixels for the third. This is a very _unwise_ way to specify your COLS because of the variety of monitor sizes being used to view web pages. The browser will almost always resize your FRAMEs in order to have them fill up the entire Window space and destroying your pixel measurements in the process.

A much better approach would be to declare them all in percentages, or if you have one FRAME that really should be a specific size, for example, the leftmost FRAME, which is often used as a table of contents, might need to be 144 pixels, but the other two FRAMEs could be designated as percentages like:

```
FRAMESET COLS="144,50%,50%"
```

which reserves the first 144 pixels for the first FRAME and then the remaining amount of the Window would be divided evenly between the last two FRAMEs.

Another way that is frequently used is:

```
FRAMESET COLS="150,*"
```

which reserves the first 150 pixels for the first FRAME, all the time, and the rest of the Window is allotted to the second FRAME. Even if the user resizes the Window, the first FRAME will remain static and still be only 150 pixels wide. The second FRAME will be scaled larger or smaller according to the user's actions.

ROWS="RowHeightNumberList" declares the Heights of the FRAMEs contained within the FRAMESET. Either ROWS or COLS must be used in each FRAMESET and you can use <u>both</u> in the same FRAMESET. You must separate each Height with a comma, and there are three types of measurements to choose from, which are: pixels, percentage, and relative: specified with the following Arguments: **numberPixels**, **number%**, and **number***. You can and usually do mix and match types of measurements in your list.

Everything that was written about the COLS Attribute is applicable to ROWS except that Height of the FRAMEs is specified instead of the Width.

numberPixels	same as for COLS but specifies Height, not Width
number%	same as for COLS but specifies Height, not Width
number*	same as for COLS but specifies Height, not Width

For instance, in the following FRAMESET:

```
FRAMESET ROWS="*,40%,15%"
```

where FRAME 1 gets 45%, FRAME 2 gets 40%, and FRAME 3 gets 15%: FRAME 1 gets 45% because that is what remains <u>after</u> the last two FRAMEs are assigned their respective percentages of the Window.

Here's a quasi-caveat example of dubious practicality:

```
FRAMESET ROWS="50%,50%,*"
```

OFFICIALLY, THIS IS IMPOSSIBLE. The browser would assign 100% of the Window to the first two FRAMEs and then try and assign the rest of the Window which would be zero% to the last FRAME.

UNOFFICIALLY, if you try it you will find that the third FRAME is invisible when the Window is initially loaded but it's actually there and hidden. If you manually change the partitioning of the FRAMEs by dragging up on the FRAMEBORDER at the very bottom of the Window, it will appear. This is undocumented behavior and not guaranteed to be available in the future. It does work in Netscape 4.0.1 for the MacIntosh, if you want to add a trap door for the curious to walk through . . .

FRAMEBORDER="YES" | "NO" designates whether the BORDERs for all the FRAMEs in a FRAMESET are to be rendered in 3D raised or 2D flat format. The default value is "YES", which indicates 3D, but it can be overridden by setting a FRAMEBORDER Attribute within a FRAME Element, which will only affect that particular FRAME. Because FRAMEs share borders, and for aesthetic reasons, the only time that a FRAME can have a 2D BORDER is when all FRAMEs that are adjacent to one another all have their FRAMEBORDERs set to "NO".

YES	creates a 3D raised BORDER.
NO	creates a 2D flat BORDER.

BORDER="pixelsThick" designates in pixels how thick the BORDERs will be for all of the FRAMEs within a FRAMESET and all of the FRAMEs in any Nested FRAMESETs. This is a global Attribute, which is only allowed in the outermost FRAMESET, so it cannot be overridden. The default value is 5 pixels, which will be rendered automatically if you don't declare this Attribute explicitly. Simply put, it you like 5-pixel-wide BORDERs, then don't bother coding it in. If you don't want any BORDERs at all for any of your FRAMEs you have to code in a setting of BORDER="0", which can be really useful if you want to make use of the functionality of FRAMEs without the obvious graphics staring you in the face and taking up precious screen space. If you check out the source code of some of the more visited websites you might be surprised at how frequently this is done. Check out the Sample435Frameset.html file for Example 3-35 on page 351, for an example of this. For the times that I do want the BORDERs to show, I like a setting of BORDER="3".

One final note; the BORDERs on FRAMEs are not like the BORDERs on TABLEs at all. First, FRAME BORDERs do not override the gray Window BORDER that surrounds the entire display area, which is a permanent feature. Therefore, the only time that a FRAME will have a colored BORDER on all four sides (other than the default gray one) is when there is another FRAME adjacent to it on each of four sides. The 3D version has a rounded feel to them, unlike the hard-edged TABLE BORDER style.

BORDERCOLOR="color" globally determines the color for all FRAMEs within that FRAMESET and any Nested FRAMESETs using a hexadecimal red-green-blue triplet or by using one of the 16 color names that are recognized by Netscape. See Appendix B.

Because of the way Navigator allocates space to FRAMEs, the BORDERS are shared, and when different colors are assigned to adjacent BORDERs, they must adhere to a hierarchy, to determine which BORDERCOLOR Attribute has priority.

Lowest Priority:	BORDERCOLOR in the outermost FRAMESET.
Next Priority:	BORDERCOLOR in a Nested FRAMESET.
Highest Priority:	BORDERCOLOR in a FRAME overrides all others.
Undefined:	Two adjacent BORDERCOLORS of equal priority.

FRAMESPACING="pixels" specifies the distance between adjacent FRAMEs. This is an undocumented Attribute that you use at your own risk.

ONLOAD="loadJavaScriptcode" executes this JavaScript code after the FRAMESET has fully loaded into the browser Window. See the advanced section on JavaScript for theory and examples dealing with Event Handlers in Chapter 6.

ONUNLOAD="unloadJavaScriptcode" executes this JavaScript code after the FRAMESET has unloaded (exited) from the browser Window. One situation that occurs frequently is when a FORM is filled out by the user and sent using a SUBMIT BUTTON, there is no default behavior supplied by the browser, so a blank page will be seen unless JavaScript code is used to take the user somewhere else. One solution to this situation is for the author to create a DIALOG BOX that usually thanks the user for the interaction, info, or transaction and gives the user some options to Link to. See the advanced section on JavaScript for theory and examples dealing with Event Handlers in Chapter 6.

ONFOCUS="focusJavaScriptcode" executes this JavaScript code when this FRAMESET gains FOCUS. FOCUS is when a component or feature of a FORM has been selected for input by the user, and in this case, that FORM would be contained inside this FRAMESET. Be very careful with that last sentence, because it's the imprecise nontechnical description. A FORM Element can never be coded directly into a FRAMESET Element. Technically speaking, the FORM would be coded into the document that is specified by the FRAME SRC Attribute, and then that FRAME would be coded into the FRAMESET. See the advanced section on JavaScript for theory and examples dealing with Event Handlers in Chapter 6. Also see the section on FORMs on pages 1004-1011, for syntax only, and see CH6.html on the CD-ROM for lots of further information.

ONBLUR="blurJavaScriptcode" executes this JavaScript code when this FRAMESET loses FOCUS. See the advanced section on JavaScript for theory and examples dealing with Event Handlers in Chapter 6.

The following very simple examples are to show the results of the various ways to code in the COLS and ROWS Attributes and the BORDER Attributes. They are not really intended to be real-world examples of using FRAMEs; however, they are intended as starting points of code for you to expand on for your own purposes to save you time and point you in some directions. I've used the exact same files for the FRAME URLs, so you can compare the different Attribute settings of the FRAMESETs with each other.

In the following example, the ROWS Attribute allocates 50% of the available Window space to each FRAME, while the BORDERCOLOR sets all the BORDERS of each FRAME to red. The file with the URL of Sample50-A.html will be loaded into the first FRAME, and the file with the URL of Sample50-B.html will be loaded into the second FRAME. The first FRAME can never be scrolled by the user, and the second FRAME will always have the scrollbars visible.

Example A5-1:   Sample50-Frameset-2.html

```
<HTML>
<HEAD>
        <TITLE>Sample 50 - FRAMESET-2 </TITLE>
</HEAD>

<FRAMESET ROWS="50%,50%" BORDERCOLOR="#ff0000">

        <FRAME SCROLLING="no" SRC="Sample50-A.html">

        <FRAME SCROLLING="yes" SRC="Sample50-B.html">

</FRAMESET>

</HTML>
```

The COLS Attribute allocates 25% of the available Window space to the first FRAME and the third FRAME, and the asterisk assigns the remaining 50% to the second FRAME. The first and the third FRAMEs will only have the scrollbars visible if they are needed, which will depend on how large the user chooses to size the browser Window, whereas the second FRAME can never be scrolled by the user.

Example A5-2:   Sample50-Frameset-3.html

```
<HTML>
<HEAD>  <TITLE>Sample 50 - FRAMESET-3 </TITLE>        </HEAD>

<FRAMESET COLS="25%,*,25%" BORDERCOLOR="#ff0000">

        <FRAME SCROLLING="auto" SRC="Sample50-E.html">

        <FRAME SCROLLING="no" SRC="Sample50-B.html">

        <FRAME SCROLLING="auto" SRC="Sample50-C.html">

</FRAMESET>
</HTML>
```

The COLS Attribute allocates 200 pixels of Window space to the first FRAME and 35% of the <u>remaining</u> Window space after subtracting the space taken by the first FRAME, to the third FRAME, while the asterisk assigns all of the remaining Window space to the second FRAME. The color of all BORDERS are globally set to red in the FRAMESET Tag but then each FRAME overrides that setting for itself. The BORDER in the first FRAME is black, the second is lime green, and the third is blue. The first FRAME will only have the scrollbars visible if they are needed, which will depend on how large the user chooses to size the browser Window, whereas the second FRAME can never be scrolled by the user, and the third FRAME will always have visible scrollbars.

Example A5-3:   Sample50-Frameset-4.html

```
<HTML>
<HEAD>  <TITLE>Sample 50 - FRAMESET-4 </TITLE>        </HEAD>

<FRAMESET COLS="200,*,35%" BORDERCOLOR="#ff0000">

        <FRAME BORDERCOLOR="#000000" SCROLLING="auto" SRC="Sample50-E.html">
        <FRAME BORDERCOLOR="#00ff00" SCROLLING="no" SRC="Sample50-E.html">
        <FRAME BORDERCOLOR="#0000ff" SCROLLING="yes" SRC="Sample50-E.html">

</FRAMESET>
</HTML>
```

Nested FRAMESETs

Nested FRAMESETs are where the real control is for creating precisely positioned, highly maneuverable, and visually complex websites. As mentioned earlier, the only time that more than one FRAMESET is allowed in one document is when one or more FRAMESETs are Nested or contained inside another FRAMESET.

You can have as many Nested FRAMESETs as you like; however, practical considerations suggest that the range is roughly 1-10. If you have three FRAMESETs that each have three to four FRAMEs in them, you've maxed out the screen real estate unless your client is planning a demonstration on an 8-foot screen or doing a demo for George Lucas at Industrial Light & Magic. For most applications two to seven FRAMEs are all you will ever need with two to four doing the bulk of that workload.

The most important concept to be clear on is how the COLS and ROWS values interact with each other in Nested FRAMESETs. If you choose COLS for your Outermost FRAMESET, then you must include an additional value in your **ColumnWidthNumberList** that will specify the Width for the entire Nested FRAMESET that is contained in the Outermost FRAMESET in addition to the Widths that you assign to the individual FRAMEs within the Outermost FRAMESET.

Think of the Nested FRAMESET in this context as just a fancy FRAME that has to have a Width value assigned to it just like all the other FRAMEs. Then, within that Nested FRAMESET, you subdivide the Width that was assigned to it even further (usually with the ROWS Attribute if COLS was used in Outermost FRAMESET and vice versa), in this case, with the ROWS Attribute. The same principle applies to the ROWS Attribute if it is used in the outermost FRAMESET.

Looking at the Example on the next page, check out the Comments and see if you understand how the code relates to the last paragraph.

Example A5-5	SAMPLE51-Frameset-DP3.html

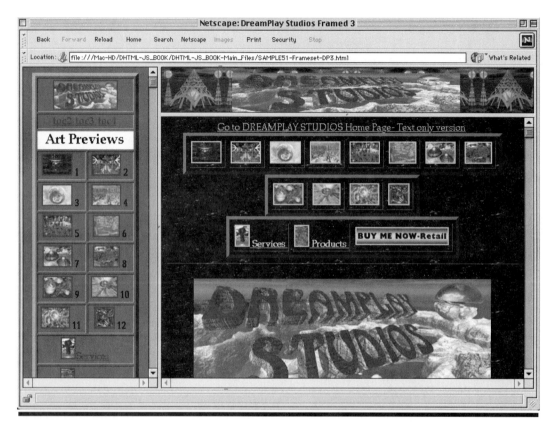

Example A5-5:   **SAMPLE51-Frameset-DP3.html**

```
<!DOCTYPE HTML PUBLIC "-//W3C//DTD HTML 3.2//EN">
<HTML>
<HEAD>
     <TITLE>DreamPlay Studios Framed 3</TITLE>
</HEAD>
```

<!-- This is the outermost Frameset. What the COLS Attribute does is divide the
Window into 2 columns where the first column gets 27% of the available Window space
and the second column gets 73% of the available Window space. The first Frame goes
into the first column of 27%. The next item is a Nested Frameset which goes into the
second column of 73%. -->

```
<FRAMESET COLS="27%,73%">
```

<!-- This is the first Frame. The 27% value in COLS is assigned to this Frame -->

```
<FRAME SCROLLING="yes" NAME="toc-icons"
SRC="dreamplay-website/DP-TABLE-OF-CONTENTS3TABLE.html">
```

<!-- This is the Nested Frameset. The 73% value in COLS is assigned to this Frameset. Now this Frameset is subdivided into two ROWS so that the first row gets the top 15% of available 73% column space and the second row gets the remaining 85% of space.-->

```
<FRAMESET ROWS="15%,85%">

        <FRAME SCROLLING="no" NAME="banner"
        SRC="dreamplay-website/BANNER1.html">

        <FRAME SCROLLING="yes" NAME="view"
        SRC="dreamplay-website/welcome2.html">

</FRAMESET>

</FRAMESET>

</HTML>
```

In order to demonstrate the creative uses of Nested FRAMESETs here are some descriptive theoretical examples and some real-world applications with code, explanations, and sample files on the CD-ROM.

If you've checked out the web at all, you probably have already seen examples of Left-Frame Navigation. Here's another example of it that also makes use of a Nested FRAMESET. Notice how the picons in the lower-left FRAME are used as master categories or table of contents that are linked to pages that actually have the content in them, which in this case are previews of paintings which are further Linked to larger images of paintings. There are also categories of text Links that take you to pages where the company's services and products are explained and to an order form where prints of the art can be purchased.

The company logo at the top of the site is stationary and in its own FRAME, which cannot be scrolled, while the main viewing FRAME starts with a lot of general information about what the site contains. There is also a generous use of graphics, color, icons, and background images.

Example A5-6:   **Sample51-Frameset-6.html**

```
<HTML>
<HEAD>
        <TITLE>        Sample51- Frameset-6        </TITLE>
</HEAD>
```

<!-- This is the outermost Frameset. What the COLS Attribute does is divide the Window into 2 columns where the first column gets 27% of the available Window space and the second column gets 73% of the available Window space. -->

```
<FRAMESET COLS="27%,73%">
```

<!-- Because the next item is a Nested Frameset it divides the first column of 27% into two rows where the first row at the top gets 7% of the first column and the second lower row gets 93% of the first column. -->

```
        <FRAMESET ROWS="7%,93%">

        <FRAME SCROLLING="no" NAME="backforward"
        SRC="dreamplay-website/BANNER10A.html">

        <FRAME SCROLLING="yes" NAME="toc-icons"
        SRC="dreamplay-website/DP-TABLE-OF-CONTENTS4TABLE.html">

         </FRAMESET>
```

<!-- Then the next item is a regular FRAME which gets all of the space reserved for the second column which is specified in the outermost FRAMESET at 73%. -->

```
            <FRAME SCROLLING="yes" NAME="view"
            SRC="dreamplay-website/welcome4inFrame.html">

</FRAMESET>

</HTML>
```

The source files for the above example are located in the "dreamplay-website" folder in the CD-ROM if you want to check out how they were coded.

The <FRAME> Element

The <FRAME> Element is where you delineate all of the Attributes and content characteristics for your FRAME, but it must be used inside of a FRAMESET Element for it to work. So what exactly is a FRAME you may ask. A FRAME is a container for an HTML web document that has the ability to be positioned with some but not complete precision inside the Navigator browser Window.

What makes it revolutionary for HTML authors is that more than one FRAME can go into that Window at the same time *AND* all of the FRAMEs are independent entities that you can individually manipulate with a remarkable amount of flexibility and control, especially when used in conjunction with JavaScript, Styles, and Layers.

Make sure you got that: Each FRAME can have its own unique web page, and you can have as many FRAMEs as you want in one browser Window, which is another way of saying that you can have multiple web pages open simultaneously.

Apparently Netscape has fixed Navigator version 4.0 so that it totally precludes any erroneous or intentional possibility of infinitely recursive FRAMEs from being rendered but not everyone is using version 4.0, so pay attention to your code so that your site doesn't get into a FRAME feedback loop and crash someone's system.

One innocuous but possibly time-consuming error to avoid having to recode is when you link to a FRAMESET with multiple FRAMEs and accidentally TARGET it into another FRAME that it wasn't intended for or have the capability to handle with any degree of proficiency. Usually this occurs when you have several slightly different versions of the same page, like multiple home pages for different browser versions or browser types, or a text-only home page.

For instance, say you have several slightly different versions of the same page and you have a Link in one of them that you wrote a year ago and forgot about that will TARGET a Nested FRAMESET with multiple pages into an existing FRAME that it wasn't designed for, so it's scrunched up in a too-small-space, but it also has that same Link in it that will scrunch an even smaller version of it into an even smaller space and so on and so on.

Now technically this isn't an infinitely recursive FRAMESET because it doesn't infinitely loop back on itself automatically until the computer runs out of memory; the user has to click on the Link each time. The first time I saw it unexpectedly happen my first thought was that it looked pretty cool; totally useless, but still fun. Somebody out there is going to try this and put a blurb in their web page that reads, "DON'T CLICK THIS LINK" just to see what happens.

Anything that you can put into a normal single HTML document can be brought into a FRAME via the SRC Attribute. Just specify the URL of the document and presto, that document is now in a FRAME.

One really intriguing stipulation is: Are you allowed to include a document that contains a FRAMESET within a FRAME? Thanks to the brilliant foresight of the hackers at Netscape you most absolutely can and it opens up all kinds of possibilities for creative panache and innovation.

Just to make sure that you understand the parameters and awesome implications of the previous paragraph, let's elaborate: Start with your interior FRAMESET and put two FRAMEs in it naming them **innerframe1** and **innerframe2**. Next create a container FRAME and NAME it **containerframe** to hold the first FRAMESET. Put the document containing that first FRAMESET into **containerframe** by using the FRAME Tag and SRC Attribute. Now create an exterior FRAMESET and put **containerframe** into it using the FRAME Tag and SRC Attribute. That's it, not too complicated: Just think of it as double nesting with a twist. Here's a graphical explanation:

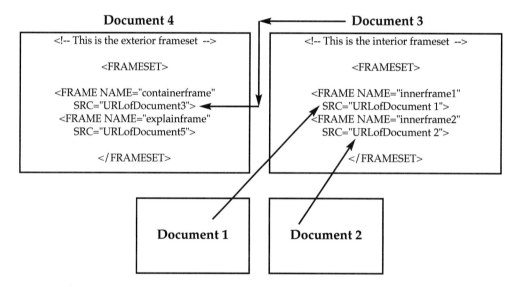

One very quick note about the above graphical example. If you looked closely at Document 4 you probably are wondering what Document 5 is for, because it hasn't been mentioned before now. It's only there because I didn't want anyone to think that <u>exterior</u> FRAMESETs can only contain one FRAME: They can't. <u>Exterior</u> FRAMESETs must always have at least two FRAMEs in them. However, an <u>interior</u> FRAMESET has the <u>option</u> of containing only one FRAME, and it can contain multiple FRAMEs.

Example A5-7 contains the bare essentials code to demonstrate the above graphic illustration of the concepts. I've only included the code for the above Document 3 and Document 4, because whatever is contained in the other two documents is incidental to the example.

Example A5-7 Part 1:   Sample52-Frameset-8D4.html

```
<!DOCTYPE HTML PUBLIC "-//W3C//DTD HTML 3.2//EN">
<HTML>
<HEAD>        <TITLE> Sample 52- Frameset-8D4 </TITLE>   </HEAD>

<FRAMESET ROWS="50%,*">

<FRAME NAME="containerframe" SRC="Sample52-Frameset-8D3.html">

<FRAME NAME="explainframe" SRC="Sample52-explain.html">

</FRAMESET>

</HTML>
```

Example A5-7 Part 2:   Sample52-Frameset-8D3.html

```
<!DOCTYPE HTML PUBLIC "-//W3C//DTD HTML 3.2//EN">
<HTML>
<HEAD>        <TITLE> Sample 52- Frameset-8D3 </TITLE>   </HEAD>

<FRAMESET COLS="20%,*">

<FRAME NAME="innerframe1" SRC="Sample51-A.html">
<FRAME NAME="innerframe2" SRC="Sample51-B.html">

</FRAMESET>

</HTML>
```

If you want to see a real-world example of this, go the folder Sample-ETOC and find the document welcomeETOC3Bkgd.html and load it into Navigator. Then look in the left FRAME and click on the Link that says Mats. Next look in the right FRAME and click on the Link that says Crescent Mats. Then click on any Link in the right FRAME that has a dull blue background color, and you will see a document with an interior FRAMESET load into the large viewing area in the middle of the screen.

Some of the really cool graphical implementations of FRAMEs are giving the surfer the option of custom designing how the website will appear while they are there. Like having several versions of art or company logos that the user can place in a banner FRAME or having several choices of background music available. These are very simple options that only require you to set up a Link for a new page for each option you want to offer and TARGET that Link to an appropriate FRAME.

Let's say you have five different company logos and you want to let the user pick a favorite one to display in your logo FRAME. Create five different web pages and put just one logo on each page. Then set up a second FRAME and create five different Links so that each Link will load a different logo into the logo FRAME. For that to happen, you need to do two things. First, when you create your two FRAMEs, assign them both a NAME using the (you guessed it) NAME Attribute. (Even though for this project you only need to name the FRAME you want to TARGET to, it's good to get in the habit of naming all your FRAMEs for easy reference and to save yourself the time of going back and doing it later when the code is less fresh in your mind.) Second, when you code in your Link to load each logo, you must set the TARGET Attribute to the NAME of the FRAME that you want the logo to load into. If your two FRAMEs are:

```
<FRAME NAME="logoFrame"  SRC="hasLogo1.html">
<FRAME NAME="toc1" SRC="TableOfContents.html">
```

and the document   "hasLogo1.html"   contains Logo version 1

and the document   "TableOfContents.html"   is your page containing the Links that will load a new logo into the FRAME named "logoFrame"

and you set up a Link with a TARGET value to load a logo into the FRAME named "logoFrame" like this:

```
<A HREF="hasLogo1.html" TARGET="logoFrame">  Go Logo 1      </A>
```

and then place that Link into the page <u>TableOfContents.html</u>, and that's it.

OK, you do have to place both FRAMEs inside a FRAMESET, but that's all been covered before. It also assumes that you have coded in your image of the logo correctly. If you want to see an outrageous example of this with lots of other bells and whistles then pop the file <u>welcomeETOC3Bkgd.html</u> into your browser, which is located in the <u>Sample-ETOC</u> folder, in the <u>DHTML-JS_BOOK-Main_Files</u> folder, in the CD-ROM. When it comes up, look at the bottom of the left-most FRAME and click on any of the Links in the table cell with the gray background color and see what happens in the top middle FRAME. Click on either of the Links "L1" or "L2" and put the mouse over the logo after it loads and see what happens. There's really cool JavaScript in it which was explained in Part II of the Book.

I guess a less-flamboyant example of the above theory would be on time right about now so here it is:

Example A5-8-Part 1:   Sample51-Frameset-7.html

```
<!DOCTYPE HTML PUBLIC "-//W3C//DTD HTML 3.2//EN">
<HTML>
<HEAD>  <TITLE>Sample 51 - FRAMESET-7 </TITLE>          </HEAD>

<FRAMESET COLS="150,*" BORDERCOLOR="#000000">

        <FRAME SCROLLING="no" NAME="toc" SRC="Sample51-toc.html">


        <FRAMESET ROWS="100,*">

        <FRAME SCROLLING="no" NAME="MiddleLogo" SRC="Sample51-C.html">

        <FRAME SCROLLING="auto" NAME="MiddleBottom" SRC="Sample51-main.html">

        </FRAMESET>

</FRAMESET>
</HTML>
```

Example A5-8-Part 2:   Sample51-toc.html

```
<!DOCTYPE HTML PUBLIC "-//W3C//DTD HTML 3.2//EN">
<HTML>
<HEAD><BASEFONT SIZE="5">
<TITLE> Sample 51 - Source File toc     </TITLE></HEAD>

<BODY><P><CENTER>

<A HREF="Sample51-A.html" TARGET="MiddleLogo">

        Load Logo 1                                </A><P>

<A HREF="Sample51-B.html" TARGET="MiddleLogo">

        Load Logo 2                                </A>
</CENTER>
</BODY>
</HTML>
```

Example A5-8-Part 3:   Sample51-main.html

```
<!DOCTYPE HTML PUBLIC "-//W3C//DTD HTML 3.2//EN">
<HTML>  <HEAD><TITLE>  Sample 51 - Source File main   </TITLE></HEAD>

<BODY BGCOLOR="#23f6ff" BACKGROUND="JPEG-FILES/Icon-Clouds.jpg">
<P><CENTER><H1>This would be the main viewing area.</H1></CENTER>
</BODY>
</HTML>
```

Example A5-8-Part 4:   Sample51-A.html

```
<!DOCTYPE HTML PUBLIC "-//W3C//DTD HTML 3.2//EN">
<HTML>
<HEAD><TITLE>  Sample 51 - Source File A      </TITLE></HEAD>

<BODY BGCOLOR="#23f6ff" BACKGROUND="JPEG-FILES/icon-BG-asteroids.jpg">
<P>
<CENTER>

<IMG SRC="Sample-ETOC/JPEG-etoc-Logo1.jpg" WIDTH="432" HEIGHT="72">

</CENTER>

</BODY>
</HTML>
```

Example A5-8-Part 5:   Sample51-B.html

```
<!DOCTYPE HTML PUBLIC "-//W3C//DTD HTML 3.2//EN">
<HTML>
<HEAD><TITLE>  Sample 51 - Source File B      </TITLE></HEAD>

<BODY BGCOLOR="#23f6ff" BACKGROUND="JPEG-FILES/icon-FieldStone-Purple.jpeg">
<P>
<CENTER>

<IMG SRC="Sample-ETOC/JPEG-etoc-Logo2.jpg" WIDTH="432" HEIGHT="72">

</CENTER>

</BODY>
</HTML>
```

Example A5-8-Part 6:   Sample51-C.html

```
<!DOCTYPE HTML PUBLIC "-//W3C//DTD HTML 3.2//EN">
<HTML>
<HEAD><TITLE>  Sample 51 - Source File C      </TITLE></HEAD>

<BODY BGCOLOR="#ff0000">
<P><CENTER>

If you want to see an image here then
click on one of the logo links in the left frame.

</CENTER>

</BODY>
</HTML>
```

One thing to keep in mind that is particularly pertinent when working with FRAMEs is that you're dealing with a lot of different pieces of a puzzle, which in this case would be HTML pages that only work when they're put together correctly. Specifically you need to pay attention to:

- Name your Frames
- Name them logically so it's easy to know what they're for
- Name your files the same way
- Target your Links correctly
- URLs and other Names or Values go inside quote marks
- Make sure you use the correct file names and URL paths
- For files or images in nested folders, make sure the name of the folder is included in the URL:, preceding the file name and separated by a / sign
- Write notes to yourself on paper: It's easier than total head storage
- Diagrams are particularly efficient for small and complex projects
- Reuse your Code: Copy and Paste with minor alterations
- FRAMESET replaces the BODY Element
- FRAMEs only go inside of a FRAMESET
- Only one <u>unnested</u> FRAMESET is allowed per document
- Unlimited <u>Nested</u> FRAMESETs are allowed in each document
- Each FRAMESET must specify either COLS or ROWS or both of them
- Each FRAME must specify exactly one SRC="URL"
- Be considerate and include a NOFRAMES Element
- Have Fun, Think Vertically, and Create Exponentially

Remember that with FRAMEs you only use a Start Tag.

Contents   None
Contained in FRAMESET

Syntax:

```
<FRAME
FRAMEBORDER="YES"|"NO"
BORDERCOLOR="#$$$$$$"|"colorName"
MARGINWIDTH="pixelsMarginWidth"
MARGINHEIGHT="pixelsMarginHeight"
SCROLLING="YES"|"NO"|"AUTO"
NORESIZE
NAME="nameYourFrame"
SRC="URL"                                required
STYLE="Property:Value; Property:Value; ..."
CLASS="nameOfClass"
ID="nameOfClassException">
```

FRAMEBORDER="YES" | "NO" designates whether the BORDER for this FRAME will be rendered in 3D raised or 2D flat format. The default value is "YES", which indicates 3D, which overrides any previous setting of a FRAMEBORDER Attribute within any FRAMESET Element. Because FRAMEs share borders, and for aesthetic reasons the only time that a FRAME can have a 2D BORDER is when all FRAMEs that are adjacent to one another, all have their FRAMEBORDERs set to "NO". The default value for FRAMEBORDER is "YES", which also includes an inherent thickness setting of 5 pixels, which cannot be altered from within the FRAME Tag.

If you want to change the thickness you have to use the global setting with the BORDER="pixelsThick" Attribute within the <u>outermost</u> FRAMESET Tag, which will affect <u>all</u> FRAMEBORDERs. It is not possible to have individual FRAMEs with different thickness settings. If you don't use the FRAMEBORDER Attribute at all, it will also by default appear in the same gray color as Navigator's outer Window border. You do have the option of changing the color of your BORDER for individual FRAMEs using the BORDERCOLOR Attribute below.

   YES creates a 3D raised BORDER.
   NO   creates a 2D flat BORDER.

BORDERCOLOR="#$$$$$$" | "colorName" determines the color for just that FRAME and overrides any global setting of any FRAMESET or Nested FRAMESET. It uses that old familiar hexadecimal red-green-blue triplet or by using one of the 16 color names that are recognized by Netscape. See the section on COLOR Theory in Appendix B.

Because of the way Navigator allocates space to FRAMEs, the BORDERs are shared and when different colors are assigned to adjacent BORDERs, they must adhere to a hierarchy to determine which BORDERCOLOR Attribute has priority.

   Lowest Priority: BORDERCOLOR in the <u>outermost</u> FRAMESET.
   Next Priority: BORDERCOLOR in a <u>Nested</u> FRAMESET.
   Highest Priority: BORDERCOLOR in a FRAME overrides all others.
   Undefined: Two adjacent BORDERCOLORs of equal priority.

When the Undefined situation occurs, Netscape will usually use the first of the BORDERCOLOR Attributes that is coded, oddly enough.

MARGINWIDTH="pixelsMarginWidth" defines the size of the margin for the left and right sides of your FRAME, which is specified in pixels. This lets you create space between the content of your FRAME and the FRAMEBORDER. You aren't allowed to use a value of 0 (zero) or a negative number because your content would touch, or even worse, it would overlap the FRAMEBORDER, causing render-nightmares. If you do inadvertently or even intentionally use a negative number, Netscape will change the number to 1 because that's the closest legal number. Any positive number from 1 on up is acceptable but remember that screen space is limited, so in practice the usual range is from about 1 to 20 pixels. If you do make the margin so large that the contents of your document won't fit inside the FRAME, Netscape will reduce the margins enough to accommodate the content but the margins won't necessarily be equal on both sides.

If you don't indicate a MARGINWIDTH, Netscape will by default create a margin that will comfortably display the content, which usually results in a size of approximately 8-10 pixels. There are definitely times when setting all the margins to 1 and turning off the borders can be the difference between visual elegance and clunkiness when you need the maximum display space available for your content.

MARGINHEIGHT="pixelsMarginHeight" defines the size of the margin for the top and bottom of your FRAME, which is specified in pixels. Everything previously mentioned for your MARGINWIDTHs is applicable to MARGINHEIGHTs except that the area affected is the space above and below the document contained within the FRAME instead of the space to the left and right of the content.

SCROLLING="YES" | "NO" | "AUTO" designates whether the optional scrollbars will be always visible, always hidden or invisible unless needed. Unless you've never used a GUI computer, you know that horizontal and vertical scrollbars are the augmented graphical versions of the arrow Keys and page-up and page-down Keys, which allow you to scroll to areas of the document that are hidden. In most computer programs they are either built-in or they don't exist at all. With HTML the choice is yours. Each option has its various applications. If you don't include the SCROLLING Attribute then Navigator will use AUTO by default.

The AUTO setting causes the browser to examine the size and contents of the FRAME and then determine if the scrollbars are required or not. If all of the contents of the FRAME can be seen at once, that is, if the contents will all fit into the size of the FRAME as the user has it sized to, then the scrollbars will be hidden. If there is more content to be displayed than the FRAME has room to visibly show, then the scrollbar that is needed will become visible automatically.

There are many instances where only the vertical scrollbar will be visible because there would be plenty of horizontal space available to display the content but not enough vertical space. Because the AUTO setting is adaptive, each time a user resizes the web page, it will change the status of the scrollbars if it's required in order to accommodate the layout of the content.

YES	specifies that the scrollbars are <u>always visible</u>.
NO	specifies that the scrollbars are <u>always hidden</u>.
AUTO	specifies that the scrollbars are invisible unless needed.
	AUTO is the default value.

NORESIZE This is a Boolean Attribute that has no assignable value. If you include it in the FRAME Tag then it is true and prevents your FRAME from being resized by the user. If you don't include it in your FRAME it is false, which is the default value, so then the user can resize the FRAME by dragging on the edge of the FRAME with the mouse. Restated, all FRAMEs are resizable by default. Because FRAME edges are shared, not two edges that touch or overlap for each FRAME, if you include NORESIZE in a FRAME that is adjacent to another FRAME that is resizable, the shared edge will still be unresizable because NORESIZE has precedence in the code hierarchy.

NAME="nameYourFrame" is a very important Attribute, which specifies an identifier for your FRAME so that it can be referenced and TARGETed with Links and JavaScript. Think of it as a nickname for your FRAME that was devised so that you could save time, space, and confusion when coding. One very useful methodology is to use NAMEs that describe what the FRAME is for or what it does. This is also very useful to remember when we get into the STYLE and JavaScript sections and start having to name Style **ids**, **classes**, and **Functions**.

SRC="URL" specifies the URL of a document or object that you want to load into this FRAME. This is the only required Attribute. Check out pages 447-452 on the **Location** Object or the CH3.html file on the CD-ROM on Links, if you need more information about URLs.

Example A5-10 contains the sample file named welcomeETOC-SAMPLE.html, which is in the folder named Sample-ETOC on the CD-ROM. It is a very involved example of a site that has four FRAMEs and two FRAMESETs. One FRAMESET is nested inside the other FRAMESET, *between* its two FRAMEs. Each FRAMESET has two FRAMEs, one with two COLS (columns) and the other with two ROWS.

What that creates is a document where the Window has a narrow column at both the left and right sides, a company logo inside a thin row at the top, and in the middle is the main viewing Window where the bulk of the documents are viewed when clicked on in the control columns. The left FRAME is used as the master table of contents and it stays there continuously. It contains the master category Links of the site, which generally are TARGETed into and thus open in the right FRAME. The right FRAME contains the subcategories that are usually TARGETed into the FRAME with the NAME Attribute set to **NAME="MiddleBottom"**, which is the large main viewing FRAME in the middle of the Window.

You really should run this sample because the visual makes the description much clearer. It also looks really cool. Feel free to reuse any of the code in the book or in the Sample HTML files on the CD-ROM. It will save you a lot of time and possibly point you in some creative directions.

When checking out the code for Part 2 be aware that there is JavaScript in it and the TABLE is contained within a FORM Element which is what makes the BUTTONs with the JavaScript work. If you are new to HTML and you started reading at Appendix A, you may need to jump to CH6.html (in HTML_BOOK-Online folder) of the online Guide, if you need clarification. For now, just be aware that to get BUTTONs to work they must be inside a FORM. If you started the book from the beginning, then this is old news.

Here's the code for the FRAMESETs, which contains the four FRAMEs, and the code for each of the pages that go into each FRAME are included afterward.

Example A5-10-Part 1-Frameset: welcomeETOC-SAMPLE.html

```
<!DOCTYPE HTML PUBLIC "-//W3C//DTD HTML 3.2//EN">
<HTML>
<HEAD>
        <TITLE>Extra Touch of Class Framed Home Page </TITLE>
</HEAD>

<FRAMESET FRAMESPACING="3" BORDER="3" COLS="145,*,155">

                        <NOFRAMES>
<P><H2>
Hey Now!!! If you are reading this you are using a Frame-Challenged-Browser.
For optimal viewing proceed immediately to
<A HREF="http://www.Netscape.com">Netscape's website</A>
 and download the current version of Navigator.
</P>
<P>
Otherwise <A HREF="ETOCmainWindow5Bkgd.html">
Enter the Non-Frames Version of the Extra Touch of Class website.</A>
</H2></P>
                        </NOFRAMES>

        <FRAME SCROLLING="no" NAME="Left" SRC="etoc-TOC8Bkgd.html">


<FRAMESET  FRAMESPACING="3" BORDER="3" ROWS="90,*">

        <FRAME SCROLLING="no" NAME="MiddleTop" SRC="ETOC-Logo8Bkgd.html">

        <FRAME SCROLLING="yes" NAME="MiddleBottom" SRC="ETOCmainWindow5Bkgd.html">

</FRAMESET>

        <FRAME SCROLLING="yes" NAME="Right" SRC="etoc-ArtByStyle3Bkgd.html">

</FRAMESET>

</BODY>
</HTML>
```

Example A5-10-Part 2:   etoc-TOC8Bkgd.html

```
<!DOCTYPE HTML PUBLIC "-//W3C//DTD HTML 3.2//EN">
<HTML>
<HEAD>    <TITLE>Window of Contents</TITLE>
        <BASE TARGET="MiddleBottom">
</HEAD>
<BODY BGCOLOR="#060dff" TEXT="#ffffff" BACKGROUND="icon-BG-stars.jpg"
VLINK="#222222" LINK="#000000" ALINK="#2826CF">
<CENTER>
<FORM>
```

```
<TABLE BORDER=3 CELLSPACING=2 CELLPADDING=2>

<TR>
<TH>
<INPUT TYPE="button" VALUE="<<B"
    onClick="parent.MiddleBottom.history.back()">
<INPUT TYPE="button" VALUE="F>>"
    onClick="parent.MiddleBottom.history.forward()">

</TH>
</TR>

<TR>
<TH>

<INPUT TYPE="button" VALUE="<<B"
    onClick="parent.Right.history.back()">
<INPUT TYPE="button" VALUE="F>>"
    onClick="parent.Right.history.forward()">
</TH>
</TR>

<TR>
<TH BGCOLOR="#dd00ff">
<A HREF="etoc-ArtByArtist3Bkgd.html" TARGET="Right">Art</A>
</TH>
</TR>

<TR>
<TD BGCOLOR="#7300dd">
<A HREF="etocWoodFrames.html" TARGET="Right"><B>Wood Frames</B></A>
</TD>
</TR>

<TR>
<TD BGCOLOR="#8300ee">
<A HREF="etocMetalFrames.html" TARGET="Right"><B>Metal Frames</B></A>
</TD>
</TR>

<TR>
<TD BGCOLOR="#9300ff">
<A HREF="etocPolymerFrames.html" TARGET="Right"><B>Polymer Frames</B></A>
</TD>
</TR>

<TR>
<TH BGCOLOR="#0066ff">
<A HREF="etocGlass.html" TARGET="Right">Glass</A>
</TH>
</TR>

<TR>
<TH BGCOLOR="#0099ff">
<A HREF="etocPlexiglass.html" TARGET="Right">Plexiglass</A>
</TH>
</TR>
```

```
<TR>
<TH BGCOLOR="#00ffff">
<A HREF="etocMats.html" TARGET="Right">Mats</A>
</TH>
</TR>


<TR>
<TH BGCOLOR="#00ff00">
<A HREF="etocMounting.html" TARGET="Right">Mounting</A>
</TH>
</TR>

<TR>
<TH BGCOLOR="#00aa00">
<A HREF="etocHardware.html" TARGET="Right">Hardware</A>
</TH>
</TR>

<TR>
<TH BGCOLOR="#ffff00">
<A HREF="Links.html" TARGET="MiddleBottom">Links</A>
</TH>
</TR>


<TR>
<TH BGCOLOR="#ffbb00">
<A HREF="Foxmans-Calendar97.html" TARGET="MiddleBottom">Calendar<BR>
of Events</A>
</TH>
</TR>


<TR>
<TH BGCOLOR="#FA5A05">
<A HREF="etoc-CompanyProfile.html" TARGET="MiddleBottom">Company Info</A>
</TH>
</TR>

<TR BGCOLOR="#F92807">
<TH>email
</TH>
</TR>

<TR BGCOLOR="#FF0000">
<TH>Order by Phone<BR>
703-354-2905
</TH>
</TR>

<TR BGCOLOR="#ff00aa">
<TH>
<A HREF="ETOC-OrderForm.html" TARGET="_blank">
<FONT SIZE=4>  Order Online</FONT></A>
</TH>
</TR>
```

```
<TR>
<TH BGCOLOR="#777777">
<A HREF="ETOC-Logo1Bkgd.html" TARGET="MiddleTop">    L1 </A>
<A HREF="ETOC-Logo2Bkgd.html" TARGET="MiddleTop">    L2 </A>
<A HREF="ETOC-Logo3Bkgd.html" TARGET="MiddleTop">    L3 </A>
<A HREF="ETOC-Logo3A-Bkgd.html" TARGET="MiddleTop">  L4 </A>

</TH>
</TR>

</TABLE>

</FORM>
</CENTER>

</BODY>
</HTML>
```

Example A5-10-Part 3:   ETOC-Logo8Bkgd.html

```
<!DOCTYPE HTML PUBLIC "-//W3C//DTD HTML 3.2//EN">
<HTML>
<HEAD>
    <TITLE>    Extra Touch of Class Logo 8 </TITLE>
</HEAD>

<BODY BGCOLOR="#23f6ff" BACKGROUND="icon-FieldStone-Purple.jpeg">
<P>
<CENTER>

<IMG SRC="JPEG-etoc-Logo3.jpg" WIDTH=432 HEIGHT=72 BORDER=0 ALIGN="MIDDLE"
NAME="roll">

</CENTER>
</BODY>
</HTML>
```

Example A5-10-Part 4:   ETOCmainWindow5Bkgd.html

```
<!DOCTYPE HTML PUBLIC "-//W3C//DTD HTML 3.2//EN">
<HTML>
<HEAD>

    <TITLE>Extra Touch of Class Main Frame</TITLE>
</HEAD>

<BODY BGCOLOR="#000000" TEXT="#FFFFFF" BACKGROUND="GIFA-EARTH-ANIMATION.gif"
VLINK="#0000FF" LINK="#000000">

<!---------------------------------------------------------------------->

<CENTER>
```

```
<TABLE BORDER=5 CELLSPACING=3 CELLPADDING=4>

<TR VALIGN=middle BGCOLOR="#755F11">
<TH COLSPAN=2>Welcome to</TH>
</TR>

<TR BGCOLOR="#755F11">
<TH COLSPAN=2 VALIGN=middle>
<FONT SIZE=7 COLOR="#000000">Extra Touch of Class</FONT><BR>
<FONT SIZE=4>Art Gallery and Framing Studio</FONT>
</TH>
</TR>

<TR VALIGN=middle BGCOLOR="#755F11">
<TH COLSPAN=2>Conservation Framing</TH>
</TR>

<TR VALIGN=middle BGCOLOR="#755F11">
<TH> * Wood * Metal * Polymer * </TH>
<TH> * Mat * Mount * Glass * Plexiglass * </TH>
</TR>

</TABLE>                 <BR>

</CENTER>

<!------------------------------------------------------------------------->

<CENTER>
<TABLE BORDER=10 CELLSPACING=10 CELLPADDING=10>

<TR>
<TH BGCOLOR="#755F11">
<A HREF="BV20-CrystalMtsWinter14.html"><IMG SRC="JPEG-EXHIBITION-1x2.jpg"
WIDTH="147" HEIGHT="103" ALIGN="BOTTOM" BORDER="10"><BR><BR>
<FONT SIZE="6">Enter the Studio</FONT></A>
</TH>
</TR>

</TABLE>                 <BR>
</CENTER>

<!------------------------------------------------------------------------->

<CENTER>
<TABLE BORDER=2 CELLSPACING=2 CELLPADDING=5>

<TR VALIGN=middle BGCOLOR="#0000FF">
<TH BGCOLOR="#FFFFFF"><FONT COLOR="#000000">Store #1</FONT></TH>
<TH BGCOLOR="#FFFFFF"><FONT COLOR="#000000">Store #2</FONT></TH>
</TR>

<TR VALIGN=middle BGCOLOR="#0000FF">
<TH>5641 -B General Washington Dr.</TH>
<TH>5641 -B General Washington Dr.</TH>
</TR>
```

```
<TR VALIGN=middle BGCOLOR="#0000FF">
<TH>Alexandria, VA  22312</TH>
<TH>Alexandria, VA  22312</TH>
</TR>

<TR VALIGN=middle BGCOLOR="#0000FF">
<TH>703-354-2905</TH>
<TH>703-354-2905</TH>
</TR>

<TR BGCOLOR="#0000FF" VALIGN=MIDDLE>
<TH BGCOLOR="#FFFFFF"><FONT COLOR="#000000">Store #3</FONT></TH>
<TH ROWSPAN=4 BGCOLOR="#00FFFF"><FONT COLOR="#000000">
Barry Broadway -- Proprietor</TH></FONT>
</TR>

<TR BGCOLOR="#0000FF" VALIGN=MIDDLE>
<TH>5641 -B General Washington Dr.</TH>
</TR>

<TR BGCOLOR="#0000FF" VALIGN=MIDDLE>
<TH>Alexandria, VA  22312</TH>
</TR>

<TR BGCOLOR="#0000FF" VALIGN=MIDDLE>
<TH>703-354-2905</TH>
</TR>

</TABLE>
</CENTER>

<!------------------------------------------------------------------------->

<BR>
<H3><CENTER><A HREF="FoxmansHELP.html"><BR>
Site Navigation Overview = HELP</A></CENTER>
</H3>

</BODY>
</HTML>
```

Example A5-10-Part 5:   etoc-ArtByStyle3Bkgd.html

```
<!DOCTYPE HTML PUBLIC "-//W3C//DTD HTML 3.2//EN">
<HTML>
<HEAD>

    <TITLE>Art by Style 3</TITLE>
</HEAD>

<BODY TEXT="#ffffff" BGCOLOR="#94bbef" BACKGROUND="icon-Paint-Palette.jpg"
ALINK="#0000ff" LINK="#ff0000" VLINK="#000000">

<CENTER>
```

```
<TABLE BORDER=5 CELLSPACING=2 CELLPADDING=1>


<TR>
<TH BGCOLOR="#ff0000">
<FONT SIZE="5"><BR>Art by<BR>Style<BR> </FONT>
</TH>
</TR>


<TR>
<TH BGCOLOR="#00ffff">
<A HREF="etoc-ArtByArtist3Bkgd.html" TARGET="Right">!!Art By Artist!!</A>
</TH>
</TR>


<TR>
<TH BGCOLOR="#00ffff">
<A HREF="etoc-ArtByTitle3Bkgd.html" TARGET="Right">!!Art By Title!!</A>
</TH>
</TR>



<TR>
<TH BGCOLOR="#0000FF">
<A HREF="etoc-3DComputerArt.html" TARGET="Right">3D</A>
</TH>
</TR>


<TR>
<TH BGCOLOR="#0000FF">
Abstract
</TH>
</TR>


<TR>
<TH BGCOLOR="#0000FF">
Cubist
</TH>
</TR>


<TR>
<TH BGCOLOR="#0000FF">
Fantasy
</TH>
</TR>


<TR>
<TH BGCOLOR="#0000FF">
Impressionism
</TH>
</TR>


<TR>
<TH BGCOLOR="#0000FF">
Industrial
</TH>
</TR>
```

```
<TR>
<TH BGCOLOR="#0000FF">
Landscapes
</TH>
</TR>

<TR>
<TH BGCOLOR="#0000FF">

</TH>
</TR>


<TR>
<TH BGCOLOR="#0000FF">
Modern
</TH>
</TR>

<TR>
<TH BGCOLOR="#0000FF">
Post Modern
</TH>
</TR>

<TR>
<TH BGCOLOR="#0000FF">
Psychedelic
</TH>
</TR>

<TR>
<TH BGCOLOR="#0000FF">
Sci-Fi
</TH>
</TR>

<TR>
<TH BGCOLOR="#0000FF">
Still Life
</TH>
</TR>

<TR>
<TH BGCOLOR="#0000FF">
<A HREF="etoc-SurrealArt.html" TARGET="Right">Surreal</A>
</TH>
</TR>

</TABLE>
</CENTER>

</BODY>
</HTML>
```

The <NOFRAMES> Element

The <NOFRAMES> Element, even though it's not required, should always be included inside one FRAMESET Element per page as a courtesy to viewers. It provides browsers that are incapable of rendering FRAMEs with alternative content that it can display to the user. Without the NOFRAMES Element, a non-Frames-capable surfer will only see a blank page because all of the page's FRAMESET content will be ignored.

Frames-capable-browsers like Navigator that can interpret FRAME content, will ignore all text, content, and Tags between the NOFRAMES Start and End Tags. One exception to this is if you create an error in your FRAME or FRAMESET code, like changing the URL or name of a file and forgetting to change the SRC=URL to match or just incorrectly typing in the URL, which will cause Navigator to be unable to reach or load the file, then the NOFRAMES content will be displayed.

Always test your code before you upload. Even if you've tested it and it works perfectly and then you decide to make one little change and you think to yourself, there's no way I could possibly have even the slightest hint of a chance of even the remotest inkling of the slimmest consideration of the infinitesimally improbable circumstance of actually coding an errrrrrrorrrrr. Don't bet your life on it. Retest that code in the browser.

There are several things that you can include in your NOFRAMES Element to show how "netiquette"-conscious you are. You could provide a Link to Netscape's homepage or software download site and let the viewer know that by downloading and using Navigator they will be able to see that site as it was intended. You should always include an entrance link into your site that doesn't have any FRAMEs in it. In fact, if you design your website around a FRAME paradigm, you should consider creating an alternative and parallel version that doesn't use FRAMEs at all. It's not an absolute, just contemplate your own unique circumstances.

Lots of web authors are creating homepages that offer the client a choice of which version of the site they want to enter, like a Frames version, a Non-Frames version, a Text-Only version, or the new Layers and Non-Layers versions that are sure to start popping up or may have been around forever depending on when you are reading this.

Contents	In HTML4.0 Transitional:	All block-level and inline Elements
	In HTML4.0 Frameset:	One BODY Element that can't contain any NOFRAMES Elements
Contained in	APPLET, BLOCKQUOTE, BODY, CENTER, DD, DIV, FORM, FRAMESET, LI, MAP, NOSCRIPT, OBJECT, TD, TH	

Syntax:

```
<NOFRAMES
LANG="ISOLanguageAbbreviation"
STYLE="Property:Value; Property:Value; ..."
CLASS="nameOfClass"
ID="nameOfClassException">
...
</NOFRAMES>
```

This is just a typical use of the NOFRAMES Element. Notice that it is inside the FRAMESET Element. Normally you would also put FRAMEs inside the FRAMESET.

```
<FRAMESET>

            <NOFRAMES>
<H2>

Hey Now!!! If you are reading this you are using a Frame-Challenged-Browser.
For optimal viewing proceed immediately to

<A HREF="http://www.Netscape.com">Netscape's website</A>

 and download the current version of Navigator.
</H2>

<H2>
Otherwise
<A HREF="welcome3.html">
Enter the Non-Frames Version of the DreamPlay Studios website.</A>
</H2>
            </NOFRAMES>

</FRAMESET>
```

Some of the possibilities for FRAMEs are, say, a Left-FRAME and Right-FRAME navigation system, where the Left-FRAME is the master control-panel containing all of the main divisions of your website that expand into the Right-FRAME control panel when clicked. In the Right-FRAME would be variable subdivisions of your site that would expand into the main viewing area in the middle FRAME. In that scenario the left and right FRAMEs would likely be narrow columns with most of the available Window space being occupied by the middle FRAME where most of the informative content would be TARGETed. Very large and data-rich sites would benefit from this scenario.

On the following page is a list of Samples that use FRAMEs and FRAMESETs in them, which are on the CD-ROM and have the code listed in this book.

Sample38frameset.html, line 5:	`<FRAMESET COLS="150,*">`
Sample50-Frameset-1.html, line 5:	`<FRAMESET COLS="40%,60%" BORDERCOLOR="#ff0000">`
Sample50-Frameset-2.html, line 5:	`<FRAMESET ROWS="50%,50%" BORDERCOLOR="#ff0000">`
Sample50-Frameset-3.html, line 5:	`<FRAMESET COLS="25%,*,25%" BORDERCOLOR="#ff0000">`
Sample50-Frameset-4.html, line 5:	`<FRAMESET COLS="200,*,35%" BORDERCOLOR="#ff0000">`
Sample50-Frameset-5.html, line 5:	`<FRAMESET COLS="200,200,200">`
Sample51-Frameset-6.html, line 10:	`<FRAMESET COLS="27%,73%">`
Sample51-Frameset-7.html, line 5:	`<FRAMESET COLS="150,*" BORDERCOLOR="#000000">`
Sample52-Frameset-8D3.html, line 5:	`<FRAMESET COLS="20%,*">`
Sample52-Frameset-8D4.html, line 5:	`<FRAMESET ROWS="50%,*">`
Sample53-Frameset-9.html, line 5:	`<FRAMESET ROWS="250,*">`
Sample54-Frameset-10.html, line 5:	`<FRAMESET BORDERCOLOR="#0000ff" COLS="25%,25%,25%,*">`
Sample56-Frameset-11.html, line 5:	`<FRAMESET BORDERCOLOR="#0000ff" COLS="25%,25%,25%,*">`
Sample56-Frameset-11.html, line 27:	`<FRAMESET BORDERCOLOR="#00ff00" ROWS="50%,25%,*">`
Sample429Frameset.html, line 5:	`<FRAMESET ROWS="150,*">`
Sample430Frameset.html, line 5:	`<FRAMESET ROWS="150,*">`
Sample432Frameset.html, line 5:	`<FRAMESET ROWS="100,*">`
Sample434Frameset.html, line 5:	`<FRAMESET ROWS="140,*">`
Sample435Frameset.html, line 4:	`<FRAMESET ROWS="24,*,24" BORDER="0">`
Sample452Frameset.html, line 5:	`<FRAMESET COLS="220,*">`
Sample453Frameset.html, line 5:	`<FRAMESET COLS="220,*">`
Sample454Frameset.html, line 5:	`<FRAMESET ROWS="130,*">`
Sample455Frameset.html, line 5:	`<FRAMESET COLS="220,*">`
Sample456Frameset.html, line 5:	`<FRAMESET COLS="200,*">`
Sample533Frameset.html, line 5:	`<FRAMESET COLS="100,*">`
Sample534.html, line 34:	`document.writeln('<FRAMESET COLS="200,*">')`
Sample718Frameset.html, line 5:	`<FRAMESET COLS="120,*">`
Sample719Frameset.html, line 5:	`<FRAMESET COLS="130,*">`
Sample724Frameset.html, line 5:	`<FRAMESET COLS="220,*">`
Sample724Frameset.html, line 10:	`<FRAMESET ROWS="100,*">`
Sample826Frameset.html, line 5:	`<FRAMESET ROWS="100,*">`
Sample899Frameset.html, line 5:	`<FRAMESET ROWS="120,*">`
Sample1014Frameset.html, line 5:	`<FRAMESET ROWS="40,*">`
Sample1015Frameset.html, line 5:	`<FRAMESET ROWS="100,*">`
Sample1016Frameset.html, line 5:	`<FRAMESET ROWS="100,*">`

Note that most Sample files with FRAMESETs in them that are on the CD-ROM, but not in the book, have the word "Frameset" as part of the file name.

The <FORM> Element

Contents   In HTML 4.0 Strict: SCRIPT or block-level Elements except FORM
                 In HTML 4.0 Transitional: block-level or inline Elements except FORM
Contained in APPLET, BLOCKQUOTE, BODY, CENTER, DD, DIV,
                 LI, MAP, NOFRAMES, NOSCRIPT, OBJECT, TD, TH

Syntax:

```
<FORM
ACTION="ServerURL"
ENCTYPE="EncodingType"
METHOD="GET" | "POST"
NAME="FormName"
TARGET="WindowName" | "FrameName"
ONRESET="resetJavaScriptCode"
ONSUBMIT="submitJavaScriptCode"
LANG="ISOLanguageAbbreviation"
STYLE="Property:Value; Property:Value; ..."
CLASS="nameOfClass"
ID="nameOfClassException">
...
</FORM>
```

The <INPUT> Element

Contents   None
Contained in All block-level or inline Elements

Syntax:

```
<INPUT
TYPE="BUTTON"|"CHECKBOX"|"FILE"|"HIDDEN"|"IMAGE"|"PASSWORD"|"RADIO"
     |"RESET"|"SUBMIT"|"TEXT"
NAME="typeName"
VALUE="displayText"
LANG="ISOLanguageAbbreviation"
STYLE="Property:Value; Property:Value; ..."
CLASS="nameOfClass"
ID="nameOfClassException">
```

BUTTON   Creates a BUTTON on a FORM that executes JavaScript code when clicked. When active it is highlighted.

RESET   Creates a BUTTON on a FORM that resets all of the Elements on the FORM to their original Values when clicked.

SUBMIT   Creates a BUTTON on a FORM that submits, that is, it transfers all of the data from the Elements on the FORM to their destination via the Server.

IMAGE   Creates a custom BUTTON on a FORM with the image as the BUTTON.

RADIO   Creates a RADIO BUTTON that lets the user choose its VALUE Value. When used in a group that all have the same NAME, they let the user choose one Value from that list.

CHECKBOX   Creates a CHECKBOX BUTTON that serves as an ON/OFF switch so that the user can decide between two alternatives.

FILE   Lets the user upload a file as part of the data submitted on the FORM.

HIDDEN   Places an invisible TEXT field on the FORM that is used to pass data to the Server when the FORM is submitted.

PASSWORD   Collects a password from the user in a TEXT field that suppresses the Characters by displaying placeholder Characters like bullets or asterisks.

TEXT   A single line TEXT field of settable length where the user can input text.

The <INPUT <u>TYPE="BUTTON"</u>> Element

Syntax:

```
<INPUT
TYPE="BUTTON"
NAME="buttonName"
VALUE="buttonText"
ONCLICK="clickJavaScriptCode"
ONBLUR="blurJavaScriptCode"
ONFOCUS="focusJavaScriptCode"
LANG="ISOLanguageAbbreviation"
STYLE="Property:Value; Property:Value; ..."
CLASS="nameOfClass"
ID="nameOfClassException">
```

The <INPUT <u>TYPE="RESET"</u>> Element

Syntax:

```
<INPUT
TYPE="RESET"
NAME="resetButtonName"
VALUE="resetButtonText"
ONCLICK="clickJavaScriptCode"
ONBLUR="blurJavaScriptCode"
ONFOCUS="focusJavaScriptCode"
LANG="ISOLanguageAbbreviation"
STYLE="Property:Value; Property:Value; ..."
CLASS="nameOfClass"
ID="nameOfClassException">
```

The <INPUT <u>TYPE="SUBMIT"</u>> Element

Syntax:

```
<INPUT
TYPE="RESET"
NAME="submitButtonName"
VALUE="submitButtonText"
ONCLICK="clickJavaScriptCode"
ONBLUR="blurJavaScriptCode"
ONFOCUS="focusJavaScriptCode"
LANG="ISOLanguageAbbreviation"
STYLE="Property:Value; Property:Value; ..."
CLASS="nameOfClass"
ID="nameOfClassException">
```

The <INPUT <u>TYPE="IMAGE"</u>> Element

Syntax:

```
<INPUT
TYPE="IMAGE"
NAME="imageName"
SRC="imageURL"
ALIGN="LEFT"|"RIGHT"|"TOP"|"TEXTTOP"|"MIDDLE"|"ABSMIDDLE"|
      "BOTTOM"|"ABSBOTTOM"|"BASELINE"
LANG="ISOLanguageAbbreviation"
STYLE="Property:Value; Property:Value; ..."
CLASS="nameOfClass"
ID="nameOfClassException">
```

The <INPUT <u>TYPE="RADIO"</u>> Element

Syntax:

```
<INPUT
TYPE="RADIO"
NAME="radioButtonName"
VALUE="radioButtonText"
CHECKED
ONCLICK="clickJavaScriptCode"
ONBLUR="blurJavaScriptCode"
ONFOCUS="focusJavaScriptCode"
LANG="ISOLanguageAbbreviation"
STYLE="Property:Value; Property:Value; ..."
CLASS="nameOfClass"
ID="nameOfClassException">
```

The <INPUT <u>TYPE="CHECKBOX"</u>> Element

Syntax:

```
<INPUT
TYPE="CHECKBOX"
NAME="checkboxName"
VALUE="checkboxValue"
CHECKED
ONCLICK="clickJavaScriptCode"
ONBLUR="blurJavaScriptCode"
ONFOCUS="focusJavaScriptCode"
LANG="ISOLanguageAbbreviation"
STYLE="Property:Value; Property:Value; ..."
CLASS="nameOfClass"
ID="nameOfClassException">
```

The <INPUT <u>TYPE="FILE"</u>> Element

Syntax:

```
<INPUT
TYPE="FILE"
NAME="fileUploadName"
VALUE="value"
ONCHANGE="changeJavaScriptCode"
ONBLUR="blurJavaScriptCode"
ONFOCUS="focusJavaScriptCode"
LANG="ISOLanguageAbbreviation"
STYLE="Property:Value; Property:Value; ..."
CLASS="nameOfClass"
ID="nameOfClassException">
```

The <INPUT <u>TYPE="HIDDEN"</u>> Element

Syntax:

```
<INPUT
TYPE="HIDDEN"
NAME="hiddenName"
VALUE="hiddenValue"
LANG="ISOLanguageAbbreviation"
STYLE="Property:Value; Property:Value; ..."
CLASS="nameOfClass"
ID="nameOfClassException">
```

The <INPUT <u>TYPE="PASSWORD"</u>> Element

Syntax:

```
<INPUT
TYPE="PASSWORD"
NAME="passwordName"
VALUE="passwordValue"
SIZE="charactersLengthInteger"
MAXLENGTH="maximumCharactersInteger"
ONSELECT="selectJavaScriptCode"
ONBLUR="blurJavaScriptCode"
ONFOCUS="focusJavaScriptCode"
LANG="ISOLanguageAbbreviation"
STYLE="Property:Value; Property:Value; ..."
CLASS="nameOfClass"
ID="nameOfClassException">
```

The <INPUT <u>TYPE="TEXT"</u>> Element

Syntax:

```
<INPUT
TYPE="TEXT"
NAME="textName"
VALUE="textValue"
SIZE="charactersLengthInteger"
MAXLENGTH="maximumCharactersInteger"
ONFOCUS="focusJavaScriptCode"
ONBLUR="blurJavaScriptCode"
ONCHANGE="changeJavaScriptCode"
ONSELECT="selectJavaScriptCode"
LANG="ISOLanguageAbbreviation"
STYLE="Property:Value; Property:Value; ..."
CLASS="nameOfClass"
ID="nameOfClassException">
```

The <TEXTAREA> Element

Contents   Plain unformatted text, which can include entities
Contained in   All block-level or inline Elements

Syntax:

```
<TEXTAREA
NAME="textareaName"
COLS="integerColumns"
ROWS="integerRows"
WRAP="OFF"|"HARD"|"SOFT"
ONFOCUS="focusJavaScriptCode"
ONBLUR="blurJavaScriptCode"
ONCHANGE="changeJavaScriptCode"
ONSELECT="selectJavaScriptCode"
LANG="ISOLanguageAbbreviation"
STYLE="Property:Value; Property:Value; ..."
CLASS="nameOfClass"
ID="nameOfClassException">

       ...  initialDisplayText  ...

</TEXTAREA>
```

The <SELECT> Element

Contents   One or more OPTION Elements
Contained in   All block-level or inline Elements

Syntax:

```
<SELECT
NAME="selectName"
SIZE="integerListLength"
MULTIPLE
ONFOCUS="focusJavaScriptCode"
ONBLUR="blurJavaScriptCode"
ONCHANGE="changeJavaScriptCode"
LANG="ISOLanguageAbbreviation"
STYLE="Property:Value; Property:Value; ..."
CLASS="nameOfClass"
ID="nameOfClassException">
                    ...
      <OPTION>     ...    </OPTION>
                    ...
</SELECT>
```

The <OPTION> Element

Contents   Plain unformatted text, which can include entities
Contained in   SELECT Element

Syntax:

```
<OPTION
VALUE="optionValue"
SELECTED
LANG="ISOLanguageAbbreviation"
STYLE="Property:Value; Property:Value; ..."
CLASS="nameOfClass"
ID="nameOfClassException">

      ...displayText...

</OPTION>
```

The <KEYGEN> Element

Used for security and encryption purposes. This is a Navigator extension and is not W3G-approved.

Syntax:

```
<KEYGEN
NAME="name"
CHALLENGE="challengeString">
```

On the CD-ROM, in CH6.html, which is in the folder named HTML_BOOK-Online, which is in the folder named DHTML-JS_BOOK-Main_Files, there is a wealth of additional information concerning FORM Elements and the Elements contained in FORMs. Here is a list of some of the Sample files on the CD-ROM, but not in the book, that are concerned with those topics as well:

Sample60.html
Sample61.html
Sample62.html
Sample63.html
Sample64.html
Sample65.html
Sample66.html
Sample67.html
Sample68.html
Sample69.html
Sample70.html
Sample71-Form1.txt
Sample71-mailsent.htm
Sample71-OrderForm.html
Sample71-SimpleForm.html
Sample72.html
Sample73.html

Note that all of the above Sample files are explained in the CH6.html file on the CD-ROM, and they are hyperlinked from that document for easy access.

The <EMBED> Element for Embedded Objects

The <EMBED> Element is used to include Objects into the web page like movies, audio files, QuickTime VR Moovies, VRML, and Shockwave multimedia files. Depending on the type of Object that is being embedded into the page, there may be additional Attributes that are passed to and can be accommodated by the Plug-in for that MIME Type. Generally you should always contact the company that creates the Plug-in for the current data. Usually all companies will have part of their website devoted to the specifics for implementing the content that use their Plug-in and the ability to download the Plug-in for free. See page 1022 for a list of URLs for some of the more popular Plug-in types to get the most updated information regarding their formats.

The appropriate Plug-in or Application must be in the Netscape Plug-ins Folder and properly configured. To configure a Plug-in, go to the Preferences Menu in the Edit Menu of Navigator. When the Preferences Window appears, go to the Navigator Category and then the Applications Category. Then scroll to the desired Plug-in and select it and click Edit or double-click the Plug-in. If there is no entry for the Plug-in you are looking for, then click the New button and start from there. Having the correct suffixes is critical both in configuring the Plug-in and in naming the File properly. This is a Navigator extension that has wide support in most browsers, even though it has been deprecated in favor of the OBJECT Element, which has poor and very buggy support at this time.

Syntax:

```
<EMBED
SRC="LocationURL"              <!--Either SRC or TYPE is required-->
TYPE="MIMEtype"
HIDDEN="TRUE|FALSE"
ALIGN="LEFT"|"RIGHT"|"TOP"|"BOTTOM"
WIDTH="width"           <!--required if TYPE unless HIDDEN="TRUE"-->
HEIGHT="height"             <!--required unless HIDDEN="TRUE"-->
UNITS="PIXELS|EN"
HSPACE="pixelsHorizontalMargin"
VSPACE="pixelsVerticalMargin"
BORDER="pixelsBorderThickness"
FRAMEBORDER="NO"
NAME="embedName|appletName|pluginName"
PALETTE="FOREGROUND"|"BACKGROUND"        <!--Windows Platform only-->
PLUGINSPAGE="instructionsURL"
PLUGINURL="pluginURL"
STYLE="Property:Value; Property:Value; ..."
CLASS="nameOfClass"
ID="nameOfClassException">
...
</EMBED>
```

SRC="LocationURL" is the URL of the file you want to load for the Plug-in to process. Because the URL must be appended with the correct suffix, the MIME type is ascertained from it. Either the SRC or TYPE Attribute is required. The SRC Attribute is usually the correct choice.

TYPE="MIMEtype" specifies the MIME type so the EMBED Element knows which Plug-in to load. You should only use the TYPE Attribute if the Plug-in procures all the required data dynamically or the Plug-in requires no data.

HIDDEN="TRUE I FALSE" specifies whether the Embedded Object is initially visible or invisible. The default value is FALSE, which means that the Object will be visible. This has more practical use than you might foresee. If you have an audio file and you don't want the audio controller, that is, the Stop-Start-Pause and Volume controls, to be visible or changeable by the user, then set HIDDEN to TRUE. You might have a movie file that you only want to hear the sound and not see the images. You can use Java and in a limited fashion use JavaScript to control various parameters of particular Plug-ins.

ALIGN="LEFT" I "RIGHT" I "TOP" I "BOTTOM" specifies the alignment of the Object with the text on that line in the document.

> **LEFT**   aligns the text flush left.
>
> **RIGHT**   aligns the text flush right.
>
> **TOP**   aligns the text flush with the top.
>
> **BOTTOM**   aligns the text flush with the bottom.

WIDTH="width" is a required Attribute if the TYPE Attribute is used, unless the HIDDEN Attribute is used. It specifies the width of the Object and is measured in either PIXELS or EN, which is specified in the UNITS Attribute (see UNITS on page 1014).

> With some Plug-ins, Navigator automatically scales the Object to fit the width. With other Objects, like a QuickTime movie, it will be cropped if a smaller width than the movie's actual width is specified and will be centered on a background if a larger width is specified. Never use a width smaller than 2 pixels or problems will occur. The default units is pixels.

HEIGHT="height" is a required Attribute unless the HIDDEN Attribute is used. It sets the height of the Object and is measured in either PIXELS or EN, which is specified in the UNITS Attribute (see UNITS on page 1014).

> If you want the controller for a QuickTime movie to be visible, you have to add an additional 24 pixels to the height of the movie. If a smaller height than the movie's actual height is specified, then it will be cropped to fit, and it will be centered on a background if a larger height is specified. Never use a height smaller than 2 pixels or problems will occur.

UNITS="PIXELS | EN" specifies the units of measurement for the WIDTH and HEIGHT Attributes. The default value is PIXELS. The value EN unit is half the height of the Point Size.

HSPACE="pixelsHorizontalMargin" specifies an invisible border or margin between the left and right sides of the Object and the surrounding text and images. It is measured in pixels.

VSPACE="pixelsVerticalMargin" specifies an invisible border or margin between the top and bottom edges of the Object and the surrounding text and images. It is measured in pixels.

BORDER="pixelsBorderThickness" specifies the thickness of a two-dimensional border surrounding the Object in the same way that an image can have a border. It is measured in pixels and inherits the foreground color of the document.

FRAMEBORDER="NO" specifies that the Object Frame will have no border. Note that this Attribute has only the one possible value of NO.

NAME="embedName | appletName | pluginName" specifies the name of the embedded Object, Applet, or Plug-in for referencing by JavaScript or Java.

PALETTE="FOREGROUND" | "BACKGROUND" is only applicable to the Windows Platform. It will have no effect on the MacIntosh or Unix Platforms. The default value is BACKGROUND and causes the Plug-in to use the background palette. If you want to use the foreground palette for the Plug-in, set the value to FOREGROUND.

PLUGINSPAGE="instructionsURL" specifies a URL that contains instructions for both downloading and installing the Plug-in if the browser determines that the required Plug-in to operate the file is not in the Plug-ins Folder of Navigator.

This is considered a courtesy to the user. The appropriate URL is always available from the company that makes the Plug-in and is usually included in the information at the company's website. Usually they have one particular URL that they want you to use, but you should update this information periodically, because it does change as companies update their websites.

For example, the PLUGINSPAGE URL for Apple's QuickTime Plug-in is currently:

```
http://quicktime.apple.com.
```

PLUGINURL="pluginURL" specifies a URL of a Java Archive file (JAR), which can be a signed collection of compressed files. PLUGINURL is recommended over and supercedes PLUGINSPAGE. See the section on Using the JAR Installation Manager in the JavaScript Guide from Netscape on the CD-ROM or from Netscape's website in the DevEdge page.

The \<NOEMBED\> Element

The \<NOEMBED\> Element is used to provide alternative content for the situations when a user does not have the ability to render the content contained in the \<EMBED\> Element.

Syntax:

```
<NOEMBED
LANG="ISOLanguageAbbreviation"
STYLE="Property:Value; Property:Value; ..."
CLASS="nameOfClass"
ID="nameOfClassException">

    ... text and/or HTML to display ...

</NOEMBED>
```

Embedding QD3D Files with the Whurlplug Plug-in

Syntax:

```
<EMBED
SRC="locationURL"
WIDTH="widthPixels"
HEIGHT="heightPixels"
SPIN="TRUE|FALSE"
ACTIVE="TRUE|FALSE"
BGCOLOR="#??????"|"colorName"
TOOLBAR="TRUE|FALSE"
ROTATE="x y z"
RENDER="interactive|wireframe"
LANG="ISOLanguageAbbreviation"
STYLE="Property:Value; Property:Value; ..."
CLASS="nameOfClass"
ID="nameOfClassException">

  ...

</EMBED>
```

The QuickTime Plug-in

QuickTime Movies and Animations

The following EMBED Syntax is for the QuickTime Plug-in to play QuickTime movies:

Syntax:

```
<EMBED
HOTSPOT n = "locationURL"
CACHE="value"
VOLUME="value"
SCALE="value"
PLUGINSPAGE="url"
WIDTH="size in pixels"
HEIGHT="size in pixels"
HIDDEN
AUTOPLAY="value"
CONTROLLER="value"
LOOP="value"
PLAYEVERYFRAME="value"
HREF="url"
TARGET="frame"
PAN="integer"
TILT="integer"
FOV="integer"
NODE="integer"
CORRECTION="value"
LANG="ISOLanguageAbbreviation"
STYLE="Property:Value; Property:Value; ..."
CLASS="nameOfClass"
ID="nameOfClassException">

    ...

</EMBED>
```

Embedding Audio Files
with the <u>LiveAudio</u> Plug-in

Syntax:

```
<EMBED
SRC="locationURL"
HIDDEN="TRUE"
AUTOSTART="TRUE"|"FALSE"
LOOP="TRUE"|"FALSE"|"quantityInteger"
STARTTIME="minutesInteger:secondsInteger"
ENDTIME="minutesInteger:secondsInteger"
VOLUME="0-100"|"MASTERVOLUME"
WIDTH="widthPixels"
HEIGHT="heightPixels"
ALIGN="TOP|BOTTOM|CENTER|BASELINE|LEFT|RIGHT
            |TEXTTOP|MIDDLE|ABSMIDDLE|ABSBOTTOM"
CONTROLS="CONSOLE|SMALLCONSOLE|PLAYBUTTON|
            PAUSEBUTTON|STOPBUTTON|VOLUMELEVER"
MASTERSOUND
NAME="unique ID to group CONTROLS to control one sound"
LANG="ISOLanguageAbbreviation"
STYLE="Property:Value; Property:Value; ..."
CLASS="nameOfClass"
ID="nameOfClassException">
   ...
</EMBED>
```

Embedding <u>VRML</u> Files
with the <u>WorldView</u> Plug-in

You can use the EMBED Element to embed VRML files directly into your web page for an interactive 3D experience with a variety of Plug-ins. The WorldView Plug-in works really well, supports VRML 2, is the fastest one available, and works on the Macintosh, Windows, and SGI Platforms. See page 1022 for the URL to download it.

VRML is the acronym for Virtual Reality Modeling Language, which saves 3D models and environments in a format that allows the user, via one of the many VRML Plug-ins or browser applications, to navigate inside of a dynamic 3D virtual world. These VRML files can contain HTML Links to other pages, movies, and images in a variety of formats in addition to the 3D models and light sources.

Many of the 3D modeling programs, like Strata Studio Pro, can save their scenes in the VRML format and some programs, even though less robust in modeling capabilities, like Virtus Walkthrough Pro, are specifically designed to create VRML files and have a built-in VRML viewer as an integral feature of the program. VRML is still in its infancy right now, but it holds a lot of promise for enriching websites, and as the web gets faster and the programs get more sophisticated, you will see it augmenting sites more frequently.

To set the MIME Type and Suffix in the browser, go to the Preferences command in the Edit Menu of Navigator. Then, click on the Applications option in the Navigator option, and after choosing a Description, click the Edit Button and enter the information. The MIME Type for VRML files is:

```
"x-world/x-vrml"
```

and the Suffix for VRML files is:

```
wrl
```

such as Sample79-VRML.wrl.

In addition to the normal Attributes that are available in all EMBED Elements, the following Attributes are interpreted by the WorldView Plug-in for VRML files.

Attribute	Value	Description
VRML_POPMENU	FALSE	Disables the right mouse button menu
SGI_POPMENU	FALSE	Disables the right mouse button menu
VRML_IMAGEQUALITY	BEST SMOOTH SMOOTHEST	Models render with "Smooth Shading" Models render with "Flat Shading" Models render in "Wireframe"
SGI_IMAGEQUALITY	BEST SMOOTH SMOOTHEST	Models render with "Smooth Shading" Models render with "Flat Shading" Models render in "Wireframe"
VRML_SPLASHSCREEN	FALSE	Disables splash screen at startup
SGI_SPLASHSCREEN	FALSE	Disables splash screen at startup
VRML_DASHBOARD	FALSE	Turns off horizontal and vertical toolbars
SGI_DASHBOARD	FALSE	Turns off horizontal and vertical toolbars

The \<APPLET\> Element for Java Applets

Contents   PARAM Elements followed by block-level Elements or inline Elements
Contained in   All block-level Elements except PRE and All inline Elements

Syntax:

```
<APPLET
CODE="classFileName"
CODEBASE="classFileDirectoryURL"
ARCHIVE="archiveFile"
ALT="alternateText"
NAME="appletName"
MAYSCRIPT
ALIGN="LEFT"|"RIGHT"|"TOP"|"ABSMIDDLE"|"ABSBOTTOM"|
            "TEXTTOP"|"MIDDLE"|"BASELINE"|"BOTTOM"
WIDTH="pixelsWidth"|"percentWidth%"
HEIGHT="pixelsHeight"|"percentHeight%"
HSPACE="horizontalPixelsMargin"
VSPACE="verticalPixelsMargin"
LANG="ISOLanguageAbbreviation"
STYLE="Property:Value; Property:Value; ..."
CLASS="nameOfClass"
ID="nameOfClassException">

        [<PARAM NAME="parameterName" VALUE="parameterValue">]
        ...

</APPLET>
```

The \<PARAM\> Element for Java Parameters

Contents   None
Contained in   Applet or Object

Syntax:

```
<PARAM
NAME="parameterName"
VALUE="parameterValue">
```

The <BASE> Element

Contents   None
Contained in   HEAD

Syntax:

```
<BASE
HREF="baseURL"
TARGET="WindowName|FrameName"
LANG="ISOLanguageAbbreviation"
STYLE="Property:Value; Property:Value; ..."
CLASS="nameOfClass"
ID="nameOfClassException">
```

The <OBJECT> Element

Contents   PARAM Elements followed by block-level Elements or inline Elements
Contained in   HEAD and All block-level Elements except PRE and All inline Elements

Syntax:

```
<OBJECT
CLASSID="classFileURL|pluginURL"
DATA="dataLocationURL"
CODEBASE="classFileDirectoryURL"
TYPE="MIMEtype"
ALIGN="LEFT"|"RIGHT"|"TOP"|"ABSMIDDLE"|"ABSBOTTOM"|
           "TEXTTOP"|"MIDDLE"|"BASELINE"|"BOTTOM"
HEIGHT="pixelsHeight"
WIDTH="pixelsWidth"
ID="objectName"
LANG="ISOLanguageAbbreviation"
STYLE="Property:Value; Property:Value; ..."
CLASS="nameOfClass"
ID="nameOfClassException">

     [<PARAM NAME="parameterName" VALUE="parameterValue">]
     ...
</OBJECT>
```

Plug-in MIME Type and Suffixes Chart

Description	Plug-in Name	MIME Type	Suffixes
QuickTime Movie	QuickTime Plug-in	video/quicktime	mov
QuickTime VR	QuickTime Plug-in	video/quicktime	snm, moov
ULAW Audio	LiveAudio Plug-in	audio/basic	au
aiff Audio	LiveAudio Plug-in	audio/aiff	aiff
WAV Audio	LiveAudio Plug-in	audio/x-wav	wav
midi Audio	LiveAudio Plug-in	audio/midi	mid
x-midi Audio	LiveAudio Plug-in	audio/x-midi	mid
QuickDraw 3D	WhurlPlug	x-world/x-3dmf	3dmf, 3dm, qd3d, qd3
VRML	WorldView	x-world/x-vrml	wrl
RealAudio Audio	RealAudio Plug-in	audio/x-pn-realaudio-plugin	rpn

For more information about the 176 currently available Plug-ins for Navigator, go to the Netscape Plug-ins page at:

`http://home.netscape.com/comprod/products/navigator/version_2.0/plugins/index.html`

For more information about the Plug-ins mentioned in this book or to download a Plug-in, visit the websites of the companies that developed them at:

```
QuickTime plug-in    http://quicktime.apple.com
WhurlPlug            http://www.apple.com/quicktime/qd3d/whurlplug.html
WorldView            http://www.intervista.com/
RealAudio            http://www.realaudio.com/
```

The <META> Element

The <META> Element goes in the HEAD of the document. This Element has no effect on the appearance of the document. There are two main categories of use for this Element. First, it can provide information about the document to external programs like search engines for categorization or description purposes. It can also be used by the browser to refresh the page, set Cookie values, update Server-Push, and Client-Pull code.

You can use as many META Tags in a document as you want. Either the NAME or the HTTP-EQUIV Attribute is required. The Value of the CONTENT Attribute depends on the Value of the NAME or the HTTP-EQUIV Attributes. There are a lot of possibilities.

For more information on the META Element see the Netscape HTML Tags Reference Documentation on the CD-ROM in the HTML-Nav4-Final-Docs Folder. For more information on Cookies, see Chapter 4 starting on page 436, or visit:

```
http://www.netscape.com/newsref/std/cookie_spec.html
```

For even more detailed information about the META Element, check out:

```
http://www.stars.com/Seminars/HTML/Head/meta.html
```

For even more detailed information about other values for the NAME and HTTP-EQUIV Attributes, see the top of page 1024, or check out:

```
http://vancouver-webpages.com/META/
```

They have quite a lot of relevant information at their site.

Contents   None
Contained in   HEAD

Syntax:

```
<META
NAME="name"
HTTP-EQUIV="fieldName"
CONTENT="value"
LANG="ISOLanguageAbbreviation"
>
```

META Element Attributes Examples Chart

This is not a complete list of all of the possibilities, but it does represent some of the more widely recognized scenarios.

NAME or HTTP-EQUIV	CONTENT example
NAME="keywords"	CONTENT="art, graphics, 3D, VRML, animation"
NAME="description"	CONTENT="A 3D art and website design company"
NAME="author"	CONTENT="Gilorien"
NAME="generator"	CONTENT="BBEdit 4.5"> //authoring program
HTTP-EQUIV="refresh"	CONTENT="5"
HTTP-EQUIV="refresh"	CONTENT="1;URL=http://www.dplay.com/nextdoc.html"
HTTP-EQUIV="expires"	CONTENT="Mon, 15 Feb 1999 11:11:22 GMT"
HTTP-EQUIV="Set-Cookie"	CONTENT="cookievalue=whatever;path=/"

The <ISINDEX> Element

The <ISINDEX> Element is a FORM Element that has no practical value unless you are using it in conjunction with a CGI Script so that the Tag is included in a page that the CGI Script generates. That's why it's included here instead of in the section on FORMs.

Theoretically, this Element provides a text field where the user can input a search-key String, and then Searching would be turned on inside the document. Because no browsers support automatic searching, it is up to the CGI Program to supply the search code (or some creative Java or JavaScript programming would do the trick too). Details for CGI Programming is beyond the scope of this book. For information on coding CGI Scripts, the following URL is a good place to start:

```
http://hoohoo.ncsa.uiuc.edu:80/cgi/overview.html
```

Contents   None
Contained in   APPLET, BLOCKQUOTE, BODY, CENTER, DD, DIV, FORM, HEAD, LI, MAP, NOFRAMES, NOSCRIPT, OBJECT, TD, TH

Syntax:

```
<ISINDEX
PROMPT="text">
```

HTML Elements by Category

Comments
        <!-- your comment here -->

Elements for Document Structure
        HTML
        HEAD
        BODY

Heading Elements
        TITLE
        BASE
        META
        STYLE
        LINK

Block-Level Text Elements
        ADDRESS
        BLOCKQUOTE
        DIV
        H1
        H2
        H3
        H4
        H5
        H6
        P
        PRE
        XMP

Formatting Elements
        BR
        CENTER
        HR
        MULTICOL
        NOBR
        SPACER
        SPAN
        WBR

Text Characteristics Elements
        B
        BASEFONT
        BIG
        BLINK
        CITE
        CODE
        EM

FONT
I
KBD
PLAINTEXT
S
SMALL
STRIKE
STRONG
SUB
SUP
TT
U
VAR

List Elements

DIR
DL
DT
DD
MENU
OL
UL
LI

Anchor and Link Elements

A

Image and Image Map Elements

IMG
AREA
MAP

Table Elements

TABLE
CAPTION
TR
TD
TH

Form Elements

FORM
INPUT
SELECT
OPTION
TEXTAREA
KEYGEN
ISINDEX

Frame and Frameset Elements
FRAME
FRAMESET
NOFRAMES
Positioning Content
LAYER
ILAYER
NOLAYER
Scripts
SCRIPT
NOSCRIPT
SERVER
Applets and Plug-ins
APPLET
PARAM
EMBED
NOEMBED
OBJECT

Part IV
Resources

Appendix B

Color Names
and Values

Color Theory

This is a short treatise on additive Color theory to help you understand the visible light spectrum and how color is handled by Navigator and the JavaScript compiler in the browser. For any of you horsehair brush artists who are making the transition, you know from mixing paints that by adding colors together you can create new colors such as adding blue and red to get purple. You also know that if you add enough wildly different colors together you will eventually get dark brown or black.

However, when working with the visible spectrum, you have to throw all that theory out the window because it works on opposite principles. Adding all light colors together gives you white and taking all color away gives you black. Think about it this way, if you turn off the all the lights in a room, it's dark because of the absence of light. If you turn the lights all the way up with a dimmer switch, you get white light. If the dimmer switch is just barely on, the light has a relatively grayish cast to it.

Now, when you break light up into its components with a prism you can see that light falls into certain broad components of red, green, and blue. By adding these three components in varying degrees of intensity, you can create millions of different colors. However, the way that is required to add them together to achieve certain colors can be very counterintuitive at times. For instance, to get the brightest, most intense yellow, you have to add full green and full red together. To get cyan, you have to add full blue and full green together. To get a darker green than lime, you have to subtract some intensity from the green component.

Fortunately, in Navigator there are a plethora of recognized color names that can be used instead of having to specify precise numbers to achieve the color you want. Just make sure that you spell them correctly. You can use either uppercase or lowercase letters or a combination of the two. Navigator interprets the sixteen universally recognized color names in addition to all of the JavaScript color names for Attribute Values in HTML code.

The sixteen universally recognized color Names are:

```
aqua, black, blue, fuchsia, gray, green, lime, maroon,
navy, olive, purple, red, silver, teal, white, yellow
```

All of the recognized JavaScript color names, along with their HEX, rgb% and rgb number value equivalents are in a chart following this overview, starting on page 1033.
This same information is contained on the CD-ROM in the Sample file: Sample1100-AllColorValues.html. If you just want to see all of the actual colors displayed along with the name of each color, then check out Sample1100-AllColorNames.html. To convert a color, or to experiment and create your own colors from scratch, go check out page 340, for a color conversion calculator contained in Sample434.html.

Hexadecimal Triplet Color

In regular HTML, you can also specify a color as a Hexadecimal Triplet, which is preceded by a hash (#) sign. In Dynamic HTML (DHTML) that uses Style Sheets with either Cascading Style Sheet (CSS) Syntax or JavaScript Syntax, you have the additional option of using the **rgb( )** Function to specify a color value.

Hexadecimal Triplet RGB color is built on Base 16 math. When you want to represent a number in Base 16 math, you can use the letters "A"-"F" or, because HTML is case-insensitive, you can also choose to use the lowercase letters "a"-"f", for the numbers 10-15 because there are no single number designations for those numbers.

In Base 16 math:

A=10, B=11, C=12, D=13, E=14, F=15
a=10, b=11, c=12, d=13, e=14, f=15

To represent a color as an RGB Hexadecimal Triplet, the first thing to know is that it is composed of six numbers in the range from 0-9 or letters from A-F or a-f. The first two values after the hash (#) character represent the Red component **RR**, the second set of two values represent the green component **GG**, and the third set of two values represent the blue component **BB**, like in the following chart:

#RRGGBB	**=**	**Color Name Equivalent**
#000000	=	black
#FFFFFF	=	white
#333333	=	darkgray
#FF0000	=	red
#00FF00	=	lime
#0000FF	=	blue
#FFFF00	=	yellow
#9300EE	=	purple

Probably the easiest way to achieve a color that isn't specified by one of the recognized color names is to look at the values next to the name in the chart that starts on page 1033 and use it as a starting point and experiment with the values until you get what you are looking for.

This is an example of specifying a magenta-ish HEX color with the TEXT Attribute of the BODY Element, noting that it is always preceded with a hash (#) sign and enclosed in quotes or double quotes, like this:

```
<BODY TEXT="#fa13de">
```

The rgb( ) Function

In CSS Syntax and JavaScript Syntax, for Style Sheet definitions you have more ways to specify the color than in regular HTML. In addition to using a recognized color Name, including all of the JavaScript color Names, or a Hexadecimal triplet, you can also express it by using the **rgb( )** Function.

The **rgb( )** Function takes the three Arguments of **redArg**, **greenArg**, and **blueArg**, which represent the Red, Green, and Blue Values of a total color. They are separated by commas and can be either numbers from 0 to 255 or a percentage from 0 to 100%. If a percentage is used, the percent (%) sign must follow the number for each Argument.

The Syntax for the **rgb( )** Function is identical for both CSS Syntax and JavaScript Syntax Style Sheets.

CSS Syntax and JavaScript Syntax:

```
rgb(redArg, greenArg, blueArg)
rgb(redArg%, greenArg%, bluerg%)
```

The numbers used in the 0-255 measurement scheme go from the lowest being no color for that value to 255 being full color for that value, so that:

rgb (255, 0, 0)	means:	full red, no green, no blue	=	red
rgb (255, 0, 255)	means:	full red, no green, full blue	=	plum
rgb (0, 0, 255)	means:	no red, no green, full blue	=	blue
rgb (0, 255, 255)	means:	no red, full green, full blue	=	aqua
rgb (0, 255, 0)	means:	no red, full green, no blue	=	lime
rgb (255, 255, 0)	means:	full red, full green, no blue	=	yellow
rgb (255, 255, 255)	means:	full red, full green, full blue	=	white
rgb (0, 0, 0)	means:	no red, no green, no blue	=	black
rgb (100%, 0%, 0%)	means:	full red, no green, no blue	=	red
rgb (100%, 0%, 100%)	means:	full red, no green, full blue	=	plum
rgb (0%, 0%, 100%)	means:	no red, no green, full blue	=	blue
rgb (0%, 100%, 100%)	means:	no red, full green, full blue	=	aqua
rgb (0%, 100%, 0%)	means:	no red, full green, no blue	=	lime
rgb (100%, 100%, 0%)	means:	full red, full green, no blue	=	yellow
rgb (100%, 100%, 100%)	means:	full red, full green, full blue	=	white
rgb (0%, 0%, 0%)	means:	no red, no green, no blue	=	black

Recognized Color Names with Values Chart

Color Name	Hex Value	RGB 0-255 Value	RGB 0-100% Value
aliceblue	F0F8FF	240, 248, 255	94, 97, 100
antiquewhite	FAEBD7	250, 235, 215	98, 92, 84
aqua	00FFFF	0, 255, 255	0, 100, 100
aquamarine	7FFFD4	127, 255, 212	50, 100, 83
azure	F0FFFF	240, 255, 255	94, 100, 100
beige	F5F5DC	245, 245, 220	96, 96, 86
bisque	FFE4C4	255, 228, 196	100, 89, 77
black	000000	0, 0, 0	0, 0, 0
blanchedalmond	FFEBCD	255, 235, 205	100, 92, 80
blue	0000FF	0, 0, 255	0, 0, 100
blueviolet	8A2BE2	138, 43, 226	54, 17, 89
brown	A52A2A	165, 42, 42	65, 16, 16
burlywood	DEB887	222, 184, 135	87, 72, 53
cadetblue	5F9EA0	95, 158, 160	37, 62, 63
chartreuse	7FFF00	127, 255, 0	50, 100, 0
chocolate	D2691E	210, 105, 30	82, 41, 12
coral	FF7F50	255, 127, 80	100, 50, 31
cornflowerblue	6495ED	100, 149, 237	39, 58, 93
cornsilk	FFF8DC	255, 248, 220	100, 97, 86
crimson	DC143C	220, 20, 60	86, 8, 24
cyan	00FFFF	0, 255, 255	0, 100, 100
darkblue	00008B	0, 0, 139	0, 0, 55
darkcyan	008B8B	0, 139, 139	0, 55, 55
darkgoldenrod	B8860B	184, 134, 11	72, 53, 4
darkgray	A9A9A9	169, 169, 169	66, 66, 66
darkgreen	006400	0, 100, 0	0, 39, 0

Color Name	Hex Value	RGB 0-255 Value	RGB 0-100% Value
darkkhaki	BDB76B	189, 183, 107	74, 72, 42
darkmagenta	8B008B	139, 0, 139	55, 0, 55
darkolivegreen	556B2F	85, 107, 47	33, 42, 18
darkorange	FF8C00	255, 140, 0	100, 55, 0
darkorchid	9932CC	153, 50, 204	60, 20, 80
darkred	8B0000	139, 0, 0	55, 0, 0
darksalmon	E9967A	233, 150, 122	91, 59, 48
darkseagreen	8FBC8F	143, 188, 143	56, 74, 56
darkslateblue	483D8B	72, 61, 139	28, 24, 55
darkslategray	2F4F4F	47, 79, 79	18, 31, 31
darkturquoise	00CED1	0, 206, 209	0, 81, 82
darkviolet	9400D3	148, 0, 211	58, 0, 83
deeppink	FF1493	255, 20, 147	100, 8, 58
deepskyblue	00BFFF	0, 191, 255	0, 75, 100
dimgray	696969	105, 105, 105	41, 41, 41
dodgerblue	1E90FF	30, 144, 255	12, 56, 100
firebrick	B22222	178, 34, 34	70, 13, 13
floralwhite	FFFAF0	255, 250, 240	100, 98, 94
forestgreen	228B22	34, 139, 34	13, 55, 13
fuchsia	FF00FF	255, 0, 255	100, 0, 100
gainsboro	DCDCDC	220, 220, 220	86, 86, 86
ghostwhite	F8F8FF	248, 248, 255	97, 97, 100
gold	FFD700	255, 215, 0	100, 84, 0
goldenrod	DAA520	218, 165, 32	85, 65, 13
gray	808080	128, 128, 128	50, 50, 50
green	008000	0, 128, 0	0, 50, 0
greenyellow	ADFF2F	173, 255, 47	68, 100, 18
honeydew	F0FFF0	240, 255, 240	94, 100, 94
hotpink	FF69B4	255, 105, 180	100, 41, 71
indianred	CD5C5C	205, 92, 92	80, 36, 36
indigo	4B0082	75, 0, 130	29, 0, 51

Color Name	Hex Value	RGB 0-255 Value	RGB 0-100% Value
ivory	FFFFF0	255, 255, 240	100, 100, 94
khaki	F0E68C	240, 230, 140	94, 90, 55
lavender	E6E6FA	230, 230, 250	90, 90, 98
lavenderblush	FFF0F5	255, 240, 245	100, 94, 96
lawngreen	7CFC00	124, 252, 0	49, 99, 0
lemonchiffon	FFFACD	255, 250, 205	100, 98, 80
lightblue	ADD8E6	173, 216, 230	68, 85, 90
lightcoral	F08080	240, 128, 128	94, 50, 50
lightcyan	E0FFFF	224, 255, 255	88, 100, 100
lightgoldenrodyellow	FAFAD2	250, 250, 210	98, 98, 82
lightgreen	90EE90	144, 238, 144	56, 93, 56
lightgrey	D3D3D3	211, 211, 211	83, 83, 83
lightpink	FFB6C1	255, 182, 193	100, 71, 76
lightsalmon	FFA07A	255, 160, 122	100, 63, 48
lightseagreen	20B2AA	32, 178, 170	13, 70, 67
lightskyblue	87CEFA	135, 206, 250	53, 81, 98
lightslategray	778899	119, 136, 153	47, 53, 60
lightsteelblue	B0C4DE	176, 196, 222	69, 77, 87
lightyellow	FFFFE0	255, 255, 224	100, 100, 88
lime	00FF00	0, 255, 0	0, 100, 0
limegreen	32CD32	50, 205, 50	20, 80, 20
linen	FAF0E6	250, 240, 230	98, 94, 90
magenta	FF00FF	255, 0, 255	100, 0, 100
maroon	800000	128, 0, 0	50, 0, 0
mediumaquamarine	66CDAA	102, 205, 170	40, 80, 67
mediumblue	0000CD	0, 0, 205	0, 0, 80
mediumorchid	BA55D3	186, 85, 211	73, 33, 83
mediumpurple	9370DB	147, 112, 219	58, 44, 86
mediumseagreen	3CB371	60, 179, 113	24, 70, 44
mediumslateblue	7B68EE	123, 104, 238	48, 41, 93
mediumspringgreen	00FA9A	0, 250, 154	0, 98, 60

Color Name	Hex Value	RGB 0-255 Value	RGB 0-100% Value
mediumturquoise	48D1CC	72, 209, 204	28, 82, 80
mediumvioletred	C71585	199, 21, 133	78, 8, 52
midnightblue	191970	25, 25, 112	10, 10, 44
mintcream	F5FFFA	245, 255, 250	96, 100, 98
mistyrose	FFE4E1	255, 228, 225	100, 89, 88
moccasin	FFE4B5	255, 228, 181	100, 89, 71
navajowhite	FFDEAD	255, 222, 173	100, 87, 68
navy	000080	0, 0, 128	0, 0, 50
oldlace	FDF5E6	253, 245, 230	99, 96, 90
olive	808000	128, 128, 0	50, 50, 0
olivedrab	6B8E23	107, 142, 35	42, 56, 14
orange	FFA500	255, 165, 0	100, 65, 0
orangered	FF4500	255, 69, 0	100, 27, 0
orchid	DA70D6	218, 112, 214	85, 44, 84
palegoldenrod	EEE8AA	238, 232, 170	93, 91, 67
palegreen	98FB98	152, 251, 152	60, 98, 60
paleturquoise	AFEEEE	175, 238, 238	69, 93, 93
palevioletred	DB7093	219, 112, 147	86, 44, 58
papayawhip	FFEFD5	255, 239, 213	100, 94, 84
peachpuff	FFDAB9	255, 218, 185	100, 85, 73
peru	CD853F	205, 133, 63	80, 52, 25
pink	FFC0CB	255, 192, 203	100, 75, 80
plum	DDA0DD	221, 160, 221	87, 63, 87
powderblue	B0E0E6	176, 224, 230	69, 88, 90
purple	800080	128, 0, 128	50, 0, 50
red	FF0000	255, 0, 0	100, 0, 0
rosybrown	BC8F8F	188, 143, 143	74, 56, 56
royalblue	4169E1	65, 105, 225	25, 41, 88
saddlebrown	8B4513	139, 69, 19	55, 27, 7
salmon	FA8072	250, 128, 114	98, 50, 45
sandybrown	F4A460	244, 164, 96	96, 64, 38

Color Name	Hex Value	RGB 0-255 Value	RGB 0-100% Value
seagreen	2E8B57	46, 139, 87	18, 55, 34
seashell	FFF5EE	255, 245, 238	100, 96, 93
sienna	A0522D	160, 82, 45	63, 32, 18
silver	C0C0C0	192, 192, 192	75, 75, 75
skyblue	87CEEB	135, 206, 235	53, 81, 92
slateblue	6A5ACD	106, 90, 205	42, 35, 80
slategray	708090	112, 128, 144	44, 50, 56
snow	FFFAFA	255, 250, 250	100, 98, 98
springgreen	00FF7F	0, 255, 127	0, 100, 50
steelblue	4682B4	70, 130, 180	27, 51, 71
tan	D2B48C	210, 180, 140	82, 71, 55
teal	008080	0, 128, 128	0, 50, 50
thistle	D8BFD8	216, 191, 216	85, 75, 85
tomato	FF6347	255, 99, 71	100, 39, 28
turquoise	40E0D0	64, 224, 208	25, 88, 82
violet	EE82EE	238, 130, 238	93, 51, 93
wheat	F5DEB3	245, 222, 179	96, 87, 70
white	FFFFFF	255, 255, 255	100, 100, 100
whitesmoke	F5F5F5	245, 245, 245	96, 96, 96
yellow	FFFF00	255, 255, 0	100, 100, 0
yellowgreen	9ACD32	154, 205, 50	60, 80, 20

Part IV
Resources

Appendix C

Sample Files

Referenced

Sample Files and Topics

For Samples that are only on the CD-ROM, there is usually further information about them in the Online Guide which is in the:

<u>"DHTML-JS_BOOK-Main_Files</u>/<u>HTML_BOOK-Online</u>" folder.

<u>Page #</u>	<u>Sample File Name</u>	<u>Sample#, Example#</u>		<u>Topic</u>
CD-ROM	Sample0.html	Sample 0	Example 1-0	My Home Page or whatever
CD-ROM	Sample1.html	Sample 1	Example 1-1	My First Home Page
CD-ROM	Sample2.html	Sample 2	Example 1-2	The PRE Element
CD-ROM	Sample3.html	Sample 3	Example 1-3	The MULTICOL Element
CD-ROM	Sample4.html	Sample 4	Example 1-4	The SPACER Element Example 1
CD-ROM	Sample5.html	Sample 5	Example 1-5	The SPACER Element Example 2
CD-ROM	Sample6.html	Sample 6	Example 1-6	H1 through H6 Headings Example
CD-ROM	Sample7.html	Sample 7	Example 1-7	Line-breaks Example
CD-ROM	Sample8.html	Sample 8	Example 1-9	Horizontal Rules 1
CD-ROM	Sample9.html	Sample 9	Example 1-9	Horizontal Rules 2
CD-ROM	Sample10.html	Sample 10	Example 2-0	Text Markup Example
CD-ROM	Sample11.html	Sample 11	Example 2-1	Font Size Example 1
CD-ROM	Sample12.html	Sample 12	Example 2-2	Font Size Example 2
CD-ROM	Sample13.html	Sample 13	Example 2-3	Font Size Example 3
CD-ROM	Sample14.html	Sample 14	Example 2-4	Font Size Example 4
CD-ROM	Sample15.html	Sample 15	Example 2-5	BLOCKQUOTE and CITE Example
CD-ROM	Sample16.html	Sample 16	Example 2-6	EM Example
CD-ROM	Sample17.html	Sample 17	Example 2-7	STRONG Example
CD-ROM	Sample18.html	Sample 18	Example 2-8	Phrasal Elements Example
CD-ROM	Sample19.html	Sample 19	Example 2-9	Ordered List Example 1
CD-ROM	Sample20.html	Sample 20	Example 2-10	Ordered List Example 2
CD-ROM	Sample21.html	Sample 21	Example 2-11	Unordered List Example 1
CD-ROM	Sample22.html	Sample 22	Example 2-12	Definition List Example 1
CD-ROM	Sample23.html	Sample 23	Example 2-13	Directory List Example 1
CD-ROM	Sample24.html	Sample 24	Example 2-14	Directory List Example 1
CD-ROM	Sample30.html	Sample 30	Example 3-0	Link Example 1
CD-ROM	Sample31.html	Sample 31	Example 3-1	Link Example 2
CD-ROM	Sample32.html	Sample 32	Example 3-2	Link Example 3
943	Sample33.html	Sample 33	Example 3-3	Image Example 1
946	Sample34.html	Sample 34	Example 3-4	Image Example 2
CD-ROM	Sample35Art.html	Sample 35	Example 3-5	Displaying Art
949	Sample36.html	Sample 36	Example 3-6	Image Map Area Example 1
CD-ROM	Sample36.map	Sample 36	Example 3-6	Image Map Area Example 1- the map
CD-ROM	Sample37.html	Sample 37	Example 3-7	Image Map Area Example 2
CD-ROM	Sample38-D-MetalProfiles.html	Sample 38	Example 3-8	Metal Profiles
CD-ROM	Sample38-Glass.html	Sample 38	Example 3-8	Regular Picture Glass
CD-ROM	Sample38-Mats.html	Sample 38	Example 3-8	Bainbridge Alphamat Matboard Colors
CD-ROM	Sample38-PlexiGlass.html	Sample 38	Example 3-8	Regular Plexiglass
CD-ROM	Sample38-Polymer.html	Sample 38	Example 3-8	Eastern Polymer Frames Group 1
CD-ROM	Sample38-Wood.html	Sample 38	Example 3-8	Washington Wood Frames Group 1
CD-ROM	Sample38.html	Sample 38	Example 3-8	Image Map Area Example 3
CD-ROM	Sample38frameset.html	Frameset for Sample 38		
954	Sample40.html	Sample 40	Example 4-0	Table Example 1
955	Sample41.html	Sample 41	Example 4-1	Table Example 2
959	Sample42.html	Sample 42	Example 4-2	Table Example 3
CD-ROM	Sample43.html	Sample 43	Example 4-3	Tabled Color Chart

Page #	Sample File Name	Sample#, Example#		Topic
CD-ROM	Sample50-A.html	Sample 50	Example 5-0	External Source File A
CD-ROM	Sample50-B.html	Sample 50	Example 5-0	External Source File B
CD-ROM	Sample50-C.html	Sample 50	Example 5-0	External Source File C
CD-ROM	Sample50-D.html	Sample 50	Example 5-0	External Source File D
CD-ROM	Sample50-E.html	Sample 50	Example 5-0	External Source File E
970	Sample50-Frameset-1.html	Sample 50	FRAMESET-1	
977	Sample50-Frameset-2.html	Sample 50	FRAMESET-2	
978	Sample50-Frameset-3.html	Sample 50	FRAMESET-3	
978	Sample50-Frameset-4.html	Sample 50	FRAMESET-4	
CD-ROM	Sample50-Frameset-5.html	Sample 50	FRAMESET-5	
CD-ROM	Sample50.html	Sample 50	Example 5-0	Image Map Area
988	Sample51-A.html	Sample 51	Example 5-1	Source A
988	Sample51-B.html	Sample 51	Example 5-1	Source B
988	Sample51-C.html	Sample 51	Example 5-1	Source C
982	Sample51-Frameset-6.html	Frameset-6 for Sample 51		
987	Sample51-Frameset-7.html	Frameset-7 for Sample 51		
CD-ROM	Sample51-Frameset-DP2000.html	Frameset-DP2000 for Sample 51		Framed Welcome 2000 page
980	Sample51-Frameset-DP3.html	Frameset-DP3 for Sample 51		Framed Welcome DP3 page
987	Sample51-main.html	Sample 51	Example 5-1	Source main
987	Sample51-toc.html	Sample 51	Example 5-1	Source toc
CD-ROM	Sample52-explain.html	Sample 52	Example 5-2	explanation
985	Sample52-Frameset-8D3.html	Frameset-8D3 for Sample 52		
985	Sample52-Frameset-8D4.html	Frameset-8D4 for Sample 52		
CD-ROM	Sample53-explain.html	Sample 53	Example 5-3	explanation
CD-ROM	Sample53-Frameset-9.html	Frameset for Sample 53		
CD-ROM	Sample54-Frameset-10.html	Frameset for Sample 54		
CD-ROM	Sample55-FramesetMother.html	Frameset for Sample 55		Framed Welcome 5000 page
CD-ROM	Sample56-Frameset-11.html	Frameset for Sample 56		
CD-ROM	Sample60.html	Sample 60	Example 6-0	Button
CD-ROM	Sample61.html	Sample 61	Example 6-1	Reset Button
CD-ROM	Sample62.html	Sample 62	Example 6-2	Submit Button
CD-ROM	Sample63.html	Sample 63	Example 6-3	Input type=image
CD-ROM	Sample64.html	Sample 64	Example 6-4	Radio Button
CD-ROM	Sample65.html	Sample 65	Example 6-5	Radio Button
CD-ROM	Sample66.html	Sample 66	Example 6-6	Checkbox
CD-ROM	Sample67.html	Sample 67	Example 6-7	Input for upload
CD-ROM	Sample68.html	Sample 68	Example 6-8	Hidden Input
CD-ROM	Sample69.html	Sample 69	Example 6-9	Password Input
CD-ROM	Sample70.html	Sample 70	Example 6-10	Text Box
CD-ROM	Sample71-mailsent.htm	Sample 71	Example 6-11	Dreamplay Studio's Thank You Page
CD-ROM	Sample71-OrderForm.html	Sample 71	Example 6-11	DreamPlay Purchase Order
CD-ROM	Sample71-SimpleForm.html	Sample 71	Example 6-11	DreamPlay Purchase Order
CD-ROM	Sample72.html	Sample 72	Example 6-12	Textarea Element
CD-ROM	Sample73.html	Sample 73	Example 6-13	Select Element
CD-ROM	Sample74-Large.html	Sample 74	Example 6-14	Embed Element
CD-ROM	Sample74.html	Sample 74	Example 6-14	Embed Element
CD-ROM	Sample75-QTVR-2.html	Sample 75	Example 6-15	Embed QTVR 2
CD-ROM	Sample76-Audio.html	Sample 76	Example 6-16	Embed Audio File of Furthur Song
CD-ROM	Sample77-QD3D.html	Sample 77	Example 6-17	Embed QD3D
CD-ROM	Sample78-QD3D.html	Sample 78	Example 6-18	Embed QD3D
CD-ROM	Sample79.html	Sample 79	Example 6-19	Embed VRML
CD-ROM	Sample80.html	Sample 80	Example 6-20	Java Hello World Applet
CD-ROM	Sample81.html	Sample 81	Example 6-21	Java Applet
CD-ROM	Sample82.html	Sample 82	Example 6-22	Object Element to Embed a movie

1042   **Part IV** — *Resources*

Page #	Sample File Name	Sample#, Example#	Topic	
756	Sample900.html	Sample 900	Example 8-0	concat Method
757	Sample901.html	Sample 901	Example 8-1	concat Method
758	Sample902.html	Sample 902	Example 8-2	concat Method
760	Sample903.html	Sample 903	Example 8-3	charAt Method
761	Sample904.html	Sample 904	Example 8-4	charCodeAt Method
763	Sample905.html	Sample 905	Example 8-5	fromCharCode Method
765	Sample906.html	Sample 906	Example 8-6	fromCharCode Method
767	Sample907.html	Sample 907	Example 8-7	indexOf Method
768	Sample908.html	Sample 908	Example 8-8	indexOf Method
770	Sample909.html	Sample 909	Example 8-9	lastIndexOf Method
772	Sample910.html	Sample 910	Example 8-10	search Method
773	Sample911.html	Sample 911	Example 8-11	search Method
774	Sample912.html	Sample 912	Example 8-12	match Method
775	Sample913.html	Sample 913	Example 8-13	match Method
776	Sample914.html	Sample 914	Example 8-14	match Method
780	Sample915.html	Sample 915	Example 8-15	replace Method
781	Sample916.html	Sample 916	Example 8-16	replace Method
785	Sample917.html	Sample 917	Example 8-17	split Method
787	Sample918.html	Sample 918	Example 8-18	split Method remembered substrings
789	Sample919.html	Sample 919	Example 8-19	slice Method
791	Sample920.html	Sample 920	Example 8-20	substring Method
793	Sample921.html	Sample 921	Example 8-21	substr Method
796	Sample922.html	Sample 922	Example 8-22	anchor and link Methods
799	Sample923.html	Sample 923	Example 8-23	decorative string methods
822	Sample1000.html	Sample 1000	Example 9-0	test Method
823	Sample1001.html	Sample 1001	Example 9-1	test Method
824	Sample1002.html	Sample 1002	Example 9-2	test Method
826	Sample1003.html	Sample 1003	Example 9-3	exec Method
827	Sample1004.html	Sample 1004	Example 9-4	exec Method and input Property
828	Sample1005.html	Sample 1005	Example 9-5	exec Method
831	Sample1006.html	Sample 1006	Example 9-6	compile Method
833	Sample1007.html	Sample 1007	Example 9-7	\D and {n,m} Special Characters
834	Sample1008.html	Sample 1008	Example 9-8	{n,} Special Character
835	Sample1009.html	Sample 1009	Example 9-9	Special Character \n
837	Sample1010.html	Sample 1010	Example 9-10	matching Control Characters
838	Sample1011.html	Sample 1011	Example 9-11	match and verify phone number
840	Sample1012.html	Sample 1012	Example 9-12	exec vs. match Array Elements
843	Sample1013.html	Sample 1013	Example 9-13	match and verify name, address
845	Sample1014.html	Sample 1014	Example 9-14	Simple Search
CD-ROM	Sample1014Frameset.html	Frameset for Sample 1014		
CD-ROM	Sample1014Main.html	Sample 1014Main	Example 9-14 Main	
848	Sample1015-SearchEngine1.html	Sample 1015	Example 9-15	Search Engine 1
CD-ROM	Sample1015-SearchEngine2.html	Sample 1016	Example 9-16	Search Engine 2
CD-ROM	Sample1015-SearchEngine3.html	Sample 1016	Example 9-16	Search Engine 3
CD-ROM	Sample1015Frameset.html	Frameset for Sample 1015		
CD-ROM	Sample1015Main-hasArrayEle.html	Sample 1015	Example 9-15	Key words for search
CD-ROM	Sample1015Main.html	Sample 1015	Example 9-15 Main	
CD-ROM	Sample1016Frameset.html	Frameset for Sample 1016		
CD-ROM	Sample1016Main.html	Sample 1016Main	Example 9-16 Main	
CD-ROM	Sample1100-AllColorNames.html	Sample 1100		Display all Color Formats
CD-ROM	Sample1101-AllColorValues.html	Sample 1101		Display all Color Formats
CD-ROM	Sample-AllColorNames.html			Color Chart- All HTML Color Names
882	Sample10000.html	Sample 10000	Example 10-0	apply Method JavaScript 1.3
884	Sample10001.html	Sample 10001	Example 10-1	apply Method JavaScript 1.3
887	Sample10002.html	Sample 10002	Example 10-2	call Method JavaScript 1.3
891	Sample10003.html	Sample 10003	Example 10-3	replace Method JavaScript 1.3

Part IV
Resources

Appendix D

Language
Abbreviations

Language Abbreviations Chart

These are the Language Abbreviations to be used as the value for the LANGUAGE Attribute that is available for most HTML Elements; they are case-insensitive.

Abbreviation	Language	Abbreviation	Language
aa	Afar	fj	Fiji
ab	Abkhazian	fo	Faeroese
af	Afrikaans	fr	French
am	Amharic	fy	Frisian
ar	Arabic		
as	Assamese	ga	Irish
ay	Aymara	gd	Scots, Gaelic
az	Azerbaijani	gl	Galician
		gn	Guarani
ba	Bashkir	gu	Gujarati
be	Byelorussian		
bg	Bulgarian	ha	Hausa
bh	Bihari	hi	Hindi
bi	Bislama	hr	Croatian
bn	Bengali, Bangla	hu	Hungarian
bo	Tibetan	hy	Armenian
br	Breton		
		ia	Interlingua
ca	Catalan	ie	Interlingue
co	Corsican	ik	Inupiak
cs	Czech	in	Indonesian
cy	Welsh	is	Icelandic
		it	Italian
da	Danish	iw	Hebrew
de	German		
dz	Bhutani	ja	Japanese
		ji	Yiddish
el	Greek	jw	Javanese
en	English		
eo	Esperanto	ka	Georgian
es	Spanish	kk	Kazakh
et	Estonian	kl	Greenlandic
eu	Basque	km	Cambodian
		kn	Kannada
fa	Persian	ko	Korean
fi	Finnish	ks	Kashmiri

Abbreviation	Language	Abbreviation	Language
ku	Kurdish	sg	Sangro
ky	Kirghiz	sh	Serbo-Croatian
		si	Singhalese
la	Latin	sk	Slovak
ln	Lingala	sl	Slovenian
lo	Laothian	sm	Samoan
lt	Lithuanian	sn	Shona
lv	Latvian, Lettish	so	Somali
		sq	Albanian
mg	Malagasy	sr	Serbian
mi	Maori	ss	Siswati
mk	Macedonian	st	Sesotho
ml	Malayalam	su	Sundanese
mn	Mongolian	sv	Swedish
mo	Moldavian	sw	Swahili
mr	Marathi		
ms	Malay	ta	Tamil
mt	Maltese	te	Tegulu
my	Burmese	tg	Tajik
		th	Thai
na	Nauru	ti	Tigrinya
ne	Nepali	tk	Turkmen
nl	Dutch	tl	Tagalog
no	Norwegian	tn	Setswana
		to	Tonga
oc	Occitan	tr	Turkish
om	(Afan), Oromo	ts	Tsonga
or	Oriya	tt	Tatar
		tw	Twi
pa	Punjabi		
pl	Polish	uk	Ukrainian
ps	Pashto, Pushto	ur	Urdu
pt	Portuguese	uz	Uzbek
qu	Quechua	vi	Vietnamese
		vo	Volapuk
rm	Rhaeto-Romance		
rn	Kirundi	wo	Wolof
ro	Romanian		
ru	Russian	xh	Xhosa
rw	Kinyarwanda	yo	Yoruba
sa	Sanskrit	zh	Chinese
sd	Sindhi	zu	Zulu

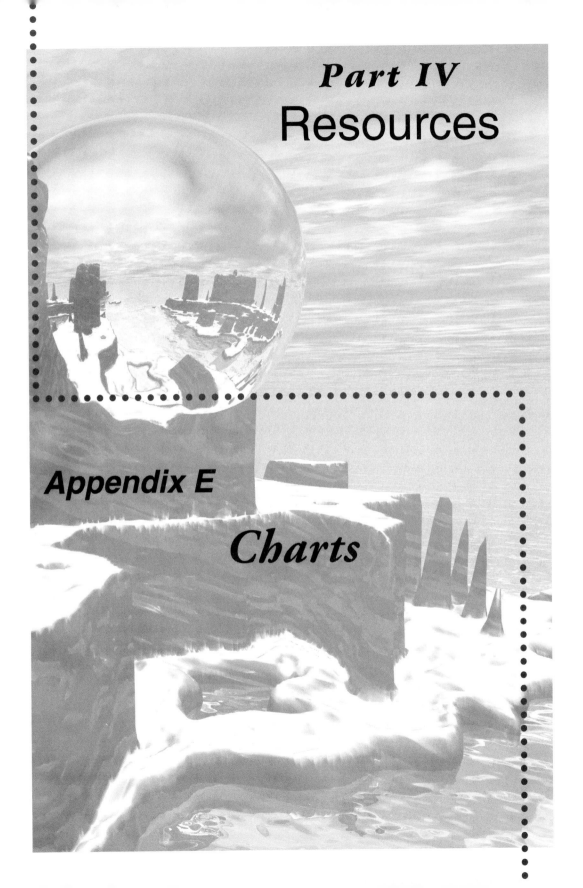

Part IV
Resources

Appendix E

Charts

∞∞

Property Name CSS Syntax	All Possible Categories	All Possible Values		
font-size	*absolute-size*	xx-small, x-small, small, medium, large, x-large, xx-large		
	relative-size	larger, smaller		
	length | percentage	10pt, 12pt, 14pt, 20pt, 24pt,... 20%, 25%, 50%, 80%, 120%,150%, 200%,...		
font-family	*any system font*	Helvetica, Times, Geneva, Courier,...		
font-weight	*keyword | number*	normal, bold, bolder, lighter | 100-900		
font-style	*keyword*	normal, italic		
line-height	*number*	multiplied by a number or decimal		
	length | percentage	em, ex, px, pt, pc, in, mm, cm	|	1%-1000%, ...n%
	keyword	normal		
text-decoration	*keyword*	none, underline, line-through, blink		
text-transform	*keyword*	capitalize, uppercase, lowercase, none		
text-align	*keyword*	left, right, center, justify		
text-indent	*length | percentage*	em, ex, px, pt, pc, in, mm, cm	|	1%-1000%, ...n%
margin	*length | percentage*	em, ex, px, pt, pc, in, mm, cm	|	1%-1000%, ...n%
	keyword	auto (is available for all 5 margin Properties)		
margin (example)		{ margin: 24pt 30pt 30pt 17pt; } sets each margin to diff. value		
		The order is: top right bottom left		
margin-top	*length | percentage*	em, ex, px, pt, pc, in, mm, cm	|	1%-1000%, ...n%
margin-right	*length | percentage*	em, ex, px, pt, pc, in, mm, cm	|	1%-1000%, ...n%
margin-bottom	*length | percentage*	em, ex, px, pt, pc, in, mm, cm	|	1%-1000%, ...n%
margin-left	*length | percentage*	em, ex, px, pt, pc, in, mm, cm	|	1%-1000%, ...n%
padding	*length | percentage*	em, ex, px, pt, pc, in, mm, cm	|	1%-1000%, ...n%
padding (example)		{ padding: 25px 20px 45px 35px; } sets each padding to diff. value		
padding-top	*length | percentage*	em, ex, px, pt, pc, in, mm, cm	|	1%-1000%, ...n%
padding-right	*length | percentage*	em, ex, px, pt, pc, in, mm, cm	|	1%-1000%, ...n%
padding-bottom	*length | percentage*	em, ex, px, pt, pc, in, mm, cm	|	1%-1000%, ...n%
padding-left	*length | percentage*	em, ex, px, pt, pc, in, mm, cm	|	1%-1000%, ...n%
color	*colorvalue*	none, <u>name</u>, #$$$$$$, rgb(0-255,0-255,0-255), rgb(?%,?%,?%)		
background-color	*colorvalue*	none, <u>name</u>, #$$$$$$, rgb(0-255,0-255,0-255), rgb(?%,?%,?%)		
the 16 color <u>names</u> are		aqua, black, blue, fuchsia, gray, green, lime, maroon,		
		navy, olive, purple, red, silver, teal, white, yellow		
background-image	*imageurl*	url( ) { background-image: url(JPEG-Images / ExampleImage.jpeg); }		
border-style	*keyword*	none, solid, double, inset, outset, groove, ridge		
border-color	*colorvalue*	none, <u>name</u>, #$$$$$$, rgb(0-255,0-255,0-255), rgb(?%,?%,?%)		
border-width	*length |percentage*	em, ex, px, pt, pc, in, mm, cm	|	1%-1000%, ...n%
border-width	*same*	{ border-width: 20px 30px 40px 50px; } sets each width to diff. value		
border-top-width	*length |percentage*	em, ex, px, pt, pc, in, mm, cm	|	1%-1000%, ...n%
border-right-width	*length |percentage*	em, ex, px, pt, pc, in, mm, cm	|	1%-1000%, ...n%
border-bottom-width	*length |percentage*	em, ex, px, pt, pc, in, mm, cm	|	1%-1000%, ...n%
border-left-width	*length |percentage*	em, ex, px, pt, pc, in, mm, cm	|	1%-1000%, ...n%
width	*length |percentage*	em, ex, px, pt, pc, in, mm, cm	|	1%-1000%, ...n%
	keyword	auto		
float	*keyword*	left, right, center, none		
clear	*keyword*	none, left, right, both		
display	*keyword*	block, inline, list-item		
list-style-type	*keyword*	disc, circle, square, decimal, lower-roman, upper-roman, lower-alpha,		
	keyword	upper-alpha, none		
white-space	*keyword*	normal, pre { white-space: pre; } { white-space: normal; }		

∞∞

CSS & JavaScript Syntax Property Comparison Chart

∞○

Property Name CSS Syntax	Property Name JavaScript Syntax	Simple CSS Syntax Examples
font-size	fontSize	{ font-size: 14pt; }
font-family	fontFamily	{ font-family: Helvetica, Times, Geneva, Courier; }
font-weight	fontWeight	{ font-weight: bold; }
font-style	fontStyle	{ font-style: italic; }
line-height	lineHeight	{ line-height: 22pt; }
text-decoration	textDecoration	{ text-decoration: underline; }
text-transform	textTransform	{ text-transform: uppercase; }
text-align	textAlign	{ text-align: right; }
text-indent	textIndent	{ text-indent: 40px; }
margin	margins( )	{ margin: 75px; } sets all 4 margins to same value
margin	margins( )	{ margin: 24pt 30pt 30pt 17pt; } sets each margin to diff. value
		The order is: top right bottom left
margin-top	marginTop	{ margin-top: 40mm; }
margin-right	marginRight	{ margin-right: 4cm; }
margin-bottom	marginBottom	{ margin-bottom: 12pc; }
margin-left	marginLeft	{ margin-left: 1in; }
padding	paddings( )	{ padding: 25px; }
padding	paddings( )	{ padding: 25pt 20px 45pt 35px; }
padding-top	paddingTop	{ padding-top:.5in; }
padding-right	paddingRight	{ padding-right: 25pt; }
padding-bottom	paddingBottom	{ padding-bottom: 15pt; }
padding-left	paddingLeft	{ padding-left: 5pt; }
color	color	{ color: blue; } { color:#0000ff; }
color	color	{ color: rgb(0%, 0%, 100%); } { color: rgb(0,20, 255); }
background-color	backgroundColor	{ background-color: maroon; } same options as color
background-image	backgroundImage	{ background-image: url(JPEG-Images/ExampleImage.jpeg); }
border-style	borderStyle	{ border-style: groove; }
border-color	borderColor	{ border-color:#335a77; }
border-color	borderColor	{ border-color: rgb(20%, 50%, 70%); }
border-color	borderColor	{ border-color: rgb(255, 20, 150); }
border-width	borderWidths( )	{ border-width: 20px; }
border-width	borderWidths( )	{ border-width: 20px 30px 40px 50px; }
border-top-width	borderTopWidth	{ border-top-width: 20px; }
border-right-width	borderRightWidth	{ border-right-width: 30px; }
border-bottom-width	borderBottomWidth	{ border-bottom-width: 40px; }
border-left-width	borderLeftWidth	{ border-left-width: 50px; }
width	width	{ width: 50%; } { width: 500px; } { width: 7in; }
float	align	{ float: left; } { float: right; } { float: center; }
clear	clear	{ clear: left; } { clear: right; } { clear: both; }
display	display	{ display: block; } { display: list-item; }
list-style-type	listStyleType	{ list-style-type: square; } { list-style-type: upper-roman; }
white-space	whiteSpace	{ white-space: pre; } { white-space: normal; }

∞○

absolute units		relative units
pt -- points	pc -- picas	em -- the height of the element's font
px -- pixels	in -- inches	ex -- half the height of the element's font
mm -- millimeters	cm -- centimeters	px -- pixels, relative to rendering surface

Note that in the chart on pages 11 and 195, for any of the Properties that have the scenario:

Possible Categories	Possible Values		
length	*percentage*	em, ex, px, pt, pc, in, mm, cm		1%-1000%, ...n%

It means that if you use a *length* type Value, then it should be a <u>number</u> suffixed by one of these units of measurement: em, ex, px, pt, pc, in, mm, cm, like this: "200px".

If you use a *percentage* type Value then it should be a <u>number</u> that is followed by a percent (%) sign, like this: "75%".

CSS Layer Properties and <LAYER> Attributes Chart

Notice that the <u>preceding</u> two charts do not include the Properties that are used to POSITION your content. Those are listed in the chart below within the Layers model.

Also note that there are no corresponding Properties in CSS Syntax for the LAYER Attributes of **PAGEX, PAGEY, ABOVE** and **BELOW** or the five Event Handlers.

∞∞

Property Name CSS Syntax	Attribute Name <LAYER> Syntax	Simple CSS Syntax Examples	Simple <LAYER> Syntax Examples
position		{ position: absolute; }	<LAYER></LAYER>
position		{ position: relative; }	<ILAYER></ILAYER>
#myLayerName	ID	{ position: absolute; }	ID="myLayerName"
left	LEFT	{ left: 40px; }	LEFT=40
top	TOP	{ top: 20px; }	TOP=20
	PAGEX		PAGEX=72
	PAGEY		PAGEY=144
width	WIDTH	{ width: 550px; }	WIDTH=550
height	HEIGHT	{ height: 400px; }	HEIGHT=400
clip	CLIP	{ clip: rect('10, 20, 30, 40'); }	CLIP="10, 20, 30, 40"
z-index	Z-INDEX	{ z-index: 3; }	Z-INDEX=3
	ABOVE		ABOVE="myLayerName5"
	BELOW		BELOW="myLayerName7"
visibility	VISIBILITY	{ visibility: show; }	VISIBILITY="SHOW"
background-color	BGCOLOR	{ background-color: purple; }	BGCOLOR="#0000ff"
layer-background-color		{ layer-background-color: blue; }	
background-image	BACKGROUND	{ background-image:url('image1.jpg'); }	BACKGROUND="image3.jpg"
layer-background-image		{ layer-background-image:url('image2.jpg'); }	
include-source	SRC	{ include-source: url('myPage.html'); }	SRC="myPage.html"
	onMouseOver		onMouseOver="JSCode"
	onMouseOut		onMouseOut="JSCode"
	onFocus		onFocus="JSCode"
	onBlur		onBlur="JSCode"
	onLoad		onLoad="JSCode"

∞∞

JavaScript Layer Object Properties Chart

∞∞∞

Layer Object Property Name JavaScript Syntax	Simple JavaScript Syntax Examples (assume there is a Layer named **myLayer1**)	Read-Only or Read/Write
document	document.write(document.myLayer1.document);	Read-Only
name	myVar=document.name;	Read-Only
left	document.myLayer1.left=20;	Read-Write
top	document.myLayer1.top=30;	Read-Write
pageX	document.myLayer1.pageX=10;	Read-Write
pageY	document.myLayer1.pageY=15;	Read-Write
zIndex	document.myLayer1.zIndex=7;	Read-Write
visibility	document.myLayer1.visibility="hide";	Read-Write
clip.top	document.myLayer1.clip.top=50;	Read-Write
clip.left	document.myLayer1.clip.left=-200;	Read-Write
clip.right	document.myLayer1.clip.right=700;	Read-Write
clip.bottom	document.myLayer1.clip.bottom=500;	Read-Write
clip.width	document.myLayer1.clip.width=640;	Read-Write
clip.height	document.myLayer1.clip.height=480;	Read-Write
background.src	document.myLayer1.background.src="myImage.jpeg";	Read-Write
bgColor	document.myLayer1.bgColor = "#ff0000";	Read-Write
	document.myLayer1.bgColor = "green";	Read-Write
	document.myLayer1.bgColor = null;	Read-Write
siblingAbove	document.myLayer1.siblingAbove;	Read-Only
siblingBelow	document.myLayer1.siblingBelow;	Read-Only
above	document.myLayer1.above;	Read-Only
below	document.myLayer1.below;	Read-Only
parentLayer	document.myLayer1.parentLayer;	Read-Only
src	document.myLayer1.src="myFile.html";	Read-Write

∞∞∞

Generic { font-family: } Names Chart

These are the *generic* Name Values for the **font-family** Property, followed by an example of each that the browser might select from the user's System Fonts:

Generic font-family Names	Example
serif	Times
sans-serif	Helvetica
cursive	Zapf-Chancery
fantasy	Western
monospace	Courier

Styles Chart for HTML Elements

This is a list of all the Elements, including those in HTML 4.0, that you can use the <u>STYLE Attribute</u> or the <u>CLASS Attribute</u> or the <u>ID Attribute</u> with:

∞∞∞

A	ACRONYM	ADDRESS	B
BIG	BLOCKQUOTE	BODY	BR
BUTTON	CAPTION	CENTER	CITE
CODE	COL	COLGROUP	DD
DEL	DFN	DIR	DIV
DL	DT	EM	FIELDSET
FORM	H1	H2	H3
H4	H5	H6	HR
I	IMG	INPUT	INS
ISINDEX	KBD	LABEL	LEGEND
LI	LINK	MAP	MENU
OBJECT	OL	OPTION	P
PRE	Q	S	SAMP
SELECT	SMALL	SPAN	STRIKE
STRONG	SUB	SUP	TABLE
TBODY	TD	TEXTAREA	TFOOT
TH	THEAD	TR	TT
U	UL	VAR	XMP

∞∞∞

You can also use them with the following Elements, but at the time of this writing, they will only work in Navigator 4.0+, but more than likely by the time you read this all the other major browsers will recognize them also. If you use cutting-edge code then you should create parallel code to include in Elements like <NOLAYER> and <NOSCRIPT> and additional pages with alternative content to cover all the cross-browser compatability issues. Note that Internet Explorer does not support Style Sheets with JavaScript Syntax.

ILAYER   LAYER

∞∞∞

Special Notice:

By default, a LAYER is transparent in the sense that other LAYERs that are beneath it will show through except in the places where the actual content, such as text or images, reside.

∞∞∞

Property Name JavaScript Syntax	Simple JavaScript Syntax Examples	
fontSize	tags.DIV.fontSize="14pt";	
fontFamily	tags.DIV.fontFamily="Helvetica, Times, Geneva, Courier";	
fontWeight	tags.DIV.fontWeight="bold";	
fontStyle	tags.DIV.fontStyle="italic";	
lineHeight	tags.DIV.lineHeight="22pt";	
textDecoration	tags.DIV.textDecoration="underline";	
textTransform	tags.DIV.textTransform="uppercase";	
textAlign	tags.DIV.textAlign="right";	
textIndent	tags.DIV.textIndent="40px";	
margins()	tags.DIV.margins("75px");	sets all 4 margins to same value
margins()	tags.DIV.margins("24pt", "30pt", "30pt", "17pt");	each margin with unique value Order is: top right bottom left
marginTop	tags.DIV.marginTop="40mm";	
marginRight	tags.DIV.marginRight="4cm";	
marginBottom	tags.DIV.marginBottom="12pc";	
marginLeft	tags.DIV.marginLeft="1in";	
paddings()	tags.DIV.paddings("25px");	
paddings()	tags.DIV.paddings("25pt", "20px", "45pt", "35px");	
paddingTop	tags.DIV.paddingTop="2in";	
paddingRight	tags.DIV.paddingRight="25pt";	
paddingBottom	tags.DIV.paddingBottom="15pt";	
paddingLeft	tags.DIV.paddingLeft="5pt";	
color	tags.DIV.color="blue";	tags.DIV.color="#0000ff";
color	tags.DIV.color="rgb(0%, 0%, 100%)";	tags.DIV.color="rgb(0,20, 255)";
backgroundColor	tags.DIV.backgroundColor="maroon";	
backgroundImage	tags.DIV.backgroundImage="JPEGImages/ExampleImage.jpeg";	
borderStyle	tags.DIV.borderStyle="groove";	
borderColor	tags.DIV.borderColor="#335a77";	
borderColor	tags.DIV.borderColor="rgb(20%, 50%, 70%)";	
borderColor	tags.DIV.borderColor="rgb(255, 20, 150)";	
borderWidths()	tags.DIV.borderWidths("20px");	
borderWidths()	tags.DIV.borderWidths("20px", "30px", "40px", "50px");	
borderTopWidth	tags.DIV.borderTopWidth="20px";	
borderRightWidth	tags.DIV.borderRightWidth="30px";	
borderBottomWidth	tags.DIV.borderBottomWidth="40px";	
borderLeftWidth	tags.DIV.borderLeftWidth="50px";	
width	tags.DIV.width="50%";	tags.DIV.width="500px";
align	tags.DIV.align="left";	tags.DIV.align="right";
align	tags.DIV.align="center";	tags.DIV.align="none";
clear	tags.DIV.clear="left";	tags.DIV.clear="right";
clear	tags.DIV.clear="both";	tags.DIV.clear="none";
display	tags.DIV.display="block";	tags.LI.display="listitem";
listStyleType	tags.LI.listStyleType="upperroman";	tags.LI.listStyleType="square";
whiteSpace	tags.DIV.whiteSpace="normal";	tags.PRE.whiteSpace="pre";

∞∞∞

∞∞∞

Property Name JavaScript Syntax	All Possible Categories	All Possible Values		
fontSize	*absolute-size*	xx-small, x-small, small, medium, large, x-large, xx-large		
	relative-size	larger, smaller		
	length | percentage	10pt, 12pt, 14pt, 20pt, 24pt,...	20%, 25%, 50%, 80%, 120%,150%, 200%,...	
fontFamily	*any system font*	Helvetica, Times, Geneva, Courier,... , (or any available Systemfont)		
fontWeight	*keyword | number*	normal, bold, bolder, lighter | 100-900		
fontStyle	*keyword*	normal, italic		
lineHeight	*number*	multiplied by a number or decimal		
	length | percentage	em, ex, px, pt, pc, in, mm, cm	|	1%-1000%, ...n%
	keyword	normal		
textDecoration	*keyword*	none, underline, line-through, blink		
textTransform	*keyword*	capitalize, uppercase, lowercase, none		
textAlign	*keyword*	left, right, center, justify		
textIndent	*length | percentage*	em, ex, px, pt, pc, in, mm, cm	|	1%-1000%, ...n%
margins()	*length | percentage*	em, ex, px, pt, pc, in, mm, cm	|	1%-1000%, ...n%
	keyword	auto (is available for all 5 margin Properties)		
margins() (example)		margins("24pt", "30pt", "30pt", "17pt");		
	sets each margin to diff. value	The order is: top right bottom left		
marginTop	*length | percentage*	em, ex, px, pt, pc, in, mm, cm	|	1%-1000%, ...n%
marginRight	*length | percentage*	em, ex, px, pt, pc, in, mm, cm	|	1%-1000%, ...n%
marginBottom	*length | percentage*	em, ex, px, pt, pc, in, mm, cm	|	1%-1000%, ...n%
marginLeft	*length | percentage*	em, ex, px, pt, pc, in, mm, cm	|	1%-1000%, ...n%
paddings()	*length | percentage*	em, ex, px, pt, pc, in, mm, cm	|	1%-1000%, ...n%
paddings() (example)		paddings("24px", "30px", "35px", "17px"); sets each padding to diff. value		
paddingTop	*length | percentage*	em, ex, px, pt, pc, in, mm, cm	|	1%-1000%, ...n%
paddingRight	*length | percentage*	em, ex, px, pt, pc, in, mm, cm	|	1%-1000%, ...n%
paddingBottom	*length | percentage*	em, ex, px, pt, pc, in, mm, cm	|	1%-1000%, ...n%
paddingLeft	*length | percentage*	em, ex, px, pt, pc, in, mm, cm	|	1%-1000%, ...n%
color	*colorvalue*	none, <u>name</u>, #$$$$$$, rgb(0-255,0-255,0-255), rgb(?%,?%,?%)		
backgroundColor	*colorvalue*	none, <u>name</u>, #$$$$$$, rgb(0-255,0-255,0-255), rgb(?%,?%,?%)		
(the 16 color <u>names</u> are)		aqua, black, blue, fuchsia, gray, green, lime, maroon, navy, olive, purple, red, silver, teal, white, yellow		
backgroundImage	*imageurl*	"url";		
backgroundImage	(example)	backgroundImage="JPEG-Images/ExampleImage.jpeg";		
borderStyle	*keyword*	none, solid, double, inset, outset, groove, ridge		
borderColor	*colorvalue*	none, <u>name</u>, #$$$$$$, rgb(0-255,0-255,0-255), rgb(?%,?%,?%)		
borderWidths()	*length | percentage*	em, ex, px, pt, pc, in, mm, cm	|	1%-1000%, ...n%
borderWidths()	*same*	borderWidths("20px", "30px", "40px", "50px");		
borderTopWidth	*length | percentage*	em, ex, px, pt, pc, in, mm, cm	|	1%-1000%, ...n%
borderRightWidth	*length | percentage*	em, ex, px, pt, pc, in, mm, cm	|	1%-1000%, ...n%
borderBottomWidth	*length | percentage*	em, ex, px, pt, pc, in, mm, cm	|	1%-1000%, ...n%
borderLeftWidth	*length | percentage*	em, ex, px, pt, pc, in, mm, cm	|	1%-1000%, ...n%
width	*length | percentage*	em, ex, px, pt, pc, in, mm, cm	|	1%-1000%, ...n%
	keyword	auto		
align	*keyword*	left, right, center,none		
clear	*keyword*	none, left, right, both		
display	*keyword*	block, inline, list-item		
listStyleType	*keyword*	disc, circle, square, decimal, lower-roman, upper-roman, lower-alpha,		
	keyword	upper-alpha, none		
whiteSpace	*keyword*	normal, pre		

∞∞∞

∞∞

Properties of the Layer Object

Here's a chart that lists all of the JavaScript **Layer** Object Properties and assumes in the Mini-Examples that **L1** is a Layer named with ID="L1" and **L2** is a Layer named with ID="L2" and is a nested Layer inside of Layer **L1**:

∞∞

Property	Mini-Example	Modifiable
document	document.L1.document.form1.text1.value= "any Text";	No
name	document.L1;	No
left	document.L1.document.L2.left=200;	Yes
top	document.L1.document.L2.top=300;	Yes
pageX	document.L1.pageX=100;	Yes
pageY	document.L1.pageX=150;	Yes
visibility	document.L1.visibility="hide";	Yes
zIndex	document.L1.document.L2.zIndex=5;	Yes
siblingAbove	document.L1.document.L2.siblingAbove;	No
siblingBelow	document.L1.document.L2.siblingBelow;	No
above	document.L1.above;	No
below	document.L1.below;	No
parentLayer	document.L2.parentLayer;	No
clip.top	document.L1.clip.top=50;	Yes
clip.left	document.L1.clip.left=30;	Yes
clip.bottom	document.L1.clip.bottom=450;	Yes
clip.right	document.L1.clip.right=690;	Yes
clip.width	document.L1.clip.width=555;	Yes
clip.height	document.L1.clip.right=444;	Yes
bgColor	document.L1.bgColor="blue";	Yes
background.src	document.L1.background.src="myImage.jpg";	Yes
src	document.L1.src="AnotherPage.html";	Yes

∞∞

Special Notice:

JavaScript **Layer** Object Property Names are case-sensitive.

∞∞

<u>Methods</u> of the Layer Object

All of the JavaScript Methods that work for **Layer** Objects can be used for Layers that are created with the LAYER Element or with JavaScript Style Sheet Syntax or CSS Style Sheet Syntax, and the Method Names are identical.

Currently, there are eight Methods that are specifically available to be invoked on a **Layer** Object to access or modify it. They are:

Method	Mini-Example
moveBy(dx, dy)	document.L1.moveBy(30, -40)
moveTo(x, y)	document.L1.moveTo(20, 90)
moveToAbsolute(x, y)	document.L1.moveToAbsolute(420, 340)
resizeBy(dwidth, dheight)	document.L1.resizeBy(-20, 30)
resizeTo(width, height)	document.L1.resizeTo(550, 350)
moveAbove(layerName)	document.L1.moveAbove(MyLayer5)
moveBelow(layerName)	document.L1.moveBelow(MyLayer3)
load("sourceURL", newPixelWidth)	document.L1.load("Sample400.html", 500)

The JavaScript Syntax to invoke a Method on a **Layer** Object is:

JavaScript Syntax:

```
layerObjectName.methodName(arguments)
```

Parameters Defined:

layerObjectName	The Name of the Layer or an expression that evaluates to a **Layer** Object
methodName	The Name of the Method
arguments	A comma-separated list of Arguments for the Method

Special Notice:

JavaScript **Layer** Object Method Names are case-sensitive.

Predefined JavaScript Objects

Here's an alphabetized list of all Predefined JavaScript Objects:

anchor			
applet			
area			
Array	See Chapter 7		
Boolean			
button			
checkbox			
Date	See Chapter 3,	page 307	
document	See Chapter 4,	page 432	
Event	See Chapter 6		
fileupload			
form			
frame			
Function	See Chapter 4,	pages 371-385, and Chapter 5,	page 505
hidden			
History	See Chapter 4,	page 452	
image			
Layer	See Chapter 3,	page 199	New in JavaScript 1.2
link			
Location	See Chapter 4,	page 447	
Math	See Chapter 3,	page 321	
mimetype			
navigator	See Chapter 4,	page 455	
Number	See Chapter 4,	page 460	
Object	See Chapter 4,	page 389	
option	See Chapter 4,	page 465	
password			
Plugin			
radio			
RegExp	See Chapter 9		
reset			
screen	See Chapter 4,	page 444	New in JavaScript 1.2
select	See Chapter 4,	page 462	
String	See Chapter 8		
submit			
text			
textarea			
window	See Chapter 4,	page 416	

Predefined JavaScript Arrays
as Object Properties

Certain JavaScript Objects have Properties that are actually Arrays of Objects, which are defined by the JavaScript compiler as the page loads, and they are based on the content that you provide. The following table specifies the Array Properties for their respective Objects where **i** is a zero-based integer **index**. These Arrays are also Core Objects.

Predefined JavaScript Arrays

Object	Property	Description
document	anchors[i]	An Array reflecting a document's <A> tags that contains a NAME attribute in source order.
	applets[i]	An Array reflecting a document's <APPLET> tags in source order.
	embeds[i]	An Array reflecting a document's <EMBED> tags in source order.
	forms[i]	An Array reflecting a document's <FORM> tags in source order.
	images[i]	An Array reflecting a document's <IMG> tags in source order. (This does not include images created with the Image() Constructor.)
	layers[i]	An Array reflecting a document's <LAYER> tags or Style Sheet Layers in source order.
	links[i]	An Array reflecting a document's <A HREF="..."> tags, <AREA HREF="..."> tags, and Link objects created with the **link()** Method in source order.
Function	arguments[i]	An Array reflecting the Arguments to a Function.
form	elements[i]	An Array reflecting a form's Elements in source order.
select	options[i]	An Array reflecting the <OPTION> tags in a Select object in source order.
window	frames[i]	An Array reflecting all the <FRAME> tags in a window containing a <FRAMESET> tag in source order.
	history[i]	An Array reflecting a window's URL history entries.
navigator	mimeTypes[i]	An Array reflecting all the MIME types supported by the client, including internal, helper applications, or plug-ins.
	plugins[i]	An Array reflecting all the plug-ins installed on the client in source order.

∞∞∞

Predefined JavaScript Core Objects

Certain JavaScript Objects are said to be "top-level" Core Objects because they are built into the language itself. They are:

Predefined Core Objects

Array	See Chapter 7
Boolean	See the JavaScript Reference
Date	See Chapter 3
Function	See Chapter 4
Math	See Chapter 3
Number	See Chapter 4
RegExp	See Chapter 9
String	See Chapter 8

∞∞∞

Predefined JavaScript Core Functions

Certain JavaScript Functions are said to be "top-level" Core Functions because they are built into the language itself. They are:

Predefined Core Functions

escape()	See Chapter 4,	page 439
unescape()	See Chapter 4,	pages 439, 442-443
eval()		
isNaN()	See Chapter 3,	page 338
Number()	See Chapter 4,	page 467
parseFloat()	See Chapter 3,	page 337
parseInt()	See Chapter 3,	page 337
String()	See Chapter 4,	page 468
taint()		
untaint()		

Window Properties

Property	Description
closed	Boolean with a value of true if a Window that you opened is now closed. Once you close a Window, you should not refer to it unless, of course, you reopen it with the **open()** Method.
defaultStatus	A settable Property that specifies the default message to be displayed in the status bar at the bottom of the Window when no priority message specified by the **status** Property is to be displayed, such as when an onMouseOver Event occurs.
document	Accesses the Properties and Methods of the **document** Object to render output to the browser. See the next section on the **document** Object.
frames[i]	An Array that reflects all the Frames in a Window in source order. You can access a Frame by its Name Attribute or by its index number. For the Frame named **myFrame3** that is the third Frame in a Frameset: `parent.frames["myFrame3"]` is equivalent to: `parent.frames[2]` and is equivalent to: `parent.myFrame3` Its **length** Property reflects the number of Frames in the Window. The **name** Property of each Array Element reflects the name of that Frame.
history[i]	An Array reflecting a Window's history of URL entries that the user has visited in source order. Accesses the **History** Object. See Example 4-33.
innerHeight	Specifies in pixels the vertical size of the space reserved for insertion of content for the Window.
innerWidth	Specifies in pixels the horizontal size of the space reserved for insertion of content for the Window.
length	A read-only integer reflecting the number of Frames in the Window. **window.length** is equivalent to **parent.frames.length**
location	Reflects the information about the current URL of the Window contained in the Window's associated **Location** Object. When referring to the **Location** Object, you must use **window.location** instead of just **location**.
locationbar	Represents the location bar of the Window where the URL of the current document is displayed. It has one Property of **visible** which can be set to **"false"** to hide the location bar and **"true"** to show it.**
menubar	Represents the menu bar of the Window where the pull-down menus such as File, Edit, View, and Go reside. It has one Property of **visible**, which can be set to **"false"** to hide the menu bar and **"true"** to show it.**
name	The unique identifier, that is, the name used to refer to a Window. This is a read/write Property as of Navigator 3.0.

** To use this Property requires that the **UniversalBrowserWrite** privilege be secured for security purposes. For more information, see the section on JavaScript Security in the JavaScript Guide or the section on the **window** Object in the JavaScript Reference.

Property	Description
opener	Specifies the name of the Window that is the calling document when the **open()** Method is used to open a new Window. Navigator allows up to 100 open Windows at the same time. To free up system resources, be sure to set the **opener** Property to **null** if you are done with the calling Window.
outerHeight	Specifies, in pixels, the vertical size of the Window's total outside edge, which includes the status bar, scroll bars, menu bar, and tool bars, which are termed the "chrome" elements of a Window.
outerWidth	Specifies, in pixels, the horizontal size of the Window's total outside edge which includes the status bar, scroll bars, menu bar and tool bars which are termed the "chrome" elements of a Window.
pageXOffset	Specifies the horizontal distance that the current position of the page is offset from the upper-left origin point of (0,0) of the document. An integer that can be positive or negative or zero and is measured in pixels.
pageYOffset	Specifies the vertical distance that the current position of the page is offset from the upper-left origin point of (0,0) of the document. An integer that can be positive or negative or zero and is measured in pixels.
parent	The generic synonym for a Frameset Window that contains the current Frame. This allows you to manipulate the contents in one Frame from within another Frame. For multiple nested Framesets use an extra **parent** for each level of nesting such as: **parent.parent.frameName** for 1 nesting.
personalbar	Represents the personal bar of the Window where the user can have easy access to bookmarks. It has one Property of **visible** which can be set to "false" to hide the personal bar and "true" to show it.**
scrollbars	Represents the scroll bars of the Window so the user can scroll the page horizontally and vertically. It has one Property of **visible**, which can be set to **"false"** to hide the scroll bars and **"true"** to show them.**
self	Refers to the current Window. This Property is identical to the **window** Property below, but with an arguably more intuitive name.
status	A settable Property that specifies the priority message to be displayed in the status bar at the bottom of the Window. This is a transient message that temporarily overrides the **defaultstatus** message when an Event such as onMouseOut occurs.
statusbar	Refers to the status bar at the bottom of the browser Window where the default status and status messages are displayed and other icons reside.
toolbar	Represents the tool bar of the Window where the back, forward, home, and other buttons reside. It has one Property of **visible**, which can be set to **"false"** to hide the tool bar and **"true"** to show it.**
top	Refers to the top-most Window, the ancestor of all other child Windows or Frames in the page.
window	Refers to the current Window.

** To use this Property requires that the **UniversalBrowserWrite** privilege be secured for security purposes. For more information see the section on JavaScript Security in the JavaScript Guide or the section on the **window** Object in the JavaScript Reference.

Window Methods

Method	Description
alert("message")	Specifies a **message** String to the user in an Alert dialog box with an OK button when no decision or user feedback is required. To custom design your own Alert dialog box, use the **open()** Method.
back()	Loads the previous URL of the top-level Window. To load the previous URL of the current Window or Frame, use **history.back()**.
blur()	Removes focus from the specified Window or Frame.
captureEvents(Event.EVENTNAME [| Event.EVENTNAME])	Causes the Window to capture all Events of the specified type. Note that the EVENTNAME such as KEYPRESS or CLICK is always specified in all uppercase and is always preceded by **Event.** and separated by (|) if more than one Event is used. See Chapter 6 on Events for details.
clearInterval(intervalID)	Cancels the timeout specified by **intervalID** that was set with the **setInterval()** Method. See pages 284, 286-287 for details.
clearTimeout(timeoutID)	Cancels the timeout specified by **timeoutID** that was set with the **setTimeout()** Method. See pages 250, 288-289 for details.
close()	Closes the Window specified by a **windowReference** like this: **myWindow.close()**. If no **windowReference** is specified, then the current Window is closed. See page 427 for details.
confirm("message")	Specifies a **message** String to the user in a Confirm dialog box with OK and Cancel buttons when a decision is required by the user.
disableExternalCapture()	Lets you disable external Event capturing that was set by the **enableExternalCapture()** Method.
enableExternalCapture()	Lets you capture Events in Frames that contain pages that have been loaded from different server locations.
find(["searchString"][, casesensitive][, backward])	Returns true if the specified **searchString** is found in the contents of the specified Window or Frame. The **backward** Argument is a Boolean that, if included, performs a search toward the start of the page and also requires the **casesensitive** Boolean to be included. See the JavaScript Reference on the CD-ROM for details.

focus()   Gives focus to the specified Window or Frame. For Frames, this is indicated by a visual cue like a cyan border on most platforms.

forward()   Simulates the user clicking on the Forward Button in the browser Navigation Bar, which is the same as loading the next URL in the history list. To load the previous URL of the current Window or Frame, use **history.forward()**.

handleEvent(eventArg) Calls the Event handler for the specified **eventArg**. This Method is always used in tandem with the **routeEvent()** Method. See Chapter 6 on pages 668-677 on Events for complete details.

home()   Loads the URL for the home page that the user specified in the preferences of the browser.

moveBy(x, y)   Moves the Window by the specified number of horizontal **x** and vertical **y** pixels, which can be positive or negative integers or zero.

moveTo(x, y)   Moves the top-left corner of the Window to the specified horizontal **x** and vertical **y** screen coordinates where (x, y) is measured down and to the right if positive and up and to the left if negative, from a (0, 0) origin at the top-left of the screen. To move any part of the Window off-screen requires that the **UniversalBrowserWrite** privilege be secured in a signed Script.

open("URL", "windowName", "windowFeatures")   Opens a new browser Window. See pages 422-428 for details.

print()   Prints the contents of the current Window or Frame that has focus.

prompt("message", [defaultInput])   Specify a **message** String to the user in a Prompt dialog box with an input field for user response data. OK and Cancel buttons respectively allow or disallow the data to be incorporated into a Script although the Script ultimately has control over how the data is used.

releaseEvents(Event.EVENTNAME | Event.EVENTNAME)   Releases the specified Event Types that were set to be captured by the **captureEvents()** Method so they will progress in the Event hierarchy. See Chapter 6 on Events for complete details.

resizeBy(x, y)   Resizes the bottom-right corner of the Window by the specified number of horizontal **x** and vertical **y** pixels, which can be positive or negative integers or zero.

resizeTo(x, y)   Resizes the entire Window by the specified number of horizontal **x** and vertical **y** pixels that represent the outer width and outer height dimensions.

routeEvent(eventArg)   Causes an Event that was captured with the **captureEvents()** Method to be passed along the normal Event hierarchy to its original target, unless another Object captures it along the way. See Chapter 6 on Events for complete details.

scroll(x, y)   Deprecated in favor of **scrollBy()** and **scrollTo()**, which have added flexibility and are more intuitively named.

scrollBy(x, y)   Scrolls the visible area of the Window by the specified number of horizontal **x** and vertical **y**, positive, negative, or zero pixels.

scrollTo(x, y)   Scrolls the visible area of the Window so that the specified (x, y) coordinate becomes the current top-left corner of the Window.

setInterval('expression', milliseconds)
setInterval('functionName()', milliseconds, [arg1, arg2, ..., argN])

The **setInterval()** Method has two syntax formats. It can evaluate an **expression** or call a Function specified by **functionName()** repeatedly after the specified number of milliseconds have elapsed.
See pages 284, 286-287 for details and examples.

setTimeout('expression', milliseconds)
setTimeout('functionName()', milliseconds, [arg1, arg2, ..., argN])

The **setTimeout()** Method has two syntax formats. It can evaluate an **expression** or call a Function specified by **functionName()** once after the specified number of milliseconds have elapsed.
See pages 250, 288-289 for details and examples.

stop()   Halts the URL that is currently being downloaded.

Document Properties

Property	Description
alinkColor	A String that contains the Value of the ALINK Attribute.
anchors[i]	An Array reflecting each Anchor in the document in source order.
applets[i]	An Array reflecting each Applet in the document in source order.
bgColor	A String that contains the Value of the BGCOLOR Attribute.
cookie	A Cookie. See pages 436-443 for details and examples.
domain	Specifies the server's domain name that served the current document.
embeds[i]	An Array reflecting each Embed in the document in source order.
fgColor	A String that contains the Value of the TEXT Attribute.
formName	For each named Form in the document, there is a **formName** Property that is specified by that Form's NAME Attribute Value. For instance, for <FORM NAME="myForm1"> the **formName** Property is set to **myForm1**. For a second Form in the document there is also a **formName** Property, so for <FORM NAME="theForm2">, the **formName** Property is **theForm2**.
forms[i]	An Array reflecting each Form in the document in source order.
images[i]	An Array reflecting each Image in the document in source order.
lastModified	A String containing the document's last modification date.
layers[i]	An Array reflecting each Layer in the document in source order.
linkColor	A String that contains the Value of the LINK Attribute.
links[i]	An Array reflecting each Link in the document in source order.
plugins[i]	An Array reflecting each plug-in in the document in source order.
referrer	A String containing the URL of the calling document.
title	A String that contains the content between the TITLE Tags.
URL	A String that contains the document's complete URL.

Document Properties (continued)

<u>Property</u>   <u>Description</u>

vlinkColor   A String that contains the Value of the VLINK Attribute.

The following Methods that are prefaced with three asterisks (***) are new for Navigator 4.0 and you can see Chapter 6 on the **Event** Object for details and examples.

Document Methods

<u>Method</u>   <u>Description</u>

captureEvents() ***Captures all Events of the specified type for the **document** Object.

close()   Closes a data stream and forces the contents of the **write()** or **writeln()** Methods to display.

getSelection() Returns a string containing the currently selected text that is highlighted by the user or selected by the Script. New for Navigator 4.0.

handleEvent()   ***Calls the Event Handler for the specified Event.

open()   Opens a data stream to collect the contents of the **write()** or **writeln()** Methods.

releaseEvents() ***Releases the specified Event Types that were set to be captured by the **captureEvents()** Method of the **document** Object so that they will progress naturally in the Event hierarchy.

routeEvent()   ***Forwards a captured Event through the normal Event hierarchy unless it is captured by another Object. Used in conjunction with **handleEvent()**.

write()   Renders HTML expressions, including Dynamic HTML and regular text to the **document** Object for the specified Window or Frame. It will also execute JavaScript code within the context of the newly created HTML. Additionally you can include JavaScript within one or more SCRIPT Elements for the page. Remember that HTML and regular text Strings must be enclosed in quotes or double quotes while executable JavaScript Expressions and Variables are not. This is an extremely useful Method.

writeln()   Same as the **write()** Method with the addition of an automatically appended new line (carriage return) character.

Screen Properties

Property	Description
availHeight	Specifies, in pixels, the height of the display screen after subtracting the space allotted for any graphical user interface (GUI) features of the operating system that are either permanent or semipermanent.
availWidth	Specifies, in pixels, the width of the display screen after subtracting the space allotted for any graphical user interface (GUI) features of the operating system that are either permanent or semipermanent.
colorDepth	If a color palette is in use, then its bit depth is specified. If no color palette is in use, then **screen.pixelDepth** provides the Value.
height	Specifies, in pixels, the height of the display screen.
pixelDepth	Specifies the resolution of the display screen in bits per pixel.
width	Specifies, in pixels, the width of the display screen.

General URL Syntax:

```
protocol//host:port/pathname#hash?search
```

Protocol	URL Type	Example
about:	Navigator info	about: (Same as about Communicator from menu) about:cache about:plugins
file:/	File	file:///myBook/testFiles/Sample22.html
ftp:	FTP	ftp://ftp.myDomainName.com/myFolder/myFile
gopher:	Gopher	gopher.myHost.com
http:	World Wide Web	http://www.myDomainName.com/
javascript:	JavaScript code	javascript:document.bgColor="blue"
mailto:	MailTo	mailto:gilorien@erols.com
news:	Usenet	news://news.erols.com/vrml
view-source:	source code viewer	view-source:wysiwyg://0/file:/cl/temp/myDoc.html

Location Properties

Property	Description
hash	A String that specifies the Anchor name part of the URL, including the hash (#) sign. Setting the **hash** Property jumps the page to that Anchor without reloading the document, but if the Anchor can't be found, you will get an error; therefore, it is safer to use the **href** Property, which only produces an Alert Window if the Anchor isn't found. The **hash** Property only applies to URLs that are of the HTTP type.
host	A String that specifies the network host, which consists of the server name, subdomain name, and domain name. This is a substring of the **hostname** Property.
hostname	A String that specifies the host:port part of the URL, including the colon.
href	A String that specifies the complete URL.
pathname	A String that specifies the pathname portion of the URL.
port	A String that specifies port part of the URL, which is the communications port that the server uses.
protocol	A String that specifies protocol part of the URL, which is the beginning of the URL, including the colon.
search	A String that specifies a search query, which begins with a question mark and is followed by **variable=value** pairs that are separated by an ampersand sign(**&**). For instance:

```
?x=2&y=5&z=7
```

The **search** Property only applies to URLs that are of the HTTP type.

Location Methods

Method	Description
reload([forceGet])	Reloads the current document into window. Same as **history(0)**. If the optional **forceGet** Boolean is set to **true**, then the server is forced to reload the page unconditionally. Otherwise, the user preferences determine whether the page is reloaded from cache or reloaded from the server.
replace("URL")	Loads the specified URL instead of the current document.

History Properties

Property	Description
current	Specifies the current URL in the **history[i]** Array.
length	Reflects the number of URL entries in the **history[i]** Array.
next	Specifies the next URL in the **history[i]** Array.
previous	Specifies the previous URL in the **history[i]** Array.

History Methods

Method	Description
back()	Loads the previous URL from the **history[i]** Array.
forward()	Loads the next URL from the **history[i]** Array.
go("location")	Loads a URL from the **history[i]** Array where **location** is a String that specifies either a full or partial URL.
go(integer)	Loads a URL from the **history** Array where **integer** is either zero or a positive or negative integer that specifies a relative position in the **history[i]** Array. If zero, the current page is reloaded. If positive, then the URL is loaded that is **integer** number of positions offset from the current URL position in the Array. If negative, the offset is in the opposite direction.

Navigator Properties

Property	Description
appCodeName	Specifies the browser's code name.
appName	Specifies the browser's name.
appVersion	Specifies Navigator's version number.
language	Specifies the language translation for the displayed content, like English.
mimeTypes[i]	An Array reflecting each MIME type supported by the user.
platform	Specifies the machine type, not OS, that Navigator was compiled for. Some possible Values are: Mac68k, MacPPC, Win16, Win32.
plugins[i]	An Array reflecting each plug-in currently configured by the user.
userAgent	Specifies the User Agent header.

Navigator Methods

Method	Description
javaEnabled()	Returns true if Java is enabled. Returns false if Java is not enabled.
plugins.refresh(false)	If **false** supplied, the newly installed plug-ins are made available.
plugins.refresh(true)	If **true** supplied, the newly installed plug-ins are made available and any open documents with EMBED Elements are reloaded.
preference("prefName")	Returns the Value of the **prefName** Preference.
preference("prefName", setValue)	Sets the Value of the **prefName** Preference with the **setValue** Argument and returns that Value. This must be set in a Signed Script.

Number Properties

Property	Description
MAX_VALUE	Has a Value that is the largest number that JavaScript can represent which is approximately 1.79E+308. It is a read-only Static Property of Number that is always invoked as **Number.MAX_VALUE** instead of as a Property of a Number Object that you have created. Larger numbers overflow to Infinity.
MIN_VALUE	Has a Value that is the smallest number <u>as it approaches zero</u> that JavaScript can represent, which is approximately 2.22E-308. Note that this is not the smallest negative number. It is a read-only Static Property of Number that is always invoked as **Number.MIN_VALUE**. Smaller numbers overflow to zero.
NaN	Has a Value of NaN that represents Not-a-Number which is a Literal that is not enclosed in quotes. It is always unequal to any number and is even unequal to itself. You can't use NaN as a test parameter in a conditional, but you can use the Global Function **isNaN(value)** to test whether a value is a number or NaN.
NEGATIVE_INFINITY	Has a Value of **"-Infinity"**, which represents and behaves like mathematical negative infinity. It is returned on overflow. It is a read-only Static Property of Number that is always invoked as **Number.NEGATIVE_INFINITY**.
POSITIVE_INFINITY	Has a Value of **"Infinity"**, which represents and behaves like mathematical positive infinity. It is returned on overflow. It is a read-only Static Property of Number that is always invoked as **Number.POSITIVE_INFINITY**.
prototype	Lets you create your own Properties for a **Number** Object.

Number Methods

Method	Description
toString([radix])	Converts the **Number** Object to a String and returns that String. The optional **radix** Argument specifies a number from 2 to 16, which is the base for the conversion. If unspecified, the default Value is 10. You can't use this Method on numeric literals.

JavaScript Syntax for Select Properties:

```
document.formName.selectName.propertyName;
document.formName.elements[index].propertyName;
```

Select Properties

Property	Description
form	A read-only Property that reflects the **form** Object that contains the current **select** Object.
length	Reflects the number of **option** Object Elements in the **options[i]** Array.
name	Reflects the NAME Attribute of the **select** Object.
options[i]	An Array that reflects an **option** Object in each Array Element.
selectedIndex	An integer that specifies the zero-based index of the currently selected **option** Object. If multiple **option** Objects are selected then the first one in the list is reflected. You can set this Property, which causes a different **option** Object to be currently selected.
type	The Value of **type** is **"select-one"** if the Object is a **select** Object. The Value of **type** is **"select-multiple"** if the Object is a **select** Object and the Boolean MULTIPLE Attribute is included in the HTML SELECT Element. This is a read-only Property.

JavaScript Syntax for Select Methods:

```
document.formName.selectName.methodName(parameters)
document.formName.elements[index].methodName(parameters)
```

Select Methods

Method	Description
blur()	Removes focus from the **select** Object.
focus()	Gives focus to the **select** Object.
handleEvent()	Invokes the Event Handler for the specified Event.

options[i] Array Properties

Property   Description

length   Reflects the number of Options in the Array.

selectedIndex Reflects the zero-based index number of the currently selected Option.

options[i] Array Element Properties

Property   Description

defaultSelected Reflects whether an **option** has the SELECTED Attribute or not. If it does the Value is **true** and **false** otherwise.

index   Reflects the zero-based **index** number of the **option**.

selected   Reflects whether the **option** is currently selected or not. This is a Boolean Property that is **true** if the **option** is selected and **false** if not selected.

text   Reflects the text String contained in the VALUE Attribute for the **option**.

value   Reflects the current VALUE Attribute of the **option**, which is returned to the server as a VALUE=value pair if the form is submitted.

option Object Properties

Property   Description

defaultSelected Specifies the **option**'s initial selection state with a Value of **true** if selected or **false** if it isn't selected.

index   Specifies the zero-based **index** number of the **option**.

prototype   Lets you create new Properties for the **option** Object.

selected   Specifies the **option** 's current selection state. This is a Boolean Property that has a Value of **true** if the **option** is selected and **false** if not selected.

text   Specifies a text String for the **option** that is displayed in the **select** Object.

value   Specifies the current VALUE Attribute of the **option** which is returned to the server as a Value=value pair if the form is submitted.

∞∞

Chart of all JavaScript Statements

Statement	Terse Definition
break	Ends the current **while** or **for** Loop that contains it and transfers program control to the statement immediately following the terminated Loop.
comment	Explanatory author's notes that are ignored by the JavaScript interpreter.
continue	Halts the block of Statements in a **while** Loop and jumps back to the condition. Halts the block of Statements in a **for** Loop and jumps back to the update Expression.
delete	Destroys the Property of an Object or an Element in an Array.
do...while	As long as the test condition is true, the preceding block of Statements are executed and always executed at least once by preceding the condition.
export	Provides Functions, Objects, and Properties within a Signed Script to other Signed or Unsigned Scripts.
for	Loop Statement that executes a block of Statements based on the parameters of its three optional Expressions, which are inside paretheses and separated by a semicolon.
for...in	Object Manipulation Statement that executes a block of Statements for each Property of an Object using a specified variable.
function	Statement that defines comma-separated, parenthesed Arguments and a named block of Statements that are enclosed in curly braces, which are executed as a unit when called. Arguments can be Strings, Numbers, or Objects. See pages 371-385, 505.
if	Statement that executes a block of statements once, if a specified condition is true or an Expression evaluates to true. If false, nothing happens.
if...else	Statement that executes a block of Statements once, if a specified condition is true or an Expression evaluates to true. If the condition is false, an alternative block of Statements is executed.
? :	Conditional Operator Statement. Shorthand for **if ()...else**.
import	Statement used by a Script to import Functions, Objects, and Properties from a Signed Script that has previously exported them.
labeled	A named Statement with its name separated from its block of Statements by a colon. The **break** or **continue** Statements use this name as the jump point for the program's continuation of Statement execution.
return	Statement specifying the value to be returned by a Function call.
switch	Conditional Statement that executes alternative Statements based on whether an evaluated Expression matches the value of the case labels.
var	Statement declaring a Variable, optionally assigning a value to it.
while	Loop Statement that executes a block of Statements as long as the determining Expression evaluates to true.
with	Statement identifying a default Object to apply a block of Statements to.

Event Objects and Event Handlers

The following is a list of the JavaScript **Event** Objects and **Event** Handlers. Remember that JavaScript is case-sensitive; if you are writing code specifically for versions of JavaScript prior to version 1.2, then both the **Event** Object and the **Event** Handler must be in all lowercase. Netscape claims that since JavaScript1.2 you can write the **Event** Handlers in the more familiar interCap way as seen below, but I've found it buggy and unreliable to do so for Events that are assigned by Property Assignment. For Events that are assigned by Attribute Assignment, it is still fine. See pages 530-533 for information on Property Assignment and Attribute Assignment of Events. Note that the **dblclick** Event is not implemented on the Macintosh platform.

Event Object	Event Handler	Objects the Event is built-in for, (uncaptured):
abort	onAbort	images
blur	onBlur	windows (<BODY>), layers, form elements
change	onChange	text fields, textareas, select lists
click	onClick	all types of buttons
		documents, links, checkboxes
dblclick	onDblClick	documents, areas, links
dragdrop	onDragDrop	windows
error	onError	images, windows
focus	onFocus	windows (<BODY>), layers, form elements
keydown	onKeyDown	documents, images, links, textareas
keypress	onKeyPress	documents, images, links, textareas
keyup	onKeyUp	documents, images, links, textareas
load	onLoad	windows (<BODY>), images, layers
mousedown	onMouseDown	documents, buttons, links
mousemove	onMouseMove	nothing by default
mouseout	onMouseOut	areas, links, layers
mouseover	onMouseOver	areas, links, layers
mouseup	onMouseUp	documents, buttons, links
move	onMove	windows
reset	onReset	forms
resize	onResize	windows
select	onSelect	text fields, textareas
submit	onSubmit	forms
unload	onUnload	windows (<BODY>)

Event Properties Summaries Chart

Event Properties:

Property	Description
type	Returns a String that represents the type of Event like **"click"**, **"mousedown"**, or **"keypress"**.
target	Returns a Reference that represents the Object to which the Event was originally sent. For a Button named "b1", (**event.target.name == "b1"**) would return true when that Button is clicked. Note that you access the **target** Property via its **name** Property.
layerX	Returns a Number that specifies the cursor's horizontal **x**-coordinate in pixels relative to the <u>Layer</u> in which the Event occurred, unless the **resize** Event occurs. In that case, it passes the Object's Width when passed along with the **resize** Event.
layerY	Returns a Number that specifies the cursor's vertical **y**-coordinate in pixels relative to the <u>Layer</u> in which the Event occurred, unless the **resize** Event occurs. In that case it passes the Object's Height when passed along with the **resize** Event.
width	Same as **layerX** but more intuitive syntax for the **resize** Event.
height	Same as **layerY** but more intuitive syntax for the **resize** Event.
x	Same as **layerX**.
y	Same as **layerY**.
pageX	Returns a Number that specifies the cursor's horizontal **x**-coordinate in pixels, relative to the page.
pageY	Returns a Number that specifies the cursor's vertical **y**-coordinate in pixels relative to the page.
screenX	Returns a Number that specifies the cursor's horizontal **x**-coordinate in pixels, relative to the screen.
screenY	Returns a Number that specifies the cursor's vertical **y**-coordinate in pixels, relative to the screen.
data	Returns an Array of Strings consisting of the URLs of all Objects that are dropped into the Window and passes them with the **dragdrop** Event.
which	Returns an Integer that specifies the ASCII Value of a Key that was pressed or the ASCII Value of the mouse button that was pressed.
modifiers	Returns an Integer that specifies the ASCII Value of the **modifiers** Key that was pressed in association with a mouse or Key Event. The **modifiers** Key Constant Values are: ALT_MASK, CONTROL_MASK, SHIFT_MASK, and META_MASK. Their associated ASCII Integer Values when used both individually and in various combinations are listed in the following chart.

∞∞∞

Available Event Properties for each Event Object

The following Chart specifes the **Event** Object Properties that are available for each **Event** Object. Once again, the **dblclick** Event is not implemented on the Macintosh.

Event Object   Available Event Properties

abort   type, target
blur   type, target
change   type, target
click   type, target, which, modifiers
               Note: When a Link, Layer or the Document or Window is clicked, the
               following six Properties represent the mouse cursor location,
               but are unused if a Button is clicked:
               layerX, layerY, pageX, pageY, screenX, screenY

dblclick   type, target, which, modifiers,
               layerX, layerY, pageX, pageY, screenX, screenY
dragdrop   type, target, data
error   type, target
focus   type, target
keydown   type, target, which, modifiers,
               layerX, layerY, pageX, pageY, screenX, screenY
keypress   type, target, which, modifiers,
               layerX, layerY, pageX, pageY, screenX, screenY
keyup   type, target, which, modifiers,
               layerX, layerY, pageX, pageY, screenX, screenY
load   type, target
mousedown   type, target, which, modifiers,
               layerX, layerY, pageX, pageY, screenX, screenY
mousemove   type, target, layerX, layerY, pageX, pageY, screenX, screenY
mouseout   type, target, layerX, layerY, pageX, pageY, screenX, screenY
mouseover   type, target, layerX, layerY, pageX, pageY, screenX, screenY
mouseup   type, target, which, modifiers,
               layerX, layerY, pageX, pageY, screenX, screenY
move   type, target, screenX, screenY
reset   type, target
resize   type, target, width, height
select   type, target
submit   type, target
unload   type, target

Modifiers Keys and ASCII Values Chart

This chart shows the ASCII Value that is returned to the **modifiers** Property when a mouse or keystroke Event occurs. If no Modifiers Key is used, then **modifiers=0**.

Modifiers Key and/or combination			ASCII Value
ALT_MASK	(the Apple Option Key)	=	1
CONTROL_MASK		=	2
ALT_MASK + CONTROL_MASK		=	3
SHIFT_MASK		=	4
ALT_MASK + SHIFT_MASK		=	5
CONTROL_MASK + SHIFT_MASK		=	6
ALT_MASK + CONTROL_MASK + SHIFT_MASK		=	7
META_MASK	(the Apple Command Key)	=	8
META_MASK + ALT_MASK		=	9
META_MASK + CONTROL_MASK		=	10
META_MASK + ALT_MASK + CONTROL_MASK		=	11
META_MASK + SHIFT_MASK		=	12
META_MASK + SHIFT_MASK + ALT_MASK		=	13
META_MASK + SHIFT_MASK + CONTROL_MASK		=	14
META_MASK + SHIFT_MASK + CONTROL_MASK + ALT_MASK		=	15
If no Modifiers Keys are used for an Event, then **modifiers**		=	0

Array Property Summaries

Property	Description
index	The zero-based integer index of the match to a String for an Array that is created as a result of a Regular Expression match.
input	Represents the original String that matched the Regular Expression for an Array that is created as a result of a Regular Expression match.
length	An Integer representing the precise number of Elements in an Array. It can be set to truncate Elements but not to extend the number of Elements.
prototype	Used to create your own Properties for all **Array** Objects in a Script.

Array Method Summaries

Method	Description
concat()	Combines two Arrays and returns a new Array that's "one level deep".
join()	Takes all Elements of an Array and converts them into one String where each Element is separated by a comma or, optionally, your own separator.
pop()	Removes and returns the last Element of an Array, changing its **length**.
push()	Adds Element(s) to the end of an Array, returns the last added Element, and changes the **length** of the Array.
reverse()	Reverses the physical order of the Elements in an Array.
shift()	Extracts the first Element of an Array and returns that Element.
slice()	Extracts a selectable portion of an Array and returns a new Array.
splice()	Optionally adds, removes, or adds and removes Elements from an Array.
sort()	Sorts the Elements of an Array lexicographically or by your Function.
toString()	Returns a String that represents the calling **Array** Object or Element.
unshift()	Adds one or more Elements before the first Element of an Array and returns the new **length** of the Array. Does not return the first Element.

String Object Property Summaries

<u>Property</u>	<u>Description</u>
length	Reflects the number of Characters in a String. This is <u>read-only</u>.
prototype	Lets you create your own Properties for the **String** Object.

String Object Method Summaries

<u>Method</u>	<u>Description</u>
anchor()	Parallels the <A> Tag creating an anchor that is used as a hypertext target.
big()	Parallels the <BIG> Tag to display a bigger String.
blink()	Parallels the <BLINK> Tag to display a blinking String.
bold()	Parallels the <B> Tag to display a boldface String.
charAt()	Returns a String containing the Character at the specified **index** within the calling String.
charCodeAt()	Returns a number that specifies the ISO-Latin-1 codeset Value of the Character at the indicated **index** within the calling String.
concat()	Returns a String that is the combination of two specified Strings.
fixed()	Parallels the <TT> Tag to display a fixed-width String.
fontcolor()	Parallels the <FONT COLOR="color"> Tag to change the color of the specified String.
fontsize()	Parallels the <FONT SIZE=size> Tag to change the size of the specified String.
fromCharCode()	Converts one or more numbers that are ISO-Latin-1 codeset Values into ASCII Characters and returns them as a String.
indexOf()	Returns a numeric String that is the **index** number within the calling String for the *first* occurrence of the specified pattern that is found inside that calling String.

italics() Parallels the <I> Tag to display an italicized String.

lastIndexOf() Returns a numeric String that is the **index** number within the calling String for the *last* occurrence of the specified pattern that is found inside that calling String.

link() Parallels the <A> Tag transforming a String into an HTML hypertext link to a specified URL.

match() Matches a Regular Expression pattern against the calling String and returns an Array of Strings reflecting the matches.

replace() Matches a Regular Expression pattern against the calling String and replaces the matched Substring with a new Substring.

search() Matches a Regular Expression pattern against the calling String and returns the **index** within the calling String of the match.

slice() Returns a new String that consists of a part of the calling String.

small() Parallels the <SMALL> Tag to display a smaller String.

split() Returns an Array of Substrings resulting from splitting up the calling String based on a separator that can be a String or a Regular Expression.

strike() Parallels the <STRIKE> Tag to display a strikeout String.

sub() Parallels the <SUB> Tag to display a subscripted String.

substr() Returns a String consisting of Characters that are specified by a starting **index** and an optional number that specifies the quantity of Characters to extract from the calling String.

substring() Returns a String consisting of Characters that are specified by a starting **index** and an optional ending **index** that specifies the Characters to extract from the calling String.

sup() Parallels the <SUP> Tag to display a superscripted String.

toLowerCase() Converts the calling String to lowercase Characters and returns it.

toUpperCase() Converts the calling String to uppercase Characters and returns it.

Property Summaries
of the Predefined RegExp Core Object

Six of the following Properties are duplicates; that is, the same Property has two different names that refer to exactly the same Value. The first is the spelled-out, longhand version, and the other is the abbreviated, shorthand, "Perl-esque", name (paralleling the Perl programming language). Make sure to remember that these are Properties of the Predefined **RegExp** Core Object and are *not* available to Individual Regular Expressions even though they carry information *about* Individual Regular Expressions. You access these Properties by prepending **RegExp** to them like this: **RegExp.input**

Property	Status	Description
$_	Read/Write	Same as **input**.
$*	Read/Write	Same as **multiline**.
$&	Read-only	Same as **lastMatch**.
$+	Read-only	Same as **lastParen**.
$`	Read-only	Same as **leftContext**.
$'	Read-only	Same as **rightContext**.
input	Read/Write	Contains the String that a **RegExp** attempts to match.
multiline	Read/Write	Boolean Property designating a search across multiple lines of text if true and a single line of text if false.
lastMatch	Read-only	String containing the last matched Characters.
lastParen	Read-only	String containing the last Parenthesized SubString match.
leftContext	Read-only	Contains the SubString before the most recent match.
rightContext	Read-only	Contains the next SubString after the most recent match.
$1, $2, $3, $4, $5, $6, $7, $8, $9	Read-only	The last nine Parenthesized SubString matches, if any. To access any additional matches, use the indexed Elements of the returned Array from the **exec()** Method. **$9** is the last match. If less than ten matches are made, **$1** will have the first match. The number of possible Parenthesized SubString matches is unlimited, but the Predefined **RegExp** Core Object can only hold the last nine for easy access.

Chart of all Special Characters
for Regular Expressions

On the next few pages are the listings for all of the Special Characters that can be used in Regular Expressions. The Special Character is listed on the left, with a description on the right. Then several Mini-Examples are given.

Special Character	Description

\   This Character has a dual purpose. If the Character it precedes is normally *not* a Special Character, then it changes it so that it *is* a Special Character and is *not* to be interpreted literally.

For instance:
/d/   Normally matches the Character 'd'
/\d/   Matches any number from 0 to 9
because the backslash Character '\' precedes 'd'

---or alternatively---

If the Character it precedes *is* normally a Special Character, then it changes it so that it is *not* a Special Character and it *should be* interpreted literally.

For instance:
+   Normally means match the preceding Character occurring one or more times.
/A+/   Normally means match the Character 'A' occurring one or more times.
/A\+/   Matches the Literal Characters 'A+' as in: "I got an A+ on my report."

---

^   Matches the start of an input or a new line.
For instance: /^A/
matches: 'A'   in   "An apple for the teacher."
doesn't match: 'A'   in   "I got an A on my report."

$ Matches the end of an input or the end of a line.
For instance: /a$/
matches: 'a'   in   "On the sea"
doesn't match: 'a'   in   "Sailing on water"

---

*   Matches the preceding Character zero or more times.
For instance: /he*/
matches: 'heeeee'   in   "heeeeey there"
matches: 'h'   in   "those musicians"
matches nothing: in   "See bears be free"   (Hint: no "h")

+   Matches the preceding Character one or more times. Same as {1,}.

For instance: /o+/

matches:	'o'	in	"Turn on the light"
matches:	'oooo'	in	"Varoooom"
doesn't match:	'O'	in	"An Orange"

?   Matches the preceding Character zero or one time.

For instance: /su?/

matches:	'su'	in	"submarine"
matches:	's'	in	"song"
matches:	'su'	in	"Black Holes suuuuuck"

.   (Period) Matches any individual Character except the newline Character.

For instance: /.m/

matches:	'om'	in	"Go home Trevor."
matches:	'am'	in	"A dog named Toby."
doesn't match:	'^m'	in	"^meager delineation."

(x)   Matches 'x' being any sequence of Characters and remembers the match.

For instance: /(her)/

matches and remembers:		'her'	in	"red herring"

The matched SubString can be referenced from the
<u>returnedArray</u> Elements **[1]** to **[n]**, or from the
<u>Predefined</u> **RegExp** Object's Properties **$1** to **$9**.

---

x | y   Matches either 'x' or 'y', which can be any sequence of Characters.
For more options just separate each one with a vertical bar Character " | ".

For instance: /blue | black/

matches:	'blue'	in	"I had blueberry pie."
matches:	'black'	in	"I had blackberry cobbler."
doesn't match:	'Black'	in	"Caution, Black ice ahead."

{n}   Matches exactly 'n' occurrences of the preceding Character where 'n' is a positive integer.

For instance: /yu{3}/

matches:	'yuuu'	in	"Pineapple on pizza is yuuucky."
matches:	'yuuu'	in	"yuuuuuuuuum."
doesn't match:	'yu' or 'yuu'	in	"To yum or not to yuum."

{n,}	Matches at least 'n' occurrences of the preceding Character where 'n' is a positive integer.			
	For instance:	/u{3,}/		
	matches:	'uuu'	in	"Pineapple on pizza is yuuucky."
	matches:	'uuuuuuu'	in	"yuuuuuuum."
	doesn't match:	'u' or 'uu'	in	"To yum or not to yuum."

{n,m}	Matches at least 'n' and no more than 'm' occurrences of the preceding Character where 'n' and 'm' are positive integers.			
	For instance:	/u{2,4}/		
	matches:	'uu'	in	"yuucky."
	matches:	'uuu'	in	"yuuum."
	matches:	'uuuu'	in	"yuuuum."
	doesn't match:	'u' or 'uuuuu'	in	"To yum or not to yuuuuum."

[xyz]	Matches any single Character of the bracketed Character Set. To specify a range of Characters, use a hyphen between the start and end Characters.			
	For instance:	/[abcdefg]/	is equivalent to:	/[a-g]/
	matches:	'e'	in	"prose"
	matches:	'g'	in	"goo"

[^xyz]	Oppositional Character Set. Matches any Character that is not specified in the enclosing brackets after the '^' Character. To specify a range of Characters, use a hyphen between the start and end Characters, after '^'.			
	For instance:	/[^abcdefg]/	is equivalent to:	/[^a-g]/
	matches:	'r'	in	"bear"
	matches:	'y'	in	"bye"

[\b]	Matches a backspace Character (Don't confuse with \b).			

\b	Matches a word boundary, like tab or space (Don't confuse with [\b]). Note that spaces, etc., get deleted out of the Strings in the <u>returned Array</u>.			
	For instance:	/\bg/		
	matches:	' g'	in	"elliptical galaxy"
	doesn't match:	'g'	in	"the shaggy dog"
	For instance:	/g\b/		
	matches:	'g '	in	"the dog barked"
	doesn't match:	'g'	in	"the shaggy pup"

\B	Matches a non-word boundary.			
	For instance:	/\Bg/		
	matches:	'g'	in	"Shagrat was an Ork"
	For instance:	/g\B\w/		
	matches:	'gg'	in	"the shaggy pup"

\cX	Matches a Control Character, where X is a Control Character. For instance: /\cE/ matches the Control Key + the 'E' or 'e' Key in a String. See Example 9-6.
\d	Matches a numerical Character. Same as [0-9]. For instance: /\d/ or /[0-9]/ matches: '5' in "Babylon 5"
\D	Matches any non-numerical Character. Same as [^0-9]. For instance: /\D/ or /[^0-9]/ matches: 'B' in "Babylon 5"
\f	Matches the first form feed.
\n	Matches a line feed.
\r	Matches a carriage return.
\s	Matches any single white space Character like space, tab, vertical tab, carriage return, form feed, and line feed. Same as [\f\n\r\t\v]. For instance: /\s\w+/ matches: ' name' in "The name of the place is"
\S	Matches any single Character other than white space Characters. Same as [^ \f\n\r\t\v]. For instance: /\S/ matches: 'T' in "The name of the place is" matches: 'r' in "rock"
\t	Matches a tab.
\v	Matches a vertical tab.
\w	Matches any alphanumeric Character and the underscore Character '_'. Same as [A-Za-z0-9_]. For instance: /\w/ or /[A-Za-z0-9_]/ matches: 'b' in "blue" matches: '2' in "#2300fe" matches: '_' in "_top"
\W	Matches any non-alphanumeric Character except the underscore. Same as [^A-Za-z0-9_]. For instance: /\W/ or /[^A-Za-z0-9_]/ matches: '#' in "#8800ff"

\n   <u>Where 'n' is a positive integer</u>. When you enclose a SubSection of the
                    Regular Expression within parentheses, that SubSection is remembered
                    and can be referenced as a SubString. The parenthesized SubSections of
                    the Regular Expression are counted from left to right starting at 1.
                    Therefore, 'n' is the nth parenthesized SubSection back-reference to the last
                    SubString that is remembered.

                    (The simple explanation is that if you want to match text that you know is
                    going to be repeated in the String, then you can use the '\n' to look for it
                    instead of repeating the syntax explicitly in the Regular Expression.)

For instance:	/(red)\1/		
matches:	'red red '	in	"The colors blue red red green."
For instance:	/(3)(+)4\2/		
matches:	'3+4+'	in	"1+2+3+4+5+6+7"
For instance:	/eagle(\sand)\shawk\1/		
matches:	'eagle and hawk and '	in	"eagle and hawk and emu"

                    Notice that if the number of parenthesized SubSections is less than the
                    number specified in 'n', then 'n' is interpreted as an octal escape Value that
                    is defined next.

                    See <u>Sample1009.html</u> on pages 835-836 for a working example of this
                    Special Character.

\ooctal   Matches 'ooctal' where 'ooctal' is any octal escape Value. Lets you include
                    ASCII code Values directly into Regular Expressions.

\xhex   Matches 'xhex' where 'xhex' is any hexadecimal escape Value. Lets you
                    include ASCII code Values directly into Regular Expressions.

\dec   Matches 'dec' where 'dec' is any decimal escape Value. Lets you
                    include ASCII code Values directly into Regular Expressions.

∞∞

Method Summary of
<u>Individual</u> RegExp Objects

The Methods of <u>Individual</u> **RegExp** Objects that you create are:

<u>Method</u>	<u>Description</u>
test()	Used to search for a match between the Regular Expression and the specified String. Returns **true** if a match is found and **false** if no match is found.
exec()	Used to search for a match between the Regular Expression and the specified String. If a match is found, the Method returns an Array of SubStrings and updates the Properties of both the <u>Individual</u> Regular Expression and the <u>Predefined</u> **RegExp** Object. Returns '**null**' if no match is found.
compile()	Used for efficiency to force compilation of a Regular Expression created with the **RegExp** Constructor Function so that it is not continually recompiled during execution. Also used to change the Regular Expression during execution.

Summary of <u>String</u> <u>Methods</u> used with
<u>Individual</u> RegExp Objects

The Methods of **<u>String Objects</u>** that you can use to interact with and manipulate <u>Individual</u> **RegExp** Objects are:

<u>Method</u>	<u>Description</u>
search()	Matches a Regular Expression **pattern** against the calling String and returns the **index** within the calling String of the match.
match()	Matches a Regular Expression **pattern** against the calling String and returns an Array of Strings reflecting the matches.
replace()	Matches a Regular Expression **pattern** against the calling String and replaces the matched SubString with a new SubString.
split()	Returns an Array of SubStrings resulting from splitting up the calling String, based on a **separator** that can be a String or a Regular Expression.

Property Summary of Individual RegExp Objects

The Properties of <u>Individual</u> **RegExp** Objects that you create are:

<u>Property</u>	<u>Description</u>
global	A <u>read-only</u> Boolean Property that has a Value of '**true**' if the **g flag** was used in the Regular Expression and '**false**' if it wasn't. The **g flag** specifies that the Regular Expression must find all the possible matches in the String. Without the **g flag**, the Regular Expression stops after the first match. Note that this Property cannot be changed explicitly, but it may possibly be changed as a result of calling the **compile()** Method.
ignoreCase	A <u>read-only</u> Boolean Property that has a Value of '**true**' if the **i flag** was used in the Regular Expression and '**false**' if it wasn't. The **i flag** specifies that the Regular Expression should ignore case, so the search is case-insensitive when looking for a match in a String. Note that this Property cannot be changed explicitly, but it may possibly be changed as a result of calling the **compile()** Method.
lastIndex	A <u>read/write</u> integer Property that is only applicable and set if the **g flag** is set to specify a global search. It indicates the **index** where the Regular Expression should start the next search. See page 832 for more information.
source	A <u>read-only</u> Property that contains the **pattern** Argument of the Regular Expression. Note that this does <u>*not*</u> include either of the enclosing forward slashes '/' or the suffixed **i** or **g flags**. Note that this Property cannot be changed explicitly, but it may possibly be changed as a result of calling the **compile()** Method. See page 828 for an example.

∞∞∞

Date Object
Property and Method Summaries

The Property and Methods of the **Date** Object that are available for JavaScript1.2 are listed below. Note that in Chapter 10, there are additional Methods available for the **Date** Object in JavaScript1.3.

Date Property	Property Description
prototype	Allows you to add and assign your own Properties and Methods when creating a new instance of the **Date** Object.

Date Method	Method Description/Results
getDate()	Returns the day of the month for the specified **Date** Object.
getDay()	Returns the day of the week for the specified **Date** Object.
getHours()	Returns the hour of the specified **Date** Object.
getMinutes()	Returns the minutes of the specified **Date** Object.
getMonth()	Returns the month of the specified **Date** Object.
getSeconds()	Returns the seconds of the specified **Date** Object.
getTime()	Returns the numeric value corresponding to the time for the specified **Date** Object.
getTimezoneOffset()	Returns the time-zone offset in minutes of the specified **Date** Object for the current geographic locale.
getYear()	Returns the year of the specified **Date** Object.
parse()	Returns the number of milliseconds of a **Date** Object String since January 1, 1970, 00:00:00, local time.
setDate(integer)	Sets the day of the month for a specified **Date** Object.
setHours(integer)	Sets the hours for a specified **Date** Object.
setMinutes(integer)	Sets the minutes for a specified **Date** Object.
setMonth(integer)	Sets the month for a specified **Date** Object.
setSeconds(integer)	Sets the seconds for a specified **Date** Object.
setTime(integer)	Sets the value of a **Date** object.
setYear(integer)	Sets the year for a specified **Date** Object.
toGMTString()	Converts a **Date** Object to a String, using the Internet GMT conventions.
toLocaleString()	Converts a **Date** Object to a String, using the current geographic locale's conventions.
UTC()	Returns the number of milliseconds of a **Date** Object since January 1, 1970, 00:00:00, Universal Coordinated Time (GMT).

Math Object Property Summaries

Math Properties	Description	Approximate Value
E	Euler's constant	2.718281828459045091
LN10	Natural logarithm of 10	2.302585092994045901
LN2	Natural logarithm of 2	0.6931471805599452862
LOG10E	Base 10 logarithm of E	0.4342944819032518167
LOG2E	Base 2 logarithm of E	1.442695040888963387
PI	Ratio of the circumference of a circle to its diameter	3.141592653589793116
SQRT1_2	Square root of 1/2	0.7071067811865475727
SQRT2	Square root of 2	1.414213562373095145

Math Object Method Summaries

Math Methods	Description
abs(x)	Returns the absolute value of x.
acos(x)	Returns the arc cosine of x in radians.
asin(x)	Returns the arc sine of x in radians.
atan(x)	Returns the arc tangent of x in radians.
atan2(y,x)	Returns the arc tangent of the quotient of its Arguments, that is, y/x. This is another way of saying it returns the angle of the Polar Coordinate (y,x).
ceil(x)	Returns the smallest integer greater than or equal to x.
cos(x)	Returns the cosine of x.
exp(x)	Returns e^x, where x is the Argument and e is Euler's constant, the base of the natural logarithms.
floor(x)	Returns the largest integer less than or equal to x.
log(x)	Returns the natural logarithm (base E) of x.
max(x,y)	Returns the greater of the two numbers x and y.
min(x,y)	Returns the lesser of the two numbers x and y.
pow(x,y)	Returns x^y, traditionally base to the exponent power, that is, $base^{exponent}$.
random()	Returns a pseudo-random number between 0 and 1.
round(x)	Returns the value of x rounded to the nearest integer with .50 as cutoff.
sin(x)	Returns the sine of x.
sqrt(x)	Returns the square root of x.
tan(x)	Returns the tangent of x.

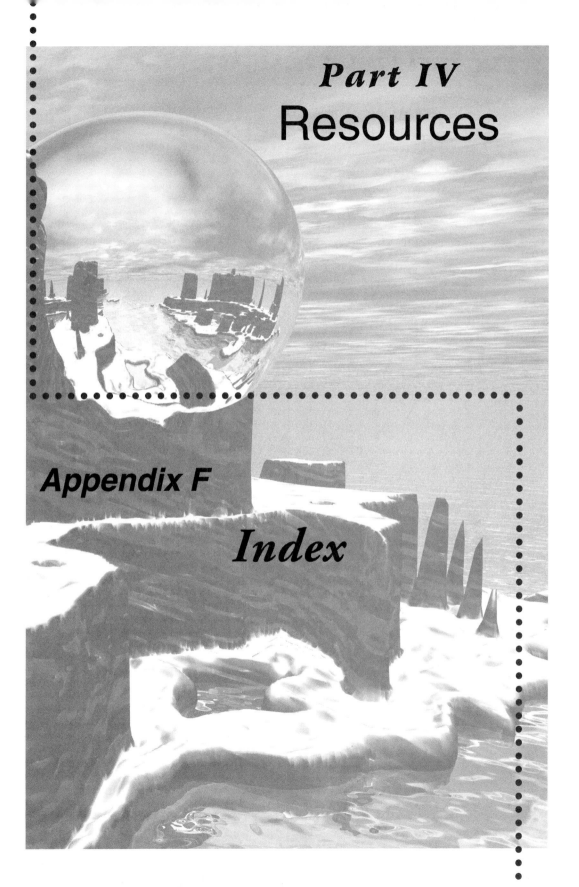

Part IV
Resources

Appendix F

Index

Index

Page numbers that use a **bold** font indicate the page(s) that are most important to that topic (main definitions/descriptions).

Note that the Appendix page numbers start at 900 and proceed to the end of the book.

For more information and examples of HTML Elements, see Chapters 1-6 in the Online Guide on the CD-ROM, which is an expanded version of the HTML Primer.

B

G

H

K

L

O

P

X

LICENSE AGREEMENT AND LIMITED WARRANTY

READ THE FOLLOWING TERMS AND CONDITIONS CAREFULLY BEFORE OPENING THIS DISK PACKAGE. THIS LEGAL DOCUMENT IS AN AGREEMENT BETWEEN YOU AND PRENTICE-HALL, INC. (THE "COMPANY"). BY OPENING THIS SEALED DISK PACKAGE, YOU ARE AGREEING TO BE BOUND BY THESE TERMS AND CONDITIONS. IF YOU DO NOT AGREE WITH THESE TERMS AND CONDITIONS, DO NOT OPEN THE DISK PACKAGE. PROMPTLY RETURN THE UNOPENED DISK PACKAGE AND ALL ACCOMPANYING ITEMS TO THE PLACE YOU OBTAINED THEM FOR A FULL REFUND OF ANY SUMS YOU HAVE PAID.

1.   **GRANT OF LICENSE:** In consideration of your purchase of this book, and your agreement to abide by the terms and conditions of this Agreement, the Company grants to you a nonexclusive right to use and display the copy of the enclosed software program (hereinafter the "SOFTWARE") on a single computer (i.e., with a single CPU) at a single location so long as you comply with the terms of this Agreement. The Company reserves all rights not expressly granted to you under this Agreement.

2.   **OWNERSHIP OF SOFTWARE:** You own only the magnetic or physical media (the enclosed disk) on which the SOFTWARE is recorded or fixed, but the Company and the software developers retain all the rights, title, and ownership to the SOFTWARE recorded on the original disk copy(ies) and all subsequent copies of the SOFTWARE, regardless of the form or media on which the original or other copies may exist. This license is not a sale of the original SOFTWARE or any copy to you.

3.   **COPY RESTRICTIONS:** This SOFTWARE and the accompanying printed materials and user manual (the "Documentation") are the subject of copyright. You may <u>not</u> copy the Documentation or the SOFTWARE, except that you may make a single copy of the SOFTWARE for backup or archival purposes only. You may be held legally responsible for any copying or copyright infringement which is caused or encouraged by your failure to abide by the terms of this restriction.

4.   **USE RESTRICTIONS:** You may <u>not</u> network the SOFTWARE or otherwise use it on more than one computer or computer terminal at the same time. You may physically transfer the SOFTWARE from one computer to another provided that the SOFTWARE is used on only one computer at a time. You may <u>not</u> distribute copies of the SOFTWARE or Documentation to others. You may <u>not</u> reverse engineer, disassemble, decompile, modify, adapt, translate, or create derivative works based on the SOFTWARE or the Documentation without the prior written consent of the Company.

5.   **TRANSFER RESTRICTIONS:** The enclosed SOFTWARE is licensed only to you and may <u>not</u> be transferred to any one else without the prior written consent of the Company. Any unauthorized transfer of the SOFTWARE shall result in the immediate termination of this Agreement.

6.   **TERMINATION:** This license is effective until terminated. This license will terminate automatically without notice from the Company and become null and void if you fail to comply with any provisions or limitations of this license. Upon termination, you shall destroy the Documentation and all copies of the SOFTWARE. All provisions of this Agreement as to warranties, limitation of liability, remedies or damages, and our ownership rights shall survive termination.

7.   **MISCELLANEOUS:** This Agreement shall be construed in accordance with the laws of the United States of America and the State of New York and shall benefit the Company, its affiliates, and assignees.

8.   **LIMITED WARRANTY AND DISCLAIMER OF WARRANTY:** The Company warrants that the SOFTWARE, when properly used in accordance with the Documentation, will operate in substantial conformity with the description of the SOFTWARE set forth in the Documentation. The Company does not warrant that the SOFTWARE will meet your requirements or that the operation of the SOFTWARE will be uninterrupted or error-free. The Company warrants that the media on which the SOFTWARE is delivered shall be free from defects in materials and workmanship under normal use for a period of thirty (30) days from the date of your purchase. Your only remedy and the

Company's only obligation under these limited warranties is, at the Company's option, return of the warranted item for a refund of any amounts paid by you or replacement of the item. Any replacement of SOFTWARE or media under the warranties shall not extend the original warranty period. The limited warranty set forth above shall not apply to any SOFTWARE which the Company determines in good faith has been subject to misuse, neglect, improper installation, repair, alteration, or damage by you. EXCEPT FOR THE EXPRESSED WARRANTIES SET FORTH ABOVE, THE COMPANY DISCLAIMS ALL WARRANTIES, EXPRESS OR IMPLIED, INCLUDING WITHOUT LIMITATION, THE IMPLIED WARRANTIES OF MERCHANTABILITY AND FITNESS FOR A PARTICULAR PURPOSE. EXCEPT FOR THE EXPRESS WARRANTY SET FORTH ABOVE, THE COMPANY DOES NOT WARRANT, GUARANTEE, OR MAKE ANY REPRESENTATION REGARDING THE USE OR THE RESULTS OF THE USE OF THE SOFTWARE IN TERMS OF ITS CORRECTNESS, ACCURACY, RELIABILITY, CURRENTNESS, OR OTHERWISE.

IN NO EVENT, SHALL THE COMPANY OR ITS EMPLOYEES, AGENTS, SUPPLIERS, OR CONTRACTORS BE LIABLE FOR ANY INCIDENTAL, INDIRECT, SPECIAL, OR CONSEQUENTIAL DAMAGES ARISING OUT OF OR IN CONNECTION WITH THE LICENSE GRANTED UNDER THIS AGREEMENT, OR FOR LOSS OF USE, LOSS OF DATA, LOSS OF INCOME OR PROFIT, OR OTHER LOSSES, SUSTAINED AS A RESULT OF INJURY TO ANY PERSON, OR LOSS OF OR DAMAGE TO PROPERTY, OR CLAIMS OF THIRD PARTIES, EVEN IF THE COMPANY OR AN AUTHORIZED REPRESENTATIVE OF THE COMPANY HAS BEEN ADVISED OF THE POSSIBILITY OF SUCH DAMAGES. IN NO EVENT SHALL LIABILITY OF THE COMPANY FOR DAMAGES WITH RESPECT TO THE SOFTWARE EXCEED THE AMOUNTS ACTUALLY PAID BY YOU, IF ANY, FOR THE SOFTWARE.

SOME JURISDICTIONS DO NOT ALLOW THE LIMITATION OF IMPLIED WARRANTIES OR LIABILITY FOR INCIDENTAL, INDIRECT, SPECIAL, OR CONSEQUENTIAL DAMAGES, SO THE ABOVE LIMITATIONS MAY NOT ALWAYS APPLY. THE WARRANTIES IN THIS AGREEMENT GIVE YOU SPECIFIC LEGAL RIGHTS AND YOU MAY ALSO HAVE OTHER RIGHTS WHICH VARY IN ACCORDANCE WITH LOCAL LAW.

ACKNOWLEDGMENT

YOU ACKNOWLEDGE THAT YOU HAVE READ THIS AGREEMENT, UNDERSTAND IT, AND AGREE TO BE BOUND BY ITS TERMS AND CONDITIONS. YOU ALSO AGREE THAT THIS AGREEMENT IS THE COMPLETE AND EXCLUSIVE STATEMENT OF THE AGREEMENT BETWEEN YOU AND THE COMPANY AND SUPERSEDES ALL PROPOSALS OR PRIOR AGREEMENTS, ORAL, OR WRITTEN, AND ANY OTHER COMMUNICATIONS BETWEEN YOU AND THE COMPANY OR ANY REPRESENTATIVE OF THE COMPANY RELATING TO THE SUBJECT MATTER OF THIS AGREEMENT.

Should you have any questions concerning this Agreement or if you wish to contact the Company for any reason, please contact in writing at the address below.

Robin Short
Prentice Hall PTR
One Lake Street
Upper Saddle River, New Jersey 07458

About the CD-ROM

First and foremost, the entire book is contained in both HTML and PDF formats, along with the source code for every example used in the book. These Sample files were created in BBEdit, but they can be opened in any text editor for perusal or copying of chunks of source code for your own pages. They have been fully tested in Navigator on the MacIntosh Platform and all Samples will work in Navigator 4.06+. My understanding is that they should work on the Windows Platform in Navigator, but I can't absolutely say they will, because I didn't personally test them on it. All of the Samples except those in Chapter 10 will work on any version of Navigator from 4.0+. The Samples from Chapter 10 were coded with JavaScript 1.3 and require that at least Navigator 4.06 be used.

Check out Appendix C for a listing of Sample and example files, including the topic covered and the page number in the book where the example starts.

Additionally, there are hundreds of Sample files on the CD-ROM that aren't in the book for you to explore.

Here are descriptions of the contents of the major folders on the CD-ROM:

Folder Name	Contents Description
DHTML_JavaScript_Book-Online	Final version of the book in one long PDF file.
HTML_BOOK-Online	Contains the original version of the Book, in HTML format, with color coded terms. Note that <u>CH1.html</u> to <u>CH6.html</u> are longer versions of the information contained in Appendix A of the final version of the book. <u>CH7.html</u> to <u>CH16.html</u> contain the information for Chapters 1 to 10 of the final book version.
Docs_for_Book	Main Documentation Folder
html-Character-Codes	Character Codes for HTML
html40 -W3C Specification	HTML 4.0 Documentation from W3C
HTML 4.0 -Reference	HTML 4.0 Reference Documentation
HTML-Nav4-Final-Docs	Netscape's HTML 4.0 Documentation for Navigator
CSS 1.1-All-Docs-97	Cascading Style Sheet White Papers
Dynamic HTML Communicator	Netscape's DHTML Guide
JavaScript 1.2 Docs	
JS1.2-Guide	Netscape's JavaScript 1.2 Guide
JS1.2-Reference	Netscape's JavaScript 1.2 Reference

About the CD-ROM continued

JavaScript 1.3 Docs
        JavaScript Guide 1.3   Netscape's JavaScript 1.3 Guide
        JavaScript Reference 1.3   Netscape's JavaScript 1.3 Reference
     More Cookie Docs   Cookie Property Documentation
     NetscapeOneDevGuide   Netscape's Developer Guide
     Plugin-DevGuide   Netscape's Plug-in Guide
     Book-Plugins-Info   Additional Plug-in Resources
     Composer-Plugin-Guide   Netscape's Composer Plug-in Guide
     JAR-Installation-Manager-Docs   Netscape's JAR Guide
     Netcaster-DevGuide   Netscape's Netcaster Developer Guide
     META-Tags-Docs   META Tags Documentation

dreamplay-website   Original website for DreamPlay Studios.
                             It has a lot of additional code files.
JPEG-FILES   Images used in Sample files.
Sample-ETOC   Original website for Extra Touch of Class.
VRML-Textures   Collection of image Textures for VRML files
ChessImages   Images used for the Chess Game Example.

There's lots of other goodies on the CD-ROM, so poke around.

Prentice Hall does not offer technical support for this software. However, if there is a problem with the media, you may obtain a replacement copy by e-mailing us with your problem at:

disc_exchange@prenhall.com

The author also has a website where you can view even more images of his art and you can also hear excerpts from the two CDs of music he composed and recorded. Framed and unframed dye-sublimation and firey prints of the art and the music CDs can also be purchased at the website at:

http://www.erols.com/gilorien

You can contact Gilorien at:

gilorien@erols.com